"An Index
to Book Reviews
in the Humanities "

Volume 28
1987

Phillip Thomson
Williamston, Michigan

This volume of the Index contains data collected up to 31 December 1987.

This is an index to book reviews in humanities periodicals. Beginning with volume 12 of this Index (dated 1971), the former policy of selectively indexing reviews of books in certain subject categories only was dropped in favor of a policy of indexing all reviews in the periodicals indexed, with the one exception of children's books – the reviews of which will not be indexed.

The form of the entries used is as follows:

Author.   Title.

Reviewer.   Identifying Legend.

The author's name used is the name that appears on the title-page of the book being reviewed, as well as we are able to determine, even though this name is known to be a pseudonym. The title only is shown; subtitles are included only where they are necessary to identify a book in a series. The identifying legend consists of the periodical, each of which has a code number, and the date and page number of the periodical where the review is to be found. PMLA abbreviations are also shown (when a periodical has such an abbreviation, but such abbreviations are limited to four letters) immediately following the code number of the periodical. To learn the name of the periodical in which the review appears, it is necessary to refer the code number to the numerically-arranged list of periodicals beginning on page iii. This list also shows the volume and number of the periodical issues indexed in this volume.

Reviews are indexed as they appear and no attempt is made to hold the title until all the reviews are published. For this reason it is necessary to refer to previous and subsequent volumes of this Index to be sure that the complete roster of reviews of any title is seen. As an aid to the user, an asterisk (*) has been added immediately following any title that was also indexed in Volume 27 (1986) of this Index.

Authors with hyphenated surnames are indexed under the name before the hyphen, and the name following the hyphen is not cross-indexed. Authors with more than one surname, but where the names are not hyphenated, are indexed under the first of the names and the last name is cross-indexed. When alphabetizing surnames containing umlauts, the umlauts are ignored. Editors are always shown in the author-title entry, and they are cross-indexed (except where the editor's surname is the same as that of the author). Translators are shown only when they are necessary to identify the book being reviewed (as in the classics), and they are not cross-indexed unless the book being reviewed has no author or editor. Certain reference works and anonymous works that are known primarily by their title are indexed under that title and their editors are cross-indexed.

A list of abbreviations used is shown on page ii.

ABBREVIATIONS

Anon	Anonymous
Apr	April
Aug	August
Bk	Book
Comp(s)	Compiler(s)
Cont	Continued
Dec	December
Ed(s)	Editor(s) [or] Edition(s)
Fasc	Fascicule
Feb	February
Jan	January
Jul	July
Jun	June
Mar	March
No	Number
Nov	November
Oct	October
Prev	Previous volume of this Index
Pt	Part
Rev	Revised
Sep	September
Ser	Series
Supp	Supplement
Trans	Translator(s)
Vol	Volume
* (asterisk)	This title was also shown in the volume of this Index immediately preceding this one

ii

The periodicals in which the reviews appear are identified in this Index by a number. To supplement this number, and to promote ready identification, PMLA abbreviations are also given following this number. Every attempt will be made to index those issues shown here as "missing" in a later volume of this Index.

The following is a list of the periodicals indexed in volume 28:

2(AfrA) – African Arts. Los Angeles.
    Nov85 thru Aug86 (vol 19 complete)
4 – Agenda. London.
    Spring86 thru Autumn86 (vol 24 no 1-3)
9(AlaR) – Alabama Review. University.
    Jan86 thru Oct86 (vol 39 complete)
16 – American Art Journal. New York.
    Vol 18 complete
18 – American Film. Washington.
    Oct86 thru Apr87, Jun87 thru Sep87 (vol 12 no 1-6 and no 8-10) [issue dated May87 missing]
24 – American Journal of Philology. Baltimore.
    Spring86 thru Winter86 (vol 107 complete)
26(ALR) – American Literary Realism, 1870-1910. Arlington.
    Fall86 thru Spring87 (vol 19 complete)
27(AL) – American Literature. Durham.
    Mar86 thru Dec86 (vol 58 complete)
29(APR) – The American Poetry Review. Philadelphia.
    Jan/Feb87 thru Nov/Dec87 (vol 16 complete)
30 – American Poetry. Jefferson.
    Fall86 thru Spring87 (vol 4 complete)
31(ASch) – American Scholar. Washington.
    Winter85/86 thru Autumn86 (vol 55 complete)
35(AS) – American Speech. University.
    Spring86 thru Winter86 (vol 61 complete)
37 – The Américas. Washington.
    Jan-Feb86 thru Nov-Dec86 (vol 38 complete)
38 – Anglia. Tübingen.
    Band 104 complete
39 – Apollo. London.
    Jan86 thru Dec86 (vols 123 & 124 complete)
40 – AEB: Analytical and Enumerative Bibliography. De Kalb.
    Vol 8 no 4
41 – Ancient Philosophy. Pittsburgh.
    Spring85, Fall85 and Vol 6 (vols 5 & 6 complete)
42(AR) – Antioch Review. Yellow Springs.
    Winter86 thru Fall86 (vol 44 complete)
43 – Architectura. München.
    Band 16 complete
44 – Architectural History. London.
    Vol 29
45 – Architectural Record. New York.
    Jan86 thru Dec86 (vol 174 complete)

46 – Architectural Review. London.
    Jan86 thru Dec86 (vols 179 & 180 complete)
48 – Archivo Español de Arte. Madrid.
    Jan-Mar86 thru Oct-Dec86 (vol 59 complete)
49 – Ariel. Calgary.
    Jan86 thru Oct86 (vol 17 complete)
50(ArQ) – Arizona Quarterly. Tucson.
    Spring86 thru Winter86 (vol 42 complete)
52 – Arcadia. Berlin.
    Band 21 complete
53(AGP) – Archiv für Geschichte der Philosophie. Berlin.
    Band 68 complete
54 – Art Bulletin. New York.
    Mar86 thru Dec86 (vol 68 complete)
55 – Art News. New York.
    Jan86 thru Dec86 (vol 85 complete)
57 – Artibus Asiae. Ascona.
    Vol 47 complete [no reviews indexed]
59 – Art History. London.
    Mar86 thru Dec86 (vol 9 complete)
60 – Arts of Asia. Hong Kong.
    Jan-Feb86 thru Nov-Dec86 (vol 16 complete)
61 – Atlantic Monthly. Boston.
    Jan87 thru Dec87 (vols 259 & 260 complete)
62 – Artforum. New York.
    Sep86 thru Summer87 (vol 25 complete)
63 – Australasian Journal of Philosophy. Bundoora.
    Mar86, Jun86 & Dec86 (vol 64 no 1, 2 & 4) [issue dated Sep86 missing]
64(Arv) – ARV: Scandinavian Yearbook of Folklore. Stockholm.
    Vol 41
67 – AMULA [Journal of the Australasian Universities Language and Literature Assn.] Nedlands
    May86 & Nov86 (no 65 & 66)
71(ALS) – Australian Literary Studies. St. Lucia.
    May86 & Oct86 (vol 12 no 3 & 4)
72 – Archiv für das Studium der neueren Sprachen und Literaturen. Berlin.
    Band 223 complete
77 – Biography. Honolulu.
    Winter86 thru Fall86 (vol 9 complete)
78(BC) – Book Collector. London.
    Spring86 thru Winter86 (vol 35 complete)
81 – Boundary 2. Binghamton.
    Fall85/Winter86 (vol 14 no 1/2) [no reviews indexed]
83 – The British Journal for Eighteenth-Century Studies. Oxford.
    Spring86 & Autumn86 (vol 9 complete)
84 – The British Journal for the Philosophy of Science. Oxford.
    Mar86 thru Dec86 (vol 37 complete)
85(SBHC) – Studies in Browning and His Circle. Waco.
    Vol 14

86(BHS) – Bulletin of Hispanic Studies. Liverpool.
Jan86 thru Oct86 (vol 63 complete)
87(BB) – Bulletin of Bibliography. Westport.
Mar86 thru Dec86 (vol 43 complete)
88 – Blake, An Illustrated Quarterly. Rochester
Summer86 & Fall86 (vol 20 no 1 & 2)
89(BJA) – The British Journal of Aesthetics. Oxford.
Winter86 thru Autumn86 (vol 26 complete)
90 – Burlington Magazine. London.
Jan86 thru Dec86 (vol 128 complete)
91 – The Black Perspective in Music. Cambria Heights.
Winter86 thru Fall86 (vol 14 complete)
92(BH) – Bulletin Hispanique. Bordeaux.
Jan–Jun85 & Jul–Dec85 (vol 87 complete)
95(CLAJ) – CLA Journal. Atlanta.
Sep86 thru Jun87 (vol 30 complete)
97(CQ) – The Cambridge Quarterly. Cambridge.
Vol 15 complete
98 – Critique. Paris.
Jan–Feb86 thru Dec86 (vol 42 complete)
99 – Canadian Forum. Toronto.
Apr86 thru Mar87 (vol 66 complete)
102(CanL) – Canadian Literature. Vancouver.
Winter85 thru Fall86 (no 107–110)
104(CASS) – Canadian–American Slavic Studies/Revue canadienne–américaine d'études slaves. Irvine.
Spring–Summer86 (vol 20 no 1/2)
105 – Canadian Poetry. London, Ontario.
Spring/Summer86 & Fall/Winter86 (no 18 & 19)
106 – The Canadian Review of American Studies. Winnipeg.
Spring86 thru Winter86 (vol 17 complete)
107(CRCL) – Canadian Review of Comparative Literature/Revue Canadienne de Littérature Comparée. South Edmonton.
Dec85 thru Dec86 (vol 12 no 4, vol 13 complete)
108 – Canadian Theatre Review. Toronto.
Spring86 thru Winter86 (no 46–49)
110 – Carolina Quarterly. Chapel Hill.
Fall86 thru Spring87 (vol 39 complete)
111 – Cauda Pavonis. Pullman.
Spring87 & Fall87 (vol 6 complete)
112 – Celtica. Dublin.
Vol 18
114(ChiR) – Chicago Review. Chicago.
Vol 35 no 4 [no reviews indexed]
115 – The Centennial Review. East Lansing.
Winter86 thru Fall86 (vol 30 complete)
116 – Chinese Literature: Essays, Articles, Reviews. Madison.
Jul85 (vol 7 complete)

121(CJ) – Classical Journal. Greenville.
Oct–Nov86 thru Apr–May87 (vol 82 complete)
122 – Classical Philology. Chicago.
Jan86 thru Oct86 (vol 81 complete)
123 – Classical Review. Oxford.
Vol 36 complete
124 – Classical World. Pittsburgh.
Sep–Oct86 thru Jul–Aug87 (vol 80 complete)
125 – Clio. Ft. Wayne.
Fall85 thru Summer86 (vol 15 complete)
126(CCC) – College Composition and Communication. Urbana.
Feb86 thru Dec86 (vol 37 complete)
128(CE) – College English. Urbana.
Jan86 thru Oct86 & Dec86 (vol 48 no 1–6 & 8) [Nov86 issue missing]
130 – Comparative Drama. Kalamazoo.
Spring86 thru Winter86/87 (vol 20 complete)
131(CL) – Comparative Literature. Eugene.
Winter86 thru Fall86 (vol 38 complete)
133 – Colloquia Germanica. Bern.
Band 18 Heft 4 & Band 19 complete
134(CP) – Concerning Poetry. Bellingham.
Vol 19
138 – Conjunctions. Boston.
No 9 & no 10
139 – American Craft. New York.
Jun/Jul86 (vol 46 no 3) [all other vol 46 issues missing]
140(CH) – Crítica Hispánica. Johnson City.
Vol 8 no 1 [no reviews indexed]
141 – Criticism. Detroit.
Winter86 thru Fall86 (vol 28 complete)
143 – Current Musicology. New York.
Issue 39 & no 40
145(Crit) – Critique. Washington.
Fall86 thru Spring87 (vol 28 no 1–3)
148 – Critical Quarterly. Manchester.
Spring/Summer86 & Autumn86 (vol 28 no 1/2 & 3)
149(CLS) – Comparative Literature Studies. Urbana.
Spring86 thru Winter86 (vol 23 complete)
150(DR) – Dalhousie Review. Halifax.
Fall85 thru Fall86 (vol 65 no 3 & 4, vol 66 no 1/2 & 3)
151 – Dancemagazine. New York.
Jan86 thru Dec86 (vol 60 complete)
152(UDQ) – The Denver Quarterly. Denver.
Fall86 thru Spring87 (vol 21 no 2–4)
153 – Diacritics. Baltimore.
Spring86, Fall86 & Winter86 (vol 16 no 1, 3 & 4) [Summer86 issue missing]
154 – Dialogue. Waterloo.
Spring86 thru Winter86 (vol 25 complete)
155 – The Dickensian. London.
Spring86 thru Autumn86 (vol 82 complete)
156(ShJW) – Deutsche Shakespeare-Gesellschaft West Jahrbuch. Bochum.
Jahrbuch 1986

157 – Drama/The Quarterly Theatre Review. London.
No 159 thru no 162
158 – Dickens Quarterly. Amherst.
Mar86 thru Dec86 (vol 3 complete)
159 – Diachronica. Hildesheim.
Spring86 & Fall86 (vol 3 complete)
160 – Diálogos. Río Piedras.
Jan86 & Jul86 (vol 21 no 47 & 48)
161(DUJ) – Durham University Journal. Durham.
Dec85 & Jun86 (vol 78 complete)
165(EAL) – Early American Literature. Chapel Hill.
Spring87 thru Vol 22 no 3 (vol 22 complete)
167 – Erkenntnis. Dordrecht.
Jan86 thru Nov86 (vols 24 & 25 complete)
168(ECW) – Essays on Canadian Writing. Toronto.
Summer86 & Fall86 (no 32 & 33)
172(Edda) – Edda. Oslo.
1986/1 thru 1986/4 (vol 86 complete)
173(ECS) – Eighteenth-Century Studies. Northfield.
Fall86 thru Summer87 (vol 20 complete)
174(Éire) – Éire-Ireland. St. Paul.
Spring86 thru Winter86 (vol 21 complete)
175 – English. Oxford.
Spring86 thru Autumn86 (vol 35 complete)
176 – Encounter. London.
Dec86 thru Dec87 (vol 67 no 5, vols 68 & 69 complete)
177(ELT) – English Literature in Transition. Greensboro.
Vol 29 complete
178 – English Studies in Canada. Edmonton.
Mar86 thru Dec86 (vol 12 complete)
179(ES) – English Studies. Lisse.
Feb86 thru Dec86 (vol 67 complete)
181 – Epoch. Ithaca.
Vol 35 no 2 & 3, Vol 36 complete
183(ESQ) – ESQ: A Journal of the American Renaissance. Pullman.
Vol 32 no 1-3
184(EIC) – Essays in Criticism. Oxford.
Jan86 thru Jul86 (vol 36 no 1-3)
185 – Ethics. Chicago.
Oct86 thru Jul87 (vol 97 complete)
186(ETC.) – Etc. San Francisco.
Spring86 thru Winter86 (vol 43 complete)
187 – Ethnomusicology. Ann Arbor.
Winter87 thru Fall87 (vol 31 complete)
188(ECr) – L'Esprit Créateur. Baton Rouge.
Spring86 thru Winter86 (vol 26 complete)
189(EA) – Etudes Anglaises. Paris.
Jul-Sep86 & Jan-Mar87 thru Oct-Dec87 (vol 39 no 3, vol 40 complete)
191(ELN) – English Language Notes. Boulder.
Sep86 thru Jun87 (vol 24 complete)
192(EP) – Les Études Philosophiques. Paris.
Jan-Jun86 thru Oct-Dec86

193(ELit) – Études Littéraires. Québec.
Spring86 thru Winter86/87 (vol 19 complete)
196 – Fabula. Berlin.
Band 27 complete
198 – The Fiddlehead. Fredericton.
Spring86 thru Fall86 (no 147-149)
199 – Field. Oberlin.
Fall86 (no 35) [no reviews indexed]
201 – Fifteenth-Century Studies. Detroit.
Vol 11
203 – Folklore. London.
Vol 97 complete
204(FdL) – Forum der Letteren. Den Haag.
Mar86 thru Dec86 (vol 27 complete)
205(ForL) – Forum Linguisticum. Lake Bluff.
Apr84 (vol 8 no 1)
206(FoLi) – Folia Linguistica. The Hague.
Vol 20 complete
207(FR) – French Review. Champaign.
Oct86 thru May87 (vol 60 complete)
208(FS) – French Studies. London.
Jan86 thru Oct86 (vol 40 complete)
209(FM) – Le Français Moderne. Paris.
Apr86 & Oct86 (vol 54 complete)
210(FrF) – French Forum. Lexington.
Jan86 thru Sep86 (vol 11 complete)
215(GL) – General Linguistics. University Park.
Vol 26 complete
219(GaR) – Georgia Review. Athens.
Spring86 thru Winter86 (vol 40 complete)
220(GL&L) – German Life and Letters. Oxford.
Oct86 thru Jul87 (vol 40 complete) [no reviews indexed]
221(GQ) – German Quarterly. Cherry Hill.
Winter86 thru Fall86 (vol 59 complete)
222(GR) – Germanic Review. Washington.
Winter86 thru Fall86 (vol 61 complete)
223 – Genre. Norman.
Spring86 thru Winter86 (vol 19 complete)
224(GRM) – Germanisch-Romanische Monatsschrift. Heidelberg.
Band 36 complete
228(GSLI) – Giornale storico della letteratura italiana. Torino.
Vol 163 complete
234 – The Hemingway Review. Ada.
Fall86 & Spring87 (vol 6 complete)
236 – The Hiram Poetry Review. Hiram.
Spring-Summer86 & Fall-Winter86/87 (no 40 & 41)
238 – Hispania. University.
Mar86 thru Dec86 (vol 69 complete)
240(HR) – Hispanic Review. Philadelphia.
Winter86 thru Autumn86 (vol 54 complete)
241 – Hispanófila. Chapel Hill.
Jan86 thru Sep86 (no 86-88)
244(HJAS) – Harvard Journal of Asiatic Studies. Cambridge.
Jun86 & Dec86 (vol 46 complete)
249(HudR) – Hudson Review. New York.
Spring86 thru Winter87 (vol 39 complete)

250(HLQ) – The Huntington Library Quarterly. San Marino.
Winter86 thru Autumn86 (vol 49 complete)
257(IRAL) – IRAL: International Review of Applied Linguistics in Language Teaching. Heidelberg.
Feb86 thru Nov86 (vol 24 complete)
258 – International Philosophical Quarterly. New York and Namur.
Mar86 thru Dec86 (vol 26 complete)
259(IIJ) – Indo-Iranian Journal. Dordrecht.
Jan86 thru Oct86 (vol 29 complete)
260(IF) – Indogermanische Forschungen. Berlin.
Band 91
262 – Inquiry. Oslo.
Mar86 thru Dec86 (vol 29 complete)
263(RIB) – Revista Interamericana de Bibliografía/Inter-American Review of Bibliography. Washington.
Vol 36 complete
264(I&L) – Ideologies and Literature. Minneapolis/Valencia.
Vol 2 no 1 [no reviews indexed]
268(IFR) – The International Fiction Review. Fredericton.
Winter87 & Summer87 (vol 14 complete)
269(IJAL) – International Journal of American Linguistics. Chicago.
Jan86 thru Oct86 (vol 52 complete)
271 – The Iowa Review. Iowa City.
Winter86 thru Fall86 (vol 16 complete)
272(IUR) – Irish University Review. Dublin.
Spring86 & Autumn86 (vol 16 complete)
275(IQ) – Italian Quarterly. New Brunswick.
Fall85 thru Summer86 (vol 26 no 102, vol 27 no 103-105)
276 – Italica. Madison.
Spring86 thru Winter86 (vol 63 complete)
278(IS) – Italian Studies. London.
Vol 41
279 – International Journal of Slavic Linguistics and Poetics. Columbus.
Vol 31/32 & Vol 33
284 – The Henry James Review. Baton Rouge.
Winter85, Fall85 thru Spring87 (vol 6 no 2, vols 7 & 8 complete)
285(JapQ) – Japan Quarterly. Tokyo.
Jan-Mar86 thru Oct-Dec86 (vol 33 complete)
287 – Jewish Frontier. New York.
Jan86 thru Oct86 (vol 53 no 1-5)
289 – The Journal of Aesthetic Education. Urbana.
Spring86 thru Winter86 (vol 20 complete)
290(JAAC) – Journal of Aesthetics and Art Criticism. Greenvale.
Fall86 thru Summer87 (vol 45 complete)
292(JAF) – Journal of American Folklore. Washington.
Jan/Mar86 thru Oct/Dec86 (vol 99 complete)

293(JASt) – Journal of Asian Studies. Ann Arbor.
Nov85 thru Aug86 (vol 45 complete)
294 – Journal of Arabic Literature. Leiden.
Vol 17
295(JML) – Journal of Modern Literature. Philadelphia.
Mar86 thru Nov86 (vol 13 complete)
296(JCF) – Journal of Canadian Fiction. Montreal.
No 35/36
297(JL) – Journal of Linguistics. Cambridge.
Mar86 & Sep86 (vol 22 complete)
298 – Journal of Canadian Studies/Revue d'études canadiennes. Peterborough.
Spring86 thru Winter86/87 (vol 21 complete)
300 – Journal of English Linguistics. Whitewater.
Apr86 & Oct86 (vol 19 complete)
301(JEGP) – Journal of English and Germanic Philology. Champaign.
Jan86 thru Oct86 (vol 85 complete)
302 – Journal of Oriental Studies. Hong Kong.
Vol 21 no 2, vol 22 no 1 [entries wholly in Chinese are not indexed]
303(JoHS) – Journal of Hellenic Studies. London.
Vol 106
304(JHP) – Journal of Hispanic Philology. Tallahassee.
Winter86 thru Fall86 (vol 10 no 2 & 3, vol 11 no 1)
305(JIL) – The Journal of Irish Literature. Newark.
Jan86 thru Sep86 (vol 15 complete)
307 – Journal of Literary Semantics. Heidelberg.
Apr86 thru Dec86 (vol 15 complete)
308 – Journal of Music Theory. New Haven.
Spring86 & Fall86 (vol 30 complete)
309 – Journal of Musicological Research. London.
Vol 7 no 1
311(JP) – Journal of Philosophy. New York.
Jan86 thru Dec86 (vol 83 complete)
313 – Journal of Roman Studies. London.
Vol 76
314 – Journal of South Asian Literature. East Lansing.
Winter-Spring86 & Summer-Fall86 (vol 21 complete)
316 – Journal of Symbolic Logic. Pasadena.
Mar86 thru Dec86 (vol 51 complete)
317 – Journal of the American Musicological Society. Philadelphia.
Spring86 thru Fall86 (vol 39 complete)
318(JAOS) – Journal of the American Oriental Society. New Haven.
Jan/Mar85 thru Oct/Dec85 (vol 105 complete)
319 – Journal of the History of Philosophy. St. Louis.
Jan87 thru Oct87 (vol 25 complete)
320(CJL) – Canadian Journal of Linguistics. Ottawa.
Spring86 thru Winter86 (vol 31 complete)

487 — Phoenix. Toronto.
Spring86 & Summer86 (vol 40 no 1 & 2)
488 — Philosophy of the Social Sciences. Waterloo.
Mar86 thru Dec86 (vol 16 complete)
489(PJGG) — Philosophisches Jahrbuch. Freiburg.
Band 93 complete
490 — Poetica. Amsterdam.
Band 18 complete
491 — Poetry. Chicago.
Apr86 thru Mar87 (vols 148 & 149 complete)
493 — Poetry Review. London.
Jun86 & Oct86 (vol 76 no 1/2 & 3)
495(PoeS) — Poe Studies. Pullman.
Jun86 & Dec86 (vol 19 complete)
496 — Poet Lore. Washington.
Spring86 & Summer86 (vol 81 no 1 & 2)
497(PolR) — Polish Review. New York.
Vol 31 complete
498 — Popular Music and Society. Bowling Green.
Vol 10 no 3 [no reviews indexed]
500 — Post Script. Jacksonville.
Fall86 thru Spring/Summer87 (vol 6 complete)
502(PrS) — Prairie Schooner. Lincoln.
Spring86 thru Winter86 (vol 60 complete)
503 — The Private Library. Pinner.
Spring86 thru Autumn86 (vol 9 no 1–3)
505 — Progressive Architecture. Cleveland.
Jan86 thru Dec86 (vol 67 complete)
506(PSt) — Prose Studies. London.
May86 thru Dec86 (vol 9 complete)
507 — Print. New York.
Jan/Feb86 thru Jul/Aug86 & Nov/Dec86 (vol 40 no 1–4 & 6) [issue dated Sep/Oct86 missing]
510 — The Piano Quarterly. Wilmington.
Winter86/87 thru Fall87 (vol 35 complete)
513 — Perspectives of New Music. Seattle.
Fall-Winter85 & Spring-Summer86 (vol 24 complete)
517(PBSA) — Papers of the Bibliographical Society of America. New York.
Vol 80 complete
518 — Philosophical Books. Oxford.
Jan86 thru Oct86 (vol 27 complete)
519(PhS) — Philosophical Studies. Dordrecht.
Jan86 thru Nov86 (vols 49 & 50 complete)
520 — Phronesis. Assen.
Vol 31 complete
521 — Philosophical Investigations. Oxford.
Jan86 thru Oct86 (vol 9 complete)
526 — Quarry. Kingston.
Winter86 thru Autumn86 (vol 35 complete)
529(QQ) — Queen's Quarterly. Kingston.
Spring86 thru Winter86 (vol 93 complete)
532(RCF) — The Review of Contemporary Fiction. Elmwood Park.
Spring86 thru Fall86 (vol 6 complete)

533 — Raritan. New Brunswick.
Summer86 thru Spring87 (vol 6 complete)
534(RALS) — Resources for American Literary Study. College Park.
Spring-Autumn84 (vol 14 complete)
535(RHL) — Revue d'Histoire Littéraire de la France. Paris.
Jan-Feb86 thru Nov-Dec86 (vol 86 complete)
536(Rev) — Review. Charlottesville.
Vol 8
537 — Revue de Musicologie. Paris.
Vol 72 complete
538(RAL) — Research in African Literatures. Austin.
Spring86 thru Winter86 (vol 17 complete)
539 — Renaissance and Reformation/Renaissance et Réforme. Toronto.
Nov86 thru Spring87 (vol 10 no 4, vol 11 no 1 & 2)
540(RIPh) — Revue Internationale de Philosophie. Wetteren.
Vol 40 complete
541(RES) — Review of English Studies. Oxford.
Feb86 thru Nov86 (vol 37 complete)
542 — Revue Philosophique de la France et de l'Étranger. Paris.
Jan-Mar86 thru Oct-Dec86 (vol 176 complete)
543 — Review of Metaphysics. Washington.
Sep86 thru Jun87 (vol 40 complete)
544 — Rhetorica. Berkeley.
Winter86 thru Autumn86 (vol 4 complete)
545(RPh) — Romance Philology. Berkeley.
Aug86 thru May87 (vol 40 complete)
546(RR) — Romanic Review. New York.
Jan86 thru Nov86 (vol 77 complete)
547(RF) — Romanische Forschungen. Frankfurt am Main.
Band 98 complete
548 — Revista Española de Lingüística. Madrid.
Jan-Jun86 & Jul-Dec86 (vol 16 complete)
549(RLC) — Revue de Littérature Comparée. Paris.
Jan-Mar86 thru Oct-Dec86 (vol 60 complete)
550(RusR) — Russian Review. Cambridge.
Jan86 thru Oct86 (vol 45 complete)
551(RenQ) — Renaissance Quarterly. New York.
Spring86 thru Winter86 (vol 39 complete)
552(REH) — Revista de estudios hispánicos. Poughkeepsie.
Jan86 thru Oct86 (vol 20 complete)
553(RLiR) — Revue de Linguistique Romane. Strasbourg.
Jan-Jun86 & Jul-Dec86 (vol 50 complete)
554 — Romania. Paris.
Vol 105 no 4, vol 106 no 1
555 — Revue de Philologie. Paris.
Vol 59 fasc 2
556 — Russell. Hamilton.
Summer86 (vol 6 no 1)

558(RLJ) – Russian Language Journal. East Lansing.
> Winter86 & Spring/Fall86 (vol 40 complete)

559 – Russian Linguistics. Dordrecht.
> Vol 10 complete

560 – Salmagundi. Saratoga Springs.
> Spring-Summer86 & Fall86 (no 70/71 & 72)

561(SFS) – Science-Fiction Studies. Montréal.
> Mar86 thru Nov86 (vol 13 complete)

562(Scan) – Scandinavica. Norwich.
> May86 & Nov86 (vol 25 complete)

563(SS) – Scandinavian Studies. Lawrence.
> Winter86 thru Autumn86 (vol 58 complete)

564 – Seminar. Toronto.
> Feb86 thru Nov86 (vol 22 complete)

565 – Stand Magazine. Newcastle upon Tyne.
> Winter85/86 thru Autumn86 (vol 27 complete)

566 – The Scriblerian. Philadelphia.
> Autumn86 & Spring87 (vol 19 complete)

567 – Semiotica. Amsterdam.
> Vols 59–63 complete

568(SCN) – Seventeenth-Century News. University Park.
> Spring-Summer86 thru Winter86 (vol 44 complete)

569(SR) – Sewanee Review. Sewanee.
> Winter86 thru Fall86 (vol 94 complete)

570(SQ) – Shakespeare Quarterly. Washington.
> Spring86 thru Winter86 (vol 37 complete)

571(ScLJ) – Scottish Literary Journal. Aberdeen.
> May86 thru Winter86 (vol 13 complete & supps 24 & 25)

572 – Shaw: The Annual of Bernard Shaw Studies. University Park.
> Vol 7

573(SSF) – Studies in Short Fiction. Newberry.
> Winter86 thru Fall86 (vol 23 complete)

574(SEEJ) – Slavic and East European Journal. Tucson.
> Spring86 thru Winter86 (vol 30 complete)

575(SEER) – Slavonic and East European Review. London.
> Jan86 thru Oct86 (vol 64 complete)

576 – Journal of the Society of Architectural Historians. Philadelphia.
> Mar86 thru Dec86 (vol 45 complete)

577(SHR) – Southern Humanities Review. Auburn.
> Winter86 thru Fall86 (vol 20 complete)

578 – Southern Literary Journal. Chapel Hill.
> Spring87 & Fall87 (vol 19 no 2, vol 20 no 1)

579(SAQ) – South Atlantic Quarterly. Durham.
> Winter86 thru Autumn86 (vol 85 complete)

580(SCR) – The South Carolina Review. Clemson.
> Fall86 & Spring87 (vol 19 complete)

581 – Southerly. Sydney.
> Mar86 thru Dec86 (vol 46 complete)

583 – Southern Speech Communication Journal. Tampa.
> Fall86 thru Summer87 (vol 52 complete)

584(SWR) – Southwest Review. Dallas.
> Winter86 thru Autumn86 (vol 71 complete)

585(SoQ) – The Southern Quarterly. Hattiesburg.
> Fall86 thru Summer87 (vol 25 complete)

587(SAF) – Studies in American Fiction. Boston.
> Spring86 (vol 14 no 1)

588(SSL) – Studies in Scottish Literature. Columbia.
> Vol 21

589 – Speculum. Cambridge.
> Jan86 thru Oct86 (vol 61 complete)

590 – Studies in the Humanities. Indiana.
> Dec86 & Jun87 (vol 13 no 2, vol 14 no 1)

591(SIR) – Studies in Romanticism. Boston.
> Spring86 thru Winter86 (vol 25 complete)

592 – Studio International. London.
> Vol 199 complete

593 – Symposium. Washington.
> Spring86 thru Winter86/87 (vol 40 complete)

594 – Studies in the Novel. Denton.
> Spring86 thru Winter86 (vol 18 complete)

595(ScS) – Scottish Studies. Edinburgh.
> Vol 28

596(SL) – Studia Linguistica. Malmö.
> Vol 40 complete

597(SN) – Studia Neophilologica. Stockholm.
> Vol 58 complete

598(SoR) – The Southern Review. Baton Rouge.
> Winter87 thru Autumn87 (vol 23 complete)

599 – Style. De Kalb.
> Spring86 thru Winter86 (vol 20 complete)

600 – Simiolus. Utrecht.
> Vol 16 complete

601(SuF) – Sinn und Form. Berlin.
> Jul-Aug85 thru Nov-Dec86 (vol 37 no 4-6, vol 38 complete)

602 – Sprachkunst. Vienna.
> Band 17 complete

603 – Studies in Language. Amsterdam.
> Vol 10 complete

604 – Spenser Newsletter. Chapel Hill.
> Winter86 thru Fall86 (vol 17 complete)

605(SC) – Stendhal Club. Grenoble.
> 15Oct86 thru 15Jul87 (vol 29 complete)

606 – Synthese. Dordrecht.
> Jan86 thru Oct86 & Dec86 (vols 66–68 complete, vol 69 no 1 & 3) [Nov86 issue missing]

607 – Tempo. London.
> Mar86 thru Dec86 (no 156–159)

Each year we are unable (for one reason or another) to index the reviews appearing in all of the periodicals scanned. The following is a list of the periodicals whose reviews were not included in this volume of the Index. Every attempt will be made to index these reviews in the next volume of the Index:

36 – The Americas Review. Houston.
70 – American Notes and Queries. Owings-ville.
127 – Art Journal. New York.
136 – Conradiana. Lubbock.
142 – Philosophy and Social Criticism. Chestnut Hill.
162(TDR) – The Drama Review. Cambridge.
202(FMod) – Filología Moderna. Madrid.
214 – Gambit. London.
229 – Gnomon. München.
239 – Hispanic Linguistics. Pittsburgh.
261 – Indian Linguistics. Pune.
283 – Jabberwocky – The Journal of the Lewis Carroll Society. Burton-on-Trent.
299 – Journal of Beckett Studies. London.
310 – The Journal of Musicology. Berkeley.
339(KSMB) – The Keats-Shelley Memorial Assn. Bulletin. Heslington.
359 – Linguistics and Philosophy. Dor-drecht.
367(L&P) – Literature and Psychology. Normal.
445 – Nineteenth-Century Literature. Berkeley.
457(NRFH) – Nueva Revista de Filología Hispánica. Mexico City.
459 – Obsidian II. Raleigh.
464 – Orbis. Louvain.
469 – Parabola. New York.
471 – Pantheon. München.
472 – Parnassus: Poetry in Review. New York.
508 – Prooftexts. Baltimore.
511 – Plays and Players. London.
582(SFQ) – Southern Folklore Quarterly. Gainesville.
608 – TESOL Quarterly. Washington.
678(YCGL) – Yearbook of Comparative and General Literature. Bloomington.
701(SinN) – Sin Nombre. San Juan.
702 – Shakespeare Studies. New York.

Achebe, C. Anthills of the Savannah.
  E. Battersby, 362:15Oct87–29
  D. Pryce–Jones, 617(TLS):9–15Oct87–
  1106
Acheson, T.W. Saint John.
  W.T. Matthews, 529(QQ):Autumn86–713
Achinstein, P. The Nature of Explanation.*
  D–H. Ruben, 84:Sep86–377
Achinstein, P. & O. Hannaway, eds. Obser-
  vation, Experiment and Hypothesis in
  Modern Physical Science.
  T.C. Holyoke, 42(AR):Winter86–117
  T.H. Maddock, 63:Dec86–533
  R. Woller, 543:Dec86–365
Achtert, W.S. & J. Gibaldi – see "The MLA
  Style Manual"
Acker, B. El cuento mexicano contempo-
  ráneo.
  H.L. Rosser, 238:Mar86–116
Ackerley, C. & L.J. Clipper. A Companion
  to "Under the Volcano."*
  A. Blayac, 189(EA):Apr–Jun87–237
  P.M. St. Pierre, 168(ECW):Fall86–190
Ackerley, J.R. My Dog Tulip.
  E. Hawes, 441:8Feb87–9
  P. Parker, 362:12Nov87–29
Ackerman, R.W. & R. Dahood, eds & trans.
  Ancrene Riwle. (Introduction & Pt 1)
  L. Georgianna, 589:Oct86–1014
Ackermann, R.J. Data, Instruments, and
  Theory.
  J. Woodward, 486:Sep86–455
Ackert, P. Please Write.
  T. Plaister, 399(MLJ):Winter86–450
Ackroyd, P. Chatterton.
  R. Christiansen, 362:10Sep87–22
  M. Dodsworth, 617(TLS):11–17Sep87–976
Ackroyd, P. The Diversions of Purley.
  M. Ford, 617(TLS):20–26Nov87–1276
Ackroyd, P. T.S. Eliot.*
  W. Harmon, 569(SR):Summer86–510
Ackroyd, P. Hawksmoor.*
  P. Lewis, 565:Spring86–38
  42(AR):Spring86–252
"Actes du colloque international de
  Valenciennes, 1983."
  A. Pagès, 535(RHL):Nov–Dec86–1145
"Actes du VIIIe Congrès des Romanistes
  scandinaves."
  P. Larthomas, 209(FM):Apr86–124
Adachi, B.C. Backstage at Bunraku.
  K. Brazell, 407(MN):Spring86–124
Adam, H. & K. Moodley. South Africa With-
  out Apartheid.*
  P.B., 185:Apr87–708
  D.F. Gordon, 385(MQR):Summer87–553
Adam, J. Employment and Wage Policies in
  Poland, Czechoslovakia and Hungary since
  1950.*
  J.L. Porket, 575(SEER):Apr86–309
Adam, P. Eileen Gray.
  P. Goldberger, 441:6Dec87–22
Adam de la Halle. The Lyrics and Melodies
  of Adam de la Halle. (D.H. Nelson, ed &
  trans)
  N. Wilkins, 208(FS):Jul86–312
Adamova, A.T. & L.T. Gyuzalian. Miniatyuri
  rukopisi poemi Shahnama 1333 goda.
  B.W. Robinson, 463:Winter86/87–413
Adams, A. Return Trips.*
  M. Boruch, 434:Autumn86–98

Adams, A., ed & trans. The Romance of
  Yder.*
  B.N. Sargent–Baur, 589:Jan86–118
Adams, A. Trees in Sheep Country.
  J. Mole, 176:Mar87–59
Adams, A., with M.S. Alinder. Ansel
  Adams.* (British title: An Autobiogra-
  phy.)
  M.L. Kotz, 55:Sep86–37
  H. Martin, 507:Mar/Apr86–122
Adams, C. American Lithographers, 1900–
  1960.
  B. Reilly, 658:Spring86–90
Adams, C.L. – see Waters, F.
Adams, D. Dirk Gently's Holistic Detective
  Agency.
  M. Coward, 362:25Jun87–29
Adams, D.J. Diderot, Dialogue and Debate.
  R. Niklaus, 83:Autumn86–292
Adams, D.W. & E.J. Deveau. Coping with
  Childhood Cancer.
  P.R. Galbraith, 529(QQ):Spring86–190
Adams, E.C.L. Tales of the Congaree.
  (R.G. O'Meally, ed)
  V.W. Wesley, 441:11Oct87–56
Adams, G. Dancing on Coral.
  R. Friedman, 441:24May87–12
Adams, H. The Letters of Henry Adams.
  (Vols 1–3) (J.C. Levenson & others, eds)
  L. Willson, 569(SR):Winter86–131
Adams, H. Philosophy of the Literary
  Symbolic.*
  S. Bagchee, 405(MP):Nov86–239
  W. Keach, 340(KSJ):Vol35–213
Adams, H. When Rich Men Die.
  P–L. Adams, 61:Jul87–98
Adams, J. The Financing of Terror.*
  S. Bakhash, 453(NYRB):24Sep87–12
  L. Robinson, 441:1Feb87–21
Adams, J.C. Sir Charles God Damn.
  B.N.S. Gooch, 376:Dec86–143
  T. Ware, 105:Fall/Winter86–117
Adams, R.J.Q. & P.P. Poirier. The Con-
  scription Controversy in Great Britain
  1900–18.
  J. Ramsden, 617(TLS):10Jul87–738
Adams, R.M. The Land and Literature of
  England.
  E.G. Stanley, 447(N&Q):Mar85–89
Adams, W. & J.W. Brock. The Bigness Com-
  plex.
  R. Lekachman, 441:11Jan87–10
Adamson, G. My Pride and Joy.
  B. Webster, 441:30Aug87–27
Adamson, J. Graham Greene and Cinema.
  H–P. Breuer, 395(MFS):Winter86–665
Adamson, M.J. Not Till a Hot January.
  N. Callendar, 441:3May87–46
Adcock, F., ed. The Faber Book of Twen-
  tieth–Century Women's Poetry.
  B. Hardy, 617(TLS):29May87–574
Adcock, F. The Incident Book.
  S. Dobyns, 441:18Oct87–46
  M. Hofmann, 617(TLS):13Feb87–165
  J. Mole, 176:Mar87–62
Adcock, F., ed. The Oxford Book of Contem-
  porary New Zealand Poetry.
  B. King, 577(SHR):Winter86–94
Addison, L. Letters from Latvia. (R.
  Chave, ed)
  V.L. Smith, 617(TLS):17Jul87–761

Addiss, S., ed. Japanese Ghosts and Demons.
    L. Fenwick, 60:Sep–Oct86–131
Addiss, S. The World of Kameda Bōsai.*
    B. Sweet, 60:Sep–Oct86–129
Adereth, M. Aragon.
    C. Geoghegan, 402(MLR):Oct87–979
    S.B. John, 208(FS):Oct86–488
Adkins, A.W.H. Poetic Craft in the Early Greek Elegists.
    J. Herington, 124:Jan–Feb87–226
Adler, D.R. Thomas Dekker.
    M.R. Woodhead, 447(N&Q):Dec85–521
Adler, J. The Jews of Paris and the Final Solution.
    H.R. Lottman, 441:20Sep87–24
Adler, K. Manet.
    P–L. Adams, 61:Mar87–95
Adler, L. It Ain't Necessarily So.
    P. Bloom, 441:28Jun87–25
Adler, M.J. A Guidebook to Learning.
    639(VQR):Summer86–104
Adler, R. Reckless Disregard.*
    R. Dworkin, 453(NYRB):26Feb87–27
Adler, W. Landscapes.
    C. White, 380:Summer86–249
Adorno, F. & others. Protagora, Antifonte, Posidonio, Aristotele.
    J. Barnes, 520:Vol31No2–183
Adorno, T.W. Aesthetic Theory.* (G. Adorno & R. Tiedemann, eds)
    R. Geuss, 311(JP):Dec86–732
    J.M. Hodge, 89(BJA):Winter86–79
    M.T. Jones, 221(GQ):Summer86–464
    W.G. Regier, 400(MLN):Apr86–705
    H.L. Shapiro, 482(PhR):Apr86–288
Adrian, A.A. Dickens and the Parent–Child Relationship.*
    S. Hudson, 577(SHR):Winter86–74
Advani, R. E.M. Forster as Critic.
    E. Heine, 395(MFS):Summer86–317
    K.M. Newton, 89(BJA):Winter86–88
Aélion, R. Euripide héritier d'Eschyle.
    A. Lebeau, 555:Vol59fasc2–277
Aelius Aristides. The Complete Works. (Vol 2) (C.A. Behr, ed & trans)
    A.H.M. Kessels, 394:Vol39fasc1/2–174
Aers, D. Chaucer.
    B. O'Donoghue, 617(TLS):29May87–587
Aeschylus. Septem contra Thebas. (G.O. Hutchinson, ed)
    A.F. Garvie, 123:Vol36No2–191
    W.G. Thalmann, 124:Jul–Aug87–462
Affron, C. Cinema and Sentiment.
    I.C. Jarvie, 488:Jun86–265
Affron, M.J. & E. Rubinstein. The Last Metro.
    E. Benson, 207(FR):May87–896
"After Apocalypse." (D.G. Goodman, trans)
    T.T. Takaya, 407(MN):Winter86–514
"After the War Was Over."*
    639(VQR):Spring86–63
Agard, F.B. A Course in Romance Linguistics.* (Vols 1 & 2)
    S. Fleischman & J.S. Turley, 350:Dec87–895
    C. López-Morillas, 238:Sep86–563
    Y. Malkiel, 215(GL):Vol26No1–38
Agde, G. – see Geschonneck, E.
Agee, J. James Agee: Selected Journalism. (P. Ashdown, ed)
    K. Byrd, 585(SoQ):Winter87–143

Agee, P. On the Run.
    T. Powers, 441:2Aug87–7
Agha, S.A. T.S. Eliot as Editor.
    G.W. Clift, 389(MQ):Winter87–283
Agheana, I.T. The Prose of Jorge Luis Borges.*
    D.L. Shaw, 86(BHS):Oct86–380
Agius, P. Ackermann's Regency Furniture and Interiors.
    F. Collard, 39:Jan86–66
    G.J. Stops, 90:Jul86–517
Agnew, J–C. Worlds Apart.
    125:Winter86–237
Agosin, M. Pablo Neruda.
    H. Galilea, 295(JML):Nov86–517
Agrawal, M.M. The Philosophy of Non-Attachment.
    M. Mehta, 318(JAOS):Apr/Jun85–382
Agrawal, O.P. Conservation of Manuscripts and Paintings of South-east Asia.
    U. Roberts, 60:Mar–Apr86–123
Aguilar Piñal, F. La biblioteca de Jovellanos (1778).
    J.H.R. Polt, 240(HR):Winter86–98
Aguilera-Malta, D. Babelandia.
    L.A. Díez, 238:Sep86–555
Aguirre, J.M. – see de Valdivielso, J.
Aharoni, A. The Second Exodus.
    L. Goldman, 390:Feb86–61
Aharoni, A. & T. Wolf. Thea.
    L. Goldman, 390:Apr86–63
Ahearn, B. Zukofsky's "A."*
    G. Clarke, 447(N&Q):Dec85–557
Ahl, F. Metaformations.
    N. Gross, 124:Jan–Feb87–219
    S.J. Harrison, 123:Vol36No2–236
    N. Horsfall, 313:Vol76–322
    B.R. Nagle, 121(CJ):Apr–May87–340
Ahlberg-Cornell, G. Herakles and the Sea-Monster in Attic Black-Figure Vase-Painting.
    J. Boardman, 123:Vol36No1–166
    S. Woodford, 303(JoHS):Vol106–259
Ahlbrecht, W.H. Paul Celans späte Gedichte.
    H. Bekker, 221(GQ):Fall86–634
Ahlstrom, S.E. & J.S. Carey, eds. An American Reformation.
    A. Delbanco, 432(NEQ):Jun86–285
Ahmad, A. Agricultural Stagnation Under Population Pressure.
    J.P. Thorp, 293(JASt):Aug86–789
Ahmad, K. & others. Computers, Language Learning and Language Teaching.
    J. Walz, 207(FR):Mar87–567
Ahmad, V. & R. Amjad. The Management of Pakistan's Economy, 1947–1982.
    I–D. Pal, 293(JASt):May86–621
Ai. Sin.*
    A. Ostriker, 491:Jan87–231
Aiken, J. Deception.
    R. Kaveney, 617(TLS):31Jul87–817
Aikin, J.P. German Baroque Drama.*
    R.E. Schade, 406:Fall86–395
Aikins, S. petals on the stream.
    404:Autumn86–56
Airal, J–C. & M. Rieuneau – see Martin du Gard, R.
"Les Aires de la Chanson Québécoise."
    M. Lacombe, 102(CanL):Spring86–147
Aitken, M. A Girdle Round the Earth.
    J. Crowley, 362:14May87–30

3

Aitken, W.R. Scottish Literature in English and Scots.*
   J.H. Alexander, 677(YES):Vol16-231
Aiton, E.J. Leibniz.
   G.H.R. Parkinson, 706:Band18Heft1-101
   C.L. Reid, 518:Oct86-216
Ajami, F. The Vanished Imam.*
   D.C. Gordon, 42(AR):Fall86-486
Ajami, M. The Neckveins of Winter.
   J.C. Bürgel, 318(JAOS):Oct/Dec85-740
Akello, G. Iteso Thought Patterns in Tales.
   J. Lamphear, 538(RAL):Summer86-298
Akenson, D.H. A Protestant in Purgatory.
   R.S. Pomeroy, 544:Winter86-72
Akiyama, N. & C. Japanese at a Glance.
   Y-H. Tohsaku, 399(MLJ):Summer86-191
van den Akker, W.J. Een dichter schreit niet.
   J. Goedegebuure, 204(FdL):Sep86-226
Akmajian, A., R.A. Demers & R.M. Harnish. Linguistics.* (2nd ed)
   R. Penny, 402(MLR):Jan86-153
Akrigg, G.P.V. - see King James VI & I
Akšina, A.A. & N.I. Formanovskaja. Etiket russkogo pis'ma.
   L.A. Kozlik, 558(RLJ):Winter86-219
Akšina, A.A. & N.I. Formanovskaja. Russkij rečevoj ètiket.
   L.A. Kozlik, 558(RLJ):Winter86-221
Aksyonov, V. In Search of Melancholy Baby.
   R. Lingeman, 441:19Jul87-5
Alain-Fournier. The Lost Domain: Le Grand Meaulnes.* Towards the Lost Domain. (W.J. Strachan, ed & trans) Lettres au petit B. Lettres à sa famille. Le Grand Meaulnes. Miracles. Le Grand Meaulnes; Miracles.
   R. Gibson, 617(TLS):3Apr87-363
Alas, L. Clarín, Treinta relatos. (C. Richmond, ed)
   F. García Sarriá, 86(BHS):Jan86-106
Alas, L. La Regenta. (M. Baquero Goyanes, ed)
   E.A. Southworth, 86(BHS):Jan86-104
Alas, L. La Regenta. (J. Oleza, ed)
   N.M. Valis, 86(BHS):Jan86-103
Alas, L. La Regenta.* (J. Rutherford, trans)
   M. Mudrick, 249(HudR):Spring86-141
   N.M. Valis, 86(BHS):Jan86-102
   N.M. Valis, 396(ModA):Summer/Fall86-333
Albarosa, N. & others. Amilcare Ponchielli 1834-1886.
   J. Budden, 410(M&L):Oct86-433
Albert, G. Goten in Konstantinopel.
   J.H.W.G. Liebeschuetz, 123:Vol36No1-157
Alberts, L. Tempting Fate.
   D. Kirk, 441:7Jun87-30
   442(NY):20Jul87-91
Alborg, C. Temas y técnicas en la narrativa de Jesús Fernández Santos.
   D.K. Herzberger, 240(HR):Autumn86-489
Albrecht, D. Designing Dreams.*
   A. Saint, 617(TLS):25-31Dec87-1425
Albrecht, E. & G. Asser - see Kondakow, N.I.
Albrecht, M. - see Wolff, C.
Albright, D. Tennyson.*
   R.B. Martin, 453(NYRB):22Oct87-17

Alburger, M.A. Scottish Fiddlers and Their Music.
   H.R.N. Macdonald, 187:Winter87-134
Alciati, A. Alciato: "Emblemas." (S. Sebastián, ed)
   D.A.I., 48:Jul-Sep86-348
Alciati, A. Andreas Alciatus: "Index Emblematicus." (Vol 1 ed by P.M. Daly & V. Callahan, with S. Cuttler; Vol 2 ed by P.M. Daly, with S. Cuttler)
   S. Gottlieb, 365:Spring/Summer86-181
   J.B. Trapp, 617(TLS):14Aug87-879
Alcock, A. - see Isaac the Presbyter
Alcosser, S. A Fish to Feed All Hunger.*
   A. Ostriker, 491:Jan87-231
Alcott, L.M. The Selected Letters of Louisa May Alcott. (J. Myerson & D. Shealy, eds)
   P-L. Adams, 61:Nov87-123
   B.L. Packer, 441:25Oct87-45
Alcuin. The Bishops, Kings, and Saints of York.* (P. Godman, ed)
   A.B.E. Hood, 123:Vol36No1-52
Alden, J.R. George Washington.
   P. Marshall, 83:Autumn86-214
Alderson, A.D. & F. Iz - see "The Oxford Turkish-English Dictionary"
Aldiss, B.W. The Year Before Yesterday.
   G. Jonas, 441:7Jun87-18
Aldridge, A.O. Thomas Paine's American Ideology.*
   R. Asselineau, 549(RLC):Apr-Jun86-240
   J.D. Krugler, 125:Fall85-95
Aldridge, J.W. The American Novel and the Way We Live Now.*
   E. Pifer, 402(MLR):Oct87-942
Alegre Cudós, J.L. La alegre noche de don Francisco de Goya y de Quevedo.
   J.C. Wilcox, 238:May86-313
Alegría, F. Changing Centuries.
   S. White, 448:Vol24No1-110
Aleichem, S. From the Fair. (C. Leviant, ed and trans)
   H. Schmelzer, 390:Oct86-57
Aleixandre, V. A Bird of Paper.
   A. Bush, 403(MLS):Summer86-341
Aleksandrov, V.A. Obychnoe pravo krepostnoi derevni Rossii XVIII-nachalo XIX v.
   P. Kolchin, 550(RusR):Oct86-439
Alekseev, M.P. Mnogojazyčie i literaturnoe tvorčestvo.
   G. Schaarschmidt, 107(CRCL):Mar86-101
Alekseev, M.P. Sravnitel'noe literaturovedenie. (G.V. Stepanov, ed)
   C. & M. Mervaud, 535(RHL):Sep-Oct86-964
Aleksić, B., ed. La Poésie surréaliste de Yougoslavie.
   L. Kovacs, 450(NRF):Feb86-115
Aler, J., ed. duitse kroniek.
   U.K. Goldsmith, 222(GR):Summer86-135
Alexakis, E.P. The Bride-price.
   F.K. Litsas, 292(JAF):Oct/Dec86-476
Alexander, C. The Early Writings of Charlotte Brontë.*
   W.A. Craik, 447(N&Q):Dec85-535
   K. Sutherland, 402(MLR):Oct87-927
Alexander, C., with others. The Production of Houses.*
   P. Tabor, 46:Feb86-86

Alexander, G.I. Fortis and Lenis in Germanic.*
  A. Braun, 685(ZDL):2/1986–239
  A. Liberman, 215(GL):Vol26No2–144
Alexander, I.W. French Literature and the Philosophy of Consciousness. (A.J.L. Busst, ed)
  C. Smith, 402(MLR):Jan87–195
Alexander, J.H. & D. Hewitt, eds. Scott and his Influence.
  I. Campbell, 588(SSL):Vol21–318
Alexander, J.J.G. & E. Temple. Illuminated Manuscripts in Oxford College Libraries, the University Archives and The Taylor Institution.
  F. Chevillet, 189(EA):Oct–Dec87–462
  78(BC):Summer86–145
Alexander, J.W. Ranulf of Chester.
  J.A. Meisel, 589:Jul86–615
Alexander, M. Old English Literature.*
  J. Roberts, 402(MLR):Apr87–434
Alexander, P. Roy Campbell.
  C.J. Rawson, 677(YES):Vol16–360
Alexander, P. Ideas, Qualities and Corpuscles.
  E. Matthews, 479(PhQ):Jul86–420
  J. Somerville, 518:Oct86–211
  J.W. Yolton, 173(ECS):Winter86/87–235
Alexander, P. – see Campbell, R.
Alexander, R.J. Das deutsche Barockdrama.
  J.P. Aikin, 221(GQ):Summer86–477
Alexander, R.M. The Collins Encyclopedia of Animal Biology.
  J. Serpell, 617(TLS):16Jan87–70
Alexander, T. A Little of All These.
  V.L. Smith, 617(TLS):17Jul87–761
Alexander, T.G. Mormonism in Transition.
  C.S. Peterson, 250(HLQ):Autumn86–421
Alexander, Z. & A. Dewjee, eds. Wonderful Adventures of Mrs. Seacole in Many Lands.
  K. Williamson, 541(RES):Feb86–113
Alexander of Aphrodisias. Alexander of Aphrodisias on Fate.* (R.W. Sharples, ed and trans)
  R.B. Todd, 41:Fall85–341
Alexander of Aphrodisias. Alexandre d'Aphrodise: "Traité du destin." (P. Thillet, ed & trans)
  R.W. Sharples, 123:Vol36No1–33
Alexandrescu, S., F. Drijkoningen & W. Noomen – see van den Boogaard, N.
Alexandrov, V.E. Andrei Bely.
  M.B., 295(JML):Nov86–444
  J.D. Elsworth, 402(MLR):Apr87–537
  D.E. Peterson, 395(MFS):Summer86–329
  R.E. Peterson, 574(SEEJ):Summer86–291
Alexiadis, M. The Greek Variants of the Dragon-Slaying Hero.
  F.K. Litsas, 292(JAF):Oct/Dec86–476
Alexiou, S. Basileios Digenēs Akritēs (kata to cheirographo toy Eskorial) kai to Asma toy Armoyrē.
  R. Beaton, 303(JoHS):Vol106–271
Alfieri, V. Scritti politici e morali. (Vol 3) (C. Mazzotta, ed)
  A. Battistini, 276:Spring86–59
Alföldi, G. Römische Statuen in Venetia et Histria.
  M.A.R. Colledge, 123:Vol36No2–343

Alföldy, G. The Social History of Rome. (German title: Römische Sozialgeschichte.)
  R.K. Sherk, 124:Mar–Apr87–320
  M.S. Spurr, 123:Vol36No2–331
Alfonsi, F. Poeti Italo-Americani/Italo-American Poets.
  R.B. Green, 276:Winter86–395
Alfonso X. Calila e Dimna.* (J.M. Cacho Blecua & M.J. Lacarra, eds)
  J.E. Keller, 86(BHS):Oct86–366
  L. Mendia Vozzo, 379(MedR):Apr86–154
Alfonso XI. Libro de la montería – Based on Escorial MS Y-II-19.* (D.P. Seniff, ed)
  P.E. Russell, 345:Nov86–503
Alford, C.F. Science and the Revenge of Nature.
  D.R., 185:Jan87–500
Alford, J.A. & D.P. Seniff. Literature and Law in the Middle Ages.*
  M.N. Pavlović, 402(MLR):Jul86–697
  R.J. Schoeck, 191(ELN):Mar87–68
Alfroy, J–M. Le Professeur est nu.
  R.J.B. Maples, 207(FR):Mar87–553
Ali, A.S. T.S. Eliot as Editor.
  R.S. Kennedy, 295(JML):Nov86–461
Ali, M.J. Scheherazade in England.
  M. Manzalaoui, 677(YES):Vol16–334
Ali, S. The Fall of a Sparrow.
  J. Buxton, 617(TLS):2–8Oct87–1087
Ali, T. Street Fighting Years.
  S. Khilnani, 617(TLS):27Nov–3Dec87–1312
  C. Sigal, 362:12Nov87–30
Alifano, R. Twenty-Four Conversations with Borges, Including a Selection of Poems.
  E. Skinner, 395(MFS):Winter86–647
Alighieri, D. – see under Dante Alighieri
Aline, Countess of Romanones. The Spy Wore Red.
  M. Gross, 441:21Jun87–10
  442(NY):1Jun87–111
Alinei, M. & others – see "Atlas Linguarum Europae (ALE)"
Alink, M.J. De Vogels van Aristophanes.
  W. Kassies, 394:Vol39fasc3/4–475
Alissandratos, J. Medieval Slavic and Patristic Eulogies.
  F.C.M. Wigzell, 575(SEER):Jan86–126
Alkazi, R. Ancient Indian Costume.
  M.W. Meister, 318(JAOS):Oct/Dec85–806
Al Khalifa, H.A. & M. Rice, eds. Bahrain Through the Ages.
  M. Roaff, 617(TLS):20Feb87–193
Alkire, L.G., Jr., ed. Periodical Title Abbreviations. (5th ed)
  K.B. Harder, 424:Dec86–405
Allain, L. Dostoievski et l'Autre.*
  M.V. Jones, 575(SEER):Oct86–594
Allain, M. & P. Souvestre. The Silent Executioner.
  P–L. Adams, 61:Sep87–102
Allaire, S. Le Modèle syntaxique des systèmes corrélatifs.*
  A. Lorian, 545(RPh):Nov86–238
Allan, G. The Importances of the Past.
  C.M. Sherover, 543:Mar87–559
Allan, P. & others – see Helvétius, C.A.
Allan, S. The Heir and the Sage.
  K–C. Chang, 318(JAOS):Jan/Mar85–175

5

Allan, T. Don't You Know Anybody Else?
P. Demers, 102(CanL):Winter85-163
Allanbrook, W.J. Rhythmic Gesture in
Mozart.*
C. Ford, 411:Mar86-108
Allegretto, M. Death on the Rocks.
N. Callendar, 441:30Aug87-29
442(NY):19Oct87-122
Allen, A.T. Satire and Society in Wil-
helmine Germany.
E.F. Timms, 402(MLR):Jan87-252
H. Zohn, 301(JEGP):Apr86-312
Allen, B. Francis Hayman.
G. Reynolds, 617(TLS):21Aug87-902
Allen, B., M. Kittel & K.J. Jewell, eds.
The Defiant Muse: Italian Feminist Poems
from the Middle Ages to the Present.
D. Ackerman, 441:3May87-38
Allen, C. - see Kipling, R.
Allen, D. Finally Truffaut.*
J. Forbes, 707:Winter85/86-68
Allen, D. & B. Jay, eds. Critics: 1840-
1880.
J.F. Scott, 637(VS):Autumn86-144
Allen, D.E. The Botanists.
D. King-Hele, 617(TLS):6Mar87-239
Allen, E. Territories.
G. Johnston, 298:Fall86-133
Allen, E. A Woman's Place in the Novels of
Henry James.*
P. Boumelha, 301(JEGP):Apr86-290
A. Trodd, 366:Autumn86-263
Allen, E.D., & others. ¿Habla español? An
Introductory Course. (3rd ed)
A. Dias, 238:Mar86-124
R.H. Gilmore, 399(MLJ):Winter86-437
Allen, E.D., T. Méndez-Faith & M.M. Gill.
¿Habla español? Essentials. (3rd ed)
C.M. Cherry, 399(MLJ):Winter86-439
Allen, F., E. Antczak & P. Shea. Vermont
Trout Streams.
K.B. Harder, 424:Mar86-121
Allen, G.W. The New Walt Whitman Hand-
book.
R. Asselineau, 189(EA):Jul-Sep87-371
E. Folsom, 646(WWR):Spring87-32
Allen, G.W. The Solitary Singer.
E. Folsom, 646(WWR):Spring87-32
Allen, G.W. & R. Asselineau. St. John de
Crevecoeur.
A. Delbanco, 441:13Sep87-35
Allen, I.L. The Language of Ethnic Con-
flict.*
J.C. Scott, 35(AS):Summer86-172
Allen, J.J. The Reconstruction of a
Spanish Golden Age Playhouse.*
C. Bandera, 552(REH):May86-134
C. Davis, 611(TN):Vol40No1-44
D. Fox, 400(MLN):Mar86-434
J.M. Ruano de la Haza, 402(MLR):Apr86-
509
J.E. Varey, 86(BHS):Apr86-163
Allen, J.L. Yeats's Epitaph.
A. Parkin, 675(YER):Vol8No1/2-137
Allen, M.D. The Faust Legend.
A.J. Swensen, 395(MFS):Summer86-334
Allen, M.J.B. Marsilio Ficino and the
Phaedran Charioteer.
L. Panizza, 278(IS):Vol41-116
Allen, M.J.B. The Platonism of Marsilio
Ficino.*
C.H. Clough, 402(MLR):Jul87-753
[continued]

[continuing]
A.B. Collins, 589:Oct86-884
J. Kraye, 319:Oct87-596
L. Panizza, 278(IS):Vol41-116
J.A. Quitslund, 604:Winter86-3
R.B. Waddington, 276:Spring86-62
Allen, M.J.B. & K. Muir - see Shakespeare,
W.
Allen, O.E. Gardening with the New Small
Plants.
A. Lacy, 441:31May87-14
Allen, P. The Concept of Woman.
M.E. Irwin, 627(UTQ):Fall86-84
M. Tiles, 483:Jul86-414
Allen, P.G., ed. Studies in American
Indian Literature.
A. Krupat, 447(N&Q):Sep85-431
Allen, R.C. Symbolic Experience.
R.G. Havard, 86(BHS):Apr86-180
Allen, R.C. & D. Gomery. Film History.
T. Elsaesser, 707:Autumn86-246
Allen, R.E. The Attalid Kingdom.*
A.J.L. van Hooff, 394:Vol39fasc3/4-529
Allen, R.E. Plato's "Parmenides."*
P. Thom, 63:Mar86-117
Allen, R.F. Literary Life in German
Expressionism and the Berlin Circles.
R.C. Reimer, 406:Fall86-415
Allen, R.F. A Stylo-Statistical Study of
"Adolphe."
C.P. Courtney, 208(FS):Apr86-218
Allen, R.R., ed. The Pocket Oxford Dic-
tionary. (7th ed)
M. Benson, 603:Vol10No1-265
Allen, T.B. War Games.
W. Mendl, 362:26Nov87-32
Allen, T.B. & N. Polmar. Ship of Gold.
N. Callendar, 441:7Jun87-25
Allen, W.R. Walker Percy.
M. Pearson, 578:Spring87-108
Allen-Weber, K. & M-L. Mauger. Raconte-
moi tout!
K.E. Kintz, 207(FR):Dec86-305
Allende, I. The House of the Spirits.*
(German title: Das Geisterhaus.)
H. Herlinghaus, Jr., 654(WB):2/1986-296
K. Laabs, 601(SuF):Jul-Aug86-888
S. White, 448:Vol24No1-110
Allende, I. Of Love and Shadows.* (Span-
ish title: De amor y de sombra.)
A. Beevor, 617(TLS):10Jul87-740
G.H. Bell-Villada, 441:12Jul87-23
L. Heron, 362:17Sep87-25
J. Updike, 442(NY):24Aug87-84
Allerton, D.J. Valency and the English
Verb.
A. Kakouriotis, 257(IRAL):Feb86-80
T. Thrane, 603:Vol10No2-485
Allison, H.E. Kant's Transcendental Ideal-
ism.*
J.V. Buroker, 449:Dec86-577
R. Meerbote, 53(AGP):Band68Heft3-319
R.B. Pippin, 342:Band77Heft3-365
Allison, L. Right Principles.*
J.P. Day, 518:Jan86-61
"The Alliterative Morte Arthure." (V.
Krishna, trans)
M. Mills, 402(MLR):Oct87-910
Allman, T.D. Miami.
J.A. Lukas, 441:10May87-12
Allnutt, G. Beginning the Avocado.
J. O'Grady, 617(TLS):18-24Sep87-1024

Alloula, M. The Colonial Harem.
C. Shloss, 441:11Jan87-24
"Almanach Banlieue."
A. Prévos, 207(FR):Oct86-152
Almansi, G. & C. Béguin, eds. Theatre of
Sleep.*
362:27Aug87-22
Almansi, G. & S. Henderson. Harold Pinter.
S.H. Gale, 397(MD):Mar86-143
P. Miles, 447(N&Q):Dec85-547
Almeida, J., S.C. Mohler & R.R. Stinson.
Descubrir y crear. (3rd ed)
C.L. McKay, 399(MLJ):Winter86-441
Almon, B. Deep North.*
G. Johnston, 298:Fall86-133
B. Whiteman, 526:Summer86-98
Alon, G. The Jews in their Land in the
Talmudic Age.
E.M. Smallwood, 313:Vol76-317
Alonso, C.H. - see under Hernández Alonso,
C.
Alpern, S. Freda Kirchwey.
R.G. Davis, 441:9Aug87-14
Alpers, A. - see Mansfield, K.
Alpert, H. Fellini.
S. Laschever, 441:11Jan87-19
Alston, R.C. & M.J. Crump - see "The
Eighteenth Century Short Title Cata-
logue"
Alston, S., with K. Evans, eds. A Bibliog-
raphy of Canadiana. (2nd supp, Vol 2)
R. Landon, 470:Vol24-113
Altbach, E.H. & others, eds. German
Feminism.
A.F. Grant, 564:Nov86-339
Alter, R. The Art of Biblical Poetry.
R.T. Anderson, 115:Fall86-531
M. Bal, 153:Winter86-71
Alter, R. & F. Kermode, eds. The Literary
Guide to the Bible.
E.S. Malbon, 441:20Dec87-1
Alter, S. The Godchild.
A. Bery, 617(TLS):29May87-588
Altick, R.D. Evil Encounters.
R. Ashton, 362:23Apr87-25
R. Shannon, 617(TLS):28Aug87-919
Altick, R.D. Paintings from Books.*
M. Hancher, 637(VS):Spring87-421
R.B. Martin, 453(NYRB):12Feb87-29
Altieri, C. Self and Sensibility in Con-
temporary American Poetry.*
S. Fredman, 191(ELN):Sep86-98
T. Gardner, 219(GaR):Winter86-1016
J.M. Reibetanz, 106:Summer86-257
R.D. Sell, 541(RES):Nov86-603
Altieri Biagi, M.L., ed. Il Resto del
Carlino in un secolo di storia.
V. Della Valle, 708:Vol12fasc2-271
Altinel, A.S. Thackeray and the Problem of
Realism.
P. Coustillas, 189(EA):Oct-Dec87-476
Altman, L.K. Who Goes First?
F. Mullan, 441:28Jun87-9
Altomonte, A. Una stagione sull'altra.
G. Pandini, 275(IQ):Winter86-112
Al'tshuller, M. Predtechi slavyanofil'stva
v russkoy literature (Obschestvo "Beseda
lyubiteley russkogo slova").
A. Levitsky, 550(RusR):Jul86-344
I.Z. Serman, 575(SEER):Jan86-129
Alvar, M. & B. Pottier. Morfología his-
tórica del español.
F. Nuessel, 545(RPh):May87-521

Alvarez, J.F. - see under Fernández
Alvarez, J.
Alvarez, L.W. Alvarez.
J. Trefil, 441:7Jun87-14
Alvarez, P.F. - see under Fernández
Alvarez, P.
Alvarez-Altman, G. & F. Burelbach - see
"Literary Onomastic Studies"
Alvarez Barrientos, J. - see de Cañizares,
J.
Alvarez-Detrell, T. & M.G. Paulson, eds.
The Gambling Mania On and Off the Stage
in Pre-Revolutionary France.*
A. Boës, 535(RHL):Jan-Feb86-150
Alverson, M. Under African Sun.
A. Kuper, 617(TLS):16-22Oct87-1146
Alvey, R.G. Dulcimer Maker.*
D. Kettlewell, 415:Jun86-338
D.W. Steel, 650(WF):Jul86-223
Amador, R. Aproximación histórica a los
Comentarios reales.
M. Zamora, 238:Sep86-551
Amalric, J-P. & others. Aux Origines du
retard économique de l'Espagne: XVIe-
XIXe siècles.
J. Harrison, 86(BHS):Apr86-173
Amann, K. P.E.N.: Politik, Emigration,
Nationalsozialismus.
A. Obermayer, 564:May86-178
Amann, K. & A. Berger, eds. Österreich-
ische Literatur der dreissiger Jahre.
W.E. Yates, 402(MLR):Jul86-804
Amastae, J. & L. Elías-Olivares, eds.
Spanish in the United States.*
J. Yli-Vakkuri, 439(NM):1986/2-311
Ambirajan, S. Political Economy and Mone-
tary Management.
A. Heston, 293(JASt):Aug86-870
Ambrazas, V. & others. Grammatika litov-
skogo jazyka.
B. Comrie, 350:Dec87-918
Ambrose, S.E. Nixon.
V. Bogdanor, 176:Nov87-52
A. Brinkley, 453(NYRB):16Jul87-10
R. Steel, 441:26Apr87-3
P. Whitehead, 362:30Jul87-22
G. Wills, 617(TLS):25-31Dec87-1424
Saint Ambrose. Les Devoirs. (Vol 1, Bk 1)
(M. Testard, ed & trans)
N.B. McLynn, 123:Vol36No1-138
Ambrosini, R. Momenti e problemi di storia
della linguistica, I.
J.E. Joseph, 350:Mar87-180
Amell, S. La narrativa de Juan Marsé,
contador de aventis.
D. Henn, 402(MLR):Jul87-767
M.C. Peñuelas, 238:Sep86-549
C. Rojas, 552(REH):Oct86-126
"American Literary Scholarship, 1979." (J.
Woodress, ed)
E. Gallafent, 677(YES):Vol16-314
"American Literary Scholarship, 1980."*
(J.A. Robbins, ed)
E. Gallafent, 677(YES):Vol16-314
Ames, F. The Kashmir Shawl.
V.M., 90:Nov86-837
B. Scott, 39:Oct86-378
Ames, K.L. & others. Material Culture.
G. Finley, 658:Winter86-332
Ames, R.T. The Art of Rulership.*
K.T. Gottschang, 293(JASt):Feb86-370

Anderson, S. Sherwood Anderson: Selected Letters.* (C.E. Modlin, ed)
L. Willson, 569(SR):Winter86-131
Anderson, S. Letters to Bab.* (W.A. Sutton, ed)
M.B., 295(JML):Nov86-438
E.T. Carroll, 395(MFS):Summer86-273
J.H. Maguire, 27(AL):Mar86-142
Anderson, S.R. Phonology in the Twentieth Century.
D.C. Walker, 320(CJL):Summer86-199
Anderson, W., with C. Hicks. The Rise of the Gothic.
P. Draper, 46:Jul86-84
P. Hetherington, 39:May86-366
Anderson, W.C. Between the Library and the Laboratory.*
W.R. Albury, 173(ECS):Spring87-362
R. Fox, 402(MLR):Oct86-1005
R. Porter, 208(FS):Jan86-79
Andersson, G., ed. Rationality in Science and Politics.
R.E.G., 185:Jan87-499
Andersson, S-G. & S. Kvam. Satzverschränkung im heutigen Deutsch.
B. Comrie, 353:Vol24No6-1133
Andolsen, B.H. Daughters of Jefferson, Daughters of Bootblacks.
I.M.Y., 185:Jul87-896
de Andrade, C.D. - see under Drummond de Andrade, C.
André, R. - see Stendhal
Andreasen, U. - see Heiberg, J.L.
Andreev, A.M. Mestnye sovety i organy burzhuaznoi vlasti (1917 g.).
Z. Galili y Garcia, 550(RusR):Jan86-83
Andrei, O. A. Claudius Charax di Pergamo.
A.J.S. Spawforth, 313:Vol76-327
Andreozzi, G. Amleto.
B.L. Glixon, 143:Issue39-74
Andreski, S. Max Weber's Insights and Errors.
P.B., 185:Apr87-694
Andrew, D.S. Louis Sullivan and the Polemics of Modern Architecture.
M. Filler, 453(NYRB):29Jan87-30
Andrew, J. & C. Pike, eds. The Structural Analysis of Russian Narrative Fiction.
S. Le Fleming, 402(MLR):Oct86-1048
A. Shukman, 575(SEER):Apr86-273
Andrews, K. Catalogue of Netherlandish Drawings in the National Gallery of Scotland.
M. Royalton-Kisch, 39:May86-362
C. White, 90:Feb86-151
Andrews, K.R. Trade, Plunder and Settlement.
J. Axtell, 656(WMQ):Apr86-296
W.T. MacCaffrey, 551(RenQ):Summer86-302
R. Tittler, 539:Spring87-192
Andrews, W.L. To Tell a Free Story.*
G. Early, 344:Summer87-146
Andreyev, L. Visions. (O.A. Carlisle, ed)
D. Fanger, 441:27Dec87-8
Andrieux, N. & E. Baumgartner. Manuel du français du moyen âge. (Vol 3)
H. van den Bussche, 597(SN):Vol58No1-107
M. Offord, 208(FS):Oct86-495

Andrieux, N. & E. Baumgartner. Systèmes morphologiques de l'ancien français.* (Vol A)
G. Price, 545(RPh):Nov86-241
E.M. Rutson, 382(MAE):1986/2-308
Andrup, B. Kaere baronesse.
E. Cederborg, 172(Edda):1986/1-92
Andrusz, G.D. Housing and Urban Development in the USSR.
J.L. Porket, 575(SEER):Jan86-153
H.J. Raimondo, 550(RusR):Jul86-306
Anesko, M. Friction with the Market.*
J. Sutherland, 617(TLS):19Jun87-672
Anfimov, A.M. Ekonomicheskoe polozhenie i klassovaia bor'ba krest'ian Evropeiskoi Rossii, 1881-1904.
C.A. Frierson, 550(RusR):Jul86-332
Anfossi, P. Adriano in Siria.
B.L. Glixon, 143:Issue39-74
Angel, A. & F. Macintosh. The Tiger's Milk.
362:24Sep87-30
Angel, R. Anxious Latitudes.
D. Shapiro, 491:Mar87-344
Angelo, I. The Tower of Glass.
J. Gledson, 617(TLS):27Feb87-207
Angelou, M. All God's Children Need Travelling Shoes.*
J. Neville, 617(TLS):28Aug87-922
Angier, C. Jean Rhys.
A. Crozier, 395(MFS):Winter86-671
Anglès, A. André Gide et le premier groupe de la "Nouvelle Revue Française."* (Vol 2)
K.D. Levy, 207(FR):Apr87-709
V. Wackenheim, 450(NRF):Jul-Aug86-177
Anglès, A. André Gide et le premier groupe de la "Nouvelle Revue Française." (Vol 3)
P. Fawcett, 617(TLS):2-8Oct87-1071
"The Anglo-Saxon Chronicle: A Collaborative Edition; MS B."* (Vol 4) (S. Taylor, ed)
M. Griffith, 382(MAE):1986/2-271
D.G. Scragg, 38:Band104Heft3/4-471
Angulo, D. and A.E. Pérez Sánchez. A Corpus of Spanish Drawings.* (Vol 3)
P. Troutman, 90:Feb86-153
E. Young, 39:Feb86-139
Angulo Iñiguez, D. & others. La catedral de Sevilla.
E. Bermejo, 48:Jan-Mar86-108
Anisfeld, M. Language Development from Birth to Three.
P. Pupier, 320(CJL):Fall86-298
Anisimov, E.V. Podatnaia reforma Petra I.
J. Cracraft, 550(RusR):Jan86-71
Ankerson, D. Agrarian Warlord.
A. Hennessy, 617(TLS):29May87-575
Anna, T.E. Spain and the Loss of America.
D. Cahill, 86(BHS):Apr86-184
"Annales Benjamin Constant 5."
M.A. Wegimont, 446(NCFS):Spring87-341
D. Wood, 402(MLR):Oct87-962
Annas, J. & J. Barnes. The Modes of Scepticism.*
D.W. Hamlyn, 518:Apr86-77
Anneke, M.F. Die gebrochenen Ketten. (M.M. Wagner, ed)
T.G. Gish, 221(GQ):Summer86-504

Anninger, A. Spanish and Portuguese 16th
Century Books in the Department of Print-
ing and Graphic Arts [in the Houghton
Library].
   D.W. Cruickshank, 354:Jun86–174
   M.E. Greco, 517(PBSA):Vol80No3–387
"Annual Review of Applied Linguistics,
1983."* (R.B. Kaplan & others, eds)
   J.E. Spratt, 355(LSoc):Dec86–564
"Annual Review of Jazz Studies." (Vols 1–
3) (D. Morgenstern, C. Nanry & D.A.
Cayer, eds)
   L. Porter, 91:Spring86–195
Annwn, D. Inhabited Voices.
   A. Swarbrick, 148:Autumn86–109
Anouilh, J. Eurydice [and] Médée. (E.
Freeman, ed)
   W. Scott, 208(FS):Apr86–237
Anreiter, P.P. Bemerkungen zu den Reflexen
indogermanischer Dentale im Tocharischen.
   W. Thomas, 260(IF):Band91–368
Anscombe, I. A Woman's Touch.*
   C. Buckley, 59:Sep86–400
Anson, R.S. Best Intentions.
   R. Coles, 441:17May87–3
   N. Lemann, 453(NYRB):16Jul87–20
Antczak, F.J. Thought and Character.
   J.I. McClintock, 115:Fall86–532
Antczak, J. Science Fiction.
   P. Nodelman, 561(SFS):Jul86–216
Anthony, P.D. John Ruskin's Labour.*
   M.E. Rose, 366:Spring86–135
Antler, J. Lucy Sprague Mitchell.
   E. Chesler, 441:22Mar87–39
   M. Lefkowitz, 617(TLS):22May87–538
Antoine, M. Le dur Métier de roi.
   J. Rogister, 617(TLS):18–24Dec87–1411
Antoine, R. Les écrivains français et les
Antilles, des premiers Pères Blancs aux
Surréalistes Noirs.
   G. Cesbron, 356(LR):Feb86–91
Antokoletz, E. The Music of Béla Bartók.*
   D. Jarman, 410(M&L):Jul86–321
   P. Wilson, 308:Spring86–113
Antola, A. & others. Dizionario di infor-
matica.
   C. Costa, 708:Vol12fasc2–265
Anton, J.P. & A. Preus, eds. Essays in
Ancient Greek Philosophy. (Vol 2)
   J. Owens, 41:Spring85–153
Antonioni, M. That Bowling Alley on the
Tiber.
   639(VQR):Summer86–94
Antonius, S. Where the Jinn Consult.
   R. Irwin, 617(TLS):25–31Dec87–1428
Antosh, R.B. Reality and Illusion in the
Novels of J–K. Huysmans.
   E.F. Gray, 395(MFS):Winter86–677
   A.H. Pasco, 446(NCFS):Spring87–330
Antúnez de Dendia, R. Augusto Roa Bastos.
   J. Gledson, 86(BHS):Oct86–397
Anyidoho, K. & others, eds. Interdiscipli-
nary Dimensions of African Literature.
   C.L. Innes, 538(RAL):Fall86–449
Anz, T., ed. Phantasien über den Wahnsinn.
(2nd ed)
   W. Paulsen, 133:Band19Heft3/4–365
Anzelewsky, F. Dürer–Studien.
   J.S. Held, 551(RenQ):Spring86–119
Anzelewsky, F. & H. Mielke. Albrecht
Dürer.
   J.S. Held, 551(RenQ):Spring86–119
   P. Strieder, 380:Spring86–90

Anzilotti, G.I. Four English/Italian
Stories.
   T. Wlassics, 205(ForL):Apr84–89
Aoun, J. A Grammar of Anaphora.
   H. Contreras, 350:Sep87–626
Apel, F. Sprachbewegung.
   E. Sallager, 343:Heft13–109
Apel, K–O. The Rationality of Human Com-
munication.
   P. Livet, 98:Jun–Jul86–692
Apel, K–O. Understanding and Explanation.
   S. Fuller, 486:Mar86–152
van Apeldoorn, J. Pratiques de la descrip-
tion.
   F. van Rossum–Guyon, 535(RHL):Jan–
   Feb86–169
Apitz, R. Hexenzeit.
   M. Krumrey, 654(WB):4/1986–654
Aplin, G., S.G. Foster & M. McKernan, eds.
Australians: Events and Places. Austra-
lians: A Historical Dictionary.
   A. Sykes, 617(TLS):27Nov–3Dec87–1322
Apollinaire, G. The Poet Assassinated and
Other Stories.* (R. Padgett, trans)
   I. Malin, 573(SSF):Fall86–462
Apostolidès, J–M. Le Prince sacrifié.
   H.B. McDermott, 207(FR):Mar87–534
Appalacharyulu, S. S. Appalacharyulu's
Sree Tiruppavai.
   M.R. & U. Parameswaran, 314:Summer–
   Fall86–243
Appel, B. The People Talk.
   M.H. Rikard, 9(AlaR):Jul86–227
Appel, W. Grundzüge der kausalen Phonetik.
   M. Pétursson, 685(ZDL):1/1986–81
Appelfeld, A. To the Land of the Cat-
tails.* (British title: To the Land of
the Reeds.)
   D.J. Enright, 453(NYRB):15Jan87–40
   G. Josipovici, 617(TLS):27Feb87–207
   442(NY):5Jan87–85
Appelt, D.E. Planning English Sentences.
   S. Cumming, 350:Mar87–176
Appiah, A. Assertion and Conditionals.
   P. Carruthers, 479(PhQ):Oct86–566
Appiah, A. For Truth in Semantics.
   S. Blackburn, 617(TLS):27Feb87–221
Appian. Appiani Bellorum Civilium Liber
Tertius. (D. Magnino, ed & trans)
   K. Brodersen, 313:Vol76–334
Appignanesi, R. Destroying America.
   A. Beevor, 617(TLS):31Jul87–817
Appignanesi, R. Italia Perversa.* (Pt 1)
   L. Hutcheon, 102(CanL):Spring86–159
Apple, M. The Propheteers.
   R. Kaveney, 617(TLS):9–15Oct87–1106
   C. McFadden, 441:15Mar87–13
Apple, R.W., Jr. Apple's Europe.
   C. Michener, 61:Jan87–88
Applebee, A.N. Contexts for Learning to
Write.
   G.M. Pradl, 126(CCC):Oct86–369
Appleman, R.E. East of Chosin.
   B.E. Trainor, 441:19Apr87–13
Appleyard, B. Richard Rogers.*
   D.F. Anstis, 324:Feb87–251
   S. Gardiner, 364:Jun86–80
   M. Pawley, 46:Jun86–79
Apte, M.L. Humor and Laughter.*
   C. Davies, 616:Spring/Summer86–54
   L.E. Mintz, 292(JAF):Jul/Sep86–339
   E. Oring, 650(WF):Jul86–231

Arntzen, H.   Der Literaturbegriff.
    R. Koester, 564:Nov86-340
Arntzen, S. - see Ikkyū
Aron, P.   Les Écrivains belges et le
    socialisme (1880-1913).
    D. Blampain, 356(LR):Aug-Nov86-325
    J. Roach, 208(FS):Oct86-493
Aronson, J.L.   A Realist Philosophy of
    Science.*
    L. Sklar, 482(PhR):Jul86-444
Aronson, N.   Mlle de Scudéry ou le voyage
    au pays de tendre.
    P.J. Wolfe, 568(SCN):Winter86-64
Aronson, R.   Sartre's Second Critique.
    J. Weightman, 453(NYRB):13Aug87-42
Arpino, G.   Passo d'addio.
    J. Hunt, 617(TLS):3Apr87-362
Arrabal, F.   El entierro de la sardina.
    P.L. Podol, 238:Mar86-108
Arrau, S.   Digo que norte sur corre la
    tierra.
    L.F. Cofresí, 352(LATR):Spring87-142
Arrian.   History of Alexander and Indica.*
    (Vol 2: Anabasis Alexandri, Bks 5-7)
    (P.A. Brunt, ed & trans)
    G. Schepens, 394:Vol39fasc3/4-499
Arrighetti, G. & others.   Aspetti di
    Hermann Usener, filologo della religione.
    J.N. Bremmer, 394:Vol39fasc3/4-561
Arrington, L.J.   Brigham Young.*
    N.O. Hatch, 432(NEQ):Sep86-434
    D.R. Perry, 649(WAL):Aug86-137
Arrivé, M., F. Gadet & M. Galmiche.   La
    Grammaire d'aujourd'hui.
    A. Valdman, 207(FR):May87-883
Arrowsmith, J.   The Reformation.
    J. Hérou, 189(EA):Jul-Sep87-371
"Art of Our Time - The Saatchi Collec-
    tion."*
    A. Payne, 324:Feb87-249
Arthur, E.   Bad Guys.*
    442(NY):9Feb87-103
"Arthurian Literature, I."*   (R. Barber,
    ed)
    V. Krishna, 38:Band104Heft1/2-195
"Arthurian Literature III."*   (R. Barber,
    ed)
    J.M. Cowen, 447(N&Q):Sep85-388
    P.J.C. Field, 541(RES):Feb86-136
    E.D. Kennedy, 38:Band104Heft3/4-481
"Le arti in Sicilia nel settecento/Studi in
    memoria di Maria Accascina."
    D. Garstang, 90:Aug86-613
Artley, A.   Hoorah for the Filth-Packets!
    D.J. Enright, 617(TLS):18-24Dec87-1399
Artmann, H.C.   Under Cover of a Hat/Green-
    Sealed Messages.*
    M. Kenyon, 376:Sep86-152
"Arts du spectacle et Histoire des idées."*
    V. Kapp, 547(RF):Band98Heft3/4-416
Arumaa, P.   Urslavische Grammatik.   (Vol 3)
    D. Huntley, 159:Fall86-233
Aschan, U.   The Man Whom Women Loved.
    D. Ackerman, 441:23Aug87-1
Aschenbrenner, K.   The Concept of Coher-
    ence in Art.
    R. Stecker, 290(JAAC):Winter86-209
Ascher, C.   The Flood.
    R. Hoffman, 441:26Jul87-16
Ascher, K.   The Politics of Privatisation.
    V. Borooah, 617(TLS):6-12Nov87-1221

Ascheri, M., A. Forzini & C. Santini, eds.
    Il Caleffo Vecchio del comune di Siena,
    4.
    W.M. Bowsky, 589:Jul86-724
Ash, J.   Disbelief.
    D.W. Hartnett, 617(TLS):20-26Nov87-
    1276
Ashbee, A.   Records of English Court
    Music.   (Vol 1) (rev ed)
    C.A. Price, 617(TLS):17Apr87-409
Ashbee, A.   Records of English Court Music.
    (Vol 2)
    C. Price, 617(TLS):23-29Oct87-1170
Ashbery, J.   Selected Poems.*
    G. Frumkin, 138:No9-258
    M. Jarman, 249(HudR):Summer86-341
    L. Mackinnon, 493:Jun86-100
    D. Spurr, 491:Jul86-228
    639(VQR):Summer86-99
Ashbery, J. & J. Schuyler.   A Nest of Nin-
    nies.
    A. Dannatt, 362:2Jul87-30
    A.H.G. Phillips, 617(TLS):24Jul87-801
Ashbrook, W.   The Operas of Puccini.   (2nd
    ed)
    J. Budden, 415:Feb86-93
Ashby, L.   Saving the Waifs.
    D. Macleod, 106:Summer86-235
Ashby-Beach, G.   The Song of Roland.
    W.G. van Emden, 208(FS):Oct86-443
Ashcraft, R.   Locke's "Two Treatises of
    Government."
    A. Ryan, 617(TLS):10Jul87-739
Ashcraft, R. Revolutionary Politics and
    Locke's "Two Treatises of Government."
    D. Braybrooke, 150(DR):Fall86-382
    A. Ryan, 617(TLS):10Jul87-739
Ashdown, P. - see Agee, J.
Asher, M.   A Desert Dies.
    J. Swift, 617(TLS):10Jul87-753
Ashford, D.E.   The Emergence of the Wel-
    fare States.
    A. Wooldridge, 617(TLS):5Jun87-600
Ashley, P.J., ed.   Dictionary of Literary
    Biography.   (Vol 23)
    S. Bush, Jr., 677(YES):Vol16-344
Ashmore, R.A.   Building a Moral System.
    A.M.S., 185:Jul87-884
Asholt, W.   Gesellschaftskritisches Theater
    im Frankreich der Belle Epoque (1887-
    1914).
    K. Beaumont, 208(FS):Oct86-484
Ashton, D., ed.   Twentieth Century Artists
    on Art.
    R. Arnheim, 290(JAAC):Spring87-321
Ashton, R.   George Eliot.
    E.M. Eigner, 402(MLR):Oct87-932
    R. Noll-Wiemann, 38:Band104Heft1/2-249
Ashton, R.   Little Germany.*
    S. Atkins, 637(VS):Summer87-544
Ashworth, M.   Beyond Methodology.
    J.M. Purcell, 399(MLJ):Winter86-413
Ashworth, W.   The History of the British
    Coal Industry.   (Vol 5)
    R. Waller, 617(TLS):30Jan87-105
Aslet, C.   Quinlan Terry.
    H. Potts, 617(TLS):13Feb87-152
Aslin, E.   E.W. Godwin.
    N. Powell, 39:Sep86-226
Asmis, E.   Epicurus' Scientific Method.
    W.G. Englert, 487:Spring86-102
    D.P. Fowler, 303(JoHS):Vol106-227
[continued]

[continuing]

B. Inwood, 122:Oct86-349
D. Konstan, 41:Spring85-121
J.E. Rexine, 24:Summer86-290

Asor Rosa, A. Storia della letteratura italiana.
P.S. Griffith, 402(MLR):Apr87-486

"Aspects de la vie traditionnelle en Wallonie."
R. Debrie, 553(RLiR):Jul-Dec86-621

Asper, U. Aspekte zum Werden der deutschen Liedsätze in Johann Walters "Geistlichem Gesangbüchlein" (1524-1551).
C. Meyer, 537:Vol72No1-144

Asquith, C. The Diaries 1915-1918.
E.S. Turner, 617(TLS):2-8Oct87-1064

Assaf, F. Lesage et le picaresque.
C.J. Stivale, 207(FR):Dec86-256

"Assays." (Vol 3) (P.A. Knapp, ed)
T. Hunt, 402(MLR):Apr87-426

Asselin, P.Y. Musique et tempérament.
H.A. Kellner, 537:Vol72No2-294

Assouline, P. Gaston Gallimard.
P. Kolb, 31(ASch):Autumn86-557

Astarita, M.L. Avidio Cassio.*
J-P. Callu, 555:Vol59fasc2-333

Asterisk. Isles of Illusion. (B. Lynch, ed)
617(TLS):30Jan87-120

Astley, T. It's Raining in Mango.
R. Brown, 441:22Nov87-14

Astrada, E. Autobiography at the Trigger.
M. Cota-Cárdenas, 238:May86-321

Astre, G-A. & P. Lépinasse. La Démocratie contrariée.
S. Ricard, 106:Fall86-361

Asún, R. - see Cela, C.J.

Athill, D. After a Funeral.*
J. Le Bas, 364:Apr/May86-176

Atil, E., W.T. Chase & P. Jett. Islamic Metalwork in the Freer Gallery of Art.
B.W. Robinson, 90:May86-361

Atiyah, P.S. Essays on Contract.
P. Birks, 617(TLS):23-29Oct87-1173

Atiyah, P.S. Pragmatism and Theory in English Law.
A.W.B. Simpson, 617(TLS):11-17Sep87-998

Atkins, A. & L.J. Schaaf. Sun Gardens, Victorian Photographs.
I.L. & A. Moor, 78(BC):Winter86-530

Atkins, B. and others, eds. Collins-Robert Paperback French-English English-French Dictionary.
R.H. Crawshaw, 402(MLR):Jul86-733

Atkins, C.D. & M.L. Johnson. Writing and Reading Differently.
L.H. Peterson, 126(CCC):Oct86-357

Atkins, G.D. Quests of Difference.
D. Nokes, 617(TLS):20Feb87-182
639(VQR):Autumn86-115

Atkins, G.D. Reading Deconstruction/Deconstructive Reading.*
R. Selden, 402(MLR):Jul86-690

Atkins, J. Sex in Literature.
C.H. Flynn, 402(MLR):Oct87-920

Atkinson, A. & M. Aveling, eds. Australians: 1838.
A. Sykes, 617(TLS):27Nov-3Dec87-1322

Atkinson, J.M. & J. Heritage, eds. Structures of Social Action.
D.H., 355(LSoc):Mar86-130
M. Owen, 307:Dec86-230

Atkinson, M. Plotinus, "Ennead" V.1.*
J.S. Lee, 124:Sep-Oct86-51
S.K. Strange, 482(PhR):Jan86-99

Atlan, L. Le Rêve des animaux rongeurs. L'amour élémentaire.
B.L. Knapp, 207(FR):Oct86-158

Atlas, J. The Great Pretender.*
R. Kaveney, 617(TLS):6Mar87-246
639(VQR):Autumn86-128

"Atlas Linguarum Europae (ALE)."* (Vol 1, fasc 1 & 2) (M. Alinei & others, eds)
V. Marrero, 548:Jul-Dec86-447

Atroshenko, V.I. and J. Collins. The Origins of the Romanesque.
T.A.H., 90:Jul86-520
P. Hetherington, 39:Feb86-137

Attal, P. & C. Muller, eds. De la syntaxe à la pragmatique.
M. Mahler, 207(FR):Mar87-572

Attali, J. A Man of Influence.* (French title: Un Homme d'influence.)
J.E. Garten, 441:6Sep87-9

Attallah, N. Women.
L. Sage, 617(TLS):16-22Oct87-1129

Attebery, L.W., ed. Idaho Folklife.
J.A. Anderson, 649(WAL):Feb87-367
T. Cochrane, 650(WF):Jul86-226

Attig, J.C., comp. The Works of John Locke.
J.S. Yolton, 354:Dec86-381

Attridge, D. The Rhythms of English Poetry.*
C. Norris, 577(SHR):Spring86-173

Attridge, D. & D. Ferrer, eds. Post-Structuralist Joyce.*
M.B., 295(JML):Nov86-493
P.F. Herring, 659(ConL):Spring87-104
C. Peake, 97(CQ):Vol15No2-141

Attuel, J., ed. L'Autorité.
V.D.L., 605(SC):15Jul87-386

Attwood, W. The Twilight Struggle.
L. Garrison, 441:30Aug87-12
442(NY):5Oct87-127

Atwood, M. Bluebeard's Egg.*
J. Clute, 617(TLS):12Jun87-626
V. Shaw, 362:11Jun87-29
D. Staines, 102(CanL):Summer86-103

Atwood, M. Bodily Harm.*
C. McLay, 296(JCF):No35/36-130

Atwood, M. The Handmaid's Tale.*
D. Flower, 249(HudR):Summer86-318

Atwood, M. Lady Oracle.
E. Jensen, 168(ECW):Fall86-29

Atwood, M. Life before Man.
C. McLay, 296(JCF):No35/36-122

Atwood, M., ed. The New Oxford Book of Canadian Verse in English.*
D. McDuff, 565:Winter85/86-72

Atwood, M. & R. Weaver, eds. The Oxford Book of Canadian Short Stories in English.
J. Clute, 617(TLS):12Jun87-626

Atwood, W.G. Fryderyk Chopin.
J. Machlis, 441:26Apr87-28
C. Rosen, 453(NYRB):28May87-9

Auberlen, E. The Commonwealth of Wit.
É. Cuvelier, 189(EA):Oct-Dec87-467
J.E. Howard, 570(SQ):Summer86-273

Aubert, E. Journal d'un collabo.
A.D. Barry, 207(FR):Oct86-159

Aubreton, R., with F. Buffière, eds. Anthologie grecque. (Pt 2)
P.A. Hansen, 123:Vol36No2-205

14

Aubrun, M–M. Henri Lehmann, 1814–1882.
R. Thomson, 59:Mar86–108
Auburger, L. Russland und Europa.
L. Hughes, 575(SEER):Oct86–651
Auchard, J. Silence in Henry James.
J.W. Tuttleton, 395(MFS):Winter86–597
Auchincloss, L. Diary of a Yuppie.*
J. Mellors, 362:19Feb87–24
Auchincloss, L. Skinny Island.
P. Cameron, 441:24May87–5
Aucouturier, M. – see "Cahiers Léon Tolstoï"
Audi, R. & W.J. Wainwright, eds. Rationality, Religious Belief, and Moral Commitment.
C.C., 185:Jul87–905
von Aue, H. – see under Hartmann von Aue
Auerbach, N. Romantic Imprisonment.*
E.A. Daniels, 637(VS):Winter87–272
E.B. Jordan, 395(MFS):Summer86–358
Auerbach, N. Ellen Terry.
B. Brophy, 617(TLS):6–12Nov87–1215
M. Peters, 441:26Jul87–11
Auerbach, N. Woman and the Demon.*
V.C. Fowler, 158:Dec86–189
E. Leites, 473(PR):Vol53No1–117
Augarde, T. The Oxford Guide to Word Games.
A. Burgess, 617(TLS):8May87–494
Saint Augustine. Saint Augustin, "La vera religione." (A. Lamacchia & P. Porro, eds)
M. Adam, 542:Oct–Dec86–496
Auletta, K. Greed and Glory on Wall Street.*
J.H.C. Leach, 617(TLS):3Jul87–708
Aulotte, R. La Comédie française de la Renaissance et son chef-d'oeuvre: "Les Contens" d'Odet de Turnèbe.
C. Mazouer, 535(RHL):Mar–Apr86–263
Aulotte, R. Mathurin Régnier: Les Satires.
J. Trethewey, 535(RHL):Jan–Feb86–141
Aulotte, R. – see de Ronsard, P.
Aune, B. Metaphysics.*
K. Dorter, 543:Dec86–367
Auroux, S. & others, eds. La linguistique fantastique.
J–J. Courtine, 400(MLN):Sep86–954
H. Ormsby-Lennon, 355(LSoc):Dec86–571
Auroux, S. & others, eds. Matériaux pour une histoire des théories linguistiques/Essays Toward a History of Linguistic Theories/Materialien zu einer Geschichte der sprachwissenschaftlichen Theorien.
P. Swiggers, 553(RLiR):Jul–Dec86–550
Ausmus, H.J. Will Herberg.
R.W. Fox, 441:30Aug87–15
"Aussprachebuch der aserbaidshanischen Sprache."
G.F. Meier, 682(ZPSK):Band39Heft2–293
Aust, S. The Baader-Meinhof Group.
A. Glees, 617(TLS):16–22Oct87–1130
Auster, P. In the Country of Last Things.
P. Powell, 441:17May87–11
Auster, P. The Locked Room.
S. Schiff, 441:4Jan87–14
442(NY):18May87–116
Auster, P. The New York Trilogy.
P. Driver, 362:31Dec87–23
C. Greenland, 617(TLS):11–17Dec87–1375

Austin, Garland, Heath & Woodcock. The Spectator Cartoon Book.
D.J. Enright, 617(TLS):18–24Dec87–1399
Austin, D.J. After the Garden.
R.G. O'Meally, 441:16Aug87–20
Austin, F. Robert Clift of Bodmin, Able Seaman 1790–1799.
J. Rowe, 83:Autumn86–232
Austin, L. Poetic Principles and Practice.
G.W. Ireland, 617(TLS):11–17Dec87–1381
Austin, R.G. – see Vergil
Austin, S. Parmenides.*
J. Barnes, 520:Vol31No3–281
E.E. Benitez, 543:Mar87–562
Austin, T.R. Language Crafted.*
R.D. Cureton, 307:Apr86–70
Autant-Lara, C. La Rage dans le coeur. Hollywood Cake-Walk.
C. Lindsay, 207(FR):May87–899
Autret, J., W. Burford & P.J. Wolfe – see Proust, M.
Auty, M. & N. Roddick, eds. British Cinema Now.*
J. Boorman, 707:Winter85/86–55
Avalle-Arce, J.B., ed. "La Galatea" de Cervantes – cuatrocientos años después.
E. Rhodes, 304(JHP):Spring86–255
Avalle-Arce, J.B. & G. Cervantes Martín – see de Vega Carpio, L.
Averill, J. – see Wordsworth, W.
Averoff-Tossizza, E. Lost Opportunities.
C.M. Woodhouse, 617(TLS):3Jul87–709
Avery, M. Northern Comfort.
T. Gerry, 102(CanL):Winter85–167
Avesani, R. & others, eds. Vestigia.
M. Lentzen, 547(RF):Band98Heft1/2–213
S. Prete, 551(RenQ):Spring86–71
Avezzù, G. Lisia.
D.M. MacDowell, 123:Vol36No2–212
Avigdor, E., with E. Labrousse, eds. Lettres fraternelles d'un prisonnier.
E.D. James, 208(FS):Jul86–329
Avila, W. Jean Stafford.
C. Goodman, 534(RALS):Spring-Autumn84–246
Avilés, M. Sueños ficticios y lucha ideológica en el Siglo de Oro.
F.A. de Armas, 552(REH):Jan86–135
Avineri, S. Moses Hess.
D. Stone, 390:Aug/Sep86–58
Avis, P. Ecumenical Theology and the Elusiveness of Doctrine.
P. Baelz, 617(TLS):27Feb87–223
Avni, O. Tics, Tics et Tics.*
R. Pickering, 208(FS):Apr86–230
S. Winspur, 188(ECr):Fall86–100
Avrich, P. The Haymarket Tragedy.
M. Tane, 639(VQR):Winter86–168
Avril, F. & others. Manuscrits enluminés de la Péninsule Ibérique.
J.J.G. Alexander, 90:Apr86–292
Avril, F., X. Barral i Altet & D. Gaborit-Chopin. Le temps des Croisades. Les royaumes d'Occident.
M.W. Cothren, 589:Jul86–617
Avril, F. & M-T. Gousset, with C. Rabel. Manuscrits enluminés d'origine italienne.* (Vol 2)
A. Stones, 589:Oct86–886
Avyžius, J. Die Farben des Chamäleons.
P. Kirchner, 654(WB):1/1986–134
Awret, I. Days of Honey.
J. Roumani, 287:Apr–May86–28

Awwad, H. Arab Causes in the Fiction of Ghâdah al-Sammân, 1961-1975.
  A. Wasmine & M.A. Karym, with J. Voisine, 549(RLC):Jan-Mar86-123
Axelrad, A.S. Meditations of a Maverick Rabbi.
  B.W. Varon, 390:Jan86-59
Axelrad, E. Marie Casse-Croûte.
  G.R. Besser, 207(FR):Feb87-421
Axelrod, S.G. & H. Deese, eds. Robert Lowell.
  M. Hofmann, 617(TLS):10Jul87-746
Axmatova, A. Socinenija. (Vol 3) (G.P. Struve, N.A. Struve & B.A. Filippov, eds)
  S. Driver, 558(RLJ):Winter86-227
Axtell, J. The Invasion Within.*
  A.T. Vaughan, 656(WMQ)Oct86-660
Ayala, F. Usurpers.
  W. Ferguson, 441:21Jun87-22
de Ayala, P.L. - see under López de Ayala, P.
de Ayala, R.P. - see under Pérez de Ayala, R.
Ayala Mallory, N. Bartolomé Esteban Murillo.*
  E.H., 90:Jan86-49
Ayer, A.J. Philosophy in the Twentieth Century.
  A. Janik, 319:Apr87-314
Ayer, A.J. Voltaire.*
  D. Flower, 364:Nov86-96
Ayer, A.J. Wittgenstein.*
  M. Budd, 393(Mind):Jul86-389
  D. Rashid, 521:Oct86-320
  G. Stock, 518:Apr86-96
Ayers, D.M. English Words from Latin and Greek Elements. (2nd ed) (T.D. Worthen, with R.L. Cherry, eds)
  E.A. Ebbinghaus, 215(GL):Vol26No3-214
Ayers, J. - see Krahl, R., with N. Erbahar
Ayerst, D. Garvin of the Observer.
  T. Lloyd, 635(VPR):Summer86-70
Ayling, R. - see O'Casey, S.
Aylmer, G.E. Rebellion or Revolution?*
  L. Stone, 453(NYRB):26Feb87-38
Aylward, E.T. Cervantes.
  A.F. Lambert, 86(BHS):Apr86-162
Aylward, E.T. Martorell's "Tirant lo Blanch."
  P. Kenworthy, 238:Dec86-862
Aymes, J-R., E-M. Fell & J-L. Guereña, eds. École et société en Espagne et en Amérique Latine (XVIIIe-XXe siècles).
  N.M. Valis, 238:Dec86-893
Ayrault, R. - see von Goethe, J.W.
Ayres, J. The Artist's Craft.
  J. Burr, 39:Jan86-62
  E.H, 90:Jul86-520
Ayuso, I.A. - see under Arellano Ayuso, I.
Azam, G. & others. La Femme dans la pensée espagnole.
  G.M. Scanlon, 402(MLR):Oct86-1017
Azarpay, G., with others. Sogdian Painting.
  E.N. Berthrong, 302:Vol22No1-113
Aziz, M. - see James, H.
Azoulay-Vicente, A. Les tours comportant l'expression DE + adjectif.
  G. Kleiber, 553(RLiR):Jul-Dec86-597
  L. Zaring, 207(FR):May87-885
Azoy, G.W. Buzkashi.
  A. Ghani, 318(JAOS):Jan/Mar85-167

van Baak, J.J., ed. Signs of Friendship.
  C.R. Pike, 402(MLR):Jul86-808
  O.T. Yokoyama, 574(SEEJ):Fall86-434
van Baal, J., ed. Jan Verschueran's Description of Yei Nan Culture.
  J.M. Blythe, 293(JASt):Aug86-797
van Baal, J., K.W. Galis & R.M. Koentjaraningrat. West Irian.
  Giok Po Oey, 293(JASt):Feb86-471
Baatz, S. "Venerate the Plough."
  D.G.C.A., 324:Mar87-334
Babbitt, I. Democracy and Leadership.
  J. Parini, 249(HudR):Summer86-322
Babbitt, M. Words about Music. (S. Dembski & J.N. Straus, eds)
  P. Griffiths, 617(TLS):23-29Oct87-1170
Babbitt, S.M. Oresme's "Livre de politiques" and the France of Charles V.
  J.B. Henneman, 589:Oct86-890
Babcock, A.E. Portraits of Artists.
  D.H. Walker, 208(FS):Oct86-486
Babcock, B.A., G. Monthan and D. Monthan. The Pueblo Storyteller.
  L. Milazzo, 584(SWR):Autumn86-538
Babel, I. Le Moulin chinois et autres scénarios.
  J. Blot, 450(NRF):Jul-Aug86-189
Babin, R. The Nuclear Power Game.
  M. Love, 529(QQ):Spring86-218
Babson, M. Reel Murder.
  G. Kaufman, 362:7May87-26
Bach, H. Handbuch der Luthersprache. (Vol 2)
  H. Wolf, 685(ZDL):2/1986-220
Bachleitner, N. Form und Funktion der Verseinlagen bei Abraham a Sancta Clara.
  E. Moser-Rath, 196:Band27Heft3/4-325
Bachmann, I. The Thirtieth Year.
  M. Gordon, 441:29Nov87-14
Bachofer, W., W. von Hahn & D. Möhn, eds. Rückläufiges Wörterbuch der mittelhochdeutschen Sprache.*
  A. Rowley, 684(ZDA):Band115Heft2-89
Bachorski, H-J., ed. Lektüren.
  A.C., 400(MLN):Apr86-731
Bacigalupo, M., ed. Ezra Pound: Un Poeta a Rapallo.
  P. Makin, 402(MLR):Jul87-720
Bacigalupo, M. - see Pound, E.
Baciu, S. Centroamericanos.
  J.E. Vargas, 263(RIB):Vol36No1-58
Back, D.M. Eine buddhistische Jenseitsreise.
  R. Kaschewsky, 259(IIJ):Oct86-326
Backes, H. Die Hochzeit Merkurs und der Philologie.
  P.W. Tax, 680(ZDP):Band105Heft1-130
Bäckman, S. & G. Kjellmer, eds. Papers on Language and Literature.
  J. Paccaud, 189(EA):Jul-Sep86-326
Backscheider, P.R. A Being More Intense.*
  W.R. Owens, 366:Autumn86-253
Backscheider, P.R. Daniel Defoe.
  P.N. Furbank, 617(TLS):1May87-471
Backus, R.L. - see "The Riverside Counselor's Stories"
Bacon, F. Francis Bacon's Natural Philosophy. (G. Rees, with C. Upton, eds)
  M. Le Doeuff, 192(EP):Apr-Jun86-235
Bacon, F. The Essayes or Counsels, Civill and Morall. (M. Kiernan, ed)
  M. Dodsworth, 175:Spring86-107
    [continued]

[continuing]
H. Durel, 189(EA):Jan-Mar87-84
F.J. Levy, 551(RenQ):Winter86-796
R. Robbins, 617(TLS):6Mar87-247
Bacon, F. Essays. (J. Pitcher, ed)
M. Dodsworth, 175:Spring86-107
R. Robbins, 617(TLS):6Mar87-247
Bacon, F. La Nouvelle Atlantide [suivi de]
Voyage dans la pensée baroque. (M. Le
Doeuff & M. Llasera, eds & trans)
P.F. Moreau, 540(RIPh):Vol40fasc4-446
Bacon, F. Le "Valerius Terminus" (de l'in-
terprétation de la Nature). (F. Vert, ed
& trans) Récusation des doctrines phil-
osophiques et autres opuscules. (D.
Deleule, ed & trans)
A. Minazzoli, 540(RIPh):Vol40fasc4-448
Bacon, M. Ernest Flagg.
T. Matthews, 45:Oct86-73
Bacon, M.H. Mothers of Feminism.
E. Griffith, 441:1Feb87-28
Bacou, R. Odilon Redon.
J. Russell, 441:6Dec87-89
Bacqué-Grammont, J-L. & P. Dumont, eds.
Économie et Sociétés dans l'Empire
Ottoman (Fin du XVIIIe-Debut du XXe
siècle).
R. Murphey, 318(JAOS):Jan/Mar85-167
Badash, L. Kapitza, Rutherford, and the
Kremlin.*
M.B. Adams, 550(RusR):Jan86-93
B.W. Sargent, 529(QQ):Winter86-940
Badcock, C.R. The Problem of Altruism.
J.E.J. Altham, 617(TLS):19Jun87-665
Badel, P-Y., ed. Le Dit du Prunier.
G. Roques, 553(RLiR):Jan-Jun86-293
Bader, R. Anthony Powell's "Music of
Time" as a Cyclic Novel of Generations.
G. Festerling, 72:Band223Heft1-184
Baebius Italicus. Baebii Italici "Ilias
Latina." (M. Scaffai, ed & trans)
G.J.M. Bartelink, 394:Vol39fasc3/4-519
F.R.D. Goodyear, 123:Vol36No2-317
Baez, J. And a Voice to Sing With.
B. Goldsmith, 441:21Jun87-30
Bage, R. Robert Bage's "Hermsprong; or,
Man As He Is Not." (S. Tave, ed)
C.A. Howells, 447(N&Q):Jun86-274
Bage, R. Hermsprong, or Man as He is Not.
(P. Faulkner, ed)
T.W. Craik, 83:Autumn86-270
Baggley, J. Doors of Perception.
H. Chadwick, 617(TLS):24Apr87-448
Bagni, P. Guercino a Cento.*
D.S-T., 90:Jul86-520
Baguley, D., ed. Critical Essays on Emile
Zola.
C. Thomson, 446(NCFS):Spring87-328
Bahlow, H. Abhandlungen zur Namenfor-
schung und Buchgeschichte.
H. Weinacht, 685(ZDL):1/1986-107
Baiardi, G.C., G. Chittolini & P. Floriani
- see under Cerboni Baiardi, G., G.
Chittolini & P. Floriani
Baier, A. Postures of the Mind.
K. Lennon, 518:Jul86-183
D. Locke, 479(PhQ):Oct86-571
Bail, M. The Drover's Wife.
R. Stevenson, 617(TLS):19Jun87-668
Bail, M., ed. The Faber Book of Contempo-
rary Australian Short Stories.
H. Jacobson, 617(TLS):27Nov-3Dec87-
1307

Bail, M. Holden's Performance.
H. Jacobson, 617(TLS):27Nov-3Dec87-
1307
Bailey, A. Major André.
E. Wright, 441:5Jul87-10
Bailey, A.C. England, First and Last.*
42(AR):Winter86-121
Bailey, C-J.N. & K. Maroldt. Grundzüge der
englischen Phonetologie.
W.H. Veith, 685(ZDL):2/1986-250
Bailey, D.R.S. - see under Shackleton
Bailey, D.R.
Bailey, F.G. The Tactical Uses of Passion.
W.L. Nothstine, 480(P&R):Vol19No1-73
Bailey, P. Gabriel's Lament.*
J. Johnston, 441:18Oct87-34
J. Mellors, 364:Oct86-91
362:26Nov87-30
Bailey, P.J. Reading Stanley Elkin.*
I. Malin, 532(RCF):Spring86-218
L.D. Stewart, 395(MFS):Summer86-289
Bailey, R. - see Wagner, R.
Bailey, R.W. & R.M. Fosheim, eds. Literacy
for Life.
D.A. Jolliffe, 126(CCC):Oct86-363
Bailey, R.W. & M. Görlach, eds. English as
a World Language.*
H.F. Nielsen, 300:Apr86-132
Bailey, T. The Ambrosian Alleluia.*
M. Huglo, 537:Vol72No1-139
Bailey, V. Delinquency and Citizenship.
T. Campbell, 617(TLS):3Jul87-710
Ballyn, B. The Peopling of British North
America.* Voyagers to the West.
N. Bliven, 442(NY):23Feb87-133
T.H. Breen, 453(NYRB):29Jan87-27
K.G. Davies, 617(TLS):4-11Sep87-959
Bainbridge, B. Forever England.
J. Dunn, 617(TLS):24Apr87-442
Bainbridge, B. Mum and Mr. Armitage.*
E. Fishel, 441:30Aug87-20
442(NY):14Sep87-134
Bainbridge, B. Watson's Apology.
42(AR):Spring86-250
Bainbridge, W.S. Dimensions of Science
Fiction.
J. Sutherland, 617(TLS):20Mar87-302
Baines, B.J. Thomas Heywood.
D.J. McDermott, 568(SCN):Spring-
Summer86-17
Baird, E. Classic Canadian Cooking.
Elizabeth Baird's Favourites.
T. Whittaker, 529(QQ):Autumn86-547
Baird-Smith, R. - see "Winter's Tales"
Baker, C. The Echoing Green.*
R.H. Fogle, 340(KSJ):Vol35-218
D. Perkins, 591(SIR):Summer86-295
F.W. Shilstone, 577(SHR):Fall86-374
Baker, C.J. An Indian Rural Economy, 1880-
1955.
D. Ludden, 293(JASt):Aug86-870
Baker, D. Haunts.
S. Brady, 649(WAL):Nov86-273
T.R. Hummer, 651(WHR):Spring86-69
Baker, D. Summer Sleep.
J. Carter, 219(GaR):Summer86-532
Baker, D.C., J.L. Murphy & L.B. Hall, Jr.,
eds. The Late Medieval Religious Plays
of Bodleian MSS. Digby 133 and e Museo
160.*
G.C. Britton, 447(N&Q):Dec85-513

Baker, D.Z. Mythic Masks in Self-Reflexive
Poetry.
S.A.S., 295(JML):Nov86-423
Baker, G.P. & P.M.S. Hacker. Frege.*
J. Weiner, 482(PhR):Oct86-617
Baker, G.P. & P.M.S. Hacker. Language,
Sense and Nonsense.*
R. Eldridge, 521:Jul86-229
M.A.P., 185:Jan87-498
Baker, G.P. & P.M.S. Hacker. Scepticism,
Rules and Language.*
R. Eldridge, 521:Jul86-229
S. Romaine, 297(JL):Mar86-244
Baker, H.A., Jr. Blues, Ideology, and
Afro-American Literature.*
K. Benston, 115:Winter86-109
J.E. Butler, 454:Fall86-90
J. Cooley, 27(AL):May86-290
M.C. Gwin, 301(JEGP):Jul86-476
Baker, H.A., Jr. Modernism and the Harlem
Renaissance.
T.B. Davis, 441:4Oct87-29
Baker, J.H. The Legal Profession and the
Common Law.
E.W. Ives, 617(TLS):28Aug87-920
Baker, J.H. Mary Todd Lincoln.
P. Longsworth, 441:13Sep87-38
442(NY):9Nov87-156
Baker, L.F. & others. Collage.* (2nd ed)
R. Danner, 399(MLJ):Winter86-424
Baker, P. & C. Corne. Isle de France
Creole.*
G. Aub-Buscher, 547(RF):Band98Heft1/2-
179
P. Stein, 260(IF):Band91-318
Baker, P.S. & others - see Boswell, J.
Baker, R.A. & M.T. Nietzel. Private Eyes.
L.D. Harred, 395(MFS):Summer86-370
Baker, S. 5001 Names for Cats.
K.B. Harder, 424:Mar86-107
Baker, T.L. and B.R. Harrison. Adobe
Walls.
L. Milazzo, 584(SWR):Autumn86-538
Baker, W. Mountain Blood.
L. Milazzo, 584(SWR):Summer86-402
K.R. Stafford, 344:Spring87-119
"Baker's Dozen: Stories by Women."*
S. Posesorski, 102(CanL):Summer86-110
Bakhtin, M.M. The Dialogic Imagination.
(M. Holquist, ed) Rabelais and His
World.
D.H. Richter, 599:Fall86-411
Bakhtin, M.M. Problems of Dostoevsky's
Poetics.* (C. Emerson, ed & trans)
D.H. Richter, 599:Fall86-411
Bakhtin, M.M. Speech Genres and Other
Late Essays. (C. Emerson & M. Holquist,
eds)
S. Stewart, 441:22Mar87-31
J. Sturrock, 617(TLS):21Aug87-892
Bakhtin, M.M./P.N. Medvedev. The Formal
Method in Literary Scholarship.
J. O'Brien, 402(MLR):Jan87-263
Bakker, B.H., with C. Becker - see Zola, É.
Bakker, J. Ernest Hemingway in Holland
1925-1981.
G. Hily-Mane, 189(EA):Jul-Sep87-368
Bakker, T., with C. Dudley. I Gotta Be Me.
Run to the Roar.
M. Gardner, 453(NYRB):13Aug87-17
Bal, M. Lethal Love.
M. Furlong, 617(TLS):6-12Nov87-1232

Bal, M. Narratology.
P. Stoicheff, 627(UTQ):Winter86/87-375
Balayé, S. - see Madame de Staël
Balbert, P. & P.L. Marcus, eds. D.H.
Lawrence.*
R.M. Davis, 223:Spring86-90
É. Delavenay, 189(EA):Apr-Jun87-230
J. Meyers, 395(MFS):Summer86-309
Balbir, N., ed & trans. Dānāṣṭakathā.
W.L. Smith, 318(JAOS):Oct/Dec85-781
Bald, W. On the Left Bank 1929-1933. (B.
Franklin 5th, ed)
A. Barnet, 441:1Mar87-21
Baldan, P. Metamorfosi di un orco.
M. Davie, 402(MLR):Jan86-224
Baldassarri, M. Introduzione alla logica
stoica.
J. Barnes, 123:Vol36No1-143
Balderston, D. El precursor velado.
G.H. Bell-Villada, 238:Sep86-553
Baldi, M.L. David Hume nel Settecento
italiano.
C. Rosso, 549(RLC):Jan-Mar86-101
L.A. Zaina, 83:Spring86-112
Baldi, P. An Introduction to the Indo-
European Languages.
B.D. Joseph, 350:Mar87-147
Baldick, C. The Social Mission of English
Criticism 1848-1932.*
J. Goode, 402(MLR):Jul87-717
Baldinger, K. Dictionnaire étymologique de
l'ancien français. (fasc G1-G4)
R. de Gorog, 545(RPh):Aug86-82
Baldinger, K. Vers une sémantique mod-
erne.*
O. Ducháček, 682(ZPSK):Band39Heft6-707
R. Hawkins, 402(MLR):Jul86-688
Balduino, A. Boccaccio, Petrarca e altri
poeti del trecento.
C. Calenda, 379(MedR):Apr86-147
J.L. Smarr, 551(RenQ):Autumn86-515
Baldwin, B. Suetonius.*
R.C. Lounsbury, 121(CJ):Dec86-Jan87-
159
Baldwin, B. - see "Timarion"
Baldwin, J. Jimmy's Blues.
639(VQR):Summer86-99
Baldwin, J.W. The Government of Philip
Augustus.
M. Vale, 617(TLS):16-22Oct87-1148
Bale, J. The Complete Plays of John Bale.
(P. Happé, ed)
J. Wasson, 130:Fall86-283
Balis, A. & others. Rubens and his World.
C. White, 90:Dec86-906
Balk, C. Bindweed.*
S.S. Moorty, 649(WAL):Feb87-369
639(VQR):Summer86-101
Ball, D. & J. Richelson, eds. Strategic
Nuclear Targeting.
R. Bulkeley, 617(TLS):13Mar87-266
Ball, H. Justice Downwind.
639(VQR):Autumn86-130
Ball, J. Indonesian Legal History, 1602-
1848. Indonesian Legal History: British
West Sumatra, 1685-1825.
M.C. Hoadley, 293(JASt):Feb86-436
Ballaira, G. Per il catalogo dei codici di
Prisciano.
P. Flobert, 555:Vol59fasc2-327
Ballantine, C. Music and its Social Mean-
ings.*
M.M., 412:Aug85-212

Ballard, J.G. The Day of Creation.
D.J. Enright, 617(TLS):11-17Sep87-977
C. MacCabe, 362:10Sep87-22
Ballard, R.D., with R. Archbold. The Discovery of the Titanic.
T. Bay, 441:27Dec87-19
Ballester, G.T. - see under Torrente Ballester, G.
Ballet, R. - see Vailland, R.
Balletto, L. Genova nel duecento.
S.A. Epstein, 589:Apr86-489
Balliett, W. American Musicians.*
E.J. Hobsbawm, 453(NYRB):12Feb87-11
Ballstadt, C., E. Hopkins & M. Peterman - see Moodie, S.
Balmas, E. Il buon selvaggio nella cultura francese del Settecento.
E. Chevallier, 549(RLC):Jul-Sep86-360
U. Schulz-Buschhaus, 72:Band223Heft2-439
Balmas, N.C. - see under Clerici Balmas, N.
Balme, C.B. The Reformation of Comedy.
G. Fischer, 67:May86-111
C.N. Genno, 564:May86-181
Balmelle, C. & others. Le Décor géométrique de la mosaïque romaine.
R. Ling, 123:Vol36No2-346
Balmès, M. Peri hermenias.
M. Adam, 542:Jan-Mar86-99
Balslev, A.N. A Study of Time in Indian Philosophy.
W. Halbfass, 318(JAOS):Oct/Dec85-803
Baltà, J.B. - see under Bonet i Baltà, J.
Baly, M.E. Florence Nightingale and the Nursing Legacy.
F.B. Smith, 637(VS):Summer87-539
de Balzac, H. La Comédie humaine. (P-G. Castex, ed)
C. Rosen, 453(NYRB):17Dec87-22
Balzer, W. Empirische Theorien.
H. Kliemt, 167:Nov86-403
Bamber, L. Comic Women, Tragic Men.*
B. Hatlen, 536(Rev):Vol8-241
Bame, K.N. Come to Laugh.
A. Ricard, 538(RAL):Summer86-287
Bammesberger, A. Beiträge zu einem etymologischen Wörterbuch des Altenglischen.
K. Toth, 38:Band104Heft1/2-174
Bammesberger, A. English Etymology.*
E.A. Ebbinghaus, 215(GL):Vol26No4-301
S.M. Embleton, 320(CJL):Fall86-303
Bammesberger, A., ed. Das etymologische Wörterbuch, Fragen der Konzeption und Gestaltung.
E.A. Ebbinghaus, 215(GL):Vol26No1-67
Bammesberger, A. Lateinische Sprachwissenschaft.*
P. Swiggers, 553(RLiR):Jul-Dec86-559
Bammesberger, A., ed. Problems of Old English Lexicography.*
R.C. St.-Jacques, 159:Spring86-97
R.L. Thomson, 215(GL):Vol26No3-217
Bammesberger, A. A Sketch of Diachronic English Morphology.*
A. Bliss, 447(N&Q):Dec85-508
Bammesberger, A. Studien zur Laryngaltheorie.
F.O. Lindeman, 260(IF):Band91-349
Banarjee, K. Regional Political Parties in India.
O. Varkey, 293(JASt):Aug86-879

Bance, A. Theodor Fontane: The Major Novels.*
M. Totten, 406:Fall86-411
Bancquart, M-C. Anatole France.*
R. Lethbridge, 208(FS):Jan86-93
Bancquart, M-C. - see France, A.
Bandem, I.M. & F.E. de Boer. Kaja and Kelod.*
P.B. Zarrilli, 615(TJ):Dec86-493
Bandle, O., W. Baumgartner & J. Glauser, eds. Strindbergs Dramen im Lichte neuerer Methodendiskussionen.
Y. Chevrel, 549(RLC):Jan-Mar86-71
Bandy, A.C. - see Lydus, J.
Banerji, S. Cobwebwalking.
R.F. Dew, 441:18Oct87-26
442(NY):7Dec87-191
Banerji, S. The Wedding of Jayanthi Mandel.
A. Ross, 617(TLS):2-8Oct87-1074
Banfield, A. Unspeakable Sentences.*
M-T. Mathet, 535(RHL):Jul-Aug86-807
P. Violi, 567:Vol60No3/4-361
Banfield, S. Sensibility and English Song.*
T.H., 412:May85-142
M. Hurd, 410(M&L):Jan86-59
N. Temperley, 637(VS):Autumn86-131
Bangs, L. Psychotic Reactions and Carburetor Dung. (G. Marcus, ed)
K. Tucker, 441:22Nov87-15
Banham, M. - see Taylor, T.
Banham, R. A Concrete Atlantis.*
R. Kimball, 45:Aug86-71
Banier, F-M. Balthazar, fils de famille.
M. Rosello, 207(FR):Apr87-719
Bank, C. & A. Dundes. First Prize: Fifteen Years!
E.F. Hellberg, 64(Arv):Vol41-141
Bank, J. Katholieken en de Indonesische Revolutie.
R. Van Niel, 293(JASt):Nov85-187
Banks, I. Espedair Street.
B. Kaveney, 617(TLS):13-19Nov87-1249
Banks, J.M., comp. Books in Native Languages in the Rare Book Collections of the National Library of Canada/Livres en langues autochtones dans les collections de livres rares de la Bibliothèque nationale du Canada. (rev)
B. Edwards, 470:Vol24-105
Banks, L.R. The Warning Bell.
K. Olson, 441:18Jan87-18
Banks, R. Success Stories.*
W.H. Pritchard, 249(HudR):Winter87-648
Bann, S. The Clothing of Clio.*
L. Gossman, 402(MLR):Jan86-203
"The Bannatyne Manuscript."
K. Bitterling, 72:Band223Heft2-405
Banner, L.W. American Beauty.*
D. Janiewski, 579(SAQ):Summer86-309
Bannon, M.J., ed. The Emergence of Irish Planning.
D. Clark, 637(VS):Winter87-273
Baño, J.S. - see under Servera Baño, J.
Banowetz, J. The Pianist's Guide to Pedaling.*
P. Whitmore, 410(M&L):Apr86-198
Banta, M. Imaging American Women.
J. Tompkins, 441:30Aug87-18
Banville, J. The Newton Letter.
M. Hite, 441:19Jul87-19
442(NY):27Apr87-104

19

Barnao, J. HammerLocke.
N. Callendar, 441:8Feb87-20
Barnard, H.F. - see Durr, V.F.
Barnard, J. John Keats.
D. Davie, 617(TLS):19Jun87-651
Barnard, M. Time and the White Tigress.
E. Grosholz, 441:4Jan87-22
R. McDowell, 249(HudR):Winter87-678
Barnard, R. The Cherry Blossom Corpse.
N. Callendar, 441:27Sep87-27
Barnard, R. Death in Purple Prose.
T.J. Binyon, 617(TLS):9-15Oct87-1124
G. Kaufman, 362:2Apr87-24
Barner, W., E. Lämmert and N. Oellers, eds.
Unser Commercium.
L. Sharpe, 402(MLR):Jul86-785
G.A. Wells, 301(JEGP):Oct86-624
Barner, W. & A.M. Reh, eds. Nation und
Gelehrtenrepublik.
R. Baasner, 224(GRM):Band36Heft4-469
H. Beck, 173(ECS):Winter86/87-251
P. Chevallier, 549(RLC):Jul-Sep86-366
H.B. Nisbet, 402(MLR):Jul86-782
Barnes, B.K. The Pragmatics of Left De-
tachment in Spoken Standard French.
J.E. Joseph, 350:Sep87-677
C. Laeufer, 207(FR):Apr87-736
Barnes, C. - see Pasternak, B.
Barnes, D. Fumée.
F. de Martinoir, 450(NRF):Nov86-112
Barnes, D. "I Could Never Be Lonely With-
out a Husband."
A.H.G. Phillips, 617(TLS):20Mar87-302
Barnes, D. Interviews.* (A. Barry, ed)
M.J. Hoffman, 395(MFS):Winter86-611
Barnes, D. Smoke and Other Early Stories.*
(D. Messerli, ed)
L. Curry, 534(RALS):Spring-Autumn84-
222
Barnes, J. Flaubert's Parrot.*
W.N., 102(CanL):Fall86-198
Barnes, J. Metroland.
J. Parini, 441:3May87-26
Barnes, J. Staring at the Sun.*
C. Fuentes, 441:12Apr87-3
D. Lodge, 453(NYRB):7May87-21
J. Mellors, 364:Oct86-91
Barnes, J. - see Aristotle
Barnes, M. Murder in Print.
J. Symons, 617(TLS):20Feb87-183
Barnes, P., ed. A Companion to Post-War
British Theatre.
B. Nightingale, 617(TLS):21Aug87-908
Barnes, P., ed. Dead Funny.
D.J. Enright, 617(TLS):18-24Dec87-1399
Barnes, T.D. Constantine and Eusebius.
R. van den Broek, 394:Vol39fasc1/2-218
Barnes, T.D. Early Christianity and the
Roman Empire.
G. Clarke, 487:Summer86-247
Barnett, A. The Resting Bell.
J. Harding, 617(TLS):18-24Dec87-1394
Barnett, C. The Audit of War.*
K. Middlemas, 324:Jun87-532
Barnett, C. The Pride and the Fall.
C.P. Kindleberger, 441:12Jul87-35
Barnett, G.K. Histoire des bibliothèques
publiques en France de la Révolution à
1939.
E. Weber, 617(TLS):2-8Oct87-1069
Barnett, R. Jade and Fire.
T. Fleming, 441:26Jul87-16

Barnhart, J.E. The Southern Baptist Holy
War.
K. Northcott, 441:1Feb87-16
Barnhart, M.A. Japan Prepares for Total
War.
W.G. Beasley, 617(TLS):14Aug87-868
Barnwell, J. Love of Order.
L. Shore, 106:Summer86-219
Barny, R. Prélude idéologique à la Révolu-
tion française.
K.M. Baker, 173(ECS):Summer87-488
Barocchi, P. & D. Gallo, eds. L'accademia
etrusca.
N. Spivey, 313:Vol76-281
Barocchi, P. & G. Ragionieri, eds. Gli
Uffizi.
M. Campbell, 551(RenQ):Winter86-755
Barolini, T. Dante's Poets.*
L. Pertile, 402(MLR):Jul87-752
R.A. Shoaf, 589:Oct86-1016
K. Taylor, 551(RenQ):Summer86-282
Baron, D. Grammar and Gender.*
639(VQR):Summer86-90
Baron, D.E. Grammar and Good Taste.*
F. Anshen, 35(AS):Spring86-89
L. Moskovit, 126(CCC):Feb86-105
U. Oomen, 38:Band104Heft1/2-159
Baron, F. Faustus.
F.L. Borchardt, 680(ZDP):Band105Heft2-
299
Baron, F., ed. Rilke and the Visual Arts.
U.K. Goldsmith, 406:Winter86-540
Baron, H. Petrarch's "Secretum."
F.E. Cranz, 551(RenQ):Winter86-731
F.R. Hausmann, 72:Band223Heft1-225
M. Palumbo, 379(MedR):Dec86-456
Baron, N.S. Speech, Writing, and Sign.
R. Harweg, 567:Vol61No3/4-285
Barone, P. The Wind.
L.B. Osborne, 441:28Jun87-24
Baroni, M. & L. Callegari, eds. Musical
Grammars and Computer Analysis.*
S.W. Smoliar, 308:Spring86-130
Barr, C., ed. All Our Yesterdays.*
C. Peachment, 707:Autumn86-291
Barr, M. & N.D. Smith, eds. Women and
Utopia.
S. Gubar, 561(SFS):Mar86-79
Barr, R. Selected Stories of Robert Barr.
(J. Parr, ed)
D. Williamson, 296(JCF):No35/36-186
Barratt, A., ed. The Book of Tribulation
ed. from MS Bodley 423.*
B. Millett, 382(MAE):1986/1-132
C.C. Morse, 589:Apr86-490
Barreau, H., ed. L'Explication dans les
sciences de la vie.
M. Espinoza, 160:Jan86-196
Barrell, J. The Political Theory of Paint-
ing from Reynolds to Hazlitt.*
D. Carrier, 290(JAAC):Summer87-420
G. Reynolds, 39:Dec86-568
P. Rogers, 617(TLS):9Jan87-44
Barrett, J.W. Impulse to Revolution in
Latin America.
S. Andreski, 396(ModA):Winter86-73
Barrett, W. Death of the Soul.*
R.E. Lauder, 543:Dec86-369
Barrientos, J.A. - see under Alvarez
Barrientos, J.
Barriga Casalini, G. Los dos mundos del
"Quijote."
E. Williamson, 86(BHS):Oct86-387

Barroll, J.L. Shakespearean Tragedy.
  W.L. Godshalk 301(JEGP):Jul86-445
  E.H. Hageman, 570(SQ):Summer86-256
Barroll, J.L., 3d, ed. Medieval and Ren-
  aissance Drama in England.* (Ser 3, Vol
  1)
  A. Lancashire, 541(RES):Aug86-402
  M.E. Mooney, 130:Spring86-85
Barron, J. Breaking the Ring.
  C.C. Davis, 441:7Jun87-31
Barrow, A. The Great Book of Small Talk.
  D.J. Enright, 617(TLS):18-24Dec87-1399
Barrow, J.D. & F.J. Tipler. The Anthropic
  Cosmological Principle.*
  M. Heller, 543:Mar87-564
  W. McCrea, 617(TLS):2Jan87-5
Barrow, J.W. Gibbon.
  M. Reinhold, 124:Sep-Oct86-56
Barry, A. - see Barnes, D.
Barry, N. & others. Hayek's "Serfdom"
  Revisited.
  P. Johnson, 521:Oct86-350
Barry, N.P. The New Right. On Classical
  Liberalism and Libertarianism.
  D. Miller, 617(TLS):4-10Dec87-1344
Barry, S. The Engine of Owl-Light.
  L. Gordon, 441:1Nov87-24
  S. Rae, 617(TLS):30Oct-5Nov87-1192
Barry, S., ed. The Inherited Boundaries.
  M. Harmon, 272(IUR):Autumn86-234
Barry, S., J. Bradley & A. Empey. A Worthy
  Foundation.
  G. Eogan, 272(IUR):Spring86-96
Barski, O. L'Entorse.
  J.R. Scott, 207(FR):Oct86-160
Barsness, L. Heads, Hides & Horns.
  L. Milazzo, 584(SWR):Spring86-257
Barstow, B. - see Sneyd, B.
Barstow, S. B-Movie.
  J. Mellors, 362:9Apr87-25
Bartels, H. Epos.*
  E.R. Haymes, 406:Fall86-382
Barth, F. The Last Wali of Swat.
  C. Lindholm, 293(JASt):Aug86-872
Barth, J. The Tidewater Tales.
  W. Pritchard, 441:28Jun87-7
Barthélemy, D. Les deux âges de la seig-
  neurie banale.
  T. Evergates, 589:Oct86-893
Barthelme, D. Forty Stories.
  C. James, 441:25Oct87-14
Barthelme, F. Chroma.
  B. Pesetsky, 441:3May87-12
Barthelme, F. Tracer.*
  639(VQR):Winter86-22
Barthelme, S. And He Tells the Little
  Horse the Whole Story.
  T. Le Clair, 441:20Dec87-8
Barthes, R. Criticism and Truth. (K.P.
  Keureman, ed & trans) Incidents.
  J. Sturrock, 617(TLS):3Jul87-713
Barthes, R. Michelet.
  442(NY):16Mar87-105
Barthes, R. The Responsibility of Forms.*
  R. Roth, 560:Fall86-236
Bartholemew, D.A. & L.C. Schoenhals. Bilin-
  gual Dictionaries for Indigenous Lan-
  guages.*
  J.E. Grimes, 269(IJAL):Oct86-422
Bartholomeusz, D. "The Winter's Tale" in
  Performance in England and America 1611-
  1976.*
  T.R. Griffiths, 402(MLR):Jan87-159

Bartled, F. Albert Camus ou le mythe et le
  mime.*
  G. Cesbron, 356(LR):Feb86-87
Bartlett, E. The Czar is Dead.
  P. Forbes, 362:5Mar87-28
Bartlett, L. William Everson.
  R.L. Gale, 649(WAL):Aug86-182
Bartlett, M.D., ed. The New Native
  American Novel.
  G. Ronnow, 649(WAL):Nov86-261
Bartlett, R., ed. Russian Thought and
  Society, 1800-1917.
  M. Banarjee, 574(SEEJ):Spring86-106
  J. Zimmerman, 550(RusR):Jul86-333
Bartlett, R. Trial by Fire and Water.
  J. Sumption, 617(TLS):17Apr87-416
Barton, A. Ben Jonson, Dramatist.*
  J. Barish, 570(SQ):Winter86-522
  R.A. Cave, 610:Summer86-159
  A. Fowler, 536(Rev):Vol8-93
  N.H. Platz, 156(ShJW):Jahrbuch1986-205
Barton, J. Oracles of God.
  J.R. Porter, 617(TLS):13Mar87-278
Barton, J. Playing Shakespeare.*
  R. Gross, 615(TJ):May86-241
  W.T. Liston, 570(SQ):Autumn86-413
  D.G. Watson, 536(Rev):Vol8-59
Bartov, O. The Eastern Front, 1941-45,
  German Troops and the Barbarisation of
  Warfare.
  G. Best, 617(TLS):3Apr87-367
Bartram, A. The English Lettering Tradi-
  tion.
  J.I. Whalley, 617(TLS):29May87-592
Bartram, G. & A. Waine, eds. Brecht in
  Perspective.
  P. Mudford, 447(N&Q):Dec85-572
Bartram, M. The Pre-Raphaelite Camera.
  B. Jay, 637(VS):Spring87-439
  V. Powell, 39:Mar86-219
Bartsch, K., D. Goltschnigg & G. Melzer,
  eds. Für und wider eine österreichische
  Literatur.
  J. Koppensteiner, 406:Summer86-232
Bartsch, R. Sprachnormen.
  G. Bourcier, 189(EA):Oct-Dec87-461
Barty-King, H. Her Majesty's Stationery
  Office.
  B. Crutchley, 324:May87-468
Barwise, J. & J. Perry. Situations and
  Attitudes.*
  J. Butterfield, 479(PhQ):Apr86-292
  N.B. Cocchiarella, 316:Jun86-470
  N. Hornstein, 311(JP):Mar86-168
  G. Leech, 355(LSoc):Sep86-431
Bary, D. Nuevos estudios sobre Huidobro y
  Larrea.
  M. Camurati, 238:Mar86-112
Barzun, J. A Word or Two Before You Go...
  D.J. Enright, 176:Dec87-91
Basarab, J. Pereiaslav 1654.
  F.E. Sysyn, 575(SEER):Jan86-100
Baselt, B. Händel-Handbuch. (Vol 2)
  M.A. Parker-Hale, 317:Fall86-655
Bashevkin, S.B. Toeing the Lines.
  R. Hamilton, 529(QQ):Autumn86-706
Basil of Caesarea. Basilio di Cesarea,
  "Discorso ai Giovani." (M. Naldini, ed)
  W.H.C. Frend, 123:Vol36No1-132
Basilakes, N. Nicephorus Basilicae,
  "Orationes et epistolae." (A. Garzya,
  ed)
  A. Kazhdan, 589:Oct86-895

Basile, B. Poëta Melancholicus, Tradizione classica e follia nell'ultimo Tasso.
 F. Pivont, 356(LR):May86−170
Baslez, M−F. L'étranger dans la Grèce antique.
 I. Joseph, 98:Mar86−244
 D. Whitehead, 303(JoHS):Vol106−237
Bass, R. The Deer Pasture.
 N. Williams, 649(WAL):May86−72
Bassan, F. Alfred de Vigny et la Comédie−Française.*
 F.W.J. Hemmings, 208(FS):Oct86−474
Bassein, B.A. Women and Death.*
 S. O'Brien, 395(MFS):Summer86−353
Bassett, J.E. Faulkner.*
 N. Polk, 40(AEB):Vol8No4−279
Bassin, J. Architectural Competitions in Nineteenth−Century England.
 R. Warde, 637(VS):Summer87−520
Basso, A., ed. Dizionario enciclopedico universale della musica e dei musicisti.
 H. Sachs, 617(TLS):9−15Oct87−1101
Bastet, N. & others. Paul Valéry, Le Pouvoir de l'esprit. (H. Laurenti, ed)
 R. Pietra, 535(RHL):Mar−Apr86−335
Bastos, A.R. − see under Roa Bastos, A.
Bataille, G. Eroticism.
 362:31Dec87−22
Batchelor, J. H.G. Wells.
 J. Huntington, 561(SFS):Jul86−200
 P. Parrinder, 177(ELT):Vol29No2−220
 G.K. Wolfe, 395(MFS):Spring86−133
Batchelor, J.C. American Falls.
 M. Childress, 617(TLS):20−26Nov87−1274
Batchelor, R. Bearings.
 R. Anderson, 102(CanL):Summer86−148
Batchelor, R.E. & M.H. Offord. A Guide to Contemporary French Usage.*
 J−P.Y. Montreuil, 207(FR):Dec86−304
Bate, J. Shakespeare and the English Romantic.
 A. Leighton, 617(TLS):31Jul87−814
Bateman, H.M. The Best of H.M. Bateman.
 E.S. Turner, 617(TLS):29May87−580
Bates, M.J. Wallace Stevens.*
 T. Armstrong, 617(TLS):10Jul87−747
 A. Filreis, 639(VQR):Summer86−543
 L.M. Kawada, 405(MP):Feb87−343
 J.N. Serio, 141:Summer86−354
 H. Vendler, 432(NEQ):Dec86−549
 K.T. Wallingford, 27(AL):May86−274
Bateson, G. & M.C. Angels Fear.
 D.L. Miller, 441:15Nov87−48
Batho, G.R. Thomas Harriot and the North−umberland Household.
 W. Sharratt, 161(DUJ):Dec85−180
Batllori, M. − see Gracián, B.
Batra, R. The Great Depression of 1990.
 E. Janeway, 441:12Jul87−11
Batsleer, J. & others. Rewriting English.*
 S. Scobie, 376:Jun86−128
Batson, B.A. The End of Absolute Monarchy in Siam.
 K.P. Landon, 293(JASt):Feb86−438
Batson, E.B. John Bunyan.
 W.R. Owens, 366:Autumn86−253
Battestin, M.C., ed. Dictionary of Liter−ary Biography. (Vol 39)
 P. Sabor, 529(QQ):Winter86−907
Battestin, M.C. − see Fielding, H.
Battin, W. In the Solar Wind.*
 S.P. Estess, 577(SHR):Winter86−84

Baudelaire, C. The Complete Verse. (Vol 1) (F. Scarfe, trans)
 S. Romer, 617(TLS):3Apr87−364
Baudot, G. − see de Motolinía, T.
Baudouin de Courtenay, J. Ausgewählte Werke in deutscher Sprache. (J. Mugdan, ed)
 F. Häusler, 682(ZPSK):Band39Heft1−121
 A. Liberman, 361:Dec86−376
Baudrillard, J. La Gauche divine.
 C.J. Stivale, 207(FR):Apr87−742
Baudusch, R. Punkt, Punkt, Komma, Strich.
 K. Noke, 682(ZPSK):Band39Heft6−709
Bauer, C. & K. Bohnen, eds. Arthur Schnitzler.
 E. Schwarz, 406:Fall86−414
Bauer, G. & H.F. Pfanner − see Graf, O.M.
Bauer, H.H. The Enigma of Loch Ness.
 P−L. Adams, 61:Feb87−94
Bauer, K.J. Zachary Taylor.
 639(VQR):Summer86−82
Bauer, L. Vertical Hold.
 A. Gelb, 441:8Feb87−24
Bauer, N. Wise−Ears.
 A. Mitcham, 198:Spring86−101
Bauer, R. & J. Wertheimer, eds. Das Ende des Stegreifspiels − Die Geburt des Nationaltheaters.*
 W. Theile, 52:Band21Heft1−94
Bäuerle, R., C. Schwarze & A. von Stechow, eds. Meaning, Use, and Interpretation of Language.
 B. Peeters, 603:Vol10No2−449
Baugh, J. & J. Sherzer, eds. Language in Use.
 W.F. Edwards, 35(AS):Summer86−165
Baughman, R., ed. American Poets.
 B.F. Engel, 115:Fall86−543
"Bauhaus Photography."
 J. Iovine, 45:May86−75
Baum, J. The Calculating Passion of Ada Byron.*
 R. Porter, 617(TLS):3Apr87−347
Baum, V. Shanghai '37.
 A. Sattin, 617(TLS):31Jul87−817
Bauman, R. Verbal Art as Performance.
 D. Jones, 650(WF):Jan86−34
Bauman, R.A. Lawyers in Roman Republican Politics.
 B.W. Frier, 122:Jul86−257
Baumann, G. Robert Musil.
 B. Pike, 406:Spring86−116
Baumann, G. The Written Word.
 A. Rosenheim, 617(TLS):13Mar87−265
Baumann, U. Die Antike in den Epigrammen und Briefen Sir Thomas Mores.
 R.J. Schoeck, 551(RenQ):Winter86−760
Baumann, W. Der Widerspenstigen Zähmung.*
 L. Hughes, 575(SEER):Jan86−127
 N.W. Ingham, 550(RusR):Jan86−51
Baumbach, J. The Life and Times of Major Fiction.
 E. Toynton, 441:7Jun87−22
Baumgarten, A.G. Philosophische Betrach−tungen über einige Bedingungen des Gedichtes.* (H. Paetzold, ed & trans) Texte zur Grundlegung der Ästhetik.* (H.R. Schweizer, ed & trans) Theoret−ische Ästhetik.*
 W. Henckmann, 489(PJGG):Band93Heft2−420

Baumgarten, A.I. The Phoenician History of Philo of Byblos.*
　　J. Mansfeld, 394:Vol39fasc3/4-486
Baumol, W. Superfairness.
　　J.E. Roemer, 185:Apr87-661
Baurmann, J. & O. Hoppe, eds. Handbuch für Deutschlehrer.
　　H. Harnisch, 682(ZPSK):Band39Heft1-142
Baurmeister, U. & others - see "Bibliothèque Nationale, Catalogue des incunables"
Bausch, K-R. & others, eds. Arbeitspapiere der 1., 2., 3. Frühjahrskonferenz zur Erforschung des Fremdsprachenunterrichts. Arbeitspapiere der 4. Frühjahrskonferenz zur Erforschung des Fremdsprachenunterrichts.
　　C. Kramsch, 399(MLJ):Summer86-169
Bausch, R. Spirits.
　　M.S. Bell, 441:14Jun87-16
Bautier, R-H., ed. La France de Philippe Auguste.
　　A.W. Lewis, 589:Apr86-382
Bautier, R-H. & J. Sornay, with F. Muret. Les sources de l'histoire économique et sociale du moyen âge. (Vol 1, Pt 2)
　　B. Lyon, 589:Jan86-122
Bauzá Ochogavía, M. - see Lull, R.
Bawden, C.R. Shamans, Lamas and Evangelicals.
　　G. Lewinson, 575(SEER):Oct86-612
Bawden, N. Circles of Deceit.
　　L. Graeber, 441:29Nov87-20
　　J. McKay, 362:10Sep87-23
　　J. Neville, 617(TLS):17Jul87-766
Bawer, B. The Middle Generation.
　　L. Mackinnon, 617(TLS):6Feb87-128
Bax, M.M.H. Oordelen in taal.
　　A. Braet, 204(FdL):Jun86-143
Baxandall, M. Giotto and the Orators.
　　M. Kemp, 324:Aug87-709
Baxandall, M. Patterns of Intention.
　　A.C. Danto, 90:Jun86-441
　　C. Gould, 39:Oct86-380
　　A.D. Rifkin, 59:Jun86-275
　　M. Sirridge, 290(JAAC):Fall86-94
　　M. Warner, 324:Sep87-781
　　S. Whitfield, 176:Feb87-49
Baxmann, I., E. Laudowicz & A. Menzel. Texte, Taten, Träume.
　　I. Dölling, 654(WB):1/1986-169
Baxter, C. Bangladesh.
　　J.P. Thorp, 293(JASt):Aug86-789
Baxter, C. First Light.
　　M. Mifflin, 441:4Oct87-18
Baxter, C. Through the Safety Net.*
　　J. Brock, 573(SSF):Fall86-459
　　T. McGonigle, 532(RCF):Summer86-155
Baxter, J. Shakespeare's Poetic Styles.
　　D.M. Burton, 599:Spring86-115
Bayer, E. & D. Endler. Bulgarische Literatur im Überblick.
　　D. Witschew, 654(WB):5/1986-873
Bayer, R. Homosexuality and American Psychiatry.
　　M. Lavin, 488:Jun86-252
Bayer, W. Pattern Crimes.
　　T.J. Binyon, 617(TLS):20-26Nov87-1274
　　G. Kaufman, 362:26Nov87-29
Bayer-Berenbaum, L. The Gothic Imagination.
　　M.T. Chialant, 677(YES):Vol16-308

Bayle, M-C. "Cherie" d'Edmond de Goncourt.
　　P. Cogny, 535(RHL):Mar-Apr86-318
Bayle, P. Pensées diverses sur la comète. (A. Prat, ed; rev by P. Rétat)
　　E.J. Campion, 207(FR):May87-859
　　J. Le Brun, 535(RHL):Sep-Oct86-914
Bayley, J. The Order of Battle at Trafalgar and Other Essays.
　　B. Bergonzi, 176:Jul/Aug87-41
　　C. Brown, 617(TLS):24Jul87-790
　　C. Emerson, 441:12Jul87-21
　　V. Shaw, 362:23Jul87-23
Bayley, J. Selected Essays.
　　F. McCombie, 447(N&Q):Dec85-559
Bayley, J. Shakespeare and Tragedy.
　　V. Bourgy, 189(EA):Apr-Jun87-206
Bayley, P. Selected Sermons of the French Baroque (1600-1650).
　　J. Hennequin, 535(RHL):Mar-Apr86-272
Baylis, S. Utrillo's Mother.
　　L. Ellmann, 617(TLS):21Aug87-896
Baym, N. Novels, Readers, and Reviewers.*
　　A. Habegger, 301(JEGP):Jul86-472
Baym, N. & others, eds. The Norton Anthology of American Literature. (2nd ed)
　　M. Dodsworth, 175:Summer86-196
　　W.S., 148:Autumn86-119
Baynes, K., J. Bohman & T. McCarthy, eds. After Philosophy.
　　C. Larmore, 441:8Mar87-21
Bazán, E.P. - see under Pardo Bazán, E.
Bazin, A. Le Cinéma français de la Libération à la Nouvelle Vague (1945-1958).
　　M. Cottenet-Hage, 207(FR):Oct86-157
Bazire, J. & J.E. Cross, eds. Eleven Old English Rogationtide Homilies.*
　　H. Sauer, 38:Band104Heft1/2-184
Beacco, J-C. & S. Lieutaud. Tours de France.
　　P.J. Edwards, 399(MLJ):Autumn86-305
Beach, I. & others. Swedish.
　　M.J. Blackwell, 399(MLJ):Summer86-203
Beadle, R. & P.M. King, eds. York Mystery Plays.*
　　P. Meredith, 402(MLR):Jul87-699
Beagle, P.S. The Folk of the Air.
　　G. Jonas, 441:18Jan87-33
Beal, B. & R. Macleod. Prairie Fire.*
　　J. Doyle, 649(WAL):May86-89
　　J.H. Thompson, 529(QQ):Winter86-917
Beale, J. Women in Ireland.
　　G. Meaney, 272(IUR):Autumn86-248
Beales, D. Joseph II. (Vol 1)
　　D. McKay, 617(TLS):2-8Oct87-1068
Bean, J., with L. Turčić. 15th-18th Century French Drawings in the Metropolitan Museum of Art.
　　K. Andrews, 617(TLS):30Jan87-121
　　J.B. Shaw, 380:Summer86-247
Bear, G. Eon.
　　C. Greenland, 617(TLS):6Feb87-134
Beard, G. Stucco and Decorative Plasterwork in Europe.
　　C. Thon, 683:Band49Heft3-416
Beard, M. & M. Crawford. Rome in the Late Republic.
　　M. Griffin, 123:Vol36No2-270
　　J.C. Traupman, 124:Jul-Aug87-449
　　639(VQR):Spring86-53
Beards, V. - see Somerville, E.O. & M. Ross
Beardsley, M.C. The Aesthetic Point of View. (M.J. Wreen & D.M. Callen, eds)
　　H. Osborne, 289:Spring86-97

Beardsley, M.C. Aesthetics. (2nd ed)
  H. Osborne, 289:Spring86-97
Bearman, J. Qadhafi's Libya.
  J. Wright, 617(TLS):27Mar87-314
Beasley, J.C. Novels of the 1740s.
  O. Izumiya, 677(YES):Vol16-272
Beattie, A. Alex Katz.
  L. Liebmann, 441:28Jun87-24
Beattie, A. Love Always.*
  639(VQR):Winter86-20
Beattie, A. Where You'll Find Me.*
  L. Taylor, 617(TLS):14Aug87-873
Beattie, S. The New Sculpture.*
  D. James, 54:Dec86-687
Beatty, B. Byron's "Don Juan."
  N. Berry, 617(TLS):23Jan87-80
  P. Morgan, 179(ES):Dec86-571
  148:Autumn86-118
Beaty, F.L. Byron the Satirist.
  W.P. Elledge, 661(WC):Autumn86-240
  C.T. Goode, 191(ELN):Dec86-71
Beauchamp, H. Le Théâtre pour enfants au
  Québec: 1950-1980.
  N. Rewa, 108:Winter86-136
Beauchemin, N., P. Martel & M. Theoret.
  Vocabulaire du québécois parlé en Estrie.
  R. Pellen, 553(RLiR):Jul-Dec86-604
Beauchemin, Y. The Alley Cat.
  B. Coleman, 441:11Jan87-14
  M. Fee, 376:Dec86-132
Beaufret, J. Entretiens avec Frédéric de
  Towarnicki.
  P. Trotignon, 542:Jan-Mar86-134
Beaulieu, M. Kaléidoscope ou les aléas du
  corps grave.
  P.G. Lewis, 207(FR):Dec86-287
Beaulieu, M. Robert Le Lorrain (1661-
  1743).
  D. Walker, 54:Sep86-496
Beaulieu, V-L. Monsieur Melville.
  E-M. Kröller, 102(CanL):Fall86-137
Beauman, N. Cynthia Asquith.
  E.S. Turner, 617(TLS):2-8Oct87-1064
Beauman, S. Destiny.
  D. Fitzpatrick, 441:12Apr87-26
  H. Wackett, 362:30Jul87-23
de Beaumarchais, J-P., D. Couty & A. Rey.
  Dictionnaire des littératures de langue
  française.
  A.D. Ketchum, 207(FR):Mar87-525
de Beaumarchais, P.A.C. Le Mariage de
  Figaro. (R. Niklaus, ed)
  A. Boës, 535(RHL):Mar-Apr86-293
Beaumont, A. Busoni the Composer.*
  D. Puffett, 415:Jan86-29
Beaumont, A. - see Busoni, F.
Beaumont, B. - see Flaubert, G. & I.S. Tur-
  genev
Beaumont, K. Alfred Jarry.
  W.D. Howarth, 208(FS):Jan86-100
  D. Whitton, 402(MLR):Jul86-751
Beaune, C. Naissance de la nation France.
  J-P. Guinle, 450(NRF):Apr86-101
de Beauregard, O.C. - see under Costa de
  Beauregard, O.
de Beaurepaire, F. Les Noms de communes
  et anciennes paroisses de la Seine-
  Maritime. Dictionnaire topographique
  du département de Seine-Maritime. (J.
  Laporte & others, eds)
  F.R. Hamlin, 424:Jun86-206
Beausoleil, C. Les Livres parlent.
  M.A. Parmentier, 627(UTQ):Fall86-193

de Beauvoir, S. Adieux.*
  E.F. Bertoldi, 154:Winter86-777
Beaver, H. The Great American Masquerade.
  M.B., 295(JML):Nov86-403
  W.E. Lenz, 27(AL):Oct86-430
  D. Seed, 541(RES):Nov86-604
Bec, C. Les livres des florentins (1413-
  1608).
  M. Grendler, 551(RenQ):Summer86-286
  P.F. Grendler, 589:Jul86-725
Bec, C. & I. Mamczarz, eds. Le théâtre
  italien et l'Europe, XVe-XVIIe siècles.
  P. Trivero, 549(RLC):Jul-Sep86-364
Bec, C. & I. Mamczarz - see Petrocchi, G.
Beccaria, G.L. La guerra e gli asfodeli.
  E. Saccone, 400(MLN):Jan86-189
Beck, H. - see Joyce, J.
Beck, K.K. The Body in the Volvo.
  N. Callendar, 441:6Dec87-79
Becker, C. & others - see Hegel, G.W.F.
Becker, G. Neuzeitliche Subjektivität und
  Religiosität.
  F.W. Graf, 489(PJGG):Band93Heft1-217
Becker, J. Bronsteins Kinder.
  M. Kane, 617(TLS):15May87-524
Becker, J. & A.H. Feinstein, eds. Karawi-
  tan. (Vol 1)
  N. Sorrell, 410(M&L):Apr86-172
  J.M. Suyenaga, 293(JASt):Feb86-439
Becker, L.F. Françoise Mallet-Joris.
  S. Rava, 207(FR):May87-876
Becker, V. Art Nouveau Jewelry.
  C. Gere, 39:Jun86-440
Becker, W. Selbstbewusstsein und Erfah-
  rung.
  P. Rohs, 687:Jul-Sep86-439
  W. Steinbeck, 342:Band77Heft4-501
Becker, W. - see Kant, I.
Becker-Cantarino, B., ed. Martin Opitz.
  R. Paulin, 447(N&Q):Jun86-262
Becker-Cantarino, B. - see Heinsius, D.
Beckett, M. Give Them Stones.
  A-M. Conway, 617(TLS):25Sep-1Oct87-
  1052
Beckett, S. Catastrophe et autres dramat-
  icules.
  B. Clément, 98:Oct86-1016
Beckford, J.A. Cult-Controversies.
  R.H. Roberts, 161(DUJ):Jun86-400
Beckford, J.A., ed. New Religious Move-
  ments and Rapid Social Change.
  B. Wilson, 617(TLS):11-17Sep87-997
Beckson, K. Arthur Symons.
  E. White, 617(TLS):13-19Nov87-1239
Becq, A. Genèse de l'esthétique française
  moderne.
  F.P. Bowman, 210(FrF):Sep86-374
  N. Cronk, 208(FS):Oct86-469
Bédard, E. & J. Maurais, eds. La norme
  linguistique.*
  J-P. Beaujot, 209(FM):Oct86-250
Bedient, C. In the Heart's Last Kingdom.*
  W.H. Pritchard, 560:Fall86-250
Bedriomo, E. Proust, Wagner et la coïnci-
  dence des arts.*
  A. Henry, 72:Band223Heft2-474
  E.R. Jackson, 210(FrF):May86-243
  A. Montandon, 535(RHL):Jul-Aug86-786
Bee, O.J. The Petroleum Resources of Indo-
  nesia.
  R. Kessler, 293(JASt):Nov85-189
Beecher, J. Charles Fourier.
  E. Weber, 441:17May87-22

Beehler, M.   T.S. Eliot, Wallace Stevens,
and the Discourses of Difference.
   M. Lebowitz, 344:Fall87-142
Beekes, S.P.   The Origins of the Indo-
European Nominal Inflection.
   J. Haudry, 159:Spring86-101
Beeman, R.R.   The Evolution of the Southern
Backcountry.*
   T.D. Clark, 585(SoQ):Winter87-153
Beer, G.   George Eliot.
   K.M. Rogers, 637(VS):Summer87-541
Beer, G. & M. Harris - see Meredith, G.
Beer, J., ed.   "A Passage to India."*
   A.W., 295(JML):Nov86-472
Beerbohm, M.   The Illustrated Zuleika
Dobson.
   I. Grushow, 177(ELT):Vol29No3-322
   S. Pickering, 569(SR):Summer86-lix
   V.S. Pritchett, 453(NYRB):5Nov87-3
Beerbohm, M.   Rossetti and His Circle.
   P-L. Adams, 61:Nov87-122
   V.S. Pritchett, 453(NYRB):5Nov87-3
Beery, C.   Making It Easy.
   R.A. Hartzell, 207(FR):Apr87-733
Beeston, A.F.L. & others, eds.   Arabic
Literature to the End of the Umayyad
Period.*
   F. Rosenthal, 589:Apr86-491
van Beethoven, L.   Ludwig van Beethoven:
Der Briefwechsel mit dem Verlag Schott.
(S. Brandenburg & others, eds)
   W. Drabkin, 415:Dec86-689
Beetz, K.H.   Tennyson, a Bibliography,
1827-1982.
   P.G. Scott, 536(Rev):Vol8-101
Beffroy de Reigny, L.A.   Nicodème dans la
Lune ou La Révolution pacifique, folie en
prose en trois actes.*   (M. Sajous, ed)
   M-E. Diéval, 535(RHL):Mar-Apr86-292
   W.D. Howarth, 208(FS):Oct86-468
"Before Hollywood."
   P. Brunette, 441:7Jun87-31
Bego, M.   The Best of "Modern Screen."
   D. Gallagher, 18:Dec86-61
Bégou, G.   Le Ciel luisait d'étoiles.
   L. di Benedetto, 207(FR):Feb87-422
Behaghel, O., ed.   Heliand und Genesis.
(9th ed) (revised by B. Taeger)
   H. Maxwell, 589:Jan86-224
Béhague, G., ed.   Performance Practice.*
   J.C. Dje Dje, 91:Fall86-306
Béhar, H., ed.   Cahiers du Centre de
recherches sur le Surréalisme, Mélusine.
(No 5)
   P. Plouvier, 535(RHL):Mar-Apr86-333
Behar, R.   Santa María del Monte.*
   S. Ott, 617(TLS):16Jan87-64
Behler, E.   Die Zeitschriften der Brüder
Schlegel.*
   M.P. Bullock, 222(GR):Spring86-77
Behounde, E.   Dialectique de la ville et de
la campagne chez Gabrielle Roy et chez
Mongo Beti.
   M. Mortimer, 538(RAL):Winter86-572
Behr, C.A. - see Aelius Aristides
Behrens, K.   Friedrich Schlegels Ge-
schichts philosophie (1794-1808).
   R.B. Bottigheimer, 221(GQ):Summer86-
483
Bei Dao.   Waves.
   L. Pan, 176:Nov87-47

Beidelman, T.O.   Moral Imagination in
Kaguru Modes of Thought.
   A. Kuper, 617(TLS):27Feb87-224
Beier, A.L.   Masterless Men.*
   P. Hyland, 568(SCN):Fall86-47
   W.T. MacCaffrey, 551(RenQ):Winter86-
767
Beierwaltes, W.   Denken des Einen.
   A.H. Armstrong, 123:Vol36No2-322
Beik, W.   Absolutism and Society in Seven-
teenth-Century France.
   J. Davies, 208(FS):Apr86-209
   O. Ranum, 551(RenQ):Winter86-775
Beilharz, P.   Trotsky, Trotskyism and the
Transition to Socialism.
   R. Service, 617(TLS):6-12Nov87-1213
Beissel, H.   Season of Blood.*
   B. Pirie, 102(CanL):Winter85-172
Beit-Hallahmi, B.   The Israeli Connection.
   S. Hoffmann, 453(NYRB):8Oct87-8
Beja, M., S.E. Gontarski & P. Astier, eds.
Samuel Beckett.*
   J. Fletcher, 208(FS):Jan86-105
   C. Zilliacus, 397(MD):Mar86-137
Belchem, J.   "Orator" Hunt.*
   J.A. Epstein, 637(VS):Winter87-264
Belfrage, S.   Living With War.
   J. Thomas, 441:20Sep87-15
   442(NY):16Nov87-160
Bell, D.   And We Are Not Saved.
   V. Harding, 441:11Oct87-7
   442(NY):7Dec87-192
Bell, I.A.   Defoe's Fiction.*
   P. Alkon, 173(ECS):Winter86/87-220
   W.R. Owens, 179(ES):Dec86-567
   G. Sill, 566:Spring87-182
Bell, I.F.A.   Critic as Scientist.*
   W. Baumann, 38:Band104Heft3/4-529
Bell, I.F.A., ed.   Henry James.*
   V. Jones, 541(RES):Nov86-589
   D. Kirby, 150(DR):Fall86-380
   R. Posnock, 141:Spring86-222
Bell, I.F.A., ed.   Ezra Pound.*
   P. Makin, 402(MLR):Jan87-189
Bell, J.L.   Boolean-Valued Models and
Independence Proofs in Set Theory.   (2nd
ed)
   J.E. Baumgartner, 316:Dec86-1076
Bell, M.   Old Snow Just Melting.*   Drawn by
Stones, by Earth, by Things That Have
Been in the Fire.*
   T. Swiss, 639(VQR):Winter86-173
Bell, M.   The Sentiment of Reality.*
   T. Braun, 447(N&Q):Sep85-422
Bell, M., with W. Stafford.   Segues.
   T. Swiss, 639(VQR):Winter86-173
Bell, M.J.   The World from Brown's Lounge.
   R.A. Banes, 106:Spring86-93
Bell, M.S.   The Year of Silence.
   R. Kaveney, 617(TLS):6-12Nov87-1227
   R. Silman, 441:15Nov87-15
Bell, M.S.   Zero db.
   A. Bernays, 441:15Feb87-15
   R. Kaveney, 617(TLS):6-12Nov87-1227
Bell, Q.   The Brandon Papers.
   J. Hamard, 189(EA):Jul-Sep86-362
   639(VQR):Spring86-55
Bell, R.M.   Holy Anorexia.*
   D.O. Hughes, 385(MQR):Winter87-266
   G.G. May, 529(QQ):Winter86-931
   E.F. Rice, Jr., 551(RenQ):Winter86-733
Bell, S.   IF ... Bounces Back.
   D.J. Enright, 617(TLS):18-24Dec87-1399

Bell, S.H. Across the Narrow Sea.
  P. Craig, 617(TLS):24Jul87-802
de Bellaigue, G. Sèvres Porcelain in the
  Collection of Her Majesty the Queen: The
  Louis XVI Service.
  R. Savill, 90:Jun86-424
  G. Wills, 39:Jun86-441
Bellamy, J. Robin Hood.
  R. Wadge, 203:Vol97No1-114
Bellamy, J.D., ed. American Poetry Ob-
  served.*
  B. Almon, 102(CanL):Spring86-177
Bellan, R. The Unnecessary Evil.
  L. Robinson, 99:Feb87-38
Bellandi, F., F. Berti & M. Mantovani, eds.
  Statuti della Lega del Borgo a San
  Lorenzo di Mugello (1374).
  D.J. Osheim, 589:Jul86-726
du Bellay, J. Oeuvres poétiques. (Vol 7)
  (G. Demerson, ed & trans)
  J-P. Beaulieu, 539:Nov86-382
  K.J. Evans, 208(FS):Apr86-198
  M. Quainton, 402(MLR):Apr87-471
  L.V.R., 568(SCN):Spring-Summer86-31
Bellen, H. Metus Gallicus-Metus Punicus.
  A.M. Eckstein, 121(CJ):Apr-May87-335
de Belleperche, G. Le fragment de la
  Chevalerie de Judas Machabee. (J.R.
  Smeets, ed)
  G. Roques, 553(RLiR):Jan-Jun86-282
Bellet, R. - see Vallès, J.
Belletto, R. L'Enfer.*
  L.K. Penrod, 207(FR):May87-903
Bellini, G. Historia de la literatura
  hispanoamericana.
  J.S. Brushwood, 240(HR):Summer86-361
  H.M. Cavallari, 238:Dec86-879
  D.L. Shaw, 402(MLR):Jul87-768
Bellis, F. Gardening and Beyond.
  A. Lacy, 441:31May87-14
Bellman, B. The Language of Secrecy.
  W.P. Murphy, 538(RAL):Summer86-296
Bellow, S. The Dean's December.
  M.G. Yetman, 477(PLL):Fall86-429
Bellow, S., ed. Great Jewish Short
  Stories.
  S. Minot, 455:Mar86-76
Bellow, S. More Die of Heartbreak.
  R. Davies, 362:29Oct87-29
  W. Gaddis, 441:24May87-1
  A. Kazin, 453(NYRB):16Jul87-3
  T. Rafferty, 442(NY):20Jul87-89
  G. Strawson, 617(TLS):23-29Oct87-1157
Bellringer, A.W. "The Ambassadors."*
  N. Bradbury, 541(RES):May86-272
  J. Preston, 402(MLR):Oct87-936
Bellver, C. Rafael Alberti en sus horas de
  destierro.
  J. Nantell, 238:Sep86-548
  N. Toscano Liria, 552(REH):Oct86-118
Beloff, H. Camera Culture.*
  N. Warburton, 89(BJA):Autumn86-408
Beloff, N. Tito's Flawed Legacy.*
  R.J. Crampton, 161(DUJ):Jun86-372
Belting, H. The End of the History of Art?
  A.C. Danto, 617(TLS):18-24Sep87-1015
Belting, H. & D. Eichberger. Jan van Eyck
  als Erzähler.*
  P. Reutersward, 341:Vol55No1-40
Bely, A. The Dramatic Symphony.*
  A. McMillin, 402(MLR):Jul87-810

Bely, A. Selected Essays.* (S. Cassedy,
  ed & trans)
  T.R. Beyer, Jr., 574(SEEJ):Winter86-578
Belyea, B. & E. Dansereau, eds. Driving
  Home.*
  J.H. Ferres, 168(ECW):Fall86-185
Bemrose, J. Imagining Horses.
  G. Boire, 102(CanL):Fall86-130
Bemrose, S. Dante's Angelic Intelligence.*
  J.C. Barnes, 278(IS):Vol41-125
  R. Kay, 589:Apr86-384
Ben-Dov, M. In the Shadow of the Temple.
  42(AR):Winter86-125
Benabou, E-M. La Prostitution et la police
  des moeurs au 18e siècle.
  D. Coward, 617(TLS):11-17Sep87-984
Benacchio, R. Modalità allocutive pronom-
  inali nella società moscovita del sec.
  XVII.
  H. Leeming, 575(SEER):Jul86-449
Benacerraf, P. & H. Putnam, eds. Philoso-
  phy of Mathematics.* (2nd ed)
  G.E. Rosado Haddock, 160:Jan86-151
Benardete, S. - see Plato
Bence-Jones, M. Clive of India.
  J. Ridley, 617(TLS):11-17Sep87-996
Bencivenga, E. Il primo libro di logica.
  F. Previale, 316:Sep86-827
Bendazzi, G. The Films of Woody Allen.
  362:31Dec87-21
Bender, B. The Archaeology of Brittany,
  Normandy and the Channel Islands.*
  A. Burl, 617(TLS):20Feb87-193
Bender, T. New York Intellect.
  R. Boyers, 441:26Jul87-18
  442(NY):13Jul87-89
Bender, W., ed. Rastafari-Kunst aus
  Jamaica.
  D.J. Crowley, 2(AfrA):Feb86-89
Bendixen, A., ed. The Whole Family.
  A. Diamond, 357:Spring87-53
Benedetti, M.T. Dante Gabriel Rossetti.
  J.A. Gere, 39:Jan86-58
Benedetti, S. Fuori dal Classicismo.
  D. Moore, 576:Jun86-171
Benedict, P. Town Smokes.
  D. McWhorter, 441:12Jul87-13
Benedict, P.K. Toppakō.
  R.A. Miller, 350:Sep87-643
Benenson, F.C. Probability, Objectivity
  and Evidence.*
  R. Foley, 484(PPR):Mar87-515
  D. Miller, 479(PhQ):Oct86-536
  P. Milne, 84:Mar86-123
Benes, P. & J.M., eds. American Speech.*
  J.L. Dillard, 292(JAF):Jul/Sep86-347
Benes, P., with J.M. Benes, eds. Foodways
  in the Northeast.*
  E.J. Reitz, 656(WMQ):Jul86-496
Benfey, C.E.G. Emily Dickinson and the
  Problem of Others.*
  J.F. Diehl, 651(WHR):Autumn86-281
  J. Loving, 183(ESQ):Vol32No3-201
Bénichou-Safar, H. Les tombes puniques de
  Carthage.
  J-P. Thuillier, 555:Vol59fasc2-337
Benjamin, R. & R.T. Kudrle, eds. The
  Industrial Future of the Pacific Basin.
  M.G. Untawale, 293(JASt):Aug86-809
Benjamin, S.M., ed. Occasional Papers of
  the Society for German-American Studies.
  (Pts 1-11)
  K. Kehr, 685(ZDL):1/1986-114

Benjamin W. Le concept de critique.
Gesammelte Schriften. (Vol 6)
R. Rochlitz, 98:Dec86-1182
Benjamin, W. Moscow Diary. (G. Smith, ed)
442(NY):9Feb87-104
Ben Jelloun, T. Les Amandiers sont morts
de leurs blessures, [suivi de] A l'insu
du souvenir.
M-L. Little, 207(FR):Apr87-720
Benko, S. Pagan Rome and the Early Chris-
tians.*
R.P.C. Hanson, 123:Vol36No2-333
A. Wasserstein, 313:Vol76-302
Benn, T. Out of the Wilderness.
P. Hennessy, 362:22Oct87-26
Bennet, G. The Wound and the Doctor.
R. Porter, 362:9Apr87-24
Bennett, A. Kafka's Dick.
M. Billington, 176:Jan87-54
Bennett, A. The Letters of Arnold Bennett.
(Vol 4) (J. Hepburn, ed)
J. Sutherland, 617(TLS):31Jul87-815
Bennett, A.A. Missionary Journalist in
China.
K.S. Vee-Sui, 302:Vol22No1-71
Bennett, B., A. Kaes & W.J. Lillyman.
Probleme der Moderne.
I. Hoesterey, 221(GQ):Winter86-119
J.F. Reynolds, 400(MLN):Apr86-706
Bennett, J. The Hunger Machine.
P. Pullman, 441:23Aug87-17
Bennett, J. A Study of Spinoza's Ethics.*
R. Ariew, 484(PPR):Jun87-649
E.J. Bond, 483:Jan86-125
E.J. Lowe, 83:Spring86-116
F. Mathews, 63:Dec86-520
P. Winch, 521:Apr86-140
Bennett, J.A.W. Middle English Literature.
(D. Gray, ed)
A.J. Minnis, 617(TLS):6Feb87-140
Bennett, L. Dangerous Wives and Sacred
Sisters.
E. Friedlander, 293(JASt):Nov85-160
Bennett, M. The Battle of Bosworth.
A.L. Rowse, 551(RenQ):Winter86-759
Bennett, T. & J. Woollacott. Bond and
Beyond.
J. Wolff, 362:21May87-28
Bennett, W.I., S.E. Goldfinger & G.T.
Johnson, eds. Your Good Health.
Y. Baskin, 441:27Sep87-37
Bennington, G. Sententiousness and the
Novel.*
P. Kamuf, 173(ECS):Summer87-483
Benoit, J., with S. Baker. Running Tide.
J.D. Cain, 441:1Nov87-28
Benrekassa, G. Fables de la personne.
P. Frantz, 208(FS):Oct86-492
Bensick, C.M. La Nouvelle Beatrice.
M. Hallissy, 573(SSF):Winter86-133
C.D. Johnson, 27(AL):Mar86-129
Benson, C.D. Chaucer's Drama of Style.
B. O'Donoghue, 617(TLS):29May87-587
Benson, J., ed. The Working Class in
England 1875-1914.
L.J. Satre, 637(VS):Summer87-560
Benson, M. Nelson Mandela.*
C. Hope, 364:Jun86-103
Benson, P. The Levels.
N. Irving, 617(TLS):11-17Sep87-976
Benson, R. German Expressionist Drama.*
L. Sharpe, 402(MLR):Jan86-257

Benstock, B., ed. Art in Crime Writing.
E.S. Lauterbach, 395(MFS):Summer86-364
Benstock, B., ed. Critical Essays on James
Joyce.*
272(IUR):Spring86-109
Benstock, B., ed. Essays on Detective Fic-
tion.
J.S. Whitley, 447(N&Q):Dec85-568
Benstock, B. James Joyce.*
J. Hurt, 301(JEGP):Jul86-470
J. Voelker, 573(SSF):Spring86-216
Benstock, B., ed. James Joyce and his
Contemporaries.
R. Mason, 447(N&Q):Sep85-407
Benstock, B., ed. The Seventh of Joyce.
P. Lawley, 402(MLR):Jan87-187
Benterrak, K., S. Muecke & P. Roe. Reading
the Country.
L. Ryan, 381:Mar86-49
Bentini, J., ed. Bastianino e la pittura a
Ferrara nel secondo cinquecento.
C. Gould, 39:Jun86-441
Bentley, E. The Brecht Memoir.
R. Hornby, 615(TJ):Oct86-379
Bentley, E. Monstrous Martyrdoms.
B. Grantham, 157:No159-47
Bentley, E. Thinking About the Playwright.
R. Bryden, 441:5Jul87-21
Bentley, G.E. The Profession of Player in
Shakespeare's Time, 1590-1642.*
A.J. Cook, 570(SQ):Autumn86-412
N.B. Hansen, 125:Fall85-89
M. Jones, 541(RES):May86-250
Bentley, U. Private Accounts.*
J. Mellors, 364:Aug/Sep86-147
Benvenisti, M. Conflicts and Contradic-
tions.*
D. Stone, 390:Jun/Jul86-61
Benvenuti, A.T. - see under Tissoni Ben-
venuti, A.
Beny, R. The Romance of Architecture.
B. Boucher, 39:Mar86-219
Benziman, U. Sharon.*
D. Isaac, 390:Dec86-49
"Beowulf."* (M. Osborn, trans)
E.G. Stanley, 541(RES):May86-304
"Beowulf." (G. Roberts, trans)
M.C. Seymour, 179(ES):Aug86-364
Berardi, P. L'Antica Maiolica di Pesaro
dal XIV al XVII secolo.
J.V.G. Mallet, 90:Jun86-424
Berberova, N. The Accompanist.
B. Heldt, 617(TLS):28Aug87-932
Berberova, N. L'Accompagnatrice.
F. de Martinoir, 450(NRF):Apr86-117
Bercé, Y-M. & others, eds. Destins et
enjeux du XVIIe siècle.
J. Lough, 475:Vol13No24-365
Bercovitch, S., ed. Reconstructing Amer-
ican Literary History.*
P.F. Gura, 27(AL):Dec86-620
T. Kent, 141:Fall86-470
M.D.O., 295(JML):Nov86-354
S. Olster, 357:Spring87-50
Bercuson, D. & D. Wertheimer. A Trust
Betrayed.
G.W., 102(CanL):Summer86-150
Bere, C. Pennod yn Hanes Milwr.
T.A. Watkins, 112:Vol18-209
Beregovski, M. Old Jewish Folk Music. (M.
Slobin, ed & trans)
J. Spector, 187:Winter87-163

Berenson, B. Le Voyageur passionné.
G. Quinsat, 450(NRF):Jun86-95
Berenson, B. & I.S. Gardner. The Letters
of Bernard Berenson and Isabella Stewart
Gardner, 1887-1924. (R.V. Hadley, ed)
D.C. McGill, 441:22Nov87-33
Berg, A. & A. Schoenberg. The Berg-
Schoenberg Correspondence. (J. Brand,
C. Hailey & D. Harris, eds)
L. Kuhn, 441:8Nov87-27
R. Craft, 453(NYRB):5Nov87-30
Berg, A.M., L. Frost & A. Olsen, eds.
Kvindfolk.
M.F. Metcalf, 563(SS):Winter86-93
van den Berg, G.P. Organisation und Ar-
beitsweise der sowjetischen Regierung.
M. McCauley, 575(SEER):Oct86-637
van den Berg, G.P. The Soviet System of
Justice.
P.B. Maggs, 550(RusR):Oct86-451
van den Berg, K.T. Playhouse and Cosmos.*
A.F. Kinney, 250(HLQ):Summer86-283
Berg, M. Aspects of Time.
B. Kiernan, 71(ALS):May86-417
Berg, S. The Body Labyrinth.
R. Anderson, 102(CanL):Summer86-148
Berg, S. In It.
455:Dec86-64
Bergen, J.J. & G.D. Bills, eds. Spanish
and Portuguese in Social Context.
M.M. Azevedo, 545(RPh):Feb87-387
Bergenholtz, H. & J. Mugdan, eds. Lexiko-
graphie und Grammatik.
F.W. Gester, 38:Band104Heft3/4-453
Berger, A.L. Crisis and Covenant.
L. Field, 395(MFS):Summer86-279
Berger, C. Forms of Farewell.*
S.S. Baskett, 115:Winter86-123
D.H. Hesla, 27(AL):Oct86-470
Berger, C. Science, God and Nature in
Victorian Canada.*
C.G. Holland, 150(DR):Fall86-393
Berger, F.R. Happiness, Justice and
Freedom.*
R.W. Hoag, 449:Mar86-81
Berger, G. Der komisch-satirische Roman
und seine Leser.
A. Niderst, 475:Vol13No24-367
Berger, J. Once in Europa.
P-L. Adams, 61:May87-95
R. Critchfield, 441:5Apr87-9
Berger, M., E. Berger & J. Patrick. Benny
Carter.
E. Southern, 91:Spring86-192
Berger, R.W. In the Garden of the Sun
King.
T. Hodgkinson, 39:Jun86-442
Berger, T. Being Invisible.
F. Prose, 441:12Apr87-9
Bergeron, D.M., ed. Pageantry in the
Shakespearean Theater.*
M. Charney, 579(SAQ):Autumn86-401
M. Jones, 541(RES):Nov86-560
A. Lancashire, 627(UTQ):Spring87-463
Bergeron, D.M. Shakespeare's Romances and
the Royal Family.
T.L. Berger, 579(SAQ):Autumn86-402
E.A.J. Honigmann, 551(RenQ):Autumn86-
561

Bergeron, D.M. & S. Lindenbaum, eds.
Research Opportunities in Renaissance
Drama, XVII (1984).
D.W. Pearson, 568(SCN):Spring-Summer86-
18
Bergeron, P.H. Antebellum Politics in
Tennessee.
L. Shore, 106:Summer86-219
Bergess, W.F., B.R.M. Riddell & J. Whyman,
eds. Bibliography of British Newspapers:
Kent.
J. Feather, 447(N&Q):Sep85-399
Bergez, D. - see Daudet, A.
Bergh, T. & others. Growth and Develop-
ment.
K. Smemo, 563(SS):Winter86-68
Berghahn, K.L. & H.U. Seeber, eds. Lit-
erarische Utopien von Morus bis zur
Gegenwart.
D. Dowdey, 221(GQ):Winter86-168
W. Füger, 38:Band104Heft1/2-214
Berghaus, G. Die Quellen zu Andreas
Gryphius' Trauerspiel "Carolus Stuardus."
J.P. Aikin, 221(GQ):Winter86-134
G. Dünnhaupt, 301(JEGP):Jan86-76
J. Hardin, 564:Feb86-89
P. Skrine, 402(MLR):Jul86-780
Bergin, J. Cardinal Richelieu.
R. Briggs, 617(TLS):6-12Nov87-1220
Bergman, D. Cracking the Code.
D. Shapiro, 491:Mar87-346
Bergner, H. - see Chaucer, G.
Bergonzi, B. The Myth of Modernism and
Twentieth Century Literature.
M.P.L., 295(JML):Nov86-362
Bergougnioux, P. Ce pas et le suivant.
J. Garreau, 207(FR):Mar87-554
Bergreen, L. James Agee.*
E.T. Carroll, 395(MFS):Summer86-273
Berinstein, A. Evidence for Multiattach-
ment in K'ekchi Mayan.
L. Campbell, 350:Jun87-444
Berjonneau, G. & J-L. Sonnery, eds. Redis-
covered Masterpieces of Mesoamerica.
R.V. Childs, 2(AfrA):May86-24
Berk, S.M. Year of Crisis, Year of Hope.
M. Stanislawski, 550(RusR):Jul86-336
Berkeley, G. The Notebooks of George Berk-
eley, Bishop of Cloyne, 1685-1753. (D.
Park, ed)
B. Belfrage, 319:Jul87-448
Berkeley, G. Oeuvres I. (G. Brykman, ed)
B. Belfrage, 542:Jul-Sep86-367
T. Cordellier, 450(NRF):Jul-Aug86-175
Berkeley, G. Viaggio in Italia. (T.E.
Jessop & M. Fimiani, eds)
J. Black, 275(IQ):Summer86-117
Berkow, I. The Man Who Robbed the Pierre.
D. Murray, 441:26Jul87-17
Berkson, W. & J. Wettersten. Learning from
Error. (German title: Lernen aus dem
Irrtum.)
G. Botterill, 518:Apr86-98
M. Schmid, 488:Jun86-260
Berkvam, M.L., with P.L. Smith - see
Hennin, P.M.
Berlanstein, L.R. The Working People of
Paris 1871-1914.*
J.F. Godfrey, 150(DR):Winter85/86-608
Berlin, I. Against the Current. (H.
Hardy, ed)
J.G. Hanink, 438:Spring86-246

Berlin, I. & others, eds. Freedom.*
(Ser 1, Vol 1)
　　G.M. Fredrickson, 617(TLS):9Jan87-31
Berlin, J.A. Writing Instruction in Nine-
teenth-Century American Colleges.
　　R.J. Connors, 126(CCC):May86-247
Berliner, N.Z. Chinese Folk Art.
　　A.B. Hadler, 441:16Aug87-17
Berlinger, R. & W. Schräder, eds.
Nietzsche-kontrovers.
　　R. Margreiter, 489(PJGG):Band93Heft2-
375
Berlinger, R. & W. Schräder - see Seidl, H.
Berlo, J.C. The Art of Pre-Hispanic Meso-
america.
　　H. Barnet-Sanchez, 2(AfrA):Aug86-80
Berman, J. The Talking Cure.*
　　M.B., 295(JML):Nov86-362
　　D.W. Ross, 395(MFS):Winter86-700
Berman, M. Time Capsule.
　　F. Howe, 441:22Mar87-38
Berman, R.A. Modern Hebrew Structure.
　　A.S. Kaye, 205(ForL):Apr84-77
Berman, R.A. The Rise of the Modern Ger-
man Novel.
　　U.S., 295(JML):Nov86-375
　　J. Schmidt, 268(IFR):Summer87-108
　　42(AR):Fall86-491
Bermant, C. The Companion.
　　G. Mangan, 617(TLS):18-24Sep87-1027
Bermant, C. Titch.
　　J. Mellors, 362:9Apr87-25
Bermingham, A. Landscape and Ideology.
　　J.D. Hunt, 617(TLS):16-22Oct87-1133
Bernadelli, G. Tre studi su Tristan
Corbière.
　　S. Meitinger, 535(RHL):Mar-Apr86-322
　　M. Tilby, 208(FS):Jan86-95
Bernáldez Montalvo, J.M. Las tarascas de
Madrid.
　　J.E. Varey, 86(BHS):Apr86-163
Bernanos, G. Journal d'un curé de cam-
pagne. (M. Milner, ed)
　　J. Chabot, 535(RHL):Sep-Oct86-955
Bernard, B. - see van Gogh, V.
Bernard, C. Poèmes intempestifs.
　　B. Hourcade, 207(FR):Mar87-565
Bernard, G.W. War Taxation and Rebellion.
　　D. Starkey, 617(TLS):6Mar87-250
Bernard, J. Aragon.
　　M. Sheringham, 208(FS):Jul86-357
Bernard, J. Low Life.*
　　M. Coward, 362:15Jan87-23
Bernard, J-A. L'Inde.
　　H. Cronel, 450(NRF):May86-104
Bernard, K. The Maldive Chronicles.
　　L. Gordon, 441:15Nov87-43
Bernardo, A.S. & A.L. Pellegrini, eds.
Dante, Petrarch, Boccaccio.*
　　F. Chiappelli, 276:Autumn86-291
　　J.H. McGregor, 545(RPh):Feb87-421
Bernardt, G. Dramen. (Vol 1) (F. Rädle,
ed & trans)
　　P. Skrine, 402(MLR):Jul87-774
Bernasconi, R. The Question of Language in
Heidegger's History of Being.
　　D. Pollard, 89(BJA):Winter86-78
Bernd, C.A. German Poetic Realism.
　　M.S. Fries, 406:Spring86-109
Bernd, C.A. & others, eds. Goethe Proceed-
ings.*
　　H. Henning, 301(JEGP):Apr86-305
　　　　　　　　　　　　　　　　　　[continued]

[continuing]
　　W. Koepke, 564:Feb86-92
　　I.H. Solbrig, 173(ECS):Fall86-110
Berndt, R. A History of the English Lan-
guage.* (2nd ed)
　　G. Kristensson, 179(ES):Aug86-378
Berner, O. Soviet & Norden.
　　B. Sundelius, 563(SS):Winter86-91
Bernhard, T. Béton.
　　R. Millet, 450(NRF):Feb86-112
　　C. Thomas, 98:May86-562
Bernhard, T. Gathering Evidence.*
　　A. Otten, 42(AR):Spring86-244
Bernhard, T. Le naufragé.
　　C. Thomas, 98:Nov86-1075
Bernhard, T. Wittgenstein's Nephew.*
(French title: Le Neveu de Wittgenstein.)
　　S. Plaice, 617(TLS):28Aug87-933
Bernhard-Walcher, A. Corpus Vasorum Anti-
quorum. (Wien, Kunsthistorisches Museum,
Vol 4)
　　V.T-B., 90:Jul86-519
Bernhardt, R. Polis und römische Herr-
schaft in der späten Republik (149-31 v.
Chr.).
　　J. Briscoe, 123:Vol36No2-267
Bernheimer, C. Flaubert and Kafka.*
　　F.J. Beharriell, 406:Summer86-250
　　R. Wilcocks, 107(CRCL):Mar86-152
Berns, E., S. IJsseling & P. Moyaert.
Denken in Parijs.
　　H. Sonneville, 356(LR):Feb86-90
Berns, J.B. Namen voor ziekten van het
vee.
　　A. Barteloot, 685(ZDL):3/1986-422
Berns, J.J., ed. Höfische Festkultur in
Braunschweig-Wolfenbüttel 1590-1666.
　　J. Hardin, 406:Winter86-528
Bernstein, C. Content's Dream.
　　M. Perloff, 385(MQR):Spring87-404
Bernstein, D.J. The Mystery of the Bayeux
Tapestry.
　　P-L. Adams, 61:Dec87-110
　　R. Minkoff, 441:11Oct87-57
Bernstein, J. The Life It Brings.
　　D.G. Stork, 441:5Apr87-20
Bernstein, J.A. Shaftesbury, Rousseau and
Kant.
　　S. Goyard-Fabre, 342:Band77Heft3-380
Bernstein, J.M. The Philosophy of the
Novel.*
　　E.L. Corredor, 478:Oct86-338
　　S. Derwin, 400(MLN):Dec86-1253
　　A.C. Leidner, 221(GQ):Summer86-462
Bernstein, L.F., ed. La Couronne et fleur
des chansons a troys.
　　R.J. Agee, 317:Fall86-642
Bernstein, R.B., with K.S. Rice. Are We to
Be a Nation?
　　M. Cunliffe, 441:3May87-26
Bernstein, R.J. Beyond Objectivism and
Relativism.*
　　N.O. Bernsen, 449:Dec86-574
　　R.R. Sullivan, 488:Dec86-513
Bernstein, R.J., ed. Habermas and Moder-
nity.
　　A. Reix, 542:Jan-Mar86-132
　　J.S., 185:Apr87-690
Bernstein, R.J. Philosophical Profiles.
　　W.M.S., 185:Apr87-681
Béroalde de Verville. Le Moyen de Parven-
ir. (H. Moreau & A. Tournon, eds)
　　I. Zinguer, 535(RHL):Nov-Dec86-1123

Berres, T. Die Entstehung der Aeneis.*
  S.J. Harrison, 313:Vol76-318
Berrian, B.F. Bibliography of African
Women Writers and Journalists.
  T.N. Hammond, 207(FR):Dec86-251
Berriault, G. The Descent.
  T. Broderick, 532(RCF):Fall86-136
Berridge, V. & G. Edwards. Opium and the
People.
  J. Ryle, 617(TLS):23-29Oct87-1163
Berrigan, D. The Mission.
  G. Johnson, 441:4Jan87-19
Berriot, F. Athéismes et athéists au XVIe
siècle en France.
  C. Lauvergnat-Gagnière, 535(RHL):Sep-
  Oct86-905
Berriot, F. & others - see Bodin, J.
Berriot, K. Louise Labé.
  I.D. McFarlane, 617(TLS):13Feb87-157
Berrong, R.M. Every Man for Himself.
  J. Parkin, 402(MLR):Apr87-472
Berry, C. Chuck Berry.
  D. McLeese, 441:18Oct87-13
Berry, C.J. Human Nature.
  D. Miller, 617(TLS):22May87-544
  A. Ryan, 617(TLS):7Aug87-854
Berry, D. The Creative Vision of Guillaume
Apollinaire.*
  E. Leube, 547(RF):Band98Heft1/2-212
Berry, J., J. Foose & T. Jones. Up from
the Cradle of Jazz.*
  E.J. Hobsbawm, 453(NYRB):12Feb87-11
  H. Williams, 617(TLS):19Jun87-656
Berry, R. Shakespeare and the Awareness
of the Audience.*
  G.E. Bentley, 570(SQ):Winter86-539
  J.R. Brown, 615(TJ):May86-242
Berry, R.J. & A. Hallam. The Collins Ency-
clopedia of Animal Evolution.
  J. Serpell, 617(TLS):16Jan87-70
Berry, W. Collected Poems 1957-1982.*
  639(VQR):Winter86-27
Berry, W. Home Economics.
  L. Hyde, 441:27Sep87-30
Berry, W. The Wild Birds.*
  G.L. Morris, 502(PrS):Winter86-102
  J. Parini, 617(TLS):26Jun87-698
Berryman, J.B. Circe's Craft.
  S.J. Adams, 106:Fall86-367
Berryman, P. Liberation Theology.
  A. Riding, 441:14Jun87-15
Bers, V. Greek Poetic Syntax in the Clas-
sical Age.*
  G.L. Koniaris, 122:Oct86-343
  J.W. Poultney, 24:Summer86-287
  C.J. Ruijgh, 394:Vol39fasc3/4-443
  P.T. Stevens, 303(JoHS):Vol106-225
Bersani, L. & U. Dutoit. The Forms of
Violence.
  G.G. Harpham, 141:Spring86-232
Berschin, W. Griechisch-lateinisches Mit-
telalter von Hieronymus zu Nikolaus von
Kues.*
  M. Lapidge, 38:Band104Heft3/4-461
Berschin, W., ed. Lateinische Dichtungen
des X. und XI. Jahrhunderts.
  G. Bernt, 684(ZDA):Band115Heft2-86
  P. Godman, 382(MAE):1986/1-131
Berschin, W., ed & trans. Vitae sanctae
Wiboradae.*
  J.F.T. Kelly, 589:Jan86-224

Berta, M. De l'androgynie dans les
"Rougon-Macquart" et deux autres études
sur Zola.
  R.B. Antosh, 446(NCFS):Spring87-326
Bertela, M. Stendhal et l'autre.
  M. Arrous, 605(SC):15Jan87-212
  E. Williamson, 208(FS):Oct86-471
Bertelli, I. La poesia di Guido Guiniz-
zelli e la poetica del "dolce stil
nuovo."
  Z.G. Barański, 545(RPh):May87-551
Bertelsen, L. The Nonsense Club.
  C. Fierobe, 189(EA):Jul-Sep87-352
  P. Rogers, 617(TLS):20Feb87-182
Berthier, P. Barbey d'Aurevilly et l'imag-
ination.
  J-L. Pire, 356(LR):Feb86-80
Berthier, P., ed. Stendhal.
  G. De Wulf, 356(LR):Feb86-79
  G. Strickland, 208(FS):Apr86-220
Berthier, P. - see Mérimée, P.
Berthoff, A.E. The Making of Meaning.
  T.Y. Booth, 126(CCC):Dec86-494
Berthold, D. & K.M. Price - see Whitman,
T.J.
Berthold, R.M. Rhodes in the Hellenistic
Age.*
  J.E. Coleman, 124:Sep-Oct86-49
  É. Will, 555:Vol59fasc2-291
Bertholf, R.J. - see Niedecker, L.
Berthoud, R. The Life of Henry Moore.
  F. Spalding, 362:12Nov87-31
Bertini, L.C. Andrea Zanzotto o la sacra
menzogna.
  V. Hand, 402(MLR):Jul87-759
Berwick, R.C. & A.S. Weinberg. The Gram-
matical Basis of Linguistic Performance.
  S. Carroll, 320(CJL):Summer86-163
  N.V. Smith, 297(JL):Mar86-222
Besas, P. Behind the Spanish Lens.
  D. Wilson, 707:Summer86-217
Besch, W. & others, eds. Dialektologie.
  G. Bellmann, 680(ZDP):Band105Heft1-147
Besch, W. & others. Sprachverhalten in
ländlichen Gemeinden. (Vol 1)
  A. Pauwels, 355(LSoc):Dec86-547
Besch, W., O. Reichmann & S. Sonderegger,
  eds. Sprachgeschichte.* (Vols 1 & 2)
  N. Voorwinden, 402(MLR):Oct87-1012
Beser, S. Pío Baroja: "El árbol de la
ciencia."
  C.A. Longhurst, 86(BHS):Apr86-176
van Besien, F. Kindertaal.
  H. Hulshof, 204(FdL):Dec86-310
Besse, H. & R. Porquier. Grammaires et
didactique des langues.
  A. Barrera-Vidal, 209(FM):Apr86-117
Bessinger, J.B., Jr. & R.F. Yeager, eds.
Approaches to Teaching "Beowulf."
  L.J. Leff, 365:Spring/Summer86-159
Besson, P. Dara.
  J. Mellors, 362:28May87-26
Best, C. & C. Boisset, eds. Leaves From
the Garden.
  P. Hobhouse, 617(TLS):3Jul87-728
  A. Lacy, 441:31May87-14
Best, D. Feeling and Reason in the Arts.*
  T. Pateman, 89(BJA):Spring86-172
Best, O.F., ed. Das Groteske in der Dich-
tung.
  M. Rother, 72:Band223Heft1-137
Besterman, T. - see de Voltaire, F.M.A.

Bethell, L., ed. The Cambridge History of
Latin America.* (Vols 1 & 2)
P.T. Bradley, 86(BHS):Oct86-378
Bethell, L., ed. Cambridge History of
Latin America. (Vols 3-5)
A. Pagden, 617(TLS):17Apr87-406
Bethell, U. Collected Poems. (V. O'Sulli-
van, ed)
J. Penberthy, 617(TLS):31Jul87-823
Betken, W.T. - see Shakespeare, W.
Bettelheim, B. A Good Enough Parent.
B. Ehrenreich, 441:24May87-3
Betts, C.J. Early Deism in France.
J. Cruickshank, 402(MLR):Oct86-1004
M.C. Horowitz, 319:Apr87-296
H. Mason, 208(FS):Jan86-73
Betts, R.K. Nuclear Blackmail and Nuclear
Balance.
P. Williams, 617(TLS):20-26Nov87-1270
Betz, H.D., ed. The Greek Magical Papyri
in Translation.* (Vol 1)
C.A. Faraone, 124:Mar-Apr87-325
Betz, J., comp. Alsace.
J.R. Paas, 221(GQ):Summer86-476
Beversluis, J. C.S. Lewis and the Search
for Rational Religion.*
P.B. McElwain, 590:Dec86-118
R.L. Purtill, 258:Jun86-200
Bevilacqua, A. La Grande Giò.
T. Parks, 617(TLS):14Aug87-881
Bevington, D. Action Is Eloquence.*
M. Axton, 130:Spring86-76
R. Jacobs, 175:Summer86-164
M. Jones, 541(RES):Aug86-413
D.G. Watson, 536(Rev):Vol8-59
Beyer, A. Deutsche Einflüsse auf die
englische Sprachwissenschaft im 19.
Jahrhundert.
K-H. Jäger, 406:Summer86-215
de Bèze, T. Pseaumes mis en vers français
(1551-1562). (P. Pidoux, ed)
P. Chilton, 208(FS):Oct86-450
O. Millet, 535(RHL):Sep-Oct86-902
Béziau, R. - see de Gobineau, A.
"The Bhagavad Gītā." (W. Sargeant, trans;
C. Chapple, ed)
J.W. de Jong, 259(IIJ):Jan86-53
Bhalla, A.S. Economic Transition in Human
and Southern China.
E.A. Winckler, 293(JASt):Nov85-104
Bhandarkar, D.R. - see Chhabra, B. & G.S.
Gai
Bhaskar, R. Scientific Realism and Human
Emancipation.
M. Tiles, 617(TLS):7Aug87-836
Bhat, M.R. - see "Varāhamihira's Bṛhat
Saṃhitā"
Bhat, P.N.M., S. Preston & T. Dyson. Vital
Rates in India, 1961-1981.
A.W. Clark, 293(JASt):Nov85-162
Bhatt, N.R. Rauravottarāgama.
S. Pollock, 318(JAOS):Oct/Dec85-804
Bhatt, N.R., ed. Sārdhatriśatikālottāgama
avec le commentaire de Bhaṭṭa Rāmakaṇṭha.
Mataṅgapārameśvarāgama (Kriyāpāda, Yoga-
pāda et Cayāpāda) avec le commentaire de
Bhaṭṭa Rāmakaṇṭha.* Rauravottarāgama.
J.W. de Jong, 259(IIJ):Jan86-51
Bhaṭṭācārya, R. The "Divyatattva" of
Raghunandana Bhaṭṭācārya. (R.W.
Lariviere, ed & trans)
W.H. Maurer, 318(JAOS):Apr/Jun85-379

Bhattacharya, G. Yajñapati Upādhyāya's
Tattvacintāmaṇiprabhā (Anumānakhaṇḍaḥ).
S. Pollock, 318(JAOS):Oct/Dec85-805
Bhayani, H.C., ed. Ratnacūḍa Rāsa.
E. Bender, 318(JAOS):Oct/Dec85-813
Bhayani, H.C., with N.M. Kansara, eds.
Jinaratna's Līlāvatī-sāra.
E. Bender, 318(JAOS):Oct/Dec85-813
Bhayani, H.C., R.M. Shah & Gitabahen, eds.
Merusundaragaṇi-viracita Śilopadeśamālā-
bālāvabodha.
E. Bender, 318(JAOS):Oct/Dec85-813
Biagi, M.L.A. - see under Altieri Biagi,
M.L.
Biagini, H.E., comp. El movimiento posi-
tivista argentino.
D.E. Zalazar, 263(RIB):Vol36No2-180
Bialer, S. The Soviet Paradox.*
A.B. Ulam, 617(TLS):6Feb87-129
Bialostosky, D.H. Making Tales.*
P.J. Manning, 401(MLQ):Mar85-96
W.J.B. Owen, 541(RES):May86-273
J.W. Page, 405(MP):Feb87-326
D.H. Richter, 599:Fall86-411
Bianchi, L. L'errore di Aristotele.*
R.C. Dales, 589:Oct86-897
A.G. Molland, 319:Apr87-291
Bianciotti, H. Sans la miséricorde de
Dieu.
D.H. McKeen, 207(FR):Mar87-555
F. de Martinoir, 450(NRF):Jan86-91
Bianciotto, G. & M. Salvat, eds. Epopée
animale, fable, fabliau.*
M. Eusebi, 547(RF):Band98Heft1/2-199
E. Suomela-Härmä, 439(NM):1986/1-160
Bianconi, L. - see Il Verso, A.
Bianconi, L. - see Marsolo, P.M.
Biard-Millerioux, J. L'esthétique d'Elie-
Catherine Fréron, 1739-1776.
J. Voisine, 549(RLC):Jul-Sep86-368
Biasin, G-P. Il vento di Debussy.
C.D.L. Huffman, 276:Winter86-398
Biasin, G-P. Italian Literary Icons.*
A.L. Lepschy, 278(IS):Vol41-152
G.L. Lucente, 276:Winter86-399
von Biberach, R. Rudolf von Biberach: "De
septem itineribus aeternitatis." Rudolf
von Biberach: "Die siben strassen zu
got." (M. Schmidt & H. Riedlinger, eds
of both)
H-J. Spitz, 72:Band223Heft2-372
"La biblioteca del cardinale Bernardo
Clesio."
D.E. Rhodes, 354:Jun86-176
"Bibliotheca Trinitariorum." (Vol 1) (E.
Schadel, ed)
F. Courth, 489(PJGG):Band93Heft1-211
"Bibliothek zur historischen deutschen
Studenten- und Schülersprache." (Vols 1-
6) (H. Henne & G. Objartel, eds)
N. Nail, 685(ZDL):2/1986-227
"Bibliothèque Nationale, Catalogue des
incunables." (Vol 2, fasc 4) (U. Baur-
meister & others, eds)
B.M. Rosenthal, 517(PBSA):Vol80No3-381
Bickerton, D. Roots of Language.*
A. Bollée, 545(RPh):May87-484
J.M. Lipski, 205(ForL):Apr84-69
Bickman, M., ed. Approaches to Teaching
Melville's "Moby-Dick."
L.J. Leff, 365:Spring/Summer86-159

Biddle, G. Great Railway Stations of Britain.
  R. Lemon, 324:Jul87-618
Bidermann, J. Jakob Bidermanns "Utopia." (M. Schuster, ed)
  H. Jaumann, 680(ZDP):Band105Heft2-300
Bidler, R.M., ed. "La Confessions et Testament de l'amant trespassé de deuil" de Pierre de Hauteville.
  J. Cerquiglini, 545(RPh):Nov86-272
Biebuyck, D.P. and N. Van den Abbeele. The Power of Headdresses.
  M.C. Berns, 2(AfrA):May86-14
Bielfeldt, H.H. Deutsch-Russisches Wörterbuch. (R. Lötzsch, ed)
  G.F. Meier, 682(ZPSK):Band39Heft2-268
Biely, A. The Dramatic Symphony [and] The Forms of Art.
  A. Woronzoff, 441:4Oct87-22
Biembiel, A. Rodnaje słova i maralnaestetyčny prahres.
  P. Mayo, 402(MLR):Jul87-813
Bienek, H. September Light.
  J.A. Snead, 441:22Feb87-35
Bierds, L. Flights of the Harvest-Mare.
  D.A. Carpenter, 649(WAL):Aug86-170
Bierds, L. Off the Aleutian Chain.
  639(VQR):Summer86-100
Bierfert, H. Automatische Spracherkennung.
  W. Tscheschner, 682(ZPSK):Band39Heft5-620
Bierhorst, J., ed & trans. Cantares Mexicanos.*
  F. Karttunen, 350:Jun87-442
  J.M. Taggart, 292(JAF):Oct/Dec86-483
Bierhorst, J., ed. Four Masterworks of American Indian Literature.
  R.M. Adams, 453(NYRB):26Mar87-32
Bierhorst, J. A Nahuatl-English Dictionary and Concordance to the "Cantares Mexicanos."*
  F. Karttunen, 350:Jun87-442
  J.M. Taggart, 292(JAF):Oct/Dec86-483
Biermann, K. Literarisch-politische Avantgarde in Frankreich 1830-1870.
  W. Drost, 224(GRM):Band36Heft2-247
Bietenholz, P. & T.B. Deutscher, eds. Contemporaries of Erasmus.* (Vol 1)
  G. Thompson, 627(UTQ):Fall86-87
Bigazzi, R. Fenoglio.
  E. Saccone, 400(MLN):Jan86-189
Bigelow, G.E. & L.V. Monti - see Rawlings, M.K.
Bigler, N. & R. Schläpfer, with R. Börlin - see Hotzenköcherle, R.
Bigsby, C.W.E. A Critical Introduction to Twentieth Century American Drama. (Vol 1)
  R.S. Smith, 106:Winter86-469
Bigsby, C.W.E. A Critical Introduction to Twentieth-Century American Drama.* (Vol 2)
  B. Murphy, 27(AL):Oct86-463
  R. Simard, 615(TJ):Mar86-123
Bigsby, C.W.E. A Critical Introduction to Twentieth-Century American Drama. (Vol 3)
  B. Murphy, 27(AL):Oct86-463
Bikaki, A.H. Ayia Irini: the Potters' Marks.
  R.L.N. Barber, 123:Vol36No1-163

Billanovich, G. La tradizione del testo di Livio e le origini dell'umanesimo.* (Vol 1, Pt 1)
  N.M., 382(MAE):1986/1-150
Billcliffe, R. The Glasgow Boys.*
  K. McConkey, 90:Jun86-438
  B.C. Rezelman, 637(VS):Summer87-549
Billeskov Jansen, F.J. Ludvig Holberg i tekst og billeder.
  G.S. Argetsinger, 563(SS):Spring86-215
Billetdoux, R. Night Without Day.
  D. Mason, 441:27Dec87-18
Billington, D. The Tower and the Bridge.
  E.C. Robison, 576:Sep86-307
Billington, M. Alan Ayckbourn.
  P. Mudford, 447(N&Q):Dec85-542
  M. Page, 397(MD):Dec86-634
  S.H. White, 610:Spring86-83
Billington, S. A Social History of the Fool.*
  H.R.E. Davidson, 203:Vol97No1-116
Billot, C., with J. di Crescenzo. Chartes et documents de la Sainte-Chapelle de Vincennes (XIVe et XVe siècles.)
  D.F. Bigras, 589:Oct86-898
"Billy Boy." Barbie.
  G. Steinem, 441:13Dec87-27
Bilstein, R. & J. Miller. Aviation in Texas.
  L. Milazzo, 584(SWR):Winter86-123
Binder, H. Franz Kafka.*
  I.C. Henel, 406:Fall86-412
Binder, W., ed. Entwicklungen im karibischen Raum 1960-1985.
  J. Martini, 343:Heft13-125
Bindman, D., ed. William Blake's Illustrations of the Book of Job. Colour Versions of Blake's Book of Job Designs from the Circle of John Linnell.
  A. Wilton, 617(TLS):14Aug87-879
Bindman, D., ed. The Thames and Hudson Encyclopaedia of British Art.*
  R. Kingzett, 39:Apr86-292
  90:Jan86-49
Binford, H.C. The First Suburbs.
  C. McShane, 432(NEQ):Dec86-597
von Bingen, H. - see under Hildegard von Bingen
Binh, T.T. - see under Tran Tu Binh
Bini, D. A Fragrance from the Desert.
  M. Caesar, 402(MLR):Jan86-229
Binkert, P.J. Generative Grammar Without Transformations.
  D.A. Dinneen, 350:Sep87-672
Binney, M. Sir Robert Taylor.
  M. McCarthy, 576:Sep86-300
Binnie, E. The Theatrical Designs of Charles Ricketts.
  R.A. Cave, 610:Autumn86-264
Binns, J.W. - see Rusticans, M.
Binns, R. Malcolm Lowry.
  E. Cameron, 298:Winter86/87-133
  G.E. Henderson, 627(UTQ):Fall86-167
Binyan, L. - see under Liu Binyan
"Biographical Dictionaries and Related Works." (2nd ed)
  K.B. Harder, 424:Dec86-405
Bion, D. Bertrand Tavernier, cinéaste de l'émotion.
  S. Fischer, 207(FR):Apr87-750
Bion, W.R. The Long Week-End 1879-1919. (F. Bion, ed)
  D. Hibberd, 617(TLS):31Jul87-828

Birault, H. Heidegger et l'expérience de
la pensée.
P. Trotignon, 542:Jan–Mar86–132
Birch, D.L. Job Creation in America.
J. Ciulla, 441:25Oct87–39
Birch–Jones, S. A First Class Funeral.
P. Klovan, 102(CanL):Winter85–144
Bircher, M., J–U. Fechner & G. Hillen, eds.
Barocker Lust–Spiegel.
P. Hess, 133:Band19Heft3/4–333
G.R. Hoyt, 221(GQ):Spring86–304
M.K. Kremer, 564:Sep86–257
Bird, C. The Woodpecker Toy Fact and
Other Stories.
H. Jacobson, 617(TLS):27Nov–3Dec87–
1307
Bird, G. William James.
S.P. Stich, 617(TLS):27Nov–3Dec87–1315
Bird, H.W. Sextus Aurelius Victor.*
J.C. Traupman, 124:Jul–Aug87–455
Bird, I. The Yangtze Valley and Beyond.
E. Newby, 441:31May87–48
Bird, R.K. Wright Morris.*
T. Hansen, 649(WAL):Feb87–374
Birdsall, E., with P.M. Zall – see Words-
worth, W.
Birdsall, V.O. Defoe's Perpetual Seekers.*
P. Alkon, 173(ECS):Winter86/87–220
Birgersson, B.O. & others, eds. Sverige
efter 1900. (10th ed)
J.B. Board, 563(SS):Spring86–209
Birkerts, S. An Artificial Wilderness.
D. Hall, 441:8Nov87–16
Birley, A.R. The "Fasti" of Roman Britain.
P. Bartholomew, 123:Vol36No2–277
Birmingham, S. America's Secret Aristoc-
racy.
E.D. Baltzell, 441:27Sep87–24
Birnbaum, H. & M.S. Flier, eds. Medieval
Russian Culture.*
P. Kosta, 559:Vol10No1–121
R. Lachmann, 559:Vol10No1–116
R. Lachmann, 559:Vol10No1–119
W. Lehfeldt, 559:Vol10No1–115
W. Lehfeldt, 559:Vol10No1–124
G. Lenhoff, 550(RusR):Jan86–49
U. Schweier, 559:Vol10No1–122
Birnbaum, H. & P.T. Merrill. Recent
Advances in the Reconstruction of Common
Slavic (1971–1982).
H. Leeming, 575(SEER):Oct86–579
Birnbaum, J.H. & A.S. Murray. Showdown at
Gucci Gulch.
R. Lekachman, 441:5Jul87–9
442(NY):7Sep87–112
Birney, E. Essays on Chaucerian Irony.
(B. Rowland, ed)
S.R. Reimer, 627(UTQ):Fall86–93
Birney, E. Words on Waves.*
J.H. Kaplan, 102(CanL):Fall86–126
M.J. Miller, 108:Fall86–137
Birringer, J.H. Marlowe's "Dr. Faustus"
and "Tamburlaine."*
D. Feldmann, 156(ShJW):Jahrbuch1986–
261
Birus, H., ed. Hermeneutische Positionen.
B. Bennett, 406:Fall86–383
Bischoff, B. Anecdota Novissima.
R. McKitterick, 354:Jun86–165
Biser, E. Gottsucher oder Antichrist?
R. Margreiter, 489(PJGG):Band93Heft2–
375

Biser, E. Nietzsche für Christen.
R. Margreiter, 489(PJGG):Band93Heft2–
375
Bishop, A.H. & J.R. Scudder, Jr., eds.
Caring, Curing, Hoping.
T.M.R., 185:Oct86–310
Bishop, D.H., ed. Thinkers of the Indian
Renaissance.*
L. Gupta, 485(PE&W):Oct86–436
Bishop, E. The Collected Prose of Eliza-
beth Bishop.* (R. Giroux, ed)
T. Martin, 534(RALS):Spring–Autumn84–
252
Bishop, J. Joyce's Book of the Dark.
R.M. Adams, 441:18Jan87–14
S. Brivic, 329(JJQ):Summer87–477
Bishop, J.P. & A. Tate. The Republic of
Letters in America. (T.D. Young & J.J.
Hindle, eds)
D. Aaron, 677(YES):Vol16–350
Bishop, L. The Romantic Hero and His Heirs
in French Literature.*
L. Jones, 210(FrF):Jan86–114
H.P. Lund, 535(RHL):Nov–Dec86–1146
Bishop, M. The Contemporary Poetry of
France.
B.L. Knapp, 188(ECr):Fall86–103
Bishop, O.B. Publications of the Province
of Upper Canada and of Great Britain
Relating to Upper Canada, 1791–1840.
E.L. Swanick, 470:Vol24–112
Bishop, P. & E. Mallie. The Provisional
IRA.
T. Hadden, 617(TLS):28Aug87–916
C. Townshend, 362:9Jul87–27
Bisky, L. & D. Wiedemann. Der Spielfilm.
E.M. Scherf, 654(WB):2/1986–346
Bissell, C. The Imperial Canadian.
M. Horn, 99:Feb87–37
Bissett, B. canada gees mate for life.
S. Scobie, 376:Jun86–122
Bisson, T.N. The Medieval Crown of Aragon.
J. Edwards, 617(TLS):13Mar87–276
Bissoondath, N. Digging Up the Mountains.*
A. Boxill, 198:Fall86–82
D. Brydon, 102(CanL):Spring86–160
J. Mellors, 364:Jun86–98
M. Thorpe, 176:May87–45
Bitov, A. Pushkin House.
J. Bayley, 453(NYRB):22Oct87–9
Bittler, P. & P–L. Mathieu. Catalogue des
dessins de Gustave Moreau.
R. Thomson, 59:Mar86–108
Bittman, L. The KGB and Soviet Disinforma-
tion.
J. Horton, 390:Dec86–54
Bix, H.P. Peasant Protest in Japan, 1590–
1884.
C. Totman, 407(MN):Winter86–507
Bixler, J.S. German Recollections.
Y. Hudson, 258:Jun86–198
Bjalik, B.A., ed. Russkaja literatura i
žurnalistika načala XX veka, 1905–1917.
T. Pogacar, 574(SEEJ):Fall86–445
Bjarvall, A. & S. Ullstrom. The Mammals of
Britain and Europe.
D.W. Macdonald, 617(TLS):8May87–498
Björk, L.A. – see Hardy, T.
Björkman, S. Le type "avoir besoin."
I. Boström, 597(SN):Vol58No2–281
Björkvall, G. Corpus Troporum V.
M. Huglo, 537:Vol72No2–285

Björkvall, G. & others. Tropes du propre
de la messe. (Vol 2)
  J. Perret, 555:Vol59fasc2–342
Bjornson, R., ed. Approaches to Teaching
Cervantes' "Don Quixote."
  R.D. Reck, 128(CE):Sep86–484
Bjørnvig, T. The Pact.*
  C.B. Black, 538(RAL):Spring86–155
  E. Bredsdorff, 562(Scan):Nov86–242
Black, A. Guilds and Civil Society in
European Political Thought from the
Twelfth Century to the Present.
  P. Riesenberg, 589:Oct86–900
Black, E. The Transfer Agreement.
  R. Wolfe, 390:Mar86–55
Black, E. & M. Black. Politics and Society
in the South.
  C.V. Woodward, 453(NYRB):11Jun87–7
Black, H.L. & E. Mr. Justice and Mrs.
Black.*
  639(VQR):Summer86–83
Black, J., ed. Britain in the Age of Wal-
pole.
  G. Holmes, 83:Autumn86–227
Black, J. The British and the Grand Tour.*
  M. Duffy, 83:Autumn86–234
  J.R. Hale, 275(IQ):Spring86–122
  I.R. Scott, 566:Autumn86–69
Black, J. British Foreign Policy in the
Age of Walpole.
  P.K. Monod, 173(ECS):Fall86–66
  G.M. Townend, 566:Autumn86–69
Black, J. The English Press in the Eigh-
teenth Century.
  D. Womersley, 617(TLS):1May87–470
Black, J. The Italian Romantic Libretto.*
  J. Budden, 410(M&L):Apr86–216
  D.R.B. Kimbell, 278(IS):Vol41–156
  G. Martin, 465:Summer86–174
Black, J. Natural and Necessary Enemies.
  R. Mettam, 617(TLS):27Feb87–220
Black, M.H. Cambridge University Press:
1584–1984.*
  J. Feather, 354:Sep86–283
Blackall, E.A. The Novels of the German
Romantics.*
  L.R. Furst, 131(CL):Spring86–205
Blackburn, G.W. Education in the Third
Reich.*
  R.P. Roth, 396(ModA):Summer/Fall86–321
Blackburn, S. Spreading the Word.*
  P. Engel, 542:Jul–Sep86–385
  B. Hale, 479(PhQ):Jan86–65
  O. Hanfling, 521:Jan86–78
Blackford, J. & N. Talbot, with others,
eds. Contrary Modes.
  M. Leahy, 561(SFS):Nov86–402
Blackham, H.J. The Fable as Literature.
  566:Autumn86–83
Blackmore, C. In the Footsteps of Lawrence
of Arabia.
  R. Whitney, 617(TLS):30Jan87–107
Blackmore, H.L. A Dictionary of London
Gunmakers 1350–1850.
  A.V.B. Norman, 617(TLS):6Mar87–249
Blackmore, S. The Adventures of a Parapsy-
chologist.
  K. Sabbagh, 362:26Mar87–31
Blackmore, T. Catalogue of the Burney Par-
abaiks in the India Office Library.
  V. Lieberman, 293(JASt):May86–644

Blackmur, R.P. Selected Essays of R.P.
Blackmur.* (D. Donoghue, ed)
  M. Wood, 453(NYRB):7May87–28
Blackmur, R.P. Studies in Henry James.
(V. Makowsky, ed)
  K. Lindberg, 284:Winter87–145
Blackwelder, J.K. Women of the Depression.
  C. Miller, 577(SHR):Summer86–290
Blackwell, K. The Spinozistic Ethics of
Bertrand Russell.*
  E.R.E., 185:Oct86–302
Blackwell, M.J. C.J.L. Almqvist and Roman-
tic Irony.*
  B. Romberg, 462(OL):Vol41No4–384
Blackwell, M.J., ed. Structures of Influ-
ence.
  Y. Chevrel, 549(RLC):Jan–Mar86–71
Blackwood, C. In the Pink.
  N. Andrew, 362:8Oct87–25
  R. Longrigg, 617(TLS):25Sep–1Oct87–
1057
Blainey, A. Immortal Boy.*
  D.R. Cheney, 340(KSJ):Vol35–199
Blair, D. Senegalese Literature.
  M.B. Cham, 538(RAL):Winter86–567
Blair, F. Isadora.*
  M. Denko, 151:Sep86–76
Blais, M–C. Anna's World.*
  D.W. Russell, 102(CanL):Winter85–137
Blais, M–C. The Day Is Dark [and] Three
Travellers.
  S. Posesorski, 102(CanL):Summer86–110
Blais, M–C. Deaf to the City.
  P. West, 441:20Sep87–12
Blais, M.J. La logique.
  D. Laurier, 154:Summer86–385
  A. Reix, 542:Jul–Sep86–387
Blais, S. Apport de la toponymie ancienne
aux études sur le français québécois et
nord–américain.*
  A. Lapierre, 424:Jun86–209
Blaise, C. Resident Alien.*
  K. Tudor, 198:Fall86–94
Blake, D.E. Two Political Worlds.
  T. Morley, 529(QQ):Winter86–915
Blake, K. Love and the Woman Question in
Victorian Literature.*
  M. Burgan, 301(JEGP):Apr86–278
  S.M. Smith, 402(MLR):Jul87–712
Blake, N.F. Shakespeare's Language.*
  B.D.H. Miller, 541(RES):May86–252
Blake, N.F. The Textual Tradition of the
"Canterbury Tales."*
  S. Knight, 67:Nov86–311
Blake, N.F. – see Chaucer, G.
Blake, R. The Decline of Power 1915–1964.*
  639(VQR):Spring86–54
Blake, R. & H. Cecil, eds. Salisbury.
  R. Foster, 617(TLS):25Sep–1Oct87–1038
Blakely, A. Russia and the Negro.
  W.C. Fuller, Jr., 441:28Jun87–25
Blakiston, G. – see Russell, C.
Blakiston, J.M.G. Reminiscing in the
Seventeenth Century.
  H.T. Barnwell, 208(FS):Jul86–330
  J.A. Schmidt, 207(FR):Apr87–707
Blamberger, G. Versuch über den deutschen
Gegenwartsroman.
  W.G. Sebald, 402(MLR):Oct87–1042
Blamires, A. "The Canterbury Tales."
  D. Trotter, 617(TLS):17Apr87–419

Blamires, H., ed. A Guide to Twentieth Century Literature in English.
G.D. Killam, 538(RAL):Fall86-430

Blanc, A. F.C. Dancourt (1661-1725).
J. Morel, 475:Vol13No24-370

Blanc, O. Last Letters.* (French title: La Dernière lettre.)
D.C., 617(TLS):28Aug87-933
P. Johnson, 362:26Feb87-22
442(NY):12Oct87-146

Blanch, J.M.L. - see under Lope Blanch, J.M.

Blanch, L. Pierre Loti, the Legendary Romantic.
M. Fougères, 207(FR):May87-870

Blanch, R.J. "Sir Gawain and the Green Knight."*
R.E. Hamilton, 40(AEB):Vol8No4-255
J. Roberts, 402(MLR):Oct87-911

Blanchard, A. Essai sur la compostion des comédies de Ménandre.*
J.C.B. Lowe, 123:Vol36No2-309

Blanchard, M.E. In Search of the City.*
R. Bowlby, 402(MLR):Oct87-970
J. Ricouart, 207(FR):Oct86-126

Blanchard, S. Walking Up & Down in the World.
L.L. Peterson, 649(WAL):Aug86-143

Blanche-Benveniste, C. & others. Pronom et syntaxe.
F.M. Jenkins, 207(FR):Dec86-271
G. Kleiber, 553(RLiR):Jan-Jun86-262
M.E. Winters, 350:Mar87-186

Blanchet, P. La langue provençale.
C. Rostaing, 553(RLiR):Jan-Jun86-231

Blanchot, M. Michel Foucault tel que je l'imagine.
T. Cordellier, 450(NRF):Dec86-99

Blanchot, M. The Last Man.
S. Ungar, 441:11Oct87-56

Blanchot, M. The Space of Literature.
T. Broderick, 532(RCF):Fall86-139

Blanchot, M. When the Time Comes.*
J. Byrne, 532(RCF):Fall86-129

Blanco, A. & C. Blanco Aguinaga - see Pérez Galdós, B.

Bland, L.I. - see Marshall, G.C.

Blank, D.L. Ancient Philosophy and Grammar.*
D. Langslow, 123:Vol36No1-148
D.J. Taylor, 41:Vol6-245

Blanke, D. Esperanto und Wissenschaft.
F. Häusler, 682(ZPSK):Band39Heft4-490

Blanke, D. Internationale Plansprachen.
F. Häusler, 682(ZPSK):Band39Heft6-736

Blanke, D. Plansprache und National-sprache.
G.F. Meier, 682(ZPSK):Band39Heft3-384

Blanning, T.C.W. The Origins of the French Revolutionary Wars.
W. Scott, 617(TLS):13Feb87-158

Blanpied, J.W. Time and the Artist in Shakespeare's English Histories.*
R. Quinones, 570(SQ):Summer86-260
E.W. Tayler, 551(RenQ):Spring86-145

Blaser, R. Syntax.*
D. McCarthy, 168(ECW):Fall86-198

Blaser, W. Schweizer Holzbrücken.
E.C. Robison, 576:Sep86-309

Blasier, C. The Giant's Rival.*
H. Desfosses, 550(RusR):Jul86-321

Blasing, M.K. American Poetry.
M. Ford, 617(TLS):23-29Oct87-1174

Blasucci, L. Leopardi e i segnali dell'-Infinito.
E. Bonora, 228(GSLI):Vol163fasc521-145

Blau, J.R. Architects and Firms.
R.D. Perl, 45:Jan86-71

Blauert, J. Räumliches Hören.
W. Kraak, 682(ZPSK):Band39Heft4-515

Blaukopf, H. - see Mahler, G.

Blaukopf, H. - see Mahler, G. & R. Strauss

Blavier, A. Les Fous littéraires.
M. Angenot, 193(ELit):Autumn86-135

Blayney, P.W.M. The Texts of "King Lear" and their Origins.* (Vol 1)
J. McLaverty, 447(N&Q):Mar85-112

Blázquez, J.M. Religiones Prerromanas.
M. Ní Dhonnchadha, 112:Vol18-210

Blázquez, J.M., R. Contreras & J.J. Urruela. Castulo IV.
N. Mackie, 123:Vol36No1-167

Bleasdale, A. "Are You Lonesome Tonight?"
B. Grantham, 157:No159-47

Blecua, A. Manual de crítica textual.*
I.A. Corfis, 240(HR):Spring86-207
F.W. Hodcroft, 86(BHS):Apr86-149

Blecua, J.M., ed. Poesía de la edad de oro, II.
A.M. Snell, 238:May86-308

Blecua, J.M.C. & M.J. Lacarra - see under Cacho Blecua, J.M. & M.J. Lacarra

Bles, M. & R. Low. The Kidnap Business.
C. Moorehead, 617(TLS):12Jun87-632

Blevins, R.W. Franz Xaver Kroetz.
I. Walther, 397(MD):Mar86-141

Blewer, E. - see Drouet, J.

Blewer, E. & J. Gaudon - see Hugo, V.

Bleznick, D.W., ed. Studies on "Don Quijote" and Other Cervantine Works.*
E. Williamson, 402(MLR):Jan87-222

Blickle, P., H-C. Rublack & W. Schulze. Religion, Politics and Social Protest.
G. Strauss, 551(RenQ):Spring86-96

Blight, J. Holiday Sea Sonnets.
C. James, 617(TLS):27Nov-3Dec87-1327

Blimes, M.E. & R. Sproat. More Dialing, More Dollars.
K. Marshall, 476:Fall86-92

Blind, H. - see Knauss, J. & others

Blinder, A.S. Hard Heads, Soft Hearts.
R. Lekachman, 441:25Oct87-30

Blinderman, C. The Piltdown Inquest.
E. Eckholm, 441:15Mar87-17

Blinn, H., ed. Shakespeare-Rezeption.
G. Bersier, 406:Spring86-81

Bliss, E. Saraband.
R. Bromley, 441:3May87-44

Blitzer, W. Between Washington and Jeru-salem.*
639(VQR):Summer86-96

Blixen, K. La Ferme africaine.
L. Kovacs, 450(NRF):Sep86-119

Blixen, K. Lettres d'Afrique (1914-1931). (F. Lasson, ed)
L. Kovacs, 450(NRF):Apr86-116

Blobaum, R. Feliks Dzierżyński and the SDKPil.
B.T. Lupack, 497(PolR):Vol31No1-90

Bloch, C. Spelling the Word.*
J.S. Coolidge, 405(MP):Feb87-316
M.E. Rickey, 551(RenQ):Summer86-351
M. Woodworth, 391:Oct86-111

Bloch, D. Passing Through.
J. Mellors, 362:1Jan87-22
N. Shack, 617(TLS):9Jan87-42

Bloch, E. Briefe 1903-1975.* (U. Opolka & others, eds)
R. Rochlitz, 98:May86-539
Bloch, E. Essays on the Philosophy of Music.
S. Hinton, 410(M&L):Oct86-423
G. Josipovici, 607:Jun86-31
E. Lippman, 451:Fall86-190
R.A.S., 412:Nov85-314
W. Truitt, 290(JAAC):Summer87-421
Bloch, E. Natural Law and Human Dignity.
B.J.S., 185:Apr87-680
Bloch, E. The Principle of Hope.*
R. Roderick, 185:Jul87-864
Bloch, E.M. The Paintings of George Caleb Bingham.
A. Staley, 617(TLS):13-19Nov87-1247
"Ernst Bloch/Romain Rolland, Lettres (1911-1933)." (J-F. Tappy, ed)
M. Faure, 535(RHL):Sep-Oct86-948
Bloch, H. Monte Cassino in the Middle Ages.
H.E.J. Cowdrey, 617(TLS):5Jun87-614
Bloch, M. From Blessing to Violence.
M. Douglas, 617(TLS):14Aug87-870
Bloch, O. Le matérialisme.
M. Conche, 542:Jan-Mar86-81
Bloch, R.H. The Scandal of the Fabliaux.
R.R. Edwards, 219(GaR):Winter86-1047
N.J. Lacy, 207(FR):Mar87-531
L. Scanlon, 400(MLN):Dec86-1260
Block, J. Les XX and Belgian Avant-Gardism, 1868-1894.
E. Hoffmann, 90:May86-362
Block, L. When the Sacred Ginmill Closes.*
T.J. Binyon, 617(TLS):17Apr87-411
Block, N. Imagery.
V. Cobb-Stevens, 258:Mar86-87
Blockley, R.C., ed & trans. The Fragmentary Classicizing Historians of the Later Roman Empire. (Vol 2)
B. Croke, 487:Spring86-118
Blok, F.F., ed. Seventy-seven Neo-Latin Letters.
M.C. Davies, 123:Vol36No2-290
D. Robin, 551(RenQ):Summer86-291
Blomfield, R. The Formal Garden in England.
J. Lees-Milne, 39:Oct86-381
Blondel, E. Nietzsche, le corps et la culture.
J. Granier, 542:Oct-Dec86-485
Bloom, A. The Closing of the American Mind.
R. Kimball, 441:5Apr87-7
K. Minogue, 617(TLS):24Jul87-786
B. Morton, 362:25Jun87-26
M. Nussbaum, 453(NYRB):5Nov87-20
442(NY):6Jul87-81
Bloom, A. Prodigal Sons.*
P. Gottfried, 396(ModA):Spring86-168
J.M.M., 295(JML):Nov86-354
W. Phillps, 473(PR):Vol53No4-629
Bloom, H. Agon.*
M. Perloff, 402(MLR):Apr86-431
Bloom, H., ed. Seamus Heaney.
M. Parker, 617(TLS):18-24Sep87-1023
Bloom, H. - see Ruskin, J.
Bloom, J.D. The Stock of Available Reality.
B. Duffey, 579(SAQ):Spring86-204

Bloomfield, M.W., ed. Allegory, Myth, and Symbol.*
T.A. Shippey, 402(MLR):Oct86-967
Blotner, J. Faulkner.*
C.S. Brown, 569(SR):Winter86-167
Blotner, J. & N. Polk - see Faulkner, W.
Blotnick, S. Ambitious Men.
K. Ray, 441:8Feb87-25
Blottière, A. Le Point d'eau.
F-E. Dorenlot, 207(FR):Feb87-423
Bluche, F. La despotisme éclairé.
J-F. Solnon, 192(EP):Apr-Jun86-238
Blue, W.R. The Development of Imagery in Calderón's "Comedias."
J. Bryans, 86(BHS):Jul86-286
D.W. Cruickshank, 402(MLR):Jan86-238
Blühm, E., J. Garber & K. Garber, eds. Hof, Staat und Gesellschaft in der Literatur des 17. Jahrhunderts.
J. Hardin, 406:Winter86-528
Bluhm, W.T. Force or Freedom?*
A. Taylor, 543:Sep86-108
Blum, C. Rousseau and the Republic of Virtue.
A.M., 125:Spring86-341
J.H. Mason, 617(TLS):27Feb87-220
Blum, C. & F. Moureau, eds. Etudes montaignistes en hommage à Pierre Michel.
R.D. Cottrell, 207(FR):Oct86-117
Blum, D.S. Walter Lippmann.*
P. Roazen, 529(QQ):Summer86-442
Blum, H. I Pledge Allegiance...
M. Kempton, 453(NYRB):19Nov87-24
J.A. Lukas, 441:11Oct87-11
Blum, J. & V. Rich. The Image of the Jew in Soviet Literature.
A. McMillin, 575(SEER):Apr86-280
A. Nakhimovsky, 550(RusR):Oct86-437
Blum, R. Die Literaturverzeichnung im Altertum und Mittelalter.
W. Berschin, 684(ZDA):Band115Heft4-151
Blum, W. The CIA.
J. Symons, 617(TLS):30Jan87-101
Blume, H. & W. Wunderlich, eds. Hermen Bote.
O. Ehrismann, 680(ZDP):Band105Heft1-143
Blümel, A. J-M-G. Le Clézios Ideenwelt in seinen Romanen und ihre kunstlerische Verwicklichung.
R. Brütting, 72:Band223Heft1-222
Blümel, W. Die aiolischen Dialekte.*
J.H.W. Penney, 123:Vol36No1-147
C.J. Ruijgh, 394:Vol39fasc1/2-145
W.P. Schmid, 260(IF):Band91-385
Blumenberg, H. The Legitimacy of the Modern Age.
R.B. Pippin, 543:Mar87-535
Blumenberg, H. Die Lesbarkeit der Welt.
J. Villwock, 224(GRM):Band36Heft1-83
Blumenberg, H. Work on Myth.
W.G. Regier, 400(MLN):Dec86-1242
Blumenkranz, B., ed. Documents modernes sur les Juifs: XVIe-XXe siècles. (Vol 1)
N. Perry, 83:Autumn86-243
Blumenson, M. Patton.
639(VQR):Spring86-45
Blumenthal, E. Joseph Chaikin.*
S.E. Wilmer, 610:Summer86-174
Blumenthal, G.R. Thresholds.
F.C. St. Aubyn, 207(FR):Apr87-710

van Boheemen, F.C. & T.C.J. van der Heij-
den. De Westlandse Rederijkerskamers in
de 16e en 17e eeuw.
E. Strietman, 402(MLR):Jul87-802
Böhler, D. Rekonstruktive Pragmatik.
T. Gil, 679:Band17Heft1-162
V. Hösle, 687:Oct-Dec86-644
Bohm, R. Notes on India.
D. Allen, 293(JASt):Aug86-873
Bohn, W. Apollinaire et l'homme sans vis-
age.*
C. Gandelman, 549(RLC):Apr-Jun86-251
R.W. Greene, 210(FrF):May86-246
T. Mathews, 208(FS):Jul86-354
M. Rainbow-Vigourt, 593:Fall86-237
Bohnen, K., ed. Lessings "Nathan der
Weise."
W. Goetschel, 221(GQ):Fall86-647
H.B. Nisbet, 402(MLR):Jan86-250
Bohnen, K. - see Jacobsen, J.P.
Bohnen, K. - see Lessing, G.E.
Bohnen, K., S-A. Jørgensen & F. Schmöe,
eds. Literatur und Psychoanalyse.
H. Ammerlahn, 406:Spring86-89
Bohnert, C. Brechts Lyrik im Kontext.
S. Mews, 221(GQ):Spring86-333
Bohren, C.F. Clouds in a Glass of Beer.
T. Bay, 441:27Sep87-36
Bohstedt, J. Riots and Community Politics
in England and Wales 1790-1810.
M. Philp, 83:Spring86-83
Boileau-Despréaux, N. Satires, Epîtres,
Art poétique. (J.P. Collinet, ed)
B. Beugnot, 475:Vol13No24-372
Bois, G. The Crisis of Feudalism.
E.A.R. Brown, 551(RenQ):Spring86-88
du Bois, P. History, Rhetorical Descrip-
tion and the Epic from Homer to Spenser.*
M. Desmond, 131(CL):Winter86-96
de Boisrobert, A.G. - see under Goulley de
Boisrobert, A.
Boitani, P. Chaucer and the Imaginary
World of Fame.
J.D. Burnley, 179(ES):Feb86-82
S. Ellis, 278(IS):Vol41-135
Boitani, P., ed. Chaucer and the Italian
Trecento.*
G.H. McWilliam, 278(IS):Vol41-131
D. Mehl, 72:Band223Heft1-161
Boitani, P. & A. Torti, eds. Literature in
Fourteenth-Century England.
S.S. Hussey, 402(MLR):Apr87-437
Boitani, P. & A. Torti, eds. Medieval and
Pseudo-Medieval Literature.
J.D. Burnley, 402(MLR):Jul86-696
Boixo, J.C.G. - see under González Boixo,
J.C.
Bojani, G.C., C. Ravanelli Guidotti & A.
Fanfani. La Donazione Galeazzo Cora,
Ceramiche dal Medioevo al XIX Secolo.
(Vol 1)
90:Jun86-443
Bok, D. Higher Learning.*
T.M.R., 185:Jul87-902
Bokamba, E.G., ed. Language in African
Culture and Society.
D.K. Nylander, 350:Jun87-438
Böker, H.J. Englische Sakralarchitektur
des Mittelalters.
W. Haas, 43:Band16Heft2-208
Böker, U. Loyale Illoyalität.
H. Zapf, 72:Band223Heft1-232

Bol, P.C. Antike Bronzetechnik.
M. Vickers, 123:Vol36No2-284
Bol, R. Das Statuenprogramm des Herodes-
Atticus-Nymphäums.
M.A.R. Colledge, 123:Vol36No2-342
Bolan, B.J. & I. Farjon. Islam in Indone-
sia.
W.R. Roff, 318(JAOS):Apr/Jun85-364
Boland, E. The Journey and Other Poems.
A. Libby, 441:22Mar87-23
L. Mackinnon, 617(TLS):21Aug87-904
Bolaños Donoso, P. La obra dramática de
Felipe Godínez Manrique (Trayectoria de
un dramaturgo marginado).
H.W. Sullivan, 240(HR):Spring86-222
Bold, A., ed. W.H. Auden.*
A. Haberer, 189(EA):Jan-Mar87-96
Bold, A., ed. The Sexual Dimension in
Literature.
J.C. Beasley, 402(MLR):Oct86-989
Bold, A., ed. Smollett.
G.S. Rousseau, 677(YES):Vol16-275
Bold, A. Summoned by Knox.
K. McCarra, 571(ScLJ):Winter86-37
Bold, A. - see MacDiarmid, H.
Bold, C. Selling the Wild West.
M. Abley, 617(TLS):22May87-552
Boldman, B. Heart and Bones.
A. Kenny, 404:Winter-Spring86-60
Bolduan, V. Minne zwischen Ideal und Wirk-
lichkeit.
H. Heinen, 406:Fall86-388
Boles, J.B. Black Southerners, 1619-1869.*
P. Lachance, 106:Winter86-449
Bolger, D. Internal Exiles.
272(IUR):Autumn86-252
Bolinger, D. Intonation and Its Parts.*
D.R. Ladd, 350:Sep87-637
Böll, H. The Casualty.
R.A. Berman, 441:23Aug87-29
Böll, H. Die Fähigkeit zu trauern.
M. Butler, 617(TLS):15May87-521
Böll, H. The Stories of Heinrich Böll.*
P. Lewis, 364:Jul86-99
P. Lewis, 565:Summer86-57
A. Otten, 42(AR):Fall86-487
Böll, H. The Train Was on Time.* What's
to Become of the Boy? A Soldier's Leg-
acy.
P. Lewis, 565:Summer86-57
Boll, M.M. Cold War in the Balkans.
R.J. Crampton, 575(SEER):Jul86-481
Bollacher, M. Wackenroder und die Kunst-
auffassung der frühen Romantik.
E. Waniek, 406:Fall86-401
Bollack, J. L'Agamemnon d'Eschyle, 1.
W.J. Verdenius, 394:Vol39fasc1/2-165
Bollenbeck, G. Till Eulenspiegel.
W. Wunderlich, 196:Band27Heft3/4-329
"Bollettino dei Classici." (Ser 3, fasc 1)
P. Petitmengin, 555:Vol59fasc2-353
Bollinger, L.C. The Tolerant Society.*
G.R.S., 185:Apr87-700
Bolster, R., ed. Documents littéraires de
l'époque romantique.*
D. Bryant, 402(MLR):Oct86-1009
Bolter, J.D. Turing's Man.*
W.E. Rivers, 577(SHR):Spring86-196
Bolton, H.P. Dickens Dramatized.
A. Sanders, 617(TLS):21Aug87-908
Bolton, W.F. The Language of 1984.*
P. Chilton, 402(MLR):Jul87-723

Boon, K.G. L'epoque de Lucas de Leyde et Pierre Bruegel.
  H. Mielke, 380:Spring86-75
Boon, P. "Spiegel der armen sündigen Seele."
  P.A. Giangrosso, 133:Band19Heft2-162
Boorman, J. Money into Light.
  J. Richards, 176:Jan87-49
Boorman, S., ed. Studies in the Performance of Late Medieval Music.
  M. Bent, 551(RenQ):Autumn86-528
  D.N. Klausner, 589:Jul86-618
  C. Page, 382(MAE):1986/1-154
Boorsch, S., M. Lewis & R.E. Lewis. The Engravings of Giorgio Ghisi.
  I. Cheney, 551(RenQ):Autumn86-531
  D. Landau, 90:Jan86-41
Booss, C., ed. Scandinavian Folk and Fairy Tales.
  A. Liberman, 563(SS):Spring86-217
Booth, E. Aristotelian Aporetic Ontology in Islamic and Christian Thinkers.
  I. Backus, 53(AGP):Band68Heft3-300
  G. Böwering, 318(JAOS):Oct/Dec85-739
  D.B. Burrell, 438:Spring86-243
  C.L. Hancock, 319:Oct87-587
Booth, M. British Poetry 1964 to 1984.*
  A. Swarbrick, 148:Autumn86-109
Booth, M. Carpet Sahib.*
  R. Mayne, 176:Apr87-52
Booth, P. Relations.*
  M. Boruch, 29(APR):Mar/Apr87-22
  R.B. Shaw, 491:Nov86-102
  P. Stitt, 219(GaR):Winter86-1021
Booth, S. "King Lear," "Macbeth," Indefinition, and Tragedy.*
  M. Goldman, 570(SQ):Spring86-121
  D. Mehl, 38:Band104Heft3/4-514
Boothroyd, B. A Shoulder to Laugh On.
  P. Oakes, 617(TLS):24Jul87-791
Booty, J. Meditating on "Four Quartets."
  R. Beum, 569(SR):Winter86-124
Borah, W. & others. El gobierno provincial en la Nueva España.
  W.B. Taylor, 263(RIB):Vol36No3-333
Boralevi, L.C. - see under Campos Boralevi, L.
Borawska, T. Tiedemann Giese (1480-1550) w życiu wewnętrznym Warmii i Prus Królewskich.
  E. Hilfstein, 497(PolR):Vol31No4-328
Borbély, A. Secrets of Sleep.
  B. Morton, 362:7May87-27
Borchmeyer, D. Das Theater Richard Wagners.*
  T.S. Hansen, 406:Winter86-538
Borck, J.S. - see "The Eighteenth Century: A Current Bibliography"
Borden, G.F. Easter Day, 1941.
  A. Krystal, 441:29Mar87-22
Bordes, P. Le Serment du Jeu de Paume de Jacques-Louis David.
  T. Crow, 54:Sep86-497
Bording, A. Den Danske Mercurius. (P. Ries, ed)
  G. Albeck, 562(Scan):Nov86-229
Bording, A. Samlede skrifter. (P. Ries, ed)
  C.S. Hale, 563(SS):Spring86-216
Bordman, G. The Oxford Companion to American Theatre.*
  C.W.E. Bigsby, 610:Spring86-81
  R.A. Martin, 115:Summer86-419

Borel, P. Champavert.* (J-L. Steinmetz, ed)
  R. Pearson, 208(FS):Oct86-473
Borer, H. Parametric Syntax.
  A.C. Battye, 361:Nov86-220
  R. Salkie, 297(JL):Sep86-502
Borg, A.J. A Study of Aspect in Maltese.
  P. Cachia, 318(JAOS):Oct/Dec85-744
Borgeaud, W.A. Fasti Vmbrici.
  J.H.W. Penney, 123:Vol36No1-149
Borgen, R. Sugawara no Michizane and the Early Heian Court.
  W. McCullough, 407(MN):Winter86-491
Borges, J.L. Textos Cautivos. (E. Sacerio-Gari & E. Rodriguez Monegal, eds)
  Y. Bronowski, 617(TLS):4-11Sep87-961
Borges, J.L., with M. Kodama. Atlas.* (A. Kerrigan, ed and trans)
  J. Byrne, 532(RCF):Summer86-151
  A. Ross, 364:Aug/Sep86-140
Borgeson, P.W., Jr. Hacia el hombre nuevo.*
  J.M. Oviedo, 238:Dec86-885
Borghi Cedrini, L. Via de lo paraiso.
  M.R. Harris, 589:Oct86-901
  E. Radtke, 553(RLiR):Jul-Dec86-566
Borgmann, A. Technology and the Character of Contemporary Life.*
  A.C. Michalos, 449:Dec86-573
Borgmeier, R. The Dying Shepherd.
  D. Rolle, 38:Band104Heft1/2-237
Borie, J. Mythologies de l'hérédite au XIXe siècle.
  R. Reid, 188(ECr):Spring86-99
Borie, J. - see Renard, J.
Borillo, M. Informatique pour les sciences de l'homme.
  G. Stahl, 542:Jul-Sep86-388
Boris, E. Art and Labor.
  R. Winter, 637(VS):Spring87-417
Borisoff, D. & L. Merrill. The Power to Communicate.
  C.A. Roach, 583:Fall86-98
Born, J., with others, eds. Franz Kafka: Kritik und Rezeption 1924-1938.
  M.L. Caputo-Mayr, 221(GQ):Winter86-154
Born, N., J. Manthey & D. Schmidt, eds. Nietzsche.
  R. Margreiter, 489(PJGG):Band93Heft2-375
Bornecque, J-H. - see Daudet, A.
Bornstein, G., ed. Ezra Pound Among the Poets.
  W. Harmon, 569(SR):Fall86-630
  M. North, 577(SHR):Summer86-267
Bornstein, G. - see Yeats, W.B.
Borodin, L. Partings.
  J. Bayley, 453(NYRB):22Oct87-9
  J. Dalley, 617(TLS):28Aug87-932
  D.M. Thomas, 441:4Oct87-30
Borowitz, A. The Thurtell-Hunt Murder Case.
  P-L. Adams, 61:Nov87-122
  P. Clinton, 441:18Oct87-30
Borowitz, H.O. The Impact of Art on French Literature from de Scudéry to Proust.
  J.A. Fleming, 446(NCFS):Spring87-336
  D. O'Connell, 207(FR):Dec86-250
  J.H. Rubin, 90:Apr86-298
Borque, J.M.D. - see under Díez Borque, J.M.
Borràs, M.L. Picabia.*
  L. Cooke, 90:Mar86-227

41

Borrás, M.R., ed. Textos de Filosofía: Kant.
M. Caimi, 342:Band77Heft3–383
Borrás Gualís, G.M. Arte mudéjar aragonés.
D. Angulo Iñiguez, 48:Oct–Dec86–424
Borri, A.P. – see under Picchioni Borri, A.
Borsetto, L. – see Muzio, G.
Borsi, F. Gian Lorenzo Bernini Architekt.
K. Güthlein, 683:Band49Heft2–248
Borsi, F., ed. Fortuna degli Etruschi.
N. Spivey, 313:Vol76–281
Borsi, F. The Monumental Era.
P. Goldberger, 441:6Dec87–22
Borsieri, P. Avventure letterarie di un giorno o Consigli di un galatuomo a vari scrittori. (W. Spaggiari, ed)
V.D.L., 605(SC):15Apr87–306
Borson, R. A Sad Device.
C.R. Steele, 102(CanL):Summer86–119
Borson, R. & K. Maltman. The Transparence of November/Snow.
E. Woods, 376:Sep86–156
Borsten, R. The Great Equalizer.
A. Giardina, 441:8Feb87–24
Bortoni-Ricardo, S.M. The Urbanization of Rural Dialect Speakers.
M.M. Azevedo, 263(RIB):Vol36No4–486
K. Fitch, 350:Jun87–450
Borum, P. Danish Literature.
F. Hugus, 563(SS):Winter86–93
Borum, P. Digteren Grundtvig.
J.I. Jensen, 562(Scan):Nov86–231
N.L. Jensen, 563(SS):Summer86–326
Bosch, H. Die Nürnberger Hausmaler.
G.R. von Bock, 683:Band49Heft2–252
Bosch, P. Agreement and Anaphora.
M.S. Rochemont, 603:Vol10No1–201
M. Strong-Jensen, 320(CJL):Winter86–367
Boschetti, A. Sartre et "Les Temps Modernes."
K. Gore, 208(FS):Oct86–490
A. van den Hoven, 628(UWR):Spring–Summer86–74
Bose, S. Agrarian Bengal.
D. Arnold, 617(TLS):1May87–469
Bosence, S. Hand Block Printing and Resist Dyeing.
E. Marx, 324:Dec86–80
Boskin, J. Sambo.
L. Alster, 362:24Sep87–27
R.G. O'Meally, 441:4Jan87–8
Boskovits, M. The Fourteenth Century: The Painters of the Miniaturist Tendency.
E. Fahy, 90:Jan86–40
de Bosque, A. Mythologie et Manièrisme aux Pays-Bas 1570–1630, Peinture-Dessins.
N. Powell, 39:Jul86–66
Bostock, D. Plato's "Phaedo."
C. Rowe, 617(TLS):3Apr87–368
Bostock, W.W. The Organisation and Co-ordination of "La Francophonie."*
C. May, 208(FS):Jan86–122
Boswell, J. Boswell: The Applause of the Jury 1782–1785. (I.S. Lustig & F.A. Pottle, eds)
W.C. Dowling, 677(YES):Vol16–285
Boswell, J. Boswell: The English Experiment, 1785–1789. (I.S. Lustig & F.A. Pottle, eds)
K. Walker, 617(TLS):3Apr87–347

Boswell, J. The Correspondence of James Boswell. (Vol 4) (P.S. Baker & others, eds)
P. Rogers, 617(TLS):23–29Oct87–1165
Boswell, J. Theodore Dreiser and the Critics, 1911–1982.
R.W. Dowell, 26(ALR):Winter87–92
Boswell, R. Crooked Hearts.
W. Balliett, 442(NY):17Aug87–71
S.S. Stark, 441:5Jul87–12
Boswell, R. Dancing in the Movies.
M. Kreyling, 573(SSF):Fall86–461
Boswell, S.G. The Book of Boswell.
362:22Oct87–33
Bosworth, R. & G. Rizzo, eds. Altro Polo.
D. Robey, 278(IS):Vol41–168
von Bothmer, D. The Amasis Painter and his World.*
R. Higgins, 39:Nov86–453
von Bothmer, D. & others. Wealth of the Ancient World.
L. Burn, 303(JoHS):Vol106–257
Bothwell, R. Eldorado.
P.E. Roy, 298:Fall86–146
Bott, G. & others. Gothic and Renaissance Art in Nuremberg 1300–1550.
J.M. Massing, 617(TLS):27Mar87–337
Bottigheimer, R.B. Fairy Tales and Society.
J. Westwood, 617(TLS):1May87–472
Bottigheimer, R.B. Grimms' Bad Girls and Bold Boys.
J.A. Smith, 453(NYRB):3Dec87–22
A. Wawn, 617(TLS):20–26Nov87–1282
Bottignole, S., ed & trans. Un angolo d'Africa.
J. Wilkinson, 538(RAL):Spring86–142
Botwinick, A. Ethics, Politics and Epistemology.
L. Krüger, 53(AGP):Band68Heft2–212
Boucé, P-G., ed. Sexuality in Eighteenth-Century Britain.*
J.C. Beasley, 402(MLR):Oct86–989
Bouchard, D. On the Content of Empty Categories.
R.D. Borsley, 297(JL):Mar86–237
Bouchelle, J.H., ed. With Tennyson at the Keyboard.*
S. Banfield, 415:Oct86–562
Boucicault, D. London Assurance. (J.L. Smith, ed)
M.R. Booth, 541(RES):Aug86–438
Boucicault, D. Plays by Dion Boucicault. (P. Thomson, ed)
M.R. Booth, 541(RES):Aug86–438
B. Murphy, 536(Rev):Vol8–197
L. Potter, 161(DUJ):Dec85–195
Boudar, G. & M. Décaudin, eds. Catalogue de la Bibliothèque de Guillaume Apollinaire.
B. Veck, 535(RHL):Mar–Apr86–329
Boudarel, G. and others. La bureaucratie au Vietnam.
A. Woodside, 302:Vol22No1–116
Boudet-Lamotte, E. – see Stendhal
Bougerol, J-G. La théologie de l'espérance aux XIIe et XIIIe siècles.
D.N. Bell, 589:Jul86–620
Bouillon, J-P. Art Nouveau 1870–1914.*
J. Polster, 139:Jun/Jul86–14
N. Powell, 39:May86–365
B.C. Rezelman, 637(VS):Summer87–549
90:Jun86–445

Boulter, C.G. & K.T. Luckner. Corpus Vasorum Antiquorum: The Toledo Museum of Art. (fasc 2)
J. Boardman, 123:Vol36No1-165
Boulton, C.A. I Fought Riel. (H. Robertson, ed)
T. Flanagan, 298:Summer86-157
C.P. Stacey, 529(QQ):Autumn86-658
Boulton, J.T. & A. Robertson - see Lawrence, D.H.
Boulton, M.B.M., ed. The Old French "Evangile de l'Enfance."*
K. Busby, 382(MAE):1986/2-313
Boumelha, P. Thomas Hardy and Women.*
V. Shaw, 402(MLR):Jan86-184
Bouquet, H. The Papers of Henry Bouquet. (Vol 3 ed by D.H. Kent, L.M. Waddell & A.L. Leonard, Vols 4 & 5 ed by L.M. Waddell, J.L. Tottenham & D.H. Kent)
G.L. Schaaf, 656(WMQ):Jan86-147
Bourchier, D. Dynamics of Dissent in Indonesia.
R.W. Liddle, 293(JASt):Feb86-441
Bourcier, G. L'orthographie de l'anglais.
P. Mertens-Fonck, 597(SN):Vol58No2-271
Bourdier, J-P. & T.T. Minh-ha. African Spaces.
J.M. Vlach, 2(AfrA):May86-21
Bourdieu, P. Distinction.*
A. Giddens, 473(PR):Vol53No2-300
Bourdieu, P. Die feinen Unterschiede.
I. Dölling, 654(WB):4/1986-700
Bourdieu, P. Homo Academicus.*
T. Suck, 188(ECr):Winter86-101
Boureau, A. La légende dorée.
B. Cazelles, 589:Oct86-903
Bourgeade, P. La Fin du monde.
G.R. Montbertrand, 207(FR):Oct86-161
de Bourges, G. - see under Guillaume de Bourges
Bourjaily, V. The Great Fake Book.
P-L. Adams, 61:Feb87-94
R.P. Brickner, 441:18Jan87-35
Bourne, J. & others. Lacquer.*
G. Wills, 39:Mar86-221
Bourne, M.A., with L.T. Bourne. The Ladies of Castine.
A.M. Boylan, 432(NEQ):Sep86-439
Boursier, N. Le Centre et la Circonférence.*
J. Campbell, 208(FS):Jan86-72
Boussinot, R. Des enfants dans les arbres.
S. Keane, 207(FR):Oct86-162
Boutelle, A.E. Thistle and Rose.
A. Noble, 677(YES):Vol16-358
Boutry, F. Faire part.
M. Moscovici, 98:Dec86-1237
Boutry, P. & J. Nassif. Martin l'Archange.
H. Cronel, 450(NRF):Apr86-112
Bouvier, J-C., ed. Tradition orale et identité culturelle.*
G. Straka, 553(RLiR):Jul-Dec86-609
Bouvier, N. The Scorpion-Fish.
S. Vogan, 441:27Sep87-18
Bova, B. The Kinsman Saga.
G. Jonas, 441:20Dec87-18
Bove, E. Un Homme qui savait.
L.K. Penrod, 207(FR):Dec86-288
Bove, E. Le Piège.
W. de Spens, 450(NRF):Nov86-99
Bové, P.A. Intellectuals in Power.
D. O'Hara, 290(JAAC):Summer87-416

Bowden, B. Performed Literature.
C.R. Finlay, 107(CRCL):Sep86-512
Bowden, C. Frog Mountain Blues.
E. Trout, 441:5Jul87-14
Bowen, B.C. Words and the Man in French Renaissance Literature.*
M. Gutwirth, 535(RHL):Jul-Aug86-727
Bowen, J. The Girls.*
J. Mellors, 364:Apr/May86-139
R. Weinreich, 441:26Apr87-24
Bowen, J.D., H. Madsen & A. Hilferty. TESOL Techniques and Procedures.
M.E. Call, 399(MLJ):Summer86-163
Bowen, M. Michael Tippett.
D. Clarke, 410(M&L):Jul86-302
Bower, W. Scotichronicon. (Vol 8) (D.E.R. Watt, ed)
G.W.S. Barrow, 617(TLS):16-22Oct87-1148
Bowering, G. Craft Slices.*
D. Leahy, 529(QQ):Summer86-412
Bowering, G. Seventy-One Poems for People.
D. Leahy, 529(QQ):Summer86-412
S. Scobie, 376:Mar86-125
Bowers, N. James Dickey.*
S. Wright, 569(SR):Spring86-292
Bowers, N. Theodore Roethke.
R. Marsack, 447(N&Q):Dec85-556
Bowersock, G.W. Roman Arabia.*
I. Shadîd, 318(JAOS):Oct/Dec85-748
M.P. Speidel, 122:Jul86-262
Bowlby, R. Just Looking.*
G. Cunningham, 541(RES):Nov86-601
L. Fletcher, 177(ELT):Vol29No4-455
J.A. Grimshaw, Jr., 395(MFS):Winter86-697
R.B. Henkle, 454:Winter87-171
E. Langland, 529(QQ):Autumn86-686
27(AL):Oct86-478
Bowle, J. - see Evelyn, J.
Bowler, G. - see Eckhardt, F.
Bowles, P., ed & trans. She Woke Me Up So I Killed Her.
I. Malin, 532(RCF):Fall86-147
Bowles, P.L. Anglais chic, anglais choc.
R. Buss, 617(TLS):31Jul87-812
Bowles, S. & H. Gintis. Democracy and Capitalism.*
A. Ryan, 176:Sep/Oct87-55
M.W., 185:Apr87-684
Bowman, R. Star Wars.
Lord Zuckerman, 453(NYRB):7May87-42
Bowman, S. A Fashion for Extravagance.
B. Scott, 39:Mar86-220
Bowron, E.P. - see Clark, A.M.
Box, J.B.H. García Márquez: "El coronel no tiene quien le escriba."
H.D. Oberhelman, 238:May86-319
Boxill, A. V.S. Naipaul's Fiction.
M. Fabre, 189(EA):Jan-Mar87-104
Boyce, M. A Persian Stronghold of Zoroastrianism.
N. Sims-Williams, 259(IIJ):Apr86-128
Boyce, M. Zoroastrians.
J. Duchesne-Guillemin, 259(IIJ):Oct86-322
Boycott, G. Boycott.
N. Andrew, 362:3Dec87-34
Boyd, B. Nabokov's "Ada."
D.B. Johnson, 574(SEEJ):Winter86-583
Boyd, J.M. Fraser Darling's Islands.
J.R.G. Turner, 617(TLS):10Apr87-396

Boyd, M. Bach.
H.T.E.M., 412:Feb85-56
Boyd, M. The Reflexive Novel.
J. Preston, 402(MLR):Jul87-689
Boyd, S.R., ed. The Whiskey Rebellion.
B. Karsky, 656(WMQ):Jul86-507
Boyd, W. The New Confessions.
A. Beevor, 617(TLS):25Sep-1Oct87-1051
J. Sutherland, 362:1Oct87-22
Boyd, W. Stars and Bars.*
C. Yates, 148:Autumn86-114
Boyde, P. Night Thoughts on Italian Poetry
and Art.
F.J. Jones, 278(IS):Vol41-136
J.R. Woodhouse, 402(MLR):Apr86-505
Boyde, P. Predisposition and Prevenience.
P. Armour, 278(IS):Vol41-126
Boyeldieu, P. Deux études Laal (Moyen-
Chari, Tchad).
G.F. Meier, 682(ZPSK):Band39Heft5-602
Boyer, E.L. College.
P. Brooks, 441:8Mar87-26
Boyer, R. Eléments de grammaire de
l'islandais ancien.
H. Fix, 680(ZDP):Band105Heft1-128
Boyers, R. Atrocity and Amnesia.*
J. Klinkowitz, 594:Fall86-320
S. Pinsker, 219(GaR):Winter86-1043
M.A. Sperber, 395(MFS):Winter86-696
Boyle, A.J., ed. Seneca Tragicus.*
M. Colakis, 124:Sep-Oct86-57
Boyle, K. & T. Hadden. Ireland.*
T. Garvin, 272(IUR):Autumn86-243
Boyle, L.E. Medieval Latin Palaeography.
B. Ross, 589:Jul86-623
Boyle, N. Goethe: "Faust," Part I.
C.H. Sisson, 617(TLS):17Apr87-419
Boyle, N. & M. Swales, eds. Realism in
European Literature.
A.S. Byatt, 617(TLS):16Jan87-65
Boyle, T.C. World's End.
P-L. Adams, 61:Nov87-122
B. De Mott, 441:27Sep87-1
442(NY):16Nov87-159
de Boylesve, P.F. - see under Faucon de
Boylesve, P.
de Brabant, S. - see under Siger de Bra-
bant
Bracciolini, G.F.P. - see under Poggio
Bracciolini, G.F.
Braches, E. Engel en afrond over "The
Turn of the Screw" van Henry James.
M. Hewitt, 395(MFS):Summer86-252
Brachin, P. The Dutch Language.*
R. Vismans, 402(MLR):Apr86-538
Brack, O.M., Jr. - see "Studies in Eigh-
teenth-Century Culture"
Bracken, H.M. Mind and Language.*
F. D'Agostino, 84:Jun86-249
D. Sievert, 543:Dec86-374
Brackenbury, R. Sense and Sensuality.
J. Olshan, 441:15Feb87-20
Brackman, A.C. The Other Nuremberg.
G. Smith, 441:5Apr87-12
Bradbrook, M. The Collected Papers of
Muriel Bradbrook. (Vol 1)
R. Miles, 402(MLR):Oct86-978
Bradbrook, M.C. Women and Literature 1779-
1982.*
R. Ashton, 402(MLR):Apr86-455

Bradbury, M. Cuts.
A. Davies, 362:16Apr87-38
T. Eagleton, 617(TLS):12Jun87-627
L. Moore, 441:18Oct87-9
Bradbury, M. Mensonge.
C. Baldick, 617(TLS):6-12Nov87-1217
Bradbury, M. The Modern American Novel.*
R. Haas, 38:Band104Heft1/2-271
Bradbury, M. No, Not Bloomsbury.
B. Bergonzi, 176:Jul/Aug87-43
T. Eagleton, 617(TLS):12Jun87-627
Bradbury, M. Rates of Exchange.*
R.S. Burton, 145(Crit):Winter87-101
Bradbury, M. & D. Palmer, eds. Shakespear-
ian Tragedy.
P. Bement, 541(RES):May86-255
L. Scragg, 148:Autumn86-102
Bradby, D. Modern French Drama, 1940-
1980.*
M. Autrand, 535(RHL):Mar-Apr86-344
A. Callen, 402(MLR):Apr86-495
N. Lane, 207(FR):Dec86-269
Braden, G. Renaissance Tragedy and the
Senecan Tradition.*
J. Crewe, 400(MLN):Dec86-1267
K.E. Maus, 551(RenQ):Summer86-330
R.S. Miola, 570(SQ):Summer86-267
Bradford, J.C., ed. Command under Sail.
I.H. King, 656(WMQ):Jan86-155
Bradford, M.E. Remembering Who We Are.
T.D. Clark, 579(SAQ):Autumn86-392
639(VQR):Spring86-46
Bradley, B. James Joyce's Schooldays.
E. Kennedy, 174(Éire):Fall86-145
Bradley, D. The Chaneysville Incident.
I. Bamforth, 617(TLS):16Jan87-56
Bradley, D.E. Africa and the Americas.
A.P. Bourgeois, 2(AfrA):Aug86-84
Bradley, G. Terms to Be Met.
J. Ash, 441:1Mar87-26
J.D. McClatchy, 491:Oct86-31
639(VQR):Autumn86-132
Bradley, I.C. Enlightened Entrepreneurs.
D. Stein, 362:15Oct87-29
Bradley, J. Muzhik and Muscovite.
J.H. Bater, 550(RusR):Oct86-443
Bradley, J.F.N. Czech Nationalism in the
Nineteenth Century.
P. Brock, 575(SEER):Jan86-137
Bradley, J.L., ed. Ruskin: The Critical
Heritage.*
C. Brooks, 326:Autumn86-55
M. Hardman, 402(MLR):Jul87-711
M. Lutyens, 39:Oct86-377
Bradley, K.R. Slaves and Masters in the
Roman Empire.
T. Wiedemann, 123:Vol36No2-276
Bradley, M.Z. The Firebrand.
M. Lefkowitz, 441:29Nov87-27
Bradley, S.A.J., ed & trans. Anglo-Saxon
Poetry.*
N.F. Blake, 402(MLR):Apr86-440
Bradshaw, G. The Beacon at Alexandria.
G. Phillips, 617(TLS):30Jan87-108
Bradshaw, G. Shakespeare's Scepticism.
J. Wilders, 617(TLS):30Oct-5Nov87-1197
Bradstock, A. Saints and Sandinistas.
E. Norman, 617(TLS):29May87-576
Brady, F. James Boswell: the Later Years
1769-1795.*
R.D. Altick, 401(MLQ):Jun85-208
D. Crane, 83:Autumn86-247
[continued]

[continuing]

T. Crawford, 571(ScLJ):Winter86-13

O.W. Ferguson, 579(SAQ):Autumn86-399

I. Grundy, 402(MLR):Apr86-453

C. Lamont, 541(RES):Aug86-422

W.A. Speck, 366:Spring86-114

Brady, M.K. "Some Kind of Power."

C.R. Farrer, 650(WF):Jan86-48

Braet, H. & W. Verbeke, eds. Death in the Middle Ages.

D.P. Seniff, 345:Nov86-489

Bragg, M. The Maid of Buttermere.

R. Ashton, 362:23Apr87-25

A. Vaux, 617(TLS):24Apr87-434

Brague, R. Du temps chez Platon et Aristote.

S.W. Broadie, 53(AGP):Band68Heft3-296

S. Rosen, 543:Jun87-759

Brahm, O. & G. Hauptmann. Otto Brahm - Gerhart Hauptmann, Briefwechsel 1889-1912. (P. Sprengel, ed)

H. Claus, 610:Autumn86-255

R.C. Cowen, 406:Winter86-514

P. Skrine, 402(MLR):Jul87-793

Brahms, C. & N. Sherrin. Too Dirty for the Windmill.*

A. Cornish, 157:No161-48

Brahms, C. & S.J. Simon. No Bed for Bacon [and] Bullet in the Ballet.

A. Cornish, 157:No161-48

Brǎiloiu, C. Problems of Ethnomusicology. (A.L. Lloyd, ed & trans)

J.R. Baldwin, 575(SEER):Jul86-466

A. Schuursma, 187:Winter87-150

Brain, P. - see Galen

Braitenberg, V. Vehicles.

D.C. Dennett, 482(PhR):Jan86-137

Brall, H. Gralsuche und Adelsheil.*

B. Schirok, 684(ZDA):Band115Heft4-163

Bramann, J.K. Wittgenstein's "Tractatus" and the Modern Arts.

D. Collinson, 89(BJA):Summer86-286

Brams, S.J. Superpower Games.*

A.C., 185:Jan87-508

Bramsbäck, B. Folklore and W.B. Yeats.*

D. Ó hÓgáin, 272(IUR):Spring86-93

Branca, V., ed. Mercanti scrittori.

D. Abulafia, 617(TLS):5Jun87-614

Branca, V. & C. Ossola, eds. Cultura e società nel Rinascimento tra riforme e manierismi.*

A. Millen, 402(MLR):Apr86-502

Brancacci, A. Rhetorike Philosophousa.

J. Barnes, 520:Vol31No3-283

Brancaforte, C.L., ed. Fridericus Berghius' Partial Latin Translation of "Lazarillo de Tormes" and its Relationship to the Early "Lazarillo" Translations in Germany.

P. Hess, 406:Fall86-394

Brand, J., C. Hailey & D. Harris - see Berg, A. & A. Schoenberg

Brand, M. Intending and Acting.

F.A., 185:Jul87-888

R.W. Binkley, 486:Sep86-459

L.H. Davis, 484(PPR):Mar87-506

J. Hornsby, 482(PhR):Apr86-261

Brand, S. The Media Lab.

L. Hunter, 441:27Sep87-38

Branden, B. The Passion of Ayn Rand.*

A. Chisholm, 617(TLS):21Aug87-893

S. Maitland, 362:18Jun87-24

Brandenburg, S. & others - see van Beethoven, L.

Brandes, U. Zitat und Montage in der neueren DDR-Prosa.

M. Eifler, 221(GQ):Winter86-167

Brandt, F.R. Late 19th and Early 20th Century Decorative Arts.

N. Powell, 39:Sep86-226

Brandt, R. Die Interpretation philosophischer Werke.

R. Fornet-Betancourt, 160:Jul86-224

Brandt, R., ed. Rechtsphilosophie der Aufklärung.

S. Fabbri Bertoletti, 489(PJGG):Band93 Heft1-190

Brandt, W. Die Abschiedsrede.

G.A. Craig, 453(NYRB):8Oct87-38

Brang, P. & M. Züllig, with K. Brang. Kommentierte Bibliographie zur Slavischen Soziolinguistik.

G. Stone, 402(MLR):Apr86-539

D.S. Worth, 279:Vol33-151

Branigan, E. Point of View in the Cinema.

B. Salt, 89(BJA):Spring86-185

F.P. Tomasulo, 290(JAAC):Spring87-309

Brans, J., with M.T. Smith. Mother, I Have Something to Tell You.

C. Carmichael, 441:25Jan87-29

Brantenberg, G. The Daughters of Egalia.

A. Born, 562(Scan):Nov86-250

Brantley, R.E. Locke, Wesley, and the Method of English Romanticism.*

R. Fadem, 478:Apr86-120

A.J. Sambrook, 402(MLR):Oct87-922

Brantlinger, P. Bread and Circuses.

T. Erwin, 385(MQR):Spring87-413

T. Gibbons, 627(UTQ):Winter86/87-372

G. Woodcock, 569(SR):Fall86-644

Brasas Egido, J.C. La pintura del siglo XIX en Valladolid.

E. Arias Anglés, 48:Apr-Jun86-199

Braselmann, P.M.E. Konnotation - Verstehen - Stil.

J. Langenbacher-Liebgott, 72:Band223 Heft1-220

Brass, P.R. Caste, Faction and Party in Indian Politics.

H. Blair, 293(JASt):Aug86-874

Brassaï. Paris by Night.

A. Grundberg, 441:6Dec87-20

Brassell, T. Tom Stoppard.*

J. Harty, 615(TJ):Mar86-127

J. Morris, 397(MD):Sep86-492

Brata, S. India.

639(VQR):Spring86-59

Brathwaite, E.K. Third World Poems.

T. Eagleton, 565:Autumn86-76

Brathwaite, E.K. X/Self.

L. James, 617(TLS):4-11Sep87-946

Brattin, J.J. & B.G. Hornback. "Our Mutual Friend."

M. Cotsell, 158:Sep86-136

Bratton, J.S., ed. Plays in Performance: "King Lear."

J. Wilders, 617(TLS):30Oct-5Nov87-1197

Braudeau, M. Naissance d'une passion.

F. de Martinoir, 450(NRF):Feb86-95

Braudel, F. Civilization and Capitalism. (Vol 3)

L. Coser, 473(PR):Vol53No1-137

Braudel, F. L'identité de la France.*

F. George, 98:Jun-Jul86-583

Braudy, L. The Frenzy of Renown.*
  D.J. Enright, 617(TLS):3Jul87-721
  T. Erwin, 385(MQR):Spring87-413
Braudy, S. What the Movies Made Me Do.
  D. Johnson, 18:Sep87-67
Braue, D.A. "Māyā" in Radhakrishnan's
Thought.
  B. Gupta, 293(JASt):Aug86-885
Brauer-Figueiredo, M.D.V. - see under
Viegas Brauer-Figueiredo, M.D.
Brault, G.J. The French-Canadian Heritage
in New England.
  A. Prévos, 207(FR):Feb87-414
Brault, J. Fragile Moments/Moments Frag-
iles.*
  J. Harrison, 529(QQ):Winter86-889
Braun, P., ed. Deutsche Gegenwartssprache.
  N. Nail, 685(ZDL):3/1986-383
Braun, W. Die Musik des 17. Jahrhunderts.
  G.J. Buelow, 410(M&L):Jan86-62
Braun, Y. Hinze-Kunze-Roman.*
  H. Kähler, 601(SuF):Mar-Apr86-435
Braund, D.C. Augustus to Nero.
  B. Burrell, 124:Jan-Feb87-225
Brauner, S., ed. Verkehrs- und National-
sprachen in Afrika.
  R. Lötzsch, 682(ZPSK):Band39Heft5-615
Braungart, W., ed. Bänkelsang.
  R.W. Brednich, 196:Band27Heft3/4-331
Braunmuller, A.R., ed. A Seventeenth-
Century Letter-Book.
  I. Donaldson, 402(MLR):Jan87-161
Braunmuller, A.R. & J.C. Bulman, eds.
Comedy from Shakespeare to Sheridan.
  T. Hawkes, 617(TLS):10Apr87-390
Bravo, M-E. Faulkner en España.
  R. Johnston, 552(REH):Jan86-145
Brawne, M. Arup Associates.
  D.F. Anstis, 324:Feb87-251
Bray, F. The Rice Economies.
  R. McVey, 617(TLS):31Jul87-826
Brayfield, C. Pearls.
  H. Wackett, 362:30Jul87-23
Braynard, F.O. Picture History of the
Normandie.
  R.F. Shepard, 441:10May87-21
Brebach, R. Joseph Conrad, Ford Madox
Ford and the Making of "Romance."
  M.B., 295(JML):Nov86-391
  R.L. Caserio, 637(VS):Summer87-537
Brecht, B. Gesammelte Werke. (Supplement-
band 3 & 4) (H. Ramthun, ed)
  S. Mews, 301(JEGP):Apr86-319
Brecht, B. Poems 1913-1956. (J. Willett &
R. Manheim, eds)
  J. Mole, 176:Jul/Aug87-45
Brecht, R.D., D.E. Davidson & M. Sendich,
eds. Soviet-American Contributions to
the Study and Teaching of Russian.
  G.L. Ervin, 574(SEEJ):Winter86-600
Breckenridge, J. Civil Blood.
  E. Grosholz, 441:4Jan87-22
Bredekamp, H. & W. Janzer. Vicino Orsini
und der heilige Wald von Bomarzo.
  J. Bury, 90:Sep86-679
Bredin, J-D. The Affair.* (French title:
L'Affaire.)
  D. Coward, 617(TLS):28Aug87-933
  M. Cranston, 362:19Mar87-27
Bredin, J-D. Un coupable.
  J. Laroche, 207(FR):Oct86-163
Bredin, J-D. L'Absence.
  R. Buss, 617(TLS):3Apr87-362

Brednich, R.W. & J.R. Dow, eds. Interna-
tionale Volkskundliche Bibliographie/
International Folklore Bibliography/
Bibliographie Internationale d'Ethnologie
für die Jahre 1979 und 1980 mit Nachträ-
gen für die vorausgehenden Jahre.
  M. Taft, 292(JAF):Jul/Sep86-365
Bredsdorff, E. Min egen kurs.
  T. Munch-Petersen, 562(Scan):May86-88
  K.H. Ober, 563(SS):Winter86-94
Bredsdorff, E. Mit engelske liv.
  N.L. Jensen, 562(Scan):May86-89
Breen, T.H. Tobacco Culture.*
  P.S. Onuf, 656(WMQ):Oct86-664
Breen, W.J. Uncle Sam at Home.
  D. Macleod, 106:Summer86-235
Bregman, J. Synesius of Cyrene.*
  R.T. McClelland, 41:Spring85-127
Bregoli-Russo, M. Renaissance Italian
Theater.
  E.B. Weaver, 276:Summer86-185
Breit, H. & M.B. Lowry - see Lowry, M.
Breit, W. & R.W. Spencer, eds. Lives of
the Laureates.
  A. Walters, 617(TLS):30Jan87-105
Breitwieser, M.R. Cotton Mather and
Benjamin Franklin.*
  T.H. Breen, 31(ASch):Spring86-279
  H.J. Dawson, 656(WMQ):Jan86-141
  J.A.L. Lemay, 27(AL):Mar86-127
  639(VQR):Winter86-7
Breivik, L.E. Existential "There."*
  J. Haiman, 320(CJL):Spring86-88
  B. Jacobsen, 179(ES):Jun86-250
  K. Reichl, 72:Band223Heft1-228
Brekke, T. The Jacaranda Flower.
  J-A. Goodwin, 617(TLS):28Aug87-929
Bremer, J. On Plato's Polity.
  J.F. Finamore, 124:Sep-Oct86-59
Bremner, G. Diderot: "Jacques le fatal-
iste."
  G. May, 402(MLR):Oct87-960
  R. Niklaus, 208(FS):Apr86-213
Bremner, G. Order and Chance.*
  J.C. Hayes, 345:Feb86-127
  M.L. Perkins, 535(RHL):Jan-Feb86-148
Brémond, J. & others. Initiation econo-
mique et sociale.
  E.C. Knox, 207(FR):Oct86-148
Brend, R.M., ed. From Phonology to Dis-
course.
  D. Payne, 350:Jun87-444
Brendon, P. Ike.*
  R. Mayne, 176:Apr87-53
Brennan, A. Shakespeare's Dramatic Struc-
tures.*
  S. Hazell, 157:No161-50
"Christopher Brennan."* (T. Sturm, ed)
  J.J. O'Carroll, 67:May86-119
Brennan, J.W., ed. "Building the Co-opera-
tive Commonwealth."
  N. Wiseman, 298:Spring86-144
Brennan, R. The Walking Wounded.
  M. Harmon, 272(IUR):Spring86-77
  J. Lanchester, 493:Jun86-113
Brent, R. Liberal Anglican Politics.
  T. Hoppen, 617(TLS):30Oct-5Nov87-1185
Brentano, C. Der Goldfaden. (K-H. Haber-
setzer, ed)
  A. Hölter, 196:Band27Heft3/4-327
Brentano, C. Die Märchen vom Rhein. (B.
Schillbach, ed)
  H.M.K. Riley, 133:Band19Heft1-82

Brereton, J., ed. Traditions of Inquiry.
    639(VQR):Winter86-17
Brereton, J.M. The British Soldier.*
    M.R.D. Foot, 176:Feb87-46
Bresenhan, K.P. & N.O. Puentes. Lone
    Stars.
    L. Milazzo, 584(SWR):Autumn86-538
Breslauer, B.H. & R. Folter, comps. Bibli-
    ography.
    R.C. Alston, 354:Sep86-279
Breslauer, S.D. Contemporary Jewish
    Ethics.
    J.G.H., 185:Apr87-679
Breslin, C. First Ladies.
    A. McCarthy, 441:14Jun87-12
Breslin, J.E.B. From Modern to Contempo-
    rary.*
    A. Golding, 405(MP):Nov86-235
    D.L. Macdonald, 106:Fall86-381
    W.H. Pritchard, 31(ASch):Autumn86-553
Breslin, J.E.B. - see Williams, W.C.
Breton, A. Mad Love.
    M. Ward, 441:26Jul87-17
Breton, S. Deux mystiques de l'excès.
    M. Adam, 542:Oct-Dec86-511
Brett, B. Smoke Without Exit.
    D.A. Macdonald, 102(CanL):Winter85-157
Brett, P., comp. Benjamin Britten: "Peter
    Grimes."*
    C. Floyd, 465:Autumn86-128
Brett, S. A Nice Class of Corpse.*
    P-L. Adams, 61:Feb87-94
    N. Callendar, 441:8Mar87-29
Brett, S. What Bloody Man is That?
    T.J. Binyon, 617(TLS):18-24Sep87-1027
    N. Callendar, 441:11Oct87-24
Brettell, R. & others. A Day in the
    Country.
    K. Adler, 59:Sep86-376
Breuer, D., ed. Frömmigkeit in der frühen
    Neuzeit.
    E. Bernstein, 221(GQ):Spring86-302
    P.A. Giangrosso, 133:Band18Heft4-368
Breuer, H-P. - see Butler, S.
Breuer, R., H. Gundel & W. Huber, eds.
    Beckett Criticism in Germany.
    J.C.C. Mays, 272(IUR):Autumn86-240
Brevda, W. Harry Kemp.
    P. Wild, 50(ArQ):Summer86-187
    27(AL):Oct86-479
Brewer, D. English Gothic Literature.*
    C. Gauvin, 189(EA):Apr-Jun87-197
Brewer, D. An Introduction to Chaucer.*
    A. Crépin, 189(EA):Jan-Mar87-113
Brewin, B. & S. Shaw. Vietnam on Trial.
    K. Evans, 441:5Apr87-13
Brewster, E. Selected Poems of Elizabeth
    Brewster 1944-1977. Selected Poems of
    Elizabeth Brewster 1977-1984.
    M. Harry, 198:Spring86-104
Brey de Rodríguez Moñino, M. - see Valera,
    J.
Brezik, V.S., ed. Thomistic Papers, I.
    J.J. Haldane, 518:Apr86-79
Brezzi, P. & M. Lorch, eds. Umanesimo a
    Roma nel Quattrocento.*
    J. O'Malley, 551(RenQ):Spring86-78
Briceño Perozo, M. La poesía y el derecho.
    M.L. Miller, 552(REH):May86-128
Bridges, M.E. Generic Contrast in Old
    English Hagiographical Poetry.
    D.G. Calder, 589:Jul86-624
                                [continued]

[continuing]
    M. Clayton, 541(RES):Aug86-401
    A. Crépin, 189(EA):Oct-Dec87-463
Bridges, R. A Choice of Bridges's Verse.
    (D. Cecil, ed)
    R. Wells, 617(TLS):14Aug87-864
Bridges, R. The Selected Letters of Robert
    Bridges.* (Vols 1 & 2) (D.E. Stanford,
    ed)
    A. Brown, 639(VQR):Autumn86-741
    C. Phillips, 541(RES):Aug86-440
Bridgland, F. Jonas Savimbi.
    R. Oliver, 617(TLS):13-19Nov87-1241
Bridgman, N. La Musique à Venise.*
    S. Mamy, 537:Vol72No1-135
Bridgwater, P. The German Poets of the
    First World War.
    E.A. McCobb, 402(MLR):Oct86-1044
Briegleb, C. & C. Rauschenberg - see von
    Eichendorff, J.
Brien, A. Lenin.
    E. Battersby, 362:22Oct87-30
    Z. Zinik, 617(TLS):20-26Nov87-1273
Brierly, D. "Der Meridian."
    R.E. Lorbe, 221(GQ):Fall86-628
Brigg, P. J.G. Ballard.
    G.K. Wolfe, 395(MFS):Spring86-133
Briggs, A. The Collected Essays of Asa
    Briggs.*
    P. Stigant, 366:Autumn86-262
Briggs, J. This Stage-Play World.*
    D.F. Bratchell, 447(N&Q):Mar85-103
    H-J. Weckermann, 156(ShJW):Jahr-
    buch1986-240
Briggs, J. A Woman of Passion.
    N. Andrew, 362:12Nov87-32
    C. Tomalin, 617(TLS):20-26Nov87-1281
Briggs, J. - see Crompton, D.
Briggs, R. Unlucky Wally.
    M. Coward, 362:16Apr87-39
Briggs, W.W., Jr. & H.W. Benario, eds.
    Basil Lanneau Gildersleeve.
    H. Lloyd-Jones, 123:Vol36No2-357
Bright, W. Bibliography of the Languages
    of Native California including Closely
    Related Languages of Adjacent Areas.
    M. Langdon, 269(IJAL):Jan86-85
Brighton, C. Lincoln Cathedral Cloister
    Bosses.
    N. Coldstream, 90:Oct86-758
Brijder, H.A.G. Siana Cups I and Komast
    Cups.*
    T.H. Carpenter, 303(JoHS):Vol106-251
Brincard, M-T., ed. Beauty by Design.
    J. Perani, 2(AfrA):Nov85-23
Brind'Amour, P. Le Calendrier romain.*
    J. Briscoe, 313:Vol76-289
Bringéus, N-A. Volkstümliche Bilderkunde.
    E. Moser-Rath, 196:Band27Heft1/2-95
Bringle, M. Death of an Unknown Man.
    G. Kaufman, 362:8Oct87-23
Brink, A. & J.M. Coetzee, eds. A Land
    Apart.
    362:8Oct87-24
Brinkmann, R. & others, eds. Theatrum
    Europaeum.
    R.J. Alexander, 406:Fall86-379
Brinkmeyer, R.H., Jr. Three Catholic
    Writers of the Modern South.*
    W.J. Stuckey, 395(MFS):Winter86-610
    T.D. Young, 392:Spring86-126
Brinnin, J.M. Truman Capote.
    J. Melmoth, 617(TLS):17Apr87-404

47

Briolet, D. Le Langage poétique.
  I. Higgins, 208(FS):Jul86-369
Brisson, L. & others. Porphyre, "La Vie de
  Plotin."* (Vol 1)
  R. Ferwerda, 394:Vol39fasc3/4-505
Bristiger, M., R. Scruton & P. Weber-
  Bockholdt, eds. Karol Szymanowski in
  seiner Zeit.
  K. Campbell, 607:Dec86-35
Bristol, M.D. Carnival and Theater.*
  V. Comensoli, 539:Nov86-384
  S.K. Fischer, 612(ThS):May/Nov86-174
Britain, I. Fabianism and Culture.
  J. Stokes, 677(YES):Vol16-345
Britten, B. On Receiving the First Aspen
  Award.
  W. Ashbrook, 465:Autumn86-147
Britton, B.K. & J.B. Black, eds. Under-
  standing Expository Prose.
  E.B. Bernhardt, 399(MLJ):Autumn86-294
Britton, J. Prospect and Retrospect.
  (G.M. Pradl, ed)
  S. Blau, 126(CCC):Oct86-364
Brivic, S. Joyce the Creator.*
  P.F. Herring, 659(ConL):Spring87-104
Brizzi, G. I sistemi informativi dei
  Romani.
  P. Jal, 555:Vol59fasc2-328
Brizzolara, J. Wirecutter.
  N. Callendar, 441:15Mar87-24
Broad, C.D. Ethics.* (C. Lewy, ed)
  J. Deigh, 185:Apr87-655
Broad, W.J. Star Warriors.*
  639(VQR):Spring86-58
Broadie, A. The Circle of John Mair.
  J.M.G. Hackett, 588(SSL):Vol21-355
  E. & F. Michael, 518:Jul86-144
Broch, H. Hugo von Hofmannsthal and his
  Time.* (M.P. Steinberg, ed & trans)
  W. Riemer, 221(GQ):Fall86-664
Broch, H. The Spell.
  D.J. Enright, 617(TLS):28Aug87-930
  E. Heller, 441:25Jan87-31
Brochu, A. L'Evasion tragique.
  G. Pascal, 627(UTQ):Fall86-195
Brock, D.H. A Ben Jonson Companion.
  R. Dutton, 402(MLR):Oct87-913
Brock, P. A Theology of Church Design.
  J. Thomas, 46:Feb86-86
Brockbank, P., ed. Players of Shake-
  speare.*
  T.W. Craik, 161(DUJ):Jun86-374
  P. Holland, 611(TN):Vol40No2-86
  M. Jones, 541(RES):Nov86-560
  M. Rosenberg, 610:Autumn86-271
  D.G. Watson, 536(Rev):Vol8-59
Brockett, A.A. The Spoken Arabic of Khā-
  būra on the Bāṭina of Oman.
  A.S. Kaye, 350:Jun87-438
Brockett, O. - see Rokem, F.
Brockington, J.L. The Sacred Thread.
  W.H. Maurer, 318(JAOS):Apr/Jun85-378
Brockliss, L.W.B. French Higher Education
  in the Seventeenth and Eighteenth Cen-
  turies.
  P. & A. Higonnet, 617(TLS):30Oct-
  5Nov87-1183
Broder, D.S. Behind the Front Page.
  T. Griffith, 441:26Apr87-14
Broder, P.J. The American West.*
  B.W. Dippie, 649(WAL):Aug86-136
Broderick, J. The Flood.
  C.D. Kennedy, 441:27Dec87-18

Broderick, J.C., ed. George Orwell and
  "Nineteen Eighty-Four."
  R.J. Voorhees, 395(MFS):Winter86-668
Brodeur, P. Restitution.
  F.P. Prucha, 432(NEQ):Mar86-131
Brodey, V., ed. Las Coplas de Mingo
  Revulgo.
  A. MacKay, 304(JHP):Spring86-251
Brodkey, H. Women and Angels.
  B. Lyons, 573(SSF):Fall86-456
  I. Malin, 532(RCF):Spring86-220
Brodsky, J. Less Than One.*
  C. Cavanagh, 115:Fall86-534
  D. Dunn, 493:Oct86-4
Brodsky, L.D. & R.W. Hamblin, eds. Faulk-
  ner.* (Vols 3 & 4)
  C.S. Brown, 569(SR):Winter86-167
Brodsky, M. Xman.
  H. Marten, 441:15Nov87-31
Brodsky, P.P. Russia in the Works of
  Rainer Maria Rilke.*
  B.L. Bradley, 222(GR):Spring86-83
  J.A. Taubman, 574(SEEJ):Summer86-290
Brodwin, S., ed. The Old and New World
  Romanticism of Washington Irving.
  D.C. Irving, 165(EAL):Vol22No3-326
Brody, J. A Coven of Women.
  C. Dragonwagon, 441:30Aug87-20
Brody, J.J., C.J. Scott & S.A. Le Blanc.
  Mimbres Pottery.
  R.M. Adams, 453(NYRB):26Mar87-32
van den Broek, M.A. - see Suevus, S.
van den Broek, M.A. & G.J. Jaspers, eds.
  In Diutscher Diute.
  P.W. Tax, 133:Band18Heft4-356
Brogan, J.V. Stevens and Simile.
  T. Armstrong, 617(TLS):10Jul87-747
de Broglie, G. Le français, pur gu'il
  vive.
  J. Weightman, 617(TLS):31Jul87-812
Brogyanyi, B. & T. Krömmelbein, eds. Ger-
  manic Dialects.
  J.B. Voyles, 159:Fall86-237
Broich, U. & others - see Schirmer, W.F.
Broich, U., T. Stemmler & G. Stratmann,
  eds. Functions of Literature.
  P. Coustillas, 189(EA):Oct-Dec87-456
Broido, V. Lenin and the Mensheviks.
  R. Service, 617(TLS):6-12Nov87-1213
Brokoph-Mauch, G., ed. Beiträge zur Musil-
  Kritik.
  S. Imhoof, 133:Band19Heft1-90
Brombert, V. Victor Hugo and the Visionary
  Novel.* (French title: Victor Hugo et le
  roman visionnaire.)
  M. Eigeldinger, 535(RHL):Nov-Dec86-
  1132
  C.A. Mossman, 210(FrF):Jan86-113
  C. Prendergast, 208(FS):Apr86-222
  K. Wren, 402(MLR):Jan86-208
Brome, R. The English Moore; or The Mock-
  Marriage. (S.J. Steen, ed)
  T.W. Craik, 161(DUJ):Dec85-190
Bromley, L. - see Frederic, H.
Brommer, F. Herakles II.
  J. Boardman, 123:Vol36No2-337
Bromwich, D. Hazlitt.*
  M. Del Sapio, 677(YES):Vol16-298
Bromwich, R. Aspects of the Poetry of
  Dafydd ap Gwilym.*
  T.A. Watkins, 112:Vol18-205

Brondy, R., B. Demotz & J-P. Leguay. La
Savoie de l'an mil à la Réforme.
E.L. Cox, 589:Jul86-626
Bronner, E.B. & D. Fraser, eds. William
Penn's Published Writings, 1660-1726.
D.A. Saar, 165(EAL):Fall87-225
Bronner, S.E. - see Pachter, H.
Bronner, S.J., ed. American Folk Art.*
J.I. Deutsch, 650(WF):Jan86-59
Bronner, S.J. Chain Carvers.
F.W. Childrey, Jr., 650(WF):Jul86-228
Bronner, S.J. Grasping Things.
42(AR):Fall86-491
Brontë, C. The Poems of Charlotte Brontë.
(V.A. Neufeldt, ed)
F.T. Flahiff, 627(UTQ):Fall86-106
Brontë, C. The Poems of Charlotte Brontë.*
(T. Winnifrith, ed)
K. Sutherland, 402(MLR):Oct87-927
P. Thomson, 541(RES):May86-280
639(VQR):Winter86-29
Brontë, C. Villette. (H. Rosengarten & M.
Smith, eds)
J. Butler, 301(JEGP):Oct86-577
F.T. Flahiff, 627(UTQ):Fall86-106
E. Hollahan, 594:Summer86-206
K. Sutherland, 402(MLR):Oct87-927
P. Thomson, 541(RES):Nov86-583
Brontë, P.B. The Poems of Patrick Branwell
Brontë.* (T. Winnifrith, ed)
K. Sutherland, 402(MLR):Oct87-927
Brook, E. Land of the Snow Lion.
C. von Fürer-Haimendorf, 617(TLS):
17Jul87-777
Brook, P. The Shifting Point.
F. King, 441:18Oct87-15
Brook-Shepherd, G. Royal Sunset.
S. Runciman, 617(TLS):10Jul87-750
Brooke, F. The History of Emily Montague.
(M.J. Edwards, ed)
L. McMullen, 627(UTQ):Fall86-163
C.R. Steele, 470:Vol24-111
C. Thomas, 529(QQ):Autumn86-659
T. Ware, 102(CanL):Fall86-113
Brooke, J. - see Walpole, H.
Brooke, R. The Poems of Rupert Brooke.
(T. Rogers, ed) The Collected Poems.
Letters from America.
D. Hibberd, 617(TLS):27Nov-3Dec87-
1310
P. Parker, 362:6Aug87-21
Brookner, A. A Friend from England.
H. Neill, 362:20Aug87-18
D. Singmaster, 617(TLS):21Aug87-897
Brookner, A. Hotel du Lac.*
J. Waelti-Walters, 376:Mar86-120
Brookner, A. The Misalliance.* (British
title: A Misalliance.)
F. Eberstadt, 441:29Mar87-10
J. Neville, 364:Oct86-98
442(NY):18May87-115
Brooks, C. William Faulkner: First
Encounters.*
K.L. Fulton, 106:Spring86-119
I. Jackson, 447(N&Q):Dec85-553
I.D. Lind, 587(SAF):Spring86-109
Brooks, C. The Language of the American
South.
M.J. Bolsterli, 395(MFS):Winter86-609
M.K. Spears, 453(NYRB):7May87-38

Brooks, C. On the Prejudices, Predilec-
tions, and Firm Beliefs of William
Faulkner.
E. Sundquist, 441:15Nov87-27
Brooks, D. - see Hamilton, E.
Brooks, D.R. & E.O. Wiley. Evolution as
Entropy.
J.E. Earley, 543:Jun87-760
Brooks, H.A., ed. Le Corbusier.
J. Iovine, 441:11Oct87-56
Brooks, H.F. & R. Selden - see Oldham, J.
Brooks, J. The Takeover Game.
S.B. Shepard, 441:25Oct87-28
Brooks, J. When Russia Learned to Read.*
C.A. Moser, 574(SEEJ):Winter86-568
639(VQR):Summer86-78
Brooks, P. The Melodramatic Imagination.*
R. Chambers, 210(FrF):Jan86-116
Brooks, P. Reading for the Plot.*
T. Docherty, 541(RES):Aug86-450
P.K. Garrett, 301(JEGP):Jan86-87
Brooks-Davies, D. Pope's "Dunciad" and
the Queen of Night.
D. Bulckaen-Messina, 189(EA):Jul-
Sep86-345
T.D. Faulkner, 566:Autumn86-55
P. Rogers, 541(RES):Nov86-575
D.H. White, 173(ECS):Fall86-76
Broome, H. Faces of the Wilderness.
D. Scheese, 649(WAL):May86-92
Broomhead, F. The Zaehnsdorfs (1842-
1947).
A. Hobson, 617(TLS):14Aug87-878
Brooten, B.J. Women Leaders in the An-
cient Synagogue.
D.J. Halperin, 318(JAOS):Apr/Jun85-343
Brophy, B. Baroque 'n' Roll and Other
Essays.
A.S. Byatt, 617(TLS):13Mar87-269
M. Wandor, 362:26Feb87-21
Brophy, J. & C. Smart, eds. Women in Law.
C.C., 185:Oct86-305
D.G. Réaume, 529(QQ):Summer86-417
Brophy, J.D. & R.J. Porter, eds. Contempo-
rary Irish Writing.*
A.E. McGuinness, 402(MLR):Oct87-947
Brose, D.S., J.A. Brown & D.W. Penney.
Ancient Art of the American Woodland
Indians.
A. Trevelyan, 2(AfrA):May86-80
Brosio, V. Ritratto segreto di Aldo
Palazzeschi.
A.J. Tamburri, 276:Winter86-402
Brossard, C. Closing the Gap.
S. Moore, 532(RCF):Fall86-134
Brosse. Les songes des hommes esveillez,
comédie (1646).* (G. Forestier, ed)
E.J. Campion, 475:Vol13No24-375
G.J. Mallinson, 208(FS):Apr86-206
J. Morgan, 402(MLR):Apr86-480
Brostrom, K.N. Russian Literature and
American Critics.
N. Cornwell, 575(SEER):Oct86-650
M. Futrell, 104(CASS):Spring-Summer86-
184
L. Milne, 402(MLR):Jul87-811
Brostrøm, T. Fantasi og Dokument.
P. Houe, 562(Scan):Nov86-247
Brostrøm, T. & M. Winge, eds. Danske
digtere i det 20. århundrede. (Vols 2-5)
F. Hugus, 563(SS):Winter86-87

Broszat, M. Nach Hitler. (H. Graml & K-D. Henke, eds)
G.A. Craig, 453(NYRB):15Jan87-16
R. Knight, 617(TLS):15May87-520
Brothwell, D. The Bog Man and the Archaeology of People.*
J.G. Deaton, 441:27Sep87-37
Broughton, V. Black Gospel.
A.P., 91:Spring86-191
Browder, C. The Money Game in Old New York.
639(VQR):Summer86-83
Brown, A. The Almond Tree.
P.M. St. Pierre, 102(CanL):Summer86-121
Brown, A., ed. Political Culture and Communist Studies.
R. Walker, 575(SEER):Apr86-310
Brown, A. Winter Journey.
B. Whiteman, 102(CanL):Summer86-124
Brown, A. & F.M. Cheney — see Tate, A.
Brown, A.C. "C."
K. Follett, 441:27Dec87-5
Brown, A.P. Performing Haydn's "Creation."
D. McCaldin, 415:Oct86-560
Brown, C., ed. The Portable Twentieth-Century Russian Reader.
K. Bushnell, 574(SEEJ):Fall86-444
Brown, C. Louis Spohr.*
N. Temperley, 410(M&L):Apr86-205
Brown, C. Van Dyck.
J.R. Martin, 54:Dec86-678
Brown, C.B. Clara Howard; in a Series of Letters with Jane Talbot. (S.J. Krause & S.W. Reid, eds)
B.R. Voloshin, 165(EAL):Vol22No3-331
Brown, C.C. John Milton's Aristocratic Entertainments.*
W.B. Hunter, 391:May86-55
D.A. Loewenstein, 568(SCN):Fall86-33
Brown, C.C. — see Townshend, A.
Brown, C.V., ed. West African Textiles.
R.A. Dunbar, 2(AfrA):Nov85-84
Brown, D. Conspiracy of Knaves.
T. Fleming, 441:11Jan87-12
Brown, D. Flight of the Old Dog.
G.A. Gross, 441:26Jul87-16
Brown, D. Tchaikovsky.* (Vol 3)
E. Garden, 410(M&L):Oct86-392
H. MacDonald, 415:Aug86-441
Brown, D., G. Abraham & D. Lloyd-Jones. Russian Masters 1.
L. Salter, 415:Aug86-441
Brown, D.E. The Grizzly in the Southwest.*
D. Peacock, 649(WAL):Aug86-160
Brown, E. Landscaping with Perennials.
A. Lacy, 441:31May87-14
Brown, F.B. Transfiguration.*
G. Smith, 402(MLR):Apr87-461
Brown, G. Maxton.
K.O. Morgan, 617(TLS):2Jan87-11
Brown, G. & G. Yule. Discourse Analysis.*
I. Kenesei, 603:Vol10No1-204
M. Toolan, 307:Apr86-74
K. Wikberg, 596(SL):Vol40No1-96
Brown, G.M. The Golden Bird.
J. Parini, 617(TLS):30Oct-5Nov87-1192
Brown, G.M. A Time to Keep.
S. Gordon, 441:22Mar87-9
Brown, H.M., ed. A Florentine Chansonnier from the Time of Lorenzo the Magnificent.*
I. Fenlon, 415:Jul86-386

Brown, I.G. Poet & Painter.
G.R.R., 588(SSL):Vol21-371
Brown, J. Lanning Roper.
A. Lacy, 441:31May87-14
Brown, J. Velázquez.*
J. Ferguson, 324:Mar87-337
Brown, J. Vita's Other World.
N. Miller, 42(AR):Spring86-242
Brown, J.C. Immodest Acts.*
P. Dickinson, 364:Jun86-111
D.O. Hughes, 385(MQR):Winter87-266
Brown, J.D. Henry Miller.
P.R.J., 295(JML):Nov86-512
Brown, J.E., ed. Clearings in the Thicket.
L.N. Allen, 9(AlaR):Apr86-147
R.M. Canfield-Reisman, 577(SHR):Fall86-400
Brown, J.L. & H.F. Pizer. Living Hungry in America.
T. Clarke, 441:15Nov87-20
Brown, J.R., ed. Marlowe: "Tamburlaine the Great," "Edward the Second" and "The Jew of Malta."
T.W. Craik, 677(YES):Vol16-239
Brown, J.W. Fictional Meals and their Function in the French Novel 1798-1848.*
C. Dickson, 207(FR):Feb87-397
A. Fischler, 446(NCFS):Fall-Winter 86/87-199
D. Knight, 208(FS):Jul86-346
Brown, L. Alexander Pope.*
M.A. Doody, 566:Spring87-179
C. Koralek, 175:Autumn86-293
F. Rosslyn, 97(CQ):Vol15No2-164
R. Wolfs, 204(FdL):Dec86-303
Brown, L. Victorian News and Newspapers.*
J.J. Barnes, 637(VS):Winter87-275
Brown, L.C., ed. State of the World 1987.
T. O'Riordan, 617(TLS):18-24Sep87-1011
Brown, L.K. & K. Mussell, eds. Ethnic and Regional Foodways in the United States.
C. Camp, 650(WF):Jul86-229
E. Wachs, 440:Summer-Fall86-172
Brown, M.E. Burns and Tradition.*
L. Haring, 650(WF):Jan86-44
C. MacLachlan, 571(ScLJ):Winter86-10
K.A. Thigpen, 292(JAF):Oct/Dec86-489
Brown, M.H., ed. Russian and Soviet Music.
G.R. Seaman, 575(SEER):Oct86-605
Brown, M.H. The Toxic Cloud.
P. Shabecoff, 441:27Dec87-19
Brown, M.H. & R.J. Wiley, eds. Slavonic and Western Music.
L. Botstein, 414:Vol72No1-138
Brown, P. Society and the Holy in Late Antiquity.* (French title: La Société et le Sacré dans l'Antiquité tardive.)
F. Trémolières, 450(NRF):Oct86-95
Brown, P.D.G. Oskar Panizza.
M. Soceanu, 133:Band19Heft1-85
Brown, P.H. & J. Pinkston. Oskar Dearest.
J. Hoberman, 441:29Mar87-23
Brown, R., ed. The Architectural Outsiders.*
E. McParland, 90:Jan86-45
J.M. Robinson, 39:Jan86-64
Brown, R. James Joyce and Sexuality.*
M.B., 295(JML):Nov86-494
P.F. Herring, 659(ConL):Spring87-104
M. Magalaner, 395(MFS):Summer86-308
V. Mahaffey, 177(ELT):Vol29No2-230

Brugnatelli, V. Questioni di morfologia e
sintassi die numerali cardinali semi-
tici.*
   S. Segert, 318(JAOS):Oct/Dec85-730
de Bruijn, J.T.P. Of Piety and Poetry.
   W.C. Chittick, 318(JAOS):Apr/Jun85-347
Brumbaugh, R.S. The Philosophers of
Greece.
   C. Weller, 41:Spring85-144
Brumbaugh, R.S. Unreality and Time.
   R.C. Hoy, 449:Sep86-441
Brumfield, W.C. Gold in Azure.
   J. Kollmann, 550(RusR):Jan86-79
Brumfit, C. Communicative Methodology in
Language Teaching.
   J.A. Muyskens, 399(MLJ):Winter86-414
Brumfit, C., H. Lunt & J. Trim, eds.
Second Language Learning.
   M-A. Reiss, 399(MLJ):Winter86-415
ten Brummelhuis, H. & J.H. Kemp, eds.
Strategies and Structures in Thai Soci-
ety.
   E.B. Ayal, 293(JASt):May86-663
Brundell, B. Pierre Gassendi.
   S. James, 617(TLS):23-29Oct87-1177
Brunel, J. - see Rapin, N.
Brunel, P. & A. Guyaux, eds. Huysmans.
   C. Lloyd, 208(FS):Jan86-96
Bruner, E.M., ed. Text, Play and Story.
   V. Cobb-Stevens, 292(JAF):Apr/Jun86-
223
   E. Turner, 355(LSoc):Mar86-95
Bruner, J. Actual Minds, Possible Worlds.*
   S. Brivic, 295(JML):Nov86-404
   N. Mergler & R. Schleifer, 400(MLN):
Dec86-1279
Brunet, E. Le Vocabulaire de Proust.*
   J. Murray, 207(FR):Dec86-263
Brunet, É. Le vocabulaire de Zola.
   G. Straka, 553(RLiR):Jan-Jun86-253
Brunette, P. Roberto Rossellini.
   M. d'Amico, 441:13Sep87-42
Bruni, R.L. & D.W. Evans. Italian Seven-
teenth-Century Books.
   U.L., 278(IS):Vol41-150
Brunn, E.Z. & A. de Libera - see under Zum
Brunn, E. & A. de Libera
Brunner, E.J. Splendid Failure.*
   M.B., 295(JML):Nov86-455
Brunner, F. & others - see Maître Eckhart
"Brünner Beiträge zur Germanistik und
Nordistik." (Vols 1 & 2)
   N.R. Wolf, 685(ZDL):1/1986-76
Bruno, A. Il Castello di Rivoli: 1734-
1984.
   D. Garstang, 39:Jan86-68
Bruno, G. Le Candelaio. (J-N. Vuarnet,
ed)
   A. Clerval, 450(NRF):Sep86-117
Bruno, V.J. Hellenistic Painting Tech-
niques.
   R. Ling, 123:Vol36No2-341
Bruns, G.L. Inventions.*
   K.H. Staudt, 403(MLS):Summer86-321
Bruns, R.A. The Damndest Radical.
   P. Clinton, 441:1Feb87-17
Brunt, P.A. - see Arrian
Brunt, R.J. The Influence of the French
Language on the German Vocabulary (1649-
1735).*
   U. Püschel, 685(ZDL):3/1986-392
Brunton, M. Discipline.
   P. Raine, 617(TLS):6-12Nov87-1216

Brunvand, J.H. The Mexican Pet.*
   M.H. Brown, 583:Summer87-413
Brushwood, J.S. Genteel Barbarism.*
   K.L. Levy, 547(RF):Band98Heft1/2-235
Brushwood, J.S. La novela hispanoamericana
del siglo XX.*
   D. Janik, 547(RF):Band98Heft3/4-487
Brustein, R. Who Needs Theatre.
   J. Temchin, 441:20Sep87-27
Bruyère, N. Méthode et dialectique dans
l'oeuvre de la Ramée - Renaissance et âge
classique.*
   F.J. Hausmann, 475:Vol13No24-377
Bruzelius, C.A. The Thirteenth-Century
Church at St. Denis.
   A. Borg, 617(TLS):13Mar87-279
   N. Coldstream, 90:Aug86-608
   P. Hetherington, 39:Oct86-378
Bryan, C.D.B. The National Geographic
Society.
   P. Benchley, 441:13Dec87-27
Bryan, G.B. An Ibsen Companion.
   Y. Shafer, 610:Spring86-75
Bryan, G.B. Stage Lives.
   G.S. Argetsinger, 563(SS):Spring86-214
Bryan, J. 3d. Hodgepodge.
   P-L. Adams, 61:Jan87-91
Bryant, A. A History of Britain and the
British People. (Vol 2)
   B. Fothergill, 617(TLS):1May87-470
Bryant, J., ed. A Companion to Melville
Studies.
   S.C. Tracy, 95(CLAJ):Jun87-509
Bryant, J.A., Jr. Shakespeare and the Uses
of Comedy.
   T. Hawkes, 617(TLS):10Apr87-390
Bryce Echenique, A. & others. Gabriel
García Márquez.
   G. Pontiero, 86(BHS):Oct86-395
Bryer, J.R. The Critical Reputation of F.
Scott Fitzgerald.
   W. White, 87(BB):Sep86-182
Bryer, J.R. - see O'Neill, E.
Bryers, P. Coming First.
   S. Fry, 362:21May87-23
   J. Melmoth, 617(TLS):17Jul87-766
Brykczynski, T. & D. Reuther, eds. The
Armchair Angler.
   639(VQR):Autumn86-137
Brykman, G. Berkeley.*
   J-M. Beyssade, 542:Jul-Sep86-377
   P. Engel, 98:Jan-Feb86-150
Brykman, G. - see Berkeley, G.
Brym, R.J., ed. The Structure of the Cana-
dian Capitalist Class.
   W. Clement, 529(QQ):Summer86-399
Bryson, J. Evil Angels.*
   P-L. Adams, 61:May87-94
   L. Wolfe, 441:22Mar87-43
Bryson, N. Vision and Painting.
   N. Carroll, 533:Summer86-138
Bryson, N. Word and Image.*
   T. Crow, 54:Sep86-497
Bubeník, V. The Phonological Interpreta-
tion of Ancient Greek.
   D.G. Miller, 487:Spring86-104
Buber-Neumann, M. Milena.
   A. Clerval, 450(NRF):May86-107
Buch, H.C. The Wedding at Port-au-Prince.*
   D. Walder, 362:26Nov87-31
   J.J. White, 617(TLS):28Aug87-933

Buchan, D., ed. A Book of Scottish Ballads.
G.R.R., 588(SSL):Vol21-368
Buchan, D., ed. Scottish Tradition.*
W.F.H. Nicolaisen, 196:Band27Heft3/4-333
K. Young, 292(JAF):Jul/Sep86-341
Buchan, J. Davy Chadwick.
R. Deveson, 617(TLS):18-24Sep87-1027
Buchan, J. A Parish of Rich Women.
639(VQR):Winter86-23
Buchan, U., ed. A Bouquet of Garden Writing.
A. Lacy, 441:31May87-14
Buchan, U. & N. Colborn. The Classic Horticulturist.
C. Lloyd, 617(TLS):18-24Dec87-1400
Buchanan, A. Ethics, Efficiency, and the Market.
J. Christman, 185:Jan87-479
D. Gordon, 258:Mar86-96
Buchanan, A.E. Marz and Justice.
M.J. De Nys, 543:Jun87-761
Buchanan, E. The Corpse Had a Familiar Face.
A. Rice, 441:13Dec87-23
Buchanan, P.H. Margaret Tudor, Queen of Scots.*
M. Lee, Jr., 551(RenQ):Winter86-762
639(VQR):Summer86-86
Buchanan, R. A Weaver's Garden.
A. Lacy, 441:6Dec87-32
Buchignani, N. & D.M. Indra, with R. Srivastiva. Continuous Journey.
G.W., 102(CanL):Fall86-197
Büchner, G. The Complete Plays. (M. Patterson, ed)
J. Hilton, 617(TLS):9-15Oct87-1098
Büchner, G. Complete Works and Letters. (W. Hinderer & H.J. Schmidt, eds)
42(AR):Fall86-493
"Georg Büchner Jahrbuch 1." (T. M. Mayer, ed) "Georg Büchner Jahrbuch 2." (H. Gersch, T.M. Mayer & G. Oesterle, eds)
I. Diersen, 654(WB):7/1986-1226
"Georg Büchner Jahrbuch 3." (H. Gersch & others, eds)
I. Diersen, 654(WB):7/1986-1226
D.G. Richards, 564:Sep86-261
Buchwald, A. I Think I Don't Remember.
E. O'Shaughnessy, 441:8Nov87-27
Buchwald, W., A. Hohlweg & O. Prinz, eds. Tusculum-Lexikon griechischer und lateinischer Autoren des Altertums und des Mittelalters. (3rd ed)
R.J. Tarrant, 589:Apr86-480
Buck, J.J. Daughter of the Swan.
W.J. Harding, 441:4Oct87-14
Buck, R.J. Agriculture and Agricultural Practice in Roman Law.*
R.P. Duncan-Jones, 313:Vol76-296
Buckler, W.E. Matthew Arnold's Prose.*
S. Monod, 402(MLR):Oct87-934
Buckler, W.E. Man and His Myths.*
S. Lavabre, 189(EA):Jul-Sep86-374
Buckler, W.E. On the Poetry of Matthew Arnold.*
C.D. Ryals, 402(MLR):Apr86-460
Buckler, W.E. The Poetry of Thomas Hardy.*
R.P. Draper, 541(RES):Feb86-121
Buckler, W.E. - see Pater, W.
Buckley, G.L. The Hornes.*
R. Koenig, 617(TLS):10Jul87-749

Buckley, J.H. The Turning Key.*
R.E. Fitch, 301(JEGP):Jan86-136
A.F.T. Lurcock, 541(RES):May86-299
I.B. Nadel, 506(PSt):May86-85
A. Nichols, 577(SHR):Fall86-371
E.L. Stelzig, 340(KSJ):Vol35-207
Buckley, R. Japan Today.
G.J. Kasza, 293(JASt):Aug86-841
Suzuki Sunao, 285(JapQ):Jan-Mar86-100
Buckley, R. Occupation Diplomacy.
E.W. Edwards, 302:Vol22No1-102
Buckley, V. Memory Ireland.
M. Finnane, 381:Sep86-379
M. Koenig, 272(IUR):Spring86-86
Buckley, W.F., Jr. Racing Through Paradise.
T. Foote, 441:31May87-34
Buckner, P.A. The Transition to Responsible Government.
R. Adelson, 637(VS):Autumn86-136
Bucur, M. Jules Michelet et les revolutionnaires roumains.
O. Séjourné, 535(RHL):Jan-Feb86-156
Buczacki, S. Ground Rules for Gardeners.
A. Urquhart, 617(TLS):27Feb87-225
Buczkowski, P. & A. Klawiter. Theories of Ideology and Ideology of Theories.
J-M. Gabaude, 542:Apr-Jun86-277
Budd, J. Henry James.*
A.W. Bellringer, 402(MLR):Oct87-938
Budd, L.J., ed. New Essays on "Adventures of Huckleberry Finn."
R.B. Hauck, 395(MFS):Winter86-595
Budd, M. Music and the Emotions.*
P. Kivy, 479(PhQ):Jul86-434
M. Mothersill, 393(Mind):Oct86-513
R.A. Sharpe, 89(BJA):Autumn86-397
Budden, J. Verdi.*
R. Parker, 410(M&L):Apr86-214
Budiardjo, C. & L.S. Liong. The War Against East Timor.
J.R. Bowen, 293(JASt):Feb86-442
Budick, E.M. Emily Dickinson and the Life of Language.
G. Johnson, 219(GaR):Winter86-1009
J. Loving, 183(ESQ):Vol36No3-201
Budick, S. The Dividing Muse.
T. Healy, 402(MLR):Oct87-915
M.A. Radzinowicz, 301(JEGP):Apr86-267
Budrys, A. Benchmarks.
G.K. Wolfe, 395(MFS):Spring86-133
Budziszewski, J. The Resurrection of Nature.
H. Arkes, 543:Jun87-762
D. Miller, 617(TLS):22May87-544
Buechner, F. Brendan.
P-L. Adams, 61:Jul87-99
J. O'Faolain, 441:9Aug87-15
442(NY):28Sep87-97
Buell, L. New England Literary Culture.
P.F. Gura, 183(ESQ):Vol32No1-68
Buell, L. & S.A. Zagarell - see Stoddard, E.
Buelow, G.J. & H.J. Marx, eds. New Mattheson Studies.*
S. Wollenberg, 410(M&L):Jan86-74
Bueno, B.L. - see under López Bueno, B.
Bueno, J.L. La sotana de Juan Ruiz.*
J. England, 86(BHS):Jul86-273
Buero Vallejo, A. La doble historia del doctor Valmy. (W. Giuliano, ed)
D.R. McKay, 399(MLJ):Winter86-440

Buero Vallejo, A. Three Plays.
  B. Grantham, 157:No159-47
  P.W. O'Connor, 552(REH):Oct86-117
Buganov, V. Pugachev.
  J.T. Alexander, 550(RusR):Jan86-74
Buhle, P., ed. C.L.R. James.
  S. Collini, 617(TLS):25Sep-1Oct87-1057
Buhle, P. Marxism in the United States.
  A. Brinkley, 617(TLS):18-24Sep87-1021
Buhlmann, J.A. & D. Gilman - see Le Caron,
  L.
Bühnemann, G. Budha-Kauśika's Rāmarak-
  ṣāstotra.
  M. Hara, 259(IIJ):Oct86-315
  S. Oleksiw, 318(JAOS):Apr/Jun85-385
Buhofer, A. Der Spracherwerb von phraseo-
  logischen Wortverbindungen.
  A. Lötscher, 685(ZDL):1/1986-92
Buisine, A. Proust et ses lettres.
  B. Brun, 535(RHL):Mar-Apr86-330
  R. Gibson, 208(FS):Jul86-352
Bukofzer, M. L'État baroque 1610-1652.
  (H. Méchoulan, ed)
  S. Goyard-Fabre, 154:Winter86-806
  M-A. Lescourret, 98:Jun-Jul86-668
  P.F. Moreau, 540(RIPh):Vol40fasc3-337
Bukofzer, M. La musique baroque 1600-
  1750. (H. Méchoulan, ed)
  M-A. Lescourret, 98:Jun-Jul86-668
Bukovski, C. Au sud de nulle part.
  J. Stéfan, 450(NRF):May86-110
Bukowczyk, J.J. And My Children Did Not
  Know Me.
  A. Paolucci, 441:15Feb87-21
Bukowski, C. & A. Purdy. The Bukowski/
  Purdy Letters, 1964-74.* (S. Cooney, ed)
  M. Peterman, 168(ECW):Fall86-181
Bulanin, D.M. Perevody i poslaniya Maksima
  Greka.
  J.J. Haney, 575(SEER):Apr86-291
Bulatović, M. Gullo Gullo.
  L. Kovacs, 450(NRF):Feb86-114
Bulciolu, M.T. L'école saint-simonienne et
  la femme.
  G. Fraisse, 192(EP):Apr-Jun86-239
Bulgakov, M.A. Sobranie sočinenij. (Vol
  2) (E. Proffer, ed)
  E.C. Haber, 574(SEEJ):Winter86-582
Bull, F. Bjørnstjerne Bjørnson.
  L. Isaacson, 563(SS):Winter86-96
Bull, J. New British Political Dramatists.
  G. Bas, 189(EA):Jan-Mar87-103
Bull, T. Lesing og Barns Talemal.
  A. Lindhe, 355(LSoc):Sep86-435
Bull, V., M. Guillet-Rydell & R. Switzer.
  A Vous de Choisir.
  L.L. Harlow, 399(MLJ):Winter86-425
Bullchild, P. The Sun Came Down.
  M. Abley, 617(TLS):1May87-460
  R.A. Roripaugh, 649(WAL):Feb87-382
Bullert, G. The Politics of John Dewey.
  T.V. Kaufman-Osborn, 396(ModA):
    Summer/Fall86-304
"Bulletin de la Commission Royale de Top-
  onymie & Dialectologie." (Vol 55, 1981)
  H.J. Wolf, 547(RF):Band98Heft3/4-399
"Bulletin d'Etudes Indiennes." (No. 1 & 2)
  E. Bender, 318(JAOS):Oct/Dec85-812
Bullier, A-J. & J-M. Racault, eds. Visages
  de la féminité.
  J.L. Pallister, 568(SCN):Winter86-72

Bulloch, A.W., ed. Callimachus: "The Fifth
  Hymn."
  J. Clack, 124:Jan-Feb87-217
  M.L. West, 123:Vol36No1-27
Bullock, A. - see Colonna, V.
Bullock, M. The Man With Flowers Through
  His Hands.
  B. Almon, 102(CanL):Spring86-177
Bullough, V.L. & J. Brundage. Sexual
  Practices and the Medieval Church.
  C.T. Wood, 589:Apr86-386
Bulygin, E. & J-L. Gardies, eds. Man, Law
  and Modern Forms of Life.
  T.D.E., 185:Apr87-689
Bumke, J., ed. Literarisches Mäzenaten-
  tum.*
  F.G. Gentry, 406:Fall86-386
Bumke, J. Mäzene im Mittelalter.
  P. Johanek, 224(GRM):Band36Heft2-209
"Bungaku ni okeru "mukōgawa."
  J. Cohn, 293(JASt):Aug86-847
Bungarten, T., ed. Wissenschaftssprache.
  K. Kehr, 685(ZDL):1/1986-102
Bungay, S. Beauty and Truth.*
  J.M. Bernstein, 518:Apr86-90
  W. Desmond, 319:Apr87-307
  S. Priest, 89(BJA):Winter86-76
Bunge, M. Treatise on Basic Philosophy.
  (Vol 7)
  M. Espinoza, 160:Jul86-213
  M. Espinoza, 542:Jul-Sep86-389
Bunin, I. Long Ago.
  J. Woodward, 402(MLR):Jan86-268
Buning, M. T.F. Powys.
  M. Pouillard, 189(EA):Jul-Sep87-361
  P.F. Schmitz, 204(FdL):Dec86-312
Bunt, G.H.V., ed. William of Palerne.
  J.D. Burnley, 179(ES):Aug86-368
Bunting, B. & M.H. Floyd. Harvard.
  T. Matthews, 45:Apr86-65
Buñuel, L., with J-C. Carrière. My Last
  Sigh.* (French title: Mon Dernier
  Soupir; British title: My Last Breath.)
  T. Doherty, 77:Fall86-365
  V. Higginbotham, 500:Winter87-63
Bunyan, J. Good News for the Vilest of
  Men; The Advocateship of Jesus Christ.
  (R.L. Greaves, ed)
  J.B.H. Alblas, 179(ES):Oct86-453
Buraselis, K. Das hellenistische Makedon-
  ien und die Ägäis.
  G.J.D. Aalders H. Wzn., 394:Vol39
    fasc3/4-527
  F.W. Walbank, 303(JoHS):Vol106-243
Burbidge, J.W. & G. di Giovanni - see
  Hegel, G.W.F.
Burchfield, R. The English Language.*
  B. Cottle, 541(RES):Aug86-400
  D.E. Eskey, 399(MLJ):Spring86-89
Burchfield, R., ed. Studies in Lexicogra-
  phy.
  J.A.C. Greppin, 617(TLS):17Jul87-773
Burchfield, R.W. - see "A Supplement to the
  Oxford English Dictionary"
Burck, F.W. Mothers Talking.*
  639(VQR):Autumn86-137
Burdon, E. I Used to Be an Animal, But I'm
  All Right Now.*
  A. Barnet, 441:3May87-45
Burger, E. Franz Liszt.
  A. Walker, 617(TLS):10Jul87-737
Burger, H.G. The Wordtree.
  J. Algeo, 35(AS):Winter86-355

Bürger, P., ed. Surrealismus.
H.T. Siepe, 72:Band223Heft1-219
Bürger, P. Theory of the Avant-Garde.*
S. Bonnycastle, 529(QQ):Spring86-198
M.T. Jones, 221(GQ):Summer86-463
M. Perloff, 402(MLR):Apr86-426
Burger, R. The "Phaedo."*
D. Frede, 24:Spring86-121
C. Gill, 123:Vol36No1-141
Burgess, A. But Do Blondes Prefer Gentle-
men?*
42(AR):Fall86-489
Burgess, A. A Clockwork Orange: A Play
(With Music).
D.A.N. Jones, 362:26Feb87-20
Burgess, A. Flame into Being.*
P. Boytinck, 529(QQ):Spring86-201
R.M. Davis, 223:Spring86-90
D.K. Dunaway, 639(VQR):Summer86-548
J. Meyers, 395(MFS):Summer86-309
H. Mills, 175:Summer86-173
T. Vichy, 189(EA):Apr-Jun87-233
Burgess, A. Ernest Hemingway and His
World.*
S.P., 295(JML):Nov86-482
Burgess, A. Little Wilson and Big God.
R. Davies, 441:22Feb87-9
D.A.N. Jones, 362:26Feb87-20
D. Lodge, 617(TLS):27Feb87-203
R. Mayne, 176:Apr87-53
G. Vidal, 453(NYRB):7May87-3
Burgess, A. The Pianoplayers.*
J. Diski, 364:Oct86-99
Burgess, G.S. & R.A. Taylor, eds. The
Spirit of the Court.
A.H. Diverres, 208(FS):Jul86-317
Bürgin, H. & H-O. Mayer. Die Briefe Thom-
as Manns: Regesten und Register. (Vol 3)
(Y. Schmidlin & others, eds)
H.R. Vaget, 406:Summer86-243
Burgin, V. The End of Art Theory.
C. Gould, 39:Oct86-380
Burgos, E. & R. Menchu. I, Rigoberta Men-
chu. (Spanish title: Me Llamo Rigoberta
Menchú y así Me Nació la Conciencia.)
E. Moya-Raggio, 385(MQR):Winter87-272
Burgos, F. La novela moderna hispanoameri-
cana.
R. de Vallbona, 263(RIB):Vol36No4-487
Burgos, J. Pour une Poétique de l'imagi-
naire.
S. Sarkany, 107(CRCL):Sep86-474
Burgos-Debray, E. - see Menchú, R.
Burguière, A. & others, eds. Histoire de
la famille.
E. Weber, 617(TLS):11-17Sep87-984
Burian, P., ed. Directions in Euripidean
Criticism.
C. Collard, 303(JoHS):Vol106-213
D. Konstan, 130:Spring86-82
Buridan, J. John Buridan on Self-Refer-
ence.* (G.E. Hughes, ed & trans)
A.J. Freddoso, 449:Mar86-77
Buridan, J. Jean Buridan's Logic.
A.R. Perreiah, 543:Mar87-565
Buridant, C., ed. La Traduction de
l'Historia Orientalis de Jacques de
Vitry.
G. Roques, 553(RLiR):Jan-Jun86-283
Burke, E. Selected Letters of Edmund
Burke.* (H.C. Mansfield, Jr., ed)
W.B. Carnochan, 506(PSt):May86-76

Burke, J.G. Cosmic Debris.
J. Meadows, 617(TLS):29May87-585
Burke, J.G., ed. The Uses of Science in
the Age of Newton.
J.M. Hill, 566:Autumn86-74
Burke, J.J., Jr. & D. Kay, eds. The
Unknown Samuel Johnson.*
J.T. Boulton, 447(N&Q):Mar85-132
Burke, J.L. The Convict.*
D. Madden, 598(SoR):Summer87-731
Burke, J.L. The Lost Get-Back Boogie.
R. Weinreich, 441:11Jan87-18
Burke, J.L. The Neon Rain.
N. Callendar, 441:21Jun87-36
Burke, P. The Historical Anthropology of
Early Modern Italy.
L. Martines, 617(TLS):11-17Sep87-982
Burke, P. Vico.
J.H. Whitfield, 402(MLR):Oct87-993
Burkert, W. Greek Religion.
J.E. Rexine, 124:Sep-Oct86-58
Burkert, W. Die orientalisierende Epoche
in der griechischen Religion und Litera-
tur.
P. Walcot, 123:Vol36No1-151
M.L. West, 303(JoHS):Vol106-233
Burkhardt, F. & S. Smith. A Calendar of
the Correspondence of Charles Darwin,
1821-1882.
D.J. Kevles, 442(NY):7Dec87-171
Burkhardt, F. & S. Smith - see Darwin, C.
Burkhardt, F. & S. Smith & others - see
Darwin, C.
Burkhardt, F.H., F. Bowers & I.K. Skrupske-
lis - see James, W.
Burkhart, C. The Pleasure of Miss Pym.
N. Shulman, 617(TLS):25-31Dec87-1420
Burkholder, J.P. Charles Ives.*
M.J. Alexander, 607:Jun86-35
Burkholz, H. The Sensitives.
N. Callendar, 441:30Aug87-29
Burl, A. The People of Stonehenge.
C. Chippindale, 617(TLS):4-10Dec87-
1355
Burleigh, M. Prussian Society and the
German Order.
C-P. Clasen, 589:Oct86-906
P.S. Fichtner, 551(RenQ):Autumn86-521
Burley, W.J. Wycliffe and the Winsor Blue.
T.J. Binyon, 617(TLS):11-17Sep87-978
Bürli-Storz, C. Deliberate Ambiguity in
Advertising.
M. Evans, 38:Band104Heft1/2-150
Burmeister, B. Streit um den Nouveau
Roman.*
M. Calle-Gruber, 72:Band223Heft2-452
Burne, G.S. Richard F. Burton.
J. Corwin, 637(VS):Summer87-556
Burnett, A. Milton's Style.
M.A. Radzinowicz, 402(MLR):Jan86-171
Burnett, A.P. Three Archaic Poets.*
E.L. Bowie, 303(JoHS):Vol106-221
A.J. Podlecki, 122:Apr86-159
Burnett, C. One More Time.*
M. Haskell, 453(NYRB):15Jan87-37
Burnett, J., D. Vincent & D. Mayall, eds.
The Autobiography of the Working Class.
(Vol 1)
P.S. Bagwell, 366:Autumn86-261

Burnett, J., D. Vincent & D. Mayall, eds. The Autobiography of the Working Class. (Vol 2)
  J.F.C. Harrison, 617(TLS):11-17Sep87-992
Burnett, P., ed. The Penguin Book of Caribbean Verse in English.*
  J. Figueroa, 364:Dec86/Jan87-158
  B. O'Donoghue, 493:Jun86-106
Burnett, V. A Comedy of Eros.* Towers at the Edge of a World.
  L. Ricou, 168(ECW):Fall86-129
Burney, F. The Journals and Letters of Fanny Burney (Madame d'Arblay).* (Vols 11 & 12) (J. Hemlow, with A. Douglas & P. Hawkins, eds)
  G.E. Bentley, Jr., 627(UTQ):Fall86-101
  R.L. Brett, 541(RES):Aug86-424
  P.B. Steese, 446(NCFS):Spring87-345
Burney, F. Selected Letters and Journals. (J. Hemlow, ed)
  P. Rogers, 617(TLS):3Apr87-347
Burnley, D. A Guide to Chaucer's Language.*
  E. Guy, 49:Apr86-79
  M. Markus, 38:Band104Heft3/4-489
  D. Pearsall, 402(MLR):Apr87-440
Burnley, J.D. Chaucer's Language and the Philosophers' Tradition.
  R. Copeland, 545(RPh):Aug86-135
Burns, A. Revolutions of the Night.
  R. Kaveney, 617(TLS):23Jan87-91
Burns, A.F., ed & trans. An Epoch of Miracles.
  A. Wiget, 650(WF):Jan86-46
Burns, C. Snakewrist.*
  J. Mellors, 364:Aug/Sep86-147
Burns, C.A. Henry Céard et le naturalisme.*
  Y. Chevrel, 549(RLC):Jan-Mar86-71
Burns, E. – see Stein, G. & C. Van Vechten
Burns, E.J. Arthurian Fictions.
  M.T. Bruckner, 210(FrF):Sep86-367
  K. Pratt, 208(FS):Oct86-447
  R.S. Sturges, 546(RR):Nov86-452
Burns, J. The Land That Lost Its Heroes.
  M. Deas, 617(TLS):15May87-512
Burns, J.M. The Workshop of Democracy.
  639(VQR):Spring86-50
Burns, M. Rural Society and French Politics.
  G.J. Barberet, 207(FR):May87-892
Burns, R. Any Given Day.
  P. Stitt, 491:May86-102
Burns, R. Robert Burns: The Kilmarnock Poems. (D.A. Low, ed)
  T. Crawford, 541(RES):Nov86-574
  C. MacLachlan, 571(ScLJ):Winter86-10
  P. Morère, 189(EA):Jul-Sep86-352
  G.R.R., 588(SSL):Vol21-349
Burns, R. The Letters of Robert Burns.* (J.D. Ferguson, ed; 2nd ed rev by G.R. Roy)
  M. Dodsworth, 175:Spring86-109
  D.A. Low, 588(SSL):Vol21-336
  P. Morère, 189(EA):Apr-Jun87-219
  K.G. Simpson, 571(ScLJ):Winter86-6
Burns, R. Suicide Season.
  N. Callendar, 441:16Aug87-21
  442(NY):6Jul87-82

Burns, R.D. & M. Leitenberg. The Wars in Vietnam, Cambodia and Laos, 1945-1982. (rev)
  J.W. Geary, 87(BB):Mar86-54
Burns, R.I. Muslims, Christians, and Jews in the Crusader Kingdom of Valencia.*
  J.E. Boswell, 589:Oct86-1017
Burns, T.S. A History of the Ostrogoths.*
  J.H.W.G. Liebeschuetz, 123:Vol36No1-158
Burnshaw, S. Robert Frost Himself.*
  P-L. Adams, 61:Jan87-90
Burollet, T. Catalogue of Porcelain. (Vol 2)
  A. Dawson, 90:Jun86-425
Burollet, T., D. Imbert & F. Folliot. Le Triomphe des mairies.
  C. Rosen & H. Zerner, 453(NYRB):26Feb87-21
Burr, E.E. The Journal of Esther Edwards Burr, 1754-1757.* (C.F. Karlsen & L. Crumpacker, eds)
  C. Mulford, 534(RALS):Spring-Autumn84-169
  B.S. Schlenther, 83:Spring86-91
Burra, E. Well, Dearie!* (W. Chappell, ed)
  D. Farr, 39:May86-363
Burros, M. You've Got it Made.
  W. & C. Cowen, 639(VQR):Spring86-68
Burrow, J.A. Autobiographical Poetry in the Middle Ages.
  D. Mehl, 447(N&Q):Jun85-255
  G. Morgan, 402(MLR):Jul87-701
Burrow, J.A. Essays on Medieval Literature.*
  R.B. Burlin, 589:Jul86-630
  D. Mehl, 447(N&Q):Jun85-255
  G. Morgan, 402(MLR):Jul87-701
  A.V.C.S., 382(MAE):1986/1-134
Burrow, J.A. Medieval Writers and Their Work.*
  D. Pearsall, 402(MLR):Jan86-164
Burrow, J.W. Gibbon.
  G.W. Bowersock, 123:Vol36No2-292
Burroway, J. Opening Nights.
  G. Davenport, 569(SR):Fall86-672
Burrowes, R. Essays on the Stile of Doctor Samuel Johnson (1787).
  G.J. Clingham, 83:Autumn86-248
  A. Pailler, 189(EA):Jul-Sep86-373
Burrows, W.E. Deep Black.
  J. Newhouse, 441:15Feb87-14
Burrs, M. The Blue Pools of Paradise.*
  S. Neuman, 168(ECW):Fall86-216
Burstein, S.M., ed & trans. The Hellenistic Age from the Battle of Ipsos to the Death of Kleopatra VII.
  J. Clack, 124:May-Jun87-384
Burstyn, V., ed. Women against Censorship.*
  T.C. Holyoke, 42(AR):Spring86-243
Burton, C. Eclipse.
  C. Jolicoeur, 189(EA):Jul-Sep87-366
Burton, G. Heartbreak Hotel.*
  R. Kaveney, 617(TLS):18-24Sep87-1026
Burton, N. Mellan eld och skugga.
  I. Soderblom, 563(SS):Autumn86-447
Burton, R. Eggs.
  B.B. Gordon, 441:2Aug87-17
Burton-Roberts, N. Analysing Sentences.
  L. Barratt, 350:Sep87-673

Busch, F. Sometimes I Live in the Country.*
  W.H. Pritchard, 249(HudR):Winter87-646
Busch, F. When People Publish.
  A. Becker, 441:18Jan87-19
Buschinger, D., ed. Guillaume et Willehalm.
  A.C., 400(MLN):Apr86-732
Buschinger, D. & A. Crépin, eds. Amour, mariage et transgressions au Moyen Age.
  M.E. Kalinke, 402(MLR):Apr86-423
Buschinger, D. & A. Crépin, eds. Comique, satire et parodie dans la tradition renardienne et les fabliaux.*
  R.J. Pearcy, 589:Jan86-124
Bush, G., with V. Gold. Looking Forward.
  G.M. Boyd, 441:4Oct87-29
Bush, P. - see Goytisolo, J.
Bush, R. T.S. Eliot.*
  R. Beum, 569(SR):Winter86-124
  W. Harmon, 569(SR):Summer86-510
Bush, S. & C. Murck. Theories of the Arts in China.
  R. Edwards, 54:Mar86-174
  W. Watson, 90:Feb86-155
Bush, S., Jr. & C.J. Rasmussen. The Library of Emmanuel College, Cambridge, 1584-1637.
  J.F. Fuggles, 617(TLS):14Aug87-878
Bush, S. & H-Y. Shih. Early Chinese Texts on Painting.
  S. Little, 116:Jul85-153
Bushell, R. Netsuke Masks.
  W.H. Tilley, 60:Nov-Dec86-149
Bushman, R.L. King and People in Provincial Massachusetts.*
  J.J. Waters, 656(WMQ):Oct86-669
Bushnell, J. Mutiny amid Repression.*
  J.E.O. Screen, 575(SEER):Jul86-473
Busi, A. La delfina bizantina.
  I. Thomson, 617(TLS):9-15Oct87-1115
Busoni, F. Selected Letters. (A. Beaumont, ed & trans)
  J. Deathridge, 617(TLS):19Jun87-658
Buss, G. The Bear's Hug.
  E. Norman, 617(TLS):29May87-576
Buss, H.M. Mother and Daughter Relationships in the Manawaka Works of Margaret Laurence.
  C. Thomas, 395(MFS):Winter86-641
Buss, R. Vigny: "Chatterton."*
  G. Chesters, 402(MLR):Oct86-1011
  J.J. Janc, 446(NCFS):Fall-Winter86/87-204
Bussmann, H. Lexikon der Sprachwissenschaft.*
  K-H. Jäger, 406:Summer86-215
  J. Knobloch, 260(IF):Band91-334
  W.P. Lehmann, 133:Band18Heft4-344
  K. Matzel, 684(ZDA):Band115Heft2-62
  C. Schmitt, 72:Band223Heft1-132
  C. Weiss, 38:Band104Heft1/2-132
Busst, A.J.L. - see Alexander, I.W.
de Bussy-Rabutin, R. Correspondance avec le Père René Rapin.* (C. Rouben, ed)
  M. Gérard, 535(RHL):Mar-Apr86-284
Busto Ogden, E. El creacionismo de Vicente Huidobro en sus relaciones con la estética cubista.
  E.A. Giordano, 240(HR):Winter86-113
Butala, S. Queen of the Headaches.
  H. Kirkwood, 99:Jan87-39
  C. Rooke, 376:Sep86-153

Butala, S. Two Readers Reading.
  J. Givner, 647:Fall86-105
  B. Selinger, 647:Fall86-101
Butchart, D.S. I madrigali di Marco da Gagliano.
  A. Newcomb, 317:Summer86-396
Butcher, G. Next to a Letter from Home.
  B. Case, 617(TLS):30Jan87-119
Butcher, L. Accidental Millionaire.
  J. Taylor, 441:25Oct87-32
"Solomon D. Butcher: Photographing the American Dream."* (J.E. Carter, ed)
  C.M. Wright, 649(WAL):Feb87-384
Buthlay, K. Hugh MacDiarmid.*
  J.H. Alexander, 677(YES):Vol16-231
Butler, C. Computers in Linguistics.* Statistics in Linguistics.*
  D. Biber, 350:Jun87-455
Butler, C. Interpretation, Deconstruction and Ideology.*
  H.J. Hansford, 541(RES):May86-303
  W. McKie, 184(EIC):Jul86-275
  P. Parrinder, 366:Spring86-122
  J. Patrick, 627(UTQ):Winter86/87-338
  R. Selden, 402(MLR):Oct86-960
Butler, C. & C. Seiler - see Hegel, G.W.F.
Butler, C.S. Systemic Linguistics.
  R. Hudson, 353:Vol24No4-791
Butler, D. Five to Eight.
  H. O'Donoghue, 617(TLS):20Feb87-197
Butler, F. & R. Rotert, eds. Triumphs of the Spirit in Children's Literature.
  H. O'Donoghue, 617(TLS):3Apr87-354
Butler, G., ed. The Re-interment on Buffelskop.
  C. Clayton, 538(RAL):Fall86-404
Butler, H. Escape from the Anthill.
  M. Koenig, 272(IUR):Spring86-86
Butler, J. - see Wordsworth, W.
Butler, L.S. Samuel Beckett and the Meaning of Being.*
  C. Norris, 577(SHR):Summer86-268
Butler, M. August and Rab.
  H. Carpenter, 617(TLS):11-17Sep87-974
Butler, M., ed. Burke, Paine, Godwin, and the Revolution Controversy.*
  M. Philp, 83:Autumn86-244
  W. Stafford, 366:Autumn86-255
Butler, M. The Plays of Max Frisch.
  J. Rouse, 615(TJ):May86-249
  M.E. Stewart, 402(MLR):Apr87-528
Butler, M. Theatre and Crisis, 1632-1642.*
  L. Bliss, 551(RenQ):Summer86-349
  M.G. Brennan, 447(N&Q):Dec85-525
  R.A. Cave, 610:Summer86-159
  J. Gasper, 541(RES):May86-262
  P.N. Siegel, 570(SQ):Autumn86-415
Butler, R. Balzac and the French Revolution.*
  J-H. Donnard, 535(RHL):Mar-Apr86-297
Butler, R. Zola: "La Terre."*
  C.A. Burns, 402(MLR):Jan87-205
Butler, R.O. Wabash.
  T. Nolan, 441:15Mar87-16
Butler, S. The Note-Books of Samuel Butler.* (Vol 1) (H-P. Breuer, ed)
  D.F. Howard, 40(AEB):Vol8No4-268
Butlin, M. The Paintings and Drawings of William Blake.
  M. Eaves, 591(SIR):Spring86-147

Butlin, M. & E. Joll. The Paintings of
J.M.W. Turner.* (rev)
  D. Irwin, 83:Autumn86-308
  C. Powell, 59:Mar86-99
Butlin, R. The Sound of My Voice.
  J. Melmoth, 617(TLS):30Jan87-109
Butrica, J.L. The Manuscript Tradition of
Propertius.*
  S.J. Heyworth, 123:Vol36No1-45
Butt, G. To Toslow We'll Go and Other
Plays. An Ear or a Fear.
  A. Wagner, 108:Spring86-110
Buttenwieser, P. Their Pride and Joy.
  P-L. Adams, 61:Oct87-107
  J. Conarroe, 441:4Oct87-9
Butterfield, H. The Origins of History.
(A. Watson, ed)
  N.F. Partner, 589:Jan86-90
Butterick, G.F. – see Olson, C.
Butters, H.C. Governors and Governments
in Early Sixteenth Century Florence 1502-
1519.
  D. Herlihy, 551(RenQ):Winter86-735
Butterworth, B., B. Comrie & Ö. Dahl, eds.
Explanations for Language Universals.*
  G. Bourcier, 189(EA):Jul-Sep86-325
Buttrey, T.V. & others. Greek, Roman and
Islamic Coins from Sardis.
  N.D. Nicol, 318(JAOS):Oct/Dec85-796
Butts, R.E. Kant and the Double Govern-
ment Methodology.
  M. Capozzi, 84:Sep86-371
  D.L.C. MacLachlan, 154:Autumn86-592
van Buuren, C., ed. "The Buke of the
Sevyne Sagis."*
  K. Bitterling, 38:Band104Heft3/4-503
van Buuren, M. De la Métaphore au Mythe.
  W.G. Weststeijn, 204(FdL):Jun86-155
Buxton, W. Talcott Parsons and the
Capitalist Nation-State.
  I.L. Horowitz, 432(NEQ):Dec86-569
de Buys, W. Enchantment and Exploitation.
  R.M. Adams, 453(NYRB):12Mar87-28
Byatt, A.S. Still Life.
  P. Lewis, 565:Spring86-38
  N. Miller, 42(AR):Winter86-118
Byatt, A.S. Sugar and Other Stories.
  A. Duchêne, 617(TLS):10Apr87-395
  L.S. Schwartz, 441:19Jul87-5
  L. Taylor, 362:7May87-25
Bybee, J.L. Morphology.
  M. Aronoff, 350:Mar87-115
  W.U. Dressler, 361:Nov86-197
  F. Karlsson, 353:Vol24No6-1134
  K-P. Lange, 603:Vol10No1-267
  D. Walker, 297(JL):Sep86-493
Byerly, V. Hard Times Cotton Mill Girls.
  R.L. Bray, 441:1Mar87-21
Byerman, K.E. Fingering the Jagged Grain.
  N. Harris, 395(MFS):Winter86-635
  J. Pettis, 578:Fall87-132
Bynum, C.W. Holy Feast and Holy Fast.
  J. Freccero, 441:5Apr87-26
  M. Keen, 453(NYRB):8Oct87-42
Bynum, C.W. Jesus as Mother.
  R. Boenig, 589:Oct86-907
Byrd, M. "Tristram Shandy."*
  E.W. Harries, 566:Spring87-180
  M. Rosenblum, 405(MP):Feb87-324
Byrne, A. London's Georgian Houses.
  H. Potts, 617(TLS):18-24Sep87-1013
Byrne, D. True Stories.
  J. Howell, 62:Oct86-8

Byrnes, H. & M. Canale, eds. Defining and
Developing Proficiency.
  K.E. Kintz, 207(FR):Mar87-569
Byron, H.J. Plays by H.J. Byron. (J.
Davis, ed)
  M.R. Booth, 402(MLR):Jul87-716
Lord Byron. The Complete Poetical Works.
(Vols 1-3) (J.J. McGann, ed)
  C. Rosen, 453(NYRB):17Dec87-22
Lord Byron. The Complete Poetical Works.
(Vol 4) (J.J. McGann, ed)
  N. Berry, 617(TLS):23Jan87-80
  C. Rosen, 453(NYRB):17Dec87-22
  T. Tessier, 189(EA):Apr-Jun87-221
  639(VQR):Autumn86-117
Lord Byron. The Complete Poetical Works.
(Vol 5) (J.J. McGann, ed)
  N. Berry, 617(TLS):23Jan87-80
  C. Rosen, 453(NYRB):17Dec87-22
Lord Byron. The Oxford Authors: Byron.
(J.J. McGann, ed)
  N. Berry, 617(TLS):23Jan87-80
  M. Dodsworth, 175:Summer86-195
Byström, T. Svenska komedien 1737-1754.
  J. Massengale, 563(SS):Spring86-204
Bysveen, J. Epic Tradition and Innovation
in James Macpherson's "Fingal."
  P. Rogers, 402(MLR):Jan87-172

Caballero, M. Latin America and the
Comintern 1919-1943.
  R. Carr, 617(TLS):17Apr87-406
Cabanis, J. L'Escaladieu. Pour Sainte-
Beuve.
  P. McCarthy, 617(TLS):2-8Oct87-1072
Cable, J. Political Institutions and
Issues in Britain.
  J. Campbell, 617(TLS):13-19Nov87-1244
Cabrera Infante, G. Holy Smoke.*
  639(VQR):Summer86-93
Cacciapaglia, G. Scrittori di lingua
tedesca e Venezia dal XV secolo a oggi.
  A. Hoffmann-Maxis, 52:Band21Heft3-315
Cacho Blecua, J.M. & M.J. Lacarra – see
Alfonso X
Cadogan, L. Digging.
  P. Parker, 362:17Sep87-26
  D. Singmaster, 617(TLS):26Jun87-698
Cady, E.H. Young Howells and John Brown.*
  G. Arms, 27(AL):May86-279
  E. Carter, 26(ALR):Fall86-86
  T.A. Gullason, 395(MFS):Summer86-249
  A. Habegger, 432(NEQ):Jun86-294
Çağman, F. and Z. Tandini. Topkapı: The
Albums and Miniatures. (J.M. Rogers, ed
& trans)
  G. Goodwin, 617(TLS):6Mar87-249
  J. Russell, 441:31May87-11
"Cahier Marcel Aymé, no. 2."
  J. Finné, 535(RHL):Jul-Aug86-801
"Cahiers de Littérature du XVIIe siècle:
Hommage à René Fromilhague."
  M-O. Sweetser, 535(RHL):Sep-Oct86-907
"Cahiers Léon Tolstoï.* (Vol 1) (M. Aucou-
turier, ed)
  A. Peyronie, 549(RLC):Apr-Jun86-250
  A. Woronzoff, 550(RusR):Apr86-219
"Cahiers Marcel Proust, 12."
  E. Dezon-Jones, 535(RHL):Jul-Aug86-
785
"Cahiers Paul Léautaud." (No. 1)
  A. Derasse, 605(SC):15Apr87-302

"Cahiers Paul Valéry, 4." (M. Jarrety, ed)
P-L. Rey, 450(NRF):Sep86-110
"Cahiers Stendhal."* (No 1) (J-J. Hamm,
ed)
V.D.L., 605(SC):15Jan87-211
Cahill, J. The Compelling Image.
Wen Fong, 54:Sep86-504
Cahill, P., ed. Duggals leidsla.
J. Tucker, 563(SS):Spring86-181
Cahill, T. Jaguars Ripped My Flesh.
D. Ackerman, 441:6Dec87-17
Caimi, J. Burocrazia e Diritto nel "De
Magistratibus" di Giovanni Lido.
M. Maas, 123:Vol36No2-221
Cain, H-U. Römische Marmorkandelaber.
R. Ling, 123:Vol36No2-349
Cain, W.E. The Crisis in Criticism.*
W. Martin, 131(CL):Fall86-360
E. Proffitt, 289:Summer86-116
125:Fall85-109
Caine, B. Destined to be Wives.
J. Harris, 617(TLS):10Apr87-375
Cairncross, A. Economics and Economic
Policy.
C. Johnson, 617(TLS):30Jan87-105
Cairns, C. Pietro Aretino and the Republic
of Venice.
J. Hösle, 547(RF):Band98Heft3/4-466
Caizzi, F.D. - see under Decleva Caizzi, F.
Calabresi, G. Ideals, Beliefs, Attitudes
and the Law.
K.L. Scheppele, 185:Oct86-285
Calame, C. Alcman.
D.E. Gerber, 122:Oct86-341
Calandra, D. New German Dramatists.*
L.C. De Meritt, 221(GQ):Spring86-335
H. Rorrison, 447(N&Q):Dec85-573
Calbris, G. & J. Montredon. Des Gestes et
des mots pour le dire.
T.A. Sebeok, 617(TLS):10Jul87-752
Caldenby, C. & O. Huttin, eds. Asplund.
S.R. Chao, 505:Nov86-137
J. Iovine, 45:Jul86-51
Calder, B.J. The Impact of Intervention.
A.G. Kuczewski, 639(VQR):Winter86-186
Calder, D.G. & others - see "Sources and
Analogues of Old English Poetry"
Calder, J. - see Stevenson, R.L.
Calder, W.M., 3d, H. Flashar & T. Lindken,
eds. Wilamowitz nach 50 Jahren.
J. Barnes, 520:Vol31No1-99
R.L. Fowler, 121(CJ):Oct-Nov86-67
H. Lloyd-Jones, 123:Vol36No2-295
Caldera, R-T. Le jugement par inclination
chez saint Thomas d'Aquin.
E. Wéber, 192(EP):Apr-Jun86-272
Calderón de la Barca, P. Cada uno para sí.
(J.M. Ruano de la Haza, ed)
R. ter Horst, 400(MLN):Mar86-440
W.F. Hunter, 402(MLR):Jul86-770
M. McKendrick, 86(BHS):Apr86-170
M.C. Quintero, 345:Nov86-505
Calderón de la Barca, P. Entremeses,
jácaras y mojigangas.* (E. Rodríguez &
A. Tordera, eds)
T.R.A. Mason, 402(MLR):Oct87-1001
Calderón de la Barca, P. Fieras afemina
Amor.* (E.M. Wilson, ed)
A.A. Heathcote, 402(MLR):Jul86-769
Calderón de la Barca, P. Guárdate de la
agua mansa/Beware of Still Waters.*
(D.M. Gitlitz, trans)
D.J. Pasto, 615(TJ):Mar86-118

Calderón de la Barca, P. No hay burlas con
el amor. (I. Arellano, ed)
D.W. Cruickshank, 86(BHS):Apr86-168
Calderón de la Barca, P. Una fiesta sacra-
mental barroca. (J.M. Díez Borque, ed)
R. ter Horst, 240(HR):Spring86-224
Calderwood, J.L. To Be and Not to Be.*
M. Coyle, 447(N&Q):Mar85-109
Caldwell, E. With All My Might.
D. Kaufman, 441:10May87-18
Caldwell, J. Editing Early Music.
N. Zaslaw, 415:Jan86-31
Caldwell, J. Under the Dog Star.
L. Hamalian, 441:17May87-51
442(NY):6Jul87-80
Caldwell, P. The Puritan Conversion Nar-
rative.*
S. Bush, Jr., 402(MLR):Apr87-448
Calimani, D. Radici Sepolte.
M. Anderson, 610:Spring86-82
Calimani, R. The Ghetto of Venice.*
(Italian title: Storia del Ghetto di
Venezia.)
K.B. Swett, 441:29Nov87-21
Calin, W. In Defense of French Poetry.
R. Buss, 617(TLS):13-19Nov87-1240
Calin, W. A Muse for Heroes.*
W.G. van Emden, 208(FS):Jul86-368
W.W. Kibler, 345:Nov86-491
R. Morse, 382(MAE):1986/2-306
P.H. Stablein, 207(FR):Oct86-112
Calisher, H. Age.
T. Mallon, 441:18Oct87-14
Calkins, R.G. Illuminated Books of the
Middle Ages.*
P.M. De Winter, 54:Mar86-157
Callaghan, C.A. Plains Miwok Dictionary.
H. Berman, 269(IJAL):Jul86-305
Callaghan, J. Time and Change.
P. Clarke, 617(TLS):24Apr87-427
P. Hennessy, 362:16Apr87-35
Callaghan, M. Our Lady of the Snows.
D. Flower, 249(HudR):Summer86-311
A.J. Harding, 102(CanL):Fall86-144
Callaghan, M. The Lost and Found Stories
of Morley Callaghan.
D.O. Spettique, 150(DR):Fall86-368
Callaghan, W., Jr. The Individual Heart.
P.M. St. Pierre, 102(CanL):Summer86-121
Callahan, D. Setting Limits.
E.E. Shelp, 441:27Sep87-7
Callahan, D., A.L. Caplan & B. Jennings,
eds. Applying the Humanities.
T.D.E., 185:Apr87-700
Callahan, M. Fighting for Tony.
R. Scheier, 441:27Dec87-19
Callary, E., ed. Festschrift in Honor of
Virgil J. Vogel.
M.I.M., 300:Apr86-142
R.M. Rennick, 424:Jun86-202
Callaway, N. - see O'Keeffe, G.
Calleo, D.P. Beyond American Hegemony.
P. Kennedy, 441:1Nov87-11
Callmer, C. & T. Nielsen, eds. Bibliothe-
ken der nordischen Länder in Vergangen-
heit und Gegenwart.
T. Geddes, 354:Mar86-92
Callow, P. New York Insomnia.
H. Buckingham, 565:Summer86-64
Callow, S. Charles Laughton.
J. Mortimer, 617(TLS):13-19Nov87-1255
E. Thomason, 362:24Sep87-26

Calogero, G. Scritti Minori di Filosofia Antica.
J. Barnes, 520:Vol31No1-98
Calvet, L-J. La Guerre des langues et les politiques linguistiques.
R. Harris, 617(TLS):11-17Dec87-1373
Calvin, J. Advertissement contre l'astrologie judiciaire. (O. Millet, ed)
J-P. Beaulieu, 539:Nov86-379
F. Higman, 208(FS):Apr86-198
Calvin, J. Des scandales. (O. Fatio, with C. Rapin, eds)
E. Forsyth, 535(RHL):Nov-Dec86-1122
Calvino, I. The Literature Machine. (French title: La Machine littérature.)
D. Davis, 617(TLS):14Aug87-881
G. Dyer, 362:9Apr87-26
W.F. Motte, Jr., 188(ECr):Winter86-99
Calvino, I. Mr. Palomar. (French title: Palomar.)
D. Bastianutti, 529(QQ):Summer86-409
I. Malin, 532(RCF):Fall86-130
J-Y. Pouilloux, 98:Mar86-274
M.J. Rosen, 560:Fall86-261
Calvo, J.H. - see under Huerta Calvo, J.
Calvocoressi, P. Who's Who in the Bible.
J.R. Porter, 617(TLS):25-31Dec87-1437
Calvocoressi, R., ed. Oskar Kokoschka, 1886-1980.*
C.E. Schorske, 453(NYRB):15Jan87-20
Camaj, M. Albanian Grammar, with Exercises, Chrestomathy and Glossaries.
N. Boretzky, 260(IF):Band91-381
V.A. Friedman, 574(SEEJ):Fall86-466
Camarasa, A.V. - see under Viudas Camarasa, A.
Cambiano, G. La filosofia in Grecia e a Roma.
J.M. Alonso-Núñez, 123:Vol36No1-145
Cambiano, G., ed. Storiografia e Dossografia nella filosofia antica.
J. Barnes, 520:Vol31No3-283
Cambon, G. Michelangelo's Poetry.
A.L. Lepschy, 90:Jun86-432
Cambridge, J. Clarise Cumberbatch Want to Go Home.
B. Probst, 441:12Apr87-26
Camden, W. Remains concerning Britain.* (R.D. Dunn, ed)
L.R.N. Ashley, 424:Jun86-218
F.J. Levy, 551(RenQ):Spring86-128
B. Lyon, 589:Jul86-632
Camenzind-Herzog, E. Robert Walser- "eine Art Verlorener Sohn."
G.C. Avery, 406:Spring86-119
Cameron, A. Procopius.
M. Maas, 121(CJ):Apr-May87-342
Cameron, A. Procopius and the Sixth Century.
R.S. Bagnall, 124:Mar-Apr87-329
R. McCail, 123:Vol36No2-219
Cameron, A. & A. Fuhrt, eds. Images of Women in Antiquity.*
T. Fleming, 121(CJ):Oct-Nov86-73
Cameron, A. & J. Herrin, with others, eds. Constantinople in the Early Eighth Century.
B. Baldwin, 589:Apr86-388
Cameron, A., A. Kingsmill & A.C. Amos. Old English Word Studies.*
K. Toth, 38:Band104Heft1/2-178
Cameron, D. & E. Frazer. The Lust to Kill.
P. Highsmith, 617(TLS):25-31Dec87-1427

Cameron, D.K. The Cornkister Days.
D. Buchan, 292(JAF):Jul/Sep86-343
Cameron, E. Encyclopedia of Pottery & Porcelain: The Nineteenth and Twentieth Centuries.
T. Hughes, 324:Apr87-408
G. Wills, 39:Sep86-225
Cameron, E. The Reformation of the Heretics.
R.M. Kingdon, 589:Jan86-126
Cameron, E. Irving Layton.*
P.K. Smith, 627(UTQ):Spring87-467
Cameron, J. An Indian Summer.
617(TLS):30Jan87-120
Cameron, K.C., W.S. Dodd & S.P.Q. Rahtz, eds. Computers and Modern Language Studies.
J. Walz, 207(FR):Mar87-567
Cameron, N. The Complete Poems of Norman Cameron.* (W. Hope, ed)
L. Mackinnon, 617(TLS):26Jun87-682
Cameron, S. Writing Nature.
R. Bridgman, 432(NEQ):Sep86-431
V. Norwood, 344:Winter87-129
K. Van Anglen, 27(AL):Oct86-440
639(VQR):Spring86-45
Caminero, J. Víctima o verdugo.*
P.J. Smith, 402(MLR):Jan86-237
Camm, J.C.R. & J. McQuilton, eds. Australians: A Historical Atlas.
A. Sykes, 617(TLS):27Nov-3Dec87-1322
Cammarata, J. Mythological Themes in the Works of Garcilaso de la Vega.
D.G. Burton, 345:Feb86-119
"Camoẽs à la Renaissance."
K.D. Jackson, 551(RenQ):Autumn86-512
Campailla, S. & C.F. Goffis, eds. La poesia di Eugenio Montale.
V. Lucchesi, 402(MLR):Apr87-494
Campana. D. Canti orfici.
P. Palmieri, 228(GSLI):Vol163fasc522-307
Campbell, B. The Iron Ladies.
O. O'Leary, 362:7May87-25
H. Spurling, 617(TLS):8May87-482
Campbell, D.Q. The Golden Lyre.
C. Meillier, 555:Vol59fasc2-276
Campbell, J. Nye Bevan and the Mirage of British Socialism.
M. Beloff, 176:Sep/Oct87-37
A. Calder, 362:30Apr87-27
P. Clarke, 617(TLS):24Apr87-427
K. Harris, 441:13Sep87-22
Campbell, J. Winston Churchill's Afternoon Nap.
F. Gonzalez-Crussi, 441:8Mar87-14
Campbell, J. Gate Fever.*
K. Smith, 364:Jun86-110
Campbell, K. Body and Mind. (2nd ed)
F. Jackson, 63:Mar86-104
Campbell, L. The Pictures in the Collection of Her Majesty the Queen: The Early Flemish Pictures.
K. Andrews, 39:May86-364
D. de Vos, 90:Apr86-292
Campbell, R. The Selected Poems of Roy Campbell. (P. Alexander, ed)
C.J. Rawson, 677(YES):Vol16-360
Campbell, R. The 600-Pound Gorilla.
N. Callendar, 441:3May87-46
Campbell, R.J. A Morphological Dictionary of Classical Nahuatl.
F. Karttunen, 350:Jun87-443

Campbell, T. The Left and Rights.
E.L. Pincoffs, 449:Jun86-271
Campbell, W.D. Forty Acres and a Goat.*
S.W.L., 219(GaR):Winter86-1053
Camporeale, G., ed. L'Etruria mineraria.
N. Spivey, 313:Vol76-281
Campos Boralevi, L. Bentham & the
Oppressed.*
B. Parekh, 83:Autumn86-253
Camps, C. Anthologie de Joseph-Sébastian
Pons.
H. Guiter, 553(RLiR):Jul-Dec86-570
Camps, C. Atlas linguistique du Biterrois.
H. Guiter, 553(RLiR):Jan-Jun86-232
Campsall, R. The Works of Richard Camp-
sall. (Vol 2) (E.A. Synan, ed)
S. Brown, 543:Dec86-403
Camus, A. American Journals.
K. van Praag, 441:16Aug87-17
442(NY):5Oct87-126
Cancogni, M. A Friendship.*
T. Broderick, 532(RCF):Fall86-146
Candar, G. - see "Jean Jaurès (1859-1914)"
del Candau de Cevallos, M. Historia de la
lengua española.
M. Torreblanca, 304(JHP):Winter86-194
Candaux, J-D. & others - see de Charrière,
I. [Belle de Zuylen]
Candelaria, C. Chicano Poetry.
R.G. Lint, 649(WAL):Feb87-380
27(AL):Oct86-481
Candelaria, F. Poems New and Selected.
A. Brooks, 102(CanL):Spring86-175
G.V. Downes, 376:Jun86-125
D. Precosky, 198:Spring86-91
Candelaria, N. Not by the Sword.
D. Zalacaín, 552(REH):Jan86-149
Cañedo-Argüelles, J.A. - see under Arena
Cañedo-Argüelles, J.
Canemaker, J. Winsor McCay.
L. Maltin, 441:6Dec87-16
Canet Valles, J.L. - see Tárrega, F.A.
Canetti, E. The Conscience of Words.*
(French title: La Conscience des mots.)
H.G. Pitt, 364:Apr/May86-158
de Canfield, B. La Règle de Perfection/The
Rule of Perfection. (J. Orcibal, ed)
J. Le Brun, 535(RHL):Jan-Feb86-140
de Cañizares, J. El anillo de Giges.* (J.
Alvarez Barrientos, ed)
I.L. McClelland, 86(BHS):Oct86-388
Canning, J., ed. The Illustrated Mayhew's
London.
J. Chernaik, 617(TLS):23Jan87-89
Cannon, H., ed. Cowboy Poetry.
J.C. McNutt, 651(WHR):Summer86-177
J. (Ugan) Roush, 649(WAL):Aug86-145
Cannon, J. Aristocratic Century.
J. Black, 161(DUJ):Jun86-367
E.A. Reitan, 173(ECS):Fall86-64
P.D.G. Thomas, 83:Autumn86-222
Cannon, M.W. & D.M. O'Brien, eds. Views
from the Bench.
639(VQR):Spring86-57
Cano, J.L., ed. Antología de los poetas
del 27.
A.M. Fagundo, 552(REH):Jan86-141
Cantin, P. Jacques Ferron, polygraphe.
D.M. Hayne, 470:Vol24-108
E-M. Kröller, 102(CanL):Fall86-115
M.E. Ross, 627(UTQ):Fall86-190
Cantlie, A. The Assamese.
S. Baruah, 293(JASt):Nov85-163

Cantor, P.A. Creature and Creator.*
M. Roberts, 541(RES):Feb86-103
N. Roe, 447(N&Q):Dec85-562
Cao, A.F. Federico García Lorca y las
vanguardias.
D. Harris, 402(MLR):Jan87-229
Cap, J-P. Decadence of Freedom.
H.T. Naughton, 188(ECr):Summer86-105
"Robert Capa: Photographs."* (R. Whelan &
C. Capa, eds)
H. Martin, 507:Jul/Aug86-303
Capella, M. - see under Martianus Capella
Capellán, A. Hemingway and the Hispanic
World.
M.B., 295(JML):Nov86-483
J.M. Muste, 27(AL):Dec86-656
zur Capellen, J.M. - see under Meyer zur
Capellen, J.
Caplan, G., with R.B. Arab and Jew in
Jerusalem.
R.L. Cooper, 355(LSoc):Mar86-111
Caplan, L. The Tenth Justice.
M.E. Price, 441:25Oct87-13
Capote, T. Answered Prayers.*
P-L. Adams, 61:Oct87-107
T. Brown, 441:13Sep87-13
J. Mellors, 364:Dec86/Jan87-149
T. Rafferty, 442(NY):21Sep87-113
J. Richardson, 453(NYRB):17Dec87-3
Capote, T. The Capote Reader.
J. Richardson, 453(NYRB):17Dec87-3
Capozzi, R. Bernari.
E. Licastro, 275(IQ):Spring86-115
Cappelli, A. The Elements of Abbreviation
in Medieval Latin Paleography.*
R.J. Tarrant, 589:Apr86-494
Caputo, P. Indian Country.
F. Conroy, 441:17May87-7
442(NY):7Sep87-111
Caputo-Mayr, M.L. & J.M. Herz. Franz
Kafkas Werke.*
E.M. Rajec, 406:Summer86-253
Caradec, F. La Compagnie des zincs.
B. Wright, 617(TLS):9Jan87-29
Caramaschi, E. Arts visuels et littéra-
ture.
D. de Chapeaurouge, 547(RF):Band98
Heft3/4-442
M. Détrie, 549(RLC):Oct-Dec86-467
R.A. Hartzell, 207(FR):Mar87-536
Caramello, C. Silverless Mirrors.*
J. Del Fattore, 587(SAF):Spring86-112
D.W. Fokkema, 549(RLC):Jan-Mar86-122
Carandini, A., ed. La romanizzazione
dell'Etruria.
N. Spivey, 313:Vol76-281
Caravaggi, B.B. - see Hardy, A.
Carayol, E. Thémiseul de Saint-Hyacinthe,
1684-1746.
D. Fletcher, 402(MLR):Jul87-738
Card, O.S. Wyrms.
G. Jonas, 441:18Oct87-36
Cardonne-Arlyck, E. La Métaphore Raconte.*
M. Davies, 402(MLR):Jan86-213
Cardwell, R.A. - see de Icaza, F.A.
Cardwell, R.A. & P. Coveney, eds. Visions
of Dystopia.
A. Barratt, 402(MLR):Jul87-696
Cardy, M. The Literary Doctrines of Jean-
François Marmontel.
M. Bellot-Antony, 535(RHL):Jan-Feb86-
144
G. Gargett, 208(FS):Jul86-334

Careless, J.M.S. Toronto to 1918.*
  J-C. Robert, 529(QQ):Autumn86-711
Carette, M. & D. Derouex. Carreaux de
pavement médiévaux de Flandre et d'Ar-
tois (XIIIe-XIVe siècles).
  M.W. Cothren, 589:Jul86-728
Carey, C. & R.A. Reid - see Demosthenes
Carey, G.O. Edward Payson Roe.
  M.J. Fertig, 26(ALR):Fall86-78
Carey, J., ed. The Faber Book of Report-
age.
  I. Jack, 617(TLS):13-19Nov87-1245
  P. Lennon, 362:3Dec87-39
Carey, J. Original Copy.
  D. Nokes, 617(TLS):24Jul87-790
  V. Shaw, 362:23Jul87-23
Carey, M. Different Drummers.
  D. Brydon, 102(CanL):Spring86-160
Carilla, E. Manierismo y Barroco en las
literaturas hispánicas.
  E. Dudley, 86(BHS):Oct86-369
Carl, W. Sinn und Bedeutung.*
  M. Schirn, 53(AGP):Band68Heft3-333
  R. Schmit, 687:Jan-Mar86-146
Carlé, B. Jomfru-Fortaellingen.
  B. Morris, 562(Scan):Nov86-227
Carley, L. - see Delius, F.
Carlier, P. La royauté en Grèce avant
Alexandre.
  N.R.E. Fisher, 303(JoHS):Vol106-236
Carlino, M. - see Gadda, C.E.
Carlisle, O.A. - see Andreyev, L.
Carlson, H.S. Nevada Place Names.
  K.H., 424:Sep86-337
Carlson, M. The Italian Shakespearians.
  D.J. Watermeier, 615(TJ):Dec86-499
Carlson, M. Theories of the Theatre.*
  B.S. Hammond, 541(RES):Aug86-447
  X. Mehta, 290(JAAC):Spring87-312
  R.W. Vince, 612(ThS):May/Nov86-167
Carlson, R. The News of the World.
  N. Forbes, 441:4Jan87-18
Carlson, S. Women of Grace.
  M.D. Springer, 284:Winter87-150
Carlyle, T. A Carlyle Reader.* (G.B.
Tennyson, ed)
  T.N.C., 506(PSt):May86-87
Carlyle, T. Carlyle's Latter-Day Pamph-
lets.* (M.K. Goldberg & J.P. Seigel,
eds)
  E. Lane, 588(SSL):Vol21-365
Carlyle, T. & J.W. The Collected Letters
of Thomas and Jane Welsh Carlyle.* (Vols
10-12) (C.R. Saunders & K.J. Fielding,
eds)
  C. Moore, 588(SSL):Vol21-295
Carmely, K.P. Das Identitätsproblem jüd-
ischer Autoren im deutschen Sprachraum.
  W.H. Sokel, 406:Summer86-258
  P.F. Veit, 406:Summer86-260
del Carmen Porrúa, M. La Galicia decimonó-
nica en las "Comedias bárbaras" de Valle
Inclán.
  J. Alberich, 86(BHS):Jul86-292
Carmichael, A.G. Plague and the Poor in
Renaissance Florence.*
  J. Henderson, 617(TLS):20Feb87-189
Carmichael, C.M. Law and Narrative in the
Bible.
  M. Gagarin, 124:Sep-Oct86-55
Carne-Ross, D.S. Pindar.*
  R.W.B. Burton, 123:Vol36No2-303

Carnegie, A.C. The Timeless Flow.
  J. Caird, 571(ScLJ):Summer86-20
Carner, M. Giacomo Puccini: "Tosca."
  R. Anderson, 415:Jun86-338
  M.S. Cole, 465:Summer86-193
  J. Smith, 410(M&L):Oct86-398
Carnes, P. Fable Scholarship.
  K. Dowden, 123:Vol36No2-319
  W.F. Hansen, 292(JAF):Oct/Dec86-481
  I. Köhler-Zülch, 196:Band27Heft3/4-334
  566:Spring87-206
Carney, R. American Dreaming.*
  J. Richards, 176:Jan87-52
Carney, R. American Vision.
  A. Dannatt, 362:9Apr87-27
Carnoy, M. The State and Political
Theory.*
  R. Mahon, 529(QQ):Summer86-436
Carosso, V.P., with R.C. Carosso. The
Morgans.
  M. Mayer, 441:5Apr87-18
  D. O'Keeffe, 617(TLS):9-15Oct87-1103
Carothers, J.B. William Faulkner's Short
Stories.
  M.B., 295(JML):Nov86-465
  D.H. Krause, 573(SSF):Summer86-342
  W. Taylor, 27(AL):May86-277
"August Carp, Esq."
  N. Andrew, 362:27Aug87-22
Carp, E.W. To Starve the Army at Plea-
sure.*
  E. Countryman, 83:Autumn86-213
"De Carpeaux à Matisse."
  R. Thomson, 59:Mar87-108
Carpenter, D. The Dispossessed.
  J.H. Maguire, 649(WAL):Feb87-358
Carpenter, D. Jewels.
  L. Boone, 198:Summer86-81
  C. Rooke, 376:Jun86-116
Carpenter, D. Jokes for the Apocalypse.*
  L. Boone, 198:Summer86-81
Carpenter, D.B. - see Emerson, L.J.
Carpenter, E. Edward Carpenter, Selected
Writings. (Vol 1) (D. Fernbach & N.
Greig, eds)
  T. Brown, 506(PSt):May86-81
Carpenter, H. Geniuses Together.
  B. Morton, 362:19Nov87-30
Carpenter, H. O.U.D.S.*
  G. Hunter, 612(ThS):May/Nov86-185
  G. Rowell, 611(TN):Vol40No2-95
Carpenter, H. & M. Prichard. The Oxford
Companion to Children's Literature.*
  B. Alderson, 354:Jun86-187
Carpenter, K. Desert Isles and Pirate
Islands.
  T. Wright, 161(DUJ):Jun86-380
Carpenter, L. Getting Better All the Time.
  J. O'Reilly, 441:2Aug87-10
Carpenter, W. Rain.
  P. Stitt, 491:May86-107
Carpentier, A. & others. Historia y fic-
ción en la narrativa hispanoamericana.
  S. Bacarisse, 86(BHS):Oct86-379
Carpio, L.D. - see under de Vega Carpio, L.
Carr, G.J. & E. Sagarra, eds. Fin de
siècle Vienna.
  B. McKittrick, 402(MLR):Apr87-517
Carr, I., D. Fairweather & B. Priestley.
Jazz.
  C. Fox, 617(TLS):25-31Dec87-1441
Carr, J. An Act of Immorality.
  D. Papineau, 617(TLS):21Aug87-894

Carrasco García, A. La Plaza Mayor de Llerena y otros estudios.
M. Estella, 48:Jan–Mar86–117
le Carré, J. A Perfect Spy.*
W. Lesser, 249(HudR):Autumn86–483
P. Lewis, 565:Summer86–57
Carreira, A. Documentos para a história das Ilhas de Cabo Verde e "Rios de Guiné" (Séculos XVII e XVIII).
P.E.H. Hair, 86(BHS):Jul86–298
Carreira, A. Os Portugueses nos Rios de Guiné (1500–1900).
P.E.H. Hair, 86(BHS):Jul86–298
Carrera, A. Arturo y yo.
T. Running, 238:May86–319
Carrère, E. La Moustache.
P.H. Solomon, 207(FR):May87–904
Carrick, P. Medical Ethics in Antiquity.*
S.H., 185:Apr87–705
Carrillo y Gariel, A. Grabados de la colección de la Academia de San Carlos.
M. Mena Marqués, 48:Apr–Jun86–199
Carringer, R.L. The Making of "Citizen Kane."*
D. Millar, 161(DUJ):Jun86–358
G. Millar, 707:Spring86–139
Carrington, C. Soldier at Bomber Command.
B. Bond, 617(TLS):3Apr87–366
Carrington, L., ed. Studies in Caribbean Language.
R. Sabino, 355(LSoc):Mar86–101
Carrington, L.D. St. Lucian Creole.
D.K. Nylander, 350:Jun87–447
de Carrión, S. – see under Santob de Carrión
Carrithers, M. The Forest Monks of Sri Lanka.
B. Smith, 293(JASt):Nov85–165
Carroll, D. Australian Contemporary Drama, 1909–1982.*
V. Emeljanow, 610:Autumn86–261
Carroll, J. The Cultural Theory of Matthew Arnold.*
M. Allott, 447(N&Q):Dec85–539
P. Coustillas, 189(EA):Apr–Jun87–222
Carroll, J. Forced Entries.
M. Stevens, 441:2Aug87–8
Carroll, J.M. What's in a Name?*
E.D. Lawson, 424:Dec86–387
Carroll, L. Lewis Carroll and the House of Macmillan. (M.N. Cohen & A. Gandolfo, eds)
A. Bell, 362:26Mar87–33
H. Carpenter, 617(TLS):12Jun87–645
Carroll, M.A., H.G. Schneider & G.R. Wesley. Ethics in the Practice of Psychology.
T.M.R., 185:Oct86–309
Carroll, M.P. The Cult of the Virgin Mary.
M. Warner, 617(TLS):12Jun87–638
Carroll, W.C. The Metamorphoses of Shakespearean Comedy.*
P. Bement, 541(RES):Nov86–561
L.S. Champion, 179(ES):Oct86–454
F. Teague, 130:Fall86–282
R.N. Watson, 551(RenQ):Autumn86–565
639(VQR):Winter86–18
Carruth, H. The Selected Poetry of Hayden Carruth.*
R.B. Shaw, 491:Nov86–98
639(VQR):Summer86–99
Carruth, H. Sitting In.
E.J. Hobsbawm, 453(NYRB):12Feb87–11

Carruthers, M.J. & E.D. Kirk, eds. Acts of Interpretation.
D. Pearsall, 402(MLR):Oct86–969
Carruthers, P. Introducing Persons.
G. Madell, 617(TLS):27Feb87–222
Carse, J.P. Finite and Infinite Games.
F. Kane, 441:12Apr87–32
Carson, A. Eros the Bittersweet.
A.W. Price, 617(TLS):22May87–546
Carson, T.L. The Status of Morality.
P. Boddington, 518:Apr86–115
D.O. Brink, 482(PhR):Jan86–144
Carsten, F.L. Essays in German History.
D. Blackbourn, 617(TLS):2Jan87–10
Carstensen, F.V. American Enterprise in Foreign Markets.*
S. Ricard, 106:Fall86–361
Carswell, C. Open the Door!
J.A. Scott Miller, 571(ScLJ):Winter86–17
Cartano, T. Blackbird.
S. Altinel, 617(TLS):27Nov–3Dec87–1333
Cartelle, E.M. – see under Montero Cartelle, E.
Carter, A. Saints and Strangers.*
D.J. Enright, 453(NYRB):26Feb87–15
42(AR):Fall86–495
Carter, A., ed. Wayward Girls and Wicked Women.*
J. Mellors, 362:1Jan87–22
Carter, D.T. When the War Was Over.*
R.N. Current, 9(AlaR):Jul86–223
Carter, E.C. 2d, J.C. Van Horne & C.E. Brownell, eds. Latrobe's View of America, 1795–1820.
D.M. Sokol, 576:Dec86–425
Carter, E.C. 2d, J.C. Van Horne & L.W. Formwalt – see Latrobe, B.H.
Carter, J. & J. Hough, Jr. A Dream Season.
J. Oppenheimer, 441:3May87–14
Carter, J. The Blood of Abraham.*
E. Current-Garcia, 577(SHR):Fall86–394
D. Polish, 287:Oct86–19
Carter, J. Fugue State. Pincushion's Strawberry.
P. Filkins, 236:Fall–Winter86/87–50
Carter, J. & R. Everything to Gain.
L.C. Pogrebin, 441:31May87–16
Carter, J.E. – see "Solomon D. Butcher: Photographing the American Dream"
Carter, J.M. Rape in Medieval England.
J. Given, 589:Jul86–633
Carter, L.J. Nuclear Imperatives and Public Trust.
M.W. Browne, 441:27Sep87–37
Carter, M. On Other Days While Going Home.
J. Bass, 441:15Nov87–27
Carter, M. George Orwell and the Problem of Authentic Existence.*
R.D.B., 295(JML):Nov86–523
Carter, M.L. & K. Schoville, eds. Sign, Symbol, Script.
M. Bernal, 318(JAOS):Oct/Dec85–736
Carter, P. The Road to Botany Bay.
P. Porter, 617(TLS):27Nov–3Dec87–1326
Carter, S. Twentieth Century Type Designers.
J. Lewis, 617(TLS):28Aug87–936
Carter, S.D. Three Poets at Yuyama.
L.R. Rodd, 318(JAOS):Oct/Dec85–771
Cartiér, X.W. Be-Bop, Re-Bop.
V. Smith, 441:13Dec87–12

Castor, G. & T. Cave, eds. Neo-Latin and the Vernacular in Renaissance France.*
    O. Millet, 535(RHL):Jul-Aug86-735
    F. Rigolot, 210(FrF):May86-227
Castro, E. & F. Betto. Fidel and Religion.
    A. Riding, 441:14Jun87-15
Cataldi, S. Symbolai e relazioni tra le città greche nel V secolo a.C.
    P.J. Rhodes, 123:Vol36No1-151
"Catalogue of Books Printed in the XVth Century now in the British Library." (Pt 12)
    P. Veneziani, 354:Jun86-171
"Catalogue of Seventeenth Century Italian Books in the British Library."
    D. McKitterick, 617(TLS):26Jun87-704
Catédra, P.M., ed. Alonso de Córdoba, Conmemoráción breve de los Reyes de Portugal [together with] Surtz, R.E., ed. Un sermón castellano del siglo XV con motivo de la fiesta del Corpus Christi.*
    G. Smolka-Koerdt, P.M. Spangenberg & D. Tillmann-Bartylla, 545(RPh):May87-554
Cátedra, P-M., ed. Poemas castellanos de cancioneros bilingües y otros manuscritos barceloneses.
    I. Macpherson, 86(BHS):Apr86-155
Cateura, L.B. Growing Up Italian.
    R.D. Heffner, 441:1Mar87-30
Cathcart, A. The Comeback.*
    H. Ritchie, 571(ScLJ):Winter86-41
Cathelat, B. & G. Mermet. Vous et les Français.
    A. Prévos, 207(FR):May87-893
Cather, W. The Troll Garden. (J. Woodress, ed)
    C. McLay, 106:Winter86-477
"Catmopolitan."
    O. de Courcy, 362:17&24Dec87-52
Catron, L.E. Writing, Producing, and Selling Your Play.
    R. Cornish, 615(TJ):Mar86-131
Catto, J.I., with R. Evans, eds. The History of the University of Oxford. (Vol 1)
    L. Colley, 617(TLS):13Mar87-261
    V.H.H. Green, 382(MAE):1986/2-275
Catullus. Versions of Catullus. (H. Clucas, trans)
    W.G. Shepherd, 4:Spring86-35
Caudet, F. – see Pérez Galdós, B.
Caudwell, C. Collected Poems.* (A. Young, ed) Scenes and Actions. (J. Duparc & D. Margolies, eds)
    J-J. Lecercle, 189(EA):Jul-Sep87-360
    E. Mendelson, 617(TLS):16Jan87-63
Caudwell, S. The Shortest Way to Hades.*
    639(VQR):Winter86-20
Caunitz, W.J. Suspects.*
    T.J. Binyon, 617(TLS):21Aug87-910
Causey, A. Edward Burra.
    D. Farr, 39:May86-363
Caute, D. News from Nowhere.*
    J. Mellors, 364:Nov86-102
Cauvain, J-P. Henri Bosco et la poétique du sacré.
    J. Hansel, 356(LR):Feb86-82
Cauville, S. Le Théologie d'Osiris à Edfu.
    A. Spalinger, 318(JAOS):Apr/Jun85-341

Cavalcanti, G. The Poetry of Guido Cavalcanti. (L. Nelson, ed & trans)
    C. Calenda, 379(MedR):Dec86-447
    M. Marti, 228(GSLI):Vol163fasc524-604
Cavalcanti, G. Pound's Cavalcanti.* (E. Pound, trans; D. Anderson, ed)
    M. Bacigalupo, 402(MLR):Jan86-220
    T. Redman, 405(MP):Feb87-340
    D. Smith, 106:Winter86-509
"El cavallero Pláçidas (MS Esc. h-I-13)." (R.M. Walker, ed)
    J.K. Walsh, 86(BHS):Apr86-154
Cavalli-Björkman, G., ed. Netherlandish Mannerism.
    L.W. Nichols, 90:Apr86-294
Cavanaugh, C. Love and Forgiveness in Yeats's Poetry.
    R.W.B., 295(JML):Nov86-558
Cave, R. The Private Press.* (2nd ed)
    P.S. Koda, 87(BB):Jun86-114
Cave, R.A., ed. The Romantic Theatre.
    A. Leighton, 617(TLS):20Mar87-300
Caveing, M. Zénon d'Élée.
    C. Osborne, 303(JoHS):Vol106-226
Cavell, S. Pursuits of Happiness.
    C. Zucker, 106:Summer86-251
Cavell, S. Themes Out of School.*
    J.M. Hodge, 89(BJA):Autumn86-404
Cavillac, C. L'Espagne dans la trilogie "picaresque" de Lesage.
    H. Klüppelholz, 356(LR):Feb86-75
Caviness, M. & others. Stained Glass before 1700 in American Collections.
    T. Husband, 90:Jul86-512
Cavini, W. & others. Studi su papiri greci di logica e medicina.
    J. Barnes, 520:Vol31No1-93
Cavitch, D. My Soul and I.*
    C.C. Hollis, 27(AL):Oct86-445
    V.R. Pollak, 646(WWR):Summer86-44
Cawelti, J.G. & G.A. Rosenberg. The Spy Story.
    J. Sutherland, 617(TLS):11-17Sep87-1001
Cawley, A.C. & others. The Revels History of Drama in English.* (Vol 1)
    H-J. Diller, 38:Band104Heft3/4-506
    C. Gauvin, 189(EA):Oct-Dec87-465
    A.F. Johnston, 447(N&Q):Mar85-89
    P. Meredith, 402(MLR):Jul87-699
Cawley, A.C. & B. Gaines, eds. The Yorkshire Tragedy.
    M. Dodsworth, 175:Spring86-107
Caws, M.A. Yves Bonnefoy.*
    S. Winspur, 546(RR):Mar86-155
Caws, M.A. Reading Frames in Modern Fiction.*
    W. Gibson, 128(CE):Dec86-832
    G. Joseph, 536(Rev):Vol8-189
    A. Kennedy, 627(UTQ):Spring87-443
    V. Kling, 191(ELN):Dec86-83
    D. Meakin, 208(FS):Apr86-241
    D.T.O., 295(JML):Nov86-415
    M. Tison-Braun, 188(ECr):Summer86-106
Caws, M.A., ed. Writing in a Modern Temper.*
    J.D. Suther, 345:May86-247
    Y. Vadé, 535(RHL):Sep-Oct86-965
    R.A. York, 402(MLR):Jan86-214
de Cayeux, J. Les Hubert Robert de la Collection Veyrenc au Musée de Valence.
    P. Conisbee, 90:Apr86-295
Cazaux, Y. – see Palma-Cayet, P-V.

Cazden, N., H. Haufrecht & N. Studer, eds.
Folk Songs of the Catskills.*
   D.J. Dyen, 187:Spring/Summer87-363
   N. Groce, 440:Summer-Fall86-159
Cazden, N., H. Haufrecht & N. Studer.
Notes and Sources for "Folk Songs of
the Catskills."*
   D.J. Dyen, 187:Spring/Summer87-363
   N. Groce, 440:Summer-Fall86-159
Cazden, R.E. A Social History of the Ger-
man Book Trade in America to the Civil
War.*
   C.L. Dolmetsch, 221(GQ):Fall86-676
   H. Froeschle, 133:Band19Heft3/4-376
   C. Sammons, 301(JEGP):Jan86-81
Cazemajou, J., ed. Les Minorités hispan-
iques en Amérique du Nord (1960-1980).
   S. Rodriguez del Pino, 189(EA):Oct-
   Dec87-487
Cazenave, A. & J-F. Lyotard, eds. L'art
des confins.
   A. Reix, 542:Oct-Dec86-512
Cèbe, J-P. - see Varro
Cebik, L.B. Fictional Narrative and
Truth.*
   L. Foreman-Peck, 289:Fall86-118
   A.W. Hayward, 290(JAAC):Winter86-205
   P. Lamarque, 478:Apr86-115
de Ceccatty, R. L'Extrémité du monde.
   M. Fougères, 207(FR):Dec86-291
de Ceccatty, R. L'Or et la poussière.*
   R. Millet, 450(NRF):Apr86-93
Cecchetti, G. - see Leopardi, G.
Cecchi, E. Fiorentinità e altri saggi.
   (M. Ghilardi, ed)
   M. Bacigalupo, 402(MLR):Jan87-220
Cecchi, E. & M. Praz. Carteggio Cecchi-
Praz. (F.B. Crucitti Ullrich, ed)
   M. Bacigalupo, 402(MLR):Jan87-220
Cecil, D. - see Bridges, R.
Cedering, S. Letters from the Floating
World.
   455:Dec86-64
Cedrini, L.B. - see under Borghi Cedrini,
L.
Cela, C.J. La colmena. (R. Asún, ed)
   D. Henn, 402(MLR):Apr87-509
   J-L. Marfany, 86(BHS):Oct86-376
   G. Roberts, 240(HR):Spring86-233
Celaya, G. The Poetry of Gabriel Celaya.
   J. Mandrell, 552(REH):Jan86-143
Celeyrette-Pietri, N. "Agathe," genèse et
exégèse d'un conte de l'entendement.
   P. Jourdan, 535(RHL):Jan-Feb86-161
Céline, L.F. Conversations with Professor
Y.*
   D. Flower, 364:Dec86/Jan87-134
Célis, R., ed. Littérature et musique.
   R. Farnsworth, 107(CRCL):Jun86-282
Cell, J. The Highest Stage of White
Supremacy.
   W.G. James, 529(QQ):Autumn86-484
Cellard, J. Anthologie de la littérature
argotique des origines à nos jours.
   G. Sartoris, 450(NRF):Nov86-96
Cellard, J. & A. Rey. Dictionnaire du
français non conventionnel.
   G. Sartoris, 450(NRF):Nov86-96
Cendrars, B. Dan Yack. The Astonished
Man.
   P. Reading, 617(TLS):29May87-582

Censer, J.T. North Carolina Planters and
Their Children, 1800-1860.
   F.M. Heath, 9(AlaR):Jan86-68
Cerboni Baiardi, G., G. Chittolini & P.
Floriani, eds. Federico di Montefeltro.
   M. Pozzi, 228(GSLI):Vol163fasc523-452
Cereteli, K. Aramejskij jazyk.
   S. Segert, 318(JAOS):Oct/Dec85-731
Cerezo Galán, P. La voluntad de aventura.*
   J. López-Morillas, 240(HR):Spring86-231
Cerny, L. - see Hutton, L.
Cerny, L. - see Snelling, T.
Cerny, P.G. & M.A. Schain. Socialism, The
State and Public Policy in France.
   D. O'Connell, 207(FR):Oct86-149
Cerquiglini, J. "Un engin si soutil."
   D. Ingenschay, 547(RF):Band98Heft3/4-
   423
del Cerro, J.L.R. - see under Román del
Cerro, J.L.
Cersowsky, P. Phantastische Literatur im
ersten Viertel des 20. Jahrhunderts.*
   H.A. Pausch, 107(CRCL):Dec86-680
   O.R. Spittel, 654(WB):1/1986-157
de Certeau, M. The Practice of Everyday
Life.
   R. Bogue, 131(CL):Fall86-367
de Cervantes Saavedra, M. The Adventures
of Don Quixote de la Mancha.* (T. Smol-
lett, trans)
   J.J. Allen, 304(JHP):Fall86-84
   566:Spring87-212
Cervigni, D.S. Dante's Poetry of Dreams.
   M. Marti, 228(GSLI):Vol163fasc522-266
Ceserani, R. La Narrazione fantastica.
   P. Pelckmans, 535(RHL):Jul-Aug86-806
Cetti Marinoni, B., G. Cusatelli & M.
Secchi. Ricerche Halleriane.
   J. Hösle, 52:Band21Heft2-213
de Cevallos, M.D. - see under del Candau de
Cevallos, M.
Chabot, D. Moon Country.*
   M. Body, 102(CanL):Winter85-142
Chabot, J. L'Autre Moi.*
   A. Fonyi, 535(RHL):Nov-Dec86-1131
Chadeour, A.B. & R. Joppien. Kataloge des
Kunstgewerbemuseums Köln. (Vol 10)
   H.H., 90:Jun86-444
Chadwick, O. Britain and the Vatican
during the Second World War.
   D.M. Smith, 617(TLS):23Jan87-77
Chadwick, W. Women Artists and the Surre-
alist Movement.
   A.G. Robins, 90:May86-365
Chaïkin, N. Celestin Nanteuil (1813-1873).
   C. Hartley, 39:Jul86-65
Chaimowicz, T. Freiheit und Gleichgewicht
im Denken Montesquieus und Burkes.
   P. Gottfried, 173(ECS):Fall86-115
Chaisson, E The Life Era.
   G. Johnson, 441:16Aug87-17
Chalfont, A. Star Wars.*
   42(AR):Summer86-378
Challis, C. Quest for Kerouac.
   L.K. Barnett, 395(MFS):Summer86-276
Chamberlain, A. & R. Steele. Guide pra-
tique de la communication.
   D.M. Schulze, 207(FR):May87-880
Chamberlin, J.E. & S.L. Gilman, eds.
Degeneration.
   T. Gibbons, 627(UTQ):Winter86/87-372

Charlton, M. The Star Wars History.
K. Booth, 617(TLS):13Mar87-266
Charmley, J. Duff Cooper.*
B. Alison, 364:Oct86-103
Charnassé, H. La guitare.
J. Bran-Ricci, 537:Vol72No2-284
Charney, L.H. Special Counsel.
D. Polish, 287:Oct86-19
Charnon-Deutsch, L. The Nineteenth-
Century Spanish Story.
C.A. McBride, 593:Winter86/87-337
N.M. Valis, 405(MP):May87-441
Charpentier, F. - see Labé, L.
Charpentier, F. & S. Perrier, eds.
Montaigne: Les Derniers Essais.
J.J. Supple, 402(MLR):Apr87-473
Charpigny, F., A-M. Grenouiller & J-B.
Martin. Marius Champailler, paysan de
Pélussin.
G. Straka, 553(RLiR):Jul-Dec86-609
Charpin, D. Archives familiales et pro-
priété privée en Babylonie ancienne.
J. Renger, 318(JAOS):Apr/Jun85-331
de Charrière, I. [Belle de Zuylen] Oeuvres
complètes. (Vols 1-3) (J-D. Candaux &
others, eds)
B. Bray, 549(RLC):Jan-Mar86-103
de Charrière, I. [Belle de Zuylen] Oeuvres
complètes.* (Vol 5) (J-D. Candaux &
others, eds)
M. Mat, 535(RHL):Jan-Feb86-153
Charteris, R. Critical Commentary and
Additional Material for the "Opera omnia"
of Alfonso Ferrabosco the Elder. Alfonso
Ferrabosco the Elder (1543-1588).
P. Macey, 317:Fall86-650
Charteris, R. - see Ferrabosco, A.
Charters, A., ed. Dictionary of Literary
Biography. (Vol 16)
P. Makin, 402(MLR):Apr87-463
Charters, S. Louisiana Black.*
W. Ferris, 441:11Jan87-22
Chartier, R. Lectures et lecteurs dans la
France d'Ancien Régime.
E. Weber, 617(TLS):2-8Oct87-1069
Chartier, R., ed. Pratiques de la lec-
ture.*
H-J. Lüsebrink, 547(RF):Band98Heft3/4-
430
Chartier, R., ed. Les Usages de l'imprimé
(XVe-XIXe siècle).
E. Weber, 617(TLS):2-8Oct87-1069
Charyn, J. Paradise Man.
R. Rosen, 441:29Mar87-11
Chase, C. Decomposing Figures.
P. Miers, 400(MLN):Dec86-1290
Chase, J. During the Reign of the Queen of
Persia.
J. Jacobson, 271:Spring-Summer86-193
Chase, J. Exterior Decoration.*
C. Robertson, 658:Winter86-315
Chase, K. Eros and Psyche.*
K. Blake, 594:Spring86-89
P. Boumelha, 175:Spring86-78
M. Steig, 158:Jun86-95
K. Sutherland, 402(MLR):Oct87-927
Chassagnol, M. La Fantaisie dans les
récits pour la jeunesse en Grande-
Bretagne de 1918 à 1968.
M. Fisher, 189(EA):Jul-Sep87-363
Chasseguet-Smirgel, J. Ethique et esthé-
tique de la perversion.
S. Lebovici, 192(EP):Apr-Jun86-241

Château, J. L'humanisation ou les premiers
pas des valeurs humaines.
J-M. Gabaude, 542:Apr-Jun86-259
Chatelain-Courtois, M. Le Mots du vin et
de l'ivresse.
L.R.N. Ashley, 424:Sep86-336
Chatham, J.R. & S.M. Scales, with others.
Western European Dissertations on the
Hispanic and Luso-Brazilian Languages
and Literatures.
A.J. Cárdenas, 552(REH):Oct86-129
Chatterjee, M. Gandhi's Religious
Thought.*
G. Richards, 485(PE&W):Jan86-61
Chatterji, R. Working Class and the
Nationalist Movement in India.
D.M. Laushey, 293(JASt):Aug86-876
Chatterji, S. Shrikanto.
J-L. Gautier, 450(NRF):May86-113
Chatwin, B. The Songlines.
P-L. Adams, 61:Nov87-122
R. Clarke, 362:9Jul87-29
A. Harvey, 441:2Aug87-1
D. Malouf, 617(TLS):4-11Sep87-948
Chaucer, G. The Book of the Duchess.* (H.
Phillips, ed)
A.I. Dickerson, 589:Jan86-128
J.O. Fichte, 38:Band104Heft1/2-207
Chaucer, G. The Canterbury Tales. (N.F.
Blake, ed)
M. Görlach, 72:Band223Heft1-159
Chaucer, G. The Canterbury Tales/Die
Canterbury-Erzählungen.* (H. Bergner,
ed)
W. Sauer, 38:Band104Heft3/4-487
Chaucer, G. Les Contes de Cantorbéry. (Pt
2) (J. de Caluwé-Dor, trans)
J. Bidard, 189(EA):Jul-Sep87-347
Chaucer, G. The Nun's Priest's Tale.* (D.
Pearsall, ed)
M.C. Seymour, 179(ES):Apr86-186
S. Wenzel, 447(N&Q):Mar85-95
Chaucer, G. St. John's College, Cambridge,
Manuscript L.1.
E.G. Stanley, 447(N&Q):Sep85-391
Chaucer, G. Troilus and Criseyde.* (B.A.
Windeatt, ed)
N.F. Blake, 402(MLR):Oct86-974
H. Cooper, 541(RES):May86-243
H.J.C. Langley, 97(CQ):Vol15No2-120
D. Mehl, 72:Band223Heft2-398
D. Pearsall, 382(MAE):1986/2-281
Chauchadis, C. Honneur, morale et société
dans l'Espagne de Philippe II.
B.M. Damiani, 240(HR):Summer86-333
Chaudenson, R. Textes créoles anciens (La
Réunion et Ile Maurice).*
P. Stein, 72:Band223Heft1-190
Chaudhuri, K.N. Trade and Civilization in
the Indian Ocean.*
S.F. Dale, 293(JASt):Aug86-878
Chaudhuri, N.C. Thy Hand, Great Anarch!
The Autobiography of an Unknown Indian.
T. Raychaudhuri, 617(TLS):27Nov-
3Dec87-1311
Chaudhuri, S. Contemporary Buddhism in
Bangladesh.
B. Smith, 293(JASt):Nov85-166
K.G. Zysk, 318(JAOS):Jan/Mar85-180
Chauleau, L. La Vie quotidienne aux
Antilles françaises au temps de Victor
Schoelcher.
M.G. Paulson, 207(FR):Feb87-412

Child, H., ed. The Calligrapher's Handbook.
  W. Gardner, 324:Feb87-249
Child, H. & others. More Than Fine Writing.
  J.I. Whalley, 617(TLS):29May87-592
Child, H. & J. Howes, eds. Edward Johnston.
  W. Gardner, 324:Aug87-711
Child, L.M. Lydia Maria Child Selected Letters, 1817-1880. (M. Meltzer & P.G. Holland, eds)
  G.A. Schultz, 106:Fall86-327
Child, L.M. - see Jacobs, H.A.
Childers, T., ed. The Formation of the Nazi Constituency, 1919-1933.
  B. Blackbourn, 617(TLS):15May87-522
Childress, M. A World Made of Fire.*
  A. Hughes, 617(TLS):6Mar87-246
Childs, D. The GDR.
  T.C. Fox, 221(GQ):Summer86-511
Chilton, J. Sidney Bechet.
  B. Morton, 362:15Oct87-30
Chilton, L. & K. and others. New Mexico.
  R.M. Adams, 453(NYRB):12Mar87-28
Chilver, G.E.F., with G.B. Townend. A Historical Commentary on Tacitus' "Histories" IV and V.
  R.J.A. Talbert, 123:Vol36No1-137
Chinery, M. Collins Guide to the Insects of Britain and Western Europe.
  J.R.G. Turner, 617(TLS):8May87-498
Chinery, M. Garden Creepy-Crawlies.
  M. Ridley, 617(TLS):27Feb87-225
Ch'ing-chao, L. - see under Li Ch'ing-chao
Chini, E. La Chiesa e il convento dei Santi Michele e Gaetano a Firenze.
  B. Boucher, 39:Mar86-219
Chinweizu. Decolonising the African Mind.
  R. Harms, 617(TLS):25Sep-1Oct87-1040
Chinweizu, O.J. & I. Madubuike. Toward the Decolonization of African Literature.
  B.D. Killam, 529(QQ):Summer86-428
Chion, M. La Voix au cinéma. Le Son au cinéma.
  H. Charley, 207(FR):Mar87-550
Chipasula, F., ed. When My Brothers Come Home.
  639(VQR):Autumn86-133
Chiquart, M. Du fait de cuisine (1420). (T. Scully, ed)
  G. Roques, 553(RLiR):Jul-Dec86-644
Chisman, F. & A. Pifer. Government for the People.
  C.R. Morris, 441:25Oct87-48
Chitham, E. & T. Winnifrith. Brontë Facts and Brontë Problems.
  W.A. Craik, 447(N&Q):Dec85-534
  K. Sutherland, 402(MLR):Oct87-927
Chitham, E. & T. Winnifrith, eds. Selected Brontë Poems.
  C. Alexander, 67:Nov86-303
  J. Le Guern, 189(EA):Jul-Sep86-356
  K. Sutherland, 402(MLR):Oct87-927
  639(VQR):Autumn86-135
Chitnis, A.C. The Scottish Enlightenment and Early Victorian English Society.*
  S.J. Brown, 637(VS):Summer87-522
Chitty, S. Gwen John.
  L. Tillman, 441:5Jul87-15
Chocheyras, J. & others. Autour de l'impersonnel.
  J.A. Brill, 207(FR):Oct86-142

Chochon, B. Structure du "Noeud de Vipères" de Mauriac, une haine à entendre.
  M. Autrand, 535(RHL):Mar-Apr86-337
Chojnacki, W. & W., eds. Bibliografia Kalendarzy Polonijnych 1838-1982.
  T.L. Zawistowski, 497(PolR):Vol31No4-339
Choldin, M.T. A Fence Around the Empire.
  P. Doyle, 402(MLR):Oct87-1054
  L. McReynolds, 550(RusR):Jul86-335
Chollet, R. Balzac journaliste.
  D. Bellos, 535(RHL):Jan-Feb86-153
  A. Kleinert, 224(GRM):Band36Heft2-244
Cholokian, R.C. Deflection/Reflection in the Lyric Poetry of Charles d'Orléans.
  D.A. Fein, 207(FR):Feb87-390
  J. Fox, 402(MLR):Oct87-952
Chomarat, J. Grammaire et Rhetorique chez Erasme.*
  J. Lindhardt, 544:Spring86-183
Chōmin, N. A Discourse by Three Drunkards on Government. (N. Tsukui & J. Hammond, eds)
  A. Walthall, 407(MN):Summer86-243
Chomsky, N. Lectures on Government and Binding. (2nd ed)
  J. McCloskey, 316:Mar86-238
Chomsky, N. Some Concepts and Consequences of the Theory of Government and Binding.
  M. Owen, 402(MLR):Jul86-687
Chopra, P.N., ed. Contributions of Buddhism to World Civilization and Culture.
  B.G. Gokhale, 318(JAOS):Oct/Dec85-806
Chotiner, B.A. Khrushchev's Party Reform.*
  M. McCauley, 575(SEER):Oct86-634
Chou, M-C. Hu Shih and Intellectual Choice in Modern China.
  P.G. Pickowicz, 293(JASt):Nov85-105
Choudhary, K.P.S. Modern Indian Mysticism.
  K.G. Zysk, 318(JAOS):Oct/Dec85-807
Choudhry, P. Punjab Politics.
  S.R. Wasti, 293(JASt):May86-623
Chouillet, A-M. & J., eds. Traitements informatiques de texts du 18ème siècle.
  D.J. Adams, 83:Autumn86-279
Choyce, L. Billy Botzweiler's Last Dance and Other Stories.
  R.M. Nischik, 102(CanL):Spring86-173
Chraibi, D. The Butts.
  42(AR):Winter86-124
Chrétien, G. - see Nonnus
Chrétien, J. Straight From the Heart.
  W. Christian, 298:Fall86-153
Chrétien, J-L. Lueur du secret.*
  F. George, 98:Apr86-308
Chrétien de Troyes. The Knight with the Lion, or Yvain (Le Chevalier au lion). (W.W. Kibler, ed & trans)
  T. Hunt, 208(FS):Autumn86-444
Chrétien de Troyes. Perceval.* (R.H. Cline, trans)
  D. Staines, 589:Apr86-495
Christ, C.T. Victorian and Modern Poetics.*
  A. Nichols, 577(SHR):Winter86-80
  D.G. Riede, 301(JEGP):Jan86-140
Christensen, M. Mortal Belladaywic.
  P. Rudnick, 441:20Sep87-26
Christensen, P. Weights and Measures.
  R. Peters, 703:No17-142
Christhilf, M. W.S. Merwin the Mythmaker.
  S.A.S., 295(JML):Nov86-512

Christian, C., ed. Bernard Bolzano.
J. Sinnreich, 687:Jan–Mar86–156
Christian, S. Nicaragua.
639(VQR):Winter86–25
Christianson, G.E. In the Presence of the
Creator.
G.S. Rousseau, 566:Spring87–212
Christie, G.C. Laws, Norms and Authority.
G. Haarscher, 540(RIPh):Vol40fasc1/2–
187
Christie, I.R. Stress and Stability in
Late Eighteenth–Century Britain.*
M. Philp, 83:Spring86–86
Christie, W.M., Jr. Preface to a Non-
Firthian Linguistics.
E. Steiner, 205(ForL):Apr84–80
Christodoulou, K.E. De Molière à Beaumar-
chais.
J–P. Collinet, 475:Vol13No24–381
Christol, H. & S. Ricard, eds. Hyphenated
Diplomacy.
G–J. Forgue, 189(EA):Jan–Mar87–108
Christopher, G.B. Milton and the Science
of the Saints.*
A. Burnett, 677(YES):Vol16–253
Christopher, N. A Short History of the
Island of Butterflies.*
J.P. White, 491:Dec86–176
455:Dec86–63
Chu, D. – see Huang Liu–hung
Chu, J–H. & C. Brown. The Elegant Brush.
L. Fenwick, 60:Nov–Dec86–146
Chukovsky, K.I. The Art of Translation.*
(L.G. Leighton, ed & trans)
R. Sobel, 399(MLJ):Spring86–96
Church, F.F. Entertaining Angels.
J. Sullivan, 441:5Jul87–21
Church, R., with A. Hall & J. Kanefsky.
The History of the British Coal Industry.
(Vol 3)
T.C. Barker, 617(TLS):9Jan87–33
Churchill, C. Fen.
V.M. Patraka, 385(MQR):Winter87–285
Churchill, E.A. Simple Forms and Vivid
Colors.
J. Hutchinson, 658:Spring86–83
Churchill, L.R. Rationing Health Care in
America.
D. Mechanic, 441:12Jul87–21
Churchland, P.M. Matter and Conscious-
ness.*
K. Gunderson, 486:Mar86–145
C. Hookway, 518:Apr86–110
R.M. Martin, 529(QQ):Spring86–211
Churchland, P.S. Neurophilosophy.
K. Campbell, 262:Jun86–143
C. McGinn, 617(TLS):6Feb87–131
G. Madell, 262:Jun86–153
M. Sereno, 262:Jun86–217
C.A. Skarda, 262:Jun86–187
A. Smith, 262:Jun86–203
K.V. Wilkes, 262:Jun86–169
Chvany, C.V. & R.D. Brecht, eds. Morpho-
syntax in Slavic.*
W.W. Derbyshire, 558(RLJ):Winter86–218
Chwast, S. The Left–Handed Designer.
T. Reese, 507:Nov/Dec86–118
Ciampoli, D. Il capitano del popolo a
Siena nel primo Trecento con il rubri-
cario dello statuto del comune di Siena
del 1337.
W.M. Bowsky, 589:Oct86–1019

Ciardi, R.P. & L. Tongiorgi Tomasi – see
under Paolo Ciardi, R. & L. Tongiorgi
Tomasi
Cicero. M. Tulli Ciceronis "Epistulae,"
Tomus I. (W.S. Watt, ed)
F.R.D. Goodyear, 123:Vol36No2–241
Cielens, I. Trois fonctions de l'exil
dans les oeuvres de fiction d'Albert
Camus.
M. Zobel–Finger, 72:Band223Heft2–474
Cierlińska, H., ed. A Panorama of Polish
History.
F. Lachowicz, 497(PolR):Vol31No1–87
Cifoletti, G. Il Vocabolario della Lingua
Franca.
C. Schmitt, 72:Band223Heft1–235
Cigar, N. – see al–Qādirī, M.
Ciment, M. John Boorman.*
M. Le Fanu, 707:Summer86–214
A. Sarris, 18:Dec86–62
Cioran, E.M. Exercices d'admiration.
M. Jarrety, 450(NRF):May86–85
Cioran, E.M. History and Utopia.
442(NY):7Sep87–112
Cioranescu, A. Le Masque et le visage.*
J–P. Leroy, 549(RLC):Apr–Jun86–236
D–H. Pageaux, 107(CRCL):Dec86–663
L. Picciola, 535(RHL):Jul–Aug86–738
J.E. Varey, 86(BHS):Oct86–368
Ciplijauskaité, B. La mujer insatisfecha.
S. Bacarisse, 86(BHS):Jan86–94
D. Henn, 402(MLR):Jul86–702
R. Schmidt, 240(HR):Winter86–100
Cipolla, G. – see Tasso, T.
Cipriano, P. Templum.
J. Linderski, 122:Oct86–330
Cisneros, A. At Night the Cats.
S. White, 448:Vol24No2–95
639(VQR):Spring86–61
Citati, P. Tolstoy.
H. Benedict, 441:8Feb87–25
Citron, P. – see Giono, J. & L. Jacques
Čivikov, G. Interpretationsprobleme mod-
erner Lyrik am Beispiel Paul Celans.*
H. Bekker, 221(GQ):Fall86–633
Cixous, H. Angst.*
C. Duchen, 402(MLR):Jan87–214
Claiborne, R. Our Marvelous Native
Tongue.
R. Overstreet, 583:Spring87–333
Clammer, J. Singapore.
P.G. Altbach, 293(JASt):May86–646
Clampitt, A. Archaic Figure.
M. Rudman, 441:20Dec87–12
Clampitt, A. What the Light Was Like.*
C. Bedient, 569(SR):Fall86–657
S. Birkerts, 473(PR):Vol53No1–144
N. Jenkins, 493:Jun86–102
Clanchy, M.T. England and its Rulers,
1066–1272.
T. Callahan, 377:Jul86–141
Clancy, L. The Novels of Vladimir Nabo-
kov.*
P. Meyer, 550(RusR):Jan86–100
Clancy, T. Patriot Games.
R. Thomas, 441:2Aug87–11
Clare, J. The Later Poems of John Clare,
1837–1864.* (E. Robinson & D. Powell,
with M. Grainger, eds)
R.L. Brett, 541(RES):May86–278
P.M.S. Dawson, 402(MLR):Jan86–178
M. Minor, 591(SIR):Winter86–576
R.K.R. Thornton, 161(DUJ):Dec85–200

Clare, J. The Letters of John Clare.* (M. Storey, ed)
  M. Dodsworth, 175:Spring86-108
  P. Morgan, 179(ES):Dec86-568
  R. Raimond, 189(EA):Oct-Dec87-472
Clare, J. The Natural History Prose Writings of John Clare.* (M. Grainger, ed)
  A. London, 541(RES):Feb86-108
  R.K.R. Thornton, 161(DUJ):Dec85-200
Clare, J. The Oxford Authors: John Clare.* (E. Robinson & D. Powell, eds)
  B. Beatty, 83:Spring86-109
  P. Drew, 402(MLR):Apr87-454
  M. Minor, 591(SIR):Winter86-576
Clare, J. The Parish.* (E. Robinson & D. Powell, eds)
  R.L. Brett, 541(RES):Aug86-455
Clare, L. La Quintaine, la course de bague et le jeu des têtes.
  L. Godard de Donville, 535(RHL):Mar-Apr86-270
  P. Heugas, 92(BH):Jan-Jun85-195
  J.E. Varey, 86(BHS):Jul86-280
Clareson, T.D., ed. Science Fiction in America, 1870s-1930s.
  D.M. Hassler, 87(BB):Dec86-260
  C. Petty, 106:Fall86-395
Clareson, T.D. Some Kind of Paradise.
  G.K. Wolfe, 395(MFS):Spring86-133
  27(AL):Oct86-482
"Clarín" - see under Alas, L.
Clark, A.M. Pompeo Batoni.* (E.P. Bowron, ed)
  B. Ford, 39:Feb86-135
  D. Irwin, 83:Autumn86-309
Clark, A.R. La France dans l'Histoire selon Bernanos.*
  C. Lépineux, 535(RHL):Jul-Aug86-791
Clark, B.R., ed. The School and the University.
  639(VQR):Spring86-59
Clark, C. Vulgar Rabelais.
  A.L. Prescott, 551(RenQ):Autumn86-552
Clark, D.H. The Cosmos from Space.
  D. Meredith, 441:27Sep87-37
Clark, E. Camping Out.*
  I. Malin, 532(RCF):Fall86-135
Clark, G. Symbols of Excellence.
  P.A. Clayton, 324:May87-471
  B. Scott, 39:Dec86-572
Clark, G. & E. Zimmerman. Educating Artistically Talented Students.
  D.M. Miller, 709:Fall86-53
Clark, J.C.D. English Society, 1688-1832.*
  D. Szechi, 566:Spring87-214
Clark, J.C.D. Revolution and Rebellion.
  M. Goldie, 617(TLS):23Jan87-88
Clark, J.K. Goodwin Wharton.
  R.F., 391:May86-59
Clark, K. & M. Holquist. Mikhail Bakhtin.*
  R.F. Christian, 575(SEER):Jul86-463
  L. Gossman, 131(CL):Fall86-337
  C. Howes, 77:Spring86-180
  N. Perlina, 550(RusR):Oct86-435
  D.H. Richter, 599:Fall86-411
  A. White, 473(PR):Vol53No4-634
Clark, L.H. The Deadly Swarm and Other Stories.
  S. Brady, 649(WAL):Aug86-186
Clark, L.L. Schooling the Daughters of Marianne.
  M.C. Weitz, 207(FR):Feb87-406

Clark, M. Michel Foucault, An Annotated Bibliography.
  R. Wilcocks, 107(CRCL):Jun86-274
Clark, M. Modern Italy 1871-1982.
  J. Pollard, 278(IS):Vol41-163
Clark, M.H. Weep No More, My Lady.
  K. Olson, 441:28Jun87-24
Clark, P., ed. The Transformation of English Provincial Towns 1600-1800.
  A. McInnes, 83:Spring86-85
Clark, R.D. Yeats at Songs and Choruses.*
  G. Bornstein, 403(MLS):Spring86-82
Clark, R.H. & M. Pause. Precedents in Architecture.
  M. Gelernter, 46:Oct86-8
Clark, S.R.L. The Mysteries of Religion.
  S. Collins, 617(TLS):12Jun87-638
Clark, T. The Exile of Céline.
  F. Sauzey, 441:8Feb87-28
Clark, T. Jack Kerouac.*
  L.K. Barnett, 395(MFS):Summer86-276
  J. Lititz, 649(WAL):Aug86-151
Clark, T. Paradise Resisted.
  B. Christophersen, 50(ArQ):Winter86-370
Clark, T.D. The Greening of the South.
  D.R. Jamieson, 9(AlaR):Jan86-77
Clark, T.J. The Painting of Modern Life.*
  P. Dickens, 89(BJA):Summer86-294
  B. Farwell, 54:Dec86-684
  J. House, 90:Apr86-296
Clark, W. Cataclysm.
  T.M. Shaw, 150(DR):Fall86-398
Clark, W. From Three Worlds.
  R. Hope, 617(TLS):25Sep-1Oct87-1045
Clark, W.B. & W.C. Turner, eds. Critical Essays on American Humor.
  L.J. Budd, 587(SAF):Spring86-115
Clarke, A. Nine Men Who Laughed.
  V.W. Wesley, 441:23Aug87-16
Clarke, A. Proud Empires.*
  M. Thorpe, 176:May87-44
Clarke, A. When Women Rule.
  D. Brydon, 102(CanL):Spring86-160
Clarke, A.C. "2061: Odyssey Three."
  G. Jonas, 441:20Dec87-18
Clarke, G. Selected Poems.*
  H. Buckingham, 565:Summer86-64
Clarke, H. The Archaeology of Medieval England.
  K. Biddick, 589:Apr86-395
Clarke, L. Sunday Whiteman.
  S. Rae, 617(TLS):18-24Dec87-1409
  D. Walder, 362:26Nov87-31
Clarke, M. The Cutting Season.*
  J. Carlsen, 102(CanL):Winter85-165
Clarke, P. Hell and Paradise.
  P-L. Adams, 61:Oct87-106
Clarke, P. & J.S. Gregory, eds. Western Reports on the Taiping.
  W.S.K. Waung, 302:Vol22No1-70
Claudel, P. & J. Rivière. Correspondance Paul Claudel/Jacques Rivière 1907-1924. (P. de Gaulmyn, ed)
  H.T. Naughton, 188(ECr):Summer86-105
Claudel, P.L.C. Art poétique. (G. Gadoffre, ed)
  M. Autrand, 535(RHL):Sep-Oct86-953
Claudon, F. Le voyage romantique.
  V.D.L., 605(SC):15Apr87-306
Clausen, W. Virgil's "Aeneid" and the Tradition of Hellenistic Poetry.
  D.C. Feeney, 617(TLS):3Jul87-722

Clausing, S. German Grammar.
M.P. Alter, 399(MLJ):Winter86-427
Claussen, H. & N. Oellers, eds. Beschädig-
tes Erbe.
H.J. Schmidt, 221(GQ):Summer86-457
Claxton, G., ed. Beyond Therapy.
A.D. Jones, 617(TLS):24Apr87-448
Clay, C.G.A. Economic Expansion and Social
Change: England 1500-1700.
S. Rappaport, 551(RenQ):Autumn86-524
Clay, D. Lucretius and Epicurus.*
W. Englert, 41:Fall85-334
Clay, H. The Papers of Henry Clay. (Vol
7) (R. Seager 2d, ed)
G.A. Schultz, 106:Fall86-327
Clayton, B. Forgotten Prophet.*
M. Lebowitz, 639(VQR):Winter86-162
Clayton, B., with N.M. Elliott. Buck
Clayton's Jazz World.
C. Fox, 617(TLS):30Jan87-119
Clayton, J.D. Ice and Flame.
A.D.P. Briggs, 575(SEER):Oct86-590
Clayton, M. Christie's Pictorial History
of English and American Silver.
G. Wills, 39:Aug86-140
Clayton, P. & P. Gammond. The Guinness
Jazz A-Z.
B. Fantoni, 362:15Jan87-24
Cleary, J.J., ed. Proceedings of the
Boston Area Colloquium in Ancient Phi-
losophy. (Vol 1)
J. Barnes, 520:Vol31No2-188
Cleary, T.R. Henry Fielding: Political
Writer.*
J. Gray, 178:Dec86-468
Cleaver, D.G. Art. (4th ed)
M. Travis, 709:Fall86-58
Cleland, J. Memoirs of a Woman of Plea-
sure.* (P. Sabor, ed)
P. Wagner, 83:Autumn86-274
Clemen, W. Shakespeares Monologe.
U. Suerbaum, 156(ShJW):Jahrbuch1986-
245
Clemens, R., with P. Gammons. Rocket Man.
D. Cole, 441:26Apr87-24
Clemens, S. Papa.* (C. Neider, ed)
H. Hill, 26(ALR):Winter87-90
Clement, H. Still River.
G. Jonas, 441:2Aug87-25
Clements, K. Henry Lamb.
D. Farr, 39:May86-363
90:Feb86-157
Clements, P. Baudelaire and the English
Tradition.
D. Bouchard, 627(UTQ):Fall86-140
J.F. Jones, Jr., 446(NCFS):Spring87-343
G.A.O., 295(JML):Nov86-424
N. Rogers, 637(VS):Winter87-277
H.W., 636(VP):Autumn86-345
Clements, W.M. & F.M. Malpezzi, comps.
Native American Folklore, 1879 to 1979.
R. Turpin, 203:Vol97No2-235
T.P. Wilson, 649(WAL):Nov86-262
Clemo, J. A Different Drummer.
J. Mole, 176:Mar87-63
Clemoes, P., ed. Anglo-Saxon England 14.
C. Gauvin, 189(EA):Oct-Dec87-464
Clendenning, J. The Life and Thought of
Josiah Royce.*
R. Burch, 619:Fall86-467
27(AL):Oct86-477

Clerici Balmas, N. Un poète du XVIe
siècle: Marc Papillon de Lasphrise.*
C. Dédéyan, 535(RHL):Jan-Feb86-135
J. Della Neva, 551(RenQ):Autumn86-548
Clews, H. The Only Teller.
C. Caramello, 395(MFS):Summer86-345
Cliffe, J.T. The Puritan Gentry.*
B. Donagan, 250(HLQ):Spring86-175
Clifford, C.E. In the Deep Heart's Core.
L. Rodenberger, 649(WAL):Nov86-245
Clifford, J. & G.E. Marcus, eds. Writing
Culture.
N. Barley, 617(TLS):27Feb87-224
Clifford, N.K. The Resistance to Church
Union in Canada 1904-1939.
D.F. Campbell, 529(QQ):Summer86-403
Clifton, T. Music as Heard.*
F. Mauk, 317:Spring86-205
L. Rowell, 289:Spring86-119
Cline, S. & D. Spender. Reflecting Men at
Twice Their Natural Size.
J. McKay, 362:30Apr87-29
Clitandre, P. Cathedral of the August
Heat.
R. Burgin, 441:5Jul87-14
Clive, H.P. Marguerite de Navarre.
P. Chilton, 208(FS):Jul86-322
O. Millet, 535(RHL):Mar-Apr86-262
Clive, H.P. Clément Marot.*
J. Pineaux, 535(RHL):Mar-Apr86-261
Cloonan, W. Michel Tournier.*
S. Dunn, 207(FR):Mar87-546
Close, D. & C. Bridge, eds. Revolution.
D.J. Manning, 161(DUJ):Jun86-394
Clothier, P. Dirty-Down.
N. Callendar, 441:13Sep87-46
Cloutier, C. & C. Seerveld, eds. Opuscula
aesthetica nostra.
S. Foisy, 627(UTQ):Fall86-184
Clover, C.J. The Medieval Saga.*
P. Foote, 562(Scan):Nov86-222
Clubb, O. KAL Flight 007.
R. Klein & W.B. Warner, 153:Spring86-2
Clubbe, J. & E.J. Lovell, Jr. English
Romanticism.*
L.M. Findlay, 447(N&Q):Sep85-401
Clutterbuck, R. Conflict and Violence in
Singapore and Malaysia, 1945-1983.
Cheah Boon Kheng, 293(JASt):May86-647
Clyman, T.W., ed. A Chekhov Companion.
K.D. Kramer, 574(SEEJ):Winter86-576
T.G. Marullo, 395(MFS):Winter86-681
Clyne, M.G. Language and Society in
German-Speaking Countries.*
R.W. Dunbar, 399(MLJ):Summer86-189
E.G. Fichtner, 133:Band19Heft3/4-321
H. Kahane, 350:Mar87-169
Coale, S. Anthony Burgess.
J.L. Halio, 677(YES):Vol16-364
Coale, S.C. In Hawthorne's Shadow.*
E. Ammons, 27(AL):Dec86-630
J. Humphries, 385(MQR):Fall87-788
H. McNeil, 617(TLS):22May87-553
L. Waldeland, 395(MFS):Summer86-248
639(VQR):Summer86-89
Coarelli, F. Il foro romano.*
T.P. Wiseman, 313:Vol76-307
Coates, D. & J. Hillard, eds. The Economic
Decline of Modern Britain.*
B. Supple, 617(TLS):13-19Nov87-1243
Coates, J. Armed and Dangerous.
W. King, 441:29Nov87-22

Cohen, I.B.   Revolution in Science.*
  J.R. Hofmann, 529(QQ):Summer86-443
Cohen, J. - see Bruce, L.
Cohen, J. & H. Snitzer.   Reprise.
  E. Roche, 415:Mar86-154
Cohen, M.   Café Le Dog.
  J-P. Durix, 102(CanL):Summer86-130
Cohen, M.   Nadine.
  L. Leith, 99:Nov86-39
  C. Matthews, 376:Dec86-134
  K. Rile, 441:9Aug87-20
Cohen, M.   The Spanish Doctor.*
  H. Dahlie, 168(ECW):Fall86-125
  J. Yanofsky, 390:Aug/Sep86-63
Cohen, M.N. & A. Gandolfo - see Carroll, L.
Cohen, M.R.   Jewish Self-Government in
  Medieval Egypt.
  S. Gellens, 318(JAOS):Jan/Mar85-165
Cohen, N. - see Randolph, V.
Cohen, R., ed.   Studies in Eighteenth-Cen-
  tury British Art and Aesthetics.
  A. Bermingham, 173(ECS):Fall86-104
  L. Lipking, 566:Autumn86-78
  C. MacLachlan, 89(BJA):Autumn86-396
Cohen, R.I.   The Burden of Conscience.
  B. Wasserstein, 441:24May87-7
Cohen, R.S., R.M. Martin & M. Westphal,
  eds.   Studies in the Philosophy of J.N.
  Findlay.
  D. Moran, 323:May86-200
  483:Jul86-425
Cohen, R.S. & M.W. Wartofsky, eds.   Episte-
  mology, Methodology, and the Social
  Sciences.*
  A. Lugg, 488:Sep86-383
Cohen, S.D.   Uneasy Partnership.
  J.N. Huddleston, Jr., 293(JASt):May86-
  588
Cohen, S.F.   Rethinking the Soviet Exper-
  ience.*
  R.B. Day, 529(QQ):Summer86-447
  P.H. Solomon, Jr., 550(RusR):Apr86-229
Cohen, S.F.   Sovieticus.*
  W. Taubman, 550(RusR):Jul86-324
Cohen, S.P.   The Pakistan Army.
  L.D. Hayes, 293(JASt):Nov85-166
Cohen, S.S. & J. Zysman.   Manufacturing
  Matters.
  R.M. Solow, 441:12Jul87-36
Cohen, T.   Remaking Japan.   (H. Passin, ed)
  C. Johnson, 441:9Aug87-12
Cohen, W.   Drama of a Nation.*
  S. Mullaney, 570(SQ):Winter86-512
  L. Salingar, 551(RenQ):Winter86-812
Cohen-Mushlin, A.   The Making of a Manu-
  script.*
  K.E. Haney, 589:Apr86-396
Cohen-Solal, A.   Sartre.*   (N. MacAfee, ed)
  S. Hoffmann, 441:26Jul87-3
  A. van den Hoven, 628(UWR):Spring-
    Summer86-74
  D. Lindenberg, 450(NRF):Mar86-95
  D.A. MacLeay, 207(FR):Mar87-547
  H.W. Wardman, 402(MLR):Jul87-750
  J. Weightman, 453(NYRB):13Aug87-42
Cohen-Tanugi, L.   Le droit sans l'Etat.
  K.S., 185:Oct86-296
Cohn, A.M. & K.K. Collins.   The Cumulated
  Dickens Checklist 1970-1979.
  S. Monod, 677(YES):Vol16-321
Coirault, Y. - see Duc de Saint-Simon

Coke, T.   Vice Chamberlain Coke's Theatri-
  cal Papers 1706-1715.*   (J. Milhous &
  R.D. Hume, eds)
  C.H. Shattuck, 677(YES):Vol16-258
Coke-Enguidanos, M.   Word and Work in the
  Poetry of Juan Ramón Jiménez.*
  R.A. Cardwell, 86(BHS):Jul86-293
Colacurcio, M.J., ed.   New Essays on "The
  Scarlet Letter."
  H. McNeil, 617(TLS):22May87-553
Colacurcio, M.J.   The Province of Piety.*
  N. Baym, 301(JEGP):Jan86-150
Colás, M.D.E. - see under Errazu Colás,
  M.D.
Colbert, J.   Profit and Sheen.*
  S. Dunant, 362:24Sep87-22
Colchie, T. & M. Strand - see Drummond de
  Andrade, C.
Cole, D.   Captured Heritage.
  S. Jones, 658:Winter86-321
  Z. Pearlstone, 2(AfrA):Feb86-19
Cole, G.H.A.   Inside a Planet.
  H. Couper, 324:Sep87-785
Cole, H.   The Marble Queen.
  L. McMahon, 441:19Apr87-20
Cole, H.C.   The "All's Well" Story from
  Boccaccio to Shakespeare.
  J. Barish, 677(YES):Vol16-227
Cole, H.M., ed.   I Am Not Myself.
  D.J. Cosentino, 2(AfrA):Nov85-81
Cole, J.   The Thatcher Years.
  J. Campbell, 617(TLS):5Jun87-597
  P. Preston, 362:30Apr87-30
Cole, J.A.   The Potosí Mita, 1573-1700.
  J. Lynch, 263(RIB):Vol36No4-488
Cole, J.H.   The People Versus the Taipings.
  K. Bernhardt, 293(JASt):Aug86-834
Cole, M. - see Dickens, C.
Cole, R.C.   Irish Booksellers and English
  Writers 1740-1800.
  J. Raven, 617(TLS):2Jan87-22
Cole, S.L.   The Absent One.
  W.B. Worthen, 615(TJ):Dec86-504
Colegate, I.   Glimpses of Sion's Glory.
  639(VQR):Summer86-93
Coleman, A.   Utopia on Trial.*
  R. Wiedenhoeft, 45:Mar86-71
Coleman, F.X.J.   Neither Angel nor Beast.
  D. Lee, 617(TLS):5Jun87-613
Coleman, J.A. - see de La Péruse, J.
Coleman, J.A. & C.M. Scollen-Jimack, eds.
  Rabelais in Glasgow.
  K.M. Hall, 208(FS):Jan86-62
  A.L. Prescott, 551(RenQ):Autumn86-552
Coleman, P.   Rousseau's Political Imagina-
  tion.*
  M-H. Cotoni, 535(RHL):Jul-Aug86-762
  R. Grimsley, 173(ECS):Fall86-118
  J.A. Perkins, 478:Apr86-135
Coleman, R.R.   Renaissance Drawings from
  the Ambrosiana.
  G. Naughton, 39:Jan86-61
Coleman, W.D.   The Independence Movement
  in Quebec 1945-1980.
  W.P. Irvine, 529(QQ):Winter86-927
Coleridge, S.T.   The Collected Works of
  Samuel Taylor Coleridge.*   (Vol 7: Bio-
  graphia Literaria.)   (J. Engell & W.J.
  Bate, eds)
  D. Jasper, 161(DUJ):Dec85-199

Coleridge, S.T. The Collected Works of
Samuel Taylor Coleridge.* (Vol 12:
Marginalia, Pt 2) (G. Whalley, ed)
  A.J. Harding, 661(WC):Autumn86-217
  G. Lindop, 617(TLS):16-22Oct87-1143
  W.J. Owen, 627(UTQ):Fall86-103
Coleridge, S.T. The Collected Works of
Samuel Taylor Coleridge. (Marginalia, Pt
1) (G. Whalley, ed)
  G. Lindop, 617(TLS):16-22Oct87-1143
Coleridge, S.T. The Oxford Authors: Cole-
ridge. (H.J. Jackson, ed)
  M. Dodsworth, 175:Summer86-195
Coles, B. & J. Sweet Track to Glaston-
bury.*
  P.J. Fowler, 324:Dec86-77
Coles, D. Landslides.
  J. Ditsky, 628(UWR):Spring-Summer86-67
Coles, R. Dorothy Day. Simone Weil.
  K.L. Woodward, 441:6Sep87-10
Coles, R. The Political Life of Children.*
  639(VQR):Autumn86-129
Coles, R. - see Williams, W.C.
Coles, W.E., Jr. & J. Vopat. What Makes
Writing Good.
  P. Bizzell, 126(CCC):May86-244
Colesanti, M. & others, eds. Stendhal,
Roma, l'Italia.
  V.D.L., 605(SC):15Apr87-298
Colet, L. Lui.
  E. O'Brien, 441:5Apr87-3
Colette. Lettres à Moune et au Toutounet
(Hélène Jourdan-Morhange et Luc-Albert
Moreau), 1929-1954. (B. Villaret, ed)
  C. Slawy-Sutton, 207(FR):Apr87-712
Colette. Oeuvres.* (Vol 1) (C. Pichois,
with others, eds)
  M. Picard, 535(RHL):Mar-Apr86-326
Coletti, V. Parole dal pulpito.*
  D.R. Lesnick, 589:Jul86-635
Coley, J.S. - see "Le Roman de Thèbes
(The Story of Thebes)"
Colish, M.L. The Mirror of Language.
  J. Simpson, 382(MAE):1986/1-123
Colish, M.L. The Stoic Tradition from
Antiquity to the Early Middle Ages.
  J. Barnes, 520:Vol31No2-193
Coll, S. The Taking of Getty Oil.
  E. Bailey, 441:20Sep87-27
Collard, F. Regency Furniture.
  90:Jun86-444
Collas, I.K. "Madame Bovary."
  L.M. Porter, 446(NCFS):Spring87-324
Collet, A. Stendhal et Milan.
  V.D.L., 605(SC):15Apr87-300
Collette, J.Y. The Death of André Breton.
  B. Pirie, 102(CanL):Winter85-172
Colli, G. Nach Nietzsche. Distanz und
Pathos.
  R. Margreiter, 489(PJGG):Band93Heft2-
375
Collie, M. George Borrow, Eccentric.*
  H. Reinhold, 677(YES):Vol16-316
Collie, M. George Gissing.
  P. Coustillas, 189(EA):Jan-Mar87-94
  B. Lake, 78(BC):Autumn86-385
Collie, M. & A. Fraser. George Borrow.*
  J.F. Fuggles, 354:Jun86-186
Collier, J.L. Duke Ellington.
  E.J. Hobsbawm, 453(NYRB):19Nov87-3
  D. Morgenstern, 441:22Nov87-22
Collier, M. - see under Duck, S.

Collier, P. & D. Horowitz. The Fords.
  J. Nocera, 441:25Oct87-35
  442(NY):28Dec87-125
Collin, F. Theory and Understanding.*
  J-M. Gabaude, 542:Jan-Mar86-155
Collinet, J.P. - see Boileau-Despréaux, N.
Collinet, J-P. - see Molière
Collinge, N.E. The Laws of Indo-European.
  D.A. Ringe, Jr., 159:Spring86-107
Collings, M. Stephen King as Richard
Bachman.
  G.K. Wolfe, 395(MFS):Spring86-133
Collings, M. & D. Engbretson. The Shorter
Works of Stephen King.
  G.K. Wolfe, 395(MFS):Spring86-133
Collingwood, P. Textile and Weaving Struc-
tures.
  M. Straub, 324:Sep87-786
Collins, A.W. Thought and Nature.*
  S.E., 185:Apr87-699
Collins, B. White Society in the Antebel-
lum South.
  M. O'Brien, 9(AlaR):Apr86-152
Collins, D. Sartre as Biographer.
  A. Otten, 345:Nov86-496
Collins, H.M. Changing Order.
  G. Myers, 128(CE):Oct86-595
Collins, H.M. & T.J. Pinch. Frames of
Meaning.
  A. Brannigan, 488:Dec86-520
Collins, J. Musicmakers of West Africa.
  J.C. Dje Dje, 91:Fall86-306
Collins, J. Spinoza on Nature.*
  D. Garrett, 482(PhR):Apr86-295
Collins, J. Trust Your Heart.
  D. Mason, 441:29Nov87-17
Collins, L., ed. Anglo-Bulgarian Sympo-
sium, London, July 1982.
  R.F. Hoddinott, 575(SEER):Jul86-478
Collins, L. Going to See the Leaves.*
  T. De Pietro, 249(HudR):Autumn86-490
Collins, M. The Catastrophe of Rainbows.
  G. Kuzma, 491:Sep86-342
Collins, M. Minnesota Strip.
  442(NY):10Aug87-80
Collins, M. - see Scarlatti, A.
Collins, M.A. Midnight Haul.
  N. Callendar, 441:8Feb87-20
Collins, P. Radios: The Golden Age.
  R. Barber, 441:13Dec87-27
Collins, R. The Basques.
  R. Fletcher, 617(TLS):13Mar87-276
Collins, R. Max Weber.
  P.B., 185:Apr87-695
Collins, R. Weberian Sociological Theory.
  B.M.D., 185:Jan87-501
Collins, S. Selfless Persons.*
  M. Kapstein, 485(PE&W):Jul86-259
Collis, J.S. Living with a Stranger.
  362:10Sep87-24
Collis, L. Impetuous Heart.
  P. Branscombe, 415:Jan86-29
Colman, G. & T. Morton. Plays by George
Colman the Younger and Thomas Morton.
(B. Sutcliffe, ed)
  E. Burns, 83:Spring86-110
Colmer, J. Patrick White.
  B. Kiernan, 71(ALS):May86-417
Colodny, R.G. - see Nalimov, V.V.
Colombani, H.G. - see under Giauffret
Colombani, H.
Colonna, G., ed. Santuari d'Etruria.
  N. Spivey, 313:Vol76-281

Colonna, V. Vittoria Colonna: Rime. (A. Bullock, ed)
    P.B. Diffley, 402(MLR):Jul87−755
Colonnese, T. & L. Owens. American Indian Novelists.
    J. Ramsey, 649(WAL):Nov86−263
Colquhoun, R. Raymond Aron.
    V. Bogdanor, 176:Apr87−45
Colton, T.J. The Dilemma of Reform in the Soviet Union. (rev)
    A. Brown, 617(TLS):27Mar87−313
Colverson, T. & D. Hall. A Catalogue of Fine Press Printers in the British Isles.
    S. Carter, 617(TLS):17Apr87−424
Colvert, J.B. Stephen Crane.*
    R.G. Deamer, 649(WAL):May86−77
Colville, D. The Teaching of Words-worth.
    P.H. Parry, 161(DUJ):Dec85−198
Colvin, H. Calke Abbey, Derbyshire.*
    J.M. Robinson, 39:Apr86−291
Colvin, H. Unbuilt Oxford.
    M.H. Port, 447(N&Q):Mar85−83
Colvin, H.M., ed. The History of the King's Works. (Vols 1−6)
    A. Gomme, 44:Vol29−197
Colwin, L. Another Marvelous Thing.*
    T. De Pietro, 249(HudR):Autumn86−489
    L. Duguid, 617(TLS):27Feb87−206
    42(AR):Summer86−380
Comas, A. − see Maragall, J.
Combs, E., ed. Modernity and Responsibility.
    W. Cragg, 154:Spring86−191
de Comes, P. & M. Marmin, eds. Le Cinéma français 1930−1960.
    H.A. Garrity, 207(FR):May87−902
Comfort, A. Imperial Patient.
    P. Howell, 617(TLS):18−24Sep87−1027
Comfort, A. Reality and Empathy.
    E. von der Luft, 543:Dec86−376
"Coming to Terms."
    A. Greene, 615(TJ):Mar86−126
Comini, A. The Changing Image of Beethoven.
    M. Kimmelman, 441:13Sep87−44
Comisso, G. Vento felice. (N. Naldini, ed)
    U. Varnai, 402(MLR):Jul86−760
Comito, T. In Defense of Winters.
    R. Asselineau, 189(EA):Jul−Sep87−369
    T. Parkinson, 27(AL):Dec86−650
    C. Wilmer, 617(TLS):25Sep−1Oct87−1043
Comley, N.R. & others. Fields of Writing.
    B.C. Mallonee, 126(CCC):Dec86−501
Compañy, F.D. − see under Dominguez Compañy, F.
Compère, M−M. & D. Julia. Les Collèges français, XVIe−XVIIIe siècles. (Vol 1)
    F. Waquet, 535(RHL):Jul−Aug86−737
Compitello, M.A. Ordering the Evidence.*
    M. Lentzen, 72:Band223Heft2−460
    N.M. Valis, 345:May86−242
Comrie, B. Tense.
    C. Bache, 307:Apr86−66
Comte-Sponville, A. Le mythe d'Icare.*
    M. Fattal, 192(EP):Apr−Jun86−231
Comyns, B. Mr. Fox.
    P. Craig, 617(TLS):5Jun87−610
Comyns, B. The Skin Chairs.* Sisters by a River.
    L.A. Walker, 441:22Mar87−22

Comyns, B. Who Was Changed and Who Was Dead.
    P. Craig, 617(TLS):18−24Sep87−1026
Con, H. & others. From China to Canada. (E. Wickberg, ed)
    S. Chan, 293(JASt):Feb86−371
Conaway, J. The Kingdom in the Country.
    442(NY):7Dec87−193
de la Concha, V.G. − see under García de la Concha, V.
Conche, M. − see Heraclitus
Concheff, B.J., comp. Bibliography of Old Catalan Texts.
    C.J. Wittlin, 304(JHP):Winter86−177
"The Concise Oxford French Dictionary." (2nd ed) (H. Ferrar, J.A. Hutchinson & J−D. Biard, eds)
    W. Ayres−Bennett, 208(FS):Oct86−499
    R.H. Crawshaw, 402(MLR):Jul86−733
Condé, M. Pays mêlé.
    A.M. Rea, 207(FR):May87−905
Condé, M. Segu.* (French title: Ségou.)
    C.R. Larson, 441:31May87−47
Conder, J.J. Naturalism in American Fiction.*
    L. Buell, 569(SR):Winter86−x
    D. Pizer, 301(JEGP):Apr86−291
Condon, A.G. The Envy of the American States.*
    D. Duffy, 627(UTQ):Fall86−232
    G.T. Stewart, 656(WMQ):Apr86−323
Condon, J. A Half Step Behind.
    639(VQR):Summer86−97
Condon, P. & others. In Pursuit of Perfection.
    R. Thomson, 59:Mar86−108
"Conference on the Acquisition and Bibliography of Commonwealth and Third World Literatures in English, 21−22 October 1982."
    N.J. Schmidt, 538(RAL):Fall86−439
Congdon, L. The Young Lukács.*
    I. Deak, 453(NYRB):12Mar87−39
Conisbee, P. Chardin.*
    M. Kemp, 617(TLS):20Feb87−195
    J. Sweetman, 324:May87−467
Conkin, P.K., with H.L. Swint & P.S. Miletich. Gone with the Ivy.
    R.F. Durden, 579(SAQ):Summer86−315
Conley, E.A. Bread and Stones.
    W. Herbert, 441:4Jan87−18
Conley, J. & others, eds & trans. The Mirror of Everyman's Salvation.
    A.H. Olsen, 589:Oct86−1019
    R. Potter, 130:Summer86−177
Conley, V.A. Hélène Cixous.*
    E. Marks, 402(MLR):Jan87−215
    C.J. Murphy, 210(FrF):Jan86−125
Conlon, D.J., ed. G.K. Chesterton.
    A. Bell, 362:19Feb87−25
    S. Medcalf, 617(TLS):25−31Dec87−1419
Conlon, P.M. Le Siècle des Lumières.* (Vol 2)
    C.J. Betts, 402(MLR):Oct87−957
Conlon, P.M. Le Siècle des Lumières.* (Vol 3)
    C.J. Betts, 402(MLR):Oct87−957
    P. Jansen, 535(RHL):Sep−Oct86−918
Conn, P. The Divided Mind.*
    V. Bischoff, 72:Band223Heft2−423
    J.A.L. Lemay, 402(MLR):Oct87−939
Connell, C. They Gave Us Shakespeare.*
    A.J. Cook, 402(MLR):Jul86−714

Connell, E. Points for a Compass Rose.
   M. Jarman, 249(HudR):Summer86-342
Connell, E.S. Son of the Morning Star.*
   P.A. Hutton, 649(WAL):Feb87-355
   B. Maine, 577(SHR):Spring86-194
   A. Shapiro, 31(ASch):Winter85/86-136
Connellan, L. The Clear Blue Lobster-
   Water Country.
   R. Peters, 30:Spring87-91
Connelly, B. Arab Folk Epic and Identity.
   I.J. Boullata, 268(IFR):Summer87-105
Connelly, J. Man's Work.
   S. Mernit, 441:22Mar87-28
Conner, D., with B. Stannard. Comeback.
   B. Lloyd, 441:31May87-32
Conner, P. The China Trade, 1600-1860.
   J. Rawson, 90:Nov86-836
Connolly, B. & R. Anderson. First Contact.
   M.F. Brown, 441:2Aug87-17
Connor, S. Charles Dickens.*
   C. Koralek, 175:Autumn86-293
   L. Lane, Jr., 268(IFR):Summer87-92
   F. Rosslyn, 97(CQ):Vol15No2-164
   R. Wolfs, 204(FdL):Dec86-303
Connor, T. Spirits of the Place.
   S. Knight, 364:Dec86/Jan87-131
   S. O'Brien, 617(TLS):13Mar87-275
Connor, W. The National Question in
   Marxist-Leninist Theory and Strategy.
   R. Pearson, 575(SEER):Jan86-147
Connor, W.R. Thucydides.*
   D.G. Kyle, 125:Fall85-102
   C. Orwin, 31(ASch):Winter85/86-128
Connors, L. The Emperor's Adviser.
   W.G. Beasley, 617(TLS):14Aug87-868
Connors, R.J., L.S. Ede & A.A. Lunsford,
   eds. Essays on Classical Rhetoric and
   Modern Discourse.*
   J.D. Lyons, 478:Apr86-102
Conoley, G. Woman Speaking Inside Film
   Noir.
   J. Carter, 219(GaR):Summer86-532
Conover, T. Coyotes.
   T.D. Allman, 441:13Sep87-7
Conquest, R. The Harvest of Sorrow.*
   G.A. Hosking, 617(TLS):20Feb87-191
   P. Wiles, 453(NYRB):26Mar87-43
Conrad, B. Referring and Non-Referring
   Phrases.*
   Y. Putseys, 603:Vol10No2-492
Conrad, J. The Collected Letters of Joseph
   Conrad.* (Vol 1) (F.R. Karl & L. Davies,
   eds)
   S. Hynes, 569(SR):Fall86-639
   C.J. Rawson, 402(MLR):Jan86-187
Conrad, J. The Collected Letters of Joseph
   Conrad.* (Vol 2) (F.R. Karl & L. Davies,
   eds)
   L. Menand, 441:25Jan87-16
   S. Monod, 189(EA):Jul-Sep87-356
Conrad, J. "Typhoon" and Other Tales. (C.
   Watts, ed)
   S. Monod, 189(EA):Jul-Sep87-359
Conrad, P. The Everyman History of En-
   glish Literature.
   M. Dodsworth, 175:Spring86-102
   S. Monod, 189(EA):Jul-Sep86-317
Conrad, P. A Song of Love and Death.
   E. Downes, 441:8Nov87-15
Conradi, P.J. Iris Murdoch.
   A. Malak, 268(IFR):Summer87-114
Conrady, K.O. Goethe.
   D. Roberts, 67:May86-108

Conran, S. Savages.
   K. Fitzgerald, 441:18Oct87-30
Conroy, F. Midair.
   T. De Pietro, 249(HudR):Autumn86-491
   639(VQR):Spring86-55
Conroy, H., S.T.W. Davis & W. Patterson,
   eds. Japan in Transition.*
   N.L. Waters, 293(JASt):Feb86-396
Conroy, J. Belfast Diary.
   M.F. Nolan, 441:20Dec87-14
Conroy, M. Modernism and Authority.*
   T.K. Bender, 141:Spring86-226
   E. Hollahan, 594:Winter86-438
   W. Sypher, 569(SR):Summer86-497
   I.V., 295(JML):Nov86-452
   E. Wasiolek, 405(MP):Aug86-104
Consolino, F.E. Claudiano, "Elogio di
   Serena."
   J.B. Hall, 123:Vol36No2-238
Constantine, D. Early Greek Travellers and
   the Hellenic Ideal.
   R. Richer, 549(RLC):Apr-Jun86-254
   P. Warren, 83:Autumn86-236
   J.E. Ziolkowski, 124:Jul-Aug87-456
Constantine, K.C. Upon Some Midnights
   Clear.
   T.J. Binyon, 617(TLS):9Jan87-42
Constantine the African. Liber de coitu.
   (E. Montero Cartelle, ed & trans)
   L. Demaitre, 589:Jan86-229
"Contacts de langues."
   G. Price, 208(FS):Oct86-502
Contamine, P. War in the Middle Ages.
   C. Allmand, 382(MAE):1986/1-125
   42(AR):Winter86-123
Conte, C. Maya Culture and Costume.
   J.S.N. Eisenlauer, 2(AfrA):Nov85-83
Contejean, C. Glossaire du patois de
   Montbéliard.* (M. Thom, with C. Duvernoy
   & G. Pourchot, eds)
   C. Schmitt, 72:Band223Heft2-428
Contini, G. - see Dante Alighieri
Contorbia, F., ed Eugenio Montale.
   E. Bonora, 228(GSLI):Vol163fasc523-460
Contreni, J.J. Codex Laudunensis 468.
   G.B. Blumenshine, 589:Jul86-636
Convenevole da Prato. Regia Carmina
   dedicati a Roberto d'Angio re di Sicilia
   e di Gerusalemme. (C. Grassi, ed)
   N.M., 382(MAE):1986/1-144
"La Conversion au XVIIe siècle."
   N. Ferrier-Caverivière, 535(RHL):Jul-
   Aug86-746
Conway, A. The Principles of the Most
   Ancient and Modern Philosophy. (P.
   Loptson, ed)
   E.J. Ashworth, 154:Winter86-821
Conway, W.E. & R. Stevenson. William
   Andrews Clark, Jr.
   S. Soupel, 189(EA):Jan-Mar87-114
Coogan, J.W. The End of Neutrality.
   G. Martel, 106:Spring86-81
Coogan, T.P. The IRA.
   J. Ridley, 617(TLS):11-17Sep87-996
Cook, A. Changing the Signs.
   C. Dempsey, 551(RenQ):Summer86-307
   C. Gould, 39:Apr86-292
Cook, A. Thresholds.
   A. Janowitz, 125:Spring86-326
Cook, B. Disorderly Elements.*
   442(NY):5Jan87-87

Coox, A.D. Nomonhan.
  J.J. Stephan, 407(MN):Summer86-250
Cope, E.S. Politics Without Parliaments,
  1629-1640.
  K. Sharpe, 617(TLS):5Jun87-602
Cope, J.I. Robert Coover's Fictions.
  T. Dooley, 617(TLS):13Feb87-164
Cope, J.I. Dramaturgy of the Daemonic.
  R. Storey, 612(ThS):May/Nov86-176
Cope, W. Making Cocoa for Kingsley Amis.*
  W. Bedford, 4:Summer86-85
  E. Larrissy, 493:Jun86-108
Copeland, J.E., ed. New Directions in Lin-
  guistics and Semiotics.*
  K. Arnold, 320(CJL):Summer86-157
  E. Haugen, 355(LSoc):Dec86-568
  R. Schreyer, 260(IF):Band91-339
Copernicus, N. Minor Works. (P. Czartory-
  ski, ed)
  J. North, 617(TLS):2Jan87-6
Coplan, D.B. In Township Tonight!
  C.A. Waterman, 187:Winter87-152
Copland, A. & V. Perlis. Copland: 1900
  through 1942.*
  A.W., 412:May85-147
Copleston, F.C. Philosophy in Russia.
  A. Besançon, 617(TLS):20Mar87-295
Copley, I. Robin Milford.
  S. Banfield, 415:Apr86-210
Copley, S., ed. Literature and the Social
  Order in Eighteenth-Century England.*
  S. Sim, 83:Spring86-97
  W.A. Speck, 366:Spring86-114
Coppel, A. Show Me a Hero.
  442(NY):10Aug87-80
Coppel, C.A. Indonesian Chinese in Crisis.
  M.F.S. Heidhues, 293(JASt):Nov85-191
Copplestone, T. Modern Art.
  J. Burr, 39:Aug86-143
Coquillat, M. Qui sont-elles?
  M.C. Weitz, 207(FR):Feb87-406
Coquillette, D.R., ed. Law in Colonial
  Massachusetts, 1630-1800.
  P.F. Gura, 639(VQR):Autumn86-734
Corazzo, N. - see Hinterthür, P.
Corballis, R. Stoppard.*
  J. Harty, 397(MD):Mar86-144
Corbett, G.G. Hierarchies, Targets and
  Controllers.*
  K. Vamling, 559:Vol10No1-126
Corbin, A. The Foul and the Fragrant.*
  T. Judt, 617(TLS):24Apr87-430
Corbin, H. Philosophie iranienne et phi-
  losophie comparée. Hamann philosophe
  du lutheranisme.
  A. Reix, 542:Jan-Mar86-87
Corboz, A. Canaletto, una Venezia immagin-
  aria.
  W.L. Barcham, 90:Aug86-614
Corcella, A. Erodoto e l'analogia.
  D. Fehling, 123:Vol36No2-310
  S. West, 303(JoHS):Vol106-209
Corcoran, N. Seamus Heaney.
  A. Haberer, 189(EA):Jan-Mar87-111
  M. Parker, 617(TLS):18-24Sep87-1023
  272(IUR):Autumn86-254
Cordasco, F. Junius.
  D. McCracken, 173(ECS):Summer87-517
Cordasco, F. & G. Simonson. Junius and His
  Works.
  D. McCracken, 173(ECS):Summer87-517
Cordero, F. Savonarola.
  F. Gilbert, 617(TLS):20Feb87-189

Cordero, N-L. Les Deux Chemins de Par-
  ménide.*
  M.R. Wright, 123:Vol36No1-63
Cordingly, D. Nicholas Pocock, 1740-1821.
  M. Butlin, 90:Nov86-834
Corea, G. The Mother Machine.
  C. Overall, 529(QQ):Spring86-193
Coren, A. Bin Ends.
  D.J. Enright, 617(TLS):18-24Dec87-1399
Corfis, I.A. Diego de San Pedro's Tractado
  de amores de Arnalte y Lucenda.
  R. Rohland de Langbehn, 304(JHP):
  Fall86-81
Corish, P. The Irish Catholic Experience.
  D.N. Doyle, 272(IUR):Spring86-102
Cork, R. David Bomberg.
  J. Collins, 362:16Apr87-37
  F. Spalding, 617(TLS):6Feb87-133
Corkery, C.J. Blessing.
  S. Birkerts, 473(PR):Vol53No1-144
  P. Stitt, 491:May86-99
Corl, K.A., B.S. Jurasek & R.T. Jurasek.
  Sprechen wir Deutsch!
  G.S. Mazur, 399(MLJ):Winter86-427
Corley, N.T. Resources for Native Peoples
  Studies/Ressources sur les études autoch-
  tones.
  B. Edwards, 470:Vol24-105
Cormack, M. Constable.
  L. Herrmann, 637(VS):Summer87-527
  L. Parris, 90:Oct86-753
  G. Reynolds, 39:Aug86-140
  D. Scrase, 617(TLS):9Jan87-44
Cormack, R. Writing in Gold.*
  C. Mango, 90:Sep86-679
Corman, A. 50.
  L.J. Davis, 441:23Aug87-9
Corman, C. - see Niedecker, L.
Cormeau, C. - see Kuhn, H.
Cormeau, C. & W. Störmer. Hartmann von
  Aue.*
  D.H. Green, 402(MLR):Oct86-1034
  M.E. Kalinke, 301(JEGP):Oct86-636
Corn, A. The Metamorphoses of Metaphor.
  B.F. Williamson, 441:29Mar87-23
Corneille, P. Théâtre complet.* (Vol 1)
  (A. Niderst, ed)
  G. Couton, 535(RHL):Mar-Apr86-274
  J-P. Dens, 356(LR):May86-174
Corneille, P. Théâtre complet. (Vol 2)
  (A. Niderst, ed)
  J-P. Dens, 356(LR):May86-174
Cornell, L.L. - see Kipling, R.
Cornell, P. & others, eds. Bildanalys.
  J. Gavel, 341:Vol55No2-83
Cornford, J. Collected Writings.* (J.
  Galassi, ed)
  E. Mendelson, 617(TLS):16Jan87-63
Cornforth, J. The Inspiration of the Past.
  J.M. Robinson, 39:Mar86-217
Corngold, S. The Fate of the Self.
  C. Koelb, 395(MFS):Winter86-684
Cornish, R. & V. Ketels. The Plays of the
  Sixties. The Plays of the Seventies.
  M. Billington, 176:Jan87-55
  M.P.L., 295(JML):Nov86-430
de Cornulier, B. Théorie du vers.
  J.S.T. Garfitt, 208(FS):Jan86-98
Cornuz, J-L. Hugo, l'homme des Misérables.
  Y. Gohin, 535(RHL):Nov-Dec86-1135
Corones, E.J. The Portrayal of Women in
  the Fiction of Henry Handel Richardson.
  E. Webby, 71(ALS):Oct86-534

Corradini, D. Ideologie e Lotte Politiche in Italia (1887–1903).
    A. Formis, 402(MLR):Apr86–507
Correa, C. The New Landscape.
    B. Richards, 46:Nov86–116
Corrie, J. Plays, Poems and Theatre Writings.* (L. Mackenney, ed)
    D. Hutchison, 571(ScLJ):Summer86–15
Corrington, J.W. All My Trials.
    P. Morrice, 441:11Oct87–56
Corrington, J.W. & J.H. A Project Named Desire.
    N. Callendar, 441:22Feb87–24
Corris, P. The Empty Beach.
    N. Callendar, 441:3May87–46
Corriveau, H. Rose Marie Berthe.
    R. Labonte, 296(JCF):No35/36–147
Corsten, T. Die Inschriften von Kios.
    A.E. Raubitschek, 24:Winter86–601
de Cortázar, C.S. – see under Sabor de Cortázar, C.
Cortázar, J. Around the Day in Eighty Worlds.*
    J. Ditsky, 628(UWR):Spring–Summer86–68
    L. Kerr, 344:Spring87–115
Cortazzi, H. Dr. Willis in Japan, 1862–1877.*
    M. Cooper, 407(MN):Autumn86–366
    H. Fruchtbaum, 637(VS):Spring87–428
    Yokoyama Toshio, 285(JapQ):Jul–Sep86–330
Cortazzi, H. – see Mitford, A.B.
Cortelazzo, M. & U. Cardinale. Dizionario di parole nuove 1964–1984.
    M. Chiesa, 228(GSLI):Vol163fasc523–462
Cortese, G. & S. Potestà. Lingue per scopi accademici.
    H.K. Moss, 278(IS):Vol41–169
Corti, M. La felicità mentale.
    M. Bacigalupo, 402(MLR):Jan86–220
Cortina Orts, A. Dios en la Filosofía Trascendental de Kant.
    M.P.M. Caimi, 342:Band77Heft2–253
Cortinez, C. Pablo Neruda.
    M. Agosin, 263(RIB):Vol36No3–334
Cortner, R.C. A "Scottsboro" Case in Mississippi.
    N.R. McMillen, 585(SoQ):Winter87–152
Corvetto, I.L. L'italiano regionale di Sardegna.
    G. Rovere, 72:Band223Heft1–200
Cosby, B. Time Flies.
    J. Viorst, 441:20Sep87–7
Coser, L.A. Refugee Scholars in America.*
    W.M. McClay, 31(ASch):Winter85/86–119
Cosgrove, A., ed. A New History of Ireland. (Vol 2)
    R. Frame, 617(TLS):21Aug87–905
Cosmacini, G. Gemelli.
    M. Clark, 617(TLS):23Jan87–78
Cossar, C.D.M., ed. The German Translation of Niccolò da Poggibonsi's "Libro d'oltramare."
    E.J. Morrall, 402(MLR):Jul87–771
Cosslett, T., ed. Science and Religion in the Nineteenth Century.*
    A.O.J. Cockshut, 447(N&Q):Sep85–403
Cosslett, T. The "Scientific Movement" and Victorian Literature.*
    R. Ashton, 402(MLR):Apr86–455
Costa, C.D.N. Lucretius: "De Rerum Natura V."*
    E.S. de Angeli, 124:Jul–Aug87–466

Costa, D. Irenic Apocalypse.
    G. Costa, 545(RPh):Nov86–215
Costa, G.J. Atlas linguistique "Sacaze" des confins catalano-languedociens.
    H. Guiter, 553(RLiR):Jul–Dec86–572
de Costa, R. Vicente Huidobro.
    P.W. Borgeson, Jr., 238:Mar86–111
    R.K. Britton, 402(MLR):Jan87–231
    M. Camurati, 240(HR):Spring86–240
    J. Higgins, 86(BHS):Oct86–381
Costa de Beauregard, O. La notion de temps équivalence avec l'espace. (2nd ed)
    H. Barreau, 192(EP):Apr–Jun86–242
Costantini, H. The Long Night of Francisco Sanctis.*
    639(VQR):Winter86–21
Coste, D., ed. Aspects d'une politique de diffusion du français langue étrangère depuis 1945.
    N. Gueunier, 209(FM):Apr86–128
Costigliola, F. Awkward Dominion.*
    S. Ricard, 106:Fall86–361
Cotensin, P. Souvenirs alphabétiques d'un amant cosmopolite.
    J-L. Fabiani, 98:Mar86–283
Cotoni, M-H. L'exégèse du nouveau testament dans la philosophie française du dix-huitième siècle.
    C.J. Betts, 402(MLR):Oct87–958
    B.E. Schwarzbach, 173(ECS):Summer87–491
    D.C. Spinelli, 207(FR):May87–860
Cotsell, M. The Companion to "Our Mutual Friend."
    P. Collins, 617(TLS):16Jan87–66
    A. Sadrin, 189(EA):Oct–Dec87–475
Cott, J. & H. El Zeini. The Search for Omm Sety.
    J.A. West, 441:26Jul87–7
Cotta, M. Les Miroirs de Jupiter.
    A. Prévos, 207(FR):Apr87–747
Cotta, S. Why Violence?
    N.G., 185:Oct86–293
Cotten, J. Vanity Will Get You Somewhere.
    B.J. Stein, 441:13Sep87–47
Cottingham, J. Descartes.
    R. Malpas, 617(TLS):10Apr87–380
Cottingham, J., R. Stoothoff & D. Murdoch – see Descartes, R.
Cottle, B. The Language of Literature.
    W. Hutchings, 568(SCN):Winter86–65
Cottom, D. The Civilized Imagination.*
    K.L. Fowler, 661(WC):Autumn86–235
Cotton, M.A. & G.P.R. Métraux. The San Rocco Villa at Francolise.
    T.W. Potter, 123:Vol36No2–286
Cottrell, R. Blood on their Hands.
    C. Hitchens, 617(TLS):27Feb87–211
Cottret, B. Terre d'exil.
    J. Blondel, 189(EA):Jul–Sep86–335
Coughlin, E.V. Poems by Robert Sosa.
    D. Garrison, 238:Mar86–123
Coulet, H. & M. Gilot – see de Marivaux, P.C.D.
Coulet du Gard, R. Dictionary of French Place Names in the U.S.A.
    K.B. Harder, 424:Sep86–312
Coulet du Gard, R. Dictionary of Spanish Place Names in the U.S.A. (Vol 5)
    K.B. Harder, 424:Sep86–321
Coulmas, F., ed. Conversational Routine.
    J.T. Irvine, 355(LSoc):Jun86–241

Craige, B.J. Literary Relativity.
   J. Preston, 402(MLR):Jul87-689
Craik, E.M., ed. Marriage and Property.
   P. Stafford, 366:Autumn86-248
Crampe-Casnabet, M. Condorcet lecteur des
   Lumières.
   A. Reix, 542:Jan-Mar86-116
Crampton, J. The Spider. The Snake.
   B.B. Gordon, 441:17May87-53
Cramsie, H.F. Teatro y censura en la
   España franquista.
   P. Zatlin, 238:Dec86-876
Crane, J. Willa Cather.
   D.H. Keller, 87(BB):Mar86-56
   C. McLay, 106:Winter86-477
Crane, J.K. The Root of all Evil.*
   R.K. Morris, 536(Rev):Vol8-231
   F.C. Watkins, 395(MFS):Winter86-623
   W. Zacharasiewicz, 27(AL):Oct86-459
Cranston, M. Jean-Jacques.
   N. O'Sullivan, 617(TLS):4-10Dec87-1344
   362:20Aug87-22
Cranston, M. Philosophers and Pamphle-
   teers.
   J.H. Mason, 617(TLS):27Feb87-220
Cranz, F.E. A Bibliography of Aristotle
   Editions, 1501-1600.* (2nd ed) (C.B.
   Schmitt, ed)
   W.A. Wallace, 319:Oct87-586
Cranz, F.E., with P.O. Kristeller, eds.
   Catalogus translationum et commentar-
   iorum.* (Vol 5)
   J.F. D'Amico, 589:Apr86-399
Crapanzano, V. Waiting.
   D.F. Gordon, 385(MQR):Summer87-553
Crapotta, J. Kingship and Tyranny in the
   Theater of Guillén de Castro.
   W. Floeck, 547(RF):Band98Heft3/4-479
   A.R. Lauer, 238:Sep86-540
   A.L. Mackenzie, 402(MLR):Oct87-999
Crary, J.W., Sr. Reminiscences of the Old
   South 1834 to 1866.
   J. White, 9(AlaR):Jul86-217
Crassweller, R.D. Peron and the Enigmas of
   Argentina.
   M. Falcoff, 441:18Jan87-22
Craven, W. Colonial American Portraiture.
   A. Staley, 617(TLS):14Aug87-867
Crawford, A. C.R. Ashbee.*
   P. Davey, 46:Nov86-115
   N. Gray, 39:Jun86-437
   R. Winter, 637(VS):Spring87-417
Crawford, D. The Lay of the Land.
   D. Leimbach, 441:11Jan87-18
Crawford, E. The Beginnings of the Nobel
   Institution.
   H. Petroski, 579(SAQ):Summer86-308
Crawford, J.W. M. Tullius Cicero: the Lost
   and Unpublished Orations.*
   A.E. Douglas, 313:Vol76-334
Crawford, M. Lords of the Plain.
   T. Pilkington, 649(WAL):Feb87-353
Crawford, T. Walter Scott.*
   J.H. Alexander, 677(YES):Vol16-231
Crawshaw, B.E. & others. Jouez le jeu!
   J.J. Smith, 207(FR):Apr87-735
Crean, J.E., Jr. & others. Deutsche
   Sprache und Landeskunde.* (2nd ed)
   P.F. Dvorak, 399(MLJ):Autumn86-311
Creed, J.L. - see Lactantius
Creel, B.L. The Religious Poetry of Jorge
   de Montemayor.
   S. Hernández-Araico, 345:Feb86-122

Creeley, R. Memories.
   R. Pybus, 565:Spring86-71
Creeley, R. Memory Gardens.
   S. Scobie, 376:Dec86-139
Creighton, J.V. Margaret Drabble.
   W.H., 148:Autumn86-118
Cremona, V. La poesia civile di Orazio.*
   J. den Boeft, 394:Vol39fasc3/4-515
Crepeau, P. Parole et Sagesse.
   C. Taylor, 292(JAF):Jul/Sep86-332
Crespo, A. - see Duque de Rivas
Cresswell, M.J. Structured Meanings.
   K. Allan, 350:Mar87-195
   W.D. Hart, 518:Oct86-231
Crevel, R. Difficult Death.
   H. Davies, 441:4Jan87-14
van Creveld, M. Command in War.
   A.C., 185:Jan87-509
Crews, F. Skeptical Engagements.
   C. Baldick, 617(TLS):1-12Nov87-1217
Crews, H. All We Need of Hell.
   R. Banks, 441:1Feb87-9
   442(NY):23Feb87-135
Crichton, M. Sphere.
   R. McKinley, 441:12Jul87-18
Crichton, R. - see Smyth, E.
Crick, B. - see Orwell, G.
Crick, B. & J. Ferns - see Whalley, G.
Crickillon, J. L'Indien de la Gare du
   Nord.
   J. Decock, 207(FR):Apr87-722
Criddle, J.D. & T.B. Mam. To Destroy You
   Is No Loss.
   B. Crossette, 441:2Aug87-8
Crider, B. Shotgun Saturday Night.
   N. Callendar, 441:27Dec87-13
Crisell, A. Understanding Radio.
   L. Taylor, 362:12Feb87-25
Crisp, N.J. In the Long Run.
   G. Krist, 441:26Jul87-17
Crispin, K. The Dingo Baby Case.
   362:19Nov87-37
Crispolti, E. Il futurismo e la moda.
   R. Cardinal, 617(TLS):9-15Oct87-1099
Crist, L.L. - see Davis, J.
Crist, T.J. - see Wing, D.
Cristescu, S. Descintece din Cornova-
   Basarabia.
   M. Bratulescu, 292(JAF):Jul/Sep86-336
Cristofani, M., ed. Civiltà degli Etrus-
   chi.
   N. Spivey, 313:Vol76-281
Critchley, J. Heseltine.
   J. Campbell, 617(TLS):4-11Sep87-944
   G. Kaufman, 362:3Sep87-30
"Critica testuale ed esegesi del testo."
   G. Roques, 553(RLiR):Jan-Jun86-198
"La Critique artistique, un genre littér-
   aire."
   P. Chardin, 549(RLC):Jan-Mar86-91
Cro, S. Realidad y utopía en el descubri-
   miento y conquista de la América Hispana
   (1492-1682).
   P.T. Bradley, 86(BHS):Jul86-301
   R. Chang-Rodríguez, 593:Spring86-84
Crocker, D.A. Praxis and Democratic
   Socialism.*
   R. Riemer, 488:Dec86-523
Croft, P.J. - see Sidney, R.
de la Croix, H. & R.G. Tansey. Gardner's
   Art through the Ages. (8th ed)
   W.C. Archer, 709:Spring87-188

Croke, B. & A. Emmett, eds. History and
Historians in Late Antiquity.*
    R.J. Penella, 124:May–Jun87–391
Croll, E., D. Davin & P. Kane, eds.
China's One–Child Family Policy.
    J. Wasserstrom, 293(JASt):Aug86–813
Crombie, W. Discourse and Language Learn-
ing.
    L. Woytak, 399(MLJ):Winter86–433
Crompton, D. A View from the Spire.* (J.
Briggs, ed)
    E.F. Shields, 529(QQ):Autumn86–685
    H.H. Watts, 395(MFS):Summer86–321
Crompton, L. Byron and Greek Love.*
    V.A. De Luca, 627(UTQ):Summer87–575
    S. Kleinberg, 536(Rev):Vol8–139
    L.A. Marchand, 340(KSJ):Vol35–190
    P.L. Thorslev, Jr., 661(WC):Autumn86–
    229
Crone, P. Meccan Trade and the Rise of
Islam.
    R. Irwin, 617(TLS):11–17Sep87–990
Crone, P. & M. Hinds. God's Caliph.
    F.M. Donner, 617(TLS):3Jul87–727
Cronin, A.K. Great Power Politics and the
Struggle Over Austria, 1945–1955.
    639(VQR):Autumn86–121
Crooke, W. – see Yule, H. & A.C. Burrell
Cropper, E. The Ideal of Painting.
    J. Gash, 59:Dec86–516
    J. Montagu, 90:Mar86–222
    C.R. Puglisi, 551(RenQ):Summer86–309
Cros, E. Théorie et pratique sociocri-
tiques.
    M–P. Malcuzynski, 107(CRCL):Jun86–265
Crosby, A.W. Ecological Imperialism.*
    D. Arnold, 617(TLS):27Feb87–208
Crosby, E.U., C.J. Bishko & R.L. Kellogg.
Medieval Studies.
    A. Gier, 72:Band223Heft2–364
Crosby, J. One Touch of Shakespeare.
(J.W. Velz & F.N. Teague, eds)
    T. Hawkes, 617(TLS):10Apr87–390
Cross, A.G., ed. Russia and the West in
the Eighteenth Century.
    J. Cracraft, 550(RusR):Jan86–69
Cross, A.G. The Russian Theme in English
Literature from the Sixteenth Century to
1980.
    P.J. O'Meara, 402(MLR):Oct87–1048
Cross, C.W. Magister ludens.
    K.J. Campbell, 221(GQ):Winter86–128
    G. Gillespie, 402(MLR):Oct86–1038
Cross, N. The Common Writer.*
    I. Britain, 637(VS):Spring87–425
    S. Gill, 155:Summer86–110
    L. James, 635(VPR):Winter86–159
"Cross Currents." (Vols 1, 2 & 4) (L.
Matejka & B. Stolz, eds)
    R.B. Pynsent, 279:Vol33–131
"Cross Currents." (Vol 3) (L. Matejka & B.
Stolz, eds)
    R.B. Pynsent, 279:Vol33–131
    R.B. Pynsent, 402(MLR):Jul86–816
Crossley, C. Musset: "Lorenzaccio."*
    W. Moser, 535(RHL):Mar–Apr86–297
    K. Wren, 402(MLR):Apr86–487
Crossley, C. Edgar Quinet (1803–1875).*
    S. Bernard–Griffiths, 535(RHL):Sep–
    Oct86–932
Crossley–Holland, K. British Folk Tales.
    J. Westwood, 617(TLS):13–19Nov87–1261

Crossley–Holland, K., ed. The Oxford Book
of Travel Verse.*
    P. Levi, 493:Oct86–37
Crossley–Holland, K. Waterslain and Other
Poems.*
    H. Lomas, 364:Jul86–86
    L. Sail, 493:Oct86–46
"El Crotalón." (Vol 1)
    J. Weiss, 86(BHS):Jul86–271
Crouch, M. & R. Porter, eds & trans.
Understanding Soviet Politics through
Literature.*
    J.R. Howlett, 402(MLR):Oct86–1052
    O. Matich, 550(RusR):Jan86–61
Crouzet, F. The First Industrialists.
    T. Kemp, 83:Autumn86–237
Crouzet, M. Nature et société chez
Stendhal.
    P. Berthier, 605(SC):15Oct86–56
    C.J. Stivale, 446(NCFS):Fall–Winter
    86/87–191
    E.J. Talbot, 210(FrF):May86–239
    C. Weiand, 547(RF):Band98Heft3/4–443
Crouzet, M. La Poétique de Stendhal.
    L. Le Guillou, 535(RHL):Mar–Apr86–301
Crow, J. – see Chappuzeau, S.
Crow, J.A. Spain. (3rd ed)
    F. Nuessel, 399(MLJ):Spring86–84
Crow, T.E. Painters and Public Life in
Eighteenth–Century Paris.*
    P.V. Conroy, Jr., 207(FR):Mar87–580
    J.E. Mitchell, 173(ECS):Summer87–475
    J. Sweetman, 324:Dec86–79
    R. Wrigley, 59:Sep86–380
Crowe, M.J. The Extraterrestrial Life
Debate 1750–1900.
    J. North, 617(TLS):23Jan87–75
Crowley, E.T. & H.E. Sheppard, eds. Acro-
nyms, Initialisms, and Abbreviations
Dictionary. (9th ed)
    K.B. Harder, 424:Mar86–116
Crowley, E.T. & H.E. Sheppard, eds. Inter-
national Acronyms, Initialisms, and
Abbreviations Dictionary.
    K.B. Harder, 424:Sep86–333
Crowley, J. AEgypt.
    J. Clute, 441:3May87–9
    J. Peake, 617(TLS):20–26Nov87–1274
Crowley, J.W. The Black Heart's Truth.*
    K.E. Eble, 27(AL):Oct86–447
    T.A. Gullason, 395(MFS):Summer86–249
    A. Habegger, 432(NEQ):Jun86–294
    K. Vanderbilt, 26(ALR):Fall86–89
Crowther, P. – see Perelman, S.J.
Crozier, A. & T. Longville, eds. A Various
Act.
    J. Harding, 617(TLS):18–24Dec87–1394
Crozier, B., ed. The Grenada Documents.
    T. Thorndike, 617(TLS):27Nov–3Dec87–
    1313
Crozier, M. Etat modeste, Etat moderne.
    J–F. Revel, 176:Nov87–40
Cruciani, F. Teatro nel Rinascimento, Roma
1450–1550.
    M. Lorch, 551(RenQ):Autumn86–518
Crucitti Ullrich, F.B. – see Cecchi, E. &
M. Praz
Cruden, S. Scottish Medieval Churches.
    H.G. Slade, 617(TLS):12Jun87–639
Cruickshank, C. SOE in Scandinavia.
    M.R.D. Foot, 617(TLS):13Feb87–169

Cruickshank, D, ed. Timeless Architecture: 1.
  P. Smithson, 46:Apr86-119
Cruikshank, B. Filipiniana in Madrid.
  B.L. Fenner, 293(JASt):Feb86-445
Crump, G.M., ed. Approaches to Teaching Milton's "Paradise Lost."
  L.J. Leff, 365:Spring/Summer86-159
Crump, R.W. Charlotte and Emily Brontë, 1846-1915.
  T.J. Winnifrith, 677(YES):Vol16-326
Cryle, P.M. The Thematics of Commitment.
  M. Adereth, 402(MLR):Oct87-974
  B. Nelson, 208(FS):Jul86-372
Crystal, D., ed. Linguistic Controversies.
  B. Korte, 402(MLR):Jan86-154
Crystal, D. Linguistic Encounters with Language Handicap.
  F. Nuessel, 361:Jul86-287
Csoma de Kőrös, A. Collected Works of Alexander Csoma de Kőrös. (J. Terjék, ed)
  J.W. de Jong, 259(IIJ):Apr86-150
Cuartero Sancho, M.P. Fuentes clásicas de la literatura paremiológica española del siglo XVI.*
  J. Chomarat, 555:Vol59fasc2-346
Cubillo de Aragón, A. Auto sacramental de "La muerte de Frislán."* (M.F. Schmidt, ed)
  A.A. Heathcote, 402(MLR):Jan87-223
Cudós, J.L.A. - see under Alegre Cudós, J.L.
Cuesta Dutari, N. Historia de la invencion del analisis infinitesimal y de su introduccion en España.
  E. Knobloch, 706:Band18Heft1-113
Cuevas García, C. - see de Zabaleta, J.
Cugusi, P. Evoluzione e forme dell'epistolografia latina nella tarda repubblica e nei primi due secoli dell'impero.*
  J. André, 555:Vol59fasc2-318
Culicover, P.W. & W.K. Wilkins. Locality in Linguistic Theory.*
  D.W. Lightfoot, 297(JL):Sep86-480
Cullen, E.J. Our War.
  M. Chernoff, 441:21Jun87-38
Cullen, P. & T.P. Roche, Jr. - see "Spenser Studies"
Culler, A.D. The Victorian Mirror of History.*
  G.A. Cevasco, 324:Feb87-252
  J.P. Farrell, 637(VS):Spring87-430
  G.H. Ford, 191(ELN):Dec86-82
  M. Stone, 150(DR):Fall86-354
  H.W., 636(VP):Autumn86-346
  639(VQR):Summer86-81
Culler, J. On Deconstruction.*
  J. Patrick, 627(UTQ):Winter86/87-338
Culleton, B. April Raintree. Spirit of the White Bison.
  A. Cameron, 102(CanL):Spring86-164
Culley, M., ed. A Day at a Time.*
  V.W. Beauchamp, 357:Fall86-62
Cullinan, M. Susan Ferrier.
  W.A. Craik, 571(ScLJ):Summer86-13
Cullingford, E., ed. Yeats: Poems, 1919-1935.* [shown in prev under Yeats, W.B.]
  D. Kiberd, 617(TLS):13Feb87-166
  A. Swarbrick, 148:Autumn86-109
Cummings, E.E. Etcetera. Hist Whist.
  R. Pybus, 565:Spring86-71

Cummings, M. & R. Simmons. The Language of Literature.
  P-G. Boucé, 189(EA):Jul-Sep86-369
Cummins, J. The Whole Truth.
  R. McDowell, 249(HudR):Winter87-680
Cummins, J.S. & A. Soons - see de Sigüenza y Góngora, C.
Cummins, R. The Nature of Psychological Explanation.*
  R. Van Gulick, 486:Dec86-616
  J. Leiber, 543:Sep86-109
  K. Neander, 63:Mar86-104
Cunningham, N.E., Jr. In Pursuit of Reason.
  R.J. Margolis, 441:14Jun87-29
Cunningham, V., ed. Spanish Front.*
  B. Knox, 453(NYRB):26Mar87-21
  E. Mendelson, 617(TLS):16Jan87-63
Cupers, J-L. Aldous Huxley et la musique.
  J. Aplin, 410(M&L):Oct86-421
  A. Dommergues, 189(EA):Apr-Jun87-236
"Curial and Guelfa." (P. Waley, trans)
  J.N.H. Lawrance, 382(MAE):1986/1-148
"Der curieuse Passagier."
  M. Maurer, 224(GRM):Band36Heft1-103
Curl, D.W. Mizner's Florida.
  J.V. Iovine, 45:Feb86-77
  S.K. Robinson, 658:Spring86-92
Curl, J.S. The Life and Work of Henry Roberts, 1803-1876.
  R. Kimball, 505:Feb86-162
Curl, J.S. The Londonderry Plantation 1609-1914.
  A. Ling, 324:Jul87-613
  E. McParland, 617(TLS):12Jun87-639
Curley, D. Living With Snakes.
  H. Anderson, 573(SSF):Spring86-215
  G. Kearns, 249(HudR):Spring86-133
  D. Madden, 598(SoR):Summer87-729
Curley, D. Mummy.
  P-L. Adams, 61:Apr87-91
  R. Plunket, 441:26Apr87-11
Curley, E. - see Spinoza, B.
Curnow, A. The Loop in Lone Kauri Road.
  J. Penberthy, 617(TLS):31Jul87-823
"Current Research in Britain (1986): The Humanities."
  S. Collini, 617(TLS):3Apr87-349
Current-Garcia, E. The American Short Story Before 1850.
  D.K. Jeffrey, 577(SHR):Fall86-398
  R.F. Marler, Jr., 27(AL):Summer86-433
  P.T. Nolan, 573(SSF):Winter86-123
Currie, E. Confronting Crime.
  T.C. Holyoke, 42(AR):Summer86-376
  C. Jencks, 453(NYRB):12Feb87-33
  639(VQR):Spring86-59
Curry, P., ed. Astrology, Science and Society.
  J. Henry, 617(TLS):27Nov-3Dec87-1316
Curteis, I. The Falklands Play.
  M. Deas, 617(TLS):15May87-512
Curtin, P.D. Cross-Cultural Trade in World History.
  E.L. Will, 124:Sep-Oct86-53
Curtis, A. & J. Whitehead, eds. W. Somerset Maugham: The Critical Heritage.
  J. Bayley, 617(TLS):23-29Oct87-1155
Curtis, D. Descartes: "Discours de la Méthode."
  E. Jacobs, 208(FS):Jan86-68
  C. Smith, 402(MLR):Apr86-481

Curtis, J., ed. Fifty Years of Mesopotamian Discovery.
  H. Weiss, 318(JAOS):Apr/Jun85-327
Curtis, J. Nush-i Jan III.
  O.W. Muscarella, 318(JAOS):Oct/Dec85-729
Curtis, J.M. Solzhenitsyn's Traditional Imagination.*
  C.N. Lee, 574(SEEJ):Spring86-115
  M. Nicholson, 402(MLR):Oct86-1051
Curtis, L.A. The Elusive Daniel Defoe.*
  P. Alkon, 173(ECS):Winter86/87-220
  P-G. Boucé, 189(EA):Jul-Sep86-341
  A. Varney, 447(N&Q):Dec85-528
Curtis, R.L., ed. Le roman de Tristan en prose. (Vol 3)
  P.E. Bennett, 402(MLR):Apr87-468
  A. Scolari, 379(MedR):Apr86-125
Curtis, T. Selected Poems 1970-1985.
  H. Lomas, 364:Dec86/Jan87-127
  N. Murray, 617(TLS):24Jul87-805
Curtis, W.J.R. Le Corbusier.
  W.H. Jordy, 617(TLS):13Feb87-151
Curtler, H., ed. What is Art?
  H. Osborne, 289:Spring86-97
Cush, G. God Help the Queen.
  M. Casserley, 617(TLS):24Jul87-802
Cushman, K. D.H. Lawrence at Work.
  J. Donnerstag, 38:Band104Heft1/2-265
Cushman, S. William Carlos Williams and the Meanings of Measure.*
  C.S. Abbott, 599:Spring86-113
  M.B., 295(JML):Nov86-553
  G. Sibley, 27(AL):May86-275
  639(VQR):Spring86-44
Cutler, A. & R.D. Ladd, eds. Prosody.*
  R. Bannert, 685(ZDL):2/1986-245
Cutrer, T.W. Parnassus on the Mississippi.*
  J.E. Brown, 392:Winter85/86-79
Cuvelier, E. Thomas Lodge.
  A.F. Kinney, 551(RenQ):Winter86-794
Cuvillier, J-P. L'Allemagne médiévale. (Vol 2)
  S. Rowan, 589:Jan86-131
Czartoryski, P. - see Copernicus, N.
Czigány, L. The Oxford History of Hungarian Literature from the Earliest Times to the Present.
  G.F. Cushing, 402(MLR):Jan87-270
  J. Pál, 549(RLC):Jul-Sep86-347
Czyba, L. Mythes et idéologie de la femme dans les romans de Flaubert.*
  G. Sagnes, 535(RHL):Mar-Apr86-308

d'Ablis, G. - see under Geoffroy d'Ablis
Dabney, L.M. - see Wilson, E.
Dabydeen, D. Hogarth's Blacks.
  H.M. Atherton, 566:Spring87-216
Dabydeen, D. Slave Song.
  A. Shucard, 125:Fall85-111
D'Accone, F.A. The History of a Baroque Opera.
  M. Boyd, 415:May86-277
  W. Dean, 410(M&L):Jul86-312
  S. Mamy, 537:Vol72No2-291
Dacey, P. & D. Jauss, eds. Strong Measures.
  B. King, 598(SoR):Winter87-224
  P. Wild, 219(GaR):Winter86-1052
  639(VQR):Summer86-101

Da Costa Fontes, M. Romanceiro Da Ilha De S. Jorge.
  I. Cardozo-Freeman, 292(JAF):Jul/Sep86-334
Dadié, B.B. The Black Cloth.
  R.F. Thompson, 441:28Jun87-9
Dadson, T.J., ed. "Avisos a un cortesano."
  J. Gornall, 402(MLR):Jul87-761
Dadson, T.J. The Genoese in Spain: Gabriel Bocángel y Unzueta (1603-1658).*
  G.A. Davies, 86(BHS):Oct86-371
  A. Mackay, 402(MLR):Oct86-1020
Daemmrich, H.S. Wilhelm Raabe.
  R.L. Jamison, 406:Spring86-111
Al-Daffa, A.A. & J.J. Stroyls. Studies in the Exact Sciences in Medieval Islam.
  J.P. Hogendijk, 84:Dec86-516
Dagenhardt, C. Dark Leaves.
  G.C. Little, 404:Autumn86-55
Dagerman, S. Notre besoin de consolation est impossible à rassasier.
  T. Cordellier, 450(NRF):Mar86-108
Dagognet, F. Le nombre et le lieu.
  J. Ecole, 192(EP):Apr-Jun86-244
D'Agostino, J. Une Femme si sage.
  L. Rosmarin, 207(FR):Mar87-556
Dagron, G. Constantinople imaginaire.
  B. Baldwin, 589:Apr86-388
  A. Cameron, 303(JoHS):Vol106-266
D'Aguiar, F. Mama Dot.*
  H. Buckingham, 565:Summer86-64
Dahan, G. - see Guillaume de Bourges
Dahl, N.O. Practical Reason, Aristotle, and Weakness of the Will.*
  M.L. Homiak, 482(PhR):Jul86-467
Dahl, P., ed. Om at skrive den dansk ånds historie.
  S.A. Aarnes, 172(Edda):1986/4-374
Dahl, R. Going Solo.*
  442(NY):12Jan87-104
Dahlhaus, C. Realism in Nineteenth-Century Music.
  C. Hatch, 451:Fall86-187
  R. Hollinrake, 410(M&L):Apr86-212
Dahlhaus, C. Schoenberg and the New Music.
  P. Griffiths, 617(TLS):25-31Dec87-1440
Dahlie, H. Varieties of Exile.
  R. Smith, 150(DR):Fall86-377
Dahood, R., ed. The Avowing of King Arthur.
  R. Hanna 3d, 589:Jan86-132
Dahrendorf, E. - see Schapiro, L.
Daiches, D. Robert Fergusson.
  J.H. Alexander, 677(YES):Vol16-231
  D.A. Low, 447(N&Q):Mar85-132
Daiches, D. God and the Poets.*
  P. Levi, 541(RES):May86-295
  H.J. Levine, 639(VQR):Spring86-366
  R.C. Murfin, 301(JEGP):Jan86-131
Daiches, D. Literature and Gentility in Scotland.
  J.H. Alexander, 677(YES):Vol16-250
Daikichi, I. - see under Irokawa Daikichi
Dailey, J. Heiress.
  B.A. Bannon, 441:14Jun87-28
Dailly, C. & B. Kotchy. Propos sur la littérature négro-africaine.
  J. Ngaté, 538(RAL):Winter86-565
Dakers, C. The Countryside at War 1914-18.
  P. Parker, 362:10Dec87-31

Dal Co, F. & G. Mazzariol, eds. Carlo
Scarpa: The Complete Works.
    P. Tabor, 46:Sep86-107
Dal Corso, M. & L. Borghi Cedrini, eds.
Vertuz e altri scritti (manoscritto Ge
206).
    M.R. Harris, 589:Jan86-134
d'Alcripe, P. La nouvelle fabrique des
excellents traicts de verité.* (F.
Joukovsky, ed)
    C. Clark, 208(FS):Jan86-63
    M. Magnien, 535(RHL):Mar-Apr86-259
Dale, P. Narrow Straits.
    S. Romer, 617(TLS):3Apr87-364
    D. Stanford, 4:Spring86-39
Dale, P. & L. Poms. English Pronunciation
for Spanish Speakers: Vowels.
    R.M. Carter, 399(MLJ):Autumn86-330
Dale, P.N. The Myth of Japanese Unique-
ness.
    B. Moeran, 617(TLS):17Apr87-407
Dale, S.F. Islamic Society on the South
Asian Frontier.
    A.S. Asani, 318(JAOS):Oct/Dec85-750
Dalen, A. Skognamålet.
    E. Haugen, 563(SS):Spring86-197
van Dalen, D. Logic and Structure. (2nd
ed)
    M. Fitting, 316:Sep86-826
Daleski, H.M. The Divided Heroine.*
    M. Allott, 541(RES):Feb86-130
    M. Burgan, 301(JEGP):Apr86-278
Daleski, H.M. Unities.
    D. David, 637(VS):Winter87-279
    J. Halperin, 395(MFS):Summer86-300
    E. Langland, 594:Fall86-322
D'Alessandro, J.M.E. Hues of Mutability.
    J. Stokes, 677(YES):Vol16-338
Daley, H. This Small Cloud.
    P.D. James, 617(TLS):27Feb87-205
    P. Parker, 362:19Feb87-24
Daley, J. All Good Men.
    T.J. Binyon, 617(TLS):21Aug87-910
    T.J. Binyon, 617(TLS):9-15Oct87-1124
Daley, S. High Cotton.
    S. Bolotin, 441:5Jul87-8
Dallaire, L., ed. Edward Sapir's Corre-
spondence.
    V. Golla, 269(IJAL):Apr86-196
Dällenbach, L. & J. Ricardou, eds. Prob-
lèmes actuels de la lecture.
    G. Cesbron, 356(LR):Feb86-67
Dalli'Acqua, M. Correggio e il suo tempo.
    C. Gould, 39:Jan86-67
Dallin, A. Black Box, KAL 007 and the
Superpowers.
    R. Klein & W.B. Warner, 153:Spring86-2
Dallmayr, F. Language and Politics.
    R.B. Gregg, 480(P&R):Vol19No3-205
    J.S., 185:Oct86-293
Dalsimer, K. Female Adolescence.
    E.C.R., 295(JML):Nov86-405
    D.W. Ross, 395(MFS):Winter86-700
Dalton, H. The Political Diary of Hugh
Dalton, 1918-40, 1945-60. (B. Pimlott,
ed)
    P. Clarke, 617(TLS):6Feb87-130
Daly, A. Plays by Augustin Daly. (D.B.
Wilmeth & R. Cullen, eds)
    B. Murphy, 536(Rev):Vol8-197
Daly, I. A Singular Attraction.
    D. Singmaster, 617(TLS):13-19Nov87-
1248

Daly, J.P. — see Rolle, R.
Daly, L.W. — see Philoponus, J.
Daly, P.M. & V. Callahan, with S. Cuttler —
see Alciati, A.
Daly, P.M., with S. Cuttler — see Alciati,
A.
Dalyell, T. Misrule.
    J. Campbell, 617(TLS):5Jun87-597
Dalzell, R.F., Jr. Enterprising Elite.
    N.W. Aldrich, Jr., 441:25Oct87-42
Damiani, B.M. "La Diana" of Montemayor as
Social and Religious Teaching.*
    E.R. Primavera, 400(MLN):Mar86-432
Damiani, P. Die Briefe des Petrus Damiani.
(Vol I) (K. Reindel, ed)
    K.F. Morrison, 589:Jan86-138
Damico, H. Beowulf's Wealhtheow and the
Valkyrie Tradition.*
    D.G. Calder, 301(JEGP):Jul86-441
    J. Harris, 589:Apr86-400
D'Amico, R. & F. Gozzi. La Pinacoteca
Civica di Pieve di Cento.
    C. Gould, 39:Jan86-67
D'Amico, R. & M. Medica. Vitale da Bolo-
gna.
    R. Gibbs, 90:Nov86-830
Damisch, H. Fenêtre jaune cadmium ou les
dessous de la peinture.
    Y-A. Bois, 98:May86-487
Dammers, R.H. Richard Steele.
    A. Graziano, 677(YES):Vol16-261
    M. Jones, 447(N&Q):Mar85-122
Damrosch, L., Jr. God's Plot and Man's
Stories.
    639(VQR):Winter86-16
Damsholt, N. Kvindebilledet i dansk
højmiddelalder.
    J.M. Jochens, 563(SS):Summer86-317
    E. Mundal, 172(Edda):1986/4-370
Dan, U. Blood Libel.
    K. Evans, 441:5Apr87-13
Dan-Cohen, M. Rights, Persons, and Organi-
zations.
    J.R.D., 185:Jul87-900
Dana, R., ed. Against the Grain.
    G.W. Clift, 389(MQ):Spring87-416
Dance, D.C. Folklore from Contemporary
Jamaicans.
    G.K. Zalazar, 37:Mar-Apr86-56
Danchev, A. Very Special Relationship.
    D. Reynolds, 617(TLS):3Apr87-366
Dancourt, F.C. Le Chevalier à la mode.
(R.H. Crawshaw, ed)
    B. Norman, 475:Vol13No24-379
Dancy, J. An Introduction to Contemporary
Epistemology.
    A. Avramides, 393(Mind):Apr86-260
    M. McGinn, 479(PhQ):Oct86-574
    P.K. Moser, 543:Sep86-110
    T.E. Wilkerson, 518:Jul86-161
Danek, J. Etoiles et horizon du domicile.
    M. Renault, 154:Summer86-371
Daneshvari, A., ed. Essays in Islamic Art
and Architecture (In Honor of Katharina
Otto-Dorn).
    L. Komaroff, 318(JAOS):Oct/Dec85-751
Danesi, M. Loanwords and Phonological
Methodology.
    J-D. Choi, 350:Jun87-451
Dangel, E. Wiederholung als Schicksal.
    W. Nehring, 680(ZDP):Band105Heft4-630
    M. Swales, 402(MLR):Apr87-522

D'Angelo, R.M. Fra trimetro e senario giambico.*
   C.J. Ruijgh, 394:Vol39fasc3/4-432
Daniel, A. - see under Arnaut Daniel
Daniel, C., ed-in-chief. Chronicle of the 20th Century.
   O. Fuerbringer, 441:13Dec87-28
Daniel, E.R. - see Joachim of Fiore
Daniel, E.V. Fluid Signs.
   M. Moffatt, 293(JASt):Feb86-420
   P.B. Zarrilli, 615(TJ):Dec86-493
Daniel, F. Discovery of the North.
   P. Puxley, 99:Aug/Sep86-25
Daniel, L.J. Cannoneers in Gray.
   H. Hattaway, 9(AlaR):Jul86-222
Daniel, N. Heroes and Saracens.*
   D. Evans, 447(N&Q):Jun85-258
   P.H. Stablein, 589:Jul86-729
Daniel, P. Standing at the Crossroads.
   639(VQR):Autumn86-118
Daniel, S.H. John Toland.*
   566:Autumn86-81
Daniel, V.J. - see Éluard, P.
Daniels, N. Just Health Care.
   E. Telfer, 518:Jul86-187
Daniels, R.V. Russia.
   W.G. Rosenberg, 550(RusR):Jul86-338
Danielson, D.R. Milton's Good God.*
   R. Lejosne, 402(MLR):Jul86-717
Danilova, A. Choura.
   J. Dunning, 441:4Jan87-13
Dankleff, R. Westerns.*
   B. Christophersen, 50(ArQ):Winter86-370
Dankoff, R. - see Hājib, Y.K.
Danky, J.P., M.E. Hady & A. Bowles, eds. Native American Periodicals and Newspapers 1928-1982.*
   B. Katz, 87(BB):Jun86-115
Danlos, L. Génération automatique de textes en langues naturelles.
   S. Cumming, 350:Mar87-176
Danly, R.L. In the Shade of Spring Leaves.
   B.C. Mckillop, 302:Vol22No1-108
Dann, J.V. and J., eds. In the Field of Fire.
   D. Bradley, 441:3May87-25
Dann, P. Mermaids.*
   442(NY):19Jan87-92
Danner, R. Patterns of Irony in the Fables of La Fontaine.
   H. Peyre, 207(FR):Oct86-119
   J.M. Zarucchi, 210(FrF):Sep86-373
Danon, R. Work in the English Novel.*
   I. Williams, 637(VS):Summer87-557
Danson, L., ed. On "King Lear."
   F.D. Hoeniger, 402(MLR):Apr86-442
Dantanus, U. Brian Friel.
   C. Murray, 272(IUR):Spring86-84
Dante Alighieri. Dante's Inferno.* (T. Phillips, trans and illustrator)
   J. Burr, 39:Aug86-143
   639(VQR):Spring86-62
Dante Alighieri. Dante's "Purgatory."* (M. Musa, trans)
   G. Costa, 545(RPh):Nov86-215
Dante Alighieri. La Divina Commedia: Inferno. (A. Vallone & L. Scorrano, eds)
   R. Wis, 439(NM):1986/1-155
Dante Alighieri. The Divine Comedy.* (Vol 1: Inferno; Vol 2: Purgatorio) (A. Mandelbaum, trans)
   C.S. Ross, 275(IQ):Winter86-59

Dante Alighieri. The Divine Comedy.* (Vol 3: Paradiso.) (A. Mandelbaum, trans)
   M. Chiarenza, 276:Autumn86-300
   R.H. Lansing, 589:Apr86-495
   C.S. Ross, 275(IQ):Winter86-59
Dante Alighieri. Il "Fiore" e il "Detto d'Amore" attribuibili a Dante Alighieri.* (G. Contini, ed)
   L. Lazzarini, 379(MedR):Apr86-133
"Dante Studies." (Vol 1) (A. Caso, ed)
   G. Costa, 545(RPh):Nov86-215
Dantinne, J. La splendeur de l'inébranlable (Akṣobhyavyūha). (Vol 1)
   J.W. de Jong, 259(IIJ):Jan86-60
Danto, A.C. Narration and Knowledge.
   L.B. Cebik, 125:Summer86-429
Danto, A.C. The Philosophical Disenfranchisement of Art.
   P. Guyer, 441:1Feb87-23
   G. Wilson, 617(TLS):9Jan87-28
Danto, A.C. The State of the Art.
   W. Feaver, 617(TLS):24Jul87-797
   F. Schier, 441:5Apr87-21
D'Antuono, N.L. Boccaccio's "Novelle" in the Theater of Lope de Vega.*
   V. Dixon, 86(BHS):Apr86-165
Danziger, S.H. & D.H. Weinberg, eds. Fighting Poverty.
   639(VQR):Autumn86-131
Dao, B. - see under Bei Dao
Daphinoff, D. - see Echlin, E.
D'Aponte, M.G. Teatro religioso e rituale della penisola sorrentina e la costiera amalfitana.
   F. Cerreta, 276:Summer86-187
Darby, P. Three Faces of Imperialism.
   M. Beloff, 176:Jul/Aug87-30
Dardess, J.W. Confucianism and Autocracy.*
   F.W. Mote, 244(HJAS):Jun86-302
Dargan, J. Balzac and the Drama of Perspective.
   L.R. Schehr, 446(NCFS):Fall-Winter 86/87-195
   G. Woollen, 402(MLR):Oct87-965
d'Argencourt, L. & others. William Bouguereau, 1825-1905.
   R. Thomson, 59:Mar86-108
Darío, R. Azul. (A.P. Debicki & M.J. Doudoroff, eds)
   J.A. Feustle, Jr., 238:Dec86-881
Darío, R. Prosa profanas y otros poemas. (I.M. Zuleta, ed)
   R.A. Cardwell, 402(MLR):Jul86-773
Darmon, A. Les corps immatériels.
   A. Reix, 542:Oct-Dec86-525
Darst, D.H. Imitatio.
   F.A. de Armas, 304(JHP):Winter86-189
Darvill, T. Prehistoric Britain.
   A. Burl, 617(TLS):2-8Oct87-1086
Darwall, S.L. Impartial Reason.*
   O. O'Neill, 311(JP):Jan86-60
Darwin, C. The Correspondence of Charles Darwin. (Vol 1) (F. Burkhardt & S. Smith & others, eds)
   D.J. Kevles, 442(NY):7Dec87-171
   G. Levine, 637(VS):Winter87-253
Darwin, C. The Correspondence of Charles Darwin. (Vol 2) (F. Burkhardt & S. Smith, eds)
   J.W. Burrow, 617(TLS):12Jun87-623
   D.J. Kevles, 442(NY):7Dec87-171
Darwin, J. The Triumphs of Big Ben.
   A.C. Davies, 324:Sep87-784

Das, R.P. – see Neisser, W.

Dasenbrock, R.W. The Literary Vorticism of Ezra Pound and Wyndham Lewis.*
  M.B., 295(JML):Nov86-363
  T. Materer, 301(JEGP):Apr86-298
  W. Sypher, 569(SR):Summer86-497

Dash, I.G. Wooing, Wedding, and Power.
  B. Hatlen, 536(Rev):Vol8-241

Dasilva, F., A. Blasi & D. Dees. The Sociology of Music.*
  C.C. Ford, 89(BJA):Spring86-187

Daskalova, L. & others, eds. Narodna proza ot Blagoevgradski okrŭg.
  I. Köhler–Zülch, 196:Band27Heft1/2-101

Dassmann, E. & K.S. Frank, eds. Pietas.
  J–M. Rondeau, 555:Vol59fasc2-350

Dassonville, M. Ronsard: Etude historique et littéraire.* (Vol 4)
  E. Armstrong, 551(RenQ):Summer86-319
  P. Ford, 208(FS):Jul86-325
  F. Joukovsky, 535(RHL):Jul–Aug86-723

d'Aubigné, A. Histoire Universelle. (Vol 3) (A. Thierry, ed)
  I.D. McFarlane, 402(MLR):Jul87-735
  R. Zuber, 535(RHL):Jul–Aug86-733

Daudet, A. Lettres de mon moulin. (D. Bergez, ed)
  F. Garavini, 535(RHL):Jul–Aug86-777

Daudet, A. Lettres de mon moulin. (J–H. Bornecque, ed)
  F. Garavini, 535(RHL):Mar–Apr86-318
  J.R. Williams, 207(FR):Dec86-261

Dauer, A.M. Tradition afrikanischer Blasorchester und Entstehung des Jazz.
  L. Porter, 91:Fall86-314

Daugherty, T. Desire Provoked.
  R. Loewinsohn, 441:1Feb87-24

Daugird, G. Pretty Personal.
  D.J. Enright, 617(TLS):18–24Dec87-1399

Daum, W. Ursemitische Religion.
  U. Marzolph, 196:Band27Heft3/4-336

Daunton, M.J. The Royal Mail.
  J. Pellew, 637(VS):Winter87-287

Dave, J.C. The Human Predicament in Hardy's Novels.
  R.K. Anderson, 395(MFS):Winter86-656
  K. Brady, 637(VS):Winter87-283

d'Avennes, E.P. – see under Prisse d'Avennes, E.

Davenport, G. Apples and Pears and Other Stories.
  J. Klinkowitz, 532(RCF):Spring86-216

Davenport, G. Cities on Hills.
  S.J. Adams, 106:Fall86-367

Davenport, G. Thasos and Ohio.
  639(VQR):Autumn86-134

Davenport, G. The Jules Verne Steam Balloon.
  H. Coale, 441:22Nov87-32

Davenport, M., E. Hansen & H.F. Nielsen, eds. Current Topics in English Historical Linguistics.*
  W. Elmer, 260(IF):Band91-405

Davey, F. Margaret Atwood.*
  D. Bennett, 627(UTQ):Fall86-175
  L. Irvine, 102(CanL):Winter85-120

Davey, F. The Louis Riel Organ and Piano Company.
  S. Scobie, 376:Mar86-125

Daviau, D.G. Hermann Bahr.
  W.E. Yates, 402(MLR):Jan87-253
  H. Zohn, 133:Band19Heft3/4-360

Daviau, D.G., J.B. Johns & J.B. Berlin – see Zweig, S., R. Auernheimer & R. Beer-Hofmann

David, E. Aristophanes and Athenian Society of the Early Fourth Century B.C.*
  M. Golden, 487:Summer86-242

David, E. An Omelette and a Glass of Wine.
  T. Whittaker, 529(QQ):Autumn86-547

David, J. & G. Kleiber, eds. La notion sémantico–logique de modalité.
  O. Eriksson, 209(FM):Oct86-244

David, L. & I. Bobby Kennedy.
  M. Tolchin, 441:1Mar87-20

David, R. and D. Pugsley, with F. Grivart de Kerstrat. Les Contrats en droit anglais.
  S. Dreyfus, 189(EA):Jul–Sep86-325

David, W. Hund unterm Tisch Gedanken zur Literaturkritik.
  G. Krieger, 654(WB):4/1986-695

David–Hillel, R. The Metaphysics of the Social World.
  K.S., 185:Jul87-890

Davidoff, L. & C. Hall. Family Fortunes.
  J. Burnett, 617(TLS):11–17Sep87-995

Davidson, A. Jean Rhys.
  A. Crozier, 395(MFS):Winter86-672

Davidson, A.E. Conrad's Endings.*
  B.E. Teets, 177(ELT):Vol29No1-101

Davidson, A.E. Mordecai Richler.*
  K. McSweeney, 168(ECW):Fall86-172

Davidson, A.E. – see Hildegard von Bingen

Davidson, B. Subway.
  K. Ryan, 441:1Feb87-21

Davidson, C. From Creation to Doom.*
  R. Beadle, 382(MAE):1986/2-299

Davidson, C.N. The Experimental Fictions of Ambrose Bierce.*
  M.E. Grenander, 649(WAL):Nov86-253
  B.L. St. Armand, 573(SSF):Winter86-119

Davidson, C.N. Revolution and the Word.
  J. Tompkins, 357:Spring87-49

Davidson, D. Inquiries into Truth and Interpretation.*
  S. Pradhan, 153:Spring86-66

Davidson, H. T.S. Eliot and Hermeneutics.
  W. Harmon, 569(SR):Summer86-510
  M. Moran, 27(AL):Mar86-114

Davidson, H.R.E. Katharine Briggs.
  A. Hayter, 617(TLS):12Jun87-645

Davie, D. Czeslaw Milosz and the Insufficiency of Lyric.*
  D.E. Stanford, 598(SoR):Summer87-736

Davie, M. The Titanic.*
  P–L. Adams, 61:Sep87-102
  S. Silvers, 364:Nov86-109
  442(NY):10Aug87-80

Davie, M. & S., eds. The Faber Book of Cricket.
  N. Andrew, 362:3Dec87-34
  M. Imlah, 617(TLS):26Jun87-686

Davies, A. An Annotated Critical Bibliography of Modernism.*
  M. Perloff, 402(MLR):Oct86-993

Davies, A. A Very Peculiar Practice.
  J. Barron, 362:19Nov87-31

Davies, F. – see Powys, J.C.

Davies, H. Catching the Conscience.*
  R.A. Lasseter, 569(SR):Spring86-279

Davies, H. Like Angels from a Cloud.
  J. Drury, 617(TLS):27Mar87-316

Davis, S.M. Apartheid's Rebels.
A. Cowell, 441:15Nov87-30
Davis, T.J. A Rumor of Revolt.
W.D. Jordan, 656(WMQ):Apr86-315
Davis, T.M. Faulkner's "Negro."
C. Werner, 403(MLS):Summer86-329
Davis, T.M. & T. Harris, eds. Afro-
American Writers after 1955: Dramatists
and Prose Writers.
E. Hill, 615(TJ):Oct86-383
Davis, W. The Serpent and the Rainbow.*
H.L. Goodall, Jr., 583:Winter87-215
K.G. Millar, 529(QQ):Winter86-914
Davis, W.C., with W.A. Frassanito, eds.
Touched by Fire. (Vol 2)
442(NY):16Feb87-110
Davis, W.E. The Celebrated Case of Esther
Waters.*
J. Noël, 189(EA):Jul-Sep86-375
Davis, W.E. & H.E. Gerber, eds. Thomas
Hardy. (Vol 2)
D.R. Schwarz, 177(ELT):Vol29No4-435
Davison, G., J.W. McCarty & A. McLeary,
eds. Australians: 1888.
A. Sykes, 617(TLS):27Nov-3Dec87-1322
Davison, I.H. Lloyd's.
J.H.C. Leach, 617(TLS):11-17Dec87-1372
Davison, P. Praying Wrong.*
W. Scammell, 364:Jun86-61
Davison, P., ed. Sheridan: Comedies.*
J. Hamard, 189(EA):Apr-Jun87-243
D. Mills, 157:No161-49
Davison, R. Diderot et Galiani.
A. Strugnell, 208(FS):Oct86-467
Dawe, B. Sometimes Gladness.
C. James, 617(TLS):27Nov-3Dec87-1327
Dawe, D. Organists of the City of London,
1666-1850.*
G. Reynolds, 415:Mar86-171
Dawe, G. The Lundys Letter.
M. Harmon, 272(IUR):Spring86-77
J. Lanchester, 493:Jun86-113
Dawe, G. & E. Longley, eds. Across a
Roaring Hill.
B. Dolan, 305(JIL):May86-59
Dawe, R.D. - see Sophocles
Dawes, N.M. Lalique Glass.
B. Scott, 39:Dec86-572
Dawson, A. Masterpieces of Wedgwood in the
British Museum.
G. Wills, 39:Jan86-68
Dawson, R.L. Additions to the Bibliogra-
phies of French Prose Fiction 1618-1806.
D.J. Adams, 402(MLR):Oct87-956
Day, D. Journey of the Wolf.
A. Beevor, 617(TLS):22May87-559
Day, D. The Whale War.
D. McCaig, 441:20Sep87-27
Day, G. From Fiction to the Novel.
J. Mullan, 617(TLS):24Jul87-803
Day, M.L., ed & trans. The Rise of Gawain,
Nephew of Arthur (De ortu Walwanii
nepotis Arturi).
K. Busby, 589:Oct86-913
Day, M.S. The Many Meanings of Myth.
M.E. Workman, 292(JAF):Apr/Jun86-228
Day, R.C. When in Florence.*
D. Flower, 249(HudR):Summer86-315
Day, W.P. In the Circles of Fear and
Desire.
P. Arnaud, 189(EA):Jan-Mar87-89
P. Brantlinger, 141:Spring86-220
[continued]

[continuing]
G.L. Green, 223:Fall86-329
K.P. Ljungquist, 573(SSF):Spring86-222
J.B. Twitchell, 454:Winter87-186
G.K. Wolfe, 395(MFS):Spring86-133
639(VQR):Summer86-89
"A Day in the Life of America."
A. Trachtenberg, 441:25Jan87-13
"A Day in the Life of the Soviet Union."
A. Grundberg, 441:6Dec87-21
Dayan, P. Mallarme's "Divine Transposi-
tion."
G.W. Ireland, 617(TLS):11-17Dec87-1381
Daydí-Tolson, S. Voces y ecos en la poesía
de José Angel Valente.*
D. Cañas, 240(HR):Spring86-236
Dayer, R.A. Bankers and Diplomats in
China 1917-1925.
W.K.K. Chan, 302:Vol22No1-92
Dayley, G. Rose's Story. (M. Wandor, ed)
V.M. Patraka, 385(MQR):Winter87-285
Daymond, D.M. & L.G. Monkman, eds. To-
wards a Canadian Literature. (Vol 1)
T. Ware, 150(DR):Winter85/86-566
G. Warkentin, 102(CanL):Fall86-109
Daymond, D.M. & L.G. Monkman, eds. To-
wards a Canadian Literature. (Vol 2)
T. Ware, 150(DR):Winter85/86-566
Daymond, M.J., J.U. Jacobs & M. Lenta, eds.
Momentum.
P.V. Shava, 49:Apr86-94
Dazai Osamu. Return to Tsugaru.* (J.
Westerhoven, trans)
P.I. Lyons, 293(JASt):May86-590
d'Azevedo, W.L., ed. Straight With the
Medicine.*
F. Papovich, 292(JAF):Oct/Dec86-481
Deagon, A. The Diver's Tomb.
B. Dixson, 577(SHR):Summer86-295
Deahl, J. Blue Ridge.
F.K. Robinson, 404:Summer86-42
Deahl, J. No Cold Ash.
C. Wiseman, 168(ECW):Fall86-210
Dean, I. Memory and Desire.
639(VQR):Winter86-23
Dean, J. Watershed in Europe.
L. Freedman, 441:23Aug87-19
Lord Zuckerman, 453(NYRB):7May87-42
Dean, J. & others. Full House.
S. McCarthy, 4:Spring86-57
Dean, W. & J.M. Knapp. Handel's Operas:
1704-1726.
E.T. Harris, 441:8Nov87-24
De Andrea, W.L. Azrael.
N. Callendar, 441:27Sep87-27
Deane, J.F. Winter in Meath.
M. Harmon, 272(IUR):Spring86-77
J. Lanchester, 493:Jun86-113
Deane, S. Celtic Revivals.*
D. O'Brien, 329(JJQ):Fall86-106
Dearborn, M.V. Pocahontas's Daughters.
L.L. Doan, 395(MFS):Winter86-627
De Bardeleben, J. The Environment and
Marxism-Leninism.
D. Weiner, 550(RusR):Apr86-231
Debax, J.P. & Y. Peyre, eds. "Coriolan."
M. Grivelet, 570(SQ):Autumn86-406
Debicki, A.P. & M.J. Doudoroff - see Darío,
R.
De Blois, A.D. & A. Metallic. Micmac Lex-
icon.*
C.F., with D.H., 355(LSoc):Mar86-131

Delaisement, G. Guy de Maupassant, le
témoin, l'homme, le critique.
R. Bismut, 535(RHL):Mar–Apr86–320
De Lamarter, R.T. Big Blue.*
S. Fry, 362:2Jul87–28
De–la–Noy, M. – see Welch, D.
Delany, P. Lawrence's Nightmare.
J. Donnerstag, 38:Band104Heft1/2–265
Delany, P. The Neo–Pagans.
J. Bayley, 453(NYRB):17Dec87–32
D. Hibberd, 617(TLS):27Nov–3Dec87–
1310
S. Hynes, 441:13Sep87–20
P. Parker, 362:6Aug87–21
Delaporte, F. Disease and Civilization.
R.A. Hartzell, 207(FR):May87–891
Delaty, S. – see de Heredia, J–M.
Delaveau, A. & F. Kerleroux. Problèmes et
exercices de syntaxe française.
G. Kleiber, 553(RLiR):Jan–Jun86–260
Delay, C. Le Hammam.
J. Moss, 207(FR):Feb87–425
Delay, J. Avant Mémoire, IV.
M. Mohrt, 450(NRF):Jul–Aug86–168
Delbanco, N. Group Portrait.
C.J. Rawson, 402(MLR):Jan86–187
Delbanco, N. – see Gardner, J.
Delbouille, P. Poésie et sonorités II.*
R. Lewis, 208(FS):Apr86–242
Delbourg–Delphis, M. Masculin singulier.
F. Coblence, 98:Apr86–341
Delbrück, M. Mind from Matter?
T.C. Holyoke, 42(AR):Summer86–376
Delclos, J–C. Le Témoignage de Georges
Chastellain, historiographe de Philippe
le Bon et de Charles le Téméraire.
D. Poirion, 545(RPh):Feb87–416
Del Corno, D. & M. Cavalli – see Plutarch
Deletant, A. & B. Walker, eds & trans. An
Anthology of Contemporary Romanian
Poetry.
D. McDuff, 565:Winter85/86–72
Deletant, A. & B. Walker, eds. Silent
Voices.
M. Parker, 617(TLS):2Jan87–20
Deletant, A. & B. Walker – see Dinescu, M.
Deleule, D. – see Bacon, F.
Deleuze, G. Cinéma 2.
D. Caron, 98:Jun–Jul86–678
Deleuze, G. Kant's Critical Philosophy.*
R. Meerbote, 342:Band77Heft3–347
De Ley, H. The Movement of Thought.
K. Lloyd–Jones, 125:Winter86–231
J.D. Lyons, 551(RenQ):Winter86–784
I. Maclean, 208(FS):Oct86–456
P.A. Wadsworth, 207(FR):Mar87–533
Delgado, M. Tiranía y derecho de resisten-
cia en el teatro de Guillén de Castro.
W. Floeck, 547(RF):Band98Heft3/4–479
Delgado, R. Acting With Both Sides of Your
Brain.
T. Dorfman, 615(TJ):May86–240
Delhez–Sarlet, C. & M. Catani, eds. Indi-
vidualisme et autobiographie en Occi-
dent.*
C. Abastado, 535(RHL):Sep–Oct86–969
C. Miething, 72:Band223Heft1–140
Delibes, M. La Mortaja. (G. Sobejano, ed)
C. Richmond, 238:Mar86–107
Dellège, C. Les fondements de la musique
tonale.
J.P. Swain, 308:Spring86–122

De Lillo, D. White Noise.*
P. Iyer, 473(PR):Vol53No2–292
Delius, F. Delius: a Life in Letters.
(Vol 1) (L. Carley, ed)
C. Butler, 410(M&L):Jan86–78
Delius, F. & E. Munch. Frederick Delius
and Edvar Munch. (J.B. Smith, ed)
C. Butler, 410(M&L):Jan86–78
Del Litto, V., ed. La Création romanesque
chez Stendhal.
K. Ringger, 605(SC):15Oct86–52
Del Litto, V. & K. Ringger, eds. Stendhal
et le Romantisme.*
F.W.J. Hemmings, 402(MLR):Jan86–207
G. Strickland, 208(FS):Apr86–220
Dello Vicario, A.A. Il richiamo di Vir-
gilio nella poesia italiano.
C. Di Biase, 275(IQ):Winter86–117
Del Mar, N. A Companion to the Orchestra.
C. Matthews, 617(TLS):22May87–564
Del Mar, N. Richard Strauss.
W. Huck, 465:Summer86–200
Delmas, C., ed. Recueil de tragédies à
machines sous Louis XIV (1657–1672).
V. Kapp, 475:Vol13No24–384
Delsol, M. Cause, loi, hasard en biologie.
J. Largeault, 542:Jul–Sep86–393
Del Valle Rodriguez, C. La Escuela Hebrea
de Córdoba.
É. Levine, 318(JAOS):Jan/Mar85–156
I.P. Rothberg, 552(REH):May86–126
Delvendahl, I., comp. Die Frauenfrage in
Deutschland. (new ser, Vol 1)
P. Herminghouse, 406:Summer86–228
Delvendahl, I., with D. Marek, comps.
Die Frauenfrage in Deutschland. (Vol 10)
P. Herminghouse, 406:Summer86–228
Demaizière, C. La grammaire française au
XVIe siècle.
P. Rickard, 545(RPh):Feb87–379
C. Schmitt, 553(RLiR):Jul–Dec86–588
Demand, N.H. Thebes in the Fifth Century.
G. Huxley, 123:Vol36No1–89
De' Mantelli di Canobio detto Tartaglia, G.
Versi d'amore. (N. Saxby, ed)
M. Marti, 228(GSLI):Vol163fasc522–289
De Maria, R., Jr. Johnson's "Dictionary"
and the Language of Learning.
A. Pailler, 189(EA):Apr–Jun87–216
K. Walker, 617(TLS):30Jan87–123
De Matteis, C. Il romanzo italiano del
Novecento.
A. Formis, 402(MLR):Apr87–498
Dembowski, P.F. Jean Froissart and his
"Meliador."*
R. Morse, 382(MAE):1986/2–316
Dembski, S. & J.N. Straus – see Babbitt,
M.
Demers, J. & L. McMurray. L'enjeu du mani-
feste/le manifeste en jeu.
P. Ouellet, 193(ELit):Autumn86–153
Demerson, G. Dorat et son temps.*
J. Pineaux, 535(RHL):Jan–Feb86–137
Demerson, G. – see du Bellay, J.
De Michelis, E. Francesi in Italia.
E. Chevallier, 549(RLC):Jul–Sep86–358
Demko, G.J. & R.J. Fuchs, eds. Geographi-
cal Studies on the Soviet Union.
R.D. Liebowitz, 550(RusR):Jul86–310
Demosthenes. Selected Private Speeches.
(C. Carey & R.A. Reid, ed)
H.L. Hudson–Williams, 123:Vol36No2–313

De Mott, R.J. Steinbeck's Reading.*
   Tetsumaro Hayashi, 577(SHR):Summer86–
   292
Dempsey, H.A. Big Bear.
   T. Flanagan, 298:Summer86–157
   D.C. Jones, 102(CanL):Summer86–140
Demus, O., with R.M. Kloos & K. Weitzmann.
   The Mosaics of San Marco in Venice.*
   A.W. Epstein, 589:Oct86–915
Denbigh, K.G. & J.S. Entropy in Relation
   to Incomplete Knowledge.
   M.J. Zenzen, 486:Sep86–451
Denby, E. The Complete Poems.* (R. Pad-
   gett, ed)
   639(VQR):Autumn86–135
Denby, E. Dance Writings.
   S. Schwartz, 61:Sep87–97
de Dendia, R.A. – see under Antúnez de
   Dendia, R.
Dendle, B.J. Galdós: The Mature Thought.
   J.B. Avalle–Arce, 241:Jan86–77
Denecke, L., ed. Brüder Grimm Gedenken.*
   (Vol 4)
   E. Moser–Rath, 196:Band27Heft1/2–103
De Neef, A.L. Spenser and the Motives of
   Metaphor.*
   G. Morgan, 402(MLR):Oct86–980
Denis, H. Logique hégélienne et systèmes
   économiques.*
   H. Faes, 542:Jan–Mar86–124
Denis, J. Treatise on Harpsichord Tuning.
   (V.J. Panetta, Jr., ed & trans)
   R. Donington, 617(TLS):9–15Oct87–1101
Denison, M. Double Act.
   S. Morley, 157:No159–48
Dennett, D.C. Elbow Room.*
   P.S. Greenspan, 482(PhR):Apr86–257
   D. Locke, 518:Jul86–178
   D.H. Sanford, 483:Oct86–547
   M. Slote, 484(PPR):Jun87–674
   R. Squires, 479(PhQ):Apr86–308
   G. Watson, 311(JP):Sep86–517
Denning, C. Adventures with Julia.*
   442(NY):23Feb87–135
Denning, M. Mechanic Accents.
   R. Rosenzweig, 617(TLS):4–10Dec87–1358
Dennis, M. No Savior and No Special
   Grace. Poems for Jessica–Flynn.
   M. Helwig, 526:Autumn86–84
Dennis, N. El aposento en el aire.
   R. Warner, 86(BHS):Jul86–297
Dennis, N. Diablo Mundo.
   M.A. Compitello, 238:Mar86–103
Dennis, N. Perfume and Poison.
   D. Harris, 402(MLR):Jul87–765
   M.A. Salgado, 238:Sep86–547
Dennison, P., ed. The Richard Wagner
   Centenary in Australia.
   R. Anderson, 415:Feb86–92
Dennison, S. [Alternative] Literary Pub-
   lishing.*
   S.S. Baskett, 115:Summer86–422
Dent, E.J. Edward J. Dent: Selected
   Essays. (H. Taylor, ed)
   A.F.L.T., 412:Feb85–69
Dent, N.J.H. The Moral Psychology of the
   Virtues.
   D. Charles, 393(Mind):Apr86–268
   R.C. Roberts, 482(PhR):Oct86–636
Dent, P., ed. The Full Note.
   R. Pybus, 565:Spring86–71
Dentan, M. Le Texte et son lecteur.*
   M. Picard, 535(RHL):Jan–Feb86–168

Dentith, S. George Eliot.
   K.M. Rogers, 637(VS):Summer87–541
Denuzière, M. Les Trois–Chênes.
   L.J. Iandoli, 207(FR):Feb87–426
Denvir, B. The Early Nineteenth Century.*
   I. Small, 89(BJA):Winter86–83
Déon, M. Un déjeuner de soleil.
   N.S. Hellerstein, 207(FR):Oct86–164
Depew, D.J. & B.H. Weber, eds. Evolution
   at a Crossroads.
   J. Collier, 486:Dec86–614
D'Epiro, P. A Touch of Rhetoric.*
   S.J. Adams, 106:Fall86–367
Deprez, K., ed. Sociolinguistics in the
   Low Countries.
   D.H., 355(LSoc):Mar86–133
De Prospo, R.C. Theism in the Discourse of
   Jonathan Edwards.*
   27(AL):Oct86–477
De Quincey, T. Les Derniers Jours d'Emman-
   uel Kant.
   G. Sartoris, 450(NRF):Jun86–92
Derbyshire, D.C. Hixkaryana.
   M.H. Klaiman, 361:Mar86–283
Deri, S.K. Symbolization and Creativity.
   M. Bal, 567:Vol63No3/4–317
De Rienzo, G., E. Del Boca & S. Orlando,
   eds. Concordanze dei "Promessi sposi."
   (Vols 1 & 2)
   A. Castellani, 708:Vol12fasc2–264
   G. Lepschy, 617(TLS):8May87–494
   C. Marello, 547(RF):Band98Heft3/4–405
De Rienzo, G., E. Del Boca & S. Orlando,
   eds. Concordanze dei "Promessi sposi."
   (Vols 3–5)
   G. Lepschy, 617(TLS):8May87–494
Der Nister. The Family Mashber.
   I. Howe, 61:Jun87–80
   D. Malouf, 453(NYRB):24Sep87–38
   R.R. Wisse, 441:12Jul87–15
Derré, J–R. & C. Giesen – see Heine, H.
Derrick, T.J. – see Wilson, T.
Derricourt, R. Man on the Kafue.
   B.M. Fagan, 2(AfrA):May86–27
Derrida, J. The Ear of the Other.
   C. Norris, 153:Winter86–61
Derrida, J. Glas.
   C. Norris, 617(TLS):18–24Dec87–1407
   J. Sturrock, 441:13Sep87–3
Derrida, J. Limited Inc: A B C.
   S. Pradhan, 153:Spring86–66
Derrida, J. Memoires (for Paul de Man).
   N. Fusini, 290(JAAC):Summer87–431
   M. Sprinker, 400(MLN):Dec86–1226
Derrida, J. Spurs.
   A. Argyros, 153:Fall86–47
Derrida, J. & M. Tlili, eds. For Nelson
   Mandela.
   S.R. Cudjoe, 441:1Nov87–35
Dervillez–Bastuji, J. Structures des rela-
   tions spatiales dans quelques langues
   naturelles.
   E.C. Traugott, 545(RPh):Aug86–75
Dervin, B. & M.J. Voight, eds. Progress in
   Communication Sciences. (Vol 4)
   D.L. Freshley, 583:Spring87–334
Desai, A. In Custody.*
   V. Kirpal, 49:Oct86–127
Desai, T. The East India Company.
   H.V. Bowen, 83:Autumn86–229
De Salvo, L.A. – see Woolf, V.

Descartes, R. The Philosophical Writings.*
(J. Cottingham, R. Stoothoff & D.
Murdoch, eds & trans)
　　D.M. Clarke, 706:Band18Heft1-94
　　J.R. Milton, 208(FS):Apr86-204
　　R.A. Watson, 319:Oct87-600
Deschaux, R., ed. Les oeuvres de Pierre
Chastellain et de Vaillant, poètes du XVe
siècle.*
　　N. Andrieux, 547(RF):Band98Heft3/4-428
Deschodt, E. Eugénie, les larmes aux yeux.
　　R.M. Henkels, Jr., 207(FR):Mar87-557
Descombes, V. Objects of All Sorts.
　　P. Lamarque, 617(TLS):7Aug87-853
Descotes, M. Victor Hugo et Waterloo.
　　K. Wren, 402(MLR):Jan86-208
Désert, G. La Vie quotidienne sur les
plages normandes du Second Empire aux
Années Folles.
　　J-L. Douchin, 535(RHL):Mar-Apr86-316
Desgraves, L. Répertoire des ouvrages de
controverse entre Catholiques et Protes-
tants en France (1598-1685).* (Vol 1)
　　J-P. Beaulieu, 539:Nov86-381
Deshpande, C.R. Transmission of the
Mahābhārata Tradition.
　　R. Lariviere, 318(JAOS):Apr/Jun85-383
Deslandres, Y., with D. Lalanne. Poiret.
　　O. Cassini, 441:13Dec87-27
Desmond, R. A Celebration of Flowers.
　　B. Elliott, 617(TLS):3Jul87-728
Desmond, W. Art and the Absolute.
　　M. Donougho, 543:Mar87-567
Desmons, G. - see Mailer, C. & P. Musgrave
Desnickaja, A.V. Sravnitel'noe jazykoz-
nanie i istorija jazykov.
　　W.R. Schmalstieg, 215(GL):Vol26No3-196
Desowitz, R.S. The Thorn in the Starfish.
　　M.F. Perutz, 453(NYRB):8Oct87-35
d'Espagnat, B. Une incertaine réalité.
　　J. Largeault, 542:Jul-Sep86-395
Des Périers[?], B. Cymbalum Mundi. (3rd
ed) (P.H. Nurse, ed)
　　P. Hendrick, 402(MLR):Apr87-470
　　H. Ingman, 208(FS):Jan86-63
　　O. Millet, 535(RHL):Jul-Aug86-736
Dessen, A.C. Elizabethan Stage Conventions
and Modern Interpreters.*
　　D. Bevington, 570(SQ):Winter86-520
　　H.C. Cole, 301(JEGP):Apr86-260
　　A. Gurr, 402(MLR):Jul87-702
　　R. Jacobs, 175:Summer86-164
　　C. Saunders, 541(RES):Aug86-409
　　D.G. Watson, 536(Rev):Vol8-59
Dessen, A.C. Shakespeare and the Late
Moral Plays.*
　　D. Bevington, 570(SQ):Winter86-520
Dessert, D. Fouquet.
　　R. Briggs, 617(TLS):6-12Nov87-1220
"Dessins Florentins et Romains de la Col-
lection Frits Lugt."
　　G. Naughton, 39:Jan86-61
De Stefanis, G.O. Bassani entro il cerchio
delle sue mura.
　　F. Ricci, 276:Spring86-67
Desző, L. Studies in Syntactic Typology
and Contrastive Grammar.
　　H. Hecker, 682(ZPSK):Band39Heft5-624
Detemmerman, J. & R. Fayt. Inventaire de
la bibliothèque de Michel de Ghelderode
léguée à l'Université Libre de Bruxelles.
　　J. Decock, 207(FR):Mar87-528

De Tommaso, P. Il Giorno e l'ideologia
agraria del Parini.
　　E. Bonora, 228(GSLI):Vol163fasc522-300
Detrez, C. La Mélancolie du voyeur.
　　C. Michael, 207(FR):May87-906
Detsch, R. Georg Trakl's Poetry.*
　　M.A. Weiner, 406:Winter86-547
Deudon, E.H. Nietzsche en France.*
　　R. Bessède, 535(RHL):Jan-Feb86-158
Deug-Su, I. - see under I Deug-Su
de Deugd, C., ed. Spinoza's Political and
Theological Thought.
　　E.G.E. van der Wall, 319:Oct87-602
Deuse, W. Untersuchungen zur mittelplaton-
ischen und neuplatonischen Seelenlehre.*
　　P. Louis, 555:Vol59fasc2-287
Deutsch, C. Frauenbilder bei Robbe-Grillet
(1970-1976).*
　　H.J. Neyer, 224(GRM):Band36Heft4-477
Deutsch, M. Distributive Justice.
　　F.E. Ellrod 3d, 543:Sep86-116
　　C.M., 185:Oct86-291
Deutschle, P. The Two Year Mountain.
　　G. Lewis, 617(TLS):10Apr87-396
Dev, A. The Idea of Comparative Litera-
ture in India.
　　M. Détrie, 549(RLC):Jul-Sep86-350
Devall, B. & G. Sessions. Deep Ecology.
　　M.E. Zimmerman, 258:Jun86-195
Devaulx, N. Le Visiteur insolite.
　　A. Nabarra, 207(FR):Feb87-427
Devereux, E.J. Renaissance English Trans-
lations of Eramus.
　　C.F. Robinson, 447(N&Q):Dec85-528
Devereux, G. The Character of the Euripi-
dean Hippolytos.
　　M. Lloyd, 123:Vol36No2-198
　　E.M. Thury, 124:Mar-Apr87-328
Devine, A.M. & L.D. Stephens. Language
and Metre.*
　　J. Diggle, 123:Vol36No2-325
De Vito, J.A., ed. The Communication Hand-
book.
　　J. Klein, 186(ETC.):Winter86-427
Devitt, M. Designation.*
　　U. Niklas, 567:Vol61No1/2-163
Devitt, M. Realism and Truth.*
　　P. Gasper, 482(PhR):Jul86-446
　　P. Madigan, 543:Sep86-117
Devlin, A. The Way-Paver.
　　A. Haverty, 617(TLS):16Jan87-56
　　J. Mellors, 362:1Jan87-22
Devlin, A.J., ed. Welty.
　　C. Cook, 441:11Oct87-63
Devlin, D.D. De Quincey, Wordsworth and
the Art of Prose.
　　J. Wilner, 591(SIR):Winter86-590
Devlin, J. The Superstitious Mind.
　　E. Weber, 617(TLS):24Apr87-430
Devroey, J-P. L'Ame de cristal.
　　C. Jolicoeur, 189(EA):Jul-Sep87-362
Devroey, J-P., ed. Le polyptyque et les
listes de cens de l'Abbaye de Saint-Remi
de Reims (IXe-XIe siècles).
　　C.B. Bouchard, 589:Oct86-918
Dev Sen, N. Counterpoints.
　　M. Détrie, 549(RLC):Jul-Sep86-350
Dewar, M. The British Army in Northern
Ireland.
　　M.R.D. Foot, 176:Feb87-46
Dewdney, A.K. The Planiverse.
　　E. Godfrey, 102(CanL):Spring86-149

Dewey, J. Types of Thinking.*
J.W. Allard, 482(PhR):Jan86-121
Dewhurst, C.K., B. MacDowell & M. Mac-
Dowell. Religious Folk Art in America.*
V.A. Chittenden, 440:Winter-Spring86-
113
De Witt, D.J. & E.R. Modern Architecture
in Europe.
P.G., 441:6Dec87-24
De Woskin, K.J. - see "Doctors, Diviners,
and Magicians of Ancient China"
Dews, P. - see Habermas, J.
Dexter, C. The Secret of Annexe 3.
T.J. Binyon, 617(TLS):17Apr87-411
Dexter, H. Student's Dictionary of Music.
B. Newbould, 415:Apr86-210
Dexter, P. Deadwood.*
M.A. Lukens, 649(WAL):Feb87-360
Dezalay, A. L'Opéra des "Rougon-Mac-
quart."*
R. Lethbridge, 208(FS):Jul86-341
d'Haen, T., ed. Linguistics and the Study
of Literature.
P-G. Boucé, 189(EA):Jul-Sep87-327
d'Haussy, C. La Vision du monde chez G.K.
Chesterton.*
M. Bottrall, 189(EA):Apr-Jun87-228
Dherbey, G.R. Les choses mêmes.
R. Brague, 192(EP):Apr-Jun86-266
d'Heur, J.M. & A. Nivelle, eds. Autour de
Paul Gérardy.
M. Otten, 356(LR):Aug-Nov86-333
Dhôtel, A. Vaux étranges.
T. Dey, 450(NRF):Oct86-91
Diamant, A. The New Jewish Wedding.
A.B. Carb, 287:Apr-May86-26
Diamond, E. Pinter's Comic Play.
A.E. Quigley, 615(TJ):Dec86-513
Diamonstein, B. American Architecture Now
II.*
S. Gutterman, 45:Oct86-71
L. Karafel, 55:Mar86-44
Diamonstein, B. Remaking America.*
P-L. Adams, 61:Jan87-91
Díaz, A.E. - see under Espinós Díaz, A.
Díaz, J.S. - see under Simón Díaz, J.
Díaz Castañón, C. - see Manrique, J.
Díaz y Díaz, G. & C. Santos Escudero. Bib-
liografía filosofica hispánica (1901-
1970).
C. Strosetzki, 72:Band223Heft2-462
Díaz y Díaz, M.C. - see Egeria
Dibdin, M. A Rich Full Death.
I. Thomson, 362:14May87-31
Di Benedetto, V. Sofocle.*
C. Segal, 122:Jul86-245
Dick, B.F. The Star-Spangled Screen.
J.M. Clum, 579(SAQ):Autumn86-389
639(VQR):Spring86-64
Dick, P.K. Humpty Dumpty in Oakland.
J. Clute, 617(TLS):6Feb87-134
Dick, P.K. Mary and the Giant.
N. Forbes, 441:26Apr87-24
Dick, S. - see Woolf, V.
Dickason, C. Indochine.
W. Smith, 441:20Dec87-16
Dickens, A.G. & J.M. Tonkin, with K.
Powell. The Reformation in Historical
Thought.*
M.E. Hussey, 42(AR):Summer86-374
Dickens, C. American Notes.*
L.R. Leavis, 396(ModA):Summer/Fall86-
299

Dickens, C. A Christmas Carol. (illus-
trated by M. Cole)
M. Slater, 155:Summer86-106
Dickens, C. Charles Dickens' Book of
Memoranda. (F. Kaplan, ed)
R.J. Dunn, 403(MLS):Spring86-80
A. Sanders, 155:Autumn86-180
Dickens, C. Dickens' Working Notes for his
Novels. (H. Stone, ed)
R. Altick, 617(TLS):7Aug87-841
D. Walder, 362:18Jun87-22
Dickens, C. Impressioni di Napoli. (S.
Manferlotti, ed)
J. McRae, 155:Spring86-55
Dickens, C. The Pickwick Papers. (J.
Kinsley, ed)
S. Monod, 189(EA):Oct-Dec87-473
A. Sanders, 617(TLS):16Jan87-66
Dickens, C. Selected Letters of Charles
Dickens.* (D. Paroissien, ed)
E. Power, 155:Autumn86-181
Dickens, C. George Silverman's Explana-
tion. (H. Stone, ed)
M. Slater, 155:Summer86-106
"Dickens Studies Annual."* (Vol 10) (M.
Timko, F. Kaplan & E. Guiliano, eds)
R. Bennett, 541(RES):Feb86-139
"Dickens Studies Annual."* (Vols 11 & 12)
(M. Timko, F. Kaplan & E. Guiliano, eds)
R. Bennett, 541(RES):Feb86-114
A. Easson, 155:Summer86-100
"Dickens Studies Annual." (Vol 14) (M.
Timko, F. Kaplan & E. Guiliano, eds)
R.L. Patten, 637(VS):Spring87-413
Dickey, C. With the Contras.*
639(VQR):Summer86-96
Dickey, J. Alnilam.
P-L. Adams, 61:Jul87-98
R. Towers, 441:21Jun87-7
Dickhoff, W.W. Zur Hermeneutik des
Schweigens.
M. Winkler, 221(GQ):Summer86-494
Dickie, G. The Art Circle.*
A. Fine, 449:Jun86-281
G. McFee, 89(BJA):Winter86-72
Dickie, M. On the Modernist Long Poem.*
V.S., 295(JML):Nov86-424
Dickie, R.B. & L.S. Rouner, eds. Corpora-
tions and the Common Good.
J.B.C., 185:Apr87-704
Dickinson, A. & M.L. Todd. Austin and
Mabel.* (P. Longsworth, ed)
R. Miller, 534(RALS):Spring-Autumn84-
191
L. Willson, 569(SR):Winter86-131
Dickinson, C. With or Without.
R. Perry, 441:21Jun87-35
Dickinson, E. The Master Letters of Emily
Dickinson. (R.W. Franklin, ed)
G. Johnson, 219(GaR):Winter86-1009
J. Loving, 183(ESQ):Vol32No3-201
Dickinson, P. Tefuga.*
42(AR):Summer86-378
639(VQR):Autumn86-126
Dickson, C.B. fragrance of frost grapes.
R. Spiess, 404:Autumn86-55
Dickson, G.R. Way of the Pilgrim.
G. Jonas, 441:2Aug87-25
Dickson, P. Names.
K.B. Harder, 424:Dec86-384
Dickson, P.G.M. Finance and Government
Under Maria Theresia 1740-1780.
D. McKay, 617(TLS):2-8Oct87-1068

Dickson, W.J. – see Scarron, P.
"Dictionary of American Regional English."*
(Vol 1) (F.G. Cassidy, ed–in–chief)
  G–J. Forgue, 189(EA):Jan–Mar87–106
  W.F. Klein, 344:Spring87–112
  T.K. Pratt, 320(CJL):Summer86–179
  W. Wolfram, 35(AS):Winter86–345
"Dictionary of Canadian Biography/Diction-
naire Biographique du Canada." (Vol 8)
(F.G. Halpenny, ed)
  R. Landon, 470:Vol24–115
  529(QQ):Winter86–949
"Dictionnaire actuel de la langue fran-
çaise."
  C. Muller, 209(FM):Apr86–97
"Dictionnaire des littératures." (P. van
Tieghem, ed)
  H. Lemaitre, 535(RHL):Sep–Oct86–972
"Diderot Studies XXI." (O. Fellows & D.G.
Carr, eds)
  A. Strugnell, 208(FS):Jan86–76
Didier, B. Le Journal intime.
  S. Rendall, 153:Fall86–57
Didier, B. La Musique des Lumières.
  S. Bernstein, 400(MLN):Sep86–959
  A. Suied, 450(NRF):Feb86–116
Didier, B. Senancour romancier.
  J–M. Monnoyer, 98:Dec86–1204
Didier, B. – see Sand, G.
Didion, J. Miami.
  J. Chace, 441:25Oct87–3
Didsbury, P. The Classical Farm.
  W. Scammell, 617(TLS):18–24Sep87–1024
Diebold, A.R., Jr. The Evolution of Indo-
European Nomenclature for Salmonid Fish.
  E.B. Holtsmark, 350:Mar87–183
Dieckmann, F. Die Zauberflöte.
  H–J. Irmer, 601(SuF):Nov–Dec86–1302
Diederich, W. Strukturalistische Rekon-
struktionen.
  W. Balzer, 167:Sep86–265
de Diego, V.G. – see under García de Diego,
V.
Diehl, J.F. Dickinson and the Romantic
Imagination.
  J. Loving, 183(ESQ):Vol32No3–201
Diem, B., with D. Chanoff. In the Jaws of
History.
  A. Tonelson, 441:13Sep87–16
Dierks, K. Handlungsstrukturen im Werk
von Charles Dickens.*
  H. Reinhold, 677(YES):Vol16–323
Diersch, M., ed. Fortschrittliche deutsche
Literaturkritik 1890–1918.
  T. Wohlfahrt, 654(WB):12/1986–2095
Diesing, M. Lokatoren.
  K–H. Jäger, 406:Summer86–215
Diesing, P. Science and Ideology in the
Policy Sciences.
  H.T. Wilson, 488:Sep86–397
Dieter, W. Beyond the Mountain.
  K. Ahearn, 649(WAL):Nov86–237
Dietiker, S.R. En Bonne Forme. (3rd ed)
  M–N. Little, 207(FR):Dec86–307
Dietrich, W. Die erotische Novelle in
Stanzen.
  U. Schulz–Buschhaus, 52:Band21Heft1–90
Dietrick, L. Prisons and Idylls.
  J.M. McGlathery, 564:Sep86–263
  W. Wittkowski, 133:Band19Heft3/4–354
Dietz, L. Franz Kafka.
  H.H.H. Remak, 406:Fall86–413

Dietz, S., ed & trans. Die Buddhistische
Briefliteratur Indiens.
  C. Lindtner, 318(JAOS):Oct/Dec85–802
  B. Pāsādika, 259(IIJ):Jul86–203
Dietze, G. Liberalism Proper and Proper
Liberalism.
  E. Spitz, 173(ECS):Fall86–107
Díez, C.E. & others – see under Estepa
Díez, C. & others
Díez, G.M., with J.M. Ruiz Asencio – see
under Martínez Díez, G., with J.M. Ruiz
Asencio
Díez Borque, J.M. – see Calderón de la
Barca, P.
Diffey, T.J. Tolstoy's "What Is Art?"
  R.W. Beardsmore, 89(BJA):Autumn86–399
  R.F. Christian, 402(MLR):Apr87–535
Diffloth, G. The Dvaravati Old Mon Lan-
guage and Nyah Kur.
  M. Durie, 350:Jun87–440
Digby, A. Madness, Morality and Medicine.*
  C.M. McGovern, 637(VS):Spring87–433
  C.K. Warsh, 529(QQ):Winter86–910
Digges, T.A. Letters of Thomas Atwood
Digges, 1742–1821. (R.H. Elias & E.D.
Finch, eds)
  G.A. Schultz, 106:Fall86–327
Diggins, J.P. The Lost Soul of American
Politics.
  J.J. Ellis, 656(WMQ):Jan86–133
  R.S., 185:Oct86–298
Diggle, J. – see Euripides
Diggory, T. Yeats and American Poetry.*
  R. Belflower, 541(RES):Feb86–133
  J.M. Reibetanz, 675(YER):Vol8No1/2–136
Di Giovanni, C.M., ed. Italian Canadian
Voices.*
  E. Padolsky, 298:Winter86/87–138
Dignan, D. The Indian Revolutionary Prob-
lem in British Diplomacy, 1914–1919.
  E.C. Brown, 293(JASt):Feb86–421
Dihle, A. The Theory of Will in Classical
Antiquity.*
  A. MacIntyre, 41:Vol6–242
van Dijk, T.A. Handbook of Discourse
Analysis.
  W. Frawley, 350:Jun87–361
  J.F. Kess, 320(CJL):Winter86–386
Dijkstra, B. Idols of Perversity.
  A. Comini, 441:1Feb87–13
Diliberto, G. Debutante.
  L. Braudy, 441:23Aug87–18
Dilke, O.A.W. Greek and Roman Maps.
  J.A.S. Evans, 529(QQ):Winter86–883
  M. Reinhold, 124:Mar–Apr87–319
  639(VQR):Summer86–104
Dillard, A. An American Childhood.
  N. Perrin, 441:27Sep87–7
Dillard, H. Daughters of the Reconquest.
  K. Kish, 238:May86–315
  J.E. Salisbury, 589:Apr86–403
Dillard, J.L. Toward a Social History of
American English.
  P. Beade, 361:Sep86–67
Diller, A–M. La pragmatique des questions
et des réponses.*
  J.E. Gombert, 353:Vol24No2–457
  C. Vandeloise, 209(FM):Apr86–108
Diller, G.T. Attitudes chevaleresques et
réalités politiques chez Froissart.*
  T. Evergates, 589:Jul86–730
  A.T. Harrison, 201:Vol11–163
[continued]

[continuing]

G. Roques, 553(RLiR):Jan–Jun86–276

M. Vale, 382(MAE):1986/2–314

Dillingham, W.B. Melville's Later Novels.

R.B. Bickley, Jr., 27(AL):Dec86–628

L. Buell, 569(SR):Fall86–lxxxiv

H. Cohen, 617(TLS):22May87–554

Dillman, K.J. The Subject in Rimbaud from Self to "Je."*

M. Davies, 208(FS):Apr86–232

Dillon, D. Dallas Architecture 1936–1986.

L. Milazzo, 584(SWR):Winter86–123

Dillon, E. The Interloper.

P. Craig, 617(TLS):13–19Nov87–1248

Dillon, M.L. Ulrich Bonnell Phillips.

639(VQR):Summer86–85

Dilman, İ. Freud and Human Nature.*

M. Brearley, 521:Oct86–333

Dilman, İ. Freud and the Mind.*

A.E. Pitson, 521:Oct86–341

Dilman, İ. Love and Human Separateness.

V. Held, 441:5Apr87–28

Dilman, İ. Quine on Ontology, Necessity and Experience.*

M. Ring, 521:Oct86–345

Dilthey, W. Selected Works.* (Vol 5) (R.A. Makkreel & F. Rodi, eds)

J.J. Kockelmans, 319:Jul87–458

Dilthey, W. Die Wissenschaften vom Menschen, der Gesellschaft und der Geschichte. Grundlegung der Wissenschaften vom Menschen, der Gesellschaft und der Geschichte. (H. Johach & F. Rodi, eds of both)

W. Henckmann, 489(PJGG):Band93Heft2–425

Dilworth, T. – see Jones, D.

Dimitriu, C. Tanner.

L. Spaas, 207(FR):Mar87–551

Dimler, R.G. Friedrich Spee von Langenfeld.

A.J. Harper, 402(MLR):Jul87–774

Dimter, M. Textklassenkonzepte heutiger Alltagssprache.

M. Philipp, 685(ZDL):2/1986–286

Din, G.C. & A.P. Nasatir. The Imperial Osages.

J. Fisher, 86(BHS):Oct86–396

d'India, S. Ottavo libro dei madrigali a cinque voci (1624). (G. Watkins, ed)

A. Newcomb, 317:Summer86–396

"Diné Bahane': The Navajo Creation Story." (P.G. Zolbrod, trans)

R.M. Adams, 453(NYRB):26Mar87–32

Dinescu, M. Exile on a Peppercorn. (A. Deletant & B. Walker, eds & trans)

M. Parker, 617(TLS):2Jan87–20

Dinesen, I. Letters from Africa: 1914–1931.

R. Harper, 396(ModA):Winter86–75

Dinesen, W. Boganis.

J. Feeney, 441:3May87–45

Dinnage, R. Annie Besant.

J. Harris, 617(TLS):10Apr87–375

"Diogene Laerzio, storico del pensiero antico."

J. Barnes, 520:Vol31No3–282

Diogenes Laertius. Diogene Laerzio, Vite dei filosofi. (3rd ed) (M. Gigante, trans)

M. Marcovich, 41:Fall85–351

Dionne, R., ed. Le Québécois et sa littérature.*

E–M. Kröller, 102(CanL):Fall86–115

Di Piero, W.S. Early Light.

T. Swiss, 569(SR):Spring86–302

Di Pietro, R.J. & E. Ifkovic, eds. Ethnic Perspectives in American Literature.

A.O. Aldridge, 107(CRCL):Jun86–319

Dircks, P.T. David Garrick.

H.W. Pedicord, 611(TN):Vol40No2–89

J.R. Roach, 615(TJ):Mar86–120

Dirven, R. & others. Die Leistung der Linguistik für den Englischunterricht.

G. Bourcier, 189(EA):Apr–Jun87–195

Di Salvo, J. War of Titans.*

A. Lincoln, 541(RES):Feb86–105

Di Scanno, T. – see Rousseau, J–B.

Di Scipio, G.C. The Symbolic Rose in Dante's "Paradiso."

R. Jacoff, 276:Autumn86–303

J.F. Took, 402(MLR):Apr86–499

"Disegni Antichi." [Galeria Rossella Gilli]

G. Naughton, 39:Jan86–61

Diski, J. Nothing Natural.*

T. Davis, 441:26Apr87–33

J. Neville, 364:Jun86–96

Disraeli, B. Benjamin Disraeli: Letters. (Vols 1 & 2) (J.A.W. Gunn & others, eds)

D. Sultana, 447(N&Q):Jun85–281

Disraeli, B. Benjamin Disraeli: Letters. (Vol 3) (M.G. Wiebe & others, eds)

B. Hilton, 617(TLS):16–22Oct87–1128

Ditlevsen, T. Early Spring.

I. Claréus, 563(SS):Autumn86–442

D'Itri, P.W. Damon Runyon.

J. Newman, 677(YES):Vol16–356

Dittmar, J. & O. Holzapfel, eds. Deutsche Volkslieder. (Pt 7)

R. Wehse, 196:Band27Heft1/2–105

Diviš, K. Kommunikative Strukturen im tschechischen Drama der 60er Jahre.

A. Měšťan, 688(ZSP):Band45Heft2–444

Dix, M.A. La lectura inteligente "en el tiempo que es turbio."

M.S. Brownlee, 238:Mar86–97

Dixon, K. Freedom and Equality.

A. Ryan, 176:Sep/Oct87–52

M.D.S., 185:Apr87–679

Dixon, P. – see Farquhar, G.

Dixon, P.B. Reversible Readings.

S. Magnarelli, 395(MFS):Autumn86–477

C. Slater, 240(HR):Winter86–114

Dixon, S. Fall & Rise.

J. Klinkowitz, 580(SCR):Fall86–90

Dixon, W.W. The Cinematic Vision of F. Scott Fitzgerald.

M. Sacharoff, 295(JML):Nov86–470

Diz, M.A. Patronio y Lucanor.*

J. England, 402(MLR):Apr86–508

Djupsund, G. & L. Karvonen. Fascismen i Finland.

P.K. Hamalainen, 563(SS):Spring86–208

Djuric, M. & J. Simon, eds. Zur Aktualität Nietzsches.

R. Margreiter, 489(PJGG):Band93Heft2–375

Doane, J.L. Silence and Narrative.

M.J. Hoffman, 395(MFS):Winter86–611

I.B.N., 295(JML):Nov86–541

Dobat, K–D. Musik als romantische Illusion.*

J.M. McGlathery, 221(GQ):Spring86–321

Dobbin, M. Going Live.
  D. Cole, 441:22Feb87-28
Doble, G. & G. Griffiths, eds. Oral Skills
  in the Modern Languages Degree.
  S.S. Toliver, 399(MLJ):Winter86-416
Dobler, P. Talking to Strangers.
  C. Muske, 441:21Jun87-13
Dobrée, B. - see Pope, A.
Dobyns, S. Black Dog, Red Dog.*
  S.P. Estess, 577(SHR):Winter86-84
Dobyns, S. A Boat Off the Coast.
  M. Childress, 441:6Dec87-30
Dobyns, S. Cemetery Nights.
  P. Hampl, 441:7Jun87-15
Dobyns, S. Cold Dog Soup.*
  J. Humphries, 385(MQR):Fall87-788
Docherty, T. On Modern Authority.
  J. Lucas, 617(TLS):18-24Dec87-1406
Docherty, T. Reading (Absent) Character.*
  A. Bony, 189(EA):Apr-Jun87-167
Doctorow, E.L. Lives of the Poets.*
  P. Iyer, 473(PR):Vol53No1-132
  P. Lewis, 565:Summer86-57
Doctorow, E.L. World's Fair.*
  D. Flower, 249(HudR):Summer86-310
  P. Lewis, 565:Summer86-57
  639(VQR):Spring86-56
"Doctors, Diviners, and Magicians of
  Ancient China." (K.J. De Woskin, trans)
  J.M. Boltz, 293(JASt):Nov85-109
  C.T. Fisher, 302:Vol22No1-65
  R.B. Mather, 244(HJAS):Dec86-635
  D. Obenchain, 485(PE&W):Jul86-302
Dod, E. Die Vernünftiqkeit der Imagination
  in Aufklärung und Romantik.
  J. Engell, 191(ELN):Mar87-77
Dodd, A. Francis Bacon's Personal Life-
  Story.
  R. Robbins, 617(TLS):6Mar87-247
Dodd, P., ed. The Art of Travel.*
  H. Beaver, 677(YES):Vol16-221
  J. Martini, 49:Jan86-104
Doder, D. Shadows and Whispers.*
  P. Reddaway, 453(NYRB):28May87-21
  442(NY):2Feb87-101
Dodge, C. & T.A. Jerse. Computer Music.
  M. Zuckerman, 513:Spring-Summer86-420
Dodge, J. Not Fade Away.
  R. Keyes, 441:1Nov87-33
Dodge, R.K. & J.B. McCullough, eds. New
  and Old Voices from Wah'kon-tah.
  P.C. Smith, 649(WAL):Nov86-279
Dodwell, C.R. Anglo-Saxon Art.
  R. Deshman, 54:Jun86-329
Doering, B. Jacques Maritain and the
  French Catholic Intellectuals.
  J. Onimus, 535(RHL):Jul-Aug86-793
Doern, G.B. & G. Toner. The Politics of
  Energy.
  P.E. Roy, 298:Fall86-146
Doerner, K. Madmen and the Bourgeoisie.
  C. Howell, 529(QQ):Spring86-19
Doherty, M. Epistemische Bedeutung.*
  G. Zybatow, 682(ZPSK):Band39Heft2-289
Doig, I. Dancing at the Rascal Fair.
  L.K. Abbott, 441:1Nov87-20
Doinas, S.A. Vînàtoare cu şoim.
  V. Nemoianu, 617(TLS):2Jan87-20
Dolamore, C.E.J. Ionesco: "Rhinocéros."
  D. Knowles, 402(MLR):Oct87-983
Dolan, J.P. The American Catholic Exper-
  ience.
  J.M. O'Toole, 432(NEQ):Dec86-585

Dolan, T.P. - see Dunning, T.P.
Dolezal, F. Forgotten But Important Lexi-
  cographers.*
  H. Käsmann, 38:Band104Heft1/2-154
Dolfi, L. Il Teatro di Góngora.*
  J. Gornall, 86(BHS):Jul86-285
Dollenmayer, D.B., T. Hansen & R. Hiller.
  Neue Horizonte.
  D.L. Hoffmeister, 399(MLJ):Autumn86-
  312
Dollimore, J. Radical Tragedy.*
  J. Drakakis, 447(N&Q):Dec85-515
  J. Goldberg, 405(MP):Aug86-71
  R. Markley, 223:Spring86-84
  W. Weiss, 156(ShJW):Jahrbuch1986-198
Dollimore, J. & A. Sinfield, eds. Politi-
  cal Shakespeare.*
  P. Erickson, 570(SQ):Summer86-251
  C. Hoover, 529(QQ):Summer86-421
  P.C. McGuire, 615(TJ):Dec86-501
  G.M. Ridden, 366:Autumn86-250
  P. Sahel, 189(EA):Jul-Sep86-333
  P.N. Siegel, 125:Fall85-86
  N. Smith, 175:Spring86-57
Dolmetsch, C.L. The German Press of the
  Shenandoah Valley.
  J. Tanis, 656(WMQ):Jul86-510
Dombroski, R.S. L'apologia del vero.
  C. Fahy, 402(MLR):Jan87-217
Dombroski, R.S. L'esistenza ubbidiente.
  D. Forgacs, 402(MLR):Jan86-235
  S. Knaller, 547(RF):Band98Heft3/4-470
Domenach, J-L. Aux Origines du Grand
  Bond en Avant.
  R.H. Myers, 293(JASt):Feb86-373
Dominguez Compañy, F. Política de pobla-
  miento de España en América.
  D. Ramos, 263(RIB):Vol36No3-335
Domínguez Rodríguez, A. Astrología y arte
  en el "Lapidario" de Alfonso X el Sabio.
  A.J. Cárdenas, 589:Apr86-405
Dominicis, M.C. & J.A. Cussen. Casos y
  cosas. (2nd ed)
  M.E. Beeson, 399(MLJ):Autumn86-330
Dominicy, M. La Naissance de la Grammaire
  moderne.*
  F. Beets, 540(RIPh):Vol40fasc1/2-183
Dömötör, T. Hungarian Folk Beliefs.
  M.D. Birnbaum, 650(WF):Jan86-75
Donald, D.H. Look Homeward.
  H. Bloom, 441:8Feb87-13
  H. Kenner, 617(TLS):17Apr87-403
  M.K. Spears, 453(NYRB):24Sep87-34
Donald, M. Diplomacy.
  N. Callendar, 441:27Sep87-27
Donaldson, E.T. The Swan at the Well.*
  L.S. Champion, 179(ES):Oct86-454
  P.S. McKinney, 570(SQ):Autumn86-404
  D. Pearsall, 191(ELN):Dec86-69
  A.C. Spearing, 551(RenQ):Winter86-804
Donaldson, G. Scottish Church History.
  J.K. Cameron, 617(TLS):16Jan87-68
Donaldson, I., ed. Jonson and Shake-
  speare.*
  J. Arnold, 568(SCN):Fall86-35
  P. Hyland, 447(N&Q):Sep85-396
  W. Weiss, 156(ShJW):Jahrbuch1986-198
Donaldson, I. The Rapes of Lucretia.*
  L.G. Bromley, 570(SQ):Spring86-136
  M. Mueller, 107(CRCL):Mar86-116
Donaldson, I. - see Jonson, B.
Donaldson, S. Fool for Love.*
  J.L.W. West 3d, 587(SAF):Spring86-117

Donaldson, S. Hold On, Mr. President!
  J. Jarvis, 441:29Mar87-9
  D. Schorr, 18:Jul/Aug87-60
Donaldson, W. Is This Allowed?
  T. Fitton, 617(TLS):14Aug87-872
Donaldson-Evans, L.K. - see de Selve, L.
Donat, H. & K. Holl, eds. Die Friedensbe-
  wegung.
  S. Bock, 654(WB):12/1986-2106
Donawerth, J. Shakespeare and the Six-
  teenth-Century Study of Language.*
  H. Cooper, 447(N&Q):Dec85-519
  G.T. Wright, 570(SQ):Summer86-270
Donchenko, A. Russian.
  G.F. Holliday, 399(MLJ):Spring86-73
Doni, R. Servo inutile.
  F. Zangrilli, 275(IQ):Winter86-113
Donington, R. Baroque Music.
  J.A. Sadie, 410(M&L):Jan86-65
Donker, M. & G.M. Muldrow. Dictionary of
  Literary-Rhetorical Conventions of the
  English Renaissance.
  P. Mack, 402(MLR):Oct86-973
Donleavy, J.P. Are You Listening Rabbi
  Löw?
  J. Naughton, 362:29Oct87-32
"J.P. Donleavy's Ireland."
  A. Higgins, 364:Aug/Sep86-142
Donne, J. The Complete English Poems of
  John Donne.* (C.A. Patrides, ed)
  J.P. Baumgaertner, 541(RES):Nov86-565
Donne, J. Selected Prose. (N. Rhodes, ed)
  617(TLS):10Apr87-397
Donne, J. The Songs and Sonnets of John
  Donne. (2nd ed) (T. Redpath, ed)
  D.F. Bratchell, 447(N&Q):Mar85-113
  L. Carrive, 549(RLC):Apr-Jun86-235
Donnedieu de Vabres, J. Vent d'espoir sur
  la démocratie.
  M. Chefdor, 207(FR):Dec86-279
Donnell, D. The Blue Ontario Hemingway
  Boat Race.
  W. Connor, 198:Summer86-88
  R. Seamon, 102(CanL):Fall86-152
Donnelly, G. Holy Mother.
  D. Singmaster, 617(TLS):25Sep-1Oct87-
  1052
Donno, E.S. - see Shakespeare, W.
Donoghue, D. Reading America.
  L. Graver, 441:27Sep87-11
Donoghue, D. We Irish.*
  E. Longley, 617(TLS):5Jun87-612
Donoghue, D. - see Blackmur, R.P.
Donohue, A.M. Hawthorne.*
  N. Baym, 301(JEGP):Apr86-288
  M. Hollister, 50(ArQ):Spring86-92
  H. McNeil, 617(TLS):22May87-553
  D.O. Tomlinson, 27(AL):Mar86-143
  K. Verduin, 432(NEQ):Mar86-149
Donoso, J. A House in the Country.
  P.R. Beardsell, 86(BHS):Jul86-305
  R. Christ, 473(PR):Vol53No2-305
Donoso, P.B. - see under Bolaños Donoso, P.
Donoughue, B. Prime Minister.
  R. Skidelsky, 617(TLS):5Jun87-598
Donovan, A.J., Jr. & B. Drury. Fatso.
  J.F. Clarity, 441:15Nov87-27
Donovan, D.G., M.G.H. Herman & A.E. Imbrie,
  comps. Sir Thomas Browne and Robert
  Burton.
  D.S. Smith, 568(SCN):Spring-Summer86-
  19

Donovan, K., ed. Cape Breton at 200.
  J. Fingard, 150(DR):Fall86-379
Donovan, P.J., ed. Ysgrifeniadau Byrion
  Morgan Llwyd.
  T.A. Watkins, 112:Vol18-207
Donskov, A. Mixail Lentovskij and the Rus-
  sian Theatre.
  L. Hecht, 574(SEEJ):Winter86-575
Doody, M.A. The Daring Muse.*
  F. Doherty, 83:Autumn86-251
  E. Rothstein, 405(MP):May87-434
Doolittle, J., ed. Eight Plays for Young
  People.*
  M. Mulholland, 102(CanL):Fall86-124
Dopsch, H., ed. Geschichte Salzburgs,
  Stadt und Land. (Vol 1, Pts 2 & 3)
  J.B. Freed, 589:Apr86-409
Dorandi, T., ed & trans. Filodemo, Il buon
  re secondo Omero.
  D.P. Fowler, 123:Vol36No1-81
Dore, C. Theism.
  G.B. Matthews, 484(PPR):Jun87-678
  R. Swinburne, 518:Jul86-191
Dore, R. Flexible Rigidities.
  B. Moeran, 617(TLS):17Apr87-407
Dorfman, A. The Last Song of Manuel Sen-
  dero.
  E. Shorris, 441:15Feb87-9
Doria, C., ed. Russian Samizdat Art.
  J. Gambrell, 617(TLS):27Mar87-336
Döring-Smirnova, J.R. & I.P. Smirnov.
  Ocherki po istoricheskoy tipologii
  kul'tury ...
  J. Graffy, 575(SEER):Jan86-117
Dorion, G. & M. Voisin, eds. Littérature
  québécoise.
  C. May, 402(MLR):Oct87-986
Dorment, R. British Painting in the Phil-
  adelphia Museum of Art, from the Seven-
  teenth through the Nineteenth Century.
  G. Reynolds, 617(TLS):27Mar87-334
Dorment, R. Alfred Gilbert.*
  C. Gere, 39:Jan86-67
  B. Read, 90:Oct86-754
  S. Whitfield, 176:Feb87-50
  A. Yarrington, 59:Dec86-530
Dorment, R., ed. Alfred Gilbert.
  B.C. Rezelman, 637(VS):Autumn86-140
  A. Yarrington, 59:Dec86-530
d'Ormesson, J. Tous les hommes en sont
  fous.
  A. Bosquet, 450(NRF):Sep86-108
Dorris, M. A Yellow Raft in Blue Water.
  A. Broyard, 441:7Jun87-7
Doshi, S., ed. Symbols and Manifestations
  of Indian Art.
  S. Aryan, 60:May-Jun86-142
Dostoevsky, F. The Double. (E. Harden,
  trans)
  P. Debreczeny, 574(SEEJ):Summer86-285
Dostoevsky, F. Selected Letters. (J. Frank
  & D.I. Goldstein, eds)
  J.L. Rice, 617(TLS):30Oct-5Nov87-1188
Dotoli, G. Bibliografia critica di Ricci-
  otto Canudo. Paris ville visage-du-
  monde chez Ricciotto Canudo et l'avant-
  garde italienne.
  H. Béhar, 535(RHL):Mar-Apr86-336
Dotoli, G. Lo Scrittore totale.
  M. Jakob, 549(RLC):Oct-Dec86-482

Doty, C.S. The First Franco-Americans.
N.J. Martin-Perdue, 292(JAF):Jul/Sep86-
345
E.J. Talbot, 207(FR):Feb87-413
Doty, W.G. Mythography.
N. Barley, 617(TLS):18-24Dec87-1392
"Le Double dans le romantisme anglo-améri-
cain."
J-R. Watson, 189(EA):Jul-Sep86-319
Doucette, L.E. Theatre in French Canada:
Laying the Foundations 1606-1867.*
P.V. Davies, 610:Spring86-72
Douchin, J-L. Le Bourreau de soi-même,
essai sur l'itinéraire intellectual de
Gustave Flaubert.
P. Cogny, 535(RHL):Sep-Oct86-937
Douchin, J-L. La Vie érotique de Flaubert.
R. Bismut, 535(RHL):Sep-Oct86-938
Dougherty, D., ed. Un Valle-Inclán
olvidado.
J. Lyon, 402(MLR):Jan86-239
V. Smith, 86(BHS):Oct86-391
Douglas, C. Hazards of the Profession.
J. Barron, 362:19Nov87-31
Douglas, G.H. Edmund Wilson's America.*
T. De Pietro, 569(SR):Winter86-160
S. Fogel, 106:Spring86-109
Douglas, K. A Prose Miscellany.* (D.
Graham, ed)
A. Head, 175:Summer86-180
R. Smith, 150(DR):Winter85/86-585
Douglas, M., ed. Essays in the Sociology
of Perception.
D.M. Lowe, 488:Jun86-281
Douglas, M. How Institutions Think.
M.O., 185:Apr87-688
Douglas, M. Risk Acceptability According
to the Social Sciences.
P. Seabright, 617(TLS):20Mar87-290
Douglas, M. & T. Arthur. See You at the
Movies.
H. Nissenson, 441:18Jan87-16
Douglas, M.S., with J. Rothchild. Marjory
Stoneman Douglas.
L. Mansnerus, 441:4Oct87-29
Douglass, M. Regional Integration on the
Capitalist Periphery.
D. Feeny, 293(JASt):Nov85-190
Doutrelant, P-M. La bonne cuisine et les
autres.
J-F. Revel, 176:Dec86-38
Dove, G.N. The Boys from Grover Avenue.
E.S. Lauterbach, 395(MFS):Summer86-364
Dove, R. Fifth Sunday.
E. McGraw, 455:Mar86-69
Dove, R. Thomas and Beulah.*
L.M. Steinman, 385(MQR):Spring87-428
P. Stitt, 219(GaR):Winter86-1021
Dowden, W.S. - see Moore, T.
Dowden, W.S., with B.G. Bartholomew & J.L.
Linsley - see Moore, T.
Dowell, C. The Houses of Children.
L. Moore, 441:24May87-17
Dowell, P.W. - see Mencken, H.L.
Dowell, R.W., J.L.W. West 3d & N.M.
Westlake - see Dreiser, T.
Dowling, D. Bloomsbury Aesthetics and the
Novels of Forster and Woolf.*
E. Heine, 395(MFS):Summer86-317
R. Shusterman, 89(BJA):Winter86-87
Dowling, D. Fictions of Nuclear Disaster.
A. Barnett, 617(TLS):24Jul87-803

Dowling, D., ed. Novelists on Novelists.
P. Faulkner, 447(N&Q):Sep85-415
Dowling, W.C. Jameson, Althusser, Marx.
E. Cobley, 376:Sep86-158
T. Eagleton, 541(RES):May86-308
D. Lloyd, 188(ECr):Spring86-100
P. Parrinder, 402(MLR):Jan86-157
Downes, D.A. Hopkins' Sanctifying Imagina-
tion.
J.J. Feeney, 637(VS):Summer87-532
Downes, K. Sir John Vanbrugh.
P. Taylor-Martin, 362:1Oct87-26
Downey, T. A Splendid Executioner.
N. Callendar, 441:29Mar87-25
Downie, J.A. Jonathan Swift.*
S. Varey, 83:Spring86-93
N. Wood, 161(DUJ):Jun86-376
Downing, A.B. & B. Smoker. Voluntary
Euthanasia.*
J.G.H., 185:Apr87-706
Dowty, A. Closed Borders.
R.M. Smith, 617(TLS):25-31Dec87-1422
Dowty, D.R., L. Karttunen & A.M. Zwicky,
eds. Natural Language Parsing.
J.E. Hoard, 350:Mar87-170
Doyle, C., ed. Wallace Stevens: The
Critical Heritage.
M. Schaum, 705:Fall86-116
Doyle, E.G. - see Sedulius Scottus
Doyle, J. North of America.*
R. Brown, 529(QQ):Winter86-897
Doyle, J., ed. Yankees in Canada.
R. Thacker, 106:Spring86-51
Doyle, J.T. Deadly Resurrection.
N. Callendar, 441:12Jul87-29
Dozier, R.E. For King, Constitution, and
Country.
M. Fitzpatrick, 83:Autumn86-229
Drabble, M., ed. The Oxford Companion to
English Literature.* (5th ed)
P-G. Boucé, 189(EA):Jan-Mar87-79
B. Cottle, 541(RES):Nov86-620
A.E. Davidson, 115:Summer86-416
P. Dickinson, 410(M&L):Jul86-306
H. Fromm, 31(ASch):Summer86-410
Drabble, M. The Radiant Way.
L. Duguid, 617(TLS):1May87-458
M. Robinson, 441:1Nov87-12
L. Taylor, 362:7May87-25
J. Updike, 442(NY):16Nov87-153
Drabeck, B.A. & H.E. Ellis - see "Archibald
MacLeish: Reflections"
Drache, D. & D. Cameron, eds. The Other
Macdonald Report.
F. Vaillancourt, 529(QQ):Spring86-216
Drachenberg, E. Die mittelalterliche
Glasmalerei im Erfurter Dom.
V. Raguin, 589:Apr86-411
Drachenberg, E., K-J. Maercker & C.
Schmidt. Die mittelalterliche Glas-
malerei in den Ordenskirchen und im
Angermuseum zu Erfurt.
V. Raguin, 589:Apr86-411
Drage, C.L. Russian and Church Slavonic
Books 1701-1800 in United Kingdom Lib-
raries.*
W.G. Jones, 402(MLR):Apr86-540
Dragland, S. Journeys through Bookland.
R. Brown, 627(UTQ):Fall86-156
Dragnich, A.N. & S. Todorovich. The Saga
of Kosovo.
M. Wheeler, 575(SEER):Jan86-155

Draheim, J. & G. Wille. Horaz-Vertonungen vom Mittelalter bis zur Gegenwart.
P.G.M. Brown, 123:Vol36No1-183
M. Huglo, 537:Vol72No1-137
Drakakis, J., ed. Alternative Shakespeares.*
R. Berry, 529(QQ):Summer86-423
P. Erickson, 570(SQ):Winter86-516
D.I. Rabey, 610:Summer86-167
N. Smith, 175:Spring86-57
Drake, D.B. & F. Viña. Don Quijote (1894-1970). (Vol 4)
W.W. Mosely, 238:Mar86-99
Drake, P.W. & E. Silva, eds. Elections and Democratization in Latin America, 1980-1985.
M.A. Seligson, 263(RIB):Vol36No4-490
Drake, W. The First Wave.
K. Hellerstein, 441:25Oct87-25
Draper, R.P. "The Winter's Tale."
M. Willems, 189(EA):Jan-Mar87-82
Dreher, D.E. Domination and Defiance.
P. Rackin, 615(TJ):Dec86-498
Dreiser, T. An Amateur Laborer.* (R.W. Dowell, J.L.W. West 3d & N.M. Westlake, eds)
S. Bush, Jr., 402(MLR):Apr87-458
Dreiser, T. & H.L. Mencken. Dreiser-Mencken Letters. (T.P. Riggio, ed)
A. Kazin, 453(NYRB):26Feb87-8
R. King, 617(TLS):17Jul87-760
Drescher, H.W., ed. Thomas Carlyle 1981.
P. Morère, 189(EA):Jul-Sep86-355
Dresner, S.H. - see Heschel, A.J.
Dressler, M.R. & M.R. Michelsen, eds. Women and Work.
E. Janeway, 441:3May87-45
Dressler, W.U. Morphonology.*
A. Carstairs, 297(JL):Sep86-489
D.H., 355(LSoc):Mar86-132
G. Kleiber, 553(RLiR):Jan-Jun86-200
S. Scalise, 350:Dec87-892
M. Shapiro, 574(SEEJ):Fall86-458
R. Singh, 320(CJL):Winter86-343
Dretske, F.I. Knowledge and the Flow of Information.*
J. Leiber, 543:Mar87-569
P.K. Moser, 438:Winter86-116
"Drevneyshiye gosudarstva na territorii SSSR: Materialy i issledovaniya, 1983 god."
W.F. Ryan, 575(SEER):Jan86-158
Drew, E. Campaign Journal.
639(VQR):Winter86-24
Drewal, H.J. & M.T. Gẹlẹdẹ.*
P.B. Zarrilli, 615(TJ):Dec86-493
Drewe, R. Fortune.
H. Jacobson, 617(TLS):27Nov-3Dec87-1307
Drewett, R. & M. Redhead. The Trial of Richard III.
K.M. Eising, 156(ShJW):Jahrbuch1986-261
Drews, P. Die slawische Avantgarde und der Westen.*
S. Baranczak, 550(RusR):Jan86-62
Drews, R. Basileus.*
N.R.E. Fisher, 303(JoHS):Vol106-236
Dreyer, E.L. Early Ming China.*
J.D. Langlois, Jr., 318(JAOS):Oct/Dec85-766

Dreyfus, H.L. & P. Rabinow. Michel Foucault.* (2nd ed)
C.D. Battershill, 488:Sep86-394
R. McGowen, 131(CL):Spring86-181
Dreyfus, K. - see Grainger, P.
"Driff's Guide to all the Secondhand & Antiquarian Bookshops in the UK, September 1986 to September 1987, together with Auction Houses and Cataloguers." (3rd ed)
D. Chambers, 503:Summer86-94
Drinka, G.F. The Birth of Neurosis.*
M.S. Micale, 31(ASch):Winter85/86-131
Drinnon, R. Keeper of Concentration Camps.
P.S. Washburn, 441:22Feb87-33
Driscoll, J.P. & J.K. Howat, eds. John Frederick Kensett.*
E. McKinsey, 432(NEQ):Mar86-145
Driskell, L.V. Passing Through.
E. Morin, 219(GaR):Summer86-579
Driver, P. - see Kipling, R.
Drochner, K-H. & D. Föhr. Eindrücke-Einblicke.
R.W. Dunbar, 399(MLJ):Autumn86-313
Droixhe, D. & P-P. Gossiaux, eds. Études sur le XVIIIe siècle.
V. Santi, 549(RLC):Oct-Dec86-477
Dronke, P. Dante and Medieval Latin Traditions.
M. Marti, 228(GSLI):Vol163fasc522-266
D. Robey, 617(TLS):6Feb87-140
Dronke, P. Women Writers of the Middle Ages.
J.M. Ferrante, 551(RenQ):Spring86-67
R. Schieffer, 72:Band223Heft2-363
M.T. Tavormina, 115:Winter86-111
Droste, F.G., ed. Stromingen in de hedendaagse linguistiek.
H. Bennis, 204(FdL):Dec86-305
Drouet, J. Lettres à Victor Hugo, 1833-1882. (E. Blewer, ed)
P.L. Horn, 446(NCFS):Fall-Winter86/87-220
Drumbl, J. Quem Quaeritis.
A. Davril, 130:Spring86-65
Drummond de Andrade, C. Travelling in the Family. (T. Colchie & M. Strand, eds)
D.H. Rosenthal, 441:13Dec87-32
Drüppel, C.J. Altfranzösische Urkunden und Lexicologie.*
R. de Gorog, 589:Oct86-919
L. Löfstedt, 439(NM):1986/2-303
Drury, E., ed. Antiques.
B. Scott, 39:Dec86-572
Dryden, J. The Oxford Authors: John Dryden. (K. Walker, ed)
D. Hopkins, 617(TLS):12Jun87-637
Dryden, J. The Works of John Dryden. (Vol 13) (M.E. Novak & G.R. Guffey, eds)
A.B. Gardiner, 566:Autumn86-57
J.V. Guerinot, 568(SCN):Spring-Summer86-1
Drysdale, H. Alone through China and Tibet.
J. Mirsky, 617(TLS):16Jan87-57
Du, N. The Tale of Kiều.* (H.S. Thong, ed & trans)
S. O'Harrow, 302:Vol22No1-117
Dubal, D. The World of the Concert Pianist.
J. Methuen-Campbell, 415:May86-280

Dube, S.W.D., ed. Proceedings of the Symposium on Afro-American and African Poetry and the Teaching of Poetry in Schools.
　E. Mathabela, 538(RAL):Spring86-133
Duberman, M.B. About Time.
　A.N. Williams, 441:22Feb87-29
Duberstein, L. The Marriage Hearse.
　C.D.B. Bryan, 441:10May87-12
Dubie, N. The Springhouse.*
　P. Stitt, 219(GaR):Summer86-557
Dubiel, H. Theory and Politics.
　F.H. Adler, 42(AR):Winter86-116
Dubin, L.S. The History of Beads.
　M. Douglas, 441:29Nov87-12
Dubnick, R.K. The Structure of Obscurity.*
　A. White, 301(JEGP):Apr86-295
Dubois, C-G. L'Imaginaire de la Renaissance.
　J.C. Nash, 207(FR):Dec86-253
　F. Rigolot, 551(RenQ):Spring86-123
Dubois, C-G., ed. L'Imaginaire du changement en France au XVIe siècle.
　R. Zuber, 535(RHL):Mar-Apr86-269
Du Bois, E.C. & others. Feminist Scholarship.
　K. Fishburn, 115:Fall86-537
　M.A.W., 185:Oct86-299
Du Bois, W.E.B. Against Racism. (H. Aptheker, ed)
　L.O. McMurry, 9(AlaR):Jul86-238
　639(VQR):Winter86-14
Du Bois, W.E.B. Newspaper Columns by W.E.B. Du Bois. (H. Aptheker, ed)
　D.F. Dorsey, Jr., 95(CLAJ):Dec86-254
Duboy, P. Lequeu.*
　M. Filler, 441:12Apr87-13
Du Bruck, E. - see Rivière, P.
"Jean Dubuffet."
　90:Jun86-445
Duby, G. Guillaume le Maréchal ou le meilleur chevalier du monde.
　J.W. Baldwin, 589:Jul86-640
Duby, G. William Marshal.*
　639(VQR):Summer86-82
Duchen, C. Feminism in France from May '68 to Mitterand.
　A. Smyth, 402(MLR):Oct87-990
Duchêne, J. Françoise de Grignan ou le mal d'amour.*
　H.T. Barnwell, 208(FS):Oct86-454
　J. Leiner, 475:Vol13No24-386
Duchêne, R. L'Imposture littéraire dans les "Provinciales" de Pascal.*
　A. McKenna, 535(RHL):Mar-Apr86-279
Duchêne, R. Ninon de Lenclos.*
　N.A. Peacock, 208(FS):Jan86-71
　J. Prévot, 535(RHL):Sep-Oct86-913
Duchesneau, F. La Physiologie des Lumières.
　R. Nadeau, 540(RIPh):Vol40fasc3-331
Duck, S. The Thresher's Labour (1736) [together with] Collier, M. The Woman's Labour (1739).
　P-G. Boucé, 189(EA):Jul-Sep86-371
Duckworth, C. The D'Antraigues Phenomenon.
　J. Rogister, 617(TLS):13Feb87-158
Ducornet, R. Entering Fire.*
　O. Conant, 441:7Jun87-30
Dudden, A.P., ed. American Humor.
　E. O'Shaughnessy, 441:17May87-51

Dudley, W.S., ed. The Naval War of 1812. (Vol 1)
　T.G. Martin, 432(NEQ):Sep86-444
"Due Bronzi da Riace."
　J. Boardman, 123:Vol36No2-282
Duff, J.H. & others. An American Vision.
　P-L. Adams, 61:Aug87-84
Duff, R.A. Trials and Punishments.*
　J.D., 185:Jul87-887
Duffey, B. A Poetry of Presence.
　P. Christensen, 191(ELN):Jun87-82
　P.R.Y., 295(JML):Nov86-553
Duffy, B. The World as I Found It.
　P. Meisel, 441:11Oct87-18
Duffy, C.A. Selling Manhattan.
　P. Forbes, 362:12Nov87-30
Duffy, C.A. Standing Female Nude.*
　W. Scammell, 364:Jun86-61
Duffy, J.J. & H.N. Muller 3d. An Anxious Democracy.
　D.P. Peeler, 106:Summer86-201
Duffy, M. Change.
　W. Brandmark, 362:16Apr87-36
　J.K.L. Walker, 617(TLS):15May87-515
Duffy, M. Soldiers, Sugar and Seapower.
　J. Ward, 617(TLS):23-29Oct87-1161
Dufournet, J., ed. Approches du Lancelot en prose.
　E. Kennedy, 382(MAE):1986/2-311
Dufournet, J., ed. Relire le "Roman d'Enéas."
　E. Suomela-Härmä, 439(NM):1986/2-305
Dufournet, J. - see Villon, F.
Dufty, A.R. Morris Embroideries.*
　J. Marsh, 90:Jun86-437
Dugan, A. New and Collected Poems, 1961-1983.
　J.F. Cotter, 249(HudR):Spring86-159
Dugas, G. Albert Memmi.
　J. Roumani, 188(ECr):Spring86-96
Duggan, J.J., ed. A Fragment of Les Enfances Vivien.
　G. Roques, 553(RLiR):Jan-Jun86-283
Duggan, W. Lovers of the African Night.
　S.S. Klass, 441:20Dec87-11
Duhamel, A. Le Complexe d'Astérix.
　H.B. Sutton, 207(FR):Apr87-741
Duhamel, G. Souvenirs de la Grande Guerre. (T. Evans, ed)
　J. Cruickshank, 402(MLR):Oct87-972
Duhem, P. Medieval Cosmology. (R. Ariew, ed & trans)
　J. North, 617(TLS):23Jan87-75
Duhoux, Y. Introduction aux dialectes grecs anciens.
　R. Schmitt, 260(IF):Band91-383
Duke, P. & K. Turan. Call Me Anna.
　H. Rubin, 441:4Oct87-29
Duke, S. US Defence Bases in the United Kingdom.
　R. Bulkeley, 617(TLS):13Mar87-266
Dukore, B.F. American Dramatists 1918-1945 Excluding O'Neill.*
　B.L. Knapp, 397(MD):Mar86-146
Dukore, M.M. Bloom.
　K. Burke, 532(RCF):Spring86-202
Dull, J.R. A Diplomatic History of the American Revolution.*
　A.H. Bowman, 173(ECS):Spring87-356
　G. Clarfield, 656(WMQ):Oct86-682

Dulles, J.W.F. The Sao Paulo Law School and the Anti-Vargas Resistance (1938-1945).
R.M. Levine, 263(RIB):Vol36No2-181
Dumézil, G. Heur et malheur du guerrier.
J-P. Guinle, 450(NRF):Dec86-96
Dummett, M. Voting Procedures.
F. Schick, 311(JP):Jul86-398
Dumont, L. Affinity as a Value.*
I. White, 318(JAOS):Oct/Dec85-793
Dumouchel, P., ed. Violence et vérité.
N. Lukacher, 400(MLN):Sep86-949
Dumville, D., ed. The Historia Brittonum: 3.
J.D. Burnley, 179(ES):Oct86-450
Dunaway, J.M. Simone Weil.
I. de Courtivron, 207(FR):Feb87-403
Duncan, A.B., ed. Claude Simon.
E.J. Smyth, 208(FS):Jul86-361
N. Soelberg, 462(OL):Vol41No4-388
A. Thiher, 395(MFS):Winter86-679
Duncan, D. Out West.
E. Newby, 441:31May87-48
442(NY):10Aug87-79
Dundas, J. The Spider and the Bee.
D. Cheney, 551(RenQ):Winter86-798
J. Norton-Smith, 541(RES):Nov86-557
L.S. Young, 568(SCN):Fall86-40
Dundes, A. Life is Like a Chicken Coop Ladder.*
N.M. Decker, 221(GQ):Spring86-343
D. Rancour-Laferriere, 567:Vol63No3/4-371
Dundes, A., ed. Sacred Narrative.*
J.F. Nagy, 650(WF):Jan86-36
J. Wall, 64(Arv):Vol41-133
M. Weigle, 292(JAF):Jan/Mar86-91
Dunham, V.C. & T.L. Kelly. The Hidden Himalayas.
D. Ackerman, 441:6Dec87-17
Dunkling, L. & W. Gosling. Everyman's Dictionary of First Names.
C.K. Evans, 424:Mar86-105
Dunleavy, J.E., ed. George Moore in Perspective.*
B. Dolan, 305(JIL):May86-59
Dunlop, J.B., R.S. Haugh & M. Nicholson, eds. Solzhenitsyn in Exile.
D.C. Gillespie, 402(MLR):Oct87-1053
Dunlop, L., ed & trans. A Late Chrysanthemum.*
442(NY):12Jan87-102
Dunmore, H. The Sea Skater.
J. O'Grady, 617(TLS):18-24Sep87-1024
Dunmore, T. Soviet Politics, 1945-1953.*
B.A. Ruble, 550(RusR):Jul86-341
Dunn, D. Elegies.*
W. Bedford, 4:Summer86-76
L. Rector, 249(HudR):Autumn86-501
Dunn, D. Selected Poems 1964-1983.
J. Mole, 176:Mar87-56
Dunn, J. Locke.*
P. Carrive, 192(EP):Oct-Dec86-555
J. Egan, 568(SCN):Spring-Summer86-20
J. Sprute, 706:Band18Heft1-96
Dunn, J. The Political Thought of John Locke.
192(EP):Oct-Dec86-554
Dunn, J. The Politics of Socialism.
J. Farr, 185:Jan87-478
Dunn, J. Rethinking Modern Political Theory.*
D.H., 185:Apr87-680

Dunn, J.C. The War the Infantry Knew 1914-1919.
B. Bond, 617(TLS):4-10Dec87-1347
Dunn, R.D. - see Camden, W.
Dunn, R.E. The Adventures of Ibn Battuta.
E. Newby, 441:31May87-48
Dunn, S. Local Time.*
M. Boruch, 29(APR):Mar/Apr87-22
L. Rector, 249(HudR):Autumn86-503
J.P. White, 491:Dec86-171
455:Dec86-64
639(VQR):Autumn86-134
Dunne, C. Hooligan.
T.J. Binyon, 617(TLS):13-19Nov87-1262
Dunne, J.G. The Red White and Blue.
T.R. Edwards, 453(NYRB):13Aug87-50
C. Hitchens, 617(TLS):16-22Oct87-1135
A. Tyler, 441:1Mar87-3
Dunne, S., ed. Poets of Munster.*
M. Harmon, 272(IUR):Spring86-77
Dunnett, D. The Ringed Castle. Checkmate.
A. Short, 571(ScLJ):Summer86-17
Dunning, S.N. Kierkegaard's Dialectic of Inwardness.
J. Donnelly, 543:Mar87-570
Dunning, T.P. "Piers Plowman." (2nd ed) (T.P. Dolan, ed)
K. Bitterling, 72:Band223Heft2-400
Dunphy, J. "Dear Genius..."
G. Pool, 441:6Sep87-17
Dunphy, W. - see Siger de Brabant
Dunwoodie, P. Camus: "L'Envers et l'endroit" and "L'Exil et le royaume."
J. Cruickshank, 208(FS):Jul86-362
L. Day, 402(MLR):Oct87-981
Duparc, J. & D. Margolies - see Caudwell, C.
Dupèbe, J. - see Nostradamus, M.
Dupee, F.W. - see James, H.
Du Plessis, R.B. Writing Beyond the Ending.*
E.E. Berry, 454:Fall86-78
K. Fishburn, 115:Summer86-420
W. Gibson, 128(CE):Dec86-832
Dupré, G. Les Mamantes.
A. Clerval, 450(NRF):Jun86-76
Dupree, R.S. allen Tate and the Augustinian Imagination.
M.R. Winchell, 106:Winter86-483
Dupuy, H., A. Bothorel & L. Brunet, eds. Recherches linguistiques.
K-H. Jäger, 406:Summer86-215
Duquette, J-P. Colette.
Y. Resch, 535(RHL):Jul-Aug86-787
Duquoc, C. Provisional Churches.
P. Baelz, 617(TLS):27Feb87-223
Durand, F. Influssi Greci nel dialetto Ligure.*
W. Hupka, 685(ZDL):1/1986-127
Durand, G. Les structures anthropologiques de l'imaginaire.
P. Somville, 542:Apr-Jun86-268
Durand, J., ed. Gaceta de Lima.
S. García Castañeda, 345:May86-244
Durant, A. Conditions of Music.
W. Mellers, 415:Apr86-212
Durant, A. Ezra Pound.*
L. Surette, 675(YER):Vol8No1/2-144
Durant, P. Jean-Paul Belmondo.
J. Van Baelen, 207(FR):May87-903
Duranti, F. The House on Moon Lake.*
I. Thomson, 362:14May87-31

Duras, M. La Douleur.*
  B.L. Knapp, 207(FR):Feb87-428
Duras, M. The Lovers.* (French title:
  L'Amant.)
  J. Byrne, 532(RCF):Fall86-131
Duras, M. The Vice-Consul.
  D. Bair, 441:23Aug87-16
Duras, M. The War.*
  G. Brée, 268(IFR):Winter87-58
  639(VQR):Autumn86-128
Duras, M. Les Yeux bleus cheveux noirs.
  The Sea Wall.
  J. Pilling, 617(TLS):10Jul87-741
Durcan, P. The Selected Paul Durcan.* (E.
  Longley, ed) The Berlin Wall Café.*
  M. O'Neill, 493:Jun86-110
Durden, R.F. The Self-Inflicted Wound.
  P.H. Bergeron, 585(SoQ):Winter87-151
  639(VQR):Spring86-53
Durie, M. A Grammar of Acehnese.
  S.A. Thompson, 350:Dec87-919
Du Rocher, R.J. Milton and Ovid.*
  A.C. Labriola, 391:May86-57
  S.P. Revard, 191(ELN):Jun87-74
  R.P. Sonkowsky, 124:May-Jun87-392
  639(VQR):Summer86-89
Durr, V.F. Outside the Magic Circle.
  (H.F. Barnard, ed)
  B. Brandon, 9(AlaR):Oct86-303
  P.A. Sullivan, 639(VQR):Summer86-535
Durrell, L. Quinx, or The Ripper's Tale.*
  639(VQR):Spring86-57
Durrell, L. The State of the Ark.
  S. Mills, 617(TLS):5Jun87-615
Durusoy, G. L'incidence de la littérature
  et de la langue tchèques sur les nou-
  velles de Franz Kafka.
  H. Jechova-Voisine, 549(RLC):Jul-Sep86-
  369
von Dusburg, P. - see under Peter von
  Dusburg
Dusinberre, J. Alice to the Lighthouse.
  A. Davies, 362:10Sep87-24
van der Dussen, W.J. History as a Science.
  L.J. Goldstein, 488:Jun86-267
Düsterdieck, P. & others. Die Sammlung
  Hobrecker der Universitätsbibliothek
  Braunschweig.
  B. Alderson, 617(TLS):23Jan87-90
Dusun, M. - see under Mpu Dusun
Dutari, N.C. - see under Cuesta Dutari, N.
Duterme, R. Alain-Fournier ou le fantasme
  amoureux.
  R. Gibson, 617(TLS):3Apr87-363
Dutourd, J. Contre les dégoûts de la vie.
  J. Théodorides, 605(SC):15Jan87-215
Dutt, S. India and the Third World.
  R. Harshé, 293(JASt):Nov85-168
  R.J. Young, 318(JAOS):Oct/Dec85-810
Dutt, V.P. India's Foreign Policy.
  S. Chawla, 293(JASt):Nov85-169
Dutton, G. Snow on the Saltbush.
  H. Priessnitz, 490:Band18Heft1/2-192
Dutton, R. Ben Jonson.*
  S. van den Berg, 551(RenQ):Summer86-
  346
  N.H. Platz, 156(ShJW):Jahrbuch1986-205
Dutton, R. - see Jonson, B.
Dutton, R.R. Saul Bellow.
  J. Newman, 677(YES):Vol16-356
Duțu, A. Literatura comparată și istoria
  mentalităților.
  A. Marino, 107(CRCL):Sep86-469

Duval, A. Place Jacques-Cartier, ou quar-
  ante ans de théâtre français à Québec,
  1871-1911.*
  M.A. Fitzpatrick, 207(FR):Mar87-529
Duval, P-M., ed. Recueil des Inscriptions
  Gauloises. (Vol 1)
  G. MacEoin, 112:Vol18-226
Duverger, E. Antwerpse kunstinventarissen
  uit de zeventiende eeuw.
  H. Vlieghe, 90:Nov86-832
Duverger, M. Bréviaire de la cohabita-
  tion.
  A. Prévos, 207(FR):Apr87-745
Düwel, K. Werkbezeichnungen der mittel-
  hochdeutschen Erzählliteratur (1050-
  1250).
  U. Schulze, 684(ZDA):Band115Heft1-39
Düwel, K., with others, eds. Der Reinhart
  Fuchs des Elsässers Heinrich.
  S. Jefferis, 589:Jan86-141
Dwork, D. War is Good for Babies and
  Other Young Children.
  J. Turner, 617(TLS):10Apr87-376
Dworkin, A. Ice and Fire.*
  C. Sternhell, 441:3May87-3
Dworkin, A. Intercourse.
  A. Coles, 362:2Jul87-32
  L. Sage, 617(TLS):16-22Oct87-1129
  C. Sternhell, 441:3May87-3
Dworkin, R. Law's Empire.*
  T.C. Grey, 453(NYRB):12Mar87-32
  K. Kress, 185:Jul87-834
  R. Scruton, 176:Jul/Aug87-66
Dworkin, R. A Matter of Principle.
  A.A. Morris, 185:Jan87-481
  639(VQR):Winter86-25
Dworkin, S. Miss America, 1945.
  E. Goodman, 441:15Nov87-12
Dworkin, S. Stolen Goods.
  C.D. Kennedy, 441:19Jul87-20
Dworkin, S.N. Etymology and Derivational
  Morphology.
  A.S. Allen, 350:Jun87-434
  Y. Malkiel, 215(GL):Vol26No4-282
  C. Schmitt, 553(RLiR):Jul-Dec86-576
Dyck, J., with others - see "Rhetorik, Ein
  internationales Jahrbuch"
Dyer, G. War.
  M.R.D. Foot, 176:Feb87-44
Dyer, G. Ways of Telling.
  L. Cooke, 617(TLS):24Apr87-449
  B. Morton, 362:1Jan87-19
Dyer, R. Heavenly Bodies.
  D. Coward, 617(TLS):24Jul87-792
Dyer, T.G. The University of Georgia.
  L.M. Crawford, 577(SHR):Fall86-401
  M.M. Thomas, 9(AlaR):Jul86-230
Dyhr, M. Zwei Beiträge zur Untersuchung
  der Valenzklassen und Satzbaupläne im
  Dänischen und Deutschen.
  R. Baudusch, 682(ZPSK):Band39Heft1-125
Dyker, D.A. The Future of the Soviet
  Economic Planning System.
  J.P. Bonin, 550(RusR):Jul86-309
  S. Estrin, 575(SEER):Oct86-644
Dyker, D.A. The Process of Investment in
  the Soviet Union.*
  A.H. Smith, 575(SEER):Jan86-150
Dykstra, L., with M. Noble. Nails.
  J. Oppenheimer, 441:3May87-14
Dykstra, Y.K. - see "Miraculous Tales of
  the Lotus Sutra from Ancient Japan"

Echevarría, R.G. – see under González Echevarría, R.
Echeverria, D. The Maupeou Revolution.
　H. Cohen 207(FR):Mar87–581
Echlin, E. An Alternative Ending to Richardson's "Clarissa." (D. Daphinoff, ed)
　J. Harris, 677(YES):Vol16–268
"Echos."
　E.C. Knox, 207(FR):Oct86–148
Eck, D.L. Banaras.*
　A. Tagore, 314:Summer–Fall86–245
Ecker, G., ed. Feminist Aesthetics.
　M. Hjort, 529(QQ):Winter86–943
Eckert, R., E. Crome & C. Fleckenstein. Geschichte der russischen Sprache.
　H. Leeming, 575(SEER):Oct86–576
Eckhardt, C.D., ed. The "Prophetia Merlini" of Geoffrey of Monmouth.*
　J.M. Cowen, 447(N&Q):Sep85–389
　V.M. Lagorio, 589:Apr86–497
Eckhardt, F. Music from Within. (G. Bowler, ed)
　R. Elliott, 529(QQ):Autumn86–694
Eckhardt, J. Das epische Theater.
　U. Weisstein, 133:Band18Heft4–376
Maître Eckhart. "Le commentaire de la Genèse," précédé des "Prologues." (F. Brunner & others, eds & trans)
　M.L. Führer, 589:Jan86–230
Eckley, G. Children's Lore in "Finnegans Wake."*
　P.F. Herring, 659(ConL):Spring87–104
　K. Reisman, 292(JAF):Jul/Sep86–350
Eckman, F.R., L.H. Bell & D. Nelson, eds. Universals of Second Language Acquisition.*
　J. Vizmuller–Zocco, 320(CJL):Summer86–196
Eckstut, S. & D. Scoulos. Real to Reel.
　B.W. Robinett, 399(MLJ):Winter86–454
Eco, U. Art and Beauty in the Middle Ages.*
　C.H. Clough, 324:Nov87–947
Eco, U. Travels in Hyperreality.*
　A.O. Aldridge, 396(ModA):Summer/Fall86–323
　M. Kozloff, 62:Sep86–4
　M. Perloff, 385(MQR):Spring87–404
Eco, U. & T.A. Sebeok, eds. The Sign of Three.*
　J.G. Kennedy, 478:Apr86–122
　P. Thagard, 567:Vol60No3/4–289
Ecole, J. – see Lavelle, L.
"Les Écrivains et la politique dans le Sud–Ouest de la France autour des années 1580."
　G–A. Pérouse, 535(RHL):Jul–Aug86–732
Eddings, D. Guardians of the West.
　D. Hartwell, 441:5Jul87–14
Edds, M. Free at Last.
　T. Chaffin, 441:4Oct87–38
Ede, J. A Way of Life: Kettle's Yard.*
　D. Armstrong, 97(CQ):Vol15No3–268
Edel, L. Henry James: A Life.
　M. Banta, 27(AL):Dec86–639
　R.E.F., 26(ALR):Winter87–95
　M.P.L., 295(JML):Nov86–489
　A.R. Tintner, 395(MFS):Winter86–599
Edel, L. – see James, H.
Edel, L. – see Wilson, E.
Edel, L. & D.H. Laurence, with J. Rambeau. A Bibliography of Henry James.* (3rd ed)
　A.W. Bellringer, 677(YES):Vol16–336

Edel, L. & L.H. Powers – see James, H.
Edel, L., with M. Wilson – see James, H.
Edel, M., E.D. Sclar & D. Luria. Shaky Palaces.
　C. McShane, 432(NEQ):Dec86–597
Edelman, M.W. Families in Peril.
　D. Wycliff, 441:7Jun87–12
Edelson, M. Hypothesis and Evidence in Psychoanalysis.*
　N. Bruss, 567:Vol60No1/2–129
　M. Lavin, 486:Jun86–300
Edelstein, S.J. The Sickled Cell.*
　R. Beddington, 617(TLS):18–24Sep87–1011
Eden, D. Gilbert and Sullivan.*
　A. Lamb, 415:Sep86–500
Eden, P.T. – see Seneca
Eden, R. Political Leadership and Nihilism.*
　R. Beiner, 529(QQ):Summer86–439
　P. Milbouer, 221(GQ):Fall86–684
　G.J. Stack, 319:Apr87–309
Edgar, W.B., ed. A Southern Renascence Man.*
　M.R. Winchell, 106:Winter86–483
Edgerton, C. Walking Across Egypt.
　K. Morton, 441:29Mar87–17
Edgerton, H. Stopping Time. (G. Kayafas, ed)
　A. Grundberg, 441:6Dec87–20
Edgerton, S.Y., Jr. Pictures and Punishment.*
　M. Kemp, 90:Feb86–147
　L. Martines, 551(RenQ):Spring86–109
　R.C. Trexler, 589:Jul86–642
Edgeworth, M. Patronage. Helen.
　P. Raine, 617(TLS):6–12Nov87–1216
Edison, C.A., ed. Cowboy Poetry from Utah.
　J.C. McNutt, 651(WHR):Summer86–177
　Z. Reisner, 649(WAL):Aug86–172
Edmiston, W.F. Diderot and the Family.
　G. Bremner, 208(FS):Oct86–466
　R. Davison, 173(ECS):Spring87–365
　C. Michael, 207(FR):May87–861
Edmond, L. Seasons and Creatures.
　J. Penberthy, 617(TLS):31Jul87–823
Edmond, M. Rare Sir William Davenant.
　S. Schoenbaum, 617(TLS):13–19Nov87–1255
Edmonds, F. Cricket XXXX Cricket.
　N. Andrew, 362:3Dec87–34
Edmonds, R. Setting the Mould.
　J.L. Gaddis, 617(TLS):8May87–479
Edmondson, R. Rhetoric in Sociology.
　R. Keat, 518:Jul86–189
Saint Edmund of Abingdon. "Mirour de Seinte Eglyse."* (A.D. Wilshere, ed)
　J. Beck, 589:Jul86–719
　J.H. Marshall, 402(MLR):Oct86–998
Edmunds, L. & A. Dundes, eds. Oedipus.*
　J. Bremmer, 303(JoHS):Vol106–233
Edmunds, R.D. Tecumseh and the Quest for Indian Leadership.* The Shawnee Prophet.
　O.P. Dickason, 106:Winter86–459
Edsall, N.C. Richard Cobden.
　N. Gash, 617(TLS):11–17Sep87–993
Edson, L. Henri Michaux and the Poetics of Movement.
　P. Broome, 208(FS):Oct86–489
　R.W. Greene, 188(ECr):Fall86–102
Edson, R. The Wounded Breakfast.
　639(VQR):Spring86–62

Eduards, J., ed. Linguistic Minorities, Policies and Pluralism.
J.A. Fishman, 399(MLJ):Spring86-57
Edwardes, M. The Myth of the Mahatma.*
J. Mellors, 364:Aug/Sep86-153
Edwards, A. Early Reagan.
V. Bogdanor, 176:Nov87-55
P. French, 362:15Oct87-27
R. Sklar, 441:26Jul87-7
Edwards, A. Road to Tara.
S.I. Bellman, 534(RALS):Spring-Autumn84-236
Edwards, A.S.G., ed. Middle English Prose.
A.E. Hartung, 589:Jul86-644
S.M. Horrall, 178:Sep86-336
S.J. Ogilvie-Thomson, 541(RES):Aug86-403
S. Wenzel, 38:Band104Heft3/4-478
Edwards, C.L. & K.E.B. Manley, eds. Narrative Folksong - New Directions.
M. Herndon, 650(WF):Oct86-297
Edwards, G. Dramatists in Perspective.
D. Gagen, 402(MLR):Jul87-763
P. Zatlin, 615(TJ):Oct86-386
Edwards, G. El teatro de Federico García Lorca.*
M. Laffranque, 92(BH):Jan-Jun85-208
J. Lyon, 86(BHS):Jul86-296
Edwards, J. Language, Society and Identity.*
R.B. Le Page, 353:Vol24No2-461
Edwards, J. Positive Discrimination, Social Justice, and Social Policy.
S. Green, 617(TLS):31Jul87-827
Edwards, J. The Works of Jonathan Edwards.* (Vol 7) (N. Pettit, ed)
W.R. Ward, 83:Autumn86-275
Edwards, M. Towards a Christian Poetics.*
R.A. Lasseter, 569(SR):Spring86-279
Edwards, M. & S. Usher, eds & trans. Greek Orators. (Vol 1)
M. Gagarin, 124:Jan-Feb87-218
Edwards, M.J. - see Brooke, F.
Edwards, P. Shakespeare.*
M. Dodsworth, 175:Summer86-189
S. Hazell, 157:No161-50
Edwards, P. Threshold of a Nation.
R.W. Desai, 675(YER):Vol8No1/2-128
Edwards, P. - see Lewis, W.
Edwards, P. - see Shakespeare, W.
Edwards, R.A. And the Glory.
P.M. Young, 415:Oct86-560
Edwards, R.D. Victor Gollancz.
H. Benedict, 441:27Dec87-19
D. Caute, 362:15Jan87-21
V. Cunningham, 617(TLS):13Feb87-156
442(NY):7Dec87-192
Edwards, V. Language in a Black Community.
V. Benmaman, 399(MLJ):Winter86-417
W.N. Francis, 350:Mar87-192
van Effenterre, H. La Cité grecque.
A.M. Snodgrass, 123:Vol36No2-261
Effinger, G.A. When Gravity Fails.
G. Jonas, 441:8Mar87-30
Egan, D. Collected Poems.*
T. Eagleton, 565:Autumn86-76
Egan, R.C. The Literary Works of Ou-yang Hsiu (1007-72).
K-I.S. Chang, 244(HJAS):Jun86-273
D.J. Levy, 293(JASt):Aug86-814
S. Sargent, 116:Jul85-174

Egan, S. Patterns of Experience in Autobiography.*
H.P. Abbott, 402(MLR):Apr86-421
R. Bell, 401(MLQ):Jun85-191
A. Brink, 178:Jun86-240
S. Vice, 506(PSt):May86-83
Egeria. Égérie, Journal de voyage. (P. Maraval, ed & trans) [together with] Valérius du Bierzo, lettre sur la Bse Égérie. (M.C. Díaz y Díaz, ed & trans)
A.P. Orbán, 394:Vol39fasc1/2-211
Egido, J.C.B. - see under Brasas Egido, J.C.
Egli, A. Weinbau im Deutschwallis.
W. Kleiber, 685(ZDL):2/1986-252
Ehnbom, D.J., with R. Skelton & P. Chandra. Indian Miniatures.
M. Archer, 39:Aug86-140
T. Wilcox, 90:Dec86-910
Ehrenpreis, I. Swift.* (Vol 3)
C. Rawson, 541(RES):Feb86-96
Ehrenstein, D. Film: The Front Line 1984.
G. Adair, 707:Spring86-141
Ehrlich, C. The Music Profession in Britain Since the Eighteenth Century.
S. Banfield, 415:Oct86-560
S. Norquist, 637(VS):Autumn86-132
P. Waller, 410(M&L):Oct86-411
Ehrlich, G. The Solace of Open Spaces.*
J.B. Cannon, 649(WAL):Nov86-255
Ehrlich, S. Dreaming the Ark.
C. Mandel, 502(PrS):Winter86-104
Ehrlichman, J. The China Card.*
639(VQR):Autumn86-127
Eibel, D. Streets Too Narrow for Parades.
P.M. St. Pierre, 102(CanL):Summer86-121
von Eichendorff, J. Sämtliche Werke des Freiherrn Joseph von Eichendorff. (Vol 3) (C. Briegleb & C. Rauschenberg, eds)
J. Purver, 402(MLR):Jul87-784
Eichler, E. & H. Walther. Ortsnamenbuch der Oberlausitz.
H. Weinacht, 685(ZDL):1/1986-110
Eichmann, R. & J. Du Val, eds & trans. The French Fabliau, B.N. MS 837. (Vol 1)
J. Tattersall, 208(FS):Jul86-318
Eichner, H. & N. Lelless - see Schlegel, F.
Eidelberg, N. Teatro experimental hispano-americano 1960-1980.
K.F. Nigro, 238:Dec86-887
Eidel'man, N. Poslednii letopisets.
P. Debreczeny, 550(RusR):Oct86-427
Eidus, J. Faithful Rebecca.
D. Leimbach, 441:21Jun87-22
Eifler, M. Die subjektivistische Romanform seit ihren Anfängen in der Frühromantik.
T.F. Barry, 221(GQ):Summer86-499
Eifring, H. Høy eller stein?
L-G. Andersson, 452(NJL):Vol9No2-199
E. Haugen, 563(SS):Autumn86-429
Eigeldinger, F.S., ed. Table de concordance rythmique et syntaxique de "Une Saison en Enfer" d'Arthur Rimbaud.
C.A. Hackett, 208(FS):Jul86-350
Eigeldinger, F.S., D. Godet & E. Wehrli, comps. Table de concordances rythmique et syntaxique des "Poésies" de Paul Verlaine.
C. Chadwick, 208(FS):Jul86-350
Eigeldinger, J-J. Chopin. (R. Howat, ed)
C. Rosen, 453(NYRB):28May87-9

Eigeldinger, M. Suite pour Odilon Redon.
  P.O. Walzer, 535(RHL):Mar–Apr86–323
Eigeldinger, M. – see Gautier, T.
"The Eighteenth Century: A Current Bibliog-
  raphy."* (Vol 5: 1979) (P.J. Korshin,
  ed)
    A.J. Sambrook, 402(MLR):Apr86–424
    R. Van Dusen, 403(MLS):Summer86–325
"The Eighteenth Century: A Current Bibliog-
  raphy." (Vol 6: 1980) (J.S. Borck, ed)
    A.J. Sambrook, 402(MLR):Apr86–424
"The Eighteenth Century: A Current Bibliog-
  raphy."* (Vol 7: 1981) (J.S. Borck, ed)
    P–G. Boucé, 189(EA):Jan–Mar87–86
"The Eighteenth Century Short Title Cata-
  logue." (R.C. Alston & M.J. Crump, eds)
    C.Y. Ferdinand, 40(AEB):Vol8No4–242
Eigner, E.M. The Metaphysical Novel in
  England and America.
    A. Hornung, 38:Band104Heft1/2–254
Eigner, E.M. & G.J. Worth, eds. Victorian
  Criticism of the Novel.*
    A. Jumeau, 189(EA):Jul–Sep86–358
Eimer, G. Bernt Botke.
    P.C., 90:Aug86–615
Einaudi, P.F. A Grammar of Biloxi.
    R.L. Rankin, 269(IJAL):Jan86–77
Einhorn, E.S. & J. Logue. A Selective Bib-
  liography of Scandinavian Politics and
  Policy.
    C.K. Rogers, 563(SS):Winter86–91
Einstein, A. The Collected Papers of
  Albert Einstein. (Vol 1) (J. Stachel,
  ed)
    J. Bernstein, 442(NY):6Jul87–77
    R. McCormmach, 441:27Sep87–33
Eire, C.M.N. War against the Idols.
    H.A. Oberman, 617(TLS):14Aug87–884
Eisele, U. Die Struktur des modernen
  deutschen Romans.*
    O. Durrani, 402(MLR):Oct86–1043
Eiseley, L. The Lost Notebooks of Loren
  Eiseley. (K. Heuer, ed)
    R. Finch, 441:20Sep87–14
Eisen, J. & F. Dine, with K. Eisen, eds.
  Unknown California.
    P.D. Morrow, 649(WAL):Aug86–161
Eisenberg, D. Transactions in a Foreign
  Currency.*
    T. De Pietro, 249(HudR):Autumn86–488
    J. Mellors, 364:Jun86–98
Eisenberg, D. & T.L. Wright. Encounters
  with Qi.
    R. Porter, 617(TLS):30Jan87–118
Eisenhower, D. Eisenhower at War 1943–
  1945.*
    D. Fraser, 617(TLS):3Apr87–365
Eisenman, P., M. Tafuri & R. Kraus. Peter
  Eisenman: Houses of Cards.
    P. Goldberger, 441:6Dec87–22
Eisenman, R. Maccabees, Zadokites,
  Christians and Qumran.
    J.C. Vander Kam, 318(JAOS):Oct/Dec85–
    798
Eisenstadt, J. From Rockaway.
    D. Kirk, 441:4Oct87–29
    442(NY):5Oct87–126
Eisenstein, S. The Inner Garden.
    S. Vogan, 441:3May87–43
Eisenzweig, U. Les Jeux le l'écriture dans
  "L'Etranger" de Camus.
    J. Sarocchi, 535(RHL):Jul–Aug86–795

Eisenzweig, U. Le Récit impossible.
    J.D. Erickson, 188(ECr):Summer86–110
Eisermann, D. Crèvecoeur oder die Erfin-
  dung Amerikas.
    C. Gerbaud, 189(EA):Oct–Dec87–483
Eisler, R. The Chalice and the Blade.
    E. Fox–Genovese, 441:4Oct87–32
Eitner, L. An Outline of 19th Century
  European Painting.
    P. Conisbee, 617(TLS):25–31Dec87–1426
van Ek, J.A., & N.J. Robat. The Student's
  Grammar of English.*
    J. Lavédrine, 189(EA):Jul–Sep87–329
Ekelöf, G. En Mölna Elegi – Metamorfoser.
    R. Shideler, 563(SS):Winter86–95
Ekelund, L. Rabbe Enckell, lyriker av den
  svåra skolan.
    G.C. Schoolfield, 563(SS):Winter86–76
Elam, K. Shakespeare's Universe of Dis-
  course.*
    W.T. MacCary, 301(JEGP):Oct86–561
    R.P. Wheeler, 551(RenQ):Spring86–141
Elbaum, B. & W. Lazonick, eds. The Decline
  of the British Economy.*
    B. Supple, 617(TLS):13–19Nov87–1243
Elder, J. Imagining the Earth.
    D. Robinson, 27(AL):Oct86–475
Elderfield, J. Kurt Schwitters.
    D. Ades, 90:Apr86–301
Eldredge, N. Life Pulse.
    C. Verderese, 441:12Apr87–27
Elegant, R. From a Far Land.
    J. Fast, 441:20Sep87–39
Elgin, S.H. The Judas Rose.
    G. Jonas, 441:8Mar87–30
"El Greco: Italy and Spain."
    E. Young, 39:Mar86–219
Eliade, M. Briser le toit de la maison.*
    T. Cordellier, 450(NRF):Oct86–96
Eliade, M. A History of Religious Ideas.*
  (Vols 1–3)
    S.H. Phillips, 485(PE&W):Apr86–177
Elias, A.C., Jr. Swift at Moor Park.*
    E.J. Rielly, 403(MLS):Summer86–316
Elias, J.A. Plato's Defense of Poetry.*
    R.P. Bond, 478:Apr86–117
    J. Bussanich, 41:Vol6–210
    J.B. Waugh, 290(JAAC):Fall86–99
Elias, R.H. & E.D. Finch – see Digges, T.A.
Eliassen, K.A. & M.N. Pedersen. Skandi-
  naviske politiske institutioner og
  politisk adfaerd 1970–1984.
    J. Logue, 563(SS):Autumn86–453
Eliot, G. Daniel Deronda. (G. Handley,
  ed)
    A.W. Bellringer, 179(ES):Oct86–462
    E. Hollahan, 594:Summer86–206
Eliot, G. Scenes of Clerical Life. (T.A.
  Noble, ed)
    A.W. Bellringer, 179(ES):Oct86–462
    A. Jumeau, 189(EA):Jul–Sep86–358
Eliot, G. Selections from George Eliot's
  Letters.* (G.S. Haight, ed)
    W.W. Fairey, 639(VQR):Spring86–369
    S. Hudson, 577(SHR):Winter86–76
    M. Wolff, 637(VS):Winter87–297
    529(QQ):Spring86–222
Elkann, A. Piazza Carignano.
    W. Grimes, 441:4Jan87–18
Elkar, R.S., ed. Europas unruhige Reg-
  ionen.
    Ž. Muljačić, 685(ZDL):2/1986–276

Elkin, S. The Rabbi of Lud.
  W. Pritchard, 441:8Nov87−12
Elkington, J. The Poisoned Womb.
  R. Doyle, 441:5Apr87−34
Elkins, A.J. A Deceptive Clarity.
  N. Callendar, 441:31May87−45
Elliot, A. On the Appian Way.*
  H. Buckingham, 565:Summer86−64
Elliot, B. Victorian Gardens.
  J.S. Curl, 324:Oct87−858
  P. Hobhouse, 617(TLS):27Feb87−225
Elliot, V., ed. Dear Mr. Shaw.
  P. Taylor−Martin, 362:10Dec87−28
Elliott, A., L. McAuley & C. O'Driscoll.
  Trio 4.
  T. Eagleton, 565:Autumn86−76
Elliott, A.G. The "Vie de Saint Alexis" in
  the Twelfth and Thirteenth Centuries.*
  M.E. Winters, 207(FR):Oct86−114
Elliott, A.G. − see "Seven Medieval Latin
  Comedies"
Elliott, D. New Worlds.
  N. Lynton, 617(TLS):27Mar87−335
Elliott, J. The Italian Lesson.
  442(NY):23Mar87−100
Elliott, J. The Sadness of Witches.
  J. Melmoth, 617(TLS):18−24Sep87−1025
  L. Taylor, 362:10Dec87−30
Elliott, J.H. The Count−Duke of Olivares.*
  N. Bliven, 442(NY):31Aug87−95
Elliott, J.P. − see Cooper, J.F.
Elliott, M. Heartbeat London.
  J. Chernaik, 617(TLS):23Jan87−89
Elliott, R.C. The Literary Persona.
  H. Pagliaro, 403(MLS):Spring86−91
Elliott, R.W.V. Thomas Hardy's English.*
  P. Ingham, 541(RES):May86−283
Elliott, S.L. Waiting for Childhood.
  A.R. Gurney, 441:6Sep87−5
  442(NY):19Oct87−119
Elliott, T.G. Ammianus Marcellinus and
  Fourth Century History.*
  J.M. Alonso−Núñez, 313:Vol76−328
Ellis, A.T. The Clothes in the Wardrobe.
  A. Duchêne, 617(TLS):16−22Oct87−1136
  J. McKay, 362:8Oct87−24
Ellis, A.T. Home Life.*
  S. Silvers, 364:Jul86−106
Ellis, A.T. More Home Life.
  D.J. Enright, 617(TLS):18−24Dec87−1399
Ellis, A.T. Unexplained Laughter.
  W. Gimbel, 441:18Oct87−22
Ellis, B.E. The Rules of Attraction.
  T. Rafferty, 442(NY):26Oct87−142
  S. Spencer, 441:13Sep87−14
Ellis, C.J. Aboriginal Music.
  R.M. Moyle, 187:Winter87−155
Ellis, D. Wordsworth, Freud and the Spots
  of Time.
  D. Gervais, 97(CQ):Vol15No2−148
  R.E. Matlak, 661(WC):Autumn86−224
  J. Woolley, 175:Spring86−73
Ellis, D.F. & E. Spong. Just Enough Serbo−
  Croat for Yugoslavia.
  C.E. Gribble, 399(MLJ):Spring86−76
Ellis, D.L. & K.S. McLaughlin. Just Enough
  Portuguese.
  R.D. Dennis, 399(MLJ):Spring86−72
Ellis, F.H., ed. Swift vs. Mainwaring.
  P. Danchin, 189(EA):Jul−Sep86−344
  J.A. Downie, 506(PSt):Dec86−103
  J.I. Fischer, 566:Spring87−194
  J.C.C. Mays, 272(IUR):Spring86−99

Ellis, J. The Russian Orthodox Church.
  G.A. Hosking, 617(TLS):9Jan87−35
Ellis, J. The Social History of the
  Machine Gun.
  362:8Oct87−24
Ellis, J.M. One Fairy Story Too Many.*
  F. Bergmann, 107(CRCL):Sep86−480
  D.P. Deneau, 573(SSF):Fall86−469
Ellis, M. Towards a Jewish Theology of
  Liberation.
  362:1Oct87−25
Ellis, P.B. Celtic Inheritance.
  B. Ó Cuív, 112:Vol18−220
Ellis, R. Classroom Second Language
  Development.
  R.J. Alexander, 257(IRAL):Feb86−82
Ellis, R. Patterns of Religious Narrative
  in the "Canterbury Tales."
  B. O'Donoghue, 617(TLS):29May87−587
Ellis, S. Dante and English Poetry.*
  K.M. Lea, 541(RES):Feb86−134
Ellis, S. Home and Away.
  J. Horder, 362:14May87−33
Ellison, D.R. The Reading of Proust.*
  J. Cruickshank, 208(FS):Oct86−487
  J−Y. Tadié, 549(RLC):Apr−Jun86−251
Ellison, H.J. Soviet Policy toward Western
  Europe.*
  H. Hanak, 575(SEER):Apr86−311
Ellison, J. Another Little Drink.
  P. Humphries, 362:15Oct87−28
  J.K.L. Walker, 617(TLS):16−22Oct87−
  1136
Ellison, J. Emerson's Romantic Style.*
  W−C. Dimock, 219(GaR):Summer86−572
  D. Simpson, 301(JEGP):Jan86−148
Ellman, M. Collectivisation, Convergence
  and Capitalism.
  P.G. Toumanoff, 550(RusR):Jul86−311
Ellmann, M. Thinking about Women.
  E.B. Voigt, 344:Summer87−127
Ellmann, R. Oscar Wilde.
  N. Lewis, 362:8Oct87−21
  G. Vidal, 617(TLS):2−8Oct87−1063
Ellmann, R. W.B. Yeats's Second Puberty.
  C. Rawson, 617(TLS):24Jul87−783
Ellroy, J. The Black Dahlia.
  N. Callendar, 441:8Nov87−62
Elm, K., ed. Norbert von Xanten.
  C.L. Smetana, 589:Jul86−733
Elm, T. & G. Hemmerich, eds. Zur Ges−
  chichtlichkeit der Moderne.
  S. Bogumil, 107(CRCL):Sep86−495
van Els, T. & others. Applied Linguistics
  and the Learning and Teaching of Foreign
  Languages.*
  P. Meara, 402(MLR):Apr86−415
El Saffar, R. Beyond Fiction.*
  S.J. Fajardo, 551(RenQ):Spring86−126
  D. Fox, 478:Apr86−127
  A.S. Trueblood, 405(MP):Nov86−222
  E. Williamson, 402(MLR):Apr87−506
Elsen, A.E. "The Gates of Hell" by Auguste
  Rodin.*
  P.W.J., 90:Jun86−445
  A.A. McLees, 207(FR):Mar87−578
Elsen, A.E. Rodin's "Thinker" and the
  Dilemmas of Modern Public Sculpture.*
  D. Carrier, 90:Aug86−614
  S. Whitfield, 176:Feb87−52

van der Elst, G., E. Leiss & B. Naumann.
Syntaktische Analyse.
  C. Thim-Mabrey, 684(ZDA):Band115Heft2-
  77
Elster, J. An Introduction to Karl Marx.
  A. Ryan, 617(TLS):13Feb87-155
Elster, J. Making Sense of Marx.*
  A. Levine, 311(JP):Dec86-721
  D. Tucker, 63:Dec86-515
Elster, J. - see "Karl Marx: A Reader"
Elstun, E.N. Richard Beer-Hofmann.*
  S. Bauschinger, 406:Winter86-549
Elsworth, J.D. Andrey Bely.*
  R.P. Hughes, 550(RusR):Jan86-53
Elton, G.R. F.W. Maitland.*
  B.M.D., 185:Oct86-302
  639(VQR):Winter86-12
Elton, G.R. The Parliament of England,
  1559-1581.
  J. Loach, 617(TLS):5Jun87-602
Éluard, P. Capitale de la douleur. (V.J.
  Daniel, ed)
  J.H. Matthews, 593:Spring86-83
  C. Scott, 402(MLR):Oct87-974
Elvers, R., ed. Festschrift Albi Rosen-
  thal.
  S. Roe, 410(M&L):Apr86-192
Elvin, L. Family Enterprise.
  N. Thistlethwaite, 415:Dec86-709
Elwitt, S. The Third Republic Defended.
  S. Englund, 617(TLS):3Jul87-725
Ely, S. Starlight.
  R. Burgin, 441:19Apr87-16
Emanuel, L. Hotel Fiesta.*
  T.R. Hummer, 651(WHR):Spring86-69
van Emden, W. & P.E. Bennett, with A. Kerr,
  eds. Guillaume d'Orange and the "Chanson
  de Geste."
  I. Short, 208(FS):Jan86-57
Emecheta, B. Head Above Water.
  A. Grimshaw, 617(TLS):27Feb87-204
Emeis, H. L'Ame prisonnière.
  A. Daspre, 535(RHL):Mar-Apr86-339
Emerson, C. Boris Godunov.
  S. Karlinsky, 617(TLS):17Jul87-762
Emerson, C. - see Bakhtin, M.M.
Emerson, C. & M. Holquist - see Bakhtin,
  M.M.
Emerson, E. The Authentic Mark Twain.*
  R.H. Cracroft, 649(WAL):Nov86-251
  J.W. Gargano, 573(SSF):Spring86-219
Emerson, E.T. The Letters of Ellen Tucker
  Emerson.* (E.E.W. Gregg, ed)
  L. Willson, 569(SR):Winter86-131
Emerson, E.W. Fat Tuesday.
  N. Callendar, 441:8Mar87-29
Emerson, L.J. The Selected Letters of
  Lidian Jackson Emerson. (D.B. Carpenter,
  ed)
  M. Walker, 441:29Nov87-24
Emerson, R.L., G. Girard & R. Runte, eds.
  Man and Nature/L'Homme et la Nature.*
  (Vol 1)
  R.J. Merrett, 107(CRCL):Mar86-125
Emerson, R.L., W. Kinsley & W. Moser, eds.
  Man and Nature/L'Homme et la Nature.
  (Vol 2)
  W.H. Barber, 402(MLR):Apr87-427
  K.W. Graham, 178:Sep86-351
  J. Gray, 107(CRCL):Mar86-128
Emerson, S. Fire Child.
  J. Abbott, 617(TLS):22May87-559
  M. Pacey, 362:4Jun87-46

Emerton, N.E. The Scientific Reinterpreta-
  tion of Form.
  E. Feuerwerker, 486:Dec86-612
Emery, E. & M. The Press and America.
  (5th ed)
  M. Distad, 635(VPR):Spring86-38
Emiliani, A. Federico Barocci (Urbino
  1535-1612).*
  C. Gould, 39:Jun86-441
Emmerich, U. & E. Pick - see Seghers, A. &
  W. Herzfelde
Emmet, D. The Effectiveness of Causes.*
  M. Tiles, 483:Apr86-279
Emond, M. La Femme à la fenêtre.
  R. Benson, 627(UTQ):Fall86-208
  G. Merler, 102(CanL):Fall86-120
Emonds, J.E. A Unified Theory of Syntactic
  Categories.
  W.N. Elliott, 350:Sep87-620
Emons, R. Englische Nominale.
  K. Reichl, 72:Band223Heft1-153
Empedocles. Empedocles: The Extant Frag-
  ments.* (M.R. Wright, ed and trans)
  D. Sider, 41:Fall85-314
Empson, W. Essays on Shakespeare.*
  M. Dodsworth, 175:Summer86-191
Empson, W. The Royal Beasts and Other
  Works.* (J. Haffenden, ed)
  P. Dickinson, 364:Dec86/Jan87-157
Emsley, C. & J. Walvin, eds. Artisans,
  Peasants, and Proletarians, 1760-1860.
  J.A. Epstein, 637(VS):Winter87-264
Enchi, F. Masks.
  B.L. Knapp, 532(RCF):Spring86-219
del Encina, J. Obras completas IV. (A.M.
  Rambaldo, ed)
  N. Griffin, 86(BHS):Oct86-386
"Encyclopaedia Iranica." (Vol 1, fasc 1-4)
  (E. Yarshater, ed)
  M.J. Dresden, 318(JAOS):Jan/Mar85-164
"Encyclopedia of Ukraine." (Vol 1) (V.
  Kubijovyč, ed)
  W.T. Zyla, 574(SEEJ):Fall86-431
Engberg, S. Pastorale.
  J. Jacobson, 271:Spring-Summer86-193
Engberg-Pedersen, T. Aristotle's Theory of
  Moral Insight.*
  J.L. Creed, 303(JoHS):Vol106-215
  D.B. Robinson, 518:Jan86-16
Engel, B.F. & P.W. Julius, eds. A New
  Voice for a New People.
  R.H. Behm, 649(WAL):Nov86-275
Engel, E. & M.F. King. The Victorian Novel
  before Victoria.*
  R. Day, 155:Spring86-53
Engel, H. A City Called July.
  T.J. Binyon, 617(TLS):17Jul87-778
  N. Callendar, 441:8Mar87-29
Engel, M. The Tattooed Woman.*
  E. McNamara, 529(QQ):Winter86-886
  M. Micros, 198:Spring86-98
  G. Whitlock, 102(CanL):Fall86-157
Engel, P. Identité et référence.
  J-L. Gardies, 542:Oct-Dec86-529
Engelberg, E. Bismarck, Urpreusse und
  Reichsgründer.*
  N. Stone, 617(TLS):16Jan87-53
Engell, J. & W.J. Bate - see Coleridge,
  S.T.
Engelmann, B. In Hitler's Germany.
  G.A. Craig, 453(NYRB):16Jul87-32
  S.M. Halpern, 441:8Mar87-21

Faas, E. Shakespeare's Poetics.
S. Hazell, 157:No161-50
639(VQR):Autumn86-117
Faas, E. Tragedy and After.
C. Garton, 402(MLR):Jan87-158
C. Watts, 89(BJA):Spring86-177
Fabbri, P. Monteverdi.
T. Carter, 410(M&L):Apr86-169
I. Fenlon, 415:Feb86-92
Faber, R. Young England.
D. Cannadine, 617(TLS):25Sep-1Oct87-
1039
C. Mosley, 362:9Jul87-30
di Fabio, C. Scultura romanica a Genova.
A. Franco, 48:Jul-Sep86-349
Fabre, G. Drumbeats, Masks, and Metaphor.*
L. Sanders, 397(MD):Mar86-148
Fabre, M. La rive noire.
A. Kom, 343:Heft13-124
C. Zimra, 538(RAL):Winter86-601
Fabre, P., ed. Les suffixes en Onomas-
tique.
H. Guiter, 553(RLiR):Jul-Dec86-544
de Fabry, A.S. Jeux de miroirs.
J. Terrasse, 107(CRCL):Mar86-135
Fadia, B. State Politics in India.
O. Varkey, 293(JASt):Aug86-879
Fadiman, C., ed. The World of the Short
Story.
J. Bayley, 617(TLS):27Mar87-317
Faerch, C. & G. Kasper, eds. Foreign Lan-
guage Learning Under Classroom Condi-
tions.
S. Ehrlich, 350:Dec87-920
Fagan, B.M. The Great Journey.
J. Hemming, 441:6Dec87-46
Fagot-Largeault, A. L'homme bioéthique.
C. Debru, 542:Jul-Sep86-397
Fagundo, A.M. Como quien no dice voz
alguna al viento.
M-E. Bravo, 552(REH):Oct86-122
Fahs, A. Grammatik des Pali.
W. Morgenroth, 682(ZPSK):Band39Heft4-
493
Faigley, L. & S. Witte. Evaluating College
Writing Programs.
S. Thomas, 126(CCC):Oct86-355
Failler, A. - see Pachymérès, G.
Fairbank, J.K. The Great Chinese Revolu-
tion, 1800-1985.*
L. Pan, 176:Nov87-48
S.R. Schram, 617(TLS):9Jan87-30
Fairbank, W. - see Liang Ssu-ch'eng
Fairbanks, C. Prairie Women.*
V. Norwood, 344:Winter87-129
C. Thomas, 395(MFS):Winter86-641
Fairbanks, C. & S.B. Sundberg. Farm Women
on the Prairie Frontier.
C. Hlus, 106:Fall86-347
Fairclough, A. To Redeem the Soul of
America.
G.M. Fredrickson, 617(TLS):17Jul87-759
Fairer, D. Pope's Imagination.*
H. Erskine-Hill, 541(RES):Aug86-420
N. Wood, 83:Autumn86-277
Fairley, B. Barker Fairley: Selected
Essays on German Literature.* (R.
Symington, ed)
S. Atkins, 564:May86-186
Fairman, P.S. España vista por los
ingleses del siglo XVII.
A.L. MacKenzie, 86(BHS):Oct86-388

Faivre, A. Accès de l'Ésotérisme Occiden-
tal.
J.S. Bentley, 111:Fall87-6
Faivre, A. & F. Tristan, eds. L'Androgyne.
J.S. Bentley, 111:Fall87-6
Fáj, A. I Karamazov tra Poe e Vico.*
C. De Grève, 549(RLC):Jan-Mar86-110
Fajardo, E.M. - see under Molina Fajardo,
E.
Falassi, A. Italian Folklore.
W.E. Simeone, 292(JAF):Jul/Sep86-364
Falcoff, M. & F.B. Pike, eds. The Spanish
Civil War.
J. Fisher, 86(BHS):Oct86-392
Faldbakken, K. The Honeymoon.
I. Kapp, 441:21Jun87-38
Falk, C. Love, Anarchy, and Emma Goldman.
W.L. Frazer, 534(RALS):Spring-Autumn84-
198
Falk, Q. & D. Prince. Last of a Kind.
P. Fox, 362:2Apr87-25
Falk, W. Handbuch der literarwissen-
schaftlichen Komponentenanalyse.
S. Hoefert, 107(CRCL):Jun86-280
Falk, W.D. Ought, Reasons, and Morality.*
A. Gewirth, 185:Apr87-654
Falkiner, S. Rain in the Distance.
442(NY):27Apr87-105
Falla, P.S. - see "The Oxford English-
Russian Dictionary"
Falli Bonet, J. - see Aristotle
Fallon, I. & J. Srodes. Takeovers.
R. Davenport-Hines, 617(TLS):25-
31Dec87-1421
Fallon, R.T. Captain or Colonel.*
J. Morrill, 541(RES):May86-258
H.M. Richmond, 301(JEGP):Oct86-565
639(VQR):Winter86-18
Faludy, G. Selected Poems 1933-1980. (R.
Skelton, ed & trans)
J. Stoffman, 376:Jun86-123
Falvey, J.F. Diderot: "Le Neveu de
Rameau."
R. Niklaus, 208(FS):Apr86-213
A. Strugnell, 402(MLR):Jul87-740
Falwell, J. Strength for the Journey.
R. Reed, 441:27Dec87-6
Fane, J. Memories of My Mother.
F. Partridge, 617(TLS):8May87-486
Fanelli, G. & E. Godoli. Art Nouveau
Postcards.
J. Russell, 441:6Dec87-86
Fang, T.H. Chinese Philosophy.
S.A. Wawrytko, 485(PE&W):Jan86-72
Fanizza, L. Giuristi crimini leggi nell'
età degli Antonini.*
W.M. Gordon, 123:Vol36No2-260
Fant, L. Estructura informativa en
español.*
H. Contreras, 361:Mar86-281
Fante, J. The Wine of Youth.* 1933 Was
a Bad Year.* The Road to Los Angeles.
Ask The Dust. Wait Until Spring,
Bandini. Dreams from Bunker Hill.
G. Mangan, 617(TLS):20Mar87-303
Fanthorpe, U.A. Selected Poems.*
C.A. Duffy, 493:Oct86-50
H. Lomas, 364:Jul86-86
Fantini, A.E. Language Acquisition of a
Bilingual Child.
R.C. Major, 350:Jun87-417

al-Fārābī. Al-Farabi's Commentary and Short Treatise on Aristotle's "De Interpretatione." (F.W. Zimmermann, ed & trans)
  J. Talanga, 53(AGP):Band68Heft3-302
Faragher, J.M. Sugar Creek.
  H. Brogan, 617(TLS):1May87-460
  G.M. Fredrickson, 453(NYRB):23Apr87-37
  A. Zito, 441:15Mar87-17
Farah, N. Maps.
  C. Hope, 441:15Nov87-40
  A. Maja-Pearce, 364:Jun86-109
Faranda, L.P. - see Niedecker, L.
Farber, B. Making People Talk.
  J. Jarvis, 441:1Nov87-22
Farber, M. The Search for an Alternative.*
  W.L. McBride, 323:Jan86-95
Farel, G. Le Pater Noster et le Credo en françoys. (F. Higman, ed)
  G. Bedouelle, 535(RHL):Jan-Feb86-133
Farella, J.R. The Main Stalk.
  R. Bunge, 619:Winter86-83
Farina, L.S. Glossario Semantico Dialettale luganese computerizzato.
  R.C. Melzi, 275(IQ):Summer86-109
Faris, W.B. Carlos Fuentes.
  R. Fiddian, 402(MLR):Jan86-241
Farmer, D., L. Vasey & J. Worthen - see Lawrence, D.H.
Farmer, N.K., Jr. Poets and the Visual Arts in Renaissance England.*
  G. Reynolds, 39:Jan86-65
Farmer, P. Away From Home.
  L. Duguid, 617(TLS):24Jul87-802
Farnell, S. The Political Ideas of the "Divine Comedy."
  R.B. Herzman, 276:Autumn86-306
  A. Wingell, 627(UTQ):Fall86-142
Farquhar, G. The Recruiting Officer. (P. Dixon, ed)
  M. Dodsworth, 175:Spring86-107
  J. Hamard, 189(EA):Apr-Jun87-213
Farr, J. The Life and Art of Elinor Wylie.*
  L.S. Boren, 534(RALS):Spring-Autumn84-218
Farrell, M.J. Mad Puppetstown. Two Days in Aragon.*
  272(IUR):Autumn86-255
Farris, F.B. From Rattlesnakes to Road Agents. (C.L. Sonnichsen, ed)
  R. Moseley, 649(WAL):Aug86-139
Farris, J. The Abiding Gospel of Claude Dee Moran, Jr.
  442(NY):28Sep87-96
Farris, W.W. Population, Disease, and Land in Early Japan, 645-900.
  D. Morris, 407(MN):Spring86-109
  E.S. Sato, 293(JASt):May86-593
Farrokhzad, F. Bride of Acacias.
  R. Sandler, 318(JAOS):Oct/Dec85-795
Farson, D. Soho in the Fifties.
  D.A.N. Jones, 362:19Nov87-32
Farwell, B. The Great War in Africa, 1914-1918.
  C.D. May, 441:9Aug87-21
Fasold, R. The Sociolinguistics of Society.*
  R. Hudson, 361:Mar86-286
Fasske, H., H. Jentsch & S. Michalk. Sorbischer Sprachatlas. (Vol 9)
  G. Stone, 575(SEER):Jan86-124

Fast, H. The Dinner Party.
  A. McCarthy, 441:29Mar87-22
Fatio, O., with C. Rapin - see Calvin, J.
Fattori, M., ed. Francis Bacon.
  M-T. Belin, 540(RIPh):Vol40fasc4-453
Fauchereau, S. Les Peintres révolutionnaires mexicains.
  J. Barnitz, 617(TLS):13Mar87-273
Faucon de Boylesve, P. Etre et Savoir.
  P-J. About, 542:Oct-Dec86-514
Fauconnier, G. Mental Spaces. (French title: Espaces Mentaux.)
  S. McConnell-Ginet, 350:Mar87-142
  C. Vandeloise, 209(FM):Apr86-105
Faulhaber, C.B., comp. Medieval Manuscripts in the Library of the Hispanic Society of America.*
  D.S. Severin, 86(BHS):Jul86-272
  J.T. Snow, 240(HR):Winter86-85
Faulkes, A. - see Snorri Sturluson
Faulkner, P. - see Bage, R.
Faulkner, P. - see "Jane Morris to Wilfrid Scawen Blunt"
Faulkner, T.C., with R. Blair - see Crabbe, G.
Faulkner, W. Father Abraham.* (J.S. Meriwether, ed) The Sound and the Fury.* (N. Polk, ed) Vision in Spring.* (J.L. Sensibar, ed)
  C.S. Brown, 569(SR):Winter86-167
Faulkner, W. Novels, 1930-1935. (J. Blotner & N. Polk, eds)
  A.F. Kinney, 395(MFS):Winter86-616
Fauré, C. La démocratie sans les femmes.
  F. Guery, 542:Jan-Mar86-157
Faure, M. Musique et société du Second Empire aux années vingt.
  H. Dufourt, 98:Apr86-316
  D.A. Powell, 207(FR):Mar87-577
Fauskevag, S.E. Sade dans le Surréalisme.
  M. Delon, 535(RHL):Jul-Aug86-789
Faust, I. The Year of the Hot Jock and Other Stories.
  639(VQR):Winter86-22
Faust, L.L., ed. American Women Writers. (abridged)
  B.H. Gelfant, 106:Fall86-355
Favre, R., ed. La Fin dernière.
  L. Andries, 535(RHL):Jul-Aug86-761
Favre, Y-A., ed. André Suarès, 3.
  H. Bouillier, 535(RHL):Jul-Aug86-788
Favre-Lejeune, C. Les Secrétaires du Roi de la grande chancellerie de France: Dictionnaire biographique et généalogique 1672-1789.
  J. Rogister, 617(TLS):3Jul87-725
Fawcett, B. Capital Tales.*
  N. Besner, 102(CanL):Spring86-162
Faÿ-Halle, A. & B. Mundt. Europäisches Porzellan vom Klassizismus bis zum Jugendstil.
  I. von Treskow, 683:Band49Heft4-591
de Fayyoum, G.S. Commentaire sur le "Sefer Yetsira" ou "Livre de la création." (M. Lambert, trans)
  P. Trotignon, 542:Oct-Dec86-520
Feagin, C. Variation and Change in Alabama English.
  W. Viereck, 685(ZDL):2/1986-272
Feather, J. The Provincial Book Trade in Eighteenth-Century England.*
  P-G. Boucé, 189(EA):Apr-Jun87-214
  I. Maxted, 78(BC):Summer86-249

Feaver, G. & F. Rosen, eds. Lives, Liberties and the Public Good.
  N. O'Sullivan, 617(TLS):4-10Dec87-1344
Fedeli, P. Properzio: Il libro terzo delle Elegie.
  G.O. Hutchinson, 123:Vol36No2-234
Fedeli, P. - see Propertius
Fedeli, P. and P. Pinotti. Bibliografia Properziana (1946-1983).
  S.J. Heyworth, 123:Vol36No1-48
Federhofer, H. Heinrich Schenker.
  W. Pastille, 317:Fall86-667
Federici, C. & C.L. Riga. Ciao!
  R.J. Di Pietro, 399(MLJ):Autumn86-319
Federman, R. Smiles on Washington Square.*
  M. Corniş-Pop, 455:Mar86-67
Fee, E. Disease and Discovery.
  R. Porter, 617(TLS):7Aug87-843
Feferman, S. & others - see Gödel, K.
Feher, F. & A. Heller. Eastern Left, Western Left.
  A. Nove, 617(TLS):29May87-577
Fehr, B. Bewegungsweisen und Verhaltensideale.
  A. Stewart, 303(JoHS):Vol106-248
Fehr, K. Conrad Ferdinand Meyer.*
  T.S. Evans, 406:Winter86-537
  G. Reinhardt, 222(GR):Spring86-75
Fehrle, R. Cato Uticensis.
  P. Jal, 555:Vol59fasc2-331
  D.R. Shackleton Bailey, 124:Jan-Feb87-216
Feibleman, J.K. Justice, Law and Culture.
  R.E.G., 185:Jan87-495
Fein, E. Speak for Yourself, Books 1 and 2.
  S. Plann, 399(MLJ):Winter86-454
Feinberg, J. Harm to Others.
  S.L. Darwall, 484(PPR):Jun87-691
  R.A. Duff, 518:Jan86-54
Feinberg, J. The Moral Limits of the Criminal Law.
  G.J. Postema, 185:Jan87-414
Feinberg, J. Offense to Others.
  M. Clark, 518:Oct86-252
Feinstein, E. Badlands.
  T. Dooley, 617(TLS):17Jul87-767
Feinstein, E. A Captive Lion.
  J. Bayley, 453(NYRB):8Oct87-20
  L. Chamberlain, 617(TLS):31Jul87-822
  D. Hughes, 362:21May87-29
  E. Proffer, 441:27Sep87-22
Feinstein, J. A Season on the Brink.
  D. Whitford, 441:8Feb87-25
Feirstein, F. Family History.
  R. McDowell, 249(HudR):Winter87-676
Fejcher, K., ed. Tola Korian.
  A. Iwańska, 497(PolR):Vol31No4-341
Fekete, É. & É. Karádi, comps. Georg Lukács.*
  I. Deak, 453(NYRB):12Mar87-39
Fekete, J., ed. The Structural Allegory.
  D. O'Hara, 290(JAAC):Fall86-96
Feld, B. Blood Relations.
  N. Callendar, 441:29Mar87-25
Feld, S. Sound and Sentiment.
  C.H. Berndt, 567:Vol61No3/4-347
Feldhaus, A., ed & trans. The Deeds of God in Ṛddhipur.
  M.L. Apte, 293(JASt):Nov85-170
Feldman, E. All of Us Here.*
  R. Asselineau, 189(EA):Jul-Sep87-371
  J.P. White, 491:Dec86-177

Feldman, L.H. Josephus and Modern Scholarship (1937-1980).*
  S.W. Hirsch, 24:Summer86-298
Feldman, M. Morton Feldman: Essays.* (W. Zimmermann, ed)
  P. Griffiths, 415:Apr86-209
Feldman, P.R. & D. Scott-Kilvert - see Shelley, M.
Fell, M. The Persistence of Memory.*
  S.P. Estess, 577(SHR):Winter86-84
Feller, D. The Public Lands in Jacksonian Politics.
  C. Hanyan, 106:Summer86-189
  J.L. Wright, Jr., 9(AlaR):Apr86-149
Fellman, S. The Japanese Tattoo.
  D. Ackerman, 441:5Apr87-34
Fellows, O. & D.G. Carr - see "Diderot Studies XXI"
Fellows-Jensen, G. Scandinavian Settlement Names in the North-West.
  W.F.H. Nicolaisen, 424:Dec86-402
Felman, S. Writing and Madness.*
  G.C. Gill, 290(JAAC):Spring87-314
Felner, M. Apostles of Silence.
  A. Lust, 615(TJ):Mar86-128
  J. Seager, 157:No159-51
Felperin, H. Beyond Deconstruction.
  D.H. Bialostosky, 454:Winter87-175
  M.P. Gillespie, 594:Winter86-441
  K. Hart, 381:Mar86-107
  R.R. Wilson, 107(CRCL):Dec86-645
  639(VQR):Winter86-19
Fel'shtinskii, I.G. Bol'sheviki i levye esery, oktiabr' 1917 - iiul' 1918.
  V. Brovkin, 550(RusR):Jan86-105
"Le Femme dans la pensée espagnole."
  K. Kish, 240(HR):Summer86-325
Fender, S. American Literature in Context. (Vol 1: 1620-1830)
  J.A.L. Lemay, 402(MLR):Oct87-939
Fender, S. Plotting the Golden West.
  R. Thacker, 106:Spring86-51
Fenik, B. Homer and the "Nibelungenlied."
  R.D. Dawe, 121(CJ):Apr-May87-331
Fenlon, I., ed. Early Music History. (Vol 4)
  F.W. Sternfeld, 410(M&L):Apr86-166
Fenoll, M.D.S-R. - see under Sánchez-Rojas Fenoll, M.D.
Fenton, A., with H. Cheape & R.K. Marshall - see "ROSC: Review of Scottish Culture"
Fenton, A. & H. Pálsson, eds. The Northern and Western Isles in the Viking World.
  S. Margeson, 562(Scan):Nov86-218
Fenton, J. Hybrid Buildings.
  P. Borsook, 45:Jul86-79
Fenton, J. - see May, S.
Fenton, J. & J. Fuller. Partingtime Hall.
  P. Forbes, 362:30Apr87-32
  B. Leithauser, 617(TLS):8May87-487
Féral, J., J.L. Savona & E.A. Walker, eds. Théâtralité, écriture et mise en scène.
  S.B. Dieckman, 615(TJ):Oct86-376
Ferber, M. The Social Vision of William Blake.
  K. Shabetai, 141:Summer86-343
Ferber, R. Platos Idee des Guten.*
  R.W. Jordan, 123:Vol36No1-65
  G.B. Kerferd, 303(JoHS):Vol106-214
  I. Robins, 41:Vol6-213

117

Ferguson, A.B. The Chivalric Tradition in Renaissance England.
R.C. McCoy, 191(ELN):Mar87-68
D.M. Michie, 125:Winter86-213
Ferguson, J. Catullus.
R. Boughner, 124:Jan-Feb87-216
Ferguson, J. Papa Doc, Baby Doc.
D. Nicholls, 617(TLS):27Nov-3Dec87-1313
Ferguson, J.D. - see Burns, R.
Ferguson, J.M., Jr. The Summerfield Stories.
R.L. Johnson, 649(WAL):Aug86-166
Ferguson, M., ed. First Feminists.
L. Austin, 568(SCN):Spring-Summer86-14
M. Mulvihill, 566:Spring87-207
Ferguson, N. Bars of America.*
C.J. Fox, 364:Aug/Sep86-160
Ferguson, P. Indefinite Nights.
J-A. Goodwin, 617(TLS):17Jul87-766
V. Shaw, 362:11Jun87-29
Ferguson, R. Enigma.
T. Clark, 441:7Jun87-28
M. Hofmann, 617(TLS):2-8Oct87-1080
B. Morton, 362:26Mar87-30
Ferguson, R. The Unbalanced Mind.
D. Nokes, 617(TLS):20Feb87-182
Ferguson, R.A. Law and Letters in American Culture.*
D. Greenberg, 656(WMQ):Apr86-325
J.A. Stein, 31(ASch):Spring86-264
J.J. Waldmeir, 115:Winter86-116
Ferguson, S. & B. Groseclose, eds. Literature and the Visual Arts in Contemporary Society.
H.T.B., 295(JML):Nov86-406
Ferguson, T.J. & E.R. Hart, eds. A Zuni Atlas.
L. Milazzo, 584(SWR):Winter86-123
Fergusson, P. Architecture of Solitude.*
F. Bucher, 589:Apr86-413
S. Chaplin, 59:Sep86-388
J.P. McAleer, 54:Sep86-489
M. Thurlby, 576:Dec86-411
Fermor, P.L. Between the Woods and the Water.*
P-L. Adams, 61:Mar87-94
G. Gibson, 441:8Feb87-30
A. Hartley, 176:Apr87-59
G. Moorhouse, 364:Nov86-100
Fernandez, J., M. Spiro & M. Singer. On Symbols in Anthropology.
J.L. Peacock, 567:Vol61No1/2-187
Fernández, J.B. & N. García. ¿Qué hay de nuevo?
S.E. Torres, 238:Mar86-125
Fernández, L.G. - see under Gil Fernández, L.
Fernández, L.R. - see under Rubio Fernández, L.
Fernández, M.V. - see under Valdés Fernández, M.
Fernández, P.H. Ideario etimológico de Miguel de Unamuno.*
I. Soto, 402(MLR):Oct86-1026
R. Wright, 86(BHS):Oct86-391
Fernández, P.H. La paradoja en Ortega y Gasset.
T. Mermall, 238:Dec86-873
N.R. Orringer, 240(HR):Autumn86-481
Fernández Alvarez, J. El subjuntivo.
M. Torreblanca, 238:May86-326

Fernández Alvarez, P. El Argólico occidental y oriental en las inscripciones de los siglos VII, VI y V a.C.
C.J. Ruijgh, 394:Vol39fasc3/4-452
Fernandez-Cañadas de Greenwood, P. Pastoral Poetics.*
M. Jakob, 52:Band21Heft3-312
Fernández Jiménez, J., ed. Tratado notable de amor.
P.E. Grieve, 304(JHP):Spring86-247
Fernbach, D. & N. Greig - see Carpenter, E.
Fernie, E. The Architecture of the Anglo-Saxons.
C.B. McClendon, 576:Jun86-169
Ferrabosco, A. [the Elder] Opera omnia. (Vol 1) (R. Charteris, ed)
P. Macey, 317:Fall86-650
Ferrán, J. Lope de Vega.
A. Carreño, 86(BHS):Oct86-369
Ferrante, J.M. The Political Vision of the "Divine Comedy."*
R.B. Herzman, 276:Autumn86-306
G. Holmes, 382(MAE):1986/2-326
J.K. Hyde, 366:Spring86-131
R. Kay, 589:Oct86-925
R.H. Lansing, 141:Winter86-105
Ferrante, J.M. & R.W. Hanning - see Jackson, W.T.H.
Ferrar, H., J.A. Hutchinson & J-D. Biard - see "The Concise Oxford French Dictionary"
Ferrar, H. & J. Spencer. Use of French.
F.G. Healey, 402(MLR):Jul87-730
Ferrars, E. Come and Be Killed.
G. Kaufman, 362:8Oct87-23
Ferrary, J. & L. Fiszer. The California-American Cookbook.
W. & C. Cowen, 639(VQR):Spring86-68
Ferrell, K. Ernest Hemingway.
R.P. Weeks, 395(MFS):Summer86-265
Ferreras, J.I. and others. Narrativa de la Restauración.*
D. Henn, 402(MLR):Jul86-773
Ferrero, M.V. - see under Viale Ferrero, M.
Ferretti, G. Il secondo libro delle canzoni a sei voci (1575). (R.I. De Ford, ed)
A. Newcomb, 317:Summer86-395
Ferretto, C. La città dissipatrice.
J.M. Alonso-Núñez, 303(JoHS):Vol106-217
Ferreyrolles, G. Pascal et la raison du politique.*
M-H. Belin, 192(EP):Oct-Dec86-556
N. Ferrier-Caverivière, 535(RHL):Mar-Apr86-278
Ferrier, C., ed. Gender, Politics and Fiction.
D. Brydon, 268(IFR):Winter87-45
S. Gingell, 49:Oct86-154
E. Webby, 71(ALS):Oct86-534
Ferrier, S. Marriage.
J.A. Scott Miller, 571(ScLJ):Winter86-17
Ferrier-Caverivière, N. Le Grand Roi à l'aube des Lumières: 1715-1751.
M-O. Sweetser, 207(FR):Dec86-274
Ferrill, A. The Origins of War.
M.R.D. Foot, 176:Feb87-44
Ferris, P. Dylan Thomas.*
D. Rigal, 189(EA):Apr-Jun87-238
Ferris, P. - see Thomas, D.

118

Ferro, M. Pétain.
R.O. Paxton, 617(TLS):13-19Nov87-1257
Ferron, J. Selected Tales of Jacques Ferron.
D. Carpenter, 102(CanL):Spring86-166
Ferry, A. The "Inward" Language.*
J.H. Ottenhoff, 568(SCN):Spring-Summer86-10
D.L. Peterson, 401(MLQ):Mar85-89
Ferry, L. Philosophie politique, 1.
J. Rivelaygue, 192(EP):Apr-Jun86-246
Ferry, L. Philosophie politique, 2.
J. Rivelaygue, 192(EP):Apr-Jun86-247
Ferry, L. & A. Renaut. La pensée 68.*
J. Largeault, 542:Jan-Mar86-144
C.J. Stivale, 207(FR):Apr87-742
Ferry, L. & A. Renaut. 68-86: Itinéraires de l'individu.
R.W. Johnson, 617(TLS):31Jul87-811
Ferster, J. Chaucer on Interpretation.
A.C. Spearing, 184(EIC):Jan86-68
Fessler, C.F., ed. Daring to Dream.
S. Gubar, 561(SFS):Mar86-79
Fest, J.C. Hitler.
J. Ridley, 617(TLS):11-17Sep87-996
Festa-McCormick, D. Proustian Optics of Clothes.*
W.C. Carter, 207(FR):Dec86-264
A. Henry, 535(RHL):Jul-Aug86-785
A.H. Pasco, 345:May86-255
W.A. Strauss, 210(FrF):May86-244
"Festschrift für Robert Muth."
P. Flobert, 555:Vol59fasc2-351
Fet, J. New Norse Literature in English Translation 1880-1982.
M. Sandberg, 563(SS):Spring86-217
S. Walton, 562(Scan):Nov86-240
Fetherling, D. The Blue Notebook.
A.L. Amprimoz, 105:Fall/Winter86-120
Fetherling, D. Variorum.
T. Whalen, 102(CanL):Summer86-126
Feuchtwanger, L. & A. Zweig. Lion Feuchtwanger – Arnold Zweig: Briefwechsel 1938-1958. (H. von Hofe, ed)
L. Kahn, 221(GQ):Winter86-155
Feuerwerker, Y-T.M. Ding Ling's Fiction.
J.L. Faurot, 293(JASt):Nov85-116
Fewsmith, J. Party, State, and Local Elites in Republican China.
P. Duara, 293(JASt):Nov85-117
Feyerabend, L. Die Rigaer und Revaler Familiennamen im 14. und 15. Jahrhundert.
J.I. Press, 575(SEER):Oct86-652
Feynman, R.P. QED.*
J. Roche, 617(TLS):30Jan87-103
Ffinch, M. G.K. Chesterton.*
H. Kenner, 441:22Feb87-18
ffolliott, S. Civic Sculpture in the Renaissance.
B. Boucher, 278(IS):Vol41-149
Fichte, J.G. Essais philosophiques choisis (1794-1795). (A. Philonenko, ed)
J-L. Vieillard-Baron, 192(EP):Jul-Sep86-416
Fichter, A. Poets Historical.*
M. Stocker, 161(DUJ):Dec85-186
Ficken, C. God's Story and Modern Literature.
G. Meeter, 395(MFS):Winter86-690
Fickett, H. & D.R. Gilbert. Flannery O'Connor.
M. Sidone, 590:Jun87-55
Fideler, D. – see Porphyry

Fidjestøl, B. Det norrøne fyrstediktet.
R. McTurk, 562(Scan):May86-74
Fido, M. The Crimes, Detection and Death of Jack the Ripper.
P. Highsmith, 617(TLS):25-31Dec87-1427
Fiedel, S.J. Prehistory of the Americas.
N. Hammond, 617(TLS):2-8Oct87-1086
Field, A. Djuna Barnes.
L. Curry, 534(RALS):Spring-Autumn84-224
F. de Martinoir, 450(NRF):Nov86-112
Field, A. VN.*
B. Boyd, 617(TLS):24Apr87-432
Fieldhouse, D.K. Black Africa 1945-80.
D. Lal, 617(TLS):1May87-469
Fielding, H. Amelia.* (M.C. Battestin, ed)
P-G. Boucé, 189(EA):Jul-Sep86-347
M. Irwin, 541(RES):Feb86-100
Fields, D. & A. Furst. "One Smart Cookie."
M. Dowd, 441:25Oct87-39
de Fieux, C. [Chevalier de Mouhy] Le Masque de Fer ou les aventures admirables du père et du fils.
P. Clancy, 535(RHL):Mar-Apr86-288
"Fifty Years of American Poetry."
J. Lynen, 529(QQ):Summer86-425
Figes, E. Little Eden.
L. Segal, 441:16Aug87-14
Figes, E. The Seven Ages.*
P-L. Adams, 61:Feb87-94
A. Goreau, 441:22Feb87-7
Figl, J. Interpretation als philosophisches Prinzip. Dialektik der Gewalt.
R. Margreiter, 489(PJGG):Band93Heft2-375
Figueroa, A. El Roman de Renart documento critico de la sociedad medieval.
R. Bellon, 553(RLiR):Jul-Dec86-638
Figueroa, M. Spanish Resources and Activities for Clubs, Class and Extracurricular Activities.
J.G. Sager, 399(MLJ):Winter86-442
Figurski, J. The Stevensdaughter Poems.
B. Almon, 102(CanL):Spring86-177
Filby, P.W., with D.M. Lower. Passenger and Immigration Lists Index: 1986 Supplement.
K.B. Harder, 424:Dec86-405
Filby, P.W. & M.K. Meyer, eds. Passenger and Immigration Lists Index: 1983 Supplement.
K.B. Harder, 424:Mar86-116
Filby, P.W. & M.K. Meyer, eds. Passenger and Immigration Lists Index: 1984 Supplement.
K.B. Harder, 424:Sep86-333
Filedt Kok, J.P. & others. 's Levens felheid.
H. Bevers, 600:Vol16No1-62
Filipović, R. Teorija jezika u kontaktu.
H. Birnbaum, 350:Jun87-450
Fillaudeau, B. L'Univers ludique d'André Gide.
S.G. Stary, 546(RR):Nov86-458
Fillion-Lahille, J. Le "De ira" de Sénèque et la philosophie stoïcienne des passions.
R. Bodéüs, 154:Summer86-382
Filonov, P. Pavel Filonov: A Hero and His Fate. (N. Misler & J.E. Bowlt, eds & trans)
H. Martin, 55:Jan86-48

Filtzer, D. Soviet Workers and Stalinist Industrialization.
  G. Hosking, 617(TLS):29May87-577
Finch, A. Stendhal: "La Chartreuse de Parme."*
  A. Fairlie, 535(RHL):Jul-Aug86-768
  G.M. Godfrey, 207(FR):Dec86-262
Findlater, J. & M. Crossriggs.
  J.A. Scott Miller, 571(ScLJ):Winter86-17
Findlay, J.M. People of Chance.*
  A. Sinclair, 617(TLS):13Mar87-268
Findlay, J.N. Wittgenstein.
  K.T. Fann, 319:Oct87-614
  J. Llewelyn, 262:Sep86-363
  A. Manser, 518:Jan86-38
Findley, T. Famous Last Words.
  J. Melmoth, 617(TLS):24Apr87-435
Fine, A. The Killjoy.*
  442(NY):18May87-119
Fine, E.C. The Folklore Text.*
  G.E. Parsons, 292(JAF):Jul/Sep86-361
Fine, K. Reasoning with Arbitrary Objects.
  G. Stahl, 542:Jul-Sep86-402
Fine, R.E. Gemini G.E.L.
  R. Cohen, 55:Jan86-48
Fineman, J. Shakespeare's Perjured Eye.*
  G. Bradshaw, 617(TLS):30Oct-5Nov87-1199
  D. Donoghue, 533:Summer86-123
  M. de Grazia, 570(SQ):Winter86-529
Finer, D.L. The Formal Grammar of Switch-Reference.
  B. Comrie, 353:Vol24No2-439
"Fingerprints."
  W.N., 102(CanL):Spring86-202
Fink, I. A Scrap of Time.
  J. Kaplan, 441:12Jul87-7
Fink, K.J. & M.L. Baeumer, eds. Goethe as a Critic of Literature.
  H. Henning, 301(JEGP):Apr86-305
  I.H. Solbrig, 173(ECS):Fall86-110
Finke, P. & S.J. Schmidt, eds. Analytische Literaturwissenschaft.
  M. Flacke, 679:Band17Heft1-165
Finkenstaedt, T. Kleine Geschichte der Anglistik in Deutschland.
  E.G. Stanley, 447(N&Q):Mar85-98
Finkielkraut, A. La Défaite de la pensée.
  R.W. Johnson, 617(TLS):31Jul87-811
Finlayson, I. Writers in Romney Marsh.
  J. Kelly, 617(TLS):27Feb87-217
Finley, M.I., D.M. Smith & C. Duggan. A History of Sicily.*
  442(NY):20Jul87-92
Finn, D. Byzantium.
  S.B., 675(YER):Vol8No1/2-147
Finn, F. Out On The Plain.
  L. Irvine, 102(CanL):Spring86-170
Finnegan, W. Crossing the Line.*
  D. Papineau, 617(TLS):21Aug87-894
Finneran, R.J., ed. Critical Essays on W.B. Yeats.
  C. Rawson, 617(TLS):24Jul87-783
Finneran, R.J. Editing Yeats's Poems.
  G. Bornstein, 403(MLS):Spring86-82
Finneran, R.J. - see Yeats, W.B.
Finneran, R.J. - see "Yeats Annual"
Finney, B. The Inner Eye.
  A. Louvre, 506(PSt):Dec86-110
  I.B.N., 295(JML):Nov86-407
Finney, B. - see Lawrence, D.H.

Finney, G. The Counterfeit Idyll.*
  D.G. Richards, 221(GQ):Fall86-658
Finnis, J., J.M. Boyle, Jr. & G. Grisez. Nuclear Deterrence, Morality and Realism.
  J.M. Cameron, 453(NYRB):5Nov87-38
Finson, J.W. & R.L. Todd, eds. Mendelssohn and Schumann.
  L. Botstein, 414:Vol72No1-138
  C. Brown, 410(M&L):Apr86-179
  J.H., 412:May85-138
Finsterwalder, K. Tiroler Namenkunde.
  G. Koss, 685(ZDL):3/1986-407
Finucane, R.C. Soldiers of the Faith.
  J. Johns, 382(MAE):1986/1-126
Fiore, P.A. Milton and Augustine.
  J.M. Evans, 541(RES):May86-260
  J.J. Smith, 447(N&Q):Mar85-118
Fiore, R.L. Lazarillo de Tormes.*
  R.W. Truman, 86(BHS):Jul86-280
Fiorioli, E. Céline e la Germania.
  E. Chevallier, 549(RLC):Jan-Mar86-121
Fiorioli, E. Madame de Staël et A.W. Schlegel.
  E. Chevallier, 549(RLC):Jan-Mar86-103
  A. Montandon, 535(RHL):Sep-Oct86-927
Fioroni, T. Lettere artistiche e familiari (1830-1855). (F. Petrucci Nardelli, ed)
  M. Palermo, 708:Vol12fasc2-269
Firmicus. Firmicus Maternus, "L'erreur des religions païennes."* (R. Turcan, ed & trans)
  A.A.R. Bastiaensen, 394:Vol39fasc1/2-191
  M. Reydellet, 555:Vol59fasc2-322
"First Fictions Introduction 9."
  J. Mellors, 364:Oct86-108
Fisch, A. A Remembered Future.
  E. Alexander, 390:May86-52
  G. Josipovici, 402(MLR):Jul87-687
Fischer, D. Der Rätselcharakter der Dichtung Kafkas.
  P-A. Alt, 680(ZDP):Band105Heft4-627
Fischer, H. Georg Büchner und Alexis Muston.
  J. Hilton, 617(TLS):9-15Oct87-1098
Fischer, M. Does Deconstruction Make Any Difference?*
  D.H. Bialostosky, 454:Winter87-175
  E. Cobley, 376:Dec86-144
  W.V. Harris, 30:Winter87-91
  A. Louch, 478:Oct86-325
  J. Stillinger, 301(JEGP):Oct86-550
Fischer, S.K. Econolingua.
  G. Monsarrat, 189(EA):Apr-Jun87-200
Fischer, W.C., W.M. Gibson & C.K. Lohmann - see Howells, W.D.
Fischer-Lichte, E., with K. Schwind. Heinrich von Kleist: "Prinz Friedrich von Homburg."
  D. Horton, 402(MLR):Oct86-1042
Fishbein, L. Rebels in Bohemia.
  S. Fogel, 106:Spring86-109
Fishburn, K. The Unexpected Universe of Doris Lessing.
  B. Draine, 594:Fall86-323
  E.C.R., 295(JML):Nov86-506
Fisher, A. Let Us Now Praise Famous Women.
  M. Slavin, 362:11Jun87-28
Fisher, A. The Three Passions of Countess Natalya.
  639(VQR):Winter86-21

Fisher, B. & B. Ross. The America's Cup 1987.
  B. Lloyd, 441:31May87-32
Fisher, C. Postcards from the Edge.
  H. Rubin, 441:16Aug87-16
  362:22Oct87-33
Fisher, D.E. A Race on the Edge of Time.
  H. Knight, 441:18Oct87-31
Fisher, J., ed. Essays on Aesthetics.
  H. Osborne, 289:Spring86-97
Fisher, J. The Lindbergh Case.
  J. Katzenbach, 441:11Oct87-48
  F. Russell, 453(NYRB):5Nov87-4
Fisher, J. Wild Flowers in Danger.
  U. Buchan, 617(TLS):3Jul87-728
Fisher, J.H., M. Richardson & J.L. Fisher, eds. An Anthology of Chancery English.
  M. Andrew, 179(ES):Oct86-452
  L.M. Matheson, 589:Jul86-646
Fisher, J.M. The Prints of Edouard Manet.
  A. Griffiths, 90:Jan86-46
Fisher, P.K. Los Alamos Experience.
  J.W. Grove, 529(QQ):Autumn86-674
Fisher, R. The City of Refuge. (J. McCluskey, Jr., ed)
  S.C. Miller, 441:20Dec87-16
Fisher, R. A Furnace.*
  S. Rae, 364:Aug/Sep86-132
Fisher, S.T. The Merchant-Millers of the Humber Valley.
  G.W., 102(CanL):Fall86-197
Fishkin, J.S. Beyond Subjective Morality.*
  A. Duff, 483:Jan86-133
  T. McConnell, 449:Mar86-87
Fishkin, J.S. Justice, Equal Opportunity, and the Family.
  A. Duff, 483:Jan86-133
Fishkin, S.F. From Fact to Fiction.*
  M.B., 295(JML):Nov86-355
  W. Balassi, 26(ALR):Spring87-92
  J. Steinbrink, 27(AL):May86-281
  R. Weber, 639(VQR):Winter86-142
  J.B. Wittenberg, 594:Fall86-326
Fishman, J.A. & others. The Rise and Fall of the Ethnic Revival.
  M. Clyne, 350:Sep87-659
Fisiak, J., ed. Papers from the 6th International Conference on Historical Linguistics.
  K. Shields, 159:Fall86-243
Fiske, R. Scotland in Music.
  H.R.N. Macdonald, 187:Winter87-134
Fitch, B.T., ed. Albert Camus, 11.*
  G. Cesbron, 356(LR):Feb86-85
Fitch, N.R. Sylvia Beach and the Lost Generation.*
  D.E. Schoonover, 534(RALS):Spring-Autumn84-234
Fitch, R.E. The Poison Sky.*
  M. Hardman, 677(YES):Vol16-328
Fitchen, J. Building Construction Before Mechanization.
  S. Pepper, 617(TLS):31Jul87-825
Fite, D. Harold Bloom.
  V.A. De Luca, 627(UTQ):Summer87-575
  A. Fairweather, 295(JML):Nov86-445
Fite, G.C. Cotton Fields No More.
  W.W. Rogers, 9(AlaR):Apr86-154
  L. Shore, 529(QQ):Autumn86-671
Fitting, M. Fundamentals of Generalized Recursion Theory.
  P.G. Hinman, 316:Dec86-1078

Fitton, J.L., ed. Cycladica.*
  S. Hood, 123:Vol36No1-161
Fittschen, K. & P. Zanker. Katalog der römischen Porträts in den Capitolinischen Museen und den anderen kommunalen Sammlungen der Stadt Rom. (Vol 1)
  M.A.R. Colledge, 123:Vol36No2-345
  R.R.R. Smith, 313:Vol76-313
Fitz, J. L'administration des provinces pannoniennes sous le Bas-Empire romain.
  J-P. Callu, 555:Vol59fasc2-334
Fitz Gerald, E. The Letters of Edward Fitz Gerald. (A.K. & A.B. Terhune, eds)
  P. Morgan, 403(MLS):Fall86-75
Fitzgerald, E. A Nickel an Inch.
  639(VQR):Spring86-50
Fitz Gerald, F. Cities on a Hill.*
  C. Hitchens, 617(TLS):18-24Sep87-1022
  D. Johnson, 453(NYRB):29Jan87-3
Fitzgerald, F.S. F. Scott Fitzgerald on Writing. (L.W. Phillips, ed)
  M.D.O., 295(JML):Nov86-471
Fitzgerald, J.T. & L.M. White. The Tabula of Cebes.*
  J. Mansfeld, 394:Vol39fasc3/4-484
Fitzgerald, M.J. Connection.
  R. Rusher, 617(TLS):31Jul87-817
Fitzgerald, M.J. Rope-Dancer.* Concertina.
  R. Ratner, 441:12Apr87-26
Fitzgerald, P. Innocence.*
  E. Leider, 441:10May87-20
  J. Mellors, 364:Oct86-91
  442(NY):27Jul87-77
Fitzgerald, P. Charlotte Mew and Her Friends.
  B. Leithauser, 453(NYRB):15Jan87-25
Fitzgerald, P. Offshore.
  B.F. Williamson, 441:13Sep87-51
Fitzgerald, R. & E. O'Brien. Vanishing Ireland.
  P-L. Adams, 61:Jun87-83
Fitz Lyon, A. Maria Malibran.
  R. Christiansen, 617(TLS):17Jul87-772
Flack, B.L. With a Sudden and Terrible Clarity.
  E.B. Gose, 102(CanL):Fall86-143
  T.B. Vincent, 198:Summer86-83
Flagg, F. Fried Green Tomatoes at the Whistle Stop Cafe.
  J. Butler, 441:18Oct87-14
Flaherty, G. Filthy the Man.*
  L. White, 573(SSF):Summer86-334
Flake, C. Tarnished Crown.
  W. Tower, 441:26Apr87-26
Flam, J. Matisse.*
  N. Bryson, 617(TLS):27Mar87-328
Flammini, G., ed. De conceptu. (Vol 1) (rev by I. Mazzini)
  G. Sabbah, 555:Vol59fasc2-324
Flanagan, M. Bad Girls.
  T. De Pietro, 249(HudR):Autumn86-492
  R.L. Johnson, 573(SSF):Summer86-330
Flanagan, M. Trust.
  W. Brandmark, 362:16Apr87-36
  R. Kaveney, 617(TLS):3Apr87-361
Flanagan, R. Naked to Naked Goes.
  D. Madden, 598(SoR):Summer87-730
Flanders, P. & K.B. Monteath - see Pallavicino, B.
Flanders, W.A. Structures of Experience.*
  I. Konigsberg, 403(MLS):Summer86-363

Flanner, H. Brief Cherishing.
J.R. Hepworth, 649(WAL):Nov86-280
Flasch, K., ed. Von Meister Dietrich zu
Meister Eckhart.
K. Ruh, 684(ZDA):Band115Heft1-7
Flasche, H., ed. Hacia Calderón.
P.W. Evans, 86(BHS):Apr86-168
Flashar, H. - see Ueberweg, F.
Flater, L., A. Van Herk & R. Wiebe, eds.
West of Fiction.*
G. McWhirter, 102(CanL):Summer86-135
Flaubert, G. L'Éducation sentimentale.
(P.M. Wetherill, ed)
L. Bottineau, 535(RHL):Jul-Aug86-773
C. Wake, 402(MLR):Jan86-211
Flaubert, G. & G. Sand. Correspondance
Flaubert-Sand.* (A. Jacobs, ed)
B.F. Bart, 535(RHL):Sep-Oct86-935
Flaubert, G. & I.S. Turgenev. A Friend-
ship in Letters.* (B. Beaumont, ed &
trans)
W. Fowlie, 569(SR):Summer86-lvi
Flay, J.C. Hegel's Quest for Certainty.*
R. Bernasconi, 518:Jan86-26
D. Janicaud, 192(EP):Oct-Dec86-557
Fleeman, J.D. A Preliminary Handlist of
Copies of Books Associated with Dr.
Samuel Johnson.*
D. Wheeler, 83:Autumn86-254
Fleeman, J.D. - see Johnson, S.
Fleetwood, H. The Past.
R. Deveson, 617(TLS):23Jan87-91
B. Morton, 362:5Feb87-25
Fleig, H. Literarischer Vampirismus.
J.L. Sammons, 221(GQ):Fall86-651
Fleischer, C.H. Bureaucrat and Intellec-
tual in the Ottoman Empire.
C. Woodhead, 617(TLS):25-31Dec87-1439
Fleischer, W. Phraseologie der deutschen
Gegenwartssprache.
J. Scharnhorst, 682(ZPSK):Band39Heft6-
716
Fleischer, W. & others, eds. Kleine Enzy-
klopädie "Deutsche Sprache."
D. Nerius, W. Hofrichter & I. Rahnen-
führer, 682(ZPSK):Band39Heft4-504
Fleishman, A. Figures of Autobiography.*
L.M. Shires, 403(MLS):Summer86-351
Fleishman, L. Boris Pasternak v tridt-
satyye gody.*
G.A. Hosking, 575(SEER):Jul86-462
G.S. Smith, 402(MLR):Jul86-810
Flejšman, L. Boris Pasternak v tridcatye
gody.
B.P. Scherr, 574(SEEJ):Summer86-292
Fleming, G. Hitler and the Final Solu-
tion.*
M. Silberman, 221(GQ):Spring86-341
Fleming, J. - see Negri, A.
Fleming, J.V. From Bonaventure to Bel-
lini.*
E. Peters, 54:Mar86-163
Fleming, J.V. Reason and the Lover.*
C.H.L. Bodenham, 382(MAE):1986/1-145
H.R. Runte, 150(DR):Winter85/86-597
E.B. Vitz, 401(MLQ):Jun85-202
Fleming, T. Time and Tide.
W. Lord, 441:13Sep87-7
Fleming-Williams, I. & L. Parris. The
Discovery of Constable.*
C. Powell, 59:Mar86-99

Fleschner, J. Im Kampf gegen das ideo-
logisch geknebelte Denken.
L. Milne, 402(MLR):Jan87-270
Fletcher, A. Reform in the Provinces.
D. Underdown, 617(TLS):23Jan87-88
Fletcher, A. & J. Stevenson, eds. Order
and Disorder in Early Modern England.*
L. Stone, 453(NYRB):26Feb87-38
Fletcher, G.A. The Keynesian Revolution
and Its Critics.
A.P. Thirlwall, 617(TLS):24Jul87-800
Fletcher, I., ed. British Poetry and Prose
1870-1905.
J. Lucas, 617(TLS):3Jul87-724
Fletcher, J. Alain Robbe-Grillet.*
E. Smyth, 535(RHL):Jan-Feb86-167
Fletcher, J. A Wife for a Moneth. (D.R.
Miller, ed)
M.R. Woodhead, 447(N&Q):Dec85-524
Fletcher, P. A Child's Learning of
English.
B.G. Blount, 350:Jun87-454
Flew, A. David Hume.
D.W.D. Owen, 617(TLS):6Mar87-237
Flew, A. Thinking about Social Thinking.
R.G., 185:Oct86-295
Flexner, S.B. Listening to America.
G-J. Forgue, 189(EA):Jan-Mar87-105
Fliege, H., ed. "Bekenntnis und Erfah-
rung."
K. Lebedewa, 654(WB):10/1986-1756
Fliegel, R. The Next to Die.
N. Callendar, 441:3May87-46
Fliegelman, J. Prodigals and Pilgrims.
J.A.L. Lemay, 402(MLR):Apr86-451
Flint, H. Return Journey.
P. Craig, 617(TLS):14Aug87-872
P. Parker, 362:17Sep87-26
Flint, K., ed. Impressionists in England.
R.S., 90:Jun86-445
Flint, W. & N. Pío Baroja: "Camino de per-
fección."
C.A. Longhurst, 86(BHS):Jul86-292
J.J. Macklin, 402(MLR):Jul86-774
Flitner, W. Goethe im Spätwerk.
S. Atkins, 406:Fall86-369
Flood, J.L., ed. Modern Swiss Literature.
P. Skrine, 402(MLR):Jan87-258
Flood, R. & M. Lockwood, eds. The Nature
of Time.
M. Talbot, 441:3May87-16
Flook, M. Reckless Wedding.*
C. Wright, 363(LitR):Fall86-118
Flora, J.M., ed. The English Short Story,
1880-1945.*
J.V. Hagopian, 573(SSF):Winter86-125
Flora, J.M. Hemingway's Nick Adams.*
I. Jackson, 447(N&Q):Dec85-551
Florby, G. The Painful Passage to Virtue.*
A.R. Braunmuller, 677(YES):Vol16-238
Florence, M.S., C. Marshall & C.K. Ogden.
Militarism versus Feminism. (M. Kamester
& J. Vellacott, eds)
J. Hornsby, 617(TLS):4-10Dec87-1345
Florence, P. Mallarmé, Manet and Redon.
S. Bann, 617(TLS):6Feb87-141
Flores, A. & K., eds. The Defiant Muse:
Hispanic Feminist Poems from the Middle
Ages to the Present.
D. Ackerman, 441:3May87-38
Flores, D.L., ed. Jefferson and Southwest-
ern Exploration.
C. Hanyan, 106:Summer86-189

Flores, R. The Rhetoric of Doubtful Authority.*
   N. Johnson, 544:Spring86-187
Florey, K.B. Duet.
   R.D. MacDougall, 441:29Nov87-20
Flori, J. L'essor de la Chevalerie (XIe-XIIe siècles).
   G. Roques, 553(RLiR):Jan-Jun86-270
Flori, J. L'Idéologie du glaive.
   M. Keen, 382(MAE):1986/1-118
Flower, J.E. Literature and the Left in France.*
   J.S.T. Garfitt, 402(MLR):Jul87-746
Flower, J.R. & C.H.R. Niven - see Vailland, R.
Flower, K. Serving Secretly.
   D. Caute, 617(TLS):13-19Nov87-1242
Floyd, V. The Plays of Eugene O'Neill.
   S.A. Black, 27(AL):Dec86-652
   J.H. Stroupe, 130:Summer86-171
Flückiger-Studer, T. Quantifikation in natürlichen Sprachen.
   J.N. Green, 208(FS):Apr86-248
   R. Martin, 209(FM):Apr86-113
   C. Schwarze, 545(RPh):Aug86-78
Flügge, C.W. Versuch einer historisch-kritischen Darstellung des bisherigen Einflusses der Kantischen Philosophie auf alle Zweige der wissenschaftlichen und praktischen Theologie.
   R. Malter, 342:Band77Heft3-385
Flukinger, R. The Formative Decades.
   J.F. Scott, 637(VS):Autumn86-144
Flusche, D.M. & E.H. Korth. Forgotten Females.
   P.E.H. Hair, 86(BHS):Apr86-185
Flydal, E. Oljespråk.
   E. Haugen, 563(SS):Autumn86-429
Flynn, C.H. Samuel Richardson.
   J. Harris, 677(YES):Vol16-268
Flynn, J., ed. Understanding Céline.
   N. Hewitt, 208(FS):Jul86-358
Flynn, R. Wanderer Springs.
   D. McWhorter, 441:11Oct87-55
Flynn, T.R. Sartre and Marxist Existentialism.*
   M.J. De Nys, 543:Jun87-767
   R. Santoni, 258:Jun86-183
Flynt, C. Mother Love.
   J. Markus, 441:28Jun87-13
Fo, D. Manuale minimo dell'attore.
   L. Fontana, 617(TLS):18-24Dec87-1398
Foakes, R.A. Illustrations of the English Stage 1580-1642.
   T.W. Craik, 161(DUJ):Jun86-374
   D. George, 570(SQ):Autumn86-408
   W. Habicht, 156(ShJW):Jahrbuch1986-220
   P. Hollindale, 541(RES):Nov86-566
   D. Mann, 354:Mar86-87
   J. Milhous, 615(TJ):Mar86-115
   M. Rosenberg, 610:Autumn86-250
   R. Studing, 568(SCN):Fall86-36
Foakes, R.A. - see Shakespeare, W.
Fodor, A. Tolstoy and the Russians.*
   N.O. Warner, 550(RusR):Apr86-218
Fodor, J.A. & others. Against Definitions.
   F. Recanati, 98:Jan-Feb86-128
Fog, D. Musikhandel og Nodetryk i Danmark efter 1750.
   J.H., 412:Feb85-71
Fogel, A. Coercion to Speak.
   T.K. Bender, 141:Spring86-226
[continued]

[continuing]
   R.L. Caserio, 637(VS):Summer87-537
   J. Feaster, 395(MFS):Summer86-305
Fogel, J.A. Politics and Sinology.*
   L. Hurvitz, 318(JAOS):Oct/Dec85-769
Fogel, S. A Tale of Two Countries.
   R. Brown, 529(QQ):Winter86-897
   S. Solecki, 627(UTQ):Fall86-159
Fogelin, R.J. Hume's Skepticism in the "Treatise of Human Nature."*
   S. Arnold, 319:Jul87-450
   D. McQueen, 518:Jan86-24
   P. Russell, 393(Mind):Jul86-392
Fohrmann, J. Abenteuer und Bürgertum.
   G. Bersier, 406:Spring86-99
Fokkema, D.W. Literary History, Modernism and Post-Modernism.
   U. Margolin, 107(CRCL):Sep86-518
Folena, G. - see Pasquali, G.
Foley, B. Telling the Truth.
   A.S. Byatt, 617(TLS):16Jan87-65
   J. Humphries, 385(MQR):Fall87-788
   C. Plantinga, 290(JAAC):Spring87-316
Foley, B.H. Listen to Me.
   P.J. Sharpe, 399(MLJ):Winter86-455
Foley, H.P., ed. Reflections of Women in Antiquity.
   T. Fleming, 121(CJ):Oct-Nov86-73
Foley, H.P. Ritual Irony.
   N. Marinatos, 121(CJ):Dec86-Jan87-154
   D. Roberts, 124:Sep-Oct86-65
Foley, J.M. Oral-Formulaic Theory and Research.*
   F.H. Bäuml, 589:Jul86-650
   D. Ben-Amos, 538(RAL):Summer86-309
   N.K. Moyle, 292(JAF):Jul/Sep86-364
   W. Parks, 574(SEEJ):Summer86-309
Foley, S.M. & C.H. Miller - see More, T.
Foley, W.A. & R.D. Van Valin, Jr. Functional Syntax and Universal Grammar.
   A.M. Bolkestein, 297(JL):Mar86-216
   D.E. Gulstad, 399(MLJ):Summer86-192
   D.H., 355(LSoc):Mar86-132
   P. Schachter, 361:Jun86-172
Folkenflik, R., ed. The English Hero, 1660-1800.*
   J.A.V. Chapple, 447(N&Q):Jun85-263
"Le folklore du corps humain."
   R. Debrie, 553(RLiR):Jul-Dec86-623
Folse, H.J. The Philosophy of Niels Bohr.
   E. MacKinnon, 486:Sep86-458
Folse, K.S. Intermediate Reading Practices.
   J.M. Fayer, 399(MLJ):Autumn86-337
Foltinek, H. George Eliot.
   R. Ashton, 402(MLR):Apr86-455
   K. Tetzeli von Rosador, 72:Band223-Heft1-231
Fonda, A., with C. Thurlow. Never Before Noon.
   A. Shapiro, 441:14Jun87-29
Foner, P. History of Black Americans. (Vols 2 & 3)
   P. Lachance, 106:Winter86-449
Fongaro, A. Sur Rimbaud.
   C.A. Hackett, 208(FS):Jan86-97
Fontes, M.D. - see under Da Costa Fontes, M.
Foot, M. Loyalists and Loners.*
   H.G. Pitt, 364:Jun86-88
Foot, M. & I. Kramnick - see Paine, T.
Foote, C.S. Selected Poems.
   D.A. Carpenter, 649(WAL):Aug86-170

Foote, P. Aurvandilstá.*
  A. Liberman, 563(SS):Spring86-179
Foote, S. & A. Murphy. Plays by Samuel
  Foote and Arthur Murphy. (G. Taylor, ed)
  E. Burns, 83:Spring86-110
  R.D. Hume, 402(MLR):Jul87-708
Forbes, B. The Endless Game.*
  639(VQR):Autumn86-127
Forbes, C. Cover Story.
  442(NY):12Jan87-104
Forbes, E. Mario and Grisi.*
  T.G. Kaufman, 465:Spring86-123
Forbes, G. The Metaphysics of Modality.*
  B. Garrett, 518:Apr86-65
Forbes, H.D., ed. Canadian Political
  Thought.
  W. Christian, 298:Fall86-153
  G.W., 102(CanL):Fall86-198
Forbes, P. & M.H. Smith - see "Harrap's
  Concise French and English Dictionary"
Force, J.E. William Whiston.
  G.S. Rousseau, 566:Spring87-212
Forcione, A.K. Cervantes and the Mystery
  of Lawlessness.*
  R. El Saffar, 405(MP):Aug86-78
  S. Gilman, 240(HR):Winter86-91
Ford, A. Edward Hicks.
  R.E. Ahlborn, 658:Winter86-312
Ford, A.E., ed. "La Vengeance de Nostre-
  Seigneur."*
  B.A. Pitts, 207(FR):Feb87-389
Ford, B., with C. Chase. Betty.
  M. Sandmaier, 441:1Mar87-9
Ford, E.B. & J.S. Haywood. Church Trea-
  sures in the Oxford District.
  J.H.W.P., 90:Feb86-156
Ford, F.L. Political Murder.*
  639(VQR):Spring86-60
Ford, H. Four Lives in Paris.
  H. Goldgar, 441:15Feb87-16
  H. Goldgar, 598(SoR):Summer87-719
Ford, J. The Lover's Melancholy. (R.F.
  Hill, ed)
  T.W. Craik, 161(DUJ):Jun86-374
  M. Dodsworth, 175:Spring86-107
Ford, J. The Selected Plays of John Ford.
  (C. Gibson, ed)
  K. Duncan-Jones, 617(TLS):20Feb87-188
Ford, P. - see Hardy, A.
Ford, R. A Piece of My Heart.
  R. Kaveney, 617(TLS):19Jun87-669
Ford, R. Rock Springs.
  A. Kazin, 453(NYRB):5Nov87-12
  J. Wideman, 441:20Sep87-1
Ford, R. The Sportswriter.*
  C.J. Fox, 364:Oct86-108
Ford, R.I., ed. The Ethnographic American
  Southwest.
  C. Kaut, 292(JAF):Oct/Dec86-482
Ford, W., with P. Pepe. Slick.
  E. Cohen, 441:19Jul87-21
Forer, L.G. A Chilling Effect.
  H. Simons, 441:14Jun87-12
Forester, J., ed. Critical Theory and
  Public Life.
  R.H., 185:Apr87-684
Forester, T. High-Tech Society.
  R. Kling, 441:27Sep87-43
Forestier, G. - see Brosse
Foreville, R. & G. Keir, eds. The Book of
  St. Gilbert.
  B. Golding, 617(TLS):25-31Dec87-1439

Forgacs, D. & G. Nowell-Smith - see
  Gramsci, A.
Forget, P., ed. Text und Interpretation.
  R.C. Holub, 221(GQ):Summer86-467
Forkner, B. & P. Samway, eds. A Modern
  Southern Reader.
  M. Kreyling, 578:Spring87-102
Forman, E. - see de Montfleury, A.J.
Fornara, C.W. The Nature of History in
  Ancient Greece and Rome.*
  R. Drews, 122:Apr86-164
Fornaro, P. La voce fuori scena.
  P.W. van der Horst, 394:Vol39fasc3/4-
  482
"Maria Irene Fornes: Plays."
  C.A. Schuler, 615(TJ):Dec86-514
Forni, P.M., with G. Cavallini - see
  Chiappelli, F.
Forrer, R. Theodicies in Conflict.
  M.I. Lowance, Jr., 165(EAL):Vol22No3-
  324
Forrest, J. Morris and Matachin.
  J.D. Sweet, 650(WF):Jan86-45
  B.J. Ward, 292(JAF):Jul/Sep86-338
Forrest, J.F. & R.L. Greaves. John Bunyan.
  N.H. Keeble, 447(N&Q):Mar85-125
Forsgren, K-A. Die Deutsche Satzgliedlehre
  1780-1830.
  L. van Driel, 204(FdL):Jun86-151
Forsmann, B., S. Koster & E. Pöhlmann -
  see Heubeck, A.
Forster, E.M. Avec vue sur l'Arno.
  A. Clerval, 450(NRF):Dec86-103
Forster, E.M. E.M. Forster's "Commonplace
  Book."* (P. Gardner, ed)
  S. Bick, 42(AR):Spring86-243
  C. Hawtree, 364:Apr/May86-148
  E. Heine, 395(MFS):Winter86-661
  J.S. Herz, 177(ELT):Vol29No4-443
  F.P.W. McDowell, 177(ELT):Vol29No3-311
  J.H. Stape, 627(UTQ):Fall86-115
Forster, E.M. The Longest Journey. (E.
  Heine, ed)
  T. Brown, 541(RES):Aug86-441
  F.P.W. McDowell, 177(ELT):Vol29No3-311
Forster, E.M. Selected Letters of E.M.
  Forster.* (Vol 2) (M. Lago & P.N. Fur-
  bank, eds)
  F.P.W. McDowell, 177(ELT):Vol29No3-311
  42(AR):Winter86-121
Forster, E.M. & R. Masood. Forster-Masood
  Letters. (J.A. Kidwai, ed)
  S.P. Rosenbaum, 177(ELT):Vol29No2-219
Forster, H. Edward Young.
  P. Rogers, 617(TLS):20Mar87-287
Forster, K.W. & M. Kubelik, eds. Palladio,
  Ein Symposium.
  C. Kolb, 576:Dec86-415
Forster, L. Christoffel van Sichem in
  Basel und die frühe deutsche Alexand-
  riner.
  A.J. Harper, 402(MLR):Jul87-773
Forsyth, J. Back to the Barn.
  E. Shorter, 157:No162-50
Forsyth, K. "Ariadne auf Naxos" by Hugo
  von Hofmannsthal and Richard Strauss.*
  C.R. Finlay, 107(CRCL):Sep86-507
  M.A. Weiner, 406:Summer86-237
Forsyth, M. Buildings for Music.*
  A. Betsky, 505:Oct86-117
  D. Vaughan, 415:Aug86-439
Forsyth, P.Y. The Poems of Catullus.
  M.B. Skinner, 124:Jul-Aug87-450

Fortenbaugh, W.W. Quellen zur Ethik
Theophrasts.
P. Louis, 555:Vol59fasc2-287
C.J. Rowe, 123:Vol36No2-321
Fortenbaugh, W.W., P.M. Huby & A.A. Long,
eds. Theophastus of Eresus.
P. Pellegrin, 542:Oct-Dec86-503
Fortescue, M. West Greenlandic.
M. Bittner, 355(LSoc):Jun86-269
D.R.F. Collis, 320(CJL):Summer86-171
Fortescue, S. The Communist Party and
Soviet Science.
L. Graham, 617(TLS):18-24Sep87-1009
Fortescue, W. Alphonse de Lamartine.
F. Letessier, 535(RHL):Mar-Apr86-295
C.F. Robinson, 447(N&Q):Dec85-533
Fortin, C. Au coeur de l'instant.
A. Moorhead, 207(FR):Apr87-725
Fortin, G. & B. Richardson. Life of the
Party.
N. Wiseman, 298:Spring86-144
Foscolo, U. Studi su Dante. (Pt 2) (G.
Petrocchi, ed)
G. Costa, 545(RPh):Nov86-215
Fossestøl, B. & others, eds. Festskrift
til Einar Lundeby, 3 oktober 1984.
H. Fix, 563(SS):Spring86-199
Foster, B.R. Umma in the Sargonic Period.
M.A. Powell, 318(JAOS):Jan/Mar85-144
Foster, C.H.W. The Cape Cod National
Seashore.
L. Arnberger, 432(NEQ):Sep86-461
Foster, D.W. Alternate Voices in the Con-
temporary Latin American Narrative.
M. Camurati, 263(RIB):Vol36No3-336
S. Magnarelli, 395(MFS):Autumn86-477
Foster, D.W., comp. Cuban Literature.*
J.J. Rodriguez-Florido, 263(RIB):
Vol36No3-337
Foster, D.W. Estudios sobre teatro
mexicano contemporáneo.
R.D. Burgess, 263(RIB):Vol36No1-59
Foster, G.W., with D.J. Hufford. The World
was Flooded with Light.
T.E. Graves, 292(JAF):Oct/Dec86-487
Foster, H., ed. The Anti-Aesthetic.*
K. Tölölyan, 454:Fall86-84
Foster, H., ed. Postmodern Culture.
C. Dilnot, 59:Jun86-245
Foster, J. A.J. Ayer.*
D.M. Armstrong, 393(Mind):Jul86-387
Foster, J. The Case for Idealism.*
P. Engel, 98:Jan-Feb86-150
H.M. Robinson, 323:May86-208
Foster, J. & H. Robinson, eds. Essays on
Berkeley.*
D.G., 185:Apr87-699
M. Phillips, 542:Jul-Sep86-373
Foster, K. Petrarch.*
N. Mann, 402(MLR):Jan86-219
S. Sturm-Maddox, 276:Spring86-64
Foster, K. & P. Boyde, eds. Cambridge
Readings in Dante's "Comedy."
G. Costa, 545(RPh):Nov86-215
Foster, S. Victorian Women's Fiction.
N. Armstrong, 637(VS):Winter87-292
S. Morgan, 594:Summer86-207
A. Trodd, 366:Autumn86-263
Fothergill, B. The Strawberry Hill Set.*
M. Kallich, 173(ECS):Summer87-509
Fothergill, R. Private Chronicles.
S. Rendall, 153:Fall86-57

Fotion, N. & G. Elfstrom. Military Ethics.
M.R.D. Foot, 176:Feb87-45
Foucault, M. The Care of Self.* (French
title: Histoire de la sexualité. (Vol 3))
J. Boswell, 441:18Jan87-31
A. Cameron, 313:Vol76-266
Foucault, M. Histoire de la sexualité.*
(Vol 2)
A. Cameron, 313:Vol76-266
D.M. Halperin, 24:Summer86-274
Foucault, M. La Pensée du dehors.
T. Cordellier, 450(NRF):Nov86-103
Foulkes, R., ed. Shakespeare and the Vic-
torian Stage.
T. Hawkes, 617(TLS):10Apr87-390
Foulkes, R. The Shakespeare Tercentenary
of 1864.*
M.J. Pringle, 611(TN):Vol40No1-43
Fouqué, F.D. Der Zauberring. (G. Schulz,
ed)
P. Wagner, 83:Spring86-122
"Four Dubliners."
C. Rawson, 617(TLS):24Jul87-783
Fout, J., ed. German Women in the Nine-
teenth Century.
J.M. Bailey, 221(GQ):Winter86-172
Fowke, E. & C.H. Carpenter, eds. Explora-
tions in Canadian Folklore.
L. Munk, 627(UTQ):Fall86-242
I.S. Posen, 440:Summer-Fall86-175
Fowler, D. & A.J. Abadie, eds. Faulkner
and Humor.*
W.R., 295(JML):Nov86-465
27(AL):Oct86-487
Fowler, D. & A.J. Abadie, eds. New
Directions in Faulkner Studies.*
C.S. Brown, 569(SR):Winter86-167
Fowler, D.C. The Bible in Middle English
Literature.
D.L. Jeffrey, 178:Dec86-452
Fowler, M. Below the Peacock Fan.
J. McKay, 362:24Sep87-24
J. Motion, 617(TLS):23-29Oct87-1160
Fowler, M. Redney.*
J.S. Grant, 178:Mar86-114
Fowler, R. Linguistic Criticism.
E.L. Epstein, 617(TLS):12Jun87-628
J. Paccaud, 189(EA):Jul-Sep87-328
Fowler, V.C. Henry James's American Girl.*
J.E. Funston, 115:Winter86-121
C.B. Torsney, 284:Winter85-136
Fowlie, W. Sites.
M. Peckham, 441:5Jul87-15
Fox, A. German Intonation.*
H.F. Taylor, 221(GQ):Winter86-126
Fox, C. Londoners.
J.M. Crook, 617(TLS):29May87-580
Fox, J. Villon: Poems.*
N.J. Lacy, 589:Oct86-927
G.M. Sutherland, 402(MLR):Jul86-735
Fox, M. Illuminations of Hildegard of
Bingen.
G.J. Lewis, 564:Nov86-324
Fox, M.A. The Case for Animal Experimen-
tation.*
M.M., 185:Apr87-702
Fox, M.A. & L. Groarke, eds. Nuclear War.*
W.E. Steinkraus, 529(QQ):Summer86-453
Fox, M.V. The Song of Songs and the
Ancient Egyptian Love Songs.
R. Couffignal, 549(RLC):Apr-Jun86-253
Fox, M.W. Agricide.
T.C. Holyoke, 42(AR):Fall86-487

French, D. British Strategy and War Aims 1914-1916.
J. Gooch, 617(TLS):10Apr87-378
French, E. Emily. (J. Lecompte, ed)
E.K. Rothman, 441:10May87-21
French, H.D. Bookbinding in Early America.
N. Barker, 617(TLS):2Jan87-22
639(VQR):Autumn86-138
French, H.D. Early American Bookbindings from the Collection of Michael Papantonio. (2nd ed)
N. Barker, 617(TLS):2Jan87-22
French, M. Her Mother's Daughter.
A. Hoffman, 441:25Oct87-7
A. Summers, 617(TLS):23-29Oct87-1158
French, M. Shakespeare's Division of Experience.
B. Hatlen, 536(Rev):Vol8-241
I. Schabert & others, 156(ShJW):Jahrbuch1986-223
Frend, W.H.C. The Rise of Christianity.
S.J.D. Cohen, 124:Jul-Aug87-465
E.D. Hunt, 313:Vol76-301
Frenz, H. & S. Tuck, eds. Eugene O'Neill's Critics.*
S. Fayad, 149(CLS):Summer86-178
R.S. Smith, 106:Winter86-469
Frere, S. Verulamium Excavations. (Vol 3)
S.E. Cleary, 123:Vol36No2-352
Frescobaldi, G. Il primo libro de' madrigali a cinque voci (1608). (C. Jacobs, ed)
A. Newcomb, 317:Summer86-395
Frescoln, W. - see Guillaume le Clerc
Freud, S. The Complete Letters of Sigmund Freud to Wilhelm Fliess, 1887-1904. (J.M. Masson, ed & trans)
S.A. Black, 529(QQ):Spring86-207
W.B. Warner, 533:Winter87-122
Freud, S. L'homme Moïse et la religion monothéiste.
J. le Hardi, 450(NRF):Jul-Aug86-183
Freund, G. Gisele Freund: Photographs.
H. Martin, 507:Jul/Aug86-303
Freund, J. La décadence.
A. Reix, 542:Jan-Mar86-155
Freund, S., ed. Deutsche Tagelieder.
H-G. Richert, 133:Band19Heft1-70
Freund, W. & K-A. Hellfaier - see "Grabbe-Jahrbuch 1-4"
Frey, R.G. Rights, Killing, and Suffering.*
E. Johnson, 482(PhR):Apr86-277
Frey, R.G., ed. Utility and Rights.
T. Christiano, 185:Jan87-477
Frey, W. - see "Otte, 'Eraclius'"
Freytag, H. Die Theorie der allegorischen Schriftdeutung und die Allegorie in deutschen Texten besonders des 11. und 12. Jahrhunderts.*
E.R. Hintz, 406:Fall86-386
E.C. Lutz, 680(ZDP):Band105Heft1-134
P.W. Tax, 133:Band18Heft4-358
Friar, K. - see Decavalles, A.
Frías, M.R. - see under Romero Frías, M.
Fricke, H. Aphorismus.
R.J. Rundell, 221(GQ):Winter86-124
Fricke, H. Norm und Abweichung.
B. Bennett, 406:Fall86-383
Fricke, R. 1876 Richard Wagner auf der Probe.
L.R. Shaw, 406:Fall86-409

Fridh-Haneson, B.M. Le Manteau symbolique.
C.E. Vafopoulou-Richardson, 123:Vol36No2-340
Fried, M. Absorption and Theatricality.*
D.W. Crawford, 543:Sep86-120
Fried, M. Realism, Writing, Disfiguration.
H. Goldgar, 441:5Jul87-15
J. Malcolm, 442(NY):5Oct87-121
Friedberg, M. Russian Culture in the 1980s.
M. Futrell, 104(CASS):Spring-Summer86-191
de Friedemann, N.S. & C. Patiño Rosselli. Lengua y Sociedad en el Palenque de San Basilo.
M. Perl, 682(ZPSK):Band39Heft5-603
Frieden, K. Genius and Monologue.
D. Robinson, 495(PoeS):Dec86-35
Friedenreich, K., ed. "Accompaninge the Players."*
M. Garrett, 541(RES):Feb86-89
A. Gurr, 402(MLR):Jul87-702
Friedheim, R.L., & others. Japan and the New Ocean Regime.
M.A. McKean, 293(JASt):May86-594
Friedman, C. & G. Giddins. A Moment's Notice.
G.L. Starks, Jr., 91:Fall86-312
Friedman, E.G. Joan Didion.
B. Gelfant, 649(WAL):May86-51
Friedman, I.S. Toward World Prosperity.
M. Kahler, 441:3May87-53
Friedman, J.E. The Enclosed Garden.
D.G. Mathews, 579(SAQ):Autumn86-407
639(VQR):Winter86-10
Friedman, K. A Case of Lone Star.
N. Callendar, 441:11Oct87-24
Friedman, L.M. Total Justice.
R.E.G., 185:Jan87-505
Friedman, M. Foundations of Space-Time Theories.
A. Heathcote, 63:Jun86-224
A.L. Hiskes, 167:Jul86-111
S.F. Savitt, 154:Summer86-388
R. Weingard & G. Smith, 486:Jun86-286
Friedman, M. Abraham Joshua Heschel and Elie Wiesel.
A. Goldman, 441:6Sep87-17
Friedman, M. The Venetian Mask.
442(NY):13Jul87-90
Friedman, R. To Live in Peace.
J. Neville, 617(TLS):10Apr87-394
Friedman, R.E. Who Wrote the Bible?
R. Davidson, 441:9Aug87-9
Friedmann, Y., ed. Islam in Asia. (Vol 1)
S.F. Dale, 293(JASt):May86-624
Friedrich, O. City of Nets.*
N. Lemann, 453(NYRB):15Jan87-23
Friel, J. Left of North.
J-A. Goodwin, 617(TLS):10Apr87-395
J. Mellors, 362:9Apr87-25
Friend, D. Family Laundry.
R. Robinson, 441:18Jan87-10
Frier, B.W. The Rise of the Roman Jurists.
M.C. Alexander, 124:Jan-Feb87-213
Fries, F.R. Verlegung eines mittleren Reiches.
J. Grambow, 654(WB):8/1986-1385
Fries, N. Syntaktische und semantische Studien zum frei verwendeten Infinitiv.
H. Janssen, 603:Vol10No1-247

Fries, U. Einführung in die Sprache
Chaucers.
G. Bourcier, 189(EA):Apr-Jun87-196
Friesen, G. The Canadian Prairies.*
J.H. Thompson, 529(QQ):Winter86-917
Friesen, G., ed. Nachrichten aus den
Staaten.
W. Grünzweig, 602:Band17Heft1-120
von Friesen, O. - see Moberg, V.
Friesen, P. Unearthly Horses.
C. Wiseman, 168(ECW):Fall86-210
Frigge, R. Das erwartbare Abenteuer.
M.T. Peischl, 221(GQ):Summer86-489
Frisch, M. L'homme apparaît au quater-
naire.
J-Y. Pouilloux, 98:Mar86-274
Frisch, W. Brahms and the Principle of
Developing Variation.*
J. Dunsby, 410(M&L):Jan86-88
M.T.R., 412:Aug85-221
W. Rothstein, 308:Fall86-284
Fritz, G. & M. Muckenhaupt. Kommunikation
und Grammatik.
F. Hundsnurscher, 685(ZDL):2/1986-284
Fritz, J.M., G. Mitchell & M.S. Nagaraja
Rao. When Kings and Gods Meet.
C.B. Asher, 293(JASt):Feb86-422
Frizzell, A. & A. Westell. The Canadian
General Election of 1984.
L. Leduc, 529(QQ):Autumn86-699
Frois, L. Historia de Japam. (Vols 3 & 4)
(J. Wicki, ed)
M. Cooper, 407(MN):Winter86-506
Froitzheim, C. Artikulationsnormen der
Umgangssprache in Köln.
A. Pauwels, 355(LSoc):Dec86-547
W.H. Vieregge, 685(ZDL):2/1986-255
Fromentin, E. Oeuvres complètes. (G.
Sagnes, ed)
B. Wright, 535(RHL):Sep-Oct86-941
Fromentin, E. & P. Bataillard. Etude sur
l'"Ahasvérus" d'Edgar Quinet.* (B.
Wright & T. Mellors, eds)
D. Weidenhammer, 72:Band223Heft1-213
Fromkin, V., ed. Phonetic Linguistics.
R.F. Port, 350:Mar87-135
Froula, C. To Write Paradise.*
G. Bornstein, 301(JEGP):Apr86-301
B. Goldensohn, 676(YR):Autumn86-128
P. Makin, 402(MLR):Jul87-720
A. Woodward, 541(RES):Nov86-594
Frow, J. Marxism and Literary History.
G. Leroy, 295(JML):Nov86-355
M. Sprinker, 617(TLS):16Jan87-65
Früh, S. & R. Wehse, eds. Die Frau im
Märchen.
R.B. Bottigheimer, 196:Band27Heft1/2-
111
Frühwald, W., ed. Gedichte der Romantik.
H.M.K. Riley, 133:Band18Heft4-375
"Adrian Frutiger, Gutenberg-Preisträger
1986 der Stadt Mainz und der Gutenberg-
Gesellschaft."
J. Dreyfus, 617(TLS):2-8Oct87-1088
Fruzzetti, L. & A. Östör. Kinship and Rit-
ual in Bengal.
P.J. Bertocci, 293(JASt):May86-625
Fry, C.B. Life Worth Living.*
D. Durrant, 364:Aug/Sep86-156
Fry, J. Visions and Models.
N.I. Nooter, 2(AfrA):Feb86-89
Fry, P.H. The Reach of Criticism.*
W. Keach, 340(KSJ):Vol35-213

Fryde, E.B. - see Treharne, R.F.
Frye, J.S. Living Stories, Telling Lives.
L.L. Doan, 395(MFS):Winter86-627
Frye, N. Northrop Frye on Shakespeare.*
(R. Sandler, ed)
M. Billington, 176:Jan87-56
K.L. Edwards, 344:Spring87-122
T. Hawkes, 617(TLS):10Apr87-390
Frye, N. The Great Code.*
G. Gillespie, 131(CL):Summer86-289
Frye, R.M. The Renaissance "Hamlet."*
R.A. Foakes, 405(MP):Aug86-69
H. Jenkins, 570(SQ):Summer86-258
J.W. Saunders, 541(RES):Feb86-88
S. Zitner, 627(UTQ):Winter86/87-367
Fryer, J. Felicitous Space.*
E.W.C., 295(JML):Nov86-391
Fuchs, D. Saul Bellow.
D. Seed, 447(N&Q):Dec85-575
Fuchs, E., ed. J.G. Fichte im Gespräch.
C. Cesa, 53(AGP):Band68Heft2-221
Fuchs, R.H. Richard Long.
T. Godfrey, 617(TLS):13Mar87-273
Fuchs, V. The Health Economy.
639(VQR):Autumn86-138
Fučić, B. Glagoljski natpisi.
A.R. Corin, 574(SEEJ):Fall86-460
Fudge, E.C. English Word-Stress.*
A.R. James, 257(IRAL):Feb86-77
Fuentes, C. A Change of Skin.
K. Duchêne, 176:Sep/Oct87-58
Fuentes, C. Distant Relations.
R. Christ, 473(PR):Vol53No2-305
Fuentes, C. Cristóbal Nonato.
A. González, 268(IFR):Summer87-91
Fuentes, C. The Old Gringo.*
M.A. Foster, 649(WAL):Nov86-281
G. Kearns, 249(HudR):Spring86-129
D. Mason, 448:Vol24No3-85
Fuentes, N. Hemingway in Cuba.*
R.A. Martin, 115:Fall86-530
Fugard, S. A Revolutionary Woman.
G. Kearns, 249(HudR):Spring86-125
Fühmann, F. Essays, Gespräche, Aufsätze
1964-1981.
H-G. Werner, 601(SuF):Jul-Aug85-894
Fuhrmann, H. Germany in the High Middle
Ages c 1050-1200.
S. Airlie, 617(TLS):5Jun87-614
Fujiwara no Sadaie. The Little Treasury of
One Hundred People, One Poem Each. (T.
Galt, trans)
J. Pigeot, 549(RLC):Apr-Jun86-187
Fuks, A. Social Conflict in Ancient
Greece.
N.R.E. Fisher, 303(JoHS):Vol106-237
"Fukuzawa Yukichi on Education." (E.
Kiyooka, ed & trans)
D.A. Dilworth, 407(MN):Autumn86-372
Fuller, E.E. Milton's Kinesthetic Vision
in "Paradise Lost."*
D. Benet, 391:Oct86-110
Fuller, J. Our Fathers' Shadows.
N. Callendar, 441:22Nov87-45
Fuller, J. Selected Poems 1954-1982.*
R. Richman, 441:29Nov87-25
Fuller, J. - see Gay, J.
Fuller, J.G. Tornado Watch #211.
S. Blakeslee, 441:27Sep87-40

[continuing]

P. Lewis, 364:Apr/May86-164

P. Lewis, 565:Summer86-57

Gaddis, W. The Recognitions.*

D. La Capra, 153:Winter86-33

Gadenne, P. Scènes dans le château.

R. Buss, 617(TLS):2-8Oct87-1072

Gadet, F. & M. Pêcheux. La langue introuvable.

A. Soulez, 192(EP):Oct-Dec86-559

Gado, F. The Passion of Ingmar Bergman.

J.R. Taylor, 617(TLS):2Jan87-16

Gadoffre, G. - see Claudel, P.L.C.

Gadoffre, G. - see de Ronsard, P.

Gaeffke, P. & D.A. Utz, eds. Identity and Division in Cults and Sects in South Asia.

O. von Hinüber, 318(JAOS):Oct/Dec85-801

Gaehde, U. T-Theoretizität und Holismus.

W. Balzer, 167:Sep86-265

Gaehtgens, T.W., ed. Johann Joachim Winckelmann 1717-1768.

H.B. Nisbet, 402(MLR):Oct87-1024

Gaeng, P.A. Collapse and Reorganization of the Latin Nominal Flection as Reflected in Epigraphic Sources.

M. Iliescu, 553(RLiR):Jan-Jun86-207

Gage, J. J.M.W. Turner.

R. Dorment, 617(TLS):10Jul87-735

J. Russell, 441:31May87-11

Gage, N. Hellas.

J.S. Bowman, 441:18Jan87-19

442(NY):23Feb87-136

Gagnier, R.A. Idylls of the Marketplace.

R.B. Henkle, 454:Winter87-171

J. Sutherland, 617(TLS):19Jun87-672

Gagnon, A. L'Absente-et-voilà/Le Quaternaire initiatique.

P.G. Lewis, 207(FR):Dec86-287

Gagnon, J.C. - see under Chapdelaine Gagnon, J.

Gai, L. L'altare argenteo di San Iacopo nel Duomo di Pistoia.

J. Beck, 551(RenQ):Spring86-107

D. Garstang, 39:Apr86-293

Gaier, U. - see Herder, J.G.

Gailey, A. Rural Houses of the North of Ireland.*

S. Bonde, 589:Jan86-148

Gaines, J.F. Social Structures in Molière's Theater.*

J. Cairncross, 475:Vol13No24-389

G. Forestier, 535(RHL):Jul-Aug86-742

H. Phillips, 208(FS):Apr86-207

R.W. Tobin, 210(FrF):Jan86-106

Gaite, C.M. - see under Martín Gaite, C.

Gál, G. & R. Wood - see Ockham, William of

Galan, F.W. Historic Structures.*

W. Martin, 599:Fall86-432

M. Sosa, 574(SEEJ):Summer86-278

Galán, P.C. - see under Cerezo Galán, P.

Galassi, J. - see Cornford, J.

Galbiati, F. P'eng P'ai and the Hai-Lu-feng Soviet.

G.W. Berkley, 293(JASt):Aug86-816

Galbraith, J.K. Economics in Perspective.

R. Heilbroner, 453(NYRB):5Nov87-44

L. Silk, 441:25Oct87-27

442(NY):28Dec87-126

Galbraith, J.K. A History of Economics.

D. Winch, 617(TLS):18-24Dec87-1393

Galbraith, J.K. A View from the Stands.*

(A.D. Williams, ed)

J. Freeman, 617(TLS):13Mar87-260

442(NY):12Jan87-103

Galdós, B.P. - see under Pérez Galdós, B.

Gale, P. Kansas in August.

M. Casserley, 617(TLS):24Jul87-802

S. Fry, 362:21May87-23

Gale, R.L. Louis L'Amour.

J.D. Nesbitt, 649(WAL):Nov86-258

Galeano, E. Memory of Fire.

T. Broderick, 532(RCF):Fall86-144

O. Conant, 441:1Mar87-20

S. White, 448:Vol24No2-95

Galen. Galen on Bloodletting. (P. Brain, ed & trans)

J. Barnes, 520:Vol31No3-283

Galen. On Respiration and the Arteries. (D.J. Furley & J.S. Wilkie, eds)

J. Longrigg, 303(JoHS):Vol106-218

J.T. Vallance, 123:Vol36No1-31

Galen. Three Treatises on the Nature of Science. (M. Frede, ed & trans)

J. Barnes, 520:Vol31No2-193

Galerstein, C., ed. Women Writers of Spain.

J. Gold, 365:Spring/Summer86-187

Galford, E. The Fires of Bride.*

L. Taylor, 362:8Jan87-22

Galisson, R. Les Mots mode d'emploi.

Y. de la Quérière, 207(FR):May87-879

Galkins, R.G. Monuments of Medieval Art.

P. Hetherington, 39:Feb86-137

Gallacher, T. Portugal.

B. Lomax, 86(BHS):Jul86-301

Gallagher, C. The Industrial Reformation of English Fiction.*

R.J. Dunn, 594:Fall86-328

J. Hawthorn, 175:Autumn86-273

R.B. Henkle, 637(VS):Winter87-261

J. Kucich, 141:Summer86-347

J.P. McGowan, 577(SHR):Spring86-171

639(VQR):Spring86-43

Gallagher, C. & T. Laqueur, eds. The Making of the Modern Body.

R. Porter, 617(TLS):28Aug87-919

Gallagher, D. - see Waugh, E.

Gallagher, M. Political Parties in the Republic of Ireland.

T. Garvin, 272(IUR):Autumn86-243

Gallagher, P., ed. Aditi.

H.L. Seneviratne, 292(JAF):Oct/Dec86-474

Gallagher, T. John Ford.*

J. Richards, 176:Jan87-51

Gallagher, T. Journeyman.

362:1Oct87-25

Gallant, M. Home Truths.*

639(VQR):Winter86-20

Gallant, M. Overhead in a Balloon.*

L. Duguid, 617(TLS):25Sep-1Oct87-1052

P. Rose, 441:15Mar87-7

Gallant, M. Paris Notebooks.

L. Leith, 99:Oct86-33

Gallardo, M.A.G. - see under Garrido Gallardo, M.A.

Gallegos, R. Canaima.

W.W. Megenney, 238:May86-317

Gallenkamp, C. & R.E. Johnson, eds. Maya.

M. Graham, 2(AfrA):May86-78

Gallese, L.R. Women Like Us.

639(VQR):Winter86-25

Gallet, M. & Y. Bottineau, eds. Les Gabriel.
   R. Neuman, 576:Jun86-174
Galli, P.V. - see under Vecchi Galli, P.
Galli de' Paratesi, N. Lingua toscana in bocca ambrosiana.
   L. Repetti, 275(IQ):Summer86-111
Gallico, C. - see Verdi, G.
Gallo, F.A. Music of the Middle Ages II.
   J. Caldwell, 410(M&L):Jul86-308
Gallo, L. Alimentazione e demografia della Grecia antica.
   S. Hornblower, 123:Vol36No2-328
Gallois, J. Haendel.
   C.M.B., 412:Aug85-217
Gallop, D. - see Parmenides
Gallop, J. The Daughter's Seduction.*
   P. Barrish, 153:Winter86-15
Gallop, J. Reading Lacan.*
   P. Barrish, 153:Winter86-15
   A. Thiher, 207(FR):May87-874
   E. Wright, 402(MLR):Jul87-685
Galloway, D., ed. Records of Early English Drama: Norwich 1540-1642.
   W. Tydeman, 610:Summer86-154
   D. Wyatt, 611(TN):Vol40No2-90
Gallup, D. - see Wilder, T.
Gally, M. & C. Marchello-Nizia. Littératures de l'Europe médiévale.
   G.T. Diller, 207(FR):Oct86-135
Galt, J. The Entail: or the Lairds of Grippy. (I.A. Gordon, ed)
   T.W. Craik, 83:Spring86-112
Galt, J. Ringan Gilhaize or The Covenanters.* (P.J. Wilson, ed)
   W.R. Aitken, 541(RES):Nov86-579
   I.A. Gordon, 588(SSL):Vol21-333
Galton, A. The Logic of Aspect.
   J. van Benthem, 482(PhR):Jul86-434
Galvin, J. God's Mistress.*
   S.P. Estess, 577(SHR):Winter86-84
Gamal, A.S. - see Ibn Riḍwān
Gambaro, G. Teatro.
   C. Kaiser-Lenoir, 352(LATR):Fall86-119
Gamberini, F. Stylistic Theory and Practice in the Younger Pliny.*
   J.G.F. Powell, 123:Vol36No1-56
Gambon, C-F. Dans les bagnes de Napoléon III. (J-Y. Mollier, ed)
   M-L. Terry, 535(RHL):Jan-Feb86-156
Gamkrelidze, T.V. & V.V. Ivanov. Indoevropejskij jazyk i indoevropejcy.*
   W.R. Schmalstieg, 159:Spring86-81
Gandelman, C. Le Regard dans le texte.
   S. Bann, 617(TLS):6Feb87-141
Gandhi, M. The Moral and Political Writings of Mahatma Gandhi. (Vol 2) (R. Iyer, ed)
   S. Khilnani, 617(TLS):6Feb87-142
de Gandillac, M. - see Nicholas of Cusa
Gandy, C.I. & P.J. Stanlis. Edmund Burke.
   L. Mitchell, 447(N&Q):Mar85-135
Gangemi, K. Olt.
   J. Byrne, 532(RCF):Spring86-199
Ganim, J.M. Style and Consciousness in Middle English Narrative.*
   H. Cooper, 382(MAE):1986/2-278
   S.S. Hussey, 402(MLR):Apr87-437
   S. Mapstone, 541(RES):Feb86-74
Ganivet, A. Los trabajos del infatigable creador Pío Cid. (L. Rivkin, ed)
   D.L. Shaw, 86(BHS):Oct86-391

Gannon, F. Yo, Poe.
   S.S. Stark, 441:9Aug87-21
Gans, D. The Le Corbusier Guide.
   M. Filler, 453(NYRB):17Dec87-49
   P.G., 441:6Dec87-24
Ganser, W.G. Die niederländische Version der Reisebeschreibung Johanns von Mandeville.
   E.J. Morrall, 402(MLR):Jul87-770
Gansleweit, K-D. Untersuchungen zur Namenkunde und Siedlungsgeschichte der nordöstlichen Niederlausitz.
   J. Udolph, 685(ZDL):1/1986-112
Gantner, J. - see "Heinrich Wölfflin: Autobiographie, Tagebücher und Briefe"
Ganz, A. George Bernard Shaw.*
   G.M. Crane, 615(TJ):Dec86-511
   P. Mudford, 447(N&Q):Dec85-542
Ganz, P.F., ed. Johann Wolfgang von Goethe.
   J.R. Williams, 402(MLR):Jan86-251
Gao Yuan. Born Red.
   T. Tung, 441:3May87-34
Garavaglia, L.A. & C.G. Worman. Firearms of the American West, 1866-1894.
   L. Milazzo, 584(SWR):Winter86-123
Garavelli, B.M. - see under Mortara Garavelli, B.
Garavini, F. Itinerari a Montaigne.*
   D. Maskell, 208(FS):Apr86-202
Garavini, F. & L. Lazzerini, eds. Macaronee provenzali.
   J. Hösle, 52:Band21Heft3-311
Garber, F. The Autonomy of the Self from Richardson to Huysmans.
   R. Ellrodt, 549(RLC):Apr-Jun86-245
Garber, S.D. The Urban Naturalist.
   T. Ferrell, 441:27Sep87-37
Garbus, M. Traitors and Heroes.
   M.E. Gale, 441:30Aug87-21
Garci-Gómez, M. El Burgos de Mio Cid.*
   G. West, 86(BHS):Apr86-152
García, A.C. - see under Carrasco García, A.
García, A.G. - see under González García, A.
García, C.C. - see under Cuevas García, C.
Garcia, J. & others, eds. Philosophical Analysis in Latin America.
   F. Recanati, 192(EP):Oct-Dec86-561
García, J.L.D. - see under de Tomás García, J.L.
Garcia, W. Mothers and Others.
   R.F. Franklin, 27(AL):May86-289
García de Diego, V. Diccionario etimológico español e hispánico. (2nd ed)
   H. Meier, 547(RF):Band98Heft3/4-407
García de la Concha, V. - see de Jesús, T.
Garcia i Sanz, A. & M-T. Ferrer i Mallol. Assegurances i canvis marítims medievals a Barcelona.
   C. Estow, 589:Apr86-416
García Iglesias, J.M. El pintor de Banga.
   I. Mateo Gómez, 48:Jan-Mar86-116
García Márquez, G. Clandestine in Chile.
   J. Updike, 442(NY):24Aug87-85
   M. Wood, 441:9Aug87-10
García Márquez, G. Crónica de una muerte anunciada.
   R. Muñoz, 241:Sep86-81
García Vega, B. El grabado del libro español.
   D.A.I., 48:Jul-Sep86-348

García y García, A., ed. Constitutiones Concilii quarti Lateranensis una cum commentariis glossatorum.
  C. Donahue, Jr., 589:Jan86-149
du Gard, R.C. - see under Coulet du Gard, R.
du Gard, R.M. - see under Martin du Gard, R.
Gardam, J. Crusoe's Daughter.*
  42(AR):Summer86-380
Gardella, P. Innocent Ecstasy.
  529(QQ):Autumn86-720
Garden, E. Tchaikovsky. (rev)
  412:May85-140
Gardette, P. Études de géographie linguistique.* (B. Horiot, M-R. Simoni & G. Straka, eds)
  D. Evans, 208(FS):Jan86-120
  P. Fabre, 545(RPh):May87-507
Gardies, J-L. Rational Grammar.
  G. Stahl, 542:Jul-Sep86-403
Gardiner, S.C. Old Church Slavonic.*
  T.A. Greenan, 402(MLR):Oct86-1054
  H. Leeming, 575(SEER):Jul86-448
Gardner, A. Angus Wilson.
  J.H. Stape, 627(UTQ):Fall86-116
Gardner, H. Frames of Mind.
  M.H. Bornstein, 289:Summer86-120
Gardner, J. No Deals, Mr. Bond.
  N. Callendar, 441:7Jun87-25
von Gardner, J. Russian Church Singing. (Vol 1)
  S.H., 412:Nov85-306
Gardner, J. Stillness [and] Shadows.* (N. Delbanco, ed)
  A.H.G. Phillips, 617(TLS):17Apr87-410
  W.H. Pritchard, 249(HudR):Winter87-654
Gardner, J. & N. Tsuki - see Itaya, K.
Gardner, J.B. & G.R. Adams, eds. Ordinary People and Everyday Life.
  D.D. Fanelli, 658:Summer/Autumn86-211
Gardner, L.C. Safe for Democracy.
  G. Martel, 106:Spring86-81
Gardner, M. Keeping Warm.
  C. Goodrich, 441:18Jan87-8
Gardner, M. - see Chesterton, G.K.
Gardner, P. - see Forster, E.M.
Gardyne, J.B. Ministers and Mandarins.
  D. Howell, 617(TLS):24Apr87-447
Garebian, K. Hugh Hood.*
  E. Cameron, 298:Winter86/87-133
Garfagnini, G.C., ed. Giorgio Vasari.
  P. Rubin, 90:Jun86-431
  J. Satkowski, 576:Dec86-416
Garfer, J.L. & C. Fernandez, eds. Adivinancero Popular Español.
  T.T. Folley, 86(BHS):Oct86-385
Garfield, E.P. Women's Voices from Latin America.
  E. Skinner, 395(MFS):Winter86-646
Garfitt, J.S.T. The Work and Thought of Jean Grenier (1898-1971).
  J. Kohn-Étiemble, 535(RHL):Mar-Apr86-338
Gariano, C. Juan Ruiz, Boccaccio, Chaucer.
  G.S. Daichman, 238:Sep86-538
Gariel, A.C. - see under Carrillo y Gariel, A.
Garin, E. - see Verde, A.F.
Garland, R. The Greek Way of Death.
  J. Boardman, 123:Vol36No2-338
  F. Litsas, 124:Jul-Aug87-445

Garneau, M. & T. Hendry, eds. The School/ L'Ecole.
  D. Gardner, 627(UTQ):Fall86-182
Garner, H. Postcards from Surfers.*
  H. Jacobson, 617(TLS):27Nov-3Dec87-1307
  442(NY):2Feb87-99
Garner, J.S. The Model Company Town.*
  D. Herrin, 658:Spring86-84
Garnett, A. Deceived with Kindness.*
  F. Gallix, 189(EA):Apr-Jun87-236
  M. Goldstein, 569(SR):Summer86-lxi
Garnett, H. Family Skeletons.*
  P-L. Adams, 61:May87-94
  N. Auerbach, 441:14Jun87-32
Garnham, B.G. Robbe-Grillet: "Les Gommes" and "Le Voyeur."*
  C. Britton, 208(FS):Jan86-104
  E. Smyth, 535(RHL):Jan-Feb86-167
Garniron, P. - see Hegel, G.W.F.
Garnsey, P. & R. Saller. The Roman Empire.
  N. Purcell, 617(TLS):4-11Sep87-962
Garrard, J., ed. The Russian Novel from Pushkin to Pasternak.*
  W.F. Kolonosky, 574(SEEJ):Fall86-440
  F.C.M. Wigzell, 575(SEER):Jan86-130
Garratt, R.F. Modern Irish Poetry.
  C. Wills, 617(TLS):5Jun87-612
Garrett, G. An Evening Performance.*
  P. La Salle, 573(SSF):Spring86-205
  639(VQR):Spring86-54
Garrido Gallardo, M.A., ed. Teoría Semiótica.
  A. Sánchez Rey, 548:Jul-Dec86-453
Garrioch, D. Neighbourhood and Community in Paris 1740-1790.
  A. Forrest, 617(TLS):27Feb87-220
Garro, E. Recollections of Things to Come.
  D. Kirk, 441:25Jan87-20
Garrow, D.J. Bearing the Cross.*
  G.M. Fredrickson, 617(TLS):17Jul87-759
  B. McKibben, 442(NY):6Apr87-102
  C.V. Woodward, 453(NYRB):15Jan87-3
Garsi, J-F., ed. Cinémas homosexuels.
  N. Greene, 207(FR):May87-898
Garstang, D. Giacomo Serpotta and the Stuccatori of Palermo.
  N. Penny, 90:Mar86-225
Garthoff, R.L. Detente and Confrontation.
  R. Dallek, 550(RusR):Jul86-322
Garton, J. Jens Bjørneboe.
  J.B. Harris, 563(SS):Summer86-336
  L. Longum, 562(Scan):May86-92
Garton, J., ed. Faces of European Modernism.
  P.T. Andersen, 172(Edda):1986/4-377
Garvin, H.R., ed. Science and Literature.
  J.J. Maier, 478:Apr86-132
Garvin, J.L. & D-B. Instruments of Change.
  D.B. Wing, 432(NEQ):Dec86-594
Garwood, E. The Undying Flame.
  C. García-Gody, 37:Nov-Dec86-59
Gary-Prieur, M-N. De la grammaire à la linguistique.
  B.K. Barnes, 207(FR):Oct86-143
Garzelli, A. Miniatura Fiorentina del Rinascimento 1440-1525.
  78(BC):Summer86-145
Garzya, A. - see Basilakes, N.
Gascar, P. Humboldt l'explorateur.
  J. Blot, 450(NRF):Sep86-105

Gasché, R. The Tain of the Mirror.
 C. Norris, 617(TLS):18-24Dec87-1407
 M. Sprinker, 400(MLN):Dec86-1226
Gascoigne, B. Cod Streuth.*
 P-L. Adams, 61:May87-94
 G. Krist, 441:3May87-44
Gascoigne, B. How to Identify Prints.
 R. Lister, 324:Nov87-950
Gascou, J. Suétone historien.
 A. Wallace-Hadrill, 123:Vol36No2-243
Gash, J. Moonspender.
 N. Callendar, 441:12Apr87-34
Gash, N. Pillars of Government.
 M. Brock, 617(TLS):1May87-470
Gaskill, H. Hölderlin's "Hyperion."
 R. Harrison, 402(MLR):Jul87-780
 M. Roche, 221(GQ):Fall86-650
Gaspar, L. Feuilles d'observation.
 D. Leuwers, 450(NRF):Nov86-95
Gaspard, F. & C. Servan-Schreiber. La Fin
 des immigrés.
 M-C.W. Koop, 207(FR):Dec86-281
Gasparov, B. Poetika "Slova o polku
 Igoreve."*
 G. Lenhoff, 550(RusR):Jan86-47
 I.P. Smirnov, 559:Vol10No1-133
Gass, S.M. & C.G. Madden, ed. Input in
 Second Language Acquisition.
 R.B. Bottigheimer, 399(MLJ):Summer86-
 172
Gass, W. In the Heart of the Heart of the
 Country.
 C. Brown, 389(MQ):Autumn86-147
Gasset, J.O. - see under Ortega y Gasset,
 J.
Gastaldelli, F. - see William of Lucca
Gasteyger, C. Searching for World Secur-
 ity.
 Lord Zuckerman, 453(NYRB):7May87-42
Gaston, G.M.A. The Pursuit of Salvation.*
 M. Luetkemeyer, 396(ModA):Summer/
 Fall86-328
Gaston, P.M. Women of Fair Hope.*
 B. Brandon, 9(AlaR):Jan86-64
Gates, W.C., Jr. & D.E. Ormerod. The East
 Liverpool, Ohio, Pottery District.
 G.L. Miller, 658:Spring86-87
Gaudes, R. Wörterbuch Khmer-Deutsch.
 (Vols 1 & 2)
 G.F. Meier, 682(ZPSK):Band39Heft2-270
Gaudet, G. Voix d'écrivains.
 P. Collet, 627(UTQ):Fall86-210
Gaudon, J. Victor Hugo et le théâtre.
 P.W.M. Cogman, 208(FS):Jul86-339
 B.L. Murphy, 446(NCFS):Spring87-349
Gaudon, J. - see Hugo, V.
Gauger, H-M., W. Oesterreicher & R. Win-
 disch. Einführung in die romanische
 Sprachwissenschaft.*
 R. Rohr, 72:Band223Heft1-187
Gaugh, H.F. The Vital Gesture.
 A. Kingsley, 90:Apr86-300
de Gaulmyn, P. - see Claudel, P. & J.
 Rivière
Gault, P. Goldenrod.*
 R. Thacker, 102(CanL):Winter85-136
Gaur, A. A History of Writing.*
 78(BC):Summer86-145
Gauthier, D. Morals by Agreement.
 D. Braybrooke, 185:Jul87-750
 A. Gibbard, 617(TLS):20Feb87-177
 [continued]

[continuing]
 J.S. Kraus & Jules L. Coleman,
 185:Jul87-715
 J. Mendola, 185:Jul87-765
Gauthier, H. L'Image de l'homme intérieur
 chez Balzac.*
 D. Bellos, 208(FS):Oct86-475
 A. Michel, 535(RHL):Sep-Oct86-930
Gauthier, M-M. Les routes de la foi.
 E.A.R. Brown, 589:Apr86-498
Gautier, T. Correspondance générale de
 Théophile Gautier.* (Vol 1) (C. Lacoste-
 Veysseyre, ed)
 I.H. Smith, 67:May86-125
 P. Whyte, 402(MLR):Jul86-747
 F. Wolfzettel, 547(RF):Band98Heft3/4-
 447
Gautier, T. Correspondance générale de
 Théophile Gautier.* (Vol 2) (C. Lacoste-
 Veysseyre, ed)
 F. Wolfzettel, 547(RF):Band98Heft3/4-
 447
Gautier, T. Gautier on Dance. (I. Guest,
 ed & trans)
 R. Snell, 617(TLS):26Jun87-701
Gautier, T. Mademoiselle Dafné. (M.
 Eigeldinger, ed)
 H. Cockerham, 208(FS):Jul86-340
Gauvin, L. Lettres d'une autre.
 M. Parmentier, 102(CanL):Spring86-182
Gay, J. John Gay: Dramatic Works.* (J.
 Fuller, ed)
 C.J. Rawson, 402(MLR):Jul86-720
 P.M. Spacks, 477(PLL):Winter86-100
Gay, P. The Bourgeois Experience.* (Vol
 1)
 E. Leites, 473(PR):Vol53No1-111
 R. O'Kell, 529(QQ):Autumn86-679
Gay, P. The Bourgeois Experience.* (Vol
 2)
 M. Lynch, 627(UTQ):Spring87-451
 W.H. Pritchard, 249(HudR):Autumn86-495
Gay, P. Freud for Historians.*
 T.T. Lewis, 125:Winter86-216
 D.R. Woolf, 529(QQ):Autumn86-677
Gay, P. A Godless Jew.
 J.C. Marshall, 441:11Oct87-39
Gay-Lussac, B. Mère et fils.
 A. Clerval, 450(NRF):Jul-Aug86-171
Gaynor, E. Scandinavia.
 P. Goldberger, 441:6Dec87-24
Gealt, A.M. Italian Portrait Drawings,
 1400-1800, from North American Collec-
 tions.
 A.S. Harris, 380:Spring86-94
Gealt, A.M. Domenico Tiepolo: The Punch-
 inello Drawings.*
 M. Levey, 39:Dec86-572
 D. Rosand, 617(TLS):27Mar87-333
Geanakoplos, D.J. Byzantium.*
 E.A. Hanawalt, 589:Jul86-653
Gearhart, S. The Open Boundary of History
 and Fiction.*
 M. Hobson, 402(MLR):Jul86-740
 N. Le Coat, 400(MLN):Sep86-956
 R. Ouellet, 535(RHL):Sep-Oct86-925
Geary, C. & A.N. Njoya. Mandou Yenou.
 M. Wittmer, 2(AfrA):Aug86-23
Gebhard, W., ed. Friedrich Nietzsche.
 F.R. Love, 221(GQ):Spring86-340
 R. Margreiter, 489(PJGG):Band93Heft2-
 375

Gebhard, W. Nietzsches Totalismus.*
  R. Margreiter, 489(PJGG):Band93Heft2–
  376
Gébler, C. August in July.*
  272(IUR):Autumn86–255
Gébler, C. Work and Play.
  M. Pacey, 362:4Jun87–46
  R. Rusher, 617(TLS):3Jul87–715
Geck, E. Grundzüge der Geschichte der
  Buchillustration.
  P.M. Daly, 107(CRCL):Sep86–483
Geddes, G. Changes of State.
  N. Besner, 647:Fall86–112
Geddes, G. The Terracotta Army.*
  J. Cook, 529(QQ):Summer86–414
  R. Gibbs, 102(CanL):Spring86–180
Geddes, P. Inside the Bank of England.
  M. Panić, 617(TLS):24Jul87–800
Geddes, V.G. "Various Children of Eve."
  B. af Klintberg, 64(Arv):Vol41–136
Geddes, W. – see "Kara Monogatari"
Gee, M. Prowlers.
  T. Aitken, 617(TLS):30Oct–5Nov8–1193
Geering, R.G. – see Stead, C.
Geerts, G. & others, eds. ANS: Algemene
  Nederlandse Spraakkunst.*
  C. Pankow, 439(NM):1986/2–319
  P. Swiggers, 350:Jun87–432
Geffriaud Rosso, J. Etudes sur la féminité
  aux XVIIe et XVIIIe siècles.
  N. Mallet, 475:Vol13No24–414
Geherin, D. The American Private Eye.
  A. Boyer, 395(MFS):Winter86–631
  M. Roth, 536(Rev):Vol8–265
Gehrts, H. & G. Lademann–Priemer, eds.
  Schamanentum und Zaubermärchen.
  A. Hartmann, 196:Band27Heft3/4–338
Geis, M.L. The Language of Television
  Advertising.
  E.E. Davies, 361:Mar86–257
Geiser, C. Prisoners of the Good Fight.
  B. Knox, 453(NYRB):26Mar87–21
Gelb, A. Playgrounds.
  M. Rubin, 441:12Jul87–20
Gelb, N. The Berlin Wall.*
  P. Graves, 617(TLS):27Feb87–210
  J.M. Markham, 441:8Feb87–21
Geldof, B., with P. Vallely. Is That It?
  A. Schmitz, 441:22Mar87–29
Gelfand, E.D. & V.T. Hules. French Femi-
  nist Criticism.
  J.H. Stewart, 207(FR):Feb87–384
Gelfant, B.H. Women Writing in America.*
  S.M. Gilbert, 454:Fall86–82
  P. Petrick, 649(WAL):Aug86–157
  F.G. See, 27(AL):Mar86–124
Gélis, J. L'Arbre et le fruit.
  H.R. Allentuch, 475:Vol13No24–392
Gellert, C.F. Christian Fürchtegott Gel-
  lerts Briefwechsel. (Vol 1) (J.F.
  Reynolds, ed)
  W.A. Little, 400(MLN):Apr86–709
  W.D. Wilson, 221(GQ):Fall86–644
Gellhorn, M. A Stricken Field.
  P. Craig, 617(TLS):18–24Sep87–1026
Gellinek, C. Pax optima rerum.
  J. Strelka, 133:Band19Heft3/4–341
Gellinek–Schellekens, J.E. The Voice of
  the Nightingale in Middle English Poems
  and Bird Debates.
  A. Squires, 161(DUJ):Jun86–373
Gelling, M. Place–Names in the Landscape.*
  M. Wakelin, 382(MAE):1986/2–274

Gellner, E. The Psychoanalytic Movement.
  Z. Lewczuk, 479(PhQ):Apr86–303
Gellner, E. Relativism in the Social
  Sciences.*
  S. Körner, 84:Sep86–367
Gellrich, J.M. The Idea of the Book in the
  Middle Ages.*
  M.L. Colish, 125:Fall85–83
  J.A. Dane, 627(UTQ):Winter86/87–365
Gelman, H. The Brezhnev Politburo and the
  Decline of Détente.
  H. Hanak, 575(SEER):Oct86–635
Gelpi, A., ed. Wallace Stevens.
  T. Armstrong, 617(TLS):10Jul87–747
  R.W.B., 295(JML):Nov86–542
  D. Emerson & F. Doggett, 705:Fall86–
  118
  H. Vendler, 432(NEQ):Dec86–549
Gendron, F. La Jeunesse sous Thermidor.*
  A. Forrest, 208(FS):Jan86–80
Genet, J. Un Captif amoureux.
  H. Cronel, 450(NRF):Dec86–81
  M. Gilsenan, 617(TLS):12Jun87–629
Genette, G. Palimpsestes.
  G. Cesbron, 356(LR):May86–165
  C. Thomson, 193(ELit):Spring86–159
Genette, G. Seuils.
  P. Brooks, 617(TLS):25–31Dec87–1436
Geng, V. Partners.
  S. Pinsker, 573(SSF):Spring86–209
Genicot, L. Les lignes de faîte du moyen
  âge. (9th ed) Le XIIIe siècle européen.
  (2nd ed)
  G. Constable, 589:Apr86–417
Madame de Genlis. Inès de Castro.
  A. Clerval, 450(NRF):Feb86–93
Genouvrier, E. Naitre en français.
  M. Léon, 207(FR):Apr87–739
Génsbøl, B. Collins Guide to the Birds of
  Prey of Britain and Europe, North Africa
  and the Middle East.
  E. Dunn, 617(TLS):8May87–498
Gentili, B. Poesia e pubblico nella Grecia
  antica da Omero al V secolo.*
  R.M. Harriott, 303(JoHS):Vol106–223
  J.T. Hooker, 123:Vol36No1–61
Genton, E. La Vie et les Opinions de Hein-
  rich Leopold Wagner (1747–1779).
  P. Grappin, 549(RLC):Apr–Jun86–242
  H. Reiss, 133:Band18Heft4–371
Gentry, M.B. Flannery O'Connor's Religion
  of the Grotesque.
  R.H. Brinkmeyer, Jr., 578:Fall87–145
  M.D.O., 295(JML):Nov86–518
Gentsch, G. Faulkner zwischen Schwarz und
  Weiss.
  U. Riese, 654(WB):3/1986–516
Geoffroy d'Ablis. L'inquisiteur Geoffroy
  d'Ablis et les cathares du comté de Foix
  (1308–1309). (A. Pales–Gobilliard, ed &
  trans)
  J.H. Mundy, 589:Oct86–883
George, D. Teatro e Antropofagia.
  M. Milleret, 352(LATR):Spring87–141
George, F. Sillages.
  Y. Hersant, 98:Dec86–1239
Geraci, G. Genesi della Provincia Romana
  d'Egitto.*
  J. Rowlandson, 123:Vol36No2–274
Geraets, T.F., ed. Hegel.
  D.J.M., 185:Jan87–503
Geraghty, T. March or Die.
  A. Mockler, 617(TLS):30Jan87–117

Gérard, A. Essais d'histoire littéraire africaine.
  M. Kane, 538(RAL):Winter86-563
  J. Riesz, 52:Band21Heft3-304
Gerard, V. De castillo a palacio.
  A. Bustamante García, 48:Jul-Sep86-346
Gerato, E.G. Guido Gustavo Gozzano.*
  G.R. Bussino, 275(IQ):Spring86-112
Gerber, A. Rumor of an Elephant.
  W. Cloonan, 441:30Aug87-24
Gerber, D. Snow on the Backs of Angels.
  455:Dec86-64
  639(VQR):Summer86-100
Gerber, M., ed. Studies in GDR Culture and Society 4.
  T.C. Fox, 221(GQ):Summer86-511
Gerber, M.J. Honeymoon.*
  C. Hardesty, 455:Mar86-73
Gerber, P.L. Robert Frost.
  R. Gray, 677(YES):Vol16-352
Gerber, W. Serenity.
  M. Marsh, 543:Dec86-378
Gerbi, A. Nature in the New World.
  F. Provost, 165(EAL):Vol22No3-322
Gere, A.R. Writing and Learning.
  R. Fulkerson, 126(CCC):Dec86-495
Gerhardi, G.C. Geld und Gesellschaft im Theater des Ancien Régime.*
  W.D. Howarth, 208(FS):Jul86-337
Gerhardt, C., N.F. Palmer & B. Wachinger, eds. Geschichtsbewusstsein in der deutschen Literatur des Mittelalters.
  D.H. Green, 402(MLR):Jan87-239
Gerlach, J. Toward the End.*
  L. Butts, 573(SSF):Winter86-135
  J. Eis, 219(GaR):Summer86-587
German, T.J. Hamann on Language and Religion.*
  U. Rainer, 406:Spring86-101
Gernet, J. China and the Christian Impact.*
  D. Helliwell, 617(TLS):20Feb87-181
Gernet, J. A History of Chinese Civilization.*
  E.S.K. Fung, 302:Vol22No1-61
Gerould, D., ed. Doubles, Demons, and Dreamers.
  H. Filipowicz, 574(SEEJ):Winter86-571
  M.L. Hoover, 615(TJ):May86-244
Gersbach, B. & R. Graf. Wortbildung in gesprochener Sprache I.
  C. Römer, 682(ZPSK):Band39Heft1-141
Gersch, H. & others - see "Georg Büchner Jahrbuch"
Gersch, H., T.M. Mayer & & G. Oesterle - see "Georg Büchner Jahrbuch"
Gershon, K. The Fifth Generation.
  L. Chamberlain, 617(TLS):30Jan87-108
Gersi, D. Explorer.
  D. Ackerman, 441:6Dec87-17
Gerson, L.P., ed. Graceful Reason.*
  N. Kretzmann, 154:Autumn86-564
  A. Madison, 41:Spring85-136
  E.P. Mahoney, 319:Oct87-594
Gerson, P.L., ed. Abbot Suger and St. Denis.
  A. Borg, 617(TLS):13Mar87-279
Gersonides - see under Levi ben Gershom
Gerszi, T. Paulus van Vianen Handzeichnungen.
  E.H-B., 380:Autumn86-416
Gertler, T. Elbowing the Seducer.
  G. Davenport, 569(SR):Spring86-296

Geschonneck, E. Meine unruhigen Jahre. (G. Agde, ed)
  R. Richter, 601(SuF):Sep-Oct86-1104
Gesensway, D. & M. Roseman. Beyond Words.
  F. Kometani, 441:19Jul87-9
Gesick, L., ed. Centers, Symbols, and Hierarchies.
  K.R. Hall, 293(JASt):Feb86-448
Gessa, V. Sulla politica in Germania.
  A. Stanguennec, 542:Jan-Mar86-117
Gessel, V.C. & Tomone Matsumoto, eds. The Shōwa Anthology.* (Vols 1 & 2)
  S.M. Strong, 407(MN):Winter86-499
  Tsuruta Kinya, 285(JapQ):Jul-Sep86-328
van Gestel, F.C. X-bar Grammar.
  D.J. Napoli, 350:Dec87-916
Gethers, P. Getting Blue.
  R.F. Shepard, 441:26Apr87-24
Getty, J.A. Origins of the Great Purges.*
  B. Bennett, 104(CASS):Spring-Summer86-188
  A.G. Meyer, 550(RusR):Oct86-444
  639(VQR):Winter86-9
Ghalib, M. Urdu Letters of Mirza Asadu'llah Khan Ghalib. (D. Rahbar, ed & trans)
  J.A.C. Greppin, 617(TLS):23-29Oct87-1160
Gherman, K. Black Flamingo.
  P.K. Smith, 99:Apr86-40
Ghidetti, E., ed. Il caso Svevo.*
  B. Maier, 228(GSLI):Vol163fasc521-148
  B. Moloney, 402(MLR):Jan86-231
Ghilardi, M. - see Cecchi, E.
Ghiselli, A. Orazio, Ode 1, 1, Saggio di analisi formale.
  S. Franchet d'Esperey, 555:Vol59fasc2-319
Giacomelli, G. La Merope.
  B.L. Glixon, 143:Issue39-74
Giacomelli, R. Graeca Italica.
  D. Briquel, 555:Vol59fasc2-312
  C.J. Ruijgh, 394:Vol39fasc3/4-507
Giamatti, A.B. Exile and Change in Renaissance Literature.*
  M.G. Brennan, 447(N&Q):Jun85-260
Giancotti, E., A. Matheron & M. Walther, eds. Studia Spinozana. (Vol 1)
  G.H.R. Parkinson, 483:Apr86-276
Giangrande, C. Down to Earth.
  529(QQ):Autumn86-715
Giannangeli, O. Il popolo sotto i lumi.
  F. Mouret, 549(RLC):Apr-Jun86-241
Giannantoni, G., ed. Lo scetticismo antico.
  G. Striker, 41:Spring85-145
Giannantoni, G. Socraticorum Reliquiae.
  J. Barnes, 520:Vol31No2-184
Giannantoni, G. & M. Vegetti, eds. La Scienza Ellenistica.
  D. Fowler, 41:Vol6-239
Giannantonio, P. Endiadi.
  J.F. Took, 402(MLR):Apr86-498
Giannetto, N. Bernardo Bembo umanista a politico veneziano.
  M.P. Mussini Sacchi, 547(RF):Band98 Heft3/4-461
  L.V.R., 568(SCN):Winter86-78
Giardina, D. Storming Heaven.
  D. Bauer, 441:20Sep87-39
Giauffret Colombani, H. Rhétorique de Jules Vallès.
  C. Dédéyan, 535(RHL):Mar-Apr86-319

Giazotto, R. Le due patrie di Giulio
  Caccini, musico medíceo (1551-1618).
    T. Carter, 410(M&L):Apr86-191
Gibaldi, J. & W.S. Achtert – see "MLA
  Handbook for Writers of Research Papers"
Gibault, F. Céline.* (Vols 1-3)
    J. Aeply, 450(NRF):Apr86-98
Gibb, R. The Winter House.
    S.C. Behrendt, 502(PrS):Spring86-109
Gibbon, D. & H. Richter, eds. Intonation,
  Accent and Rhythm.*
    G. Brown, 353:Vol24No4-817
Gibbons, B. Dragonflies and Damselflies of
  Britain and Northern Europe.
    J.R.G. Turner, 617(TLS):8May87-498
Gibbons, K. Ellen Foster.
    A. Hoffman, 441:31May87-13
Gibbs, A.M. The Art and Mind of Shaw.*
    N. Grene, 447(N&Q):Jun85-286
Gibian, G. – see Seifert, J.
Gibson, A. Biblical Semantic Logic.
    E.L. Greenstein, 318(JAOS):Oct/Dec85-
    735
Gibson, C. – see Ford, J.
Gibson, D. & J.K. Baldwin, eds. Law in a
  Cynical Society?
    J.R. Matheson, 529(QQ):Winter86-896
Gibson, J. – see Hardy, T.
Gibson, J.W. The Perfect War.
    R. Halloran, 441:24May87-13
Gibson, M. Dancing with Mermaids.
    442(NY):13Jul87-89
Gibson, M. Vinegar Soup.
    C. Hawtree, 617(TLS):21Aug87-897
Gibson, R. Tropism.
    A. Grundberg, 441:6Dec87-21
Gicovate, B., ed. Garcilaso y su escuela
  poética.
    D.G. Walters, 86(BHS):Jul86-281
Giddens, A. The Nation State and Violence.
    B.M.D., 185:Apr87-688
Giddings, R., ed. The Changing World of
  Charles Dickens.*
    S. Shatto, 402(MLR):Oct87-925
Giddings, R., ed. Mark Twain.
    R.B. Hauck, 395(MFS):Summer86-255
Giddins, G. Celebrating Bird.
    J. Berry, 441:11Jan87-19
Giddins, G. Rhythm-a-Ning.*
    G.L. Starks, Jr., 91:Spring86-187
Gide, A. Correspondance avec Francis
  Vielé-Griffin. (H. de Paysac, ed)
    R. Millet, 450(NRF):Nov86-93
Giedymin, J. Science and Convention.*
    J. Largeault, 542:Jul-Sep86-404
Giegerich, H.J. Metrical Phonology and
  Phonological Structure.*
    B. Hayes, 297(JL):Mar86-229
    E. Standop, 38:Band104Heft3/4-445
Gielgud, J. Early Stages.
    362:8Oct87-24
Gies, F. The Knight in History.
    B.B. Rezak, 589:Jul86-654
Gies, M., with A.L. Gold. Anne Frank
  Remembered.
    T. Des Pres, 441:10May87-7
Gifford, H. Poetry in a Divided World.*
    H. Lomas, 364:Aug/Sep86-154
    S.A.S., 295(JML):Nov86-424
Gifford, P., ed. The Treaty of Paris
  (1783) in a Changing States System.
    G. Clarfield, 656(WMQ):Oct86-682

Gignoux, P. & R. Gyselen. Sceaux sasanides
  de diverses collections privées.
    D.N. MacKenzie, 259(IIJ):Apr86-129
Giguère, R. Exil, révolte et dissidence.
    B. Godard, 627(UTQ):Fall86-197
    D.G. Jones, 529(QQ):Spring86-179
    E-M. Kröller, 102(CanL):Fall86-115
Giguère, R.G. Le Concept de la réalité
  dans la poésie d'Yves Bonnefoy.
    R. Little, 402(MLR):Jan87-211
Gikandi, S. Wole Soyinka's "The Road."
    J. Gibbs, 538(RAL):Winter86-617
Gil, M. Palestine During the First Muslim
  Period (634-1009).
    J. Shatzmiller, 287:Apr-May86-23
Gil-Albert, J. Fuentes de la constancia.
  (J.C. Rovira, ed)
    S. Daydí-Tolson, 238:Sep86-549
Gil Fernández, L. Estudios de humanismo y
  tradición clásica.
    T. O'Reilly, 402(MLR):Apr87-502
Gilardino, S.M. La Scuola romantica.
    A. Grewe, 72:Band223Heft1-238
    M. Verdicchio, 107(CRCL):Mar86-142
Gilbert, B.B. David Lloyd George.
    P. Clarke, 617(TLS):24Apr87-427
Gilbert, G.N. & M. Mulkay. Opening
  Pandora's Box.*
    G. Myers, 128(CE):Oct86-595
Gilbert, M. Winston S. Churchill.* (Vol
  7: Road to Victory).
    T.G. Ash, 453(NYRB):7May87-22
    A. Horne, 617(TLS):13Feb87-169
    442(NY):19Jan87-92
Gilbert, M. The Holocaust.*
    R. Clements, 99:Aug/Sep86-28
Gilbert, M. Trouble.
    T.J. Binyon, 617(TLS):21Aug87-910
    S. Dunant, 362:11Jun87-26
Gilbert, R.A. A.E. Waite.
    H. Ormsby-Lennon, 677(YES):Vol16-354
Gilbert, W.S. Plays by W.S. Gilbert. (G.
  Rowell, ed)
    M.R. Booth, 677(YES):Vol16-335
Gilbert-Lecomte, R. Lettre à Benjamin
  Fondane.
    J. Stéfan, 450(NRF):Mar86-89
Gilchrist, E. Drunk with Love.*
    J. Cooke, 362:19Mar87-26
    J. Melmoth, 617(TLS):6Mar87-246
Gildea, R. Barricades and Borders.
    M.S. Anderson, 617(TLS):18-24Dec87-
    1411
Gilder, E. The Dictionary of Composers and
  their Music.
    B. Newbould, 415:Apr86-210
Gilderhus, M.T. Pan American Visions.
    L.D. Langley, 263(RIB):Vol36No4-492
Gildner, G. A Week in South Dakota. The
  Second Bridge.
    R. Goodman, 441:26Apr87-18
Gilead, Z. & D. Krook. Gideon's Spring.
    E. Alexander, 390:Oct86-52
Giles, F. Sundry Times.*
    A. Hartley, 176:Apr87-58
Giles, M. Rough Translations.*
    K. Cushman, 573(SSF):Summer86-329
Giles, R.F., ed. Hopkins among the Poets.
    J.J. Feeney, 637(VS):Summer87-532
    C. Lock, 627(UTQ):Fall86-111
Giliberti, G. Servus quasi colonus.
    R.P. Duncan-Jones, 313:Vol76-295

Gilks, A. & G. Segal. China and the Arms Trade.
H. Jencks, 293(JASt):Aug86-817
Gill, A. The Early Mallarmé.* (Vol 2)
A.J. Steele, 402(MLR):Oct87-971
Gill, B. Many Masks.
M. Filler, 441:13Dec87-15
Gill, D. & L. Levidow, eds. Anti-Racist Science Teaching.
A. Wooldridge, 617(TLS):4-10Dec87-1341
Gill, S. - see Wordsworth, W.
Gille, P. Bernanos et l'Angoisse.
J. Chabot, 535(RHL):Jul-Aug86-792
Gillespie, A.K. Folklorist of the Coal Fields.
J.D.A. Widdowson, 203:Vol97No2-233
Gillespie, M.A. Hegel, Heidegger, and the Ground of History.*
D. Magurshak, 125:Fall85-105
Gillespie, M.P., with E.B. Stocker. James Joyce's Trieste Library.
M.T. Reynolds, 329(JJQ):Summer87-483
Gillespie, R. Colonial Ulster.
K.S. Bottigheimer, 656(WMQ):Jul86-478
Gillis, C.M. The Paradox of Privacy.*
J. Harris, 402(MLR):Apr87-450
Gillmeister, H. Chaucer's Conversion.
J. Dean, 589:Jan86-151
Gilman, C. Where Two Worlds Meet.
R. Thacker, 106:Spring86-51
Gilman, E.B. Iconoclasm and Poetry in the English Reformation.
J.N. King, 604:Fall86-55
Gilman, R. Faith, Sex, Mystery.
M. Gordon, 441:18Jan87-1
Gilman, S.L., ed. Begegnungen mit Nietzsche.
R. Margreiter, 489(PJGG):Band93Heft2-375
Gilman, S.L. Difference and Pathology.
J.R. Reed, 637(VS):Spring87-410
R. Stott, 529(QQ):Autumn86-697
Gilmore, D.D. Aggression and Community.
R. Carr, 453(NYRB):28May87-41
Gilmore, M.T. American Romanticism and the Marketplace.
N. Baym, 301(JEGP):Oct86-600
S. Bercovitch, 617(TLS):9Jan87-40
P.F. Gura, 183(ESQ):Vol32No1-68
E.A. Meese, 141:Spring86-216
B. Menikoff, 250(HLQ):Autumn86-414
J. Myerson, 432(NEQ):Jun86-308
M.R. Patterson, 594:Fall86-330
W.H. Shurr, 27(AL):May86-282
Gilmore, R. The Novel in the Victorian Age.
A.L. Harris, 268(IFR):Winter87-34
Gilmore, R.K. Ozark Baptizings, Hangings, and Other Diversions.
R. Cochran, 650(WF):Jan86-62
Gilmour, P. Ken Tyler, Master Printer.
J. Burr, 39:Nov86-455
J. Lewison, 90:Sep86-686
Gilpin, R., with J.M. Gilpin. The Political Economy of International Relations.
R. Rosecrance, 441:16Aug87-22
Gilroy, P. There Ain't no Black in the Union Jack.
D. Edgar, 362:4Jun87-44
Gilson, D. A Bibliography of Jane Austen.*
B. Southam, 677(YES):Vol16-293
Gindin, J. John Galsworthy's Life and Art.
A.H.G. Phillips, 617(TLS):3Jul87-723

Ginet, C. & S. Shoemaker, eds. Knowledge and Mind.*
J.C. Edwards, 543:Sep86-122
Gingerich, O., ed. Astrophysics and Twentieth-Century Astronomy to 1950.
D.J. Raine, 84:Dec86-510
Giniger, H. Reasons of the Heart.
M. Childress, 441:19Apr87-16
Ginori-Lisci, L. The Palazzi of Florence.
L. Berti, 39:Oct86-380
Ginsberg, A. Collected Poems 1947-1980.*
R. Roark, 30:Winter87-93
Ginsberg, B. The Captive Public.
M.C. Miller, 441:8Feb87-32
Ginsberg, H.L. The Israelian Heritage of Judaism.
M. Fishbane, 318(JAOS):Jan/Mar85-157
Ginsberg, W. The Cast of Character.*
J. Marenbon, 447(N&Q):Mar85-93
Ginzburg, C. The Enigma of Piero della Francesca: The Baptism, The Arezzo Cycle, The Flagellation.*
C. Gould, 39:Apr86-292
Ginzburg, C. Spurensicherungen.
H-O. Boström, 341:Vol55No2-77
Ginzburg, N. The City and the House.
A. Cornelisen, 441:13Sep87-30
442(NY):10Aug87-78
Ginzburg, N. The Little Virtues.*
442(NY):16Feb87-111
Ginzburg, N. The Manzoni Family.
D. Davis, 617(TLS):28Aug87-933
I. Thomson, 362:1Oct87-25
Giobbi, E. & R. Wolff. Eat Right, Eat Well - the Italian Way.
W. & C. Cowen, 639(VQR):Autumn86-141
Gioia, D. Daily Horoscope.*
R.E. Knoll, 502(PrS):Fall86-122
J.D. McClatchy, 491:Oct86-31
R. McDowell, 249(HudR):Winter87-673
639(VQR):Autumn86-132
Giono, J. & L. Jacques. Correspondance Jean Giono-Lucien Jacques, 1930-1961. (P. Citron, ed)
R. Ricatte, 535(RHL):Mar-Apr86-342
Giordano, E. La teatralización de la obra dramática.
M.A. Giella, 352(LATR):Spring87-139
Giovannini, A. Consulare imperium.
J.A. Crook, 313:Vol76-286
Giovannini, L., ed. Lettere di Ottavio Falconieri a Leopoldo de' Medici.
E.K.W., 90:Jan86-48
Gioviale, F. La poetica narrativa di Pirandello.
A.L. Lepschy, 402(MLR):Apr86-506
Gippius, Z. Stixotvorenija.
O. Zuevskij, 558(RLJ):Spring/Fall86-241
Girard, G. Les Vrais Principes de la Langue françoise.
J. Bourguignon, 553(RLiR):Jan-Jun86-310
Girard, R. Le Bouc émissaire.
G. Gillespie, 131(CL):Summer86-289
Girard, R. La Route antique des hommes pervers.
N. Lukacher, 400(MLN):Sep86-949
Girard, R. The Scapegoat.
P. Winch, 617(TLS):20Mar87-290
Girard, R. La violenza e il sacro.
C. Di Biase, 275(IQ):Spring86-118
Girardet, K.M. Die Ordnung der Welt.*
G. Gawlick, 53(AGP):Band68Heft3-298

Girardin, R.G.   L'Oeil de Palomar.
  K. Meadwell, 102(CanL):Winter85-158
Girardot, N.J.   Myth and Meaning in Early Taoism.*
  S.L. Field, 293(JASt):Aug86-819
Giraud, Y., N. King & S. de Reyff, eds. Trois jeux des rois (XVIe-XVIIe siecles).
  M. McGowan, 208(FS):Oct86-455
Girgus, S.B.   The New Covenant.*
  R.A. Burchell, 447(N&Q):Dec85-576
Girodet, J.   Le Tour du mot.
  A.D. Ketchum, 207(FR):Oct86-136
de la Gironière, P.   Journey to Majayjay.
  J.A. Larkin, 293(JASt):Feb86-456
Girouard, M.   Cities and People.*
  A. Betsky, 505:Jul86-139
  N. Powell, 39:Apr86-291
  639(VQR):Spring86-54
Giroux, R. - see Bishop, E.
Giroux, R. - see Lowell, R.
Gish, T.G. & S.G. Frieden, eds.   Deutsche Romantik and English Romanticism.
  L.R. Furst, 107(CRCL):Dec86-669
Gíslason, K.   Bréf Konráds Gíslasonar.   (A. Kristjánsson, ed)
  K. Wolf, 563(SS):Autumn86-432
Gissing, G.   Veranilda.   (P. Coustillas, ed)
  D. Grylls, 617(TLS):25Sep-1Oct87-1044
Gisslen, W.   Professional Cooking.
  W. & C. Cowen, 639(VQR):Spring86-69
Gitlin, T.   The Sixties.
  J. Miller, 441:8Nov87-13
Gitlin, T., ed.   Watching Television.
  B. Staples, 441:8Feb87-7
Gittings, R. & J. Manton.   Dorothy Wordsworth.*
  B. Darlington, 661(WC):Autumn86-227
  V.N. Paananen, 115:Summer86-429
  R. Sheets, 637(VS):Autumn86-145
Giudicelli, C.   Station balnéaire.
  R. Buss, 617(TLS):3Apr87-362
Giudici, G.   La dama non cercata.
  M. Bacigalupo, 402(MLR):Apr87-501
Giuliano, G. & D. Pellizzaro.   Il grande dizionario Jackson di elettronica e informatica.
  C. Costa, 708:Vol12fasc2-265
Giuliano, W. - see Buero Vallejo, A.
Given-Wilson, C.   The English Nobility in the Middle Ages.
  N. Saul, 617(TLS):25-31Dec87-1439
Givner, J.   Tentacles of Unreason.*
  C. Hardesty, 455:Mar86-73
Givon, T., ed.   Topic Continuity in Discourse.*
  K. Allan, 350:Mar87-160
  G. Thurgood, 351(LL):Dec86-533
Gjertsen, D.   The Newton Handbook.
  J. Henry, 617(TLS):13Mar87-281
Gladstein, M.R.   The Indestructible Woman in Faulkner, Hemingway, and Steinbeck.
  P.R.J., 295(JML):Nov86-392
Gladstone, W.E.   The Gladstone Diaries. (Vol 9) (H.C.G. Matthew, ed)
  A. Hartley, 176:Apr87-57
Glancy, R.F.   Dickens's Christmas Books, Christmas Stories, and Other Short Fiction.
  D.A. Thomas, 158:Sep86-139
Glaser, E.   Graphische Studien zum Schreibsprachwandel vom 13. bis 16. Jahrhundert.
  H. Penzl, 350:Mar87-158

Glasgow, J., ed.   George Sand.
  J.M. Vest, 446(NCFS):Spring87-353
Glass, F.W.   The Fertilizing Seed.
  R.L.J., 412:Feb85-59
Glass, J.M.   Play Memory.
  V.M. Patraka, 385(MQR):Winter87-285
Glasser, P.   Singing on the Titanic.
  E. Gleick, 441:13Sep87-34
Glassman, P.   J.S. Mill.*
  J. Stillinger, 637(VS):Autumn86-141
Glatthaar, J.T.   The March to the Sea and Beyond.
  J.G. Dawson 3d, 9(AlaR):Oct86-307
Glatzer, N.N.   The Loves of Franz Kafka.*
  R.D. Fulton, 594:Winter86-443
  M.P.L., 295(JML):Nov86-499
Glauser, B.   A Phonology of Present-Day Speech in Grassington (North Yorkshire).
  C.M. Barrack, 685(ZDL):1/1986-133
Glaysher, F. - see Hayden, R.
Glazebrook, P.   Captain Vinegar's Commission.
  E. Munro, 441:15Nov87-11
Glazier, L.P. - see under Pequeño Glazier, L.
Gleason, A., P. Kenez & R. Stites, eds. Bolshevik Culture.
  L. Mally, 550(RusR):Jul86-343
Gleason, J.B., ed.   The Development of Language.
  A.M. Peters, 350:Jun87-454
Gleckner, R.F.   Blake and Spenser.
  S.C. Behrendt, 173(ECS):Winter86/87-257
  F. Piquet, 189(EA):Jul-Sep87-355
  I. Tayler, 551(RenQ):Winter86-802
Gledhill, C., ed.   Home is Where the Heart Is.
  362:22Oct87-33
Gledson, J.   The Deceptive Realism of Machado de Assis.*
  R.J. Oakley, 402(MLR):Oct86-1028
  J. Parker, 86(BHS):Jan86-108
  B.M. Woodbridge, Jr., 240(HR):Spring86-239
Glees, A.   The Secrets of the Service.
  N. Annan, 453(NYRB):24Sep87-47
  N. Hiley, 617(TLS):22May87-539
  Z. Steiner, 441:13Dec87-9
Glei, R.   Die Batrachomyomachie.*
  M. Menu, 555:Vol59fasc2-298
Gleick, J.   Chaos.
  J. Maddox, 441:25Oct87-11
  442(NY):16Nov87-160
Gleize, J-M.   Poésie et Figuration.*
  S. Lévy, 188(ECr):Fall86-104
Glen, D.   The Stones of Time.
  A. Smith, 571(ScLJ):Winter86-33
Glendinning, R.J. & H. Bessason, eds. Edda.
  P. Foote, 562(Scan):Nov86-221
Glendinning, V.   Rebecca West.
  J. Kaplan, 441:18Oct87-3
  P. Kemp, 617(TLS):24Apr87-431
  M. Laski, 176:Dec87-82
  S. Maitland, 362:18Jun87-24
  V.S. Pritchett, 442(NY):21Dec87-132
Glenn, C.W.   Jim Dine: Drawings.*
  E. Turner, 55:Jan86-47
Glickman, G.   Year From Now.
  R. Houston, 441:18Oct87-20
Glickman, R.L.   Russian Factory Women.*
  L. Edmondson, 575(SEER):Oct86-616

Goetsch, P., ed. Englische Literatur zwischen Viktorianismus und Moderne.
  G. Schmitz, 72:Band223Heft1-181
Goetschel, R. La Kabbale.
  A. Reix, 542:Jan-Mar86-88
Goetz, R. Chez les fous.
  M. Alhau, 450(NRF):Mar86-112
Goetz, W.R. Henry James and the Darkest Abyss of Romance.*
  A.R. Tintner, 395(MFS):Winter86-599
Goetzmann, W.H. New Lands, New Men.
  W. Kittredge, 441:11Jan87-22
Goetzmann, W.H. & J.C. Porter. The West as Romantic Horizon.
  R. Thacker, 106:Spring86-51
Goffen, R. Piety and Patronage in Renaissance Venice.
  F. Gilbert, 453(NYRB):16Jul87-37
  C. Gould, 39:Nov86-451
  P. Humfrey, 324:May87-465
  G. Robertson, 617(TLS):22May87-560
van Gogh, V. Vincent by Himself. (B. Bernard, ed)
  M. Clarke, 39:Aug86-141
Gohin, Y. - see Hugo, V.
Göhler, H. Franz Kafka.*
  G. Benda, 406:Summer86-252
Goines, D.L. Goines Posters.
  C. Hess, 507:Mar/Apr86-125
Goitein, S.D. Letters of Medieval Jewish Traders.
  I. Joseph, 98:Mar86-244
Goitein, S.D. A Mediterranean Society. (Vol 4)
  I. Joseph, 98:Mar86-244
  A.L. Udovitch, 589:Jul86-656
Golby, J.M. & A.W. Purdue. The Civilization of the Crowd.
  639(VQR):Winter86-8
Gold, J.J. - see Johnson, S.
Gold, P.S. The Lady and the Virgin.
  R.H. Bloch, 405(MP):Nov86-209
  J.A. McNamara, 589:Oct86-930
Goldbarth, A. Art & Sciences.
  E. Grosholz, 441:4Jan87-22
Goldberg, J. La culpabilité.
  J-M. Gabaude, 542:Jan-Mar86-153
Goldberg, J. James I and the Politics of Literature.*
  R.A. Anselment, 402(MLR):Apr87-445
  W. Weiss, 156(ShJW):Jahrbuch1986-198
Goldberg, J. Voice Terminal Echo.
  E.J. Bellamy, 604:Fall86-60
  L.S. Marcus, 141:Fall86-459
  J. Pitcher, 617(TLS):27Mar87-316
Goldberg, L. A Commentary on Plato's "Protagoras."*
  P. Mitsis, 124:Jan-Feb87-213
  F. Sparshott, 41:Spring85-95
Goldberg, L. In Siberia It Is Very Cold.
  P-L. Adams, 61:Jul87-98
  O. Conant, 441:2Aug87-13
Goldberg, M.K. & J.P. Seigel - see Carlyle, T.
Goldberg, R. Sex and Enlightenment.*
  I. Grundy, 566:Autumn86-66
  J. Harris, 402(MLR):Apr87-450
  P. Sabor, 173(ECS):Fall86-70
  C. Sherman, 207(FR):Feb87-396
  M. Smith, 83:Spring86-95
  S. Soupel, 549(RLC):Apr-Jun86-239
Goldberg, S.M. Understanding Terence.
  E. Segal, 617(TLS):6Mar87-253

Goldberg, V. Margaret Bourke-White.*
  A. Graham-Dixon, 362:26Feb87-19
  A. Hopkinson, 617(TLS):19Jun87-655
Goldblatt, R. Topoi. (rev)
  P.J. Scott, 316:Dec86-1077
Goldemberg, I. Tiempo al tiempo.
  F.H. Schiminovich, 238:Mar86-117
Golden, J. A List of the Papers and Correspondence of Henry Clark Barlow, M.D. (1806-1876) Held in the Manuscripts Room, University College London Library.
  J. Lindon, 278(IS):Vol41-158
  J.R. Woodhouse, 402(MLR):Apr87-492
Goldhill, S. Language, Sexuality, Narrative.*
  A.F. Garvie, 303(JoHS):Vol106-206
  M.R. Kitzinger, 24:Spring86-115
Goldin, J. Les Comices agricoles de Gustave Flaubert.
  G. Bonaccorso, 535(RHL):Sep-Oct86-935
  A.W. Raitt, 402(MLR):Apr87-479
Goldin, N. The Ballad of Sexual Dependency.
  J. Howell, 62:Oct86-8
Golding, R. Idiolects in Dickens.*
  M.G. Miller, 594:Winter86-444
  N. Page, 155:Spring86-52
  K.C. Phillipps, 158:Dec86-181
Golding, W. Äquatortaufe.* Herr der Fliegen. The Paper Men.
  W. Wicht, 601(SuF):Sep-Oct86-1109
Golding, W. Close Quarters.
  R.M. Adams, 441:31May87-44
  R. Ashton, 362:11Jun87-25
  D. Nokes, 617(TLS):19Jun87-653
Goldman, A.I. Epistemology and Cognition.
  D. Papineau, 617(TLS):20Apr87-294
Goldman, J. James Rosenquist.*
  E. Heartney, 55:Mar86-44
Goldman, L. The Part of Fortune.
  L. Heron, 362:31Dec87-24
  C. Pelletier, 441:25Jan87-10
  A. Vaux, 617(TLS):4-10Dec87-1348
Goldman, L. Talk Never Dies.
  A. Rumsey, 355(LSoc):Jun86-250
Goldman, M. Acting and Action in Shakespearean Tragedy.*
  L.S. Champion, 179(ES):Oct86-454
  S. Homan, 301(JEGP):Apr86-263
  R. Jacobs, 175:Summer86-164
  H. Keyishian, 130:Summer86-183
Goldman, M.I. Gorbachev's Challenge.
  W. Leontief, 441:21Jun87-9
Goldman, P.B., ed. Conflicting Realities.
  G.M. Scanlon, 402(MLR):Oct87-1006
  J. Whiston, 86(BHS):Jan86-100
Goldman, R.P. & S.J. Sutherland - see "The Rāmāyaṇa of Vālmīki"
Goldman, W. Brothers.
  S. Dobyns, 441:15Feb87-18
Goldsborough, R. Murder in E Minor.*
  T.J. Binyon, 617(TLS):9-15Oct87-1124
Goldschmidt, A. L'Espoir barbelé.
  J. Kolbert, 207(FR):May87-908
Goldsmith, B. Johnson v. Johnson.
  J. Allen, 441:8Mar87-15
Goldsmith, J. - see Spender, S.
Goldsmith, M.M. Private Vices, Public Benefits.
  T.A. Horne, 566:Spring87-187
  G. Vichert, 173(ECS):Winter86/87-226

Goldstein, D. Hebrew Incunables in the British Isles: A Preliminary Census.*
A.K. Offenberg, 354:Mar86-70
Goldstein, J.A., ed & trans. II Maccabees.
S.J.D. Cohen, 318(JAOS):Oct/Dec85-799
Goldstein, L. A Mask for the General.
G. Jonas, 441:20Dec87-18
Goldthorpe, R. Sartre.*
K. Gore, 208(FS):Jan86-103
C. Rigolot, 207(FR):Feb87-404
H.W. Wardman, 402(MLR):Apr86-493
Göller, K.H., ed. Spätmittelalterliche Artusliteratur.
P. Ganz, 541(RES):Aug86-406
S. Kohl, 224(GRM):Band36Heft2-234
Göller, K.H. & T. Stemmler - see Schirmer, W.F.
Golley, J., with F. Whittle. Whittle.
T. Ferrell, 441:8Nov87-27
Gollin, R.K. Portraits of Nathaniel Hawthorne.*
J. Kestner, 477(PLL):Spring86-221
Golomb, L. An Anthropology of Curing in Multiethnic Thailand.
P.F. Laird, 293(JASt):Aug86-903
Gomba, S. & G. Haiman, eds. Tótfalusi Kis Miklós az Amszterdami Biblia kiadásának háromszázadik évfordulója alkalmából Debrecen 1985.
B. Guzner, 354:Jun86-181
Gombrich, E.H. Meditations on a Hobby Horse.
L. Dunlap, 532(RCF):Summer86-147
Gombrich, E.H. Tributes.*
M. Podro, 59:Mar86-84
Gombrich, E.H. Aby Warburg.*
G. Steiner, 442(NY):2Feb87-95
Gómez, A.L. & others - see under López Gómez, A. & others
Gómez, E.A. - see under Abreu Gómez, E.
Gómez de Orozco, F. El mobiliaro y la decoración en la Nueva España en el siglo XVI.
C. Esteras, 48:Jul-Sep86-347
Gómez de Silva, G. Elsevier's Concise Spanish Etymological Dictionary.
R. de Gorog, 159:Fall86-255
Y. Malkiel, 240(HR):Summer86-323
D.A. Pharies, 238:Dec86-895
Gómez Lance, B.R. Vendimia del tiempo.
C. Rovira, 238:Mar86-118
Gomez-Lobo, A. - see "Parmenides"
Gomi, T. Wirtschaftstexte der Ur III–Zeit aus dem British Museum.
M. Sigrist, 318(JAOS):Apr/Jun85-334
Goncharov, I.A. The Frigate Pallada.
A. Tyler, 441:20Sep87-9
Goncharov, I.A. Oblomov.
J. Blot, 450(NRF):Dec86-105
Gonda, J. Prajāpati and the Year.
K. Mylius, 259(IIJ):Oct86-313
Góngora, C.D. - see under de Sigüenza y Góngora, C.
de Góngora, L. La firmezas de Isabela.
(R. Jammes, ed)
W.J. Weaver 3d, 240(HR):Summer86-336
Gontarski, S.E. The Intent of Undoing in Samuel Beckett's Dramatic Texts.
M.B., 295(JML):Nov86-441
T. Postlewait, 610:Autumn86-273
González, A. La crónica modernista hispanoamericana.*
F. Dauster, 240(HR):Winter86-111

González, A. Formas y funciones de los principios en el Romancero viejo.
L. Mirrer, 238:Sep86-540
González, A., T. Holzapfel & A. Rodríguez, eds. Estudios sobre el Siglo de Oro en homenaje a Raymond R. MacCurdy.
J.M. Ruano de la Haza, 86(BHS):Apr86-157
R.E. Surtz, 240(HR):Winter86-95
González, A.N. - see under Navarro González, A.
González, C. "El Cavallero Zifar" y el reino lejano.*
S.D. Kirby, 238:May86-303
González, J.M.C. - see under Caso González, J.M.
Gonzalez, M. Louis Souris et ses amis.
L. Schryver, 207(FR):Oct86-137
González Boixo, J.C. - see Rulfo, J.
Gonzalez Casanova, P., ed. Cultura y creación intelectual en América Latina.
I.M. Zuleta, 263(RIB):Vol36No1-60
González-del-Valle, L.T. & D. Villanueva, eds. Estudios en honor a Ricardo Gullón.
B.B. Aponte, 240(HR):Winter86-83
F. Wyers, 238:May86-313
González Echevarría, R., comp. Historia y ficción en la narrativa hispanoamericana.
J.J. Hassett, 240(HR):Summer86-358
J. Walker, 238:Dec86-888
González Echevarría, R. Los pasos perdidos.
E. González, 400(MLN):Mar86-424
González Echevarría, R. The Voice of the Masters.
P.G. Earle, 263(RIB):Vol36No3-339
González García, A. - see de Holanda, F.
González-Grano de Oro, E. El español de José L. Castillo-Puche.
R. Penny, 86(BHS):Jul86-271
M. Ruggeri Marchetti, 548:Jan-Jun86-218
González Herrán, J.M. La obra de Pereda ante la crítica literaria de su tiempo.
M.E. Barbieri, 240(HR):Spring86-227
A.H. Clarke, 86(BHS):Jan86-95
S. García Castañeda, 345:Nov86-506
M. Montes-Huidobro, 238:Mar86-101
E. Rodgers, 402(MLR):Oct86-1025
González Muñiz, M.A. Quevedo.
R.M. Price, 86(BHS):Oct86-387
González-Palacios, A. Il Tempio del Gusto.*
P. Thornton, 39:Jan86-66
Goodall, J. The Chimpanzees of Gombe.*
S.J. Gould, 453(NYRB):25Jun87-20
M. Ridley, 617(TLS):1May87-473
42(AR):Fall86-489
Goodden, A. Actio and Persuasion.*
B.A. Brown, 173(ECS):Summer87-478
Goode, P. & M. Lancaster, eds. The Oxford Companion to Gardens.
A. Paterson, 617(TLS):27Feb87-225
Gooders, J. The New Where to Watch Birds.
E. Dunlon, 617(TLS):13Mar87-280
Goodheart, E. The Skeptic Disposition in Contemporary Criticism.*
D.H. Bialostosky, 454:Winter87-175
T. Docherty, 541(RES):Nov86-619
M. Fischer, 560:Fall86-267
E.K. Kaplan, 210(FrF):May86-252
R. Selden, 402(MLR):Oct86-961

Goodin, R.E. Protecting the Vulnerable.
  J. Abramson, 185:Apr87-659
  M.E. Winston, 543:Dec86-379
Goodison, J.W. Catalogue of the Portraits
  in Christ's, Clare and Sidney Sussex
  Colleges.
  J.I., 90:Sep86-689
Goodkin, R.E. The Symbolist Home and the
  Tragic Home.*
  C. Chadwick, 402(MLR):Apr86-490
  R. Lloyd, 208(FS):Apr86-229
  M.C. Olds, 210(FrF):Jan86-120
Goodman, D.G. - see "After Apocalypse"
Goodman, J. Murder in High Places.
  E.S. Turner, 617(TLS):20Mar87-289
Goodman, J. The Slaying of Joseph Bowne
  Elwell.
  J. Clay, 617(TLS):4-10Dec87-1346
Goodman, J. - see Heppenstall, R.
Goodman, M. State and Society in Roman
  Galilee, A.D. 132-212.*
  A. Wasserstein, 123:Vol36No1-108
Goodman, N. Of Mind and Other Matters.*
  A. Margalit, 311(JP):Sep86-500
  J.N. Safran, 84:Jun86-242
Goodwin, D.K. The Fitzgeralds and the
  Kennedys.
  D. Adams, 617(TLS):17Jul87-760
  L. McTaggart, 362:9Jul87-28
  F. Russell, 453(NYRB):23Apr87-3
  G.C. Ward, 441:15Feb87-11
Goodwin, J. Caught in the Crossfire.
  B. Woffinden, 362:27Aug87-18
Goodwin, K. A History of Australian Lit-
  erature.
  B. Bennett, 71(ALS):Oct86-542
Gooneratne, Y. Relative Merits.*
  E. Nissan, 617(TLS):12Jun87-631
Gooneratne, Y. Silence, Exile and Cunning.
  M.M. Mahood, 402(MLR):Jul87-728
Gopal, S. Jawaharlal Nehru. (Vol 3)
  A.T. Embree, 293(JASt):Nov85-171
Gopal, S. - see Nehru, J.
Gorbachev, M. Perestroika.
  A. Beaton, 362:31Dec87-20
  R. Legvold, 441:13Dec87-3
Gorbachev, M. Socialism, Peace and Democ-
  racy.
  A. Beaton, 362:31Dec87-20
Gordimer, N. A Sport of Nature.
  W. Brandmark, 362:16Apr87-36
  P. Craig, 617(TLS):17Apr87-411
  M. Howard, 441:3May87-1
  D. Johnson, 453(NYRB):16Jul87-8
  J. Thurman, 442(NY):29Jun87-87
Gordon, A. The Evolution of Labor Rela-
  tions in Japan.*
  C. Johnson, 407(MN):Summer86-245
Gordon, C. The Southern Mandarins.* (S.
  Wood, ed)
  G. Core, 534(RALS):Spring-Autumn84-
  212
  M.R. Winchell, 106:Winter86-483
Gordon, G. & D. Hughes, eds. Best Short
  Stories 1986.
  J. Mellors, 362:1Jan87-22
Gordon, I. & F. Weitzenhoffer - see Rewald,
  J.
Gordon, I.A. - see Galt, J.
Gordon, J.C.B., ed. German History and
  Society 1870-1920.
  S. Olsen, 399(MLJ):Summer86-187

Gordon, J.S. The Golden Guru.
  M.E. Marty, 441:13Sep87-15
Gordon, K. Untersuchungen zum russischen
  romantischen Versmärchen.
  J.D. Clayton, 107(CRCL):Sep86-487
Gordon, K.E. The Transitive Vampire.*
  E.J. Higgins, 95(CLAJ):Dec86-252
Gordon, L. Cossack Rebellions.
  F.E. Sysyn, 575(SEER):Jan86-100
Gordon, L. Virginia Woolf.*
  M. Beja, 454:Fall86-88
Gordon, M. Temporary Shelter.
  R. Billington, 441:19Apr87-8
  H. Lee, 617(TLS):17Jul87-765
Gordon, P. - see Spencer, J.P.
Gordon, R. Breeds.
  R.M. Davis, 573(SSF):Summer86-333
Gordon, R. Jazz West Coast.
  B. Case, 617(TLS):19Jun87-656
Gordon, S. Seduction Lines.
  D.J. Enright, 617(TLS):18-24Dec87-1399
Gorgias. Encomium of Helen. (D.M.
  MacDowell, ed & trans)
  H.L. Hudson-Williams, 123:Vol36No1-131
Gorgias, J. [alias Veriphantor] Betroge-
  ner Frontalbo. (H. Rölleke, ed)
  A.J. Harper, 402(MLR):Apr87-775
  H. Wagener, 133:Band19Heft3/4-336
Goriushkin, L.M. & N.A. Minenko. Istorio-
  grafiia Sibiri dooktiabr'skogo perioda
  (konets XVI-nachalo XX v.).
  A.P. Allison, 550(RusR):Jul86-331
Gorki, M. Briefwechsel mit sowjetischen
  Schriftstellern. (I. Idzikowski, ed)
  N. Thun, 654(WB):1/1986-163
Gorky, M. Philistines. (D. Hughes, trans)
  P. Storfer, 157:No162-46
Görlach, M., ed. Focus on: Scotland.
  F. Chevillet, 189(EA):Jul-Sep86-331
Gorman, E. Murder on the Aisle.
  N. Callendar, 441:30Aug87-29
Gorn, E.J. The Manly Art.
  D. Kelly, 441:11Jan87-8
  E.S. Turner, 617(TLS):18-24Dec87-1412
Gornick, V. Fierce Attachments.
  M. Simpson, 441:26Apr87-7
Gorny, Y. Zionism and the Arabs 1882-
  1948.
  E. Salmon, 617(TLS):4-11Sep87-943
Gorodetsky, G. Stafford Cripps' Mission to
  Moscow, 1940-42.
  S. White, 575(SEER):Jul86-480
de Gorog, R. Dictionnaire inverse de
  l'ancien français.
  J.H. Marshall, 208(FS):Jan86-119
van Gorp, H. & others, eds. Lexicon van
  literaire termen.*
  J. Voisine, 549(RLC):Jul-Sep86-349
Görtzen, R. Jürgen Habermas.
  J. Grondin, 98:Jan-Feb86-40
Goscilo, H., ed & trans. Russian and
  Polish Women's Fiction.
  M.G. Levine, 574(SEEJ):Fall86-441
  B.T. Lupack, 497(PolR):Vol31No2/3-206
  E.M. Thompson, 402(MLR):Apr87-539
Gose, E.B., Jr. The World of the Irish
  Wonder Tale.
  J. Dutka, 627(UTQ):Fall86-144
Gosling, J.C.B. & C.C.W. Taylor. The
  Greeks on Pleasure.*
  D. Pralon, 542:Oct-Dec86-504

Gracián, B. Obras de Baltasar Gracián
(Selección). (M. Batllori, ed)
   J.B. Hall, 86(BHS):Jul86-289
Gracq, J. La forme d'une ville.*
   L.A. MacKenzie, Jr., 207(FR):May87-890
   J. Taylor, 532(RCF):Fall86-137
Grade, C. My Mother's Sabbath Days.*
   442(NY):9Feb87-105
Grady, J. Just a Shot Away.
   N. Callendar, 441:12Apr87-34
Graefe, R. Vela erunt.
   A. Hoffmann, 43:Band16Heft2-207
Graf, O.A. Otto Wagner, Das Werk des
Architekten.
   A.J. Sarnitz, 576:Sep86-302
Graf, O.M. Oskar Maria Graf in seinen
Briefen. (G. Bauer & H.F. Pfanner, eds)
   S.K. Johnson, 221(GQ):Fall86-667
Graff, G. Professing Literature.
   C. Baldick, 617(TLS):6-12Nov87-1217
Graff, G. & R. Gibbons, eds. Criticism in
the University.*
   J. Hunter, 434:Winter86-242
   J. Stillinger, 301(JEGP):Oct86-550
   639(VQR):Winter86-19
Graffagnino, K. Vermont in the Victorian
Age.
   M. McCorison, 432(NEQ):Dec86-602
de Graffigny, F. Correspondance de Madame
de Graffigny.* (Vol 1) (E. Showalter,
ed)
   E.C. Goldsmith, 207(FR):Apr87-708
   P. Le Clerc, 627(UTQ):Fall86-138
   D. Wood, 402(MLR):Jul86-739
Grafton, A. & L. Jardine. From Humanism
to the Humanities.
   J.B. Trapp, 617(TLS):24Jul87-787
Grafton, A., G.W. Most & J.E.G. Zetzel –
see Wolf, F.A.
Grafton, C. & A. Permaloff. Big Mules and
Branchheads.
   D.W. Grantham, 585(SoQ):Winter87-154
Grafton, D. Red, Hot and Rich!
   S. McCauley, 441:21Jun87-14
Graham, D., ed. South by Southwest.
   L. Milazzo, 584(SWR):Summer86-402
   E.P. Sewell, 649(WAL):Feb87-363
Graham, D. Texas.
   L. Milazzo, 584(SWR):Spring86-257
   R.C. Reynolds, 649(WAL):Feb87-363
Graham, D. The Truth of War.
   M. Standen, 565:Summer86-18
Graham, D. – see Douglas, K.
Graham, D. & S. Bidwell. Tug of War.*
   R. Trevelyan, 617(TLS):23Jan87-78
Graham, G. Politics in Its Place.*
   R.E.G., 185:Apr87-687
Graham, J. The End of Beauty.
   M. Boruch, 29(APR):Mar/Apr87-22
   J.D. McClatchy, 441:26Jul87-9
   H. Vendler, 442(NY):27Jul87-74
Graham, J. Lavater's Essays on Physiog-
nomy.
   E. Heier, 107(CRCL):Mar86-138
Graham, L.R. Science, Philosophy, and
Human Behavior in the Soviet Union.
   C. Sagan, 441:27Sep87-34
Graham, M. New World Architecture.
   M. Jarman, 249(HudR):Summer86-336
   455:Dec86-63
Graham, P.W. – see Hobhouse, J.C.

Graham, S.D. The Lyric Poetry of A.K.
Tolstoi.
   R. Lane, 402(MLR):Oct86-1049
   A. McMillin, 575(SEER):Oct86-600
Graham, W. A Green Flash.
   S. Offit, 441:25Oct87-20
Grainger, M. – see Clare, J.
Grainger, P. The Farthest North of Human-
ness.* (K. Dreyfus, ed)
   S. Banfield, 415:Nov86-624
   M. Hurd, 410(M&L):Oct86-437
Gram, M.S., ed. Interpreting Kant.*
   M. Kuehn, 154:Winter86-797
Graml, H. & K-D. Henke – see Broszat, M.
Gramsci, A. Antonio Gramsci: Selections
from Cultural Writings.* (D. Forgacs &
G. Nowell-Smith, eds)
   M.A. Finocchiaro, 543:Jun87-770
   B. Tonkin, 366:Spring86-116
Granaas, R.C. & others. Kvinnesyn –
tvisyn.*
   P. Bjørby, 563(SS):Summer86-308
Granatstein, J.L. Canada 1957-1967.
   R. Whitaker, 99:Aug/Sep86-31
Grancsay, S.V. Arms and Armor.
   A.V. Norman, 39:Dec86-571
   G. Wilson, 617(TLS):6Mar87-249
de Granda, G. Estudios de lingüística
afro-románica.
   C. Schmitt, 547(RF):Band98Heft3/4-411
Grandbois, A. Poèmes inédits.
   C. Cloutier, 627(UTQ):Fall86-201
Grandin, N. Le Soudan Nilotique et l'Ad-
ministration Britannique (1898-1956).
   P.R. Woodward, 318(JAOS):Oct/Dec85-747
de Grandsaigne, J., ed. African Short
Stories in English.
   A. Maja-Pearce, 538(RAL):Winter86-620
Granger, G-G. Formal Thought and the Sci-
ences of Man.
   R. Harré, 543:Mar87-575
Granier, J. Penser la praxis.
   T.R. Flynn, 543:Jun87-772
Grannes, A., A. Lillehammer & E. Pettersen.
Documents russes sur la pêche et le com-
merce russes en Norvège au XVIIIe
siècle.*
   R.P. Bartlett, 562(Scan):May86-77
Gransden, K.W. Virgil's "Iliad."*
   S.J. Harrison, 123:Vol36No1-38
   T. Van Nortwick, 24:Summer86-293
   A.J. Woodman, 161(DUJ):Dec85-174
Grant, B.K., ed. Film Genre Reader.
   M. Sidone, 590:Jun87-57
Grant, J. Stella Benson.
   L. Gerend, 617(TLS):8May87-486
   S. Maitland, 362:18Jun87-24
Grant, J.S. – see Davies, R.
Grant, K.S. Dr. Burney as Critic and His-
torian of Music.
   C.M.B., 412:Aug85-217
Grant, M. The Roman Emperors.
   M. Hammond, 124:May-Jun87-383
   639(VQR):Winter86-14
Grant, P. Literature and the Discovery
Method in the English Renaissance.
   D. Freake, 627(UTQ):Fall86-96
Grant, P. Literature of Mysticism in West-
ern Tradition.
   A. Louth, 447(N&Q):Mar85-141
Grant, P.R. Ecology and Evolution of Dar-
win's Finches.
   C. Perrins, 617(TLS):5Jun87-615

Grant, Z. Over the Beach.
R. Witkin, 441:11Jan87-25
Grant-Adamson, L. Wild Justice.
G. Kaufman, 362:2Jul87-31
Grantham, D.W. Southern Progressivism.
D.E. Alsobrook, 9(AlaR):Jul86-224
Granville-Barker, H.G. Granville Barker
and His Correspondents. (E. Salmon, ed)
L.H. Hugo, 572:Vol7-351
Grass, G. On Writing and Politics, 1967-
1983.
M.N. Love, 395(MFS):Summer86-335
Grass, G. The Rat.* (German title: Die
Rättin.)
P-L. Adams, 61:Sep87-102
G.P. Butler, 617(TLS):28Aug87-933
D.J. Enright, 453(NYRB):24Sep87-45
J. Grambow, 601(SuF):Nov-Dec86-1292
J.T. Hospital, 441:5Jul87-6
D.A.N. Jones, 362:9Jul87-30
Grasselli, M.M. & P. Rosenberg, with N.
Parmantier. Watteau, 1684-1721.*
M. Eidelberg, 380:Spring86-102
Grassi, C. - see Convenevole da Prato
Grassi, E. Heidegger and the Question of
Renaissance Humanism.*
G. Shapiro, 478:Apr86-106
Grassl, H. Sozialökonomische Vorstellungen
in der kaiserzeitlichen griechischen
Literatur (1.-3. Jh. n. Chr.).
E.L. Bowie, 313:Vol76-294
Grau, S.A. Nine Women.*
639(VQR):Summer86-92
de Grauwe, L. De Wachtendonckse psalmen
en glossen.*
W. Sanders, 684(ZDA):Band115Heft1-45
Gravel, F. La note de passage.
J. Viswanathan, 102(CanL):Fall86-148
Graver, S. George Eliot and Community.*
M. Halliday, 405(MP):Nov86-228
C.A. Martin, 635(VPR):Fall86-112
Graves, D.H. Writing.
G.E. Cook, 126(CCC):Dec86-490
Graves, J.T. The Fighting South.
M.E. Armbrester, 9(AlaR):Jul86-213
Graves, R.P. Robert Graves.* (Vol 1)
P-L. Adams, 61:Apr87-91
J. Wain, 453(NYRB):25Jun87-8
Grawe, C. Theodor Fontane: "Effi Briest."
H.R. Klieneberger, 402(MLR):Oct87-1030
Gray, A. The Fall of Kelvin Walker.*
D.J. Enright, 453(NYRB):26Feb87-15
Gray, A. 1982, Janine.
R. Buckeye, 532(RCF):Spring86-204
Gray, A.X.D. - see under White, P.
Gray, C. The Russian Experiment in Art
1863-1922.
N. Lynton, 617(TLS):27Mar87-335
Gray, D., ed. The Oxford Book of Late
Medieval Verse and Prose.
N.F. Blake, 179(ES):Feb86-73
Gray, D. - see Bennett, J.A.W.
Gray, D. & E.G. Stanley, eds. Middle
English Studies Presented to Norman
Davis in Honour of his Seventieth
Birthday.*
S.S. Hussey, 402(MLR):Apr87-435
D. Mehl, 447(N&Q):Mar85-92
Gray, F.D. Adam and Eve and the City.
J. Alter, 441:30Aug87-13
Gray, J. Hayek on Liberty.*
J.E.J. Altham, 483:Jan86-130
P. Johnson, 521:Oct86-350

Gray, J. Liberalism.
J.C., 185:Jul87-897
A. Ryan, 617(TLS):7Aug87-854
Gray, J. Park. (P. Healy, ed)
I. Murray, 161(DUJ):Dec85-207
Gray, J.M. Thro' the Vision of the Night.
P.J.C. Field, 382(MAE):1986/2-306
Gray, N. A History of Lettering.
C. Gere, 39:Nov86-459
J.I. Whalley, 617(TLS):29May87-592
Gray, R., ed. American Fiction.*
K. Carabine, 447(N&Q):Sep85-429
Gray, R. Writing the South.*
M. Kreyling, 578:Spring87-102
Gray, S. Douglas Blackburn.
M. Chapman, 538(RAL):Fall86-406
Gray, S., ed. The Penguin Book of Southern
African Stories.
442(NY):26Jan87-85
Gray, S. An Unnatural Pursuit and Other
Pieces.*
S. Morley, 157:No159-48
Grayling, A.C. The Refutation of Scepti-
cism.
J. Dancy, 393(Mind):Apr86-263
A. Morton, 518:Jul86-163
R.C.S. Walker, 479(PhQ):Oct86-564
Grayson, D.A. The Genesis of Debussy's
"Pelléas et Mélisande."
R.L. Smith, 617(TLS):23-29Oct87-1170
Grazia Profeti, M. - see de Vega Carpio, L.
Greaves, D.D. - see Sextus Empiricus
Greaves, R.L. Saints and Rebels.
B. Donagan, 250(HLQ):Spring86-175
Greaves, R.L. - see Bunyan, J.
Greeley, A.M. The Communal Catholic.
J. Newman, 390:Jan86-44
Greeley, A.M. Patience of a Saint.
J. Sullivan, 441:8Feb87-31
Green, C. Cubism and Its Enemies.
R. Cork, 362:3Dec87-38
Green, G. & C. Kahn, eds. Making a Differ-
ence.
S. Scobie, 376:Jun86-128
Green, H.M. A History of Australian Lit-
erature. (rev by D. Green)
B. Bennett, 71(ALS):Oct86-542
Green, J. God's Fool.
639(VQR):Winter86-12
Green, J. & S. Lefanu, eds. Despatches
from the Frontier of the Female Mind.
J.L. Gomez, 441:28Jun87-23
Green, J.A. The Government of England
under Henry I.
F. Barlow, 617(TLS):6Mar87-250
Green, J.A. - see Schwob, M.
Green, L.C. Essays on the Modern Law of
War.
A.C., 185:Jan87-508
Green, M. The English Novel in the Twen-
tieth Century.
A. Blayac, 189(EA):Jul-Sep86-360
Green, M., ed. The Old English Elegies.*
S.A.J. Bradley, 402(MLR):Jul87-697
R. Gleissner, 38:Band104Heft3/4-468
B. O'Donoghue, 541(RES):May86-237
Green, M. The Origins of Nonviolence.
M. Ceadel, 617(TLS):6Feb87-142
Green, M., ed & trans. The Russian Symbol-
ist Theatre.
T.J. Binyon, 617(TLS):31Jul87-822
J. Freedman, 574(SEEJ):Winter86-579

Green, M.J. Fiction in the Historical Present.
P. McCarthy, 617(TLS):18-24Sep87-1029
Green, P. Retrieving Democracy.*
B.H. Baxter, 518:Oct86-244
Green, R. The "Sissy Boy Syndrome" and the Development of Homosexuality.
P. Lomas, 617(TLS):27Mar87-321
Green, R., ed. That's What She Said.
P. Petrick, 649(WAL):Aug86-157
Green, S. The Great Clowns of Broadway.
T.G. Dunn, 615(TJ):Mar86-130
Green, S. Who Owns London?
J. Chernaik, 617(TLS):23Jan87-89
Green-Pedersen, N.J. The Tradition of the Topics in the Middle Ages.
J-L. Gardies, 542:Jan-Mar86-108
A.R. Perreiah, 319:Jul87-442
Greenbaum, S., ed. The English Language Today.*
O. Alexandrova, 257(IRAL):Aug86-261
S.J. Gaies, 399(MLJ):Autumn86-338
Greenbaum, S., G. Leech & J. Svartvik, eds. Studies in English Linguistics for Randolph Quirk.
G. Tottie, 597(SN):Vol58No1-115
Greenberg, C. The Collected Essays and Criticism.* (J. O'Brian, ed)
T. Hilton, 617(TLS):27Mar87-330
Greenberg, J. Age of Consent.
M.J. Gerber, 441:27Dec87-11
Greenberg, K.S. Masters and Statesmen.
639(VQR):Summer86-80
Greenberg, M. Biblical Prose Prayer as a Window to the Popular Religion of Ancient Israel.
J.H. Tigay, 318(JAOS):Jan/Mar85-155
Greenberg, M. Corneille, Classicism and the Rules of Symmetry.
I. Maclean, 617(TLS):5Jun87-613
Greenberg, M. Detours of Desire.*
M. Giordano, 141:Winter86-107
J.L. Pallister, 568(SCN):Spring-Summer86-21
C.H. Winn, 210(FrF):Jan86-103
Greenberg, M. The Hamlet Vocation of Coleridge and Wordsworth.
A. Leighton, 617(TLS):31Jul87-814
Greenberg, M.H., ed. Touring Nam.*
R.G. Topp, 569(SR):Fall86-lxxxvii
Greenberg, S.B. Legitimating the Illegitimate.
W.G. James, 529(QQ):Autumn86-484
Greenberg, W.N. The Power of Rhetoric.
R.T. Denommé, 207(FR):May87-866
L.W. Marvick, 188(ECr):Fall86-101
J.R. Williams, 446(NCFS):Spring87-319
Greenblatt, S., ed. The Power of Forms in the English Renaissance.*
K. Muir, 402(MLR):Jul86-706
Greene, A.C. Texas Sketches.
L. Milazzo, 584(SWR):Winter86-123
Greene, B. Be True to Your School.
J. Kaufman, 441:7Jun87-31
Greene, D. - see Johnson, S.
Greene, D.B. Mahler, Consciousness and Temporality.*
S.M. Filler, 309:Vol7No1-124
Greene, D.B. Temporal Processes in Beethoven's Music.*
M.M., 412:Feb85-58

Greene, D.M. Greene's Biographical Encyclopedia of Composers.
G. Martin, 465:Spring86-101
Greene, G. The Tenth Man.*
W.N., 102(CanL):Winter85-195
K. Wilson, 529(QQ):Spring86-203
Greene, G. The Third Man. (B. Lenz, ed)
C. Jansohn, 72:Band223Heft1-185
Greene, G.K., ed. Polyphonic Music of the Fourteenth Century. (Vols 18-20)
L. Koehler, 317:Fall86-633
Greene, T.M. The Light in Troy.*
M. Mueller, 107(CRCL):Sep86-484
Greenfeld, H. The Devil and Dr. Barnes.
A.C. Danto, 441:22Nov87-13
Greenfeld, J. A Client Called Noah.
S. Kenney, 441:15Feb87-1
Greenfield, S.B. & D.G. Calder. A New Critical History of Old English Literature.
M-M. Dubois, 189(EA):Jul-Sep87-345
Greenfield, T.N. The Eye of Judgment.*
K. Duncan-Jones, 677(YES):Vol16-236
"Elizabeth Greenhill, Bookbinder."
A. Hobson, 617(TLS):14Aug87-878
Greenland, C. The Hour of the Thin Ox.
J. Clute, 617(TLS):25-31Dec87-1428
Greenleaf, S. Beyond Blame.*
G. Kaufman, 362:4Jun87-45
Greenleaf, S. Toll Call.
442(NY):27Apr87-106
Greenspoon, L.J. Textual Studies in the Book of Joshua.
E. Tov, 318(JAOS):Jan/Mar85-148
Greenwald, D.S. & S.J. Zeitlin. No Reason to Talk About It.
E. Rhodes, 441:26Apr87-25
Greenwald, M. Directions by Indirections.
A. Cornish, 157:No162-48
Greenwald, R. - see Jacobsen, R.
Greenwood, L.B. Sherlock Holmes and the Case of the Raleigh Legacy.
442(NY):19Jan87-93
de Greenwood, P.F-C. - see under Fernandez-Cañadas de Greenwood, P.
Greenya, J. Blood Relations.
M. Jones, 441:13Sep87-28
Greer, G. The Madwoman's Underclothes.
L. Blandford, 441:11Oct87-14
Greer, G. Shakespeare.*
M. Dodsworth, 175:Summer86-190
M. Willems, 189(EA):Apr-Jun87-204
Greetham, D.C. & W.S. Hill - see "Text"
Greger, D. And.*
J.D. McClatchy, 491:Oct86-31
639(VQR):Summer86-101
Gregg, E.E.W. - see Emerson, E.T.
Gregg, K.C. An Index to the Spanish Theatre Collection in the London Library.
A.J.C. Bainton, 402(MLR):Jul86-765
Gregg, L. Alma.*
C. Bedient, 569(SR):Fall86-657
L. Rector, 249(HudR):Autumn86-506
455:Dec86-63
639(VQR):Summer86-98
Gregg, R.J. The Scotch-Irish Dialect Boundaries in the Province of Ulster.
J.K. Chambers, 627(UTQ):Fall86-251
Gregory, M.L. Equal to Princes.
D. Johnson, 18:Sep87-67
Gregory, P.R. Russian National Income, 1885-1913.
G. Jones, 575(SEER):Jul86-473

Griffiths, P. New Sounds, New Personalities.
R. Christiansen, 617(TLS):9Jan87–39
H. Halbreich, 607:Sep86–57
C. Shaw, 607:Mar86–31
A. Whittall, 410(M&L):Oct86–425
Griffiths, P., ed. Philosophy and Literature.
P. Somville, 542:Apr–Jun86–268
Griffiths, P. The Thames and Hudson Encyclopaedia of 20th–Century Music.
R. Christiansen, 617(TLS):9Jan87–39
Griffiths, P.J. On Being Mindless.
S. Collins, 617(TLS):17Jul87–776
Griffiths, R. Fellow Travellers of the Right.
C. Jolicoeur, 189(EA):Jul–Sep87–363
Grigorieva, I., Y. Kuznetsov & I. Novoselskaja. Disegni dell'Europa Occidentale dall'Ermitage di Leningrado.
380:Autumn86–417
Grigoryeva, T.P., ed. Chelovek i mir v yaponski kulture.
H. Plutschow, 407(MN):Summer86–259
Grigson, G. The Englishman's Flora.
J. Buxton, 617(TLS):14Aug87–885
Grigson, G. Persephone's Flowers.
J. Loveday, 493:Oct86–53
Grigson, J. The Observer Guide to British Cookery.
T. Whittaker, 529(QQ):Autumn86–547
Grillandi, M. Lucrezia Borgia.
C. Di Biase, 275(IQ):Spring86–109
Grillo, P., ed. La Chrétienté Corbaran.
M.B. Speer, 589:Jul86–660
Grimal, P. Les jardins romains. (3rd ed)
P. Flobert, 555:Vol59fasc2–341
Grimald, N. Christus Redivivus. (K. Tetzeli von Rosador, ed)
G. Schmitz, 72:Band223Heft2–409
Grimaud, M., ed. Victor Hugo: "Approches critiques contemporaines."*
W.J.S. Kirton, 402(MLR):Apr86–488
Grimaud, M. – see "Victor Hugo, I."
Grimes, L.E. The Religious Design of Hemingway's Early Fiction.
M.B., 295(JML):Nov86–483
S.R. Portch, 573(SSF):Summer86–344
Grimes, M. The Five Bells and Bladebone.
E. Jolley, 441:13Sep87–53
Grimes, R.L. Beginnings in Ritual Studies.
P.B. Zarrilli, 615(TJ):Dec86–493
Grimes, R.L. Research in Ritual Studies.
S. Drury, 203:Vol97No2–234
Grimm, G.E. Literatur und Gelehrtentum in Deutschland.*
H. Jaumann, 400(MLN):Apr86–710
Grimm, G.E. & H–P. Bayerdörfer, eds. Im Zeichen Hiobs.
S.S. Prawer, 402(MLR):Jul86–798
Grimm, J. Das avantgardistische Theater Frankreichs 1895–1930.*
M. Cranston, 207(FR):Oct86–130
Grimm, J. & W. Deutsches Wörterbuch von Jacob Grimm und Wilhelm Grimm.
H. Schmitt, 682(ZPSK):Band39Heft6–712
Grimm, J. & W. Volkslieder. (Vol 1) (C. Oberfeld & others, eds)
R.W. Brednich, 196:Band27Heft3/4–342
Grimm, R., ed. Hans Magnus Enzensberger: Materialien.
C. Melin, 406:Winter86–551
H.D. Osterle, 221(GQ):Spring86–279

Grimm, R. Love, Lust, and Rebellion.
R.C. Cowen, 221(GQ):Fall86–653
Grimm, R. Texturen.
I. Eggers, 222(GR):Spring86–74
H.D. Osterle, 221(GQ):Spring86–279
C. Melin, 406:Winter86–550
Grimm, R. & B. Armstrong – see Enzensberger, H.M.
Grimshaw, A. – see James, C.L.R.
Grimshaw, J.A., Jr., ed. Robert Penn Warren's "Brother to Dragons."
M.R. Winchell, 106:Winter86–483
Grimson, T. Within Normal Limits.
E. Gleick, 441:19Jul87–20
442(NY):10Aug87–78
Grimwood, K. Replay.
A. Krystal, 441:25Jan87–20
Grin, A. Selected Short Stories.
H. Robinson, 441:20Dec87–10
Grinde, O. – see Jacobsen, R.
Grindle, J. & S. Gatrell – see Hardy, T.
Grinspoon, L., ed. The Long Darkness.*
R.E.G., 185:Apr87–707
639(VQR):Autumn86–131
Grisé, Y. Le suicide dans la Rome antique.
M. Billerbeck, 487:Summer86–233
M. Ducos, 555:Vol59fasc2–342
Grissell, E. Thyme on My Hands.
A. Lacy, 441:6Dec87–34
Griswold, C.L., Jr. Self-Knowledge in Plato's "Phaedrus."
M. Nussbaum, 617(TLS):7Aug87–850
Groarke, L. & C. Tindale. Informal Logic.
M. Richardson, 154:Winter86–787
Grob, G.N. Mental Illness and American Society 1875–1940.
C. Howell, 529(QQ):Spring86–19
Groce, N.E. Everyone Here Spoke Sign Language.*
H. Lane, 432(NEQ):Jun86–281
Grodecki, L., with C. Brisac. Gothic Stained Glass 1200–1300.*
P. Hetherington, 39:Apr86–290
Grodecki, L., with A. Prache & R. Recht. Gothic Architecture.
J.S. Curl, 324:Apr87–405
Groening, M. Love is Hell. Work is Hell.
M. Richler, 441:3May87–35
Groffin, R., M. Vanhelleputte & M. Weyembrogh-Boussart, eds. Littérature et culture allemandes.
G. van de Louw, 549(RLC):Oct–Dec86–471
Groh, R. Ironie und Moral im Werk Diderots.
P.H. Meyer, 173(ECS):Fall86–73
"The Grolier Club 1884–1984."*
R.C. Alston, 354:Sep86–279
Grönbald, G. Der Buddhistische Kanon.
J.P. McDermott, 318(JAOS):Oct/Dec85–815
von Gronicka, A. The Russian Image of Goethe. (Vol 2)
E.C. Barksdale, 221(GQ):Fall86–679
P.P. Brodsky, 574(SEEJ):Winter86–573
C.V. Ponomareff, 627(UTQ):Summer87–592
V. Terras, 301(JEGP):Oct86–628
Grønstøl, S.B. Songen og barnet.
B. Holm, 172(Edda):1986/2–189

Grønvik, O. Die dialektgeographische Stellung des Krimgotischen und die krimgotische "cantilena."
K. Matzel, 685(ZDL):3/1986-366
Groover, D.L. & C.C. Conner, Jr. Skeletons from the Opera Closet.*
B. Holland, 441:11Jan87-15
Gros, P. & others. Fouilles de l'École Française de Rome à Bolsena (Poggio Moscini). (Vols 1-6)
J.R. Patterson, 313:Vol76-308
Gröschel, B. Sprachnorm, Sprachplanung und Sprachpflege.
K. Kehr, 685(ZDL):1/1986-132
Gross, J.T. - seee Staniszkis, J.
Gross, K. Arbeit als literarisches Problem.
H.G. Klaus, 224(GRM):Band36Heft3-366
Gross, K. Spenserian Poetics.
E.J. Bellamy, 111:Fall87-8
J. Goldberg, 141:Summer86-341
J.N. King, 604:Fall86-55
639(VQR):Autumn86-116
Gross, M. The Red President.
R. Smith, 441:18Jan87-19
Gross, N. Amatory Persuasion in Antiquity.
T. Conley, 544:Autumn86-424
Gross, N. From Gesture to Idea.
L.W. Riggs, 345:Feb86-125
Gross, P. Cat's Whisker.
P. Forbes, 362:12Nov87-30
Gross, P. The Ice Factory.
J. Loveday, 4:Spring86-54
J. Saunders, 565:Summer86-74
Gross, S. - see Maeterlinck, M.
"Der Grosse Duden." (18th ed)
D. Herberg, 682(ZPSK):Band39Heft4-491
Grossir, C. L'Islam des Romantiques. (Vol 1)
G. Bonaccorso, 535(RHL):Jan-Feb86-155
Grossklaus, G. & E. Oldemeyer, eds. Natur als Gegenwelt.
M. Dierks, 680(ZDP):Band105Heft2-293
Grosskurth, P. Melanie Klein.*
D. Ingleby, 617(TLS):1May87-467
D.M. Mendes, 176:Apr87-59
Grosskurth, P. - see Symonds, J.A.
Grossman, A. The Bright Nails Scattered on the Ground.
J.D. McClatchy, 491:Oct86-31
Grossman, J.D. Valery Bryusov and the Riddle of Russian Decadence.*
P. Davidson, 402(MLR):Oct87-1049
Grossmann, R. Phenomenology and Existentialism.
L.N. Oaklander, 484(PPR):Sep86-160
Groth, R. Die französische Kompositionslehre im 19. Jahrhunderts.
R.W. Wason, 308:Fall86-295
Grothusen, K-D., ed. Jugoslawien.
C.W. Bracewell, 575(SEER):Apr86-302
Groult, B. - see de Gouges, O.
"The Group of Discourses (Suttanipāta)." (Vol 1) (K.R. Norman, with I.B. Horner & W. Rahula, trans)
W.B. Bollée, 259(IIJ):Oct86-323
Grout, P.B. & others, eds. The Legend of Arthur in the Middle Ages.*
E.D. Kennedy, 38:Band104Heft1/2-192
M. Mills, 402(MLR):Oct87-910
R. Morris, 382(MAE):1986/2-304

Grove, L. & C. Daniels, eds. State and Society in China.
J.A. Fogel, 293(JASt):May86-566
Groves, D. - see Hogg, J.
Grübel, R., ed. Russische Erzählung, Russian Short Story, Russkiy rasskaz.
L. Burnett, 402(MLR):Jan87-265
P. Henry, 575(SEER):Apr86-272
Gruber, J. Die Dialektik des Trobar.
F. Goldin, 589:Apr86-422
Grucza, F. Zagadnienia metalinguistyki.
R. Sadziński, 682(ZPSK):Band39Heft4-495
Grudzińska-Gross, I. The Art of Solidarity.
G. Gumpert, 497(PolR):Vol31No4-325
Gruen, E.S. The Hellenistic World and the Coming of Rome.*
J. Briscoe, 123:Vol36No1-91
E. Will, 487:Summer86-212
Gruending, D. Emmett Hall.*
D.M. Schurman, 529(QQ):Autumn86-650
Grumbach, D. The Magician's Girl.
P. Deitz, 441:1Feb87-22
M. Wiggins, 617(TLS):19Jun87-669
de Grummond, N.T. A Guide to Etruscan Mirrors.
L.B. van der Meer, 394:Vol39fasc3/4-559
von der Grün, M. Die Lawine.
C. Russ, 617(TLS):15May87-524
Grünbaum, A. The Foundations of Psychoanalysis.
N. Bruss, 567:Vol60No1/2-129
M.N. Eagle, 486:Mar86-65
H. Ruttenberg, 185:Jan87-491
R.A. Sharpe, 262:Mar86-121
Grunchec, P. Les Concours d'esquisses peintes, 1816-1863.
C. Rosen & H. Zerner, 453(NYRB): 26Feb87-21
Grunchec, P. The Grand Prix de Rome.
R. Thomson, 59:Mar86-108
Grundberg, A. & K.M. Gauss. Photography and Art.
V. Goldberg, 441:6Dec87-21
Gründer, K. Reflexion der Kontinuitäten.
R. Specht, 489(PJGG):Band93Heft1-200
"Grundkurs Philosophie." (Vols 1-5, 8 & 9)
R.F. Harvanek, 258:Sep86-297
Grundy, I., ed. Samuel Johnson.*
D. Wheeler, 83:Autumn86-254
Grundy, M. Venice.
J.G. Links, 90:May86-365
Grunebaum, J.O. Private Ownership.
A. Ryan, 176:Sep/Oct87-55
Grünendahl, R. Viṣṇudharmāḥ.
J.W. de Jong, 259(IIJ):Jan86-64
Grunewald, M. Klaus Mann 1906-1949.
K.W. Jonas, 222(GR):Summer86-131
Grunfeld, F.V. Rodin.
B. Read, 441:13Dec87-1
Grünzweig, W. Charles Sealsfield.
R.L. Gale, 649(WAL):Aug86-182
Grushkin, P.D. The Art of Rock.
E. Sanders, 441:13Dec87-13
Grylls, D. The Paradox of Gissing.
P. Coustillas, 189(EA):Jul-Sep87-356
J. Symons, 617(TLS):24Jul87-803
Grypdonck, A., ed. Nederlands als taal van de wetenschap.
J. de Jong, 204(FdL):Sep86-237

Gryphius, A.   Die Übersetzungen der Erbauungsschriften Sir Richard Bakers.*   (H. Powell, ed)
  B.L. Spahr, 133:Band19Heft2-166
Grzebieniowski, T. – see "Langenscheidt's Pocket Polish Dictionary"
Grzegorek, M.   Thematization in English and Polish.
  N.J.C. Gotteri, 402(MLR):Oct86-1055
Gsell, O.   Gegensatzrelationen im Wortschatz romanischer Sprachen.
  G.F. Meier, 682(ZPSK):Band39Heft2-280
Gsteiger, M.   Wandlungen Werthers und andere Essays zur vergleichenden Literaturgeschichte.
  A. Nivelle, 549(RLC):Oct-Dec86-459
Gualís, G.M.B. – see under Borrás Gualís, G.M.
"The Guardian."*   (J.C. Stephens, ed)
  S. Varey, 677(YES):Vol16-260
Guchmann, M.M. & N.N. Semenjuk.   Zur ausbildung der Norm der deutschen Literatursprache im Bereich des Verbs (1470-1730).
  H. Penzl, 685(ZDL):2/1986-223
  C. Walther, 682(ZPSK):Band39Heft3-389
Guenancia, P.   Descartes.
  A.A. Azar, 98:Nov86-1149
"René Guénon."
  A. Calame, 450(NRF):May86-95
Guerard, A.J.   Christine/Annette.
  D. Levin, 639(VQR):Spring86-344
  I. Malin, 532(RCF):Summer86-149
Guerdan, R.   Corneille ou la vie méconnue du Shakespeare français.
  A. Couprie, 535(RHL):Jul-Aug86-740
Guérin, C. & D. Courvoisier.   Manuscrits et livres.
  F. de Marez Oyens, 517(PBSA):Vol80No1-125
de Guérin, M.   Poésie.
  C. Gely, 535(RHL):Nov-Dec86-1130
Guerlac, R. – see Hutton, J.
Gueroult, M.   Descartes' Philosophy Interpreted According to the Order of Reasons. (Vol 2)
  C. Wolf-Devine, 543:Dec86-380
Gueroult, M.   Histoire de l'histoire de la philosophie.
  A. Doz, 192(EP):Apr-Jun86-251
Guerra, J.A., ed & trans. Livro dos Cantares.
  R. Ptak, 318(JAOS):Oct/Dec85-757
Guerrero, M.J.S. – see under Sanz Guerrero, M.J.
Guers-Villate, Y.   Continuité/discontinuité de l'oeuvre durassienne.
  B.L. Knapp, 207(FR):May87-875
Guest, B. & J.M. Sellers, eds.   Enterprise and Exploitation in a Victorian Colony.
  K. Ingham, 617(TLS):20Feb87-190
Guest, I. – see Gautier, T.
Guest, J.S.   The Yezidis.
  R. Irwin, 617(TLS):22May87-543
Guglielminetti, M.   La "scuola dell'ironia."
  M. Mari, 228(GSLI):Vol163fasc523-458
  S. Vinall, 402(MLR):Jan86-232
Gugnier, G. & others.   Jean-Léon Gérôme, 1824-1904.
  R. Thomson, 59:Mar86-108
Guha, R.   Elementary Aspects of Peasant Insurgency in Colonial India.
  W. Hauser, 293(JASt):Nov85-174

Guha, R., ed.   Subaltern Studies II.
  A.A. Yang, 293(JASt):Nov85-177
Guichemerre, R. – see Scarron, P.
Guild, T.S. & H.L. Carter.   Kit Carson.*
  C. Hanyan, 106:Summer86-189
Guilhou, D.P. & others – see under Perez Guilhou, D. & others
Guillaume, G.   Foundations for a Science of Language.*
  Y. Tobin, 361:Nov86-231
Guillaume, J. & C. Pichois.   Gérard de Nerval.*
  N. Rinsler, 208(FS):Jan86-90
Guillaume de Bourges.   Livre des guerres du Seigneur et deux homélies.   (G. Dahan, ed & trans)
  M. Reydellet, 555:Vol59fasc2-343
Guillaume de Machaut.   The Judgment of the King of Bohemia (Le Jugement dou Roy de Behaingne).   (R.B. Palmer, ed and trans)
  A. Dzelzainis, 382(MAE):1986/2-322
  H.B. Garey, 589:Jan86-153
  N. Wilkins, 208(FS):Jul86-313
Guillaume le Clerc.   The Romance of Fergus.*   (W. Frescoln, ed)
  A. Gier, 72:Band223Heft2-433
Guillaumont, F.   Philosophe et augure.
  J. Linderski, 122:Oct86-330
Guillermin, J.H. & L.L. Holmstrom.   Mixed Blessings.
  G.E.J., 185:Jul87-901
Guinet, L.   Les emprunts gallo-romans au germanique (du Ier à la fin du Ve siècle).
  N.C.W. Spence, 208(FS):Jan86-119
Guinizzelli, G.   Poesie.   (E. Sanguineti, ed)
  C. Di Girolamo, 379(MedR):Dec86-446
"The Guinness Book of Records 1988."   (A. Russell, ed)
  L. Alster, 362:17&24Dec87-51
Guiraud-Weber, M.   Les Propositions sans nominatif en russe moderne.
  J.M. Kirkwood, 575(SEER):Apr86-261
Guissard, L.   Les Chemins de la nuit.
  F. de Martinoir, 450(NRF):Mar86-91
Guitarte, G.L.   Siete estudios sobre el español de América.*
  M.T. Ward, 240(HR):Winter86-106
Guitton, E. – see de Saint-Pierre, B.
Gula, R.M.   What Are They Saying about Euthanasia?
  S.P., 185:Jul87-902
Guldbrandsen, T.   Med fireflaiten åffsjår.
  E. Haugen, 563(SS):Autumn86-429
Gullón, G.   La novela como acto imaginativo.*
  P.B. Goldman, 86(BHS):Jan86-93
Gulyga, A.   Immanuel Kant.
  R. George, 484(PPR):Mar87-485
  R. Malter, 342:Band77Heft3-355
Gumpel, L.   Metaphor Reexamined.*
  D. McArthur, 323:May86-206
Gumpert, G.   Talking Tombstones.
  N. Postman, 441:8Mar87-23
Gunn, B.   The Timetables of History.
  W.N., 102(CanL):Spring86-203
Gunn, G.   The Culture of Criticism and the Criticism of Culture.
  C. Baldick, 617(TLS):6-12Nov87-1217
  C. Ricks, 441:10May87-14
Gunn, J.A.W. & others – see Disraeli, B.

Haiman, J. Hua.
E-D. Cook, 320(CJL):Fall86-285
Haiman, J., ed. Iconicity in Syntax.
D. Justice, 350:Sep87-632
Haines, J. Living off the Country.*
D. Engel, 649(WAL):Aug86-168
Haines, J. Stories We Listened To.
D. Murray, 441:29Mar87-23
Haines, J. & P. Donnelly - see Jackson, J.
Haines, M. The "Sacrestia delle Messe" of
the Florentine Cathedral.
B. Preyer, 54:Sep86-493
Hainhofer, P. Der Briefwechsel zwischen
Philipp Hainhofer und Herzog August d.J.
von Braunschweig-Lüneburg. (R. Gobiet,
ed)
H-O. Boström, 341:Vol55No2-78
T. Hausmann, 683:Band49Heft1-105
Hajdú, M. & others, eds. Tolna megye
földrajzi nevei.
T. Kesztyüs, 685(ZDL):1/1986-133
Hajdú, P. & L. Honti, eds. Studien zur
phonologischen Beschreibung uralischer
Sprachen.
H. Zikmund, 682(ZPSK):Band39Heft5-623
Ḥājib, Y.K. Wisdom of Royal Glory (Kutadgu
Bilig).* (R. Dankoff, ed & trans)
A. Schimmel, 318(JAOS):Apr/Jun85-356
Hakuta, K. Mirror of Language.*
L. Spitzer, 350:Jun87-452
Halberstam, D. The Reckoning.*
T. Fitzgerald, 385(MQR):Summer87-535
Halbfass, W. Studies in Kumārila and
Śaṅkara.*
R.V. De Smet, 318(JAOS):Apr/Jun85-373
Haldane, S. Couple Dynamics.
639(VQR):Spring86-64
Haldeman, J. Tool of the Trade.
G. Jonas, 441:7Jun87-18
Hale, N. and F. Bowers, eds. Leon Kroll.
M.S. Young, 39:Jan86-69
Hales, C. Underground.
J.W. Clark, 649(WAL):Feb87-370
Haley, S. Getting Married in Buffalo Jump.
S. Hubbell, 441:16Aug87-22
Haley, S.C. A Nest of Singing Birds.*
J. Giltrow, 102(CanL):Fall86-140
Haliczer, S., ed. Inquisition and Society
in Early Modern Europe.
A. Hamilton, 617(TLS):17Apr87-416
Halio, J.L., ed. Critical Essays on Angus
Wilson.
J.H. Stape, 189(EA):Jul-Sep86-361
Halka, C.S. Melquíades, Alchemy and
Narrative Theory.*
J. Labanyi, 402(MLR):Oct87-1011
Halkin, F. & A-J. Festugière, eds. Dix
textes inédits tirés du ménologe impérial
de Koutloumous.
J.A. Munitiz, 303(JoHS):Vol106-268
Hall, A.R. & B.A. Bembridge. Physic and
Philanthropy.
R.P.T. Davenport-Hines, 617(TLS):
20Feb87-192
Hall, D. Joyce Cary.
C. Cook, 447(N&Q):Sep85-409
Hall, D. The Happy Man.
W. Logan, 441:18Jan87-13
R. McDowell, 249(HudR):Winter87-681
L.M. Steinman, 385(MQR):Spring87-428
D. Wilson, 617(TLS):6-12Nov87-1229
Hall, D. The Ideal Bakery.
J. Casey, 441:2Aug87-14

Hall, D., J.M. Murrin & T.W. Tate, eds.
Saints and Revolutionaries.
F. Anderson, 658:Spring86-71
B.S. Schlenther, 83:Autumn86-211
Hall, D. & C.C. Olds. Winter.*
639(VQR):Summer86-105
Hall, D.D. & D.G. Allen, eds. Seventeenth-
Century New England.*
P.F. Gura, 639(VQR):Autumn86-734
C.L. Heyrman, 656(WMQ):Jul86-487
Hall, D.J. Imaging God.
B.J.T., 185:Jul87-906
Hall, G.E. Four Leagues of Pecos.
R.M. Adams, 453(NYRB):12Mar87-28
Hall, H.G. Comedy in Context.*
H.C. Knutson, 402(MLR):Oct86-1003
D.L. Rubin, 210(FrF):Jan86-108
Hall, J.H. Powers and Liberties.
B.M.D., 185:Jan87-505
Hall, J.W. Under Cover of Daylight.
C. Willeford, 441:1Nov87-18
Hall, K.M. & M.B. Wells. Du Bellay: Poems.
D.G. Coleman, 402(MLR):Jan87-198
K. Ley, 547(RF):Band98Heft3/4-429
G.H. Tucker, 208(FS):Apr86-199
Hall, N.J., with N. Burgis - see Trollope,
A.
Hall, O. The Coming of the Kid.
M. Washington, 649(WAL):Feb87-357
Hall, P. Governing the Economy.
J. Hayward, 617(TLS):20Mar87-292
Hall, P. - see Orwell, G.
Hall, R. My Life With Tiny.
R. Davenport-Hines, 617(TLS):25-
31Dec87-1421
Hall, R.A., Jr. Comparative Romance
Grammar, 3.
R. de Dardel, 603:Vol10No2-501
Hall, R.A., Jr. Proto-Romance Morphology.*
R. Wright, 545(RPh):Nov86-227
Hall, R.V. A Spy's Revenge.
N. Hiley, 617(TLS):22May87-539
Hall, S. The Fourth World.
442(NY):7Sep87-111
Hall, S., with J. Ramsey, eds. Approaches
to Teaching Wordsworth's Poetry.
L.J. Leff, 365:Spring/Summer86-159
Hall, S.S. Invisible Frontiers.
D.J. Kevles, 441:27Sep87-41
Hall, W.E. Shadowy Heroes.
J. Ronsley, 675(YER):Vol8No1/2-127
Hallberg, P. Diktens bildspråk.
N.L. Jensen, 562(Scan):May86-99
von Hallberg, R. American Poetry and Cul-
ture, 1945-1980.*
T. Gardner, 219(GaR):Winter86-1016
A. Golding, 27(AL):Oct86-468
S. Paul, 301(JEGP):Oct86-602
W.H. Pritchard, 31(ASch):Autumn86-553
von Hallberg, R., ed. Canons.*
D.E. Latané, Jr., 577(SHR):Spring86-175
L.A. Renza, 659(ConL):Summer87-257
R. Shusterman, 290(JAAC):Fall86-97
de la Halle, A. - see under Adam de la
Halle
Halle, D. America's Working Man.
B. Greenberg, 658:Winter86-330
Halle, M. & others, eds. Semiosis.
D. Shepherd, 575(SEER):Jul86-453
A. Shukman, 402(MLR):Jan87-261
Haller, H., ed. Il Panfilo veneziano.*
P. Frassica, 275(IQ):Winter86-107

Haller, R., ed. Schlick und Neurath, ein Symposion.*
  G. Siegwart, 53(AGP):Band68Heft3-339
Halleran, M.R. Stagecraft in Euripides.*
  E.M. Craik, 303(JoHS):Vol106-212
  J. Wilkins, 123:Vol36No2-305
Hallett, J.P. Fathers and Daughters in Roman Society.*
  S. Dixon, 24:Spring86-125
  T. Fleming, 121(CJ):Oct-Nov86-73
  S. Martin, 313:Vol76-293
  R.P. Saller, 122:Oct86-354
  S. Treggiari, 123:Vol36No1-102
Hallett, M. Cantorian Set Theory and Limitation of Size.
  P. Clark, 393(Mind):Oct86-523
  J. Mayberry, 479(PhQ):Jul86-429
Halleux, R. Les Alchimistes grecs. (Vol 1)
  J. Dillon, 123:Vol36No1-35
Halliday, J. - see Hoxha, E.
Halliday, M.A.K. An Introduction to Functional Grammar.
  R. Hudson, 353:Vol24No4-791
  G.D. Morley, 361:Jun86-186
Hallin, D.C. The Uncensored War.*
  639(VQR):Autumn86-132
Halliwell, L. Seats in All Parts.*
  B. Weeks, 18:Nov86-63
Halliwell, S. Aristotle's "Poetics."
  A. Nehamas, 617(TLS):9Jan87-27
Halloran, R. To Arm a Nation.*
  442(NY):26Jan87-86
Hallowell, J.H. - see Voegelin, E.
Halmøy, J-O. Le gérondif.*
  M.J. Albalá, 548:Jul-Dec86-445
Halpenny, F.G. - see "Dictionary of Canadian Biography/Dictionnaire Biographique du Canada"
Halperin, C.J. Russia and the Golden Horde.
  639(VQR):Spring86-53
Halperin, D.M. Before Pastoral.
  M.C. Howatson, 447(N&Q):Mar85-88
  C. Segal, 131(CL):Winter86-92
  G.J. de Vries, 394:Vol39fasc3/4-481
  G.B. Walsh, 122:Jan86-85
Halperin, J. The Life of Jane Austen.*
  A.S. Grossman, 31(ASch):Spring86-272
  P. Honan, 83:Spring86-99
  D. Le Faye, 541(RES):Aug86-426
  K.B. Mann, 579(SAQ):Summer86-301
  L.D. Mitchell, 95(CLAJ):Sep86-104
  R.W. Rogers, 301(JEGP):Oct86-569
  B. Roth, 594:Summer86-209
  J. Thompson, 536(Rev):Vol8-21
Halperin, M.H. Nuclear Fallacy.
  G. Overholser, 441:3May87-12
  P. Williams, 617(TLS):20-26Nov87-1270
Halpern, D., ed. The Art of the Tale.
  J. Bayley, 617(TLS):27Mar87-317
Halpern, D., ed. On Nature.
  J. Tallmadge, 441:14Jun87-29
Haltunnen, K. Confidence Men and Painted Women.
  R.A. Banes, 106:Spring86-93
Hamann, B. The Reluctant Empress.
  H. Pakula, 441:8Feb87-25
Hambro, C. Arnulf Øverland.
  S. Lyngstad, 563(SS):Summer86-335
Hambuch, W. Der Weinbau von Pusztavám.
  K. Manherz, 685(ZDL):1/1986-96

Hamburg, G.M. Politics of the Russian Nobility 1881-1905.*
  D. Lieven, 575(SEER):Jul86-472
Hamburger, K. Liszt.
  A. Walker, 617(TLS):10Jul87-737
Hamburger, K. Logique des genres littéraires.
  M. Jarrety, 450(NRF):Sep86-112
Hamburger, M. After the Second Flood.
  G.P. Butler, 617(TLS):13Mar87-269
de Hamel, C. A History of Illuminated Manuscripts.*
  B. Cron, 503:Autumn86-140
  C. Reynolds, 90:Nov86-835
  78(BC):Summer86-145
de Hamel, C. Western Manuscripts and Minatures.
  F. de Marez Oyens, 517(PBSA):Vol80No1-125
de Hamel, C.F.R. Glossed Books of the Bible and the Origins of the Parisian Book Trade.
  M. Gibson, 354:Jun86-166
  C.M. Kauffmann, 39:Feb86-140
  78(BC):Summer86-145
Hamer, M. Writing by Numbers.
  J. Adlard, 617(TLS):19Jun87-672
Hamid, S. Disastrous Twilight.
  W.R. Louis, 617(TLS):28Aug87-915
Hamill, D. Pig in the Middle.
  M.R.D. Foot, 176:Feb87-46
Hamill, S. Fatal Pleasure.
  L.L. Lee, 649(WAL):Aug86-169
Hamilton, D.M. "The Tools of My Trade."
  S.I. Gatti, 590:Jun87-60
Hamilton, E. The Destruction of Lord Rosebery. (D. Brooks, ed)
  R. Foster, 617(TLS):25Sep-1Oct87-1038
Hamilton, N. Monty: Final Years of the Field Marshal, 1944-1976.*
  442(NY):27Apr87-105
Hamilton, P. Coleridge's Poetics.*
  L.M. Findlay, 447(N&Q):Jun85-276
Hamilton, P. Mr. Stimpson and Mr. Gorse.
  362:1Oct87-25
Hamilton, P. Twenty Thousand Streets Under the Sky.
  D. Lessing, 362:17Sep87-23
  D. Thomas, 176:Jul/Aug87-32
Hamilton, P. Wordsworth.
  L. Newlyn, 617(TLS):15May87-525
Hamilton, R.F. & J.D. Wright. The State of the Masses.
  S.F., 185:Apr87-690
Hamilton, R.G. Literatura Africana Literatura Necessária, II.
  G. Moser, 538(RAL):Spring86-144
Hamilton-Paterson, J. Playing with Water.
  D. Chandler, 617(TLS):14Aug87-883
  A. Eames, 362:3Sep87-29
Hamilton-Paterson, J. The View From Mount Dog.
  J. Mellors, 362:1Jan87-22
Hamlyn, D.W. A History of Western Philosophy.
  J. Waldron, 617(TLS):10Apr87-380
Hamlyn, D.W. Metaphysics.*
  J.E.J. Altham, 479(PhQ):Jul86-443
Hamm, J. - see Križanić, J.
Hamm, J-J. - see "Cahiers Stendhal"
Hammel, E. Guadalcanal: The Carrier Battles.
  R. Sherrod, 441:20Dec87-17

Hammer, A. & N. Lyndon. Hammer.
T. Morgan, 441:24May87-6
A.J. Sherman, 617(TLS):21Aug87-893
Hammer, G. Good Faith and Credit.
M.S. Chertoff, 390:May86-56
Hammer, G. & K-H. zur Mühlen, eds. Luth-
eriana.
S.H. Hendrix, 551(RenQ):Winter86-740
Hammer, R. The CBS Murders.
H. Weil, 441:21Jun87-23
Hammerly, H. Synthesis in Second Language
Teaching.* An Integrated Theory of Lan-
guage Teaching and Its Practical Con-
sequences.
T.S. Parry, 399(MLJ):Summer86-165
Hammick, G. People for Lunch.
L. Duguid, 617(TLS):17Jul87-766
Hammond, B.S. Pope and Bolingbroke.*
F.M. Keener, 401(MLQ):Mar85-81
Hammond, G. - see Ralegh, W.
Hammond, J.R. - see Wells, H.G.
Hammond, N. Twentieth Century Wildlife
Artists.
E. Dunn, 617(TLS):5Jun87-615
Hammond, N.G.L. Three Historians of Alex-
ander the Great.*
A.M. Devine, 24:Spring86-123
C.R. Rubincam, 487:Summer86-208
Hammond, P. John Oldham and the Renewal
of Classical Culture.*
P.E. Hewison, 447(N&Q):Jun85-265
Hammond, R.M. Cocteau reflects for Me/I
reflect for Him.
J. Decock, 207(FR):Dec86-282
Hammond, T.T., ed. Witnesses to the
Origins of the Cold War.
J.L. Gaddis, 617(TLS):8May87-479
Hamon, H. & P. Rotman. Génération. (Vol
1)
R.W. Johnson, 617(TLS):31Jul87-811
Hamon, P. Texte et idéologie.*
R. Ripoll, 535(RHL):Jul-Aug86-805
Hamowy, R. Canadian Medicine.
D. Coburn, 529(QQ):Spring86-205
Hampl, P. Spillville.
N. Willard, 441:26Jul87-6
442(NY):14Sep87-135
Hampshire, S. Morality and Conflict.*
L. Code, 154:Winter86-773
Hampson, N. Will and Circumstance.*
K.M. Baker, 173(ECS):Summer87-488
Hampson, R. - see Kipling, R.
Hampton, C. Les Liaisons dangereuses.
L. Sante, 453(NYRB):13Aug87-28
Hampton, S. & K. Llewellyn, eds. The
Penguin Book of Australian Women Poets.
M. Bradstock, 67:Nov86-307
C. James, 617(TLS):27Nov-3Dec87-1327
Hancock, G., ed. Moving Off the Map.
F. Davey, 99:Nov86-40
Hancock, I. The Pariah Syndrome.
A. Codrescu, 441:16Aug87-29
Hand, J.O. & others. The Age of Bruegel.
L. Campbell, 617(TLS):6-12Nov87-1230
"Handbook of Latin American Studies: No.
44." (D. Moyano Martin, ed)
J.H. Valdivieso, 238:May86-323
"Handbook of Latin American Studies." (No.
45 & 46) (D. Moyano Martin, ed)
N. Sfeir de Gonzalez, 263(RIB):
Vol36No4-498

Handke, P. Die Abwesenheit. Nachmittag
eines Schriftstellers.
M. Hofmann, 617(TLS):9-15Oct87-1113
Handke, P. Le Chinois de la douleur.
A. Andreucci, 450(NRF):Dec86-107
Handke, P. Slow Homecoming.
K. Agena, 473(PR):Vol53No3-468
van Handle, D.C. "Das spiel vor der
Menge."
S. McMullen, 402(MLR):Oct87-1038
Handler, D. Kiddo.
D. Freeman, 441:3May87-37
Handley, G. - see Eliot, G.
Handlin, J.F. Action in Late Ming
Thought.*
J. Berling, 244(HJAS):Jun86-269
C. Brokaw, 293(JASt):Feb86-375
Chu Hung-Lam, 302:Vol2No1-66
Handscombe, J., R.A. Orem & B.P. Taylor,
eds. On TESOL '83.
F.J. Bosco, 399(MLJ):Spring86-58
Handwerk, G.J. Irony and Ethics in Narra-
tive.
R. Chambers, 141:Fall86-484
W. Gibson, 128(CE):Dec86-832
S.A.H., 185:Jul87-895
Hankey, J., ed. Plays in Performance:
"Othello."
J. Wilders, 617(TLS):30Oct-5Nov87-1197
Hankey, R. & D. Little, eds. Essays in
Honour of Agathe Thornton.
D.A. Kidd, 67:May86-114
Hankins, T.L. Science & the Enlightenment.
W. Hackmann, 83:Autumn86-300
639(VQR):Winter86-8
Hänlein-Schäfer, H. Veneratio Augusti.
S.R.F. Price, 313:Vol76-300
E.T. Salmon, 124:Jul-Aug87-461
Hanley, S.B. & A.P. Wolf, eds. Family and
Population in East Asian History.
C. Mosk, 293(JASt):May86-563
Hanlon, J. Beggar Your Neighbours.*
A. Sheps, 617(TLS):16Jan87-54
"Forman Hanna: Pictorial Photographer of
the Southwest."
J. Harris, 649(WAL):Feb87-385
Hanna, R. 3d, ed. The Index of Middle
English Prose: Handlist I.*
R. Beadle, 617(TLS):24Jul87-808
S.S. Hussey, 402(MLR):Apr87-435
O.S. Pickering, 72:Band223Heft2-392
Hannah, B. Captain Maximus.*
T. McGonigle, 532(RCF):Summer86-155
Hannah, B. Hey Jack!
T.R. Edwards, 441:1Nov87-26
Hannay, A. Kierkegaard.
R. Schacht, 482(PhR):Apr86-302
Hannay, M. English Existentials in Func-
tional Grammar.
P. Erdmann, 257(IRAL):Aug86-262
Hannay, M.P., ed. Silent But for the
Word.*
R.P. Batteiger, 568(SCN):Winter86-72
E. Rosenberg, 551(RenQ):Winter86-769
639(VQR):Summer86-88
Hannigan, J.P. As I Have Loved You.
S.P., 185:Jan87-497
Hansen, B. and others. Englische Lexikol-
ogie.*
H. Ulherr, 300:Apr86-137
Hansen, C. Language and Logic in Ancient
China.*
W.G. Boltz, 318(JAOS):Apr/Jun85-309

Hardy, T. The Collected Letters of Thomas
Hardy.* (Vol 5) (R.L. Purdy & M. Mill-
gate, eds)
P. Coustillas, 189(EA):Jan–Mar87–90
J. Halperin, 395(MFS):Summer86–300
H. Orel, 177(ELT):Vol29No1–92
639(VQR):Spring86–50
Hardy, T. The Collected Letters of Thomas
Hardy. (Vol 6) (R.L. Purdy & M. Mill-
gate, eds)
G. Cavaliero, 617(TLS):3Jul87–723
Hardy, T. The Complete Poetical Works of
Thomas Hardy.* (Vol 1) (S. Hynes, ed)
P. Coustillas, 189(EA):Jan–Mar87–93
J. Grundy, 402(MLR):Jul86–727
529(QQ):Summer86–459
Hardy, T. The Complete Poetical Works of
Thomas Hardy.* (Vols 2 & 3) (S. Hynes,
ed)
P. Coustillas, 189(EA):Jan–Mar87–93
J. Grundy, 402(MLR):Jul86–727
K. Wilson, 177(ELT):Vol29No4–431
529(QQ):Summer86–459
Hardy, T. Far from the Madding Crowd. (J.
Gibson, ed)
P. Coustillas, 189(EA):Jan–Mar87–91
Hardy, T. Far from the Madding Crowd.
(R.C. Schweik, ed)
P. Coustillas, 189(EA):Jan–Mar87–92
Hardy, T. Thomas Hardy: Selected Poems.*
(W. Davies, ed)
P. Coustillas, 189(EA):Jan–Mar87–114
Hardy, T. The Life and Work of Thomas
Hardy by Thomas Hardy.* (M. Millgate,
ed)
J. Halperin, 395(MFS):Summer86–300
K. Wilson, 177(ELT):Vol29No4–431
Hardy, T. The Literary Notebooks of Thomas
Hardy.* (L.A. Björk, ed)
J. Halperin, 395(MFS):Summer86–300
D. Kramer, 536(Rev):Vol8–1
Hardy, T. The Oxford Authors: Thomas
Hardy. (S. Hynes, ed)
P. Coustillas, 189(EA):Jan–Mar87–93
P. Drew, 402(MLR):Apr87–454
529(QQ):Summer86–459
Hardy, T. Tess of the d'Urbervilles.* (J.
Grindle & S. Gatrell, eds)
K.M. Hewitt, 447(N&Q):Jun85–283
"Thomas Hardy Annual." (No 3) (N. Page,
ed)
K. Brady, 637(VS):Winter87–283
R.K. Anderson, 395(MFS):Winter86–656
Hare, D. Plenty.
B. Grantham, 157:No160–47
Hare, J.E. & C.B. Joynt. Ethics and Inter-
national Affairs.
N. Dower, 518:Apr86–118
Hare, P.H. A Woman's Quest for Science.
B.N. Chiñas, 650(WF):Oct86–298
Hare, R.M. Plato.
M. Narcy, 192(EP):Apr–Jun86–255
Hare, T.B. Zeami's Style.
M.J. Nearman, 407(MN):Winter86–512
Hare, W. In Defence of Open-Mindedness.*
M. Schiralli, 529(QQ):Spring86–185
Lord Harewood, ed. Kobbé's Complete Opera
Book. (10th ed)
J. Rosselli, 617(TLS):17Apr87–409
Hargreaves, J. Sport, Power and Culture.
S. Green, 617(TLS):10Apr87–388
Harig, L. Ordnung ist das ganze Leben.
J.J. White, 617(TLS):15May87–524

Haring, L. Malagasy Tale Index.*
D.J. Crowley, 538(RAL):Summer86–308
Harker, D. Fakesong.
D.K. Wilgus, 637(VS):Autumn86–133
Harle, J.C. The Art and Architecture of
the Indian Subcontinent.
A. Robinson, 362:15Jan87–22
"Harlem Renaissance."
J. Haskins, 441:1Mar87–21
Harlen, E. Unterschiedliche Versuche vor-
nehmlich an Paul Ernst. (K.A. Kutzbach,
ed)
K. Hanson, 221(GQ):Summer86–453
Harley, B. Age in Second Language Acquisi-
tion.
W.D. Davies, 350:Sep87–680
Harley, J.B. & D. Woodward, eds. The His-
tory of Cartography. (Vol 1)
J.C. Stone, 617(TLS):30Oct–5Nov87–1204
J.N. Wilford, 441:20Sep87–13
Harlow, R. Felice.
L.K. MacKendrick, 99:May86–38
Harman, G. Change in View.
M. Hollis, 617(TLS):6Feb87–132
Harman, I.M., ed. National Directory of
Latin Americanists. (3rd ed)
M.S. Sable, 263(RIB):Vol36No2–182
Harman, P.M., ed. Wranglers and Physi-
cists.
H.W. Becher, 637(VS):Spring87–440
Harmening, D. Der Anfang von Dracula.*
F. Shaw, 402(MLR):Jan86–245
Harmon, M., ed. The Irish Writer and the
City.*
R.E. Ward, 174(Éire):Spring86–150
Harms, W. & M. Schilling, with others, eds.
Deutsche illustrierte Flugblätter des 16.
und 17. Jahrhunderts. (Vol 1, Pt 1)
W.A. Coupe, 402(MLR):Apr87–510
Harneit, R. Die handschriftlichen Unter-
lagen der französischen Buchverwaltung
im Ancien Régime (1700–1750).*
J. Lough, 208(FS):Jul86–336
Harner, J.L. On Compiling an Annotated
Bibliography.*
87(BB):Jun86–120
Harney, M.J. Intentionality, Sense and the
Mind.
D. Bell, 518:Apr86–107
R. Grigg, 63:Jun86–229
Harnoncourt, N. Le Dialogue musical.
A. Suied, 450(NRF):Mar86–118
Harper, G.M. The Making of Yeats's "A
Vision."
C. Rawson, 617(TLS):24Jul87–783
Harper, G.M. W.B. Yeats and W.T. Horton.
H. Summerfield, 675(YER):Vol8No1/2–139
Harper, H. Between Language and Silence.*
S. McNichol, 402(MLR):Apr86–462
Harpham, G.G. On the Grotesque.*
D.W. Crawford, 289:Summer86–119
Harrán, D. "Maniera" e il madrigale.
J. Chater, 410(M&L):Apr86–169
"Harrap's Concise French and English Dic-
tionary." (P. Forbes & M.H. Smith, eds;
rev by H. Knox)
J.E. Joseph, 399(MLJ):Autumn86–306
"Harrap's Slang Dictionary: English–
French/French–English."* (rev) (G.A.
Marks & C.B. Johnson, comps; J. Pratt,
ed)
L. Vines, 399(MLJ):Spring86–62

Harrison, G.A. The Enthusiast.*
  R.S. Smith, 106:Winter86-469
Harrison, J. The Theory and Practice of
  Rivers.
  J. Rohrkemper, 115:Fall86-535
Harrison, J.A. - see Horace
Harrison, K. After Six Days.
  K. Tudor, 198:Fall86-96
Harrison, L.E. Underdevelopment is a State
  of Mind.
  A. Riding, 441:22Feb87-28
Harrison, P. Seabirds of the World.
  C. Perrins, 617(TLS):2-8Oct87-1087
Harrison, P.A. Behaving Brazilian.
  F. Tarallo, 355(LSoc):Dec86-560
Harrison, R. Bentham.*
  J. Kidder, 484(PPR):Jun87-681
Harrison, R. Deathwatch.
  639(VQR):Summer86-93
Harrison, R. Lessing: "Minna von Barn-
  helm."
  H.B. Nisbet, 402(MLR):Oct87-1026
Harrison, R.L. Aviation Lore in Faulkner.
  C.S. Brown, 569(SR):Winter86-167
Harrison, T. Dramatic Verse 1973-1985.*
  B. Grantham, 157:No160-47
Harrison, T. Selected Poems.*
  D. McDuff, 565:Winter85/86-72
  R. Richman, 441:29Nov87-25
Harrison, T. V.
  T. Eagleton, 493:Jun86-20
  A.Y., 148:Autumn86-119
Harshav, B. & B., eds. American Yiddish
  Poetry.
  A. Brumberg, 617(TLS):23-29Oct87-1174
Hart, D. Guardians of the Khaibar Pass.
  C. Lindholm, 293(JASt):Aug86-872
Hart, G. The Strategies of Zeus.
  B. O'Reilly, 441:25Jan87-20
Hart, H. The Poetry of Geoffrey Hill.
  V.S., 295(JML):Nov86-486
Hart, H.L.A. Essays on Bentham, Jurispru-
  dence and Political Theory.*
  J. King, 543:Jun87-777
Hart, H.L.A. & T. Honore. Causation in the
  Law. (2nd ed)
  L.C. Becker, 185:Apr87-664
  J.P.W. Cartwright, 518:Oct86-254
Hart, J.D. The Concise Oxford Companion
  to American Literature.
  M. Couturier, 189(EA):Oct-Dec87-483
Hart, J.D. The Oxford Companion to
  American Literature.
  P. Preston, 447(N&Q):Sep85-428
Hart, L. The Complete Lyrics of Lorenz
  Hart.* (D. Hart & R. Kimball, eds)
  442(NY):2Feb87-101
Hart, M. Act One.
  617(TLS):10Apr87-397
Hart, R. Seascape with Dead Figures.
  T.J. Binyon, 617(TLS):12Jun87-626
Hart-Davis, D. Hitler's Games.*
  639(VQR):Autumn86-119
Hart-Davis, D. - see Lascelles, A.
Hart-Davis, R. - see Sassoon, S.
Hart-Davis, R. - see Wilde, O.
Harte, N. The University of London 1836-
  1986.
  T.J. Reed, 617(TLS):13Mar87-262
Harter, E.C. The Lost Colony of the Con-
  federacy.
  O. Marshall, 617(TLS):4-11Sep87-959

Harth, E. Ideology and Culture in Seven-
  teenth-Century France.*
  H. Mydlarski, 345:May86-251
  N. Nahra, 125:Fall85-93
Harth, H. - see Poggio Bracciolini, G.F.
Hartigan, F.X., ed. The Accounts of
  Alphonse of Poitiers, 1243-1248.
  W.C. Jordan, 589:Jan86-233
Hartigan, K.V., ed. The Many Forms of
  Drama.
  K. Worth, 402(MLR):Apr87-426
Hartigan, K.V., ed. To Hold a Mirror to
  Nature. (Vol 1)
  S. Williams, 107(CRCL):Jun86-296
Härtl, H., ed. "Die Wahlverwandtschaften."
  A. Klingenberg, 654(WB):12/1986-2102
Hartle, A. The Modern Self in Rousseau's
  "Confessions."*
  J. Voisine, 535(RHL):Sep-Oct86-922
Härtling, P. Waiblingers Augen.
  J.J. White, 617(TLS):9-15Oct87-1114
Hartman, E. French Romantics on Progress.*
  C. Crossley, 535(RHL):Mar-Apr86-302
Hartman, G.H., ed. Bitburg in Moral and
  Political Perspective.*
  G. Eley, 385(MQR):Spring87-439
Hartman, G.H. Easy Pieces.
  E.P. Nassar, 396(ModA):Spring86-170
von Hartmann, L-M. Modalitäten des
  Nichtstuns.
  F.J. Hausmann, 257(IRAL):May86-171
Hartmann, R.R.K. Contrastive Textology.
  D. Sternemann, 682(ZPSK):Band39Heft4-
  500
Hartmann, R.R.K., ed. LEXeter '83 Proceed-
  ings.
  M. Görlach, 72:Band223Heft2-381
  G. Kempcke, 682(ZPSK):Band39Heft6-724
Hartmann von Aue. Der arme Heinrich. (H.
  Paul, ed; 15th ed rev by U. Pretzel)
  B. Plate, 133:Band19Heft3/4-332
Hartmann von Aue. Erec. (J.W. Thomas,
  trans)
  K.J. Meyer, 406:Spring86-95
Hartmann von Aue. Gregorius. (H. Paul,
  ed; 13th ed rev by B. Wachinger)
  S. Jefferis, 589:Jan86-156
  B. Plate, 133:Band19Heft2-160
Hartmann von Aue. Iwein. (W. Mohr, trans)
  W.C.M., 400(MLN):Apr86-733
Hartnett, M. O Bruadair.
  J. Lanchester, 493:Jun86-113
Hartnoll, P., comp. Plays and Players.
  J. Reading, 611(TN):Vol40No1-47
Hartog, D. Candy from Strangers.
  S. Thesen, 376:Dec86-139
Hartsfield, L.K. The American Response to
  Professional Crime, 1870-1917.
  M.T. Inge, 27(AL):May86-308
Hartshorne, C. Omnipotence and Other
  Theological Mistakes.*
  D.W. Viney, 389(MQ):Autumn86-144
Hartung, G. Literatur und Ästhetik des
  deutschen Faschismus.
  L. Krenzlin, 654(WB):11/1986-1928
Hartung, W. Süddeutschland in der frühen
  Merowingerzeit.
  I. Boba, 589:Jul86-735
Hartwell, D. Age of Wonders.
  L. Leith, 561(SFS):Mar86-87
  G.K. Wolfe, 395(MFS):Spring86-133

160

Haugen, E. Scandinavian Language Structure.
  W.P. Lehmann, 320(CJL):Fall86-290
Haugen, E. Die skandinavischen Sprachen.
  A. Liberman, 563(SS):Spring86-191
  J. Orešnik, 215(GL):Vol26No1-68
Haugen, E.L. A Bibliography of Scandinavian Dictionaries.
  M.J. Blackwell, 399(MLJ):Spring86-75
  K. Brookfield, 562(Scan):May86-105
  P.L. Hjorth, 301(JEGP):Oct86-606
  L.E. Janus, 563(SS):Spring86-189
Haule, J.M. & P.H. Smith, Jr. Concordances to the Novels of Virginia Woolf.
  J. Marcus, 40(AEB):Vol8No4-272
Hauptman, P.C., R. Leblanc & M.B. Wesche. Second Language Performance Testing/ L'Evaluation de la performance en langue seconde.
  E.J. Matte, 399(MLJ):Winter86-418
Hauptman, R. The Pathological Vision.*
  T. Dawson, 161(DUJ):Jun86-388
Hauptmeier, H. & S.J. Schmidt. Einführung in die Empirische Literaturwissenschaft.
  J. Strutz, 602:Band17Heft2-305
von Hausen, F. Lieder. (G. Schweikle, ed & trans)
  O. Sayce, 680(ZDP):Band105Heft1-137
Hauser, T. The Black Lights.
  P. Smith, 617(TLS):18-24Dec87-1412
Hausman, C.R. A Discourse on Novelty and Creation.
  P.C.L. Tang, 289:Fall86-113
Hausmann, F.J., ed. Die französische Sprache von heute.
  J.N. Green, 208(FS):Oct86-498
  B. Henschel, 682(ZPSK):Band39Heft2-295
  D. Nehls, 257(IRAL):May86-177
Madame du Hausset. Mémoires sur Louis XV et Madame de Pompadour.
  J. Aeply, 450(NRF):Mar86-88
Havard, W.C. The Recovery of Political Theory.*
  D. Germino, 396(ModA):Summer/Fall86-307
Havel, V. Vaclav Havel: or Living in Truth. (J. Vladislav, ed)
  T. Venclova, 441:19Jul87-12
Havemann, E. Bloodsong.
  M. Bloom, 441:23Aug87-16
Havens, T.R.H. Artist and Patron in Post-War Japan.
  B. Powell, 161(DUJ):Dec85-211
Haverkamp, A. Aufbruch und Gestaltung: Deutschland, 1056-1273.
  J.M. Powell, 589:Oct86-933
Haverkate, H. Speech Acts, Speakers and Hearers.
  K. Aijmer, 596(SL):Vol40No2-186
Hawes, D.S. - see Hubbard, K.
Hawes, G. The Philippine State and the Marcos Regime.
  D. Chandler, 617(TLS):14Aug87-883
Hawkes, J. Adventures in the Alaskan Skin Trade.*
  P. Lewis, 565:Summer86-57
  639(VQR):Spring86-56
Hawkes, J. Innocence in Extremis.
  J. Byrne, 532(RCF):Fall86-127
Hawkes, T. That Shakespeherean Rag.*
  M. Dodsworth, 175:Summer86-192

Hawkesworth, C. Ivo Andrić.
  E.D. Goy, 575(SEER):Apr86-285
  D.A. Norris, 402(MLR):Jan87-272
  F. Rosslyn, 97(CQ):Vol15No1-89
Hawkey, R. It.
  N. Callendar, 441:8Feb87-20
Hawkins, D. The Tess Opera.
  A.F.L.T., 412:May85-140
Hawkins, H. The Devil's Party.*
  M. Charney, 551(RenQ):Winter86-810
  T.W. Craik, 541(RES):Nov86-563
  M. Dodsworth, 175:Summer86-192
  M. Willems, 189(EA):Jul-Sep86-334
Hawkins, J.A. Word Order Universals.
  J. Aitchison, 361:Nov86-191
Hawkins, J. Introducing Phonology.*
  R. Penny, 402(MLR):Jan86-153
Hawkins, R.E. Common Indian Words in English.
  G. Bourcier, 189(EA):Jan-Mar87-112
Hawks, E.H. A Woman Doctor's Civil War. (G. Schwartz, ed)
  K.C. Berkeley, 579(SAQ):Summer86-317
Hawley, H. Grasshopper.
  P.M. St. Pierre, 102(CanL):Summer86-121
Hawthorn, J., ed. The British Working-Class Novel in the Twentieth Century.
  W.K. Buckley, 594:Summer86-211
  C. Pawling, 366:Spring86-134
Hawthorn, J., ed. Narrative.
  H. Bredin, 89(BJA):Spring86-176
  A. Morvan, 189(EA):Jul-Sep87-326
Hawthorne, N. The Letters, 1813-1843.* The Letters, 1843-1853.* (T. Woodson, L.N. Smith & N.H. Pearson, eds of both)
  R.H. Fogle, 27(AL):Oct86-441
  J.L. Idol, Jr., 301(JEGP):Oct86-586
  H. McNeil, 617(TLS):22May87-553
Haxton, B. Dominion.*
  M. Boruch, 29(APR):Mar/Apr87-22
  B. Raffel, 363(LitR):Summer87-636
Haxton, B. The Lay of Eleanore and Irene.
  455:Dec86-64
Hay, E.K. T.S. Eliot's Negative Way.
  D.S. Bonds, 301(JEGP):Jan86-153
  G. Reeves, 402(MLR):Jan87-191
Hay, J. The Immortal Wilderness.
  S. Salisbury, 441:8Feb87-25
Hay, M.V. The Life of Robert Sidney, Earl of Leicester.
  G.F. Waller, 539:Spring87-185
Hayashi, T. James Joyce.
  R.B., 295(JML):Nov86-495
Hayden, D. Redesigning the American Dream.*
  S. McMurry, 658:Spring86-96
Hayden, R. Collected Poems. (F. Glaysher, ed)
  J.F. Cotter, 249(HudR):Spring86-158
  P. Stitt, 219(GaR):Winter86-1021
Haydon, G., ed. Education and Values.
  A. Wooldridge, 617(TLS):4-10Dec87-1341
Hayes, J. The Rural Communities of Hong Kong.
  J. Strauch, 302:Vol22No1-95
Hayes, J.W. Greek and Italian Black-Gloss Wares and Related Wares in the Royal Ontario Museum.
  D.W.J. Gill, 313:Vol76-312
  S.I. Rotroff, 487:Summer86-250
Hayes, P. Industry and Ideology.
  B.A. Carroll, 441:7Jun87-31

Hayles, N.K. The Cosmic Web.*
  C.E., 561(SFS):Jul86-209
  S. Peterfreund, 301(JEGP):Jan86-156
Hayley, B. Carleton's "Traits and Stories"
  and the 19th Century Anglo-Irish Tradi-
  tion.
  H. Pyle, 541(RES):Feb86-109
Hayman, D. - see Sollers, P.
Hayman, P., J. Marchant & T. Prater.
  Shorebirds.
  E. Dunn, 617(TLS):16Jan87-70
Hayman, R. Brecht.*
  S. Mews, 221(GQ):Winter86-106
Hayman, R. Günter Grass.
  J.W. Rohlfs, 402(MLR):Apr87-530
Hayman, R. Sartre.
  T. Bishop, 441:7Jun87-11
  J. Weightman, 453(NYRB):13Aug87-42
Haymes, E., ed. Ortnit und Wolfdietrich.
  A.C., 400(MLN):Apr86-736
  J.L. Flood, 402(MLR):Oct86-1037
Haymon, S.T. Death of a God.
  N. Callendar, 441:26Apr87-37
  G. Kaufman, 362:7May87-26
Hayne, P.H. A Man of Letters in the Nine-
  teenth-Century South.* (R.S. Moore, ed)
  L. Willson, 569(SR):Winter86-131
Haynes, A. The White Bear.
  P. Collinson, 617(TLS):13-19Nov87-1256
Haynes, J.I. William Faulkner.
  M. Millgate, 392:Spring86-133
Haynes, S. Etruscan Bronzes.
  B. Cook, 90:Nov86-827
  R. Higgins, 39:Nov86-453
Hays, M. - see Szondi, P.
Hayward, D. & A. Duhaime, eds. Haïku.
  M. Parmentier, 102(CanL):Spring86-182
Haywood, C.R. Trails South.
  L. Milazzo, 584(SWR):Autumn86-538
Haywood, E. The History of Miss Betsy
  Thoughtless.
  P. Raine, 617(TLS):6-12Nov87-1216
Haywood, E. & B. Jones, eds. Dante Com-
  parisons.
  G. Cambon, 276:Autumn86-311
  J. Took, 278(IS):Vol41-129
Haywood, I. Faking It.
  T. Phillips, 617(TLS):27Mar87-336
  442(NY):31Aug87-98
de la Haza, J.M.R. - see under Ruano de la
  Haza, J.M.
Hazas, A.R. - see under Rey Hazas, A.
Hazen, M.H. & R.M. The Music Men.
  P. Kountz, 441:5Jul87-10
Head, R. The Indian Style.*
  B.C. Bloomfield, 324:Sep87-784
  P.C., 90:Nov86-837
  T. Wilcox, 39:Nov86-454
Headings, P.R. T.S. Eliot. (rev)
  A.V.C. Schmidt, 402(MLR):Jan86-188
Headington, C. Britten.
  V. Montgomery, 465:Autumn86-135
Heald, T. The Character of Cricket.
  N. Andrew, 362:3Dec87-34
  D. Durrant, 364:Aug/Sep86-156
Healey, E.C. & K. Cushman - see Lawrence,
  D.H. and A. Lowell
Healy, P. - see Gray, J.
Heaney, S. The Haw Lantern.
  N. Corcoran, 617(TLS):26Jun87-681
  P. Forbes, 362:9Jul87-29
  M. Rudman, 441:20Dec87-12

Heaney, S. Preoccupations.
  G. O'Brien, 97(CQ):Vol15No1-70
Heaney, S. Station Island.*
  J. Cobley, 376:Mar86-128
  A. Haberer, 189(EA):Jul-Sep86-365
  E.G. Ingersoll, 174(Éire):Spring86-139
  D. McDuff, 565:Winter85/86-72
  G. O'Brien, 97(CQ):Vol15No1-70
  D. Tall, 473(PR):Vol53No3-478
Heaney, S. Sweeney Astray.*
  D. McDuff, 565:Winter85/86-72
  G. O'Brien, 97(CQ):Vol15No1-70
Heaps, L. A Boy Called Nam.
  P. Demers, 102(CanL):Winter85-163
Heaps, L. The Rebel in the House.
  N. Wiseman, 298:Spring86-144
Hearn, M.F. Ripon Minster.
  M. Thurlby, 576:Mar86-68
Hearne, V. Adam's Task.*
  S.R.L. Clark, 617(TLS):20Feb87-175
  S.J. Gould, 453(NYRB):25Jun87-20
Hearnshaw, L.S. The Shaping of Modern Psy-
  chology.
  L. Shaffer, 617(TLS):24Jul87-798
Hearon, S. Five Hundred Scorpions.
  L. Pei, 441:10May87-7
Heath, C., ed. Double Bond.
  S. Gingell, 102(CanL):Summer86-111
  C. Matyas, 168(ECW):Fall86-140
Hebert, B. - see Hoffmann, E.T.A.
Hebert, E. The Passion of Estelle Jordan.
  D. Smith, 441:1Mar87-30
Hechinger, F.M., ed. A Better Start.
  S. Mernit, 441:25Jan87-31
van Heck, A. - see Piccolomini, E.S.
Heckscher, M.H. American Furniture in the
  Metropolitan Museum of Art. (Vol 2)
  (M-A. Rogers, ed)
  P.D. Zimmerman, 658:Winter86-307
Heckscher, W.S. Art and Literature. (E.
  Verheyen, ed)
  H. Andreadis, 568(SCN):Winter86-57
Hedberg, J. Pieces on Joyce.
  R.M. Kain, 329(JJQ):Summer87-492
Hedges, I. Languages of Revolt.*
  M. Bonnet, 535(RHL):Mar-Apr86-334
Hedges, J.W. Tomb of the Eagles.
  P-L. Adams, 61:Dec87-111
Hedin, R. Country O.
  J. Gurley, 649(WAL):Aug86-171
Hedley, L.W. XYZ and Other Stories.
  J. Byrne, 532(RCF):Summer86-153
Heelan, P.A. Space-Perception and the
  Philosophy of Science.*
  S. Fuller, 488:Sep86-391
  C.A. Hooker, 167:May86-399
Heers, J. Espaces publics, espaces privés
  dans la ville.
  R.A. Goldthwaite, 589:Oct86-1023
Heesakkers, C.L. & W.G. Kamerbeek, eds.
  Carmina Scholastica Amstelodamensia.
  L.V.R., 568(SCN):Spring-Summer86-32
Heffer, E.S. Labour's Future.
  J. Dunn, 617(TLS):2Jan87-11
Heffernan, C.W. Choral Music.
  L. Halsey, 289:Summer86-114
Heffernan, G. Bedeutung und Evidenz bei
  Edmund Husserl.
  K. Rosen, 53(AGP):Band68Heft3-327
Heffernan, J.A.W. The Re-Creation of the
  Landscape.*
  J.E. Jordan, 536(Rev):Vol8-47
  W. Walling, 661(WC):Autumn86-197

Heffernan, M. Central States.
J. Carter, 219(GaR):Summer86–532
Heffernan, T.J., ed. The Popular Litera-
ture of the Middle Ages.
H. O'Donoghue, 617(TLS):14Aug87–880
Hegel, G.W.F. Hegel: The Letters.* (C.
Butler & C. Seiler, eds & trans)
L.W. Beck, 319:Jul87–456
J. McCumber, 529(QQ):Autumn86–637
Hegel, G.W.F. Introduction to the Lectures
on the History of Philosophy.
S. Sayers, 518:Jul86–146
Hegel, G.W.F. The Jena System, 1804–5.
(J.W. Burbidge & G. di Giovanni, eds)
W. Patt, 543:Jun87–778
Hegel, G.W.F. Leçons sur l'histoire de la
philosophie. (Vol 6) (P. Garniron, ed &
trans)
C. Juillet–Burnod, 540(RIPh):Vol40
fasc4–451
Hegel, G.W.F. Philosophie des Rechts.*
(D. Henrich, ed) Vorlesungen über Natur-
recht und Staatswissenschaft. (C. Becker
& others, eds) Die Philosophie des
Rechts. (K–H. Ilting, ed)
E.E. Harris, 319:Apr87–304
Hegel, G.W.F. Three Essays, 1793–1795.
(P. Fuss & J. Dobbins, eds & trans)
H.S. Harris, 482(PhR):Jan86–113
Hegel, G.W.F. Vorlesungen über die Philos-
ophie der Religion. (W. Jaeschke, ed)
P–P. Druet, 258:Dec86–409
F. Wagner, 687:Oct–Dec86–631
Heggoy, A.A., ed. Through Foreign Eyes.
A.E. Hilliard, 538(RAL):Winter86–584
Heiberg, J.L., ed. Kjøbenhavns flyvende
Post. (new ed) (U. Andreasen, ed)
T. Petersen, 562(Scan):May86–63
Heidegger, M. Concepts fondamentaux.
T. Cordellier, 450(NRF):Apr86–95
Heidegger, M. The Metaphysical Founda-
tions of Logic.
D. Willard, 482(PhR):Oct86–628
Heidegger, M. Les problèmes fondamentaux
de la phénoménologie.* (F–W. von Her-
mann, ed)
M. Haar, 192(EP):Apr–Jun86–256
Heidelberger–Leonard, I. Alfred Andersch.
H. Höller, 602:Band17Heft2–302
Heidtmann, H. Utopisch-phantastische
Literatur in der DDR.
H. Müssener, 406:Summer86–256
van der Heijden, H.A.M. The Oldest Maps
of the Netherlands.
S. Tyacke, 617(TLS):30Oct–5Nov87–1204
Heil, J. Perception and Cognition.*
M.E. Winston, 543:Sep86–124
Heilbut, A. Exiled in Paradise.*
M. Kuxdorf, 107(CRCL):Dec86–692
Heilbut, A. The Gospel Sound. (rev)
A.P., 91:Spring86–191
Heim, M., Z. Meyerstein & D. Worth. Read-
ings in Czech.
C.E. Townsend, 574(SEEJ):Winter86–603
Heimer, C.A. Reactive Risk and Rational
Action.
R.G., 185:Oct86–311
Heiming, O., ed. Liber sacramentorum
Augustodunensis.
J.M. McCulloh, 589:Jul86–663
Heimpel, H. Die Vener von Gmünd und
Strassburg 1162–1447.
A. Wolf, 684(ZDA):Band115Heft3–108

Hein, H.K. & P. Pedersen. Romanske Stenar-
bejder 3.
L. Kennerstedt, 341:Vol55No4–170
Hein, R. The Harmony Within.
D.S. Robb, 49:Jan86–98
Heine, B. & U. Claudi. On the Rise of
Grammatical Categories.
B. Comrie, 350:Dec87–918
Heine, E. – see Forster, E.M.
Heine, H. Deutschland.
T. Ziolkowski, 617(TLS):21Aug87–903
Heine, H. Historisch-kritische Gesamtaus-
gabe der Werke. (Vol 4) (W. Woesler, ed)
W. Grab, 224(GRM):Band36Heft4–475
Heine, H. Historisch-kritische Gesamtaus-
gabe der Werke. (Vol 12, Pts 1 & 2)
(J–R. Derré & C. Giesen, eds)
W. Grab, 224(GRM):Band36Heft3–362
M. Werner, 98:May86–522
Heine, H. Werke, Briefe, Lebenszeugnisse.
(Vols 7 & 7K) (F. Mende, ed)
S. Atkins, 301(JEGP):Jan86–79
M. Werner, 98:May86–522
Heine, S. Existential and Ontological
Dimensions of Time in Heidegger and
Dōgen.
T.P. Kasulis, 407(MN):Winter86–521
Y. Saito, 293(JASt):Aug86–843
Heine, S. Women and Early Christianity.
M. Furlong, 617(TLS):6–12Nov87–1232
Heineman, H. Mrs. Trollope.
R.H. Super, 403(MLS):Summer86–336
Heineman, H. Frances Trollope.
R. Sheets, 637(VS):Autumn86–145
Heinemann, L. Paco's Story.
C. Benfey, 441:8Nov87–19
V. Geng, 442(NY):11May87–111
Heinemann, W. Negation und Negierung.
H. Harnisch, 682(ZPSK):Band39Heft4–501
Heinen, H., with K. Stroheker & G. Walser,
eds. Althistorische Studien Hermann
Bengtson zum 70. Geburtstag.
J–C. Richard, 555:Vol59fasc2–349
Heinesen, W. Laterna Magica.
A. Paolucci, 441:24May87–12
Heinle, E–M. Hieronymus Freyers Anwei-
ung zur Teutschen Orthographie.
H. Schmidt, 682(ZPSK):Band39Heft3–390
Heinlein, R.A. To Sail Beyond the Sunset.
G. Jonas, 441:18Oct87–36
Heinrich, B. One Man's Owl.
B.B. Gordon, 441:29Nov87–20
Heinrich, I. Ravenna unter Erzbischof
Wibert (1073–1100).
R. Schumann, 589:Apr86–425
Heinrich von Kalkar. Die Korrespondenz
und der "Liber exhortacionis" des
Heinrich von Kalkar. (A.P. Orbán, ed)
P.L. Nyhus, 589:Jan86–236
Heinsius, D. Nederduytsche Poemata. (B.
Becker–Cantarino, ed)
M.R. Sperberg–McQueen, 221(GQ):
Spring86–300
Heinze, D. & L. Hoffmann – see "Konrad
Wolf im Dialog"
Heinze, R–I. Tham khwan.
S. Piker, 302:Vol22No1–119
Heiple, D.L. Mechanical Imagery in Spanish
Golden Age Poetry.*
J. Olivares, 400(MLN):Mar86–437
A. Terry, 131(CL):Fall86–388
D.G. Walters, 86(BHS):Jul86–282

Henderson, J.B. The Development and
Decline of Chinese Cosmology.
 W.J. Peterson, 244(HJAS):Dec86-657
Henderson, K.U. & B.F. McManus. Half
Humankind.
 L. Austin, 568(SCN):Spring-Summer86-14
Henderson, M.C. Theater in America.
 M. Gussow, 441:22Mar87-29
Henderson, N. Inside the Private Office.
 J. Spalter, 441:21Jun87-23
Henderson, T. & P. Knobler. Out of
Control.
 D. Rudd, 441:18Oct87-31
Hendley, B.P. Dewey, Russell, Whitehead.
 E.H.C., 185:Apr87-693
Hendrick, G. - see Jones, S.A.
Hendrickson, D.C. The Future of American
Strategy.
 M. Howard, 617(TLS):18-24Sep87-1007
Hendry, J. The Creation of Quantum
Mechanics and the Bohr-Pauli Dialogue.
 H.R. Brown, 84:Dec86-497
Hendry, J.F. The Sacred Threshold.*
 C.S. Brown, 569(SR):Summer86-504
Hendy, M.F. Studies in the Byzantine Mon-
etary Economy c 300-1453.
 J. Kent, 617(TLS):19Jun87-666
Heng, L. & J. Shapiro - see under Liang
Heng & J. Shapiro
Henke, R. Studien zum Romanushymnus des
Prudentius.
 J-P. Callu, 555:Vol59fasc2-327
Henle, R.J. Theory of Knowledge.
 D. Foster, 543:Sep86-126
Henley, P. Friday Night at Silver Star.*
 D. Olson, 649(WAL):Feb87-354
Henman, A., R. Lewis and T. Malyon. Big
Deal.
 J. Ryle, 617(TLS):23-29Oct87-1163
Henne, H., ed. Praxis der Lexikographie.*
 M. Hornung, 685(ZDL):1/1986-82
Henne, H. & G. Objartel - see "Bibliothek
zur historischen deutschen Studenten-
und Schülersprache"
Hennebo, D., ed. Gartendenkmalpflege.
 R. von Schopf, 683:Band49Heft4-596
Hennin, P.M. Correspondence and Collected
Papers of Pierre Michel Hennin.* (Pt 1)
(M.L. Berkvam, with P.L. Smith, eds)
 A. Billaz, 535(RHL):Jan-Feb86-144
Henningsen, G. The Witches' Advocate.
 J.F. Baumhauer, 196:Band27Heft1/2-112
Hennock, E.P. British Social Reform and
German Precedents.
 R. Pinker, 617(TLS):30Oct-5Nov87-1185
Henri, A. Collected Poems 1967-85.
 R. Sheppard, 617(TLS):23Jan87-92
Henri, F. The Southern Indians and
Benjamin Hawkins, 1796-1816.
 P. Galloway, 585(SoQ):Winter87-149
Henrich, D. - see Hegel, G.W.F.
Henrich, D. & R-P. Horstmann, eds. Hegels
Logik der Philosophie.
 P. Schaber, 687:Oct-Dec86-636
Henriksen, A. De ubaendige.
 C.B. Black, 538(RAL):Spring86-155
Henry, A. Métonymie et métaphore.*
 F. Moreau, 535(RHL):Sep-Oct86-959
Henry, A., ed. The Mirour of Mans Salua-
cioune.
 R. Morse, 617(TLS):25-31Dec87-1439

Henry, A. Proust romancier.*
 A. Corbineau-Hoffmann, 72:Band223
Heft1-218
 P-L. Rey, 535(RHL):Mar-Apr86-331
Henry, A. - see Perse, S.
Henry, D. The Listener's Guide to Medieval
and Renaissance Music.
 H.T.E.M., 412:May85-133
Henry, D. & E. The Mask of Power.*
 G.W.M. Harrison, 124:Jan-Feb87-223
Henry, D.P. That Most Subtle Question
(Quaestio Subtilissima).*
 K. Arnold, 320(CJL):Spring86-83
Henry, F.G. Le Message humaniste des
"Fleurs du Mal."*
 J.A. Hiddleston, 210(FrF):Jan86-119
Henry, M. Généalogie de la psychanalyse.*
 T. Cordellier, 450(NRF):Feb86-108
 A. Himy, 542:Apr-Jun86-257
Henry, M.M. Menander's Courtesans and the
Greek Comic Tradition.
 L.P. Wencis, 124:Jul-Aug87-452
Henry, W. The Gates of the Mountains.
 S. Jenkins, 649(WAL):May86-85
Henry-Hermann, G. Die Überwindung des
Zufalls.
 L. Geldsetzer, 679:Band17Heft2-384
Henrysson, H. & J.W. Porter. A Jussi Björ-
ling Phonography.
 W. Ashbrook, 465:Spring86-114
Hensley, T. - see Link, O.W.
Hentoff, N. Boston Boy.*
 42(AR):Fall86-491
Heny, F. & B. Richards, eds. Linguistic
Categories.* (Vols 1 & 2)
 B. Rigter, 361:Aug86-355
 A. Warner, 353:Vol24No4-841
Hepburn, F. Portraits of the Later Plan-
tagenets.
 G. Reynolds, 39:Nov86-460
Hepburn, J. Critic into Anti-Critic.
 S. Pickering, 569(SR):Winter86-xiv
Hepburn, J. - see Bennett, A.
Hepburn, K. The Making of "The African
Queen."
 C. James, 441:13Sep87-35
Hepokoski, J.A. Giuseppe Verdi: "Otello."
 J. Rosselli, 617(TLS):9-15Oct87-1101
Heppenstall, R. The Master Eccentric. (J.
Goodman, ed) The Pier.
 N. Williams, 362:1Jan87-20
Hepworth, J. & G. McNamee, eds. Resist
Much, Obey Little.
 A. Ronald, 649(WAL):Nov86-254
Heraclitus. Héraclite - Fragments.* (M.
Conche, ed)
 J. Barnes, 520:Vol31No2-182
Hérail, R.S. & E.A. Lovatt, eds. Diction-
ary of Modern Colloquial French.*
 G. Bourcier, 189(EA):Jul-Sep86-370
 P.M. Sewell, 208(FS):Oct86-499
Herbers, K. Der Jacobuskult des 12. Jahr-
hunderts und der "Liber Sancti Jacobi."
 J. Howe, 589:Oct86-934
 H-W. Klein, 547(RF):Band98Heft1/2-192
Herbert, B. Prisoners of Arionn.
 G. Jonas, 441:2Aug87-25
Herbert, F. The Maker of Dune. (T.
O'Reilly, ed)
 E. Stumpf, 441:30Aug87-21

Herbert, G. & H. Vaughan. The Oxford
Authors: George Herbert and Henry
Vaughan. (L.L. Martz, ed)
    M. Dodsworth, 175:Summer86-195
    A. Rudrum, 617(TLS):27Mar87-316
Herbert, J. Approaching Snow.
    J. Saunders, 565:Summer86-74
Herbert, J. & J. Varenne. Vocabulaire de
l'hindouisme.
    A. Reix, 542:Jan-Mar86-90
Herbert, P.A. & T. Chiang. Chinese Studies
Research Methodology.
    Ho Peng Yoke, 302:Vol22No1-125
Herbert, Z. Report from the Besieged City
and Other Poems.*
    D. Finnell, 152(UDQ):Winter87-113
    P. Forbes, 362:25Jun87-31
Herbst, T. Untersuchungen zur Valenz
englischer Adjektive und ihrer Nominal-
isierungen.
    E. von Randow, 38:Band104Heft1/2-144
Herbstrith, W. Edith Stein.*
    P. O'Connor, 42(AR):Summer86-375
Herd, E.W. & A. Obermayer, eds. A Glossary
of German Literary Terms.
    D. Hayman, 406:Winter86-523
Herdeg, K. The Decorated Diagram.*
    R. Wesley, 576:Sep86-310
Herder, J.G. Werke. (Vol 1) (U. Gaier,
ed)
    H.B. Nisbet, 402(MLR):Jan87-245
Herder, J.G. Werke. (Vol 1) (W. Pross,
ed)
    W. Henckmann, 489(PJGG):Band93Heft2-
    424
Herdmann, U. Die Südlichen Poeme A.S.
Puškins.*
    J.D. Clayton, 107(CRCL):Sep86-487
    U. Jekutsch, 38:Band104Heft1/2-246
de Herdt, A. Dessins genevois de Liotard à
Hodler.
    G. Apgar, 380:Summer86-254
Herdt, G.H., ed. Ritualized Homosexuality
in Melanesia.
    J.M. Blythe, 293(JASt):Aug86-797
de Heredia, J-M. Oeuvres poétiques complètes de José-Maria de Heredia. (Vol 1)
(S. Delaty, ed)
    W.N. Ince, 208(FS):Apr86-228
    R. Killick, 402(MLR):Jan87-206
    D.W.P. Lewis, 446(NCFS):Fall-Winter
    86/87-201
    E. Pich, 535(RHL):Nov-Dec86-1149
de Heredia, J-M. Oeuvres poétiques com-
plètes de José-Maria de Heredia.* (Vol
2) (S. Delaty, ed)
    W.N. Ince, 208(FS):Apr86-228
    R. Killick, 402(MLR):Jan87-206
    E. Pich, 535(RHL):Nov-Dec86-1149
Herf, J. Reactionary Modernism.*
    V. Jirat-Wasiutyński, 529(QQ):Summer86-
    339
Hergenhan, L., ed. The Australian Short
Story.
    R. Stevenson, 617(TLS):19Jun87-668
Hergenhan, L. Unnatural Lives.
    T. Goldie, 49:Jan86-102
Herget, W. & K. Ortseifen, eds. The Tran-
sit of Civilization from Europe to
America.
    H.J. Dawson, 165(EAL):Vol22No3-320

Heriti, P. Književni jezik Emanuila
Jankovića.
    A. Albijanić, 279:Vol33-153
van Herk, A. No Fixed Address.
    H. Kirkwood, 99:Aug/Sep86-40
    C. Rooke, 376:Sep86-156
Herken, G. Counsels of War.
    639(VQR):Spring86-58
Herland, J. "Cinna" ou le péché et la
grâce.
    J. Moravcevich, 475:Vol13No24-397
Herlihy, D. & C. Klapisch-Zuber. Tuscans
and their Families.*
    D.O. Hughes, 385(MQR):Winter87-266
    N. Rubinstein, 278(IS):Vol41-138
Herlin, H. Assassins.
    S. Dunant, 362:24Sep87-22
Hermand, J., H. Peitsch & K.R. Scherpe,
eds. Nachkriegsliteratur in Westdeutsch-
land. (Vol 2)
    R.W. Williams, 402(MLR):Jul86-805
von Hermann, F-W. – see Heidegger, M.
Hermann, J.P. & J.J. Burke, Jr., eds.
Signs and Symbols in Chaucer's Poetry.
    J.M. Fyler, 677(YES):Vol16-230
Hermann, U. Knaurs etymologisches Lexikon.
    K. Müller, 682(ZPSK):Band39Heft1-145
Hermans, T. The Structure of Modernist
Poetry.*
    E.F. Gal, 447(N&Q):Dec85-563
Hermenegildo, A. – see Lasso de la Vega, G.
Hermerén, G. Aspects of Aesthetics.*
    B. Dziemidok, 290(JAAC):Winter86-214
    P. Somville, 542:Apr-Jun86-269
Hernadi, P. Interpreting Events.
    C. Perricone, 125:Winter86-219
    M.G. Rose, 130:Fall86-285
    L. Stern, 290(JAAC):Winter86-201
    639(VQR):Summer86-89
Hernández, F.J., ed. Los Cartularios de
Toledo.
    A. Mackay, 617(TLS):3Jul87-726
Hernández, J.A. Studien zum religiös-
ethischen Wortschatz der deutschen
Mystik.*
    E. Glaser, 680(ZDP):Band105Heft3-463
    J.F. Poag, 301(JEGP):Apr86-303
Hernández Alonso, C. Gramática funcional
del español.
    T.A. Lathrop, 238:Sep86-566
    E. Martinell, 548:Jan-Jun86-220
Hernández Araico, S. Ironía y tragedia en
Calderón.
    D. Fox, 304(JHP):Spring86-263
Hernández Sacristán, C. Oraciones
reflejas y estructuras actanciales en
español.
    M. Suñer, 238:Dec86-894
Herodotus. The History. (D. Grene, trans)
    J. Griffin, 453(NYRB):9Apr87-11
    S. Hornblower, 617(TLS):3Jul87-722
    P. Levi, 441:28Jun87-13
Herraiz, J.L. & J. Fernández Jiménez – see
under Labrador Herraiz, J. & J. Fernández
Jiménez
Herrán, J.M.G. – see under González Herrán,
J.M.
Herrick, W. That's Life.
    G.R. Grund, 573(SSF):Spring86-213
Herrity, P. – see under Heriti, P.
Herrmann, L. Paul and Thomas Sandby.
    J. Egerton, 90:Oct86-755
    G. Reynolds, 617(TLS):19Jun87-664

Herrmann, P. Tituli Lydiae linguis Graeca et Latina conscripti. (fasc 1)
  H.W. Pleket, 394:Vol39fasc3/4−556
Herrmann-Fiore, K. Disegni degli Alberti.*
  D. De Grazia, 380:Autumn86−405
Hersey, J. Blues.
  P−L. Adams, 61:Jul87−99
  V. Klinkenborg, 441:31May87−12
  442(NY):18May87−118
Hershbell, J.P. Pseudo-Plato, "Axiochus."
  J.P. Kenney, 41:Spring85−143
Herslund, M., O. Mørdrup & F. Sørensen, eds. Analyses grammaticales du français.
  D. Gaatone, 545(RPh):Feb87−369
Herstein, S.R. A Mid-Victorian Feminist, Barbara Leigh Smith Bodichon.*
  E.A. Daniels, 637(VS):Winter87−272
Herteig, A. The Bryggen Papers. (Main Ser, Vol 1)
  D.J. Shepherd, 563(SS):Summer86−313
Herttrich, E. & H. Schneider, eds. Festschrift Rudolf Elvers zum 60. Geburtstag.
  A. Rosenthal, 410(M&L):Oct86−406
Hertz, N. The End of the Line.
  M. Sprinker, 400(MLN):Dec86−1226
Herwig, H.H. Germany's Vision of Empire in Venezuela 1871−1914.
  M. Deas, 617(TLS):10Jul87−738
Herwig, W., ed. Goethes Gespräche. (Vol 3, Pt 2)
  S. Atkins, 406:Summer86−235
Herwig, W. Goethes Gespräche. (Vol 4)
  S. Atkins, 406:Summer86−235
Herz, G. Bach-Quellen in Amerika/Bach Sources in America.
  R. Stinson, 143:Issue39−86
Herz, G. Essays on J.S. Bach.
  G.B. Stauffer, 414:Vol72No2−272
Herzen, A. Who Is to Blame?
  K.J. McKenna, 574(SEEJ):Summer86−283
Herzhaft-Marin, Y. Ravenscourt Road.
  R.R. Morton, 189(EA):Oct−Dec87−479
Herzog, A. Vesco.
  R. Rosenbaum, 441:25Oct87−37
Herzog, K. Women, Ethnics, and Exotics.*
  B.H. Gelfant, 106:Fall86−355
Heschel, A.J. The Circle of the Baal Shem Tov.* (S.H. Dresner, ed)
  H. Goldberg, 390:Jan86−61
Heseltine, M. Where There's a Will.
  J. Dunn, 617(TLS):24Apr87−442
  G. Kaufman, 362:3Sep87−30
Hess, A. Googie.
  J. Blanton, 505:Dec86−107
  P.M.S., 45:May86−71
Hess-Gabriel, B. Zur Didaktik des Deutschunterrichts für Kinder türkischer Muttersprache.
  G. Koss, 685(ZDL):3/1986−402
Hess-Lüttich, E.W.B. Soziale Interaktion und literarischer Dialog. (Vol 2)
  R.C. Cowen, 406:Winter86−514
Hesse, E.W. The Comedia and Points of View.
  J.A. Castañeda, 238:Sep86−541
Hesse, M.G. Gabrielle Roy.* (French title: Gabrielle Roy par elle-même.)
  J. Marshall, 102(CanL):Summer86−107
Hessen, B. Der historische Infinitiv im Wandel der Darstellungstechnik Sallusts.
  S.P. Oakley, 123:Vol36No2−319
Hessenberg, I., ed. London in Detail.
  J. Chernaik, 617(TLS):23Jan87−89

Hesson, E.C. Twentieth Century Odyssey.
  A.C. Ulmer, 406:Fall86−416
Hester, M.T. "Kinde Pitty" and "Brave Scorn."*
  R. Selden, 402(MLR):Jan87−165
Heubeck, A. Kleine Schriften zur griechischen Sprache und Literatur. (B. Forsmann, S. Koster & E. Pöhlmann, eds)
  J.B. Hainsworth, 123:Vol36No2−360
Heubner, H. Kommentar zum "Agricola" des Tacitus.
  R.H. Martin, 123:Vol36No1−136
Heuer, K. − see Eiseley, L.
Heukenkamp, U. & R. Karl Mickel.
  K. Werner, 654(WB):9/1986−1570
Heus, W.E. Claudianus, Laus Serenae (carm. min. 30).
  H. Hofmann, 394:Vol39fascl/2−193
Heuser, A. − see MacNeice, L.
Hevia, A.M. − see under Miranda Hevia, A.
Hewison, R. Footlights!*
  G. Hunter, 612(ThS):May/Nov86−185
  W. Kendall, 611(TN):Vol40No1−37
  A.F. Sponberg, 615(TJ):May86−248
Hewison, W., ed. Spaced Out. Party Pieces. Crooked Smiles.
  D.J. Enright, 617(TLS):18−24Dec87−1399
Hewitt, D. & M. Spiller, eds. Literature of the North.
  D. Groves, 588(SSL):Vol21−346
Hewitt, J. Freehold.
  S. O'Brien, 617(TLS):21Aug87−904
Hewitt, N. The Golden Age of Louis-Ferdinand Céline.
  P. McCarthy, 617(TLS):25−31Dec87−1436
Hewitt, N. Henri Troyat.
  A. Demaitre, 207(FR):Oct86−133
Hewlett, S.A. A Lesser Life.*
  A.S. Grossman, 617(TLS):27Mar87−321
Hewton, E. Education in Recession.
  R. Floud, 617(TLS):13Mar87−263
Heyblon, R. Le Cas du juge.
  R.T. Cargo, 207(FR):Dec86−293
Heydenreich, T., ed. Denis Diderot 1713−1784.
  G. Bremner, 208(FS):Jan86−74
  M. Delon, 547(RF):Band98Heft3/4−438
Heyen, W. The Chestnut Rain.
  R. von Hallberg, 441:15Feb87−42
Heyer, P. Nature, Human Nature, and Society.
  G. Jones, 488:Jun86−255
Heynen, J. You Know What Is Right.*
  D. Duer, 455:Sep86−78
Heyrman, C.L. Commerce and Culture.*
  G.B. Nash, 656(WMQ):Jan86−138
Heywood, J. The Berkut.
  S. Kellerman, 441:29Nov87−20
  442(NY):28Sep87−98
Heywood, T. A Woman Killed with Kindness. (B. Scobie, ed)
  M. Grivelet, 189(EA):Jan−Mar87−113
Heyworth, P., ed. Conversations with Klemperer. (rev)
  D.R.P., 412:Aug85−230
Hiatt, H.H. America's Health in the Balance.
  M. Freudenheim, 441:5Apr87−35
Hibbard, G.R., ed. The Elizabethan Theatre VIII.
  R.S. White, 541(RES):Feb86−137
Hibbert, C. Cities and Civilizations.
  442(NY):12Jan87−103

Hibbert, C. The English.
P. Collinson, 617(TLS):11–17Sep87–991
M. Quilligan, 441:12Apr87–11
Hibbert, C. The Grand Tour.
J. Keates, 617(TLS):11–17Sep87–988
Hibbert, C. Rome.
362:10Dec87–29
Hickin, N. Bookworms.*
A.D. Baynes-Cope, 78(BC):Autumn86–384
Hickman, C.R. & M.A. Silva. The Future 500.
E. Bailey, 441:25Oct87–38
Hickman, H. Robert Musil and the Culture of Vienna.*
W.E. Yates, 402(MLR):Jan86–258
Hicks, D. A Maternal Religion.
J.C. Kuipers, 293(JASt):Feb86–449
Hidalgo-Serna, E. Das ingeniöse Denken bei Baltasar Gracián.
U. Schulz-Buschhaus, 547(RF):Band98 Heft1/2–229
Hiddleston, J.A. Baudelaire and "Le Spleen de Paris."
G.W. Ireland, 617(TLS):11–17Dec87–1381
Higbie, R. Character and Structure in the English Novel.*
J. Chalker, 566:Spring87–197
R.J. Dunn, 594:Summer86–214
L. Speirs, 179(ES):Aug86–376
M. Steig, 158:Jun86–95
Higdon, D.L. Shadows of the Past in Contemporary British Fiction.*
L.L. Doan, 395(MFS):Summer86–324
Higginbotham, D. George Washington and the American Military Tradition.
L. Kennett, 173(ECS):Spring87–355
639(VQR):Autumn86–121
Higgins, G.V. Impostors.*
W.H. Pritchard, 249(HudR):Winter87–644
Higgins, G.V. Outlaws.
P-L. Adams, 61:Oct87–106
T.J. Binyon, 617(TLS):19Jun87–668
G. Kaufman, 362:8Oct87–23
W. Walker, 441:1Nov87–24
442(NY):12Oct87–145
Higgins, J. A History of Peruvian Literature.
G. Brotherston, 617(TLS):4–11Sep87–961
Higgins, J. Night of the Fox.
R. Lourie, 441:18Jan87–15
442(NY):23Feb87–135
Higgins, L.A. Parables of Theory.
E.J. Smyth, 208(FS):Apr86–240
Higgins, T. The Perfect Failure.
S. Hoffmann, 441:29Nov87–3
Higginson, W.J., with P. Harter. The Haiku Handbook.*
639(VQR):Winter86–19
Higgs, D. Nobles in 19th-Century France.
J.F. McMillan, 617(TLS):9–15Oct87–1096
Higham, R. Diary of a Disaster.
C.M. Woodhouse, 617(TLS):3Jul87–709
Highfill, P.H., Jr., K.A. Burnim & E.A. Langhans. A Biographical Dictionary of Actors, Actresses, Musicians, Dancers, Managers, and Other Stage Personnel in London, 1660–1800. (Vols 7 & 8)
S. Wells, 402(MLR):Apr86–435
Highfill, P.H., Jr., K.A. Burnim & E.A. Langhans. A Biographical Dictionary of Actors, Actresses, Musicians, Dancers, Managers, and Other Stage Personnel in

London, 1660–1800.* (Vols 9 & 10)
J. Milhous, 610:Summer86–170
S. Wells, 402(MLR):Apr86–435
Highsmith, P. Found in the Street.*
R. Burgin, 441:1Nov87–24
Highsmith, P. Leute, die an die Tür klopfen.
I. Skotnicki, 654(WB):5/1986–846
Highsmith, P. Tales of Natural and Unnatural Catastrophes.
J. Melmoth, 617(TLS):6–12Nov87–1227
Higman, F. – see Farel, G.
Hignett, S. Brett.*
D.K. Dunaway, 639(VQR):Summer86–548
90:Feb86–157
Higonnet, M.R. & others, eds. Behind the Lines.
C. Moorehead, 362:6Aug87–22
Hihara Toshikuni, ed. Chūgoku shisō jiten.
B.A. Elman, 293(JASt):Nov85–120
Hilberg, R. The Destruction of the European Jews. (rev)
J.M. Masson, 390:Apr86–51
Hildebidle, J. Thoreau.*
R.W. Harvey, 106:Summer86–211
Hildebrand, K. The Third Reich.
M.W. Roche, 221(GQ):Summer86–509
Hildebrandt, K. Naturalistische Dramen Gerhart Hauptmanns.
R.C. Cowen, 406:Winter86–514
Hildebrandt, R., ed. Summarium Heinrici. (Vol 2)
W. Kleiber, 685(ZDL):2/1986–216
J. Splett, 680(ZDP):Band105Heft3–458
Hildebrandt, R. & H. Friebertshäuser, eds. Sprache und Brauchtum.
H. Schwedt, 685(ZDL):2/1986–257
Hildebrandt, W. The Battle of Batoche.
T. Flanagan, 298:Summer86–157
Hildegard von Bingen. The Ordo Virtutum of Hildegard von Bingen. (A.E. Davidson, ed)
F. Collins, Jr., 130:Spring86–81
Hildesheimer, W. The Collected Stories of Wolfgang Hildesheimer.
D. Aldan, 441:10May87–20
Hilen, A. – see Longfellow, H.W.
Hilfiker, D. Healing the Wounds.
639(VQR):Summer86–105
Hilg, H. Das "Marienleben" des Heinrich von St. Gallen.*
T.R. Jackson, 402(MLR):Jan87–244
Hill, A.G. – see Wordsworth, D.
Hill, A.G. – see Wordsworth, W. & D.
Hill, B. Eighteenth-Century Women.*
M. Smith, 83:Spring86–95
Hill, B.M. Wakeful in the Sleep of Time.
D. McDuff, 565:Winter86/86–72
Hill, C. The Collected Essays.* (Vol 1)
R. Howell, Jr., 366:Spring86–132
Hill, C. The Collected Essays.* (Vol 2)
639(VQR):Autumn86–122
Hill, C. The Collected Essays.* (Vol 3)
D. Underdown, 617(TLS):23Jan87–88
Hill, D. Constable's English Landscape Scenery.
G. Reynolds, 39:Apr86–288
Hill, D. A History of Engineering in Classical and Medieval Times.*
K.D. White, 123:Vol36No1–175
Hill, D. In Turner's Footsteps.
A. Adams, 161(DUJ):Dec85–171
C. Powell, 59:Mar86–99

Hill, D.E. – see Ovid

Hill, D.I. Canterbury Cathedral.
N. Coldstream, 90:Oct86–758

Hill, E. Shakespeare in Sable.*
D.W. Beams, 130:Spring86–90
R. Cowhig, 538(RAL):Summer86–284
G.J. Williams, 570(SQ):Summer86–276

Hill, G. Collected Poems.*
A. Stevenson, 493:Oct86–42

Hill, G. The Lords of Limit.*
D. Gervais, 97(CQ):Vol15No3–236
M. Standen, 565:Summer86–18

Hill, G. The Mystery of the Charity of
Charles Péguy.*
L. Lerner, 569(SR):Spring86–312

Hill, J. The Letters and Papers of Sir
John Hill 1714–1775. (G.S. Rousseau, ed)
H. Ormsby-Lennon, 677(YES):Vol16–270

Hill, J., ed. Old English Minor Heroic
Poems.
P.S. Baker, 589:Jan86–237
D.G. Scragg, 382(MAE):1986/2–269
C. Sisam, 541(RES):Feb86–69

Hill, J. Sex, Class and Realism.
A. Stanbrook, 617(TLS):17Apr87–408

Hill, J.M. Celtic Warfare 1595–1763.
J. Black, 566:Autumn86–81

Hill, R. Child's Play.
T.J. Binyon, 617(TLS):30Oct–5Nov87–
1192
N. Callendar, 441:15Mar87–24
442(NY):13Apr87–106

Hill, R.F. – see Ford, J.

Hill, S. Saying Hello at the Station.
J. Saunders, 565:Summer86–74

Hill, T. The Gardener's Labyrinth. (R.
Mabey, ed)
C. Lloyd, 617(TLS):18–24Dec87–1400

Hill, W.S. – see Hooker, R.

Hillabold, J. & T. Poirier. Double Visions.
C. Tapping, 102(CanL):Winter85–155

Hillen, W. & L. Rheinbach. Einführung in
die bibliographischen Hilfsmittel für das
Studium der Romanistik. (Vol 1)
H. Fuchs, 547(RF):Band98Heft3/4–392
P. Swiggers, 553(RLiR):Jul–Dec86–555

Hillenbrand, R. – see Pedersen, J.

Hiller, M.P. Krisenregion Nahost.
B. Jelavich, 104(CASS):Spring–Summer86–
185

Hiller, U. – see Maugham, W.S.

Hillerman, T. The Ghostway.
R. Evans, 649(WAL):May86–63

Hillerman, T. Skinwalkers.
P-L. Adams, 61:Feb87–95
N. Callendar, 441:18Jan87–23
442(NY):2Feb87–102

Hillesum, E. Letters from Westerbork.
(J.G. Gaarlandt, ed)
P-L. Adams, 61:Feb87–95
N. Ascherson, 453(NYRB):28May87–29

Hillgruber, A. Zweierlei Untergang.
G.A. Craig, 453(NYRB):15Jan87–16
R. Knight, 617(TLS):15May87–520

Hilliard, S.S. The Singularity of Thomas
Nashe.
H.R. Woudhuysen, 617(TLS):6Mar87–247

Hillier, B. John Betjeman.
B. Sewell, 161(DUJ):Dec85–166

Hillier, J., ed. Cahiers du Cinéma.* (Vol
1)
J. Forbes, 208(FS):Oct86–495

Hillier, M. The History of Wax Dolls.
V. Powell, 39:Apr86–288

Hillis, D. Voices and Visions.
P. Denham, 627(UTQ):Fall86–151

Hills, P. The Light of Early Italian
Painting.
J.B. Shaw, 324:Nov87–948

Hilmar, R., ed. Katalog der Schriftstücke
von der Hand Alban Bergs, der fremd-
schriftlichen und gedruckten Dokumente
zur Lebensgeschichte und zu seinem Werk.
D. Jarman, 410(M&L):Oct86–438

Hilmy, S.S. The Later Wittgenstein.
M. Budd, 617(TLS):4–10Dec87–1356

Hilpinen, R. New Studies in Deontic Logic.
M. Forrester, 449:Sep86–421

Hilton, J.B. Passion in the Peak.
639(VQR):Spring86–57

Hilton, J.B. Slickensides.
T.J. Binyon, 617(TLS):23–29Oct87–1175

Hilton, N. Literal Imagination.*
D. Fuller, 83:Autumn86–269

Hilton, T. John Ruskin: The Early Years,
1819–1859.*
C. Brooks, 326:Autumn86–55
M. Brooks, 576:Jun86–177
P. Fuller, 90:Mar86–226
R. Kimball, 45:Apr86–63

Hilty, S.L. & W.L. Brown. A Guide to the
Birds of Colombia.
A.F. Skutch, 617(TLS):13Mar87–280

Himes, C. Lonely Crusade.
I. Bamforth, 617(TLS):16Jan87–56

Himmel, H. Wirkungen Rilkes auf den öster-
reichischen Roman.
B.L. Bradley, 406:Spring86–117

Himmelfarb, G. The Idea of Poverty.*
J. Annette, 366:Autumn86–259
F.S. Schwarzbach, 158:Jun86–100

Himmelfarb, G. Marriage and Morals Among
the Victorians.*
K. Thomas, 453(NYRB):28May87–26

Himmelfarb, G. The New History and the
Old.
L. Stone, 453(NYRB):17Dec87–59

Hinchliff, P. Benjamin Jowett and the
Christian Religion.
O. Chadwick, 617(TLS):25–31Dec87–1437

Hinchliffe, A.P., ed. T.S. Eliot: Plays.
W. Harmon, 569(SR):Summer86–510

Hinchliffe, A.P. "Volpone."*
R.L. Smallwood, 611(TN):Vol40No3–137

Hinchman, L.P. Hegel's Critique of the
Enlightenment.*
Q. Lauer, 258:Mar86–93
H. Williams, 518:Jan86–28

Hinde, W. Richard Cobden.
H. Benedict, 441:12Jul87–21
N. Gash, 617(TLS):11–17Sep87–993
G.S. Jones, 362:14May87–32

Hinderer, W., ed. Geschichte der deutschen
Lyrik vom Mittelalter bis zur Gegenwart.*
R. Dove, 402(MLR):Oct86–1040

Hinderer, W. & H.J. Schmidt – see Büchner,
G.

Hindley, A. & B.J. Levy, eds. The Old
French Epic.*
M. Heintze, 547(RF):Band98Heft1/2–195

Hinds, H.E., Jr. & C.M. Tatum, eds. Hand-
book of Latin American Popular Culture.
D.W. Foster, 238:Dec86–891
K. Shaw, 37:Nov–Dec86–60

Hindus, M. The Crippled Giant.
  D. Flower, 364:Dec86/Jan87-134
Hine, D. Academic Festival Overtures.
  M. Jarman, 249(HudR):Summer86-344
Hine, T. Populuxe.*
  442(NY):12Jan87-104
Hines, D.M. Tales of the Nez Perce.
  A.G. Marshall, 292(JAF):Jul/Sep86-322
Hinkkanen-Lievonen, M-L. British Trade
  and Enterprise in the Baltic States,
  1919-1925.
  G. Maude, 575(SEER):Oct86-619
Hinnenkamp, V. Foreigner Talk und Tarzan-
  isch.
  A. Mihm, 685(ZDL):3/1986-400
Hinojosa, R. The Rolando Hinojosa Reader.
  (J.D. Saldívar, ed) Der Rafe. Partners
  in Crime.
  C. Tatum, 238:Sep86-560
Hinrichs, J.P. Zum Akzent im Mittelbul-
  garischen. (A.A. Barentsen, B.M. Groen &
  R. Sprenger, eds)
  C.M. MacRobert, 402(MLR):Oct87-1047
Hinrichs, K. Stars & Stripes.
  M. Lida, 441:6Sep87-16
von Hinten, W. "Der Franckforter."
  V. Honemann, 684(ZDA):Band115Heft1-14
Hinterthür, P. Modern Art in Hong Kong.
  (N. Corazzo, ed)
  L. Fenwick, 60:Jan-Feb86-118
Hintikka, M.B. & J. Investigating Wittgen-
  stein.
  M. Budd, 617(TLS):13Mar87-277
Hinton, L. & L.J. Watahomigie, eds. Spirit
  Mountain.
  K.I. Periman, 292(JAF):Jul/Sep86-323
  W. Ude, 649(WAL):Aug86-142
Hinton, N. The Heart of the Valley.
  J. Reed, 364:Jul86-111
Hinxman, M. The Sound of Murder.
  G. Kaufman, 362:7May87-26
Hippisley, A. The Poetic Style of Simeon
  Polotsky.
  L. Hughes, 402(MLR):Apr87-533
Hippocrates. Hippocrate, "Maladies II."
  (J. Jouanna, ed & trans)
  P. Potter, 487:Summer86-245
  G. Sabbah, 555:Vol59fasc2-279
Hirbour, L. - see Varèse, E.
Hirsch, E. Wild Gratitude.*
  R.S. Gwynn, 434:Autumn86-111
  L. Rector, 249(HudR):Autumn86-507
  P. Stitt, 491:May86-105
  639(VQR):Summer86-100
Hirsch, E.D., Jr. Cultural Literacy.
  G. Steiner, 442(NY):1Jun87-106
  R. Stevens, 441:26Apr87-36
Hirson, D. The House Next Door to Africa.
  G. Blooston, 441:27Dec87-18
  A. Sattin, 617(TLS):13-19Nov87-1248
  D. Walder, 362:26Nov87-31
Hirst, D. Authority and Conflict.*
  L. Stone, 453(NYRB):26Feb87-38
Hirst, D.L. Edward Bond.
  G. Bas, 189(EA):Jan-Mar87-101
Hirst, D.L. Tragicomedy.*
  G. Bas, 189(EA):Jul-Sep87-323
  R.P. Lessenich, 343:Heft13-119
Hirt, G. & S. Wonders, eds. Kulturpalast.
  G. Janecek, 574(SEEJ):Winter86-586
Hirtle, W.H. Number and Inner Space.*
  S. Levin, 215(GL):Vol26No3-205

Hirukawa, A. Transition entre le Person-
  nage de Jean Santeuil et le Narrateur de
  Marcel Proust.
  B. Brun, 535(RHL):Jul-Aug86-787
"A Historical Guide to the United States."
  H. Brogan, 617(TLS):16-22Oct87-1147
Hitchcock, H.W. & S. Sadie, eds. The New
  Grove Dictionary of American Music.*
  W. Mellers, 617(TLS):9Jan87-39
Hitchcock, J. Years of Crisis.
  C.D. Murphy, 396(ModA):Winter86-61
Hitchens, C. The Elgin Marbles.
  M. Lefkowitz, 617(TLS):14Aug87-865
Hite, M. Class Porn.
  C. Dragonwagon, 441:12Jul87-20
Hite, S. Women and Love.
  A.R. Hochschild, 441:15Nov87-3
Hitt, R.F. What Does Your Name Mean?
  K.B. Harder, 424:Jun86-201
Hjartarson, P., ed. A Stranger to My Time.
  A. Knoenagel, 268(IFR):Summer87-115
Hoad, T.F., ed. The Concise Oxford Dic-
  tionary of English Etymology.
  A. Tellier, 189(EA):Jul-Sep87-341
Hoagland, E. Seven Rivers West.*
  J. Updike, 442(NY):30Mar87-120
Hoagwood, T.A. Prophecy and the Philoso-
  phy of Mind.
  A. Robinson, 541(RES):Nov86-576
Hoban, R. The Medusa Frequency.
  P-L. Adams, 61:Nov87-122
  S. Erickson, 441:8Nov87-11
  D. Kennedy, 362:13Aug87-19
  E. Korn, 617(TLS):4-11Sep87-949
Hobart, M.E. Science and Religion in the
  Thought of Nicolas Malebranche.
  R. McRae, 543:Mar87-577
Hobbs, R. Edward Hopper.
  J. Russell, 441:6Dec87-89
Hoberg, R., ed. Rechtschreibung im Beruf.
  D. Herberg, 682(ZPSK):Band39Heft6-721
Hobhouse, H., ed. Survey of London. (Vol
  42)
  J.M. Crook, 617(TLS):15May87-514
  J. Hayes, 324:Apr87-402
Hobhouse, J. November.*
  J. Motion, 617(TLS):27Mar87-319
  442(NY):9Feb87-103
Hobhouse, J.C. Byron's Bulldog.* (P.W.
  Graham, ed)
  R.F. Gleckner, 579(SAQ):Spring86-209
  L.M. Jones, 340(KSJ):Vol35-188
Hobhouse, P. The Private Gardens of
  England.
  R.I. Ross, 617(TLS):14Aug87-885
Hobsbawm, E. The Age of Empire 1875-
  1914.
  R. Silver, 362:26Nov87-28
Hobson, A., ed. Remembering America.
  J. Seelye, 432(NEQ):Jun86-267
Hobson, F. - see Johnson, G.W.
Hobson, L.Z. Laura Z.
  D. Goldberg, 441:8Feb87-25
Hoch, E.D. Leopold's Way.
  P. Wolfe, 573(SSF):Summer86-332
Hochberg, H. Logic, Ontology, and Lan-
  guage.
  J-L. Gardies, 542:Jul-Sep86-407
Hoche, H-U. & W. Strube. Analytische
  Philosophie.
  D. Birnbacher, 679:Band17Heft2-387

Hochman, B. Character in Literature.
　W.B. Bache, 395(MFS):Winter86-686
　S. Connor, 155:Summer86-108
　42(AR):Winter86-120
Hochman, J. The Soviet Union and the
Failure of Collective Security, 1934-38.
　H. Hanak, 575(SEER):Apr86-307
　V. Mastny, 550(RusR):Jan86-102
Hochstein, W. Die Kirchenmusik von Niccolò
Jommelli (1714-1774).
　D. Arnold, 410(M&L):Apr86-203
Hock, H.H. Principles of Historical Lin-
guistics.
　S.M. Embleton, 159:Fall86-203
Höckmann, O. Antike Seefahrt.
　G.E. Rickman, 123:Vol36No2-354
Hockney, D. Martha's Vineyard and Other
Places.
　M.L., 90:Sep86-688
Hodder, I. Reading the Past.
　P. Fowler, 617(TLS):20Feb87-193
de Hodenc, R. - see under Raoul de Hodenc
Hodges, D.L. Renaissance Fictions of
Anatomy.
　R. Boenig, 568(SCN):Winter86-57
　D. Novarr, 551(RenQ):Summer86-339
Hodges, L.S., Jr. Portrait of an Expatri-
ate.
　N. McKay, 27(AL):Dec86-662
　C. Werner, 395(MFS):Winter86-638
Hodges, S. Lorenzo Da Ponte.
　J. Black, 278(IS):Vol41-151
　D. Heartz, 415:Jul86-389
　A. Steptoe, 410(M&L):Oct86-417
Hodgson, P., ed. "The Cloud of Unknowing"
and Related Treatises on Contemplative
Prayer.*
　W. Riehle, 72:Band223Heft2-402
Hödl, G. & P. Classen, eds. Die Admonter
Briefsammlung.
　J.M. Powell, 589:Jul86-665
Hodne, Ø. The Types of Norwegian Folk-
tale.*
　B. Holbek, 563(SS):Spring86-188
　W.E. Richmond, 301(JEGP):Oct86-637
　J. Simpson, 203:Vol97No1-117
Hodson, P. Under a Sickle Moon.
　I. Jack, 617(TLS):8May87-483
　B. Woffinden, 362:27Aug87-18
Hoelscher-Obermaier, H-P. Das lyrische
Werk Antoni Langes.
　P. Coates, 575(SEER):Oct86-649
Hoermann, R. Achim von Arnim.*
　R. Burwick, 222(GR):Fall86-178
von Hofe, H. - see Feuchtwanger, L. & A.
Zweig
Hoff, U. The Art of Arthur Boyd.
　A. Ross, 364:Aug/Sep86-140
Höffe, O. Strategien der Humanität. Ethik
und Politik. Sittlich-politische Dis-
kurse.
　K. Schuhmann, 489(PJGG):Band93Heft1-
194
Hoffer, P.C. Revolution and Regeneration.
　J.E. Illick, 656(WMQ):Apr86-321
Hoffman, A. Illumination Night.
　G. Cravens, 441:9Aug87-7
　L. Taylor, 362:10Dec87-30
　442(NY):28Sep87-96
Hoffman, A., with J. Silvers. Steal this
Urine Test.
　H.M. Schmeck, Jr., 441:29Nov87-21

Hoffman, D. Paul Bunyan.
　G. Boyes, 203:Vol97No1-119
Hoffman, D., ed. Ezra Pound and William
Carlos Williams.
　D. Smith, 106:Winter86-509
Hoffman, M.J. Critical Essays on Gertrude
Stein.*
　I.B.N., 295(JML):Nov86-541
Hoffman, P.T. Church and Community in the
Diocese of Lyon, 1500-1789.*
　C. Jones, 83:Autumn86-238
Hoffman, R. & P.J. Albert, eds. Peace and
the Peacemakers.
　G. Clarfield, 656(WMQ):Oct86-682
Hoffmann, C. Die Pfosten sind, die Bretter
aufgeschlagen, und jedermann erwartet
sich ein Fest.
　R. Dressler, 654(WB):3/1986-509
Hoffmann, E.T.A. Écrits sur la musique.
(B. Hebert, ed)
　F. Claudon, 537:Vol72No2-300
Hoffmann, G. Heinrich Böll.
　M. Butler, 617(TLS):15May87-521
Hoffmann, J. Die Geschichte der Wlassow-
Armee.
　F.L. Carsten, 575(SEER):Jan86-146
Hoffmann, L-F. Essays on Haitian Litera-
ture.
　M.A. Lubin, 538(RAL):Winter86-593
Hoffmann, L-F. Le Français en français,
niveau intermédiaire.*
　T.M. Scanlan, 399(MLJ):Spring86-61
Hoffmann, P. The Anatomy of Idealism.
　M.S. Gram, 543:Sep86-128
Hoffmann, R. Figuren des Scheins.
　M.W. Jennings, 221(GQ):Summer86-466
Hoffmann, W. "Ansturm gegen die letzte
irdische Grenze."
　J. Hibberd, 133:Band19Heft3/4-358
　J. Rolleston, 301(JEGP):Oct86-632
Hoffmann, Y., ed. Japanese Death Poems.
　J. Kirkup, 617(TLS):27Mar87-320
Hoffmeister, G. Byron und der europäische
Byronismus.*
　R.P. Lessenich, 72:Band223Heft1-170
　H.N. Rohloff, 38:Band104Heft1/2-240
Hoffmeister, G., ed. Fortunatus.
　H.G. Rötzer, 133:Band19Heft2-169
Hoffmeister, G., ed. German Baroque Lit-
erature.*
　R.D. Hacken, 406:Fall86-396
Hoffmeister, G. Goethe und die europäische
Romantik.*
　H. Dunkle, 221(GQ):Summer86-480
　H.A. Pausch, 107(CRCL):Mar86-140
　H. Reiss, 133:Band19Heft3/4-344
Hoffpauir, R. Romantic Fallacies.
　R. Tetreault, 150(DR):Winter85/86-601
Hofmann, E., ed. Benjamin Constant, Madame
de Staël, et le groupe de Coppet.
　M. Zobel-Finger, 72:Band223Heft1-211
Hofmann, G. The Spectacle at the Tower.*
　A. Smith, 617(TLS):15May87-524
Hofmann, M. Acrimony.
　A. Coles, 362:8Jan87-23
　H. Haughton, 617(TLS):20Mar87-301
　S. Knight, 364:Dec86/Jan87-131
von Hofmannsthal, H. Sämtliche Werke III.
(G.E. Hübner, K-G. Pott & C. Michel, eds)
Sämtliche Werke XXX. (M. Pape, ed)
　G. Finney, 406:Summer86-238

Hofstadter, D.R. Metamagical Themas.*
617(TLS):10Apr87-397

Hogan, D. A Curious Street.
R. Tracy, 174(Eire):Spring86-143

Hogan, J.C. A Commentary on The Complete
Greek Tragedies: Aeschylus.
J.M. Walton, 610(Autumn86-247

Hogan, R. "Since O'Casey" and Other Essays
on Irish Drama.*
E. Kraft, 177(ELT):Vol29No1-105

"The Hogarth Letters."*
639(VQR):Autumn86-123

Hogenson, G.B. Jung's Struggle with Freud.
D. Bakan, 488:Sep86-404

Höger, A. Hetärismus und bürgerliche
Gesellschaft im Frühwerk Frank Wedekinds.
A.B. Willeke, 406:Spring86-115

Hogg, J. James Hogg: Anecdotes of Sir
Walter Scott. (D.S. Mack, ed)
I. Campbell, 447(N&Q):Jun85-275

Hogg, J. James Hogg: Selected Stories and
Sketches.* (D.S. Mack, ed)
G.H. Hughes, 447(N&Q):Mar85-140

Hogg, J. A Shepherd's Delight. (J. Steel,
ed)
G.H. Hughes, 571(ScLJ):Summer86-9

Hogg, J. Tales of Love and Mystery.* (D.
Groves, ed)
H.B. de Groot, 627(UTQ):Fall86-109
G.H. Hughes, 571(ScLJ):Summer86-9

Hogg, J. - see Keller, H.

Hoggart, R. & D. Johnson. An Idea of
Europe.
C. Tugendhat, 176:Dec87-77

Hoglund, A.W. Immigrants and Their
Children in the United States.
L. Schelbert, 563(SS):Autumn86-441

Hogrefe, J. "Wholly Unacceptable."*
A. Howard, 617(TLS):16Jan87-58
639(VQR):Autumn86-137

Hogwood, B.W. From Crisis to Complacency?
V. Bogdanor, 617(TLS):16-22Oct87-1131

Hogwood, C. Handel.*
P.M. Young, 410(M&L):Apr86-162

Hohenberg, P.M. & L.H. Lees. The Making
of Urban Europe, 1000-1950.
R.C. Hoffmann, 589:Oct86-1024

Hohendahl, P.U. Literarische Kultur im
Zeitalter des Liberalismus 1830-1870.*
A. Bohm, 400(MLN):Apr86-713
J. Osborne, 402(MLR):Apr87-516

Hohendahl, P.U., ed. Literaturkritik.*
(Vol 4)
J.L. Sammons, 221(GQ):Spring86-325

Hohendahl, U., ed. Geschichte der deutsch-
en Literaturkritik.
H. Kähler, 654(WB):1/1986-159

Hohler, R.T. "I Touch the Future..."
M.S. Kennedy, 441:15Mar87-23

Hoisington, W.A., Jr. The Casablanca Connection.
E. Morot-Sir, 207(FR):May87-895

de Holanda, F. Da Pintura Antiga. (A.
González García, ed)
J. Bury, 90:Nov86-832

Holcot, R. Exploring the Boundaries of
Reason.
E.D. Sylla, 589:Apr86-501

Holden, A.J., ed. Le Roman de Waldef.
G. Roques, 553(RLiR):Jan-Jun86-290

Holden, J. Style and Authenticity in Post-
modern Poetry.
M. Ford, 617(TLS):22May87-557
W. Woessner, 441:22Mar87-29

Holden, U. Tin Toys.*
J. Neville, 364:Jun86-96

Holder, E. Manfred ou l'hésitation.
M-F. Hilgar, 207(FR):Mar87-558

Holder, R.W., comp. A Dictionary of American and British Euphemisms.
617(TLS):8May87-493

Holdheim, W.W. The Hermeneutic Mode.*
J. Alter, 207(FR):Apr87-700
H. Bertens, 549(RLC):Jan-Mar86-98
J. Goodliffe, 478:Apr86-105
M-T. Mathet, 535(RHL):Nov-Dec86-1151

Holeczek, H. Erasmus Deutsch. (Vol 1)
P.G. Bietenholz, 551(RenQ):Summer86-
297

Holinger, W. The Fence-Walker.
G. Davenport, 569(SR):Fall86-672

Holland, A. "Manon Lescaut" de l'abbé
Prévost, 1731-1759.
J-P. Sermain, 535(RHL):Jul-Aug86-755

Holland, A.J., ed. Philosophy.
G.H.R. Parkinson, 483:Oct86-550

Holland, B., ed. Soviet Sisterhood.
W.Z. Goldman, 550(RusR):Oct86-452
639(VQR):Winter86-26

Holland, J. The American Connection.
M.F. Nolan, 441:22Mar87-12
C.C. O'Brien, 61:Apr87-89

Holland, N.N. The I.*
H. Kellner, 400(MLN):Dec86-1249
H. Rapaport, 478:Oct86-344

Hollander, J. In Time and Place.
R. von Hallberg, 441:15Feb87-42
J. Parini, 617(TLS):17Jul87-767

Hollander, J. Vision and Resonance.*
A. Haberer, 189(EA):Jan-Mar87-111

Hollander, N. The Whole Enchilada.
M. Richler, 441:3May87-35

Hollander, S. Classical Economics.
T.W. Hutchison, 617(TLS):11-17Dec87-
1372

Hollander, S. The Economics of John Stuart
Mill.
S. Rashid, 637(VS):Spring87-429

Holliday, J.C. Land at the Centre.
S. Alderson, 324:Jun87-534

Hollier, D. The Politics of Prose.*
(French title: Politique de la Prose.)
J. Weightman, 453(NYRB):13Aug87-42

Hollingsworth, M. Willful Acts.
R. Fraticelli, 108:Summer86-149

Hollis, C.C. Language and Style in "Leaves
of Grass."*
D. Babington, 106:Fall86-337
S. Hutchinson, 447(N&Q):Dec85-548

Hollis, M. Invitation to Philosophy.
A. Holland, 518:Jul86-156
P. Lamarque, 479(PhQ):Oct86-540
T.M.R., 185:Oct86-294

Hollis, M. & S. Lukes, eds. Rationality
and Relativism.*
A. Boyer, 542:Jul-Sep86-413
I.C. Jarvie & J. Agassi, 488:Sep86-367

Hollist, W.L. & F.L. Tullis, eds. An
International Political Economy.
K.K.T., 185:Apr87-710

Hollister, C.W. Monarchy, Magnates and
Institutions in the Anglo-Norman World.
J.R. Maddicott, 617(TLS):27Feb87-219

173

Holloway, J., ed. The Oxford Book of Local Verses.
P. Beer, 617(TLS):17Jul87-764
Holloway, J. The Slumber of Apollo.*
F. McCombie, 447(N&Q):Sep85-420
J. Voelker, 577(SHR):Winter86-79
Holly, M.A. Panofsky and the Foundations of Art History.*
D. Dahlstrom, 543:Mar87-579
C. Gould, 39:Mar86-221
M. Iversen, 59:Jun86-271
R.A. Smith, 709:Spring87-176
Holm, B. The Box of Daylight. Smoky Top.
A. Wardwell, 39:Sep86-226
Holm, B. Romanens mödrar 2.
J.E. Bellquist, 563(SS):Autumn86-443
Holm, J., ed. Central American English.*
H. Ulherr, 38:Band104Heft1/2-170
Holman-Hunt, D. My Grandmothers and I.
617(TLS):10Apr87-397
Holmes, G. Florence, Rome and the Origins of Renaissance.
L. Martines, 617(TLS):22May87-560
Holmes, G. Politics, Religion and Society in England, 1679-1742.
M. Goldie, 617(TLS):6Feb87-143
Holmes, J.S. & W.J. Smith, eds. Dutch Interior.
J.C. Prins, 222(GR):Summer86-133
Holmes, M. The Country House Described.
T. Russell-Cobb, 324:Aug87-708
Holmes, P. The Green Road.
S. Knight, 364:Dec86/Jan87-131
Holmes, P. Resistance and Compromise.
R.A. Anselment, 677(YES):Vol16-234
Holmes, R. Firing Line.
M.R.D. Foot, 176:Feb87-45
Holmquist, I. & E. Witt-Brattström, eds. Kvinnornas litteraturhistoria. (Pt 2)
B. Steene, 562(Scan):May86-101
Holquist, M. - see Bakhtin, M.M.
Holst, I. Britten. (3rd ed)
F.E. Peterson, 465:Autumn86-139
Holt, G. French Country Kitchen.
A. Davidson, 617(TLS):18-24Dec87-1401
Holt, J.C. Robin Hood.*
R. Wadge, 203:Vol97No1-114
Holt, M.P., ed. Drama Contemporary: Spain.
C. De Oliveira, 399(MLJ):Autumn86-332
Holt, R.L. Good Friday.
N. Callendar, 441:6Dec87-79
Höltgen, K.J. Aspects of the Emblem.
J.B. Trapp, 617(TLS):14Aug87-879
A.R. Young, 150(DR):Winter85/86-598
Holton, G. The Advancement of Science, and Its Burdens.*
B. Pippard, 617(TLS):17Jul87-774
Holtus, J., ed. La versione franco-italiana della "Bataille d'Aliscans."
G. Roques, 553(RLiR):Jan-Jun86-287
Holtus, G. & E. Radtke, eds. Varietäten-linguistik des Italienischen.*
H. Stammerjohann, 72:Band223Heft1-197
Holtzman, H. & M.S. James - see Mondrian, P.
Holub, M. The Fly.
P. Forbes, 362:25Jun87-31
Holub, R.C. Heinrich Heine's Reception of German Grecophilia.
M. Geisler, 406:Spring86-108
Holub, R.C. Reception Theory.*
S. Rendall, 478:Apr86-139

Holum, K.G. Theodosian Empresses.*
H.C. Teitler, 394:Vol39fasc3/4-533
Holyoake, J. Montaigne: "Essais."
M.B. McKinley, 402(MLR):Oct86-1000
Holz, H. & E. Wolf-Gazo, eds. Whitehead und der Prozessbegriff.*
D. Birnbacher, 489(PJGG):Band93Heft2-427
Holzberger, W.G. & H.J. Saatkamp, Jr. - see Santayana, G.
Holzel, T. & A. Salkeld. First on Everest.* (British title: The Mystery of Mallory and Irvine.)
D. Murphy, 617(TLS):30Jan87-106
J. Wickwire, 441:1Feb87-21
Holzermayr, K. Historicité et conceptualité de la littérature médiévale.
A.J. Holden, 554:Vol105No4-580
R. Pensom, 208(FS):Jul86-321
Holzhey, H. & G. Kohler, with C. Gabnebin, eds. Eigentum und seine Gründe.
K. Homann, 687:Jul-Sep86-448
Homan, S. Beckett's Theaters.*
H.P. Abbott, 301(JEGP):Oct86-598
Homans, M. Women Writers and Poetic Identity.
J. Loving, 183(ESQ):Vol32No3-201
Homberger, E. American Writers and Radical Politics, 1900-39.
J. Moynahan, 617(TLS):14Aug87-882
A. Ryan, 362:5Feb87-25
Homer. Pope's "Iliad."* (A. Pope, trans; F. Rosslyn, ed)
F.C. Blessington, 566:Spring87-196
Homer, A. What We Did After Rain.*
R. Robbins, 271:Spring-Summer86-190
Homer, F.X.J. & L.D. Wilcox, eds. Germany and Europe in the Era of the Two World Wars.
639(VQR):Autumn86-120
Homolya, I. Valentine Bakfark.
R. Spencer, 410(M&L):Jan86-82
Honan, P. Matthew Arnold.
R. Shaw, 289:Spring86-121
Honan, P. Jane Austen.
D. Nokes, 617(TLS):6-12Nov87-1216
T. Tanner, 362:22Oct87-30
Honderich, T., ed. Morality and Objectivity.*
J.C. Klagge, 185:Oct86-278
I.G. McFetridge, 483:Oct86-542
Hondros, J.L. Occupation and Resistance.
S. Wichert, 575(SEER):Jul86-480
Honey, M. Creating Rosie the Riveter.
S.C. Koppelman, 115:Winter86-110
Hong Lysa. Thailand in the Nineteenth Century.
C.M. Wilson, 293(JASt):Aug86-906
Honig, E., ed. The Poet's Other Voice.*
639(VQR):Spring86-43
Honig, E. & S.M. Brown - see Pessoa, F.
Honigmann, E.A.J. Shakespeare: The "Lost Years."*
D. George, 570(SQ):Winter86-525
Honigmann, E.A.J. Shakespeare's Impact on His Contemporaries.*
W. Weiss, 156(ShJW):Jahrbuch1986-198
Honigmann, E.A.J. John Weever.
K. Duncan-Jones, 617(TLS):23-29Oct87-1165
Honko, L. & P. Laaksonen, eds. Trends in Nordic Tradition Research.
K. Grimstad, 650(WF):Jan86-52

Houlihan, P.F., with S.H. Goodman. The Birds of Ancient Egypt.
  J.A.C. Greppin, 617(TLS):6Feb87-144
Houppermans, S. Raymond Roussel.
  C. Toloudis, 207(FR):Apr87-711
Hourani, G. Reason and Tradition in Islamic Ethics.
  O. Leaman, 483:Jul86-420
House, J. Monet.
  E. Cowling, 617(TLS):27Mar87-331
House, J. & S. Blum-Kulka, eds. Interlingual and Intercultural Communication.
  H. Lindquist, 596(SL):Vol40No2-190
House, K.S. - see Cooper, J.F.
Houseman, J. Unfinished Business.
  P. Brunette, 617(TLS):2Jan87-16
  J. Richards, 176:Jan87-50
Houston, D. With the Offal Eaters.*
  J. Mole, 176:Mar87-60
Houston, J., ed. Is it Reasonable to Believe in God?
  A. Millar, 479(PhQ):Jan86-103
Houston, J.D. Love Life.
  N.O. Nelson, 649(WAL):Nov86-239
Houston, J.D. One Can Think About Life After the Fish Is In the Canoe.
  J.W. Byrkit, 649(WAL):Aug86-184
Houston, J.W. Beyond Manzanar.
  J.W. Byrkit, 649(WAL):Aug86-184
Houston, R.A. Scottish Literacy and the Scottish Identity.
  B.N. Gonul, 568(SCN):Winter86-60
van Houts, E.M.C. Gesta Normannorum ducum.
  B.M. Kaczynski, 589:Jan86-219
Houtzagers, H.P. The Čakavian Dialect of Orlec on the Island of Cres.*
  G. Thomas, 402(MLR):Apr87-542
Hovde, C.F., W.L. Howarth & E.H. Witherell - see Thoreau, H.D.
Hovi, K. Interessensphären im Baltikum.
  J. Hiden, 575(SEER):Apr86-303
Howard, A. Rab.
  D. Cannadine, 453(NYRB):17Dec87-63
  N. Gash, 617(TLS):13Mar87-259
  J. Ramsden, 362:19Mar87-23
Howard, D. From Marx to Kant.
  H. van der Linden, 319:Oct87-612
Howard, D., ed. Philip Massinger.
  M. Dodsworth, 175:Spring86-105
Howard, D. & A. Duhaime, eds. Haiku.
  R. Spiess, 404:Winter-Spring86-58
Howard, D.R. Chaucer.
  P-L. Adams, 61:Nov87-122
  C. Rawson, 441:13Dec87-43
Howard, D.R. Chaucer and the Medieval World.
  D. Pearsall, 362:19Nov87-37
Howard, F. Wilbur and Orville.
  T. Ferrell, 441:19Jul87-8
Howard, J. Form and History in American Literary Naturalism.
  R.A. Cassell, 395(MFS):Summer86-257
  V. Fitzpatrick, 27(AL):Dec86-644
Howard, J.E. Shakespeare's Art of Orchestration.*
  R. Berry, 301(JEGP):Jan86-121
  M. Cheney, 551(RenQ):Autumn86-563
  P. Gaudet, 615(TJ):Mar86-116
  K. Newman, 570(SQ):Autumn86-402
  D.H. Ogden, 610:Spring86-67
  D.G. Watson, 536(Rev):Vol8-59

Howard, M. The Early Tudor Country House.
  J. Summerson, 617(TLS):18-24Sep87-1013
Howard, M. The Wisdom of the Runes.
  J.S. Ryan, 67:May86-117
Howard, P., ed. Benjamin Britten: "The Turn of the Screw."*
  P. Evans, 410(M&L):Oct86-399
  A. Whittall, 415:Aug86-443
Howard, P. The Operas of Benjamin Britten.
  D.W. Wakeling, 465:Autumn86-145
Howarth, D. Lord Arundel and his Circle.*
  M. Bence-Jones, 324:Jan87-168
Howarth, P. Intelligence Chief Extraordinary.
  A. Glees, 617(TLS):30Jan87-102
Howat, R. - see Eigeldinger, J-J.
Howatch, S. Glittering Images.
  L. Dickstein, 441:18Oct87-30
Howe, I. The American Newness.*
  R. Coles, 432(NEQ):Dec86-564
  S.T. Gutman, 27(AL):Dec86-631
  B. Lee, 617(TLS):2Jan87-8
  L. Marx, 453(NYRB):12Mar87-36
Howe, I. Socialism and America.*
  G. McKenna, 396(ModA):Summer/Fall86-315
  639(VQR):Spring86-60
Howe, N. The Old English Catalogue Poems.
  B. Mitchell, 541(RES):Nov86-624
Howell, M. & P. Ford. Medical Mysteries.
  J.F. Watkins, 617(TLS):30Jan87-118
Howells, M. & K. Skinner. The Ripper Legacy.
  P. Highsmith, 617(TLS):25-31Dec87-1427
  B. Woolley, 362:17&24Dec87-54
Howells, R.J. Pierre Jurieu.
  B. Cottret, 535(RHL):Mar-Apr86-287
Howells, R.J. & others, eds. Voltaire and his World.
  J.H. Brumfitt, 208(FS):Oct86-461
Howells, W.D. Selected Letters.* (Vols 5 & 6) (W.C. Fischer, W.M. Gibson & C.K. Lohmann, eds)
  E. Wagenknecht, 402(MLR):Apr87-457
Hower, E. Wolf Tickets.
  L.B. Osborne, 441:18Jan87-18
Howie, J., ed. Ethical Principles for Social Policy.
  T.Y. Henderson, 154:Autumn86-584
Howlett, J. Murder of a Moderate Man.
  N. Callendar, 441:22Feb87-24
  442(NY):18May87-120
Hoxha, E. The Artful Albanian. (J. Halliday, ed)
  G. Chamberlain, 441:18Oct87-34
  R. Clogg, 617(TLS):19Jun87-667
Hoy, A.H. Fabrications.
  A. Grundberg, 441:6Dec87-21
Hoy, C. Bill Davis.
  G.W., 102(CanL):Spring86-203
Hoy, C.M. A Philosophy of Individual Freedom.
  P.F., 185:Oct86-301
Hoy, D.C., ed. Foucault.
  J. Boswell, 441:18Jan87-31
de Hoz, J. On Aeschylean Composition I.
  D. van Nes, 394:Vol39fasc3/4-472
Hrabal, B. Proluky.
  I. Hájek, 617(TLS):2-8Oct87-1067
Hribal, C.J. Matty's Heart.*
  A. Arthur, 649(WAL):Aug86-168

Hsiao Tseng, ed. Ti-cheng ta-tz'u-tien.
    R.H. Myers, 293(JASt):May86-571
Hsieh Hai-p'ing. T'ang-tai shih-jen jü
    tsai-hua wai-kuo-jen chih wen-tzu-chiao.
    F.K.H. So, 116:Jul85-209
Hsu, T-C. The Chinese Conception of the
    Theatre.*
    W.J. Meserve, 612(ThS):May/Nov86-182
    K. Rea, 157:No162-51
Hsu, V.L., ed. Stories of Modern Chinese
    Women.
    T.E. Barlow, 116:Jul85-193
Huang Liu-hung. A Complete Book Concern-
    ing Happiness and Benevolence. (D. Chu,
    ed & trans)
    L.A. Struve, 318(JAOS):Oct/Dec85-768
    M. Zelin, 293(JASt):Nov85-111
Huang Mei-ling. T'ang-tai shih-p'ing-chung
    feng-ke-lun chih yen-chiu.
    F.K.H. So, 116:Jul85-209
Huang, P.C.C. The Peasant Economy and
    Social Change in North China.*
    P. Duara, 244(HJAS):Jun86-283
    S. Mann, 293(JASt):May86-572
Huang Wei-liang, comp. Huo-yü te feng-
    huang.
    S.S.J. Hou, 116:Jul85-201
Hubbard, B.A.F. & E.S. Karnofsky. Plato's
    "Protagoras."
    A.R. Mele, 449:Jun86-269
    R.K. Sprague, 122:Jan86-85
Hubbard, F.A. Theories of Action in Con-
    rad.*
    B.E. Teets, 177(ELT):Vol29No1-101
Hubbard, K. The Best of Kin Hubbard.
    (D.S. Hawes, ed)
    G. Weales, 569(SR):Winter86-xvi
Huber, R.E. & R. Rieth - see under "Glos-
    sarium artis (deutsch-französische
    englisch)."
Hubin, A.J. Crime Fiction, 1749-1980.
    B.C. Bloomfield, 354:Mar86-96
    W.P. Kenney, 365:Spring/Summer86-180
Hubka, T.C. Big House, Little House, Back
    House, Barn.*
    J.M. Vlach, 440:Summer-Fall86-166
Hübler, A. Einander verstehen.
    M. Görlach, 355(LSoc):Sep86-439
Hübler, A. Understatements and Hedges in
    English.*
    J. Holmes, 355(LSoc):Jun86-245
Hübner, G.E., K-G. Pott & C. Michel - see
    von Hofmannsthal, H.
Hübner, K. & J. Vuillemin, eds. Wissen-
    schaftliche und nichtwissenschaftliche
    Rationalität.*
    R. Zimmer, 53(AGP):Band68Heft3-346
Huchel, P. Peter Huchel: Gesammelte Werke
    in zwei Bänden.* (A. Vieregg, ed)
    H.A. Hesse, 67:May86-126
    P. Hutchinson, 402(MLR):Apr86-536
Hucke, K-H. Jene "Scheu vor allem Mercan-
    tilischen."
    H.S. Daemmrich, 564:Sep86-258
    L. Sharpe, 402(MLR):Apr86-533
Hucker, C.O. A Dictionary of Official
    Titles in Imperial China.
    H. Bielenstein, 244(HJAS):Dec86-611
Huddleston, R. Introduction to the Grammar
    of English.*
    G. Ayres, 350:Sep87-635
    K. Brown, 297(JL):Sep86-501
    J. Lavédrine, 189(EA):Jul-Sep87-335

Hudgins, A. Saints and Strangers.*
    M. Jarman, 249(HudR):Summer86-346
    R.B. Shaw, 491:Apr86-41
    L. Skipper, 502(PrS):Fall86-125
    455:Dec86-64
Hudson, A., ed. English Wycliffite
    Sermons.* (Vol 1)
    J.A. Alford, 405(MP):Aug86-67
    K. Bitterling, 38:Band104Heft3/4-493
    S. Wenzel, 447(N&Q):Mar85-98
Hudson, H. A Temporary Residence.
    M. Buck, 441:27Dec87-18
Hudson, N. Mobile Homes.
    C. Rooke, 376:Sep86-153
Hudson, P. The Genesis of Industrial
    Capital.
    S. Pollard, 617(TLS):27Mar87-322
Hudson, R. Word Grammar.*
    R.D. Borsley, 361:Jul86-283
    M.B. Kac, 603:Vol10No2-507
    D.J. Napoli, 297(JL):Mar86-187
Hudson, S.D. Human Character and Morality.
    D. Miller, 617(TLS):22May87-544
Hudson, W.H. & G. Gissing. Landscapes and
    Literati. (D. Shrubsall & P. Coustillas,
    eds)
    M.S. Vogeler, 177(ELT):Vol29No4-453
Hudspeth, R.N. - see Fuller, M.
Huebert, R. - see Shirley, J.
Huelsenbeck, R. Reise bis ans Ende der
    Freiheit.* (U. Karthaus & H. Krueger,
    eds)
    W. Paulsen, 133:Band19Heft3/4-370
Huerta Calvo, J. El teatro medieval y
    renacentista.
    J.C. Temprano, 238:Sep86-539
Huf, L. A Portrait of the Artist as a
    Young Woman.
    C. McLay, 106:Winter86-477
    S. O'Brien, 395(MFS):Summer86-353
    J. Todd, 402(MLR):Apr87-464
Huff, R. Shore Guide to Flocking Names.
    J. Carter, 219(GaR):Summer86-532
Hufschmidt, J. & others. Sprachverhalten
    in ländlichen Gemeinden. (Vol 2)
    A. Pauwels, 355(LSoc):Dec86-547
Huggan, I. The Elizabeth Stories.*
    E. Currie, 441:12Jul87-11
    442(NY):31Aug87-97
Huggett, F.E. Teachers.
    R. Floud, 617(TLS):13Mar87-263
Hughes, A. & D. Porter, eds. Current
    Developments in Language Testing.*
    D.G. Brodkey, 355(LSoc):Sep86-440
    W. Grabe, 361:Sep86-61
Hughes, D. Bishop Sahib.
    B. Fothergill, 617(TLS):30Jan87-107
Hughes, D. The Joke of the Century.*
    442(NY):5Jan87-85
Hughes, D. The Pork Butcher.
    P. Lewis, 565:Spring86-38
Hughes, E.J. Marcel Proust.*
    M. Spencer, 345:Nov86-500
Hughes, G., ed. Papers Given at the First
    James Hogg Society Conference (Stirling,
    1983).*
    A. Fraser, 588(SSL):Vol21-370
Hughes, G. The Poetry of Francisco de la
    Torre.*
    L. Cerrón Puga, 403(MLS):Spring86-89
Hughes, G. The Rape of the Rose.
    S. Altinel, 617(TLS):18-24Sep87-1027
Hughes, G.E. - see Buridan, J.

Hunger, H., ed. Prochoros Kydones, Über-
setzung von acht Briefen des Hl. Augus-
tinus.*
   A. Kazhdan, 589:Jan86-238
Hunnicutt, E. In the Music Library.
   K. Weber, 441:11Oct87-56
Hunt, J.D. Garden and Grove.*
   J. Lees-Milne, 39:Oct86-381
Hunt, J.D. & F.M. Holland, eds. The Ruskin
Polygon.
   M. Brooks, 576:Jun86-177
Hunt, L. Politics, Culture, and Class in
the French Revolution.*
   J. Klancher, 250(HLQ):Autumn86-409
Hunt, M.H. Ideology and U.S. Foreign
Policy.
   D.M. Kennedy, 441:14Jun87-30
Hunt, M.H. The Making of a Special Rela-
tionship.
   C.W. Hayford, 293(JASt):Aug86-821
"Myron Hunt, 1868-1952."
   C. Robertson, 658:Winter86-315
Hunt, R.W. The Schools and the Cloister.
   A.G. Rigg, 589:Jul86-666
Hunt, S. Collected Poems, 1963-1980.
   B. King, 577(SHR):Winter86-94
Hunter, A. Joseph Conrad and the Ethics
of Darwinism.*
   C. Watts, 402(MLR):Jul86-730
   K. Williamson, 447(N&Q):Sep85-406
Hunter, C. The Life and Letters of Alex-
ander Wilson.
   G.R.R., 588(SSL):Vol21-342
   D-J.S. Ridge, 588(SSL):Vol21-339
Hunter, G.K. & C.J. Rawson - see "The
Yearbook of English Studies"
Hunter, I. Nothing to Repent.
   A. Bell, 362:19Feb87-25
   F. Raphael, 617(TLS):31Jul87-816
Hunter, J. The Hallamshire Glossary.
   N. Philip, 203:Vol97No1-119
Hunter, J.D. Evangelicalism.
   A. Swidler, 441:10May87-33
Hunter, J.E., comp. Concise Dictionary of
Modern Japanese History.*
   W.D. Kinzley, 293(JASt):Feb86-399
Hunter, J.F.M. Understanding Wittgenstein.
   T.S. Champlin, 518:Oct86-219
Hunter, L. Rhetorical Stance in Modern
Literature.
   D. Bogdan, 289:Summer86-111
Hunter, R. The Fourth Angel.
   G.M. Henry, 441:18Jan87-18
Hunter, R.L. The New Comedy of Greece and
Rome.
   W.S. Anderson, 124:Mar-Apr87-321
   J. Barsby, 67:Nov86-298
   J.M. Walton, 610:Autumn86-247
   N. Zagagi, 123:Vol36No2-252
Hunter-Lougheed, R. Die Nachtwachen von
Bonaventura.
   W. Paulsen, 564:Sep86-264
Huntingdon, E. The Unsettled Account.
   V.L. Smith, 617(TLS):17Jul87-761
Huntington, J. The Logic of Fantasy.
   R.G. Hampson, 447(N&Q):Jun85-284
   P. Parrinder, 402(MLR):Jul86-731
Huntington, S.L. The "Pāla-Sena" Schools
of Sculpture.*
   R. Morris, 318(JAOS):Oct/Dec85-788
Hüppauf, B., ed. Ansichten vom Krieg.
   A. Obermayer, 564:Nov86-333

Huppé, B.F. The Hero in the Earthly City.
   E.B. Irving, Jr., 589:Jul86-668
Hüpper-Dröge, D. Schild und Speer.
   W.H. Jackson, 402(MLR):Oct86-1032
Huré, J.S. I Mary, Daughter of Israel.
   T. Rajak, 617(TLS):21Aug87-896
Hurford, D. The Right Moves.
   G. Chin, 441:16Aug87-17
Hurst, A., O. Reverdin & J. Rudhardt, eds &
trans. Papyrus Bodmer XXIX.*
   D. van Berchem, 303(JoHS):Vol106-264
Hurst, H.R. Kingsholm.
   S.E. Cleary, 123:Vol36No2-351
Hurwit, J.M. The Art and Culture of Early
Greece, 1100-480 B.C.
   639(VQR):Summer86-104
Huse, N. & W. Wolters. Venedig.
   B. Boucher, 617(TLS):30Oct-5Nov87-
1202
Huseboe, A.R. Herbert Krause.
   R.L. Gale, 649(WAL):Aug86-182
Huser, F. La Chambre ouverte.
   M. Naudin, 207(FR):May87-909
Huskey, E. Russian Lawyers and the Soviet
State.
   639(VQR):Autumn86-121
Husserl, E. Einleitung in die Logik und
Erkenntnistheorie. (U. Melle, ed)
   R. Sokolowski, 543:Jun87-779
Husserl, E. Logische Untersuchungen.
   B. Grünewald, 687:Apr-Jun86-297
Hussey, E. - see Aristotle
Hussey, J.M. The Orthodox Church in the
Byzantine Empire.
   G. Fowden, 617(TLS):16Jan87-68
Hussey, S.S. The Literary Language of
Shakespeare.*
   B.D.H. Miller, 541(RES):May86-252
   J. Schäfer, 402(MLR):Oct86-985
Hussman, L.E., Jr. Dreiser and His Fic-
tion.
   S.C. Brennan, 403(MLS):Summer86-327
Hutcheon, L. Formalism and the Freudian
Aesthetic.*
   D. Morton, 651(WHR):Autumn86-287
   R.R. Wilson, 178:Dec86-491
   E. Wright, 208(FS):Jan86-107
Hutcheon, L. A Theory of Parody.*
   D. Collinson, 89(BJA):Spring86-181
   D.J. Dooley, 616:Spring/Summer86-57
   M. Głowiński, 549(RLC):Oct-Dec86-464
   K. Kuiper, 478:Oct86-343
   M.E. O'Connor, 627(UTQ):Fall86-117
   C. Shorley, 208(FS):Oct86-491
   R. Terry, 184(EIC):Apr86-160
   C. Thomson, 193(ELit):Spring86-163
Hutchings, B. The Poetry of William Cow-
per.*
   R. Bradford, 447(N&Q):Sep85-398
Hutchings, R. The Structural Origins of
Soviet Industrial Expansion.
   D.A. Dyker, 575(SEER):Jan86-152
Hutchings, R.L. Soviet-East European Rela-
tions.
   H. Hanak, 575(SEER):Jul86-485
Hutchinson, D.S. The Virtues of Aristotle.
   M. Schofield, 617(TLS):3Apr87-368
Hutchinson, G.O. - see Aeschylus
Hutchinson, P. Climbing the Light.
   J. Lanchester, 493:Jun86-113
Hutchinson, P. Games Authors Play.*
   R.J. Dingley, 447(N&Q):Sep85-427

Hutchison, B. The Unfinished Country.
G.W., 102(CanL):Fall86-197
Hütter, E. & H. Magirius. Der Wechsel-
burger Lettner.
W. Haas, 43:Band16Heft2-209
Hutter, I., ed. Byzanz und der Westen.
R.S. Nelson, 589:Oct86-936
Hüttinger, E. & others, eds. Künstler
Häuser von der Renaissance bis zur Gegen-
wart.
J. Anderson, 90:Jun86-440
Hutton, J. Themes of Peace in Renaissance
Poetry.* (R. Guerlac, ed)
B.C. Ewell, 301(JEGP):Oct86-559
E.V. George, 124:Jul-Aug87-460
G.W. Pigman 3d, 551(RenQ):Spring86-82
R. Pooley, 539:Spring87-202
J.M. Steadman, 131(CL):Fall86-382
Hutton, L. Bellum Grammaticale sive Nom-
inum Verborumque Discordia Civilis.
[together with] Snelling, T. Thibaldus
sive Vindictae Ingenium. (L. Cerny, ed
of both)
G. Schmitz, 72:Band223Heft2-409
Hutton, P.A. Phil Sheridan and His Army.
J.W. Bailey, 649(WAL):Aug86-149
R.L. Nichols, 250(HLQ):Autumn86-419
W.M. Sarf, 31(ASch):Autumn86-565
Hutton, R. The Restoration.
J.V. Guerinot, 568(SCN):Fall86-46
Hutton, W. The Revolution that Never Was.*
R. Skidelsky, 617(TLS):25Sep-1Oct87-
1035
Huxley, E. Out in the Midday Sun.*
L. Dawkins, 441:22Mar87-20
442(NY):13Apr87-104
Huyser, R.E. Mission to Tehran.*
R. Jervis, 441:22Feb87-14
Huysmans, J-K. Lettres à Théodore Hannon
(1876-1886). (P. Cogny & C. Berg, eds)
A. Kies, 356(LR):Aug-Nov86-319
Hvížďala, K., ed. Generace 35-45.
V. Písecký, 617(TLS):9-15Oct87-1112
Hyatte, R. - see "Laughter for the Devil"
Hyde, D. The Songs of Connacht. (B.
O'Conaire, ed)
P. Craig, 617(TLS):21Aug87-904
Hyde, E. Two Dialogues.
P-G. Boucé, 189(EA):Jul-Sep86-372
Hyde, H.M. Lord Alfred Douglas.
R. Beum, 569(SR):Summer86-lxvi
K. Powell, 637(VS):Summer87-558
Hyde, L., ed. On the Poetry of Allen Gins-
berg.*
R. Roark, 30:Winter87-93
Hyde, R. Selected Poems. (L. Wevers, ed)
J. Penberthy, 617(TLS):31Jul87-823
Hye-gu, L. - see under Lee Hye-gu
Hyland, W.G. Mortal Rivals.
D. Holloway, 441:5Jul87-3
Hyltenstam, K. & M. Peinemann, eds. Mod-
elling and Assessing Second Language
Acquisition.
M.D. Finnemann, 399(MLJ):Summer86-175
Hyman, B.D. & J. Narrow Is the Way.
H. Rubin, 441:26Apr87-16
Hyman, H.M. & W.M. Wiecek. Equal Justice
Under Law.
D. Gibson, 106:Fall86-375
Hyman, L.M. A Theory of Phonological
Weight.*
D.H., 355(LSoc):Mar86-133
F. Katamba, 297(JL):Sep86-497

Hynes, S. - see Hardy, T.
Hyvernaud, G. Le Wagon à vaches.
L. Arénilla, 450(NRF):Apr86-86

I Deug-Su. L'opera agiografica di Alcuino.
J.J. Contreni, 589:Apr86-427
Ianin, V.L., ed. Zakonodatel'stvo Drevnei
Rusi.
D.H. Kaiser, 550(RusR):Jul86-328
Iannace, G.A. Interferenza linguistica ai
confini fra Stato e Regno.*
R.C. Melzi, 275(IQ):Spring86-101
Iannucci, A.A. Forma ed evento nella
"Divina Commedia."
P.C. Viglionese, 276:Autumn86-313
Ibáñez Martínez, P.N. & M.D. Pérez García.
El retablo de Valdecabras.
I. Mateo Gómez, 48:Jan-Mar86-117
Ibn Riḍwān. Medieval Islamic Medicine.
(A.S. Gamal, ed)
G. Leiser, 589:Jan86-159
Ibn Sīnā. Remarks and Admonitions. (Pt 1)
(S.C. Inati, trans)
B.H. Zedler, 589:Jan86-239
de Icaza, F.A. Efímeras y lejanías.*
(R.A. Cardwell, ed)
D.L. Shaw, 86(BHS):Oct86-390
Ichien, M. - see Mujū Ichien
Ickler, T. Deutsch als Fremdsprache.*
B.S. Jurasek, 133:Band19Heft1-94
Ide, R.S. & J. Wittreich, eds. Composite
Orders.*
M. Fixler, 541(RES):May86-307
Idone, C. Glorious American Food.
W. & C. Cowen, 639(VQR):Spring86-67
Idzikowski, I. - see Gorki, M.
Ife, B.W. Reading and Fiction in Golden-
Age Spain.
B.W. Wardropper, 551(RenQ):Winter86-
786
Ifri, P.A. Proust et son narrataire dans
"A la Recherche du Temps perdu."*
G. Prince, 535(RHL):Mar-Apr86-332
Iga, M. The Thorn in the Chrysanthemum.
B. Moeran, 617(TLS):17Apr87-407
Ōhara Kenshirō, 285(JapQ):Oct-Dec86-
444
de la Iglesia, M.R.S. - see under Saurín
de la Iglesia, M.R.
Iglesias, J.M.G. - see under García
Iglesias, J.M.
Iglesias, M. & W. Meiden. Spanish for Oral
and Written Review. (3rd ed)
M.E. Beeson, 399(MLJ):Winter86-442
Ignatieff, G. The Making of a Peacemonger.
T.P. Socknat, 529(QQ):Summer86-455
Ignatieff, M. The Needs of Strangers.
D. Allen, 627(UTQ):Fall86-254
D. Braybrooke, 150(DR):Winter85/86-609
Ignatieff, M. The Russian Album.
B. Chatwin, 453(NYRB):24Sep87-17
S. Massie, 441:23Aug87-8
R. Scruton, 617(TLS):17Jul87-761
442(NY):28Sep87-97
Ignatius, D. Agents of Innocence.
J. Koslow, 441:13Sep87-34
Ignatow, D. New and Collected Poems, 1970-
1985.
H. Lazer, 639(VQR):Summer86-553
R.B. Shaw, 491:Nov86-100
V. Sherry, 617(TLS):6-12Nov87-1229
P. Stitt, 441:11Jan87-30

Ihimaera, W. The Matriarch.
  M. Thorpe, 176:May87-45
Ihrie, M. Skepticism in Cervantes.*
  F. Pierce, 86(BHS):Apr86-161
Ikkyū. Ikkyū and the Crazy Cloud Anthology. (S. Arntzen, comp & trans)
  J. Kirkup, 617(TLS):27Mar87-320
Iknayan, M. The Concave Mirror.*
  M. Hobson, 208(FS):Jul86-343
  B. Juden, 535(RHL):Jul-Aug86-765
  J.S. Patty, 345:Nov86-492
  U. Schöning, 72:Band223Heft2-442
"Il 'Giuliano l'Apostata' de Augusto Rostagni."
  R. Braun, 555:Vol59fasc2-335
Iliescu, M. & H. Siller-Runggaldier. Rätoromanische Bibliographie.
  P. Swiggers, 553(RLiR):Jan-Jun86-215
Ilting, K-H. - see Hegel, G.W.F.
Il Verso, A. Madrigali a tre e a cinque voci (1605 e 1619). (L. Bianconi, ed)
  A. Newcomb, 317:Summer86-396
Imaeda, Y. Catalogue du Kanjur tibétain de l'édition de 'Jang sa-tham.
  H. Eimer, 259(IIJ):Apr86-153
"Images de La Rochefoucauld."*
  Y. Coirault, 535(RHL):Mar-Apr86-281
Imbach, R. & M-H. Méléard, eds. Philosophes médiévaux.
  J. Jolivet, 542:Oct-Dec86-515
Imber, N.H. Master of Hope. (J. Kabakoff, ed)
  G. Nahshon, 390:May86-57
Imbert, P. Roman québécois contemporain et clichés.*
  A. Wall, 193(ELit):Spring86-166
Imhof, H. Rilkes "Gott."
  U.K. Goldsmith, 406:Winter86-539
Imhof, R., ed. Alive Alive O!*
  M.D.O., 295(JML):Nov86-522
Imhof, R. Contemporary Metafiction.
  W. Wolf, 490:Band18Heft3/4-368
"Imprimeurs et libraires parisiens du XVIe siècle." (Fasc Cavellat-Marnef et Cavellat) (I. Pantin, comp)
  D.J. Shaw, 617(TLS):19Jun87-673
"In Pursuit of Beauty."
  C. Vogel, 441:22Feb87-29
Ince, W., ed. Colloque Paul Valéry.
  R. Pietra, 535(RHL):Sep-Oct86-949
  N. Suckling, 208(FS):Jan86-101
"Indian Floral Patterns."
  S. Braybrooke, 507:Nov/Dec86-125
Infante, G.C. - see under Cabrera Infante, G.
Ing, N., ed. Winter Plum.*
  P.G. Pickowicz, 302:Vol22No1-83
Ingalls, R. The End of Tragedy.
  L. Taylor, 617(TLS):16-22Oct87-1135
Ingalls, R. The Pearlkillers.*
  U.K. Le Guin, 441:15Nov87-24
  J. Mellors, 364:Jun86-98
Ingamells, J. The Wallace Collection Catalogue of Pictures. (Vol 1)
  E. Fahy, 90:Jul86-516
Ingarden, R. Man and Value.*
  E.L. Corredor, 478:Apr86-108
Ingarden, R. Selected Papers in Aesthetics. (P.J. McCormick, ed)
  E.F. Kaelin, 290(JAAC):Fall86-89

Ingarden, R. The Work of Music and the Problem of Its Identity. (J.G. Harrell, ed)
  P. Kivy, 290(JAAC):Summer87-413
Ingdahl, K. The Artist and the Creative Act.*
  V. Peppard, 558(RLJ):Winter86-225
Inge, M.T., ed. Huck Finn among the Critics.
  D.L. Vanderwerken, 616:Spring/Summer86-59
  27(AL):Mar86-146
van Ingen, F. & G. Labroisse, eds. Luther-Bilder im 20. Jahrhundert.
  H.G. Haile, 133:Band19Heft2-164
Ingham, K. Jan Christian Smuts.*
  J.F. Burns, 441:15Mar87-15
Ingle, M. The Mayan Revival Style.
  P. Borsook, 45:May86-73
  D. Gebhard, 576:Sep86-313
Ingle, S. The British Party System.
  J. Campbell, 617(TLS):13-19Nov87-1244
Inglis, B.L.S., ed. Une nouvelle collection de poésies lyriques et courtoises du XVe siècle.
  O. Merisalo, 439(NM):1986/1-156
Inglis, T. Moral Monopoly.
  E. Norman, 617(TLS):29May87-576
Ingram, A. Intricate Laughter in the Satire of Swift and Pope.
  D. Nokes, 617(TLS):20Feb87-182
Ingram, D.H. - see Horney, K.
Ingram, E., ed. National and International Politics in the Middle East.
  D. Pryce-Jones, 617(TLS):3Jul87-709
Ingram, F., ed. Russian without a Dictionary.
  D.K. Jarvis, 574(SEEJ):Winter86-602
Ingrams, R. John Stewart Collis.*
  D. Flower, 364:Oct86-87
  R. Mayne, 176:Apr87-53
Ingrams, R. & J. Wells. Mud in Your Eye!
  D.J. Enright, 617(TLS):18-24Dec87-1399
Ingstad, A.S. & H. The Norse Discovery of America.
  J. Graham-Campbell, 617(TLS):19Jun87-654
Iñiguez, D.A. & others - see under Angulo Iñiguez, D. & others
Inman, A.C. The Inman Diary.* (D. Aaron, ed)
  J.P. Diggins, 432(NEQ):Jun86-282
  F. Hobson, 344:Winter87-139
Inman, R. Home Fires Burning.
  T. Wicker, 441:25Jan87-17
Innes, C. Edward Gordon Craig.*
  P. Hollindale, 541(RES):Feb86-124
Innes, C. Holy Theatre.
  M.X. Zelenak, 130:Spring86-88
Innes, M. Appleby and the Ospreys.
  G. Kaufman, 362:19Feb87-26
Innis, J. & others. Intermediate and Advanced Russian Reader.
  H.H. Keller, 574(SEEJ):Summer86-303
Innocenti, M.D. - see under Degli Innocenti, M.
Inoue, M. Space in Japanese Architecture.
  Ishikawa Kiyoshi, 285(JapQ):Jul-Sep86-333
"Interlinguistica Tartuensis." (Vols 1 & 2)
  G.F. Meier, 682(ZPSK):Band39Heft4-517

Jaccottet, P. Une Transaction secrète.
R. Buss, 617(TLS):25-31Dec87-1436
Jachmann, G. Textgeschichtliche Studien.
(C. Gnilka, ed)
J. Schneider, 555:Vol59fasc2-307
Jack, I. Before the Oil Ran Out.
T. Gould, 617(TLS):5Jun87-598
Jack, I. The Poet and his Audience.*
D. Birch, 541(RES):May86-298
Jack, I. & M. Smith - see Browning, R.
Jack, R.D.S. Alexander Montgomerie.
A.M. Kinghorn, 588(SSL):Vol21-310
Jack, R.D.S. Scottish Literature's Debt to
Italy.
T. Crawford, 617(TLS):23Jan87-80
Jack, R.D.S. & R.J. Lyall - see Urquhart,
T.
Jack, R.D.S. & A. Noble, eds. The Art of
Robert Burns.*
D.W. Lindsay, 677(YES):Vol16-288
Jackendoff, R.S. Semantics and Cognition.*
H.J. Verkuyl, 361:Jan86-59
Jackson, A.A. London's Metropolitan Rail-
way.
P.S. Bagwell, 324:Sep87-780
Jackson, B., ed. Teaching Folklore.
J. Bunch, 292(JAF):Apr/Jun86-233
P.B. Mullen, 650(WF):Oct86-302
J.M. Vlach, 440:Summer-Fall86-157
Jackson, B.S. Semiotics and Legal Theory.
S. Levinson, 185:Apr87-666
Jackson, C.H.W. Ships and Shipbuilders of
a West Country Seaport.
R. Goold-Adams, 324:Aug87-710
Jackson, H.H. and P. Spalding, eds. Forty
Years of Diversity.
R.S. Lambert, 656(WMQ):Jan86-144
R.G. Mitchell, 9(AlaR):Jul86-215
Jackson, H.J. - see Coleridge, S.T.
Jackson, I.V., ed. More Than Drumming.
More Than Dancing.
L.P. Monts, 2(AfrA):May86-76
R.B. Winans, 292(JAF):Jul/Sep86-358
Jackson, J. Malice in Wonderland. (J.
Haines & P. Donnelly, eds)
R. Twisk, 362:22Jan87-25
Jackson, J.R.D. Annals of English Verse,
1770-1835.
A. McWhir, 627(UTQ):Fall86-99
Jackson, K. Control.
N. Callendar, 441:27Sep87-27
Jackson, K. Necessary.
N. Callendar, 441:4Jan87-35
Jackson, K.T. Crabgrass Frontier.*
C.E. Clark, Jr., 658:Winter86-328
D.R. Goldfield, 432(NEQ):Dec86-611
Jackson, L.R. The Poems of Laura Riding.
J. Mole, 176:Jul/Aug87-48
Jackson, M.P. & M. Neill - see Marston, J.
Jackson, M.P. & V. O'Sullivan, eds. The
Oxford Anthology of New Zealand Writing
Since 1945.
B. King, 577(SHR):Winter86-94
Jackson, R.A. Vive le Roi!*
S. Hanley, 589:Oct86-940
R. Oresko, 208(FS):Jan86-117
Jackson, S.W. Melancholia and Depression.
M. Critchley, 453(NYRB):12Feb87-5
R.M.A. Hirschfeld, 441:5Apr87-32
M. Ignatieff, 617(TLS):4-11Sep87-939
Jackson, T.W. On a Slow Train Through
Arkansaw.
W.M. Clements, 650(WF):Oct86-292

Jackson, W. Altars of Unhewn Stone.
L. Hyde, 441:27Sep87-30
Jackson, W. Vision and Re-Vision in Alex-
ander Pope.*
D. Fairer, 83:Spring86-103
Jackson, W. & T.P. Cleave. The Mediter-
ranean and Middle East. (Vol 6, Pt 2)
D. Hunt, 617(TLS):7Aug87-844
Jackson, W.A., F.S. Ferguson & K.F. Pantzer
- see "A Short-Title Catalogue of Books
Printed in England, Scotland and Ireland
and of English Books Printed Abroad 1475-
1640"
Jackson, W.T.H. The Challenge of the
Medieval Text. (J.M. Ferrante & R.W.
Hanning, eds)
T. Hunt, 208(FS):Apr86-192
N.J. Lacy, 207(FR):Feb87-387
A.J. Minnis, 617(TLS):6Feb87-140
Jackson, W.T.H., ed. The Interpretation of
Medieval Lyric Poetry.
E.W. Poe, 545(RPh):Nov86-274
Jackson-Stops, G. & J. Pipkin. The Country
House Garden.
A. Lacy, 441:6Dec87-34
Jacob, F. La statue intérieure.
J-F. Revel, 176:Jul/Aug87-26
Jacob, M. & J., eds. The Origins of Anglo-
American Radicalism.*
S.W. Baskerville, 366:Spring86-123
J. Cannon, 83:Spring86-81
Jacob, S. Laura Laur.
P. Merivale, 102(CanL):Summer86-108
Jacobs, A. Arthur Sullivan.*
D.B. Levy, 451:Fall86-194
Jacobs, A. - see Flaubert, G. & G. Sand
Jacobs, B.D. Black Politics and Urban
Crisis in Britain.
M.B. Carter, 617(TLS):24Apr87-445
Jacobs, C. - see Frescobaldi, G.
Jacobs, D. The Brutality of Nations.
C. Campbell, 441:29Mar87-15
Jacobs, E.M., ed. Soviet Local Politics
and Government.*
P.H. Juviler, 550(RusR):Jan86-96
Jacobs, H.A. Incidents in the Life of a
Slave Girl. (L.M. Child, ed; new ed rev
by J.F. Yellin)
E. Fox-Genovese, 617(TLS):4-10Dec87-
1340
H.L. Gates, Jr., 441:22Nov87-12
Jacobs, J. Aus bewusster Bosheit.
D.A. Wells, 402(MLR):Apr86-525
Jacobs, J. Der deutsche Schelmenroman.
R.D. Hacken, 406:Fall86-398
Jacobs, J. Syntax und Semantik der
Negation im Deutschen.
J. Hoeksema, 350:Jun87-432
Jacobs, J.C. - see Odo of Cheriton
Jacobs, M. The Good and Simple Life.
F. Spalding, 90:May86-361
D. Sutton, 39:Aug86-75
Jacobs, M. & P. Stirton. France.
N. Powell, 39:Aug86-142
Jacobs, R. Slow Burn.
B.A. Franklin, 441:4Jan87-16
Jacobsen, J.P. Niels Lyhne. (K. Bohnen,
ed)
S.R. Cerf, 133:Band19Heft2-179
Jacobsen, R. Breathing Exercises. (O.
Grinde, ed & trans)
S. Øksenholt, 563(SS):Summer86-339

James, H. Tales of Henry James. (C. Wegelin, ed)
 J.W. Gargano, 573(SSF):Winter86-128
James, H. The Tales of Henry James.*
 (Vol 3) (M. Aziz, ed)
 A. Duperray, 189(EA):Jul-Sep86-366
 J.W. Gargano, 573(SSF):Winter86-128
James, J. Chartres.
 N.C., 90:Feb86-156
James, K.I. & D.J. Shaw - see McLeod, M.S.G. & others
James, M. Society, Politics and Culture.
 C.S.L. Davies, 617(TLS):16Jan87-67
James, M.R. A Warning to the Curious - The Ghost Stories of M.R. James. (R. Rendell, ed)
 P. Craig, 617(TLS):25-31Dec87-1428
James, R.R. Anthony Eden.*
 D. Cannadine, 453(NYRB):22Oct87-35
 A. Hartley, 176:Apr87-54
 G. Smith, 441:23Aug87-12
James, W. The Varieties of Religious Experience. (F.H. Burkhardt, F. Bowers & I.K. Skrupskelis, eds)
 T.R. Martland, 619:Fall86-487
James, W.P. & W. Tatton-Brown. Hospitals.
 H. Winterbotham, 617(TLS):12Jun87-639
King James VI & I. Letters of King James VI & I.* (G.P.V. Akrigg, ed)
 M.C. Fissel, 377:Mar86-72
 A. Morvan, 189(EA):Jul-Sep86-333
 A. Pritchard, 178:Mar86-105
King James VI & I. Minor Prose Works of King James VI & I. (J. Craigie & A. Law, eds)
 M.P. McDiarmid, 571(ScLJ):Winter86-3
Jameson, F. The Political Unconscious.*
 S. Corngold & M. Jennings, 403(MLS): Summer86-367
Jameson, F., ed. Sartre after Sartre.
 H.W. Wardman, 402(MLR):Jul87-749
Jameson, S. Company Parade.
 T.C. Holyoke, 42(AR):Winter86-119
Jamie, K. & A. Gregg. A Flame in Your Heart.
 J. Mole, 176:Mar87-63
Jamieson, A.G., ed. A People of the Sea.
 N.A.M. Rodger, 617(TLS):1May87-470
Jamieson, R.A. Thin Wealth.*
 H. Ritchie, 571(ScLJ):Winter86-41
Jamison, S.W. Function and Form in the -áya-Formations of the Rig Veda and Atharva Veda.
 E. Seebold, 260(IF):Band91-358
Jammes, R. - see de Góngora, L.
Janaš, P. Niedersorbische Grammatik. (2nd ed)
 G. Stone, 575(SEER):Apr86-263
Janeček, G. The Look of Russian Literature.*
 A. Lawton, 574(SEEJ):Spring86-111
 C.A. Lodder, 90:Dec86-908
 G.S. Smith, 402(MLR):Jan87-269
Janelli, R.L. & D.Y. Ancestor Worship and Korean Society.*
 P.S. Sangren, 302:Vol22No1-112
Janeway, E. Improper Behavior.
 D. English, 441:5Jul87-13
Jangenäs, B. The Swedish Approach to Labor Market Policy.
 J. Logue, 563(SS):Summer86-338
Jangfeldt, B. - see Mayakovsky, V.

Janicaud, D. La Puissance du rationnel.
 J-P. Guinle, 450(NRF):Feb86-100
 J-L. Marion, 192(EP):Apr-Jun86-258
Jänicke, G. Edith Södergran.
 G.C. Schoolfield, 563(SS):Winter86-73
Janik, A. Essays on Wittgenstein and Weininger.
 R.H. Popkin, 319:Jul87-461
Janke, J. & H. Schumann, eds. Nachbarn.
 H. Olschowsky, 601(SuF):Nov-Dec86-1283
Janke, W. & R. Weyers - see Volkmann-Schluck, K.H.
Janko, R. Aristotle on Comedy.*
 L. Golden, 24:Fall86-440
Janko, R. Homer, Hesiod and the Hymns.*
 A. Hoekstra, 394:Vol39fasc1/2-158
Jann, R. The Art and Science of Victorian History.
 A.D. Culler, 637(VS):Winter87-263
Janni, P. Greco o "italiota"?
 L. Serianni, 708:Vol12fasc2-276
Janni, P. Il nostro greco quotidiano.
 L. Serianni, 708:Vol12fasc2-276
Jannini, P.A., G. Dotoli & E.P. Carile, eds. Scritti sulla Nouvelle-France nel Seicento.
 C.E.J. Caldicott, 535(RHL):Sep-Oct86-915
Janovy, J., Jr. Fields of Friendly Strife.
 K. Stabiner, 441:14Jun87-11
Janowitz, T. A Cannibal in Manhattan.
 F. Prose, 441:4Oct87-12
 T. Rafferty, 442(NY):26Oct87-142
Janowitz, T. Slaves of New York.*
 T. De Pietro, 249(HudR):Autumn86-489
Jansen, F.J.B. - see under Billeskov Jansen, F.J.
Janssen, O., comp. Lemmatisierte(n) Konkordanz zu den Schweizer Minnesängern.
 M. Schiendorfer, 680(ZDP):Band105Heft1-114
Janssens, G.A.M. & F.G.A.M. Aarts, eds. Studies in Seventeenth-Century English Literature, History and Bibliography.
 M.G. Brennan, 447(N&Q):Dec85-527
Janta, A. A History of Nineteenth-Century American-Polish Music.
 G.J. Lerski, 497(PolR):Vol31No1-81
Janusko, R. The Sources and Structures of James Joyce's "Oxen."
 J.V. Card, 329(JJQ):Winter87-230
Jao Tsung-i, ed. Inscriptions tombales des dynasties T'ang et Song.
 P.W. Kroll, 318(JAOS):Jan/Mar85-174
"Japanese Business Language."
 J. McMullen, 617(TLS):30Oct-5Nov87-1200
Japp, U. Theorie der Ironie.*
 D. Kaiser, 224(GRM):Band36Heft2-229
Jardin, A. Alexis de Tocqueville, 1805-1859.
 L. Groopman, 31(ASch):Spring86-267
Jardine, A. & P. Smith, eds. Men in Feminism.
 M. Hussey, 441:19Jul87-8
Jardine, A.A. Gynesis.*
 J. Curtis, 627(UTQ):Fall86-125
 A. Herrmann, 659(ConL):Summer87-271
 N. Segal, 208(FS):Jul86-370
Jardine, L. Still Harping on Daughters.
 I. Schabert & others, 156(ShJW):Jahrbuch1986-223

Jardine, N. The Birth of History and Phi-
losophy of Science.*
  P. Catton, 486:Sep86-453
  J.V. Field, 84:Jun86-255
Jardine, N. The Fortunes of Inquiry.
  B. Barnes, 617(TLS):15May87-528
Jarman, D. The Last of England.
  S. Burt, 617(TLS):6-12Nov87-1225
Jarman, M. Far and Away.
  J.F. Cotter, 249(HudR):Spring86-154
Jarman, M.A. Dancing Nightly in the Tav-
ern.
  R.W. Harvey, 102(CanL):Winter85-170
Jarrell, R. Fly by Night. The Lost World.
  J.A. Bryant, Jr., 569(SR):Fall86-lxxvi
Jarrell, R. Randall Jarrell's Letters.*
  (M. Jarrell, ed)
  J. Applewhite, 27(AL):Mar86-117
  D. Donoghue, 473(PR):Vol53No1-126
  S. Ferguson, 659(ConL):Spring87-129
  J. Mazzaro, 569(SR):Winter86-143
  J. Meyers, 639(VQR):Spring86-348
  H.R. Miller, 31(ASch):Summer86-423
Jarrell, R. Pictures from an Institution.
  362:20Aug87-22
Jarrety, M. - see "Cahiers Paul Valéry, 4"
Jarvi, R. - see Landelius, O.R.
Jarvie, I.C. Rationality and Relativism.
  F.A. Hanson, 488:Dec86-489
  J.J., 185:Oct86-295
Jarvis, B., ed. Trafod Cerddi.
  T.A. Watkins, 112:Vol18-208
Jarvis, D.K. & E.D. Lifschitz. Viewpoints.
  (3rd ed)
  P.M. Mitchell, 399(MLJ):Winter86-436
Jarvis, G.A., ed. The Challenge for Ex-
cellence in Foreign Language Education.
  S.N. Gynan, 399(MLJ):Autumn86-296
Jarvis, S., ed. Inside Outer Space.
  G.K. Wolfe, 395(MFS):Spring86-133
Jarzębski, J. Zufall und Ordnung.
  F. Rottensteiner, 561(SFS):Nov86-393
Jasani, B., ed. Space Weapons and Interna-
tional Security.
  Lord Zuckerman, 453(NYRB):9Apr87-35
de Jasay, A. The State.
  K.S., 185:Oct86-292
Jasinski, B. - see Madame de Staël
Jasinski, R. Autour de l'"Esther" racin-
ienne.
  R.J. Howells, 402(MLR):Apr87-476
Jason, K. - see Landolfi, T.
Jasper, D. Coleridge as Poet and Religious
Thinker.
  M. Jarrett-Kerr, 161(DUJ):Jun86-379
Jasper, D., ed. Images of Belief in Lit-
erature.
  R.A. Lasseter, 569(SR):Spring86-279
Jaspers, K. Nietzsche.
  R. Margreiter, 489(PJGG):Band93Heft2-
375
Jaspers, K. Philosophie.
  J. Hersch, 192(EP):Oct-Dec86-566
Jauffret, R. - Cet extrême amour.
  C. Mackey, 207(FR):May87-910
"Jean Jaurès (1859-1914)." (G. Candar, ed)
  E. Cahm, 208(FS):Apr86-232
Jauss, H.R. Aesthetic Experience and
Literary Hermeneutics.* (German title:
Ästhetische Erfahrung und literarische
Hermeneutik.)
  M.E. Blanchard, 567:Vol61No3/4-307
  M. Jackson, 545(RPh):May87-470

Jay, G.S. T.S. Eliot and the Poetics of
Literary History.
  R. Beum, 569(SR):Winter86-124
  S. Fogel, 106:Spring86-109
Jay, M. Adorno.*
  W. Goetschel, 221(GQ):Spring86-291
  J.J. Stuhr, 478:Apr86-103
Jay, P. Being in the Text.*
  R.E. Fitch, 301(JEGP):Jan86-136
  J.M. Todd, 131(CL):Summer86-298
Jay, P. & M. Stewart. Apocalypse 2000.
  A. Cairncross, 617(TLS):3Jul87-707
Jay, R. Learned Pigs and Fireproof Women.*
  442(NY):5Jan87-87
Jayasree, S. Nītidvisaṣṭikā of Sundara-
pāṇḍya.
  E. Bender, 318(JAOS):Oct/Dec85-813
Jean-Charles, J. La Nuit de l'engoulevent.
  R.C. White, 207(FR):Mar87-559
Jeay, M. Savoir faire.
  G. Hasenohr, 547(RF):Band98Heft3/4-426
Jebb, M. Walkers.
  J. Reed, 364:Nov86-110
Jeffares, A.N. - see Yeats, W.B.
Jeffers, R. "What Odd Expedients" and
Other Poems. (R.I. Scott, ed)
  D. Bromwich, 677(YES):Vol16-362
Jeffrey, D.L., ed. Chaucer and Scriptural
Tradition.
  M.T. Tavormina, 301(JEGP):Jan86-99
Jeffrey, F. Jeffrey's Criticism.* (P.F.
Morgan, ed)
  J.H. Alexander, 677(YES):Vol16-292
  L.M. Findlay, 447(N&Q):Mar85-138
Jeffries, R. Relatively Dangerous.
  T.J. Binyon, 617(TLS):17Jul87-778
Jehl, R. Melancholie und Acedia.
  C. Flüeler, 687:Oct-Dec86-641
  T. Reist, 589:Oct86-1026
Jehlen, M. American Incarnation.
  M. Gonnaud, 189(EA):Oct-Dec87-485
  A. Kolodny, 165(EAL):Spring87-144
Jelavich, B. Russia and the Formation of
the Romanian National State, 1821-1878.*
  S. Fischer-Galati, 550(RusR):Jul86-337
Jelavich, P. Munich and Theatrical Modern-
ism.*
  W.R. Elwood, 615(TJ):Dec86-509
  J.L. Hibberd, 402(MLR):Apr87-519
  M.X. Zelenak, 130:Winter86/87-378
Jeletzky, T.F., ed. Russian Canadians.*
  M.B. Thompson, 558(RLJ):Spring/Fall86-
247
Jellicoe, G. & others, eds. The Oxford
Companion to Gardens.
  442(NY):16Feb87-110
ben Jelloun, T. The Sand Child.
  B. Harlow, 441:25Oct87-49
Jencks, C. Post-Modernism.
  P. Goldberger, 441:6Dec87-22
Jencks, C. Symbolic Architecture.
  A. McIntyre, 46:Oct86-6
Jencks, C. Towards a Symbolic Architec-
ture.
  J. Lichtblau, 45:Jul86-79
Jendryschik, M. Anna, das zweite Leben.
  (G. Rothbauer, ed)
  K. Schuhmann, 601(SuF):May-Jun86-673
Jenkins, A., ed. The Isle of Ladies or The
Ile of Pleasaunce.
  R. Evans, 72:Band223Heft1-164
Jenkins, A. - see Reading, P.

Jenkins, D. Suharto and His Generals.
J.A. MacDougall, 293(JASt):May86–650
Jenkins, H. – see Shakespeare, W.
Jenkins, J.H. Basic Texas Books.*
S.A. Grider, 649(WAL):Aug86–147
Jenkins, L. Faulkner and Black–White Relations.
C. Werner, 403(MLS):Summer86–329
Jenkins, M. Writing.
J.J. Kohn, 399(MLJ):Winter86–452
Jenkins, R. Baldwin.
J. Grigg, 362:12Mar87–26
J. Turner, 617(TLS):6Mar87–233
Jenn, P. Georges Méliès cinéaste.
J. Paulhan, 207(FR):Feb87–415
Jenner, P.N., ed. Mon–Khmer–Studies XI.
G.F. Meier, 682(ZPSK):Band39Heft5–607
Jenner, W.J.F. & D. Davin – see Zhang
Xinxin & Sang Ye
Jennings, B. & D. Callahan, eds. Representation and Responsibility.
N.E. Bowie, 185:Jan87–485
Jennings, E. Collected Poems.*
J. Forth, 364:Oct86–82
Jennings, G. Spangle.
P–L. Adams, 61:Dec87–111
S.S. Wells, 441:27Dec87–18
Jennings, H. Pandaemonium 1660–1886.*
(M–L. Jennings & C. Madge, eds)
M. Yorke, 324:Jan87–165
566:Spring87–219
Jennings, L.B. Justinus Kerners Weg nach
Weinsberg (1809–1819).*
H. Slessarev, 406:Spring86–107
Jenny, M. – see Luther, M.
Jensen, E.J. Ben Jonson's Comedies on the
Modern Stage.
F. Teague, 130:Winter86/87–376
Jensen, F. Provençal Philology and the
Poetry of Guillaume of Poitiers.
G.A. Bond, 545(RPh):Aug86–130
Jensen, J. Loosening the Bonds.
639(VQR):Autumn86–121
Jensen, L. Shelter.*
M. Boruch, 29(APR):Mar/Apr87–22
Jensen, R.G., Theodore Shabad & A.W.
Wright, eds. Soviet Natural Resources in
the World Economy.
D. Yergin, 550(RusR):Jul86–312
Jenstad, T.E. Sunndalsmålet.
C. Creider, 350:Mar87–187
E. Haugen, 563(SS):Spring86–194
Jernakoff, N. – see "Transactions of the
Association of Russian–American Scholars
in the U.S.A."
Jerome, J. Mr. Speaker.
W. Christian, 298:Fall86–154
Saint Jerome. Saint Jerôme, "Apologie
contre Rufin." (P. Lardet, ed & trans)
G.J.M. Bartelink, 394:Vol39fasc3/4–525
Jervis, S. Furniture of about 1900 from
Austria and Hungary in the Victoria and
Albert Museum.
P. Vergo, 90:Oct86–756
Jesenská, M. Vivre.
A. Clerval, 450(NRF):May86–107
Jeske, W. Bertolt Brechts Poetik des
Romans.
S. Mews, 221(GQ):Winter86–106
Jeske, W. & P. Zahn. Lion Feuchtwanger
oder Der arge Weg der Erkenntnis.
W. Koepke, 221(GQ):Summer86–497

Jessop, B. Nicos Poulantzas.
T.M., 185:Oct86–301
Jessop, T.E. & M. Fimiani – see Berkeley,
G.
Jessup, L. The Mandika Balafon.
J.C. Dje Dje, 91:Fall86–306
Jestaz, B. La Chapelle Zen à Saint–Marc de
Venise.
B. Boucher, 617(TLS):30Oct–5Nov87–
1202
de Jesús, T. Libro de las fundaciones.
(V. García de la Concha, ed)
F–A. Lapuente, 552(REH):Oct86–130
Jeyifo, B. The Truthful Lie.
E.S. Fido, 538(RAL):Summer86–273
Jhabvala, R.P. Out of India.*
W.H. Pritchard, 249(HudR):Winter87–651
J. Rees, 617(TLS):24Apr87–434
L. Williams, 396(ModA):Summer/Fall86–
335
Jhabvala, R.P. Three Continents.
P. Ackroyd, 441:23Aug87–3
A. Duchêne, 617(TLS):13–19Nov87–1248
R. Towers, 453(NYRB):8Oct87–45
Jiang Yang. Six Chapters from My Life
"Downunder."
J.K. Kallgren, 293(JASt):Nov85–121
Jiaqian, W. & others – see under Wu Jiaqian
& others
Jie, Z. – see under Zhang Jie
Jiles, P. Celestial Navigation.*
M.T. Lane, 198:Spring86–94
Jiménez, J.F. – see under Fernández
Jiménez, J.
Jiménez, J.O. & D. Cañas – see under Olivio
Jiménez, J. & D. Cañas
Jiménez–Fajardo, S. & J.C. Wilcox, eds. At
Home and Beyond.*
L. Close, 86(BHS):Apr86–178
Jing, Z. – see under Zhuang Jing
Jirgens, K. Strappado.
D. Ingham, 102(CanL):Fall86–156
Joachim of Fiore. Liber de concordia Novi
ac Veteris Testamenti. (E.R. Daniel, ed)
S.L. Zimdars–Swartz, 589:Apr86–429
Joachimedes, C.M., N. Rosenthal & W.
Schmied, eds. German Art in the Twentieth Century: Painting and Sculpture 1905–
1985.
H. Boorman, 59:Sep86–363
Joannes Secundus. The Kisses of Joannes
Secundus: Basia & Epithalamium.
L.V.R., 568(SCN):Fall86–56
Joas, H. G.H. Mead.*
G.A. Cook, 619:Summer86–338
Job, A., M.L. Laureati & C. Ronchetta.
Botteghe e Negozi.
D. Garstang, 39:Jan86–68
Jobe, B. & M. Kaye. New England Furniture:
The Colonial Era.*
F.J. Puig, 658:Spring86–75
Jocano, F.L., ed. Filipino Muslims.
T.M. Kiefer, 293(JASt):Aug86–907
Joensuu, M. Harjunpaa and the Stone
Murders.
T.J. Binyon, 617(TLS):30Jan87–108
Joensuu, M. The Stone Murders.
N. Callendar, 441:8Nov87–62
Joffe, C. The Regulation of Sexuality.
M. Sandmaier, 441:8Feb87–25
Johach, H. & F. Rodi – see Dilthey, W.

Johannisson, T., ed. Språkliga signale-
ment.
R. McTurk, 562(Scan):Nov86-225
Johansen, J.D. & M. Nøjgaard, eds. Danish
Semiotics.
A. Lange-Seidl, 567:Vol61No1/2-171
Johanssen, T., ed. 20 Contemporary Norwe-
gian Poets.
E. Rokkan, 562(Scan):May86-103
F. Shackelford, 563(SS):Summer86-338
Johansson, S., ed. Computer Corpora in
English Language Research.
C.F. Meyer, 35(AS):Winter86-357
John, A.V., ed. Unequal Opportunities.*
E. Yeo, 637(VS):Summer87-529
John, N., ed. English National Opera
Guide. (No 24)
K. Pendle, 465:Autumn86-131
John, N., ed. English National Opera
Guides. (No. 33-36)
R. Anderson, 415:Aug86-442
John, S.B. Anouilh: "L'Alouette" and
"Pauvre Bitos."*
W.D. Howarth, 208(FS):Jan86-104
J. Rothenberg, 402(MLR):Jul86-752
John of Salisbury. Le "Policratique" de
Jean de Salisbury.* (Bk 4) (D. Foule-
chat, trans; C. Brücker, ed)
J.C. Laidlaw, 208(FS):Apr86-193
Johne, K-P., J. Köhn & V. Weber. Die
Kolonen in Italien und den westlichen
Provinzen des römischen Reiches.
R.P. Duncan-Jones, 313:Vol76-296
Johns, E. Thomas Eakins.
H. Adams, 54:Jun86-345
Johnson, A. Long Road to Nowhere.
T. Eagleton, 565:Autumn86-76
Johnson, B. The Four Days of Courage.
D.H. Bain, 441:14Jun87-9
Johnson, B. True Correspondence.*
S. Gatrell, 541(RES):Feb86-120
Johnson, B.C. Lost in the Alps.*
P.R. Harris, 354:Sep86-272
Johnson, B.S. House Mother Normal.*
I. Malin, 532(RCF):Fall86-132
Johnson, C. Song for Three Voices.
J. Byrne, 532(RCF):Spring86-212
Johnson, C. The Sorcerer's Apprentice.*
P. La Salle, 573(SSF):Fall86-455
42(AR):Summer86-381
Johnson, C.B. Madness and Lust.*
R. El Saffar, 131(CL):Winter86-73
E. Williamson, 86(BHS):Jul86-283
Johnson, D. Angels.
P. Lewis, 565:Spring86-38
Johnson, D. Fiskadoro.*
T. McGonigle, 532(RCF):Summer86-155
Johnson, D. Persian Nights.
R. Dinnage, 453(NYRB):23Apr87-14
R. Irwin, 617(TLS):3Jul87-714
J.A. Phillips, 441:5Apr87-8
Johnson, D. The Stars at Noon.*
A. Beevor, 617(TLS):27Mar87-319
J. Mellors, 362:28May87-26
Johnson, D. The Veil.
S. Dobyns, 441:18Oct87-46
Johnson, D., A. Tyson & R. Winter. The
Beethoven Sketchbooks.* (D. Johnson, ed)
W. Drabkin, 415:Dec86-688
H. Lenneberg, 309:Vol7No1-95
M. Staehelin, 537:Vol72No2-298
Johnson, D.B. Worlds in Regression.*
J.W. Connolly, 574(SEEJ):Summer86-295

Johnson, E. Dreams of Roses and Fire.*
G. Orton, 562(Scan):Nov86-246
Johnson, E.D.H. Paintings of the British
Social Scene from Hogarth to Sickert.*
D. Sutton, 39:Aug86-74
Johnson, G. Emily Dickinson.*
J. Loving, 183(ESQ):Vol32No3-201
L. Munk, 627(UTQ):Summer87-590
Johnson, G.N. Weaving Rag Rugs.
Y.J. Milspaw, 292(JAF):Jul/Sep86-355
Johnson, G.W. South Watching. (F. Hobson,
ed)
T.G. Dyer, 9(AlaR):Jul86-229
Johnson, H.C. The Midi in Revolution.
W. Scott, 617(TLS):13Feb87-158
Johnson, J.G. Women in Colonial Spanish
American Literature.
A. McDermott, 86(BHS):Oct86-395
L.T. Valdivieso, 552(REH):Oct86-125
Johnson, K. Doing Words.
C. Strum, 441:28Jun87-25
Johnson, K. Waves of Drifting Snow.
W. Swist, 404:Autumn86-52
Johnson, K. - see "A Nation of Poets"
Johnson, K.K. When Orchids Were Flowers.
M. McGovern, 344:Fall87-131
Johnson, L. The Chicago Home.
K. West, 502(PrS):Winter86-109
Johnson, L. The Paintings of Eugène Dela-
croix. (Vols 3 & 4)
L. Eitner, 617(TLS):29May87-583
Johnson, L.S. The Voice of the "Gawain"-
Poet.*
R.J. Blanch, 589:Oct86-942
J. Roberts, 402(MLR):Oct87-911
Johnson, M.P. and J.L. Roark, eds. No
Chariot Let Down.
H.A. Reed, 115:Summer86-417
J. White, 9(AlaR):Apr86-151
Johnson, P. A History of the Jews.
T. Endelman, 617(TLS):26Jun87-684
A. Hertzberg, 441:19Apr87-11
A. Momigliano, 453(NYRB):8Oct87-7
Johnson, P. Saving and Spending.*
E. Taplin, 637(VS):Spring87-437
"Philip Johnson/John Burgee Architecture
1979-1985."
S.R. Chao, 505:Nov86-137
Johnson, R. The American Table.*
T. Whittaker, 529(QQ):Autumn86-547
Johnson, R. Ark 50: Spires 34-50.*
S.P. Estess, 577(SHR):Winter86-84
Johnson, S. Johnson on Johnson. (J. Wain,
ed)
J.T. Boulton, 447(N&Q):Mar85-132
Johnson, S. A Journey to the Western
Islands of Scotland.* (J.D. Fleeman, ed)
M. Jannetta, 354:Sep86-284
Johnson, S. The Oxford Authors: Samuel
Johnson.* (D. Greene, ed)
G.J. Clingham, 97(CQ):Vol15No1-77
D. Wheeler, 83:Autumn86-254
Johnson, S. A Voyage to Abyssinia. (J.J.
Gold, ed)
A. Pailler, 189(EA):Jul-Sep86-346
639(VQR):Winter86-18
Johnson, S. & C. Planning for Liturgy.
J. Thomas, 46:Feb86-86
Johnson, U. Anniversaries II.
T. Ziolkowski, 441:8Nov87-61
Johnson, W. The Girl Who Would Be Rus-
sian.*
M. Boruch, 434:Autumn86-98

Johnston, A. – see Noe, S.P.
Johnston, C. Jack London – An American Radical?*
  G. Beauchamp, 106:Spring86–69
Johnston, C. Selected Poems II or Writers on the Edge.
  P. Levi, 4:Autumn86–93
  J. Mole, 176:Mar87–62
Johnston, C., G.V. Shepherd & M. Worsdale. Vatican Splendour.
  R.F. Swain, 529(QQ):Autumn86–668
Johnston, D. The Rhetoric of "Leviathan."
  R. Tuck, 617(TLS):17Apr87–420
Johnston, D. Up the Hill.
  W. Christian, 298:Fall86–154
Johnston, G. Ask Again.*
  529(QQ):Autumn86–719
Johnston, J. Fool's Sanctuary.
  A–M. Conway, 617(TLS):1May87–458
Johnston, J.F., Jr. The Limits of Government.
  S.J. Sniegoski, 396(ModA): Summer/Fall86–316
Johnston, J.H. The Poet and the City.*
  M. Birnbaum, 396(ModA):Spring86–177
Johnston, K.R. Wordsworth and "The Recluse."*
  V.A. De Luca, 627(UTQ):Summer87–575
  J.E. Jordan, 536(Rev):Vol8–47
Johnston, W. The Story of Bobby O'Malley.
  R.P. Knowles, 198:Fall86–92
Johnston, W.J., ed. Education on Trial.
  P. Rothman, 42(AR):Winter86–116
Johnston, W.R. The Nineteenth Century Paintings in the Walters Art Gallery.
  R. Thomson, 59:Mar86–108
Johnstone, R. The Will to Believe.
  M. Stannard, 677(YES):Vol16–360
Join–Dieterle, C. Musée du Petit Palais, Catalogue de Céramiques I.
  J.V.G. Mallet, 90:Aug86–610
Jokl, N. Sprachliche Beiträge zur Paläo-Ethnologie der Balkanhalbinsel.
  B.D. Joseph, 350:Jun87–435
Jollès, B. – see Aquinas, T.
Jolles, C. Fontane und die Politik.
  D. Sommer, 654(WB):11/1986–1933
Jolley, E. Milk and Honey.*
  H. Jacobson, 617(TLS):27Nov–3Dec87–1307
Jolley, E. The Newspaper of Claremont Street.
  R.P. Sinkler, 441:20Dec87–16
Jolley, E. Palomino.*
  J. Hendin, 441:19Jul87–11
  442(NY):14Sep87–134
Jolley, N. Leibniz and Locke.*
  J. Bennett, 449:Mar86–108
  M. Kulstad, 706:Band18Heft1–99
  P. Remnant, 482(PhR):Apr86–297
Jonas, H. The Imperative of Responsibility.*
  G. Niemeyer, 396(ModA):Spring86–157
Jones. The Brave Never Write Poetry.
  S. Scobie, 376:Jun86–125
Jones, B.W. & A.L. Vinson. The World of Toni Morrison.
  W.J. Goggans, 95(CLAJ):Mar87–395
  N. Harris, 395(MFS):Winter86–635
Jones, C. The Case of the Fragmented Woman.
  C. Salzberg, 441:18Jan87–18

Jones, C., ed. Party and Management in Parliament 1660–1784.*
  J. Black, 161(DUJ):Dec85–181
  P.D.G. Thomas, 83:Spring86–93
Jones, C. & G. Holmes – see Nicolson, W.
Jones, C., M. Newitt & S. Roberts, eds. Politics and People in Revolutionary England.
  D. Underdown, 617(TLS):23Jan87–88
Jones, C., G. Wainwright & E. Yarnold, eds. The Study of Spirituality.
  H. Chadwick, 617(TLS):12Jun87–638
Jones, D. Inner Necessities.* (T. Dilworth, ed)
  N. Jacobs, 541(RES):Aug86–443
  S. Kane, 529(QQ):Autumn86–683
Jones, D.C. Gone the Dreams and Dancing.
  R. Tuerk, 649(WAL):May86–66
Jones, D.R. Great Directors at Work.*
  J. Peter, 617(TLS):20Mar87–300
Jones, E. Industrial Architecture in Britain 1750–1939.
  J.S. Curl, 324:Jan87–167
  J.M. Richards, 46:Jan86–80
Jones, E. Scenic Form in Shakespeare.
  D.I. Rabey, 610:Summer86–167
  K. Tetzeli von Rosador, 156(ShJW):Jahrbuch1986–258
Jones, E.D., ed. African Literature Today No. 14.
  L.A. Johnson, 538(RAL):Fall86–442
Jones, E.T. Following Directions.*
  D.J. Watermeier, 615(TJ):May86–243
Jones, G. Divine Endurance.
  G. Jonas, 441:26Apr87–29
Jones, G. Social Darwinism in English Thought.
  P. Heyer, 488:Jun86–233
Jones, H. Mutiny on the Amistad.
  D.B. Davis, 453(NYRB):5Nov87–34
  W.S. McFeely, 441:18Jan87–9
Jones, J. & J. Australian Fiction.*
  B. Kiernan, 71(ALS):May86–417
Jones, J. & W. Wilson. An Incomplete Education.
  J. Kaufman, 441:18Oct87–31
Jones, J.R. Charles II.
  R. Beddard, 617(TLS):24Jul87–789
Jones, J.T. Wayward Skeptic.*
  M. Wood, 453(NYRB):7May87–28
Jones, L. Minstrel of the Appalachians.
  D.E. Whisnant, 292(JAF):Jan/Mar86–95
Jones, L.E. Sad Clowns and Pale Pierrots.*
  F.P. Bowman, 210(FrF):May86–240
  M.G. Rose, 130:Summer86–175
  C.W. Thompson, 402(MLR):Apr86–486
Jones, L.M. The Life of John Hamilton Reynolds.*
  R.M. Wardle, 340(KSJ):Vol35–205
Jones, M. Chances.
  D.A.N. Jones, 617(TLS):20–26Nov87–1277
  K.O. Morgan, 362:15Oct87–32
Jones, M. Getting It On.
  E. Sanders, 441:13Dec87–13
Jones, M.E.W. The Contemporary Spanish Novel, 1939–1975.
  I. Lamartina–Lens, 552(REH):Oct86–128
  R.C. Spires, 238:May86–311
Jones, M.P. Conrad's Heroism.*
  B.E. Teets, 177(ELT):Vol29No1–101
Jones, M.S. "Der Sturm."*
  M. Adams, 67:May86–112
  S.L. Gilman, 564:Sep86–265

Jones, P. Hume's Sentiments.*
F. Wilson, 449:Jun86-274
Jones, R. Innocent Things.
639(VQR):Summer86-98
Jones, R. Julia Paradise.
W. Herbert, 441:11Oct87-12
Jones, R., ed. Poetry and Politics.
L.M. York, 102(CanL):Spring86-157
Jones, R. The Unborn.
T.R. Hummer, 651(WHR):Spring86-69
P. Stitt, 219(GaR):Summer86-557
T. Swiss, 569(SR):Spring86-302
Jones, R. & N. Penny. Raphael.
S. Ferino-Pagden, 90:Mar86-221
Jones, R.E. H-R. Lenormand.
G.J. Barberet, 207(FR):Feb87-402
Jones, R.E. Provincial Development in
Russia.*
J. Black, 161(DUJ):Jun86-365
Jones, R.L. Wild Onions.
J.R. Hepworth, 649(WAL):Aug86-177
Jones, S. Cambridge Introduction to the
History of Art: The Eighteenth Century.
C. Ezell, 566:Spring87-218
Jones, S. It All Began with Daisy.
B. Coleman, 441:21Jun87-33
Jones, S. Two Centuries of Overseas Trad-
ing.*
D.K. Fieldhouse, 617(TLS):6-12Nov87-
1221
Jones, S.A. Thoreau Amongst Friends and
Philistines and Other Thoreauviana.*
(G. Hendrick, ed)
R.W. Harvey, 106:Summer86-211
Jones, S.H., Jr. - see Takeda Izumo &
others
Jones, S.S. Folklore and Literature in the
United States.
R.W. Brednich, 196:Band27Heft1/2-117
Jones, T. The Improbable Voyage.
E. Newby, 441:31May87-49
Jones, T.L. Lee's Tigers.
P-L. Adams, 61:Aug87-84
Jones, V. James, the Critic.
M.B., 295(JML):Nov86-489
C.B. Cox, 27(AL):May86-273
A.R. Kaminsky, 177(ELT):Vol29No3-335
J. Rambeau, 395(MFS):Winter86-604
Jones, W.G. Nikolay Novikov.*
N. Buhks, 402(MLR):Jan86-263
M. Hughes, 83:Spring86-123
A. Levitsky, 550(RusR):Jul86-346
K.J. McKenna, 574(SEEJ):Spring86-108
Jones-Davies, M-T., ed. Les Mythes
poétiques au temps de la Renaissance.
L. Salingar, 189(EA):Apr-Jun87-199
Jong, E. Serenissima.
P. Binding, 362:24Sep87-29
V. Cunningham, 617(TLS):18-24Sep87-
1025
M. Malone, 441:19Apr87-12
de Jong, W.R. The Semantics of John Stuart
Mill.*
I. Angelelli, 53(AGP):Band68Heft2-225
de Jonge, A. Stalin and the Shaping of the
Soviet Union.*
639(VQR):Autumn86-120
Jongen, R. & others, eds. Akten des 17.
Linguistischen Kolloquiums.
K.H. Schmidt, 685(ZDL):1/1986-74
de Jongh, E. Portretten van echt en trouw.
H-J. Raupp, 600:Vol16No4-254

Jönsjö, J. Studies on Middle English Nick-
names. (Vol 1)
E. Felder, 685(ZDL):3/1986-411
Jonson, B. Ben Jonson: "Epigrams" and "The
Forest." (R. Dutton, ed)
J.P. Vander Motten, 179(ES):Dec86-566
Jonson, B. The Oxford Authors: Ben
Jonson.* (I. Donaldson, ed)
M. Dodsworth, 175:Summer86-195
639(VQR):Autumn86-115
Jonson, B. Volpone or the Fox.* (R.B.
Parker, ed)
J. Creaser, 447(N&Q):Dec85-522
I. Donaldson, 402(MLR):Jan87-161
Joós, E. Lucács's Last Autocriticism.
J. Amstutz, 154:Autumn86-599
Jordan, D.P. The Revolutionary Career of
Maximilien Robespierre.*
W. Scott, 617(TLS):13Feb87-158
Jordan, F., ed. The English Romantic
Poets. (4th ed)
J. Blondel, 189(EA):Apr-Jun87-220
Jordan, J.E. - see Wordsworth, W.
Jordan, K. Henry the Lion.
S. Airlie, 617(TLS):5Jun87-614
Jordan, L., B. Kortländer & F. Nies, eds.
Interferenzen - Deutschland und Frank-
reich.*
B. Bray, 535(RHL):Jul-Aug86-809
Jordan, R.A. & S.J. Kalčik, eds. Women's
Folklore, Women's Culture.
C.R. Farrer, 650(WF):Jan86-40
Jordan, R.W. Plato's Arguments for Forms.*
P. Louis, 555:Vol59fasc2-285
Jordan, S. Decision Making for Incompetent
Persons.
A.S. Cua, 543:Sep86-130
Jordan, T.G. American Log Buildings.*
S.G. Del Sordo, 658:Summer/Autumn86-201
H. Kirker, 585(SoQ):Winter87-144
Jordan, T.G. Texas Graveyards.
R.E. Meyer, 650(WF):Jan86-71
Jordanova, L.J. Lamarck.
D. Knight, 83:Spring86-113
Jordanova, L.J., ed. Languages of Nature.*
R. Porter, 617(TLS):8May87-489
Jörg, C.J.A. The Geldermalsen.
C.R. Boxer, 617(TLS):6Mar87-249
Jorgens, E.B. The Well-Tun'd Word.*
F.W. Sternfeld, 551(RenQ):Spring86-132
Jose, V.R., ed. Mortgaging the Future.
G. Hawes, 293(JASt):May86-652
Joseph, G. Clément Marot.
H.H. Glidden, 551(RenQ):Winter86-782
Joseph, H. Side by Side.
S. Mufson, 441:30Aug87-37
Joseph, J.R. Crébillon fils.*
G.P. Bennington, 208(FS):Oct86-464
P.V. Conroy, Jr., 173(ECS):Fall86-82
D. Coward, 402(MLR):Jan87-200
Joseph, M. To Kill the Potemkin.
S. Dunant, 362:24Sep87-22
Joseph, R. Michael Joseph.
V. Cunningham, 617(TLS):13Feb87-156
Joset, J. Gabriel Garcia Márquez.
L. Pollmann, 547(RF):Band98Heft3/4-489
E. Williamson, 402(MLR):Oct87-1011
Joshi, L.M. Discerning the Buddha.
J.W. de Jong, 259(IIJ):Apr86-151
Josipovici, G. Contre-Jour.*
C. Baranger, 189(EA):Jul-Sep87-365
Josipovici, G. In the Fertile Land.
P. Driver, 362:31Dec87-23

Josipovici, G. The Mirror of Criticism.
  J. Preston, 402(MLR):Jul87–689
Jost, U. Die französischen Entlehnungen im
  Englischen von 1750 bis 1759.
  W.J. Jones, 685(ZDL):3/1986–394
Jouanna, J. – see Hippocrates
Joubert, C–H. Le fil d'or.
  A. Corbineau-Hoffmann, 72:Band223
  Heft1–217
Joubert, J. Joseph Joubert, "Essais,"
  1779–1821.* (R. Tessonneau, ed)
  A. Michel, 535(RHL):Mar–Apr86–293
Joukovsky, F. – see d'Alcripe, P.
Jourdan, S. The Sparrow and the Flea.
  L. Cerny, 156(ShJW):Jahrbuch1986–230
Jovanovski, M. Cousins.
  B.G. Yovovich, 441:15Feb87–20
de Jovellanos, G.M. Obras completas. (Vol
  1) (J.M. Caso González, ed)
  J.H.R. Polt, 240(HR):Autumn86–475
Jowell, R., S. Witherspoon & L. Brook, eds.
  British Social Attitudes.
  J. Dunn, 617(TLS):24Apr87–442
Jowett, B. Dear Miss Nightingale. (E.V.
  Quinn & J.M. Prest, eds)
  A. Summers, 617(TLS):11–17Sep87–994
Joyce, J. Dubliners. (H. Beck, ed)
  C. Jansohn, 72:Band223Heft1–185
Joyce, J. Ulysses.* (H.W. Gabler, with W.
  Steppe & C. Melchior, eds)
  R. Ellmann, 219(GaR):Summer86–548
  A. Hammond, 354:Dec86–382
  P.F. Herring, 659(ConL):Spring87–104
  C. Jacquet, 189(EA):Jul–Sep87–294
  I.B. Nadel, 659(ConL):Spring87–111
Joyce, W.L. and others, eds. Printing and
  Society in Early America.*
  P.F. Gura, 639(VQR):Autumn86–734
Joyner, C. Down by the Riverside.*
  C.L. Perdue, Jr., 650(WF):Jan86–57
  K. Walters, 355(LSoc):Mar86–109
Jozsa, P. & J. Leenhardt. Lire la Lecture.
  S. Sarkany, 107(CRCL):Jun86–269
Judd, A. The Noonday Devil.
  E. Battersby, 362:6Aug87–24
  J. Burnham, 617(TLS):26Jun87–697
Judkins, D.C. The Nondramatic Works of
  Ben Jonson.
  A. Leggatt, 677(YES):Vol16–245
Juel-Christiansen, C. Monument and Niche.
  D. Gosling, 46:Oct86–8
Juergensmeyer, M. Fighting with Gandhi.
  R. Church, 293(JASt):May86–628
Juhasz, S., ed. Feminist Critics Read
  Emily Dickinson.*
  J. Loving, 183(ESQ):Vol32No3–201
Juhasz, S. The Undiscovered Continent.*
  J. Loving, 183(ESQ):Vol32No3–201
Juhl, M. & B.H. Jørgensen. Diana's
  Revenge.
  S.H. Aiken, 563(SS):Winter86–89
Julier, J. Studien zur spätgotischen
  Baukunst am Oberrhein.
  W. Müller, 576:Mar86–69
Jung, F. Werke in Einzelausgaben. (Vol
  1, Pts 1 & 2; Vol 2, Pt 1; Vol 8) (L.
  Schulenburg, ed) Der tolle Nikolaus.
  (C.M. Jung & F. Mierau, eds)
  W. Paulsen, 133:Band19Heft3/4–365
Jung, J. Altes und Neues zu Thomas Manns
  Roman "Doktor Faustus."
  H. Siefken, 402(MLR):Apr87–525
Jung, K.D. – see under Kim Dae Jung

Jung, W. Theorie und Praxis des Typischen
  bei Honoré de Balzac.
  D. Bellos, 208(FS):Oct86–475
  R. Klein, 547(RF):Band98Heft3/4–445
  D. Rounsaville, 446(NCFS):Fall–Winter
  86/87–196
  A. Vanoncini, 535(RHL):Mar–Apr86–299
Junge, M. J.E. Stimson.
  L. Milazzo, 584(SWR):Spring86–257
Jungk, P.S. Franz Werfel.
  E. Timms, 617(TLS):9–15Oct87–1097
Jungnickel, C. & R. McCormmach. Intellec-
  tual Mastery of Nature.
  B. Pippard, 617(TLS):2Jan87–5
Junnosuke, M. – see under Masumi Junno-
  suke
Junor, P. Charles.
  C. Mosley, 362:2Jul87–27
Juntunen, A. Suomalaisten karkottaminen
  Siperiaan autonomian aikana ja karkotetut
  Siperiassa.
  A. Upton, 575(SEER):Jan86–136
Jupp, P. Lord Grenville 1759–1834.*
  J. Black, 173(ECS):Spring87–349
Juretschke, H. & others. Romanticismo I.
  R.A. Cardwell, 86(BHS):Apr86–175
Jurgensen, M. Deutsche Frauenautoren der
  Gegenwart.*
  E. Boa, 402(MLR):Jul86–806
  S. Lennox, 221(GQ):Fall86–672
  C. Poore, 406:Fall86–421
Jurgensen, M., ed. Wolf.
  R.C.Y. Smith, 133:Band19Heft3/4–373
Just, J. Meissen Porcelain of the Art
  Nouveau Period.*
  N. Powell, 39:Mar86–218
Just, W. The American Ambassador.
  R. Stone, 441:15Mar87–1
  442(NY):18May87–116
Justeson, J.S. & L. Campbell, eds. Phonet-
  icism in Mayan Hieroglyphic Writing.*
  C.A. Hofling, 269(IJAL):Jul86–309
Justice, D. The Sunset Maker.
  E. Hirsch, 441:23Aug87–20
Justus, J.H. The Achievement of Robert
  Penn Warren.
  H. Claridge, 447(N&Q):Mar85–142

Kabakoff, J. – see Imber, N.H.
Kabbani, R. Europe's Myths of Orient.
  D. Mason, 441:4Jan87–18
  N. Powell, 39:Aug86–143
Kabir. The Bijak of Kabir.* (L. Hess & S.
  Singh, trans)
  K.E. Bryant, 293(JASt):Feb86–426
Kac, M. Enigmas of Chance.
  42(AR):Winter86–122
Kachru, B.B. The Indianization of English.
  A. Jacob, 215(GL):Vol26No3–208
Kaczyński, T. Conversations with Witold
  Lutoslawski. (2nd ed)
  J. Casken, 415:Apr86–208
Kadare, I. Chronicle in Stone.
  S. Altinel, 617(TLS):3Jul87–715
Kadaré, I. Le général de l'armée morte.
  Qui a ramené Doruntine?
  V. Alleton, 98:May86–546
Kadish, A. Apostle Arnold.*
  R.N. Bérard, 637(VS):Summer87–546
Kadish, D.Y. The Literature of Images.
  T. Dawson, 268(IFR):Summer87–110

Kael, P.   State of the Art.
   M. Wood, 617(TLS):24Jul87-792
Kaempfer, M.   Wort und Wortverwendung.
   A.C., 400(MLN):Apr86-734
Kaes, A., ed.   Weimarer Republik.*
   M. Pazi, 680(ZDP):Band105Heft2-308
   E. Schürer, 133:Band19Heft1-87
Kafka, B.   Microwave Gourmet.
   A. Byrn, 441:6Dec87-44
Kafka, F.   Amtliche Schriften.   (W. Possner
   & J. Loužil, eds)
   J.J. White, 402(MLR):Oct87-1034
Kaftal, G.   Iconography of the Saints in
   the Painting of North West Italy.
   J. Pope-Hennessy, 39:Feb86-136
Kagan, D.   The Fall of the Athenian Empire.
   B. Knox, 61:Nov87-119
Kagan, J.   The Nature of the Child.
   T.C. Holyoke, 42(AR):Spring86-244
Kahan, A., with R. Hellie.   The Plow, the
   Hammer, and the Knout.
   J. Brooks, 173(ECS):Summer87-497
   I. de Madariaga, 617(TLS):2-8Oct87-
   1068
Kahan, G., ed.   George Alexander Stevens
   and "The Lecture on Heads."
   H.W. Pedicord, 611(TN):Vol40No1-41
   P. Wagner, 83:Autumn86-262
Kahn, A. & L.H. Holt.   Menopause.
   H. Wackett, 362:3Dec87-35
Kahn, E.J., Jr.   The Problem Solvers.*
   C.N. Kimball, 432(NEQ):Sep86-427
Kahn, J.   Timefall.
   G. Jonas, 441:26Apr87-29
Kahn, V.   Rhetoric, Prudence, and Skep-
   ticism in the Renaissance.*
   J.B. Altman, 551(RenQ):Summer86-314
   J.D. Lyons, 478:Oct86-334
   639(VQR):Summer86-88
von Kahn, W., ed.   Fachsprachen.
   K. Kehr, 685(ZDL):1/1986-101
Kahn-Ackermann, M.   China Within the
   Outer Gate.
   J.K. Kallgren, 293(JASt):Nov85-121
Kahsnitz, R., ed.   Veit Stoss.
   P. Crossley, 90:Jun86-428
Kaid, L.L., D. Nimmo & K.R. Sanders, eds.
   New Perspectives on Political Advertis-
   ing.
   R.K. Whillock, 583:Spring87-331
Kain, P.J.   Schiller, Hegel and Marx.
   P. Somville, 542:Jan-Mar86-124
Kainz, H.P.   Hegel's Phenomenology.*   (Pt
   2)
   192(EP):Oct-Dec86-567
Kaiser, G.   Bilder lesen.
   U. Weisstein, 107(CRCL):Jun86-285
Kajanto, I.   Porthan and Classical Scholar-
   ship.
   G.C. Schoolfield, 563(SS):Winter86-69
Kaku, M. & J. Trainer.   Beyond Einstein.
   R. Wright, 441:3May87-45
Kālidāsa.   Theater of Memory.   (B.S.
   Miller, ed)
   I.V. Peterson, 293(JASt):Feb86-428
Kalikoff, B.   Murder and Moral Decay in
   Victorian Popular Literature.
   P. Beer, 617(TLS):11-17Dec87-1380
Kalinke, M.E. & P.M. Mitchell.   Bibliogra-
   phy of Old Norse-Icelandic Romances.
   P. Foote, 562(Scan):Nov86-220
   J. Glauser, 301(JEGP):Jul86-437

Kalinowski, G.   Sémiotique et philosophie.
   J-L. Gardies, 542:Jul-Sep86-408
Kalinowski, G. & F. Selvaggi.   Les fonde-
   ments logiques de la pensée normative.
   P. Bailhache, 542:Apr-Jun86-272
von Kalkar, H. - see under Heinrich von
   Kalkar
Kalnins, M., ed.   D.H. Lawrence.
   H. Mills, 175:Summer86-173
Kalpakian, L.   Fair Augusto.
   M. Bloom, 441:1Feb87-20
Kaluza, Z. & P. Vignaux, eds.   Preuves et
   raisons à l'Université de Paris.
   A.R. Perreiah, 589:Jan86-161
Kambas, C.   Walter Benjamin im Exil.
   H.F. Pfanner, 406:Fall86-417
Kamenetsky, C.   Children's Literature in
   Hitler's Germany.*
   R.B. Bottigheimer, 221(GQ):Winter86-173
   R. Handler, 292(JAF):Jul/Sep86-352
   J. Zipes, 222(GR):Summer86-130
Kamenetz, R.   Terra Infirma.*
   42(AR):Spring86-245
Kamester, M. & J. Vellacott - see Florence,
   M.S., C. Marshall & C.K. Ogden
Kaminski, T.   The Early Career of Samuel
   Johnson.
   W.B. Carnochan, 617(TLS):18-24Dec87-
   1396
Kaminsky, S.M.   A Fine Red Rain.
   442(NY):12Oct87-146
Kamman, M.   In Madeleine's Kitchen.
   W. & C. Cowen, 639(VQR):Spring86-66
Kanda, C.G.   Shinzō.
   D.F. McCallum, 407(MN):Winter86-477
Kane, G.   Chaucer.*
   S.C.B. Atkinson, 577(SHR):Fall86-381
   D. Mehl, 38:Band104Heft1/2-204
   P.G. Ruggiers, 589:Oct86-945
Kane, H., ed.   The Prickynge of Love.
   J. Bazire, 382(MAE):1986/2-294
Kane, J.   Beyond Empiricism.
   K. Denbigh, 84:Sep86-375
Kane, J.E. - see François Ier
Kane, R.   Free Will and Values.
   T. Talbott, 258:Sep86-300
Kane, R.S.   Spain at its Best.
   J.J. Deveny, Jr., 399(MLJ):Autumn86-
   333
Kanellos, N., ed.   Hispanic Theatre in the
   United States.*
   H. Cohen, 238:Mar86-122
Kaniuk, Y.   Confessions of a Good Arab.
   H. Harris, 617(TLS):3Jul87-714
   J. Mellors, 362:28May87-26
Kanowitsch, G.   Kerzen im Wind.
   H. Conrad, 654(WB):1/1986-124
Kant, I.   La Religion dans les limites de
   la simple raison.   (M. Naar, ed; J.
   Gibelin, trans)
   J. Ferrari, 342:Band77Heft2-267
Kant, I.   Zum ewigen Frieden.   (R. Malter,
   ed) Anthropologie in pragmatischer
   Absicht.   (W. Becker, ed)
   W. Steinbeck, 342:Band77Heft3-382
Kantaris, S.   The Tenth Muse.   Time and
   Motion.
   J. O'Grady, 617(TLS):18-24Sep87-1024
Kantor, A.   The Book of Alfred Kantor.
   E. Kuryluk, 441:23Aug87-17
Kantorowitz, E.H.   Mourir pour la patrie et
   autres textes.
   J. Jolivet, 542:Oct-Dec86-517

Kelley, C.M. & J.K. Davis. Kelley.
R. Sherrill, 441:13Sep87-12
Kelley, K. His Way.*
E.J. Hobsbawm, 453(NYRB):12Feb87-11
Kelley, M. Private Woman, Public Stage.
C. Hlus, 106:Fall86-347
Kelley, M. - see Milton, J.
Kelley, P. & R. Hudson - see Browning, R. &
E.B.
Kelliher, W.H. - see Wordsworth, W.
Kellman, S.G., ed. Approaches to Teaching
Camus' "The Plague."
L.J. Leff, 365:Spring/Summer86-159
R.D. Reck, 128(CE):Sep86-484
M. Zobel-Finger, 72:Band223Heft2-474
Kellman, S.G. Loving Reading.
M.B., 295(JML):Nov86-408
D.R. Schwarz, 395(MFS):Summer86-341
Kelly, D., ed. The Romances of Chrétien de
Troyes.
C. Corley, 402(MLR):Apr87-469
P.F. Dembowski, 405(MP):May87-418
T. Hunt, 208(FS):Jul86-311
Kelly, F.E. & G.J. Etzkorn - see Ockham,
William of
Kelly, G.A. Mortal Politics in Eighteenth-
Century France.
J. Rogister, 617(TLS):18-24Dec87-1411
Kelly, H.A. Canon Law and the Archpriest
of Hita.*
J.N.H. Lawrance, 382(MAE):1986/2-336
G. Silano, 589:Jul86-670
Kelly, J. Women, History and Theory.*
S.G. Bell, 551(RenQ):Summer86-284
S. Jeffords, 577(SHR):Winter86-71
Kelly, J., with E. Domville - see Yeats,
W.B.
Kelly, L., ed. Istanbul.
J.A. Cuddon, 617(TLS):18-24Sep87-1010
Kelly, L. Women of the French Revolution.
A. Forrest, 617(TLS):11-17Sep87-983
Kelly, R. Graham Greene.
E. Hollahan, 594:Winter86-438
Kelly, W.W. Deference and Defiance in
Nineteenth-Century Japan.*
A. Walthall, 293(JASt):May86-602
Kelman, J. Greyhound for Breakfast.
T. Dooley, 617(TLS):8May87-488
Kelman, S. Making Public Policy.
M. Tolchin, 441:7Jun87-23
Kelsay, I.T. Joseph Brant, 1743-1807.*
O.P. Dickason, 106:Winter86-459
Kelso, W.M. Kingsmill Plantations, 1619-
1800.
A. Yentsch, 656(WMQ):Apr86-307
Kelton, E. The Good Old Boys.
M. Terry, 649(WAL):Aug86-140
Kelvin, N. - see Morris, W.
Kemal, S. Kant and Fine Art.
F. Schier, 617(TLS):24Apr87-449
Kemal, Y. The Birds Have Also Gone.
S. Altinel, 617(TLS):6-12Nov87-1226
Kemal, Y. Et la mer se fâcha...
H. Cronel, 450(NRF):Sep86-120
Kemal, Y. The Sea-Crossed Fisherman.*
T. McGonigle, 532(RCF):Summer86-155
Kemelman, H. One Fine Day the Rabbi
Bought a Cross.
N. Callendar, 441:26Apr87-37
Kemp, I. Tippett.*
T.B., 412:May85-145
C. Fussell, 414:Vol72No2-282

Kemp, J. American Vernacular.
P. Goldberger, 441:6Dec87-24
Kemp, P. Animus.
D. Bennett, 102(CanL):Winter85-152
Kemp, P. The Strauss Family.*
A. Jacobs, 410(M&L):Oct86-398
Kemp, P. H.G. Wells and the Culminating
Ape.*
R.G. Hampson, 447(N&Q):Jun85-284
Kemp, S. - see Kipling, R.
Kempcke, G. & others. Handwörterbuch der
deutschen Gegenwartssprache.
J. Werner, 682(ZPSK):Band39Heft2-265
Kemper, H-G. Gottebenbildlichkeit und
Naturnachahmung im Säkularisierungspro-
zess.*
W. Braungart, 224(GRM):Band36Heft1-112
Kemper, H-G. & F.R. Max - see Trakl, G.
Kempf, J.M. The Early Career of Malcolm
Cowley.*
M.B., 295(JML):Nov86-454
D.W. Faulkner, 569(SR):Winter86-ii
Kempff, M. Jordan Målare [together with]
Norrby, I. Johannes Snickares altarskåp
i Östra Ryds kyrka, Uppland.
J. von Bonsdorff, 341:Vol55No3-136
Kenaz, Y. After the Holidays.
L. Dickstein, 441:14Jun87-28
Kendall, W. The Conservative Affirmation
in America.
G.W. Carey, 396(ModA):Summer/Fall86-
294
Kendrick, B.L. - see Freeman, M.E.W.
Kendrick, W. The Secret Museum.
L. Stone, 441:3May87-3
Keneally, T. The Playmaker.
J. Atlas, 441:20Sep87-7
R. Clarke, 362:15Oct87-30
H. Jacobson, 617(TLS):27Nov-3Dec87-
1307
Kennealy, J. Polo Solo.
N. Callendar, 441:16Aug87-21
Kennedy, A.J. Christine de Pizan.*
J.C. Laidlaw, 402(MLR):Jan87-198
Kennedy, C. ICI.
J. Taylor, 324:Oct87-851
Kennedy, C. Mayfair.
J. Chernaik, 617(TLS):23Jan87-89
Kennedy, D. Granville Barker and the
Dream of Theatre.*
J. Coakley, 130:Winter86/87-371
C.M. Mazer, 615(TJ):Dec86-505
M.M. Morgan, 611(TN):Vol40No3-135
P. Storfer, 157:No160-49
Kennedy, G.A. Greek Rhetoric under
Christian Emperors.*
M.B. Cunningham, 303(JoHS):Vol106-270
Kennedy, G.A. New Testament Interpreta-
tion Through Rhetorical Criticism.*
R.L.S. Evans, 124:Jan-Feb87-222
Kennedy, H. The Prophet and the Age of
the Caliphates.
W.F. Madelung, 617(TLS):19Jun87-666
Kennedy, J.H. Relatos latinoamericanos.
P. Hunter, 399(MLJ):Winter86-443
Kennedy, L. Faces.*
B. Harvey, 441:23Aug87-16
Kennedy, M. Adrian Boult.
H. Canning, 362:16Jul87-25
A. Jacobs, 617(TLS):4-11Sep87-945
Kennedy, M. Britten.*
G. Martin, 465:Autumn86-120

Kidder, T. House.*
J. Iovine, 45:May86-75
S.T. Swank, 658:Spring86-99
Kido Takayoshi. The Diary of Kido Takayo-
shi. (Vol 2)
J.B. Leavell, 293(JASt):Aug86-839
R.M. Spaulding, 407(MN):Spring86-117
Kidwai, J.A. - see Forster, E.M. & R.
Masood
Kieckhefer, R. Unquiet Souls.*
M.E. Kalinke, 301(JEGP):Jan86-96
D. Weinstein, 589:Jul86-672
Kiefer, F. Fortune and Elizabethan Trag-
edy.*
J.M. Lyon, 402(MLR):Apr87-443
Kielhöfer, B. & S. Jonekiet. Zweisprachige
Kindererziehung.
P.R. Lutzeier, 603:Vol10No1-213
Kiely, B. A Letter to Peachtree and Nine
Other Stories.
P. Craig, 617(TLS):10Apr87-394
Kiely, B. Nothing Happens in Carmincross.*
D. Flower, 249(HudR):Summer86-314
M. Harmon, 272(IUR):Spring86-77
Kiely, R., with J. Hildebidle, eds. Mod-
ernism Reconsidered.
T. Docherty, 541(RES):May86-301
Kienlechner, S. Negativität der Erkenntnis
im Werk Franz Kafkas.
J.M. Grandin, 406:Summer86-247
Kieras, D.E. & M.A. Just, eds. New Methods
in Reading Comprehension Research.
B.A. Beatie, 399(MLJ):Autumn86-295
Kiernan, C. Daniel Mannix and Ireland.
J. McCalman, 381:Mar86-69
Kiernan, M. - see Bacon, F.
Kiernan, R.F. Gore Vidal.
D. Seed, 677(YES):Vol16-363
Kieser, R. Erzwungene Symbiose.*
J. Strelka, 133:Band18Heft4-379
Kihlman, C. All My Sons.
I. Scobbie, 562(Scan):May86-98
Kiker, D. Murder on Clam Pond.
N. Callendar, 441:4Jan87-35
442(NY):2Feb87-102
Kikuchi, Y. Mindoro Highlanders.
B.J. Wallace, 293(JASt):Nov85-194
Kilby, D. Descriptive Syntax and the
English Verb.
D.J. Allerton, 297(JL):Mar86-204
S.M. Embleton, 320(CJL):Fall86-306
Killam, G.D., ed. Critical Perspectives on
Ngugi wa Thiong'o.
D.A.M. Brown, 538(RAL):Winter86-614
Killian, J.R., Jr. The Education of a Col-
lege President.
C.N. Kimball, 432(NEQ):Mar86-123
Kilmarnock, A., ed. The Radical Challenge.
P. Clarke, 617(TLS):16-22Oct87-1131
Kilmister, C.W. Russell.
N. Griffin, 518:Jan86-32
Kilpatrick, R.S. The Poetry of Friendship.
K.J. Reckford, 121(CJ):Apr-May87-338
Kilroy, J.F., ed. The Irish Short Story.*
J.M. Cahalan, 174(Éire):Winter86-154
Kim Dae Jung. Prison Writings.
I. Buruma, 453(NYRB):29Jan87-21
C. Haberman, 441:5Jul87-13
C. Hitchens, 617(TLS):6-12Nov87-1212
Kim, G-U. Valenz und Wortbildung.
A. Greule, 685(ZDL):3/1986-391
Kimball, P. Harvesting Ballads.
D.D. Quantic, 649(WAL):May86-57

Kimbrough, R. - see Sidney, P.
Kimmerle, G. Die Aporie der Wahrheit.
R. Margreiter, 489(PJGG):Band93Heft2-
376
Kimpel, D., ed. Mehrsprachigkeit in der
deutschen Aufklärung.
R. Baasner, 52:Band21Heft1-92
Kinder, G. Light Years.
E. Dolnick, 441:19Jul87-21
Kinderman, W. Beethoven's Diabelli
Variations.
D. Matthews, 617(TLS):7Aug87-845
Kindstrand, J.F. The Stylistic Evaluation
of Aeschines in Antiquity.*
S. Perlman, 24:Fall86-436
Kiner, R., with J. Gergen. Kiner's Korner.
J. Oppenheimer, 441:3May87-14
King, A. The Bungalow.
J.V. Iovine, 45:Feb86-77
King, A.H. A Mozart Legacy.
J. Arthur, 410(M&L):Apr86-194
King, B. Starkadder.
R. Short, 441:18Oct87-31
King, D. & C. Porter. Images of Revolu-
tion.
J. Bushnell, 550(RusR):Jan86-81
King, F. Frozen Music.
L. Taylor, 362:10Dec87-30
R. Trevelyan, 617(TLS):2-8Oct87-1074
King, F.H.H., ed. Eastern Banking.
W.K.K. Chan, 302:Vol22No1-92
King, J. William Cowper.*
639(VQR):Autumn86-124
King, J. Interior Landscapes.
J. Gage, 617(TLS):16-22Oct87-1133
King, J. "Sur."
J. Wilson, 617(TLS):4-11Sep87-961
King, J. & C. Ryskamp - see Cowper, W.
King, J.A. The Irish Lumberman-Farmer.
F.M. Carroll, 174(Éire):Fall86-149
King, L.D. & C.A. Maley, eds. Selected
Papers from the XIIIth Linguistic Sympo-
sium on Romance Languages, Chapel Hill,
NC, 24-26 March 1983.
D.J. Napoli, 350:Mar87-183
F. Nuessel, 361:Apr86-351
King, L.L. Warning: Writers at Work.
J. Byrd, 649(WAL):Nov86-282
King, L.S. The Industrialization of Taste.
M. Bright, 637(VS):Spring87-424
King, M. Freedom Song.
S. Brownmiller, 441:30Aug87-12
442(NY):12Oct87-145
King, M., ed. H.D.
T.H.J., 295(JML):Nov86-458
King, M.C. The Drama of J.M. Synge.
B. Benstock, 659(ConL):Spring87-121
F. McClusky, 305(JIL):Jan86-62
King, M.L. A Testament of Hope.* (J.M.
Washington, ed)
B. McKibben, 442(NY):6Apr87-107
King, M.L. Venetian Humanism in an Age of
Patrician Dominance.*
F. Gilbert, 453(NYRB):16Jul87-37
King, M.L. & A. Rabil, Jr., eds. Her
Immaculate Hand.*
J. Lorch, 278(IS):Vol41-141
L.V.R., 568(SCN):Spring-Summer86-30
King, R. Written on a Stranger's Map.
L. Taylor, 362:9Jul87-31
King, S. The Eyes of the Dragon.
B. Tritel, 441:22Feb87-12

King, S. Misery.
  S. Dunant, 362:24Sep87-22
  J. Katzenbach, 441:31May87-20
King, S. The Tommyknockers.
  N. Auerbach, 441:20Dec87-8
Kinghorn, A.M. & A. Law – see Ramsay, A.
  & R. Fergusson
Kingsland, S.E. Modeling Nature.
  L. Shaffer, 617(TLS):16Jan87-69
Kinkley, J.C., ed. After Mao.
  M.S. Duke, 293(JASt):Feb86-377
Kinneavy, J.L., W.J. McCleary & N. Naka-
  date. Writing in the Liberal Arts Tra-
  dition.
  R.H. Haswell, 126(CCC):Dec86-500
Kinnell, G. The Past.*
  J.F. Cotter, 249(HudR):Spring86-157
  M. Ford, 617(TLS):6-12Nov87-1229
Kinney, A.F. Critical Essays on William
  Faulkner: The Sartoris Family.
  R.K. Bird, 268(IFR):Winter87-60
Kinney, A.F. Flannery O'Connor's Library.*
  M. Orvell, 534(RALS):Spring-Autumn84-
  242
Kinney, A.F. – see West, R.H.
Kinney, J.L. Amalgamation!
  C.P. Schmitt, 26(ALR):Fall86-82
  27(AL):Dec86-674
Kinnock, N. Making Our Way.
  A. Ryan, 176:Sep/Oct87-55
Kinsella, T. Her Vertical Smile.* Songs
  of the Psyche.*
  J. Lanchester, 493:Jun86-113
Kinsella, T., ed & trans. The New Oxford
  Book of Irish Verse.*
  M. Dodsworth, 175:Summer86-196
  D. Donoghue, 453(NYRB):26Feb87-25
  M. Harmon, 272(IUR):Autumn86-234
  B. O'Donoghue, 493:Oct86-51
Kinsella, V., ed. Cambridge Language
  Teaching Surveys 3.
  A.S. Kaye, 350:Sep87-679
Kinsella, W.P. Scars.
  G. Noonan, 296(JCF):No35/36-158
Kinsley, J. – see Dickens, C.
Kintzler, C. Jean-Philippe Rameau.*
  P. Henriot, 192(EP):Oct-Dec86-568
  B. Norman, 207(FR):Mar87-575
Kinzer, B.L., ed. The Gladstonian Turn of
  Mind.
  P. Stansky, 637(VS):Autumn86-147
Kipel, V. & Z., comps. Janka Kupala and
  Jakub Kolas in the West.
  J. Dingley, 402(MLR):Jul87-814
  A. McMillin, 574(SEEJ):Winter86-588
Kipling, R. Early Verse by Rudyard Kip-
  ling, 1879-1899.* (A. Rutherford, ed)
  T.J. Binyon, 617(TLS):5Jun87-608
  H.W., 636(VP):Autumn86-348
  639(VQR):Autumn86-135
Kipling, R. Kipling's Kingdom. (C. Allen,
  ed) The Illustrated Kipling. (N.
  Philip, ed) A Choice of Kipling's Prose.
  (C. Raine, ed) The Day's Work. (T.
  Pinney, ed) The Jungle Book. (W.W.
  Robson, ed) Kim. (A. Sandison, ed)
  Life's Handicap. (A.O.J. Cockshut, ed)
  The Man Who Would Be King and Other
  Stories. (L.L. Cornell, ed) Plain Tales
  from the Hills. (A. Rutherford, ed) The
  Second Jungle Book. (W.W. Robson, ed)
  [continued]

[continuing]
Stalky and Co. (I. Quigley, ed) Debits
  and Credits. (S. Kemp, ed) A Diversity
  of Creatures. (P. Driver, ed) The
  Jungle Books. (D. Karlin, ed) Just So
  Stories. (P. Levi, ed) Life's Handicap.
  (P.N. Furbank, ed) Plain Tales from the
  Hills. (H.R. Woudhuysen, with D. Trot-
  ter, eds) Puck of Pook's Hill. (S.
  Wintle, ed) Something of Myself. (R.
  Hampson, ed) Traffics and Discoveries.
  (H. Lee, ed)
  T.J. Binyon, 617(TLS):5Jun87-608
Kipury, N. Oral Literature of the Maasai.
  C.A. Okafor, 538(RAL):Summer86-301
Király, B.K., ed. The Crucial Decade.
  B.H. Reid, 575(SEER):Apr86-298
Király, P., ed. Typographia Universitatis
  Hungaricae Budae 1777-1848.
  P. Sherwood, 402(MLR):Apr86-543
Kirk, G.S., general ed. "The Iliad": A
  Commentary. (Vol 1, Bks 1-4)
  J.P. Holoka, 124:Jan-Feb87-221
  P.V. Jones, 123:Vol36No1-1
  F. Vian, 555:Vol59fasc2-275
  M.M. Willcock, 303(JoHS):Vol106-201
Kirk, J.M. & others, eds. Studies in
  Linguistic Geography.
  S.M. Embleton, 350:Jun87-429
Kirkby, R.J.R. Urbanization in China.
  D.D. Buck, 293(JASt):Feb86-379
Kirkham, M. Jane Austen, Feminism and
  Fiction.*
  F.M. Keener, 677(YES):Vol16-297
  J. Thompson, 536(Rev):Vol8-21
Kirkham, M. The Imagination of Edward
  Thomas.
  K. Bucknell, 617(TLS):27Feb87-217
Kirkland, E.H. Divine Average. Love is a
  Wild Assault. The Edge of Disrepute.
  D.C. Grover, 649(WAL):Nov86-234
Kirkland, G., with G. Lawrence. Dancing On
  My Grave.*
  R. Philp, 151:Dec86-75
Kirkpatrick, B., ed. The Original Roget's
  Thesaurus of English Words and Phrases
  in a New Edition.
  D.A.N. Jones, 362:6Aug87-23
Kirkpatrick, B.J. A Bibliography of E.M.
  Forster.
  C. Hawtree, 364:Apr/May86-148
Kirkpatrick, R. Dante: "The Divine Com-
  edy."
  C.H. Sisson, 617(TLS):17Apr87-419
Kirkpatrick, R. Early Years.
  H. Schott, 415:Jul86-389
Kirkpatrick, R. Interpreting Bach's "Well-
  Tempered Clavier."*
  G.S.J., 412:Feb85-56
Kirkpatrick, S.D. A Cast of Killers.*
  T. Milne, 707:Autumn86-292
Kirp, D.L., M.G. Yudof & M.S. Franks.
  Gender Justice.*
  C.C., 185:Apr87-703
Kisarauskas, V. Lietuvos Knygos Ženklai,
  1518-1918.
  V.E. Vengris, 574(SEEJ):Fall86-456
Kisch, K.V. & U. Ritzenhoff – see Wirsung,
  C.
Kiser, L.J. Telling Classical Tales.*
  D. Mehl, 72:Band223Heft1-161

Kishlansky, M. Parliamentary Selection.
  A. Fletcher, 617(TLS):5Jun87-602
  L. Stone, 453(NYRB):26Feb87-38
Kiso, A. The Lost Sophocles.*
  A.L. Brown, 303(JoHS):Vol106-210
  J. Wilkins, 123:Vol36No1-12
Kiss, E., ed. Hermann Broch.
  S. Dahl, 680(ZDP):Band105Heft2-310
Kitchen, M. British Policy Towards the
  Soviet Union During the Second World War.
  T.G. Ash, 453(NYRB):11Jun87-44
Kitchener, R.F. Piaget's Theory of Know-
  ledge.
  H. Furth, 543:Mar87-580
Kitcher, P. Abusing Science.*
  B.S. Baigrie, 154:Autumn86-588
Kitcher, P. The Nature of Mathematical
  Knowledge.*
  C. Parsons, 482(PhR):Jan86-129
Kitcher, P. Vaulting Ambition.*
  P. Colgan, 529(QQ):Autumn86-595
  A. Rosenberg, 486:Dec86-607
Kitromelides, P.M. Iosipos Moisiodax.
  P.J. Vatikiotis, 617(TLS):10Apr87-379
Kitson, F. Warfare as a Whole.
  H. Beach, 362:2Apr87-24
  M. Carver, 617(TLS):10Apr87-377
Kitson, N. Where Sixpence Lives.
  J.D. Battersby, 441:22Nov87-46
Kittang, A. Luft, vind, ingenting.
  H.S. Naess, 562(Scan):May86-82
Kittelson, J.M. & P.J. Transue, eds.
  Rebirth, Reform, and Resilience.
  C.B. Schmitt, 551(RenQ):Spring86-76
Kittmann, S. Kant und Nietzsche.
  J. Salaquarda, 342:Band77Heft2-264
Kivy, P. The Corded Shell.*
  R.A. Solie & E.V. Spelman, 317:
    Spring86-191
Kivy, P. Sound and Semblance.*
  S. Ross, 482(PhR):Apr86-284
  R.A.S., 412:Feb85-70
  R.A. Solie & E.V. Spelman, 317:
    Spring86-191
Kiyoko, T. – see under Takeda Kiyoko
Kiyooka, E. – see "Fukuzawa Yukichi on
  Education"
Kizer, C. The Nearness of You.
  A. Libby, 441:22Mar87-23
Kjellström, B. & others. Folkmusikvågen/
  The Folk Music Vogue.
  O.K. Ledang, 187:Spring/Summer87-361
Kjetsaa, G. Dostoevsky and His New Testa-
  ment.
  R. Freeborn, 575(SEER):Oct86-593
Kjetsaa, G. & others. The Authorship of
  "The Quiet Don."*
  E. Egeberg, 172(Edda):1986/2-189
Klaidman, S. & T.L. Beauchamp. The Virtu-
  ous Journalist.
  J. Fleming, 441:19Apr87-16
Klapisch-Zuber, C. Women, Family and
  Ritual in Renaissance Italy.
  D.O. Hughes, 385(MQR):Winter87-266
Klass, P. I Am Having an Adventure.*
  T. De Pietro, 249(HudR):Autumn86-489
Klass, P. A Not Entirely Benign Procedure.
  I. Yalof, 441:10May87-20
Klaus, H.G. The Literature of Labour.
  J. Hansford, 541(RES):Nov86-597
  I. Kovačević, 637(VS):Spring87-434

Klaus, H.G., ed. The Socialist Novel in
  Britain.*
  M. Wilding, 677(YES):Vol16-347
Klaus, K. Das Maitrakanyakāvadāna (Divyā-
  vadāna 38).
  A. Mette, 259(IIJ):Apr86-142
Klause, J. The Unfortunate Fall.*
  C. Hill, 366:Spring86-111
Kleberg, L. & N.A. Nilsson, eds. Theater
  and Literature in Russia, 1900-1930.
  E. Braun, 575(SEER):Apr86-276
Kleiman, L. Ranniaia proza Fedora Solo-
  guba.
  Z. Yurieff, 550(RusR):Apr86-222
Klein, A.M. Short Stories. (M.W. Stein-
  berg, ed)
  D.O. Spettique, 150(DR):Fall86-368
Klein, D. & M. Bishop. Decorative Art
  1880-1980.
  C. Gere, 39:Dec86-567
Klein, E. Semantic and Pragmatic Indeter-
  minacy in English Non-finite Verb Comple-
  mentation.*
  Y. Putseys, 603:Vol10No2-516
Klein, F-J. Lexematische Untersuchungen
  zum französischen Verbalwortschatz im
  Sinnbezirk von Wahrnehmung und Einschätz-
  ung.*
  L. Bauer, 209(FM):Oct86-233
Klein, G. Ninon und Hermann Hesse.
  J. Mileck, 406:Summer86-240
Klein, G. & D. Fisher. First Down and a
  Billion.
  J.F. Clarity, 441:11Jan87-19
Klein, H., with J. Flower & E. Homberger,
  eds. The Second World War in Fiction.
  B. Bergonzi, 366:Autumn86-243
Klein, H.E.M. & L.R. Stark, eds. South
  American Indian Languages.
  M.R. Key, 350:Sep87-657
  L.W. Robinson, 263(RIB):Vol36No2-183
Klein, H.S. African Slavery in Latin
  America and the Caribbean.*
  D.B. Davis, 453(NYRB):5Nov87-34
Klein, J. England zwischen Aufklärung und
  Romantik.
  K. Gamerschlag, 72:Band223Heft1-169
Klein, L.S., ed. African Literatures in
  the Twentieth Century.
  E.S., 295(JML):Nov86-377
Klein, M.M. & R.W. Howard – see Robertson,
  J.
Klein, N. American Dreams.
  C.L. Mithers, 441:29Mar87-23
Kleiner, D.E.E. The Monument of Philopap-
  pos in Athens.
  J. Pouilloux, 555:Vol59fasc2-296
Kleiner, F.S. The Arch of Nero in Rome.
  F.E. Romer, 124:Jul-Aug87-464
Kleinig, J. Paternalism.
  R. Bronaugh, 154:Winter86-800
Kleinman, A. Social Origins of Distress
  and Disease.
  R. Porter, 617(TLS):1May87-461
Kleinman, A. & B. Good, eds. Culture and
  Depression.*
  G.R. Lowe, 529(QQ):Winter86-912
Kleinman, R. Anne of Austria.
  R. Bonney, 617(TLS):9Jan87-34
  J.H. Elliott, 453(NYRB):11Jun87-40
Kleinmann, H.H. & J. Weissman. Everyday
  Consumer English.
  M. Landa, 399(MLJ):Summer86-205

von Kleist, H. Sämtliche Erzählungen.
  W. Wittkowski, 133:Band19Heft3/4-349
"Kleist-Jahrbuch 1981/82."* (H-J. Kreutzer, ed)
  B. Fischer, 221(GQ):Winter86-139
"Kleist-Jahrbuch 1984." (H-J. Kreutzer, ed)
  K. Arens, 221(GQ):Summer86-484
Klejman, L. Rannjaja proza fedora Sologuba.
  P.R. Hart, 574(SEEJ):Fall86-448
Klement, F.L. Dark Lanterns.
  A.W. Trelease, 9(AlaR):Jan86-69
Klemp, P.J. Fulke Greville and Sir John Davies.
  S.J. Steen, 568(SCN):Fall86-43
Klenin, E. Animacy in Russian.*
  F.Y. Gladney, 574(SEEJ):Spring86-127
Klibbe, L.H. Lorca's "Impresiones y paisajes."*
  A.A. Anderson, 86(BHS):Jul86-294
  G. Connell, 402(MLR):Jan87-228
Klíma, I. My First Loves.
  R. Scruton, 617(TLS):23Jan87-83
  C. Wheatley, 362:1Jan87-20
Klíma, I. Soudce z Milosti.
  R. Scruton, 617(TLS):23Jan87-83
Klíma, I. A Summer Affair.
  L. Chamberlain, 617(TLS):28Aug87-932
Klimaszewski, B., ed. An Outline History of Polish Culture.
  G.T. Kapolka, 497(PolR):Vol31No1-85
Klinkowitz, J. Literary Subversions.
  J. Humphries, 385(MQR):Fall87-788
  S. Moore, 532(RCF):Summer86-150
Klinkowitz, J. The New American Novel of Manners.
  P.T.S., 295(JML):Nov86-417
Klinkowitz, J. The Self-Apparent Word.*
  I.R. Fairley, 567:Vol62No3/4-497
  S. Moore, 532(RCF):Summer86-150
  P. Stevick, 301(JEGP):Jan86-159
Klippel, F. Keep Talking.
  E.K. Horwitz, 399(MLJ):Summer86-167
Kloek, J.J. Over Werther geschreven...
  H. Steinmetz, 204(FdL):Mar86-60
Klopstock, F.G. Werke und Briefe.
  (Briefe, Vol 2) (R. Schmidt, ed)
  H.T. Betteridge, 402(MLR):Jul86-784
  P.M. Mitchell, 301(JEGP):Oct86-623
Klopstock, F.G. Werke und Briefe.
  (Briefe, Vol 7) (H. Riege, ed)
  M. Lee, 221(GQ):Winter86-136
Klopstock, F.G. Werke und Briefe.* (Werke IV, Vol 4) (E. Höpker-Herberg, ed)
  P.M. Mitchell, 301(JEGP):Jan86-79
Kloss, H., ed. Deutsch als Muttersprache in den Vereinigten Staaten. (Pt 2)
  M.L. Huffines, 660(Word):Dec86-226
Klostermaier, K.K. Mythologies and Philosophies of Salvation in the Theistic Traditions of India.
  L. Mowry, 293(JASt):May86-630
  B.J. Stewart, 485(PE&W):Apr86-187
Klotz, H., ed. Postmodern Visions.*
  P. Goldberger, 441:6Dec87-22
Klotz, V. Das europäische Kunstmärchen.
  H. Bausinger, 196:Band27Heft1/2-118
  H-H. Ewers, 52:Band21Heft3-317
  A. Montandon, 549(RLC):Jul-Sep86-354
Kluback, W. Hermann Cohen.
  G. Haarscher, 540(RIPh):Vol40fasc1/2-185

Kluge, G., ed. Aufsätze zu Literatur und Kunst der Jahrhundertwende.
  S.M. Patsch, 133:Band19Heft2-176
  W.E. Yates, 402(MLR):Jan87-253
Knabe, P.E. & R. Trousson, eds. Émile Verhaeren.
  Y-A. Favre, 535(RHL):Sep-Oct86-945
Knape, J. "Historie" in Mittelalter und früher Neuzeit.*
  D.H. Green, 402(MLR):Jan87-239
  P. Strohschneider, 224(GRM):Band36 Heft3-348
Knapp, B.L. Archetype, Architecture, and the Writer.
  M. Danahy, 446(NCFS):Spring87-331
Knapp, B.L. Edgar Allan Poe.*
  R.P. Benton, 495(PoeS):Jun86-25
  B.F. Fisher 4th, 27(AL):Mar86-141
Knapp, B.L. Word/Image/Psyche.*
  P.N. Humble, 89(BJA):Spring86-182
  A. Nabarra, 207(FR):Feb87-385
Knapp, F.P. Chevalier errant und fin' amor.
  D.H. Green, 402(MLR):Oct87-1021
Knapp, M. Doris Lessing.
  L. Leith, 561(SFS):Jul86-220
Knapp, M.L. & G.R. Miller, eds. Handbook of Interpersonal Communication.
  G.L. Wilson, 583:Winter87-213
Knapp, P.A. - see "Assays"
Knapp, S. Personification and the Sublime.*
  L. Newlyn, 541(RES):Aug86-430
  K.G. Thomas, 173(ECS):Spring87-395
  639(VQR):Spring86-43
Knapp-Potthoff, A. & K. Knapp. Fremdsprachenlernen und -lehren.*
  W. Heindrichs & H.P. Kelz, 72:Band223-Heft1-227
Knauss, J. & others. Die Wasserbauten der Minyer in der Kopais. (H. Blind, ed)
  A.M. Snodgrass, 303(JoHS):Vol106-245
Kneale, M. Whore Banquets.
  R. Deveson, 617(TLS):30Jan87-109
Kneale, W. & M. The Development of Logic.
  B. Mates, 316:Jun86-476
Kneece, J. Family Treason.
  P. Shenon, 441:4Jan87-19
Knepler, G. Karl Kraus liest Offenbach.
  H-J. Irmer, 601(SuF):Nov-Dec86-1302
Kneppe, A. & J.W. Höfer. Friedrich Münzer, ein Althistoriker zwischen Kaiserreich und Nationalsozialismus.
  F. Millar, 123:Vol36No2-358
Knevitt, C. Connections.
  D.F. Anstis, 324:Feb87-251
Knibbeler, W. & M. Bernards, eds. New Approaches in Foreign Language Methodology.
  A. Gołębiowska, 257(IRAL):Aug86-266
Kniffka, H. Soziolinguistik und empirische Textanalyse.
  W. Viereck, 685(ZDL):3/1986-420
Kniffler, G. Die Grabdenkmäler der Mainzer Erzbischöfe vom 13. bis zum frühen 16. Jahrhundert, Untersuchungen zur Geschichte, zur Plastik und zur Ornamentik.
  W. Müller, 576:Mar86-69
Knight, A. The Mexican Revolution.
  A. Hennessy, 617(TLS):29May87-575
Knight, A. The Robert Louis Stevenson Treasury.
  A.D. Ross, 588(SSL):Vol21-372

Kofman, S. La philosophie au théâtre,
Mélancolie de l'art.
F. Proust, 192(EP):Apr–Jun86–260
Kogan, J. Nothing But the Best.
K. Gann, 441:4Oct87–31
Kogan, S. The Hieroglyphic King.
R. Gill, 617(TLS):31Jul87–814
Kogawa, J. Woman in the Woods.
S. Scobie, 376:Sep86–156
Kohfeldt, M.L. Lady Gregory.*
R.E. Ward, 174(Éire):Spring86–155
Kohl, N. Oscar Wilde.
E. Späth, 38:Band104Heft3/4–524
Kohlberg, L. The Psychology of Moral De-
velopment.
T.M. Reed, 185:Jan87–441
Köhler-Hausmann, R. Literaturbetrieb in
der DDR.
G. Klatt, 654(WB):6/1986–1039
Kohli, M. & G. Robert, eds. Biographie und
soziale Wirklichkeit.*
C. Berens, 343:Heft13–105
Kohn, A. False Prophets.
P. Reading, 617(TLS):16Jan87–69
Kohn, D., with M.J. Kottler, eds. The Dar-
winian Heritage.
C.S. Blinderman, 637(VS):Winter87–290
R. Colp, Jr., 77:Summer86–269
Kohn, M. Narcomania.
J. Ryle, 617(TLS):23–29Oct87–1163
Kojo Laing, B. – see under Laing, B.K.
de Kok, A. La place du pronom personnel
régime conjoint en français.
M. Harris, 402(MLR):Apr87–466
L. Schøsler, 553(RLiR):Jul–Dec86–594
Kok, J.P.F. & others – see under Filedt
Kok, J.P. & others
"Kokinshū."* (L.R. Rodd, with M.C. Henken-
ius, eds & trans)
J.N. Rabinovitch, 293(JASt):Feb86–414
Kokoschka, O. Briefe III. (O. Kokoschka &
H. Spielmann, eds)
N. Lynton, 617(TLS):28Aug87–923
Kolakowski, L. Bergson.
A.E. Pilkington, 402(MLR):Apr87–483
Kolatch, A.J. Complete Dictionary of
English and Hebrew First Names.
L.R.N. Ashley, 424:Dec86–415
Kolb, E., E. Roters & W. Schmied. Krit-
ische Grafik in der Weimarer Zeit.
A. Fant, 341:Vol55No1–43
Kolb, P. – see Proust, M.
Kolbert, J. The Worlds of André Maurois.
C. Toloudis, 207(FR):Apr87–715
Kolchin, P. Unfree Labor.
C.V. Woodward, 453(NYRB):19Nov87–38
Kolek, L.S. Evelyn Waugh's Writings.
R.M. Davis, 223:Fall86–334
Kolenda, P. Caste, Cult, and Hierarchy.
P.G. Hiebert, 293(JASt):May86–631
Kolin, P.C., ed. Shakespeare and Southern
Writers.
M. Frazee, 189(EA):Jan–Mar87–115
P. Lentz, 651(WHR):Autumn86–275
Kolin, P.C., ed. Shakespeare in the
South.*
R.S. White, 161(DUJ):Jun86–375
Kolkenbrock-Netz, J. Fabrikation – Experi-
ment – Schöpfung.
Y. Chevrel, 549(RLC):Jan–Mar86–71
Kolker, R.P. Bernardo Bertolucci.*
L. Kroha, 529(QQ):Autumn86–653

Kolker, R.P. A Cinema of Loneliness.
B. Testa, 106:Winter86–525
Kolko, G. Anatomy of a War.* (British
title: Vietnam.)
639(VQR):Summer86–95
Koll-Stobbe, A. Textleistung im Komplex
Bild–Sprache.
G. Bourcier, 189(EA):Apr–Jun87–243
Koller, J.M. Oriental Philosophies. (2nd
ed)
K-M. Wu, 485(PE&W):Jul86–299
Kölling, B. Kiel UB. Cod. MS. K. B. 145.
H. Tiefenbach, 260(IF):Band91–421
Kolodny, A. The Land Before Her.*
C. Fairbanks, 366:Spring86–126
C. Hlus, 106:Fall86–347
E. Kolmer, 377:Jul86–146
Kolve, V.A. Chaucer and the Imagery of
Narrative.*
H. Cooper, 382(MAE):1986/2–286
A. Crépin, 189(EA):Oct–Dec87–466
P. Hardman, 541(RES):May86–245
S. Lerer, 405(MP):Aug86–64
C. Muscatine, 589:Jul86–674
F.C. Robinson, 569(SR):Fall86–668
J.I. Wimsatt, 579(SAQ):Winter86–98
Kölving, U. & J. Carriat, eds. Inventaire
de la Correspondance littéraire de Grimm
et Meister.
D. Williams, 402(MLR):Jul86–741
Kom, A., ed. Dictionnaire des oeuvres lit-
téraires négro-africaines de langue fran-
çaise: Des Origines à 1978.
A. Gérard, 107(CRCL):Mar86–111
L-M. Ongoum, 535(RHL):Jul–Aug86–808
Komar, K.L. Pattern and Chaos.
C. Caramello, 395(MFS):Summer86–345
L.A. Rickels, 406:Winter86–553
Komesu, O. The Double Perspective of
Yeats's Aesthetic.*
D. Kiberd, 617(TLS):13Feb87–166
A. Roche, 577(SHR):Summer86–271
Komisar, L. Corazon Aquino.
I. Buruma, 453(NYRB):11Jun87–10
F.X. Clines, 441:3May87–52
Komlos, J., ed. Economic Development in
the Habsburg Monarchy in the Nine-
teenth Century.
A. Sked, 575(SEER):Apr86–299
Komunyakaa, Y. I Apologize for the Eyes in
My Head.
M. Flamm, 441:4Oct87–24
Konaté, M. L'Or du diable [suivi de] Le
Cercle au féminin.
H.A. Waters, 207(FR):Feb87–430
Kondakow, N.I. Wörterbuch der Logik. (E.
Albrecht & G. Asser, eds)
J. Dölling, 682(ZPSK):Band39Heft2–293
Kondrup, J. Livsvaerker.
S.A. Aarnes, 172(Edda):1986/4–374
Kone, A. & others. Littérature et method-
ologie.
M. Schipper, 538(RAL):Winter86–566
König-Nordhoff, U. Ignatius von Loyola.
M. Schilling, 354:Mar86–85
Konigsberg, I., ed. American Criticism in
the Poststructuralist Age.
M. Finlay, 107(CRCL):Mar86–94
Konigsberg, I. Narrative Technique in the
English Novel.
S. Soupel, 189(EA):Oct–Dec87–469

Konishi, J.   A History of Japanese Litera-
ture. (Vol 2)
   J. McMullen, 617(TLS):11–17Dec87–1382
Konner, M.   Becoming a Doctor.
   L. Thomas, 453(NYRB):24Sep87–6
   G. Weissmann, 441:26Jul87–1
Konrad, H. & W. Maderthaner, eds.   Neuere
   Studien zur Arbeitergeschichte.
   F.L. Carsten, 575(SEER):Apr86–304
Konrad von Haslau.   Der Jüngling.* (W.
   Tauber, ed)
   H. Kratz, 133:Band19Heft2–162
Konrads, M.   Wörter und Sachen im Wilden-
   burger Ländchen.
   K. Kehr, 685(ZDL):1/1986–94
Konstan, D.   Roman Comedy.*
   P.G.M. Brown, 123:Vol36No1–133
   W.T. MacCary, 24:Fall86–448
   N.W. Slater, 122:Apr86–169
Konstan, D. & C. El-Shabrawy, eds.   Pro-
   ceedings of the International Conference
   on Comparative Drama.
   M. Fayad, 149(CLS):Spring86–84
Konstantinović, Z., E. Kushner & B.
   Köpeczi, eds.   Evolution of the Novel.
   F. Meregalli, 107(CRCL):Jun86–293
Kontorini, V.   Inscriptions inédites
   relatives à l'histoire et aux cultes de
   Rhodes au IIe et au Ier s. av. J–C.:
   Rhodiaka I.*
   E.E. Rice, 303(JoHS):Vol106–263
Konwicki, T.   Moonrise, Moonset.
   N. Ascherson, 453(NYRB):17Dec87–44
   E. Kuryluk, 441:30Aug87–3
Koon, H.   Colley Cibber.
   J.L. Knowles, 173(ECS):Spring87–343
"William de Kooning; Drawings, Paintings
   and Sculpture."
   J. Burr, 39:Jan86–62
Koontz, D.R.   Watchers.
   K. Weber, 441:15Mar87–16
Koonz, C.   Mothers in the Fatherland.
   G.A. Craig, 453(NYRB):16Jul87–32
Koop, A.   Constructivist Architecture in
   the USSR.
   C. Cooke, 592:Vol199No1014–63
Koopmans, J., ed.   Quatre sermons joyeux.*
   J. Crow, 382(MAE):1986/2–320
Köpeczi, B., general ed.   Erdély Történe-
   te.
   N. Stone, 617(TLS):2–8Oct87–1066
Köpeczi, B.   Hongrois et Français.
   J. Voisine, 549(RLC):Jan–Mar86–102
Köpeczi, B. & others.   Archivum Ràkóczia-
   num. (Vol 2)
   J. Voisine, 549(RLC):Jan–Mar86–102
Köpke, W.   Lion Feuchtwanger.*
   U. Weisstein, 133:Band18Heft4–377
Koppes, C.R. & G.D. Black.   Hollywood Goes
   to War.
   W. Goodman, 441:23Aug87–15
Koppisch, M.S.   The Dissolution of Charac-
   ter.*
   W. Henning, 72:Band223Heft1–208
Koppitz, H–J. – see "Gutenberg-Jahrbuch
   1986"
Koranyi, S.   Autobiographik und Wissen-
   schaft im Denken Goethes.
   S. Atkins, 406:Fall86–369
Koren, R.   L'Anti-récit.
   J–J. Roubine, 535(RHL):Mar–Apr86–345

Korenský, J. & J. Hoffmannová, eds.   Text
   and the Pragmatic Aspects of Language.
   D.H., 355(LSoc):Mar86–134
Koreny, F.   Albrecht Dürer und die Tier-
   und Pflanzenstudien der Renaissance.
   J.M. Massing, 90:Aug86–611
Korjakinová, T., M. Nedvědová & G. Vaněč-
   ková, comps.   Marina Cvetajevová a Praha.
   S. Capus, 575(SEER):Jan86–157
Korn, D.A.   Ethiopia, the United States and
   the Soviet Union.
   C.D. May, 441:28Jun87–35
Kornblatt, J.R.   Breaking Bread.
   B. Thompson, 441:18Jan87–11
Körner, K–H. & D. Briesemeister, eds.
   Aureum Saeculum Hispanum.
   F. Pierce, 86(BHS):Jul86–277
de Kőrös, A.C. – see under Csoma de Kőrös,
   A.
Korr, C.   West Ham United.
   P. Smith, 617(TLS):30Jan87–106
Korshin, P.J., ed.   Johnson After Two Hun-
   dred Years.
   W.B. Carnochan, 617(TLS):18–24Dec87–
   1396
   O. Hedley, 324:Oct87–853
Korshin, P.J.   Typologies in England, 1650–
   1820.*
   G.S. Rousseau, 301(JEGP):Jan86–125
   E. Zimmerman, 566:Spring87–201
Korshin, P.J. – see "The Eighteenth Cen-
   tury: A Current Bibliography"
Korshin, P.J. & R.R. Allen, eds.   Greene
   Centennial Studies.
   H.W. Hamilton, 579(SAQ):Autumn86–396
   J.A. Vance, 173(ECS):Fall86–91
Kort, W.A.   Modern Fiction and Human Time.
   M.P.L., 295(JML):Nov86–418
   G. Meeter, 395(MFS):Winter86–690
Kortländer, B. & F. Nies, eds.   Franzö-
   sische Literatur in deutscher Sprache.
   W. Pöckl, 547(RF):Band98Heft3/4–418
Korzen, H.   Pourquoi et l'inversion finale
   en français.
   G. Kleiber, 553(RLiR):Jul–Dec86–601
Korzenik, D.   Drawn to Art.*
   W.M. Corn, 617(TLS):2Jan87–17
Koschmal, W.   Vom Realismus zum Symbolis-
   mus.
   E. Możejko, 558(RLJ):Spring/Fall86–227
   W. Smyrniw, 402(MLR):Jan87–267
Koschmann, J.V., Ōiwa Keibō & Yamashita
   Shinji, eds.   International Perspectives
   on Yanagita Kunio and Japanese Folklore
   Studies.
   F.G. Kavanagh, 293(JASt):May86–604
   P. Knecht, 407(MN):Spring86–119
Kosegarten, A.M.   Sienesische Bildhauer am
   Duomo Vecchio.*
   G. Kreytenberg, 90:May86–358
   E.L. Schlee, 683:Band49Heft2–236
Köseoglu, C.   Topkapı: The Treasury.
   (J.M. Rogers, ed & trans)
   G. Goodwin, 617(TLS):14Aug87–866
Koshar, R.   Social Life, Local Politics,
   and Nazism.
   B. Blackbourn, 617(TLS):15May87–522
Koshkaki, M., ed.   Qataghan et Badakhshān.
   (M. Reut, trans)
   A. Ghani, 318(JAOS):Jan/Mar85–169
Kosicka, J. & D. Gerould.   A Life of Soli-
   tude.*
   M. Meyer, 364:Dec86/Jan87–138

Koslowski, P., ed. Economics and Philosophy.
   K.S., 185:Jul87-886
Kosok, H. O'Casey the Dramatist.
   C. Murray, 272(IUR):Autumn86-238
Kossuth, K.C. & D.R. Antal. Alte Legenden und neue Literatur.
   R.H. Buchheit, 399(MLJ):Winter86-429
Köster, P. - see Turner, N.
Köster, U. Literatur und Gesellschft in Deutschland 1830-1848.
   D.C.G. Lorenz, 221(GQ):Winter86-148
Kostka, S. & D. Payne. Tonal Harmony
   A.K. McNamee, 308:Fall86-309
Kostof, S. America by Design.
   T. Hine, 441:4Oct87-43
Kostomarov, V. - see Stepanova, E.M. & others
Kosztolányi, D. Le Traducteur cleptomane. L'Oeil-de-mer.
   J-C. Dorrier, 450(NRF):Jun86-94
Kotlowitz, R. Sea Changes.*
   442(NY):16Feb87-109
Kott, J. The Bottom Translation.
   R.M. Adams, 453(NYRB):19Nov87-46
   M. Gussow, 441:14Jun87-27
   J. Wilders, 617(TLS):30Oct-5Nov87-1197
Kott, J. The Theater of Essence.
   R. Engle, 615(TJ):Mar86-122
   E. Fischer, 397(MD):Jun86-357
Kotzor, G., ed. Das altenglische Martyrologium.
   D.W. Rollason, 677(YES):Vol16-223
Kotzwinkle, W. The Exile.
   H. Gold, 441:10May87-1
Kozioł, U. Im Rhythmus der Sonne.
   G. Rothbauer, 601(SuF):Nov-Dec85-1320
Kozlov, V.A. Kul'turnaia revoliutsiia i krest'ianstvo, 1921-1927.
   R.T. Manning, 550(RusR):Jan86-86
Kraehe, E.E. Metternich's German Policy.* (Vol 2)
   P.W. Schroeder, 579(SAQ):Winter86-102
Kraggerud, E. Horaz und Actium.
   J. den Boeft, 394:Vol39fasc3/4-515
Krahl, R., with N. Erbahar. Chinese Ceramics in the Topkapi Saray Museum, Istanbul. (J. Ayers, ed)
   B. Gray, 463:Winter86/87-411
Krakel, D. 2d. Downriver.
   E. Newby, 441:31May87-48
Krakovitch, O. Hugo censuré.*
   B.T. Cooper, 210(FrF):Sep86-376
Kramer, H. The Revenge of the Philistines.*
   J. McLean, 617(TLS):13Mar87-273
Kramer, K-S. Fränkisches Alltagsleben um 1500.
   U. Heuer, 196:Band27Heft3/4-346
Kramer, L. Music and Poetry.*
   M.H. Frank, 301(JEGP):Oct86-590
   R.P. Morgan, 405(MP):Feb87-337
   S.P. Scher, 451:Spring87-290
   M. Smith, 607:Mar86-32
   A. Whittall, 308:Fall86-304
Kramer, S.N. Le Mariage Sacré.
   W. Heimpel, 318(JAOS):Apr/Jun85-325
Kramer, V.A., ed. American Critics at Work.
   W.E. Cain, 478:Oct86-337
Kramsch, C. Interaction et discours dans la classe de langue.
   E.K. Horwitz, 207(FR):Dec86-270

Kranes, D. The Hunting Years.
   J.M. Flora, 649(WAL):May86-85
Krapf, N., ed. Under Open Sky.
   J.D. Eberwein, 165(EAL):Vol22No3-330
Kraschewski-Stolz, S. Studien zu Form und Funktion der Bildlichkeit im "Tristan" Gottfrieds von Strassburg.
   D.H. Green, 402(MLR):Apr86-527
Krashen, S.D. Inquiries and Insights.
   M.E. Call, 399(MLJ):Autumn86-299
Krasnobaev, B.I. Russkaia kul'tura vtoroi poloviny XVII-nachala XIX v.
   J. Cracraft, 550(RusR):Jan86-68
Krasser, A. Let it just happen.
   404:Autumn86-57
Kratoska, P.H., ed. Honourable Intentions.
   G.P. Means, 293(JASt):Feb86-452
Krätzer, A. Studien zum Amerikabild in der neueren deutschen Literatur.*
   H.D. Osterle, 406:Fall86-422
Kratzmann, G., ed. "Colkelbie Sow" and "The Talis of the Fyve Bestes."
   S. Mapstone, 382(MAE):1986/2-301
Kraus, D. & H. The Gothic Choirstalls of Spain.
   P. Hetherington, 39:Dec86-571
Kraus, J.W. A History of Way and Williams, With a Bibliography of Their Publications: 1895-1898.* Messrs. Copeland and Day, 69 Cornhill, Boston, 1893-1899.
   R.A. Tibbetts, 87(BB):Jun86-117
Krause, B.H. Iuppiter Optimus Maximus Saturnus.
   R. Ling, 123:Vol36No2-350
Krause, E-D. Wörterbuch Deutsch-Esperanto.
   R. Lötzsch, 682(ZPSK):Band39Heft2-284
Krause, J. "Märtyrer" und "Prophet."*
   D.C. Riechel, 221(GQ):Fall86-681
Krause, J. What We Bring Home.
   M. Estok, 198:Fall86-86
Krause, S.J. & S.W. Reid - see Brown, C.B.
Krauss, H., ed. Europäisches Hochmittelalter.*
   D. Kelly, 406:Spring86-92
Krauss, R.E. The Originality of the Avant-Garde and Other Modernist Myths.*
   M.B. Wiseman, 289:Fall86-122
   P. Wood, 59:Mar86-119
Kraut, R. Socrates and the State.*
   J. Dybikowski, 482(PhR):Apr86-292
   G.B. Kerferd, 303(JoHS):Vol106-226
Krauthammer, C. Cutting Edges.*
   R. Leiter, 473(PR):Vol53No4-642
Krautheimer, R. The Rome of Alexander VII, 1655-1667.*
   B. Boucher, 39:Nov86-452
   639(VQR):Summer86-104
Krawchenko, B. Social Change and National Consciousness in Twentieth-Century Ukraine.
   R. Solchanyk, 575(SEER):Oct86-643
Krawiec, R. Time Sharing.*
   B. Cooley, 110:Fall86-88
Kreindler, I.T., ed. Sociolinguistic Perspectives on Soviet National Languages, their Past, Present and Future.
   J.I. Press, 575(SEER):Oct86-580
Kreiswirth, M. William Faulkner.*
   S. Bagchee, 178:Sep86-365
   K.L. Fulton, 106:Spring86-119
   T.D. Young, 585(SoQ):Winter87-148

Kreiter, J.A., with M-A. Burmeister.
Madame de Lafayette: "Zaïde."*
  J. Campbell, 208(FS):Apr86-208
Kreitman, E.S. Deborah.*
  A.S. Grossman, 390:Apr86-62
Kremer, J-F. Les Formes symboliques de la
musique.*
  C. Ayrey, 410(M&L):Jul86-299
Kremer, L. Grenzmundarten und Mundart-
grenzen. (Pts 1 & 2)
  W. Haas, 685(ZDL):1/1986-85
Kremer-Marietti, A. Entre le signe et
l'histoire.
  J. Walch, 192(EP):Oct-Dec86-571
Kremnitz, G., ed. Entfremdung, Selbstbe-
freiung und Norm.
  A. Bollée, 72:Band223Heft1-236
Kremnitz, G. Français et créole.
  M. Perl, 72:Band223Heft2-429
Kremnitz, G. Das Okzitanische.*
  W. Oesterreicher, 685(ZDL):1/1986-124
Kreps, M. Bulgakov i Pasternak kak
romanisty.
  E.C. Haber, 550(RusR):Jul86-348
Kreps, M. O poezii Iosifa Brodskogo.
  J. Innis, 550(RusR):Apr86-223
  A. Zholkovsky, 574(SEEJ):Spring86-117
Kretschmer, E. Die Welt der Galgenlieder
Christian Morgensterns und der viktorian-
ische Nonsense.
  D. Petzold, 52:Band21Heft1-111
Kreuder, H-D. Studienbibliographie Lin-
guistik. (2nd ed)
  P. Kühn, 685(ZDL):3/1986-365
Kreutzer, H-J. - see "Kleist Jahrbuch"
Kreuzer, I. Märchenform und Individuelle
Geschichte.*
  A. von Bormann, 224(GRM):Band36Heft1-
  116
  L. Vogel, 654(WB):5/1986-876
Krier, L. & L.O. Larsson. Albert Speer:
Architecture 1932-1942.
  J-C. Garcias, 46:Dec86-8
  J. Rykwert, 617(TLS):6Mar87-238
von Kries, F.W. - see "Thomasin von
Zerclaere, 'Der Welsche Gast'"
Krifka, M. Zur semantischen und pragmat-
ischen Motivation syntaktischer Regulari-
täten.
  S. Brauner, 682(ZPSK):Band39Heft5-604
Krinsky, C.H. Synagogues of Europe.
  B. Bergdoll, 45:Jan86-73
  A. Betsky, 505:Oct86-117
  42(AR):Winter86-125
Kripke, S.A. Wittgenstein on Rules and
Private Language.*
  H. Deutsch, 316:Sep86-819
  J. Llewelyn, 262:Sep86-363
Krishna, V. - see "The Alliterative Morte
Arthure"
Kristeller, P.O., comp. Iter italicum.*
(Vol 3)
  A. Grafton, 551(RenQ):Autumn86-508
Kristensen, A.K.G. Tacitus' germanische
Gefolgschaft.*
  P. Flobert, 555:Vol59fasc2-321
Kristensson, G. Studies on the Early 14th-
Century Population of Lindsey (Lincoln-
shire).
  E. Felder, 685(ZDL):3/1986-417

Kristeva, J. Desire in Language.* (L.S.
Roudiez, ed)
  J.F. MacCannell, 567:Vol62No3/4-325
  R. Poole, 447(N&Q):Sep85-424
  D.H. Richter, 599:Fall86-411
Kriesteva, J. Powers of Horror.
  J.F. MacCannell, 567:Vol62No3/4-325
Kristeva, J. Revolution in Poetic Lan-
guage.*
  D. Morton, 651(WHR):Spring86-91
Kristeva, J. Sēmeiōtichē.
  D.H. Richter, 599:Fall86-411
Kristeva, J. Soleil noir.
  M. Ignatieff, 617(TLS):4-11Sep87-939
Kristjánsson, A. - see Gíslason, K.
Kristol, A.M. Sprachkontakt und Mehr-
sprachigkeit in Bivio (Graubünden).*
  M. Iliescu, 553(RLiR):Jan-Jun86-220
  A. Schwegler, 545(RPh):Feb87-401
Križanić, J. Sabrana djela. (Knjiga 1 &
2) (J. Hamm, ed)
  W. Browne, 574(SEEJ):Summer86-305
Kroetsch, R. Advice to My Friends.
  D. Barbour, 376:Mar86-129
Kroetsch, R. Excerpts from the Real World.
  S. Scobie, 376:Sep86-157
Kroetsch, R. & R.M. Nischik, eds. Gaining
Ground.*
  W.J. Keith, 298:Spring86-154
  J.J. O'Connor, 627(UTQ):Fall86-152
  T. Ware, 150(DR):Winter85/86-566
Krogerus, G. Bezeichnungen für Franenkopf-
bedeckungen und Kopfschmuck im Mittelnie-
derdeutschen.
  M. Wis, 439(NM):1986/4-611
Krohane, R.O. After Hegemony.
  E. Kierans, 529(QQ):Spring86-214
Krohn, R., ed. Liebe als Literatur.*
  I. Glier, 221(GQ):Summer86-471
Kroker, A. Technology and the Canadian
Mind.*
  L. Armour, 102(CanL):Fall86-163
  J. Feeley, 529(QQ):Summer86-438
Kroll, R. Der narrative Lai als eigenstän-
dige Gattung in der Literatur des Mittel-
alters.
  K. Pratt, 382(MAE):1986/2-309
Kromer, T. Waiting for Nothing and Other
Writings. (A.D. Casciato & J.W. West 3d,
eds)
  639(VQR):Autumn86-124
Kronick, J.G. American Poetics of His-
tory.*
  J.M. Reibetanz, 106:Summer86-257
Kruberg, G. A Handbook for Translating
from English into Russian.
  J.S. Levine, 574(SEEJ):Winter86-598
Krúdy, G. N.N.
  L. Kovacs, 450(NRF):May86-115
Krull, W. Prosa des Expressionismus.*
  M. Goth, 221(GQ):Fall86-661
Krupat, A. For Those Who Come After.
  J. Thaddeus, 27(AL):Oct86-431
  A. Wiget, 649(WAL):Nov86-266
Krupnick, M., ed. Displacement.*
  S. Bretzius, 223:Spring86-86
  M. Kerkhoff, 160:Jan86-183
Krupnick, M. Lionel Trilling and the Fate
of Cultural Criticism.*
  M. Birnbaum, 396(ModA):Summer/Fall86-
  289
  D.T. O'Hara, 659(ConL):Fall87-409
  J.W. Tuttleton, 27(AL):Dec86-669

Kryger, K. Allegori og Borgerdyd.
C. Stevenson, 90:Nov86-833
Krysl, M. Mozart, Westmoreland, and Me.
E. McGraw, 455:Mar86-69
Krzyżanowski, L. & I. Nagurski, with K.M.
Olszer - see Zimmer, S.K.
Kšicová, D. Poéma za romantismu a novoro-
mantismu.
R.B. Pynsent, 575(SEER):Apr86-267
Kub'alakov'a, V. & A.A. Cruickshank. Marx-
ism and International Relations.*
M.C.D., 185:Jan87-507
Kubek, T. & T. Pluto. Sixty-One.
C. Salzberg, 441:29Mar87-23
Kubicki, J. Breaker Boys.
R. Houston, 441:25Jan87-21
Kubijovyč, V. - see "Encyclopedia of
Ukraine" (Vol 1)
Kubler, G. Studies in Ancient American and
European Art. (T.F. Reese, ed)
V. Fraser, 90:Jan86-48
Kuch, P. Yeats and A.E.
D. Kiberd, 617(TLS):13Feb87-166
Kugler, H., ed. Ambrosius Metzger, Meta-
morphosis Ovidij in Meisterthöne
gebracht.
W. Röll, 684(ZDA):Band115Heft4-189
Kühl, K. Eigentumsordnung als Freiheits-
ordnung.
W. Kersting, 687:Apr-Jun86-309
Kühlmann, W. Gelehrtenrepublik und Für-
stenstaat.
G. Hoffmeister, 406:Spring86-97
Kuhlmann, W. Reflexive Letztbegründung.*
M. Riedinger, 687:Jul-Sep86-452
Kühlwein, W., G. Thome & W. Wilss, eds.
Kontrastive Linguistik und Übersetzungs-
wissenschaft.
R. Sternemann, 682(ZPSK):Band39Heft1-
146
Kuhn, B. Hardball.
D. Okrent, 441:8Mar87-11
Kuhn, H. Minnelieder Walthers von der
Vogelweide.* (C. Cormeau, ed)
H. Heinen, 406:Fall86-388
Kühne, L. Haus und Landschaft.
H. Hirdina, 654(WB):9/1986-1562
Kühnel, H., ed. Alltag im Spätmittelalter.
R.C. Hoffmann, 589:Oct86-949
Kühnel, J. & others, eds. Psychologie in
der Mediävistik.
W.C.M., 400(MLN):Apr86-735
Kuhns, R. Psychoanalytic Theory of Art.*
W. Charlton, 483:Apr86-253
Kuhse, H. & P. Singer. Should the Baby
Live?*
J.M. Boyle, Jr., 543:Dec86-384
G.E.J., 185:Jan87-513
Kuiper, F.B.J. Ancient Indian Cosmogony.
(J. Irwin, ed)
B. Oguibenine, 617(TLS):2Jan87-18
Kuklick, B. Churchmen and Philosophers.*
J.L. Blau, 619:Spring86-217
D. Rucker, 319:Jul87-453
C. Wright, 432(NEQ):Jun86-291
Kulkarni, V.M. Studies in Sanskrit
Sāhitya-Śāstra.
S. Pollock, 318(JAOS):Jan/Mar85-184
Kully, E., ed. Codex Weimar Q 565.*
W.C. McDonald, 406:Summer86-233
Kumar, A. International Theme in the
Novels of Henry James.
M. Joseph, 284:Winter87-153

Kumar, K. Utopia and Anti-Utopia in
Modern Times.
B. Goodwin, 617(TLS):24Jul87-786
Kumer, Z. and others, eds. Slovenske
ljudske pesmi (Slovenian Folk Songs).
B. Krader, 187:Winter87-136
Kumiega, J. The Theatre of Grotowski.*
C. Innes, 610:Autumn86-277
Kumin, M. In Deep.
A.S. Barnes, 441:30Aug87-21
Kumin, M. The Long Approach.*
R.B. Shaw, 491:Apr86-36
P. Stitt, 219(GaR):Summer86-557
Kumpf, M.M. Four Indices of the Homeric
Hapax Legomena, together with Statistical
Data.
J.T. Hooker, 123:Vol36No1-126
Kundera, M. The Book of Laughter and For-
getting.
N.P. Straus, 145(Crit):Winter87-69
Kundera, M. Jacques and his Master.
P. Storfer, 157:No162-46
Kundera, M. Life is Elsewhere.*
P. Lewis, 364:Dec86/Jan87-152
G. Szirtes, 617(TLS):16Jan87-55
Kunen, K. Set Theory.
J.E. Baumgartner, 316:Jun86-462
Küng, H. Christianity and the World Reli-
gions.
A. Race, 617(TLS):25Sep-1Oct87-1056
Kunnas, T. Nietzsches Lachen.* Politik
als Prostitution des Geistes.
R. Margreiter, 489(PJGG):Band93Heft2-
376
Kuntz, P.G. Alfred North Whitehead.*
T.R. Vitali, 619:Summer86-362
Kunze, M. Highroad to the Stake.
W.D. O'Flaherty, 441:19Apr87-14
Kuo, W. Teaching Grammar of Thai.*
L.F. & W. Kenman, 399(MLJ):Summer86-
204
Kupersmith, W. Roman Satirists in Seven-
teenth-Century England.
F.C. Blessington, 566:Autumn86-70
S.N. Zwicker, 191(ELN):Mar87-71
Kupfer, F. Surviving the Seasons.
D. Fitzpatrick, 441:1Nov87-27
Kuppner, F. The Intelligent Observation of
Naked Women.
D.W. Hartnett, 617(TLS):24Jul87-805
Kuraszkiewicz, W., with R. Olesch, eds.
Der polnische Wortbestand in J. Mączyń-
skis Lexicon Latino-Polonicum aus dem
Jahre 1564. (Vol 2)
H. Leeming, 575(SEER):Oct86-581
Kurland, P.B. & R. Lerner, eds. The Foun-
ders' Constitution.
P.A. Freund, 441:15Mar87-3
Kurosawa, A. Something Like an Autobiog-
raphy.
Kazuya Sato, 500:Winter87-74
Kursunoglu, B.N. & E.P. Wigner, ed. Rem-
iniscences About a Great Physicist.
C.R. Herron, 441:27Sep87-36
Kurtz, D.C. The Berlin Painter.
A.B. Brownlee, 54:Mar86-155
Kurucz, G. & L. Szörényi, eds. Hungaria
litterata Europae filia.
J. Pál, 549(RLC):Jul-Sep86-345
Kurzke, H., ed. Stationen der Thomas-Mann-
Forschung.
H. Siefken, 402(MLR):Apr87-523

Kurzman, D. A Killing Wind.
  J.R. Luoma, 441:29Nov87-16
Kurzweil, E. & W. Phelps, eds. Literature
  and Psychoanalysis.
  N.H. Bruss, 567:Vol62No3/4-381
Kushner, D. Uncle Jacob's Ghost Story.
  P. Demers, 102(CanL):Winter85-163
Kushner, E. & M. Bishop, eds. La Poésie
  Québécoise depuis 1975.
  S.I. Lockerbie, 402(MLR):Oct87-987
Kusters, W. De killer.
  J. Goedegebuure, 204(FdL):Sep86-226
Kustow, M. One in Four.
  S. Hey, 362:5Nov87-30
Kutnik, J. The Novel as Performance.
  M.J. Friedman, 268(IFR):Winter87-55
  A.J. Sabatini, 295(JML):Nov86-393
Kuttert, R. Syntaktische und semantische
  Differenzierung der spanischen Tempusfor-
  men der Vergangenheit "perfecto simple,"
  "perfecto compuesto" und "imperfecto."*
  C. Schmitt, 72:Band223Heft1-191
Kuttner, R. The Life of the Party.
  E.J. Dionne, Jr., 441:15Nov87-9
Kuttner, S. Gratian and the Schools of
  Law, 1140-1234.
  J. Tarrant, 589:Jan86-240
Kutzbach, K.A. - see Harlen, E.
Kuwabara, T. & S. Suzuki, eds. Etudes
  stendhaliennes.
  V.D.L., 605(SC):15Jul87-383
Kuznetsov, Y., ed. The Hermitage: Western
  European Drawing.
  380:Autumn86-417
Kuznick, P.J. Beyond the Laboratory.
  S. Boxer, 441:27Sep87-37
Kvam, S. Linksverschachtelung im Deut-
  schen und Norwegischen.*
  B. Comrie, 353:Vol24No6-1133
Kvavik, R.B. Scandinavian Government and
  Politics.
  C.K. Rogers, 563(SS):Winter86-91
Kwaśniewski, J. Society and Deviance in
  Communist Poland.
  J. Woodall, 575(SEER):Apr86-314
Kwitny, J. The Crimes of Patriots.
  H. Blum, 441:6Sep87-3
Kwong, L.S.K. A Mosaic of the Hundred
  Days.
  D.C. Price, 293(JASt):Feb86-381
Kyburg, H.E., Jr. Epistemology and Infer-
  ence.
  I. Levi, 449:Sep86-417
  D. Miller, 479(PhQ):Oct86-536
  S. Spielman, 486:Mar86-149
Kyburg, H.E., Jr. Theory and Measurement.*
  W. Balzer & C.M. Dawe, 84:Dec86-506
Kyes, R.L. Dictionary of the Old Low and
  Central Franconian Psalms and Glosses.
  L. de Grauwe, 133:Band18Heft4-352
  H. Tiefenbach, 260(IF):Band91-418
Kyle, J.G. & B. Woll. Sign Language.
  B.T. Tervoort, 361:Nov86-205

Labarge, M.W. A Small Sound of the
  Trumpet.
  M. Keen, 453(NYRB):15Jan87-42
de La Barre, F.P. - see under Poullain de
  La Barre, F.
Labé, L. Oeuvres complètes. (F. Rigolot,
  ed)
  J. Stéfan, 450(NRF):Jul-Aug86-164

Labé, L. Oeuvres poétiques [together with]
  du Guillet, P. Rymes [and] Blasons du
  Corps féminin. (F. Charpentier, ed)
  F. Rigolot, 535(RHL):Jan-Feb86-131
Laberge, M. Deux tangos pour toute une
  vie.
  T. Vuong-Riddick, 102(CanL):Fall86-122
Laborde, A.M. Diderot et Madame de
  Puisieux.
  W.F. Edmiston, 207(FR):Feb87-395
  A. Strugnell, 402(MLR):Oct87-959
La Bossière, C.R., ed. Translation in
  Canadian Literature.*
  D.G. Jones, 107(CRCL):Dec86-701
Labrador, J.J., C. Angel Zorita & R.A. Di
  Franco. Cancionero de poesías varias,
  biblioteca de Palacio, Ms. No. 617
  (siglos XV y XVI).
  J. Weiss, 86(BHS):Jul86-274
Labrador Herraiz, J. & J. Fernández Jimé-
  nez, eds. Cervantes and the Pastoral.
  E. Rhodes, 304(JHP):Spring86-255
Labrie, R. James Merrill.*
  D.L. Macdonald, 134(CP):Vol19-143
Labrousse, E. "Une foi, une loi, un roi?"
  J-C. Vuillemin, 207(FR):Oct86-146
Labrune, D. Stendhal et la médecine.
  V.D.L., 605(SC):15Jan87-217
La Capra, D. History and Criticism.*
  C. Baldick, 617(TLS):6-12Nov87-1218
  P. De Bolla, 153:Winter86-49
La Capra, D. A Preface to Sartre.*
  J. Weightman, 453(NYRB):13Aug87-42
La Capra, D. Rethinking Intellectual His-
  tory.*
  P. De Bolla, 153:Winter86-49
  R. Rigney, 107(CRCL):Jun86-277
Lacey, C.A., ed. Barbara Leigh Smith
  Bodichon and the Langham Place Group.
  J. Lewis, 617(TLS):30Oct-5Nov87-1184
Lacey, S. The Startling Jungle.
  A. Urquhart, 617(TLS):3Apr87-348
La Charité, R.C., ed. A Critical Bibliog-
  raphy of French Literature.* (rev) (Vol
  2: The Sixteenth Century.)
  P. Ford, 208(FS):Jan86-66
  W.J. Kennedy, 546(RR):Nov86-455
  A. Moss, 402(MLR):Jul86-736
  G.P. Norton, 210(FrF):Jan86-96
Lachaud, J-M. Marxisme et philosophie de
  l'art.
  P. Somville, 542:Jan-Mar86-124
Lachmann, L.M. The Market as an Economic
  Process.
  C. Makin, 617(TLS):20Mar87-292
Lachmet, D. Lallia.
  I. Hill, 617(TLS):3Jul87-714
  R. Warren, 441:9Aug87-28
Lackey, D.P. Moral Principles and Nuclear
  Weapons.
  A. Cohen, 185:Jan87-457
  J. McMahan, 518:Jul86-129
"Laclos et le libertinage, 1782-1982."*
  J. Pál, 549(RLC):Jan-Mar86-102
Lacoste-Veysseyre, C. La Critique d'art de
  Théophile Gautier.
  A.G. Gann, 446(NCFS):Spring87-333
Lacoste-Veysseyre, C. - see Gautier, T.
Lacourbe, R. Nazisme et seconde guerre
  mondiale dans le cinéma d'espionnage. La
  Guerre froide dans le cinéma d'espion-
  nage.
  R.M. Webster, 207(FR):Mar87-552

Lacouture, J. Pierre Mendes France.
V. Caron, 287:Apr–May86–20
Lactantius. De mortibus persecutorum. (J.L. Creed, ed & trans)
O. Nicholson, 123:Vol36No2–246
Lacy, A. – see Lawrence, E.
Lacy, N.J. and J.C. Nash, eds. Essays in Early French Literature Presented to Barbara M. Craig.
T. Scully, 589:Jan86–240
F.P. Sweetser, 207(FR):Oct86–115
Lader, L. Politics, Power, and the Church.
P. Zaleski, 441:1Nov87–25
Ladis, A. Taddeo Gaddi.*
P.F. Watson, 54:Mar86–158
Ladrière, J. & P. Van Parijs, eds. Fondements d'une Théorie de la Justice.
K. Raes, 540(RIPh):Vol40fasc3–344
Ladurie, E.L. – see under Le Roy Ladurie, E.
Laertius, D. – see under Diogenes Laertius
La Farge, P. The Strangelove Legacy.
M. Pines, 441:22Mar87–38
Lafay, A. La sagesse de Georges Duhamel.
G. De Wulf, 356(LR):May86–187
La Fleur, W.R., ed. Dōgen Studies.
M.J. Augustine, 407(MN):Summer86–258
Tadanori Yamashita, 293(JASt):Aug86–849
La Fleur, W.R. The Karma of Words.*
T. Harper, 293(JASt):Nov85–151
La Fleur, W.R. – see Abe, M.
Lafond, J., ed. Les Formes brèves de la prose et le discours discontinu (XVIe–XVIIe siècles).
G. Verdier, 475:Vol13No24–399
de La Fontaine, J. Fables. (M. Fumaroli, ed)
D.L. Rubin, 207(FR):Dec86–256
Laforgue, J. Moral Tales.
P.M. Gathercole, 573(SSF):Summer86–337
Laforgue, J. Poems. (P. Dale, trans)
S. Romer, 617(TLS):3Apr87–364
Laforgue, J. Poems of Jules Laforgue.
P. Levi, 4:Autumn86–89
Lafortune–Martel, A. Fête noble en Bourgogne au XVe siècle.
C. Stocker, 589:Apr86–434
Lafrance, H. Yves Thériault et l'institution littéraire québécoise.
B–Z. Shek, 627(UTQ):Fall86–215
Lagercrantz, O. August Strindberg.*
M. Robinson, 562(Scan):Nov86–203
Lagerroth, E. Mot en ny vetenskap.
P. Buvik, 172(Edda):1986/4–375
Laget, T. – see Rivière, J.
Lagmay, L.A. Cruz-na-Ligas.
C.N. Nydegger, 293(JASt):Feb86–453
Lago, M., comp. Calendar of the Letters of E.M. Forster.*
F.P.W. McDowell, 177(ELT):Vol29No3–311
Lago, M. & P.N. Furbank – see Forster, E.M.
Lagorio, G. Penelope senza tela.
P. Frassica, 275(IQ):Winter86–123
La Guardia, D.M. Advance on Chaos.*
T. Whalen, 106:Winter86–495
Lahr, J. Automatic Vaudeville.
P. Storfer, 157:No160–49
Lahr, J. Prick Up Your Ears.
G. Annan, 453(NYRB):24Sep87–3
Lahr, J. – see Orton, J.

Lahusen, G. Untersuchungen zur Ehrenstatue in Rom.*
P. Flobert, 555:Vol59fasc2–340
Laine, E.W., ed. Scandinavian–Canadian Studies/Études scandinaves au Canada.
P.M. Mitchell, 562(Scan):May86–107
Laing, B.K. Search Sweet Country.* [shown in prev under Kojo Laing, B.]
A. Maja-Pearce, 364:Nov86–108
G. Packer, 441:7Jun87–30
Laing, D.A. Clive Bell.*
C. Spadoni, 470:Vol24–121
Laiou-Thomadakis, A.E. Peasant Society in the Late Byzantine Empire.
D. Jacoby, 589:Jul86–676
Laird, H. Carl Oscar Borg and the Magic Region.
P.R. Howell, 649(WAL):Feb87–385
Laird, M. English Misericords.
H. Thorold, 324:May87–469
Laitin, D.D. Hegemony and Culture.
D.H.L., 185:Jul87–892
Lake, P. Moderate Puritans and the Elizabethan Church.
R.A. Anselment, 677(YES):Vol16–234
Lakoff, G. & M. Johnson. Les Métaphores dans la vie quotidienne.
G. Bourcier, 189(EA):Oct–Dec87–490
Laks, A. Diogène d'Apollonie.
J-F. Duvernoy, 192(EP):Oct–Dec86–572
Laksmi, C.S. The Face Behind the Mask.
H.B. Reynolds, 293(JASt):May86–632
Lalande, D., ed. Le Livre des fais du bon messire Jehan le Maingre, dit Bouciquaut, mareschal de France et gouverneur de Jennes.
P. Rickard, 208(FS):Apr86–194
G. Roques, 553(RLiR):Jan–Jun86–296
Lalande, J.F. 2d, S.M. Johnson & K.P. Wilcox. Aller Anfang.
M.W. Conner, 399(MLJ):Autumn86–315
Lalonde, R. Une Belle Journée d'avance.
E. Hamblet, 207(FR):Apr87–726
Lamacchia, A. & P. Porro – see Saint Augustine
Lamadrid, E.E. & others. Communicating in Spanish: A First Course.* (2nd ed)
J.R. Gutiérrez, 238:Sep86–568
Lamar, H.R. – see Perlot, J-N.
Lamb, D. The Arabs.
J.F. Clarity, 441:5Apr87–9
442(NY):13Jul87–89
Lamb, E.S. Casting into a Cloud.
R. Bodner, 649(WAL):Nov86–276
A. Rotella, 404:Winter–Spring86–59
Lamb, R. The Failure of the Eden Government.
P. Hennessy, 362:29Oct87–30
Lamb, W. Ane Resonyng of ane Scottis and Inglis Merchand betuix Rowand and Lionis.* (R.J. Lyall, ed)
R.D.S. Jack, 541(RES):Nov86–554
Lambert, B. Crossings.
M.S. Dyment, 296(JCF):No35/36–151
Lambert, B., ed. Music in Colonial Massachusetts, 1630–1820. (Vol 2)
A.D. Shapiro, 432(NEQ):Sep86–425
Lambert, B. Three Radio Plays.
J.H. Kaplan, 102(CanL):Fall86–126
Lambert, D.H. Swamp Rice Farming.
R.D. Hill, 293(JASt):Feb86–455

Lambert, K. Meinong and the Principle of Independence.*
J. Brandl, 53(AGP):Band68Heft3-321
W.J. Rapaport, 316:Mar86-248
Lamberton, R.D. & S.I. Rotroff. Birds of the Athenian Agora.
W.G. Arnott, 123:Vol36No1-178
Lambrecht, U. Herrscherbild und Principatsidee in Suetons Kaiserbiographien.
A. Wallace-Hadrill, 313:Vol76-326
Lambton, A. Elizabeth and Alexandra.*
639(VQR):Autumn86-123
Laminger-Pascher, G. Beiträge zu den griechischen Inschriften Lykaoniens.*
A.G. Woodhead, 303(JoHS):Vol106-262
Lamis, A.P. The Two-Party South.
D.C. Colby, 579(SAQ):Spring86-196
Lammel, A. & I. Nagy. Parasztbiblia.
I. Futaky, 196:Band27Heft3/4-348
Lämmert, E., ed. Erzählforschung.*
A. Otten, 406:Spring86-105
Lamonde, Y., ed. L'Imprimé au Québec.
D.M. Hayne, 470:Vol24-109
L'Amour, L. The Haunted Mesa.
J. Sullivan, 441:2Aug87-16
L'Amour, L. Jubal Sackett.
R.L. Gale, 649(WAL):May86-68
Lampert, N. Whistleblowing in the Soviet Union.
A. McAuley, 575(SEER):Oct86-642
Lampert, V. & others. "The New Grove" Modern Masters.*
P. Dickinson, 410(M&L):Oct86-403
Lamping, D. Der Name in der Erzählung.*
H. Birus, 301(JEGP):Apr86-316
Lampugnani, V.M. - see under Magnano Lampugnani, V.
Lamy, S. Quand je lis je m'invente.*
K. Gould, 207(FR):Apr87-701
Lancashire, I., ed. Dramatic Texts and Records of Britain: A Chronological Topography of Britain to 1558.*
K.M. Ashley, 301(JEGP):Jan86-106
S. Carpenter, 541(RES):May86-238
P. Neuss, 611(TN):Vol40No1-40
W. Tydeman, 610:Summer86-154
Lancaster, C. The American Bungalow: 1880-1930.
W. Lebovich, 658:Winter86-319
Lance, B.R.G. - see under Gómez Lance, B.R.
Lancelot-Harrington, K. America Past and Present. (Vols 1-3)
B. Arnold, 399(MLJ):Winter86-456
Land, S.K. Paradox and Polarity in the Fiction of Joseph Conrad.*
C. Watts, 301(JEGP):Oct86-579
Land, S.K. The Philosophy of Language in Britain.
V. Salmon, 617(TLS):17Jul87-773
Landale, Z., ed. Shop Talk.
J. Wright, 526:Autumn86-94
Landau, N. The Justices of the Peace, 1679-1760.*
J. Black, 83:Autumn86-226
P.B. Munsche, 173(ECS):Spring87-385
Landelius, O.R. Swedish Place-Names in North America. (R. Jarvi, ed)
E. Callery, 424:Jun86-221
G. Fellows-Jensen, 301(JEGP):Oct86-614
Landesman, J. Rebel Without Applause.
J. Wood, 617(TLS):18-24Sep87-1022

Landolfi, T. Words in Commotion and Other Stories.* (K. Jason, ed & trans)
J. Bayley, 617(TLS):27Mar87-317
Landon, H.C.R. Handel and his World.*
H.D. Johnstone, 83:Autumn86-303
Landow, G.P. Ruskin.*
M. Brooks, 576:Jun86-177
P. Conner, 89(BJA):Summer86-285
Landry, B. The New Black Middle Class.
D. Wycliff, 441:7Jun87-12
Landsman, N.C. Scotland and Its First American Colony, 1683-1765.*
P.O. Wacker, 656(WMQ):Oct86-672
Landy, M. Fascism in Film.
A.M., 125:Spring86-341
Lane, B.G. The Altar and the Altarpiece.*
R. Baldwin, 539:Spring87-197
Lane, D. The End of Social Inequality?
W.D. Connor, 550(RusR):Oct86-456
Lane, D., W. Vernon & D. Carson. The Sound of Wonder.
G.K. Wolfe, 395(MFS):Spring86-133
Lane, E.N. The Other Monuments and Literary Evidence.
N.H. Ramage, 124:Jul-Aug87-461
Lane, F.C. & R.C. Mueller. Money and Banking in Medieval and Renaissance Venice.* (Vol 1)
L.B. Robbert, 589:Oct86-952
Lane, H. When the Mind Hears.*
L. Hudson, 617(TLS):29May87-584
C.A. Padden, 355(LSoc):Mar86-120
Lane, J., ed. Coventry Apprentices and their Masters, 1781-1806.
P.J. Wallis, 447(N&Q):Jun85-269
Lane, M. Architecture of the Old South: Virginia.
P. Goldberger, 441:6Dec87-24
Lane, P. A Linen Crow, A Caftan Magpie.*
R. Gibbs, 102(CanL):Spring86-180
Lang, C.Y. & E.F. Shannon - see Tennyson, A.
Lang, E. The Semantics of Coordination.
R.R. van Oirsouw, 297(JL):Mar86-239
Lang, H-J. George Orwell.
U. Böker, 72:Band223Heft2-422
Lang, M.L. Herodotean Narrative and Discourse.*
P.W. Sage, 24:Spring86-118
H.D. Westlake, 303(JoHS):Vol106-207
Lang, P.C. Literarischer Unsinn im späten 19. und frühen 20. Jahrhundert.
A. Arnold, 107(CRCL):Jun86-311
Langan, M. & B. Schwarz, eds. Crises in the British State 1880-1930.
M.J. Wiener, 637(VS):Winter87-278
de Langbehn, R.R. - see under Rohland de Langbehn, R.
Langdale, C. Gwen John.
R. Snell, 617(TLS):18-24Dec87-1397
Langdon, H. Italy.
N. Powell, 39:Aug86-142
Lange, M. The Bathing Huts.
A. Ross, 364:Apr/May86-170
Lange, W. Theater in Deutschland nach 1945.
G. Mason, 406:Fall86-418
Langendoen, D.T. & P.M. Postal. The Vastness of Natural Languages.*
G. Prószéky, 603:Vol10No2-520
H. Thompson, 297(JL):Mar86-241

"Langenscheidt's Pocket Polish Dictionary."
(T. Grzebieniowski, comp)
   R.A. Rothstein, 574(SEEJ):Fall86–463
Langer, E. Josephine Herbst.*
   J. Gilbert, 534(RALS):Spring–Autumn84–
   232
Langer, L.L. Versions of Survival.
   I. Avisar, 107(CRCL):Jun86–313
Langhorne, R., ed. Diplomacy and Intelli-
gence during the Second World War.
   F.L. Carsten, 575(SEER):Oct86–620
Langley, L. Changes of Address.
   J. Rees, 617(TLS):23–29Oct87–1175
Langley, L.D. The Banana Wars.*
   G. Martel, 106:Spring86–81
Langton, J. Good and Dead.
   442(NY):9Feb87–106
"Langue et Littérature orales dans l'Ouest
de la France."
   A–M. Thiesse, 535(RHL):Jan–Feb86–170
Lanham, R.A. Analyzing Prose.*
   D.C. Freeman, 126(CCC):Feb86–108
Lankheit, K. Die Modellsammlung der Por-
zellanmanufaktur Doccia.
   A. Klein, 683:Band49Heft2–257
Lannon, F. Privilege, Persecution, and
Prophecy.
   D. Smyth, 617(TLS):26Jun87–685
"L'Annuaire théâtral 1985."
   L–E. Doucette, 627(UTQ):Fall86–186
Lansbury, C. Felicity.
   F. Weldon, 441:8Nov87–7
Lansbury, C. The Reasonable Man.*
   R.H. Super, 403(MLS):Summer86–336
Lanser, S.S. The Narrative Act.*
   S. Cohan, 403(MLS):Summer86–345
Lanszweert, R. Die Rekonstruktion des
baltischen Grundwortschatzes.
   W.R. Schmalstieg, 159:Spring86–115
Lantz, K.A. Anton Chekhov.
   R.A. Peace, 402(MLR):Apr87–536
   L. Senelick, 550(RusR):Oct86–429
Lanz, H. Die romanischen Wandmalereien
von San Silvestro in Tivoli.
   M. Kupfer, 589:Apr86–503
Lanzmann, C. Shoah.
   R. Clements, 99:Aug/Sep86–28
   F. Lurçat, 450(NRF):Mar86–104
Laor, E. Maps of the Holy Land.
   S. Tyacke, 617(TLS):30Oct–5Nov87–1204
Laourdas, B. & L.G. Westerink – see Photius
La Palombara, J. Democracy, Italian Style.
   H.S. Hughes, 441:8Nov87–58
de La Péruse, J. La Médée. (J.A. Coleman,
ed)
   R. Griffiths, 402(MLR):Jul87–736
Lapesa, R. Estudios de historia lingüís-
tica española.
   G. Bossong, 547(RF):Band98Heft1/2–181
   Y. Malkiel, 545(RPh):Nov86–253
Lapesa, R. La trayectoria poética de
Garcilaso. Garcilaso.
   E.L. Rivers, 400(MLN):Mar86–430
Lapidge M. & H. Gneuss, eds. Learning and
Literature in Anglo-Saxon England.*
   R. Frank, 627(UTQ):Spring87–461
   B. Mitchell, 541(RES):Nov86–550
Lapierre, D. The City of Joy.* (French
title: La Cité de la joie.)
   C. Michael, 207(FR):Dec86–294
Lapierre, R. L'Été Rebecca.
   S. Petit, 207(FR):Feb87–431

de Laplace, P–S. Essai sur les probabil-
ités.
   J. Largeault, 542:Oct–Dec86–533
Laporte, J. & others – see de Beaurepaire,
F.
Laporte, R. Une Vie.*
   M–J. Renaudie, 207(FR):Apr87–727
Lapouge, G. La Bataille de Wagram.
   P–L. Rey, 450(NRF):Jun86–80
La Puma, S. The Boys of Bensonhurst.
   J. Hendin, 441:29Mar87–22
Laqueur, W. The Age of Terrorism.
   S. Bakhash, 453(NYRB):24Sep87–12
Laqueur, W., ed. The Pattern of Soviet
Conduct in the Third World.
   C.R. Saivetz, 550(RusR):Jul86–316
Laqueur, W. A World of Secrets.*
   L. Navrozov, 390:Mar86–48
Laqueur, W. & R. Breitman. Breaking the
Silence.*
   M.R. Marrus, 617(TLS):30Jan87–102
Larbaud, V. An Homage to Jerome.
   J. Byrne, 532(RCF):Fall86–138
Lardet, P. – see Saint Jerome
Lardner, J. Fast Forward.
   P. Andrews, 441:17May87–14
Lardreau, G. Discours philosophique et
discours spirituel.
   P. Guenancia, 98:Oct86–1054
Large, D.C. & W. Weber, eds. Wagnerism in
European Culture and Politics.*
   R. Hollinrake, 410(M&L):Apr86–183
Largeault, J. Critiques et Controverses.
   M. Espinoza, 160:Jan86–169
   M. Espinoza, 192(EP):Jul–Sep86–417
Largeault, J. Principes de philosophie
réaliste.
   J–L. Gardies, 542:Oct–Dec86–538
Largeault, J. Les systèmes de la nature.
   J–L. Gardies, 542:Oct–Dec86–538
   Y. Gauthier, 154:Summer86–384
Larguèche, E. L'Effet Injure.
   F. Najab, 209(FM):Oct86–242
Larissy, E. William Blake.
   N. Hilton, 88:Fall86–66
Lariviere, R.W. – see Bhaṭṭācārya, R.
Larkin, P. Required Writing.
   M.J. Rosen, 496:Spring86–51
Larkin, S. – see Marchand, P. & the
Marquis d'Argens
Larrabee, E. Commander in Chief.
   J. Keegan, 441:16Aug87–10
   442(NY):31Aug87–98
Larre, C. Le Traité VII du Houai Nan
Tseu.*
   L. Pfister, 485(PE&W):Jan86–74
Larsen, J.L. & B. Breudenheim. Interlac-
ing.
   P.L. Brown, 441:19Apr87–17
Larsen, L. Dr. Johnson's Household.
   S. Soupel, 189(EA):Oct–Dec87–491
Larsen, W. & T.T. Nga. Shallow Graves.
   639(VQR):Autumn86–135
Larsen-Freeman, D. Techniques and Prin-
ciples in Language Teaching.
   H.J. Siskin, 207(FR):Apr87–735
Larson, G. The Far Side Gallery. The Far
Side Gallery 2.
   M. Richler, 441:3May87–35
Larson, J. & R. Kerr. Guanyin.
   G. Harris, 60:Jul–Aug86–127
   J. Rawson, 90:Dec86–911

Larson, M.L. Meaning-Based Translation.*
  D.P. Verity, 399(MLJ):Spring86-95
Lary, D. Warlord Soldiers.
  E.A. McCord, 293(JASt):Aug86-822
Lasansky, J. In the Heart of Pennsylvania.
  Y.J. Milspaw, 292(JAF):Jul/Sep86-353
Lasater, M.L. The Taiwan Issue in Sino-
  American Strategic Relations.
  M. Ng-Quinn, 293(JASt):Aug86-836
Lascault, G. Eloges à Geneviève.
  A. Moeglin-Delcroix, 98:Mar86-232
  J. Taylor, 532(RCF):Fall86-128
Lascault, G. Encyclopédie abrégée de
  l'Empire Vert. Malaval. Faire et
  Défaire.
  A. Moeglin-Delcroix, 98:Mar86-232
Lascault, G., with P. Alechinsky. Arron-
  dissements.
  A. Moeglin-Delcroix, 98:Mar86-232
Lascault, G., with J. Voss. Marmottes à
  l'imparfait.
  A. Moeglin-Delcroix, 98:Mar86-232
Lascault, G., with C. Zeimert. Le Petit
  Zeimert illustré.
  A. Moeglin-Delcroix, 98:Mar86-232
Lascelles, A. End of an Era.* (D. Hart-
  Davis, ed)
  P. Parker, 364:Oct86-105
Lasch, C. The Minimal Self.*
  G. Hartley, 50(ArQ):Spring86-88
  J. Voelker, 577(SHR):Spring86-181
Lasdun, J. Delirium Eclipse and Other
  Stories.*
  W.H. Pritchard, 249(HudR):Winter87-648
  442(NY):9Feb87-103
Lasdun, J. A Jump Start.
  P. Forbes, 362:12Nov87-30
  S. Rae, 617(TLS):20-26Nov87-1275
Lasker, G.W. Surnames and Genetic Struc-
  ture.
  F.E. Johnston, 424:Jun86-200
Laski, M. From Palm to Pine.
  T.J. Binyon, 617(TLS):5Jun87-608
Laslett, P. The World We Have Lost - Fur-
  ther Explored. (3rd ed)
  M. Roberts, 83:Spring86-89
La Sorte, M. La Merica.
  L.A. Losito, 276:Winter86-405
Lass, R. Phonology.
  E. Broselow, 350:Jun87-398
  J-F. Prunet, 320(CJL):Spring86-102
Lassalle, C. Breaking the Rules.
  R. Grant, 441:1Mar87-20
Lassalle, J-P. - see Maynard, F.
Lasso de la Vega, G. Tragedia de la
  destruyción de Constantinopla. (A.
  Hermenegildo, ed)
  N. Griffin, 402(MLR):Apr87-503
Lasson, F., ed. Sophus Claussen og hans
  kreds.
  B. Glienke, 562(Scan):May86-79
Lasson, F. - see Blixen, K.
Lath, M., ed & trans. Ardhakathānaka.
  E. Bender, 318(JAOS):Oct/Dec85-779
Latham, C. The David Letterman Story.
  T. Rafferty, 441:8Mar87-21
Latham, J. From the Other Side of the
  Street.
  J. Greening, 493:Oct86-54
  W. Scammell, 364:Jun86-61
  G. Tiffin, 617(TLS):13Feb87-165

Latham, R.E. & D.R. Howlett. Dictionary of
  Medieval Latin from British Sources.
  (fasc 3)
  V. Law, 617(TLS):23Jan87-94
Lathrop, T.A. Curso de gramática histórica
  española.*
  S.L. Hartman, 545(RPh):May87-526
Latour, B. Les Microbes.
  A.C. Vila, 400(MLN):Sep86-941
Latour, B. Science in Action.
  N. Jardine, 617(TLS):20-26Nov87-1291
La Tourette, A. Cry Wolf.*
  M. Thiebaux, 441:12Jul87-20
Latrobe, B.H. The Papers of Benjamin Henry
  Latrobe. (Ser 1, Vol 3) (E.C. Carter 2d,
  J.C. Van Horne & L.W. Formwalt, eds)
  R.L. Alexander, 658:Summer/Autumn86-
  204
Latrobe, B.H. The Papers of Benjamin Henry
  Latrobe. (Ser 4, Vol 1) (J.C. Van Horne
  & L.W. Formwalt, eds)
  R.L. Alexander, 658:Summer/Autumn86-
  204
  P.F. Norton, 576:Jun86-178
de Lattre, A. La Doctrine de la réalité
  chez Proust, III.
  F.C. St. Aubyn, 207(FR):May87-871
Lau, D.C. - see "Tao Te Ching"
Lauber, J. The Making of Mark Twain.
  R.H. Cracroft, 649(WAL):Nov86-251
  R.B. Hauck, 395(MFS):Winter86-595
  H. Hill, 26(ALR):Winter87-91
  27(AL):May86-312
Laučjute, J.A. Slovar' baltizmov v
  slavjanskix jazykax.
  E. Hemmerling & K. Musteikis,
  682(ZPSK):Band39Heft2-273
Laudan, L. Science and Values.*
  H.I. Brown, 482(PhR):Jul86-439
  P. Suppes, 486:Sep86-449
Lauder, H. Over the White Wall.
  J. Penberthy, 617(TLS):31Jul87-823
Lauener, H. Willard V. Quine.
  P. Gochet, 540(RIPh):Vol40fasc3-340
Laughlin, J. Selected Poems: 1935-1985.*
  R.B. Shaw, 491:Nov86-96
"Laughter for the Devil." (R. Hyatte,
  trans)
  M.J. Freeman, 208(FS):Apr86-195
  S.M. Taylor, 201:Vol11-168
Laurence, D.H. & M. Quinn - see Shaw, G.B.
Laurence, D.H. & J. Rambeau - see Shaw,
  G.B.
Laurent, A. Cuisine Novella.
  W. Brandmark, 362:16Jul87-23
  R. Plunket, 441:13Sep87-34
Laurenti, H. - see Bastet, N. & others
de Lauretis, T. Alice Doesn't.*
  L. Hutcheon, 153:Spring86-78
Lauritzen, P. Venice Preserved.
  J.G. Links, 39:Sep86-224
Lausberg, M. Das Einzeldistichon.
  P.A. Hansen, 123:Vol36No2-207
Lautenbach, F. Die Sieben Schwerter Apol-
  linaires.
  A. Kies, 535(RHL):Jul-Aug86-781
Lauth, R. Die tranzendentale Naturlehre
  Fichtes nach den Prinzipien der Wissen-
  schaftslehre.
  T. Rockmore, 319:Jul87-455
"L'autobiographie en Espagne." "L'auto-
  biographie dans le monde hispanique."
  H.R. Picard, 547(RF):Band98Heft3/4-353

Lauvhjell, A., ed. HEIT strid om nynorsk.
K. Haugseth, 563(SS):Autumn86–455
Lavandera, B.R. Variación y significado.*
M.T. Turell, 355(LSoc):Jun86–257
Lavelle, L. Carnets de guerre 1915–1918.
192(EP):Oct–Dec86–574
Lavelle, L. De l'existence. (J. Ecole,
ed)
J. Moreau, 192(EP):Oct–Dec86–576
Lavers, A. Roland Barthes.*
G.H. Bauer, 567:Vol60No3/4–351
Lavers, N. Jerzy Kosinski.
J. Newman, 677(YES):Vol16–356
Laverty, M. No More Than Human.*
272(IUR):Autumn86–254
Lavin, I., ed. Drawings by Gianlorenzo
Bernini from the Museum der bildenden
Künste, Leipzig, German Democratic
Republic.*
W.C. Kirwin, 380:Spring86–100
Lavin, M. A Family Likeness. The Stories
of Mary Lavin. (Vol 3)
M. Harmon, 272(IUR):Spring86–77
Lavin, M. Mary O'Grady.
272(IUR):Autumn86–254
Lavis, G. & M. Stasse. Les Chansons de
Moniot d'Arras.
G. Roques, 553(RLiR):Jan–Jun86–280
Lavoie, P. Pour suivre le théâtre au
Québec.*
L–E. Doucette, 627(UTQ):Fall86–186
Law, A. To an Easy Grave.
N. Callendar, 441:18Jan87–23
Law, J. All the King's Ladies.
442(NY):19Jan87–91
"Law in Colonial Massachusetts, 1630–1800."
G.W. Gawalt, 656(WMQ):Jul86–490
Lawler, T. The One and the Many in the
"Canterbury Tales."
H. Cooper, 382(MAE):1986/2–285
Lawner, L. I Modi.
D. Ekserdjian, 90:Feb86–149
Lawner, L. Lives of the Courtesans.
A. Barnet, 441:15Feb87–21
C. Hope, 453(NYRB):28May87–35
Lawrence, D.H. Etruscan Places. (G.
Kezich & M. Lorenzini, eds)
D. Ridgway, 617(TLS):29May87–586
Lawrence, D.H. The Letters of D.H. Law-
rence. (Vol 2) (G.J. Zytaruk & J.T.
Boulton, eds)
P. Preston, 447(N&Q):Jun85–287
Lawrence, D.H. The Letters of D.H. Law-
rence.* (Vol 3) (J.T. Boulton & A.
Robertson, eds)
K.M. Hewitt, 541(RES):May86–289
S. Hynes, 569(SR):Fall86–639
Lawrence, D.H. The Letters of D.H. Law-
rence. (Vol 4) (W. Roberts, J.T. Boulton
& E. Mansfield, eds)
L. Gordon, 617(TLS):16–22Oct87–1142
Lawrence, D.H. The Lost Girl.* (J.
Worthen, ed)
J.C. Cowan, 40(AEB):Vol8No4–269
Lawrence, D.H. Mr. Noon.* (L. Vasey, ed)
K. Cushman, 517(PBSA):Vol80No2–265
K.M. Hewitt, 541(RES):May86–289
S. Smith, 366:Autumn86–245
Lawrence, D.H. "St. Mawr" and Other
Stories.* (B. Finney, ed)
H. Bonheim, 38:Band104Heft3/4–527

Lawrence, D.H. Study of Thomas Hardy and
Other Essays.* (B. Steele, ed)
R.D.B., 295(JML):Nov86–502
É. Delavenay, 189(EA):Apr–Jun87–231
D.R. Schwarz, 177(ELT):Vol29No3–324
Lawrence, D.H. The White Peacock.* (A.
Robertson, ed)
B. Korte, 38:Band104Heft1/2–263
Lawrence, D.H. Women in Love. (D. Farmer,
L. Vasey & J. Worthen, eds)
L. Gordon, 617(TLS):16–22Oct87–1142
Lawrence, D.H. & A. Lowell. The Letters of
D.H. Lawrence and Amy Lowell, 1914–1925.
(E.C. Healey & K. Cushman, eds)
P. Balbert, 177(ELT):Vol29No4–439
J. Meyers, 395(MFS):Summer86–309
Lawrence, E. Gardening for Love. (A.
Lacy, ed)
S. Kunitz, 441:11Oct87–53
Lawrence, E.A. Rodeo.
J.C. McNutt, 650(WF):Jan86–69
Lawson, L.A. & V.A. Kramer, eds. Conversa-
tions with Walker Percy.
E.T. Carroll, 395(MFS):Summer86–273
Lawson, P. George Grenville.*
A. Murdoch, 83:Spring86–88
I.K. Steele, 656(WMQ):Jan86–148
Lawson, R.H. Günter Grass.
J.W. Rohlfs, 402(MLR):Apr87–530
Lawton, T. Chinese Art of the Warring
States Period.
H–Y. Shih, 302:Vol22No1–85
Layard, R. How to Beat Unemployment.
R. Skidelsky, 617(TLS):25Sep–1Oct87–
1035
Layman, R. & M.J. Bruccoli, eds. Crime
Wave.
362:12Nov87–32
Layton, I. Waiting for the Messiah.
P.K. Smith, 627(UTQ):Spring87–467
Layton–Henry, Z. & P.B. Rich, eds. Race,
Government and Politics in Britain.
M.B. Carter, 617(TLS):24Apr87–445
Lazard, M. Images littéraires de la femme
à la renaissance.
C. Jordan, 551(RenQ):Autumn86–551
Lazenby, J.F. The Spartan Army.
T.J. Figueira, 124:Jan–Feb87–214
S. Hodkinson, 123:Vol36No2–327
Lazerowitz, M. & A. Ambrose. Necessity and
Language.
G. McFee, 518:Oct86–229
Lea, H.A. Gustav Mahler.
P. Franklin, 415:Apr86–209
J. Williamson, 410(M&L):Jul86–309
Leach, C. God, Spartacus and Miss Emily.
L. Taylor, 362:12Feb87–28
Leach, M., ed. Funk & Wagnall's Standard
Dictionary of Folklore, Mythology, and
Legend.
W.N., 102(CanL):Spring86–191
Leach, R.H. Whatever Happened to Urban
Policy?
P.L. McCarney, 529(QQ):Autumn86–709
Leacroft, R. & H. Theatre and Playhouse.*
J. Earl, 611(TN):Vol40No2–88
A. Woods, 610:Spring86–63
Leaf, M.J. Song of Hope.
R. Kurin, 293(JASt):Nov85–179
Leale, B.C. Leviathan and Other Poems.
J. Saunders, 565:Summer86–74
Leaming, B. Orson Welles.*
G. Millar, 707:Spring86–139

Lee, A.R., ed. The Nineteenth-Century American Short Story.
R. Asselineau, 189(EA):Apr–Jun87–244
Lee, B. Theory and Personality.
Rajnath, 675(YER):Vol8No1/2–140
Lee, C.H. The British Economy since 1700.
N.F.R. Crafts, 617(TLS):27Mar87–322
Lee, C–J. China and Japan.
R. Kokubun, 293(JASt):Feb86–383
Lee, D., ed. The New Canadian Poets (1970–1985).*
B. Trehearne, 105:Spring/Summer86–138
Lee, D. The Porcine Canticles.
L. Sanazaro, 649(WAL):May86–86
Lee, H. Elizabeth Bowen.
J.L. Halio, 402(MLR):Jan86–191
Lee, H., ed. The Secret Self.*
C. Larrière, 189(EA):Oct–Dec87–478
Lee, H. – see Kipling, R.
Lee Hye–gu, ed. Korean Musical Instruments.
Lu Ping–Chuan, 302:Vol22No1–125
Lee, J., ed. Ireland.
T. Garvin, 272(IUR):Autumn86–243
Lee, J.A.L. A Lexical Study of the Septuagint Version of the Pentateuch.
P.J. Parsons, 123:Vol36No2–326
Lee, K. A New Basis for Moral Philosophy.
T.L.C., 185:Jan87–493
Lee, L–Y. Rose.
M. Boruch, 29(APR):Mar/Apr87–22
M. Flamm, 441:4Oct87–24
M. McGovern, 344:Fall87–131
Lee, P. Guard Her Children.
E. Norman, 617(TLS):16Jan87–54
"Russell Lee's FSA Photographs of Chamisal and Penasco, New Mexico." (W. Wroth, ed)
L. Milazzo, 584(SWR):Winter86–123
Lee, S. ABZs of Economics.
P. O'Toole, 441:5Apr87–23
Lee, S. Camara Laye.
M.E. Mudimbe–Boyi, 207(FR):Oct86–113
Lee, S. Spike Lee's Gotta Have It.
S.S. Martin, 441:13Dec87–14
Lee, T–S. Die griechische Tradition der aristotelischen Syllogistik in den Spätantike.*
R.W. Sharples, 303(JoHS):Vol106–231
Lee, V. Supernatural Tales.
I. Thomson, 362:14May87–31
Lee, W.R. – see Poldauf, I.
Leech, G.N. Principles of Pragmatics.*
T.J. Taylor, 541(RES):Feb86–66
Leedham–Green, E.S. Books in Cambridge Inventories.
J.F. Fuggles, 617(TLS):14Aug87–878
Leeman, A.D., H. Pinkster & H.L.W. Nelson. M. Tullius Cicero, "De Oratore" Libri III. (Vol 2)
M. Winterbottom, 123:Vol36No2–318
Lees, A. Cities Perceived.*
C. Forster, 637(VS):Winter87–284
Lees, G. Singers and the Song.
P. Conrad, 441:15Nov87–1
Lees, R.A. The Negative Language of the Dionysian School of Mystical Theology.*
J.P.H. Clark, 382(MAE):1986/2–292
Leet, J. Flowering Trees and Shrubs.
A. Lacy, 441:6Dec87–32
Lefcourt, C.H., ed. Women and the Law.
M. Friedman, 185:Jan87–483

Lefebvre, J–P. & P. Macherey. Hegel et la société.
H. Faes, 542:Jan–Mar86–124
Lefevere, A. & R. Vanderauwera, eds. Vertaalwetenschap, literatuur, wetenschap, vertaling en vertalen.
A. Dussart, 107(CRCL):Sep86–472
Lefèvre, R. Jean–Luc Godard.
M–N. Little, 207(FR):Oct86–156
Leff, H.L. Playful Perception.
B. Bates, 89(BJA):Winter86–74
Lefkowitz, M.R. Heroines and Hysterics.
T. Fleming, 121(CJ):Oct–Nov86–73
Lefort, C. Essais sur le politique XIXe–XXe siècles.
P. Livet, 98:Nov86–1109
Legány, D., ed. Franz Liszt.
P. Merrick, 410(M&L):Apr86–181
Legendre, P. L'inestimable objet de la transmission.
Y. Brès, 542:Apr–Jun86–273
Leggatt, A. Ben Jonson.
I. Donaldson, 677(YES):Vol16–244
Leggett, J. Making Believe.*
P. Gifford, 271:Winter86–184
Le Goff, J. L'Imaginaire médiéval.*
J–P. Guinle, 450(NRF):Jul–Aug86–180
Legrenzi, G. The Instrumental Music of Giovanni Legrenzi; Sonate a due e tre, Opus 2, 1655. (S. Bonta, ed)
R. Boenig, 568(SCN):Spring–Summer86–22
Leguat, F. Aventures aux Mascareignes. (J–M. Racault, ed)
J–G. Prosper, 535(RHL):Sep–Oct86–916
Le Guillou, J–Y. Grammaire de Vieux Bulgare (Vieux Slave).
H. Galton, 159:Fall86–261
Le Guillou, L. Lettres inédits du baron d'Eckstein.
J. Gaulmier, 535(RHL):Mar–Apr86–303
Le Guin, U.K. Always Coming Home.*
D. Allen, 249(HudR):Spring86–135
C.L. Crow, 649(WAL):Nov86–235
"Franz Lehár: Thematic Index."
A. Lamb, 415:Jun86–337
Lehman, D. An Alternative to Speech.
J. Ash, 441:1Mar87–26
M. Ford, 617(TLS):20–26Nov87–1276
Lehman, D. & C. Berger, eds. James Merrill.*
D.L. Macdonald, 106:Fall86–381
D.L. Macdonald, 134(CP):Vol19–143
Lehmann, C. Der Relativsatz.*
J. van der Auwera, 603:Vol10No1–151
B. Comrie, 353:Vol24No2–446
J. Haiman, 297(JL):Mar86–194
H–J. Sasse, 361:Jun86–121
Lehmann, J. Christopher Isherwood.
C. Hawtree, 617(TLS):27Nov–3Dec87–1310
Lehmann, W.P. & Y. Malkiel, eds. Perspectives on Historical Linguistics.*
D. Messner, 547(RF):Band98Heft3/4–393
Lehmus, U. Attribut oder Satzglied.
H. Nikula, 597(SN):Vol58No1–128
Lehnatd, E. Urchristentum und Wohlstandsgesellschaft.
J.H. Reid, 161(DUJ):Jun86–390
Lehner, J. Poesie und Politik in Claudians Panegyrikus auf das vierte Konsulat des Kaisers Honorius.
B.S. Rodgers, 24:Fall86–445

Lehrer, K. Best Intentions.
  M. Gallagher, 441:16Aug87-16
Lehrer, K. & C. Wagner. Rational Consensus
in Science and Society.
  R.F. Bordley, 449:Dec86-565
Lehrman, W.D., D.J. Sarafinski & E. Savage.
The Plays of Ben Jonson.
  I. Donaldson, 677(YES):Vol16-244
Le Huenen, J. & R. Contes, récits et
légendes de îles Saint-Pierre et Mique-
lon.
  G. Gourdeau-Wilson, 627(UTQ):Fall86-
  249
Leiber, J. Can Animals and Machines Be
Persons?
  W.M. Schuyler, 543:Mar87-583
Leibniz, G.W. Sämtliche Schriften und
Briefe. (Ser 6, Vol 3) (H. Shepers, W.
Schneiders & W. Kabitz, eds)
  C. Wilson, 311(JP):Jul86-395
Leidhold, W. Ethik und Politik bei Francis
Hutcheson.
  W. Farr, 489(PJGG):Band93Heft2-415
Leidig, H-D. - see Gwinne, M.
Leigh, R.A. - see Rousseau, J-J.
Leighton, A. American Gardens of the 19th
Century.
  A. Lacy, 441:6Dec87-34
Leighton, A. Shelley and the Sublime.*
  V.A. De Luca, 627(UTQ):Summer87-575
Leighton, F.S. The Search for the Real
Nancy Reagan.
  M. Dowd, 441:12Jul87-20
Leighton, L.G., ed. Studies in Honor of
Xenia Gąsiorowska.*
  P. Debreczeny, 574(SEEJ):Spring86-108
Leighton, L.G. - see Chukovsky, K.
Leimbach, P.P. Harvest of Bittersweet.
  K. Ray, 441:26Jul87-17
Leimbach, R. Militärische Musterrhetorik.
  H.D. Westlake, 123:Vol36No2-311
Leimbigler, P. Fast-Track Japanese.
  P.J. Wetzel, 399(MLJ):Autumn86-321
Leiner, J., ed. Soleil eclaté.
  B. Aresu, 538(RAL):Winter86-588
Leinonen, M. Impersonal Sentences in Fin-
nish and Russian.
  J.I. Press, 575(SEER):Jul86-450
Leipman, F. The Long Journey Home.
  V.L. Smith, 617(TLS):17Jul87-761
Leiris, M. Langage tangage.
  D. Hollier, 98:Mar86-195
Leistner, B. ...dich zu treiben bis aufs
Blut.
  M. & R. Dau, 601(SuF):Mar-Apr86-442
Leitch, M. The Hands of Cheryl Boyd and
Other Stories. Chinese Whispers.
  P. Craig, 617(TLS):6-12Nov87-1226
Leitch, V.B. Deconstructive Criticism.*
  J. Patrick, 627(UTQ):Winter86/87-338
Leiter, S. Akhmatova's Petersburg.*
  H.A. Stammler, 550(RusR):Jan86-58
Leiter, S.L., with H. Hill, eds. The Ency-
clopedia of the New York Stage, 1920-
1930.
  D.B. Wilmeth, 615(TJ):May86-235
Leith, P. & P. Tyrer. Entertaining with
Style.
  W. & C. Cowen, 639(VQR):Autumn86-142
Leithauser, B. Between Leaps.
  L. Mackinnon, 617(TLS):20-26Nov87-
  1276

Leithauser, B. Cats of the Temple.*
  W. Logan, 617(TLS):9Jan87-41
  L. Rector, 249(HudR):Autumn86-509
  639(VQR):Autumn86-134
Leithe-Jasper, M. Renaissance Master
Bronzes from the Collection of the Kunst-
historisches Museum, Vienna.
  S.B. Butters, 617(TLS):27Mar87-332
Lejeune, M. Recueil des Inscriptions
Gauloises. (Vol 1)
  A. Tovar, 548:Jan-Jun86-207
Lejeune, P. Moi aussi.
  M. Erman, 98:Jun-Jul86-732
  P. France, 402(MLR):Apr87-467
Lejosne, R. La Raison dans l'oeuvre de
Milton.
  I. Simon, 189(EA):Apr-Jun87-209
Lekachman, R. Visions and Nightmares.
  M.C. Janeway, 441:29Mar87-14
Leland, C.T. The Last Happy Men.
  J. Wilson, 617(TLS):4-11Sep87-961
Leland, C.T. Mrs. Randall.
  J. Marcus, 441:5Jul87-14
Leland, M. The Little Galloway Girls.
  J. Cooke, 362:19Mar87-26
Lel'chuk, V.S. Industrializatsiia SSSR.
  H. Kuromiya, 550(RusR):Apr86-228
Lellis, G. Bertolt Brecht, "Cahiers du
Cinéma," and Contemporary Film Theory.
  F. Worth, 207(FR):Oct86-156
Lelyveld, J. Move Your Shadow.*
  D.F. Gordon, 385(MQR):Summer87-553
Lem, S. Fiasco.
  P. Delany, 441:7Jun87-1
  N. Shack, 617(TLS):4-10Dec87-1348
Lemaire, A. & J-M. Durand. Les inscrip-
tions araméennes de Sfiré et l'Assyrie de
Shamshiilu.
  W.R. Garr, 318(JAOS):Oct/Dec85-798
Lemaire, J-P. Visitation.
  R. Daillie, 450(NRF):Mar86-85
Lemaitre, H. William Blake.
  F. Piquet, 189(EA):Oct-Dec87-471
Lemaître, J-L, with J. Dufour. Les docu-
ments nécrologiques de l'Abbaye Saint-
Pierre de Solignac.
  G. Constable, 589:Apr86-436
Lemann, N. Lives of the Saints.
  T. McGonigle, 532(RCF):Summer86-155
Lemay, J.A.L. "New England's Annoyances."*
  R.D. Arner, 656(WMQ):Jul86-495
Lemelin, R. The Crime of Ovide Plouffe.
  E. Thompson, 102(CanL):Summer86-115
Le Men, S. Les abécédaires français
illustrés du XIXe siècle.
  M-P. Johnson, 517(PBSA):Vol80No1-129
Lemieux, D. Une culture de la nostalgie.
  D.M. Hayne, 627(UTQ):Fall86-219
Lemm, R. A Difficult Faith.
  B. Pirie, 102(CanL):Winter85-172
  N. Zacharin, 526:Summer86-100
Lemmon, D. Cricket Mercenaries.
  M.B. Carter, 617(TLS):18-24Dec87-1412
Lemon, J. Toronto since 1918.
  J-C. Robert, 529(QQ):Autumn86-711
Lemon, L.T. Portraits of the Artist in
Contemporary Fiction.
  M.B., 295(JML):Nov86-364
  W.B. Bache, 395(MFS):Winter86-686
  J. Gindin, 301(JEGP):Oct86-580
de Lempicka-Foxhall, K., with C. Phillips.
Passion by Design.
  R. Smith, 441:8Nov87-27

Lénard, Y.　L'Art de la conversation.
(2nd ed)
　S.K. Jackson, 399(MLJ):Summer86-183
Lendvai, E.　The Workshop of Bartók and
Kodály.
　M. Gillies, 411:Jul/Oct86-285
Lenerz, J.　Syntaktischer Wandel und Gram-
matiktheorie.
　R.P. Ebert, 603:Vol10No2-463
Leng, S. & H. Chiu.　Criminal Justice in
Post-Mao China.
　P.B. Potter, 293(JASt):Aug86-824
Lennon, N.　Mark Twain in California.
　T.J. Gordon, 649(WAL):Feb87-376
Lensing, G.S.　Wallace Stevens.*
　T. Armstrong, 617(TLS):10Jul87-747
Lentzen, M.　Der spanischen Bürgerkrieg und
die Dichter.
　M. Bertrand de Muñoz, 547(RF):Band98
Heft3/4-485
Lenz, B. - see Greene, G.
Lenz, C.R.S., G. Greene & C.T. Neely, eds.
The Woman's Part.*
　I. Schabert & others, 156(ShJW):Jahr-
buch1986-223
Leon, J.M. - see under Messer Leon, J.
Léon, P.R. & P. Perron, eds.　Le Dialogue.
(Ser 3, Vol 7)
　A. Whitfield, 627(UTQ):Fall86-131
Leonard, C.S., Jr.　Umlaut in Romance.
　J. Klausenburger, 545(RPh):Feb87-366
Leonard, E.　Bandits.
　T.J. Binyon, 617(TLS):17Jul87-778
　T.R. Edwards, 453(NYRB):13Aug87-50
　W. Percy, 441:4Jan87-7
　C. Sigal, 362:9Apr87-28
　442(NY):19Jan87-94
Leonard, E.　Touch.
　D. Ryan, 441:18Oct87-30
　442(NY):9Nov87-154
Leonard, J.K.　Wei Yuan and China's
Rediscovery of the Maritime World.
　J.A. Whitbeck, 293(JASt):Feb86-384
Leonard, N.　Jazz.
　J.P. Calagione, 441:10May87-21
　E. Hobsbawm, 617(TLS):18-24Sep87-1012
Leonard, R.　The Interpretation of English
Noun Phrase Sequences on the Computer.
　K. Allan, 350:Jun87-429
Leonard, T.C.　The Power of the Press.
　K.O. Morgan, 617(TLS):13Mar87-268
Leonhard, J-F.　Die Seestadt Ancona im
Spätmittelalter.
　L.B. Robbert, 589:Jan86-168
Leonhard, W.　The Kremlin and the West.
　M. Danner, 441:25Jan87-21
Leopardi, G.　Operette Morali.*　(G. Cec-
chetti, ed & trans)　The Moral Essays.
Pensieri.　A Leopardi Reader.　(O.
Casale, ed & trans)
　D.S. Carne-Ross, 453(NYRB):29Jan87-42
Leotta, R. - see Marbod of Rennes
Le Page, R.B. & A. Tabouret-Keller.　Acts
of Identity.
　A. Valdman, 263(RIB):Vol36No1-61
Le Pore, E. & B. MacLaughlin, eds.　Actions
and Events.
　P. Engel, 98:Nov86-1125
　G. Stahl, 542:Oct-Dec86-542
Leppmann, W.　Rilke.*
　B.L. Bradley, 406:Spring86-117
Lépront, C.　Le Retour de Julie Farnèse.
　J.C. Elliott, 207(FR):Apr87-728

Lepschy, A.L.　Narrativa e teatro fra due
secoli.
　L. Pertile, 278(IS):Vol41-161
Lequerica de la Vega, S. & C. Salazar.
Avanzando.　(2nd ed)
　M.D. Finnemann, 399(MLJ):Winter86-444
de Lerma, D-R.　Bibliography of Black
Music.　(Vol 4)
　D.E. McGinty, 91:Spring86-185
Lermontov, M.　Major Poetical Works.*　(A.
Liberman, ed & trans)
　P.M. Austin, 558(RLJ):Spring/Fall86-230
　D.D. Phillips, 399(MLJ):Spring86-74
　J.T. Shaw, 574(SEEJ):Summer86-281
Lerner, F.A.　Modern Science Fiction and
the American Literary Community.
　D. Ketterer, 561(SFS):Mar86-94
　G.K. Wolfe, 395(MFS):Spring86-133
Lerner, G.　The Creation of Patriarchy.*
　J. Tinson, 529(QQ):Winter86-945
Lerner, L.　The Literary Imagination.*
　M. Wood, 402(MLR):Apr86-428
Lerner, L., ed.　Reconstructing Litera-
ture.*
　F. McCombie, 447(N&Q):Sep85-425
　C. Norris, 577(SHR):Summer86-270
Lerner, L.　Rembrandt's Mirror.
　M. O'Neill, 617(TLS):24Jul87-805
Lerner, L.S.　Metáfora y sátira en la obra
de Quevedo.
　C. Vaíllo, 240(HR):Spring86-216
Le Roy Ladurie, E.　The French Peasantry
1450-1600.
　D. Parker, 617(TLS):3Jul87-725
Le Roy Ladurie, E.　The Mind and Method of
the Historian.
　N.F. Partner, 589:Jan86-90
Lertora Mendoza, C.A.　Bibliografía filo-
sófica argentina (1900-1975).
　J.C. Torchia Estrada, 263(RIB):
Vol36No1-62
Leschak, P.M.　Letters From Side Lake.
　J. Tallmadge, 441:28Jun87-15
Lesemann, F.　Services and Circuses.
　P.C. Findlay, 298:Summer86-164
Lesko, D.　James Ensor.*
　F. Whitford, 90:May86-364
Leskov, N.　Five Tales.*　(M. Shotton, ed &
trans)
　F. Wigzell, 402(MLR):Jan86-267
Leslie, M.　Spenser's "Fierce Warres and
Faithfull Loves."*
　G. Morgan, 541(RES):May86-249
Le Sourd, P.S.　Kolusuwakonol Peskotomuh-
kati-Wolastoqewi Naka Ikolisomani Latuwe-
wakon/Philip S. Le Sourd's Passamaquoddy-
Maliseet and English Dictionary.　(R.M.
Leavitt & D.A. Francis, eds)
　P. Proulx, 269(IJAL):Oct86-427
Lesser, W.　The Life Below the Ground.
　E. Toynton, 441:22Nov87-26
Lessing, D.　The Good Terrorist.*
　G. Kearns, 249(HudR):Spring86-121
　P. Lewis, 565:Spring86-38
　P.K. Page, 376:Mar86-123
Lessing, D.　Prisons We Choose to Live
Inside.
　S.R.L. Clark, 617(TLS):16-22Oct87-1130
Lessing, D.　The Wind Blows Away Our
Words.
　I. Jack, 617(TLS):8May87-483
　A. Kent, 362:2Apr87-22

219

Lessing, D. Winter im Juli.
H-J. Sander, 654(WB):3/1986-481
Lessing, G.E. Werke und Briefe. (Vol 6)
(K. Bohnen, ed)
H.B. Nisbet, 402(MLR):Jan87-245
"Lessing Yearbook." (Vol 16) (E.P. Harris
& R.E. Schade, eds)
K.L. Komar, 221(GQ):Fall86-648
Lessnoff, M. Social Contract.
A. Ryan, 617(TLS):7Aug87-854
Lester, G.A., ed. The Index of Middle
English Prose: Handlist II.
R. Beadle, 617(TLS):24Jul87-808
Lester, G.A. Sir John Paston's "Grete
Boke."*
N. Davis, 447(N&Q):Jun85-257
Lestringant, F. Agrippa d'Aubigné: "Les
Tragiques."
A.P. Stabler, 207(FR):Feb87-391
Lestringant, F. - see Thevet, A.
Lesure, F. & R. Nichols - see Debussy, A-C.
Lesy, M. The Forbidden Zone.
L. Harris, 441:19Jul87-10
Lethbridge, R. Maupassant: "Pierre et
Jean."*
G.M. Godfrey, 207(FR):Dec86-262
B. Nelson, 208(FS):Jan86-95
M. Weatherilt, 402(MLR):Apr86-489
"La Letteratura e l'Immaginario."
G. Cesbron, 535(RHL):Nov-Dec86-1147
"Letteratura popolare di espressione fran-
cese dall' 'Ancien Régime' all'Ottocento/
Roland Barthes e il suo metodo critico."*
M. Calle-Gruber, 72:Band223Heft2-453
Lettinck, N. Geschiedbeschouwing en
beleving van de eigen tijd in de eerste
helft van de twaalfde eeuw.
R. Ray, 589:Apr86-504
"Lettura e ricezione del testo."
F. Meregalli, 549(RLC):Jul-Sep86-351
Leutner, R.W. Shikitei Sanba and the Comic
Tradition in Edo Fiction.
R. Bowring, 407(MN):Summer86-242
Leuwers, D., ed. La Grand Meaulnes: Images
et documents.
R. Gibson, 617(TLS):3Apr87-363
Leuwers, D. Jouve avant Jouve, ou la
naissance d'un poète.
J. Chabot, 535(RHL):Jul-Aug86-794
Levao, R. Renaissance Minds and Their Fic-
tions.
A.F. Kinney, 405(MP):May87-423
F. McGee, 568(SCN):Fall86-42
R.B. Waddington, 551(RenQ):Winter86-
791
Léveillé, J.R. L'Incomparable.
K. Meadwell, 102(CanL):Winter85-158
Levenson, J.C. & others - see Adams, H.
Levenson, M.H. From Polemics to Irenics.
T. Gibbons, 67:May86-132
Levenson, M.H. A Genealogy of Modernism.*
H. Gross, 536(Rev):Vol8-33
D.D. Pearlman, 659(ConL):Fall87-394
R. Shusterman, 541(RES):Aug86-446
W. Sypher, 569(SR):Summer86-497
Levenstam, T. Almanackan som kulturbär-
are.
A. Swanson, 563(SS):Autumn86-435
Leventhal, F.M. The Last Dissenter.
M. Milne, 635(VPR):Fall86-114
Levere, T.H. Poetry Realized in Nature.*
S.M. Tave, 402(MLR):Jan86-177

Levering, D. Outcroppings from Navajoland.
A.C. Parker, 649(WAL):Aug86-174
Levertov, D. Oblique Prayers.* Selected
Poems.
M. Lomax, 617(TLS):9Jan87-41
Levey, M. Giambattista Tiepolo.
D. Posner, 441:14Jun87-34
D. Rosand, 617(TLS):27Mar87-333
J.B. Shaw, 324:Jun87-532
D. Sutton, 39:Dec86-565
Levi, A.H.T. - see Erasmus
Levi, I. Decisions and Revisions.
L.J. Cohen, 84:Jun86-252
H.E. Kyburg, Jr., 482(PhR):Jul86-441
Lévi, J. The Chinese Emperor.
J. Spence, 441:4Oct87-1
Lévi, J. Le Grand empereur et ses auto-
mates.
R.J. Hartwig, 207(FR):Dec86-286
Levi, M.A. Augusto e il suo tempo.
R. Seager, 617(TLS):3Apr87-369
Levi, P. The Echoing Green.*
H. Buck, 4:Autumn86-63
Levi, P. The Flutes of Autumn.
N.K. Sandars, 4:Autumn86-68
Levi, P. The Frontiers of Paradise.
D. Cupitt, 617(TLS):24Apr87-448
Levi, P. Grave Witness.
639(VQR):Spring86-57
Levi, P. If Not Now, When?*
J. Hunter, 249(HudR):Summer86-329
639(VQR):Winter86-21
Levi, P. If This is a Man [and] The Truce.
P. Kemp, 617(TLS):13-19Nov87-1258
Levi, P. The Monkey's Wrench.* (British
title: The Wrench.)
D.J. Enright, 453(NYRB):15Jan87-40
P. Forbes, 362:14May87-29
I. Thomson, 617(TLS):5Jun87-610
Levi, P. The Periodic Table.*
D.L. Bastianutti, 529(QQ):Winter86-887
B. Clarke, 219(GaR):Summer86-576
J. Hunter, 249(HudR):Summer86-331
Levi, P. I sommersi e i salvati. Vizio di
forma.
H. Denman, 617(TLS):2-8Oct87-1081
Levi, P. - see Kipling, R.
Levi ben Gersom (Gersonides). The Wars of
the Lord, Book One.
N.M. Samuelson, 589:Apr86-420
Lévi-Strauss, C. Anthropology and Myth.
N. Barley, 617(TLS):18-24Dec87-1392
Lévi-Strauss, C. The View from Afar.
E. Leach, 473(PR):Vol53No1-141
Leviant, C. - see Aleichem, S.
Levick, B. The Government of the Roman
Empire.
E.D. Hunt, 161(DUJ):Jun86-356
Levin, B. The Way We Live Now.
M. Bream, 364:Aug/Sep86-160
Levin, D.M. The Body's Recollection of
Being.
R. Skelton, 323:May86-201
M.E. Zimmerman, 485(PE&W):Oct86-435
Levin, G. Edward Hopper.
J-P. Naugrette, 98:Jun-Jul86-637
Levin, H. Playboys and Killjoys.
T. Tanner, 441:8Mar87-25
Levin, H.D. Categorial Grammar and the
Logical Form of Quantification.
J.T. Kearns, 482(PhR):Jan86-127
Levin, J. Shimoni's Lover.
J. Silber, 441:29Nov87-19

Levin, M. The Socratic Method.
  S. Turow, 441:27Dec87-9
Levin, M.D. The Modern Museum.
  M. Brawne, 46:Jan86-80
Levin, M.R. Republican Art and Ideology in Late Nineteenth-Century France.
  N. McWilliam, 90:Nov86-834
Levin, P.L. Abigail Adams.
  J. Fritz, 441:7Jun87-16
Levin, R.A. Love and Society in Shake-spearean Comedy.*
  R. Berry, 405(MP):May87-426
Lévinas, E. Transcendance et intelligi-bilité.
  P. de Saint-Chéron, 192(EP):Oct-Dec86-577
Levine, A. Arguing for Socialism.
  D. Little, 482(PhR):Jul86-459
Levine, D.N. The Flight from Ambiguity.
  S.A.H., 185:Jul87-886
Levine, G.R. - see Bonner, W.H.
Levine, I.A. Left-Wing Dramatic Theory in American Theatre.
  B. McConachie, 615(TJ):Dec86-502
Levine, J.M. Humanism and History.
  J.P. Kenyon, 617(TLS):24Jul87-788
Levine, L. & L.S. Hughey. Changing Times.
  J.M. Fayer, 399(MLJ):Autumn86-337
Levinson, D. Modus Vivendi.
  Y. Luria, 390:Feb86-60
Levinson, M. Wordsworth's Great Period Poems. The Romantic Fragment Poem.
  L. Newlyn, 617(TLS):15May87-525
Levinson, S.C. Pragmatics.*
  S. McConnell-Ginet, 482(PhR):Jan86-123
  M. Toolan, 307:Aug86-145
Levis, L. Winter Stars.
  P. Stitt, 491:May86-103
  455:Dec86-64
  639(VQR):Winter86-29
Levitt, S. Victorians Unbuttoned.*
  V. Powell, 39:May86-367
Le Vot, A. F. Scott Fitzgerald.
  A.H. Petry, 403(MLS):Spring86-93
Lévy, B-H. Éloge des intellectuels.
  R.W. Johnson, 617(TLS):31Jul87-811
Levy, B.J. Nine Verse Sermons by Nicholas Bozon.
  B. Cazelles, 545(RPh):Nov86-268
Lévy, C.M.L., ed. Le Roman de Floriant et Florete, ou Le Chevalier qui la nef maine.*
  N.J. Lacy, 545(RPh):Aug86-117
  D.A. Monson, 589:Apr86-438
  J.H.M. Taylor, 382(MAE):1986/2-318
Levy, D.W. Herbert Croly of "The New Republic."*
  J. Campbell, 619:Summer86-343
Levy, I.H. Hitomaro and the Birth of Japanese Lyricism.*
  M. Morris, 244(HJAS):Dec86-638
Levy, J.M. Beethoven's Compositional Choices.*
  M.M., 412:May85-138
Levy, K.D. Jacques Rivière.*
  H.T. Naughton, 188(ECr):Summer86-105
Levy, L.W. Emergence of a Free Press.*
  G.R. Stone, 185:Oct86-286
Levy, M. Liberty Style.
  N. Powell, 39:Sep86-226
Lévy, Z.H. Jérôme "agonistes."
  M. Tilby, 208(FS):Jul86-352
  D.H. Walker, 402(MLR):Jan86-212

Lewalski, B.K. "Paradise Lost" and the Rhetoric of Literary Forms.*
  T. Healy, 402(MLR):Oct87-915
  C. Kendrick, 141:Spring86-213
  M. Lieb, 405(MP):Nov86-225
  D.A. Loewenstein, 223:Summer86-203
  J. Wittreich, 551(RenQ):Autumn86-569
Lewell, J. Computer Graphics.
  M.L.V. Pitteway, 324:Feb87-254
  D. Spence, 89(BJA):Spring86-186
Lewin, I. The Jewish Community in Poland.
  I. Nagurski, 497(PolR):Vol31No2/3-197
Lewin, M. The Making of the Soviet System.*
  L. Viola, 550(RusR):Jan86-85
Lewin, R. Bones of Contention.
  P-L. Adams, 61:Oct87-106
  R. Wright, 441:20Sep87-27
Lewin, W. Federico.
  B. Leistner, 601(SuF):May-Jun86-666
  G. Müller-Waldeck, 654(WB):3/1986-473
Lewis, B. The Jews of Islam.*
  A. Levy, 589:Jul86-679
Lewis, B. Le Retour de l'Islam.
  H. Cronel, 450(NRF):Mar86-101
Lewis, B. Semites and Anti-Semites.*
  M. Curtis, 390:Nov86-50
Lewis, D. On the Plurality of Worlds.*
  D. Weissman, 543:Mar87-585
Lewis, D. Philosophical Papers.* (Vol 1)
  M. Davies, 84:Mar86-130
  P. Van Inwagen, 393(Mind):Apr86-246
Lewis, F. Europe.
  S.R. Graubard, 441:22Nov87-11
Lewis, G. Somerville and Ross.*
  V. Beards, 295(JML):Nov86-539
Lewis, G.K. Grenada.
  T. Thorndike, 617(TLS):27Nov-3Dec87-1313
Lewis, H.D. Freedom and Alienation.*
  D. Gordon, 258:Sep86-303
Lewis, I.M. Religion in Context.
  V. Skultans, 617(TLS):2Jan87-18
Lewis, J., ed. Labour and Love.
  E. Yeo, 637(VS):Summer87-529
Lewis, J. Playing for Time.
  J.K.L. Walker, 617(TLS):24Jul87-791
Lewis, J. The Pursuit of Happiness.
  B.S. Schlenther, 83:Autumn86-214
Lewis, J. The Trial of Sören Qvist.
  S. Altinel, 617(TLS):10Apr87-394
Lewis, J.S. & R.A. Space Resources.
  D.F. Salisbury, 441:27Sep87-36
Lewis, L. Henry Miller.
  P.R.J., 295(JML):Nov86-513
Lewis, L.B. The Tainted War.
  T. Myers, 395(MFS):Summer86-293
Lewis, M. Robert Cantwell.
  R.L. Gale, 649(WAL):Aug86-182
Lewis, M.A. Afro-Hispanic Poetry, 1940-1980.*
  A.A. Fernández-Vázquez, 345:May86-249
Lewis, N. Greeks in Ptolemaic Egypt.
  J.D. Ray, 617(TLS):12Jun87-640
Lewis, N. The Ides of March.
  R.L. Bates, 124:Sep-Oct86-49
Lewis, N. Jackdaw Cake.*
  442(NY):14Sep87-136
Lewis, N. The March of the Long Shadows.
  N. Shack, 617(TLS):5Jun87-610
Lewis, P.G. The Literary Vision of Gabrielle Roy.*
  C.F. Coates, 207(FR):Dec86-251

Lidtke, V.L. The Alternative Culture.*
  H. Groschopp, 654(WB):1/1986-166
Lieberman, E.J. Acts of Will.*
  R.A. Paskauskas, 529(QQ):Autumn86-645
Lieberman, V.B. Burmese Administrative
Cycles.
  D.K. Wyatt, 293(JASt):May86-654
Liebertz-Grün, U. Das andere Mittelalter.
  F. Shaw, 402(MLR):Jan87-241
  S.C. Van D'Elden, 589:Oct86-954
Liebertz-Grün, U. Seifried Helbling.
  S.C. Van D'Elden, 406:Fall86-392
Liebs, C.H. Main Street to Miracle Mile.*
  J. Iovine, 45:Jul86-81
Liedtke, W.A. Architectural Painting in
Delft.
  A.K. Wheelock, Jr., 54:Mar86-169
Liedtke, W.A. Flemish Paintings in the
Metropolitan Museum of Art.
  C. Scribner 3d, 90:Jul86-515
Liefer, M. Indonesia's Foreign Policy.
  R. Pringle, 293(JASt):Nov85-195
Liesenfeld, V.J. The Licensing Act of
1737.*
  H.T. Dickinson, 83:Autumn86-225
  T. Lockwood, 611(TN):Vol40No2-92
Lieu, S.N.C. Manichaeism in the Later
Roman Empire and Medieval China.
  R.A. Markus, 313:Vol76-305
Lieutaud, S. & J-C. Beacco. Tours de
France.
  P. Trescases, 207(FR):May87-887
Lifton, R.J. The Future of Immortality and
Other Essays for a Nuclear Age.
  T. De Pietro, 441:5Apr87-34
  L. Goldstein, 385(MQR):Summer87-578
Lifton, R.J. The Nazi Doctors.*
  N. Ascherson, 453(NYRB):28May87-29
  S. Bloch, 617(TLS):12Jun87-625
Light, F. & D. Finn. Canova.
  S.G. Lindsay, 54:Jun86-340
Lightbody, A. The Terrorism Survival
Guide.
  E. Newby, 441:31May87-48
Lightbown, R. Mantegna.*
  E.H. Ramsden, 39:Aug86-138
  A. Stewart, 324:Oct87-854
Lightfoot, D.W. The Language Lottery.*
  D. Caplan, 567:Vol59No1/2-171
Lightman, B. A Modern Day Yankee in a
Connecticut Court.
  Y. Baskin, 441:25Jan87-21
Lightner, T.M. Introduction to English
Derivational Morphology.*
  L. Bauer, 603:Vol10No1-223
de Ligne, C-J. Les Enlèvements. (B. Guy,
ed)
  J. Lough, 208(FS):Apr86-215
Likhachev, D.S., A.M. Panchenko & N.V
Ponyrko. Smekh drevnei Rusi. (2nd ed)
  D.E. Farrell, 550(RusR):Jan86-45
Lillich, M.P., ed. Studies in Cistercian
Art and Architecture.
  D.M. Gillerman, 576:Dec86-410
Lillyman, W.J., ed. Goethe's Narrative
Fiction.*
  M. Swales, 402(MLR):Jan86-255
Lima, J.L. – see under Lezama Lima, J.
Lima, R. & D. Dougherty. Dos ensayos
sobre teatro español de los '20. (C.
Oliva, ed)
  J.P. Gabriele, 238:Mar86-103
  J. Lyon, 402(MLR):Jan87-227

Limb, S. Love Forty.
  C. Hawtree, 617(TLS):24Jul87-791
Limerick, P.N. Desert Passages.
  J. Aton, 649(WAL):Aug86-162
Limerick, P.N. The Legacy of Conquest.
  A. Kolodny, 441:2Aug87-15
Limon, J. Dangerous Matter.
  L. Potter, 617(TLS):20Feb87-188
Limon, J. Gentlemen of a Company.*
  P. Brady, 611(TN):Vol40No3-139
  T. Dunn, 157:No159-52
  R.P. Knowles, 568(SCN):Fall86-38
Limonov, E. His Butler's Story.
  M. Paley, 441:5Jul87-2
Lin, F. Florence Lin's Complete Book of
Chinese Noodles, Dumplings, and Breads.
  W. & C. Cowen, 639(VQR):Autumn86-139
Lin Lu-tche. Le règne de l'empereur Hiuan-
tsong (713-756). (R. des Rotours, ed &
trans)
  P.W. Kroll, 318(JAOS):Oct/Dec85-759
Lincoln, B. Myth, Cosmos, and Society.
  N. Austin, 124:Mar-Apr87-321
  D. Pocock, 617(TLS):2Jan87-18
Lincoln, W.B. In the Vanguard of Reform.
  L. Gerstein, 377:Jul86-149
Lincoln, W.B. In War's Dark Shadow.
  T. Emmons, 550(RusR):Jan86-76
Lincoln, Y.S., ed. Organizational Theory
and Inquiry.
  M.O., 185:Apr87-688
Lind, G., H.A. Hartmann & R. Wakenhut, eds.
Moral Development and the Social Environ-
ment.
  T.M.R., 185:Apr87-683
Lind, J. The Inventor.
  S. Altinel, 617(TLS):29May87-588
  L. Taylor, 362:9Jul87-31
Lindberg, D.C. & G. Cantor. The Discourse
of Light from the Middle Ages to the
Enlightenment.
  J.M. Hill, 566:Autumn86-74
Lindbom, T. The Tares and the Good Grain.
  D. Swickard, 396(ModA):Winter86-69
Lindell, K. & others. The Kammu Year.
  F. Scholz, 196:Band27Heft3/4-349
Lindell, K., J-Ö. Swahn & D. Tayanin, eds.
Folk Tales from Kammu.* (Vol 3)
  F. Scholz, 196:Band27Heft3/4-351
Lindeman, Y. – see Macropedius, G.
Lindenberger, H. Opera.*
  C.S. Brown, 131(CL):Winter86-83
  E. Rothstein, 401(MLQ):Mar85-100
  U. Weisstein, 52:Band21Heft1-86
Linderman, G.F. Embattled Courage.
  S.W. Sears, 441:5Jul87-11
  442(NY):14Sep87-135
Lindgren, M. & others. Svensk konsthisto-
ria.
  R. Zeitler, 341:Vol55No4-168
Lindheim, N. The Structures of Sidney's
"Arcadia."*
  K. Duncan-Jones, 402(MLR):Oct86-981
Lindley, D. The Court Masque.
  R. Gill, 617(TLS):31Jul87-814
Lindley, M. Lutes, Viols and Tempera-
ments.*
  P. Gouk, 410(M&L):Jul86-313
Lindley, R. Autonomy.
  A. Ryan, 617(TLS):7Aug87-854
Lindley, R.B. Haciendas and Economic
Development.
  M.F. Lang, 86(BHS):Jul86-302

223

Lindop, G. Tourists.
  B. O'Donoghue, 617(TLS):20-26Nov87-1275
Lindow, W., ed. Plattdeutsches Wörterbuch.
  C. Prowatke, 682(ZPSK):Band39Heft2-282
Lindquist, M. Sad Movies.
  S. Schiff, 441:13Dec87-12
Lindsay, J. Turner.*
  C. Hartley, 90:May86-363
  G. Reynolds, 39:Apr86-288
Lindsey, D.L. Spiral.
  S. Dunant, 362:11Jun87-26
  442(NY):5Jan87-88
Lindström, U. Fascism in Scandinavia 1920-1940.
  M.F. Metcalf, 563(SS):Spring86-206
Lindvall, L. Jean Renart et Galeran de Bretagne.
  B. Cerquiglini, 545(RPh):Nov86-269
Lingenfelter, R.E. & K.R. Gash. The Newspapers of Nevada.
  N. Branz, 635(VPR):Spring86-38
Lingis, A. Excesses.
  F.J. Ramos, 160:Jan86-193
"Linguistique comparée et typologie des langues romanes."
  A. Lodge, 208(FS):Oct86-501
Link, A.S., ed. Woodrow Wilson and a Revolutionary World, 1913-1921.
  G. Martel, 106:Spring86-81
Link, J. Elementare Literatur und generative Diskursanalyse.
  E. Ibsch, 107(CRCL):Dec86-650
Link, O.W. Steam, Steel and Stars. (Text by T. Hensley)
  A. Grundberg, 441:6Dec87-21
Link, P. - see Liu Binyan
Linke, H.G. Das Zarische Russland und der Erste Weltkrieg.*
  L.L. Farrar, Jr., 550(RusR):Oct86-440
Linklater, A. Compton Mackenzie.
  G. Mangan, 617(TLS):29May87-572
  P. Taylor-Martin, 362:4Jun87-45
Links, R. Alfred Döblin.
  C. Poore, 406:Summer86-253
Linscott, G. Knightfall.
  T.J.B., 617(TLS):1May87-458
Linsky, L. Oblique Contexts.*
  A. Fisher, 518:Jan86-47
  J. Tienson, 316:Sep86-821
Linstedt, J. On the Semantics of Tense and Aspect in Bulgarian.
  J.I. Press, 575(SEER):Jul86-450
Linz, S.J., ed. The Impact of World War II on the Soviet Union.
  W.O. McCagg, Jr., 104(CASS):Spring-Summer86-190
  N.M. Naimark, 550(RusR):Oct86-445
Lioure, M. "Tête d'Or" de Paul Claudel.
  J-N. Segrestaa, 535(RHL):Sep-Oct86-954
Lipking, L., ed. High Romantic Argument.
  J. Beer, 402(MLR):Jan87-179
Lipman, E. Into Love and Out Again.
  S. Vogan, 441:26Apr87-24
Lipman, J. Frank Lloyd Wright and the Johnson Wax Buildings.*
  A. Saint, 617(TLS):10Apr87-381
Lipman, J., E.V. Warren & R. Bishop. Young America.*
  C. Cerny, 441:22Feb87-15
Lipman, M. Something To Fall Back On.
  D.J. Enright, 617(TLS):18-24Dec87-1399

Lipold, G. Gottschee in Jugoslawien, System, Stil und Prozess. (Pt 1)
  H. Traunmüller, 685(ZDL):1/1986-138
Lipski, J.J. KOR.*
  S.R. Burant, 497(PolR):Vol31No2/3-204
Lipstadt, D.E. Beyond Belief.*
  A. Wohl, 390:Apr86-59
  H. Ziff, 152(UDQ):Winter87-96
Lipton, E. Looking into Degas.
  E. Cowling, 617(TLS):28Aug87-923
Lipton, M. Capitalism and Apartheid.
  P.B., 185:Apr87-709
Lish, G. Peru.*
  I. Malin, 532(RCF):Summer86-153
Lisio, D.J. Hoover, Blacks, and Lily-Whites.
  639(VQR):Spring86-52
Lisle, L. Portrait of an Artist.
  R.M. Adams, 453(NYRB):26Mar87-32
  L. Ellmann, 617(TLS):18-24Dec87-1397
  B. Morton, 362:10Dec87-27
Lissorgues, Y. La Pensée philosophique et religieuse de Leopoldo Alas (Clarín) - 1875-1901.
  P.B. Goldman, 240(HR):Summer86-348
Lister, R. The Paintings of Samuel Palmer.*
  D.B. Brown, 90:Jun86-436
  G. Reynolds, 39:Apr86-288
Listfield, E. Variations in the Night.
  R. Rosen, 441:6Sep87-12
Litan, R.E. What Should Banks Do?
  N.C. Nash, 441:25Oct87-39
"Literary Onomastic Studies." (Vol 9) (G. Alvarez-Altman & F. Burelbach, eds)
  E.W. McMullen, 424:Sep86-323
"Littératures du Maghreb."
  K.W. Harrow, 188(ECr):Spring86-95
Little, B. Architecture of Norman Britain.
  E.C. Fernie, 46:Sep86-109
  P. Hetherington, 39:May86-366
Little, D. Malevolent Neutrality.
  639(VQR):Winter86-8
Little, J. Comedy and the Woman Writer.*
  J. Todd, 402(MLR):Apr87-464
Little, J. Etudes sur Saint-John Perse.*
  L. Allen, 402(MLR):Jul87-747
  C. Rigolot, 207(FR):Apr87-713
Little, R. Rimbaud: "Illuminations."*
  G. Chesters, 402(MLR):Oct86-1011
  J.E. Jackson, 535(RHL):Sep-Oct86-944
Littlefield, D.F., Jr. & J.W. Parins. American Indian and Alaska Native Newspapers and Periodicals, 1826-1924.*
  B. Katz, 87(BB):Jun86-118
Littlefield, D.F., Jr. & J.W. Parins, eds. American Indian and Alaska Native Newspapers and Periodicals 1925-1970.
  R. Dwyer, 649(WAL):Feb87-383
Littlefield, D.F., Jr. & J.W. Parins. A Biobibliography of Native American Writers 1772-1924: A Supplement.
  W.T. Hagan, 649(WAL):Nov86-267
Littlewood, I. The Writings of Evelyn Waugh.*
  M. Stannard, 402(MLR):Apr86-466
Litwak, M. Reel Power.*
  E.J. Scherick, 18:Jan/Feb87-69
Litz, A.W. & C. MacGowan - see Williams, W.C.

Liu Binyan. People or Monsters?* (P. Link, ed)
   L.S. Robinson, 116:Jul85-191
Liu, Z. Two Years in the Melting Pot.
   J.K. Kallgren, 293(JASt):Nov85-121
Liu-hung, H. – see under Huang Liu-hung
Liuzzi, D. Nigidio Figulo, "astrologo e mago."
   L. Holford-Strevens, 123:Vol36No1-135
Lively, P. Moon Tiger.
   J. McKay, 362:10Sep87-23
   J.K.L. Walker, 617(TLS):15May87-515
Liver, R. Manuel pratique de romanche: sursilvan-vallader.
   K. Baldinger, 72:Band223Heft1-236
Livesay, D. Feeling the Worlds.*
   D. Leahy, 529(QQ):Summer86-412
   R. Miles, 102(CanL):Winter85-124
Livesey, M. Learning By Heart.
   H. Kirkwood, 99:Jan87-39
   F.R. McConnel, 441:2Aug87-16
Livingston, D.W. Hume's Philosophy of Common Life.*
   R. Ginsberg, 577(SHR):Spring86-188
   D.F. Norton, 319:Apr87-300
   D.R. Raynor, 173(ECS):Spring87-389
Livingston, H. Ride a Tiger.
   R. Bromley, 441:12Apr87-26
Livingston, N. Incident at Parga.
   T.J. Binyon, 617(TLS):13-19Nov87-1262
Livingstone, A. – see Pasternak, B.
Livingstone, D. Saving Grace.
   J. O'Grady, 617(TLS):18-24Sep87-1024
Livingstone, K. If Voting Changed Anything, They'd Abolish It.
   J. Naughtie, 362:10Sep87-21
Livingstone, M. R.B. Kitaj.*
   T. Godfrey, 90:Mar86-227
Livy. Abrégés des livres de l'"Histoire romaine" de Tite-Live. (Vol 34, Pts 1 & 2) (P. Jal, ed & trans)
   J-C. Richard, 555:Vol59fasc2-316
Ljungquist, K. The Grand and the Fair.*
   D.A. Daiker, 573(SSF):Summer86-339
   P.F. Quinn, 27(AL):May86-286
Llewelyn, J. Beyond Metaphysics?*
   C. Norris, 518:Oct86-225
Llosa, M.V. – see under Vargas Llosa, M.
Lloyd, A.C. Form and Universal in Aristotle.
   W. Leszl, 53(AGP):Band68Heft2-200
Lloyd, A.L. – see Brăiloiu, C.
Lloyd, C. The Year of Great Dixter.
   A. Urquhart, 617(TLS):3Jul87-728
Lloyd, G. The Man of Reason.*
   D. Judovitz, 208(FS):Jan86-111
   D. Russell, 63:Jun86(supp)-139
   S. Shute, 319:Jul87-464
   M. Tiles, 483:Jul86-414
Lloyd, G.E.R. Science, Folklore and Ideology.*
   H. Vos, 394:Vol39fasc3/4-545
Lloyd, N. & M.E. Owen, eds. Drych yr Oesoedd Canol.
   P. MacCana, 112:Vol18-216
Lloyd, R. Mallarmé: "Poésies."*
   G. Millan, 402(MLR):Apr87-481
Lloyd, S. Chinese Characters.
   J. Mirsky, 617(TLS):11-17Sep87-973
Lloyd, S. & H.W. Müller. Ancient Architecture.
   J.S. Curl, 324:Nov87-951

Lloyd Evans, G. & B., eds. Plays in Review 1956-1980.
   A. Vivis, 157:No159-49
Llull, R. Selected Works of Ramon Llull (1232-1316). (A. Bonner, ed & trans)
   W.W. Artus, 551(RenQ):Summer86-276
   J.M. Sobré, 240(HR):Summer86-329
Lo, S.D. – see under de Mundo Lo, S.
Loader, J. Between Pictures.
   W.J. Harding, 441:8Nov87-26
Loades, D.M. The Tudor Court.
   J. Loach, 617(TLS):5Jun87-602
Loar, B. Mind and Meaning.*
   B. McLaughlin, 543:Mar87-589
Lock, F.P. Burke's "Reflections on the Revolution in France."
   M. Fuchs, 189(EA):Apr-Jun87-218
Lock, F.P. The Politics of "Gulliver's Travels."
   H.J. Real & H.J. Vienken, 38:Band104 Heft3/4-516
Locke, R.P. Music, Musicians and the Saint-Simonians.
   J. Warrack, 617(TLS):27Mar87-323
Lockett, R. Samuel Prout (1783-1852).*
   L.S., 90:Feb86-156
Lockhart, J. & S.B. Schwartz. Early Latin America.
   J. Fisher, 86(BHS):Jul86-302
Lockhart, R.B. Halfway to Heaven.
   P. Zaleski, 441:8Feb87-28
Locklin, G. The Case of the Missing Blue Volkswagen.
   J. Byrne, 532(RCF):Spring86-211
Locklin, G. Gringo and Other Poems.
   G. Haslam, 649(WAL):Nov86-246
Lockwood, L. Music in Renaissance Ferrara 1400-1505.
   R. Strohm, 410(M&L):Jul86-283
   C. Wright, 589:Oct86-956
Lockwood, L. & P. Benjamin, eds. Beethoven Essays.*
   B. Cooper, 410(M&L):Jan86-60
Lockwood, L. & C. Wolff – see Pirrotta, N.
Lockwood, W.B. The Oxford Book of British Bird Names.*
   G. Bourcier, 189(EA):Jul-Sep86-370
Lockwood, Y.R. Text and Context.*
   S. Chianis, 187:Winter87-139
   G. Monger, 203:Vol97No1-118
Lodge, D. Small World.*
   R.B. Hovey, 396(ModA):Spring86-173
Lodge, K.R. Studies in the Phonology of Colloquial English.*
   M. Picard, 320(CJL):Winter86-371
Loescher, G. & J.A. Scanlan. Calculated Kindness.*
   R.M. Smith, 617(TLS):25-31Dec87-1422
Loetscher, H. Die Papiere des Immunen.
   M. Butler, 617(TLS):9-15Oct87-1114
Loewenberg, P. Decoding the Past.*
   D.J. Fisher, 473(PR):Vol53No3-474
Loewenberg, R. An American Idol.
   L. Schweikart, 390:Aug/Sep86-60
Loewenstein, J. Responsive Readings.*
   R. Dutton, 402(MLR):Oct87-913
Loewer, P. Gardens by Design.
   A. Lacy, 441:31May87-14
Loewinsohn, R. Where All the Ladders Start.
   S. Braudy, 441:19Jul87-14
Löffler, A. The Rebel Muse.
   H.J. Real, 566:Autumn86-5

Löffler, C.M. The Voyage to the Otherworld Island in Early Irish Literature.
  J.E.C. Williams, 382(MAE):1986/1-127
Löffler, H., ed. Das Deutsch der Schweizer.
  R.E. Keller, 402(MLR):Oct87-1018
Loftus, J. L'Affreux Secret.
  V. Eskenasy, 575(SEER):Oct86-630
Logan, G.M. The Meaning of More's "Utopia."*
  H.P. Heinrich, 72:Band223Heft2-406
Logan, W. Moorhen and Other Poems.*
  T. Swiss, 569(SR):Spring86-302
Lo Giudice, A. Motivi italiani in Paul Valéry.
  E. Chevallier, 549(RLC):Jul-Sep86-358
Logue, J. Boats Against the Current.
  H. Mayer, 441:26Apr87-31
Lohafer, S. Coming to Terms with the Short Story.
  P. Miles, 447(N&Q):Dec85-561
Lohmeier, A-M. Beatus ille.
  J. Hardin, 406:Winter86-528
Lohr, C. - see Lull, R.
Loinaz, J.A.M. - see under Munita Loinaz, J.A.
Loizeaux, E.B. Yeats and the Visual Arts.
  C. Rawson, 617(TLS):24Jul87-783
Lolos, A. Der unbekannte Teil der Ilias-Exegesis des Iohannes Tzetzes.
  K. Snipes, 123:Vol36No1-179
Lomas, H. Letters in the Dark.*
  R. McDowell, 249(HudR):Winter87-686
  S. O'Brien, 493:Jun86-104
  S. Rae, 364:Aug/Sep86-132
Lomax, M. Stage Images and Traditions.
  J. Wilders, 617(TLS):30Oct-5Nov87-1197
Lombard, L.B. Events.*
  H.J.M., 185:Jul87-891
London, J. Croc-Blanc. L'Appel sauvage.
  R. Asselineau, 189(EA):Jul-Sep87-372
Londré, F.H. Federico García Lorca.*
  R. Anderson, 238:May86-310
  I.R. Hark, 130:Summer86-182
  J. Schevill, 610:Summer86-172
Lonergan, J. Video in Language Teaching.
  J. Gillespie, 399(MLJ):Summer86-167
  K.M. Pederson, 207(FR):Oct86-138
Long, C. Wishbones.
  E. Lupu, 296(JCF):No35/36-193
Long, D. The Flood of '64.
  G. Johnson, 441:5Jul87-15
Long, E. The American Dream and the Popular Novel.
  J. Dewey, 395(MFS):Summer86-292
  B.K. Horvath, 27(AL):Mar86-130
  D. Seed, 541(RES):Nov86-604
Long, E.H. & J.R. Le Master. The New Mark Twain Handbook.
  H. Hill, 26(ALR):Winter87-90
  27(AL):Dec86-682
Long, F.A., D. Hafner & J. Boutwell, eds. Weapons in Space.*
  Lord Zuckerman, 453(NYRB):9Apr87-35
Long, M. The Dark Gateway.
  T.J. Binyon, 617(TLS):13-19Nov87-1262
Long, M. Marvell, Nabokov.*
  T.N. Corns, 402(MLR):Jul87-705
Long, R.E. Henry James: The Early Novels.*
  P.B. Armstrong, 284:Winter85-148
Long, R.E. Nathanael West.
  J.F. English, 50(ArQ):Summer86-188
  G. Locklin, 573(SSF):Summer86-340

Long, S. Death without Dignity.
  R.L. Scheier, 441:19Apr87-17
Longère, J. La prédication médiévale.
  C.W. Connell, 589:Jul86-681
Longfellow, H.W. The Letters of Henry Wadsworth Longfellow. (Vols 5 & 6) (A. Hilen, ed)
  L. Willson, 569(SR):Winter86-131
Longhurst, C.A. - see de Unamuno, M.
Longley, E. Poetry in the Wars.
  N. Corcoran, 617(TLS):13Mar87-275
Longley, E. - see Durcan, P.
Longman, P. Born to Pay.
  M. Freudenheim, 441:1Nov87-25
Longree, G.H.F. L'Expérience idéocalli-grammatique d'Apollinaire.
  T. Mathews, 208(FS):Jul86-354
Longstreet, S. Storyville to Harlem.
  B. Atkinson, 441:8Feb87-24
Longsworth, P. - see Dickinson, A. & M.L. Todd
Longuenesse, B. Hegel et la critique de la métaphysique.
  P. Livet, 192(EP):Apr-Jun86-261
Longworth, P. Alexis, Tsar of All the Russias.
  R.P. Bartlett, 575(SEER):Jul86-467
Lonigan, P.R. The Early Irish Church from the Beginnings to the Two Doves.
  272(IUR):Spring86-109
Lonoff, S. Wilkie Collins and his Victorian Readers.*
  S.M. Smith, 402(MLR):Apr86-457
Lonsdale, R. Dr. Charles Burney.
  A. Pailler, 189(EA):Jul-Sep87-354
Lonsdale, R., ed. The New Oxford Book of Eighteenth-Century Verse.*
  P-G. Boucé, 189(EA):Jul-Sep86-339
  T. Lockwood, 541(RES):Feb86-94
  W.A. Speck, 366:Spring86-114
Loomis, V. & J. Ethell. Amelia Earhart.
  639(VQR):Winter86-12
Looney, R. Haunted Highways.
  R.M. Adams, 453(NYRB):12Mar87-28
Looney, S., A. Huseboe & G. Hunt, eds. The Prairie Frontier.
  C.A. Andrews, 649(WAL):May86-70
Loos, H. & G. Massenkeil, eds. Zu Richard Wagner.
  M.A. Cicora, 343:Heft13-120
  G. Jordan, 221(GQ):Spring86-338
  H.M.K. Riley, 133:Band19Heft1-83
  J. Spering, 52:Band21Heft2-216
Loos, W. The Fodor Collection.
  J.M. Roos, 380:Summer86-251
Looseley, D. A Search for Commitment.
  D. Knowles, 208(FS):Jul86-357
  N. Lane, 207(FR):Mar87-542
Loots, S. Uit de vuildoos.
  E. Hulsens, 196:Band27Heft3/4-352
Lopate, P. The Rug Merchant.
  J. Charyn, 441:8Mar87-12
  R. Towers, 453(NYRB):25Jun87-45
Lope Blanch, J.M. Estudios sobre el español de México.
  M.T. Ward, 240(HR):Winter86-106
Lope Blanch, J.M., ed. Homenaje a Andrés Bello.
  S.N. Dworkin, 240(HR):Winter86-109
Lope Blanch, J.M. - see de Texeda, J.
Lopes, H. Blutiger Ball.
  C. Serauky, 654(WB):5/1986-855

Lopes, H. The Laughing Cry.
  D.E. Westlake, 441:3May87-32
Lopez, B. Arctic Dreams.*
  B. Powell, 647:Spring86-77
  P. Puxley, 99:Aug/Sep86-25
López, J.M.R. - see under Rozas López, J.M.
López, V.S. - see under Serna López, V.
López Bueno, B. - see de Rioja, F.
López de Abiada, J.M. & A. López Berna-
  socchi, eds. De los romances-villancico
  a la poesía de Claudio Rodríguez.
  C. Strosetzki, 547(RF):Band98Heft3/4-
  473
López de Ayala, P. Corónica del rey don
  Pedro. (C.L. & H.M. Wilkins, eds)
  E.M. Gerli, 238:Dec86-861
  R.B. Tate, 304(JHP):Winter86-180
  M. Vaquero, 240(HR):Autumn86-468
López de Ayala, P. Las Décadas de Tito
  Livio.* (C.J. Wittlin, ed)
  M.J. Sconza, 545(RPh):Feb87-427
López de Mendoza, I. Los Sonetos "Al
  Itálico Modo."* (M.P.A.M. Kerkhof & D.
  Tuin, eds)
  R.G. Black, 240(HR):Summer86-331
López Gómez, A. and others. Valencia.
  D. Angulo Iñiguez, 48:Jan-Mar86-108
Lopez-Gonzaga, V. Peasants in the Hills.
  B.J. Wallace, 293(JASt):Nov85-194
López-Landy, R. El espacio novelesco en la
  obra de Galdós.
  J.B. Avalle-Arce, 241:Jan86-77
Loptson, P. - see Conway, A.
Loquai, F. Künstler und Melancholie in der
  Romantik.
  A.R. Schmitt, 221(GQ):Spring86-320
Loran, E. Cézanne's Composition.
  R. Thomson, 90:Apr86-297
Lorca, F.G. Impresiones y paisajes.
  A.A. Anderson, 86(BHS):Jul86-294
Lord, C. Education and Culture in the
  Political Thought of Aristotle.
  E.C. Halper, 41:Spring85-109
Lord, C. - see Aristotle
Lord, G.D. Trials of the Self.
  C. Rawson, 402(MLR):Jan87-157
Lord, G.D. - see Marvell, A.
Lord, J. Giacometti.*
  L. Cooke, 90:Oct86-757
  D. Farr, 39:Nov86-449
  H. Goldgar, 598(SoR):Summer87-719
  J. Silver, 55:Mar86-43
Lordereau, P., comp. Littératures afri-
  caines à la Bibliothèque nationale, 1973-
  1983.
  H.E. Panofsky, 538(RAL):Winter86-605
Lorenz, G. Das Doppelnischenportal von St.
  Emmeram in Regensburg.
  W. Haas, 43:Band16Heft1-89
Lorenz, G., ed & trans. Snorri Sturluson
  Gylfaginning.
  T. Krömmelbein, 684(ZDA):Band115Heft2-
  51
Lorenz, K. The Waning of Humaneness.
  M. Konner, 441:12Jul87-30
Lorenzoni, G., ed. Le sculture del Santo
  di Padova.
  B. Boucher, 90:Nov86-830
Lorian, A. Souplesse et complexité de la
  proposition relative en français.
  N. Gueunier, 209(FM):Apr86-125
  K. Klingebiel, 545(RPh):Nov86-232

"Claude Lorrain 1600-1682."
  E. Young, 39:Mar86-219
Loseff, L. On the Beneficence of Censor-
  ship.
  P. Doyle, 402(MLR):Oct87-1054
  A. Nakhimovsky, 574(SEEJ):Fall86-453
  A. Zholkovsky, 550(RusR):Jul86-349
Lotchin, R.W., ed. The Martial Metropolis.
  R.M. Bernard, 9(AlaR):Jan86-78
Lotman, J.M., L.I. Ginsburg & B.A. Uspen-
  skii. The Semiotics of Russian Cultural
  History.* (A.D. & A.S. Nakhimovsky, eds)
  S. Golub, 615(TJ):Dec86-508
  J.P. Mozur, 125:Spring86-340
  D. Shepherd, 575(SEER):Jul86-453
  W.M. Todd 3d, 279:Vol33-178
Lotman, J.M. & B.A. Uspenskij. The
  Semiotics of Russian Culture.* (A.
  Shukman, ed)
  D. Shepherd, 575(SEER):Jul86-453
  W.M. Todd 3d, 279:Vol33-178
  F. Wigzell, 402(MLR):Jan87-262
Lötscher, A. Satzakzent und Funktionale
  Satzperspektive im Deutschen.
  R. Pasch, 682(ZPSK):Band39Heft1-131
Lott, B. The Man Who Owned Vermont.
  L.B. Miller, 441:12Jul87-20
Lottes, W. Wie ein goldener Traum.*
  P. Goetsch, 38:Band104Heft1/2-251
  S. Reynolds, 39:May86-367
Lottman, H.R. The People's Anger.*
  D. Pryce-Jones, 617(TLS):3Apr87-367
Lotz, H-J. Die Genese des Realismus in der
  französischen Literaturästhetik.
  U. Schöning, 72:Band223Heft1-212
Lotz, J.B. Ästhetik aus der ontologischen
  Differenz.
  G. Pöltner, 489(PJGG):Band93Heft2-438
Lotze, D.P. & V. Sander, eds. German
  Satirical Writings.
  D.C. Riechel, 399(MLJ):Summer86-188
Lötzsch, R. - see Bielfeldt, H.H.
Loudon, I. Medical Care and the General
  Practitioner 1750-1850.
  J.V. Pickstone, 617(TLS):24Jul87-798
Loudon, J.C. In Search of English Gardens.
  (P. Boniface, ed)
  C. Lloyd, 617(TLS):18-24Dec87-1400
Lough, J. The Philosophes and Post-Revolu-
  tionary France.
  D. Williams, 83:Spring86-114
Lougheed, L. Listening Between the Lines.
  P.F. Whittaker, 399(MLJ):Summer86-206
Loughrey, B., ed. The Pastoral Mode.*
  M.G. Brennan, 541(RES):May86-294
Louis, P. - see Aristotle
Louis, W.R. Imperialism at Bay, 1941-1945.
  617(TLS):7Aug87-854
Louis, W.R. & H. Bull, eds. The Special
  Relationship.
  R.B. Reich, 617(TLS):6Mar87-231
Loukakis, A. Vernacular Dreams.
  H. Jacobson, 617(TLS):27Nov-3Dec87-
  1307
Lourie, R. Zero Gravity.
  C. Buckley, 441:18Oct87-12
de Louville, F. & E. Lucie-Smith. The Male
  Nude.
  90:Sep86-688
Louvish, S. The Death of Moishe-Ganef.
  J. Mellors, 364:Jul86-103

Lucash, F.S., ed. Justice and Equality Here and Now.
R.E.G., 185:Apr87-679
Lucie-Smith, E. American Art Now.*
J. Burr, 39:Nov86-455
Lucie-Smith, E. The Art of the 1930s.*
D. Farr, 39:May86-363
Luck, G. Arcana mundi.
M.J.B. Allen, 111:Fall87-8
P.W. van der Horst, 394:Vol39fasc3/4-569
M. Smith, 124:May-Jun87-388
Lucke, C. P. Ovidius Naso, Remedia Amoris: Kommentar zu Vers 397-814.
J. den Boeft, 394:Vol39fasc1/2-182
Luckham, C. Trafford Tanzi. (M. Wandor, ed)
V.M. Patraka, 385(MQR):Winter87-285
Ludlum, R. The Bourne Supremacy.*
639(VQR):Summer86-94
Lüdtke, J. Katalanisch.
A. Quintana, 547(RF):Band98Heft1/2-185
Ludwig, A.K., comp. Brazil.
E.B. Burns, 263(RIB):Vol36No1-63
Ludwig, R.M. and C.A. Nault, Jr. Annals of American Literature 1602-1983.
L.B., 30:Spring87-96
Luft, L. The Island of the Dead.
G.J. Goldberg, 441:4Jan87-18
Lug, S. Poetic Techniques and Conceptual Elements in Ibn Zaydūn's Love Poetry.
M. Ajami, 318(JAOS):Apr/Jun85-351
Luhan, M.D. Edge of Taos Desert.
R.M. Adams, 453(NYRB):26Mar87-32
Luhmann, N. A Sociological Theory of Law.
K.S., 185:Jul87-887
Luhr, W. Raymond Chandler and Film.
C. Zucker, 106:Summer86-251
Luis, W., ed. Voices from Under.*
G. Seda-Rodríguez, 238:Mar86-119
Lukacher, N. Primal Scenes.
S. Melville, 400(MLN):Dec86-1256
M.L. Shaw, 188(ECr):Winter86-102
Lukács, G. Georg Lukács: Record of a Life. (I. Eörsi, ed) Georg Lukács: Selected Correspondence, 1902-1920, Dialogues with Weber, Simmel, Buber, Mannheim, and Others. (J. Marcus & Z. Tar, eds & trans)
I. Deak, 453(NYRB):12Mar87-39
Lukas, J.A. Common Ground.*
F.J. Lally, 432(NEQ):Mar86-133
Lukes, S. Marxism and Morality.*
T. Ball, 185:Jul87-871
R. Norman, 483:Apr86-272
A. Ryan, 473(PR):Vol53No3-486
R. Sheaff, 393(Mind):Jul86-396
Lull, R. Raimundus Lullus, Opera Latina. (Vol 11 ed by C. Lohr, Vol 12 ed by A. Madre, Vol 13 ed by M. Bauzà Ochogavía)
J.N. Hillgarth, 589:Oct86-959
Lumiansky, R.M. & D. Mills, with R. Rastall. The Chester Mystery Cycle.*
R. Beadle, 382(MAE):1986/2-296
J.M. Cowen, 447(N&Q):Sep85-390
Lundquist, L. The Party and the Masses.
E. Kingston-Mann, 550(RusR):Jan86-89
Lunn, E. Marxism and Modernism.*
P. Parrinder, 366:Spring86-122
Lupaş, L. & Z. Petre. Commentaire aux "Sept contre Thèbes" d'Eschyle.*
S. Goldhill, 24:Fall86-433

Luschnig, C.A.E. & L.J. Etymidion.
D.H. Kelly, 124:Mar-Apr87-322
R. Masciantonio, 399(MLJ):Autumn86-305
Lüsebrink, H-J., ed. Histoires curieuses et véritables de Cartouche et de Mandrin.
L. Andries, 535(RHL):Jul-Aug86-761
Lustig, A. The Unloved.*
P. Lewis, 565:Autumn86-71
Lustig, I.S. & F.A. Pottle - see Boswell, J.
Lustig, M.L. Robert Hunter, 1666-1734.
Sung Bok Kim, 656(WMQ):Jan86-142
Luther, M. Luthers geistliche Lieder und Kirchengesänge. (M. Jenny, ed)
C. Meyer, 537:Vol72No2-289
Luttwak, E.N. The Pentagon and the Art of War.
639(VQR):Spring86-57
Luttwak, E.N. Strategy.
M. Howard, 617(TLS):18-24Sep87-1007
H.G. Summers, Jr., 441:30Aug87-22
Lutwack, L. The Role of Place in Literature.*
D.D. Quantic, 649(WAL):Aug86-154
Lutz, A., ed. Die Version G der Angelsächsischen Chronik.
J. Bately, 38:Band104Heft3/4-474
D.G. Calder, 589:Jan86-242
Lützeler, P.M. Hermann Broch.*
E. Schlant, 221(GQ):Fall86-662
Lützeler, P.M., ed. Brochs "Verzauberung."
W. Riemer, 221(GQ):Summer86-495
Lützeler, P.M., ed. Romane und Erzählungen zwischen Romantik und Realismus.*
R. Burwick, 406:Winter86-534
Lux, T. Half Promised Land.
L. McMahon, 441:19Apr87-20
L. Rector, 249(HudR):Autumn86-513
455:Dec86-63
Luxenberg, S. Roadside Empires.
R.S. Tedlow, 432(NEQ):Sep86-437
Luzzo [Lucio], F. Il Medoro.
B.L. Glixon, 143:Issue39-74
Lyall, F. Slaves, Citizens, Sons.
A.N. Sherwin-White, 313:Vol76-323
Lyall, R.J. - see Lamb, W.
Lycan, W.G. Logical Form in Natural Language.
M.J. Cresswell, 393(Mind):Apr86-266
G. Harman, 484(PPR):Dec86-340
J.E. Tiles, 518:Apr86-103
Lydenberg, S.D. & others. Rating America's Corporate Conscience.
R.L. Heilbroner, 441:18Jan87-29
M. Kempton, 453(NYRB):26Feb87-37
Lydon, M. How to Succeed in Show Business by Really Trying.
K. Grubb, 151:Feb86-84
Lydus, J. Ioannes Lydus: "On Powers or the Magistracies of the Roman State."* (A.C. Bandy, ed & trans)
M. Maas, 123:Vol36No2-221
Lyle, W. A Dictionary of Pianists.*
J. Methuen-Campbell, 415:Apr86-211
Lynch, B. - see Asterisk
Lynch, J.J. Henry Fielding and the Heliodoran Novel.
J. Mullan, 617(TLS):27Feb87-218
Lynch, M. Art and Artifact in Laboratory Science.
G. Myers, 128(CE):Oct86-595

Lynch, T. Skating with Heather Grace.
M. Flamm, 441:4Oct87-24
Lyne, R.O.A.M. Further Voices in Vergil's
"Aeneid."
D.C. Feeney, 617(TLS):3Jul87-722
Lynes, R. The Lively Audience.
A. Berman, 55:Nov86-56
Lyngstad, S. Sigurd Hoel's Fiction.
F. Ingwersen, 222(GR):Summer86-129
L. Longum, 172(Edda):1986/2-187
J. de Mylius, 301(JEGP):Apr86-321
Lynn, J., ed. By No Extraordinary Means.
P. Jordan, 441:1Mar87-21
Lynn, J. & A. Jay - see Hacker, J.
Lynn, K.S. The Air-Line to Seattle.*
H.W. Emerson, Jr., 366:Spring86-129
Lynn, K.S. Hemingway.
H. Beaver, 617(TLS):30Oct-5Nov87-1190
F. Crews, 453(NYRB):13Aug87-30
B. De Mott, 61:Jul87-91
D. Johnson, 441:19Jul87-3
Lynskey, E.C. Teeth of the Hydra.
G. Butcher, 236:Fall-Winter86/87-49
Lynton, R. & others. Looking into Paint-
ings.*
S. Whitfield, 176:Feb87-50
E. Young, 39:May86-367
Lyon, J. The Theatre of Valle-Inclán.*
D. Gagen, 402(MLR):Apr86-516
V. Smith, 86(BHS):Apr86-177
Lyon, R. Zolas "foi nouvelle."
F. Wolfzettel, 224(GRM):Band36Heft2-249
Lyons, A. Fast Fade.
N. Callendar, 441:13Sep87-46
Lyons, A. Three With a Bullet.
G. Kaufman, 362:8Oct87-23
Lyons, D. Ethics and the Rule of Law.*
L.C. Becker, 543:Sep86-133
Lyons, J. Artists' Books.
M. Kasper, 517(PBSA):Vol80No3-398
Lyons, J. Language and Linguistics.
R. Hickey, 72:Band223Heft1-129
Lyons, M. Le Triomphe du livre.
E. Weber, 617(TLS):2-8Oct87-1069
Lyons, P.I. The Saga of Dazai Osamu.*
V.C. Gessel, 293(JASt):Feb86-405
Lyons, W. The Disappearance of Introspec-
tion.
B.M. Ross, 543:Jun87-782
A. Woodfield, 617(TLS):7Aug87-853
Lyotard, J-F. The Postmodern Condition.*
(French title: La condition postmoderne.)
C. Dilnot, 59:Jun86-245
J.W. Murphy, 258:Sep86-305
K. Racevskis, 478:Apr86-123
Lyotard, J-F. Le Postmoderne expliqué aux
enfants.
T. Eagleton, 617(TLS):20Feb87-194
Lyotard, J-F. & J-L. Thebaud. Just Gam-
ing.
T. Eagleton, 617(TLS):20Feb87-194
Lysa, H. - see under Hong Lysa
Lytra, D., ed. Aproximación crítica a
Ignacio Aldecoa.
G. Pérez Firmat, 238:Mar86-107

"MLA Handbook for Writers of Research
Papers." (2nd ed) (by J. Gibaldi & W.S.
Achtert) "The MLA Style Manual." (by
W.S. Achtert & J. Gibaldi)
P-G. Boucé, 189(EA):Jan-Mar87-76

Maalouf, A. The Crusades Through Arab
Eyes.
639(VQR):Spring86-52
Maas, A. Azorín oder der Mensch im Zeichen
der Ebene.
A.G. Hauf, 402(MLR):Oct86-1027
H. Ramsden, 86(BHS):Oct86-374
Maas, J. Holman Hunt and the Light of the
World.
A. Woods, 97(CQ):Vol15No3-246
Mabbett, I., ed. Patterns of Kingship and
Authority in Traditional Asia.
J.S. Lansing, 293(JASt):Feb86-369
Mabey, R. - see Hill, T.
Macadam, A. Blue Guide: Rome and Environs.
90:Jul86-521
McAdams, A.J. East Germany and Détente.
R.G. Livingston, 441:22Mar87-28
Macafee, C. Glasgow.*
E.W. Schneider, 685(ZDL):3/1986-419
MacAfee, N. - see Cohen-Solal, A.
McAleer, J. Ralph Waldo Emerson.*
R.S. Corrington, 619:Spring86-225
McAllister, B. Look, No Feet!
D.J. Enright, 617(TLS):18-24Dec87-1399
McAllister, J.A. The Government of Edward
Schreyer.
N. Wiseman, 298:Spring86-144
MacAloon, J.J., ed. Rite, Drama, Festival,
Spectacle.
P.B. Zarrilli, 615(TJ):Oct86-372
McAlpin, D.W. Proto-Elamo-Dravidian.
K.V. Zvelebil, 318(JAOS):Apr/Jun85-364
Macandrew, H. Italian Drawings in The
Museum of Fine Arts, Boston.
G. Naughton, 39:Jan86-61
McAndrew, L. Idaho Aerogram.
J.R. Hepworth, 649(WAL):Aug86-177
Macann, C.E. Kant and the Foundations of
Metaphysics.
E.C. Sandberg, 342:Band77Heft3-373
MacAodha, B.S., ed. Topothesia.
N. Ó Muraíle, 112:Vol18-228
McArthur, B. Actors and American Culture,
1880-1920.*
T.L. Miller, 615(TJ):May86-237
McAuley, M., ed. The Soviet Union Under
Gorbachev.
A. McAuley, 617(TLS):14Aug87-883
McAvoy, W.C., comp. "Twelfth Night, or
What You Will."
J.A. Roberts, 40(AEB):Vol8No4-264
MacBain, B. Prodigy and Expiation.
J.A. North, 313:Vol76-251
McBain, E. Poison.
G. Kaufman, 362:4Jun87-45
442(NY):23Mar87-102
McBain, E. Puss in Boots.
G. Kaufman, 362:26Nov87-29
McBain, E. Tricks.
N. Callendar, 441:6Dec87-79
442(NY):9Nov87-156
MacBeth, G. A Child of the War.
D.A.N. Jones, 362:3Sep87-28
R. Mayne, 176:Nov87-56
J. Symons, 617(TLS):28Aug87-922
MacBeth, G. The Cleaver Garden.
H. Lomas, 364:Dec86/Jan87-127
McBriar, A.M. An Edwardian Mixed Doubles.
R. Pinker, 617(TLS):30Oct-5Nov87-1185
McCabe, R.A. Joseph Hall.*
J.W. Blench, 161(DUJ):Dec85-193
R. Selden, 161(DUJ):Dec85-192

McCaffery, L. & S. Gregory, eds. Alive and Writing.
W. Smith, 441:26Jul87-17
McCaffery, S. PANOPTICON.
E. Quigley, 102(CanL):Winter85-176
McCaig, D. The Man Who Made the Devil Glad.
P-L. Adams, 61:Jan87-90
McCandless, A. The Burke Foundation.
J. Koslow, 441:8Mar87-20
McCann, A.M. & others. The Roman Port and Fishery of Cosa.
N. Purcell, 617(TLS):4-11Sep87-962
McCann, J. From Poverty to Famine in Northeast Ethiopia.
M. Meredith, 617(TLS):4-11Sep87-942
McCardle, A.W. & A.B. Boenau, eds. East Germany, A New Nation Under Socialism?
T.C. Fox, 221(GQ):Summer86-511
McCarter, W. & R. Gilbert. Living with Art.
L.D. Milbrandt, 709:Winter87-126
McCarthy, C. Blood Meridian or The Evening Redness in the West.
B. Baines, 649(WAL):May86-59
J.L. Longley, Jr., 639(VQR):Autumn86-746
MacCarthy, D. Sailing With Mr. Belloc.*
A. Eames, 362:8Jan87-21
McCarthy, E. Up 'Til Now.
E.J. Dionne, Jr., 441:29Mar87-13
McCarthy, G. Wind River. Powder River. The Last Buffalo Hunt. Mando.
J.D. Nesbitt, 649(WAL):Feb87-349
McCarthy, J. A Papago Traveler. (J.G. Westhover, ed)
M. Loudon, 649(WAL):Feb87-381
McCarthy, M. Campaigning for the Poor.
R. Klein, 617(TLS):24Apr87-428
McCarthy, M. How I Grew.
P-L. Adams, 61:Jun87-82
R. Dinnage, 617(TLS):18-24Sep87-1022
A. Lurie, 453(NYRB):11Jun87-19
W. Sheed, 441:19Apr87-5
McCarthy, M. Occasional Prose.*
L. Williams, 651(WHR):Summer86-181
McCarthy, M. The Origins of the Gothic Revival.
J.M. Crook, 617(TLS):30Oct-5Nov87-1202
McCarthy, M.S. Balzac and His Reader.*
P. Brooks, 535(RHL):Jul-Aug86-767
McCarthy, P. A Second Skin.*
W. Scammell, 364:Jun86-61
McCarthy, S. The Banned Man.
S. Wade, 4:Spring86-61
McCarthy, T. The Non-Aligned Storyteller.*
S. Sefton, 4:Spring86-66
McCarthy, W. Hester Thrale Piozzi.*
W.R. Siebenschuh, 173(ECS):Spring87-345
42(AR):Spring86-248
639(VQR):Summer86-85
MacCary, W.T. Friends and Lovers.
C. Kahn, 551(RenQ):Summer86-343
M. Novy, 481(PQ):Spring86-278
McCauley, E.A. A.A.E. Disderi and the Carte de Visite Portrait Photograph.
J. Kelly, 446(NCFS):Spring87-347
McCauley, S. The Object of My Affection.
A.H.G. Phillips, 617(TLS):11-17Sep87-978
S.F. Schaeffer, 441:22Mar87-7
442(NY):13Apr87-103

McClain, J.L. Kanazawa.*
R.L. Edmonds, 302:Vol22No1-97
McClain, L. A Foot in Each World.
D. Camper, 441:18Jan87-19
McClanahan, E. Famous People I Have Known.
639(VQR):Summer86-86
McClatchy, J.D. Stars Principal.*
N. Jenkins, 493:Jun86-102
J. Parini, 617(TLS):9Jan87-41
J.P. White, 491:Dec86-174
McClatchy, J.D. - see Merrill, J.
McClellan, E. Woman in the Crested Kimono. Nakai Yoshiyuki, 407(MN):Autumn86-353
S. Napier, 293(JASt):Aug86-852
McClellan, J.E. 3d. Science Reorganized.
R.E. Rider, 173(ECS):Spring87-360
McClellan, W. Russia.
639(VQR):Autumn86-119
McClelland, B.W. & T.R. Donovan, eds. Perspectives on Research and Scholarship in Composition.
K. Grant-Davie, 365:Spring/Summer86-191
McClendon, C.B. The Imperial Abbey of Farfa.
R. Krautheimer, 617(TLS):22May87-560
McCloskey, D.N. The Rhetoric of Economics.*
D.S. Kaufer, 125:Spring86-330
A.R., 185:Apr87-686
McClure, J.A. Kipling and Conrad.
C.J. Rawson,. 677(YES):Vol16-341
McClure, J.D., ed. Minority Languages in Central Scotland.
M. Martin-Jones, 355(LSoc):Jun86-285
McClure, M. Selected Poems.
P. Cole, 138:No9-278
McCluskey, J., Jr. - see Fisher, R.
McCluskey, K. Reverberations.
H. Richter, 594:Winter86-447
A.W., 295(JML):Nov86-555
McClusky, P. Praise Poems.
J. Povey, 2(AfrA):Aug86-81
McCollom, J.P. The Continental Affair.
S. Kinsley, 441:8Nov87-27
McConachie, B.A. & D. Friedman, eds. Theatre for Working-Class Audiences in the United States, 1830-1980.
R.K. Bank, 610:Autumn86-269
M.K. Fielder, 615(TJ):Oct86-384
McConica, J., ed. The History of the University of Oxford. (Vol 3)
L. Colley, 617(TLS):13Mar87-261
McConkey, J., ed. Chekhov and Our Age.
A.R. Durkin, 550(RusR):Oct86-434
McConkey, J. Kayo.
M. Anania, 441:28Jun87-31
McConnell, F., ed. The Bible and the Narrative Tradition.
J.M.M., 295(JML):Nov86-418
McConnell, M. Challenger.
D. King-Hele, 617(TLS):4-11Sep87-960
McCorkle, J. Tending to Virginia.
A. McDermott, 441:11Oct87-1
McCormac, E.R. A Cognitive Theory of Metaphor.
C. Neill, 350:Mar87-196
F. Nuessel, 361:Sep86-69
C.C. Rostankowski, 290(JAAC):Summer87-418
I.K. Skrupskelis, 543:Dec86-385

McCormack, E. Inspecting the Vaults.
S. Slosberg, 441:20Sep87-26

McCormack, W.J. Ascendancy and Tradition in Anglo-Irish Literary History from 1789 to 1939.*
R. Fallis, 125:Spring86-321
H. Pyle, 541(RES):Nov86-598

McCormick, J. George Santayana.
B. Kuklick, 441:26Apr87-27
442(NY):13Apr87-106

McCormick, P.J., ed. The Reasons of Art/L'Art a ses raisons.
G. Van Cauwenberge, 290(JAAC):Summer 87-429

McCormick, P.J. - see Ingarden, R.

McCorquodale, C. The History of Interior Decoration.
90:Jun86-443

McCoubrey, H. The Development of Naturalist Legal Theory.
J. Gardner, 617(TLS):28Aug87-920

McCown, R.A., ed. The Life and Times of Leigh Hunt.*
D.R. Cheney, 340(KSJ):Vol35-199

McCoy, A.W. & E.C. de Jesus, eds. Philippine Social History.
V.L. Rafael, 293(JASt):May86-655

McCoy, M. Summertime.
E. Listfield, 441:12Jul87-36

McCracken, C.J. Malebranche and British Philosophy.*
L. Kreimendahl, 53(AGP):Band68Heft3-314

McCracken, D. Wordsworth and the Lake District.*
J.E. Jordan, 536(Rev):Vol8-47
M. Wedd, 541(RES):Feb86-107

McCrary, W.C. & J.A. Madrigal, eds. Studies in Honor of Everett W. Hesse.
R. Moore, 552(REH):May86-125
J.J. Reynolds, 403(MLS):Summer86-314

McCreary, L. Mount's Mistake.
R.E. Nicholls, 441:27Dec87-18

Maccubbin, R.P. & P. Martin. British and American Gardens in the Eighteenth Century.*
C. Fabricant, 173(ECS):Summer87-500

McCullagh, C.B. Justifying Historical Descriptions.*
L.J. O'Neill, 63:Mar86-114
D. Watson, 366:Spring86-121

McCulloch, A.M. A Tragic Vision.
J.B. Beston, 49:Apr86-91

MacCulloch, D. Suffolk and the Tudors.
C. Cross, 617(TLS):6Feb87-143

McCulloch, H.Y., Jr. Narrative Cause in the Annals of Tacitus.
R.D. Weigel, 124:Mar-Apr87-327

McCulloch, J. Black Soul, White Artifact.
H. Wylie, 538(RAL):Winter86-599

McCullough, C. The Ladies of Missalonghi.
J. Yolen, 441:26Apr87-15

McCusker, J.J. & R.R. Menard. The Economy of British America, 1607-1789.*
J.P. Greene, 656(WMQ):Jul86-474
J.R. Hanson 2d, 568(SCN):Fall86-47

McCutcheon, M.A. Guitar and Vihuela.
C. Harris, 415:Jul86-390

McDermott, A. That Night.
W. Balliett, 442(NY):17Aug87-71
D. Leavitt, 441:19Apr87-1

McDermott, J.J. Streams of Experience.
E.M. Adams, 543:Sep86-134
J.D. Moreno, 432(NEQ):Dec86-566

MacDiarmid, H. The Letters of Hugh MacDiarmid. (A. Bold, ed)
J.T.D. Hall, 588(SSL):Vol21-319

McDiarmid, L. Saving Civilization.*
V. Fitzpatrick, 639(VQR):Spring86-360
W. Harmon, 569(SR):Summer86-510
B. Quinn, 659(ConL):Spring87-133

McDiarmid, M.P. Robert Henryson.
J.H. Alexander, 677(YES):Vol16-231

McDiarmid, M.P. & J.A.C. Stevenson - see "Barbour's Bruce"

Macdonald, A. "My Dear Legs..."
N. Wiseman, 298:Spring86-144

Macdonald, A. Towards the Mystery.
P.M. St. Pierre, 102(CanL):Summer86-121
A. Smith, 571(ScLJ):Winter86-33

Macdonald, C. Alternate Means of Transport.*
J.F. Cotter, 249(HudR):Spring86-163
R.B. Shaw, 491:Apr86-44

MacDonald, C.A. Korea.
M. Carver, 617(TLS):11-17Dec87-1367

McDonald, C.V. The Dialogue of Writing.
A. Rosenberg, 627(UTQ):Fall86-137

McDonald, C.V., ed. The Ear of the Other.
E. Baer, 567:Vol63No3/4-345

Macdonald, E. Cavalier in a Roundhead School.
C. Tapping, 102(CanL):Winter85-155

MacDonald, E.E. & T.B. Inge. Ellen Glasgow.
M. Frazee, 189(EA):Oct-Dec87-492

McDonald, F. Novus Ordo Seclorum.
R.R. Beeman, 656(WMQ):Oct86-679
R. Hamowy, 173(ECS):Summer87-523
J.N. Shklar, 617(TLS):11-17Sep87-996

Mcdonald, G. Fletch, Too.*
G. Kaufman, 362:2Apr87-24

Mcdonald, G. A World Too Wide.
R. Short, 441:22Nov87-32

Macdonald, G. & C. Wright, eds. Fact, Science and Morality.
J. Foster, 617(TLS):19Jun87-665

McDonald, I. The History of The Times. (Vol 5)
C. Kent, 635(VPR):Spring86-36

MacDonald, J.D. Slam the Big Door.
442(NY):27Jul87-78

MacDonald, L.I. From Bourassa to Bourassa.
W. Irvine, 529(QQ):Autumn86-700

MacDonald, M. Mystical Bedlam.
391:May86-58

MacDonald, M. Schoenberg.
362:19Nov87-37

MacDonald, M. The Symphonies of Havergal Brian. (Vol 3)
S. Banfield, 415:Nov86-625

McDonald, W. Witching on Hardscrabble.
P. Filkins, 236:Fall-Winter86/87-50

McDonald, W.C., ed. Spectrum medii aevi.
H. Heinen, 589:Jan86-245

MacDonald, W.L. The Architecture of the Roman Empire. (Vol 2)
M. Henig, 617(TLS):3Apr87-369

Macdonnell, D. Theories of Discourse.
S.A.S., 295(JML):Nov86-408

McDonnell, J. Waugh on Women.
A. Blayac, 189(EA):Jan-Mar87-99

McDonogh, G.W. Good Families of Barcelona.
J. MacClancy, 617(TLS):14Aug87-870

McDonough, R.M. The Argument of the "Tractatus."
V.M. Cooke, 258:Dec86-403
McDonough, T.R. Space.
D. King-Hele, 617(TLS):27Nov-3Dec87-1316
MacDougall, D. Don and Mandarin.
C. Johnson, 617(TLS):27Nov-3Dec87-1314
McDougall, W.A. The Heavens and the Earth.*
D. Ehrenfeld, 249(HudR):Autumn86-368
McDowall, D. Steel at the Sault.
P.E. Roy, 298:Fall86-146
MacDowell, D.M. - see Gorgias
McDowell, F.P.W. E.M. Forster.* (rev)
E. Heine, 677(YES):Vol16-354
McDowell, J. - see Evans, G.
McDowell, R. Quiet Money.
S. Santos, 441:8Nov87-68
McDowell, R.B. & D.A. Webb. Trinity College Dublin 1592-1952.
J.C. Beckett, 677(YES):Vol16-249
Macé, G. Le Manteau de Fortuny.
J. Kirkup, 617(TLS):11-17Dec87-1381
Macé, G. Les trois coffrets.
C. Dis, 450(NRF):Apr86-85
S. Rappaport, 98:Jun-Jul86-735
McElroy, C.J. Jesus and Fat Tuesday.
C.A. Colman, 441:6Sep87-16
McElroy, J. Women and Men.
I. Gold, 441:12Apr87-18
McElvaine, R.S. The End of the Conservative Era.
K. Phillips, 441:9Aug87-10
McEvoy, S. Samuel R. Delany.*
C. Petty, 106:Fall86-395
McEwan, G.J.P. Priest and Temple in Hellenistic Babylonia.
M. Stolper, 318(JAOS):Jan/Mar85-141
McEwan, G.J.P. Texts from Hellenistic Babylonia in the Ashmolean Museum.
M.A. Dandamayev, 318(JAOS):Apr/Jun85-330
McEwan, I. The Child in Time.
J. Cooke, 362:17Sep87-24
R. Goldstein, 441:11Oct87-9
M. Neve, 617(TLS):4-11Sep87-947
MacEwen, G. Noman's Land.*
G.V. Downes, 376:Jun86-126
Macey, S.L. Money and the Novel.*
M.E. Novak, 402(MLR):Apr86-448
McFadden, D. The Art of Darkness.
L.M. York, 102(CanL):Spring86-157
N. Zacharin, 526:Summer86-100
McFadden, R. Letters to the Hinterland.
272(IUR):Autumn86-253
McFarland, D.T. & W. Van Ness - see Weil, S.
McFarland, T. Originality and Imagination.*
D.A. Dombrowski, 478:Oct86-341
J.C. McKusick, 661(WC):Autumn86-194
L. Newlyn, 541(RES):Nov86-613
McFarland, T. Shapes of Culture.
C. Baldick, 617(TLS):6-12Nov87-1217
Macfarlane, A. Marriage and Love in England 1300-1840.*
639(VQR):Autumn86-120
Macfarlane, N., with M. Herd. Sport and Politics.
S. Green, 617(TLS):10Apr87-388

McForan, D. The World Held Hostage.
S. Bakhash, 453(NYRB):24Sep87-12
McGahern, J. High Ground.*
J. Conarroe, 441:8Feb87-9
M. Harmon, 272(IUR):Spring86-77
McGann, J.J. The Beauty of Inflections.*
M. Berg, 541(RES):Nov86-617
W.E. Cain, 639(VQR):Spring86-337
J. Stillinger, 301(JEGP):Oct86-550
H.W., 636(VP):Autumn86-347
McGann, J.J. A Critique of Modern Textual Criticism.*
W.S. Hill, 340(KSJ):Vol35-229
T.J. Reiss, 107(CRCL):Dec86-652
McGann, J.J. Historical Studies and Literary Criticism.*
639(VQR):Autumn86-116
McGann, J.J. The Romantic Ideology.*
L.R. Furst, 107(CRCL):Jun86-301
A.K. Mellor, 591(SIR):Summer86-282
B.K. Mudge, 403(MLS):Fall86-78
McGann, J.J., ed. Textual Criticism and Literary Interpretation.
D.T.O., 295(JML):Nov86-409
McGann, J.J. - see Lord Byron
McGarry, J. Airs of Providence.
E. McGraw, 455:Mar86-69
R. Orodenker, 573(SSF):Summer86-331
McGarry, J. The Very Rich Hours.
L.B. Osborne, 441:11Oct87-56
442(NY):9Nov87-155
McGary, M.J. - see Tenenbaum, J.
McGee, T.J. Medieval and Renaissance Music.
R.W. Duffin, 627(UTQ):Fall86-252
D. Fallows, 415:Apr86-212
McGill, J.S. Edmund Morris.
D.C. Jones, 102(CanL):Summer86-140
McGilligan, P., ed. Backstory.
G. Mast, 441:18Jan87-37
MacGillivray, J.A. & R.L.N. Barber, eds. The Prehistoric Cyclades.
R.W.V. Catling, 123:Vol36No1-161
McGinley, P. The Red Men.
B. Morton, 362:4Jun87-49
J. Rees, 617(TLS):27Mar87-319
L. Rosenthal, 441:22Mar87-28
442(NY):13Apr87-103
McGinn, B. The Calabrian Abbot.
R.E. Lerner, 589:Oct86-965
McGinn, C. The Subjective View.*
S.E. Boer, 484(PPR):Dec86-327
S. Shoemaker, 311(JP):Jul86-407
D.D. Todd, 154:Autumn86-586
McGinn, C. Wittgenstein on Meaning.
P. Carruthers, 518:Jan86-36
J. Heal, 479(PhQ):Jul86-412
J. Llewelyn, 262:Sep86-363
D. Rashid, 521:Jul86-245
W.W. Tait, 185:Apr87-675
McGlathery, J.M. Desire's Sway.*
H. Eichner, 591(SIR):Winter86-583
W. Hoffmeister, 149(CLS):Spring86-78
W. Wittkowski, 133:Band18Heft4-372
McGlathery, J.M. Mysticism and Sexuality.
J. Kolb, 221(GQ):Winter86-145
McGonigle, T. The Corpse Dream of N. Petkov.
A. Codrescu, 441:24May87-8
McGough, R. Melting into the Foreground.
R. Sheppard, 617(TLS):23Jan87-92

McGowan, J.P. Representation and Revelation.
  K. Flint, 617(TLS):19Jun87-652
  C.R. Vanden Bossche, 637(VS):Summer87-555
McGowan, M.M. Ideal Forms in the Age of Ronsard.
  J. O'Brien, 402(MLR):Oct87-954
Macgoye, M.O. The Present Moment.
  J-A. Goodwin, 617(TLS):28Aug87-929
McGrath, F.C. The Sensible Spirit.
  J. Uglow, 617(TLS):13Feb87-166
  P. Zeitlow, 637(VS):Summer87-523
McGrath, T. Letters to an Imaginary Friend Parts Three and Four.
  F.C. Stern, 649(WAL):Nov86-229
McGregor, G. The Wacousta Syndrome.
  F. Davey, 99:Nov86-40
  A.E. Davidson, 395(MFS):Summer86-296
  M. Hurley, 529(QQ):Autumn86-665
  I.S. MacLaren, 105:Spring/Summer86-118
  C. Thomas, 627(UTQ):Fall86-147
  T. Ware, 150(DR):Winter85/86-566
McGuane, T. To Skin a Cat.*
  L. Taylor, 617(TLS):14Aug87-873
McGuckian, M. Venus and the Rain.*
  639(VQR):Autumn86-134
McGuinness, B. - see Frege, G.
McGuinness, F. Observe the Sons of Ulster Marching Towards the Somme.
  272(IUR):Autumn86-253
McGuire, D.K. & L. Fern, eds. Beatrix Jones Farrand (1872-1959), Fifty Years of American Landscape Architecture.
  N.P. Alpert, 576:Mar86-78
McGuire, J. The Making of a Colonial Mind.
  D. Kopf, 293(JASt):Feb86-427
McGuire, J.E. & M. Tamny - see Newton, I.
McGuire, M.C. Milton's Puritan Masque.*
  M. Fixler, 541(RES):Feb86-92
McGuire, P.L. Red Stars.
  C. Nicol, 561(SFS):Nov86-403
McGuire, W. Bollingen.
  R. Breugelmans, 107(CRCL):Mar86-105
McGuirk, C. Robert Burns and the Sentimental Era.*
  C.L. Caywood, 579(SAQ):Autumn86-408
  D.A. Low, 588(SSL):Vol21-315
  P. Morère, 189(EA):Jul-Sep86-351
  K.G. Simpson, 67:Nov86-294
McGurk, P. & others, eds. An Eleventh-Century Anglo-Saxon Illustrated Miscellany.*
  J.B. Friedman, 301(JEGP):Oct86-557
  R. Hamer, 382(MAE):1986/2-270
  G. Russom, 403(MLS):Summer86-356
MaccGwire, M. Military Objectives in Soviet Foreign Policy.
  J. Sherr, 617(TLS):23-29Oct87-1162
Macha, J. Dialekt - Hochsprache in der Grundschule.
  E. Bauer, 685(ZDL):1/1986-95
McHaney, T.L. - see Ohashi, K. & K. Ono
de Machaut, G. - see under Guillaume de Machaut
Machin, A. Cohérence et continuité dans le théâtre de Sophocle.
  C. Segal, 24:Winter86-594
Machin, G.I.T. Politics and the Churches in Great Britain 1869 to 1921.
  E. Norman, 617(TLS):23-29Oct87-1172

Machin, R. & C. Norris, eds. Post-Structuralist Readings of English Poetry.
  M. Edwards, 617(TLS):21Aug87-891
Machlin, P.S. Stride.
  E. Southern, 91:Spring86-192
Machlis, P., ed. Union Catalog of Clemens Letters.
  27(AL):Dec86-681
McHoul, A.W. Telling How Texts Talk.
  D. Birch, 402(MLR):Jan86-155
McHugh, P. Toronto Architecture.
  529(QQ):Summer86-458
McInerney, J. Ransom.*
  639(VQR):Summer86-91
McInerny, R. Cause and Effect.
  N. Callendar, 441:6Dec87-79
McInerny, R. Leave of Absence.*
  442(NY):12Jan87-101
McIntosh, A. & others, eds. A Linguistic Atlas of Late Medieval English.
  T.A. Shippey, 617(TLS):30Oct-5Nov87-1200
McIntosh, C. Common and Courtly Language.
  A. Lobeck, 350:Sep87-673
  R. Markley, 173(ECS):Spring87-398
McIntosh, M.K. Autonomy and Community.
  J.R. Maddicott, 617(TLS):27Feb87-219
MacIntyre, A. After Virtue.*
  F.M. Dolan, 435:Spring86-61
McJimsey, G. Harry Hopkins.
  J.A. Garraty, 441:12Jul87-28
Mack, D., ed. Richard Wagner.
  R. Hollinrake, 410(M&L):Apr86-185
Mack, D.S. Hogg's Prose.
  G.H. Hughes, 571(ScLJ):Summer86-9
Mack, D.S. - see Hogg, J.
Mack, M. Alexander Pope.*
  F. Bogel, 566:Autumn86-51
  P. Martin, 161(DUJ):Jun86-353
  P. Martin, 173(ECS):Spring87-336
  W.H. Pritchard, 249(HudR):Summer86-302
  C. Thomas, 385(MQR):Spring87-441
Mack, M. - see Pope, A.
Mackay, D.A. The Building of Manhattan.
  P. Goldberger, 441:6Dec87-22
McKay, J.H. Narration and Discourse in American Realistic Fiction.*
  B. Murphy, 403(MLS):Fall86-81
Mackay, S. Dreams of Dead Women's Handbags.
  A. Mars-Jones, 617(TLS):21Aug87-897
McKay, T. Infinitival Complements in German.*
  T. Hoekstra, 361:Mar86-263
McKee, P. Heroic Commitment in Richardson, Eliot, and James.
  A.M. Duckworth, 637(VS):Summer87-524
  A.R. Tintner, 395(MFS):Winter86-599
MacKeith, M. The History and Conservation of Shopping Arcades. Shopping Arcades.
  T. Russell-Cobb, 324:Feb87-248
McKellar, H. Matya-Mundi.
  L. Ryan, 381:Mar86-49
MacKendrick, L.K., ed. Probable Fictions.*
  T. Ware, 573(SSF):Summer86-340
Mackenney, L. - see Corrie, J.
Mackenney, L. - see McLeish, R.
Mackenney, R. Tradesmen and Traders.
  D. Abulafia, 617(TLS):5Jun87-614
Mackensen, L. Die Nibelungen.*
  E.R. Haymes, 221(GQ):Summer86-473
  H. Kratz, 133:Band19Heft2-158

Mackenzie, J. The Children of the Souls.*
P. Dickinson, 364:Jun86-92
Mackenzie, J.G. A Lexicon of the 14th-
Century Aragonese Manuscripts of Juan
Fernández de Heredia.*
S.N. Dworkin, 240(HR):Spring86-212
K.B. Harder, 589:Apr86-441
Mackenzie, J.L. & H. Wekker, eds. English
Language Research: the Dutch Contribu-
tion I.
F. Stuurman, 179(ES):Apr86-188
MacKenzie, J.M., ed. Imperialism and Pop-
ular Culture.
C.J.D. Duder, 637(VS):Summer87-528
MacKenzie, N. & J. The Life of H.G. Wells.
M. Laski, 176:Dec87-82
362:3Sep87-29
McKeown, K.R. Text Generation.
S. Cumming, 350:Mar87-176
McKercher, W.R., ed. The U.S. Bill of
Rights and the Canadian Charter of
Rights and Freedoms.
D. Gibson, 106:Fall86-375
Mackerell, A. Shawls, Stoles & Scarves.
B. Scott, 39:Oct86-378
Mackesy, P. War without Victory.
M. Duffy, 83:Spring86-84
Mackey, N. Eroding Witness.
G.F. Butterick, 138:No9-283
Mackey, S. The Saudis.
E. Sciolino, 441:12Jul87-13
Mackie, J.L. The Miracle of Theism.*
R.M. Adams, 482(PhR):Apr86-309
MacKillop, J. The British Ethical Socie-
ties.*
D.M., 185:Apr87-696
M.S. Vogeler, 637(VS):Summer87-543
MacKillop, J. Fionn Mac Cumhaill.
Z.B., 295(JML):Nov86-365
McKinley, R. Imaginary Lands.
639(VQR):Autumn86-127
MacKinnon, B., ed. American Philosophy.
K.J. Dykeman, 619:Spring86-219
MacKinnon, C. Finding Hoseyn.*
T.J. Binyon, 617(TLS):21Aug87-910
MacKinnon, C.A. Feminism Unmodified.
A.M. Jaggar, 441:3May87-3
Mackinnon, E., ed. East is East.
J.T. Brewer, 399(MLJ):Autumn86-315
McKinnon, J., ed. Music in Early Christian
Liturgy.
W. Mellers, 617(TLS):31Jul87-813
MacKinnon, J.R. & S.R. Agnes Smedley.
J.P. Diggins, 441:13Dec87-22
MacKinnon, S.R. & O. Friesen. China
Reporting.
S.F. Fishkin, 441:11Oct87-52
McKinsey, E. Niagara Falls.*
L. Goldstein, 115:Summer86-428
J.F. Stewart, 102(CanL):Summer86-142
M.S. Young, 39:Dec86-574
McKitterick, R. The Frankish Kingdoms
under the Carolingians 751-987.
D. Ganz, 382(MAE):1986/1-130
Macklin, R. Mortal Choices.
R. Rapp, 441:2Aug87-17
McKnight, G. Bitter Legacy.
N. Watkins, 617(TLS):24Jul87-797
Mackridge, P. The Modern Greek Language.
R. Beaton, 575(SEER):Oct86-585
B.D. Joseph, 350:Jun87-436
Macksey, K. Technology in War.
M.R.D. Foot, 176:Feb87-46

Macksey, R. & F.E. Moorer, eds. Richard
Wright.
J. Gillen, 400(MLN):Dec86-1283
Mackworth, C. Ends of the World.
J. Ure, 617(TLS):7Aug87-840
McLachlan, E.P. The Scriptorium of Bury
St. Edmunds in the Twelfth Century.
T.A. Heslop, 90:Nov86-828
MacLaine, A.H. Allan Ramsay.*
T. Crawford, 541(RES):Nov86-574
MacLaine, S. Out on a Limb. Dancing in
the Light.
M. Gardner, 453(NYRB):9Apr87-16
McLaughlin, J. Old English Syntax.
W. Elmer, 260(IF):Band91-415
M. Kilpiö, 589:Apr86-442
McLaughlin, M.L. Conversation.
D. Cameron, 297(JL):Mar86-245
McLaughlin, R.E. Caspar Schwenckfeld,
Reluctant Radical.
A. Hamilton, 617(TLS):8May87-500
McLaughlin, S. Schopenhauer in Russland.
J.T. Baer, 574(SEEJ):Summer86-283
McLaurin, M.A. Separate Pasts.
A. Friesinger, 441:11Oct87-57
MacLaverty, B. The Great Profundo and
Other Stories.
P. Craig, 617(TLS):11-17Dec87-1375
McLean, A. A Nun's Diary.
R. Anderson, 526:Summer86-92
C. Tapping, 102(CanL):Winter85-155
MacLean, A. Santorini.
J. Bass, 441:8Mar87-20
McLean, D. 1885.*
T. Flanagan, 298:Summer86-157
MacLean, D., ed. Values at Risk.
R.E.G., 185:Apr87-710
MacLean, S. Ris a'Bhruthaich.
E. Ní Chuilleanáin, 617(TLS):5Jun87-611
McLean, T. The Men in White Coats.
N. Andrew, 362:3Dec87-34
McLeave, H. Under the Icefall.
T.J. Binyon, 617(TLS):13-19Nov87-1262
MacLeish, A. Collected Poems: 1917-1982.
(rev)
R.B. Shaw, 491:Nov86-107
"Archibald MacLeish: Reflections."* (B.A.
Drabeck & H.E. Ellis, eds)
S.A.S., 295(JML):Nov86-510
McLeish, K. The Penguin Companion to the
Arts in the Twentieth Century.
S. Silvers, 364:Jun86-107
McLeish, R. The Gorbals Story. (L. Mac-
kenney, ed)
D. Hutchison, 571(ScLJ):Summer86-15
MacLeish, W.H. Oil and Water.
A.G. Gaines, Jr., 432(NEQ):Mar86-129
McLellan, D. Ideology.
A. Ryan, 617(TLS):7Aug87-854
McLellan, D. Marxism and Religion.
L. Kolakowski, 617(TLS):25-31Dec87-
1438
McLendon, W.L., ed. L'Hénaurme Siècle.*
R.T. Denommé, 210(FrF):Jan86-111
L. Le Guillou, 535(RHL):Sep-Oct86-943
MacLeod, A. As Birds Bring Forth the Sun.
F. Sutherland, 99:Aug/Sep86-35
Macleod, C. The Corpse in Oozark's Pond.
T.J. Binyon, 617(TLS):30Jan87-108
MacLeod, G. New Age Business.
T. Jackson, 99:Oct86-34
McLeod, K. Henry Handel Richardson.
E. Webby, 71(ALS):Oct86-534

McLeod, M. & B. Manhire, comps. Some
Other Country.
  R.L. Buckland, 573(SSF):Winter86-132
McLeod, M.S.G. & others. The Cathedral
Libraries Catalogue. (Vol 1) (K.I. James
& D.J. Shaw, eds)
  P. Morgan, 78(BC):Winter86-527
MacLeod, P.N. Daffodils in Winter.* (J.
Murray, ed)
  P. Morley, 102(CanL):Spring86-155
MacLeod, S. Lawrence's Men and Women.
  H. Mills, 175:Summer86-173
  T. Vichy, 189(EA):Apr-Jun87-234
McLynn, F. Invasion.
  N.A.M. Rodger, 617(TLS):17Jul87-775
McMahan, I. Footwork.
  D. Mason, 441:4Jan87-9
McMahon, T. Loving Little Egypt.
  P-L. Adams, 61:Mar87-95
  E. Toynton, 441:8Feb87-16
McManus, P.F. Rubber Legs and White Tail-
Hairs.
  H. Middleton, 441:29Nov87-20
McMaster, G. Scott and Society.
  P. Garside, 677(YES):Vol16-290
McMaster, J. Dickens the Designer.
  S. Wall, 617(TLS):11-17Dec87-1380
McMaster, R.D. Trollope and the Law.
  R.H.C., 125:Spring86-342
  P. Devlin, 617(TLS):20Feb87-183
  A. Sadrin, 189(EA):Oct-Dec87-477
McMeekin, D. Diego Rivera.
  J. Barnitz, 617(TLS):13Mar87-273
McMillan, C.J. The Japanese Industrial
System.
  R.S. Ozaki, 293(JASt):Nov85-138
McMillan, I. How the Hornpipe Failed.
  J. Saunders, 565:Summer86-74
MacMillan, I. Proud Monster.
  B.F. Williamson, 441:26Jul87-16
McMillan, I. Selected Poems.
  T. Dooley, 617(TLS):18-24Sep87-1024
  J. Horder, 362:14May87-33
McMillan, T. Mama.
  W. Blythe, 441:22Feb87-11
  442(NY):16Mar87-104
McMullen, L. Sinclair Ross.
  D. Raymond, 296(JCF):No35/36-142
MacMullen, R. Christianizing the Roman
Empire (A.D. 100-400).*
  T.G. Elliott, 487:Summer86-235
  J. O'Brien, 121(CJ):Dec86-Jan87-162
McMullin, E., ed. Evolution and Creation.
  J.E. Earley, 543:Dec86-389
  M. Ruse, 486:Dec86-608
McMullin, N. Buddhism and the State in
Sixteenth-Century Japan.*
  J.C. Dobbins, 244(HJAS):Dec86-625
  H. Ooms, 407(MN):Autumn86-364
  K.K. Troost, 293(JASt):May86-606
McMurray, R.M. John Bell Hood and the War
for Southern Independence.
  L. Shore, 106:Summer86-219
McMurtry, L. Film Flam.
  W. Murray, 441:31May87-35
McMurtry, L. The Last Picture Show.
  R.M. Adams, 453(NYRB):13Aug87-39
McMurtry, L. Lonesome Dove.
  R.M. Adams, 453(NYRB):13Aug87-39
  R.E. Morsberger, 649(WAL):Aug86-165
McMurtry, L. Texasville.
  R.M. Adams, 453(NYRB):13Aug87-39
           [continued]

[continuing]
  J. Clute, 617(TLS):11-17Sep87-978
  L. Erdrich, 441:19Apr87-7
  T. Rafferty, 442(NY):15Jun87-92
McNab, J.P. Raymond Radiguet.
  M. Scott, 402(MLR):Jan87-207
McNamara, R. Blundering into Disaster.*
  P. Williams, 617(TLS):20-26Nov87-1270
  Lord Zuckerman, 453(NYRB):23Apr87-8
  442(NY):5Jan87-86
MacNeacail, A., ed & trans. An seachnadh
agus dàin eile.
  E.N.C., 617(TLS):5Jun87-611
MacNeice, L. Selected Literary Criticism
of Louis MacNeice. (A. Heuser, ed)
  P. Craig, 617(TLS):3Apr87-346
  P. Forbes, 362:23Apr87-28
McNeil, B., ed. Biography and Genealogy
Master Index: 1981-85 Cumulation.
  K.B. Harder, 424:Sep86-333
McNeil, B., ed. Biography and Genealogy
Master Index 1986.
  K.B. Harder, 424:Dec86-405
McNeil, M. Under the Banner of Science.
  D. King-Hele, 617(TLS):11-17Dec87-
1370
McNeil, W.K., ed. The Charm Is Broken.
  G.E. Lankford, 650(WF):Jan86-61
  E.J. Lawless, 292(JAF):Jan/Mar86-94
McNeil, W.K., ed. Ghost Stories from the
American South.
  K. Burdick, 292(JAF):Jul/Sep86-327
MacNeilage, P.F., ed. The Production of
Speech.
  T. de Graaf, 603:Vol10No2-543
McNeill, W.H. Polyethnicity and National
Unity in World History.
  A. Kuper, 617(TLS):12Jun87-630
McNeillie, A. - see Woolf, V.
MacNelly, J. One Shoe Fits All.
  M. Richler, 441:3May87-35
McParland, E. James Gandon, Vitruvius
Hibernicus.
  K. Downes, 90:Mar86-224
McPartland, M. All in Good Time.
  P. Keepnews, 441:25Oct87-57
McPhee, J. In the Highlands and Islands.
  617(TLS):30Jan87-120
Macpherson, C.B. The Rise and Fall of
Economic Justice and Other Essays.
  W. Christian, 298:Fall86-154
  J.A.W. Gunn, 529(QQ):Summer86-432
Macpherson, J. The Spirit of Solitude.*
  L. Newlyn, 541(RES):Aug86-455
  L. Weir, 131(CL):Winter86-102
McPherson, J.M. Ordeal by Fire.
  L. Shore, 106:Summer86-219
McPherson, W. To the Sargasso Sea.
  J. Leggett, 441:14Jun87-20
McQuade, D. & others, eds. The Harper
American Literature.
  B. Lee, 617(TLS):22May87-552
MacQueen, B.D. Plato's Republic in the
Monographs of Sallust.
  F.H. Mutschler, 41:Fall85-344
MacQueen, J. The Enlightenment and Scot-
tish Literature.* (Vol 1)
  J.H. Alexander, 677(YES):Vol16-231
MacQueen, J. Numerology.
  A. Dunlop, 551(RenQ):Summer86-329
  A.C. Spearing, 541(RES):Aug86-453
  J. Took, 402(MLR):Oct86-967

McQuere, G.D., eds. Russian Theoretical Thought in Music.
  D. Brown, 411:Mar86-103
McQuillan, M. Impressionist Portraits.*
  M. Pointon, 617(TLS):16Jan87-59
Macrae-Gibson, G. The Secret Life of Buildings.*
  B. Bergdoll, 505:Sep86-213
  S.W. Ksiazek, 45:Jul86-77
Macrae-Gibson, O.D., ed. The Old English Riming Poem.
  J. Roberts, 402(MLR):Apr87-434
McRea, R.G. Philosophy and the Absolute.
  T.J. Bole, 543:Dec86-390
Macready, S. & F.H. Thompson, eds. Influences in Victorian Art and Architecture.
  D. Jones, 324:Feb87-253
  J.M. Robinson, 39:Jun86-440
Macri, G., ed. "L'Enfant prodigue."
  M. Simonin, 535(RHL):Jan-Feb86-132
McRoberts, J.P. Shakespeare and the Medieval Tradition.
  B. Cohen-Stratyner, 615(TJ):Dec86-496
Macropedius, G. Two Comedies. (Y. Lindeman, ed & trans)
  R.J. Schoeck, 539:Spring87-195
MacShane, F. Into Eternity.
  A. Boyer, 395(MFS):Winter86-631
  J.M. Flora, 27(AL):Oct86-458
MacSweeney, B. Ranter.
  R. Sheppard, 617(TLS):23Jan87-92
McSweeney, K. Four Contemporary Novelists.*
  F.M. Holmes, 49:Jul86-126
  K. Hume, 402(MLR):Jul87-726
  G.D. Killam, 178:Mar86-119
McSweeney, K. "Middlemarch."*
  R. Ashton, 541(RES):May86-282
  R. O'Kell, 178:Dec86-477
  J. Preston, 402(MLR):Oct87-936
McWatters, K.G. & R. Dénier - see Stendhal
McWhirter, G. Paula Lake.*
  M. Body, 102(CanL):Winter85-142
McWilliams, J.P., Jr. Hawthorne, Melville, and the American Character.*
  H. Tulloch, 366:Spring86-128
Madan, T.N., ed. Way of Life.
  J.F. Pugh, 293(JASt):May86-633
Madden, D. Cain's Craft.
  L.D. Harred, 395(MFS):Summer86-370
Madden, D. Hidden Symptoms.
  L. Graeber, 441:15Feb87-20
Madden, T.R. Women vs. Women.
  W. Kaminer, 441:25Oct87-38
Madden-Simpson, J., ed. Woman's Part.
  J.Z. Brown, 174(Éire):Fall86-154
Maddieson, I. Patterns of Sounds.*
  R. Lass, 297(JL):Mar86-200
  W. Pagliuca & R.D. Perkins, 361:Dec86-365
Maddox, D. Semiotics of Deceit.*
  H. Arden, 589:Jul86-684
Maddox, L.B. Nabokov's Novels in English.*
  B.L. Clark, 587(SAF):Spring86-118
Madelénat, D. La biographie.*
  G. Merle, 77:Fall86-361
Madigan, P. The Modern Project To Rigor.
  D.J. Balestra, 543:Mar87-590
Madison, G.B. Understanding.*
  C.G. Prado, 154:Spring86-200
Madison, J. The Papers of James Madison. (Vols 11-14) (R.A. Rutland & others, eds)
  R.R. Beeman, 656(WMQ):Apr86-301

Madison, J. The Papers of James Madison. (Presidential Ser, Vol 1) (R.A. Rutland & others, eds)
  R.R. Beeman, 656(WMQ):Apr86-301
Mádl, A. & A. Schwob, eds. Vergleichende Literaturforschung.
  M.C. Crichton, 133:Band19Heft2-175
Madott, D. Bottled Roses.
  K. Tudor, 526:Spring86-117
Madre, A. - see Lull, R.
Madrick, J. Marrying for Money.
  R. Davenport-Hines, 617(TLS):25-31Dec87-1421
Madrick, J. Taking America.
  M. Kandel, 441:10May87-31
Madsen, A. Cousteau.
  L. Wylie, 441:8Mar87-16
Madsen, R. Morality and Power in a Chinese Village.*
  S. Harrell, 293(JASt):May86-574
Madtes, R.E. The "Ithaca" Chapter of Joyce's "Ulysses."
  J.V. Card, 329(JJQ):Winter87-230
Maeder, T. Crime and Madness.
  639(VQR):Winter86-25
Maehler, H. Die Lieder der Bakchylides.* (Pt 1)
  M.C. Howatson, 123:Vol36No2-192
Maeno, S. & K. Inazumi, comps. A Melville Lexicon.
  C. Gerrard, 541(RES):Aug86-437
Maeterlinck, M. Introduction à une psychologie des songes (1886-1896). (S. Gross, ed)
  P. Gorceix, 356(LR):Aug-Nov86-331
Maffeo, P. Fabulario.
  W. Mauro, 275(IQ):Summer86-119
Maffesoli, M. La Connaissance ordinaire.
  P. Reumaux, 450(NRF):Oct86-103
Maffi, A. Studi di epigrafia giuridica greca.
  M. Gagarin, 124:Sep-Oct86-56
Magarey, S. Unbridling the Tongues of Women.
  B. Kingston, 71(ALS):Oct86-550
Magee, J. Loyalist Mosaic.*
  C.G. Holland, 102(CanL):Winter85-127
Maggiani, A., ed. Artigianato artistico in Etruria.
  N. Spivey, 313:Vol76-281
Maggiori, R. De la convivance.
  C. Jaquillard, 98:Nov86-1120
Magi, A.P. & R. Walser, eds. Thomas Wolfe Interviewed, 1929-1938.
  L. Field, 395(MFS):Winter86-618
  J.L. Idol, Jr., 580(SCR):Fall86-92
Magliola, R. Derrida on the Mend.
  C. Koelb, 131(CL):Fall86-366
  G. O'Sullivan, 258:Mar86-95
  L. Orr, 395(MFS):Summer86-351
Maglione, S.G. - see de Vega Carpio, L.
Magnano Lampugnani, V., general ed. The Thames & Hudson Encyclopaedia of 20th-Century Architecture.* (German title: Lexikon der Architektur des 20. Jahrhunderts.)
  D.F. Anstis, 324:Jul87-614
Magnarelli, S. The Lost Rib.
  G.R. McMurray, 240(HR):Autumn86-490
  E. Skinner, 395(MFS):Winter86-647
Magner, T.F., ed. Yugoslavia in Sociolinguistic Perspective.
  R.L. Lencek, 574(SEEJ):Fall86-465

Magnet, M. Dickens and the Social Order.*
P. Brantlinger, 405(MP):May87-444
L.R. Leavis, 396(ModA):Summer/Fall86-
299
M.G. Miller, 594:Summer86-215
D. Parker, 155:Summer86-103
Magnino, D. - see Appian
Maguire, J.H., ed. The Literature of
Idaho.
O. Siporin, 649(WAL):Feb87-372
"Magyar-román filológiai Tanulmányok."
G. Piccillo, 553(RLiR):Jan-Jun86-192
"Mahābhāṣyapradīpavyākhyānāni." (M.S.
Narasiṃhācārya, ed)
J.W. de Jong, 259(IIJ):Jan86-50
Mahadevan, T.M.P. Superimposition in
Advaita Vedānta.
B. Gupta, 293(JASt):Aug86-885
Mahapatra, J. Life Signs.
U. Parameswaran, 314:Summer-Fall86-247
Mahapatra, L.N. Voices from Within.
R.K. Singh, 314:Summer-Fall86-238
Maheshwari, S.R. Political Development in
India.
N.D. Palmer, 293(JASt):Nov85-180
Mahias, M-C. Delivrance et convivalite.
R.S. Khare, 292(JAF):Oct/Dec86-473
Mahlendorf, U.R. The Wellsprings of Lit-
erary Creation.
L.B. Jennings, 301(JEGP):Oct86-635
H.M.K. Riley, 133:Band19Heft2-173
M. Swales, 402(MLR):Jul86-792
Mahler, G. Mahler's Unknown Letters. (H.
Blaukopf, ed)
D. Mitchell, 617(TLS):19Jun87-657
Mahler, G. Symphony No. 2 in C Minor
("Resurrection") Facsimile.
D. Matthews, 617(TLS):17Jul87-772
Mahler, G. & R. Strauss. Gustav Mahler/
Richard Strauss: Correspondence, 1888-
1911.* (H. Blaukopf, ed)
B. Gilliam, 317:Summer86-418
Mahmoody, B., with W. Hoffer. Not Without
My Daughter.
M. Golden, 441:27Dec87-12
Mahon, D. Antarctica.*
M. Harmon, 272(IUR):Spring86-77
J. Lanchester, 493:Jun86-113
Mahon, D. High Time (after Molière).
M. Harmon, 272(IUR):Spring86-77
Mahon, D. The Hunt by Night. Courtyards
in Delft. Poems 1962-1978.
B. Howard, 502(PrS):Fall86-128
Mahon, R. The Politics of Industrial
Restructuring.*
M.M. Atkinson, 529(QQ):Spring86-213
Mahony, R. & B. Rizzo. Christopher Smart.
M. Walsh, 541(RES):Feb86-137
Maier, D. The Theory of Relational
Databases.
J.A. Makowsky, 316:Dec86-1079
Maier, J.R., ed. El Rrey Guillelme.
S.D. Kirby, 304(JHP):Spring86-249
Maiguashca, R.U. & others. Schede di
lavoro 1 & 2.
J.B. Funigiello, 399(MLJ):Winter86-432
Mailer, C. & P. Musgrave. The History of
the Industrial Society 1918-1986. (G.
Desmons, ed)
S. Alderson, 324:Oct87-852
Mailer, F. Josef Strauss.
A. Lamb, 415:Jun86-337

Mailhot, L., with B. Melançon. Essais qué-
bécois 1837-1983.
G. Dorion, 627(UTQ):Fall86-192
Maillard, J. Adam de la Halle.
F. Suard, 554:Vol105No4-584
Maillet, A. The Devil is Loose! Maria-
agélas.
B. Godard, 99:Oct86-36
Maillo Salgado, F. Los arabismos del cas-
tellano en la Baja Edad Media (Considera-
ciones históricas y filológicas).
F. Marcos-Marín, 86(BHS):Oct86-385
Mailloux, S. Interpretive Conventions.
R. Crosman, 131(CL):Winter86-85
J.S. Whitley, 447(N&Q):Dec85-569
Maimon, E.P. & others. Writing in the Arts
and Sciences.
E.P.J. Corbett, 126(CCC):Dec86-496
Maimonides, M. Ethical Writings of Maimon-
ides (Moses ben Maimon). (R.L. Weiss &
C. Butterworth, eds)
K.M. Craig, Jr., 438:Autumn86-501
Main, J.T. Society and Economy in Colonial
Connecticut.
L. Withey, 656(WMQ):Apr86-305
Mainer, J-C., ed. Ramón J. Sender in memo-
riam.
A.M. Trippett, 86(BHS):Oct86-392
Mainwaring, S. The Catholic Church and
Politics in Brazil, 1916-1985.
D. Lehmann, 617(TLS):20Feb87-181
Maiorano, R. & V. Brooks. Balanchine's
"Mozartiana."*
R. Bailey, 151:Feb86-84
Mair, V.H. Tun-huang Popular Narratives.
L-S. Yang, 302:Vol22No1-82
A.C. Yu, 244(HJAS):Dec86-674
de Maistre, J. Écrits maçonniques de
Joseph de Maistre et quelques-uns de
ses amis francs-maçons. (J. Rebotton,
ed)
J. Brengues, 535(RHL):Mar-Apr86-294
Maitland, B. Shopping Malls.
D. Gosling, 46:Sep86-105
Maitland, S. A Book of Spells.
L. Duguid, 617(TLS):23-29Oct87-1158
L. Heron, 362:17Sep87-25
Maitland, S. & M. Wandor. Arky Types.
L. Duguid, 617(TLS):23-29Oct87-1158
362:5Nov87-31
Maja-Pearce, A. In My Father's Country.
D.A.N. Jones, 617(TLS):14Aug87-871
Majeska, G.P. Russian Travelers to Con-
stantinople in the Fourteenth and
Fifteenth Centuries.
A. Kazhdan & C. Smith, 589:Jan86-172
Major, C. Such was the Season.
A. Young, 441:13Dec87-19
Major-Poetzl, P. Michel Foucault's
Archaeology of Western Culture.*
R. McGowen, 131(CL):Spring86-181
Majorano, M., ed. Il "Roman des eles" di
Raoul de Houdenc.*
J.M. Ferrante, 589:Apr86-455
G. Hasenohr, 554:Vol105No4-576
Makin, P. Pound's "Cantos."
I.F.A. Bell, 366:Autumn86-269
N. Corcoran, 402(MLR):Apr86-464
W. Harmon, 569(SR):Fall86-630
L. Surette, 468:Fall/Winter86-307
H. Witemeyer, 30:Winter87-90
A. Woodward, 541(RES):Aug86-442
Makkreel, R.A. & F. Rodi - see Dilthey, W.

238

Makowsky, V. – see Blackmur, R.P.
Malabre, A.L., Jr. Beyond Our Means.
  A. Smith, 441:12Apr87-7
Malachy, T. La Mort en situation dans le
  théâtre contemporain.
  R. Frickx, 535(RHL):Nov-Dec86-1141
Malan, J.P., ed. South African Music Ency-
  clopedia. (Vols 1 & 4)
  J. Joubert, 617(TLS):8May87-496
Malan, J.P., ed. South African Music
  Encyclopedia. (Vols 2 & 3)
  J. Joubert, 617(TLS):8May87-496
  R. Thackeray, 415:Jun86-337
Malandra, W.M., ed & trans. An Introduc-
  tion to Ancient Iranian Religion.
  J.R. Russell, 318(JAOS):Jan/Mar85-170
Malaspina, E. Patrizio e l'acculturazione
  latina dell'Irlanda.
  M. Winterbottom, 123:Vol36No1-159
Malaurie, J. The Last Kings of Thule.
  B. Jackson, 292(JAF):Apr/Jun86-229
Malcolm, A.H. The Canadians.
  R.H. Babcock, 529(QQ):Spring86-170
  C. Bissell, 102(CanL):Spring86-144
Malcolm, A.H. This Far and No More.
  G. Hochman, 441:26Apr87-15
Malcolm, J. Gothic Pursuit.
  T.J. Binyon, 617(TLS):22May87-559
  N. Callendar, 441:1Nov87-34
Malcolm, J. In the Freud Archives.*
  W.B. Warner, 533:Winter87-122
Malcolm, J. Whistler in the Dark.*
  N. Callendar, 441:15Mar87-24
  442(NY):16Feb87-112
Malcolm, N. De Dominis (1560-1624).
  U. Limentani, 402(MLR):Jan86-225
Malcolm, N. Nothing is Hidden.
  M. Budd, 617(TLS):13Mar87-277
Malcolm, W.K. A Blasphemer and Reformer.*
  A. Stevenson, 161(DUJ):Dec85-209
Maldiney, H. Art et existence.
  F. Wybrands, 450(NRF):Jun86-90
Maleczek, W. Papst und Kardinalskolleg von
  1191 bis 1216.
  R.C. Figueira, 589:Jan86-173
Małek, E. Historia o Meluzynie.
  H. Leeming, 575(SEER):Jul86-451
Maley, C.A. Dans le Vent.* (2nd ed)
  M.R. Gitterman, 399(MLJ):Autumn86-307
Malik, H., ed. Soviet-American Relations
  with Pakistan, Iran and Afghanistan.
  M. Hauner, 617(TLS):18-24Sep87-1009
Malik, K. 26 Poems. Negatives.
  U. Parameswaran, 314:Summer-Fall86-247
Malik, Y.K., ed. South Asian Intellectuals
  and Social Change.
  M.L. Cormack, 293(JASt):May86-634
Malinowski, B. Journal d'ethnographe.
  G.A. Tiberghien, 98:May86-576
Malitz, J. Die "Historien" des Poseidon-
  ius.*
  G.J.D. Aalders H. Wzn., 394:Vol39
    fasc3/4-488
  D.E. Hahm, 303(JoHS):Vol106-217
Malkin, L. The National Debt.
  A. Balk, 441:3May87-11
Mallarmé, S. Correspondance. (Vol 8) (H.
  Mondor & L.J. Austin, eds)
  C. Chadwick, 402(MLR):Jul86-750
  D. Leuwers, 535(RHL):Mar-Apr86-323

Mallarmé, S. Correspondance.* (Vol 9)
  (H. Mondor & L.J. Austin, eds)
  C. Chadwick, 402(MLR):Jul86-750
  D. Leuwers, 535(RHL):Jul-Aug86-780
Mallarmé, S. Correspondance.* (Vols 10 &
  11) (H. Mondor & L.J. Austin, eds)
  C. Chadwick, 402(MLR):Jul86-750
Mallat, J. The Philippines.
  J.A. Larkin, 293(JASt):Feb86-456
Mallet, J. & A. Thibaut. Le manuscrits en
  écriture bénéventaine de la Bibliothèque
  capitulaire de Bénévent. (Vol 1)
  D. Williman, 589:Jan86-243
Mallet-Joris, F. Le Rire de Laura.
  P.A. Mankin, 207(FR):Feb87-432
Mallinson, G. Rumanian.
  D.R. Ladd, 350:Sep87-678
Mallinson, G.J. The Comedies of Corne-
  ille.*
  H.C. Knutson, 402(MLR):Jan86-199
Mallory, N.A. – see Ayala Mallory, N.
Malm, W.P. Six Hidden Views of Japanese
  Music.
  D. Hughes, 617(TLS):25Sep-1Oct87-1050
Malmgreen, G. Silk Town.
  M.J. Winstanley, 637(VS):Summer87-554
Malone, B.C. Country Music, U.S.A. (rev)
  C. Seemann, 292(JAF):Jul/Sep86-356
Malone, M. Handling Sin.*
  B. Morton, 617(TLS):9Jan87-42
Maloney, E. & A. Pollak. Paisley.
  C.C. O'Brien, 362:22Jan87-23
Malory, T. Caxton's Malory.* (J.W. Spisak
  & W. Matthews, eds)
  J.M. Cowen, 382(MAE):1986/2-303
  O.D. Macrae-Gibson, 541(RES):May86-246
Malotki, E. Gullible Coyote/Una' ihu.
  B. Schöler, 649(WAL):Nov86-280
Malotki, E. & M. Lomatuway'ma. Hopi Coy-
  ote Tales: Istutuwutsi.
  L. Simms, 649(WAL):May86-64
Malouf, D. Antipodes.*
  W.N., 102(CanL):Winter85-195
Maltby, R. Harmless Entertainment.
  B. Testa, 106:Winter86-525
Maltby, R., ed. Latin Love Elegy.
  H.V. Bender, 124:Jul-Aug87-463
Malter, F., with K. Kopper – see Vorländer,
  K.
Malter, R. – see Kant, I.
Malthus, R. The Works of Robert Malthus.
  (E.A. Wrigley & D. Souden, eds)
  D. Winch, 617(TLS):12Jun87-624
Maltzoff, N. Essentials of Russian Gram-
  mar.
  M.I. Levin, 558(RLJ):Winter86-212
Maltzoff, N. Everyday Conversations in
  Russian.*
  M.I. Levin, 558(RLJ):Winter86-214
Maluschke, G. Philosophische Grundlagen
  des demokratischen Verfassungsstaates.
  V. Gerhardt, 687:Apr-Jun86-313
  H. Ottmann, 489(PJGG):Band93Heft1-209
Malvern, P. Persuaders.
  W. Christian, 298:Fall86-154
Malzhan, M. Aspects of Identity.*
  P. Morère, 189(EA):Jul-Sep86-363
Mamet, D. Writing in Restaurants.*
  442(NY):19Jan87-93
Mamonsono, L-P. La nouvelle génération
  de poètes congolais.
  D. Whitman, 538(RAL):Winter86-570

de Man, J. Recollections of a Voyage to
the Philippines.
  J.A. Larkin, 293(JASt):Feb86-456
de Man, P. The Resistance to Theory.
  C. Baldick, 617(TLS):6-12Nov87-1217
de Man, P. The Rhetoric of Romanticism.*
  L.R. Furst, 301(JEGP):Jan86-90
  W. Keach, 340(KSJ):Vol35-213
  C. Norris, 577(SHR):Winter86-53
  D. Simpson, 579(SAQ):Spring86-202
  M. Storey, 175:Spring86-67
Manceaux, M. Le Voyage en Afrique de Lara
Simpson.
  M.B. St. Onge, 207(FR):Mar87-560
Mancing, H. The Chivalric World of "Don
Quijote."
  J. Ackerman, 345:Feb86-123
  G.W. Frey, 72:Band223Heft1-224
Mancini, A.N. Romanzi e romanzieri del
Seicento.
  M. Cottino-Jones, 275(IQ):Winter86-106
Mancini, F. Scritti filologici.
  F. Bruni, 379(MedR):Apr86-151
Mancini, M. La gaia scienza dei trova-
tori.*
  H-E. Keller, 589:Oct86-962
de Mandach, A. Naissance et développe-
ment de la chanson de geste en Europe.
(Vol 4)
  A. Iker-Gittleman, 545(RPh):May87-540
Mandel, E. Delightful Murder.
  B. Benstock, 454:Winter87-184
  E.S. Lauterbach, 395(MFS):Summer86-364
  P.N. Siegel, 125:Spring86-328
Mandel, M. The Collected Poems of Miriam
Mandel.* (S. Watson, ed)
  D.A. Macdonald, 102(CanL):Winter85-157
  D. Precosky, 198:Spring86-91
Mandel, O. The Book of Elaborations.
  639(VQR):Summer86-102
Mandel, O. Philoctetes and the Fall of
Troy.
  H.C. Rutledge, 124:Mar-Apr87-318
  M. Simpson, 569(SR):Spring86-xxx
  42(AR):Spring86-247
Mandelbaum, D.G. - see Sapir, E.
Mandelbaum, M. & S. Talbott. Reagan and
Gorbachev.
  M.I. Goldman, 441:25Jan87-7
Mandelker, I.L. Religion, Society, and
Utopia in Nineteenth-Century America.
  R. Muccigrosso, 125:Spring86-324
Mandell, G.P. The Phoenix Paradox.
  P. Hobsbaum, 402(MLR):Jul87-722
  V. Mahon, 541(RES):May86-292
Manders, F.W.D., ed. Bibliography of
British Newspapers: Durham and Northum-
berland.
  J. Feather, 447(N&Q):Sep85-399
de Mandiargues, A.P. Tout disparaître.
  R. Buss, 617(TLS):9-15Oct87-1116
Manessy, G. & P. Wald. Le français en
Afrique Noire.*
  N. Gueunier, 209(FM):Apr86-126
Manferlotti, S. - see Dickens, C.
Mangan, J.A. The Games Ethic and Imperial-
ism.
  W.B. Frere, 364:Apr/May86-178
  J.S. Galbraith, 637(VS):Winter87-295
Manganyi, N.C. - see Mphahlele, E.
Manger, K. Das "Narrenschiff."*
  P. Mcardle, 447(N&Q):Mar85-100

Mango, C. Byzantine Architecture.
  J.S. Curl, 324:Apr87-405
Mango, C. Le développement urbain de
Constantinople (IVe-VIIe siècles).
  A. Cameron, 303(JoHS):Vol106-266
Mango, C. & O. Pritsak, eds. Okeanos.
  H. Birnbaum, 279:Vol33-183
  S. Franklin, 575(SEER):Jan86-134
Manin, Y.I. A Course in Mathematical
Logic.
  G. Boolos, 316:Sep86-829
Mankowitz, W. Gioconda.
  J. Melmoth, 617(TLS):27Mar87-318
  L. Taylor, 362:26Mar87-29
Manley, F. & F.C. Watkins. Some Poems and
Some Talk About Poetry.
  T. Sauret, 392:Spring86-135
Mann, C. Tinsel Town.
  639(VQR):Summer86-93
Mann, D.D. A Concordance to the Plays and
Poems of Sir George Etherege.
  C. Spencer, 130:Summer86-189
Mann, H. Man of Straw (Der Untertan).
  M.W. Roche, 221(GQ):Summer86-492
Mann, J. V poiskax živoj duši.
  L. Koehler, 574(SEEJ):Fall86-442
Mann, K. Turning Point.
  K.W. Jonas, 222(GR):Summer86-118
Mann, K.B. The Language that Makes
George Eliot's Fiction.*
  T. Braun, 447(N&Q):Dec85-537
  D.P. Deneau, 268(IFR):Winter87-45
Mann, M. Fragmente eines Lebens. (F.C. &
S.P. Tubach, eds)
  K.W. Jonas, 221(GQ):Winter86-163
Mann, N. Petrarch.*
  S.P. Coy, 589:Oct86-964
  T.G. Griffith, 402(MLR):Jan86-217
  J.L. Smarr, 551(RenQ):Spring86-80
Mann, R.G. El Greco and his Patrons.*
  E. Young, 39:Jun86-440
Mann, T. Aufsätze, Reden, Essays.* (Vols
1 & 2) (H. Matter, ed)
  H. Hatfield, 406:Summer86-269
  I.B. Jonas, 406:Summer86-267
  H.R. Vaget, 406:Summer86-243
Mann, T. Pro and Contra Wagner.* (A.
Blunden, ed & trans)
  C. Hatch, 465:Summer86-189
Manning, A., ed. The Argentaye Tract.
  W.H. Clement, 382(MAE):1986/2-324
Manning, C.S. With Ears Opening Like
Morning Glories.
  K. King, 27(AL):Dec86-664
  L. Westling, 395(MFS):Summer86-272
Manning, D.J. & T.J. Robinson. The Place
of Ideology in Political Life.
  T. Modood, 161(DUJ):Jun86-395
Manning, E. Richard Jeffries.
  J.W. Blench, 161(DUJ):Dec85-205
Manning, F. The Middle Parts of Fortune.
  M.R.D. Foot, 176:Feb87-47
Manning, F.E., ed. The World of Play.
  J. Mechling, 292(JAF):Jan/Mar86-87
Manning, P. Electronic and Computer
Music.*
  S. Emmerson, 410(M&L):Oct86-435
Manning, R. A Corridor of Mirrors.
  M. Stimpson, 617(TLS):25Sep-1Oct87-
  1045
Manning, S. "Hard Times."
  A.M. Cohn, 158:Sep86-135

Mannoni, M. Un savoir qui ne sait pas.
  A. Reix, 542:Apr–Jun86–260
Mannyng, R. Robert Mannyng of Brunne:
"Handlyng Synne." (I. Sullens, ed)
  K. Bitterling, 38:Band104Heft1/2–200
  J. Weiss, 382(MAE):1986/1–132
Manoff, R.K. & M. Schudson. Reading the
News.
  S. Sadler, 441:3May87–45
Manolikakis, Y. Eleftherios Venizelos.
  N. Clive, 617(TLS):27Feb87–211
Manrique, J. Coplas a la muerte de su
padre. (C. Díaz Castañón, ed)
  J.M. Aguirre, 86(BHS):Oct86–386
Manser, A. & G. Stock, eds. The Philosophy
of F.H. Bradley.*
  P. Butchvarov, 449:Sep86–435
  D. Campbell, 518:Apr86–91
  A.C. Grayling, 479(PhQ):Jul86–438
Mansergh, N., ed. The Transfer of Power,
1942–1947. (Vols 10–12)
  L.A. Gordon, 293(JASt):May86–635
Mansfield, H.C., Jr. – see Burke, E.
Mansfield, K. The Collected Letters of
Katherine Mansfield.* (Vol 1) (V. O'Sul-
livan & M. Scott, eds)
  P. Boumelha, 541(RES):May86–292
  D. Bradshaw, 402(MLR):Jan87–192
  S. Hynes, 569(SR):Fall86–639
Mansfield, K. The Collected Letters of
Katherine Mansfield. (Vol 2) (V. O'Sul-
livan, with M. Scott, eds)
  R. Dinnage, 617(TLS):13Feb87–156
Mansfield, K. The Stories of Katherine
Mansfield. (A. Alpers, ed)
  D. Bradshaw, 402(MLR):Jan87–192
  D.M. Davin, 541(RES):Nov86–595
Mansion, S. Études Aristotéliciennes.*
  C.C.W. Taylor, 123:Vol36No1–72
Manso, P., ed. Mailer.*
  J. Braham, 395(MFS):Winter86–619
Manson, C., with N. Emmons. Manson in his
Own Words. (British title: Without Con-
science.)
  A. Friesinger, 441:25Jan87–21
  P. Highsmith, 617(TLS):12Jun87–632
  L. Taylor, 362:30Jul87–23
Manson, J. East Sutherland and Other
Poems.
  J. Caird, 571(ScLJ):Summer86–20
Manteiga, R.C., D.K. Herzberger & M.A. Com-
pitello, eds. Critical Approaches to the
Writings of Juan Benet.*
  B. Jordan, 86(BHS):Jul86–297
  N.M. Valis, 345:May86–242
Mantel, H. Vacant Possession.*
  J. Mellors, 364:Apr/May86–139
Manthey, J. Wenn Blicke zeugen könnten.
  P.M. Lützeler, 133:Band19Heft1–68
Manthorpe, V. – see Smith, R.G.
Manto, S.H. Kingdom's End and Other
Stories.
  A. Bery, 617(TLS):23–29Oct87–1175
Mantoux, T. BCBG: le guide du bon chic
bon genre.
  A. Prévos, 207(FR):Oct86–153
Manusakas, M.I. & W. Puchner. Die verges-
sene Braut.
  M. Meraklis, 196:Band27Heft3/4–353
"Manuscript Pepys 2006." [Magdalen Col-
lege, Cambridge]
  N.F. Blake, 179(ES):Dec86–565

Manzoni, A. Il Conte di Carmagnola. (G.
Bardazzi, ed)
  G. Bezzola, 228(GSLI):Vol163fasc522–304
Manzoni, A. On the Historical Novel.
  D.M. Schurman, 529(QQ):Spring86–196
Maor, E. To Infinity and Beyond.
  M. Gardner, 453(NYRB):3Dec87–34
  B.G. Yovovich, 441:27Sep87–36
Mapanje, J. & L. White, eds. Oral Poetry
from Africa.
  O. Owomoyela, 538(RAL):Spring86–137
Mapp, A.J., Jr. Thomas Jefferson.
  J. Lewis, 441:5Jul87–11
Marable, M. Black American Politics. (Vol
1)
  639(VQR):Summer86–97
Maragall, J. Obra poética. (A. Comas, ed)
  J.M. Sobré, 240(HR):Autumn86–485
  A. Yates, 402(MLR):Jan87–232
Marani, P.C. L'Architettura fortificata
negli studi di Leonardo da Vinci.
  N. Adams, 576:Dec86–413
  M. Pollak, 551(RenQ):Winter86–749
Maratos, D.C. & M.D. Hill, comps. Escri-
tores de la diáspora cubana.
  M. Goslinga, 263(RIB):Vol36No4–494
Maraval, P. – see Egeria
Maravall, J.A. Culture of the Baroque.
  J.H. Elliott, 453(NYRB):9Apr87–26
de Marbeuf, P. Le Miracle d'Amour.
  F. Wybrands, 450(NRF):Jul–Aug86–166
Marbod of Rennes. Marbodo, "Liber decem
capitulorum." (R. Leotta, ed)
  J. Ziolkowski, 589:Jul86–686
Marceau, F. La Carriole du Père Juniet.
  W. De Spens, 450(NRF):May86–88
Marceau, F. Les Passions partagées.
  D. Coward, 617(TLS):2–8Oct87–1072
Marchal, B. Lecture de Mallarmé.
  E. Souffrin-Le Breton, 208(FS):Oct86–
478
Marchand, L.A. Byron.
  R. Clarke, 362:4Jun87–48
  617(TLS):10Apr87–397
Marchand, L.A., ed. Byron's Letters and
Journals. (Vol 12: Index)
  A. Nicholson, 677(YES):Vol16–302
Marchand, P. & the Marquis d'Argens. Cor-
respondance entre Prosper Marchand et le
marquis d'Argens. (S. Larkin, ed)
  M. Carroll, 402(MLR):Oct87–958
Marchand, R. Advertising the American
Dream.*
  S. Strasser, 432(NEQ):Dec86–613
Marchello-Nizia, C. Dire le vrai.*
  R. de Gorog, 207(FR):Oct86–145
  R. Martin, 554:Vol106No1–118
Marchesault, J. Anaïs, dans la queue de
la comète.
  J. Moss, 207(FR):Apr87–728
Marchessault, J. Saga of the Wet Hens.*
  V.M. Patraka, 385(MQR):Winter87–285
Marchi, A. Lo stendhalesco don Ferrante
Pallavicino.
  V.D.L., 605(SC):15Apr87–305
Marchi, C. Impariamo l'Italiano.
  L. Repetti, 275(IQ):Spring86–103
Marci-Gómez, M. El Burgos de "Mio Cid."
  B. Taylor, 382(MAE):1986/1–153
Marciales, M. – see de Rojas, F.
Marcil-Lacoste, L. La thématique contem-
poraine de l'égalité.*
  P. Ansart, 154:Summer86–369

Marco, M.A.L. - see under Lozano Marco, M.A.

Marcondes de Souza Filho, D. Language and Action.
K. Bookman, 350:Mar87-196

Marcos, J.M. Roa Bastos, precursor del Post-Boom.*
F. Burgos, 552(REH):Oct86-120

Marcus, C.C. & W. Sarkissian, with others. Housing As If People Mattered.
T. Fisher, 505:May86-180

Marcus, G. - see Bangs, L.

Marcus, G.E. & M.M.J. Fischer. Anthropology as Cultural Critique.
J.F., 185:Jul87-891

Marcus, J., ed. Virginia Woolf.*
A. McLaurin, 447(N&Q):Dec85-545
J.M. Paul, 223:Spring86-81

Marcus, J. & Z. Tar - see Lukács, G.

Marder, A.J. Old Friends, New Enemies.
L. Allen, 161(DUJ):Dec85-184

Marder, T., ed. The Critical Edge.
D.P. Doordan, 576:Sep86-311

Mareiner, M., ed. "Frau Minne und die Liebenden."
T. Kerth, 221(GQ):Spring86-298

Marek, E. The Children at Santa Clara.
R. Brown, 441:5Apr87-26

Marek, M.J. Ekphrasis und Herrscherallegorie.
P. Holberton, 90:Apr86-294

Marek, R. Works of Genius.
H.F. Mosher, 441:30Aug87-14

Marenzio, L. Opera omnia. (Vols 4-6) (B. Meier, ed)
A. Newcomb, 317:Summer86-396

Marenzio, L. The Secular Works.* (Vols 6, 7 & 14) (S. Ledbetter & P. Myers, eds)
A. Newcomb, 317:Summer86-396

Margitic, M.R., ed. Corneille comique.
A. Niderst, 535(RHL):Sep-Oct86-908

Margolies, D. Novel and Society in Elizabethan England.*
M. Brennan, 541(RES):Aug86-410
L.S. Champion, 179(ES):Aug86-370
M. Zell, 366:Autumn86-251

Margolis, A.T. Henry James and the Problem of Audience.
M.B., 295(JML):Nov86-490
M. Jacobson, 27(AL):Dec86-638

Margolis, J. Philosophy of Psychology.
J. Russell, 518:Jan86-48

Margolis, J. Pragmatism without Foundations.
P. Smith, 617(TLS):4-11Sep87-963

Margolis, M.L. Mothers and Such.
K. Lystra, 250(HLQ):Autumn86-423

Margulis, L. & D. Sagan. Microcosmos.*
M. Ridley, 617(TLS):10Jul87-753

Margulis, L. & D. Sagan. Origins of Sex.
R. Beddington, 617(TLS):6Mar87-239

Marías, F. La arquitectura del Renacimiento en Toledo (1541-1631). (Vols 1 & 2)
J.B. Bury, 90:Feb86-154

Marie, C.P. Le Sens sous les mots.
G. Cesbron, 535(RHL):Sep-Oct86-961

Marie de France. The Fables of Marie de France. (M.L. Martin, trans)
G.S. Burgess, 589:Jan86-244
E.J. Mickel, 545(RPh):May87-534

Marienstras, R. New Perspectives on the Shakespearean World.*
N. Grene, 189(EA):Jan-Mar87-83

Marietta, J.D. The Reformation of American Quakerism, 1748-1783.
T. Bassett, 656(WMQ):Apr86-316
B.S. Schlenther, 83:Autumn86-210

Marigny, J. Le Vampire dans la littérature anglo-saxonne.
J. Finné, 189(EA):Oct-Dec87-457

Marín, J.L.M. - see under Morales y Marín, J.L.

Marin, N., ed. The French Businessmate.
D.E. Rivas, 399(MLJ):Winter86-426

Marín, N. - see de Vega Carpio, L.

Marinoni, B.C., G. Cusatelli & M. Secchi - see under Cetti Marinoni, B., G. Cusatelli & M. Secchi

Marion, J-L., with J. Deprun, eds. La passion de la raison.
F. de Buzon, 192(EP):Jul-Sep86-415

Marius, R. Thomas More.*
B. Bickers, 161(DUJ):Jun86-351

Mariuz, A. L'opera completa del Piazzetta.
A. Binion, 54:Dec86-680

de Marivaux, P.C.D. Le Prince travesti; Le Triomphe de l'amour. (H. Coulet & M. Gilot, eds)
D.J. Culpin, 208(FS):Apr86-211

Mark, J. Zeno Was Here.
L. Duguid, 617(TLS):3Jul87-715

Mark, J.P. The Empire Builders.
J. Friedman, 441:25Oct87-39

Markels, R.B. A New Perspective on Cohesion in Expository Paragraphs.
S. Stotsky, 126(CCC):Dec86-489

Marker, G. Publishing, Printing and the Origins of Intellectual Life in Russia, 1700-1800.*
W.G. Jones, 575(SEER):Oct86-609
K.J. McKenna, 574(SEEJ):Winter86-567
M.J. Okenfuss, 550(RusR):Apr86-225
C. Thomas, 354:Dec86-379
639(VQR):Winter86-8

Markham, B. The Splendid Outcast. (M.S. Lovell, comp)
D. Ackerman, 441:23Aug87-1

Markham, E.A. Family Matters.
T. Eagleton, 565:Autumn86-76

Markham, E.J. Saibara.*
H. Burnett, 414:Vol72No1-133
A. Gatten, 293(JASt):Aug86-850

Markham, S. John Loveday of Caversham 1711-1789.
L. Mitchell, 447(N&Q):Jun85-267

Markie, P.J. Descartes's Gambit.
R. Malpas, 617(TLS):10Apr87-380

Countess Markievicz. Prison Letters of Countess Markievicz.
617(TLS):7Aug87-854

Markiewicz, H. Wymiary dzieła literackiego.
H. Jechova, 549(RLC):Apr-Jun86-231

Markkanen, R. Cross-Language Studies in Pragmatics.
L.F. Bouton, 350:Mar87-197

"Marko the Prince." (A. Pennington & & P. Levi, trans)
J. Greening, 4:Autumn86-80

Markovits, C. Indian Business and Nationalist Politics, 1931-1939.
T.A. Timberg, 293(JASt):Aug86-886

Marks, G.A. & C.B. Johnson – see "Harrap's Slang Dictionary: English–French/French–English"

Marks, P. American Literary and Drama Reviews.
J.J. Savory, 635(VPR):Summer86–73

Marks, P. Skullduggery.
P. McGrath, 441:23Aug87–11

Marks, R. Burrell.
E. Schaper, 89(BJA):Winter86–84

Marks, S. The Ambiguities of Dependence in South Africa.
I. Schapera, 617(TLS):20Feb87–190

Marlatt, D. Touch to My Tongue.
D. Bennett, 102(CanL):Winter85–152

van Marle, J. On the Paradigmatic Dimension of Morphological Creativity.*
W. Zonneveld, 204(FdL):Mar86–64

Marling, K.A. Tom Benton and His Drawings.*
T. Anderson, 709:Spring87–181

Marlow, E. & V. Morrison. A La Page.*
J.C. Evans, 399(MLJ):Spring86–63

Marlowe, C. Dr. Faustus: The A-Text. (D. Ormerod & C. Wortham, eds)
B.E. Brandt, 111:Fall87–9
J.S. Ryan, 67:Nov86–316

Marlowe, S. The Memoirs of Christopher Columbus.
P. Reading, 617(TLS):6Mar87–245

Marmo, V. Dalle fonti alle forme.*
E. Urbina, 240(HR):Winter86–87

Marmor, T.R. Political Analysis and American Medical Care.
M.J.M., 185:Jan87–513

Marnham, P. So Far from God.
639(VQR):Winter86–23

Marnham, P. Trail of Havoc.
J. Symons, 617(TLS):4–10Dec87–1346
B. Woffinden, 362:22Oct87–28

Maron, M. Flight of Ashes.
J. Lucraft, 617(TLS):28Aug87–932
C. Wheatley, 362:1Jan87–20

Marotta, K. A Piece of Earth.*
G. Davenport, 569(SR):Spring86–296

Marotti, A.F. John Donne, Coterie Poet.
A.F. Kinney, 115:Fall86–538

Marples, D.R. Chernobyl and Nuclear Power in the USSR.
R. Wilson, 441:1Feb87–31

Marqués, M.B.M. – see under Mena Marqués, M.B.

Marquess, W.H. Lives of the Poet.
E. Crichton-Miller, 617(TLS):9Jan87–43

Marquet, J-F. – see Schelling, F.J.W.

Márquez, G.G. – see under García Márquez, G.

Marqusee, M. Slow Turn.*
A. Ross, 364:Oct86–106

Marr, D. – see Tran Tu Binh

Marra, M. – see "I racconti di Ise (Ise Monogatari)"

Marras, S. Macías.
F. de Toro, 352(LATR):Spring87–144

Marriott, A. A Long Way to Oregon.
R.W. Harvey, 102(CanL):Winter85–170

Marrs, E.W., Jr., comp. A Descriptive Catalogue of the Letters of Charles and Mary Anne Lamb in the W. Hugh Peal Collection, University of Kentucky Libraries.
W.F. Courtney, 340(KSJ):Vol35–211

Marrus, M.R. The Holocaust in History.
D.S. Wyman, 441:22Nov87–38

Marrus, M.R. The Unwanted.*
R.A. Cooper, 390:Nov86–57
C. Strom, 99:Nov86–41

Mars-Jones, A. & E. White. The Darker Proof.
A. Hollinghurst, 617(TLS):10Jul87–740

Marsack, R. The Cave of Making.*
J.C. Beckett, 402(MLR):Apr86–467

Marschall, R. – see Dr. Seuss

Marsden, S. The Haunted Realm.
P-L. Adams, 61:Apr87–91

Marsh, C. M.A. Voloshin.
A. Pyman, 575(SEER):Apr86–278
R.D.B. Thomson, 402(MLR):Jan86–269

Marsh, D. Glory Days.
P. Watrous, 441:5Jul87–7

Marsh, J. Jane and May Morris.
P. Faulkner, 326:Spring87–32
R. Mander, 617(TLS):31Jul87–816

Marsh, J. Pre-Raphaelite Sisterhood.*
Q. Bell, 90:Jan86–47
B.J. Dunlap, 635(VPR):Fall86–117
R. Mander, 39:Jan86–69

Marsh, P. & P. Collett. Driving Passion.*
G. Johnson, 441:19Apr87–17

Marsh, R.J. Soviet Fiction since Stalin.
R. Bowie, 295(JML):Nov86–378

Marshal, A. Mr. Marshal's Flower Album.
V. Powell, 39:Apr86–288

Marshall, B.A. A Historical Commentary on Asconius.*
A.W. Ward, 24:Winter86–605

Marshall, F. Charlotte Deans (1768–1859).
R. FitzSimons, 611(TN):Vol40No1–36

Marshall, G.C. The Papers of George Catlett Marshall. (Vol 2) (L.I. Bland, ed)
H. Brogan, 617(TLS):2Jan87–9

Marshall, J.D. – see Powell, L.C.

Marshall, M. Gentlemen and Players.
N. Andrew, 362:3Dec87–34

Marshall, M.F. & J. Todd. English Congregational Hymns in the Eighteenth Century.
W. Hutchings, 402(MLR):Apr86–445

Marshall, P.H. William Godwin.*
J.K. Chandler, 402(MLR):Jan87–173
D. McCracken, 405(MP):Aug86–99
W. Stafford, 366:Autumn86–255
R.M. Wardle, 340(KSJ):Vol35–205

Marshall, R. Unheard Voices.
H. Goodman, 441:17May87–51

Marshall, R.C. Collective Decision Making in Rural Japan.*
W.W. Kelly, 293(JASt):Nov85–154

Marshall, T. Dance of the Particles.
B. Whiteman, 102(CanL):Summer86–124

Marshall, T. Glass Houses.
M. Goldman, 376:Jun86–117

Marshall, W. Frogmouth.
N. Callendar, 441:16Aug87–21
G. Kaufman, 362:26Nov87–29

Marshall, W. Manila Bay.
N. Callendar, 441:8Feb87–20

Marshall, W. Yellowthread Street. The Hatchet Man. Gelignite. The Faraway Man.
G. Kaufman, 362:26Nov87–29

Marsolo, P.M. Secondo libro dei madrigali a quattro voci (1614). (L. Bianconi, ed)
A. Newcomb, 317:Summer86–396

Martineau, H. Harriet Martineau on Women.
(G.G. Yates, ed)
  R. Sheets, 637(VS):Autumn86–145
Martinengo, A. La astrología en la obra de
Quevedo.
  R.M. Price, 86(BHS):Jul86–288
Martines, L. Society and History in
English Renaissance Verse.
  J.E. Van Domelen, 568(SCN):Spring–
  Summer86–13
  C. Wortham, 67:Nov86–301
  639(VQR):Summer86–87
Martinet, A. Des steppes aux océans.
  S.M. Embleton, 350:Jun87–426
  J.A.C. Greppin, 617(TLS):23Jan87–94
Martinet, A. Syntaxe générale.
  D.K. Nylander, 350:Jun87–423
Martínez, J.L. Pasajeros de Indias.
  J.S. Cummins, 86(BHS):Apr86–160
Martínez, P.N.I. & M.D. Pérez García – see
under Ibáñez Martínez, P.N. & M.D. Pérez
García
Martínez Díez, G., with J.M. Ruiz Asencio,
eds. Leyes de Alfonso X. (Vol 1)
  R.A. MacDonald, 304(JHP):Spring86–253
"Simone Martini e 'Chompagni.'"
  C. Gould, 39:Jun86–441
di Martino, F., L. Rossetti & P.P. Rosati.
Eraclito.
  J. Barnes, 520:Vol31No3–280
de Martinoir, F. Arrêt sur image.
  A. Clerval, 450(NRF):Nov86–101
Martinoni, R. Gian Vincenzo Imperiale
Politico, letterato e collezionista geno-
vese del seicento.
  T.J. Standring, 551(RenQ):Winter86–747
Martins, M.T.H-S. – see under Hundertmark-
Santos Martins, M.T.
Martinson, S.D. – see Schlegel, J.E.
Marton, K. An American Woman.
  N. Darnton, 441:24May87–12
Marty, E. L'Écriture du jour.*
  D.H. Walker, 208(FS):Jul86–351
Marty, M.E. Modern American Religion.
(Vol 1)
  J.M. Cooper, Jr., 441:4Jan87–13
Märtz, K. Sexualität und Macht.
  K. Heitmann, 72:Band223Heft2–448
Martz, L. Poverty and Welfare in Habsburg
Spain.
  R.A. Stradling, 86(BHS):Jul86–290
Martz, L.L. – see H.D.
Martz, L.L. – see Herbert, G. & H. Vaughan
Marún, G. Orígenes del costumbrismo ético-
social – Addison y Steele.
  P.J. Guinard, 547(RF):Band98Heft1/2–232
Marvell, A. Complete Poetry. (G.D. Lord,
ed)
  T.N. Corns, 402(MLR):Jul87–705
Marvick, E.W. Louis XIII.
  J.H. Elliott, 453(NYRB):11Jun87–40
Marvick, L.W. Mallarmé and the Sublime.
  U. Franklin, 115:Fall86–542
Marwedel, R. Theodor Lessing 1872–1933.
  G. Steiner, 617(TLS):26Jun87–683
Marx, H. Deutsche in der Neuen Welt.
  H. Weydt, 406:Fall86–380
Marx, J. Tiphaigne de La Roche.
  G. Cesbron, 356(LR):May86–177
"Karl Marx: A Reader." (J. Elster, ed)
  A. Ryan, 617(TLS):13Feb87–155
Marx, L. Benny Andersen.*
  B. Elbrønd-Bek, 562(Scan):May86–96

Marx, S. A Gaudy Spree.
  R. Dooley, 441:31May87–43
Marx, W. The Philosophy of F.W.J. Schel-
ling.*
  M.G. Vater, 319:Apr87–302
Marzolph, U., ed. Persische Märchen Minia-
turen.
  B. Hoffmann, 196:Band27Heft1/2–126
Marzolph, U. Der weise Narr Buhlūl.*
  W. Madelung, 294:Vol17–146
no Masafusa, Ō. – see under Ōe no Masa-
fusa
Masaoka, M., with B. Hosokawa. They Call
Me Moses Masaoka.
  D. MacEachron, 441:29Nov87–31
Masařík, Z. Die frühneuhochdeutsche
Geschäftssprache in Mähren.
  W.P. Ahrens, 350:Jun87–431
  E. Skála, 597(SN):Vol58No2–273
Mascoli, L. Le "Voyage de Naple" (1719) de
Ferdinand Delamonce.
  J. Geffriaud-Rosso, 535(RHL):Sep–Oct86–
  917
Masing-Delic, I., ed. Slavic Culture.
  H. Goscilo, 574(SEEJ):Winter86–570
Maslow, J.E. Bird of Life, Bird of Death.*
  S. White, 448:Vol24No3–95
  362:17Sep87–24
Mason, A. Ports of Entry.*
  E.U. Irving, 399(MLJ):Spring86–90
Mason, B.A. In Country.*
  T. McGonigle, 532(RCF):Summer86–155
  639(VQR):Spring86–56
Mason, C. The Poet Robert Browning and
his Kinsfolk by his Cousin Cyrus Mason.
(W.C. Turner, ed)
  P. Drew, 402(MLR):Jul87–710
Mason, H. Cyrano de Bergerac: "L'Autre
Monde."*
  G.J. Mallinson, 402(MLR):Apr87–474
Mason, H. – see "Studies on Voltaire and
the Eighteenth Century"
Mason Rinaldi, S. Palma il Giovane.
  D. Rosand, 54:Jun86–336
Mass, E. Literatur und Zensur in der
frühen Aufklärung.
  H. Mattauch, 72:Band223Heft1–209
Mass, J.P. & W.B. Hauser, eds. The Bakufu
in Japanese History.
  C. Steenstrup, 407(MN):Autumn86–361
Massara, G. Americani.
  L.A. Losito, 276:Winter86–405
Massard, J. Nous Gens de Ganchong.
  C. Laderman, 293(JASt):May86–658
Massey, E.G., ed. Bittersweet Earth.
  W.M. Clements, 650(WF):Oct86–293
Massie, A. Augustus.*
  P. Vansittart, 364:Oct86–101
Masson, J.M. The Assault on Truth.*
  J.L. De Vitis, 577(SHR):Summer86–289
  W.B. Warner, 533:Winter87–122
  J.O. Wisdom, 488:Mar86–135
Masson, J.M. – see Freud, S.
Masson, P. André Gide: Voyage et écri-
ture.*
  D. Moutote, 535(RHL):Jan–Feb86–163
de Massy, C. & C. Higham. Palace.
  H. Neill, 362:16Jul87–24
Mast, G. Howard Hawks: Storyteller.
  C. Zucker, 106:Summer86–251
Masters, A. Literary Agents.
  D.A.N. Jones, 362:29Oct87–30

Masters, H. Cooper.
  A. Bellow, 441:13Sep87-34
Masters, O. Amy's Children.
  H. Jacobson, 617(TLS):27Nov-3Dec87-
  1307
Masters, O. A Long Time Dying.
  J. Perlez, 441:15Mar87-16
Masumi Junnosuke. Postwar Politics in
  Japan, 1945-1955.
  G.D. Hook, 285(JapQ):Oct-Dec86-439
Mat, M., ed. Problèmes d'Histoire du
  Christianisme.
  R. Waller, 83:Spring86-118
Mata, A.F. - see under Franco Mata, A.
Matejka, L. & B. Stolz- see "Cross Cur-
  rents"
Materer, T. - see Pound, E. & W. Lewis
Maternicki, J. Historiografia polska XX
  wieku. (Pt 1)
  A.A. Hetnal, 497(PolR):Vol31No4-331
Mates, B. The Philosophy of Leibniz.
  S. Brown, 617(TLS):1May87-468
  I. Hacking, 543:Dec86-387
Mathabane, M. Kaffir Boy.*
  D. Papineau, 617(TLS):21Aug87-894
Matheopoulos, H. Divo.
  B. Holland, 441:11Jan87-15
Mather, C. & S. Woods. Santa Fe Style.
  R.M. Adams, 453(NYRB):26Mar87-32
Matheson, D. Stray Cat.
  N. Callendar, 441:13Sep87-46
  442(NY):28Sep87-98
Mathews, H. Cigarettes.
  L. Zeidner, 441:29Nov87-23
Mathews, N.M. Mary Cassatt.
  K. Adler, 617(TLS):28Aug87-923
Mathews, R. Blood Ties and Other Stories.*
  R.B. Endres, 102(CanL):Winter85-160
Mathias, E. & R. Raspa. Italian Folktales
  in America.
  W.E. Simeone, 292(JAF):Oct-Dec86-479
Mathias, J. & T.L. Kennedy, eds. Comput-
  ers, Language Reform, and Lexicography in
  China.
  N-P. Chan, 302:Vol22No1-84
Mathieu, J-C. La Poésie de René Char ou
  Le Sel de la splendeur.*
  M. Cranston, 207(FR):Apr87-718
  M.J. Worton, 208(FS):Jul86-360
Mathis, E. Natural Prey.
  N. Callendar, 441:11Oct87-24
Matich, O. & M. Heim, eds. The Third
  Wave.*
  M.G. Basker, 402(MLR):Jul86-814
Matos, C.A.R. - see under Rodríguez Matos,
  C.A.
Matray, J.I. The Reluctant Crusade.
  Hakjoon Kim, 293(JASt):May86-618
Matsueda, P. The Fish Catcher.
  J. Carter, 219(GaR):Summer86-532
Matte, E.J. Histoire des modes phoné-
  tiques du français.*
  F. Abel, 72:Band223Heft1-234
Matter, H. - see Mann, T.
Mattesini, E. Il "Diario" in volgare
  quattrocentesco di Antonio Lotieri de
  Pisano notaio in Nepi.
  P. Trifone, 708:Vol12fasc2-258
Matteson, M.M. Bienvenidos al español.
  W.D. Baker, 238:Sep86-567
Matthee, D. Fiela's Child.*
  42(AR):Summer86-379

Mattheier, K.J., ed. Aspekte der Dialekt-
  theorie.
  D. Stellmacher, 260(IF):Band91-353
Matthes, L. Vaudeville.*
  W. Asholt, 72:Band223Heft2-443
Matthew, H.C.G. Gladstone 1809-1874.
  A. Hartley, 176:Apr87-57
Matthew, H.C.G. - see Gladstone, W.E.
Matthews, D. Beethoven.*
  R. Anderson, 415:Jul86-387
  J. Rushton, 410(M&L):Oct86-419
Matthews, D. A Course in Nepali.
  S. Lienhard, 318(JAOS):Oct/Dec85-806
Matthews, E. The Structured World of Jorge
  Guillén.
  A.P. Debicki, 240(HR):Summer86-352
Matthews, G. Heart of the Country.*
  A. Ronald, 649(WAL):Feb87-354
Matthews, J. Crazy Women.*
  G. Locklin, 573(SSF):Spring86-212
  E. Sparkes, 376:Jun86-119
Matthews, J. Ghostly Populations.
  C. Benfey, 441:1Feb87-20
Matthews, J.H. Languages of Surrealism.
  B.L. Knapp, 593:Fall86-235
Matthews, J.H. Surrealism, Insanity, and
  Poetry.
  W. Bohn, 131(CL):Winter86-108
  M. Cottenet-Hage, 345:Feb86-124
Matthews, M. Poverty in the Soviet Union.
  R. Pearson, 362:19Feb87-27
Matthews, R.K. The Radical Politics of
  Thomas Jefferson.
  E. Cassara, 656(WMQ):Jan86-150
  F. Shuffelton, 173(ECS):Winter86/87-265
Matthews, T.S. Angels Unawares.
  639(VQR):Spring86-46
Matthews, W. Foreseeable Futures.
  J.D. McClatchy, 441:26Jul87-9
Matthias, J. Northern Summer.
  R. Pybus, 565:Spring86-71
Matthiessen, P. Nine-Headed Dragon River.*
  M. Pye, 617(TLS):17Jul87-777
  362:5Nov87-31
Matthieu, P. Clytemnestre. (G. Ernst, ed)
  H. Ingman, 208(FS):Oct86-452
Mattina, A. - see Seymour, P.J.
Matyjaszkiewicz, K., ed. James Tissot.
  R. Thomson, 59:Mar86-108
Maubrey-Rose, V. The Anti-Representa-
  tional Response.
  M-C. Pasquier, 189(EA):Jan-Mar87-110
  D. Robinson, 597(SN):Vol58No2-267
Maugham, W.S. The Letter. (U. Hiller, ed)
  C. Jansohn, 72:Band223Heft1-185
de Maupassant, G. Seven Stories of Guy de
  Maupassant. (R. Nybakken & H. Silver,
  eds)
  R.B. Grant, 207(FR):May87-882
Mauquoy-Hendrickx, M. Les estampes des
  Wierix.*
  A.E.C. Simoni, 354:Mar86-83
Maurais, J., ed. La crise des langues.
  P. Hagiwara, 399(MLJ):Autumn86-300
  E. Martin, 209(FM):Oct86-255
Maurer, A. - see Siger de Brabant
Maurer-Schmoock, S. Deutsche Theater im
  18. Jahrhundert.
  G. Bersier, 406:Spring86-81
Mauriac, C. Mauriac et fils.
  G.R. Besser, 207(FR):May87-911
Maurice. Strategikon.
  W. Treadgold, 589:Jan86-176

Mauron, C. & F-X. Emmanuelli. Textes poli-
tiques de l'époque révolutionnaire en
langue provençale. (Vol 1)
  C. Rostaing, 553(RLiR):Jan-Jun86-266
Maury, L. Piaget et l'enfant.
  E. Jalley, 542:Jan-Mar86-153
Maus, K.E. Ben Jonson and the Roman
Frame of Mind.
  D. McPherson, 481(PQ):Spring86-281
  R.S. Miola, 24:Fall86-446
  F. Teague, 130:Summer86-180
Mautner, F.H. - see Lichtenberg, G.C.
Maxmen, J.S. The New Psychiatry.
  639(VQR):Winter86-31
Maxwell, A.E. Gatsby's Vineyard.
  442(NY):14Sep87-136
Maxwell, D.E.S. A Critical History of Mod-
ern Irish Drama 1891-1980.*
  B. Benstock, 659(ConL):Spring87-121
  K. Dorn, 610:Spring86-77
  J.E. Dunleavy, 177(ELT):Vol29No2-229
  H. Hunt, 611(TN):Vol40No1-38
  S. Watt, 301(JEGP):Oct86-583
May, K.M. Ibsen and Shaw.
  C.A. Berst, 177(ELT):Vol29No3-317
  G.M. Crane, 615(TJ):Dec86-511
May, R. Law and Society East and West.
  R.W. Lariviere, 293(JASt):Aug86-811
  V.R., 185:Jan87-499
May, R.E. John A. Quitman, Old South Cru-
sader.
  K.R. Johnson, 9(AlaR):Jul86-220
May, S. Cambodian Witness.* (J. Fenton,
ed)
  P-L. Adams, 61:Feb87-95
  R. Nalley, 441:18Jan87-19
Mayakovsky, V. Love is the Heart of Every-
thing.* (B. Jangfeldt, ed)
  A. McMillin, 402(MLR):Jul87-810
Mayakovsky, V.V. The Bedbug. (R. Russell,
ed)
  P. Doyle, 402(MLR):Apr87-538
Mayakovsky, V.V. Klop. (R. Russell, ed)
  R. Aizlewood, 575(SEER):Oct86-598
Mayer, A. La persistance de l'ancien
régime.
  H. Dufourt, 98:Apr86-316
Mayer, C-A. Lucien de Samosate et la Ren-
aissance française.
  F-R. Hausmann, 72:Band223Heft1-205
Mayer, F.H., ed & trans. Ancient Tales in
Modern Japan.*
  N. Naumann, 196:Band27Heft3/4-355
  N.M. Ochner, 293(JASt):May86-608
Mayer, H. A Son of Thunder.*
  639(VQR):Autumn86-122
Mayer, H.E. Mélanges sur l'histoire du
royaume latin de Jérusalem.
  J.A. Brundage, 589:Oct86-1028
Mayer, M. Making News.
  J.H. Jaffe, 441:3May87-22
  D. Schorr, 18:Jul/Aug87-60
Mayer, T.M. - see "Georg Büchner Jahrbuch"
Mayerthaler, E. Unbetonter Vokalismus und
Silbenstruktur im Romanischen.
  E. Diekmann, 72:Band223Heft1-201
Mayerthaler, W. Morphologische Natürlich-
keit.
  J. Klausenburger, 320(CJL):Winter86-327
Mayhew, L. - see "Monkey's Raincoat
(Sarumino)"

Maynard, F. Les Lettres du Président May-
nard. (J-P. Lassalle, ed)
  P. Wolfe, 475:Vol13No24-403
Maynard, J. Charlotte Brontë and Sexual-
ity.*
  P. Boumelha, 175:Spring86-78
  J.E. Hogle, 405(MP):Feb87-331
  K. Sutherland, 402(MLR):Oct87-927
  A. Trodd, 366:Autumn86-263
  M. Vicinus, 141:Summer86-350
Maynard, J. Domestic Affairs.
  F.W. Burck, 441:19Jul87-20
Maynes, M.J. Schooling in Western Europe.
  S.S. Bryson, 207(FR):May87-894
Mayo, P.J. The Morphology of Aspect in
Seventeenth-Century Russian (Based on
the Texts of the Smutnoe Vremja).
  J.A. Dunn, 402(MLR):Apr87-532
  F.Y. Gladney, 574(SEEJ):Fall86-461
Mayrhofer, M., ed. Indogermanische Gram-
matik. (Vol 1)
  J.S. Klein, 350:Jun87-407
Mayröcker, F. Dal Anheben der Arme bei
Feuersglut.
  B. Bjorklund, 133:Band18Heft4-383
Mazouer, C. Le Personnage du naïf dans le
théâtre comique du Moyen Age à Mari-
vaux.
  C. Jordens, 356(LR):Feb86-69
Mazur, G. The Pose of Happiness.
  R. McDowell, 249(HudR):Winter87-685
Mazuzan, G.T. & J.S. Walker. Controlling
the Atom.
  A. Roland, 579(SAQ):Spring86-192
Mazzacurati, G. Il Rinascimento dei
moderni.
  M. Pozzi, 228(GSLI):Vol163fasc524-617
Mazzarella, S. & R. Zanca. Il libro delle
torri.
  W. Krönig, 683:Band49Heft3-414
Mazzaro, J. The Figure of Dante.
  G. Costa, 545(RPh):Nov86-215
  V. Tripodi, 345:Feb86-119
Mazzini, I. - see Flammini, G.
"Angiolo Mazzoni (1894-1979)."
  N. Miller, 576:Mar86-74
Mazzoni, G. On the Defense of the Comedy
of Dante.*
  C. Grayson, 402(MLR):Jan86-227
Mazzoni, S. & O. Guaita. Il teatro di Sab-
bioneta.
  M. Marti, 228(GSLI):Vol163fasc521-140
Mazzotta, C. - see Alfieri, V.
Mazzotta, G. The World at Play in Boccac-
cio's "Decameron."*
  G.L. Lucente, 400(MLN):Dec86-1263
Mdo-mkhar Tshe-ring. Mi-dbang rtogs-
brjod. (Zhuang Jing, ed)
  L.W.J. van der Kuijp, 318(JAOS):
  Apr/Jun85-321
Meacham, S. Toynbee Hall and Social
Reform, 1880-1914.
  P. Thomas, 441:27Dec87-12
Mead, W.R. Mortal Splendor.
  R. Rothenberg, 441:17May87-11
Méchoulan, H. - see Bukofzer, M.
"Medieval Latin Poems of Male Love and
Friendship." (T. Stehling, trans)
  J. Ziolkowski, 589:Jul86-706
Medina, C.D. - see under de Araújo Medina,
C.

Medvedev, P.N. The Formal Method in Literary Study.
D.H. Richter, 599:Fall86-411
Mee, C.L., Jr. The Genius of the People.
J.N. Rakove, 441:15Mar87-3
Meehan, E. Reasoned Argument in the Social Sciences.
D.P. McCaffrey, 488:Jun86-257
Meerhoff, K. Rhétorique et Poétique au XVIe siècle en France.
C. Beuermann, 210(FrF):Sep86-372
Meeropol, R. & M. We Are Your Sons.
L. Mansnerus, 441:29Mar87-23
Meese, E.A. Crossing the Double-Cross.
E.C.R., 295(JML):Nov86-366
Megged, M. Dialogue in the Void.
P. West, 473(PR):Vol53No3-471
Megill, A. Prophets of Extremity.*
D. Carrier, 89(BJA):Summer86-288
Mehl, D. Die Tragödien Shakespeares.*
M. Draudt, 38:Band104Heft1/2-222
K. Otten, 72:Band223Heft1-166
Mehlman, J. Legacies of Anti-Semitism in France.
S. Petit, 345:Nov86-493
Mehnert, K. The Russians and Their Favorite Books.
J. Brooks, 550(RusR):Jan86-101
Mehta, M.M. Gīrvāṇa-Bhāratī.
E. Bender, 318(JAOS):Oct/Dec85-812
Mehta, V. Sound Shadows of the New World.*
P. Kemp, 617(TLS):13-19Nov87-1258
362:3Sep87-29
Mei-hui, W. - see under Wen Mei-hui
Mei-ling, H. - see under Huang Mei-ling
Meid, V. Grimmelshausen.
G. Hoffmeister, 221(GQ):Winter86-131
Meid, V. & others, eds. Gedichte und Interpretationen.
R. Dove, 402(MLR):Jul86-776
Meid, W. & K. Heller. Italienische Interferenzen in der lautlichen Struktur des Zimbrischen.
K. Rein, 685(ZDL):1/1986-99
Meid, W. & K. Heller, eds. Sprachkontakt als Ursache von Veränderungen der Sprach- und Bewusstseinsstruktur.
K. Rein, 685(ZDL):1/1986-78
Meier, B. - see Marenzio, L.
Meier, H. Notas críticas al "Diccionario crítico etimológico castellano e hispánico" de Corominos/Pascual: Verba.*
Y. Malkiel, 545(RPh):Nov86-181
Meier, H. Prinzipien der etymologischen Forschung.
A. Zamboni, 547(RF):Band98Heft3/4-394
Meier, S. Animation and Mechanization in the Novels of Charles Dickens.
K. Tetzeli von Rosador, 72:Band223 Heft1-231
Meier, W. Bibliography of African Languages.
S. Brauner, 682(ZPSK):Band39Heft5-621
Meigs, A.S. Food, Sex, and Pollution.
J.M. Blythe, 293(JASt):Aug86-797
Meijer, B.W. I grandi disegni italiani del Teylers Museum di Haarlem.
J.B. Shaw, 90:Jul86-513
Meijer, E. Treasures from the Rijksmuseum Amsterdam.
E. Young, 39:May86-367

Meijer, F. A History of Seafaring in the Classical World.
G.S. Kirk, 617(TLS):15May87-527
Meijer, L.C. Eine strukturelle Analyse der Hagia Triada-Tafeln.
G.A. Rendsburg, 318(JAOS):Jan/Mar85-143
Meikle, S. Essentialism in the Thought of Karl Marx.
A. Collier, 262:Dec86-459
G. MacDonald, 518:Apr86-93
A. Reix, 542:Jan-Mar86-129
Meindl, D., ed. Zur Literatur und Kultur Kanadas.
G. Düsterhaus, 72:Band223Heft1-233
Meindl, D., F. Horlacher & M. Christadler, eds. Mythos und Aufklärung in der amerikanischen Literatur/Myth and Enlightenment in American Literature.
R. Asselineau, 189(EA):Jan-Mar87-109
Meineke, E. Saint-Mihiel Bibliothèque Municipale Ms. 25.
A. Schwarz, 685(ZDL):2/1986-215
H. Tiefenbach, 260(IF):Band91-422
Meinig, D.W. The Shaping of America.* (Vol 1)
H. Brogan, 324:Nov87-947
G. Wills, 617(TLS):17Apr87-405
Meininger, A-M. - see Monnier, H.
Meiring, D. A Talk with the Angels.
P. Lewis, 565:Spring86-38
Meisel, M. Realizations.*
G. Levine, 405(MP):Nov86-233
J. Viscomi, 591(SIR):Winter86-561
Meisel, P. The Myth of the Modern.
J.D. Bloom, 441:20Dec87-17
Meisel, P. & W. Kendrick - see Strachey, J. & A.
Meisenburg, T. Die soziale Rolle des Okzitanischen in einer kleinen Gemeinde im Languedoc (Lacaune/Tarn).
H.P. Kunert, 547(RF):Band98Heft3/4-403
Meissburger, G. Einführung in die mediävistische Germanistik.
O. Ehrismann, 680(ZDP):Band105Heft3-456
Meister, M.W., ed. Discourses on Śiva.*
G. Yocum, 293(JASt):Aug86-887
Meixner, H. & S. Vietta, eds. Expressionismus - sozialer Wandel und künstlerische Erfahrung.
W. Paulsen, 133:Band19Heft3/4-362
"Mélanges sur la littérature de la Renaissance à la mémoire de V-L. Saulnier."*
N. Kenny, 208(FS):Apr86-203
Melbin, M. Night as Frontier.
P. Hoffman, 441:5Apr87-35
Melchett, S. Someone is Missing.
R. Dinnage, 617(TLS):31Jul87-828
Melchiori, B.A. Terrorism in the Late Victorian Novel.*
P. Brantlinger, 177(ELT):Vol29No4-447
J. Newman, 161(DUJ):Jun86-381
P. Parrinder, 637(VS):Summer87-545
Mel'čuk I. & others. Dictionnaire explicatif et combinatoire du français contemporain.*
T.R. Wooldridge, 627(UTQ):Fall86-202
"Méliès et la naissance du spectacle cinématographique."
J. Paulhan, 207(FR):Feb87-415
Melin, L. & S. Lange, eds. Läsning.
J. Backman, 452(NJL):Vol9No2-203

Melis, L. & others. Les constructions de
la phrase française.
N. Corbett, 350:Mar87-184
Mellard, J.M. The Exploded Form.
S. Moore, 532(RCF):Fall86-144
Melle, U. - see Husserl, E.
Mellers, W. Beethoven and the Voice of
God.*
W. Kinderman, 451:Spring87-287
Mellers, W. A Darker Shade of Pale.*
R. Middleton, 410(M&L):Jan86-90
Mellers, W. François Couperin and the
French Classical Tradition. (rev)
P. Williams, 617(TLS):20-26Nov87-1290
Mellett, D.J. The Prerogative of Asylum-
dom.
C. Howell, 529(QQ):Spring86-19
Melnicove, M., ed. Inside Vacationland.
S. Minot, 455:Mar86-76
Melnyk, G. The Search for Community.
T. Jackson, 99:Oct86-34
G.W., 102(CanL):Summer86-173
Meltzer, M. & P.G. Holland - Child, L.M.
Meltzer, R. The Aesthetics of Rock.
J. Rees, 617(TLS):25-31Dec87-1441
Melwood, M. Reflections in Black Glass.
I. Scholes, 617(TLS):3Apr87-361
Mena Marqués, M.B. Dibujos Italianos de
los Siglos XVII y XVIII en la Biblioteca
Nacional, Madrid.* Museo del Prado,
Catálogo de Dibujos VI, Dibujos Italianos
del Siglo XVII.
A.S. Harris, 380:Autumn86-411
Menaker, D. The Old Left.
D. Stern, 441:3May87-15
Ménard, P. Les Fabliaux.*
R.H. Bloch, 545(RPh):May87-543
Menashe, S. Collected Poems.
M. Heller, 441:8Mar87-22
Menchú, R. I ... Rigoberta Menchú. (E.
Burgos-Debray, ed)
S. White, 448:Vol24No2-95
Mencken, H.L. "Ich Kuss die Hand." (P.W.
Dowell, ed)
R. King, 617(TLS):17Jul87-760
Mencken, H.L. & S. Haardt. Mencken and
Sara. (M.E. Rodgers, ed)
A. Kazin, 453(NYRB):26Feb87-8
D. Kirby, 598(SoR):Summer87-750
Mende, F. - see Heine, H.
Mendels, O. Mandela's Children.
E. Pall, 441:22Feb87-28
Mendelsohn, E. The Jews of East Central
Europe.*
S. Kassow, 550(RusR):Jan86-91
Mendelsohn, E., ed. Transformation and
Tradition in the Sciences.
C. Lawrence, 83:Autumn86-299
Mendelson, A. Secular Education in Philo
of Alexandria.
D.T. Runia, 394:Vol39fasc3/4-493
Mendelson, E. Early Auden.
C. Uhlig, 38:Band104Heft3/4-532
Mendes, O. Sobre Literatura Moçambicana.
R.G. Hamilton, 538(RAL):Fall86-422
Méndez-Faith, T. Con-Textos literarios
hispanoamericanos.
E.A. Echevarria, 399(MLJ):Autumn86-
333
R.G. Feal, 238:Dec86-897
Mendilow, J. The Romantic Tradition in
British Political Thought.
R.J. Halliday, 637(VS):Spring87-412

Mendoza, C.A.L. - see under Lertora
Mendoza, C.A.
de Mendoza, I.L. - see under López de Men-
doza, I.
Mendoza, T. Stories.
P. Watrous, 441:22Nov87-33
Menefee, S.P. Wives for Sale.
V. Shaw, 402(MLR):Jan86-184
K. Tiller, 447(N&Q):Sep85-400
Meneghetti, M.L. Il pubblico dei trova-
tori.
C. Di Girolamo, 379(MedR):Dec86-433
Menéndez Onrubia, C., ed. El dramaturgo y
los actores.
R.G. Sánchez, 240(HR):Spring86-230
Menéndez Onrubia, C. Introducción al
teatro de Benito Pérez Galdós.*
J. Lowe, 86(BHS):Jan86-99
Menestò, E., ed. Atti del Convegno Storico
Iacoponico.
Z.G. Barański, 545(RPh):Nov86-278
Ménétra, J-L. Journal of My Life.
A. Forrest, 617(TLS):27Feb87-220
Meng-ou, W. - see under Wang Meng-ou
Menichi, P. Guida a Gozzano.
S. Vinall, 402(MLR):Apr87-493
Menikoff, B. Robert Louis Stevenson and
"The Beach of Falesá."*
R.A. Boyle, 637(VS):Summer87-551
D.H. Jackson, 536(Rev):Vol8-79
K. Sutherland, 541(RES):Nov86-590
Menke, H. Das Namengut der frühen karo-
lingischen Königsurkunden.
I. Reiffenstein, 685(ZDL):3/1986-404
Mennell, S. All Manners of Food.*
639(VQR):Summer86-105
Mennemeier, F.N. Bertolt Brechts Lyrik.
S. Mews, 221(GQ):Winter86-106
Mennemeier, F.N. Literatur der Jahrhun-
dertwende I.
J. Schultz, 343:Heft14-140
M. Swales, 402(MLR):Oct87-1033
Mensching, S. Erinnerung an eine Milch-
glasscheibe.
B. Leistner, 601(SuF):Sep-Oct85-1094
Mentrup, W., ed. Konzepte zur Lexikogra-
phie.
C. Römer, 682(ZPSK):Band39Heft1-147
Menzel, B. Assyrische Tempel.
H.D. Galter, 318(JAOS):Jan/Mar85-145
Merchant, M. Jeshua.
T. Rajak, 617(TLS):21Aug87-896
Meredith, G. The Notebooks of George
Meredith.* (G. Beer & M. Harris, eds)
P.D. Edwards, 67:May86-103
S. Monod, 402(MLR):Oct87-936
Meredith, P. & J.E. Tailby, eds. The Stag-
ing of Religious Drama in Europe in the
Later Middle Ages.*
G.A. Lester, 179(ES):Aug86-366
H. Phillips, 382(MAE):1986/2-295
Merezhkovskii, D. Malen'kaia Tereza. (T.
Pachmuss, ed)
J.D. Grossman, 550(RusR):Jan86-57
Mergen, B. Play and Playthings.
R.A. Banes, 106:Spring86-93
Mérimée, P. L'Art Dramatique en Espagne
dans la Première Moitié du XVIIIe Siècle.
I.L. McClelland, 86(BHS):Jul86-291
Mérimée, P. Théâtre de Clara Gazul. (P.
Berthier, ed)
P.W.M. Cogman, 208(FS):Jul86-340

Merino, L. El Cabildo Secular.
  L. Diaz-Trechuelo, 293(JASt):Nov85-196
Meriwether, J.S. - see Faulkner, W.
Merkes, C. Wahrnehmungsstrukturen in
  Werken des Neuen Realismus.
  H.A. Pausch, 107(CRCL):Mar86-156
Merkin, D. Enchantment.*
  K. Bucknell, 617(TLS):14Aug87-873
Merlo, G.G. Valdesi e Valdismi medievali.
  R.A. Mentzer, Jr., 589:Oct86-1029
Mermall, T. Las alegorías del poder en
  Francisco Ayala.*
  J. Labanyi, 86(BHS):Jul86-296
Mermet, G. Francoscopie.*
  W. Wrage, 399(MLJ):Summer86-184
Mermin, D. The Audience in the Poems.*
  P. Drew, 85(SBHC):Vol14-148
Méron, E. Tendre et cruel Corneille.*
  A. Couprie, 535(RHL):Jul-Aug86-740
  Q.M. Hope, 207(FR):May87-858
  W.D. Howarth, 402(MLR):Apr86-481
Merrell, F. Deconstruction Reframed.
  P. Lamarque, 89(BJA):Summer86-290
Merrett, R.J., ed. Man and Nature/L'Homme
  et la Nature.* (Vol 3)
  D. Adams, 83:Spring86-117
  K.W. Graham, 178:Sep86-351
  R. Mortier, 107(CRCL):Mar86-132
Merrick, P. Revolution and Religion in the
  Music of Liszt.
  A. Walker, 617(TLS):10Jul87-737
Merrill, J. Late Settings.*
  C. Bedient, 569(SR):Fall86-657
Merrill, J. Recitative. (J.D. McClatchy,
  ed)
  H. Benedict, 441:15Feb87-21
  M. Boruch, 29(APR):Mar/Apr87-22
  D.W. Hartnett, 617(TLS):22May87-557
Merritt, A.T. - see Gabrieli, A.
Merser, C. "Grown-Ups."
  F. Klagsbrun, 441:18Oct87-11
Mersereau, J., Jr. Russian Romantic Fic-
  tion.
  H. Goscilo-Kostin, 550(RusR):Jan86-55
Mertens, D. Der Tempel von Segesta und die
  dorische Tempelbaukunst des griechischen
  Westens in Klassischer Zeit.
  R.A. Tomlinson, 303(JoHS):Vol106-247
Mertens, V. & U. Müller, eds. Epische
  Stoffe des Mittelalters.
  T.M. Andersson, 563(SS):Winter86-92
  C. Cormeau, 224(GRM):Band36Heft3-345
  S.M. Johnson, 221(GQ):Spring86-297
  M.E. Kalinke, 301(JEGP):Jan86-70
  J.W. Thomas, 133:Band19Heft2-156
Mervaud, C. Voltaire et Frédéric II.
  E. Jacobs, 208(FS):Oct86-460
van der Merwe, A., ed. Old and New Ques-
  tions in Physics, Cosmology, Philosophy
  and Theoretical Biology.
  S. Prokhovnik, 84:Jun86-257
Meschonnic, H. Les États de la poétique.
  Mallarmé au-delà du silence.
  M. Jarrety, 450(NRF):Jun86-82
Meserole, H.T., ed. American Poetry of the
  Seventeenth Century.
  A. Delbanco, 617(TLS):9Jan87-40
Messenger, J.C. An Anthropologist at
  Play.*
  D.K. Wilgus, 650(WF):Jan86-42
Messer Leon, J. The Book of the Honey-
  comb's Flow.*
  F. Talmage, 318(JAOS):Apr/Jun85-342

Messerli, D. - see Barnes, D.
Messinger, G.S. Manchester in the Victo-
  rian Age.
  F. Singleton, 637(VS):Spring87-416
Messner, D. & H.J. Müller. Ibero-Roman-
  isch.
  E. Blasco Ferrer, 379(MedR):Dec86-465
Mĕšt'an, A. Geschichte der tschechischen
  Literatur im 19. und 20. Jahrhundert.
  Z. Salzmann, 574(SEEJ):Fall86-455
  W. Schamschula, 402(MLR):Jul87-814
Metcalf, J. Adult Entertainment.
  J. Kuropatwa, 99:Dec86-37
  A. Van Herk, 376:Dec86-136
Metcalf, J. Girl in Gingham.
  M. Peterman, 296(JCF):No35/36-160
Metcalf, P. Golden Delicious.
  J. Byrne, 532(RCF):Spring86-208
Meter, J.H. The Literary Theories of
  Daniel Heinsius.*
  O.B. Hardison, Jr., 551(RenQ):Summer86-
  299
van der Meulen, J. & J. Hohmeyer.
  Chartres.
  R. Zeitler, 341:Vol55No1-39
Meurant, G. Shoowa Design.
  T. Phillips, 617(TLS):25Sep-1Oct87-1040
Mews, S., ed. "The Fisherman and His
  Wife."*
  W. Blomster, 406:Winter86-553
  W. Hoffmeister, 301(JEGP):Jul86-432
Mews, S. Carl Zuckmayer.
  H.F. Rahde, 406:Summer86-270
  H. Wagener, 406:Summer86-271
Mewshaw, M. Money to Burn.
  M. Jones, 441:13Sep87-28
Meyer, B. & B. O'Riordan, eds. In Their
  Words.*
  W.J. Keith, 298:Spring86-154
  G. Lynch, 102(CanL):Fall86-150
Meyer, C. American Folk Medicine.
  S.B. Thiederman, 650(WF):Jul86-239
Meyer, D. Sex and Power.
  K. Offen, 441:11Oct87-23
Meyer, H., comp. Bibliographie der Buch-
  und Bibliotheksgeschichte. (Vol 3)
  B.J. McMullin, 517(PBSA):Vol80No2-263
Meyer, M. Logique, langage et argumenta-
  tion.
  M. Dominicy, 209(FM):Oct86-247
Meyer, M. Meaning and Reading.*
  G. Prince, 478:Apr86-101
Meyer, M. Strindberg.*
  S. Callow, 157:No161-47
  M. Robinson, 562(Scan):Nov86-203
  R.B. Vowles, 563(SS):Summer86-329
Meyer, R., ed. Die Hamburger Oper.
  H.M.K. Riley, 133:Band19Heft3/4-337
Meyer-Krentler, E. Der Bürger als Freund.
  G. Finney, 221(GQ):Winter86-151
  R. Stauf, 224(GRM):Band36Heft4-472
Meyer zur Capellen, J. Gentile Bellini.
  P.F. Brown, 90:Dec86-905
Meyerhoff, D. Traditioneller Stoff und
  individuelle Gestaltung.
  R.L. Fowler, 123:Vol36No2-301
Meyers, D.T. Inalienable Rights.
  D.R. Knowles, 518:Oct86-246
Meyers, J. Hemingway.*
  L. Butts, 594:Fall86-333
  W. Just, 639(VQR):Summer86-524
  M.P.L., 295(JML):Nov86-484
                                    [continued]

[continuing]

T. Ludington, 27(AL):Dec86-653

G. Luthi, 365:Spring/Summer86-175

E. Mottram, 176:Dec86-46

J. Symons, 364:Jun86-85

R.P. Weeks, 395(MFS):Summer86-265

Meyers, J. D.H. Lawrence and the Experience of Italy.*
C. Caesar, 131(CL):Winter86-106

Meyers, J., ed. D.H. Lawrence and Tradition.
H. Mills, 175:Summer86-173
D.R. Schwarz, 177(ELT):Vol29No2-223
W. Young, 395(MFS):Summer86-315

Meyerson, E. The Relativistic Deduction.
J. Williamson, 518:Oct86-236

de Meyïer, K.A. & P.F.J. Obbema, comps. Codices Vossiani Latini, IV.
R.C. Barker-Benfield, 123:Vol36No1-173

Meynell, H.A. The Nature of Aesthetic Value.
D. Townsend, 290(JAAC):Spring87-305

Meynet, R. Quelle est donc cette parole? Initiation à la rhétorique biblique. Rhétorique sémitique et interprétation de la Bible et de la tradition musulmane. L'Evangile de Luc et la rhétorique biblique.
G. Mounin, 98:Dec86-1198

Meyrowitz, J. No Sense of Place.*
W.E. Coleman, 186(ETC.):Winter86-423
D.M. Davis, 583:Summer87-411

Miall, D.S., ed. Metaphor.
D.O. Nathan, 478:Apr86-136

Mianney, R. Maurice Rollinat, poète et musicien du fantastique.*
G. Cesbron, 356(LR):May86-180

Miao, R.C. Early Medieval Chinese Poetry.*
R.J. Cutter, 116:Jul85-160

Michaels, A. A Comprehensive Śulvasūtra Word Index.
K.G. Zysk, 318(JAOS):Oct/Dec85-807

Michaels, A. The Weight of Oranges.
S. Scobie, 376:Jun86-127

Michaels, J.E. Anarchy and Eros.* (German title: Anarchie und Eros.)
W. Paulsen, 133:Band19Heft3/4-365
R.C. Reimer, 406:Fall86-415

Michaelsen, A.G. "av mangel på seg selv."
E. Aadland, 172(Edda):1986/2-188

Michaud, S., ed. Un Fabuleux Destin.
E. Gelfand, 446(NCFS):Fall-Winter86/87-233

Michaud, S. Muse et madone.
B. Klingler, 52:Band21Heft2-215
E.B. Sivert, 446(NCFS):Spring87-355

Michaud, S. - see "Flora Tristan (1803-1844)"

Michaud, Y. Locke.
M. Meyer, 540(RIPh):Vol40fasc3-354

Michaux, H. Saisir. Chemins cherchés. Idéogrammes en Chine. Par des traits. Déplacements, dégagements.
S. Canadas, 98:Nov86-1092

Michel, W. Ästhetische Hermeneutik und frühromantische Kritik.
J. Ryan, 406:Fall86-403

Michelet, J. Mother Death.* (E.K. Kaplan, ed & trans)
C. Crossley, 535(RHL):Nov-Dec86-1151

Michelet, J. Oeuvres complètes. (Vol 17) (E. Kaplan, ed)
M. Bishop, 150(DR):Fall86-391
O.A. Haac, 446(NCFS):Spring87-317

Michelini Tocci, L. - see Santi, G.

Michelson, A. - see Vertov, D.

Michener, J.A. Legacy.
J. Martin, 441:6Sep87-6

Michi, D. & R. Johnston. The Knowledge Machine.
42(AR):Spring86-245

Mickler, E.M. White Trash Cooking.
S. Belk, 138:No9-281
W. & C. Cowen, 639(VQR):Autumn86-140

Middlebrook, K.J. & C. Rico, eds. The United States and Latin America in the 1980s.
B.M. Bagley, 263(RIB):Vol36No4-495

Middlemas, K. Power Competition and the State. (Vol 1)
M. Pugh, 617(TLS):20Mar87-292

Middleton, C. Two Horse Wagon Going By.
A. Corn, 441:15Nov87-32

Middleton, R. The Bells of Victory.
J. Black, 173(ECS):Summer87-514

Middleton, R. & D. Horn, eds. Popular Music. (Vol 3)
P. Dickinson, 410(M&L):Jan86-66

Middleton, S. After a Fashion.
J. Mellors, 362:9Apr87-25

Middleton, S. Valley of Decision.
442(NY):9Nov87-154

Middleton Murry, K. Beloved Quixote.*
D. Sexton, 364:Apr/May86-172

Midgley, M. Animals and Why They Matter.*
H. Lehman, 154:Autumn86-600

Midgley, M. Wickedness.*
B. Gibbs, 483:Apr86-269
R.D. Milo, 482(PhR):Apr86-279

Midgley, M. & J. Hughes. Women's Choices.
G. Tulloch, 63:Jun86(supp)-141

Miedema, H. Karel van Manders Leven der moderne, oft dees-tytsche doorluchtighe Italiaensche schilders en hun bron.
E. Grasman, 600:Vol16No1-70

Mieder, W., ed. Disenchantments.
E. Moser-Rath, 196:Band27Heft1/2-127

Mieder, W., ed. Mädchen, pfeif auf den Prinzen.*
E. Moser-Rath, 196:Band27Heft1/2-127

Migel, P., ed. Great Ballet Stars in Historic Photographs.
R. Philp, 151:Mar86-90

Mighetto, L. - see Muir, J.

Migliorini, L.P. - see Praz, M.

Mignone, M.B. Eduardo De Filippo.
U. Mariani, 275(IQ):Winter86-124
F. Zangrilli, 397(MD):Mar86-139

Miguelez, R. Science, Valeurs et Rationalité.
K.S., 185:Jul87-888

Mihailovich, V.D. & M. Matejić. A Comprehensive Bibliography of Yugoslav Literature in English, 1593-1980.*
E.C. Hawkesworth, 402(MLR):Jan86-272
A.M. Mlikotin, 574(SEEJ):Spring86-120

Mikalson, J.D. Athenian Popular Religion.*
J.N. Bremmer, 394:Vol39fasc3/4-543

Mikhail, E.H. Sean O'Casey and His Critics.*
B.L. Smith, 87(BB):Sep86-183

Mila, M. Cento anni di musica moderna.
J. Budden, 415:Oct86-563

Milbauer, A.Z. Transcending Exile.*
  M.B., 295(JML):Nov86-393
  L. Field, 395(MFS):Summer86-279
  J. Kertzer, 49:Jul86-120
Milberg-Kaye, R. Thomas Hardy.
  K. Brady, 637(VS):Winter87-283
Milburn, F. Sheltered Lives.
  S. MacDonald, 441:1Feb87-20
Mildenberg, L. The Coinage of the Bar
  Kokhba War.
  S.E. Sidebotham, 124:Jul-Aug87-453
Mileham, J.W. The Conspiracy Novel.*
  G.R. Besser, 207(FR):Oct86-125
  T. Lyons, 188(ECr):Summer86-108
Miles, J. - see Schenkar, J.
Miles, K. Bullet Hole.
  N. Callendar, 441:2Aug87-29
Miles, M.L. Logik und Metaphysik bei Kant.
  W. Steinbeck, 342:Band77Heft2-260
Miles, M.R. Image as Insight.*
  J.H. Stone, 709:Winter87-123
Miles, R. Ben Jonson.
  I. Donaldson, 617(TLS):23-29Oct87-1165
Milhous, J. & R.D. Hume. Producible Inter-
  pretation.*
  D. Barrett, 610:Spring86-71
  D. Hughes, 130:Summer86-187
  J.A. Vaughn, 615(TJ):Mar86-117
Milhous, J. & R.D. Hume - see Coke, T.
Mill, J.S. Collected Works of John Stuart
  Mill. (Vol 1: Autobiography and Literary
  Essays.) (J.M. Robson & J. Stillinger,
  eds)
  N. Masterman, 402(MLR):Jul86-726
Mill, J.S. Collected Works of John Stuart
  Mill. (Vol 20: Essays on French History
  and Historians.) (J.M. Robson, ed)
  C. Jones, 506(PSt):Dec86-105
  T. Judt, 208(FS):Oct86-485
Mill, J.S. Collected Works of John Stuart
  Mill. (Vol 22: Newspaper Writings.)
  (A.P. & J.M. Robson, eds)
  G. Himmelfarb, 617(TLS):16-22Oct87-
  1127
Millar, D. Queen Victoria's Life in the
  Scottish Highlands.
  V. Powell, 39:Apr86-288
Millar, M. Spider Webs.*
  G. Kaufman, 362:19Feb87-26
Millard, P. - see North, R.
Miller, A. Timebends.
  D. Hirson, 617(TLS):25-31Dec87-1425
  A. Kazin, 442(NY):14Dec87-150
  R. Shattuck, 441:8Nov87-1
  L. Truss, 362:5Nov87-32
Miller, A.S. Toward Increased Judicial
  Activism.
  D. Gibson, 106:Fall86-375
Miller, B. Rosario Castellanos.
  M.S. Vásquez, 238:Sep86-558
Miller, B., ed. Women in Hispanic Litera-
  ture.*
  G.M. Scanlon, 402(MLR):Oct86-1017
Miller, B.S. - see Kālidāsa
Miller, C. Who's Really Who.
  362:29Oct87-31
Miller, C. & K. Swift. The Handbook of
  Nonsexist Writing.
  B. Renshaw, 126(CCC):Feb86-111
Miller, C.L. Blank Darkness.*
  E.S., 295(JML):Nov86-379
  D. Stephens, 207(FR):Mar87-527

Miller, D.A. Narrative and Its Discon-
  tents.
  J. Frank, 569(SR):Fall86-650
Miller, D.L. - see Mumford, L.
Miller, D.N. Fear of Fiction.
  L. Field, 395(MFS):Summer86-279
  S. Pinsker, 573(SSF):Fall86-470
Miller, D.R. - see Fletcher, J.
Miller, F., with others. Batman: The Dark
  Knight Returns.
  M. Richler, 441:3May87-35
Miller, H. Dear, Dear Brenda. (G. Sin-
  dell, ed)
  639(VQR):Autumn86-123
Miller, H. Snow on the Wind.
  S. Horner, 441:28Jun87-25
Miller, H. The Time of the Assassins.
  M. Sheringham, 208(FS):Apr86-231
Miller, I. Husserl, Perception, and Tempo-
  ral Awareness.*
  D.W. Smith, 484(PPR):Mar87-500
Miller, J., ed. The Art of Alice Munro.
  T. Ware, 573(SSF):Summer86-340
Miller, J. Bourbon and Stuart.
  R. Beddard, 617(TLS):24Jul87-789
Miller, J. "Democracy is in the Streets."
  A. Brinkley, 453(NYRB):22Oct87-10
  H. Hertzberg, 441:21Jun87-1
Miller, J. One Girl's War.
  J. Symons, 617(TLS):30Jan87-101
Miller, J. Rousseau.*
  M. Cranston, 176:Feb87-41
  J.A. Perkins, 405(MP):Aug86-92
Miller, J. Semantics and Syntax.
  M.A. Covington, 350:Mar87-181
  J. Goldsmith, 297(JL):Sep86-485
  R. Salkie, 361:Sep86-57
Miller, J. Subsequent Performances.*
  V. Geng, 442(NY):26Jan87-83
  S. Gold, 441:12Apr87-27
  J. Weightman, 176:Jan87-44
Miller, J., ed. Voices Against Tyranny.
  B. Knox, 453(NYRB):26Mar87-21
Miller, J. A Will to Win.
  L. Ryan, 381:Mar86-49
Miller, J. Women Writing About Men.*
  M. Corrigan, 441:22Feb87-29
Miller, J.C., comp. Slavery.
  E. Fox-Genovese, 263(RIB):Vol36No2-
  185
Miller, J.E. Modern Greek Folklore.
  J. Dubisch, 292(JAF):Oct/Dec86-477
Miller, J.H. The Ethics of Reading.
  M. Sprinker, 400(MLN):Dec86-1226
Miller, J.H. Fiction and Repetition.*
  J. Preston, 677(YES):Vol16-319
Miller, J.H. The Linguistic Moment.*
  M.B., 295(JML):Nov86-426
  M. Fischer, 301(JEGP):Oct86-572
  M. Hancher, 661(WC):Autumn86-199
Miller, K. Doubles.*
  J. Batchelor, 175:Spring86-85
  D.R. Davis, 184(EIC):Jan86-89
  E. Langland, 594:Winter86-448
  V. Newey, 541(RES):Nov86-615
  R.B. Shuman, 573(SSF):Winter86-134
  B.E. Teets, 177(ELT):Vol29No3-338
Miller, K.A. Emigrants and Exiles.*
  D.H. Akenson, 174(Éire):Spring86-122
  D.N. Doyle, 272(IUR):Spring86-88

Miller, L. John Milton and the Oldenburg Safeguard.*
  J. Shawcross, 391:Oct86-106
  M.R. Wade, 221(GQ):Fall86-674
Miller, L.B., with S. Hart, eds. The Selected Papers of Charles Willson Peale and His Family.* (Vol 1)
  G.A. Schultz, 106:Fall86-327
Miller, M. Bliss Carman.
  E. Cameron, 298:Winter86/87-133
Miller, M. Ike the Soldier.
  R.F. Weigley, 441:20Dec87-10
Miller, M. Jazz in Canada.
  529(QQ):Autumn86-719
Miller, M.E. The Murals of Bonampak.*
  V. Fraser, 90:Nov86-826
Miller, M.Y. & J. Chance, eds. Approaches to Teaching "Sir Gawain and the Green Knight."
  L.J. Leff, 365:Spring/Summer86-159
Miller, P. - see Sheridan, A.
Miller, R. Bare-Faced Messiah.
  M. Fagg, 362:19Nov87-34
Miller, R.A. Nihongo.*
  J.D. McCawley, 350:Dec87-904
Miller, R.B., ed. Black American Literature and Humanism.
  K. Kinnamon, 677(YES):Vol16-349
Miller, R.B., ed. Black American Poets Between Worlds, 1940-1960.
  J. Pettis, 578:Fall87-132
Miller, R.F. & F. Féhér, eds. Khruschchev and the Communist World.*
  A.Z. Rubinstein, 550(RusR):Jul86-315
Miller, R.W. Analyzing Marx.
  D. Allen, 529(QQ):Summer86-434
  A. Collier, 262:Dec86-459
  C. Morgareidge, 577(SHR):Summer86-284
Miller, S. Excellence & Equity.*
  T.C. Reeves, 579(SAQ):Spring86-193
Miller, S. Inventing the Abbotts.
  R. Kaveney, 617(TLS):17Jul87-765
  P. Lively, 441:24May87-5
Miller, S. El mundo de Galdós.*
  P. Bly, 345:May86-246
  J. Labanyi, 86(BHS):Jan86-96
Miller, S. Painted in Blood.
  C. Benfey, 441:26Jul87-17
Miller, V. Between Struggle and Hope.
  G.C. Ruscoe, 263(RIB):Vol36No1-63
Miller, V., ed. Despite This Flesh.
  F. Bricklebank, 150(DR):Fall86-388
Miller, W.M., Jr., ed. Beyond Armageddon.
  P. Brians, 561(SFS):Jul86-198
Millet, O. - see Calvin, J.
Millet, R. Le Sentiment de la langue.
  T. Cordellier, 450(NRF):Jun86-85
Millett, L. The Curve of the Arch.
  M. Filler, 453(NYRB):29Jan87-30
Millett, R.W. The Vultures and the Phoenix.
  K.M. Hewitt, 541(RES):May86-307
Millgate, J. Walter Scott.*
  K. Sutherland, 541(RES):Aug86-425
  E. Wagenknecht, 591(SIR):Spring86-159
  D. Whitmore, 405(MP):Aug86-94
Millgate, M. Thomas Hardy.*
  A. Swift, 38:Band104Heft1/2-256
Millgate, M. - see Hardy, T.
Millhauser, S. In the Penny Arcade.*
  T. De Pietro, 249(HudR):Autumn86-494
  I. Malin, 532(RCF):Summer86-146
  42(AR):Summer86-381

Milligan, I. The Novel in English.*
  J. Tyler, 447(N&Q):Sep85-415
Milligan, S. The Looney.
  D.J. Enright, 617(TLS):18-24Dec87-1399
Milligan, S. War Biography. (Vols 5 & 6)
  M. Kington, 176:May87-38
Millikan, R.G. Language, Thought, and other Biological Categories.
  P.H. Salus, 350:Mar87-195
  B. Sanders, 543:Sep86-136
  J.W.M. Verhaar, 355(LSoc):Mar86-135
Millon-Delsol, C. Essai sur le pouvoir occidental.
  A. Reix, 542:Jan-Mar86-155
Mills, W. The Meaning of Coyotes.
  L. Horton, 577(SHR):Winter86-91
Milly, J. - see Proust, M.
Milne, J. Dead Birds.
  T.J. Binyon, 617(TLS):9Jan87-42
Milner, J. Vladimir Tatlin and the Russian Avant-Garde.*
  S.F. Starr, 550(RusR):Jan86-46
Milner, M. - see Bernanos, G.
Milo, R.D. Immorality.*
  B. Gibbs, 483:Apr86-269
  W. Parent, 484(PPR):Jun87-655
Milojković-Djurić, J. Tradition and Avant-Garde.*
  H.R. Cooper, Jr., 574(SEEJ):Spring86-121
Milosz, C. The Land of Ulro.*
  A.H. Burleigh, 396(ModA):Spring86-162
Milosz, C. Unattainable Earth.*
  J.P. White, 491:Dec86-168
Milton, J. The Complete Prose Works of John Milton.* (Vol 8) (M. Kelley, ed)
  A. Burnett, 447(N&Q):Mar85-120
  G. Campbell, 402(MLR):Apr86-444
Milward-Oliver, E. The Len Deighton Companion.
  P. Humphries, 362:3Dec87-36
Minc, R.S., ed. El Cono Sur.
  E. Gimbernat de González, 238:Dec86-890
Minden, M.R. Arno Schmidt.
  H. Denkler, 406:Summer86-255
Miner, E., ed. Principles of Classical Japanese Literature.
  W.P. Lammers, 293(JASt):Aug86-854
Miner, M.M. Insatiable Appetites.*
  S. O'Brien, 395(MFS):Summer86-353
Miner, R. Exes.
  C. Colman, 441:8Mar87-20
Miner, V. & H.E. Longino, eds. Competition.
  M. Dimen, 441:11Oct87-57
Mines, M. The Warrior Merchants.
  G. Rosen, 293(JASt):Feb86-429
Minetti, B. Erinnerungen eines Schauspielers.
  R. Kift, 157:No162-46
Minnis, A.J. Chaucer and Pagan Antiquity.*
  J.M. Fyler, 402(MLR):Jul86-704
Minnis, A.J., ed. Gower's "Confessio Amantis."
  P. Gradon, 447(N&Q):Jun85-259
  G. Morgan, 402(MLR):Apr87-439
  R.A. Peck, 589:Jan86-180
  H. White, 382(MAE):1986/2-289
Minnis, A.J. Medieval Theory of Authorship.*
  J. Coleman, 677(YES):Vol16-224
  [continued]

[continuing]
G.R. Evans, 541(RES):Feb86-76
C. Gauvin, 189(EA):Jul-Sep87-346
W. Ginsberg, 447(N&Q):Jun85-256
W. Wetherbee, 589:Jan86-178
Mino, Y. & J. Robinson. Beauty and Tranquility.
M.G. Neill, 293(JASt):Nov85-123
Minogue, K. & M. Biddiss, eds. Thatcherism.
J. Campbell, 617(TLS):5Jun87-597
Minot, S. Monkeys.*
W. Lesser, 249(HudR):Autumn86-480
Minsky, M. The Society of Mind.
J.W. Lance, 441:22Feb87-10
B. Williams, 453(NYRB):11Jun87-33
Minson, J. Genealogies of Morals.
J.S., 185:Apr87-693
Minta, S. Gabriel García Márquez.
K. Duchêne, 176:Sep/Oct87-57
Minter, W. King Solomon's Mines Revisited.
R. Oliver, 617(TLS):13-19Nov87-1241
L. Robinson, 441:22Mar87-29
L. Thompson, 453(NYRB):11Jun87-20
Mintz, S.W. & S. Price, eds. Caribbean Contours.
R.L. Austin, 263(RIB):Vol36No2-185
Minyard, J.D. Lucretius and the Late Republic.
D. Edwards, 124:May-Jun87-390
E. Rawson, 123:Vol36No2-314
Miola, R.S. Shakespeare's Rome.*
P. Boitani, 156(ShJW):Jahrbuch1986-238
M. Draudt, 38:Band104Heft1/2-222
J. Rees, 447(N&Q):Mar85-111
Miquet, J., ed. Fierabras.*
M.J. Ailes, 382(MAE):1986/2-317
F.P. Sweetser, 589:Apr86-444
"Miraculous Tales of the Lotus Sutra from Ancient Japan." (Y.K. Dykstra, trans)
J.R. Goodwin, 293(JASt):Nov85-143
Miralles, C. & J. Pòrtulas. Archilochus and the Iambic Poetry.
E.L. Bowie, 303(JoHS):Vol106-205
Miranda Hevia, A. Novela, discurso y sociedad.
M. Agosin, 263(RIB):Vol36No1-64
della Mirandola, G.P. – see under Pico della Mirandola, G.
Miró, G. El obispo leproso. (C. Ruiz Silva, ed)
M.G.R. Coope, 240(HR):Autumn86-483
Miró, J. Joan Miró: Selected Writings and Interviews. (M. Rowell, ed)
C. Green, 617(TLS):24Jul87-797
Mirollo, J.V. Mannerism and Renaissance Poetry.*
L. Gent, 551(RenQ):Autumn86-545
M. Roston, 301(JEGP):Apr86-256
Miron, G. Embers and Earth.
E. Dansereau, 526:Summer86-103
Misan, J. L'Italie des doctrinaires (1817-1830). Les Lettres italiennes dans la presse française (1815-1834).
M. Arrous, 605(SC):15Jan87-213
"Miscellanea archaeologica Tobias Dohrn dedicata."
J-C. Richard, 555:Vol59fasc2-349
"Miscellanea Frisica."
L-R. Howe, 682(ZPSK):Band39Heft3-393
Mishima, Y. The Temple of the Golden Pavilion.
362:13Aug87-23

Mishriky, S. Le Costume de déguisement et la théâtralité de l'apparence dans "Le Bourgeois gentilhomme."
P.A. Wadsworth, 207(FR):Dec86-255
Miskimin, H.A. Money and Power in Fifteenth-Century France.
M. Howell, 551(RenQ):Spring86-90
L.B. Robbert, 589:Jul86-688
Misler, N. & J.E. Bowlt – see Filonov, P.
Missios, C. Kalá, esý skotóthikes norís.
K. Andrews, 617(TLS):10Apr87-379
Mistler, J., ed. Kant intime.
A.A. Azar, 98:Oct86-981
Mistral, F. & P. Devoluy. Correspondance Frédéric Mistral/Pierre Devoluy (1895-1913). (C. Rostaing, ed)
S. Thiolier-Méjean, 535(RHL):Sep-Oct86-946
Mitchell, A. On the Beach at Cambridge.
J. Saunders, 565:Summer86-74
Mitchell, A. Victors and Vanquished.*
S. Wilson, 208(FS):Jul86-349
Mitchell, A. & P. Ó Snodaigh. Irish Political Documents, 1916-1949.
T. Garvin, 272(IUR):Autumn86-243
Mitchell, A.W. The Enchanted Canopy.
442(NY):23Mar87-100
Mitchell, B. Old English Syntax.
E.G. Stanley, 541(RES):May86-234
Mitchell, B. & F.C. Robinson. A Guide to Old English.* (rev)
K. Reichl, 72:Band223Heft1-229
Mitchell, D., ed. Benjamin Britten: "Death in Venice."
A. Whittall, 617(TLS):25Sep-1Oct87-1050
Mitchell, D. Britten and Auden in the Thirties: The Year 1936.*
W. Huck, 465:Autumn86-136
Mitchell, D. Gustav Mahler.* (Vol 3)
P. Franklin, 410(M&L):Oct86-412
M. Kennedy, 415:Mar86-153
Z. Roman, 414:Vol72No3-410
Mitchell, D. & G. Chaplin. The Elegant Shed.
E.M. Farrelly, 46:Jul86-84
Mitchell, D., with J. Evans, comps. Benjamin Britten, 1913-1976.
M.S. Cole, 465:Autumn86-142
Mitchell, D. & H. Keller, eds. Benjamin Britten.
F.E. Peterson, 465:Autumn86-148
Mitchell, J. Alaskan Stories.
D. McElroy, 649(WAL):May86-60
Mitchell, J. & A. Oakley, eds. What is Feminism?
A.M. Davidon, 441:15Mar87-17
J. Hornsby, 617(TLS):4-10Dec87-1345
Mitchell, J.H. Ceremonial Time.
D. Scheese, 658:Summer/Autumn86-219
Mitchell, K. Through the Nan Da Gate.
R.C. Cosbey, 647:Fall86-109
Mitchell, L.C. Witnesses to a Vanishing America.
R. Thacker, 106:Spring86-51
Mitchell, M. Margaret Mitchell's "Gone with the Wind." (R. Harwell, ed)
M. Fagg, 362:24Sep87-26
Mitchell, M.H. Hollywood Cemetery.
639(VQR):Summer86-102
Mitchell, R. The Gift of Fire.
A. Boyer, 441:13Sep87-35

Mitchell, S. & M. Rosen, eds. The Need for Interpretation.
P.A. Johnson, 488:Dec86-503
Mitchell, S.A. Job in Female Garb.
B. Morris, 562(Scan):Nov86-228
Mitchell, T. Dario Fo.
T.A. Joscelyne, 610:Spring86-84
Mitchell, W.J.T., ed. Against Theory.
P. Kamuf, 153:Winter86-3
D. Keesey, 478:Oct86-340
Mitchell, W.J.T. Iconology.*
L.B. Brown, 290(JAAC):Winter86-211
M. Conroy, 577(SHR):Fall86-365
Mitchison, R. Lordship to Patronage.
A. Murdoch, 83:Spring86-82
Mitford, A.B. Mitford's Japan. (H. Cortazzi, ed)
M. Cooper, 407(MN):Autumn86-366
Mitford, M.R. Our Village.
362:31Dec87-21
Mitford, N. A Talent to Annoy.* (C. Mosley, ed)
442(NY):20Jul87-92
Mitford, T.B. & O. Masson. The Syllabic Inscriptions of Rantidi-Paphos.*
C.J. Ruijgh, 394:Vol39fasc3/4-550
Mitgutsch, A. Three Daughters.
P-L. Adams, 61:Apr87-91
S. Winnett, 441:19Apr87-16
Mitias, M.H. The Moral Foundation of the State in Hegel's Philosophy of Right.*
C. Cordura, 160:Jan86-135
Mitsuru, Y. – see under Yoshida Mitsuru
Mitterand, H. Zola et le naturalisme.
P. Walker, 207(FR):May87-868
Mitterand, H. – see Zola, É.
Mittler, R. Theorie und Praxis des sozialen Dramas bei Gerhart Hauptmann.
R.C. Cowen, 406:Winter86-514
Mizukami Shizuo. Chūgoku kodai no shoku-butsugaku no kenkyū.
J.K. Riegel, 244(HJAS):Jun86-317
Mo, T. An Insular Possession.*
P. Vansittart, 364:Jun86-94
R.W. Winks, 441:19Apr87-2
Moatti, C. "La Condition humaine" d'André Malraux.
E. Fallaize, 208(FS):Jul86-359
F. Trécourt, 535(RHL):Jul-Aug86-790
Moberg, V. I egen sak. (O. von Friesen, ed)
R. Wright, 563(SS):Autumn86-446
Möbius, F. & E. Schubert, eds. Architektur des Mittelalters.
H.E. Kubach, 683:Band49Heft4-584
Mode, H., ed. Zigeunermärchen aus aller Welt.
I. Köhler-Zülch, 196:Band27Heft1/2-129
Modiano, P. Dimanches d'août.*
A. Clerval, 450(NRF):Dec86-89
C.A. Porter, 207(FR):May87-910
Modiano, P. Quartier perdu.* Rue des boutiques obscures. De si braves garçons.
A. Bony, 98:Jun-Jul86-653
Modiano, R. Coleridge and the Concept of Nature.*
L. Lockridge, 661(WC):Autumn86-222
Modlin, C.E. – see Anderson, S.
Moe, V.I. Deutscher Naturalismus und aus-ländische Literatur.
Y. Chevrel, 549(RLC):Jan-Mar86-71

Moelleken, W.W., ed. Dialectology, Linguistics, Literature.*
H. Sohogt, 564:May86-183
Moeller, H-B., ed. Latin America and the Literature of Exile.
A.R. Wedel, 221(GQ):Fall86-637
Moeran, B. Lost Innocence.*
R. Faulkner, 407(MN):Summer86-252
J. Kleinberg, 293(JASt):Feb86-407
H. Willett, 650(WF):Jan86-55
Moeran, B. Ōkubo Diary.
C. Blacker, 617(TLS):22May87-542
D.W. Plath, 293(JASt):Aug86-856
Moes, J. & J-M. Valentin, eds. De Lessing à Heine.
J-P. Danès, 549(RLC):Oct-Dec86-475
Moeschler, J. Argumentation et conversation.
N. Corbett, 350:Mar87-199
Moffatt, L.N. Norman Rockwell.*
C. Reid, 617(TLS):2Jan87-17
M.S. Young, 39:Nov86-458
Moffett, C.S., with others. The New Painting.*
K. Adler, 59:Sep86-376
Moffett, J. Coming on Center.
J.C. Schaefer, 126(CCC):Oct86-366
Moffett, J. James Merrill.*
D.L. Macdonald, 106:Fall86-381
D.L. Macdonald, 134(CP):Vol19-143
Moggach, D. To Have and to Hold.*
E. Feldman, 441:29Mar87-19
Mogge, B., comp. Die Sprachnorm-Diskussion in Presse, Hörfunk und Fernsehen.
N. Nail, 685(ZDL):3/1986-398
Moglen, H. Charlotte Brontë.*
K. Sutherland, 402(MLR):Oct87-927
Mohanty, J.N. Husserl and Frege.*
G. Gabriel, 687:Apr-Jun86-300
R. Schmit, 53(AGP):Band68Heft3-330
D.W. Smith, 482(PhR):Jan86-118
Mohin, L., ed. Beautiful Barbarians.
C. Wills, 617(TLS):10Jul87-748
Mohr, R.D. The Platonic Cosmology.
J. Barnes, 520:Vol31No1-97
W.J. Prior, 319:Oct87-585
Mohrt, M. La Guerre civile.*
A. Bosquet, 450(NRF):May86-89
Moi, T. Sexual/Textual Politics.
P. Barry, 175:Spring86-89
A. Caesar, 208(FS):Apr86-245
H. Forsås-Scott, 172(Edda):1986/1-87
S. Scobie, 376:Jun86-128
Mojares, R.B. Origins and Rise of the Filipino Novel.*
L. Casper, 293(JASt):Nov85-198
Mojtabai, A.G. Blessed Assurance.*
C. Sigal, 362:22Jan87-24
Mokrzycki, E. Philosophy of Science and Sociology.
R. Taras, 488:Dec86-507
Molas, J. Literatura catalana d'Avant-guarda, 1916-1938.
D. Keown, 86(BHS):Apr86-183
Moldea, D.E. Dark Victory.*
P. Dunne, 18:Mar87-63
N. Lemann, 453(NYRB):15Jan87-23
Mole, J. Homing.
D. Dunn, 176:Jun87-51
D.W. Hartnett, 617(TLS):18-24Sep87-1024
Mole, J. In and Out of the Apple.*
H. Buckingham, 565:Summer86-64

de Montfleury, A.J.   Le Mary sans femme. (E. Forman, ed)
   J. Morgan, 402(MLR):Jul87-738
Montgomerie, W.   From Time to Time.
   J. Caird, 571(ScLJ):Summer86-20
Montgomery, D.   The Fall of the House of Labor.
   B. Ehrenreich, 61:Sep87-100
   N. Lichtenstein, 441:29Nov87-30
Montgomery, J., comp.   The Kerouac We Knew.
   M. Wilding, 402(MLR):Apr86-468
Montgomery, L.M.   The Selected Journals of L.M. Montgomery.   (Vol 1) (M. Rubio & E. Waterson, eds)
   C.G. Holland, 529(QQ):Autumn86-667
Montgomery, M.   An Introduction to Language and Society.
   G.D. Bills, 399(MLJ):Winter86-435
   J. Paccaud, 189(EA):Jul-Sep87-328
Montgomery, M.   Why Poe Drank Liquor.*
   T.H. Pickett, 577(SHR):Spring86-201
Monti, N., ed.   Africa Then.
   442(NY):6Jul87-82
Monti, S. - see de Valera, D.
Montinari, M.   Nietzsche lesen.
   R. Margreiter, 489(PJGG):Band93Heft2-375
Montrose, J.H.   Tracks in the Widest Orbit.
   G. Haslam, 649(WAL):Feb87-371
Montserrat, J.   Simone Signoret.
   J. Van Baelen, 207(FR):Mar87-548
Moodie, S.   Susanna Moodie: Letters of a Lifetime.   (C. Ballstadt, E. Hopkins & M. Peterman, eds)
   J. Giltrow, 627(UTQ):Fall86-164
   C. Thomas, 529(QQ):Autumn86-659
   G. Woodcock, 102(CanL):Summer86-101
Moody, H.L.B., E. Gunner & E. Finnegan, eds.   A Teacher's Guide to African Literature.
   C. Wood, 538(RAL):Winter86-606
Moody, J. & R. Boyes.   The Priest and the Policeman.
   N. Davies, 441:15Mar87-9
Mooney, M.   Vico in the Tradition of Rhetoric.*
   J.H. Whitfield, 402(MLR):Oct87-993
Moorcock, M.   The Brothel in Rosenstrasse.
   442(NY):5Oct87-126
Moorcock, M.   Letters from Hollywood.*
   J. Richards, 176:Jan87-50
Moore, A.   Opia.*
   272(IUR):Autumn86-253
Moore, B.   Black Robe.*
   G. Lynch, 102(CanL):Fall86-150
Moore, B.   The Color of Blood.
   N. Ascherson, 453(NYRB):17Dec87-44
   E. Battersby, 362:22Oct87-30
   A-M. Conway, 617(TLS):2-8Oct87-1073
   C. Sigal, 441:27Sep87-11
   442(NY):19Oct87-120
Moore, B.   The Luck of Ginger Coffey.
   362:10Dec87-29
Moore, B.   The Wolf Whispered Death.*
   C.S. Long, 649(WAL):Feb87-357
Moore, C., A.N. Wilson & G. Stamp.   The Church in Crisis.*
   H. Lomas, 364:Oct86-89
Moore, G.   In Minor Keys.   (D.B. Eakin & H.E. Gerber, eds)
   J.E. Dunleavy, 174(Éire):Spring86-147
                 [continued]

[continuing]
   B.L. Moore, 573(SSF):Summer86-336
   J. Weaver, 177(ELT):Vol29No3-320
Moore, G.E.   The Early Essays.   (T. Regan, ed)
   S. Hampshire, 453(NYRB):26Mar87-37
Moore, G.S.   The Banker's Life.
   R.A. Bennett, 441:2Aug87-17
Moore, H. & J. Hedgecoe.   Henry Moore.
   90:Oct86-759
Moore, L.   Anagrams.*
   A. Vaux, 617(TLS):4-11Sep87-949
   442(NY):9Mar87-104
Moore, L.   Self-Help.
   T. McGonigle, 532(RCF):Summer86-155
   I. Malin, 532(RCF):Spring86-213
Moore, M.   The Complete Prose of Marianne Moore.*   (P.C. Willis, ed)
   P. Forbes, 362:12Feb87-26
   T. Gunn, 617(TLS):6Feb87-127
   J. Mole, 176:Jul/Aug87-46
   H. Vendler, 442(NY):16Mar87-94
Moore, M.   The Short Season Between Two Silences.*
   A. McLaurin, 447(N&Q):Dec85-545
Moore, P.D.   The Collins Encyclopedia of Animal Ecology.
   J. Serpell, 617(TLS):16Jan87-70
Moore, R.   Niels Bohr.
   K.R. Sopka, 529(QQ):Summer86-446
Moore, R.I.   The Formation of a Persecuting Society.
   M.T. Clanchy, 617(TLS):11-17Sep87-990
Moore, R.J.   Making the New Commonwealth.
   W.R. Louis, 617(TLS):28Aug87-915
Moore, R.S. - see Hayne, P.H.
Moore, S.   Lucan Not Guilty.
   J. Symons, 617(TLS):4-10Dec87-1346
   B. Woffinden, 362:22Oct87-28
Moore, S.   A Reader's Guide to William Gaddis's "The Recognitions."
   D. Seed, 677(YES):Vol16-363
Moore, S.R.   The Drama of Discrimination in Henry James.
   P.B. Armstrong, 284:Winter85-148
Moore, T.   The Journal of Thomas Moore.   (Vol 1) (W.S. Dowden, ed)
   P.W. Graham, 661(WC):Autumn86-219
Moore, T.   The Journal of Thomas Moore.*   (Vol 2) (W.S. Dowden, with B.G. Bartholomew & J.L. Linsley, eds)
   P.W. Graham, 661(WC):Autumn86-219
   P.J. Manning, 340(KSJ):Vol35-201
   L.A. Marchand, 591(SIR):Winter86-567
Moore-Gilbert, B., ed.   Literature and Imperialism.
   R.D. Hamner, 538(RAL):Spring86-162
Moore-Gilbert, B.J.   Kipling and "Orientalism."
   T.J. Binyon, 617(TLS):5Jun87-608
Moorehead, C.   Troublesome People.
   B. Pimlott, 617(TLS):8May87-481
   T. Powers, 61:Aug87-78
Moosa, M.   The Origins of Modern Arabic Fiction.
   R.H. Dekmejian, 318(JAOS):Oct/Dec85-745
de la Mora, G.S. - see under Schmidhuber de la Mora, G.
Mora, P., L. Mora & P. Philippot.   Conservation of Wall Paintings.
   J. White, 90:Jan86-39

Morace, R.A. & K. Van Spanckeren, eds.
John Gardner.
M.F. Schulz, 402(MLR):Apr86-470
Morain, M., ed. Enriching Professional
Skills Through General Semantics.
H. Maynard, 186(ETC.):Winter86-422
Moral, P. & others. Atlas d'Haïti.
S.B. McDonald, 263(RIB):Vol36No2-187
Morales y Marín, J.L. Diccionario de
Iconología y Simbología.
W. Rincón García, 48:Jan-Mar86-113
Moran, J.A.H. The Growth of English
Schooling 1340-1548.
M.C. Burson, 589:Oct86-971
R. O'Day, 161(DUJ):Jun86-361
Moran, J.M. & F. Checa. El Coleccionismo
en España.
R. Mulcahy, 90:Jan86-42
Moran, M. & C. Spadoni, eds. Intellect and
Social Conscience.
J.B. Schneewind, 154:Winter86-816
Moran, M.G. & R.F. Lunsford, eds. Research
in Composition and Rhetoric.
N. Shapiro, 365:Winter86-71
Morand, P. Les Extravagants.
R. Buss, 617(TLS):20Feb87-196
Morandini, G. Bloodstains.
L. Re, 441:8Nov87-26
Morante, E. Aracoeli.
S.L. Arico, 275(IQ):Spring86-116
R. West, 473(PR):Vol53No4-649
Morath, I. Portraits.
442(NY):9Feb87-105
Moraux, P. Der Aristotelismus bei den
Griechen von Andronikos bis Alexander von
Aphrodisias. (Vol 2)
P. Louis, 555:Vol59fasc2-286
Moraux, P. Galien de Pergame.
P. Pellegrin, 542:Oct-Déc86-506
Moravia, A. The Voyeur.*
L. Re, 441:29Mar87-15
Morazzoni, A.M., ed. Musorgskij.
J. Warrack, 410(M&L):Oct86-436
Morazzoni, M. La ragazza col turbante.
N.S. Thompson, 617(TLS):3Apr87-362
Mordden, E. Buddies.
J. Olshan, 441:11Jan87-18
More, T. The Complete Works of St. Thomas
More. (Vol 11) (S.M. Foley & C.H.
Miller, eds)
N. Barker, 617(TLS):17Apr87-416
Moreau, H. & A. Tournon - see Béroalde de
Verville
Moreau, J. Les Mots mode d'emploi.
Y. de la Quérière, 207(FR):May87-879
Moreau, J. La problématique kantienne.
M. Adam, 542:Jan-Mar86-117
J. Ecole, 192(EP):Apr-Jun86-262
Moreau, P. Clodiana religio.
J.A. North, 313:Vol76-251
Morejón, N. Where the Island Sleeps Like a
Wing.
S. White, 448:Vol24No1-110
Morel, J. - see Molière
Morel, J-P. Le roman insupportable.*
J. Body, 549(RLC):Oct-Dec86-483
Morell, H.R. Composición expresionista en
"El lugar sin límites" de José Donoso.
M.A. Rojos, 263(RIB):Vol36No3-341
Moreno, R. La polémica del darwinismo en
México.
J.C. Torchia Estrada, 263(RIB):
Vol36No4-496

Moreschini, A.Q. - see under Quattordio
Moreschini, A.
Moret, J-M. Oedipe, la sphinx et les
Thébains.
S. Woodford, 303(JoHS):Vol106-259
Moreton, E. & G. Segal, eds. Soviet
Strategy Toward Western Europe.*
G.H. Bolsover, 575(SEER):Jan86-154
Moretti, W. L'Ultimo Ariosto.
P. Cola, 356(LR):Feb86-71
Morford, M. Persius.*
J.P. Sullivan, 24:Winter86-608
Morgan, B., H. Porter & G. Rubia, eds.
from this place.
G. Davies, 296(JCF):No35/36-154
Morgan, D. The Mongols.
R. Irwin, 617(TLS):6Mar87-234
Morgan, E. Selected Poems.*
H. Buckingham, 565:Summer86-64
Morgan, F. The Fountain & Other Fables.*
M.K. Spears, 569(SR):Spring86-xli
Morgan, F. A Woman of No Character.
P. Lewis, 364:Aug/Sep86-151
L. Potter, 617(TLS):20Mar87-288
Morgan, H. Symbols of America.*
S. Strasser, 432(NEQ):Dec86-613
639(VQR):Autumn86-137
Morgan, J. The Arctic Herd.
L. Horton, 577(SHR):Winter86-91
Morgan, J. Agatha Christie.
639(VQR):Spring86-46
Morgan, J. Perrault's Morals for Moderns.
D. Kuizenga, 210(FrF):May86-233
W.J. Wolfe, 568(SCN):Winter86-64
Morgan, K.N. Charles A. Platt.
T. Matthews, 45:Oct86-73
W.B. Rhoads, 576:Dec86-423
B.F. Tolles, Jr., 432(NEQ):Dec86-607
Morgan, K.O. Labour People.
P. Clarke, 617(TLS):24Apr87-427
P. Hennessy, 362:16Apr87-35
Morgan, M. August Strindberg.
M. Robinson, 562(Scan):May86-84
Morgan, P.F. Literary Critics and Review-
ers in Early 19th-Century Britain.*
J. Shattock, 677(YES):Vol16-301
Morgan, P.F. - see Jeffrey, F.
Morgan, R. Dry Your Smile.
A. Becker, 441:27Sep87-16
Morgan, S. & L.J. Sears, eds. Aesthetic
Tradition and Cultural Transition in Java
and Bali.*
M.J. Kartomi, 187:Winter87-140
Morgan, T.B. Snyder's Walk.
S. Kellerman, 441:17May87-50
Lady Morgan. The Wild Irish Girl.
P. Raine, 617(TLS):6-12Nov87-1216
Morganstern, J. The Byzantine Church at
Dereağzi and its Decoration.*
A.W. Epstein, 576:Jun86-168
A.H.S. Megaw, 303(JoHS):Vol106-268
Morgenstern, D., C. Nanry & D.A. Cayer -
see "Annual Review of Jazz Studies"
Mori, E. Libretti di melodrammi e balli
del secolo XVIII.
R. Monelle, 410(M&L):Apr86-186
Morice, A. Treble Exposure.
G. Kaufman, 362:26Nov87-29
Morita, A., with E.M. Reingold & M. Shimo-
mura. Made in Japan.*
I. Buruma, 453(NYRB):12Mar87-16
J. Hardie, 617(TLS):17Apr87-407

Moritz, A. & T. Leacock.
  G. Lynch, 627(UTQ):Fall86-166
  G. Noonan, 102(CanL):Summer86-132
Morley, J. Listening and Language Learning
  in ESL.
  T. Plaister, 399(MLJ):Spring86-59
Morley, J.D. The Case of Thomas N.
  A. Hulbert, 441:13Sep87-26
Morley, J.T. Secular Socialists.*
  N. Wiseman, 298:Spring86-144
Morley, P. - see Seton, E.T.
Morley, S. Spread a Little Happiness.
  J. Gerard, 441:15Nov87-22
Morphos, E. - see Strasberg, L.
Morragh, P. Alfred Mynn.
  D. Durrant, 364:Jul86-110
Morrell, D. The League of Night and Fog.
  S. Kellerman, 441:16Aug87-16
Morrell, R.E. Sand & Pebbles.
  S. Nagatomo, 485(PE&W):Oct86-438
Morrice, K. Twal Mile Roon.
  K. McCarra, 571(ScLJ):Winter86-37
Morris, A.J.A. The Scaremongers.
  P. Stansky, 635(VPR):Summer86-71
Morris, B. Inspiration for Design.
  E. Bonython, 324:Sep87-782
  R. Watkinson, 326:Autumn86-66
Morris, B. - see Shakespeare, W.
Morris, C.B. El manifesto surrealista
  escrito en Tenerife.
  R.A. Cardwell, 86(BHS):Oct86-397
Morris, D. Catlore.
  O. de Courcy, 362:17&24Dec87-52
Morris, D. & B. Milner. Thomas Hearne
  1744-1817.
  G. Reynolds, 39:Apr86-288
Morris, D.B. Alexander Pope.*
  H. Erskine-Hill, 541(RES):Aug86-420
  F.M. Keener, 401(MLQ):Mar85-81
  P. Thorpe, 577(SHR):Winter86-72
  N. Wood, 83:Autumn86-277
Morris, G.H. Doves and Silk Handkerchiefs.
  P. Parker, 362:17Sep87-26
Morris, H. Dream Palace.
  M. Jarman, 249(HudR):Summer86-335
  J.P. White, 491:Dec86-169
Morris, H. Last Things in Shakespeare.*
  R. Battenhouse, 579(SAQ):Autumn86-416
Morris, H. Romeo and Juliet.
  T. Minter, 157:No160-50
Morris, J. Manhattan '45.
  S. Brook, 617(TLS):21Aug87-895
  R. Starr, 441:19Apr87-8
  N. Williams, 362:28May87-25
Morris, J. & others. Architecture of the
  British Empire.
  P. Davies, 39:Nov86-462
"Jane Morris to Wilfrid Scawen Blunt." (P.
  Faulkner, ed)
  R. Mander, 617(TLS):31Jul87-816
Morris, K.L. The Image of the Middle Ages
  in Romantic and Victorian Literature.*
  B. Richards, 541(RES):Aug86-434
Morris, M. The Bus of Dreams.
  M. Boruch, 434:Autumn86-98
Morris, M.L. Southwestern Fiction 1960-
  1980.
  M. Busby, 649(WAL):Feb87-382
Morris, N. Madness and the Criminal Law.
  M. Bayles, 449:Jun86-268
Morris, R.B. The Forging of the Union
  1781-1789.
  M. Kammen, 441:14Jun87-24

Morris, S.P. The Black and White Style.*
  D.C. Kurtz, 487:Spring86-122
Morris, T.V. Understanding Identity State-
  ments.*
  H.W. Noonan, 479(PhQ):Jul86-457
Morris, W. A Book of Verse.
  F.S. Boos, 637(VS):Summer87-552
Morris, W. The Collected Letters of Wil-
  liam Morris.* (Vol 1) (N. Kelvin, ed)
  F. Kirchhoff, 403(MLS):Summer86-358
  J. Rees, 402(MLR):Jan86-182
Morris, W. The Ideal Book. (W.S. Peter-
  son, ed)
  F.S. Boos, 637(VS):Summer87-552
  J. Dreyfus, 78(BC):Autumn86-387
Morris-Suzuki, T. Shōwa.
  S.H. Nolte, 293(JASt):Feb86-408
Morrison, B. The Ballad of the Yorkshire
  Ripper and Other Poems.
  M. O'Neill, 617(TLS):29May87-574
Morrison, J. The Maturing of the Arts on
  the American Campus.
  L.S. Whitesel, 709:Spring87-186
Morrison, J. This Freedom.
  R. Stevenson, 617(TLS):19Jun87-668
Morrison, J.S. & J.F. Coates. The Athenian
  Trireme.
  G.S. Kirk, 617(TLS):15May87-527
Morrison, T. Beloved.
  M. Atwood, 441:13Sep87-1
  T.R. Edwards, 453(NYRB):5Nov87-18
  L. Heron, 362:29Oct87-28
  C. Rumens, 617(TLS):16-22Oct87-1135
  J. Thurman, 442(NY):2Nov87-175
Morriss, M. & D.J. Dooley. Evelyn Waugh.
  R.M. Davis, 477(PLL):Spring86-218
Morrissette, B. Novel and Film.*
  J. Alter, 207(FR):May87-857
  R.F. Cousins, 402(MLR):Oct87-985
  W. Gibson, 128(CE):Dec86-832
Morrissey, R.J. La Rêverie jusqu'à Rous-
  seau.*
  P. Robinson, 208(FS):Apr86-214
  J.H. Stewart, 210(FrF):Jan86-109
Morrogh, A. Disegni di architetti fioren-
  tini 1540-1640.
  J. Satkowski, 576:Dec86-416
Morrow, B. - see Rexroth, K.
Morrow, J. This is the Way the World
  Ends.*
  C. Greenland, 617(TLS):31Jul87-817
Morrow, P.D., ed. Seventeen North Dakota
  Tales.
  R.L. Smith, 649(WAL):Aug86-138
Morselli, G. Divertimento 1889.
  A. Cancogni, 441:13Sep87-34
  P. Vansittart, 364:Oct86-101
Morson, G.S. The Boundaries of Genre.*
  J. Frank, 569(SR):Fall86-650
Mort, F. Dangerous Sexualities.
  362:19Nov87-37
Mortara Garavelli, B. La parola d'altri.
  N. Cronk, 617(TLS):10Jul87-752
  V. Della Valle, 708:Vol12fasc2-275
Mortier, R. & H. Hasquin, eds. Études sur
  le XVIIIe siècle. (Vol 6)
  D. Oger, 356(LR):May86-175
Mortier, R. & M. Mat, comps. Diderot et
  son temps.
  G. Bremner, 208(FS):Jan86-74
  J. Renwick, 402(MLR):Jan87-203
Mortimer, E., ed. Roosevelt's Children.
  A. Cairncross, 617(TLS):3Jul87-707

259

Mortimer, G.L. Faulkner's Rhetoric of Loss.*
  C.S. Brown, 569(SR):Winter86-167
  K.L. Fulton, 106:Spring86-119
  P. Verney, 150(DR):Winter85/86-606
Mortimer, J. Charade.
  M. Stasio, 441:8Mar87-24
Mortimer, J. Paradise Postponed.*
  42(AR):Summer86-379
  639(VQR):Autumn86-126
Mortimer, R. Stubborn Survivors.
  J. Scott, 293(JASt):Aug86-909
Mortman, D. First Born.
  L. Graeber, 441:4Oct87-28
Morton, D. A Military History of Canada.
  D.M. Schurman, 529(QQ):Spring86-174
Morton, F. Crosstown Sabbath.
  P. Lopate, 441:13Sep87-18
Morton, H.W. & R.C. Stuart. The Contemporary Soviet City.
  C. Nechemias, 550(RusR):Jul86-307
Morton, N. The Journey Is Home.*
  L.M. Getz, 618:Fall86-94
  B. Walsh, 618:Fall86-97
Morton, P. The Vital Science.*
  J.L. Epstein, 125:Fall85-100
  P. Parrinder, 366:Autumn86-265
  T.R. Wright, 161(DUJ):Dec85-204
Morvan, A., ed. La Peur.
  R.A. Day, 189(EA):Oct-Dec87-455
Morwood, J. The Life and Works of Richard Brinsley Sheridan.*
  W. Ruddick, 173(ECS):Summer87-530
Mosci, G. Mounier e Béguin.
  R. Bessède, 535(RHL):Mar-Apr86-337
Moser, H., ed. Zur Situation des Deutschen in Südtirol.
  H. Penzl, 350:Jun87-410
Moser, L.J. The Chinese Mosaic.
  D. Deal, 293(JASt):May86-576
Moser, P.K. Empirical Justification.
  A. Ward, 543:Jun87-787
Moser, W. Gitarre-Musik.
  M. Criswick, 415:Aug86-443
Moser-Rath, E. "Lustige Gesellschaft."*
  P. Brady, 402(MLR):Apr87-512
Moses, C.G. French Feminism in the 19th Century.*
  M.C. Weitz, 207(FR):Feb87-406
Moses, E. Astonishment of Heart.
  D.D. Quantic, 649(WAL):May86-57
Moses, J. The Novelist as Comedian.*
  S. Hunter, 402(MLR):Apr87-456
Moses, L.G. The Indian Man.*
  O.P. Dickason, 106:Winter86-459
Moses, L.G. & R. Wilson, eds. Indian Lives.
  L. Milazzo, 584(SWR):Summer86-402
Moses, M. Master Craftsmen of Newport.
  E.S. Cooke, Jr., 658:Spring86-78
Mosher, S.W. Journey to the Forbidden China.
  G.E. Johnson, 293(JASt):Aug86-826
  639(VQR):Winter86-24
Moskalew, W. Formular Language and Poetic Design in the "Aeneid."*
  S.J. Harrison, 313:Vol76-318
Moskalskaja, O.I. Textgrammatik. (H. Zikmund, ed & trans)
  H-W. Eroms, 684(ZDA):Band115Heft4-154

Moskoff, W. Labour and Leisure in the Soviet Union.
  J. Brine, 575(SEER):Oct86-646
  W.D. Connor, 550(RusR):Oct86-455
Moskop, J.C. & L. Kopelman, eds. Ethics and Critical Care Medicine.
  W.W., 185:Apr87-706
Moskowitz, S., ed. A. Merritt.
  G.K. Wolfe, 561(SFS):Jul86-219
Mosley, C. - see Mitford, N.
Mosley, D. Loved Ones.
  P. Dickinson, 410(M&L):Apr86-198
  B. Sewell, 161(DUJ):Dec85-166
Mosley, J. British Type Specimens Before 1831.
  D. McKitterick, 354:Dec86-377
Mosley, L. The Real Walt Disney.*
  362:15Oct87-28
Mosley, N. Judith.*
  P. Lewis, 565:Autumn86-71
  J. Mellors, 364:Aug/Sep86-147
Moss, A. Poetry and Fable.*
  C.M. Scollen-Jimack, 402(MLR):Apr86-479
  H.R. Secor, 627(UTQ):Fall86-132
Moss, H. New Selected Poems.*
  639(VQR):Winter86-29
Moss, N. Klaus Fuchs.
  Z. Steiner, 441:13Dec87-9
  S. Toulmin, 453(NYRB):19Nov87-54
  H. Whitemore, 362:23Apr87-26
Moss, R. Carnival of Spies.
  J.A.C. Greppin, 441:2Aug87-16
Moss, T. Hosiery Seams on a Bowlegged Woman.
  A. Aubert, 181:Vol36No1-91
Mossberg, B.A.C. Emily Dickinson.*
  J. Loving, 183(ESQ):Vol32No3-201
Mossman, C.A. The Narrative Matrix.*
  D.F. Bell, 210(FrF):Jan86-118
  G. Strickland, 402(MLR):Oct86-1010
Mossman, J. & J.A. Ruffner, eds. Eponyms Dictionaries Index.
  K.B. Harder, 424:Mar86-116
Mossman, T. - see Poe, E.A.
Mossmann, M. Zerfer Platt.
  J.E. Schmidt, 685(ZDL):2/1986-260
Mostyn, T. Coming of Age in the Middle East.
  N. Ryan, 617(TLS):11-17Dec87-1385
Mothersill, M. Beauty Restored.
  M. Budd, 479(PhQ):Jan86-89
  W. Charlton, 89(BJA):Winter86-71
  W. Charlton, 483:Apr86-253
  B. Falk, 518:Jan86-2
  U.H. St. Clair, 484(PPR):Jun87-660
  F. Sparshott, 482(PhR):Jul86-461
Motion, A. The Lamberts.*
  A. Arblaster, 607:Sep86-61
  J. Davidson, 381:Sep86-362
  R. Fuller, 364:Jun86-78
  V. Powell, 39:Jul86-63
  J. Rockwell, 441:2Aug87-21
  442(NY):18May87-118
Motion, A. Philip Larkin.
  R. Marsack, 447(N&Q):Sep85-412
Motion, A. Natural Causes.
  I. Hamilton, 617(TLS):9-15Oct87-1117
Motokiyo, Z. - see under Zeami Motokiyo
de Motolinía, T. Historia de los indios de la Nueva España. (G. Baudot, ed)
  A.F. Bolaños, 304(JHP):Winter86-192

Motte, W.F., Jr. The Poetics of Experiment.*
  C. Rigolot, 207(FR):Dec86-268
  J. Roudant, 535(RHL):Jul-Aug86-802
Mottram, R. Inner Landscapes.*
  M.C. Blew, 649(WAL):Aug86-163
  W.E. Kleb, 610:Summer86-175
  A. Wilson, 397(MD):Mar86-149
Moughtin, J.C. Hausa Architecture.
  V.K. Tarikhu Fahrar, 2(AfrA):Feb86-86
Moukanos, D.D. Ontologie der "Mathematica" in der Metaphysik der Aristoteles.*
  K. Gloy, 53(AGP):Band68Heft2-199
Moulinas, R. Les Juifs du Pape en France.
  N. Perry, 83:Autumn86-243
Mouline, L. Bibliques.
  A. Martin, 208(FS):Jan86-115
Mount, F. The Selkirk Strip.
  C. Hawtree, 617(TLS):13Feb87-164
Mountain, M. Pissed Off Poems and Cross Words.
  J. Kilbride, 404:Autumn86-53
Mountjoy, P.A. Four Early Mycenaean Wells from the South Slope of the Acropolis at Athens.
  O.T.P.K. Dickinson, 303(JoHS):Vol106-244
Mountjoy, P.A. Orchomenos V.
  E. Schofield, 123:Vol36No2-336
Moureau, F. & A-M. Rieu, eds. Eros philosophe.
  H. Mason, 83:Autumn86-282
  J. Rustin, 535(RHL):Nov-Dec86-1128
Moureau, F. & M. Tetel - see Tarde, J.
Moureaux, J-M. - see de Voltaire, F.M.A.
Mouriki, D. The Mosaics of Nea Moni on Chios.
  C. Mango, 617(TLS):14Aug87-866
Mouron, H. A.M. Cassandre.*
  S. Heller, 507:Mar/Apr86-120
Mousnier, R. & J. Mesnard, eds. L'Age d'or du Mécénat (1598-1661).
  A. Viala, 475:Vol13No25-143
Moutspoulos, E.A. Les structures de l'imaginaire dans la philosophie de Proclus.
  J. Brun, 192(EP):Apr-Jun86-263
  M. Lassègue, 542:Oct-Dec86-508
Mouzouni, L. Réception critique d'Ahmed Séfrioui.
  I.C. Tcheho, 188(ECr):Spring86-86
Mowat, F. Woman in the Mists.
  E. Linden, 441:25Oct87-15
Mowl, T. & B. Earnshaw. Trumpet at a Distant Gate.*
  G.A.W., 90:Feb86-156
Moyano Martin, D. - see "Handbook of Latin American Studies"
Moyles, R.G. The Text of "Paradise Lost."*
  J. Leonard, 365:Spring/Summer86-166
  C.A. Thompson, 178:Sep86-346
Moynihan, D.P. Family and Nation.*
  639(VQR):Autumn86-129
Mozart, W.A. & others. The Letters of Mozart and His Family. (E. Anderson, ed; 3rd ed rev by S. Sadie & F. Smart)
  J. Arthur, 410(M&L):Oct86-431
  M. Mudrick, 249(HudR):Autumn86-517
Mphahlele, E. Bury Me at the Marketplace. (N.C. Manganyi, ed)
  B. Worsfold, 538(RAL):Fall86-395

Mpu Dusun. Kunjarakarna Dharmakathana. (A. Teeuw & S.O. Robson, eds & trans)
  J. Errington, 293(JASt):Nov85-204
Mral, S. Frühe schwedische Arbeiterdichtung.
  M. Fahlgren, 172(Edda):1986/3-284
  B. Steene, 563(SS):Spring86-213
Mrozek, D.J. Sport and American Mentality, 1880-1910.
  D. Macleod, 106:Summer86-235
Mueller, I.J. - see Wyclif, J.
Mueller, J. Astaire Dancing.
  J.R. Acocella, 151:Sep86-77
Mueller, J.M. The Native Tongue and the Word.*
  P.J.C. Field, 506(PSt):May86-73
  A. Patterson, 301(JEGP):Jan86-104
Mueller, M. Les Idées politiques dans le roman héroïque de 1630 à 1670.*
  J. Chupeau, 535(RHL):Nov-Dec86-1127
  L.A. Gregorio, 210(FrF):Jan86-105
  W. Henning, 72:Band223Heft2-438
  K. Wine, 207(FR):Oct86-118
  E. Woodrough, 402(MLR):Jul86-737
Mueller, M. "The Iliad."*
  E.M. Jenkinson, 161(DUJ):Dec85-173
  C. Leach, 447(N&Q):Dec85-507
  G.D. Lord, 402(MLR):Jan87-153
  M.M. Willcock, 303(JoHS):Vol106-202
Muenzer, C.S. Figures of Identity.
  B. Duncan, 173(ECS):Winter86/87-255
Mugdan, J. Jan Baudouin de Courtenay (1845-1929).
  F. Häusler, 682(ZPSK):Band39Heft1-123
  A. Liberman, 361:Dec86-376
Mugdan, J. - see Baudouin de Courtenay, J.
Muggeridge, M. Picture Palace.
  C. Hawtree, 617(TLS):22May87-559
Mugo, E.N. Kikuyu People.
  S. Gikandi, 538(RAL):Summer86-299
Mühlhölzer, F. Der Zeitbegriff in der speziellen Relativitätstheorie.
  A. Kamlah, 167:Mar86-235
Mühlmann, W.F. Pfade in die Weltliteratur.
  W. Ross, 52:Band21Heft1-84
Mühlner, W. & K-E. Sommerfeldt, eds. Semantik, Valenz und Sprachkonfrontation des Russischen mit den Deutschen.
  W. Gladrow, 682(ZPSK):Band39Heft1-136
Muhr, R. Sprachwandel als soziales Phänomen.
  K. Rein, 685(ZDL):1/1986-89
Mühsam, E. Trotz allem Mensch sein. (J. Schiewe & H. Maussner, eds)
  S.M. Patsch, 133:Band19Heft2-178
Muir, E. An Autobiography.
  P. Kemp, 617(TLS):13-19Nov87-1258
Muir, J. Muir Among the Animals. (L. Mighetto, ed)
  S.J. Gould, 453(NYRB):25Jun87-20
  442(NY):9Feb87-104
Muir, K., ed. Interpretations of Shakespeare.
  V. Bourgy, 189(EA):Apr-Jun87-205
  H. Hunt, 610:Spring86-64
  L. Scragg, 148:Autumn86-102
  K. Tetzeli von Rosador, 72:Band223 Heft2-471
Muir, K. Shakespeare.*
  H. Jenkins, 570(SQ):Winter86-539
  L. Scragg, 148:Autumn86-102
Muir, R. The Miniature Man.
  A. Postman, 441:27Dec87-18

Munro, A. The Folk Music Revival in
Scotland.*
  T. Crawford, 571(ScLJ):Winter86-27
  H.B.R., 412:Feb85-68
Munro, A. The Progress of Love.*
  E.D. Blodgett, 99:Oct86-32
  A.S. Byatt, 362:29Jan87-22
  A. Duchêne, 617(TLS):30Jan87-109
Munro, C. Wild Man of Letters.*
  V. Smith, 71(ALS):May86-421
Munro, D. Alexandre Dumas père.*
  F.W.J. Hemmings, 208(FS):Apr86-222
Munro, E. On Glory Roads.
  R. Blythe, 441:26Apr87-9
  442(NY):1Jun87-112
Munro, J. The Trees Just Moved Into a
Season of Other Shapes.
  S. Scobie, 376:Dec86-140
Munson, G. The Awakening Twenties.*
  639(VQR):Winter86-10
Munson, H., Jr., ed & trans. The House of
Si Abd Allah.
  J.A. Miller, 538(RAL):Winter86-582
Münster, A. Studien zu Beethovens
Diabelli-Variationen.
  W. Drabkin, 415:Jun86-336
Munting, R. Hedges and Hurdles.
  R. Carr, 617(TLS):3Jul87-729
"Muqarnas."* (Vol 1) (O. Grabar, ed)
  Y. Tabbaa, 318(JAOS):Oct/Dec85-752
Muraro, M.T., ed. Malipiero.
  R. Fearn, 410(M&L):Apr86-190
Murase, M. Iconography of the "Tale of
Genji."*
  M. Graybill, 293(JASt):Nov85-155
Murat, M. "Le Rivage des Syrtes" de Julien
Gracq.*
  R. Amossy, 535(RHL):Sep-Oct86-956
  F. Calin, 210(FrF):May86-247
Murav'eva, L.L. Letopisanie severo-
vostochnoi Rusi kontsa XIII-nachala XV
veka.
  N.S. Kollmann, 550(RusR):Jan86-64
Muray, P. Le XIXe siècle à travers les
âges.*
  M. Pierssens, 98:Oct86-999
Murcia, M.C., ed. Beyond Basics.
  T.D. Terrell, 399(MLJ):Summer86-171
Murdoch, B. - see Remarque, E.M.
Murdoch, B.O. Old High German Literature.
  H. Mayer, 589:Jan86-184
Murdoch, I. Acastos.*
  J. Updike, 442(NY):18May87-113
Murdoch, I. The Book and the Brotherhood.
  S.R.L. Clark, 617(TLS):4-11Sep87-947
  S. Fry, 362:24Sep87-20
Murdoch, I. The Good Apprentice.*
  D. Flower, 249(HudR):Summer86-320
  P. Lewis, 565:Spring86-38
Murdoch, I. L'Élève du philosophe.
  T. Dey, 450(NRF):Mar86-110
Murdoch, J. A Bibliography of Algonquian
Syllabic Texts in Canadian Repositories.
  B. Edwards, 470:Vol24-105
Murdoch, J.E. Antiquity and the Middle
Ages.
  R.B. Thomson, 589:Apr86-445
Murfin, R.C., ed. Conrad Revisited.*
  J. Batchelor, 541(RES):Nov86-592
  P. Casagrande, 594:Spring86-96
  R. Kimbrough, 177(ELT):Vol29No3-332
  P.D. Morrow, 577(SHR):Fall86-387

Murfin, R.C. The Poetry of D.H. Lawrence.*
  J. Worthen, 447(N&Q):Sep85-407
Murgatroyd, P. Tibullus I.
  R.J. Ball, 121(CJ):Dec86-Jan87-156
Murnane, G. Landscape with Landscape.
  H. Jacobson, 617(TLS):27Nov-3Dec87-
  1307
Murphy, A.J. John Dennis.
  J.W. Johnson, 566:Autumn86-77
Murphy, A.L. Three Bluenose Plays.
  A. Wagner, 108:Spring86-110
Murphy, B. Turncoat.
  C.C. Davis, 441:19Jul87-21
Murphy, C. The Jericho Rumble.
  N. Callendar, 441:22Nov87-45
Murphy, D. Lover Man.
  N. Callendar, 441:13Sep87-46
Murphy, H. Murder Takes a Partner.
  N. Callendar, 441:19Apr87-22
  G. Kaufman, 362:26Nov87-29
Murphy, J.G. & J.L. Coleman. The Philoso-
phy of Law.
  J. Deigh, 185:Oct86-282
Murphy, J.J., ed. The Rhetorical Tradition
and Modern Writing.*
  D. Birch, 402(MLR):Jul86-732
  V.J. Vitanza, 126(CCC):Oct86-361
Murphy, J.J., ed. A Synoptic History of
Classical Rhetoric.
  R.L. Enos, 126(CCC):Oct86-360
Murphy, J.L. Darkness and Devils.
  F.W. Brownlow, 481(PQ):Winter86-131
  J. Reibetanz, 401(MLQ):Jun85-181
Murphy, K. The Autopsy.
  P. Filkins, 236:Fall-Winter86/87-50
Murphy, N.T.P. In Search of Blandings.*
  C. Hawtree, 364:Aug/Sep86-155
  362:10Dec87-29
Murphy, R.F. The Body Silent.
  M.F. Brown, 441:5Apr87-34
Murphy, S. The Life and Times of Barly
Beach.
  P. Craig, 617(TLS):27Feb87-206
Murphy, T. Appetites.
  S. Paulos, 441:20Sep87-27
Murphy, W.F. Upon this Rock.
  J. Koenig, 441:6Dec87-26
Murphy, Y. Stories in Another Language.
  A. Becker, 441:7Jun87-30
Murray, J. The Best of the Group of
Seven.*
  L.R., 102(CanL):Winter85-178
Murray, J. - see MacLeod, P.N.
Murray, L.A. Selected Poems.*
  J.P. Ward, 493:Oct86-48
Murray, M. South Africa.
  L. Thompson, 453(NYRB):11Jun87-20
Murray, P. Renaissance Architecture.
  J.S. Curl, 324:Apr87-405
Murray, P. Song in a Weary Throat.
  P. Williams, 441:29Mar87-12
Murray, S. Building Troyes Cathedral.
  P. Lindley, 617(TLS):31Jul87-825
Murray, S.O. Group Formation in Social
Science.
  W. Leeds-Hurwitz, 350:Sep87-668
Murray, T.H. & A.L. Caplan, eds. Which
Babies Shall Live?
  G.E.J., 185:Jan87-512
Murray, W. When the Fat Man Sings.
  T. Hillerman, 441:8Nov87-22
  442(NY):28Dec87-126

Murray, W.J. The Right Wing Press in the French Revolution.
 W. Scott, 617(TLS):13Feb87-158
Murrell, J. Farther West and New World.
 H. Lynn, 108:Fall86-139
Murry, K.M. - see under Middleton Murry, K.
Murthy, D.S. Just Born.
 U. Parameswaran, 314:Summer-Fall86-247
Murti, M.S.N. Vallabhadeva's Kommentar (Śaradā-Version) zum Kumārasaṃbhava des Kālidāsa.
 S. Pollock, 318(JAOS):Apr/Jun85-381
Musacchio, E. & S. Cordeschi. Il riso nelle poetiche rinascimentali.
 A. Di Benedetto, 228(GSLI):Vol163 fasc521-142
Musallam, B.F. Sex and Society in Islam.
 C. Issawi, 318(JAOS):Apr/Jun85-362
Muscatine, C. The Old French Fabliaux.
 D.D.R. Owen, 617(TLS):6Mar87-236
 42(AR):Fall86-493
Muscetta, C. Pace e guerra nella poesia contemporanea da Alfonso Gatto a Umberto Saba.
 Z.G. Barański, 402(MLR):Jan86-234
"Museo Poldi Pezzoli, Milan: Armeria I."
 S. Bevan, 90:Aug86-610
Musgrave, M. The Music of Brahms.*
 42(AR):Fall86-491
Musgrove, J., ed. Sir Banister Fletcher's "A History of Architecture." (19th ed)
 A. Saint, 617(TLS):8May87-495
"Music in Colonial Massachusetts, 1630-1820."
 G.G. Carey, 656(WMQ):Jul86-492
"Musik und lateinischer Ritus/Musique et Rite latin."
 N. Sevestre, 537:Vol72No1-138
Muskat, B.T. and M.A. Neeley. The Way It Was, 1850-1930.
 S.R. Wolfe, 9(AlaR):Jul86-214
Mussell, K. Fantasy and Reconciliation.
 S. O'Brien, 395(MFS):Summer86-353
Mustajoki, A., ed. Doklady finskoy delegatsii na IX s"yezde slavistov.
 J.I. Press, 575(SEER):Jul86-450
Mustajoki, A. Padež dopolnenija v russkix otricatel'nyx predloženijax 1.
 C.H. Chvany, 279:Vol33-164
 G. Fowler, 350:Mar87-189
 J.I. Press, 575(SEER):Jul86-450
Musumarra, C., ed. I Malavoglia di Giovanni Verga.
 G. Cecchetti, 275(IQ):Spring86-110
Muzerelle, D. Vocabulaire codicologique.
 O. Merisalo, 439(NM):1986/3-465
Muzio, G. Lettere. (L. Borsetto, ed)
 M. Pozzi, 228(GSLI):Vol163fasc524-622
Myer, V.G., ed. Laurence Sterne.*
 C.H. Flynn, 402(MLR):Oct87-920
 F. Price, 83:Spring86-101
 L.E. Warren, 566:Spring87-198
Myerowitz, M. Ovid's Games of Love.
 E. O'Connor, 124:May-Jun87-387
Myers, B.S. & T. Copplestone, eds. Landmarks of Western Art.
 C. Gould, 39:Aug86-142
Myers, G.E. William James.
 A.A. Rhodes, 441:22Mar87-29
 S.P. Stich, 617(TLS):27Nov-3Dec87-1315
 S. Sutherland, 362:15Jan87-21
Myers, J. As Long as You're Happy.
 B. Shlain, 441:25Jan87-15

Myers, N., general ed. The Gaia Atlas of Planet Management.
 J.M. Ashworth, 324:Dec86-76
Myers, P. Deadly Cadenza.*
 N. Callendar, 441:8Feb87-20
Myers, R. & M. Harris, eds. Author/Publisher Relations during the Eighteenth and Nineteenth Centuries.
 J.J. & P.P. Barnes, 517(PBSA):Vol80No1-111
 L. Madden, 447(N&Q):Dec85-558
Myers, R. & M. Harris, eds. Bibliophily.
 D. Chambers, 503:Summer86-96
Myers, R. & M. Harris, eds. Development of the English Book Trade, 1700-1899.* Sale and Distribution of Books from 1700.* Maps and Prints. Economics of the British Book Trade, 1605-1939.
 J.J. & P.P. Barnes, 517(PBSA):Vol80No1-111
Myers, R.E., ed. The Intersection of Science Fiction and Philosophy.
 P.C. Bjarkman, 395(MFS):Summer86-374
Myers, R.H. & M.R. Peattie, eds. The Japanese Colonial Empire, 1895-1945.*
 G.O. Totten 3d, 293(JASt):May86-610
Myers, W. The Teaching of George Eliot.*
 E.M. Eigner, 402(MLR):Oct87-932
 C. Viera, 577(SHR):Winter86-78
Myerson, J., ed. The Transcendentalists.*
 S.E. Marovitz, 87(BB):Sep86-183
Myerson, J. & D. Shealy - see Alcott, L.M.
Myint, T.P. - see under Thein Pe Myint
Mylius, K. Geschichte der Literatur im alten Indien.
 H. Scharfe, 318(JAOS):Oct/Dec85-817

Naar, M. - see Kant, I.
Nabhan, G.P. Gathering the Desert.*
 C. Bowden, 649(WAL):Nov86-254
Nabokov, V. The Enchanter.*
 A. Jenkins, 617(TLS):16Jan87-55
 A.R. Lee, 362:22Jan87-26
 V.S. Pritchett, 453(NYRB):12Mar87-9
 362:31Dec87-21
Nabokov, V. Perepiska s sestroj. (H. Sikorski, ed)
 D.B. Johnson, 574(SEEJ):Summer86-295
Nadel, I.B. Biography.*
 P. Allen, 627(UTQ):Fall86-124
 B. Jones, 178:Dec86-497
 J. Olney, 177(ELT):Vol29No4-429
 G. Webster, 77:Summer86-277
Nadel, I.B. & W.E. Fredeman, eds. Dictionary of Literary Biography. (Vols 18 & 21)
 S.M. Smith, 402(MLR):Jul87-714
Nadolny, S. The Discovery of Slowness.
 S. Blackburn, 441:20Dec87-15
Naess, H.E. Med Bål og brann - Trolldomsprosesser i Norge.
 K. Stokker, 563(SS):Autumn86-434
Naess, H.E. Trolldomsprosessene i Norge på 1500- og 1600-tallet.
 K. Stokker, 563(SS):Autumn86-433
Nagaraja, K.S. Khasi.
 B. Comrie, 350:Jun87-440
Nagata, J. The Reflowering of Malaysian Islam.
 R. Provencher, 293(JASt):Feb86-458

Nagel, B. Das Reimproblem in der deutschen
Dichtung.
R. Dove, 402(MLR):Oct87-1019
Nagel, P.C. The Adams Women.
J. Lewis, 441:25Oct87-23
Nagel, T. The View from Nowhere.*
J. Glover, 453(NYRB):9Apr87-31
Nagorski, A. Reluctant Farewell.
639(VQR):Winter86-26
Nagy, G. & S. Erdész, eds. Karcsai
népmesék.
T. Fazekas, 196:Band27Heft3/4-362
Naipaul, S. An Unfinished Journey.*
J.F. Avedon, 441:22Mar87-26
D.J. Taylor, 364:Aug/Sep86-135
Naipaul, V.S. The Enigma of Arrival.
J. Bayley, 453(NYRB):9Apr87-3
G. Josipovici, 362:12Mar87-24
P. Kemp, 617(TLS):7Aug87-838
F. Kermode, 441:22Mar87-11
Nairne, S. State of the Art.
R. Cork, 617(TLS):13Feb87-163
Najder, Z. Joseph Conrad.*
R. Brebach, 301(JEGP):Jan86-145
Najder, Z., ed. Conrad Under Familial
Eyes.*
J. Kertzer, 49:Apr86-89
Nakadate, N., ed. Robert Penn Warren.
H. Claridge, 447(N&Q):Mar85-143
Nakam, G. Les "Essais" de Montaigne,
miroir et procès de leur temps.*
J. Bailbé, 535(RHL):Mar-Apr86-266
A. Compagnon, 208(FS):Oct86-451
Nakamura, H. Divorce in Java.
S. Brenner, 293(JASt):Feb86-460
Nakamura, M. The Crescent Arises over the
Banyan Tree.
R.W. Hefner, 293(JASt):May86-649
Nakamura, R. & R. de Ceccatty. Mille ans
de littérature japonaise.
J. Pigeot, 549(RLC):Apr-Jun86-187
Nakamura, T. Economic Growth in Prewar
Japan.
R. Evans, Jr., 302:Vol22No1-99
Nakhimovsky, A.D. & A.S. - see Lotman,
J.M., L.I. Ginsburg & B.A. Uspenskii
Nakov, A. Avant Garde Russe.
N.D. Lobanov, 39:Nov86-459
Nalbantian, S. Seeds of Decadence in the
Late Nineteenth Century Novel.*
R. Asselineau, 549(RLC):Jan-Mar86-108
R. Crawford, 447(N&Q):Sep85-405
Naldini, M. - see Basil of Caesarea
Naldini, N. - see Comisso, G.
Naldini, N. - see Pasolini, P.P.
Nalimov, V.V. Faces of Science. (R.G.
Colodny, ed)
M. Ruse, 488:Jun86-249
Namioka, L. China.
42(AR):Spring86-247
Ñāṇamoli, B., ed & trans. The Path of Dis-
crimination (Paṭisambhidāmagga).* (rev
by A.K. Warder)
J.P. McDermott, 318(JAOS):Oct/Dec85-
784
Nanavati, R.I. Secondary Tales of the Two
Great Epics.
R. Lariviere, 318(JAOS):Apr/Jun85-383
Nanda, B.R. Gandhi and his Critics.
S. Khilnani, 617(TLS):6Feb87-142
Naoya, S. - see under Shiga Naoya
Napier, E.R. The Failure of Gothic.
C. Baldick, 617(TLS):1May87-471

Narasiṃhācārya, M.S. - see "Mahābhāṣyapra-
dīpavyākhyānāni"
Narayan, R.K. Talkative Man.*
A. Becker, 441:29Mar87-22
A. Ross, 364:Oct86-106
M. Thorpe, 176:May87-42
R. Towers, 453(NYRB):8Oct87-45
Narayan, R.K. Under the Banyan Tree &
Other Stories.*
639(VQR):Winter86-22
Nardelli, F.P. - see under Petrucci
Nardelli, F.
Nardi, C. Il battesimo in Clemente Ales-
sandrino.
É. des Places, 555:Vol59fasc2-300
Nardova, V.A. Gorodskoe samoupravlenie v
Rossii v 60-kh-nachale 90-kh godov XIX
veka.
D.R. Brower, 550(RusR):Jan86-77
Narula, U. & W.B. Pearce. Development as
Communication.
J.J. MacDougall, 583:Fall86-94
Nash, J.C., ed. Pre-Pléiade Poetry.
U. Langer, 210(FrF):May86-229
A. Moss, 208(FS):Jul86-323
G.P. Norton, 551(RenQ):Winter86-779
Nash, J.C. Veiled Images.
D. Rosand, 551(RenQ):Winter86-752
Nash, S. Paul Valéry's "Album de vers
anciens."*
U. Franklin, 131(CL):Winter86-104
Nash, W. The Language of Humour.*
A. Moulin, 596(SL):Vol40No1-98
R.S. Sharma, 257(IRAL):Nov86-341
Nashef, K. Die Orts- und Gewässernamen
der mittelbabylonischen und mittelassyr-
ischen Zeit.
T. Kwasman, 318(JAOS):Oct/Dec85-728
Nasr, R.T., ed. The Teaching of Arabic to
Adults in Europe.
A.S. Kaye, 320(CJL):Spring86-91
I. Mutlak, 682(ZPSK):Band39Heft5-613
Nassar, E.P. Essays Critical and Meta-
critical.
V.C. Fowler, 284:Winter85-144
E.M. Thompson, 396(ModA):Summer/Fall
86-326
Natalle, E.J. Feminist Theatre.
M. Hamer, 610:Autumn86-276
Nater, H.F. The Bella Coola Language.
D.H., 355(LSoc):Mar86-136
Nathan, A.J. Chinese Democracy.
B. Womack, 293(JASt):May86-577
Nathan, J. An American Folklife Cookbook.
W. & C. Cowen, 639(VQR):Spring86-67
Nathan, R.S. The White Tiger.
J.A. Cohen, 441:6Sep87-9
Nathanson, S. The Ideal of Rationality.
J.R., 185:Jan87-496
"A Nation of Poets." (K. Johnson, trans)
S. White, 448:Vol24No1-110
Natov, N. Mikhail Bulgakov.*
E.K. Beaujour, 574(SEEJ):Fall86-450
E.C. Haber, 550(RusR):Jan86-59
L. Milne, 575(SEER):Oct86-599
"Naturalismul în Literatura română."
Y. Chevrel, 549(RLC):Jan-Mar86-71
Naudé, G. Lettres de Gabriel Naudé à
Jacques Dupuy (1632-1652).* (P. Wolfe,
ed)
B. Beugnot, 107(CRCL):Jun86-298

Newman, L. Good Enough to Eat.
  H. Fensome, 617(TLS):13–19Nov87–1249
Newman, P.C. Company of Adventurers.
  (Vol 2)
  J. Barfoot, 441:20Dec87–9
Newman, R.J. Growth in the American South.
  J.L. McCorkle, Jr., 392:Spring86–119
Newmeyer, F.J. The Politics of Linguis-
  tics.
  R. Harris, 617(TLS):11–17Dec87–1373
Newton, D.J. British Labour, European
  Socialism and the Struggle for Peace
  1889–1914.*
  J. Schneer, 637(VS):Summer87–547
Newton, I. Certain Philosophical Ques-
  tions.* (J.E. McGuire & M. Tamny, eds)
  D. Shapere, 482(PhR):Jan86–102
Newton, I. Principia Mathematica. (M.F.
  Biarnais, trans)
  J. Largeault, 542:Jan–Mar86–119
Newton, I. The Sparrowhawk.
  M. Greppin, 617(TLS):13Mar87–280
Newton, J. & D. Rosenfelt, eds. Feminist
  Criticism and Social Change.
  E.C.R., 295(JML):Nov86–366
Newton–Smith, W.H. Logic.
  A.J. Dale, 518:Jul86–170
Ney, K. Rumänische Transferenzen in vier
  siebenbürgisch–sächsischen Ortsmundarten
  des Kreises Hermannstadt/Rumänien.
  T. Teaha, 685(ZDL):2/1986–262
Neyt, F., with A. Désirant. The Arts of
  the Benue.
  A. Rubin, 2(AfrA):Aug86–15
Ngal, N.A.M. & M. Steins. Césaire 70.
  A. Kom, 343:Heft14–135
Ngara, E. Teaching Literature in Africa.
  F. Stratton, 538(RAL):Fall86–451
Ngugi wa Thiong'o. Decolonizing the Mind.
  Chinweizu, 617(TLS):8May87–499
Nichol, B.P. Zygal.
  S. Scobie, 376:Sep86–157
Nicholas, D. The Domestic Life of a Medie-
  val City.
  T.C. Holyoke, 42(AR):Summer86–375
Nicholas of Cusa. Nicolas de Cues, "Let-
  tres aux moines de Tegernsee sur la docte
  ignorance" (1452–1456). (M. de Gandil-
  lac, ed & trans)
  J. Jolivet, 542:Oct–Dec86–513
Nicholl, C. A Cup of News.*
  N. Rhodes, 447(N&Q):Dec85–517
Nicholls, G. "Measure for Measure."
  M. Willems, 189(EA):Jul–Sep87–350
Nicholls, J.W. The Matter of Courtesy.
  J.D. Burnley, 179(ES):Aug86–369
Nicholls, P. Ezra Pound: Politics,
  Economics and Writing.*
  I.F.A. Bell, 366:Autumn86–269
Nichols, B. Ideology and the Image.
  F. Leibowitz, 488:Sep86–399
Nichols, G. The Fat Black Woman's Poems.
  T. Eagleton, 565:Autumn86–76
Nichols, J. & A.C. Woodbury, eds. Grammar
  Inside and Outside the Clause.
  M.S. Dryer, 320(CJL):Winter86–382
Nichols, K.D. The Road to Trinity.
  A.A. Rhodes, 441:30Aug87–21
Nichols, L. African Writers at the Micro-
  phone.
  A. Tetteh–Lartey, 538(RAL):Spring86–
  153

Nichols, S.G., Jr. Romanesque Signs.*
  J.H.M. McCash, 131(CL):Spring86–195
  C.L. Scarborough, 345:May86–238
Nicholson, G. Seeing and Reading.
  M.M. van de Pitte, 154:Winter86–782
  W.F. Vallicella, 449:Sep86–437
Nicholson, L.J. Gender and History.
  P.S.M., 185:Apr87–691
Nicholson, W. Unknown Colour.
  F. Spalding, 617(TLS):19Jun87–663
Ní Chuilleanáin, E. The Second Voyage.
  C. Wills, 617(TLS):25–31Dec87–1435
Nickel, H.L. Medieval Architecture in Eas-
  tern Europe.*
  I. Nagurski, 497(PolR):Vol31No4–342
Nickerson, C.C. & J.W. Osborne – see
  Cobbett, W.
Nicol, D.M. The Despotate of Epiros 1267–
  1479.
  J.W. Barker, 589:Jul86–689
  S. Franklin, 303(JoHS):Vol106–269
  T. Winnifrith, 575(SEER):Apr86–288
Nicol, N.D., R. el-Nabarawy & J.L. Bachar-
  ach. Catalog of the Islamic Coins, Glass
  Weights, Dies and Medals in the Egyptian
  National Library.
  H.E. Kassis, 318(JAOS):Oct/Dec85–755
Nicolaï, R. Préliminaires à une étude sur
  l'origine du Songhay.
  S. Brauner, 682(ZPSK):Band39Heft5–622
Nicolet, C., ed. Demokratia et Aristo-
  kratia.
  J. Briscoe, 123:Vol36No1–155
  P. Flobert, 555:Vol59fasc2–331
Nicolodi, F. Musica e musicisti nel
  ventennio fascista.*
  J.C.G. Waterhouse, 410(M&L):Oct86–426
Nicolson, N. Portrait d'un mariage.
  F. de Martinoir, 450(NRF):Jul–Aug86–186
Nicolson, N. & A. Two Roads to Dodge
  City.*
  K.A. Marling, 441:12Apr87–47
Nicolson, W. The London Diaries of William
  Nicolson, Bishop of Carlisle 1702–1718.*
  (C. Jones & G. Holmes, eds)
  G.M. Townend, 83:Autumn86–272
Niderst, A. – see Corneille, P.
Niderst, A. – see Goulley de Boisrobert, A.
Niebaum, H. Dialektologie.*
  K–H. Jäger, 406:Summer86–215
  P. Suchsland, 682(ZPSK):Band39Heft3–
  392
  P. Wagener, 260(IF):Band91–356
Niebuhr, R. The Essential Reinhold Nie-
  buhr. (R.M. Brown, ed)
  R. Cook, 529(QQ):Winter86–932
  J.M., 185:Jan87–500
Niedecker, L. From This Condensery.*
  (R.J. Bertholf, ed) "Between Your House
  and Mine." (L.P. Faranda, ed)
  J. Penberthy, 617(TLS):25Sep–1Oct87–
  1043
Niedecker, L. The Granite Pail.* (C.
  Corman, ed)
  639(VQR):Spring86–60
"Niederländische Zeichnungen."
  A–M.L., 380:Autumn86–422
Nield, K., ed. Victorian Social Con-
  science: Prostitution.
  J.J. Savory, 635(VPR):Fall86–116
Nielsen, H.A. Where the Passion Is.*
  A. McKinnon, 154:Winter86–786
  D.Z. Phillips, 521:Jan86–66

Nielsen, H.F. Old English and the Continental Germanic Languages.
C–D. Wetzel, 260(IF):Band91–409
Nielsen, K. Equality and Liberty.*
W.E. Cooper, 154:Summer86–303
J. Narveson, 258:Jun86–192
Nielsen, K. Philosophy and Atheism.*
B. Leftow, 258:Mar86–101
Nielsen, W.A. The Golden Donors.*
639(VQR):Summer86–98
Niessen, S.A. Motifs of Life in Toba Batak Texts and Textiles.
R.S. Kipp, 293(JASt):Aug86–911
Niesz, A.J. Dramaturgy in German Drama.
E. Catholy, 133:Band18Heft4–366
Niethammer, P–M., comp. Urkundenfindbuch zu Oswald von Wolkenstein (1400–1445).
A. Robertshaw, 402(MLR):Oct86–1039
Nietzsche, F. Human, All Too Human. (M. Faber, with S. Lehmann, trans)
A. Del Caro, 221(GQ):Summer86–506
Nigg, J. Winegold.
A. Cuelho, 649(WAL):Aug86–180
Nightingale, B. Fifth Row Center.*
B. Bergonzi, 176:Jul/Aug87–44
S. Fry, 362:23Apr87–22
Nightingale, P. Journey through Darkness.
P. Kemp, 617(TLS):7Aug87–838
Nigro, R. I fuochi del Basento.
M. d'Amico, 617(TLS):9–15Oct87–1115
Nikkilä, P. Early Confucianism and Inherited Thought in the Light of Some Key Terms of the Confucian Analects. (Vol 1)
B.B. Blakeley, 302:Vol22No1–63
Niklaus, R. Beaumarchais: "Le Mariage de Figaro."*
G. Bremner, 402(MLR):Apr86–485
Niklaus, R. – see de Beaumarchais, P.A.C.
Niles, D. Commercial Recordings of Papua New Guinea Music, 1949–1983. (1984 Supp)
S. Feld, 187:Winter87–163
Niles, J.D. "Beowulf."*
S.A.J. Bradley, 402(MLR):Jul87–697
H. Chickering, 589:Jan86–186
M.E. Goldsmith, 382(MAE):1986/2–266
S.B. Greenfield, 131(CL):Winter86–98
E.G. Stanley, 541(RES):Feb86–70
Nill, M. Morality and Self-Interest in Protagoras, Antiphon and Democritus.
J. Annas, 617(TLS):20Feb87–178
Nilsen, D.L.F. & A.P., eds. Whimsy III.
L.E. Mintz, 292(JAF):Jul/Sep86–339
Nilsson, L. & J. Lindberg, with others. The Body Victorious.
I. Poliski, 441:27Sep87–36
Nimmo, D. Not in Front of the Servants.
D.J. Enright, 617(TLS):18–24Dec87–1399
Nin, A. The Early Diary of Anaïs Nin.* (Vol 4)
639(VQR):Winter86–14
"Nineteenth Century Short Title Catalogue." (Ser 1, Phase 1)
P. Fleming, 635(VPR):Summer86–68
D. McKitterick, 617(TLS):8May87–497
D.H. Reiman, 591(SIR):Summer86–289
"Nineteenth Century Short Title Catalogue." (Ser 2, Phase 1, Vols 1–5)
D. McKitterick, 617(TLS):8May87–497
Nipperdey, T. Nachdenken über die deutschen Geschichte.
D. Blackbourn, 617(TLS):2Jan87–10
G.A. Craig, 453(NYRB):15Jan87–16

Nisbet, A–M. Littérature néo-calédonienne.
M–R. Cornu, 627(UTQ):Fall86–248
Nisbet, A–M. Le personnage féminin dans la roman maghrébin de langue français des indépendances à 1980.
C.H. Bruner, 538(RAL):Winter86–576
Nisbet, H.B., ed. German Aesthetic and Literary Criticism. (Vol 1)
H.M. Schueller, 290(JAAC):Spring87–301
J. Voisine, 549(RLC):Oct–Dec86–472
Nisbet, R. Conservatism.
A. Ryan, 617(TLS):7Aug87–854
Nisetich, F.J. Pindar's Victory Songs.
W.J. Verdenius, 394:Vol39fasc1/2–164
Nish, I., ed. Anglo–Japanese Alienation 1919–1952.
E.W. Edwards, 302:Vol22No1–102
Nishi, K. & K. Hozumi. What is Japanese Architecture? (H.M. Horton, ed & trans)
W.H. Coaldrake, 407(MN):Autumn86–374
G. Wajed, 46:Jan86–80
Nishikawa, K. & E.J. Sano. The Great Age of Japanese Buddhist Sculpture AD 600–1300.
D. Waterhouse, 302:Vol22No1–110
Nishimura Shigeo. Chūgoku kindai Tōhoku chi–ikishi kenkyū.
R. Suleski, 293(JASt):Feb86–386
Nissanka, H.S.S. Sri Lanka's Foreign Policy.
R. Oberst, 293(JASt):Aug86–884
Nissen, W. Die Brüder Grimm und ihre Märchen.
D.P. Haase, 221(GQ):Spring86–337
Nissenson, H. The Tree of Life.
C. Beyers, 649(WAL):Nov86–238
42(AR):Spring86–252
Nisula, D.C. – see Parun, V.
Nitta, Y., ed. Japanische Beiträge zur Phänomenologie.
H. Schmitz, 489(PJGG):Band93Heft1–187
Nixon, C. Lawrence's Leadership Politics and the Turn against Women.
M. Magalaner, 395(MFS):Winter86–663
Nixon, H.M., comp. Catalogue of the Pepys Library at Magdalene College, Cambridge. (Vol 5)
78(BC):Summer86–145
Nixon, I. – see "Thomas of Erceldoune"
Nizon, P. L'Année de l'amour.
J–L. Coatalem, 450(NRF):Dec86–108
Nkosi, L. Home and Exile and Other Selections.
J. Booth, 538(RAL):Fall86–398
"No Feather, No Ink."
T. Flanagan, 298:Summer86–157
W. Klooss, 376:Dec86–141
Noble, A. – see Stevenson, R.L.
Noble, A.G. Wood, Brick & Stone.*
T.C. Hubka, 432(NEQ):Mar86–152
Noble, C. Afternoon Starlight.*
G. Johnston, 298:Fall86–133
Noble, C. Banff/Breaking.
D. Bennett, 102(CanL):Winter85–152
Noble, I. Language and Narration in Céline's Writing.
P. McCarthy, 617(TLS):25–31Dec87–1436
Noble, J. & others. "The New Grove" High Renaissance Masters.
D. Arnold, 410(M&L):Apr86–192
Noble, P.S. Love and Marriage in Chrétien de Troyes.*
W.W. Kibler, 345:May86–237

Noble, P.S. & L.M. Paterson, eds. Chrétien de Troyes and the Troubadours.*
S. Kay, 382(MAE):1986/1-144
W. Rothwell, 208(FS):Oct86-446
S. Spence, 589:Jan86-246
Noble, T.A. - see Eliot, G.
Noble, T.F.X. The Republic of St. Peter.*
W.M. Daly, 589:Jan86-190
Nodier, C. Moi-même.* (D. Sangsue, ed)
R. Pearson, 208(FS):Apr86-219
Noe, S.P. The Coinage of Metapontum. (rev by A. Johnston)
A. Burnett, 303(JoHS):Vol106-258
Nogales, J.L.M. - see under Martín Nogales, J.L.
Noguez, D. Les Trois Rimbaud.
J-C. Dorrier, 450(NRF):Jul-Aug86-173
Noiray, J. Le Romancier et la machine.* (Vol 2)
J. Anzalone, 188(ECr):Winter86-100
Nokes, D. Jonathan Swift, a Hypocrite Reversed.*
P. Danchin, 189(EA):Jul-Sep86-343
F.H. Ellis, 173(ECS):Spring87-339
O.W. Ferguson, 191(ELN):Mar87-75
B.S. Hammond, 83:Autumn86-267
J.C.C. Mays, 272(IUR):Spring86-99
D.M. Vieth, 566:Spring87-185
639(VQR):Summer86-84
Nolan, C. Under the Eye of the Clock.
J. Naughton, 362:30Apr87-31
D. Singmaster, 617(TLS):31Jul87-828
Nolan, F. Red Center.
N. Callendar, 441:26Apr87-37
Nolan, P. & S. Paine, eds. Rethinking Socialist Economics.
F. Cairncross, 617(TLS):9Jan87-32
Nølke, H. Les adverbes paradigmatisants.
D. Gaatone, 545(RPh):Aug86-92
Nolte, S.H. Liberalism in Modern Japan.
W.G. Beasley, 617(TLS):14Aug87-868
de Nonno, M. La grammatica dell'Anonymus Bobiensis (G.L., I, 533-565 Keil).
A.P. Orbán, 394:Vol39fasc1/2-214
Nonnus. Nonnos de Panopolis, "Les Dionysiaques." (Vol 4) (G. Chrétien, ed)
M.L. West, 123:Vol36No2-210
Noomen, W. & N. van den Boogaard. Nouveau Recueil complet des Fabliaux.* (Vol 1)
A.J. Holden, 402(MLR):Oct86-996
T. Hunt, 208(FS):Oct86-448
R.J. Pearcy, 589:Apr86-448
M.J. Schenck, 545(RPh):Aug86-114
Noomen, W. & N. van den Boogaard, eds. Nouveau Recueil complet des Fabliaux. (Vol 2)
A.J. Holden, 402(MLR):Oct86-996
T. Hunt, 208(FS):Oct86-448
R.J. Pearcy, 589:Apr86-448
G. Roques, 553(RLiR):Jan-Jun86-281
Nooteboom, C. In the Dutch Mountains.
M. Malone, 441:11Oct87-42
Nooteboom, C. Rituale.
C. Pankow, 654(WB):2/1986-307
Nooteboom, C. A Song of Truth and Semblance.
T. McGonigle, 532(RCF):Summer86-155
Nora, P., ed. Les Lieux de mémoire.
S. Collini, 617(TLS):16Jan87-51
Norberg-Schulz, C. Baroque Architecture.
J.S. Curl, 324:Nov87-951

Norberg-Schulz, C. Late Baroque and Rococo Architecture.
J.S. Curl, 324:Apr87-405
Norbrook, D. Poetry and Politics in the English Renaissance.*
J.N. King, 250(HLQ):Summer86-277
I. Roots, 366:Autumn86-249
Nord, D.E. The Apprenticeship of Beatrice Webb.*
P. Parrinder, 506(PSt):Dec86-107
Nordland, G. Richard Diebenkorn.
J. Russell, 441:6Dec87-89
Nordström, F. Mediaeval Baptismal Fonts.*
E.C. Parker, 589:Oct86-1030
Noricks, M.L. Dime, Constanza.
P. Hunter, 399(MLJ):Spring86-85
Noriega, T.A. La novelística de Carlos Droguett.
H.M. Cavallari, 238:Mar86-114
Norman, B. Footsteps.
P.G. Bahn, 617(TLS):4-10Dec87-1355
Norman, D. Encounters.
A. Anderson, 441:28Jun87-19
Norman, D. Terrible Beauty.
C. Townshend, 617(TLS):11-17Sep87-972
Norman, E. The English Catholic Church in the Nineteenth Century.
L.F. Barmann, 377:Mar86-75
Norman, E. The Victorian Christian Socialists.
P. Butler, 617(TLS):26Jun87-680
Norman, H. In Love and Friendship.
S. Paulos, 441:8Mar87-21
Norman, H. The Northern Lights.
P-L. Adams, 61:Jun87-82
C. Cleveland, 441:12Apr87-26
442(NY):1Jun87-110
Norman, K.R. Pāli Literature.
W.B. Bollée, 318(JAOS):Jan/Mar85-178
Norman, K.R., with I.B. Horner & W. Rahula - see "The Group of Discourses (Suttanipāta)"
Norman, M. The Fortune Teller.
A. Hempel, 441:24May87-10
Norman, M. 'Night, Mother.
V.M. Patraka, 385(MQR):Winter87-285
Norman, P. Pieces of Hate.
D.J. Enright, 617(TLS):18-24Dec87-1399
Norman, P. The Skater's Waltz.*
639(VQR):Autumn86-126
Norman, T. Isolation and Contact.*
M. Pouillard, 189(EA):Jul-Sep87-370
Norrby, I. - see under Kempff, M.
Norrell, R.J. Reaping the Whirlwind.*
639(VQR):Winter86-9
Norri, M-R. & others, eds. Pietilä.
W.C. Miller, 576:Sep86-304
Norrick, N.R. How Proverbs Mean.
R.W. Dent, 599:Summer86-272
R.K.S. Macaulay, 350:Mar87-202
Norris, C. Contest of Faculties.
M. Conroy, 577(SHR):Fall86-365
C. Craig, 617(TLS):30Jan87-116
Norris, C. Deconstruction.*
42(AR):Winter86-120
Norris, C. The Deconstructive Turn.*
A. Appiah, 153:Spring86-49
B.S. Ash, 405(MP):Aug86-109
K. Hart, 381:Mar86-107
I.E. Harvey, 480(P&R):Vol19No3-201
M. Hobson, 208(FS):Apr86-247
M. Kerkhoff, 160:Jan86-183
R. Selden, 402(MLR):Oct86-961

Nwoga, D.I., ed. Critical Perspectives on
Christopher Okigbo.
　　C.O. Acholonu, 538(RAL):Winter86-613
Nyamndi, G. The West African Village
Novel with Particular Reference to Elechi
Amadi's "The Concubine."
　　E.N. Emenyonu, 538(RAL):Winter86-622
Nyberg, T. & others, eds. History and
Heroic Tale.
　　P. MacCana, 112:Vol18-214
　　J. Salmons, 563(SS):Autumn86-456
Nycz, R. Sylwy współczesne.
　　J.N. Roney, 574(SEEJ):Fall86-436
Nye, D.E. Image Worlds.
　　J.K. Smith, 432(NEQ):Sep86-452
Nye, J.S., Jr. Nuclear Ethics.*
　　G. Dworkin, 185:Jul87-876
Nye, N.S. Yellow Glove.
　　M. McGovern, 344:Fall87-131
Nyiszli, M. Auschwitz.
　　N. Ascherson, 453(NYRB):28May87-29
Nyssen, H. Lecture d'Albert Cohen.
　　L. van Delft, 535(RHL):Jul-Aug86-798

Oakes, J. Keeping Track.
　　R. Floud, 617(TLS):13Mar87-263
Oakes, J. The Ruling Class.
　　J.B. Moore, 577(SHR):Spring86-163
Oates, J.C. Marya.*
　　P. Craig, 617(TLS):16Jan87-55
　　D. Flower, 249(HudR):Summer86-309
　　D.A.N. Jones, 362:12Feb87-28
Oates, J.C. On Boxing.
　　A. Broyard, 441:15Mar87-8
　　C. Sigal, 362:18Jun87-23
　　P. Smith, 617(TLS):18-24Dec87-1412
Oates, J.C. Son of the Morning.
　　S.L. Dean, 145(Crit):Spring87-135
Oates, J.C. You Must Remember This.
　　S. Birkerts, 441:16Aug87-3
　　J. Updike, 442(NY):28Dec87-119
Oates, L.R. Populist Nationalism in Prewar
Japan.
　　M. Fletcher, 407(MN):Summer86-248
　　Kajitani Yoshihisa, 285(JapQ):Apr-
　　Jun86-219
Oates, S.B. William Faulkner.
　　B. De Mott, 61:Jul87-91
　　L.D. Rubin, Jr., 441:20Sep87-18
Oates, S.B. Let the Trumpet Sound.
　　J.B. Moore, 577(SHR):Spring86-159
Obelkevich, J., L. Roper & R. Samuel, eds.
Disciplines of Faith.
　　M. Ruthven, 617(TLS):26Jun87-685
Ober, W.B. Bottoms Up!
　　R. Selzer, 441:29Nov87-13
Oberfeld, C. & others - see Grimm, J. & W.
Oberfeld, C. & P. Assion, eds. Erzählen -
Sammeln - Deuten.
　　S. Ude-Koeller, 196:Band27Heft3/4-364
Oberhammer, G., ed. Epiphanie des Heils.
　　J.A. Taber, 318(JAOS):Oct/Dec85-792
Oberhammer, R., ed. Inklusivismus.
　　J.W. de Jong, 259(IIJ):Jan86-68
Oberman, H.A. Die Reformation.
　　A. Hamilton, 617(TLS):11-17Dec87-1384
Obeyesekere, G. The Cult of the Goddess
Pattini.*
　　S.B. Steever, 318(JAOS):Jan/Mar85-186
O'Brian, J. - see Greenberg, C.

O'Brien, C.C. The Siege.*
　　M. Beloff, 176:Dec86-30
　　E. Lipsky, 390:Jun/Jul86-59
O'Brien, D. Eminent Domain.
　　H. Zinnes, 441:26Apr87-24
O'Brien, D. Theories of Weight in the
Ancient World.* (Vol 1)
　　M.R. Wright, 41:Spring85-134
O'Brien, E. The Beckett Country.*
　　M. Billington, 176:Jan87-55
　　442(NY):9Feb87-104
O'Brien, K.D. Veganic Gardening.
　　K.E. Jermy, 324:Apr87-409
O'Brien, M. A Character of Hugh Legaré.
　　G.W. Williams, 27(AL):Dec86-633
　　639(VQR):Autumn86-122
O'Brien, M. Vince.
　　D. Rudd, 441:22Nov87-33
O'Brien, S. Willa Cather.*
　　A.S. Byatt, 617(TLS):15May87-507
　　F.W. Kaye, 357:Spring87-51
　　442(NY):23Feb87-136
O'Brien, S. The Frighteners.
　　D. Dunn, 176:Jun87-52
　　W. Scammell, 617(TLS):20-26Nov87-1275
O'Brien, T. The Nuclear Age.*
　　G. Kearns, 249(HudR):Spring86-123
　　639(VQR):Spring86-55
O'Brien, W.V. & J. Langan, eds. The Nucle-
ar Dilemma and the Just War Tradition.
　　S.L., 185:Jul87-899
Ó Broin, L. Protestant Nationalists in
Revolutionary Ireland.*
　　D. Clark, 637(VS):Winter87-273
Ó Bruadair, D. Selected Poems.
　　E. Ní Chuilleanáin, 617(TLS):21Aug87-
　　904
O'Casey, S. O'Casey: The Dublin Trilogy.
Seven Plays by Sean O'Casey. (R. Ayling,
ed of both)
　　C. Murray, 272(IUR):Autumn86-238
Occhiogrosso, P. Once a Catholic.
　　J. Leo, 441:11Oct87-15
Occhioni, N., ed. Il processo per la can-
onizzazione di S. Nicola da Tolentino.
　　J. Howe, 589:Oct86-975
Ochogavía, M.B. - see under Bauzà Ocho-
gavía, M.
Ó Ciobháin, B. Toponomia Hiberniae. (Vols
1 & 4)
　　D. Ó Sé, 112:Vol18-199
Ó Ciobháin, B. Toponomia Hiberniae. (Vols
2 & 3)
　　W.F.H. Nicolaisen, 424:Sep86-310
　　D. Ó Sé, 112:Vol18-199
Ockham, William of. Quaestiones in librum
quartum sententiarum (reportatio).* (R.
Wood & G. Gál, with R. Green, eds)
　　W.R. Thomson, 589:Apr86-483
Ockham, William of. Quaestiones in Librum
Secundum Sententiarum (Reportatio). (G.
Gál & R. Wood, eds) Quaestiones in
Librum Tertium Sententiarum (Reporta-
tio). (F.E. Kelly & G.J. Etzkorn, eds)
　　M.M. Adams, 482(PhR):Jul86-474
Ó Conaire, B. Myles na Gaeilge, Lámhleab-
har ar Shaothar Gaelige Bhrian Ó Bual-
láin.
　　E. Ó hAnluain, 272(IUR):Autumn86-249
O'Conaire, B. - see Hyde, D.

O'Connell, R. William James on the Courage to Believe.
S.M. Jordan, 543:Sep86-137
J.J. McDermott, 258:Jun86-189
O'Connor, D.J., ed. A Critical History of Western Philosophy.
483:Jan86-139
O'Connor, F. The Presence of Grace and Other Book Reviews. (L.J. Zuber, comp; C.W. Martin, ed)
M.J. Friedman, 534(RALS):Spring-Autumn84-239
O'Connor, F. & B. Cheney. The Correspondence of Flannery O'Connor and the Brainard Cheneys.* (C.R. Stephens, ed)
R.H. Brinkmeyer, Jr., 578:Fall87-145
J.F. Desmond, 396(ModA):Summer/Fall86-331
M.D.O., 295(JML):Nov86-519
O'Connor, M. The Fiesta of Men.
R. Pybus, 565:Spring86-71
O'Connor, T.E. The Politics of Soviet Culture.*
A.L. Tait, 575(SEER):Jan86-144
O'Crohan, T. Island Cross-Talk.
272(IUR):Spring86-108
O'Cuilleanáin, C.L. Religion and the Clergy in Boccaccio's "Decameron."
J.H. Whitfield, 382(MAE):1986/2-328
Odaga, A.B. Literature for Children and Young People in Kenya.*
N.J. Schmidt, 538(RAL):Winter86-609
Odo of Cheriton. The Fables of Odo of Cheriton. (J.C. Jacobs, ed & trans)
W.A. Kretzschmar, Jr., 405(MP):May87-416
M. Martin, 589:Oct86-1031
O'Donnell, C.P. Bangladesh.
J.P. Thorp, 293(JASt):Aug86-789
O'Donnell, M. Doctor! Doctor!
B. Hepburn, 617(TLS):20Feb87-192
O'Donnell, M.A. Aphra Behn.
B. Dhuicq, 189(EA):Apr-Jun87-212
O'Donnell, P. John Hawkes.
J. Newman, 677(YES):Vol16-356
O'Donnell, W.H. The Poetry of William Butler Yeats.
L.A. Cellucci, 295(JML):Nov86-559
O'Donovan, J.E. George Grant and the Twilight of Justice.*
H.L. Thomas, 102(CanL):Fall86-160
Odrowąż-Pieniążek, J., ed. Blok-Notes Muzeum Literatury im. Adama Mickiewicza.
J.T. Baer, 497(PolR):Vol31No2/3-209
O'Dwyer, W. Beyond the Golden Door. (P. O'Dwyer, ed)
M.J. O'Neill, 441:16Aug87-12
Ōe no Masafusa. Il Dio Incatenato.
M. Marra, 407(MN):Winter86-495
Oelmüller, W. Transendentalphilosophische Normenbergründungen.
P. Livet, 98:Jun-Jul86-692
Oeser, H-C., ed. Modern English Short Stories I.
C. Jansohn, 72:Band223Heft1-185
O'Faolain, J. The Irish Signorina.*
442(NY):5Jan87-85
O'Faolain, J. No Country For Young Men.
J. Moynahan, 441:1Feb87-7
442(NY):16Mar87-104
Offermans, C. De mensen zijn mooier dan ze denken.
R. Wolfs, 204(FdL):Dec86-313

Offord, D. Portraits of Early Russian Liberals.
R. Freeborn, 402(MLR):Jul87-807
O'Flaherty, J.C., T.F. Sellner & R.M. Helm, eds. Studies in Nietzsche and the Judaeo-Christian Tradition.
A. Closs, 402(MLR):Apr86-534
F.R. Love, 221(GQ):Fall86-683
O'Flaherty, L. The Wilderness.
P. MacManus, 441:30Aug87-20
O'Flaherty, W.D. Dreams, Illusions and Other Realities.*
J.P. Brereton, 318(JAOS):Oct/Dec85-777
O'Flaherty, W.D. Women, Androgynes, and Other Mythical Beasts.
W.H. Maurer, 318(JAOS):Oct/Dec85-774
O'Flynn, J.M. Generalissimos of the Western Roman Empire.
A. Demandt, 487:Spring86-115
Ogbalu, F.C. & E.N. Emenanjo, eds. Igbo Language and Culture. (Vol 2)
K. Ogbaa, 538(RAL):Summer86-291
Ogden, D.H. Actor Training and Audience Response.*
S-C. Lai, 610:Spring86-85
Ogden, E.B. — see under Busto Ogden, E.
Ogilvy, J.D.A. & D.C. Baker. Reading "Beowulf."*
W. Obst, 38:Band104Heft3/4-466
J. Roberts, 447(N&Q):Sep85-387
O'Gorman, F. British Conservatism.
J. Dunn, 617(TLS):24Apr87-442
O'Gorman, R., ed. "Les Braies au cordelier," Anonymous Fabliau of the Thirteenth Century.*
P.W. Cummins, 207(FR):Mar87-530
O'Hanlon, R. Joseph Conrad and Charles Darwin.*
J. Batchelor, 541(RES):May86-285
J. Feaster, 395(MFS):Summer86-305
C.J. Rawson, 402(MLR):Jan86-187
O'Hara, D., ed. Why Nietzsche Now?
J. McGowan, 141:Summer86-357
O'Hara, D.T. The Romance of Interpretation.
P.A. Bové, 150(DR):Winter85/86-594
639(VQR):Spring86-45
O'Hara, D.T. Tragic Knowledge.*
L. Kramer, 675(YER):Vol8No1/2-142
O'Hara, M.L., ed. Substances and Things.
L.P. Gerson, 41:Spring85-119
Ohashi, K. & K. Ono, comps. Faulkner Studies in Japan.* (T.L. McHaney, ed)
C.S. Brown, 569(SR):Winter86-167
D.L. Cook, 27(AL):Dec86-660
O'Hear, A. What Philosophy Is.
P. Gilbert, 518:Jan86-43
P. Lamarque, 479(PhQ):Oct86-540
O'Higgins, J.S.J. Yves de Vallone.*
B.E. Schwarzbach, 83:Autumn86-284
O'Higgins, M. Wells and Other Poems.
S. Toulson, 4:Spring86-63
Ohkawa, K. & G. Ranis, eds. Japan and the Developing Countries.
Hirashima Shigemochi, 285(JapQ):Apr-Jun86-217
Ohly, F. Geometria e Memoria. (L.R. Santini, ed)
P. Menard, 549(RLC):Apr-Jun86-233
Ohly, S. Literaturgeschichte und politische Reaktion im neunzehnten Jahrhundert.
E. Grunewald, 406:Fall86-409

273

Olson, C. The Maximus Poems.* (G.F. But-
terick, ed)
   J.F. Cotter, 249(HudR):Spring86-153
Olson, D.R., N. Torrance & A. Hildyard,
eds. Literacy, Language, and Learning.
   B.A. Beatie, 399(MLJ):Summer86-174
Olson, G.A., ed. Writing Centers.
   K. Moreland, 577(SHR):Spring86-199
Olson, P.R. Unamuno, "Niebla."
   I. Soto, 402(MLR):Apr87-507
   R. Wright, 86(BHS):Oct86-373
Olson, S. John Singer Sargent.*
   D. Sutton, 39:Nov86-462
   639(VQR):Autumn86-125
Olson, S., W. Adelson & R. Ormond. Sargent
at Broadway.
   O. Beckett, 324:Jul87-616
Olson, T. Utah.
   C. Johnson, 441:9Aug87-12
Olsson, A. Ekelöfs nej.*
   R. Shideler, 563(SS):Winter86-79
Olsson, H. La concurrence entre "il," "ce"
et "cela (ça)" comme sujet d'expressions
impersonnelles en français contemporain.
   J.E. Joseph, 350:Sep87-676
Omaggio, A.C., ed. Proficiency, Curricu-
lum, Articulation.*
   K. Chastain, 399(MLJ):Autumn86-297
Omaggio, A.C. Teaching Language in Con-
text.
   J-P. Berwald, 207(FR):Dec86-308
Oman, C. Nelson.
   J. Ridley, 617(TLS):11-17Sep87-996
O'Meally, R.F. The Craft of Ralph Ellison.
   J.D.A. Widdowson, 203:Vol97No2-233
O'Meally, R.G. - see Adams, E.C.L.
O'Meara, D.J., ed. Neoplatonism and Chris-
tian Thought.*
   L. Sweeny, 543:Jun87-784
O'Meara, D.J., ed. Platonic Investiga-
tions.
   J. Barnes, 520:Vol31No2-185
O'Meara, P. K.F. Ryleyev.*
   G. Barratt, 575(SEER):Jul86-470
Omond, R. The Apartheid Handbook.* (2nd
ed)
   D. Baker, 138:No9-283
Ondaatje, M. In the Skin of a Lion.
   J. Cooke, 362:22Oct87-23
   M. Hulse, 617(TLS):4-11Sep87-948
   C. Kizer, 441:27Sep87-12
Ondaatje, M. Secular Love.*
   J. Cook, 529(QQ):Summer86-414
   639(VQR):Spring86-61
O'Neal, J.C.C. Seeing and Observing.
   J.F. Jones, Jr., 207(FR):May87-863
   G. May, 402(MLR):Oct87-961
   A. Rosenberg, 173(ECS):Winter86/87-242
   J. Still, 208(FS):Oct86-466
O'Neill, E. "The Theatre We Worked For."
(J.R. Bryer, ed)
   R.S. Smith, 106:Winter86-469
O'Neill, J.M. Duffy is Dead.
   T. Dooley, 617(TLS):23Jan87-91
   B. Morton, 362:4Jun87-49
O'Neill, T.P., Jr., with W. Novak. Man of
the House.
   W. Safire, 441:6Sep87-1
O'Neill, T.R. Shades of Gray.
   P-L. Adams, 61:Jun87-82
   A. Brennan, 441:24May87-12

O'Neill, W.L. American High.
   W.E. Leuchtenburg, 61:Feb87-91
   R. Starr, 441:1Feb87-22
Ongaro, A. La partita.
   C.R-M. Pinsky, 275(IQ):Summer86-118
Onori, A.M. L'abbazia di San Salvatore a
Sesto e il Lago di Bientina.
   D.J. Osheim, 589:Jul86-740
Onrubia, C.M. - see under Menéndez Onrubia,
C.
"Ontologija jazyka kak obščestvennogo
javlenija."
   W. Mühlner, 682(ZPSK):Band39Heft6-729
Oomen, U. Die englische Sprache in den
USA. (Pt 1)
   E.W. Schneider, 685(ZDL):1/1986-118
Ooms, H. Tokugawa Ideology.
   Koyasu Nobukuni, 285(JapQ):Apr-Jun86-
214
   H. Watanabe, 293(JASt):May86-614
Oosthuizen, A., ed. Sometimes When It
Rains.
   C. Hope, 617(TLS):17Apr87-411
O'Phelan Godoy, S. Rebellions and Revolts
in Eighteenth Century Peru and Upper
Peru.
   J.R. Fisher, 263(RIB):Vol36No1-66
Opie, I. & P. The Singing Game.
   B. Sutton-Smith, 292(JAF):Apr/Jun86-
239
Mrs. Opie. Adeline Mowbray, or, The Mother
and Daughter.
   P. Raine, 617(TLS):6-12Nov87-1216
Opitz, R. Krise des Romans?
   C. Günther, 654(WB):6/1986-1043
Opland, J. Xhosa Oral Poetry.*
   L. Haring, 650(WF):Jan86-73
   J.S. Miletich, 131(CL):Fall86-395
Opolka, U. & others - see Bloch, E.
Oppenheimer, H. Lorca: The Drawings.
   H. Benedict, 441:15Mar87-16
Oppenlander, E.A. Dickens' "All the Year
Round."
   D. Paroissien, 158:Sep86-142
   A. Sanders, 155:Autumn86-180
Oppici, P. Proust e il movimento immobile.
   A. Henry, 72:Band223Heft2-473
   M. Tilby, 208(FS):Apr86-235
Opul'skij, A. Vokrug imeni l'va tolstogo.
   V. Perelesin, 558(RLJ):Winter86-236
Orange, D.M. Peirce's Conception of God.*
   M.L. Raposa, 438:Spring86-235
Oranje, H. Euripides' "Bacchae."
   R. Seaford, 123:Vol36No1-24
Orbán, J. - see Heinrich von Kalkar
Orcibal, J. - see de Canfield, B.
O'Reilly, T. - see Herbert, F.
O'Reilly, T. - see Parker, A.A.
Orel, H., ed. Kipling: Interviews and
Recollections.*
   A. Rutherford, 402(MLR):Apr87-460
Orel, H. The Literary Achievement of
Rebecca West.
   A. Crozier, 395(MFS):Winter86-671
Orel, H., ed. Victorian Short Stories.
   P. Craig, 617(TLS):18-24Sep87-1026
Orel, H. The Victorian Short Story.
   A.L. Harris, 268(IFR):Winter87-34
   P. Kemp, 617(TLS):5Jun87-609
Orenstein, H. I Shall Live.
   S. Taitz, 441:8Nov87-27

Orgland, I. & F. Raastad. Islandsk–norsk ordbok.
　E. Haugen, 563(SS):Spring86–216
Oring, E. The Jokes of Sigmund Freud.
　C. Mitchell, 650(WF):Jul86–232
　H.H. Panjwani, 616:Spring/Summer86–62
Orioli, R., ed. Fra Dolcino.
　P. McNair, 402(MLR):Jan87–216
O'Riordan, J. A Guide to O'Casey's Plays.*
　B. Benstock, 659(ConL):Spring87–121
Orlando, S., ed. Un'altra testimonianza del "Seneca" provenzale.
　M.R. Harris, 589:Oct86–901
Orlock, C. The Goddess Letters.
　M. Hawthorne, 441:9Aug87–21
Orlov, V. Danilov the Violist.
　O. Carlisle, 441:13Sep87–47
Orlova, R. Vospominaniia o neproshedshem vremeni. Memoirs.
　A. Zeide, 550(RusR):Jan86–95
Orme, N. From Childhood to Chivalry.*
　E. Clark, 589:Oct86–977
Ormerod, B. An Introduction to the French Caribbean Novel.*
　G.C. Jones, 67:May86–118
　E. Skinner, 395(MFS):Winter86–646
Ormerod, D. & C. Wortham – see Marlowe, C.
Ormsby, E.L. Theodicy in Islamic Thought.
　L.E. Goodman, 319:Oct87–589
Ormsby, F. A Northern Spring.*
　M. O'Neill, 493:Jun86–110
　272(IUR):Autumn86–253
Ormsby, F. Northern Windows.
　S. O'Brien, 617(TLS):16–22Oct87–1132
"Ornate Wallpapers."
　S. Braybrooke, 507:Nov/Dec86–125
　P. Faulkner, 326:Autumn86–67
Ornstein, R. Shakespeare's Comedies.
　T. Hawkes, 617(TLS):10Apr87–390
de Oro, E.G-G. – see under González–Grano de Oro, E.
Orosius, P. Historia contra paganos. (E. Gallego–Blanco, trans)
　J.E. Keller, 86(BHS):Apr86–150
O'Rourke, P.J. Republican Party Reptile. The Bachelor Home Companion.
　L.B. Frumkes, 441:3May87–30
de Orozco, F.G. – see under Gómez de Orozco, F.
Orr, E.W. Twice as Less.
　J. Countryman, 441:1Nov87–12
Orr, G. Stanley Kunitz.
　639(VQR):Autumn86–116
Orrell, J. The Quest for Shakespeare's Globe.*
　R.A. Cave, 610:Summer86–159
Orrell, J. The Theatres of Inigo Jones and John Webb.*
　G.C. Adams, 539:Spring87–193
　G. Barlow, 610:Spring86–70
Orrieux, C. Les papyrus de Zénon.*
　R.S. Bagnall, 122:Jul86–249
　J. Rowlandson, 123:Vol36No1–172
Orso, S.N. Philip IV and the Decoration of the Alcazar of Madrid.
　N. Glendinning, 39:Dec86–569
Ortas, F.M. The Last Pharaoh.*
　A. Beevor, 617(TLS):16Jan87–64
Ortega, J. Poetics of Change.*
　R.W. Fiddian, 402(MLR):Jan87–230
Ortega y Gasset, J. The Revolt of the Masses.* (A. Kerrigan, trans)
　G. Woodcock, 569(SR):Fall86–644

"Ortega y Gasset Centennial/Centenario Ortega y Gasset."
　B. Ciplijauskaité, 552(REH):Oct86–115
　R. Johnson, 238:May86–309
Ortese, A.M. The Iguana.
　L. Venuti, 441:22Nov87–40
Ortiz, A., ed. Handbook of North American Indians. (Vol 10)
　K. McCarty, 50(ArQ):Winter86–369
Ortiz, A. The Tewa World.
　R.M. Adams, 453(NYRB):26Mar87–32
Ortolá, M-S. Un estudio del "Viaje de Turquía."*
　H. Ettinghausen, 86(BHS):Jul86–285
Ortolani, B., ed. International Bibliography of the Theatre: 1982.
　F.H. Londré, 615(TJ):Oct86–381
Orton, H., S. Sanderson & J. Widowson, eds. The Linguistic Atlas of England.
　W. Viereck, 685(ZDL):2/1986–269
Orton, J. Head to Toe.
　G. Annan, 453(NYRB):24Sep87–3
Orton, J. The Orton Diaries.* (J. Lahr, ed)
　G. Annan, 453(NYRB):24Sep87–3
　M. Billington, 176:Jan87–54
　J. Bowen, 364:Nov86–93
　B. Nightingale, 441:10May87–9
Orts, A.C. – see under Cortina Orts, A.
Orwell, G. Animal Farm. (adapted by P. Hall)
　B. Grantham, 157:No160–47
Orwell, G. Nineteen Eighty-Four.* (B. Crick, ed)
　J. Mezciems, 402(MLR):Oct86–994
Osamu, D. – see under Dazai Osamu
Osborn, M. – see "Beowulf"
Osborn, R. – see Wordsworth, W.
Osborne, C. Giving It Away.*
　R. Fuller, 364:Nov86–98
Osborne, C. Schubert and his Vienna.*
　A.M. Hanson, 410(M&L):Oct86–396
Osborne, F. The True Tragicomedy Formerly Acted at Court.* (L. Potter, ed)
　D. Norbrook, 447(N&Q):Mar85–116
Osborne, J. A Better Class of Person [and] God Rot Tunbridge Wells.
　B. Grantham, 157:No159–47
Osborne, K.L. Carlyle Simpson.
　C. Ames, 441:1Feb87–20
Osborne, L. Ania Malina.
　A. Josephs, 441:18Oct87–52
Osborne, M.J. Naturalization in Athens.* (Vols 3 & 4)
　M.B. Walbank, 303(JoHS):Vol106–240
Osborne, R. Classical Landscape with Figures.
　L. Foxhall, 617(TLS):31Jul87–824
Osborne. R. Demos.
　D. Roessel, 124:Sep–Oct86–64
　G. Shipley, 123:Vol36No2–265
Osborne, R. Rossini.*
　R. Crichton, 415:Dec86–691
Osgood, C.E. Lectures on Language Performance.
　T. Ickler, 685(ZDL):2/1986–282
O'Sharkey, E.M. The Role of the Priest in the Novels of Georges Bernanos.
　J.C. Whitehouse, 402(MLR):Apr87–484
O'Shaughnessy, B. The Will.
　A. Morton, 482(PhR):Jul86–451
O'Shaughnessy, H. Grenada.
　A.J. Rawick, 287:Jan86–24

O'Shea, M.J. James Joyce and Heraldry.
  R.B., 295(JML):Nov86-495
  C.D. Lobner, 329(JJQ):Summer87-488
Osinski, J. Über Vernunft und Wahnsinn.*
  H. Rowland, 221(GQ):Spring86-312
Osiński, Z. Grotowski and His Laboratory.*
  (L. Vallee & R. Findlay, eds & trans)
  E.J. Czerwinski, 574(SEEJ):Winter86-591
Osmond-Smith, D. Playing on Words.*
  G.D.P., 412:Aug85-228
Ostendorf, B. Black Literature in White
  America.
  J.B. Moore, 577(SHR):Spring86-165
Ostenfeld, E. Forms Matter and Mind.
  R.W. Jordan, 41:Fall85-325
Oster, J. Nowhere Man.
  N. Callendar, 441:7Jun87-25
  442(NY):16Mar87-106
Oster, J. Saint Mike.
  N. Callendar, 441:27Dec87-13
Ostriker, A. The Imaginary Lover.
  P. Hampl, 441:7Jun87-15
  C. Wills, 617(TLS):10Jul87-748
Ostriker, A.S. Stealing the Language.*
  M. Karr, 491:Feb87-294
  K.L. Nichols, 389(MQ):Spring87-412
  C. Wills, 617(TLS):10Jul87-748
Ostrogorsky, G. History of the Byzantine
  State.
  617(TLS):30Jan87-120
Ostrovsky, E. Under the Sign of Ambiguity.
  C. Rigolot, 210(FrF):Sep86-378
Ostwald, M. Autonomia.
  G.J.D. Aalders H. Wzn., 394:Vol39
  fascl/2-216
  D. Lateiner, 41:Vol6-195
Ostwald, P.F. Schumann.*
  H. Lenneberg, 451:Summer86-80
  R. Taylor, 410(M&L):Apr86-207
O'Sullivan, V. The Butcher Papers.
  R. Pybus, 565:Spring86-71
O'Sullivan, V. - see Bethell, U.
O'Sullivan, V. & M. Scott - see Mansfield,
  K.
O'Toole, C., ed. The Encyclopaedia of
  Insects.
  M. Ridley, 617(TLS):6Feb87-144
Ott, N.H. Rechtspraxis und Heilsge-
  schichte.*
  M. Curschmann, 589:Apr86-450
"Otte, 'Eraclius.'" (W. Frey, ed)
  I. Bennewitz-Behr, 680(ZDP):Band105
  Heft3-461
  D.H. Green, 402(MLR):Apr87-509
Otten, C.F. Environ'd with Eternity.
  K.M. Swaim, 191(ELN):Sep86-100
  J.E. Van Domelen, 568(SCN):Winter86-71
Otten, C.F., ed. A Lycanthropy Reader.
  F. Huxley, 617(TLS):21Aug87-907
  A. Rice, 441:5Apr87-33
Otten, H. Die Apologie Hattusilis III.*
  H.A. Hoffner, 318(JAOS):Apr/Jun85-337
Otten, R.M. Joseph Addison.
  A. Graziano, 677(YES):Vol16-261
  G. Midgley, 447(N&Q):Mar85-124
Ottenberg, S., ed. African Religious
  Groups and Beliefs.
  P. Stevens, Jr., 650(WF):Jan86-67
Otto, F. Robert Schumann als Jean Paul-
  Leser.
  R. Taylor, 410(M&L):Apr86-180

Otto, J.S. Cannon's Point Plantation,
  1794-1860.
  J.I. Hantman & D.W. Sanford,
  292(JAF):Jan/Mar86-92
Otto, S. Rekonstruktion der Geschichte.
  (Pt 1)
  E. Simons, 489(PJGG):Band93Heft2-434
Oudot, S. Guide to Correspondence in
  French.
  D.E. Rivas, 399(MLJ):Summer86-185
Oudot, S. & D.L. Gobert. La France.*
  D.E. Rivas, 399(MLJ):Spring86-64
Ouellette, F. Lucie ou un midi en novem-
  bre.
  P. Merivale, 102(CanL):Summer86-108
Ouimette, V. José Ortega y Gasset.
  A. Román, 552(REH):May86-131
Ould, C. Road Lines.
  B. Atkinson, 441:21Jun87-22
OuLiPo. La Bibliothèque Oulipienne.
  G. Josipovici, 617(TLS):30Oct-5Nov87-
  1191
Oumano, E. Sam Shepard.*
  362:6Aug87-22
Ourliac, P. & A-M. Magnou. Le cartulaire
  de la Selve.
  A. Grafström, 553(RLiR):Jul-Dec86-628
Outram, R. Man in Love.
  R. Anderson, 102(CanL):Summer86-148
Ovenell, R.F. The Ashmolean Museum 1683-
  1894.*
  E. Esdaile, 324:May87-470
Overfield, J.H. Humanism and Scholasti-
  cism in Late Medieval Germany.
  F.L. Borchardt, 221(GQ):Winter86-130
Overholser, W.D. The Best Western Stories
  of Wayne D. Overholser. (B. Pronzini &
  M.H. Greenberg, eds)
  M.T. Marsden, 649(WAL):Aug86-141
Overing, J., ed. Reason and Morality.*
  H.O. Mounce, 518:Jul86-185
Oversteegen, J.J. Anastasio en de schaal
  van Richter.
  J.M. Hollaar, 204(FdL):Dec86-307
Ovid. Metamorphoses. (A.D. Melville,
  trans; E.J. Kenney, ed)
  W.S. Anderson, 121(CJ):Dec86-Jan87-157
Ovid. Metamorphoses I-IV. (D.E. Hill, ed
  & trans) Metamorphoses I. (A.G. Lee,
  ed)
  E. Block, 124:Jul-Aug87-445
Owen, C.R. Erich Maria Remarque.
  A.F. Bance, 402(MLR):Jul87-798
Owen, D. & D. Steel. The Time Has Come.
  J. Dunn, 617(TLS):24Apr87-442
Owen, D.I. Neo-Sumerian Archival Texts
  Primarily from Nippur, in the University
  Museum, the Oriental Institute, and the
  Iraq Museum.
  H. Neumann, 318(JAOS):Jan/Mar85-150
Owen, D.M., ed. The Making of King's Lynn.
  M. Kowaleski, 589:Oct86-1031
Owen, G.E.L. Logic, Science, and Dialec-
  tic.
  J.A., 185:Jul87-898
  D.H. Frank, 543:Mar87-594
Owen, M. Apologies and Remedial Inter-
  changes.*
  G.D. de Wolf, 320(CJL):Spring86-86
Owen, R. Crisis in the Kremlin.
  A.B. Ulam, 617(TLS):6Feb87-129

Owen, R.W. James Joyce and the Beginnings of "Ulysses."
S. Sultan, 329(JJQ):Fall86-95
Owen, S. Traditional Chinese Poetry and Poetics.
J.R. Allen 3d, 116:Jul85-143
E.H. Kaplan, 134(CP):Vol19-134
J.J.Y. Liu, 293(JASt):May86-579
Owen, W.J.B. - see Wordsworth, W.
Owen-Crocker, G. Dress in Anglo-Saxon England.
C. Walkley, 617(TLS):16Jan87-67
Owens, A. Like Birds in the Wilderness.
B. McCabe, 617(TLS):8May87-488
Owens, J. Human Destiny.
H.B.V., 185:Apr87-709
Owens, L. John Steinbeck's Re-Vision of America.*
R. Astro, 649(WAL):Aug86-148
Y. Hakutani, 27(AL):May86-303
Owings, W.A.D., E. Pribić & N. Pribić, eds & trans. The Sarajevo Trial.
M. Wheeler, 575(SEER):Oct86-650
Owusu, M. Drama of the Gods.
M.T. David, 538(RAL):Summer86-276
"The Oxford-Duden Pictorial French-English Dictionary."
J.E. Joseph, 399(MLJ):Spring86-66
"The Oxford English-Russian Dictionary."* (P.S. Falla, ed)
N.J. Brown, 402(MLR):Jan86-262
S. Lubensky, 574(SEEJ):Spring86-122
"The Oxford Russian-English Dictionary."* (2nd ed) (M. Wheeler, ed)
N.J. Brown, 402(MLR):Jan86-261
M. Heim, 574(SEEJ):Summer86-304
"The Oxford Turkish-English Dictionary." (3rd ed) (A.D. Alderson & F. Iz, eds)
D.R. Magrath, 399(MLJ):Spring86-96
Oz, A. A Perfect Peace.*
N. Aschkenasy, 390:Aug/Sep86-52
Ozdoba, J. Heuristik der Fiktion.
E. Schroeder-Buys, 72:Band223Heft1-206
Ozick, C. The Messiah of Stockholm.
H. Bloom, 441:22Mar87-1
J. Clute, 617(TLS):13-19Nov87-1249
D.J. Enright, 453(NYRB):28May87-18
J. Malcolm, 442(NY):8Jun87-102
Ozment, S. Magdalena and Balthasar.
442(NY):2Feb87-100
Ozment, S. When Fathers Ruled.
E. Leites, 473(PR):Vol53No1-121
R. Tittler, 539:Spring87-184

Pacey, D. - see Roberts, C.G.D.
Pacey, P. If Man.
J. Saunders, 565:Summer86-74
Pacheco, F. Libro de descripción de verdaderos retratos de ilustres y memorables varones.
E.H., 90:Jan86-49
Pacheco, J.E. Battles in the Desert and Other Stories.
P. Sourian, 441:24May87-12
Pachmuss, T. - see Merezhkovskii, D.
Pachoński, J. & R.K. Wilson. Poland's Caribbean Tragedy.*
R.A. Joseph, 441:22Mar87-19
Pächt, O. Buchmalerei des Mittelalters.* (D. Thoss & U. Jenni, eds)
G. Schmidt, 683:Band49Heft1-103

Pachter, H. Socialism in History. (S.E. Bronner, ed)
F. Warren, 579(SAQ):Winter86-107
Pachymérès, G. Relations historiques. (Vols 1 & 2) (A. Failler, ed)
A.E. Laiou, 589:Jul86-693
Pack, R. Affirming Limits.
D.T.O., 295(JML):Nov86-426
Pack, R. Faces in a Single Tree.*
T. Swiss, 569(SR):Spring86-302
Packer, W. & G. Levine. Henry Moore.
J. Burr, 39:Jan86-62
90:Oct86-759
Packman, D. Vladimir Nabokov.*
M. Bell, 402(MLR):Jan87-194
Padel, O.J. Cornish Place-Name Elements.
W.F.H. Nicolaisen, 424:Sep86-314
Padgett, R. - see Denby, E.
Padilla, G.M. - see Chavez, A.
Padley, G.A. Grammatical Theory in Western Europe, 1500-1700.*
M.A. Covington, 350:Jun87-422
Padoan, M. La musica in S. Maria Maggiore a Bergamo nel periodo di Giovanni Cavaccio (1598-1626).
J. Roche, 410(M&L):Jan86-76
Padučeva, E.V. Vyskazyvanie i ego sootnesennost' s dejstvitel'nost'ju.
A. Wierzbicka, 297(JL):Sep86-475
Paetzold, H. - see Baumgarten, A.G.
Pagano, S.M., with A.G. Luciani, eds. I documenti del processo di Galileo Galilei.
W.A. Wallace, 551(RenQ):Winter86-745
Page, C. Voices and Instruments of the Middle Ages.
J. Stevens, 617(TLS):28Aug87-928
Page, M. & R. Ingpen. Encyclopedia of Things That Never Were.
P-L. Adams, 61:Feb87-94
Page, N., ed. Byron.
N. Berry, 617(TLS):23Jan87-80
Page, N. A Conrad Companion.
S. Monod, 189(EA):Apr-Jun87-226
I.V., 295(JML):Nov86-453
Page, N. A.E. Housman.*
B. Gasser, 447(N&Q):Dec85-541
Page, N., ed. Dr. Johnson.
W.B. Carnochan, 617(TLS):18-24Dec87-1396
Page, N. A Kipling Companion.*
W.V. Harris, 177(ELT):Vol29No1-91
Page, N., ed. Nabokov: The Critical Heritage.
M. Bell, 402(MLR):Apr86-465
Page, N. - see "Thomas Hardy Annual"
Page, R. Northern Development.
P. Puxley, 99:Aug/Sep86-25
Page, S. The Soviet Union and the Yemens.
L.G. Martin, 550(RusR):Jan86-106
Page, T. - see Gould, G.
Pageaux, D-H. Images et mythes d'Haïti.
C. Zimra, 538(RAL):Winter86-591
Pageaux, D-H., ed. La Recherche en littérature générale et comparée en France.*
M. Schmeling, 52:Band21Heft2-203
Pagetti, C., ed. La Battaglia di Dorking, tratto dal Blackwood's Magazine, Maggio 1871.
I.F. Clarke, 561(SFS):Mar86-84

Paikeday, T.M. The Native Speaker Is Dead!*
  F. Coulmas, 355(LSoc):Dec86-573
  T.V. Higgs, 399(MLJ):Autumn86-301
  J.D. McCawley, 353:Vol24No6-1137
  P. Meara, 402(MLR):Oct86-957
Paillard, D. Énonciation et détermination en russe contemporain.
  G.G. Corbett, 575(SEER):Oct86-575
Paillet, M. Le Rendez-vous de Montavel.
  R.J. Hartwig, 207(FR):Dec86-295
Painchaud, L. Le Deuxième Traité du Grand Seth (NH VII.2).
  S. Emmel, 318(JAOS):Apr/Jun85-344
Paine, T. The Thomas Paine Reader. (M. Foot & I. Kramnick, eds)
  B. Lee, 617(TLS):11-17Sep87-996
  362:27Aug87-22
Painter, C. Into the Mother Tongue.*
  K.N. Post, 355(LSoc):Sep86-425
Painter, G.D. Studies in Fifteenth-Century Printing.
  P. Needham, 354:Sep86-274
Painter, N.I. Standing at Armageddon.
  C. Tilly, 441:4Oct87-13
Painter, P. Getting to Know the Weather.*
  J.L. Halio, 573(SSF):Spring86-212
  C. Hardesty, 455:Mar86-73
  D. Madden, 598(SoR):Summer87-730
  639(VQR):Summer86-90
Pairo, P. Winner's Cut.
  N. Callendar, 441:19Apr87-22
Pais, A. Inward Bound.
  I. Hacking, 453(NYRB):26Feb87-17
  J. Roche, 617(TLS):30Jan87-103
Pakenham, K.J. Expectations.
  M.O. James, 399(MLJ):Winter86-451
Pal, P. Art of Nepal.
  I. Alsop, 60:Jan-Feb86-121
Pal, P. & V. Dehejia. From Merchants to Emperors, 1757-1930.*
  M. Archer, 39:Nov86-453
  G. Reynolds, 617(TLS):16Jan87-59
Palencia-Roth, M. Gabriel García Márquez.*
  J. Labanyi, 86(BHS):Oct86-395
Palencia-Roth, M., ed. Perspectives on "Faust."*
  E. Feiler, 149(CLS):Spring86-71
  H. Henning, 301(JEGP):Apr86-305
Pales-Gobilliard, A. - see Geoffroy d'Ablis
Paley, G. Later the Same Day.*
  M. Dekoven, 473(PR):Vol53No2-315
Paley, G. Leaning Forward.*
  R.B. Shaw, 491:Apr86-38
Paley, M.D. The Apocalyptic Sublime.
  J. Gage, 617(TLS):27Feb87-216
  L. Goldstein, 385(MQR):Summer87-578
Paley, M.D. The Continuing City.*
  M.L. Johnson, 301(JEGP):Apr86-275
  D. Worrall, 591(SIR):Summer86-277
Paley, V.G. Boys and Girls.
  J. Powell, 658:Summer/Autumn86-218
Pallares, B. - see Tirso de Molina
Pallavicino, B. Opera omnia. (Vols 1-3) (P. Flanders & K.B. Monteath, eds)
  A. Newcomb, 317:Summer86-396
Palley, J. The Ambiguous Mirror.*
  H. Sieber, 86(BHS):Jul86-270
Pallottino, M. Storia della prima Italia.*
  T.W. Potter, 123:Vol36No1-154
Palm, A. Möten mellan konstarter.
  A. Aarseth, 172(Edda):1986/2-191
  G. Orton, 562(Scan):Nov86-246

Palma, C. Malevolent Tales.
  M. Ahern, 238:Dec86-883
Palma-Cayet, P-V. L'Histoire prodigieuse du Docteur Fauste. (Y. Cazaux, ed)
  M. Simonin, 535(RHL):Jan-Feb86-138
Palmer, A. The Banner of Battle.
  R. Blake, 441:28Jun87-33
  J. Ridley, 617(TLS):24Jul87-789
Palmer, A. & V. Who's Who in Shakespeare's England.
  E.W. Ives, 677(YES):Vol16-240
Palmer, A.S. & T.A. Rodgers, with J.W-B. Olsen. Back and Forth.
  E.U. Irving, 399(MLJ):Summer86-207
Palmer, B.R., Jr. The Twenty-Five-Year War.
  T. Ropp, 579(SAQ):Winter86-91
Palmer, C., ed. The Britten Companion.*
  S. Banfield, 410(M&L):Jul86-300
  J.K. Law, 465:Autumn86-125
Palmer, C. George Dyson.
  S. Banfield, 415:Nov86-625
Palmer, F., ed. Anti-Racism.
  A. Ryan, 617(TLS):13Mar87-264
Palmer, L.R. The Greek Language.
  E. Tucker, 303(JoHS):Vol106-224
Palmer, R., ed. Folk Songs Collected by Ralph Vaughan Williams.
  S. Banfield, 415:Nov86-625
Palmer, R.B. - see Guillaume de Machaut
Palmer, R.H. The Lighting Art.
  J.W. Clapper, 615(TJ):Dec86-515
Palmer, S. The Parting Light. (M. Abley, ed)
  G. Reynolds, 617(TLS):27Feb87-216
Palomares, F.J.D. - see under de Santiago y Palomares, F.J.
Palomero Páramo, J.M. El retablo sevillano del Renacimiento.
  F. Marías, 48:Apr-Jun86-197
Palov, V.M. Zur Ausbildung der Norm der deutschen Literatursprache im Bereich der Wortbildung (1470-1730).
  H. Penzl, 685(ZDL):2/1986-225
Pálsson, G. Bréf Gunnars Pálssonar. (Vol 1) (G. Sveinsson, ed)
  K. Wolf, 563(SS):Autumn86-432
Paludan, P.S. Victims.
  L. Shore, 106:Summer86-219
Palumbo, D., ed. Erotic Universe.
  L. Olsen, 395(MFS):Winter86-704
Palumbo, M. The Palestinian Catastrophe.
  E. Salmon, 617(TLS):4-11Sep87-943
"Le Pamphlet en France au XVIe siècle."
  M. Yardeni, 535(RHL):Jul-Aug86-727
Pan, L. The New Chinese Revolution.
  J. Mirsky, 617(TLS):1May87-461
Panagopoulos, E.P. Essays on the History and Meaning of Checks and Balances.
  W.B. Gwyn, 656(WMQ):Jul86-505
Pancake, J.S. This Destructive War.*
  R.J. Hargrove, Jr., 656(WMQ):Jan86-153
Pandey, S.M. The Hindi Oral Epic Canainī.*
  W.L. Smith, 318(JAOS):Jan/Mar85-181
Pane, A. Shackles.
  H. Sutherland, 293(JASt):Aug86-908
Panetta, V.J., Jr. - see Denis, J.
Panhuis, D.G.J. The Communicative Perspective in the Sentence.
  O. Wenskus, 260(IF):Band91-397
Panichas, G.A. The Burden of Vision.
  D.E. Peterson, 395(MFS):Summer86-329

Pannenberg, W. Anthropologie in theolog-
ischer Perspektive.
    P. Koslowski, 687:Apr–Jun86–305
Pannick, D. Judges.
    S. Lee, 362:8Oct87–22
Pannwitz, R. Eine Auswahl aus seinem Werk.
(E. Jaeckle, ed)
    K. Weissenberger, 133:Band19Heft3/4–371
Pantin, I. – see "Imprimeurs et libraires
parisiens du XVIe siècle"
Panufnik, A. Composing Myself.
    G. Abraham, 617(TLS):15May87–513
Panzenböck, E. Ein deutscher Traum.
    F.L. Carsten, 575(SEER):Oct86–623
Paolini, S.J. Confessions of Sin and Love
in the Middle Ages.
    G. Costa, 545(RPh):Nov86–215
Paolo Ciardi, R. & L. Tongiorgi Tomasi.
Immagini anatomiche e naturalistiche nei
disegni degli Uffizi, Secc. XVI e XVII.*
    M. Cazort, 380:Autumn86–408
Paolozzi, E. & others. Lost Magic Kingdoms
and Six Paper Moons from Nahuatl.
    A. Coombes & J. Lloyd, 59:Dec86–540
Papadakis, A. Crisis in Byzantium.
    N.M. Vaporis, 589:Jan86–195
Papadiamantis, A. Tales from a Greek
Island.
    G. Economou, 441:30Aug87–14
    J. Taylor, 617(TLS):18–24Dec87–1410
Pape, M. – see von Hofmannsthal, H.
Papen, J. Georges Bugnet.
    P. Imbert, 627(UTQ):Fall86–204
    G. Lecomte, 102(CanL):Summer86–134
Paper, L.J. Empire.
    J. Jarvis, 441:30Aug87–26
    442(NY):19Oct87–122
Paperno, S. & others. Intermediate Rus-
sian.
    O. Frink, 399(MLJ):Winter86–437
Papernyj, V. Kul'tura "Dva."
    J.E. Bowlt, 574(SEEJ):Summer86–297
Papetti, V. – see Pope, A.
Paque, R. Le statut parisien des nominal-
istes.
    J. Biard, 192(EP):Oct–Dec86–578
Paradis, M., Hiroko Hagiwara & N. Hilde-
brandt. Neurolinguistic Aspects of the
Japanese Writing System.
    M.P. Lorch, J. Katsuki-Nakamura, S.
      Sasanuma & L. Menn, 350:Dec87–910
    E.O. Reiman, 293(JASt):Aug86–859
Paradis, S. La Ligne bleue.
    M. Naudin, 207(FR):Mar87–566
Paraíso, I. El verso libre hispánico.
    P. Abad, 439(NM):1986/2–307
    W. Ferguson, 240(HR):Autumn86–459
    O. Rivera-Rodas, 238:Dec86–877
    I. Vallejo, 547(RF):Band98Heft3/4–484
Parameswaran, U., ed. The Commonwealth in
Canada.*
    A. Niven, 538(RAL):Fall86–435
Páramo, J.M.P. – see under Palomero Páramo,
J.M.
de' Paratesi, N.G. – see under Galli de'
Paratesi, N.
Pardo Bazán, E. Cuentos (Selección). (J.
Paredes Núñez, ed)
    D. Henn, 402(MLR):Jul87–763
    W.T. Pattison, 240(HR):Autumn86–480
Paredes Núñez, J. – see Pardo Bazán, E.
Parent, G. A Sign of the Eighties.
    D. Cole, 441:26Jul87–16

Parent, M. The Roof in Japanese Buddhist
Architecture.
    D.J. Byard, 576:Jun86–183
Parenti, M. Inventing Reality.*
    W.E. Coleman, 186(ETC.):Winter86–423
    639(VQR):Summer86–98
Parenti, M.I. – see under Isnardi Parenti,
M.
Paretsky, S. Bitter Medicine.
    T.J. Binyon, 617(TLS):13–19Nov87–1262
    N. Callendar, 441:2Aug87–29
Parfit, D. Reasons and Persons.*
    E.J. Bond, 529(QQ):Summer86–276
    B. Gruzalski, 519(PhS):Jul86–143
    M. Kapstein, 485(PE&W):Jul86–259
    J. Margolis, 484(PPR):Dec86–311
    J. Mendola, 519(PhS):Jul86–153
    L. Sowden, 479(PhQ):Oct86–514
Parfitt, G. English Poetry of the Seven-
teenth Century.*
    M. Dodsworth, 175:Spring86–103
    M. Llasera, 189(EA):Jul–Sep86–336
    A. Rudrum, 541(RES):Nov86–567
Parfitt, T. The Thirteenth Gate.
    A.J. Sherman, 617(TLS):18–24Sep87–
    1010
Pariente, J–C. L'analyse du langage à
Port-Royal.
    A. Boyer, 542:Oct–Dec86–527
Parini, J. The Patch Boys.*
    C. Hawtree, 617(TLS):14Aug87–873
"Paris au XIXe siècle: aspects d'un mythe
littéraire."
    J. Guichardet, 535(RHL):Jul–Aug86–778
Parish, W.L., ed. Chinese Rural Develop-
ment.
    G.E. Johnson, 293(JASt):Aug86–826
Park, D. – see Berkeley, G.
Park, M. & G.E. Markowitz. Democratic
Vistas.*
    F.V. O'Connor, 658:Spring86–94
Park, R. Missus.
    J. Cohen, 441:8Feb87–24
    R. Stevenson, 617(TLS):19Jun87–668
Parke, H.W. The Oracles of Apollo in Asia
Minor.
    P.J. Rhodes, 161(DUJ):Jun86–355
Parker, A.A. The Philosophy of Love in
Spanish Literature, 1480–1680. (T.
O'Reilly, ed)
    T.R.H., 131(CL):Winter86–101
    H. Merkl & K. Hawken, 72:Band223Heft1–
    222
Parker, G.L. The Beginnings of the Book
Trade in Canada.
    D.G. Lochhead, 627(UTQ):Fall86–145
    J.A. Wiseman, 470:Vol24–117
Parker, H. Flawed Texts and Verbal Icons.*
    J. McLaverty, 536(Rev):Vol8–119
    J.P. Sisk, 31(ASch):Spring86–262
    T. Ware, 102(CanL):Fall86–113
    J.L.W. West 3d, 301(JEGP):Oct86–588
Parker, H.N. Biological Themes in Modern
Science Fiction.
    M.D. Rose, 561(SFS):Nov86–398
Parker, L.C., Jr. The Japanese Police
System Today.
    W.L. Ames, 293(JASt):Nov85–157
Parker, O. Weighing the Planets.
    A. Grundberg, 441:6Dec87–21
Parker, P. The Old Lie.
    R. Blythe, 362:12Mar87–23
    D. Hibberd, 617(TLS):10Apr87–378

Parker, P. & G. Hartman, eds. Shakespeare and the Question of Theory.*
　P. Erickson, 570(SQ):Winter86-516
　P. Storfer, 157:No162-48
Parker, R. Miasma.*
　R. Garland, 303(JoHS):Vol106-234
　H.F.J. Horstmanshoff, 394:Vol39fasc3/4-538
Parker, R. The Subversive Stitch.*
　T. Garb, 59:Mar86-131
Parker, R.B. Pale Kings and Princes.
　T. Weesner, 441:31May87-26
　442(NY):13Jul87-90
Parker, R.B. Taming a Sea-Horse.*
　G. Kaufman, 362:7May87-26
Parker, R.B. - see Jonson, B.
Parker, R.D. Faulkner and the Novelistic Imagination.*
　M.B., 295(JML):Nov86-467
　D. Minter, 395(MFS):Summer86-269
　W. Taylor, 27(AL):May86-277
　639(VQR):Spring86-43
Parker, T. Soldier, Soldier.*
　362:6Aug87-22
Parker, T.H.L. Calvin's Old Testament Commentaries.
　H.A. Oberman, 617(TLS):14Aug87-884
Parkes, K.S. Writers and Politics in West Germany.
　G.P. Butler, 617(TLS):2-8Oct87-1075
Parkin, D., ed. The Anthropology of Evil.
　639(VQR):Winter86-30
Parkin, F. The Mind and Body Shop.
　E. Hawes, 441:16Aug87-9
Parkinson, G.H.R. Georg Lukács.
　S. Glynn, 518:Oct86-222
Parkinson, K. & M. Priestman, eds. Peasants and Countrymen in Literature.
　S. Hunter, 677(YES):Vol16-309
Parks, R.S. 18th Century Counterpoint and Tonal Structure.
　C.C. Judd, 411:Jul/Oct86-281
Parks, S. The Elizabethan Club of Yale University and Its Library.
　D. McKitterick, 617(TLS):6-12Nov87-1234
Parks, T. Home Thoughts.
　L. Taylor, 617(TLS):25Sep-1Oct87-1053
Parks, T. Loving Roger.*
　J. Mellors, 364:Oct86-91
Parks, T. Tongues of Flame.
　M. Wolitzer, 441:4Jan87-9
"Parlare fascista."
　C. Di Fusco, 708:Vol12fasc2-272
Parlasca, K. Syrische Grabreliefs hellenistischer und römischer Zeit.
　M.A.R. Colledge, 123:Vol36No1-166
Parmenides. Parmenides of Elea: Fragments.* (D. Gallop, ed & trans)
　D. Sider, 121(CJ):Apr-May87-333
　M.R. Wright, 123:Vol36No1-63
"Parmenides." (A. Gomez-Lobo, ed & trans)
　J. Barnes, 520:Vol31No2-182
Parmenter, R. Lawrence in Oaxaca.*
　E. Delavenay, 189(EA):Apr-Jun87-229
Parnell, M. Eric Linklater.*
　N. Curme, 571(ScLJ):Winter86-24
Paroissien, D. - see Dickens, C.
Parotti, P. The Greek Generals Talk.
　P-L. Adams, 61:Jan87-90
Parr, J. - see Barr, R.
Parra, N. Antipoems.
　639(VQR):Spring86-61

Parret, H. & J. Bouveresse, eds. Meaning and Understanding.
　W. Oesterreicher, 685(ZDL):2/1986-278
Parrinder, G. Avatar and Incarnation.
　H. Coward, 485(PE&W):Apr86-189
Parrinder, G. Encountering World Religions.
　A. Race, 617(TLS):25Sep-1Oct87-1056
Parrinder, P. The Failure of Theory.
　C. Baldick, 617(TLS):6-12Nov87-1217
Parrinder, P. James Joyce.*
　P.F. Herring, 659(ConL):Spring87-104
　J. Hurt, 301(JEGP):Jul86-470
　C. Peake, 97(CQ):Vol15No2-141
　J.P. Riquelme, 329(JJQ):Fall86-91
Parrish, S.M. - see Wordsworth, W.
Parrott, E.O., ed. How to Become Absurdly Well-Informed About the Famous and Infamous.
　D.J. Enright, 617(TLS):18-24Dec87-1399
Parrott, E.O., ed. Imitations of Immortality.
　H. Stevens, 364:Nov86-111
Parry, B. Conrad and Imperialism.*
　P. Delany, 401(MLQ):Jun85-218
　R. Hamner, 538(RAL):Spring86-158
Parry, G. The Golden Age Restor'd.
　S.J. Steen, 568(SCN):Winter86-59
Parry, G. Seventeenth-Century English Poetry.*
　A. Rudrum, 541(RES):Nov86-567
Parry, G.J.R. A Protestant Vision.
　C. Cross, 617(TLS):18-24Sep87-1014
Parry, J.P. Democracy and Religion.
　R. Foster, 617(TLS):25Sep-1Oct87-1038
Parry, L. William Morris Textiles.
　F.S. Boos, 637(VS):Summer87-552
Parsons, C. Mathematics in Philosophy.*
　W.W. Tait, 486:Dec86-588
"Partalopa saga."* (L.P. Andersen, ed)
　C.B. Hieatt, 301(JEGP):Jan86-84
Parton, J. "Air Force Spoken Here."
　J.B. McCarley, 441:12Jul87-21
Partridge, A.C. Language and Society in Anglo-Irish Literature.
　A. Roche, 577(SHR):Summer86-273
Partridge, F. Everything to Lose.*
　42(AR):Fall86-493
Partridge, M., ed. Alexander Herzen and European Culture.
　E. Acton, 402(MLR):Oct86-1050
Partridge, V.P. & R.J. Adrosko. Made in New York State.
　J.B. Reinstein, 440:Summer-Fall86-164
Parun, V. Selected Poems. (D.C. Nisula, ed & trans)
　J. Kolsti, 574(SEEJ):Winter86-593
Paskin, S., J. Ramsey & J. Silver, eds. Angels of Fire.
　B. O'Donoghue, 493:Jun86-106
　R. Sheppard, 617(TLS):23Jan87-92
Pasler, J., ed. Confronting Stravinsky.
　D. Matthews, 617(TLS):13Feb87-159
Pasolini, P.P. Lettere 1940-1954, con una cronologia della vita e delle opere. (N. Naldini, ed)
　P. McCarthy, 617(TLS):17Apr87-408
Pasolini, P.P. Roman Poems.
　L.R. Smith, 703:No17-126
Pasquali, G. Lingua nuova e antica. (G. Folena, ed)
　F. Chiappelli, 402(MLR):Apr87-499

Pellegrino, C.R. & J. Stoff. Chariots for Apollo.
639(VQR):Autumn86-130
Pelletier, C. The Funeral Makers.*
D. Montrose, 617(TLS):6Mar87-246
Pelletier, F.J. & J. King-Farlow, eds. New Essays on Aristotle.*
J. Shea, 41:Vol6-222
Pelletier, F.J. & J. King-Farlow, eds. New Essays on Plato.
R.W. Jordan, 123:Vol36No1-142
Pelletier, Y. - see Aristotle
Pelphrey, B. Love Was His Meaning.
W. Riehle, 72:Band223Heft2-403
Peltason, T. Reading "In Memoriam."*
J. Bristow, 175:Autumn86-279
E. Jordan, 184(EIC):Jul86-268
S. Lavabre, 189(EA):Jan-Mar87-90
H.W., 636(VP):Autumn86-347
Pemble, J. The Mediterranean Passion.
R. Shannon, 617(TLS):23-29Oct87-1161
Peña, L. El ente y su ser.
M.D. Diez Hoyo, 540(RIPh):Vol40fasc4-455
Peña, M. The Texas-Mexican Conjunto.*
L.K. Sommers, 650(WF):Jul86-237
de la Peña, P., ed. Antología de la poesía romántica.
D.T. Gies, 86(BHS):Oct86-372
Penčev, J. Stroež na b'lgarskoto izrečenie.
C.V. Chvany, 574(SEEJ):Summer86-306
Penelhum, T. Butler.*
J.K., 185:Apr87-697
Penelhum, T. God and Skepticism.*
C.G. Prado, 154:Summer86-375
G. Rosenkrantz, 484(PPR):Sep86-168
E. Talmor, 319:Apr87-299
Pénigault-Duhet, P. Mary Wollstonecraft-Godwin (1759-1797).
M. Baridon, 189(EA):Jul-Sep86-354
E.W. Sunstein, 340(KSJ):Vol35-203
Penn, J. Barren Revenge.
G. Kaufman, 362:7May87-26
Penna, S. This Strange Joy.
H. Haller, 275(IQ):Winter86-122
Pennaod, G. An Novelov Ancien ha Devot.
M. McKenna, 112:Vol18-213
Penniman, H.R. & E.M. Mujal-Leon, eds. Spain at the Polls, 1977, 1979, and 1982.
639(VQR):Summer86-95
Pennington, A. & P. Levi - see "Marko the Prince"
Pennington, R. A Descriptive Catalogue of the Etched Work of Wenceslaus Hollar 1607-1677.*
S.T. Fisher, 447(N&Q):Sep85-397
Pennock, J.R. & J.W. Chapman, eds. NOMOS XXVIII.
M. Davis, 185:Apr87-657
Penny, N., ed. Reynolds.*
A. Woods, 97(CQ):Vol15No2-168
Penrose, A. The Lives of Lee Miller.*
J. Bell, 55:Sep86-38
639(VQR):Spring86-48
Penrose, B. & S. Freeman. Conspiracy of Silence.
N. Annan, 453(NYRB):22Oct87-3
J. Brodsky, 617(TLS):30Jan87-99
S. Koch, 441:16Aug87-11
Pensado, J.L. & C. Pensado Ruiz. "Gueada" y "géada" gallegas.
D.A. Pharies, 545(RPh):Aug86-106

Pensado Ruiz, C. Cronología relativa del castellano.
M. Torreblanca, 240(HR):Autumn86-457
Penzkofer, G. Der Bedeutungsaufbau in den späten Erzählungen Čechovs.
A.R. Durkin, 574(SEEJ):Summer86-288
P. Henry, 575(SEER):Oct86-596
Penzl, H. Frühneuhochdeutsch.
F.G. Banta, 301(JEGP):Jan86-71
H. Wellmann, 685(ZDL):3/1986-370
Pepicello, W.J. & T.A. Green. The Language of Riddles.*
T.E. Murray, 35(AS):Spring86-93
D. Roemer, 650(WF):Jan86-39
Pepper, D.S. Guido Reni.
J. Gash, 59:Dec86-516
D. Mahon, 90:Mar86-213
Pepper, P. & T. de Araugo. The Kurnai of Gippsland.
L. Ryan, 381:Mar86-49
Pepper, S. & N. Adams. Firearms and Fortifications.
M. Mallett, 617(TLS):17Jul87-775
Pequeño Glazier, L., ed. All's Normal Here.
G. Haslam, 649(WAL):Nov86-243
Pequigney, J. Such Is My Love.*
G. Bradshaw, 617(TLS):30Oct-5Nov87-1199
D. Donoghue, 533:Summer86-123
639(VQR):Spring86-44
Peradotto, J. & J.P. Sullivan, eds. Women in the Ancient World.*
T. Fleming, 121(CJ):Oct-Nov86-73
Percival, A. Galdós and His Critics.
P.A. Bly, 593:Winter86/87-338
H. Hinterhäuser, 547(RF):Band98 Heft3/4-483
J. Sinnigen, 238:Dec86-870
Percy, A. & others. Bernardo Cavallino of Naples, 1616-1656.
R. Enggass, 54:Mar86-168
Percy, H.R. Painted Ladies.
G. Dowden, 102(CanL):Winter85-162
Percy, W. The Thanatos Syndrome.
D. Bauer, 61:Apr87-86
P. Binding, 362:29Oct87-28
G. Godwin, 441:5Apr87-1
R. Porter, 617(TLS):2-8Oct87-1074
T. Rafferty, 442(NY):15Jun87-91
R. Towers, 453(NYRB):25Jun87-45
Perdue, C., ed. Second Language Acquisition by Adult Immigrants.*
L. Selinker, 351(LL):Mar86-83
Perec, G. Life: A User's Manual.
P-L. Adams, 61:Dec87-110
P. Auster, 441:15Nov87-7
G. Josipovici, 617(TLS):30Oct-5Nov87-1191
Perec, G. Penser/Classer.*
W.F. Motte, Jr., 207(FR):Dec86-296
Perelli, L. Il movimento popolare nell'ultimo secolo della repubblica.
A.J.L. van Hooff, 394:Vol39fasc3/4-532
Perelman, S.J. Don't Tread On Me. (P. Crowther, ed)
M. Richler, 441:9Aug87-1
Perelmuter Pérez, R. Noche intelectual.*
G. Flynn, 241:Sep86-83
P. Martín, 552(REH):Jan86-148

Pérennec, R. Recherches sur le roman
arthurien en vers en Allemagne aux XIIe
et XIIIe siècles.
D.H. Green, 402(MLR):Apr86-529
Péret, B. A Marvelous World.
W.H., 148:Autumn86-118
Pérez, G.J. La novelística de J. Leyva.
L.T. González-del-Valle, 238:Dec86-877
Pérez, O.R. - see under Rodríguez Pérez, O.
Pérez, R.P. - see under Perelmuter Pérez,
R.
Pérez de Ayala, R. El ombligo del mundo.
(A. Prado, ed)
S.E. Torres, 552(REH):Jan86-140
Pérez Galdós, B. Fortunata and Jacinta.
(A.M. Gullón, trans)
J. Butt, 617(TLS):28Aug87-931
Pérez Galdós, B. Fortunata y Jacinta. (F.
Caudet, ed)
T.T. Folley, 86(BHS):Jan86-101
Pérez Galdós, B. La de Bringas. (A.
Blanco & C. Blanco Aguinaga, eds)
J. Lowe, 86(BHS):Jan86-99
Pérez Galdós, B. Our Friend Manso. (R.
Russell, trans)
J. Butt, 617(TLS):28Aug87-931
W. Ferguson, 441:22Feb87-28
Perez Guilhou, D. & others. Atribuciones
del presidente argentino.
C. Garcia Godoy, 263(RIB):Vol36No4-500
Pérez Sánchez, A. Historia del dibujo en
España.
D. Angulo Iñiguez, 48:Oct-Dec86-425
Pérez Vidal, A. Artículos.
D.E. Schurlknight, 240(HR):Spring86-226
Perfect, C. & G. Rookledge. Rookledge's
International Typefinder.
P.M. Van Wingen, 517(PSBA):Vol80No2-
276
Perfetti, C.A. Reading Ability.
W. Grabe, 350:Mar87-201
Perinbam, B.M. Holy Violence.
H. Wylie, 538(RAL):Winter86-597
Perinbanayagam, R.S. The Karmic Theater.*
S.B. Steever, 318(JAOS):Jan/Mar85-187
Perkyns, R., ed. Major Plays of the Cana-
dian Theatre, 1934-1984.*
A. Andrews, 610:Summer86-178
A. Messenger, 102(CanL):Winter85-125
B. Parker, 397(MD):Mar86-161
Perl, J.M. The Tradition of Return.*
H. Gross, 536(Rev):Vol8-33
R.D. Newman, 577(SHR):Spring86-183
Perl, M., ed. Estudios sobre el léxico del
español de América.*
J.L. Rivarola, 72:Band223Heft1-193
Perle, G. The Operas of Alban Berg.* (Vol
2: Lulu.)
M. Taylor, 410(M&L):Oct86-404
Perlina, N. Varieties of Poetic Utter-
ance.*
C. Emerson, 550(RusR):Jan86-52
Perlman, J., E. Folsom & D. Campion, eds.
Walt Whitman.
125:Fall85-111
Perlmutter, A. The Life and Times of
Menachem Begin.
G. Gottlieb, 441:21Jun87-3
Perlmutter, D.M., ed. Studies in Rela-
tional Grammar 1.
B. Comrie, 353:Vol24No4-773

Perlmutter, D.M. & C.G. Rosen, eds.
Studies in Relational Grammar 2.*
B. Comrie, 353:Vol24No4-773
J. De Chicchis, 355(LSoc):Mar86-137
Perloff, M. The Dance of the Intellect.*
G. Bornstein, 191(ELN):Jun87-80
V.S., 295(JML):Nov86-426
Perlot, J-N. Gold Seeker.* (H.R. Lamar,
ed)
D.R. Lewis, 649(WAL):Nov86-271
Perlstein, S. & others. A Stage for
Memory.
V.M. Patraka, 385(MQR):Winter87-285
Perman, M. The Road to Redemption.
D.W. Bowen, 9(AlaR):Jan86-72
C.L. Flynn, Jr., 579(SAQ):Spring86-195
Pernick, M.S. A Calculus of Suffering.
J.D.H., 185:Oct86-309
Pernot, L. Les "Discours Siciliens"
d'Aelius Aristide (Or. 5-6).*
B.P. Reardon, 24:Winter86-609
Perosa, S. American Theories of the Novel,
1793-1903.*
E.M. Eigner, 402(MLR):Oct87-941
M. Gidley, 366:Spring86-125
Perozo, M.B. - see under Briceño Perozo, M.
Perreiah, A.R. - see Paulus Venetus
Perrein, M. Les Cotonniers de Bassalane.
J.H. Stewart, 207(FR):Oct86-166
Perrier, D. Die Spanische Kleinkunst des
11. Jahrhunderts.
M. Estella, 48:Jan-Mar86-112
Perrier, F. Voyages extraordinaires en
Translacanie.*
C.J. Stivale, 207(FR):Oct86-154
Perrins, C. Birds of Britain and Europe.
R.W. Ashford, 617(TLS):2-8Oct87-1087
Perris, A. Music as Propaganda.
G. Martin, 465:Summer86-179
Perrois, L. Ancestral Art of Gabon.
J.W. Fernandez, 2(AfrA):Aug86-8
du Perron, J.D. Oraison funèbre sur la
mort de Monsieur de Ronsard (1586). (M.
Simonin, ed)
T. Allott, 402(MLR):Oct87-955
P. Ford, 208(FS):Jul86-325
Perrot, M. Une Histoire des femmes est-
elle possible?
C. Slawy-Sutton, 207(FR):Dec86-276
Perrot, M. Workers on Strike.
J.F. McMillan, 617(TLS):9-15Oct87-1096
Perrot, P. Le Travail des apparences, ou
les transformations du corps féminin,
XVIIIe-XIXe siècle.
N.W. Jouve, 208(FS):Jan86-80
Perrucci, A. Shepherd's Song.
F. Cerreta, 276:Summer86-187
Perry, E.I. Belle Moskowitz.
D. Seidman, 441:18Oct87-31
Perry, J. Le Coeur de l'escargot.
R. Linkhorn, 207(FR):Oct86-167
Perry, R. The Celebrated Mary Astell.*
F. Morgan, 617(TLS):15May87-508
Perry, T.A. A Bibliography of American
Literature.
A. Marino, 149(CLS):Spring86-80
Perry, T.A. - see Santob de Carrión
Perse, S. Anabase.* (A. Henry, ed)
H. Levillain, 535(RHL):Mar-Apr86-343
Person, J.E., Jr., ed. Literature Criti-
cism from 1400 to 1800. (Vol 3)
D.R. Anderson, 568(SCN):Winter86-65
[continued]

Peukert, H. Science, Action, and Funda-
mental Theology.
C.G. Prado, 449:Dec86–571
Peuntner, T. Büchlein von der Liebhabung
Gottes. (B. Schnell, ed)
S. Jefferis, 589:Oct86–986
H.B. Willson, 301(JEGP):Oct86–618
Peyret, J–F. & V. La Rocca – see Aretino,
P.
Peyser, J. Bernstein.
L. Botstein, 441:10May87–3
Peyser, J., ed. The Orchestra.
C. Wuorinen, 414:Vol72No4–535
Peyton, J. Zions Cause (1920–1950).
442(NY):28Dec87–123
Pfaelzer, J. The Utopian Novel in America,
1886–1896.*
K.M. Roemer, 27(AL):Mar86–132
T.H. Towers, 395(MFS):Summer86–245
Pfaff, F. The Cinema of Ousmane Sembene.*
L. de Vitry–Maubrey, 207(FR):Dec86–285
Pfahl, J. Picture Windows.
A. Grundberg, 441:6Dec87–20
von der Pfalz, L. A Woman's Life in the
Court of the Sun King.
H.M.K. Riley, 133:Band18Heft4–369
Pfanz, H.W. Gettysburg: The Second Day.
T. Wicker, 61:Dec87–108
Pfeffer, J.A., ed. Studies in Descriptive
German Grammar.*
G. Helbig, 682(ZPSK):Band39Heft4–509
Pfeffer, W. The Change of Philomel.
D.A. Fein, 207(FR):Feb87–388
Pfeifer, H. – see Bonhoeffer, D.
Pfeiffer, B.B. Treasures of Taliesin.
D. Hoffmann, 576:Dec86–422
J. Iovine, 45:Jul86–81
Pfeiffer, B.B. – see "Frank Lloyd Wright
Letters Trilogy"
Pfeiffer, H. Roman und historischer Kon-
text.
U. Schulz–Buschhaus, 547(RF):Band98
Heft1/2–208
Pfister, M. & B. Schulte–Middelich, eds.
Die 'Nineties.*
C. Daufenbach, 52:Band21Heft1–105
Phan Chu Trinh. A Complete Account of
the Peasants' Uprising in the Central
Region.
G. Gran, 293(JASt):Nov85–199
Pharr, C. Homeric Greek.
J. Williams, 124:Jul–Aug87–447
Phelan, A., ed. The Weimar Dilemma.
O. Durrani, 402(MLR):Oct86–1046
E. Harvey, 366:Autumn86–268
Phelps, L.R. & K. McCullough. Herman
Melville's Foreign Reputation.
R. Asselineau, 549(RLC):Jan–Mar86–109
"Le phénomène IXE–13."
M. Lacombe, 102(CanL):Spring86–147
Philbert, B. L'Homosexualité à l'écran.
N. Greene, 207(FR):May87–898
Philbrick, T. & C.A. Denne – see Cooper,
J.F.
Philbrick, T. & M. Geracht – see Cooper,
J.F.
Philip, I. The Bodleian Library in the
Seventeenth and Eighteenth Centuries.*
G. Walters, 447(N&Q):Mar85–106
Philip, N. – see Kipling, R.
Philippe, C–J. Le Roman du cinéma, 1.
T. Conley, 207(FR):May87–901

Philippe, C–L. Oeuvres complètes.
P. McCarthy, 617(TLS):2Jan87–7
"Philippi Cancellarii, 'Summa de Bono.'"
(N. Wicki, ed)
J. Jolivet, 542:Oct–Dec86–512
Philips, C. – see Hopkins, G.M.
Philipson, M. Somebody Else's Life.
B. De Mott, 441:15Feb87–31
Phillipps, K.C. Language and Class in
Victorian England.
H. Perkin, 637(VS):Autumn86–138
M. Vicinus, 361:Jul86–291
Phillips, C. The European Tribe.
A. Bery, 617(TLS):10Apr87–396
P. Binding, 362:12Feb87–25
A. Lee, 441:9Aug87–7
Phillips, C. A State of Independence.*
M. Thorpe, 176:May87–44
Phillips, C.R. Six Galleons for the King
of Spain.
K. Andrews, 617(TLS):17Jul87–775
Phillips, D. Letters from Windermere,
1912–1914. (R.C. Harris & E. Phillips,
eds)
F. McNeil, 102(CanL):Winter85–112
Phillips, D.L. Toward a Just Social
Order.
J. Samples, 185:Jul87–872
Phillips, D.Z. R.S. Thomas, Poet of the
Hidden God.
S. Medcalf, 617(TLS):17Apr87–418
Phillips, G. The Imagery of the "Libro de
Buen Amor."*
J.K. Walsh, 240(HR):Autumn86–465
Phillips, H. – see Chaucer, G.
Phillips, J.A. Fast Lanes.
J. McInerney, 441:3May87–7
M. Wiggins, 617(TLS):11–17Sep87–978
Phillips, J.J. Mojo Hand.
A.V. Hewat, 617(TLS):18–24Dec87–1409
Phillips, K., ed. New German Filmmakers.
F.A. Birgel, 221(GQ):Fall86–686
Phillips, L.W. – see Fitzgerald, F.S.
Phillips, M. Aspects of Text Structure.
W. Grabe, 350:Mar87–200
Phillips, R. Personal Accounts.
R.B. Shaw, 491:Nov86–105
Phillips, R. – see Schwartz, D.
Phillips, T. A Humument. (rev)
D. Bindman, 617(TLS):6–12Nov87–1230
Phillipson, M. Painting, Language, and
Modernity.*
R.N. Wynyard, 89(BJA):Summer86–299
Philmus, R.M. Into the Unknown. (2nd ed)
P. Parrinder, 402(MLR):Jul86–694
Philodemus. On Methods of Inference.
(P.H. & E.A. De Lacy, eds & trans)
E. Amis, 41:Vol6–251
Philodemus. Über die Musik IV. Buch.
(A.J. Neubecker, ed)
J. Barnes, 520:Vol31No2–192
Philonenko, A. La Théorie kantienne de
l'histoire.
G. Steiner, 617(TLS):1May87–468
Philonenko, A. – see Fichte, J.G.
Philoponus, J. De vocabulis quae diversum
significatum exhibent secundum differen-
tiam accentus. (L.W. Daly, ed)
I.C. Cunningham, 123:Vol36No1–150
Philp, M. Godwin's Political Justice.
D. Locke, 617(TLS):20Feb87–178

Photius. Epistulae et Amphilochia, 2.
(B. Laourdas & L.G. Westerink, eds)
A. Kazhdan, 589:Oct86-895
Picchi, M. Storie di casa Leopardi.
F. Donini, 617(TLS):14Aug87-881
Picchioni Borri, A. Espressioni e forme
del culto cattolico nell'opera di Flau-
bert.
G. Séginger, 535(RHL):Mar-Apr86-311
Piccolomini, E.S. [Papa Pio II]. I commen-
tarii. (L. Totaro, ed) Commentarii
rerum memorabilium que temporibus suis
contigerunt. (A. van Heck, ed)
M. Pozzi, 228(GSLI):Vol163fasc521-127
Piché, C. Das Ideal.
A.M. Hjort, 154:Winter86-804
Picherit, J-L.G., ed & trans. The Journey
of Charlemagne to Jerusalem and Constan-
tinople (Le Voyage de Charlemagne à
Jérusalem et à Constantinople).
G.S. Burgess, 208(FS):Apr86-190
Pichois, C., with others - see Colette
Pichois, C. & V., with A. Brunet, eds.
Album Colette.*
M. Picard, 535(RHL):Mar-Apr86-326
Pickard, N. No Body.
T.J. Binyon, 617(TLS):13-19Nov87-1262
Pickard, T. Custom & Exile.
R. Sheppard, 617(TLS):23Jan87-92
Picken, L., ed. Musica Asiatica 4.*
W.P. Malm, 318(JAOS):Oct/Dec85-773
Pickens, T.B., Jr. Boone.
G. Phillips, 617(TLS):11-17Dec87-1372
E. Prescott, 441:22Mar87-18
Pickering, A. Constructing Quarks.*
R. Torretti, 160:Jan86-177
Pickering, K. A Midsummer Night's Dream.
T. Minter, 157:No160-50
Pickett, T.H. The Unseasonable Democrat.
M.R. McCulloh, 221(GQ):Fall86-655
Pickles, J. Straight from the Bench.
P. Devlin, 617(TLS):12Jun87-633
Pickvance, R. Van Gogh in Saint-Rémy and
Auvers.
P-L. Adams, 61:Jul87-98
J. House, 617(TLS):6-12Nov87-1230
Pico della Mirandola, G. Commentary on a
Canzone of Benivieni. (S. Jayne, trans)
M.J.B. Allen, 276:Summer86-189
Pico della Mirandola, G. Über die Vorstel-
lung/De imaginatione.* (E. Kessler, ed &
trans)
K. Ley, 72:Band223Heft2-463
Picoche, J. Le vocabulaire psychologique
dans les "Chroniques" de Froissart.
G.S. Burgess, 589:Jul86-742
G. Roussineau, 209(FM):Apr86-119
Pidoux, P. - see de Bèze, T.
Pienkos, D.E. PNA.
J.W. Wieczerzak, 497(PolR):Vol31No4-335
Piepenbrock, M. & C.P. Fisher. Classic
Dishes Made Easy.
W. & C. Cowen, 639(VQR):Autumn86-142
Pieper, A. Albert Camus.
H.R. Schlette, 687:Apr-Jun86-303
Pieper, A. Ethik und Moral.
G.L., 185:Jul87-884
Pieper, M. Die Funktionen der Kommentie-
rung im "Frauendienst" Ulrichs von
Liechtenstein.
H. Heinen, 406:Fall86-388
Pierce, C. When Things Get Back to Normal.
J. Humphreys, 441:3May87-33

Pierce, F. Alonso de Ercilla y Zúñiga.*
D. Janik, 224(GRM):Band36Heft3-363
I. Lerner, 86(BHS):Oct86-370
Pierce-Moses, R., ed. Historic Texas.
L. Milazzo, 584(SWR):Spring86-257
Piercy, M. Gone to Soldiers.
H. Wolitzer, 441:10May87-11
Pierre, J., ed. Tracts surréalistes et
déclarations collectives.
C. Moisan, 193(ELit):Autumn86-141
Pierre, J-L., ed. C.F. Ramuz 1.
G. Cesbron, 356(LR):May86-186
Pierrot, J. The Decadent Imagination 1890-
1900.*
H. Tucker, 385(MQR):Spring87-421
Pierrot, J. Marguerite Duras.
D. Coward, 617(TLS):10Jul87-741
Pierssens, M. Lautréamont.*
J. Romney, 208(FS):Oct86-479
Pietallei-Palmarini, M., ed. Language and
Learning.
D.H., 355(LSoc):Mar86-138
Pietrangeli, C. & others. The Sistine
Chapel.*
J. Pope-Hennessy, 453(NYRB):8Oct87-16
Pietri, L. La ville de Tours du IVe au VIe
siècle.
W. Goffart, 589:Oct86-988
Pietzcker, C. Trauma, Wunsch und Abwehr.
H. Schmiedt, 680(ZDP):Band105Heft2-305
Pigman, G.W. 3d. Grief and English Renais-
sance Elegy.*
J.M. Evans, 541(RES):Aug86-408
A. Guibbory, 551(RenQ):Summer86-334
Pignatti, T. Disegni Antichi del Museo
Correr di Venezia.
G. Naughton, 39:Jan86-61
Piguet, J-C. Où va la philosophie.
R. Quilliot, 192(EP):Apr-Jun86-265
Pike, B. The Image of the City in Modern
Literature.*
R. Kieser, 406:Spring86-123
Pike, D. Lukács and Brecht.*
B. Kiralyfalvi, 615(TJ):Mar86-121
D. Steward, 125:Winter86-223
Pike, F.B. The Politics of the Miraculous
in Peru.
T.M. Davies, Jr., 263(RIB):Vol36No3-342
Pike, K.L. & E.G. Text and Tagmeme.
G.L. Huttar, 355(LSoc):Mar86-138
Pike, R. Penal Servitude in Early Modern
Spain.
M.F. Lang, 86(BHS):Apr86-159
Piker, S. A Peasant Community in Changing
Thailand.
S.H. Potter, 293(JASt):Feb86-462
Pikulik, L. Leistungsethik contra Gefühls-
kult.
E. Keller, 67:Nov86-308
C. Zelle, 72:Band223Heft1-141
Pilhes, R-V. La Pompéi.
P. Daly, 207(FR):Oct86-168
Pillay, A. An Introduction to Stability
Theory.
M. Makkai, 316:Jun86-465
Pilpel, R.H. Between Eternities.
F.C. Mench, Jr., 124:Jan-Feb87-226
Pimlott, B. Labour and the Left in the
1930s.
617(TLS):30Jan87-120
Pimlott, B. - see Dalton, H.
Pin Yathay & J. Mann. Stay Alive, My Son.
D. Pownall, 362:13Aug87-23

Piñal, F.A. – see under Aguilar Piñal, F.
Pincher, C. Traitors.
  D. Fitzpatrick, 441:13Sep87-35
  N. Hiley, 617(TLS):22May87-539
Pinciss, G.M. & others. Explorations in
the Arts.
  G.S. Plummer, 709:Fall86-57
Pindar. Pindaro: "Le Istmiche." (G.A.
Privitera, ed)
  M.C. Howatson, 123:Vol36No1-9
Pinder, L.H. Under the House.
  L. Taylor, 617(TLS):18-24Dec87-1409
Pine, L.G. A Dictionary of Nicknames.
  A. Room, 424:Jun86-211
Pineda, C. Frieze.*
  442(NY):2Feb87-98
Pinelli, G.V. Un Abozzo di Grammatica
francese del '500.* (A.M. Raugei, ed)
[shown in prev under ed]
  F.J. Hausmann, 547(RF):Band98Heft3/4-
  398
  R. Posner, 208(FS):Jan86-67
Pinget, R. The Apocrypha.
  S. Bann, 617(TLS):18-24Dec87-1410
  J. Updike, 442(NY):18May87-110
Pinget, R. Graal Flibuste.
  R.M. Henkels, 193(ELit):Winter86/87-202
Pinget, R. L'Ennemi.
  S. Bann, 617(TLS):18-24Dec87-1410
Pinget, R. Mahu ou le matériau.
  A. Robbe-Grillet, 193(ELit):Winter
  86/87-201
Pinget, R. Monsieur Songe. Le Harnais.
Charrue.
  G. Brulotte, 193(ELit):Winter86/87-203
  J-Y. Pouilloux, 98:Mar86-274
Pinget, R. Un testament bizarre.
  R. Henkels, 207(FR):May87-913
  J-Y. Pouilloux, 98:Mar86-274
Pini, P. Terra di Belgirate.
  V.D.L., 605(SC):15Jan87-218
Pinker, S. Language Learnability and Lan-
guage Development.
  E. Bialystok, 399(MLJ):Summer86-176
  M. Maratsos, 617(TLS):2Jan87-19
Pinkney, T. Women in the Poetry of T.S.
Eliot.
  G. Smith, 402(MLR):Apr87-461
Pinkster, H., ed. Latin Linguistics and
Linguistic Theory.
  O. Wenskus, 260(IF):Band91-393
Pinkus, B. The Soviet Government and the
Jews, 1948-1967.*
  A. Orbach, 550(RusR):Oct86-446
Pinney, T. – see Kipling, R.
Pinsker, S. Conversations with Contempo-
rary American Writers.
  K. Versluys, 179(ES):Oct86-463
Pintacuda, M. Interpretazioni musicale
sul teatro di Aristofane.
  A. Bélis, 555:Vol59fasc2-278
Pinter, H. Collected Poems and Prose.
  V. Cunningham, 493:Jun86-116
Piø, I. Nye veje til folkevisen.
  L. Isaacson, 563(SS):Spring86-186
  V. Ólason, 64(Arv):Vol41-138
Pipa, A. & S. Repishti, eds. Studies on
Kosova.
  M. Wheeler, 575(SEER):Jan86-155
Piperno, F. Gli "eccellentissimi musici
della città di Bologna."
  D. Butchart, 410(M&L):Apr86-196

Pippidi, D.M., ed & trans. Inscriptiones
Daciae et Scythiae Minoris Antiquae.
(Ser 2, Vol 1)
  A.G. Woodhead, 303(JoHS):Vol106-262
Pirandello, L. Lettere da Bonn. (E. Pro-
videnti, ed)
  F. Firth, 402(MLR):Oct86-1015
Pirandello, L. Tales of Madness.
  A. Paolucci, 275(IQ):Spring86-113
Pires, J.C. Ballad of Dogs' Beach.
  A. Hyde, 441:3May87-13
Pirie, D., ed. Jan Kochanowski in Glasgow.
  D.A. Frick, 497(PolR):Vol31No4-333
Pirie, D.B. William Wordsworth.*
  E. Larrissy, 402(MLR):Jan87-183
Piron, M., with M. Lemoine, eds. L'Univers
de Simenon.
  J. Fabre, 535(RHL):Jan-Feb86-166
Piroth, W. Ortsnamenstudien zur angelsäch-
sischen Wanderung.
  E. Felder, 685(ZDL):3/1986-412
Pirrotta, N. Music and Culture in Italy
from the Middle Ages to the Baroque.*
(L. Lockwood & C. Wolff, eds)
  F.J. Guentner, 377:Jul86-144
  E. Rosand, 317:Summer86-389
Pirtle, C. 3d & M.F. Cusack. The Lonely
Sentinel.
  L. Milazzo, 584(SWR):Spring86-257
Pistorius, T. Hegemoniestreben und
Autonomiesicherung in der griechischen
Vertragspolitik klassischer und hel-
lenistischer Zeit.
  P.J. Rhodes, 123:Vol36No2-329
Pitcher, J. – see Bacon, F.
Pitou, S. The Paris Opéra.* (Vol 2)
  B. Norman, 207(FR):Mar87-576
Pitt, D.G. E.J. Pratt: The Truant Years
1882-1927.*
  R.G. Moyles, 178:Dec86-487
Pitt-Kethley, F. Sky Ray Lolly.*
  E. Larrissy, 493:Jun86-108
  S. Rae, 364:Aug/Sep86-132
Pittaluga, M.G. L'Évolution de la langue
commerciale.*
  R. Arveiller, 535(RHL):Mar-Apr86-286
· Pitwood, M. Dante and the French Roman-
tics.
  S. Ellis, 208(FS):Oct86-471
  T.M. Lazzaro, 446(NCFS):Spring87-339
  J.A. Scott, 67:Nov86-290
  R. Trousson, 547(RF):Band98Heft3/4-440
  K. Wren, 402(MLR):Oct87-964
Pivato, J., ed. Contrasts.
  E. Padolsky, 298:Winter86/87-138
Pivčević, E., ed. The Cartulary of the
Benedictine Abbey of St. Peter of Gumay
(Crotia), 1080-1187.
  D. Abulafia, 575(SEER):Apr86-287
  B. Krekić, 589:Jul86-742
Pivčević, E. The Concept of Reality.
  H.M. Robinson, 617(TLS):6Feb87-132
Pizarnik, A. Les travaux et les nuits.
  A. Suied, 98:Nov86-1150
Placksin, S. American Women in Jazz, 1900
to the Present.
  B. Pennycook, 529(QQ):Autumn86-693
Plaisant, M., ed. Les Formes de l'arriv-
isme en Angleterre du XVIe siècle à
l'époque romantique.
  R.A. Day, 189(EA):Jul-Sep86-322

Plank, F., ed. Objects.*
  G. Bossong, 361:Jun86-139
  J. Miller, 297(JL):Mar86-213
Plank, F., ed. Relational Typology.
  G. Bourcier, 189(EA):Jul-Sep87-337
van der Plank, P.H. Taalsociologie.
  C.D. Grijns, 204(FdL):Mar86-71
Plant, R., ed. The Penguin Book of Modern
Canadian Drama.* (Vol 1)
  A. Andrews, 610:Summer86-178
  A. Messenger, 102(CanL):Winter85-125
  B. Parker, 397(MD):Mar86-151
Plante, D. The Native.
  J. Lucraft, 617(TLS):17Jul87-765
Plantinga, A. & N. Wolterstorff, eds.
Faith and Rationality.*
  J.E. Tomberlin, 449:Sep86-401
Plater, A. Misterioso.
  B. Morton, 617(TLS):13-19Nov87-1248
Plath, D.W., ed. Work and Lifecourse in
Japan.*
  R.E. Mouer, 302:Vol22No1-100
Plato. The Being of the Beautiful.* (S.
Benardete, ed & trans)
  D.A. Hyland, 543:Dec86-371
Plato. The Dialogues of Plato. (Vol 1)
(R.E. Allen, trans)
  J.B.W., 185:Oct86-304
Plato. Phaedrus. (C.J. Rowe, trans)
  M. Nussbaum, 617(TLS):7Aug87-850
Plato. Plato's "Euthyphro."* (I. Walker,
ed)
  R.J. Klonoski, 41:Fall85-322
Plato. Symposium of Plato. (T. Griffith,
trans)
  J.H.C. Leach, 617(TLS):7Aug87-850
"Plato and Aristophanes: Four Texts on
Socrates." (T.G. & G.S. West, trans)
  S. Forde, 41:Vol6-205
Platonov, A. Le Chemin de l'éther.
  J. Blot, 450(NRF):Jan86-109
Platt, C. The Abbeys and Priories of
Medieval England.
  L.J. Daly, 377:Jul86-140
Platt, J., H. Weber & Ho Mian Lian. The
New Englishes.
  P.H. Lowenberg, 399(MLJ):Summer86-207
  J. Williams, 355(LSoc):Jun86-264
Platt, M. Rome and Romans acccording to
Shakespeare.
  P. Boitani, 156(ShJW):Jahrbuch1986-238
Plaul, H. Illustrierte Geschichte der
Trivialliteratur.*
  H. & R. Hartmann, 654(WB):6/1986-1050
Pleines, J-E. Praxis und Vernunft.
  A. Stanguennec, 542:Jan-Mar86-120
  E. Vollrath, 489(PJGG):Band93Heft2-418
Pleket, H.W. & R.S. Stroud, eds. Supple-
mentum Epigraphicum Graecum. (Vol 31)
  P.M. Fraser, 123:Vol36No1-171
du Plessis, M. A State of Fear.
  C. Hope, 617(TLS):17Apr87-411
  J. North, 441:8Nov87-59
Plett, H.F. Englische Rhetorik und Poetik
1479-1660.
  N. Bachleitner, 602:Band17Heft2-309
Pleynet, M. Painting and System.*
  S. Scobie, 376:Mar86-136
  C. Wilde, 89(BJA):Summer86-297
Plimpton, G. The Curious Case of Sidd
Finch.
  A.B. Giamatti, 441:5Jul87-2

Plimpton, G., ed. Writers at Work. (7th
Ser)
  A.H.G. Phillips, 617(TLS):20Mar87-302
Plokker, A. Adriaen Pietersz.
  M. Royalton-Kisch, 90:Feb86-152
Plotinus. Enneads IV.* Enneads V.*
(both trans by A.H. Armstrong)
  M.J. Atkinson, 123:Vol36No1-144
Plough, A.L. Borrowed Time.
  P.L.F., 185:Apr87-705
Plowden, G.F.C. Pope on Classic Ground.*
  P. Dixon, 447(N&Q):Mar85-129
  D. Nokes, 83:Spring86-104
Plumly, S. Summer Celestial.*
  J.F. Cotter, 249(HudR):Spring86-155
Plumptre, G. The Fast Set.
  442(NY):31Aug87-98
Plutarch. Plutarco, "Iside e Osiride."
(D. Del Corno & M. Cavalli, eds & trans)
  J.G. Griffiths, 123:Vol36No2-314
Pluto, T. & J. Neuman, eds. A Baseball
Winter.*
  639(VQR):Summer86-103
Pöckl, W., ed. Europäische Mehrsprachig-
keit.
  G. Bellmann, 685(ZDL):1/1986-67
Pocock, J.G.A. Virtue, Commerce, and His-
tory.*
  J. Robertson, 83:Autumn86-219
  W.A. Speck, 566:Autumn86-82
Pocock, T. Horatio Nelson.
  N.A.M. Rodger, 617(TLS):25-31Dec87-
  1427
Podhoretz, N. The Bloody Crossroads.*
  639(VQR):Autumn86-115
Podlecki, A.J. The Early Greek Poets and
their Times.*
  J.T. Hooker, 123:Vol36No2-302
Podro, M. The Critical Historians of Art.*
  C. Gould, 39:Mar86-221
  C. Lord, 289:Spring86-117
Poe, E.A. Collected Writings of Edgar
Allan Poe. (Vol 2) (B.R. Pollin, ed)
  B.F. Fisher 4th, 27(AL):May86-284
  J.J. Moldenhauer, 495(PoeS):Dec86-44
Poe, E.A. The Collected Writings of Edgar
Allan Poe. (Vols 3 & 4) (B.R. Pollin,
ed)
  R. Asselineau, 189(EA):Oct-Dec87-484
Poe, E.A. Edgar Allan Poe: Poetry and
Tales.* (P.F. Quinn, ed) Edgar Allan
Poe: Essays and Reviews.* (G.R. Thomp-
son, ed) The Unabridged Edgar Allan Poe.
(T. Mossman, ed)
  B.F. Fisher 4th, 392:Spring86-111
Poe, E.W. From Poetry to Prose in Old
Provençal.
  J.H. Marshall, 208(FS):Apr86-191
"Poetry: A Collection of Poems Written by
Medical Students."
  C. Donley, 236:Spring-Summer86-62
Poewe, K. The Namibian Herero.
  K. Ingham, 617(TLS):20Feb87-190
Pogarell, R. Minority Languages in
Europe.*
  W. Brickman, 355(LSoc):Mar86-139
Pöggeler, O. Heidegger und die hermeneu-
tische Philosophie.
  R.R. Sullivan, 488:Dec86-516
Poggio Bracciolini, G.F. "Contratti di
compre di beni."* (R. Ristori, ed)
  B.G. Kohl, 589:Jul86-694

Poggio Bracciolini, G.F. Lettere.* (Vol 1) (H. Harth, ed)
B.G. Kohl, 589:Jul86-694
J. Kraye, 402(MLR):Apr86-499
M. Lentzen, 547(RF):Band98Heft3/4-456
L.V.R., 568(SCN):Spring-Summer86-31
Poggio Bracciolini, G.F. Lettere.* (Vol 2) (H. Harth, ed)
B.G. Kohl, 589:Jul86-694
J. Kraye, 402(MLR):Apr86-499
M. Lentzen, 547(RF):Band98Heft3/4-456
Pogue, F.C. George C. Marshall: Statesman, 1945-1959.
G.A. Craig, 453(NYRB):13Aug87-11
J.L. Gaddis, 61:Jun87-78
P. Kennedy, 441:28Jun87-3
442(NY):13Jul87-89
Pohl, F. Chernobyl.
M. Rubin, 441:15Nov87-26
Pohl, F. The Coming of the Quantum Cats.*
C. Greenland, 617(TLS):31Jul87-817
Pohl, F. & E.A. Hull, eds. Tales from the Planet Earth.
G. Jonas, 441:18Jan87-33
Poinsot, J. Tractatus de Signis.* (J.N. Deely, with R.A. Powell, eds & trans)
E.J. Furton, 543:Jun87-766
D.P. Henry, 617(TLS):30Oct-5Nov87-1201
Pointon, G.E., ed. BBC Pronouncing Dictionary of British Names. (2nd ed)
K. Forster, 38:Band104Heft1/2-157
Pointon, M. The Bonington Circle.*
M. Rosenthal, 89(BJA):Summer86-292
Pointon, M. Mulready.
L. Herrmann, 637(VS):Summer87-527
Poirier, C., ed. Trésor de la langue française au Québec.
G. Straka, 553(RLiR):Jan-Jun86-248
Poirier, C. & others. Dictionnaire du français québécois.*
T.R. Wooldridge, 627(UTQ):Fall86-202
Poirier, G. Corneille et la vertu de prudence.*
W.O. Goode, 207(FR):Feb87-392
G.J. Mallinson, 208(FS):Jan86-70
L. Picciola, 535(RHL):Jul-Aug86-741
D.A. Watts, 547(RF):Band98Heft3/4-434
Poirier, R. The Renewal of Literature.
N. Baym, 441:22Mar87-37
D. Donoghue, 453(NYRB):25Jun87-50
Pokornowski, I.M. & others. African Dress II.
H.M. Cole, 2(AfrA):Aug86-24
Polan, A.J. Lenin and the End of Politics.*
R. Gregor, 104(CASS):Spring-Summer86-188
Poldauf, I. English Word Stress. (W.R. Lee, ed)
A.R. James, 257(IRAL):Feb86-77
C.W. Kreidler, 350:Mar87-155
Polet, J-C., ed. Auteurs contemporains. (Vols 1-3)
G. Jacques, 356(LR):May86-191
Poletti, J-G. Montaigne à bâtons rompus, le désordre d'un texte.*
F. Moureau, 535(RHL):Sep-Oct86-903
Polheim, K.K., ed. Ferdinand von Saar.
A.A. Wallas, 602:Band17Heft1-102
Poliakoff, M.B. Combat Sports in the Ancient World.
P. Smith, 617(TLS):18-24Dec87-1412

de Polignac, F. La Naissance de la cité grecque.
A.M. Snodgrass, 123:Vol36No2-261
"The Politics of Alternative Defence."
M. Howard, 617(TLS):18-24Sep87-1007
Polk, N. An Editorial Handbook for William Faulkner's "The Sound and the Fury."
W.R., 295(JML):Nov86-467
Polk, N. - see Faulkner, W.
Pollack, B., ed. Popular Music, 1920-1979. (Vol 9)
D.E. McGinty, 91:Fall86-309
Pollack, D. Zen Poems of the Five Mountains.
J. Stevens, 407(MN):Autumn86-352
Pollack, F. The Adventure.
L. Rector, 249(HudR):Autumn86-505
Pollak, E. The Poetics of Sexual Myth.
N.C. Jaffe, 173(ECS):Winter86/87-244
D. Nokes, 617(TLS):20Feb87-182
Pollak, F. Prose and Cons.*
S.J. Smoller, 271:Spring-Summer86-186
Pollak, V.R. Dickinson.*
G. Johnson, 219(GaR):Winter86-1009
J. Loving, 183(ESQ):Vol32No3-201
Pollard, D. The Poetry of Keats.
D. Birch, 541(RES):Aug86-433
C. Murry, 89(BJA):Spring86-179
S. Wolfson, 340(KSJ):Vol35-193
Pollard, J.G. Medaglie Italiane del Rinascimento nel Museo Nazionale del Bargello.* (Vol 1)
J. Pope-Hennessy, 39:Jan86-63
Pollet, E. - see Schwartz, D.
Pollin, B.R. - see Poe, E.A.
Pollock, L. Forgotten Children.
E. Leites, 473(PR):Vol53No1-118
Polster, E. Every Person's Life is Worth a Novel.
S. Schneiderman, 441:1Nov87-32
Polster, J. A Guest in the Jungle.
M. Buck, 441:15Nov87-26
Polterauer, I. Die Deminutiva in der modernen russischen Schriftsprache.
S. Ettinger, 688(ZSP):Band45Heft2-438
Pomeau, R. Beaumarchais ou la bizarre destinée.
D. Coward, 617(TLS):9-15Oct87-1095
Pomeau, R. D'Arouet à Voltaire, 1694-1734.
E.D. James, 208(FS):Oct86-459
E. Showalter, Jr., 207(FR):Dec86-257
Pomerance, B. We Need to Dream All This Again.
M. Kirby, 441:23Aug87-17
Pomorska, K. & S. Rudy - see Jakobson, R.
Pompili, B. Licantropi e meteore.
R. Lloyd, 208(FS):Oct86-474
Pompilio, A. I madrigali a quattro voci di Pomponio Nenna (1613).
A. Newcomb, 317:Summer86-396
Ponge, F. L'atelier contemporain.
J-Y. Pouilloux, 98:Nov86-1063
Ponsot, M. & R. Deen. Beat Not the Poor Desk.
H.F. Dowling, 126(CCC):Oct86-370
Pontalis, J-B. L'Amour des commencements.
R. de Ceccatty, 450(NRF):Dec86-85
Pontano, G. Dialoge (Charon, Antonius, Actius, Aegidius, Asinus).*
K. Ley, 72:Band223Heft2-463

Poovey, M. The Proper Lady and the Woman Writer.*
  A. London, 541(RES):May86-270
  J. Thompson, 536(Rev):Vol8-21
Pope, A. The Last and Greatest Art.* (M. Mack, ed)
  B.S. Hammond, 83:Spring86-102
  P. Rogers, 402(MLR):Jul86-721
Pope, A. Alexander Pope: Collected Poems. (B. Dobrée, ed)
  P. Dixon, 447(N&Q):Mar85-129
Pope, A. The Prose Works of Alexander Pope.* (Vol 2) (R. Cowler, ed)
  H. Erskine-Hill, 617(TLS):12Jun87-637
Pope, A. Il riccio rapito. (V. Papetti, ed & trans)
  F. Ciompi, 566:Autumn86-8
Pope, D. A Separate Vision.*
  P. Thorpe, 401(MLQ):Mar85-103
Pope-Hennessy, J. Cellini.*
  C. Avery, 39:Jul86-61
Popham, M.R. & others. The Minoan Unexplored Mansion at Knossos.
  S. Hood, 123:Vol36No1-117
"Popol Vuh."* (D. Tedlock, ed & trans)
  N. Tarn, 138:No9-273
  S. White, 448:Vol24No3-95
Popovsky, M. The Vavilov Affair.*
  M. McCauley, 575(SEER):Oct86-625
Popowska-Taborska, H. Z dawnych podziałów słowiańszczyzny.
  H. Leeming, 575(SEER):Oct86-587
Poppe, E. C.F. Aichingers "Versuch einer teutschen Sprachlehre.
  U. Püschel, 685(ZDL):3/1986-379
Popper, K.R. L'univers irrésolu.
  A. Boyer, 542:Jan-Mar86-138
Popper, K.R. Postscript to the Logic of Scientific Discovery.* (Vols 1 & 2) (W.W. Bartley 3d, ed) Auf der Suche nach einer besseren Welt.
  P. Feyerabend, 262:Mar86-93
"Porcelain from Europe."
  G. Wills, 39:Sep86-225
Porcher, L. & others. Civilisation.
  P. Trescases, 207(FR):May87-888
Porcher, M-C., ed. Inde et littératures.
  J.W. de Jong, 259(IIJ):Jan86-49
Porges, H. Wagner Rehearsing the "Ring."
  L.R. Shaw, 406:Fall86-409
Pörnbacher, H. & I., eds. Spielmannsepen I.
  F.G. Gentry, 406:Fall86-388
  J.W. Thomas, 133:Band19Heft2-157
Porphyry. Letter to Marcella. (D. Fideler, ed)
  J. Barnes, 520:Vol31No2-194
Porras, F. Titelles, teatro popular.
  M. de Semprún Donahue, 552(REH):Jan86-146
Porrúa, M.D. - see under del Carmen Porrúa, M.
Porsché, D.C. Die Zweisprachigkeit während des primären Spracherwerbs.
  P.R. Lutzeier, 603:Vol10No1-213
Portch, S.R. Literature's Silent Language.
  J.E. Bassett, 27(AL):May86-297
  L. Waldeland, 395(MFS):Summer86-248
Porter, B.D. The USSR in Third World Conflicts.*
  S.K. Gupta, 550(RusR):Oct86-450
Porter, D. Dickinson.
  J. Loving, 183(ESQ):Vol32No3-201

Porter, E. Eliot Porter's Southwest.
  L. Milazzo, 584(SWR):Winter86-123
  A. Ross, 364:Apr/May86-178
Porter, E. & E. Auerbach, with D. Pierce. Mexican Churches.
  O. Paz, 441:20Dec87-3
Porter, J.C. Paper Medicine Man.
  L. Milazzo, 584(SWR):Summer86-402
Porter, L. Lester Young.*
  E. Southern, 91:Spring86-192
Porter, L. & L.M., eds. Aging in Literature.
  P. Pelckmans, 535(RHL):Sep-Oct86-971
Porter, M.C. Through Parisian Eyes.
  R.W. Johnson, 617(TLS):31Jul87-811
Porter, P. Fast Forward.*
  L. Lerner, 569(SR):Spring86-312
Porter, P.A., M. Grant & M. Draper. Communicating Effectively in English.
  M. Landa, 399(MLJ):Spring86-90
Porter, R. Mind-Forg'd Manacles. A Social History of Madness.
  K. Thomas, 617(TLS):4-10Dec87-1339
Portinari, F. Pari siamo!
  J. Budden, 415:Oct86-563
Pörtl, K. Das lyrische Werk des Damián Cornejo (1629-1707).
  A.L. MacKenzie, 86(BHS):Oct86-388
Porush, D. The Soft Machine.*
  C. Caramello, 395(MFS):Summer86-345
  F. Coppay, 188(ECr):Winter86-103
Posner, G.L. & J. Ware. Mengele.*
  N. Ascherson, 453(NYRB):28May87-29
  S. Bloch, 617(TLS):12Jun87-625
  639(VQR):Autumn86-125
Posner, R. Rational Discourse and Poetic Communication.*
  S.E. Larsen, 462(OL):Vol41No3-289
Posner, R.A. The Federal Courts.*
  J.M. O'Fallon, 185:Jan87-486
Posnock, R. Henry James and the Problem of Robert Browning.*
  E. Langland, 594:Spring86-102
  E. Nettels, 401(MLQ):Jun85-215
  P. Sharp, 284:Fall85-52
  A.R. Tintner, 395(MFS):Winter86-599
  A.R. Tintner, 579(SAQ):Autumn86-403
Pospielovsky, D. The Russian Church under the Soviet Regime, 1917-1982.*
  F. Sysyn, 550(RusR):Jan86-87
Possner, W. & J. Loužil - see Kafka, F.
Post, J.F.S. Henry Vaughan.*
  S.C. Seelig, 402(MLR):Jan87-169
van der Post, L., with J-M. Pottiez. A Walk with a White Bushman.
  A. Barnard, 617(TLS):23Jan87-93
Postel, M., A. Neven & K. Mankodi. Antiquites of Himachal.
  M. McCutcheon, 60:May-Jun86-141
Poster, J. - see Crabbe, G.
Poster, M. Foucault, Marxism and History.
  J. Sawicki, 125:Summer86-433
Postlethwaite, D. Making It Whole.*
  J.R. Reed, 301(JEGP):Oct86-574
Postlewait, T. Prophet of the New Drama.
  Y. Shafer, 615(TJ):Dec86-507
Postman, N. Amusing Ourselves to Death.*
  T.R. Edwards, 533:Summer86-114
  T. Erwin, 385(MQR):Spring87-413
  639(VQR):Spring86-59

Poteat, P.L. Walker Percy and the Old Modern Age.*
  M. Johnson, 478:Apr86-129
  M. Pearson, 577(SHR):Fall86-389
Poteat, W.H. Polanyian Meditations.
  P.J. Haanstad, 543:Dec86-392
Potel, J-Y. L'Etat de la France et de ses habitants.*
  W. Wrage, 399(MLJ):Autumn86-309
Potok, C. Davita's Harp.
  R. Ratner, 390:Mar86-60
Potter, D. Blackeyes.
  J. Symons, 362:1Oct87-22
Potter, J. Pretenders.
  B. Fothergill, 617(TLS):10Jul87-750
Potter, L. "Twelfth Night."*
  R.L. Smallwood, 611(TN):Vol40No3-137
Potter, L. - see Osborne, F.
Potter, N. Legacies.
  R. Atwan, 441:19Jul87-22
Potterton, H. Dutch Seventeenth and Eighteenth Century Paintings in The National Gallery of Ireland.
  M. Russell, 617(TLS):20Feb87-195
  C. White, 39:Nov86-460
Pottle, F.A. James Boswell: The Earlier Years, 1740-1769.*
  R.D. Altick, 401(MLQ):Jun85-208
  O.W. Ferguson, 579(SAQ):Autumn86-399
Potz, E. Claudian, Kommentar zu "De raptu Proserpinae," Buch I.
  J.B. Hall, 123:Vol36No2-239
Poulenc, F. Diary of My Songs.
  J. Cox, 410(M&L):Jul86-310
  T.H., 412:Nov85-312
  R. Nichols, 415:Sep86-500
Poulet, G. Exploding Poetry, Baudelaire/Rimbaud.
  S. Lawall, 131(CL):Fall86-380
Poulin, J. Spring Tides.
  J. Urbas, 99:Jan87-39
Poullain de La Barre, F. De l'Égalité des deux sexes.
  M.M. Rowan, 475:Vol13No24-407
Poulle, E., ed & trans. Les tables alphonsines avec les canons de Jean de Saxe.
  D. Pingree, 589:Jul86-743
Poullet, H., S. Telchid & D. Montbrand. Dictionnaire des expressions du créole guadeloupéen.
  R. Morgan, Jr., 207(FR):Mar87-573
Poulsen, R.C. The Mountain Man Vernacular.
  J.L. Dillard, 292(JAF):Jul/Sep86-347
Pound, E. I Cantos. (M. de Rachewiltz, trans)
  M. Bacigalupo, 468:Fall/Winter86-297
  W. Cookson, 4:Summer86-95
Pound, E. Les Cantos. (J. Darras & others, trans)
  C. Minière, 98:Oct86-1053
  G. Sartoris, 450(NRF):Oct86-105
Pound, E. Hugh Selwyn Mauberley. (M. Bacigalupo, ed)
  P. Makin, 402(MLR):Jan87-190
Pound, E. Omaggio a Sesto Properzio. (M. Bacigalupo, ed & trans)
  P. Makin, 402(MLR):Jul87-720
Pound, E. Poèmes.
  G. Quinsat, 450(NRF):Apr86-114
Pound, E. & W. Lewis. Pound/Lewis.* (T. Materer, ed)
  R.W. Dasenbrock, 468:Spring86-137
  T.C.D. Eaves, 27(AL):Mar86-112

Pound, E. and D. Shakespear. Ezra Pound and Dorothy Shakespear: Their Letters, 1909-1914.* (O. Pound and A.W. Litz, eds)
  J.T. Barbarese, 219(GaR):Summer86-590
  B. Goldensohn, 676(YR):Autumn86-128
  W. Harmon, 569(SR):Fall86-630
  C.F. Terrell, 30:Fall86-92
  L. Willson, 569(SR):Winter86-131
Pound, E. & J. Theobald. Ezra Pound-John Theobald: Letters.* (D. Pearce & H. Schneidau, eds)
  T.C.D. Eaves, 579(SAQ):Winter86-92
  W. Harmon, 569(SR):Fall86-630
Pounds, W. Paul Bowles.
  L.D. Stewart, 395(MFS):Summer86-289
Poupard, D., ed. Literature Criticism from 1400 to 1800. (Vol 2)
  S. Soupel, 189(EA):Oct-Dec87-490
Poupard, D. & M.W. Scott, eds. Literature Criticism from 1400 to 1800.* (Vol 1)
  R.F. Dolle, 568(SCN):Spring-Summer86-12
"Pierre Pourbus, Peintre brugeois 1524-1584."
  J. Woodall, 90:Jun86-432
Pouthier, P. Ops et la conception divine de l'abondance dans la religion romaine jusqu'à la mort d'Auguste.
  H.S. Versnel, 394:Vol39fasc3/4-546
Powe, B.W. A Climate Charged.*
  W.J. Keith, 298:Spring86-154
  P. Stuewe, 168(ECW):Fall86-167
Powe, L.A., Jr. American Broadcasting and the First Amendment.
  H. Dorfman, 441:19Apr87-19
Powell, A. The Fisher King.*
  J. Mellors, 364:Apr/May86-139
Powell, B. Epic and Chronicle.*
  D.G. Pattison, 382(MAE):1986/2-333
Powell, C. Turner in the South.
  R. Dorment, 617(TLS):10Jul87-735
  J. Russell, 441:31May87-11
Powell, D. Tom Paine.
  D.E. Jones, 27(AL):Dec86-624
Powell, G. Yvor Winters.*
  T. Whalen, 106:Winter86-495
Powell, H. - see Gryphius, A.
Powell, J. Restoration Theatre Production.*
  W.J. Burling, 566:Autumn86-71
  E. Burns, 83:Autumn86-263
  P. Danchin, 189(EA):Jul-Sep86-337
  R.D. Sell, 541(RES):Aug86-418
Powell, L.C. Books Are Basic. (J.D. Marshall, ed)
  L. Milazzo, 584(SWR):Autumn86-538
Powell, M. Fabula Docet.*
  S. Mapstone, 382(MAE):1986/2-300
Powell, M. A Life in Movies.*
  P. Brunette, 441:19Apr87-17
  G. O'Brien, 453(NYRB):13Aug87-14
  J.R. Taylor, 707:Autumn86-243
  442(NY):13Jul87-90
Powell, P. A Woman Named Drown.
  T.C. Boyle, 441:7Jun87-9
Powell, V. The Album of Anthony Powell's "Dance to the Music of Time."
  A. Motion, 617(TLS):23-29Oct87-1156
Power, B. The Puppet Emperor.
  R. Harris, 617(TLS):9Jan87-30
Power, M. Goblin Fruit.
  A. Carpenter, 617(TLS):4-10Dec87-1348

Power, M.S. A Darkness in the Eye.
  S. Dunant, 362:11Jun87-26
  J. Melmoth, 617(TLS):29May87-588
Powers, R. Three Farmers on Their Way to a Dance.*
  G. Kearns, 249(HudR):Spring86-133
  G.L. Morris, 502(PrS):Spring86-108
  639(VQR):Spring86-57
Powers, R.G. G-Men.
  R.A. Banes, 106:Spring86-93
Powers, R.G. Secrecy and Power.
  S.E. Ambrose, 617(TLS):30Oct-5Nov87-1189
  A. Brinkley, 453(NYRB):23Apr87-15
  N. Morris, 441:8Mar87-1
  442(NY):23Mar87-101
Powys, J.C. The Diary of John Cowper Powys, 1930. (F. Davies, ed)
  G. Cavaliero, 617(TLS):16-22Oct87-1142
Powys, J.C. Three Fantasies.
  639(VQR):Winter86-20
Powys, J.C. Wolf Solent. Weymouth Sands.
  V. Young, 31(ASch):Spring86-248
Poziemski, J. - see Wilde, O.
Pozuelo Yvancos, J.M. La lengua literaria.
  F. Vicente Gómez, 548:Jan-Jun86-209
Pradier, J. Correspondance.* (Vol 1) (D. Siler, ed)
  J-M. Bailbé, 535(RHL):Jul-Aug86-765
  B. Juden, 402(MLR):Jan86-202
Pradier, J. Correspondance. (Vol 2) (D. Siler, ed)
  J-M. Bailbé, 535(RHL):Jul-Aug86-765
  B. Juden, 402(MLR):Jan87-204
Pradl, G.M. - see Britton, J.
Prado, A. - see Pérez de Ayala, R.
Prado, C.G. Making Believe.*
  C. Crittenden, 449:Jun86-283
Prado, H. Gardens.
  G. Davenport, 569(SR):Fall86-672
Prager, E. Clea and Zeus Divorce.
  R. Plunket, 441:22Nov87-9
Prance, C.A. Companion to Charles Lamb.
  W.F. Courtney, 340(KSJ):Vol35-211
  S. Jones, 447(N&Q):Mar85-137
Prandi, J.D. Spirited Women Heroes.*
  S.L. Cocalis, 222(GR):Spring86-79
Prantera, A. Conversations with Lord Byron on Sexual Perversion 163 Years After his Death.
  R. Clarke, 362:4Jun87-48
Prasad, M.V.R. Script of Fire.
  U. Parameswaran, 314:Summer-Fall86-247
Prasad, V.S.S., ed. Indo-Australian Flowers.
  R.K. Singh, 314:Summer-Fall86-239
Prassinos, G. L'instant qui va.
  A. Morin, 98:Nov86-1151
Prat, A. - see Bayle, P.
Prater, D. A Ringing Glass.*
  M.K. Devinney, 295(JML):Nov86-534
  H. Goldgar, 249(HudR):Winter87-667
  H. Reiss, 402(MLR):Jul87-796
da Prato, C. - see under Convenevole da Prato
Pratt, A. Archetypal Patterns in Women's Fiction.*
  V. Shaw, 402(MLR):Jan86-184
Pratt, D.H., P.L. Bruner & D.G. Berrett. A Field Guide to the Birds of Hawaii and the Tropical Pacific.
  C. Perrins, 617(TLS):2-8Oct87-1087

Pratt, J. - see "Harrap's Slang Dictionary: English-French/French-English"
Pratt, S. Russian Metaphysical Romanticism.*
  C. De Grève, 549(RLC):Jan-Mar86-110
  M. Makin, 402(MLR):Jul87-808
Pratte, J. Les Persiennes.
  C.E. Noble, 207(FR):Mar87-561
Prauss, G. Einführung in die Erkenntnistheorie.
  D.E. Christensen, 543:Dec86-339
Prawer, S.S. Frankenstein's Island.
  T. Ziolkowski, 617(TLS):21Aug87-903
Prawer, S.S. Heine's Jewish Comedy.*
  L. Kahn, 390:Nov86-54
Praz, M. Lettere a Bruno Migliorini. (L.P. Migliorini, ed)
  M. Bacigalupo, 402(MLR):Jan87-220
Praz, M. Il mondo che ho visto.
  G. Cambon, 275(IQ):Winter86-109
Prédal, R. Le Cinéma français contemporain.
  H.A. Garrity, 207(FR):Feb87-418
Prendergast, C. The Order of Mimesis.*
  A. Jefferson, 208(FS):Oct86-482
Prenshaw, P.W., ed. Conversations with Eudora Welty.*
  C.S. Manning, 534(RALS):Spring-Autumn84-256
Prenshaw, P.W., ed. Women Writers of the Contemporary South.
  H.H. McAlexander, 577(SHR):Summer86-299
  J.G. Vance, 578:Spring87-113
"Présence de l'architecture et de l'urbanisme romains."
  P.F., 555:Vol59fasc2-340
Pressouyre, S. Nicolas Cordier, recherches sur la sculpture à Rome autour de 1600.
  D. Shawe-Taylor, 90:Jan86-42
Prest, W.R. The Rise of the Barristers.
  E.W. Ives, 617(TLS):28Aug87-920
Preston, G.N. Sets, Series and Ensembles in African Art.
  D.H. Ross, 2(AfrA):May86-23
Preston, P. The Spanish Civil War 1936-1939.*
  P. Parker, 364:Aug/Sep86-138
Preston, R.H. The Future of Christian Ethics.
  H. Oppenheimer, 617(TLS):11-17Dec87-1384
Pretagostini, R. Ricerche sulla poesia allessandrina.
  D.M. Schenkeveld, 394:Vol39fasc3/4-566
Preto-Rodas, R.A. & A. Hower, eds. Carlos Drummond de Andrade.
  S.J. Albuquerque, 238:Sep86-569
Prevenier, W. & W. Blockmans. The Burgundian Netherlands.
  L. Hellinga, 78(BC):Autumn86-383
  M.D.H. Larsen, 324:Apr87-407
Prévost, A.F. The Story of a Fair Greek of Yesteryear.
  J. Sgard, 535(RHL):Mar-Apr86-287
Prévot, M., Phạm Ðán Bình & Ðoàn Thiện Thuật. Parler vietnamien.
  Nguyên Ðình-Hoà, 350:Jun87-441
du Prey, D.H. - see Chekhov, M.
Price, A. For the Good of the State.
  T.J. Binyon, 617(TLS):10Apr87-394
  N. Callendar, 441:16Aug87-21

Price, A.W., ed. Shakespeare: "A Midsummer Night's Dream."
A.W. Bellringer, 447(N&Q):Dec85-520
Price, C.A. Henry Purcell and the London Stage.*
S. Lincoln, 611(TN):Vol40No1-45
J. Michon, 189(EA):Jul-Sep86-338
Price, J. Everything Must Go.*
H. Buckingham, 565:Summer86-64
Price, M. Forms of Life.*
P. Goetsch, 38:Band104Heft3/4-538
Price, N. Sleeping with the Enemy.
442(NY):18May87-115
Price, R. Kate Vaiden.*
P. Binding, 362:5Mar87-27
J. O'Faolain, 617(TLS):22May87-558
Price, R.M. Quevedo, "Los sueños."
W.B. Berg, 72:Band223Heft2-456
H. Ettinghausen, 86(BHS):Jul86-287
P.J. Smith, 402(MLR):Apr86-512
Price, S.R.F. Rituals and Power.*
D. Fishwick, 487:Summer86-225
R. Mellor, 24:Summer86-296
Price-Mars, J. So Spoke the Uncle.
M-R. Trouillot, 538(RAL):Winter86-596
Prickett, S. Words and "The Word."
C.H. Sisson, 617(TLS):30Jan87-116
Pride, J., ed. Cross-Cultural Encounters.
H.B. Allen, 351(LL):Sep86-387
Pride, N. Crow Man's People.
R.D. Ortiz, 649(WAL):Nov86-269
Priest, R. The Man Who Broke Out Of The Letter X.*
P. O'Brien, 102(CanL):Fall86-135
Priestley, G. Military Government and Popular Participation in Panama.
D.N. Farnsworth, 263(RIB):Vol36No3-344
Priestley, J.B. English Journey.*
J. Hunter, 579(SAQ):Winter86-89
Priestley, P. Victorian Prison Lives.*
D. Philips, 637(VS):Winter87-267
Priestman, M. Cowper's "Task."*
A.J. Sambrook, 402(MLR):Oct87-922
Prill, M. Bürgerliche Alltagswelt und pietistisches Denken im Werk Hölderlins.*
B. Bjorklund, 406:Fall86-400
Prince, G. Narratology.*
O. Izumiya, 402(MLR):Jul86-692
M-L. Ryan, 107(CRCL):Mar86-98
Pringle, D. Science Fiction, the 100 Best Novels.
V. Hollinger, 561(SFS):Mar86-95
Prinz, M. Das Motiv der Reise im Frühwerk von Blaise Cendrars (1910-1929).
A. Grewe, 72:Band223Heft2-447
Prioleau, E.S. The Circle of Eros.*
A. Massa, 447(N&Q):Dec85-549
Prior, M., ed. Women in English Society 1500-1800.
M.J.M. Ezell, 568(SCN):Spring-Summer86-15
Prior, W.J. Unity and Development in Plato's Metaphysics.*
P.M. Huby, 123:Vol36No2-320
J. Malcolm, 41:Vol6-218
J.P. Schiller, 319:Apr87-289
Prisse d'Avennes, E. Arab Art as Seen Through the Monuments of Cairo.
J. Sweetman, 463:Spring86-85
Pritchard, M. Spirit Seizures.
E. Tallent, 441:22Nov87-11

Pritchard, W.H. Frost.*
J.M. Cox, 569(SR):Winter86-118
R. Crawford, 184(EIC):Apr86-175
P. Davison, 473(PR):Vol53No2-313
F.L., 27(AL):Oct86-480
L.A. Renza, 579(SAQ):Summer86-303
Pritchard, W.H. Lives of the Modern Poets.
C. Doyle, 675(YER):Vol8No1/2-131
Pritchett, V.S. A Man of Letters.*
H. Fromm, 249(HudR):Winter87-690
Pritchett, W.K. The Greek State at War. (Pt 4)
P. Culham, 124:Jan-Feb87-223
Pritscher, U.F. Die Funktion der Register in den drei Versionen von "Lady Chatterley's Lover" von D.H. Lawrence.
H. Bonheim, 38:Band104Heft1/2-269
Privitera, G.A. – see Pindar
Probst, G.F. & J.F. Bodine, eds. Perspectives on Max Frisch.*
G.B. Pickar, 397(MD):Sep86-497
Proclus. Proclus, Théologie Platonicienne. (Bk 4) (H.D. Saffrey & L.G. Westerink, eds & trans)
R. Ferwerda, 394:Vol39fasc1/2-180
Proclus. Proclus, Trois études sur la providence, III. (D. Isaac, ed & trans)
R. Ferwerda, 394:Vol39fasc1/2-178
Profeti, M.G. – see under Grazia Profeti, M.
Proffer, C.R. The Widows of Russia.
C. Emerson, 441:18Oct87-31
Proffer, E. Bulgakov.*
J. Grayson, 575(SEER):Apr86-282
M. Lebowitz, 639(VQR):Winter86-162
Proffer, E. – see Bulgakov, M.A.
Pronzini, B., ed. Son of Gun in Cheek.
N. Callendar, 441:13Sep87-46
Pronzini, B. & M.H. Greenberg, eds. The Third Reel West.
L. Milazzo, 584(SWR):Autumn86-538
Pronzini, B. & M.H. Greenberg – see Frazee, S.
Pronzini, B. & M.H. Greenberg – see Overholser, W.D.
Propertius. Codex Guelferbytanus Gudianus 224 olim Neapolitanus. (P. Fedeli, ed)
S.J. Heyworth, 123:Vol36No1-48
Propp, V. Theory and History of Folklore.* (A. Liberman, ed)
R. Bendix, 650(WF):Oct86-305
S.S. Jones, 292(JAF):Apr/Jun86-225
M. Tarlinskaja, 599:Spring86-103
J. Voisine, 549(RLC):Apr-Jun86-232
F.C.M. Wigzell, 575(SEER):Apr86-266
"Propyläen Geschichte der Literatur." (Vol 4)
P. Wagner, 224(GRM):Band36Heft1-95
Prose, F. Bigfoot Dreams.*
42(AR):Summer86-380
Pross, W. – see Herder, J.G.
Prost, A. Eloge des pédagogues.
P. & A. Higonnet, 617(TLS):30Oct-5Nov87-1183
Proust, M. Correspondance.* (Vol 13) (P. Kolb, ed)
J. Murray, 207(FR):Mar87-541
Proust, M. On Reading Ruskin. (J. Autret, W. Burford & P.J. Wolfe, eds & trans)
T. Hilton, 453(NYRB):22Oct87-24
G. Josipovici, 617(TLS):25Sep-1Oct87-1044

Proust, M.   La Prisonnière.   (J. Milly, ed)
J-Y. Tadié, 535(RHL):Sep-Oct86-948
Prouty, C.   Empress Taytu and Menilek II.
D. Bates, 617(TLS):20Feb87-190
Providenti, E. - see Pirandello, L.
Provine, W.B.   Sewall Wright and Evolutionary Biology.*
J. Secord, 617(TLS):11-17Dec87-1370
Provine, W.B - see Wright, S.
Prucha, F.P.   The Indians in American Society.*
G.W. La Fantasie, 432(NEQ):Dec86-583
639(VQR):Summer86-95
Pruett, K.D.   The Nurturing Father.
A.L. Goldman, 441:8Mar87-24
Prunty, W.   What Women Know, What Men Believe.*
M. Jarman, 502(PrS):Winter86-106
Prussen, J.   Essais et conférences.
G. Kalinowski, 192(EP):Oct-Dec86-580
Prvulović, Z.K.   Religious Philosophy of Prince-Bishop Njegoš of Montenegro.
E.D. Goy, 575(SEER):Apr86-271
Pryce-Jones, A.   The Bonus of Laughter.
A. Ross, 617(TLS):9Jan87-29
Pryce-Jones, D.   The Afternoon Sun.*
G. Annan, 453(NYRB):11Jun87-28
442(NY):26Jan87-85
Pryor, E.B.   Clara Barton.
S. Reverby, 441:11Oct87-46
Pryse, M. & H. Spillers, eds.   Conjuring.*
C. Werner, 395(MFS):Winter86-639
Przeworski, A.   Capitalism and Social Democracy.
J. Dunn, 185:Jul87-867
Przybylowicz, D.   Desire and Repression.
P. O'Donnell, 223:Fall86-319
J.W. Tuttleton, 395(MFS):Winter86-597
"Le Psautier de Genève, 1562-1865."
C. Meyer, 537:Vol72No2-290
Ptolemy.   Ptolemy's "Almagest."   (G.J. Toomer, trans)
P. Brind'Amour, 487:Summer86-249
D. Pingree, 41:Fall85-348
Pückler-Muskau, H.   Pückler's Progress.
J. Keates, 617(TLS):19Jun87-659
N. Williams, 362:26Mar87-28
Puckrein, G.A.   Little England.
R. Waterhouse, 656(WMQ):Jan86-136
Pugh, A.C.   Simon: "Histoire."*
E. Smyth, 535(RHL):Jul-Aug86-801
Pugh, A.R.   The Composition of Pascal's Apologia.*
B. Beugnot, 627(UTQ):Fall86-134
J. Cruickshank, 402(MLR):Jan86-201
J-J. Demorest, 210(FrF):May86-235
Pugh, D.G.   Sons of Liberty.
D.P. Peeler, 106:Summer86-201
Pugh, P.   Educate, Agitate, Organize.
S. Kang, 637(VS):Spring87-426
Pugliatti, T.   Giulio Mazzoni e la decorazione a Roma nella cerchia di Daniele da Volterra.
P. Barolsky, 54:Jun86-334
Puig, M.   Pubis Angelical.*
J. Wilson, 617(TLS):16-22Oct87-1135
Pulaski, J.   The St. Veronica Gig Stories.
D. Cole, 441:15Mar87-16
J.H. Korelitz, 617(TLS):4-11Sep87-949
Pullan, B.S.   The Jews of Europe and the Inquisition of Venice, 1550-1670.*
U. Limentani, 402(MLR):Jan86-226

Pulleyblank, E.G.   Middle Chinese.
K. Chang, 293(JASt):Feb86-388
H.M. Stimson, 318(JAOS):Oct/Dec85-755
Pulman, S.G.   Word Meaning and Belief.*
B. Harrison, 518:Jan86-45
Punter, D.   Blake, Hegel and Dialectic.*
S. Prickett, 402(MLR):Jan86-159
Punter, D.   The Hidden Script.
D.W. Ross, 395(MFS):Winter86-700
Puppo, M.   Poetica e critica del romanticismo italiano.
W. Krömer, 547(RF):Band98Heft1/2-219
Puppo, M.   Romanticismo italiano e romanticismo europeo.
W. Krömer, 547(RF):Band98Heft3/4-467
Purcell, N. - see Frederiksen, M.
Purdy, J.   The Candles of Your Eyes.
E. Munk, 441:6Sep87-23
Purdy, J.   In the Hollow of His Hand.*
42(AR):Fall86-495
Purdy, R.L. & M. Millgate - see Hardy, T.
Purtle, C.J.   The Marian Paintings of Jan van Eyck.
C. Eisler, 54:Dec86-676
Purves, A.C. & O.S. Niles, eds.   Becoming Readers in a Complex Society.
W.H. Clark, Jr., 289:Spring86-124
Purvis, M.   Tall Storeys.
S. Markbreiter, 60:Sep-Oct86-127
Purwo, B.K. - see under Kaswanti Purwo, B.
Pusch, L.F.   Das Deutsche als Männersprache.
M. Hellinger, 353:Vol24No2-459
Pusch, L.F.   Kontrastive Untersuchungen zum italienischen "gerundio."*
G.F. Meier, 682(ZPSK):Band39Heft1-148
Pusey, J.R.   China and Charles Darwin.
A.J. Nathan, 293(JASt):Nov85-127
Pushkarev, A.N.   Iurii Krizhanich.
S.H. Baron, 550(RusR):Jan86-67
Pushkin, A.S.   Epigrams and Satirical Verse.   (C. Whittaker, ed & trans)
S. Driver, 574(SEEJ):Summer86-280
Puskas, R.   Die mittelalterlichen Mettenresponsorien der Klosterkirche Rheinau.
M. Huglo, 537:Vol72No1-140
Puttfarken, T.   Roger de Piles' Theory of Art.*
C. Gould, 39:Oct86-380
Pütz, P.   Peter Handke.
T.F. Barry, 221(GQ):Summer86-499
Putzel, M.   Genius of Place.*
C.S. Brown, 569(SR):Winter86-167
J.L. Sensibar, 115:Winter86-120
Putzel, S.   Reconstructing Yeats.
D. Kiberd, 617(TLS):13Feb87-166
Py, A.   Imitation et Renaissance dans la Poésie de Ronsard.
F. Cornilliat, 535(RHL):Jul-Aug86-724
A. Moss, 208(FS):Apr86-200
J. O'Brien, 402(MLR):Oct86-999
Pylyshyn, Z.W.   Computation and Cognition.
P.P. Hanson, 154:Winter86-811
Pym, B.   An Academic Question.*
W.H. Pritchard, 249(HudR):Winter87-654
Pym, B.   Civil to Strangers and Other Writings.
N. Shulman, 617(TLS):25-31Dec87-1420
Pym, B.   Crampton Hodnet.*
639(VQR):Winter86-23
Pynchon, T.   Slow Learner.*
J. Dugdale, 97(CQ):Vol15No2-156

Pynchon, T. Die Versteigerung von No. 49.
  U. Riese, 654(WB):10/1986-1687
Pyne, S.J. The Ice.
  R. Kirk, 441:11Jan87-11

al-Qādirī, M. Muhammad al-Qadiri's "Nashr
  al-mathami": The Chronicles. (N. Cigar,
  ed & trans)
  H.E. Kassis, 318(JAOS):Jan/Mar85-161
Quaghebeur, M. and A. Spinette, eds.
  Alphabet des lettres belges de langue
  française.
  J. Decock, 207(FR):Apr87-702
Quak, A. Die altmittel- und altnieder-
  fränkischen Psalmen und Glossen.
  A. Turner, 406:Spring86-95
Qualls, B.V. The Secular Pilgrims of Vic-
  torian Fiction.*
  S.M. Smith, 402(MLR):Apr86-457
Qualter, T.H. Opinion Control in the Demo-
  cracies.
  S.E.F., 185:Oct86-305
Quammen, D. Natural Acts.
  P. Wild, 649(WAL):Aug86-159
Quammen, D. The Soul of Viktor Tronko.
  W. Hood, 441:12Jul87-12
Quandt, R. Struktur und Funktion der
  apokalyptischen Elemente in der Lyrik
  T.S. Eliots.
  W. Riehle, 72:Band223Heft2-472
Quantrill, M. Reima Pietilä.
  W.C. Miller, 576:Sep86-304
Quarrington, P. Home Game.
  C.R. Steele, 102(CanL):Summer86-128
Quarrington, P. The Life of Hope.
  R.B. Hatch, 99:Apr86-39
Quarta, C. L'utopia platonica.*
  Y. Lafrance, 154:Autumn86-566
Quattordio Moreschini, A. Tre millenni di
  storia linguistica della Sicilia.
  A.G. Mocciaro, 545(RPh):May87-520
Queffélec, Y. Les Noces barbares.
  J.J. Smith, 207(FR):Mar87-563
de Queiroz, J.M.E. - see under Eça de
  Queiroz, J.M.
Queller, D.E. The Venetian Patriciate.
  F. Gilbert, 453(NYRB):16Jul87-37
Quemada, B., ed. Datations et documents
  lexicographiques. (2nd Ser, No 26)
  R. Arveiller, 553(RLiR):Jan-Jun86-235
Quemada, G., ed. Dictionnaire de termes
  nouveaux des sciences et des techniques.
  P. Lerat, 209(FM):Oct86-231
Queneau, R. The Blue Flowers.
  L. Gorman, 532(RCF):Fall86-146
Queneau, R. Journal 1939-1940.* (A.I.
  Queneau & J.J. Marchand eds)
  A. Calame, 450(NRF):Oct86-86
  J. Piel, 98:Dec86-1235
Quenelle, R. La France, j'aime.
  C.J. Fouillade, 207(FR):Feb87-438
  D.L. Gobert, 399(MLJ):Summer86-186
Quennell, P. Four Portraits.
  362:15Oct87-28
Quennell, P. & T. Zetterholm. An Illus-
  trated Companion to World Literature.
  J. Griffin, 617(TLS):17Apr87-419
Quested, R.K.I. Sino-Russian Relations.
  C.M. Foust, 293(JASt):Nov85-129
Quester, G.H. The Future of Nuclear Deter-
  rence.
  S.L., 185:Jul87-899

de Quevedo, F. Virtud militante contra las
  quatro pestes del mundo, inuidia, ingra-
  titud, soberbia, avarizia. (A. Rey, ed)
  W.H. Clamurro, 304(JHP):Fall86-86
  J.A. Whitenack, 240(HR):Autumn86-474
Quigley, A.E. The Modern Stage and Other
  Worlds.
  B. Johnston, 130:Fall86-270
  A. Vivis, 157:No159-49
Quigley, I. - see Kipling, R.
Quignard, P. Une gêne technique à l'égard
  du fragment.
  S. Rappaport, 450(NRF):Oct86-90
Quignard, P. Le Salon du Wurtemberg.
  D. Gunn, 617(TLS):20Feb87-196
  R. Millet, 450(NRF):Dec86-91
  J. Piel, 98:Nov86-1086
  J. Taylor, 268(IFR):Winter87-53
Quilici, V. - see Khan-Magomedov, S.O.
Quillian, W.H. "Hamlet" and the New
  Poetic.
  V.J. Cheng, 329(JJQ):Fall86-101
Quilligan, M. Milton's Spenser.*
  B.K. Lewalski, 551(RenQ):Summer86-353
Quinan, J. Frank Lloyd Wright's Larkin
  Building.
  P. Goldberger, 441:6Dec87-22
Quine, W.V. The Time of My Life.
  L.J. Cohen, 617(TLS):13-19Nov87-1259
  P. Engel, 98:Mar86-285
  T.M.R., 185:Oct86-300
Quinn, D.B. Set Fair for Roanoke.
  V.D. Anderson, 551(RenQ):Summer86-304
  N. Canny, 656(WMQ):Apr86-299
Quinn, E.V. & J.M. Prest - see Jowett, B.
Quinn, J. American Tongue and Cheek.
  D.L.F. Nilsen, 126(CCC):Feb86-107
Quinn, P.F. - see Poe, E.A.
Quinn, S. A Mind of Her Own.
  R. Dinnage, 441:29Nov87-10
  P. Grosskurth, 453(NYRB):5Nov87-14
Quinnell, A.J. In the Name of the Father.
  N. Callendar, 441:8Nov87-62
Quinnell, A.V. In the Name of the Father.
  S. Dunant, 362:24Sep87-22
Quino. The World of Quino.
  M. Richler, 441:3May87-35
Quinones, R.J. Mapping Literary Modern-
  ism.*
  M.B., 295(JML):Nov86-358
  M. Dickie, 301(JEGP):Jul86-468
  H. Gross, 536(Rev):Vol8-33
  D.D. Pearlman, 659(ConL):Fall87-394
  W. Sypher, 569(SR):Summer86-497
Quinsat, G. L'Éclipse.
  M. Le Bot, 450(NRF):May86-91
Quint, D. Origin and Originality in Ren-
  aissance Literature.*
  L.L. Carroll, 345:May86-253
  W.A. Rebhorn, 131(CL):Fall86-384
Quint-Wegemund, U. Das Theater des Absur-
  den auf die Bühne und im Spiegel litera-
  turwissenschaftlicher Kritik.
  L. Matthes, 72:Band223Heft2-450
Quirino, C. Amang.
  D.J. Steinberg, 293(JASt):Nov85-200
Quirino, C. Chick Parsons.
  G.K. Goodman, 293(JASt):Feb86-461
Quirk, R. Words at Work.
  D.J. Enright, 176:Dec87-94
  T.A. Shippey, 617(TLS):17Jul87-773

Quirk, R. and others. A Comprehensive
Grammar of the English Language.
F. Chevillet, 189(EA):Jul-Sep86-327
Quiroga, H. The Exiles.
K. Bereday, 441:16Aug87-16
Qun, S. - see under Shi Qun

"ROSC: Review of Scottish Culture." (Vol
1) (A. Fenton, with H. Cheape & R.K.
Marshall, eds)
W.F.H. Nicolaisen, 203:Vol97No2-234
Raab, M. Des Widerspenstigen Zähmung.
D. Meyer-Dinkgräfe, 612(ThS):May/Nov86-
183
K. Tetzeli von Rosador, 610:Summer86-
165
Raabe, P. Bücherlust und Lesefreuden.
M.W. Rectanus, 221(GQ):Fall86-678
Raban, J. Coasting.*
A. Eames, 362:8Jan87-21
J. Krich, 441:1Feb87-14
G. Moorhouse, 364:Oct86-85
M. Wood, 453(NYRB):22Oct87-39
442(NY):16Mar87-104
Raban, J. For Love and Money.
P. Kemp, 617(TLS):11-17Dec87-1369
D. Kennedy, 362:19Nov87-35
Raban, J. Foreign Land.*
42(AR):Spring86-250
Rabaté, J-M. James Joyce.
R.A. Day, 189(EA):Jul-Sep86-364
Rabaté, J-M. Language, Sexuality and
Ideology in Ezra Pound's Cantos.
639(VQR):Autumn86-116
Rabb, J.D., ed. Religion and Reason.
E.J. Thiessen, 154:Spring86-195
Rabinovitz, R. The Development of Samuel
Beckett's Fiction.*
J. Hansford, 541(RES):Aug86-444
Rabinowitz, S., ed. The Noise of Change.
T.J. Binyon, 617(TLS):31Jul87-822
Rabkin, E.S., M.H. Greenberg & J.D.
Olander, eds. The End of the World.*
H. Auffret, 189(EA):Jul-Sep86-322
Rabkin, N. Shakespeare and the Common
Understanding.
K. Tetzeli von Rosador, 156(ShJW):Jahr-
buch1986-258
Rable, G.C. But There Was No Peace.*
L. Shore, 106:Summer86-219
Rabourdin, D. - see Truffaut, F.
Raby, N. Kachcheri Bureaucracy in Sri
Lanka.
C. Morrison, 293(JASt):May86-637
Racault, J-M. - see Leguat, F.
"I racconti di Ise (Ise Monogatari)." (M.
Marra, trans)
V.H. Viglielmo, 407(MN):Autumn86-345
Race, H. The Classical Priamel from Homer
to Boethius.
G. Schreiner, 394:Vol39fasc1/2-143
Race, W.H. Pindar.
R. Hamilton, 124:Jul-Aug87-457
Racevskis, K. Michel Foucault and the Sub-
version of Intellect.*
R. McGowen, 131(CL):Spring86-181
Rachels, J. The End of Life.*
B. Steinbock, 185:Jul87-878
Racine, D. Léon-Gontran Damas.
B. Arescu, 207(FR):Feb87-386
M. Steins, 538(RAL):Winter86-587

Rackham, O. The History of the Country-
side.*
D. Jacques, 324:Oct87-858
Raczymow, H. Un cri sans voix.
C. Dis, 450(NRF):Jan86-96
Radden, J. Madness and Reason.
J.N., 185:Jan87-510
Rader, D. Tennessee.*
N. de Jongh, 157:No161-48
T.H. Pauly, 615(TJ):Mar86-124
Radice, G. & L. Socialists in the Reces-
sion.
J. Dunn, 617(TLS):2Jan87-11
Radice, R. Filone di Alessandria.
J. Barnes, 520:Vol31No1-99
P.W. van der Horst, 394:Vol39fasc3/4-
496
Radice, W. Louring Skies.
W.G. Shepherd, 4:Summer86-81
Radice, W. & B. Reynolds, eds. The Trans-
lator's Art.
362:10Sep87-24
Rädle, F. - see Bernardt, G.
Radnóti, M. Under Gemini.
C. Gyorgyey, 390:Nov86-56
639(VQR):Winter86-29
Radwan, S., ed. Word and Melody.
H. Bruen, 289:Summer86-113
Radway, J.A. Reading the Romance.*
R.A. Banes, 106:Spring86-93
L. Berlant, 405(MP):Feb87-346
A. Kolodny, 115:Winter86-119
S. O'Brien, 395(MFS):Summer86-353
Radzinowicz, L. & R. Hood. A History of
English Criminal Law and its Administra-
tion from 1750. (Vol 5)
P.W.J. Bartrip, 637(VS):Summer87-535
Rae, J. Letters from School.
P. Parker, 362:8Oct87-23
Raeburn, J. Fame Became of Him.*
R.A. Martin, 115:Winter86-117
J. Meyers, 50(ArQ):Summer86-190
Raeff, M. Understanding Imperial Russia.*
P. Longworth, 575(SEER):Apr86-296
Raeff, M. The Well-Ordered Police State.
H. Schnelling, 568(SCN):Spring-
Summer86-21
Raeper, W. George MacDonald.
H. Finch, 362:26Nov87-28
Raffel, B. Possum and Ole Ez in the Public
Eye.
M. Moran, 27(AL):Mar86-114
Raffler-Engel, W. Nonverbal Behaviour in
the Career Interview.
R. Wodak, 603:Vol10No1-231
Rafter, N.H. Partial Justice.
E. Freedman, 432(NEQ):Dec86-599
Ragon, M. La Louve de Mervent.
R.J. Hartwig, 207(FR):Feb87-433
Ragonese, G. Da Manzoni a Fogazzaro.*
M. Caesar, 402(MLR):Apr87-491
Ragotzky, H. Gattungserneurung und Laien-
unterweisung in den Texten des Strickers.
A. Jürging, 196:Band27Heft1/2-134
J. Margetts, 224(GRM):Band36Heft1-109
Raguin, V.C. Stained Glass in Thirteenth-
Century Burgundy.*
S. Murray, 54:Jun86-332
Rahbar, D. - see Ghalib, M.
Rahn, J. A Theory for All Music.
R. Joseph, 410(M&L):Jan86-68
Rai, A. A House Divided.
C.R. King, 293(JASt):May86-639

Raidt, E.   Einführung in die Geschichte und Struktur des Afrikaans.*
   P. Mühlhäusler, 447(N&Q):Sep85–393
Raimes, A.   Technique in Teaching Writing.*
   P. Ryan, 351(LL):Dec86–535
Raimond, J.   La Littérature anglaise.
   S. Monod, 189(EA):Apr–Jun87–242
Raimond, M.   Proust romancier.
   J–Y. Tadié, 535(RHL):Jul–Aug86–783
Raina, B.   Dickens and the Dialectic of Growth.
   J. Hawthorn, 175:Autumn86–273
   S. Monod, 189(EA):Oct–Dec87–474
Raina, P.   Poland 1981.
   A. Kemp–Welch, 575(SEER):Oct86–647
Raine, C.   Rich.*
   F. Giles, 4:Spring86–78
   L. Lerner, 569(SR):Spring86–312
Raine, C. – see Kipling, R.
Raine, K.   L'Imagination créatrice de William Blake.
   F. Piquet, 189(EA):Jul–Sep86–353
Raine, K.   Yeats the Initiate.
   C. Rawson, 617(TLS):24Jul87–783
Rainer, F.   Intensivierung im Italienischen.*
   G. Lepschy, 545(RPh):Aug86–100
Rainer, J.K.   First Do No Harm.
   A. Knopf, 441:5Apr87–34
Raines, J.C. & D.C. Day–Lower.   Modern Work and Human Meaning.
   D.C., 185:Jul87–904
Rainwater, C. & W.J. Scheick, eds.   Contemporary American Women Writers.
   L.L. Doan, 395(MFS):Winter86–627
Raitz, W.   Fortunatus.
   H.G. Rötzer, 133:Band19Heft2–164
Rajak, T.   Josephus.*
   P.W. van der Horst, 394:Vol39fasc3/4–497
   M. Stern, 313:Vol76–324
Rajan, B.   The Form of the Unfinished.
   A. Janowitz, 661(WC):Autumn86–233
   R.D. Kendall, 604:Spring/Summer86–33
   R.P. Stoicheff, 627(UTQ):Fall86–98
   639(VQR):Summer86–88
Rajchman, J. & C. West, eds.   Post–Analytic Philosophy.
   M. Fisk, 125:Summer86–435
   R.M., 185:Oct86–300
Rajic, N.   The Master of Strappado.*
   T. Gerry, 102(CanL):Winter85–167
Rakosi, C.   The Collected Poems of Carl Rakosi.
   M. Heller, 441:8Mar87–22
Ralegh, W.   Sir Walter Ralegh: Selected Writings.   (G. Hammond, ed)
   J. Rees, 541(RES):May86–306
Raleigh, D.J.   Revolution on the Volga.*
   639(VQR):Autumn86–120
Ramanujan, A.K.   Poems of Love and War.
   639(VQR):Summer86–100
Ramaswamy, E.A.   Power and Justice.
   J.G. Scoville, 293(JASt):Aug86–891
Ramat, P.   Linguistica tipologica.*
   B. Comrie, 353:Vol24No4–822
   F. Plank, 206(FoLi):Vol20No1/2–233
"The Rāmāyaṇa of Vālmīki."*   (Vol 1) (R.P. Goldman & S.J. Sutherland, eds)
   E. Gerow, 293(JASt):Feb86–424
Ramazani, R.K.   Revolutionary Iran.*
   S. Bakhash, 453(NYRB):15Jan87–10

Rambach, P. & S.   Gardens of Longevity in China and Japan.
   R. Bly, 441:13Dec87–29
Rambaldo, A.M. – see del Encina, J.
Ramet, P., ed.   Religion and Nationalism in Soviet and East European Politics.
   R. Pearson, 575(SEER):Jul86–484
Ramírez, S.   Stories
   P–L. Adams, 61:Mar87–95
Ramírez Sánchez, C.   Toponimia de Cautín.
   D.J. Gifford, 86(BHS):Oct86–396
Ramírez Trejo, A.   Heródoto, padre y creador de la historia científica.
   J.M. Alonso–Núñez, 303(JoHS):Vol106–209
Ramnefalk, M.L. & A. Westberg, eds.   Kvinnornas litteraturhistoria.   (Pt 1)
   B. Steene, 562(Scan):May86–101
Ramos, J.   Neo–Conservative Economics in the Southern Cone of Latin America, 1973–83.
   L. Whitehead, 617(TLS):9–15Oct87–1103
Ramos–Horta, J.   Funu.*
   P. Carey, 617(TLS):27Feb87–209
   H. Kamm, 441:11Jan87–26
Ramos–Kuethe, L.   Valle Inclán: Las "Comedias Bárbaras."
   A. López de Martínez, 238:Dec86–872
Rampton, D.   Vladimir Nabokov.*
   J. Armstrong, 67:Nov86–320
   J.W. Connolly, 550(RusR):Apr86–221
   J. Grayson, 402(MLR):Jan86–270
Ramras–Rauch, G.   The Protagonist in Transition.
   P. Merivale, 107(CRCL):Mar86–155
Ramsay, A. & R. Fergusson.   Poems.   (A.M. Kinghorn & A. Law, eds)
   G.R.R., 588(SSL):Vol21–361
Ramsey, D.K.   The Corporate Warriors.
   R. Davenport–Hines, 617(TLS):25–31Dec87–1421
   A. Feinberg, 441:12Apr87–30
Ramsey, J.   Reading the Fire.*
   A. Krupat, 447(N&Q):Sep85–431
Ramsey, L.C.   Chivalric Romances.*
   A. Wilson, 203:Vol97No1–115
Ramthun, H. – see Brecht, B.
Ranald, M.L.   The Eugene O'Neill Companion.
   J.E. Barlow, 612(ThS):May/Nov86–172
   T. Bogard, 610:Spring86–79
Rand, P.   Paul Rand: A Designer's Art.*
   A. Gowan, 507:Mar/Apr86–120
Randall, D.B.J.   Gentle Flame.*
   J. La Belle, 301(JEGP):Jan86–123
Randall, R.H., Jr. & others.   Masterpieces of Ivory from the Walters Art Gallery.
   P. Hetherington, 39:Aug86–139
   P. Williamson, 90:Aug86–608
Randel, D., ed.   The New Harvard Dictionary of Music.
   C. Wintle, 617(TLS):8May87–496
Randolph, V.   Ozark Folksongs.   (N. Cohen, ed)
   D.J. Dyen, 187:Spring/Summer87–363
Ranelagh, J.   The Agent.*
   J. Symons, 617(TLS):30Jan87–101
Ranelagh, J.O.   A Short History of Ireland.
   H.C.G. Matthew. 447(N&Q):Sep85–399
Ranke, K., ed.   Enzyklopädie des Märchens.   (Vol 2, fasc 5 and Vol 3)
   E. Ettlinger, 203:Vol97No2–236

Ranke, K., ed. Enzyklopädie des Märchens. (Vol 5, Pt 1)
    H. Rölleke, 52:Band21Heft1-85
Ranke, K. & others, eds. Enzyklopädie des Märchens. (Vol 4, Pt 1-3)
    A. Gier, 72:Band223Heft1-138
    M. Zender, 196:Band27Heft1/2-106
Rankin, A.C. The Poetry of Stevie Smith - "Little Girl Lost."
    J. Russell, 175:Autumn86-285
Rankin, H.D. Sophists, Socratics and Cynics.*
    J. Poulakos, 480(P&R):Vol19No2-138
Rankin, I. The Flood.*
    H. Ritchie, 571(ScLJ):Winter86-41
Rankin, N. Dead Man's Chest.
    A. Alpers, 617(TLS):7Aug87-840
Rankin, P. To the House Ghost.
    J.F. Cotter, 249(HudR):Spring86-161
Ransom, J.C. Selected Essays of John Crowe Ransom.* (T.D. Young & J. Hindle, eds)
    G. Core, 579(SAQ):Spring86-205
Ransom, J.C. Selected Letters of John Crowe Ransom.* (T.D. Young & G. Core, eds)
    D. Donoghue, 473(PR):Vol53No1-126
    J. Mazzaro, 569(SR):Winter86-143
Rao, S.R. The Decipherment of the Indus Script.
    W.H. Maurer, 318(JAOS):Apr/Jun85-374
Rapaport, H. Milton and the Postmodern.*
    J.M. Evans, 541(RES):Aug86-415
Raper, H.W. William W. Holden.
    O.H. Olsen, 9(AlaR):Jul86-231
Raphael, C. The Road from Babylon.*
    M.D. Angel, 390:Jun/Jul86-60
Raphael, D.D. Adam Smith.
    J.R., 185:Jan87-503
Rapin, N. Oeuvres.* (Vols 1 & 2) (J. Brunel, ed)
    J-P. Beaulieu, 539:Nov86-380
Rapin, N. Oeuvres.* (Vol 3) (J. Brunel, ed)
    J-P. Beaulieu, 539:Nov86-380
    P. Chilton, 208(FS):Jan86-64
Rapoport, A. General System Theory.
    R. Kapral, 186(ETC.):Winter86-421
Rapoport, L. Redemption Song.
    639(VQR):Autumn86-132
Rapp, C. William Carlos Williams and Romantic Idealism.*
    N.K. Barry, 651(WHR):Summer86-185
Rappaport, G.C. Grammatical Function and Syntactic Structure.
    G.G. Corbett, 402(MLR):Jul86-809
    R.C. De Armond, 558(RLJ):Spring/Fall86-209
    J.I. Press, 575(SEER):Apr86-262
Rappaport, R.A. Pigs for the Ancestors.
    J.M. Blythe, 293(JASt):Aug86-797
Rasch, J.J. Das Maxentius-Mausoleum an der Via Appia in Rom.
    M.A.R. Colledge, 123:Vol36No2-344
Raschel, H. Das Nietzsche-Bild im George-Kreis.*
    U.K. Goldsmith, 222(GR):Summer86-132
    R. Margreiter, 489(PJGG):Band93Heft2-375
Rashid, S.A. Mesopotamien.
    C. Homo, 537:Vol72No1-134

Rasico, P.D. Estudis sobre la fonologia del català preliterari.
    J. Llisterri, 86(BHS):Oct86-394
    N.B. Smith, 545(RPh):May87-530
Raskin, B. Hot Flashes.
    J. Rascoe, 441:27Sep87-13
Raskin, V. Semantic Mechanisms of Humor.*
    C. Davies, 616:Spring/Summer86-54
    D.H., 355(LSoc):Jun86-286
Raspa, A. The Emotive Image.
    D.R. Shore, 178:Dec86-455
Rasputin, V. You Live and Love.*
    J.H. Billington, 441:10May87-22
Rathbone, J. Greenfinger.
    442(NY):19Oct87-122
Ratiu, I. Moscow Challenges the World.
    A. Brown, 617(TLS):27Mar87-313
Ratushinskaya, I. Beyond the Limit.
    M. Carlson, 441:28Jun87-12
Ratushinskaya, I. No, I'm Not Afraid.*
    C. Rumens, 493:Oct86-60
Rau, F. Zur Verbreitung und Nachahmung des "Tatler" und "Spectator."
    B. Nugel, 38:Band104Heft3/4-522
Rau, W. Zur vedischen Altertumskunde.
    M. Sparreboom, 259(IIJ):Apr86-125
Raugei, A.M., ed. Bestiario valdese.*
    M.R. Harris, 589:Jul86-697
Raugei, A.M. Rifrazioni e metamorfosi.
    E.W. Poe, 545(RPh):Feb87-406
Raugei, A.M. - see Pinelli, G.V.
Raulet, G. Humanisation de la nature, Naturalisation de l'homme.
    M. de Gandillac, 192(EP):Oct-Dec86-583
Raulet, S. Art Deco Jewelry.
    C. Gere, 39:Jun86-440
Raupp, H-J. Untersuchungen zu Künstler-bildnis und Künstlerdarstellung in den Niederlanden im 17. Jahrhundert.
    I. Gerards-Nelissen, 600:Vol16No4-262
Rauschenbach, B. - see Schmidt, A.
Ravaisson, F. L'Art et les mystères grecs.
    F. Wybrands, 450(NRF):Apr86-107
Raval, S. The Art of Failure.
    R.L. Caserio, 637(VS):Summer87-537
    S. Monod, 189(EA):Apr-Jun87-227
Ravelli, L. Polidoro Caldara da Caravaggio.
    J.A. Gere, 380:Spring86-61
Raven, S. The Old School. Close of Play.
    P. Parker, 364:Nov86-106
Ravensdale, J. The Domesday Inheritance.*
    H.R. Loyn, 617(TLS):27Feb87-219
Rawdon, M. Green Eyes, Dukes and Kings.
    M.L. Scott, 198:Fall86-79
Rawlings, M.K. Selected Letters of Marjorie Kinnan Rawlings. (G.E. Bigelow & L.V. Monti, eds)
    S.I. Bellman, 534(RALS):Spring-Autumn84-227
Rawlyk, G.A. Ravished by the Spirit.
    C.G. Holland, 102(CanL):Winter85-127
Rawson, B., ed. The Family in Ancient Rome.*
    639(VQR):Autumn86-119
Rawson, C., ed. The Character of Swift's Satire.*
    M. Byrd, 402(MLR):Apr86-449
    M. Thackeray, 541(RES):May86-267
Rawson, C., ed. English Satire and the Satiric Tradition.*
    W.B. Carnochan, 402(MLR):Jan86-162
    M. Seidel, 173(ECS):Summer87-533

301

Rawson, C. Order from Confusion Sprung.
P-G. Boucé, 189(EA):Jan-Mar87-88
W.B. Carnochan, 566:Spring87-200
P. Harth, 402(MLR):Jul87-706
Rawson, C.J. - see "The Yearbook of English Studies"
Rawson, C.J. & J. Mezciems - see "The Yearbook of English Studies"
Rawson, E. Intellectual Life in the Late Roman Republic.*
J. Barnes, 520:Vol31No1-96
V. Hunter, 125:Spring86-333
J.E. Rexine, 24:Fall86-442
F.E. Romer, 124:Sep-Oct86-60
Ray, A.C. For Images.
R. Hogan, 41:Vol6-225
Ray, J.L. The Future of American-Israel Relations.*
639(VQR):Winter86-26
Ray, R.B. A Certain Tendency of the Hollywood Cinema, 1930-1980.*
B. Allan, 529(QQ):Winter86-893
T. Doherty, 500:Spring/Summer87-90
Ray, R.J. Murdock for Hire.
N. Callendar, 441:31May87-45
Ray, S. Stories.
J. Rees, 617(TLS):24Apr87-434
Ray, S. The Unicorn Expedition.
I. Buruma, 453(NYRB):19Nov87-12
G. Wilson, 441:20Sep87-25
Ray, W. Literary Meaning.*
W.B. Bache, 395(MFS):Winter86-686
R. Selden, 402(MLR):Oct86-961
639(VQR):Summer86-87
Raymond, D. He Died With His Eyes Open.
N. Callendar, 441:3May87-46
Raymond, J.C., ed. Literacy as a Human Problem.*
L. Ede, 126(CCC):Oct86-362
Raynaud, J-M. Voltaire, soi-disant.
N. Wagner, 535(RHL):Jan-Feb86-143
Raynaud, M., D. Laroque & S. Rémy. Michel Roux-Spitz.
J.F. Gabriel, 576:Mar86-76
Raz, J. The Morality of Freedom.
N. MacCormick, 617(TLS):5Jun87-599
Raz, S. Tigre Grammar and Texts.
J. Fellman, 318(JAOS):Oct/Dec85-814
G.F. Meier, 682(ZPSK):Band39Heft1-142
Read, B. Victorian Sculpture.
D. James, 54:Dec86-687
Read, C. & R.J. Staggs, eds. The Rebellion of 1837 in Upper Canada.
G.W., 102(CanL):Fall86-198
Read, M.K. The Birth and Death of Language.
N.G. Round, 86(BHS):Apr86-150
Read, P.P. The Free Frenchman.*
T. Fleming, 441:12Apr87-15
442(NY):1Jun87-110
Read, W.A. Indian Place Names in Alabama.* (rev)
W.F.H. Nicolaisen, 35(AS):Summer86-179
Reader, K.A. Intellectuals and the Left in France since 1968.
R.W. Johnson, 617(TLS):31Jul87-811
Reading, P. Essential Reading. (A. Jenkins, ed) Stet.
M. Imlah, 617(TLS):8May87-487
"Reallexikon für Antike und Christentum." (Pts 89-96)
J. André, 555:Vol59fasc2-348

Reames, S.L. The "Legenda aurea."
P. Menard, 549(RLC):Apr-Jun86-234
E.F. Rice, Jr., 551(RenQ):Summer86-279
Reaney, J. Imprecations.
G. Boire, 102(CanL):Fall86-130
Rearick, C. Pleasures of the Belle Epoque.*
K.J. Brady, 446(NCFS):Fall-Winter86/87-226
D. Sutton, 39:Apr86-226
639(VQR):Spring86-65
"Frank Reaugh."
L. Milazzo, 584(SWR):Winter86-123
Reay, B., ed. Popular Culture in Seventeenth-Century England.
K.E. McLuskie, 161(DUJ):Jun86-363
Reay, B. The Quakers and the English Revolution.
C.R. Davis, 568(SCN):Winter86-68
Rebelo, L.D. - see under de Sousa Rebelo, L.
Rebotton, J. - see de Maistre, J.
Reboul, J. La Liberté pour l'ombre.
B. Hourcade, 207(FR):Mar87-565
"Recherches sur le français parlé." (Vol 4)
F-X. Nève, 209(FM):Oct86-260
Réda, J. Jouer le jeu.
A. Prévos, 91:Spring86-189
Reddaway, J. Burdened with Cyprus.
C.M. Woodhouse, 617(TLS):3Jul87-709
Redfern, J., ed. Basic Terms of Business and Finance, French-English, English-French.*
D.E. Corbin, 399(MLJ):Spring86-69
Redfern, W. Puns.*
C. Davies, 616:Spring/Summer86-54
G. Price, 208(FS):Apr86-249
A.E.S., 636(VP):Autumn86-348
566:Spring87-204
Redfern, W.D. Georges Darien.
R. Carr, 208(FS):Apr86-234
C. Lloyd, 402(MLR):Oct87-968
Redfern, W.D - see Sartre, J-P.
Redgrave, M. In My Mind's I.
J.C. Trewin, 570(SQ):Summer86-278
Redgrove, P. The Black Goddess and the Sixth Sense.
R. Clarke, 362:5Nov87-28
Redgrove, P. The Mudlark Poems and Grand Buveur.
H. Davies, 617(TLS):13Feb87-165
Redmon, A. Second Sight.
L. Duguid, 617(TLS):11-17-Sep87-978
Redmon, C. Come as You Are.
C.D. May, 441:15Feb87-20
Redmond, J., ed. Drama and Symbolism.
J. Stokes, 402(MLR):Apr86-437
Redondi, P. Galileo Heretic. (French title: Galilée hérétique.)
I. Calvino, 453(NYRB):8Oct87-13
P. Corsi, 441:15Nov87-13
H. Cronel, 450(NRF):Jun86-86
442(NY):19Oct87-122
Redpath, F. To the Village.
J. Mole, 176:Mar87-60
Redpath, T. - see Donne, J.
Rée, H. Educator Extraordinary.
G.R. Batho, 161(DUJ):Dec85-176
Reece, S.C. - see Scott, P.

Reed, A. Romantic Weather.*
  D. Degrois, 549(RLC):Apr–Jun86–246
  D. Hughes, 591(SIR):Spring86–140
  R. Lloyd, 208(FS):Jan86–91
Reed, A., ed. Romanticism and Language.*
  M. Brown, 661(WC):Autumn86–200
  V.A. De Luca, 627(UTQ):Summer87–575
  S. Peterfreund, 301(JEGP):Jul86–464
  J. Raimond, 189(EA):Jul–Sep86–350
  M. Storey, 175:Spring86–67
Reed, D.K. The Novel and the Nazi Past.
  J.M. Ritchie, 366:Autumn86–247
Reed, H.H. The Reader in the Picaresque
Novel.
  F. Baasner, 547(RF):Band98Heft1/2–227
  P.N. Dunn, 593:Fall86–238
  R.L. Fiore, 238:Dec86–863
  B.W. Wardropper, 551(RenQ):Winter86–
  786
Reed, I. Reckless Eyeballing.*
  D. Pinckney, 453(NYRB):29Jan87–17
Reed, J. Blue Rock.
  R. Kaveney, 617(TLS):29May87–588
Reed, J. Nero.
  S. O'Brien, 493:Jun86–104
Reed, J. Schubert.
  E. Sams, 617(TLS):17Jul87–772
Reed, J. Selected Poems.
  J. Horder, 362:14May87–33
  M. Imlah, 617(TLS):25–31Dec87–1435
Reed, J.D. & C. Exposure.
  N. Callendar, 441:7Jun87–25
Reed, J.R. Decadent Style.*
  F.E. Court, 599:Spring86–110
  L. Kamm, 207(FR):Mar87–539
  R.K.R. Thornton, 148:Autumn86–116
  H. Tucker, 385(MQR):Spring87–421
Reed, J.R. The Natural History of H.G.
Wells.
  B. Gasser, 447(N&Q):Jun85–286
Reed, K. Catholic Girls.
  R. Weinreich, 441:1Nov87–24
Reed, R. The Leeshore.
  G. Jonas, 441:26Apr87–29
Reed, R. Personal Effects.
  D. Johnson, 18:Sep87–67
Reed, R.R., Jr. Crime and God's Judgment
in Shakespeare.*
  L. Cerny, 156(ShJW):Jahrbuch1986–230
  C. Saunders, 541(RES):May86–254
  V.M. Vaughan, 403(MLS):Fall86–86
Reed, T.J. Goethe.*
  K.F. Hilliard, 83:Autumn86–298
  C.E. Schweitzer, 301(JEGP):Apr86–304
de Reede, R., ed. Concerning the Flute.*
  A. Davis, 410(M&L):Jan86–83
Reeder, H.P. Language and Experience.
  D. Ihde, 323:May86–204
  C.W. Kneupper, 583:Winter87–212
Reedy, G. The Bible and Reason.*
  D.R. Dickson, 568(SCN):Winter86–66
  I. Simon, 173(ECS):Fall86–89
Reedy, G.E. The Twilight of the Presi-
dency.
  D. Murray, 441:29Nov87–21
Rees, A.L. and F. Borzello, eds. The New
Art History.*
  G. Reynolds, 39:Oct86–376
  C. Seerveld, 290(JAAC):Spring87–313
  S. Whitfield, 176:Feb87–48
Rees, B. A Musical Peacemaker.
  M. Kennedy, 617(TLS):24Jul87–793
Rees, G., with C. Upton – see Bacon, F.

Rees, N. The Newsmakers.
  P. Humphries, 362:15Oct87–28
Rees, R. Land of Earth and Sky.
  L.R., 102(CanL):Winter85–178
  R. Thacker, 649(WAL):May86–69
Rees–Mogg, W. How to Buy Rare Books.*
  A.G. Thomas, 354:Sep86–281
Reese, T.F. – see Kubler, G.
Reese, W. Die innere Anschauung.
  H. Rombach, 489(PJGG):Band93Heft2–406
Reeve, A. – see Erasmus
Reeves, G. Real Stories.*
  M. Hulse, 161(DUJ):Dec85–210
Reeves, M. & W. Gould. Joachim of Fiore
and the Myth of the Eternal Evangel in
the Nineteenth Century.
  F. Kermode, 617(TLS):25Sep–1Oct87–
  1054
Reeves, R. The Reagan Detour.
  639(VQR):Spring86–59
Regan, G. Someone Had Blundered...
  D. Hibberd, 617(TLS):18–24Sep87–1008
Regan, T., ed. Animal Sacrifices.
  M. Midgley, 185:Jul87–879
Regan, T. Bloomsbury's Prophet.
  S. Hampshire, 453(NYRB):26Mar87–37
Regan, T. The Case for Animal Rights.*
  L.W. Sumner, 449:Sep86–425
Regan, T. – see Moore, G.E.
Regard, M. – see Sainte-Beuve, C-A.
Regis, E. Who Got Einstein's Office?
  J. Weiner, 441:27Sep87–39
Regis, E., Jr., ed. Gewirth's Ethical
Rationalism.*
  D.M. Taylor, 483:Jan86–137
Register, C. Living with Chronic Illness.
  N. Mairs, 441:4Oct87–12
Regueiro, J.M. & A.G. Reichenberger.
Spanish Drama of the Golden Age.
  C. Stern, 240(HR):Spring86–218
  W.M. Whitby, 551(RenQ):Summer86–322
Rehnquist, W.H. The Supreme Court.
  P.B. Kurland, 441:20Sep87–3
Reich, L.S. The Making of American Indus-
trial Research.
  J.K. Smith, 432(NEQ):Sep86–452
Reich, N.B. Clara Schumann.*
  E. Brody, 415:Sep86–499
  R.A. Solie, 451:Summer86–74
  A. Walker, 410(M&L):Oct86–409
Reich, R.B. Tales of a New America.
  N. Lemann, 441:22Mar87–7
Reichardt, L. Ortsnamenbuch des Kreises
Esslingen. Ortsnamenbuch des Stadt-
kreises Stuttgart und des Landkreises
Ludwigsburg.
  T. Steiner, 685(ZDL):1/1986–108
Reid, A. Whereabouts.
  S. French, 617(TLS):16–22Oct87–1132
  E. Newby, 441:31May87–48
Reid, A., with J. Brewster, eds. Slavery,
Bondage, and Dependency in Southeast
Asia.
  J. Taylor, 293(JASt):Aug86–912
Reid, B. & R. Bringhurst. The Raven Steals
the Light.
  M. Lewis, 649(WAL):May86–65
Reid, C. Edmund Burke and the Practice of
Political Writing.
  J.C.C. Mays, 272(IUR):Spring86–99
Reid, C. The Music Monster.*
  412:Feb85–66

Renner, R.G. Peter Handke.
  L. Kersten, 67:Nov86-310
Rennolds, M.B., ed. National Museum of
Women in the Arts.
  K. Adler, 617(TLS):28Aug87-923
Rensch, B. Biophilosophical Implications
of Inorganic and Organismic Evolution.
  E. Mayr, 486:Dec86-612
Rentsch, T. Heidegger und Wittgenstein.
  R. Fornet-Betancourt, 160:Jul86-221
Rentschler, E. West German Film in the
Course of Time.
  L. Caltvedt, 221(GQ):Winter86-175
Renza, L.A. "A White Heron" and the Ques-
tion of Minor Literature.*
  J.E. Bassett, 141:Fall86-474
Requadt, P. Unbürgerliche Dichterporträts
des Expressionismus.
  J.M. Ritchie, 402(MLR):Apr87-526
Requardt, W. & M. Machatzke. Gerhart
Hauptmann und Erkner.
  E. Catholy, 221(GQ):Winter86-153
Resnick, P. Parliament vs. People.*
  E.Z. Friedenberg, 150(DR):Winter85/86-
611
Resnicow, H. The Dead Room.
  N. Callendar, 441:2Aug87-29
Ress, L. Flight Patterns.
  R. Crist, 502(PrS):Spring86-106
Reston, J. Washington.
  A. Cooke, 442(NY):9Feb87-101
"Restoration and Eighteenth Century Prose."
  A.F.T. Lurcock, 447(N&Q):Jun85-264
Reswick, I. Traditional Textiles of
Tunisia.
  R.D. Mathey, 2(AfrA):May86-81
Rétat, L. - see Renan, J.E.
Rétat, P. - see Bayle, P.
Reubart, D. Anxiety and Musical Perform-
ance.
  J.B. Hartman, 510:Winter86/87-61
Reulos, M. Comment traduire et interpréter
les références juridiques (droit romain,
droit canonique et droit coutumier) con-
tenues dans les ouvrages du XVIe siècle.
  K.J. Evans, 208(FS):Oct86-453
Reuter, H., ed. Orgelmuseum Borgentreich.
  C. Hill, 415:Jul86-390
Rewald, J. Cézanne.*
  D. Sutton, 39:Nov86-462
Rewald, J. Cézanne, the Steins and their
Circle.
  L. Ellmann, 617(TLS):19Jun87-655
  442(NY):13Apr87-105
Rewald, J. Studies in Impressionism.* (I.
Gordon & F. Weitzenhoffer, eds)
  J. House, 59:Sep86-369
  R. Thomson, 90:Apr86-297
Rexroth, K. The Selected Poems of Kenneth
Rexroth.* (B. Morrow, ed)
  M. Westbrook, 649(WAL):May86-80
Rexroth, K. World Outside the Window. (B.
Morrow, ed)
  442(NY):10Aug87-80
Rey, A. - see de Quevedo, F.
Rey, J-M. Quelqu'un danse.
  V. Kaufmann, 400(MLN):Sep86-966
Rey-Flaud, B. La Farce ou la machine à
rire.*
  E. Du Bruck, 201:Vol11-170
  N.J. Lacy, 207(FR):Dec86-252
  G.A. Runnalls, 208(FS):Jul86-319

Rey Hazas, A., ed. La vida de Lazarillo de
Tormes.
  P.J. Smith, 402(MLR):Jul86-766
Reyes, G. Polifonía textual.
  S. Bacarisse, 86(BHS):Oct86-363
Reymond, E.A.E. From the Records of a
Priestly Family from Memphis. (Vol 1)
  R. Jasnow, 318(JAOS):Apr/Jun85-339
Reynolds, C. Agatite.
  K. Rile, 441:11Jan87-18
Reynolds, C. The Vigil.*
  G. Haslam, 649(WAL):Feb87-356
Reynolds, G. The Later Paintings and Draw-
ings of John Constable.*
  L. Hawes, 54:Mar86-172
  C. Powell, 59:Mar86-99
Reynolds, H. The Defector.
  A. Hyde, 441:1Feb87-16
Reynolds, J.F. - see Gellert, C.F.
Reynolds, L.D., ed. Texts and Transmis-
sion.*
  M. Ferrari, 123:Vol36No2-287
  F. Lo Monaco, 313:Vol76-330
  J.E.G. Zetzel, 122:Jul86-270
Reynolds, M. The Young Hemingway.*
  J.M. Flora, 573(SSF):Fall86-465
  P.R.J., 295(JML):Nov86-484
  J.M. Muste, 27(AL):Dec86-656
  R.S. Nelson, 268(IFR):Summer87-111
  S. Pinsker, 395(MFS):Winter86-614
  J. Symons, 364:Jun86-85
  D. Wyatt, 569(SR):Spring86-289
Reynolds, M.D. "Uncle Tom's Cabin" and
Mid-Nineteenth Century United States.
  G.T.B., 27(AL):May86-312
Reynolds, S. The Vision of Simeon Solomon,
Stroud, Glos.*
  P. Delaney, 39:Dec86-574
Reynolds, W.H., with G. Warfield. Common-
Practice Harmony.
  D.A. Damschroder, 308:Fall86-315
Rézeau, P. Dictionnaire des régionalismes
de l'Ouest entre Loire et Gironde.*
  K. Klingebiel, 545(RPh):Feb87-383
  M. Piron, 209(FM):Apr86-96
Rézeau, P., ed. Les Prières aux saints en
français à la fin du moyen âge, 2.
  B. Cazelles, 545(RPh):Feb87-414
von Rezzori, G. The Death of My Brother
Abel.*
  T. McGonigle, 532(RCF):Summer86-155
Rheinbach, L. Die laufenden Bibliographien
zur romanischen Sprachwissenschaft.*
  P. Swiggers, 553(RLiR):Jul-Dec86-555
"Rhetorik, Ein internationales Jahrbuch."
  (Vol 4) (J. Dyck, with others, eds)
  J. Schmidt, 320(CJL):Winter86-380
Rhoades, D., comp. The Independent Mono-
logue in Latin American Theater.
  L.H. Quackenbush, 352(LATR):Spring87-
146
  G.W. Woodyard, 263(RIB):Vol36No2-188
Rhoads, J.W. The Contract.*
  42(AR):Fall86-494
Rhodes, D.E. Studies in European Printing
and Book Collecting.
  P. Needham, 354:Sep86-274
Rhodes, D.E. and D.I. Janik, eds. Studies
in Ruskin.*
  M. Hardman, 677(YES):Vol16-328
Rhodes, J.W. Keats's Major Odes.*
  D. Birch, 541(RES):Feb86-110
Rhodes, N. - see Donne, J.

Richardson, W. "Zolotoe Runo" and Russian Modernism: 1905–1910.
T.J. Binyon, 617(TLS):31Jul87–822
Riché, P. & G. Lobrichon, eds. Le moyen âge et la Bible.
J.H. Bentley, 589:Jul86–744
Riches, D., ed. The Anthropology of Violence.
P. Winch, 617(TLS):20Mar87–290
Richetti, J.J. Philosophical Writing: Locke, Berkeley, Hume.*
R.S. Pomeroy, 173(ECS):Fall86–68
R. Zimmer, 489(PJGG):Band93Heft2–411
Richie, D. The Inland Sea.
F. Tuohy, 617(TLS):3Jul87–711
Richler, M. Home Sweet Home.*
K. McSweeney, 168(ECW):Fall86–172
Richlin, A. The Garden of Priapus.*
J.H.C. Leach, 447(N&Q):Jun85–253
M.B. Skinner, 122:Jul86–252
Richmond, C. – see Alas, L.
Richmond, H.M. Puritans and Libertines.*
D.S. Kastan & N.J. Vickers, 131(CL): Spring86–197
Richmond, V.B. Muriel Spark.*
I. Malin, 268(IFR):Winter87–44
Richter, B. & S. Kotzé, comps. A Bibliography of Criticism of Southern African Literature in English.
G.E. Gorman, 538(RAL):Fall86–419
Richter, E. Lehrbuch des modernen Burmesisch (Umgangssprache).
A. Esche, 682(ZPSK):Band39Heft5–610
Richter, H., ed. Das "Rolandslied" des Pfaffen Konrad.
F.G. Gentry, 406:Fall86–388
Richter, J. Handlungsfiguren in kommunikativen Prozessen.
C. von Stutterheim, 355(LSoc):Sep86–443
Richter, L.G. Hegels begreifende Naturebetrachtung als Versöhnung der Spekulation mit der Erfahrung.
H. Faes, 542:Jan–Mar86–124
Ricken, F., ed. Lexikon der Erkenntnistheorie und Metaphysik.
M. Zelger, 489(PJGG):Band93Heft2–436
Ricken, U., ed. Französische Lexikologie.*
C. Schmitt, 72:Band223Heft1–189
Ricken, U. Sprache, Anthropologie, Philosophie in der französischen Aufklärung.
H–M. Militz, 682(ZPSK):Band39Heft6–731
Ricks, C. The Force of Poetry.*
A.V.C. Schmidt, 541(RES):May86–296
G. Stewart, 651(WHR):Autumn86–261
Ricks, C., ed. The New Oxford Book of Victorian Verse.
R. Jenkyns, 617(TLS):26Jun87–679
N. Lewis, 362:25Jun87–27
Ricks, C. – see Tennyson, A.
Rico, F. El pequeño mundo del hombre. (2nd ed)
A.V., 379(MedR):Dec86–469
Ricoeur, P. Temps et récit. (Vol 3)
J.H. Miller, 617(TLS):9–15Oct87–1104
Ricoeur, P. Le Temps raconté.
P.S. Thompson, 207(FR):May87–854
Ricoeur, P. Time and Narrative.* (French title: Temps et Récit.) (Vol 1)
J. Dunphy, 63:Jun86–232
J.H. Miller, 617(TLS):9–15Oct87–1104
K.J. Vanhoozer, 208(FS):Jul86–364
K.J. Vanhoozer, 473(PR):Vol53No4–645

Ricoeur, P. Time and Narrative. (French title: Temps et Récit.) (Vol 2)
J.M.M., 295(JML):Nov86–420
J.H. Miller, 617(TLS):9–15Oct87–1104
K.J. Vanhoozer, 208(FS):Jul86–364
Ridderbos, B. Saint and Symbol.*
H. Friedmann, 551(RenQ):Spring86–105
Riddle, J.M. Dioscorides on Pharmacy and Medicine.
P. de Lacy, 124:Mar–Apr87–317
Riddle, M–M.G. Herman Melville's "Piazza Tales."*
E. Kielland-Lund, 172(Edda):1986/4–381
Rider, R.W., with D.M. Paulsen. The Roll Away Saloon.
O. Sawey, 649(WAL):Nov86–242
Riding, A. Mexico.
L. Whitehead, 362:20Aug87–18
Ridley, M. Animal Behaviour.
T. Halliday, 617(TLS):20Feb87–176
Rieckmann, J. Aufbruch in die Moderne.
W.E. Yates, 402(MLR):Jan87–253
Riede, D.G. Dante Gabriel Rossetti and the Limits of Victorian Vision.*
R.L. Stein, 131(CL):Spring86–207
Riedel, M. Between Tradition and Revolution.*
D.R. Knowles, 518:Apr86–84
A.W. Wood, 482(PhR):Apr86–300
Riedel, V. Antikerezeption in der Literatur der Deutschen Demokratischen Republik.
R. Charbon, 72:Band223Heft2–378
D. Gelbrich, 654(WB):6/1986–1035
Riedel, W. Die Anthropologie des jungen Schiller.
L. Sharpe, 402(MLR):Oct87–1027
Riedel, W.E., ed. The Old World and the New.*
E. Herd, 564:Nov86–335
H. Ohlendorf, 627(UTQ):Fall86–239
Riedinger, M. Das Wort "Gut" in der angelsächsischen Metaethik.
L.K. Sosoe, 687:Oct–Dec86–639
Riedl, P.A. & M. Seidel. Die Kirchen von Siena. (Pt 1)
J. Pope–Hennessy, 90:Jul86–512
Rieff, D. Going to Miami.
J. Krich, 441:23Aug87–7
Rieff, P. Fellow Teachers.
B. Lang, 560:Fall86–227
Riege, H. – see Klopstock, F.G.
Riegel, M. L'Adjectif attribut.
L.R. Waugh, 207(FR):May87–886
Rieger, D. Diogenes als Lumpensammler.*
A. Grewe, 72:Band223Heft1–237
Rieger, D., ed. Das französische Theatre des 18. Jahrhunderts.
J. von Stackelberg, 535(RHL):Sep–Oct86–924
Riemenschneider, D., ed. The History and Historiography of Commonwealth Literature.*
G. Griffiths, 538(RAL):Fall86–433
di Rienzo, E. Il Sogno della Ragione, Saggi su Paul Valéry.
H. Laurenti, 535(RHL):Jan–Feb86–160
Ries, G. Prolog und Epilog in Gesetzen des Altertums.*
T. Honoré, 123:Vol36No1–146
Ries, P. – see Bording, A.

Ries, W. Nietzsche.
　　R. Margreiter, 489(PJGG):Band93Heft2–
　　375
Rieselback, H.F. Conrad's Rebels.*
　　B.E. Teets, 177(ELT):Vol29No1–101
Rietzschel, T., ed. Fortschrittliche
　　deutsche Literaturkritik 1918–1933.
　　H. Kähler, 654(WB):12/1986–2099
Riewald, J.G. & J. Bakker. The Critical
　　Reception of American Literature in the
　　Netherlands 1824–1900.
　　H. Beaver, 677(YES):Vol16–310
Rifelj, C.D. Word and Figure.
　　R. Buss, 617(TLS):13–19Nov87–1240
Riffaterre, M. Text Production.
　　J. Patrick, 627(UTQ):Winter86/87–338
Rifkin, J. Declaration of a Heretic.
　　R.G., 185:Oct86–311
　　42(AR):Winter86–123
Rifkin, J. Time Wars.
　　J. Updike, 442(NY):7Sep87–108
Rifkin, S.B. Health Planning and Community
　　Participation.
　　P. Van Esterik, 293(JASt):May86–659
Rigden, J.S. Rabi.
　　P. Hoffman, 441:10May87–13
Rigg, P. & D.S. Enright, eds. Children and
　　ESL.
　　W.D. Davies, 350:Dec87–921
Riggio, T.P. – see Dreiser, T. & H.L.
　　Mencken
Righi, G. A.M.S. Boezio, "De Syllogismo
　　Cathegorico."
　　J. Jolivet, 542:Oct–Dec86–518
Rigney, B.H. Lilith's Daughters.
　　P. Clements, 107(CRCL):Sep86–523
　　R. Miles, 677(YES):Vol16–365
Rigobello, A. Kant.
　　C. La Rocca, 342:Band77Heft3–371
Rigolot, F. Le texte de la Renaissance.*
　　E. Werner, 72:Band223Heft1–203
Rigolot, F. – see Labé, L.
Rigoni, M.A. Variations sur l'impossible.
　　M. Jarrety, 450(NRF):Dec86–100
Rihoit, C. Soleil.
　　C.F. Coates, 207(FR):Dec86–297
Rijaluddin bin Hakim Long Fakìr Kandu, A.
　　Ahmad Rijaluddin's Hikayat Perintah
　　Negeri Benggala.
　　H. Chambert-Loir, 302:Vol22No1–122
de Rijk, L.M. La philosophie au Moyen Age.
　　F. Beets, 540(RIPh):Vol40fasc3–332
　　J. Jolivet, 542:Oct–Dec86–519
Riley, D. Dry Air.
　　H. Buckingham, 565:Summer86–64
Riley, H.M.K. Clemens Brentano.
　　J.F. Fetzer, 222(GR):Fall86–177
Riley, J.C. The Eighteenth-Century Cam-
　　paign to Avoid Disease.
　　R. Porter, 617(TLS):6–12Nov87–1219
Riley, J.C. The Seven Years War and the
　　Old Régime in France.
　　J. Rogister, 617(TLS):18–24Dec87–1411
Rilke, R.M. The Astonishment of Origins.
　　The Migration of Powers. Orchards. The
　　Roses & the Windows. (A. Poulin, Jr.,
　　trans of all)
　　C.S. Brown, 569(SR):Summer86–504
Rilke, R.M. The Lay of the Love and Death
　　of Cornet Christoph Rilke. (S. Mitchell,
　　trans)
　　C.S. Brown, 569(SR):Summer86–504

Rilke, R.M. Letters on Cézanne.* (C.
　　Rilke, ed)
　　J. Byrne, 532(RCF):Fall86–134
　　H. Goldgar, 598(SoR):Summer87–719
Rilke, R.M. New Poems.* (E. Snow, trans)
　　C.S. Brown, 569(SR):Summer86–504
Rilke, R.M. The Sonnets to Orpheus.* (S.
　　Mitchell, trans)
　　C.S. Brown, 569(SR):Summer86–504
Rilke, R.M., B. Pasternak & M. Tsvetaïeva.
　　Correspondance à trois.
　　J. Aeply, 450(NRF):Nov86–110
Rimbaud, A. Oeuvres poétiques. (C.A.
　　Hackett, ed)
　　F.S. Heck, 207(FR):May87–867
Rimmon-Kenan, S. Narrative Fiction.*
　　K. Kuiper, 478:Apr86–114
　　J-M. Rabaté, 189(EA):Jul–Sep87–324
Rinaldi, S.M. – see under Mason Rinaldi, S.
Ring, F.K. Against the Current.*
　　T. Quirk, 27(AL):Oct86–455
Ringbom, S. Icon to Narrative. (2nd ed)
　　W. Hood, 90:Jun86–429
Ringe, D.A. American Gothic.
　　M.T. Chialant, 402(MLR):Jan87–177
Ringe, D.A. & L.B. – see Cooper, J.F.
Ringger, K. & C. Weiand – see "Stendhal-
　　Hefte, 1"
Ringrose, D.R. Madrid and the Spanish
　　Economy 1560–1850.
　　J. Black, 83:Spring86–92
Rinvolucri, M. Grammar Games.
　　J. Di Iuglio, 399(MLJ):Summer86–209
Rio, M. Dreaming Jungles.
　　P-L. Adams, 61:Jun87–83
　　W.W. Stowe, 441:23Aug87–11
Rio, M. Les Jungles pensives.
　　R. Linkhorn, 207(FR):Feb87–434
de Rioja, F. Poesía. (B. López Bueno, ed)
　　D.L. Heiple, 238:Dec86–867
Riordan, M. The Hunting of the Quark.
　　M. Bartusiak, 441:27Sep87–42
　　442(NY):28Dec87–125
Ripley, G. & A.V. Mercer. Who's Who in
　　Canadian Literature 1983–84.
　　D. Jackel, 168(ECW):Fall86–195
Rippy, F.M. Matthew Prior.
　　566:Spring87–208
Riskin, C. China's Political Economy.
　　L. Pan, 176:Nov87–48
Rissman, L. Love as War.
　　R.L. Fowler, 123:Vol36No2–301
Rissom, I. Der Begriff des Zeichens in den
　　Arbeiten Lev Semenovic Vygotskijs.
　　W.C.M., 400(MLN):Apr86–736
Rist, J.M. Human Value.
　　C.C.W. Taylor, 41:Vol6–234
Ristori, R. – see Poggio Bracciolini, G.F.
Ristow, W.W. American Maps and Mapmakers.
　　D. Woodward, 517(PBSA):Vol80No4–515
Ritchie, B. & W. Goldsmith. The New Elite.
　　R. Davenport-Hines, 617(TLS):20Mar87–
　　293
Ritchie, R., ed. The Joint Stock Book.
　　D. Walder, 362:29Jan87–22
Ritchie, R.C. Captain Kidd and the War
　　Against the Pirates.*
　　C. Hill, 453(NYRB):29Jan87–14
Ritchie, S. The Hollow Woman.
　　N. Callendar, 441:29Mar87–25
Ritti, T. Iscrizioni e rilievi greci nel
　　Museo Maffeiano di Verona.
　　C. Dobias-Lalou, 555:Vol59fasc2–293

Ritvo, H. The Animal Estate.
V. Hearne, 441:11Oct87-61
A. Ryan, 362:3Dec87-32
Ritz, H. Divided Soul.
C. Keil, 187:Spring/Summer87-367
Ritzel, W. Kant.
R. George, 484(PPR):Mar87-485
Rivabella, O. Requiem for a Woman's Soul.*
R. Wright, 617(TLS):27Feb87-207
639(VQR):Autumn86-128
Duque de Rivas. El moro expósito o Córdoba y Burgos en el siglo décimo. (A. Crespo, ed)
R.A. Cardwell, 402(MLR):Jul86-772
Rive, R. "Buckingham Palace," District Six.
W. Finnegan, 441:4Oct87-16
Rivera, C., ed. Communicative Competence Approaches to Language Proficiency Assessment.*
J.P. Lantolf, 399(MLJ):Summer86-173
Rivera, C., ed. Language Proficiency and Academic Achievement.
C. Edelsky, 355(LSoc):Mar86-123
A. Mirhassani, 351(LL):Dec86-523
Rivers, E.L. Fray Luis de León: The Original Poems.*
C.P. Thompson, 402(MLR):Apr86-510
A.S. Trueblood, 403(MLS):Fall86-88
Rivers, E.L. Quixotic Scriptures.*
F. Pierce, 86(BHS):Jul86-269
"The Riverside Counselor's Stories." (R.L. Backus, trans)
M. Morris, 407(MN):Autumn86-349
V. Skord, 293(JASt):May86-585
Rivière, A., J-G. Morgenthaler & F. Garcia - see Lhote, A., Alain-Fournier & J. Rivière
Rivière, J. Cahiers Marcel Proust, 13. (T. Laget, ed)
P-L. Rey, 450(NRF):Feb86-104
Rivière, P. La Nef des folz du monde. (E. Du Bruck, ed)
S. Bagoly, 553(RLiR):Jan-Jun86-299
Rivkin, L. - see Ganivet, A.
Rizzo, A. Scienza impura.
P. Petitmengin, 555:Vol59fasc2-352
Rizzo, G., ed. Fenoglio a Lecce.
L. Quartermaine, 402(MLR):Jan87-218
Roa Bastos, A. I the Supreme.*
J. Sturrock, 617(TLS):3Apr87-361
639(VQR):Autumn86-127
Roach, J.R. The Player's Passion.
S.M. Archer, 615(TJ):Oct86-377
J. Hankey, 617(TLS):20Feb87-188
L. Woods, 612(ThS):May/Nov86-169
Roach, W., ed. The Continuations of the Old French "Perceval" of Chrétien de Troyes.* (Vol 5)
A.J. Holden, 402(MLR):Jan86-193
L. Löfstedt, 439(NM):1986/4-608
M. Offord, 208(FS):Jan86-59
Roadarmel, P. Beach House 7.
442(NY):16Feb87-109
Roads, C., ed. Composers and the Computer.
J. Appleton, 414:Vol72No1-124
P.D. Manning, 415:Apr86-207
Roads, C. & J. Strawn, eds. Foundations of Computer Music.
B. Blakely, 513:Fall-Winter85-450
P.D. Manning, 415:Apr86-207

Roazen, P. Helene Deutsch.
E.H. Baruch, 473(PR):Vol53No2-308
J.E. Robinson, 152(UDQ):Fall86-112
Robb, G. - see Vitu, A.
Robbe-Grillet, A. Le miroir qui revient.*
M. Connon, 67:Nov86-313
C.A. Durham, 207(FR):Feb87-435
Robbins, B. The Servant's Hand.
D.T. O'Hara, 659(ConL):Fall87-409
639(VQR):Autumn86-117
Robbins, J.A. - see "American Literary Scholarship, 1980"
Robbins, R. - see Browne, T.
Robbins, V.K. Jesus the Teacher.
G.A. Kennedy, 544:Winter86-67
Robert, M. En haine du roman.
M.C. Olds, 446(NCFS):Spring87-322
Robert, R., ed. Il était une fois les fées, contes des XVIIe-XVIIIe siècles.
P. Hourcade, 535(RHL):Jul-Aug86-751
Roberts, C.G.D. The Collected Poems of Sir Charles G.D. Roberts. (D. Pacey, ed)
E. Jewinski, 105:Fall/Winter86-105
Roberts, G., ed. Gerard Manley Hopkins: The Critical Heritage.
T. Paulin, 617(TLS):14Aug87-863
Roberts, G. - see "Beowulf"
Roberts, J. Agenda for Canada.
W. Christian, 298:Fall86-154
Roberts, J. Ondina.
S. Pugmire, 649(WAL):Nov86-273
Roberts, J. Royal Artists.
C. Fox, 617(TLS):25-31Dec87-1426
Roberts, J.A. - see Wroth, M.
Roberts, J.R. Richard Crashaw.*
A.C. Labriola, 405(MP):May87-431
P.A. Parrish, 568(SCN):Spring-Summer86-12
Roberts, J.R. John Donne.*
W. White, 87(BB):Mar86-59
Roberts, J.W. - see Harding, S.
Roberts, L. From the Dark.
L. McKee, 448:Vol24No3-91
Roberts, L. An Infinite Number of Monkeys.
C.G. Fraser, 441:30Aug87-20
Roberts, M. Biblical Epic and Rhetorical Paraphrase in Late Antiquity.
T. Conley, 544:Autumn86-423
Roberts, M. The Book of Mrs. Noah.
J. McKay, 362:10Sep87-23
A. Vaux, 617(TLS):24Jul87-801
Roberts, M. British Poets and Secret Societies.
C. MacLachlan, 571(ScLJ):Winter86-10
Roberts, M. The Early Vasas.
G.C. Schoolfield, 568(SCN):Winter86-61
Roberts, M. The Mirror of the Mother.
C. Wills, 617(TLS):10Jul87-748
Roberts, O. Miracles of Seed-Faith. The Holy Spirit in the Now.
M. Gardner, 453(NYRB):13Aug87-17
Roberts, P. The Royal Court Theatre: 1965-1972.
D. Walder, 362:29Jan87-22
Roberts, P., with S. Andrews. Ashes to Gold.
M. Gardner, 453(NYRB):13Aug87-17
ap Roberts, R. Arnold and God.*
C. Dawson, 541(RES):Feb86-117
Roberts, R. He's the God of a Second Chance!
M. Gardner, 453(NYRB):13Aug87-17

Robreau, Y. L'Honneur et la honte.*
 B.N. Sargent-Baur, 545(RPh):Aug86-112
Robson, A.P. & J.M. - see Mill, J.S.
Robson, D.W. Educating Republicans.
 F. Rudolph, 173(ECS):Fall86-62
Robson, J.M. - see Mill, J.S.
Robson, J.M. & J. Stillinger - see Mill,
 J.S.
Robson, W.W. The Definition of Literature
 and Other Essays.*
 T. Eagleton, 402(MLR):Apr86-428
Robson, W.W. - see Kipling, R.
Roček, R. Neue Akzente.
 P.M. Lützeler, 222(GR):Summer86-125
Roche, D. The People of Paris.
 A. Forrest, 617(TLS):11-17Sep87-983
Roche, J. North Italian Church Music in
 the Age of Monteverdi.*
 J.E. Glixon, 551(RenQ):Summer86-312
 J. Steele, 410(M&L):Apr86-174
Roche-Pézard, F. L'aventure futuriste
 1909/1916.
 A. Cozea Motei, 193(ELit):Autumn86-145
Rocher, R. Orientalism, Poetry and the
 Millennium.
 S.V.R. Char, 83:Autumn86-260
 P. Mitter, 293(JASt):Feb86-430
Lord Rochester. The Poems of John Wilmot,
 Earl of Rochester.* (K. Walker, ed)
 P. Hammond, 541(RES):May86-263
 J.H. O'Neill, 250(HLQ):Summer86-280
 K. Robinson, 402(MLR):Oct86-988
 I. Simon, 179(ES):Jun86-270
Rochlin, D. Frobisch's Angel.
 C. Ames, 441:26Jul87-16
Rock, R.O., comp. The Native American in
 American Literature.
 T.N. Weissbuch, 649(WAL):Aug86-155
Rockwell, J. All American Music.*
 P. Dickinson, 607:Sep86-59
"Rococo Silks."
 S. Braybrooke, 507:Nov/Dec86-125
Röd, W. Die Philosophie der Neuzeit 2.*
 L. Kreimendahl, 687:Apr-Jun86-294
Rodd, L.R., with M.C. Henkenius - see
 "Kokinshū"
Roddaz, J-M. Marcus Agrippa.
 M. Reinhold, 24:Spring86-130
 R. Seager, 123:Vol36No1-96
Roddewig, M. Dante Alighieri.*
 M. Hardt, 547(RF):Band98Heft3/4-451
 I. Klein & C. Kleinhenz, 276:Autumn86-
 314
Rodgers, M.E. - see Mencken, H.L. & S.
 Haardt
Rodimzeva, I., N. Rachmanov & A. Raimann.
 The Kremlin.
 S. Massie, 441:13Dec87-26
Rodini, R.J. & S. Di Maria. Ludovico
 Ariosto.*
 M. Davie, 402(MLR):Apr87-488
 J. Everson, 278(IS):Vol41-147
Rodinis, G.T. - see under Toso Rodinis, G.
Rodino, R.H. Swift Studies, 1965-1980.
 M. Treadwell, 541(RES):Feb86-98
Rodley, L. Cave Monasteries of Byzantine
 Cappadocia.*
 P. Hetherington, 39:Jul86-64
Rodman, F.R. - see Winnicott, D.W.
Rodoreda, M. My Christina.
 I. Malin, 532(RCF):Spring86-221

Rodrigo, A. García Lorca el amigo de
 Cataluña.
 M. Laffranque, 92(BH):Jan-Jun85-212
Rodrigo, A. Memoria de Granada.
 M. Laffranque, 92(BH):Jan-Jun85-215
Rodrigues, M.J. Steerage and Ten Other
 Stories. (G. Monteiro, ed)
 K.H. Brower, 238:May86-316
Rodríguez, A. La estructura mítica del
 Popol Vuh.
 L.A. Daniel, 238:Dec86-880
Rodríguez, A.D. - see under Domínguez
 Rodríguez, A.
Rodríguez, A.V. - see under Vespertino
 Rodríguez, A.
Rodriguez, C.D. - see under Del Valle
 Rodríguez, C.
Rodríguez, E. & A. Tordera. Calderón y la
 obra corta dramática del siglo XVII.
 T.R.A. Mason, 402(MLR):Oct87-1001
Rodríguez, E. & A. Tordera. La escritura
 como espejo de palacio.
 P.J. Smith, 402(MLR):Jul87-762
 A. Valbuena-Briones, 238:Sep86-542
Rodríguez, E. & A. Tordera - see Calderón
 de la Barca, P.
Rodríguez, I. & M. Zimmerman, eds. Process
 of Unity in Caribbean Society.
 L. King, 86(BHS):Apr86-186
Rodríguez-Luis, J. La literatura hispano-
 americana.
 E. Gimbernat de González, 552(REH):
 May86-127
 R.L. Williams, 240(HR):Summer86-359
Rodríguez-Luis, J. Novedad y ejemplo de
 las Novelas de Cervantes.*
 P.N. Dunn, 240(HR):Spring86-214
Rodríguez Matos, C.A. El narrador pícaro.
 C.B. Johnson, 238:Dec86-864
Rodríguez Pérez, O. La novela picaresca
 como transformación textual.
 B.W. Ife, 86(BHS):Oct86-386
Rodriguez Roque, O. American Furniture at
 Chipstone.
 P. Zea, 658:Winter86-308
Rodway, A. The Craft of Criticism.
 C. Norris, 402(MLR):Apr86-429
Rodzinski, W. A History of China. (Vol 2)
 J.E. Sheridan, 302:Vol22No1-72
Roebuck, J.B. & M. Hickson 3d. The
 Southern Redneck.
 D.E. Whillock, 583:Summer87-415
Roemer, J., ed. Analytical Marxism.
 D. Schweickart, 185:Jul87-869
Rogalla, H. & W. German for Academic Pur-
 poses. Grammar Handbook for Reading
 German Texts.
 A. Galt, 399(MLJ):Winter86-431
Rogan, B. Cafe Nevo.
 R. Finn, 441:4Oct87-28
Roger, P. Roland Barthes, roman.
 E.S. Apter, 98:Oct86-967
Rogers, J. The Ice is Singing.
 J. McKay, 362:10Sep87-23
 M. Seymour, 617(TLS):24Jul87-802
Rogers, J.M. - see Çağman, F. and Z.
 Tandini
Rogers, J.M. - see Köseoglu, C.
Rogers, J.M. - see Tezcan, H. & S. Delibas
Rogers, J.N. The Country Music Message.*
 D.E. Whillock, 583:Summer87-415
Rogers, J.S. Stage by Stage.*
 O. Trilling, 157:No159-51

Romero, P.W. E. Sylvia Pankhurst.
  J. Harris, 617(TLS):10Apr87-375
Romero Frías, M. Catalogo degli antichi
  fondi spagnoli della Biblioteca Univer-
  sitaria di Cagliari, I.
  M. Johnson, 86(BHS):Oct86-385
Romeyer-Dherbey, G. Les Sophistes.
  A-M. Rieu, 542:Jan-Mar86-104
de Romilly, J. "Patience, mon coeur."
  J.H.C. Leach, 123:Vol36No1-139
de Romilly, J. A Short History of Greek
  Literature.*
  J.E. Rexine, 124:Mar-Apr87-331
Romtvedt, D. Moon.
  L. Sanazaro, 649(WAL):May86-86
Roncalli, F., ed. Scrivere etrusco.
  N. Spivey, 313:Vol76-281
Ronda, J.P. Lewis and Clark among the
  Indians.
  C. Hanyan, 106:Summer86-189
  S. Jenkins, 649(WAL):May86-71
  D.B. Nunis, Jr., 250(HLQ):Spring86-180
  F.P. Prucha, 656(WMQ):Jan86-157
de Ronsard, P. Amours de Marie; Sonnets
  pour Hélène. (R. Aulotte, ed)
  W.J. Beck, 207(FR):Mar87-532
de Ronsard, P. Les Quatre Saisons de Ron-
  sard. (G. Gadoffre, ed)
  P. Ford, 208(FS):Jul86-325
  L. Herlin, 450(NRF):Jan86-88
Ronyoung, K. Clay Walls.
  A. Engeler, 441:11Jan87-18
Ronza, R. La nuova via della seta.
  A. Formis, 402(MLR):Jul87-761
Room, A. Dictionary of Changes in Meaning.
  D.J. Enright, 176:May87-69
Rooney, C.J., Jr. Dreams and Visions.*
  K.M. Roemer, 27(AL):Mar86-132
  T.H. Towers, 395(MFS):Summer86-245
Rooney, D. Khmer Ceramics.
  W.G. Solheim 2d, 293(JASt):May86-661
  42(AR):Spring86-248
Roose-Evans, J. Experimental Theatre from
  Stanislavsky to Peter Brook.*
  G. Bas, 189(EA):Jan-Mar87-114
Root, W. The Paris Edition. (S. Abt, ed)
  S.I. Toll, 441:16Aug87-18
  442(NY):27Jul87-78
Root, W.P. Faultdancing.
  455:Dec86-64
Root-Bernstein, M. Boulevard Theater and
  Revolution in Eighteenth-Century Paris.
  W.E. Rex, 173(ECS):Spring87-375
Rooth, A.B. L.O. Från lögnsaga till
  paradis.
  J. Lindow, 650(WF):Jan86-50
Ropars-Wuilleumier, M-C. Le texte divisé.*
  L. Oswald, 567:Vol60No3/4-315
Roque, O.R. - see under Rodriguez Roque, O.
Rorem, N. The Nantucket Diary of Ned
  Rorem: 1973-1985.
  J. Feeney, 441:1Nov87-25
Rorty, A., ed. Essays on Aristotle's
  Ethics.
  J. Roberts, 41:Spring85-98
Rorty, A.O., ed. Essays on Descartes'
  "Meditations."
  A.N., 185:Apr87-698
Rorty, R. Consequences of Pragmatism.*
  Philosophy and the Mirror of Nature.
  D. Frede, 543:Jun87-733
Rorty, R. & others. Wirkungen Heideggers.
  J. Poulain, 98:Jan-Feb86-60

Rorty, R., J.B. Schneewind & Q. Skinner,
  eds. Philosophy in History.*
  T. Ball, 185:Oct86-281
  J.E.K. Secada, 483:Jul86-409
Rosa, A.A. - see under Asor Rosa, A.
von Rosador, K.T. - see under Tetzeli von
  Rosador, K.
Rosales, A-M. A Study of a Sixteenth-
  Century Tagalog Manuscript on the Ten
  Commandments.
  V.L. Rafael, 293(JASt):Feb86-465
Roscow, G.H. Syntax and Style in Chaucer's
  Poetry.
  M. Markus, 72:Band223Heft2-394
Rose, B. & others. Arikha.
  A. Ross, 364:Jun86-101
Rose, D.A. Flipping for It.
  R. Goodman, 441:22Feb87-28
  442(NY):27Apr87-105
Rose, G. Dialectic of Nihilism.
  G. Strickland, 97(CQ):Vol15No1-85
Rose, G.J. Trauma and Mastery in Life and
  Art.
  A. Brumer, 441:19Jul87-21
Rose, J. The Edwardian Temperament.
  C. Cagle, 389(MQ):Winter87-288
Rose, M.A. Marx's Lost Aesthetic.*
  P. Somville, 542:Jan-Mar86-130
Rose, M.B. The Gregs of Quarry Bank Mill.
  J. Hoppit, 617(TLS):27Mar87-322
Rose, M.E., ed. The Poor and the City.
  C. Forster, 637(VS):Winter87-284
Rose, P. Parallel Lives.
  E. Leites, 473(PR):Vol53No1-115
Rose, P. Writing of Women.
  E.B. Jordan, 395(MFS):Summer86-361
  639(VQR):Winter86-16
Rose, R. Ministers and Ministries.
  B. Pimlott, 617(TLS):4-11Sep87-944
Rose, S., R.C. Lewontin & L.J. Kamin. Not
  in Our Genes.
  P. Colgan, 529(QQ):Autumn86-595
Rosellini, J. Volker Braun.*
  D. Sevin, 406:Winter86-552
Rosen, C. Plays of Impasse.*
  G.K. Hunter, 402(MLR):Jul87-729
Rosen, D. & A. Porter, eds. Verdi's
  "Macbeth."*
  J.A. Hepokoski, 317:Summer86-408
Rosen, F. Jeremy Bentham and Representa-
  tive Democracy.
  G.J. Postema, 482(PhR):Jul86-483
Rosen, K. Ammianus Marcellinus.*
  R.J. Penella, 124:Sep-Oct86-63
Rosen, M.J. A Drink at the Mirage.
  R. Andersen, 577(SHR):Winter86-82
Rosen, R. Fadeaway.*
  E. Stumpf, 441:15Feb87-20
Rosenbaum, B. & P. White, comps. Index of
  English Literary Manuscripts. (Vol 4, Pt
  1)
  P. Coustillas, 189(EA):Apr-Jun87-223
  J. Shattock, 677(YES):Vol16-299
Rosenbaum, C.P. Italian for Educated
  Guessers.
  L. Kibler, 276:Winter86-410
Rosenbaum, J. Film: The Front Line 1983.*
  G. Adair, 707:Spring86-141
Rosenbaum, R. Manhattan Passions.
  A. Barnet, 441:21Jun87-23

Rosenberg, A. Sociobiology and the Pre-
emption of Social Science.*
   M. Ruse, 488:Mar86-141
   G.R. Weaver, 543:Sep86-138
Rosenberg, A. The Structure of Biological
Science.*
   J. Dupré, 486:Sep86-461
Rosenberg, C.E. The Care of Strangers.
   G.H. Brieger, 441:22Nov87-1
Rosenberg, D., ed. Congregation.
   E. Hirsch, 441:20Dec87-1
Rosenberg, J.D. Carlyle and the Burden of
History.
   I. Campbell, 506(PSt):May86-80
   A.D. Culler, 158:Dec86-184
   J.P. Farrell, 637(VS):Spring87-430
   R. Jann, 125:Winter86-214
   D.R.M. Wilkinson, 179(ES):Oct86-458
Rosenberg, J.H. Margaret Atwood.
   E. Cameron, 298:Winter86/87-133
   A.E. Davidson, 102(CanL):Summer86-105
Rosenblum, M. Mission to Civilize.*
   442(NY):12Jan87-103
Rosenblum, M. & D. Williamson. Squandering
Eden.
   J. Brooke, 441:29Nov87-7
Rosenblum, N. A World History of Photogra-
phy.*
   B. Pinkard, 592:Vol199No1014-64
Rosenblum, R. & H.W. Janson. 19th Century
Art.* (British title: Art of the Nine-
teenth Century, Painting and Sculpture.)
   R. Thomson, 59:Mar86-108
Rosenfield, D. Politique et liberté.
   J-F. Kervegan, 192(EP):Oct-Dec86-573
Rosengarten, H. & M. Smith - see Brontë, C.
Rosengarten, T. Tombee.*
   B. Wyatt-Brown, 453(NYRB):26Feb87-12
Rosengren, I., ed. Sprache und Pragmatik.
   G. Objartel, 133:Band19Heft3/4-323
Rosenqvist, C. Hem till historien.
   M. Robinson, 562(Scan):May86-85
   B. Steene, 563(SS):Winter86-71
Rosenthal, A.M. & A. Gelb, eds. The So-
phisticated Traveler.
   639(VQR):Winter86-30
Rosenthal, A.M. & A. Gelb, eds. The World
of New York.
   639(VQR):Summer86-105
Rosenthal, D. Studien zur Syntax und
Semantik des Verbs "bleiben" unter beson-
derer Berücksichtigung des Nieder-
deutschen und Niederländischen.
   H. Tiefenbach, 685(ZDL):1/1986-83
Rosenthal, M.L. and S.M. Gall. The Modern
Poetic Sequence.
   P. Mariani, 27(AL):Oct86-465
Rosetti, A. La linguistique balkanique.
   G.M. Messing, 350:Mar87-188
Rosinsky, N.M. Feminist Futures.
   L. Leith, 561(SFS):Mar86-92
Roskies, D. Against the Apocalypse.
   J.E. Young, 659(ConL):Summer87-278
Roskill, M. The Interpretation of Cubism.*
   B. Kennedy, 89(BJA):Summer86-295
Roskill, M. & D. Carrier. Truth and False-
hood in Visual Images.*
   C.Z. Elgin, 482(PhR):Jan86-139
Rosman, A. & P.G. Rubel. The Tapestry of
Culture. (2nd ed)
   R.D. Bethke, 292(JAF):Jul/Sep86-337
Rosmarin, A. The Power of Genre.
   S. Gillies, 290(JAAC):Spring87-307

Rosowski, S.J. The Voyage Perilous.
   A.S. Byatt, 617(TLS):15May87-507
Ross, A. Cape Summer. Through the Carib-
bean.
   D. Durrant, 364:Jul86-110
Ross, A. The Emissary.*
   T. Raychaudhuri, 617(TLS):6Feb87-142
Ross, A. - see Richardson, S.
Ross, A. & M. Cyprien. A Traveller's Guide
to Celtic Britain.
   J. Hamard, 189(EA):Oct-Dec87-461
Ross, A. & D. Woolley - see Swift, J.
Ross, A.B. The Pilgrimage.
   V. Sayers, 441:27Sep87-51
Ross, F. A Conspiracy of Angels.
   N. Callendar, 441:31May87-45
   442(NY):1Jun87-112
Ross, G.M. Leibniz.*
   E. Craig, 393(Mind):Apr86-258
   G.H.R. Parkinson, 706:Band18Heft1-101
Ross, M. The Impossible Sum of Our Tradi-
tions.
   F. Davey, 99:Nov86-40
   P. Koster, 376:Dec86-145
Ross, M., F. Cogswell & M. Maillet. The
Bicentennial Lectures on New Brunswick
Literature.
   D. Duffy, 627(UTQ):Fall86-232
Ross, R. & J. Hendry, eds. Sorley MacLean.
   E. Ní Chuilleanáin, 617(TLS):5Jun87-611
Ross, W.S. Crusade.
   H.M. Schmeck, Jr., 441:5Apr87-35
Rossanda, R. Anche per me.
   M. Clark, 617(TLS):4-10Dec87-1345
Rossen, J. The World of Barbara Pym.
   N. Shulman, 617(TLS):25-31Dec87-1420
Rosset, C. La Force majeure.* Logique du
pire. Le Réel.
   D. Bell, 400(MLN):Sep86-930
Rossetti, C. Christina Rossetti: Selected
Poems. (C.H. Sisson, ed)
   E.D. Mackerness, 447(N&Q):Jun85-283
Rossetti, G. Lettere familiari a Charles
Lyell. (P. Horne & J. Woodhouse, eds)
   C.P. Brand, 402(MLR):Jul86-759
   H.W. Smith, 278(IS):Vol41-155
Rossetti, G. Gabriele Rossetti: Carteggi.
(Vol 1) (T.R. Toscano, ed)
   C.P. Brand, 402(MLR):Jul86-759
Rossi, A., ed. Sociology and Anthropology
in the People's Republic of China.
   G.E. Johnson, 293(JASt):Aug86-826
Rossi, A., with B. Huet & P. Lombardo.
Three Cities.
   A. Betsky, 505:Jan86-159
Rossi, L. Process.
   R. Beach, 126(CCC):Dec86-493
Rossi, L., G. Garcia & S. Mulvaney. Com-
puter Notions.
   S.J. Sacco, 399(MLJ):Spring86-91
Rossi, P. The Dark Abyss of Time.*
   R. Cormier, 568(SCN):Winter86-73
Rossiter, C., W. Schmidtkunz & J. Winke.
thirds.
   W. Swist, 404:Winter-Spring86-63
Rossiter, M.L. Women in the Resistance.
   J.S. Dugan, 207(FR):Feb87-411
Rossiter, M.W. Women Scientists in Amer-
ica.
   B.F. Sloat, 385(MQR):Winter87-278
Rossiter, S. Beyond This Bitter Air.
   E. Spencer, 441:9Aug87-15

Rossiter, S. The Human Season.
    L. Dickstein, 441:17May87-50
Rosslyn, F. - see Homer
Rosso, C. Pagine al vento.*
    P. Oppici, 535(RHL):Sep-Oct86-962
Rosso, C., ed. Transhumances culturelles.
    T. de Vulpillières, 549(RLC):Jul-Sep86-
    357
Rosso, J.G. - see under Geffriaud Rosso, J.
Rossvaer, V. The Laborious Game.
    P. Thom, 63:Mar86-117
Rostad, L. Grace Stone Coates.
    N.P. Arbuthnot, 649(WAL):Feb87-361
Rostaing, C. - see Mistral, F. & P. Devoluy
Rostal, M. Beethoven: the Sonatas for
    Piano and Violin.
    W. Drabkin, 415:Jun86-336
Rostand, E. Cyrano de Bergerac. (P.
    Truchet, ed)
    J. Anzalone, 207(FR):Dec86-261
    P. Besnier, 535(RHL):Mar-Apr86-325
Roszak, T. The Cult of Information.*
    B. Lovell, 324:Jul87-612
Rotenstreich, N. Jews and German Philos-
    ophy.*
    W. Kluback, 390:Feb86-59
Rotenstreich, N. Reflection and Action.
    H.D. Lewis, 483:Oct86-541
Roth, B. An Annotated Bibliography of
    Jane Austen Studies, 1973-83.
    J.A. Dussinger, 402(MLR):Oct87-923
Roth, G. Mallī-jñāta.
    J.W. de Jong, 259(IIJ):Jan86-55
Roth, J. Hotel Savoy.
    H. Gold, 441:8Feb87-30
    A. Sattin, 617(TLS):16Jan87-56
Roth, J. Tarabas.*
    S. Lardner, 442(NY):23Nov87-154
    A. Sattin, 617(TLS):2-8Oct87-1074
Roth, M. & R. Bluglass, eds. Psychiatry,
    Human Rights and the Law.
    S.J.M., 185:Jul87-900
Roth, M.P. The Juror and the General.
    H. Goodman, 441:18Jan87-19
Roth, N. Maimonides.
    M.R. Menocal, 240(HR):Autumn86-463
Roth, P. The Counterlife.
    M. Amis, 61:Feb87-89
    W.H. Gass, 441:4Jan87-1
    E. Korn, 617(TLS):13Mar87-274
    J. Rubins, 453(NYRB):26Mar87-40
    T. Tanner, 362:12Mar87-25
    J. Updike, 442(NY):2Mar87-107
Roth, P.A., ed. Critical Essays on Vlad-
    imir Nabokov.
    J. Katsell, 574(SEEJ):Fall86-452
Roth, S. Laute Einsamkeit und bitteres
    Gluck.
    I. Hájek, 617(TLS):2-8Oct87-1067
Rothbauer, G. - see Jendryschik, M.
Rothe, W. Tänzer und Täter.
    J. Ramin, 403(MLS):Summer86-311
Rothman, W. Hitchcock.
    B. Testa, 106:Winter86-525
Rotman, B. Signifying Nothing.
    J. Sturrock, 617(TLS):18-24Dec87-1408
    362:20Aug87-22
des Rotours, R. - see Lin Lu-tche
Rouart, D. Renoir.
    M. Clarke, 39:Aug86-141

Rouart, M-F. Le mythe du Juif errant dans
    les littératures européennes du XIXe
    siècle.
    R. Trousson, 549(RLC):Oct-Dec86-480
Roubaud, J. La Belle Hortense.
    W.F. Motte, Jr., 207(FR):Oct86-170
Roubaud, J. La Fleur inverse.
    N. Mann, 617(TLS):14Aug87-880
Roubaud, J. Quelque chose noir.*
    A. Bosquet, 450(NRF):Oct86-84
    M. Rosello, 207(FR):May87-914
Rouben, C. - see de Bussy-Rabutin, R.
Roudiez, L.S. - see Kristeva, J.
Roudy, Y. A cause d'elles.
    S.I. Spencer, 207(FR):Dec86-278
de Rougemont, D. Love in the Western
    World. (rev)
    G. Woodcock, 569(SR):Spring86-272
Rougerie, R. La Fête des ânes; ou, la mise
    à mort du livre.
    L.A. Olivier, 207(FR):Mar87-526
Roughsey, L/E. An Aboriginal Mother Tells
    of the Old and the New.
    L. Ryan, 381:Mar86-49
Roulet, E. & others. L'Articulation du
    discours en français contemporain.
    C. Kramsch, 207(FR):Feb87-442
Rouner, L.S., ed. Knowing Religiously.
    L.G.J., 185:Apr87-682
Rourke, C. American Humor.
    S.P., 295(JML):Nov86-411
Rousseau, G.S. Tobias Smollett.
    J.V. Price, 677(YES):Vol16-274
Rousseau, G.S. - see Hill, J.
"Henri Rousseau."
    M. Clarke, 39:Aug86-141
Rousseau, J-B. Cantates. (T. Di Scanno,
    ed)
    D. Williams, 208(FS):Oct86-458
Rousseau, J-J. Correspondance complète.
    (Vols 39 & 40) (R.A. Leigh, ed)
    P. Lefebvre, 535(RHL):Jan-Feb86-149
Rousseau, J-J. Correspondance complète.
    (Vols 41-43) (R.A. Leigh, ed)
    J. Bloch, 208(FS):Jul86-330
    P. France, 402(MLR):Jan87-201
    P. Lefebvre, 535(RHL):Jul-Aug86-763
Rousseau, J-J. Correspondance complète.
    (Vol 44) (R.A. Leigh, ed)
    J. Bloch, 208(FS):Oct86-464
Rousseau, J-J. Correspondance complète de
    Jean-Jack Rousseau. (first 45 vols)
    (R.A. Leigh, ed)
    M. Cranston, 83:Autumn86-287
Rousseau, P. Pachomius.*
    G. Constable, 377:Jul86-138
Roussel, R. The Conversation of the Sexes.
    S.W.R. Smith, 566:Spring87-205
    639(VQR):Summer86-90
Rousset, J. Le Lecteur intime de Balzac au
    journal.
    D. Kelly, 446(NCFS):Spring87-318
Routh, S. & J., ed. Leonardo's Kitchen
    Note Books.
    E. David, 617(TLS):18-24Dec87-1401
Routley, R., with others. Relevant Logics
    and Their Rivals, 1.
    R. Bull, 63:Jun86-222
Rouveret, A. - see Reinach, A.
Röver, A. Paula Modersohn-Becker: Das
    Frühwerk.
    S. Rainbird, 90:Jun86-437

Roviello, A-M. L'institution kantienne de
la liberté.
  A. Stanguennec, 542:Jan-Mar86-121
Rovira, J.C. - see Gil-Albert, J.
Rowan, A. Designs for Castles and Country
Villas by Robert and James Adam.
  T.R. Matthews, 505:Jun86-66
  R. Middleton, 90:Mar86-224
  N. Powell, 39:Feb86-139
Rowan-Robinson, M. - see Ryle, M.
Rowe, C.J. Plato.*
  R. McKim, 124:Sep-Oct86-50
Rowe, F.W. The Smallwood Era.
  G. Panting, 529(QQ):Spring86-172
Rowe, J.C. The Theoretical Dimensions of
Henry James.*
  V. Jones, 541(RES):Nov86-589
  P. O'Donnell, 223:Fall86-319
  R. Posnock, 141:Spring86-222
Rowe, K.E. Saint and Singer.
  U. Brumm, 165(EAL):Fall87-219
Rowell, G. - see Gilbert, W.S.
Rowell, G. & A. Jackson. The Repertory
Movement.*
  A. Emmet, 611(TN):Vol40No1-32
Rowell, L. Thinking About Music.*
  S. Ross, 289:Spring86-126
  R.E. Wates, 308:Spring86-141
Rowell, M. - see Miró, J.
Rowland, B. - see Birney, E.
Rowlands, J. Holbein.*
  L. Campbell, 90:Feb86-149
  G. Reynolds, 39:Mar86-216
  A. Washton, 55:Nov86-55
Rowlands, J. Master Drawings & Watercol-
ours in the British Museum.
  G. Naughton, 39:Jan86-61
Rowley, T. The High Middle Ages, 1200-
1550.
  J.R. Maddicott, 617(TLS):27Feb87-219
Rowse, A.L. Court and Country.
  C. Haigh, 617(TLS):18-24Sep87-1014
Rowse, A.L. A Life.
  R. D'Arcy, 364:Jun86-112
Rowse, A.L. The Poet Auden.
  N. Jenkins, 617(TLS):3Jul87-717
Rowse, T. Arguing the Arts.
  J. Frow, 381:Mar86-118
Roxburgh, A. Pravda.
  A. Austin, 441:18Oct87-18
  B. Woffinden, 362:11Jun87-27
Roy, A. The Islamic Syncretistic Traditon
in Bengal.*
  A. Asani, 318(JAOS):Apr/Jun85-363
Roy, C. L'Ami lointain.
  D. Coward, 617(TLS):27Nov-3Dec87-1333
Roy, C.D. Art and Life in Africa.
  W. Dewey, 2(AfrA):Nov85-14
Roy, G. La détresse et l'enchantement.*
  P.G. Socken, 102(CanL):Winter85-129
Roy, G. Garden in the Wind.
  L. McMullen, 296(JCF):No35/36-172
Roy, G.R. - see Burns, R.
Roy, J. Hobbes and Freud.
  J. Zwicky, 154:Summer86-367
Roy, L. Entre la lumière et l'ombre.
  J-L. Backès, 535(RHL):Jul-Aug86-802
  G. Merler, 102(CanL):Fall86-120
  J.M. Paterson, 627(UTQ):Fall86-206
Royce, A.P. Movement and Meaning.
  B. Rolfe, 615(TJ):May86-250
Royle, T. The Best Years of Their Lives.*
  P. Oakes, 617(TLS):23Jan87-89

Royot, D. & C. Colmanzo. Images des U.S.A.
  R.A. Day, 189(EA):Oct-Dec87-492
Rozas López, J.M. Lope de Vega y Felipe IV
en el "Ciclo de Senectute."
  A. Soons, 86(BHS):Apr86-166
Rozett, M.T. The Doctrine of Election and
the Emergence of Elizabethan Tragedy.*
  L.S. Champion, 179(ES):Aug86-370
  R.Y. Turner, 551(RenQ):Winter86-808
Rozman, G. Population and Marketing
Settlements in Ch'ing China.
  R.H. Myers, 302:Vol22No1-68
Rozzo, U., ed. Matteo Bandello, novelliere
europeo.
  W. Hirdt, 547(RF):Band98Heft3/4-463
Ruane, K. The Polish Challenge.
  C.G. Robertson, Jr., 497(PolR):Vol31
No4-322
Ruano de la Haza, J.M. - see Calderón de la
Barca, P.
Rubel, A.J., C.W. O'Nell & R. Collado-
Ardón. Susto, A Folk Illness.
  S.B. Thiederman, 650(WF):Oct86-300
Ruben, D-H. The Metaphysics of the Social
World.
  R. Fellows, 479(PhQ):Jan86-92
  S. James, 483:Jul86-421
Rubens, B. Our Father.
  H. Neill, 362:2Apr87-22
  M. Paley, 441:27Dec87-11
  L. Taylor, 617(TLS):27Mar87-319
Rubens, B. Set on Edge. Mate in Three.
  H. Neill, 362:2Apr87-22
Rubens, G. William Richard Lethaby.*
  D. Bowen, 324:Jun87-535
  P. Davey, 46:Nov86-115
Rubenstein, C. The Honey Tree Song.
  T. Wignesan, 293(JASt):Aug86-914
Rubenstein, J. - see Stuart, L.
Rubenstein, R.E. Alchemists of Revolution.
  S. Bakhash, 453(NYRB):24Sep87-12
  D. Fromkin, 441:28Jun87-22
Rubia Barcia, J. Mascarón de Proa.
  E. Lloréns Allen, 552(REH):May86-132
Rubin, B. Modern Dictators.
  B.D. Nossiter, 441:5Apr87-17
Rubin, B. Secrets of State.
  G.S. Smith, 529(QQ):Summer86-449
Rubin, D. After the Raj.
  L. Graver, 441:15Mar87-14
Rubin, J. Injurious to Public Morals.*
  R.L. Danly, 318(JAOS):Oct/Dec85-770
Rubin, L. Frank Stella Paintings 1958 to
1965.
  J. Golding, 617(TLS):27Mar87-311
Rubin, L.B. Quiet Rage.*
  G.P. Fletcher, 453(NYRB):23Apr87-22
  C. Sigal, 362:29Oct87-31
Rubin, L.D., Jr., ed. An Apple for My
Teacher.
  W. Lesser, 441:3May87-34
Rubin, L.D., Jr. and others, eds. The
History of Southern Literature.*
  G. Core, 639(VQR):Summer86-519
  J.K. Crane, 365:Winter86-69
  M.J. Friedman, 27(AL):Oct86-427
  B. Hitchcock, 392:Summer86-417
Rubin, L.D., Jr. & J.L. Idol, Jr. - see
Wolfe, T.
Rubin, M. Charity and Community in Medie-
val Cambridge.
  R.H. Hilton, 617(TLS):21Aug87-905

Rubino, C.A. & C.W. Shelmerdine, eds.
Approaches to Homer.*
  G.J. de Vries, 394:Vol39fasc3/4-469
Rubino, G. Gide.
  A-C. Faitrop, 535(RHL):Jan-Feb86-164
Rubinstein, A.Z. Soviet Policy Toward
Turkey, Iran, and Afghanistan.
  C.R. Saivetz, 550(RusR):Jul86-316
Rubio, M. & E. Waterson - see Montgomery,
L.M.
Rubio Fernández, L. Catálogo de los manu-
scritos clásicos latinos existentes en
España.
  R. Rouse, 123:Vol36No1-173
Rubio Vela, A. Epistolari de la València
medieval.
  G. Colón, 553(RLiR):Jul-Dec86-567
de Rubrouck, G. Guillaume de Rubrouck,
envoyé de saint Louis: Voyage dans
l'empire mongol. (C. & R. Kappler, eds &
trans)
  J. Richard, 554:Vol106No1-124
Rucker, R. Mind Tools.
  M. Gardner, 453(NYRB):3Dec87-34
  G. Johnson, 441:19Apr87-17
Ruckhäberle, H-J., ed. Bildung und Organ-
isation in den deutschen Handwerks-
gesellen- und Arbeitervereinen in der
Schweiz.
  C. Siegrist, 406:Winter86-532
Rudd, N. Themes in Roman Satire.
  A.J. Woodman, 617(TLS):6Mar87-253
Rudel-Tessier, J. Roquelune.
  R. Sarkonak, 102(CanL):Summer86-113
Ruderman, J. D.H. Lawrence and the
Devouring Mother.*
  D. Bradshaw, 402(MLR):Jan87-192
  E. Delavenay, 189(EA):Apr-Jun87-229
Rudnick, L.P. Mabel Dodge Luhan.*
  M. Atlas, 534(RALS):Spring-Autumn84-
  209
  T.H. Pauly, 651(WHR):Autumn86-279
Rudnik-Smalbraak, M. Samuel Richardson.
  I. Grundy, 566:Autumn86-9
  J. Harris, 402(MLR):Apr87-450
Rudrum, A. Henry Vaughan.
  P. Palmer, 677(YES):Vol16-247
Rudrum, A., with J. Drake-Brockman - see
Vaughan, T.
Rudwick, E. W.E.B. Du Bois.
  J.B. Moore, 577(SHR):Spring86-161
Rudwick, M.J.S. The Great Devonian Contro-
versy.*
  D.H., 185:Oct86-303
  R.A. Watson, 486:Dec86-610
Rudy, S. - see Jakobson, R.
Ruegg, D.S. The Literature of the Madhya-
maka School of Philosophy in India.
  R.A.F. Thurman, 318(JAOS):Apr/Jun85-
  380
Ruell, P. Death of a Dormouse.
  442(NY):9Nov87-156
Ruelle, P., ed. Le Dialogue des Créatures.
(C. Mansion, trans)
  G. Roques, 553(RLiR):Jul-Dec86-646
  A. Sakari, 439(NM):1986/3-456
  K. Varty, 208(FS):Oct86-449
Rueschemeyer, D. Power and the Division
of Labour.
  J.H., 185:Jul87-892
Rueschemeyer, M., I. Golomshtok & J.
Kennedy. Soviet Emigré Artists.*
  J.R. Stapanian, 550(RusR):Oct86-438

Ruffolo, L. Holidays.
  J. McCulloch, 441:10May87-20
Rufino, A. Verde America.
  L.A. Losito, 276:Winter86-405
Rugama, L. The Earth Is a Satellite of the
Moon.
  S. White, 448:Vol24No2-95
Ruggiero, G. The Boundaries of Eros.
  S. Chojnacki, 551(RenQ):Summer86-288
  S. Chojnacki, 560:Fall86-278
  R. Mackenney, 278(IS):Vol41-140
Ruggiers, P.G., ed. Editing Chaucer.*
  N.F. Blake, 402(MLR):Oct86-974
  A.I. Doyle, 589:Jul86-700
  G.R. Keiser, 301(JEGP):Apr86-251
  E.G. Stanley, 447(N&Q):Sep85-393
Ruh, K. & others, ed. Die deutsche Lit-
eratur des Mittelalters.* (2nd ed) (Vol
4)
  E.A. Philippson, 301(JEGP):Jul86-426
Ruhe, D.S. Door of Hope.
  M.M. Mazzaoui, 318(JAOS):Apr/Jun85-360
Ruhlen, M. A Guide to the World's Lan-
guages. (Vol 1)
  J.A.C. Greppin, 617(TLS):18-24Sep87-
  1029
Ruipérez, G. Die strukturelle Umschichtung
der Verwandtschaftsbezeichnungen im Deut-
schen.
  D. Karch, 133:Band18Heft4-349
Ruiperez, M.S. - see under Sanchez Rui-
perez, M.
Ruiz, C.P. - see under Pensado Ruiz, C.
Ruiz, E. - see Aragon, L.
Ruiz Silva, C. - see Miró, G.
Rule, A. Small Sacrifices.
  A. Jones, 441:14Jun87-32
Rule, J. Inland Passage and Other Sto-
ries.*
  N. Besner, 102(CanL):Fall86-139
Rule, J. This Is Not For You.
  J. O'Grady, 617(TLS):26Jun87-698
Rulfo, J. Pedro Páramo. (J.C. González
Boixo, ed)
  P.R. Beardsell, 86(BHS):Jul86-304
Rumelhart, D.E., J.L. McClelland & others.
Parallel Distributed Processing.
  J.G. Greeno, 441:4Jan87-28
  G. Sampson, 350:Dec87-871
  G. Sampson, 617(TLS):12Jun87-643
Rumens, C. Plato Park. Selected Poems.
  E. Feinstein, 617(TLS):20-26Nov87-1273
  P. Forbes, 362:26Mar87-32
Rummel, E. Erasmus as a Translator of the
Classics.
  E. Fantham, 627(UTQ):Fall86-85
  J.K. Sowards, 551(RenQ):Summer86-295
Rumsey, P.L. Acts of God and the People,
1620-1730.
  A.J. von Frank, 165(EAL):Fall87-223
Runte, H.R., J.K. Wikeley & A.J. Farrell.
The Seven Sages of Rome and the Book of
Sinbad.*
  M-A. Vetterling, 589:Jan86-251
Runyon, D. Romance in the Roaring Forties
and Other Stories.
  639(VQR):Summer86-92
Runzo, J. Reason, Relativism and God.*
  R.S., 185:Jul87-905
Ruoff, A. Mundarten in Baden-Württemberg.
  K. Rein, 685(ZDL):1/1986-91

317

Rupke, N.A., ed. Vivisection in Historical Perspective.
  A. Ryan, 362:20Aug87-19
Rusch, G. Die verhinderte Mitsprache.
  S. Brauner, 682(ZPSK):Band39Heft5-612
Rüsch, L. Ironie und Herrschaft.
  G.C. Avery, 406:Winter86-546
  A. Solbach, 680(ZDP):Band105Heft4-625
Rusch, R.D. Jazz Talk.
  G.L. Starks, Jr., 91:Spring86-187
Ruse, M. Darwinism Defended.
  L. Azar, 438:Spring86-232
Rush, C. A Resurrection of a Kind.
  K. McCarra, 571(ScLJ):Winter86-37
Rush, N. Whites.*
  T. De Pietro, 249(HudR):Autumn86-493
  J. Mellors, 364:Jun86-98
Rush, R., ed. The Building Systems Integration Handbook.
  F. Wilson, 505:May86-177
Rushdie, S. The Jaguar Smile.
  J. Le Moyne, 441:8Mar87-14
Rushdie, S. Midnight's Children.
  M. Porée, 98:May86-503
Rushmore, R. The Singing Voice. (2nd ed)
  L. Green, 465:Spring86-120
Rushton, J. Classical Music.
  R. Christiansen, 617(TLS):7Aug87-845
Rushton, J. The Musical Language of Berlioz.*
  J. Ellis, 411:Jul/Oct86-270
Rushton, W. Marylebone Versus the World!
  N. Andrew, 362:3Dec87-34
Rushton, W., ed. Spy Thatcher.
  D.J. Enright, 617(TLS):18-24Dec87-1399
Rusiecki, J. Adjectives and Comparison in English.*
  F. Chevillet, 189(EA):Jul-Sep86-329
  J. Milton, 349:Summer86-309
  F.R. Palmer, 257(IRAL):May86-175
  U. Teleman, 452(NJL):Vol9No1-97
Rüskamp, W. Dramaturgie ohne Publikum.
  E. Glass, 221(GQ):Fall86-646
Ruskin, J. The Literary Criticism of John Ruskin. (H. Bloom, ed)
  R. Hewison, 617(TLS):7Aug87-842
Ruspoli, M. The Cave of Lascaux.
  J. Russell, 441:31May87-11
Russell, A. - see "The Guinness Book of Records 1988"
Russell, B. The Collected Papers of Bertrand Russell.* (Vol 7: Theory of Knowledge.) (E.R. Eames, ed)
  A. Pavkovic, 63:Dec86-514
Russell, B. The Collected Papers of Bertrand Russell. (Vol 12) (R.A. Rempel, A. Brink & M. Moran, eds)
  483:Jan86-139
Russell, C. Letters of Conrad Russell 1897-1947. (G. Blakiston, ed)
  I. Colegate, 617(TLS):3Jul87-712
Russell, C. Poets, Prophets, and Revolutionaries.*
  M.B., 295(JML):Nov86-359
  M. Little, 405(MP):May87-454
  W. Sypher, 569(SR):Summer86-497
Russell, D.S. The Emblem and Device in France.
  L.K. Donaldson-Evans, 210(FrF):Sep86-369
  N. Kenny, 208(FS):Oct86-455

Russell, F., ed. Richard Rogers + Architects.*
  M. Pawley, 46:Jun86-79
Russell, F. Sacco & Vanzetti.
  42(AR):Fall86-490
Russell, J.B. Lucifer.
  A.E. Bernstein, 589:Oct86-994
  529(QQ):Winter86-949
Russell, J.B. Mephistopheles.
  A. Burgess, 61:Jan87-84
  R. Coles, 441:8Mar87-28
Russell, L.B. Is Prevention Better than Care?
  S.P., 185:Jan87-514
Russell, L.M., ed. Feminist Interpretation of the Bible.
  S. Jeffords, 577(SHR):Fall86-376
Russell, N. The Novelist and Mammon.*
  I. Williams, 637(VS):Summer87-557
  639(VQR):Autumn86-117
Russell, R. Generi poetici medievali.
  J. Leeker, 547(RF):Band98Heft1/2-218
Russell, R. - see Mayakovsky, V.V.
Russell, W. Stags and Hens.
  B. Grantham, 157:No159-47
"Russian-English/English-Russian Military Dictionary."*
  W.W. Derbyshire, 558(RLJ):Winter86-215
Russo, R. Mohawk.*
  D. Montrose, 617(TLS):6Mar87-246
Russo, V. Il romanzo teologico.
  R. Armour, 402(MLR):Jan86-216
  L. Cassata, 379(MedR):Apr86-143
Rust, W.J. Kennedy in Vietnam.
  639(VQR):Winter86-24
Rusticans, M. Antoninus Bassianus Caracalla. (J.W. Binns, ed)
  G. Schmitz, 72:Band223Heft2-409
Rustin, M. & M. Narratives of Love and Loss.
  N. Tucker, 362:31Dec87-21
Rustow, D.A. Turkey.
  A. Cowell, 441:18Oct87-26
Ruszkiewicz, P. Aspects of Reflexivization in English.
  E. Battistella, 350:Jun87-427
Ruta, S. Stalin in the Bronx.
  E. Pall, 441:29Nov87-10
Rutelli, R. Dialoghi con il testo.
  M. Bacigalupo, 402(MLR):Apr87-501
Rutherford, A. - see Kipling, R.
Rutherford, W.E., ed. Language Universals and Second Language Acquisition.
  H. Burmeister, 603:Vol10No2-547
  G. Thurgood, 351(LL):Sep86-391
Rutherfurd, E. Sarum.
  M. Quilligan, 441:13Sep87-14
Ruthven, K.K. Feminist Literary Studies.*
  P. Barry, 175:Spring86-89
  J. Simons, 541(RES):Aug86-452
Rutland, R.A. James Madison.
  A. Todd, 441:4Oct87-20
Rutland, R.A. & others - see Madison, J.
Rutten, C. & A. Motte, eds. Aristotelica.
  J. Barnes, 520:Vol31No1-97
Rutter, C.C., ed. Documents of the Rose Playhouse.
  R.A. Foakes, 570(SQ):Summer86-275
  R. Gair, 539:Spring87-187
  W. Habicht, 156(ShJW):Jahrbuch1986-220
  P. Hollindale, 541(RES):Aug86-412
Rutter, O. The Pagans of North Borneo.
  617(TLS):30Jan87-120

Ryals, C.D.   Becoming Browning.*
P. Drew, 402(MLR):Jul87-710
Ryan, A.   Property and Political Theory.*
O. O'Neill, 262:Sep86-383
Ryan, E.B. & H. Giles, eds.   Attitudes
towards Language Variation.
R.L. Cooper, 355(LSoc):Jun86-262
Ryan, E.E.   Aristotle's Theory of Rhetori-
cal Argumentation.
J. Brunning, 627(UTQ):Fall86-83
J.D. Moss, 543:Dec86-395
Ryan, J.   The Uncompleted Past.*
G.B. Pickar, 301(JEGP):Jul86-435
Ryan, M.   Marxism and Deconstruction.*
T. Eagleton, 567:Vol63No3/4-351
K. Hart, 381:Mar86-107
I.E. Harvey, 480(P&R):Vol19No3-201
Rybakken, R. & H. Silver - see de Maupas-
sant, G.
Ryberg, A.   Per Wästbergs skrifter 1973-
1983.
J.E. Bellquist, 563(SS):Autumn86-449
Rychner, J.   Du Saint Alexis à François
Villon.
G. Roques, 553(RLiR):Jan-Jun86-191
Rychner, J. & A. Henry - see Villon, F.
Rydel, C., ed.   The Ardis Anthology of
Russian Romanticism.
L.G. Leighton, 574(SEEJ):Spring86-110
Rydén, M.   The English Plant Names in "The
Grete Herball" (1526).*
G. Bourcier, 189(EA):Jul-Sep86-332
Ryder, F.G. & E.A. McCormick.   Lebendige
Literatur.
S. Olsen, 399(MLJ):Autumn86-316
Rykwert, J. & A.   Robert and James Adam.*
(British title: The Brothers Adam.)
H. Colvin, 46:Jan86-80
T.R. Matthews, 505:Jun86-66
N. Powell, 39:Jun86-439
A. Rowan, 90:Aug86-613
Ryle, M.   Martin Ryle's Letter.   (M. Rowan-
Robinson, ed)
P. Lewis, 565:Summer86-57
Rylko, H.M., ed.   Artifical Intelligence.
R.D. Rodman & D. Kirks, 350:Jun87-456
Rzhevsky, N.   Russian Literature and Ideol-
ogy.*
A. Gleason, 550(RusR):Apr86-227

Saalbach, M.   Spanisches Gegenwartstheater.
R.D. Pope, 240(HR):Spring86-235
Saarikoski, P.   Pentti Saaikoski Poems -
1958-1980.
K.O. Dana, 563(SS):Autumn86-452
Saavedra, M.D. - see under de Cervantes
Saavedra, M.
Saba, G. - see de Viau, T.
Saba, U.   Ernesto.
G. Krist, 441:6Sep87-16
Sabar, Y.   Sefer Be-reꜣshit ha-Aramit
Hadashah be-Nivam shel Yehude Zaꜣkho
(The Book of Genesis in Neo-Aramaic in
the Dialect of the Jewish Community of
Zakho).
R.D. Hoberman, 318(JAOS):Oct/Dec85-734
Sable, B.K.   The Vocal Sound.
L. Halsey, 289:Summer86-114
Sablich, S.   Busoni.
J. Budden, 415:Oct86-563
Sablovsky, I., ed.   What They Heard.
W. Mellers, 617(TLS):9Jan87-39

Sabol, A.J., ed.   Four Hundred Songs and
Dances from the Stuart Masque.
D. Fuller, 161(DUJ):Dec85-191
F.W. Sternfeld, 447(N&Q):Dec85-526
Sabor, P. - see Cleland, J.
Sabor de Cortázar, C. - see de Vega Carpio,
L.
Sacco, G., ed.   Iscrizioni Greche d'Italia:
Porto.
A.G. Woodhead, 303(JoHS):Vol106-262
Sacerio-Gari, E. & E. Rodriguez Monegal -
see Borges, J.L.
Sachar, H.M.   Diaspora.
B. Levine, 287:Jan86-23
Sachar, H.M.   A History of Israel.   (Vol 2)
W. Reich, 441:26Jul87-13
Sachs, H.   Music in Fascist Italy.
J. Rosselli, 617(TLS):30Oct-5Nov87-1187
Sack, V.   Die Inkunabeln der Universitäts-
bibliothek und anderer öffentlicher
Sammlungen in Freiberg im Breisgau und
Umgebung.*
P. Needham, 517(PBSA):Vol80No4-500
Sacken, J.P.   "A Certain Slant of Light."
L. Westling, 395(MFS):Summer86-272
Sackett, T.A.   Galdós y las máscaras.
M. Schinas, 552(REH):Jan86-138
Sacks, O.   The Man Who Mistook His Wife
for His Hat and Other Clinical Tales.*
639(VQR):Summer86-102
Sacks, P.   In These Mountains.
P. Stitt, 219(GaR):Winter86-1021
639(VQR):Autumn86-133
Sacks, P.M.   The English Elegy.*
C.S. Hunter, 604:Winter86-6
G.W. Pigman 3d, 551(RenQ):Autumn86-
558
Sackville-West, V.   No Signposts in the
Sea.
T.C. Holyoke, 42(AR):Winter86-119
Sackville-West, V. & V. Woolf.   Correspon-
dance.
F. de Martinoir, 450(NRF):Jul-Aug86-186
Sacoto, A.   La nueva novela ecuatoriana.
A.J. Vetrano, 238:Sep86-559
Sacristán, C.H. - see under Hernández
Sacristán, C.
no Sadaie, F. - see under Fujiwara no
Sadaie
Sadat, J.   A Woman of Egypt.
B. Slavin, 441:30Aug87-15
A. Soueif, 617(TLS):23-29Oct87-1159
Saddlemyer, A. - see Synge, J.M.
Sadie, S., ed.   The New Grove Dictionary of
Musical Instruments.*
A. Baines, 410(M&L):Jul86-292
Sadie, S. & A. Latham, eds.   The Cambridge
Music Guide.
W. Sutton, 415:Dec86-692
Sadie, S. & F. Smart - see Mozart, W.A. &
others
Sadiq, M.   A History of Urdu Literature.
(2nd ed)
F.W. Pritchett, 293(JASt):Nov85-182
Sadlier, D.J.   Imagery and Theme in the
Poetry of Cecília Meireles.*
J. Parker, 86(BHS):Jul86-305
K.A. Stackhouse, 238:May86-324
Sadlier, D.J.   Cecília Meireles & João
Alphonsus.
K.A. Stackhouse, 238:Sep86-562
Saférys, F.   La Suggestopédie.   (new ed)
A. Prévos, 207(FR):Apr87-734

319

Salerno, L. La natura morta italiana 1560–1895/Still Life Painting in Italy.
    L. Vertova, 39:Jan86–67
    C.W., 90:Jan86–48
Sales, H. Os Pareceres do tempo.
    D. Patai, 238:May86–323
Salgado, F.M. – see under Maillo Salgado, F.
Salgado, G. "King Lear."*
    T. Minter, 157:No160–50
Saller, R.P. Personal Patronage under the Early Empire.
    J.H. D'Arms, 122:Jan86–95
Salles, J–F. Kition-Bamboula. (Vol 2)
    V. Tatton-Brown, 303(JoHS):Vol106–246
Salmānī, U.M. My Memories of Bahā°u'llāh.
    M.M. Mazzaoui, 318(JAOS):Apr/Jun85–360
Salmen, W., ed. The Social Status of the Professional Musician from the Middle Ages to the 19th Century.
    M.S. Keller, 317:Spring86–199
Salmon, E. – see Granville-Barker, H.G.
Salmon, J.B. Wealthy Corinth.*
    J.G. Pedley, 124:Jan–Feb87–224
Salmon, J.H.M. Renaissance and Revolt.
    J. Powis, 617(TLS):20–26Nov87–1268
Salmon, M. Women and the Law of Property in Early America.
    L. Handlin, 432(NEQ):Dec86–577
Salmons, J. & W. Moretti, eds. The Renaissance in Ferrara and its European Horizons.
    P. Burke, 208(FS):Jan86–65
    R. Catani, 278(IS):Vol41–143
    J.E. Everson, 402(MLR):Apr87–489
Salomon, B. Critical Analyses in English Renaissance Drama.
    B. Cohen-Stratyner, 615(TJ):Dec86–496
Salomon, H.P. Os primeiros portugueses de Amesterdão.
    T. Oelman, 86(BHS):Jul86–299
Salsano, F. Personaggi della "Divina Commedia."
    M. Marti, 228(GSLI):Vol163fasc522–266
Salska, A. Walt Whitman and Emily Dickinson.
    J. Loving, 183(ESQ):Vol32No3–201
Salt, B. Film Style and Technology.
    T. Elsaesser, 707:Autumn86–246
Salter, D., ed. New Canadian Drama 3.
    G. Anthony, 102(CanL):Spring86–186
Salter, E. Fourteenth-Century English Poetry.* (D. Pearsall & N. Zeeman, eds)
    J.C. Hirsh, 382(MAE):1986/2–291
    S.S. Hussey, 402(MLR):Apr87–437
    G. Schmitz, 38:Band104Heft3/4–484
Salter, M.J. Henry Purcell in Japan.*
    D. Shea, 577(SHR):Fall86–392
Saltykov-Shchedrin, M.E. The Pompadours.*
    T.H. Hoisington, 574(SEEJ):Summer86–288
Saltzman, A.M. The Fiction of William Gass.
    N. French, 395(MFS):Summer86–287
    B.K. Horvath, 27(AL):Dec86–666
    P.B. McElwain, 590:Dec86–116
    S. Moore, 532(RCF):Summer86–152
    P.T.S., 295(JML):Nov86–478
Salusinszky, I. Criticism in Society.
    C. Baldick, 617(TLS):6–12Nov87–1217
    362:13Aug87–23
Salutin, R. Marginal Notes.*
    J. Kertzer, 627(UTQ):Fall86–154

Salvador, G. Semántica y lexicología del español.
    Y. Malkiel, 545(RPh):Feb87–397
Salverda, R. Leading Conceptions in Linguistic Theory.
    J.G. Kooij, 204(FdL):Mar86–76
Salwak, D., ed. The Life and Work of Barbara Pym.
    N. Shulman, 617(TLS):25–31Dec87–1420
Salzman, M. Iron and Silk.
    D. Davin, 617(TLS):3Jul87–711
    R. Selzer, 441:1Feb87–9
Salzman, P. English Prose Fiction, 1558–1700.*
    J.J. O'Connor, 551(RenQ):Spring86–130
    H.R. Woudhuysen, 617(TLS):6Mar87–247
Sambin, G. – see Martin-Löf, P.
Sambrook, J. The Eighteenth Century.
    A. Morvan, 189(EA):Jul–Sep87–352
Sambrook, J. – see Thomson, J.
Sambucus, J. Emblemata.
    G. van de Louw, 549(RLC):Oct–Dec86–472
Sambursky, S., ed & trans. The Concept of Place in Late Neoplatonism.
    R. Brague, 192(EP):Jul–Sep86–420
Sammons, J.L. Wilhelm Raabe.
    G.P. Butler, 617(TLS):9–15Oct87–1098
Sampson, A. Black and Gold.
    A. Cowell, 441:24May87–11
    S. Jenkins, 617(TLS):3Apr87–343
    J.E. Spence, 362:19Feb87–21
    L. Thompson, 453(NYRB):11Jun87–20
Sampson, A. & S., ed. The Oxford Book of Ages.*
    639(VQR):Spring86–63
Sampson, G. Schools of Linguistics.
    A.S. Kaye, 603:Vol10No1–187
    Y. Tobin, 361:Jan86–99
Sams, E., ed. Shakespeare's Lost Play: Edmund Ironside.*
    E.A.J. Honigmann, 453(NYRB):12Feb87–23
    G. Monsarrat, 189(EA):Apr–Jun87–203
Sams, F. The Widow's Mite.
    S. Hearon, 441:13Dec87–7
Samson, J. Chennault.
    R. Schaffer, 441:29Nov87–21
Samson, J. The Music of Chopin.*
    42(AR):Fall86–491
Samuel, A.E. From Athens to Alexandria.
    P.M. Fraser, 487:Spring86–100
Samuel, H.E. The Cantata in Nuremburg during the Seventeenth Century.
    M.R. Wade, 221(GQ):Winter86–170
Samuel, R., E. MacColl & S. Cosgrove. Theatres of the Left 1880–1935.
    J. Allen, 611(TN):Vol40No3–143
    T.A. Greenfield, 130:Spring86–93
    B. McConachie, 615(TJ):Dec86–502
Samuelian, T.J. & M.E. Stone, eds. Medieval Armenian Culture.
    J.A.C. Greppin, 318(JAOS):Oct/Dec85–738
Samuels, E., with J.N. Samuels. Bernard Berenson: The Making of a Legend.
    R. Dinnage, 453(NYRB):8Oct87–3
    F. Haskell, 617(TLS):5Jun87–595
    J. Updike, 441:29Mar87–1
Samuels, S.W., ed. The Environment of the Workplace and Human Values.
    D.C., 185:Jul87–903
Samuelson, A. With Hemingway.*
    A. Josephs, 587(SAF):Spring86–119
Sánchez, A.P. – see under Pérez Sánchez, A.

321

Sánchez, C.R. - see under Ramírez Sánchez, C.

Sánchez, J.M. The Spanish Civil War as a Religious Tragedy.
   J.S. Amelang, 441:11Oct87-57

Sánchez, M.E. Contemporary Chicana Poetry.
   N.S. Grabo, 27(AL):Oct86-473
   L. Torres, 649(WAL):Feb87-378

Sánchez-Rojas Fenoll, M.D. El escultor Nicolás de Bussy.
   M. Estella, 48:Jul-Sep86-347

Sanchez Ruiperez, M. Structure du système des aspects et des temps du verbe en grec ancien.
   P. Monteil, 555:Vol59fasc2-273

Sancho, M.P.C. - see under Cuartero Sancho, M.P.

Sand, G. Correspondance. (Vol 18) (G. Lubin, ed)
   L.J. Austin, 208(FS):Jan86-87
   J. Gaulmier, 535(RHL):Mar-Apr86-306

Sand, G. Correspondance. (Vol 19) (G. Lubin, ed)
   L.J. Austin, 208(FS):Jan86-87

Sand, G. Indiana. (B. Didier, ed)
   L.J. Austin, 208(FS):Jan86-87

"George Sand."
   M. Bossis, 535(RHL):Mar-Apr86-304

"The George Sand Papers." [Conference Proceedings, 1978]
   L.J. Austin, 208(FS):Jan86-87

Sanday, P.R. Divine Hunger.
   D. Gewertz, 441:3May87-39

Sandbach, F.H. Aristotle and the Stoics.*
   B. Inwood, 482(PhR):Jul86-470

Sandberg, B. Untersuchungen zur Graphematik und Phonemik eines Tiroler Autographs aus dem Ende des 15. Jahrhunderts.
   G. Kettmann, 682(ZPSK):Band39Heft3-395

Sandel, C. The Silken Thread.
   N. Lawson, 617(TLS):20Feb87-196

Sanders, A., comp. Walter Legge.
   M. Walker, 415:Jun86-339

Sanders, J.T. The Jews in Luke-Acts.
   J.L. Houlden, 617(TLS):6-12Nov87-1232

Sanders, N. - see Shakespeare, W.

Sanders, S.R. The Paradise of Bombs.
   K.R. Stafford, 441:24May87-13

Sanders, S.R. Wilderness Plots.
   P. Lehmberg, 649(WAL):Aug86-156

Sanders, S.R. & J.A. Wolin. Stone Country.
   42(AR):Spring86-249

Sanderson, M. Educational Opportunities and Social Change in England.
   A. Wooldridge, 617(TLS):4-10Dec87-1341

Sanderson, M. From Irving to Olivier.
   J. Beryl, 615(TJ):May86-238

Sandison, A. - see Kipling, R.

Sandler, K.W. & S. Whitebook. Tour de grammaire II. (2nd ed)
   K.A. Gordon, 399(MLJ):Spring86-66

Sandler, L.F. Gothic Manuscripts, 1285-1385.
   C. de Hamel, 617(TLS):3Jul87-726

Sandler, R. - see Frye, N.

Sandmann, A.J. Wortbildung im heutigen brasilianischen Portugiesisch.
   H. Kröll, 547(RF):Band98Heft3/4-414

Sandøy, H. Norsk dialektkunnskap.
   E. Haugen, 355(LSoc):Sep86-420
   A. Liberman, 563(SS):Spring86-192

Sandqvist, S., ed. La mort du roi Souvain.
   G. Roques, 553(RLiR):Jul-Dec86-643

Sandqvist, S. Notes textuelles sur le "Roman de Tristan" de Béroul.*
   D. Beyerle, 547(RF):Band98Heft3/4-421
   M.R. Blakeslee, 589:Jan86-202
   S. Gregory, 382(MAE):1986/2-310
   L. Löfstedt, 439(NM):1986/4-605
   P.S. Noble, 208(FS):Apr86-189
   I. Short, 402(MLR):Jul87-732

Sandqvist, S., ed. Trois contes français du XIVe siècle tirés du recueil intitulé "Le tombel de Chartrose."*
   G. Hasenohr, 554:Vol105No4-578

Sandusky, M.C. America's Parallel.
   Hakjoon Kim, 293(JASt):May86-618

Sandved, A.O. Introduction to Chaucerian English.
   N. Davis, 541(RES):Nov86-551
   R. Lass, 439(NM):1986/4-599

Sandweiss, M.A. Laura Gilpin.
   L. Milazzo, 584(SWR):Spring86-257

"San Francisco Museum of Modern Art: The Painting and Sculpture Collection."
   J. Burr, 39:Jan86-62

"Sangen om Bjovulf." (A. Haarder, trans)
   B. Morris, 617(TLS):6Feb87-140

Sangster, C. The St. Lawrence and the Saguenay and Other Poems.* (rev) (F.M. Tierney, ed)
   L. Boone, 102(CanL):Fall86-128
   W.J. Keith, 168(ECW):Fall86-175

Sangster, J. Snowball.
   N. Callendar, 441:4Jan87-35

Sangsue, D. - see Nodier, C.

Sanguineti, E. - see Guinizzelli, G.

San Juan, E. Toward a People's Literature.
   S. Evangelista, 293(JASt):Feb86-466

Sansone, G.E., ed. La poesia dell'antica Provenza. (Vol 2)
   D. Rieger, 547(RF):Band98Heft3/4-420

Santamaria, B.A. Daniel Mannix.
   J. McCalman, 381:Mar86-69

Santangelo, G. Dante e la Sicilia e altre "letture" e note dantesche.
   M. Marti, 228(GSLI):Vol163fasc522-286

Santangelo, G.S. Madame Dacier, una filologa nella "Crisi" (1672-1720).
   B. Tocanne, 535(RHL):Jul-Aug86-751

Santangelo, G.S. L'officina delle ombre.
   E. Chevallier, 549(RLC):Jul-Sep86-358

Santayana, G. Persons and Places. (W.G. Holzberger & H.J. Saatkamp, Jr.)
   B. Kuklick, 441:26Apr87-27

Santí, E.M. Pablo Neruda.*
   R.O. Salmon, 552(REH):May86-123

Santi, G. La Vita e le Geste di Federico di Montefeltro, Duca d'Urbino. (L. Michelini Tocci, ed)
   C.H. Clough, 90:May86-359
   M. Pozzi, 228(GSLI):Vol163fasc523-452

de Santiago y Palomares, F.J. Selected Writings, 1776-95. (D.P. Seniff, ed)
   P. Deacon, 402(MLR):Jan87-224

Marqués de Santillana - see under López de Mendoza, I.

Santini, C. La cognizione del passato in Silio Italico.
   P. Jal, 555:Vol59fasc2-321

Santini, L.R. - see Ohly, F.

Santirocco, M. Unity and Design in Horace's Odes.
S.F. Wiltshire, 124:Jan-Feb87-215
Santob de Carrión. Proverbios morales. (T.A. Perry, ed)
J. Joset, 304(JHP):Winter86-171
Santoro, F.S. Antonello e l'Europa.
N. Penny, 617(TLS):27Mar87-332
Santoro, M. La stampa a Napoli nel Quattrocento.
D.E. Rhodes, 354:Mar86-76
Santos Torroella, R. La miel es más dulce que la sangre.
M. Laffranque, 92(BH):Jan-Jun85-219
Sanz, A.G. & M-T. Ferrer i Mallol - see under Garcia i Sanz, A. & M-T. Ferrer i Mallol
Sanz Guerrero, M.J. Antiguos dibujos de la platería sevillana.
D. Angulo Iñiguez, 48:Oct-Dec86-425
Sapieha, A. Podróże w krajach Słowiańskich odbywane.
H. Leeming, 575(SEER):Jul86-469
Sapir, E. Selected Writings in Language, Culture, and Personality. (D.G. Mandelbaum, ed)
617(TLS):10Apr87-397
Sapir, R.B. Quest.
N. Callendar, 441:27Sep87-27
Sarah, R. Anyone Skating on that Middle Ground.
N. Zacharin, 526:Summer86-100
Saramago, J. Baltasar and Blimunda.
I. Howe, 441:1Nov87-7
Saratinovska, N. & C. Wukasch. A Macedonian Reader/Makedonski Četiva.
K.E. Naylor, 574(SEEJ):Spring86-135
Sareil, J. L'Ecriture comique.
W. Redfern, 402(MLR):Apr86-473
Sargent, M. & J. Hogg, eds. The "Chartae" of the Carthusian General Chapter; Aula Dei: The Egen "Manuale" from the Charterhouse of Buxheim; Oxford: Bodleian Library MS. Rawlinson D.318.
R.B. Marks, 589:Apr86-506
Sargent, P. The Shore of Women.
G. Jonas, 441:18Jan87-33
Sarkissian, J. Catullus 68.
D.F. Bright, 394:Vol39fasc3/4-509
Sarkonak, R., ed. The Language of Difference.*
A.L. Amprimoz, 345:Nov86-502
Sarkonak, R. Claude Simon.
D.Y. Kadish, 268(IFR):Summer87-116
Saro-Wiwa, K. Songs in a Time of War.
J.F. Povey, 2(AfrA):May86-78
Sarraute, N. Childhood.*
V. Minogue, 402(MLR):Jan86-215
Sarraute, N. Do You Hear Them?
S.M. Bell, 402(MLR):Jan87-209
Sarraute, N. Martereau.
S.M. Bell, 402(MLR):Jan87-209
Sartor, M. La cittá e la conquista.
C.L. Joost-Gaugier, 54:Sep86-502
Sartor, M. & F. Ursini. Cent'anni di emigrazione.
G.M. Zilio, 545(RPh):Nov86-244
Sartorio, A. L'Orfeo.
B.L. Glixon, 143:Issue39-74
Sartre, J-P. The Family Idiot. (Vol 2)
S. Bann, 617(TLS):27Nov-3Dec87-1333
N. Bliven, 442(NY):22Jun87-94

Sartre, J-P. Lettres au Castor et à quelques autres.
M. Crouzet, 560:Fall86-292
Sartre, J-P. Les Mains sales. (W.D. Redfern, ed)
T. Keefe, 208(FS):Oct86-490
H.W. Wardman, 402(MLR):Oct87-982
Sass, E.K. Lykkens Tempel.
C. Stevenson, 90:Sep86-682
Sassoon, S. Diaries 1923-1925. (R. Hart-Davis, ed)
M. Thorpe, 179(ES):Oct86-459
Sassoon, S. Letters to Max Beerbohm from Siegfried Sassoon. (R. Hart-Davis, ed)
P. Parker, 364:Oct86-105
Satta, S. The Day of Judgment.
J. Barnes, 441:4Oct87-13
P.N. Furbank, 617(TLS):28Aug87-930
G. Steiner, 442(NY):19Oct87-115
Sattelmeyer, R. & J.D. Crowley, eds. One Hundred Years of "Huckleberry Finn."*
E. Emerson, 579(SAQ):Autumn86-394
R.B. Hauck, 395(MFS):Summer86-255
M. Oriard, 594:Spring86-104
J. Seelye, 26(ALR):Winter87-85
C.L. Sonnichsen, 649(WAL):May86-78
Sauer, H., ed. Theodulfi Capitula in England.
D.N. Dumville, 72:Band223Heft2-388
Sauer, H., ed & trans. The Owl and the Nightingale.*
D. Mehl, 72:Band223Heft2-470
Sauer, L. Marionetten, Maschinen, Automaten.*
L.R. Furst, 52:Band21Heft3-323
T. Ziolkowski, 131(CL):Summer86-301
Sauer, W. Österreichische Philosophie zwischen Aufklärung und Restauration.
R. Langthaler, 687:Jul-Sep86-435
R. Malter, 342:Band77Heft1-128
Sauerberg, L.O. Secret Agents in Fiction.
E.S. Lauterbach, 395(MFS):Summer86-364
Sauermann, E. Zur Datierung und Interpretation von Texten Georg Trakls.
R. Detsch, 564:May86-179
Saul, J.R. The Next Best Thing.*
S. Scobie, 376:Jun86-120
Saul, N. Scenes from Provincial Life.
J.R. Maddicott, 617(TLS):27Feb87-219
Saulnier, L. & N. Stratford. La sculpture oubliée de Vézelay.*
I.H. Forsyth, 589:Apr86-457
Saunders, B. Contemporary German Autobiography.
K. Bullivant, 402(MLR):Apr87-529
Saunders, C.R. & K.J. Fielding - see Carlyle, T. & J.W.
Saunders, D. The Ukrainian Impact on Russian Culture, 1750-1850.
L. Hughes, 575(SEER):Oct86-610
Saunders, E.D. Mudra.
B.G., 90:Apr86-304
Saunders, F.W. Ellen Axson Wilson.
B. Brandon, 9(AlaR):Jul86-236
Saunders, J.W. A Biographical Dictionary of Renaissance Poets and Dramatists, 1520-1650.
M. Hattaway, 541(RES):Feb86-83
Saunders, R. Ambrose Bierce.
A. Frietzsche, 649(WAL):May86-77
M. Rohrberger, 395(MFS):Summer86-260

Sauneron, S. Villes et Légendes D'Égypte. (2nd ed)
    R.S. Bianchi, 318(JAOS):Oct/Dec85-727
Saurín de la Iglesia, M.R. Reforma y reacción en la Galicia del Siglo XVIII, 1764-1798.
    J. Harrison, 86(BHS):Oct86-389
Savage, H., Jr. & E.J. André and François Michaux.
    R. Desmond, 617(TLS):14Aug87-885
    A. Huxley, 441:9Aug87-22
Savage, V.B. Western Impressions of Nature and Landscape in Southeast Asia.
    R.D. Hill, 293(JASt):Aug86-915
Savan, G. White Palace.
    M. Wolitzer, 441:13Sep87-18
Savard-Boulanger, S. - see Harvey, J-C.
Savarese, G. "Il Furioso" e la Cultura del Rinascimento.
    J.E. Everson, 402(MLR):Oct86-1013
Savary, C., ed. Les Rapports culturels entre le Québec et les Etats-Unis.
    B-Z. Shek, 627(UTQ):Fall86-235
Savary, C. & C. Panaccio, eds. L'idéologie et les stratégies de la raison.*
    H. Aronovitch, 154:Summer86-327
Savater, F. Instrucciones para olvidar et "Quijote," y otros ensayos generales.
    T. Mermall, 240(HR):Autumn86-462
"Roelant Savery in seiner Zeit (1576-1639)."
    T.D. Kaufmann, 600:Vol16No4-249
von Savigny, F.C. & S.A. Winkelmann. Der Briefwechsel zwischen Friedrich Carl von Savigny und Stephan August Winkelmann (1800-1804). (I. Schnack, ed)
    I.B. Jonas, 221(GQ):Spring86-317
Savigny, J-B.H. & A. Corréard. Narrative of a Voyage to Senegal.
    S. Callahan, 441:1Feb87-31
Saville, A. The Test of Time.
    A. Reix, 542:Apr-Jun86-269
Savoie, P. A la façon d'un charpentier.
    K. Meadwell, 102(CanL):Winter85-158
Savona, J.L. Jean Genet.*
    U. Chaudhuri, 397(MD):Dec86-629
    E. Jacquart, 535(RHL):Jul-Aug86-797
    J.G. Miller, 210(FrF):May86-251
Savory, J. & P. Marks. The Smiling Muse.*
    M. Reger, 635(VPR):Fall86-115
Savory, R.M. & D.A. Agius, eds. Logos Islamikos.
    J. Corbett, 627(UTQ):Fall86-89
Savy, N. & G. Rosa - see Hugo, V.
Sawyer, J. & D. Clines, eds. Midian, Moab and Edom.
    R.H. Dornemann, 318(JAOS):Oct/Dec85-796
Sawyer, P.L. Ruskin's Poetic Argument.*
    W.S. Johnson, 191(ELN):Dec86-76
    N. Vance, 529(QQ):Spring86-199
    639(VQR):Summer86-88
Saxby, N. - see De' Mantelli di Canobio detto Tartaglia, G.
El-Sayed, R. La Déesse Neith de Saïs.
    R.S. Bianchi, 318(JAOS):Jan/Mar85-139
Sayen, J. Einstein in America.
    S.J. Whitfield, 579(SAQ):Autumn86-388
Sayer, C. Costumes of Mexico.
    J.C. Berlo, 2(AfrA):Feb86-26

Sayers, J.E. Papal Government and England During the Pontificate of Honorius III (1216-1227).
    J.H. Lynch, 377:Jul86-142
Sayers, S. Reality and Reason.*
    M.J. Inwood, 393(Mind):Apr86-265
    D. Knowles, 518:Jul86-167
Sayers, V. Due East.
    J. Butler, 441:8Mar87-9
Sayles, J. Thinking in Pictures.
    C. James, 441:29Nov87-21
Sayre, H.M. The Visual Text of William Carlos Williams.*
    M. Dickie, 402(MLR):Oct87-944
    T. Whalen, 106:Winter86-495
Sayre, K.M. Plato's Late Ontology.*
    R. Bolton, 41:Fall85-328
    W. Prior, 53(AGP):Band68Heft3-292
Sayre, R.F. - see Thoreau, H.D.
Scaffai, M. - see Baebius Italicus
Scaglione, A., ed. The Emergence of National Languages.*
    S.N. Dworkin, 320(CJL):Winter86-365
    G. Price, 402(MLR):Oct86-957
Scalamandrè, R. Guy Lavaud.
    A. Fongaro, 535(RHL):Nov-Dec86-1139
    R. Pouilliart, 356(LR):May86-183
Scalapino, L. that they were at the beach - aeolotropic series.*
    B. Hollander, 138:No9-269
    M. Jarman, 249(HudR):Summer86-334
Scalapino, R.A. & J. Wanandi, eds. Economic, Political and Security Issues in Southeast Asia in the 1980s.
    R.S. Milne, 302:Vol22No1-115
Scales, J.I. & R. Nickson. Cause at Heart.
    W. Herrick, 441:12Jul87-26
Scalise, S. Generative Morphology.
    M.C. Jacobs, 399(MLJ):Spring86-72
Scanlan, J.P. Marxism in the USSR.*
    639(VQR):Winter86-24
Scanlon, P.A., ed. Stories from Central and Southern Africa.*
    A. Roscoe, 538(RAL):Fall86-413
Scanlon, T.F. Greek and Roman Athletics.
    H.D. Evjen, 121(CJ):Feb-Mar87-268
Scannell, V. Argument of Kings.
    G. Mangan, 617(TLS):16-22Oct87-1132
    R. Mayne, 176:Nov87-56
Scannell, V. Funeral Games.
    G. Mangan, 617(TLS):16-22Oct87-1132
    J. Mole, 176:Jul/Aug87-50
Scannell, V., ed. Sporting Literature.
    G. Ewart, 617(TLS):10Apr87-388
di Scanno, T. La Vision du monde de Le Clézio.
    A. Blümel, 535(RHL):Mar-Apr86-349
Scarborough, J., ed. Symposium on Byzantine Medicine.
    M. Angold, 617(TLS):30Jan87-118
Scarf, M. Intimate Partners.
    C. Tavris, 441:1Mar87-15
Scarlatti, A. The Operas of Alessandro Scarlatti. (Vol 8: Tigrane.) (M. Collins, ed)
    T. Griffin, 317:Spring86-186
von Scarpatetti, B.M. Die Handschriften der Stiftsbibliothek St. Gallen.
    K. Schneider, 684(ZDA):Band115Heft3-103
Scarpellini, P. Perugino, l'opera completa.
    M. Bury, 90:Oct86-750

325

Schele, L. & M.E. Miller. The Blood of
Kings.*
    V. Fraser, 90:Nov86-826
    O. Paz, 453(NYRB):26Feb87-3
Scheler, M. Shakespeares Englisch.*
    H. Reinhold, 402(MLR):Oct86-984
Schell, E. Strangers and Pilgrims.
    D.W. Robertson, Jr., 570(SQ):Spring86-
    139
Schelle, H., ed. Christoph Martin Wie-
land.*
    W. Albrecht, 654(WB):3/1986-523
    W. Paulsen, 222(GR):Summer86-117
    A.E. Ratz, 564:Nov86-329
Schellens, P.J. Redelijke argumenten.
    A. Braet, 204(FdL):Jun86-143
Schelling, F.W.J. Bruno or On the Natural
and the Divine Principle of Things
(1802). (M.G. Vater, ed & trans)
    A.A. Kuzniar, 221(GQ):Winter86-116
Schelling, F.W.J. Contribution à l'his-
toire de la philosophie moderne. (J-F.
Marquet, ed & trans)
    A.A. Azar, 98:Oct86-981
Schelling, F.W.J. Über das Verhältnis der
bildenden Künste zu der Natur.* (L.
Sziborsky, ed)
    P. David, 192(EP):Apr-Jun86-270
Schemann, H. Die portugiesischen Verbal-
periphrasen.*
    W. Dietrich, 72:Band223Heft1-196
Schemann, H. & L. Schemann-Dias. Die
portugiesischen Verbalperiphrasen und
ihre deutschen Entsprechungen.*
    W. Dietrich, 72:Band223Heft1-196
Schenk, P. Die Gestalt des Turnus in
Vergils "Aeneis."
    S.J. Harrison, 123:Vol36No1-40
Schenkar, J. Signs of Life. (J. Miles,
ed)
    V.M. Patraka, 385(MQR):Winter87-285
Schenkel, M. Lessings Poetik des Mitleids
im bürgerlichen Trauerspiel "Miss Sara
Sampson."
    E. Glass, 221(GQ):Summer86-479
Schenkluhn, W. Ordines Studentes.
    P. Crossley, 90:Mar86-220
Scheps, W. & J.A. Looney. Middle Scots
Poets.
    P. Bawcutt, 571(ScLJ):Winter86-1
Scherer, B.M. Prolegomena zu einer ein-
heitlichen Zeichentheorie.
    A. Juffras, 619:Spring86-232
Scherer, C. Comédie et société sous Louis
XIII.*
    J.S. Street, 208(FS):Jan86-69
Scherer, J. Le Théâtre de Corneille.*
    H.T. Barnwell, 208(FS):Apr86-205
    J. Clarke, 402(MLR):Jan86-197
Scherer, J. & J. Truchet, eds. Théâtre du
XVIIe siècle. (Vol 2)
    I. Maclean, 617(TLS):5Jun87-613
Scherfig, H. Stolen Spring.
    L. Goldberger, 441:15Mar87-17
Scherner, M. Sprache als Text.*
    K-H. Jäger, 406:Summer86-215
Scherpereel, J. L'Orchestre et les Instru-
mentistes de la Real Camara à Lisbonne
de 1764 à 1834.
    J. Mongrédien, 537:Vol72No1-146
Scheuermann, M. Social Protest in the
Eighteenth-Century English Novel.
    J.P. Zomchick, 173(ECS):Fall86-79

Scheven, Y., comp. Bibliographies for
African Studies, 1980-1983.
    N.J. Schmidt, 538(RAL):Spring86-145
Schick, F. Having Reasons.*
    J. Bishop, 63:Jun86-238
Schickel, R. Intimate Strangers.
    T. Erwin, 385(MQR):Spring87-413
    S. Krim, 364:Apr/May86-111
Schickel, R. & M. Walsh. Carnegie Hall.
    E. Zukerman, 441:6Dec87-18
Schideler, R. Per Olov Enquist.
    P. Holmes, 562(Scan):May86-93
Schieb, G. & others, eds. Beiträge zur
Erforschung der deutschen Sprache. (Vol
3)
    D. Herberg, 682(ZPSK):Band39Heft3-382
Schieffer, R., comp. Acta Conciliorum
Oecumenicorum IV. (Vol 3, Pt 2, fasc 1
& 2)
    A. Cameron, 122:Jan86-98
Schiendorfer, M. Ulrich von Singenberg,
Walther und Wolfram.*
    H. Heinen, 406:Fall86-388
Schiewe, J. & H. Maussner - see Mühsam, E.
Schiffman, L. Sectarian Laws in the Dead
Sea Scrolls.
    J.A. Sanders, 318(JAOS):Jan/Mar85-146
Schillbach, B. - see Brentano, C.
Schiller, F. Schillers Briefe. (E.
Streitfeld & V. Zmegac, eds)
    T. Kontje, 222(GR):Spring86-73
Schilpp, P.A., ed. The Philosophy of Jean-
Paul Sartre.
    İ. Dilman, 521:Apr86-164
Schindler, W. Voice and Crisis.
    J. Egan, 568(SCN):Fall86-34
    T. Kranidas, 551(RenQ):Spring86-148
Schiødt, N., D. Fog & H. Daneland, comps.
Registrant over Hagens Samling.
    412:Feb85-71
Schippan, T. Lexikologie der deutschen
Gegenwartssprache.*
    C. Römer, 682(ZPSK):Band39Heft2-294
Schipper, L., S. Meyers & H. Kelly. Coming
in From the Cold.
    L.M. Sommers, 563(SS):Autumn86-459
Schipper, M. Theatre and Society in
Africa.
    O. Obafemi, 538(RAL):Summer86-271
Schirmer, W.F. Geschichte der englischen
und amerikanischen Literatur.* (6th ed)
(Vol 1, Pt 1 rev by K.H. Göller & T.
Stemmler)
    E.D. Kennedy, 38:Band104Heft1/2-171
Schirmer, W.F. Geschichte der englischen
und amerikanischen Literatur.* (Vols 1 &
2) (6th ed) (U. Broich & others, eds)
    H-J. Weckermann, 156(ShJW):Jahr-
    buch1986-240
Schirok, B., ed. Wolfram von Eschenbach,
"Parzival": Die Bilder der illustrierten
Handschriften.
    M.H. Jones, 402(MLR):Oct86-1038
    W.C.M., 400(MLN):Apr86-738
Schlachter, G.A., ed. Latin American
Politics.
    M.H. Sable, 263(RIB):Vol36No1-68
Schlaffer, H. Wilhelm Meister. Faust
Zweiter Teil.
    G. Marahrens, 564:May86-165
Schlagel, R.H. From Myth to the Modern
Mind. (Vol 1)
    R. Ariew, 543:Jun87-792

Schlanger, J. L'activité théorique.
  J-C. Margolin, 192(EP):Apr-Jun86-273
Schläpfer, R. & R. Trüb - see Hotzenköch-
  erle, R.
Schlatter, M. Ich lerne Romanisch, die
  vierte Landessprache.
  P. Swiggers, 553(RLiR):Jan-Jun86-218
Schleberger, E., ed. Märchen aus Sri Lanka
  (Ceylon).
  H. Mode, 196:Band27Heft1/2-136
Schlee, A. Laing.
  L. Heron, 362:31Dec87-24
Schlegel, F. Gemälde alter Meister.* (H.
  Eichner & N. Lelless, eds)
  F. Jolles, 83:Autumn86-295
  U. Weisstein, 107(CRCL):Dec86-672
Schlegel, J.E. Vergleichung Shakespears
  und Andreas Gryphs und andere dramen-
  theoretische Schriften. (S.D. Martinson,
  ed)
  P. Hess, 133:Band19Heft1-75
Schleichert, H. Klassische Chinesische
  Philosophie.
  K. Kruger, 485(PE&W):Oct86-440
Schleier, M.N., with C.M. Goguel. Le dessin
  à Gênes du XVIe au XVIIIe siècle.
  L. Turčić, 380:Summer86-242
Schlein, S. - see Erikson, E.H.
Schleiner, L. The Living Lyre in English
  Verse.*
  D. Attridge, 551(RenQ):Spring86-134
  E.R. Cunnar, 570(SQ):Winter86-544
  H. Smith, 301(JEGP):Apr86-271
  C. Wilson, 410(M&L):Jan86-83
Schlereth, T.J., ed. Material Culture.
  J.M. Vlach, 292(JAF):Oct/Dec86-484
Schlereth, T.J. Material Culture Studies
  in America.
  P.S. Koda, 87(BB):Dec86-261
Schlesinger, A.M., Jr. The Cycles of
  American History.*
  J.N. Shklar, 617(TLS):13Mar87-267
Schlesinger, G.N. The Intelligibility of
  Nature.
  E.J. Lowe, 518:Oct86-234
Schlesinger, G.N. The Range of Epistemic
  Logic.
  G. Macdonald, 479(PhQ):Oct86-553
  R. McLaughlin, 63:Dec86-530
Schless, H.H. Chaucer and Dante.*
  P. Boitani, 447(N&Q):Dec85-511
  N.R. Havely, 589:Oct86-997
  J.L. Smarr, 301(JEGP):Jan86-97
Schlicke, P. Dickens and Popular Enter-
  tainment.*
  M.R. Booth, 610:Autmn86-256
  M. McGowan, 155:Summer86-101
  R.L. Patten, 637(VS):Spring87-413
  S. Wall, 617(TLS):11-17Dec87-1380
Schlimpert, G. Slawische Personennamen in
  mittelalterlichen Quellen zur deutschen
  Geschichte.
  J. Udolph, 685(ZDL):1/1986-110
Schlobin, R.C., ed. The Aesthetics of
  Fantasy Literature and Art.
  M.T. Chialant, 402(MLR):Jan87-177
  J. Schmidt, 107(CRCL):Sep86-479
de Schloezer, B. Scriabin.
  H. Macdonald, 617(TLS):18-24Dec87-
  1414

Schlosser, H.D. dtv-Atlas zur deutschen
  Literatur.
  U. Liebertz-Grün, 406:Fall86-378
  G. von Wilpert, 133:Band18Heft4-350
Schlossman, B. Joyce's Catholic Comedy of
  Language.*
  B. Benstock, 594:Summer86-217
Schlueter, J. The Plays and Novels of
  Peter Handke.
  L.D. Lindsay, 406:Spring86-121
Schlueter, P. & J., eds. The English
  Novel. (Vol 2)
  J.L. Halio, 677(YES):Vol16-348
Schmalfeldt, J. Berg's "Wozzeck."*
  A. Pople, 411:Jul/Oct86-265
Schmalstieg, W.R. An Introduction to Old
  Church Slavic.* (2nd ed)
  D.G. Lockwood, 558(RLJ):Winter86-222
  D.S. Worth, 159:Spring86-119
Schmid, H. & A. van Kesteren, eds. Semi-
  otics of Drama and Theater.
  M. Carlson, 567:Vol62No3/4-365
Schmid, M. Theorie Sozialen Wandels.
  A. Pickel, 488:Dec86-505
Schmid, S. & H. Schnedl, eds. Totgesch-
  wiegen.
  B. McKittrick, 402(MLR):Jul86-794
Schmid, W. & W-D. Stempel, eds. Dialog der
  Texte.*
  J. Strutz, 602:Band17Heft1-136
Schmid-Bortenschlager, S. & H. Schnedl-
  Bubeniček. Österreichische Schriftstel-
  lerinnen 1880-1938.
  B. McKittrick, 402(MLR):Jul86-794
Schmidely, J. La Personne grammaticale et
  la langue espagnole.
  R. Pellen, 553(RLiR):Jul-Dec86-579
Schmidhuber de la Mora, G. Cuarteto de mi
  gentedad.
  A.G. Labinger, 352(LATR):Spring87-143
Schmidlin, Y. & others - see Bürgin, H. &
  H-O. Mayer
Schmidt, A. Der Briefwechsel mit Alfred
  Andersch. (B. Rauschenbach, ed)
  M. Schardt, 680(ZDP):Band105Heft2-313
  R.W. Williams, 402(MLR):Jul87-801
Schmidt, D.M. Die Kunst des Dialogs in den
  Wakefield-Spielen.
  W. Riehle, 38:Band104Heft3/4-509
Schmidt, G. Die Figuren des Kaleidoskops.
  P. Somville, 542:Apr-Jun86-270
Schmidt, H. A Grand Strategy for the
  West.*
  639(VQR):Summer86-96
Schmidt, H. Quellenlexikon der Interpreta-
  tionen und Textanalysen. (2nd ed)
  R. Grimm, 406:Fall86-377
Schmidt, H-M. Sinnlichkeit und Verstand.
  G. Bersier, 406:Spring86-81
Schmidt, J. Maurice Merleau-Ponty.
  R. Boyne, 323:May86-198
  J.S., 185:Jan87-501
Schmidt, M. The Dresden Gate.*
  J. Rees, 617(TLS):9Jan87-42
Schmidt, M. - see von Simson, G.
Schmidt, M. & H. Riedlinger - see von
  Biberach, R.
Schmidt, M.F. - see Cubillo de Aragón, A.
Schmidt, P. Gebrauchstheorie der Bedeu-
  tung und Valenztheorie.
  G. Helbig, 682(ZPSK):Band39Heft2-288
Schmidt, R. - see Klopstock, F.G.

Schmidt, R.M. Die Handschriftenillustra-
tionen des "Willehalm" Wolframs von
Eschenbach.
  W. Schröder, 684(ZDA):Band115Heft3-129
Schmidt, S.J., ed. Literatur und Kunst –
Wozu?
  I. Gregori, 72:Band223Heft1-134
Schmidt, W. & others. Geschichte der
Deutschen Sprache.* (5th ed)
  J. Schildt, 682(ZPSK):Band39Heft3-387
  H-J. Solms, 680(ZDP):Band105Heft3-467
  N.R. Wolf, 684(ZDA):Band115Heft1-3
Schmidt, W-H., ed. Gattungsprobleme der
älteren slavischen Literaturen (Berliner
Fachtagung 1981).
  N.W. Ingham, 574(SEEJ):Fall86-438
Schmidt-Biggemann, W. Topica universalis.
  H. Jaumann, 224(GRM):Band36Heft3-352
  E. Kessler, 706:Band18Heft1-107
Schmidt-Künsemüller, F.A. Die abendländ-
ischen romanischen Blindstempeleinbände.
  A. Hobson, 617(TLS):6-12Nov87-1234
Schmidt-Küntzel, M. Cotgrave et sa source
rabelaisienne.
  F.J. Hausmann, 547(RF):Band98Heft1/2-
178
Schmidt-Mathy, D. Die literarische Opposi-
tion zu Juan Manuel de Rosas.
  A. de Toro, 107(CRCL):Dec86-676
Schmiechen, J.A. Sweated Industries and
Sweated Labor.
  L.J. Satre, 637(VS):Summer87-560
Schmitt, C.B. – see Cranz, F.E.
Schmitt, R. – see Schwyzer, E.
Schmitt, T. Der langsame Symphoniesatz
Gustav Mahlers.
  S.E. Hefling, 308:Spring86-145
Schmitz, N. Of Huck and Alice.*
  S.I. Bellman, 649(WAL):May86-83
Schmitz, S. Weltentwurf als Realitäts-
bewältigung in Johannes Paulis "Schimpf
und Ernst."
  G.F. Jones, 406:Winter86-526
Schnack, I. – see von Savigny, F.C. & S.A.
Winkelmann
Schnackenburg, B. Adriaen van Ostade,
Isack van Ostade – Zeichnungen und
Aquarelle.
  R. Klessmann, 90:Jun86-433
Schnackenberg, G. The Lamplit Answer.*
  H. Lomas, 364:Jul86-86
  L. Mackinnon, 617(TLS):9Jan87-41
  L. Sail, 493:Oct86-46
Schnädelbach, H. Philosophy in Germany,
1831-1933.* (German title: Philosophie
in Deutschland 1831-1933.)
  C. Larmore, 222(GR):Summer86-134
Schnapper, D. Jewish Identities in France.
  H.H. Weinberg, 390:Mar86-58
Schnedl, H., ed. Rosa Mayreder, Zur Kritik
der Weiblichkeit.
  B. McKittrick, 402(MLR):Jul86-794
Schneewind, W., ed. Numismatic Essays by
Members of the South African Numismatic
Society 1986.
  P.A. Clayton, 324:Sep87-783
Schneider, A. Entrances.*
  Y. Shafer, 615(TJ):Oct86-380
Schneider, B., ed. Das Aeneissupplement
des Maffeo Vegio.
  R. Jenkyns, 123:Vol36No2-356

Schneider, D.J. The Consciousness of D.H.
Lawrence.
  M. Magalaner, 395(MFS):Winter86-663
  D.T.O., 295(JML):Nov86-504
Schneider, E.W. Morphologische und syntak-
tische Variablen im amerikanischen Early
Black English.*
  J.P. Brewer, 35(AS):Summer86-153
Schneider, P. Matisse.*
  N. Watkins, 59:Mar86-115
Schneider, P. The Wall Jumper.
  P. Lewis, 565:Summer86-57
Schneider, R. Ain't We Got Fun?
  K.B. Harder, 424:Mar86-121
Schneider, S. Das Ende Weimars im Exil-
roman.
  K. Haberkamm, 400(MLN):Apr86-715
Schneider, U. Grundzüge einer Philosophie
des Glücks bei Nietzsche.*
  R. Margreiter, 489(PJGG):Band93Heft2-
376
Schneider, U. Die Londoner Music Hall und
ihre Songs 1850-1920.
  J. Bratton, 611(TN):Vol40No2-94
Schneider, W. Ästhetische Ontologie.
  D.E. Shannon, 543:Dec86-397
Schnell, B. – see Peuntner, T.
Schnell, R. Causa amoris.
  D.H. Green, 402(MLR):Jul87-692
Schnitzler, A. Tagebuch 1917-1919. (W.
Welzig & others, eds)
  W.E. Yates, 402(MLR):Jul86-799
Schober, R. Abbild, Sinnbild, Wertung.*
  H.A. Pausch, 107(CRCL):Sep86-458
Schöberle, W. Argumentieren – Bewerten –
Manipulieren.
  W. Zydatiss, 257(IRAL):May86-173
Schodek, D.L. Landmarks in American Civil
Engineering.
  K.A. Marling, 441:27Sep87-44
Schoelwer, S.P. Alamo Images.
  M. Westbrook, 649(WAL):Feb87-364
Schoeman, F.D., ed. Philosophical Dimen-
sions of Privacy.*
  M.A. Menlowe, 518:Apr86-121
Schoenbaum, S. William Shakespeare: A
Compact Documentary Life.
  P. Kemp, 617(TLS):13-19Nov87-1258
Schoenbaum, S. Shakespeare and Others.*
  A.R. Braunmuller, 354:Jun86-177
  L.S. Champion, 179(ES):Oct86-454
  S. Homan, 570(SQ):Spring86-132
Schoenbaum, S. William Shakespeare:
Records and Images.
  E.W. Ives, 677(YES):Vol16-240
Schoenberner, G. The Holocaust.
  R. Clements, 99:Aug/Sep86-28
Schofield, M. An Essay on Anaxagoras.
  D.K. Modrak, 41:Fall85-309
Schofield, M. & M.C. Nussbaum, eds. Lan-
guage and Logos.*
  S.W. Broadie, 53(AGP):Band68Heft1-116
  D.W. Graham, 41:Spring85-140
Schofield, M. & G. Striker, eds. The Norms
of Nature.*
  J. Barnes, 520:Vol31No2-191
Schofield, M.A. & C. Macheski, eds.
Fetter'd or Free?
  J. Richetti, 617(TLS):16Jan87-66
  J.F. Thaddeus, 173(ECS):Summer87-520
Scholes, R. Textual Power.*
  K. Moreland, 577(SHR):Fall86-379

Scholten, C.M. Childbearing in American Society, 1650-1850.
  J. Lewis, 656(WMQ):Apr86-310
Scholz, K. & D. Wojtecki — see Peter von Dusburg
Schom, A. Émile Zola.
  G. Tindall, 176:Dec87-74
Schomer, K. Mahadevi Varma and the Chhayavad Age of Modern Hindi Poetry.
  I.V. Peterson, 318(JAOS):Jan/Mar85-188
Schön, D. The Design Studio.
  A. Cunningham, 46:Sep86-109
Schönau, W., ed. Literaturpsychologische Studien und Analysen.
  S.L. Gilman, 222(GR):Spring86-76
Schöning, U. Literatur als Spiegel.
  R. Lloyd, 208(FS):Jul86-344
Schönrich, G. Kategorien und transzendentale Argumentation.
  P. Rohs, 687:Jul-Sep86-439
Schoolfield, G.C. Edith Södergran.*
  M.J. Blackwell, 221(GQ):Fall86-668
Schopf, A. Das Verzeitungssystem des Englischen und seine Textfunktion.
  G. Bourcier, 189(EA):Jul-Sep86-329
Schöppner, A. Bayerische Legenden. (E. Böck, ed)
  H. Pörnbacher, 196:Band27Heft1/2-138
Schor, N. Breaking the Chain.*
  M. Lydon, 210(FrF):May86-238
  L.M. Porter, 446(NCFS):Spring87-356
  N. Segal, 208(FS):Jul86-370
Schor, N. & H.F. Majewski, eds. Flaubert and Postmodernism.*
  D.W. Fokkema, 549(RLC):Apr-Jun86-249
  P.M. Wetherill, 402(MLR):Jan86-209
Schøsler, L. La déclinaison bicasuelle de l'ancien français.*
  H. Van den Bussche, 361:Mar86-275
Schoultz, L. National Security and United States Policy Toward Latin America.
  J. Rohwer, 441:20Sep87-34
Schouwink, W. Der wilde Eber in Gottes Weinberg.
  N. Voorwinden, 402(MLR):Oct87-1021
Schöwerling, R. Chapbooks.*
  U. Horstmann-Guthrie, 447(N&Q):Mar85-123
Schrader, W.H. Ethik und Anthropologie in der englischen Aufklärung.
  W. Farr, 489(PJGG):Band93Heft2-417
Schram, D.H. Norm en Normdoorbreking.
  H. Verschuren, 204(FdL):Sep86-233
Schram, M. The Great American Video Game.
  H. Goodman, 441:15Mar87-17
  D. Schorr, 18:Jul/Aug87-60
Schreiber, B. La Descente au berceau.*
  M. Gegerias, 207(FR):Apr87-730
Schreiber, V.T., ed. Bones for Barnum Brown.
  L. Milazzo, 584(SWR):Winter86-123
Schreiner, O. An Olive Schreiner Reader. (C. Barash, ed)
  L. Taylor, 362:4Jun87-47
Schricker, G.C. A New Species of Man.
  S. Rees, 675(YER):Vol8No1/2-133
Schröder, H.J. Kasernenzeit.
  P. Morf, 196:Band27Heft3/4-369
Schröder, W. "Arabel"-Studien III.
  M. Resler, 133:Band19Heft1-73
Schröder, W. Wolfram-Nachfolge im "Jüngeren Titurel."
  S.N. Johnson, 406:Fall86-392

Schrodt, R. System und Norm in der Diachronie des deutschen Konjunktivs.
  H. Schmidt, 682(ZPSK):Band39Heft1-134
Schroeder, A. Dustship Glory.
  G. Hancock, 99:Feb87-39
Schroeder, M.R., ed. Speech and Speaker Recognition.*
  F.J. Nolan, 353:Vol24No4-833
  W. Tscheschner, 682(ZPSK):Band39Heft6-732
Schuback, G.B. and W.M. & C.L. Senner. Land und Leute.
  J.F. Lalande 2d, 399(MLJ):Summer86-190
Schubert, D. Works and Days.
  R. Pybus, 565:Spring86-71
Schubert, W. Jupiter in den Epen der Flavierzeit.
  D.C. Feeney, 123:Vol36No1-134
  W. Liebeschuetz, 313:Vol76-333
Schubnell, M. N. Scott Momaday.
  A. Krupat, 27(AL):Dec86-667
  C.L. Woodard, 649(WAL):Feb87-373
  J.J. Wydeven, 395(MFS):Winter86-625
Schuck, P.H. Agent Orange on Trial.
  S. Mills, 617(TLS):15May87-512
Schuck, P.H. & R.M. Smith. Citizenship without Consent.*
  D.C.B., 185:Apr87-701
Schudson, M. Advertising.*
  V. Mosco, 529(QQ):Summer86-406
Schuffenhauer, H. & W., with D. Schuffenhauer, eds. Pädagogisches Gedankengut bei Kant, Fichte, Schelling, Hegel, Feuerbach.
  E. Hufnagel, 342:Band77Heft2-263
Schulenburg, L. — see Jung, F.
Schulke, F. & P.O. McPhee. King Remembered.
  R. Mayne, 176:Apr87-54
Schuller, T. Democracy at Work.
  D.C., 185:Jan87-506
Schullery, P. American Fly Fishing.
  L.A. Schreiber, 441:15Nov87-26
Schulman, G. Marianne Moore.
  W. Woessner, 441:1Feb87-21
Schulte, E. Dante Gabriel Rossetti.
  H. Brill, 326:Autumn86-61
Schulte, G. "Ich impfe euch mit dem Wahnsinn."
  R. Margreiter, 489(PJGG):Band93Heft2-376
Schultz, J. Ist Begegnung möglich?
  J. Martini, 343:Heft13-121
Schultze, B. Studien zum russischen literarischen Einakter.
  N. Worrall, 575(SEER):Apr86-274
Schultze, B-F. Der Augsburger Meistersinger Onoferus Schwartzenbach.
  H. Brunner, 680(ZDP):Band105Heft3-465
Schulz, G., ed. Lessing und der Kreis seiner Freunde.
  H.B. Nisbet, 402(MLR):Jul87-776
Schulz, G. — see Fouqué, F.D.
Schulz, K. Handwerksgesellen und Lohnarbeiter.
  S. Rowan, 589:Oct86-999
Schulz, M.F. Paradise Preserved.*
  566:Spring87-211
Schulze, F. Mies van der Rohe.*
  R.L. Castro, 529(QQ):Autumn86-648
  W.J.R. Curtis, 617(TLS):2-8Oct87-1084
  T.S. Hines, 505:Apr86-211

Schulze, J. Montales Anfänge.
H. Merkl, 72:Band223Heft2-468
Schulze, R. Höflichkeit im Englischen.
P. Westney, 257(IRAL):Nov86-338
Schulze-Busacker, E. Proverbes et expres-
sions proverbiales dans la Littérature
narrative du moyen âge français.
G. Roques, 553(RLiR):Jan-Jun86-278
Schulzinger, R.D. The Wise Men of Foreign
Affairs.
R.W. Leopold, 579(SAQ):Winter86-95
Schumacher, C. Alfred Jarry and Guillaume
Apollinaire.
F.H. Londré, 610:Autumn86-258
Schumacher, T.L. The Danteum.
D.P. Doordan, 576:Sep86-305
Schumann, A., K. Vogel & B. Voss, eds.
Hörverstehen.
C.J. James, 399(MLJ):Winter86-420
Schumann, E. Memoirs of Eugenie Schumann.
R. Anderson, 415:Jul86-389
Schumer, F. Most Likely to Succeed.
B. Lovenheim, 441:17May87-51
Schunk, S. & J. Waisbrot. Explorations.
M-N. Little, 207(FR):May87-881
Schupbach, R.D. Lexical Specialization in
Russian.*
G.G. Corbett, 402(MLR):Jul86-809
T. Priestly, 558(RLJ):Spring/Fall86-221
Schupbach, W. The Paradox of Rembrandt's
"Anatomy of Dr. Tulp."
D.A. Levine, 54:Jun86-337
Schürer, E. The History of the Jewish
People in the Age of Jesus Christ. (Vol
3, Pt 1) (G. Vermes, F. Millar & M.
Goodman, eds)
T. Rajak, 617(TLS):13Mar87-278
Schuster, M. - see Bidermann, J.
Schuster-Šewc, H. Historisch-etymolo-
gisches Wörterbuch der ober- und
niedersorbischen Sprache. (Vol 2)
G. Stone, 575(SEER):Jan86-124
Schütrumpf, E. Die Analyse der Polis durch
Aristoteles.*
M. Forschner, 53(AGP):Band68Heft2-196
Schutte, O. Beyond Nihilism.
G. Carr, 478:Apr86-138
R. Woller, 577(SHR):Spring86-184
Schutz, A. Life Forms and Meaning Struc-
tures. (H.R. Wagner, ed & trans)
P.A.Y. Gunter, 543:Jun87-793
Schütz, A.J. The Fijian Language.
N. Besnier, 350:Mar87-191
Schutz, H. The Romans in Central Europe.
R. Brilliant, 124:May-Jun87-385
Schützeichel, R. Addenda und Corrigenda
(II) zur althochdeutschen Glossensamm-
lung.
M.P. Chappell, 402(MLR):Oct86-1029
Schuyler, J. A Few Days.*
M. Jarman, 249(HudR):Summer86-339
J.D. McClatchy, 491:Oct86-31
639(VQR):Spring86-62
Schwab, A.T. - see Huneker, J.G.
Schwab, R.N., with W.E. Rex. Inventory of
Diderot's "Encyclopédie."* (Vol 7)
P.H. Meyer, 207(FR):Oct86-122
J. Proust, 535(RHL):Jul-Aug86-755
Schwabe, K. Woodrow Wilson, Revolutionary
Germany, and Peacemaking, 1918-1919.
639(VQR):Spring86-53

Schwarte, K-H. Der Ausbruch des zweiten
punischen Krieges - Rechtsfrage und Über-
lieferung.*
P. Jal, 555:Vol59fasc2-329
Schwartz, B. Swann's Way.*
639(VQR):Autumn86-131
Schwartz, B. George Washington.
L. Ziff, 441:13Sep87-12
442(NY):19Oct87-121
Schwartz, B.M. A World of Villages.*
42(AR):Fall86-489
Schwartz, D. The Letters of Delmore
Schwartz.* (R. Phillips, ed)
J. Mazzaro, 569(SR):Winter86-143
J. Meyers, 639(VQR):Spring86-348
Schwartz, D. Portrait of Delmore.* (E.
Pollet, ed)
H. Goldgar, 598(SoR):Summer87-719
Schwartz, E.A. & R. Ezawa. Everyday
Japanese.
P. Szatrowski, 399(MLJ):Winter86-433
Schwartz, G. Rembrandt.*
P.C. Sutton, 90:Sep86-680
Schwartz, G. - see Hawks, E.H.
Schwartz, H., ed. The Burger Years.
R.A. Smolla, 441:21Jun87-18
Schwartz, H. & M.M. Fisher. The New
Jersey House.
M. Pearson, 576:Sep86-314
Schwartz, J. The Sexual Politics of Jean-
Jacques Rousseau.*
M. Cranston, 176:Feb87-42
Schwartz, L.S. The Melting Pot.
P. Klass, 441:11Oct87-15
Schwartz, S. The Matrix of Modernism.*
D.D. Pearlman, 659(ConL):Fall87-394
A. Rieke, 27(AL):Dec86-648
P. Smith, 150(DR):Winter85/86-577
W. Sypher, 569(SR):Summer86-497
Schwartz, S. To Leningrad in Winter.*
R. Orodenker, 573(SSF):Fall86-458
Schwartz-Nobel, L. Engaged to Murder.
L. Franks, 441:1Mar87-12
Schwarz, D.R. The Humanistic Heritage.
V. Aarons, 395(MFS):Winter86-655
P.T.S., 295(JML):Nov86-421
Schwarz, E. Dichtung, Kritik, Geschichte.*
M. Boulby, 564:Nov86-331
M. Eifler, 221(GQ):Spring86-290
Schwarz, H. - see Trier, J.
Schwarz-Mehrens, E. Zum Funktionieren
und zur Funktion der Compassio im "Flies-
senden Licht der Gottheit" Mechthilds
von Magdeburg.
W.C.M., 400(MLN):Apr86-737
Schweickard, C. "Sobre.l vieill trobar e.l
novel" zwei Jahrhunderte Troubadourlyrik.
A. Rieger, 553(RLiR):Jul-Dec86-626
Schweickart, D. Capitalism or Worker
Control?
D. Gordon, 258:Mar86-96
Schweik, R.C. - see Hardy, T.
Schweikhart, G. Der Codex Wolfegg.
D. Ekserdjian, 617(TLS):19Jun87-664
Schweikle, G. - see von Hausen, F.
Schweikle, G. & I., eds. Metzler Literatur
Lexikon.
E.W. Herd, 67:May86-129
Schweitzer, D., ed. Discovering Stephen
King. Discovering Modern Horror Fiction.
G.K. Wolfe, 395(MFS):Spring86-133
Schweizer, H. Metaphorische Grammatik.
S. Segert, 318(JAOS):Oct/Dec85-800

Schweizer, H.R. - see Baumgarten, A.G.

Schwob, M. Chroniques. (J.A. Green, ed)
N. Wilson, 208(FS):Oct86-481

Schwob, M. Correspondance inédite. (J.A. Green, ed)
J.P. Gilroy, 446(NCFS):Fall-Winter 86/87-223
R. Stanley, 207(FR):Mar87-537
N. Wilson, 208(FS):Oct86-481

Schwoeffermann, C. Threaded Memories. Folk Artists of the Southern Tier.
N. Groce, 440:Summer-Fall86-162

Schwyzer, E. Kleine Schriften. (R. Schmitt, ed)
W. Euler, 260(IF):Band91-389

Sciascia, L. The Moro Affair [and] The Mystery of Majorana.
A. Lyttelton, 453(NYRB):25Jun87-3
W. Weaver, 441:5Apr87-10
B. Woffinden, 362:5Mar87-24

Sciascia, L. 1912 + 1.
J. Rosselli, 617(TLS):20Mar87-289

Sciascia, L. One Way or Another.
P. Binding, 362:24Sep87-29

Sciascia, L. Sicilian Uncles.*
G. Josipovici, 617(TLS):6Feb87-135

Scobie, A. Apuleius and Folklore.*
M.J. Jensen, 64(Arv):Vol41-135

Scobie, B. - see Heywood, T.

Scobie, S. Expecting Rain.
T. Whalen, 102(CanL):Summer86-126

Scobie, S. bpNichol: What History Teaches.
D. Bennett, 627(UTQ):Fall86-175
E. Quigley, 102(CanL):Winter85-176

Scott, B.K. Joyce and Feminism.
P.F. Herring, 659(ConL):Spring87-104

Scott, C. A Question of Syllables.
R. Buss, 617(TLS):13-19Nov87-1240

Scott, E.M. French Subsistence at Fort Michilimackinac, 1715-1781.
E.J. Reitz, 656(WMQ):Jul86-496

Scott, J. Fading, My Parmacheene Belle.
N. Ramsey, 441:22Mar87-28
442(NY):27Apr87-104

Scott, J. Midnight Matinees.
G. Matteo, 627(UTQ):Fall86-245

Scott, J.A. The Butterflies of North America.
M. Ridley, 617(TLS):8May87-498

Scott, J.C. Weapons of the Weak.*
B.M. Downing, 185:Jul87-875

Scott, J.S. A Knife Between the Ribs.
N. Callendar, 441:12Apr87-34

Scott, J.W. Mme de Lafayette: "La Princesse de Clèves."*
E.M.M. Woodrough, 402(MLR):Apr87-475

Scott, M. The Female Advocate.*
M. Blondel, 189(EA):Jul-Sep86-372

Scott, M. Renaissance Drama and a Modern Audience.
D.S. Smith, 568(SCN):Spring-Summer86-18

Scott, N.A., Jr. The Poetics of Belief.*
R.A. Lasseter, 569(SR):Spring86-279

Scott, P. My Appointment with the Muse. (S.C. Reece, ed)
P. Oakes, 617(TLS):27Feb87-204

Scott, P. On Writing and the Novel. (S.C. Reece, ed)
L. Graver, 441:15Mar87-14

Scott, P.H. John Galt.*
W.R. Aitken, 541(RES):Nov86-579
I.A. Gordon, 588(SSL):Vol21-333

Scott, P.J.M. Anne Brontë.*
P. Thomson, 541(RES):Feb86-116

Scott, P.J.M. E.M. Forster.*
J. Rothschild, 577(SHR):Summer86-278
J. Tyler, 447(N&Q):Dec85-545

Scott, R.I. - see Jeffers, R.

Scott-Prelorentzos, A. The Servant in German Enlightenment Comedy.*
G. Bersier, 406:Spring86-81

"Scottish Short Stories 1986."
J. Mellors, 362:1Jan87-22

Scottus, S. - see under Sedulius Scottus

Scotus, J.D. Duns Scotus on the Will and Morality. (A.B. Wolter, ed)
W.B. Ewald, 617(TLS):23Jan87-76

Scotus, J.D. A Treatise on God as First Principle.* (2nd ed) (A.B. Wolter, ed and trans)
B. Kent, 258:Sep86-298

Scragg, L. The Metamorphosis of Gallathea.
W. Weiss, 156(ShJW):Jahrbuch1986-198

Scranton, P. & W. Licht, eds. Work Sights.
S.B. Warner, Jr., 441:4Jan87-19

Scrase, D. Wilhelm Lehmann. (Vol 1)
E. Krispyn, 564:May86-182
W. Riemer, 221(GQ):Fall86-659

Scraton, P. & K. Chadwick. In the Arms of the Law.
D. Pannick, 617(TLS):3Jul87-710

"THE SCREAM."
S. Grace, 102(CanL):Spring86-152

Scribner, R.W. For the Sake of Simple Folk.
A.G. Dickens, 90:May86-360

Scrivá, L. Veneris Tribunal.* (R. Rohland de Langbehn, ed)
I. Macpherson, 86(BHS):Apr86-156

Scrivener, M.H. Radical Shelley.*
P.M.S. Dawson, 677(YES):Vol16-306

Scruggs, C.E. Charles Dassoucy.
F. Assef, 475:Vol13No24-419

Scruton, R. From Descartes to Wittgenstein.
R.A. Watson, 543:Sep86-140

Scruton, R. A Land Held Hostage.
M. Yapp, 617(TLS):4-11Sep87-943

Scruton, R. Sexual Desire.*
P. Parker, 364:Jun86-105
C. Pateman, 185:Jul87-881

de Scudéry, G. Poésies diverses.* (Vol 1) (R.G. Pellegrini, ed)
M.M. McGowan, 208(FS):Jan86-68

de Scudéry, G. Poésies diverses. (Vol 2) (R.G. Pellegrini, ed)
N. Aronson, 475:Vol13No25-150
D.L. Rubin, 207(FR):Apr87-706

Scuffil, M. Experiments in Comparative Intonation.
M. Durrell, 685(ZDL):2/1986-248
E. Weiher, 72:Band223Heft2-386

Scullard, H.H. Festivals and Ceremonies of the Roman Republic.
J.A. North, 313:Vol76-251

Sculley, J., with J.A. Byrne. Odyssey.
J. Taylor, 441:25Oct87-32

Scully, T. - see Chiquart, M.

Scupham, P. Out Late.*
J. Forth, 364:Oct86-82
P. Gross, 493:Oct86-63
J. Mole, 176:Mar87-62

Seaborg, G.T., with B.S. Loeb. Stemming the Tide.
A. Frye, 441:19Jul87-15

Seidl, H. Aristoteles, Zweite Analytiken.
P.M. Huby, 123:Vol36No1-143
C. Rutten, 489(PJGG):Band93Heft2-414
Seidl, H. Beiträge zu Aristoteles' Er-
kenntnislehre und Metaphysik.* (R.
Berlinger & W. Schräder, eds)
P.M. Huby, 123:Vol36No1-70
Seifert, A. Untersuchungen zu Hölderlins
Pindar-Rezeption.
B. Bjorklund, 406:Summer86-234
Seifert, J. The Selected Poetry of Jaro-
slav Seifert.* (G. Gibian, ed)
A. Ross, 364:Aug/Sep86-152
G. Szirtes, 493:Oct86-59
Seiler, H. Apprehension. (Pt 3)
J.L. Iturrioz, 361:Nov86-212
Seiler, H. Possession as an Operational
Dimension of Language.
P. Swiggers, 215(GL):Vol26No1-53
Seiler, T.B. & W. Wannemacher, eds. Con-
cept Development and the Development of
Word Meaning.*
A. Lehrer, 603:Vol10No1-256
B. Peeters, 685(ZDL):2/1986-281
de Seingalt, J.C. - see under Casanova de
Seingalt, J.
Seiters, D. Image Patterns in the Novels
of F. Scott Fitzgerald.
S.P., 295(JML):Nov86-471
Sekine, M., ed. Irish Writers and Society
at Large.
Z.B., 295(JML):Nov86-380
B. Dolan, 305(JIL):May86-59
Sekine, M. Ze-Ami and His Theories of Noh
Drama.
L.C. Pronko, 130:Winter86/87-368
Sekler, E.F. Josef Hoffmann, the Architec-
tural Work.*
N. Powell, 39:May86-365
I.B. Whyte, 46:Oct86-8
Sekula, A. Photography against the Grain.
S. Edwards, 59:Dec86-545
Selbmann, R. Der deutsche Bildungsroman.
L.E. Kurth-Voigt, 400(MLN):Apr86-721
Selbmann, R. Theater im Roman.
M.S. Fries, 406:Winter86-522
Selbourne, D. Left Behind.
J. Dunn, 617(TLS):24Apr87-442
Selcher, W.A., ed. Political Liberaliza-
tion in Brazil.
S.G. Bunker, 263(RIB):Vol36No3-347
Selden, R. A Reader's Guide to Contem-
porary Literary Theory.*
M.B., 295(JML):Nov86-411
T. Eagleton, 402(MLR):Oct86-959
Seldes, G. Witness to a Century.
S.I. Toll, 441:16Aug87-18
Seldon, A. Law and Lawyers in Perspective.
362:27Aug87-22
"Selections of XVII and XVIII Century Dutch
Art from the Collection of Dr. A.C.R.
Dreesmann."
380:Autumn86-421
Seleskovitch, D. & M. Lederer. Interpréter
pour traduire.
R.M.A. Allen, 355(LSoc):Sep86-429
J. Berretti, 549(RLC):Jul-Sep86-356
Self, D. Television Drama.*
E. Brater, 397(MD):Dec86-631
Self, G. The Music of E.J. Moeran.
M. Smith, 607:Sep86-58

Selkirk, E.O. Phonology and Syntax.
W.E. Cooper, 603:Vol10No1-235
C. Gussenhoven, 297(JL):Sep86-455
Sell, R.D. The Reluctant Naturalism of
"Amelia."*
H. Amory, 447(N&Q):Dec85-531
P-G. Boucé, 189(EA):Jul-Sep86-373
M. Irwin, 541(RES):Feb86-100
E. Zimmerman, 402(MLR):Apr87-452
Sellstrom, A.D. Corneille, Tasso and Mod-
ern Poetics.
I. Maclean, 617(TLS):5Jun87-613
Seltzer, M. Henry James and the Art of
Power.*
J.E. Funston, 594:Summer86-220
R. Hewitt, 395(MFS):Summer86-252
A.M., 125:Fall85-110
P. O'Donnell, 223:Fall86-319
de Selve, L. Les Oeuvres sprituelles sur
les évangiles des jours de caresme et sur
les festes de l'année. (L.K. Donaldson-
Evans, ed)
Y. Quenot, 535(RHL):Mar-Apr86-271
C.N. Smith, 208(FS):Oct86-453
Selwyn, V., ed. Poems of the Second World
War.
A. Ross, 617(TLS):27Feb87-217
Semaan, K.I., ed. Islam and the Medieval
West.
S. Gellens, 318(JAOS):Oct/Dec85-795
Semenzato, C., ed. La pitture del Santo di
Padova.
J. Richards, 90:Jun86-426
Sémon, M. Les femmes dans l'oeuvre de
Léon Tolstoi.
P. Carden, 104(CASS):Spring-Summer86-
182
A.V. Knowles, 575(SEER):Jul86-459
Semyonov, J. TASS is Authorized to
Announce...
T.J. Binyon, 617(TLS):16-22Oct87-1136
Sen, A. On Ethics and Economics.
D. Collard, 617(TLS):27Nov-3Dec87-1314
Sen, A. Resources, Values and Develop-
ment.* Choice, Welfare and Measurement.
A.B. Atkinson, 453(NYRB):22Oct87-41
Sender, R.J. Hughes y el once negro.
M.E.W. Jones, 238:Mar86-105
Sendler, H. Über Michael Kohlhaas - dam-
als und heute.
W. Wittkowski, 133:Band19Heft3/4-356
Seneca. Apocolocyntosis.* (P.T. Eden, ed)
W.J. Raschke, 124:May-Jun87-389
Senelick, L. Anton Chekhov.
R.A. Peace, 402(MLR):Apr87-536
Sen Gupta, S.C. India Wrests Freedom.
L.A. Gordon, 293(JASt):Nov85-184
Sen Gupta, S.C. A Shakespeare Manual.*
(2nd ed)
A.W. Bellringer, 447(N&Q):Dec85-520
L. Scragg, 148:Autumn86-102
Seniff, D.P. - see Alfonso XI
Seniff, D.P. - see de Santiago y Palomares,
F.J.
Sennett, R. Palais-Royal.
D.J. Enright, 453(NYRB):9Apr87-23
R. Holmes, 441:8Feb87-14
J. Keates, 617(TLS):24Jul87-801
de Sensi Sestito, G. La Calabria in età
arcaica e classica.
R.J.A. Talbert, 303(JoHS):Vol106-240

Sensibar, J.L. The Origins of Faulkner's Art.*
    C.S. Brown, 569(SR):Winter86-167
Sensibar, J.L. - see Faulkner, W.
Sentaurens, J. Séville et le théâtre, de la fin du Moyen âge à la fin du XVIIe siècle.
    J-M. Pelorson, 92(BH):Jan-Jun85-200
Sephiha, H.V. - see under Vidal Sephiha, H.
Serbat, G., ed. E. Benveniste aujourd-'hui.* (Vol 1)
    R. Martin, 209(FM):Apr86-122
Sergent, B. Homosexuality in Greek Myth. (French title: L'Homosexualité dans la mythologie grecque.
    T.J. Figueira, 24:Fall86-426
    H. King, 617(TLS):22May87-546
Sergent, B. L'homosexualité initiatique dans l'Europe ancienne.
    H. King, 617(TLS):22May87-546
Sergent, M. & K. Wilkins. A Translation Textbook.*
    O.A. Haac, 399(MLJ):Autumn86-308
Serhane, A. Messaouda.
    I. Hill, 617(TLS):3Jul87-714
Sermain, J-P. Rhétorique et roman au dix-huitième siècle.
    D.J. Culpin, 208(FS):Jul86-335
    R.A. Francis, 402(MLR):Apr87-477
Serna López, V. El teatro de Alonso Remón.
    F.B. Exum, 238:May86-307
Serpell, J. In the Company of Animals.*
    S.R.L. Clark, 617(TLS):20Feb87-175
    S.J. Gould, 453(NYRB):25Jun87-20
Serper, A. Huon de Saint-Quentin.
    U. Mölk, 547(RF):Band98Heft3/4-422
Serra, P.A. Miró and Mallorca.
    N. Watkins, 90:Dec86-909
Serravezza, A., ed. La sociologia della musica.
    M.S. Keller, 317:Spring86-199
Serres, M. Les Cinq Sens.
    T. Cordellier, 450(NRF):May86-99
    T.M. Kavanagh, 400(MLN):Sep86-937
Serres, M. Hermes.* (J.V. Harari & D.F. Bell, eds)
    S. Fuller, 488:Dec86-502
Serroy, J., ed. Jean Pellerin 1885-1921.
    V.D.L., 605(SC):15Apr87-305
Servera Baño, J. Ramón del Valle-Inclán.
    A. Sinclair, 86(BHS):Oct86-390
Servet, J-M. Nomismata.
    M. Price, 303(JoHS):Vol106-257
Service, R. Lenin. (Vol 1)
    J. Keep, 575(SEER):Oct86-624
Servodidio, M. & M.L. Welles, eds. From Fiction to Metafiction.
    M.E.W. Jones, 86(BHS):Oct86-393
Serzisko, F. Der Ausdruck der Possessivi-tät im Somali.
    C.E. Mewis, 682(ZPSK):Band39Heft4-510
Sestito, G.D. - see under de Sensi Sestito, G.
Seth, V. The Golden Gate.*
    W.A. Evans, 649(WAL):Feb87-367
    B. King, 598(SoR):Winter87-224
    H. Lomas, 364:Jul86-86
    R. McDowell, 249(HudR):Winter87-679
    639(VQR):Autumn86-133
Seth, V. The Humble Administrator's Garden.*
    B. King, 569(SR):Summer86-lxiv

Seton, E.T. Wild Animals I Have Known. Selected Stories of Ernest Thompson Seton. (P. Morley, ed)
    W. Drew, 296(JCF):No35/36-183
Settis, S., ed. The Land of the Etruscans.
    R. Higgins, 39:Apr86-289
Seung, T.K. Semiotics and Thematics in Hermeneutics.*
    L. Kintz, 478:Apr86-112
Seuren, P.A.M. Discourse Semantics.
    A. Granham, 307:Dec86-227
    R.T. Williams, 399(MLJ):Summer86-193
Dr. Seuss. The Tough Coughs as He Ploughs the Dough. (R. Marschall, ed)
    S.G. Lanes, 441:12Apr87-27
Ševčenko, N.P. The Life of Saint Nicholas in Byzantine Art.
    H. Maguire, 589:Apr86-466
"Seven Medieval Latin Comedies." (A.G. Elliott, trans)
    S.L. Wailes, 589:Jul86-733
Severin, T. The Ulysses Voyages.
    G.S. Kirk, 617(TLS):18-24Sep87-1010
Sexton, A. The Complete Poems.*
    B. Gallagher, 152(UDQ):Fall86-95
Sextus Empiricus. Against the Musicians. (D.D. Greaves, ed & trans)
    D. Hiley, 415:Dec86-692
Seyersted, P. From Norwegian Romantic to American Realist.
    E. Löfroth, 597(SN):Vol58No1-123
    O. Øverland, 179(ES):Aug86-374
Seyffert, P. Soviet Literary Structural-ism.
    F.W. Galan, 550(RusR):Jul86-349
Seymour, G. Field of Blood.
    R. Fréchet, 189(EA):Apr-Jun87-241
Seymour, J.D. China Rights Annals 1.
    P.B. Potter, 293(JASt):Aug86-824
Seymour, P.J. The Golden Woman. (A. Mattina, ed)
    A. Wiget, 292(JAF):Jul/Sep86-324
Seymour-Smith, M. The New Guide to Modern World Literature.
    M.B., 295(JML):Nov86-352
Sguaitamatti, M. L'Offrande de porcelet dans la coroplathie Géléenne.*
    C.E. Vafopoulou-Richardson, 123: Vol36No2-339
Shabtai, Y. Past Continuous.
    S.G. Kellman, 390:Feb86-57
Shabtai, Y. Past Perfect.
    R. Alter, 441:9Aug87-11
Shackle, C. An Introduction to the Sacred Language of the Sikhs.
    V. Gambhir, 318(JAOS):Oct/Dec85-808
Shackleton, K. Wildlife and Wilderness.
    E. Dunn, 617(TLS):10Apr87-396
Shackleton, K. & J. Snyder. Ship in the Wilderness.
    E. Dunn, 617(TLS):10Apr87-396
Shackleton Bailey, D.R. - see Horace
Shadbolt, M. Season of the Jew.
    T. Armstrong, 617(TLS):6Mar87-245
    C.C. O'Brien, 441:2Aug87-9
Shaddy, V.M. L'influence française et le rôle de Dryden dans l'evolution des idées générales et de la rhétorique en occi-dent.
    S. Archer, 568(SCN):Spring-Summer86-5
Shafer, Y., ed. Approaches to Teaching Ibsen's "A Doll House."
    L.J. Leff, 365:Spring/Summer86-159

Shafir, M. Romania.
   D. Deletant, 575(SEER):Oct86-632
Shah, M.B., ed. Vācaka Kamalaśekhara's Pradyumnakumāra Cupaī.
   E. Bender, 318(JAOS):Oct/Dec85-813
Shah, R.C. Yeats and Eliot.
   S. Bagchee, 107(CRCL):Dec86-689
Shah, R.M., ed. Saṃdhikāvya-samuccaya.
   E. Bender, 318(JAOS):Oct/Dec85-813
Shahar, D. Un voyage à Ur de Chaldée.
   J. Blot, 450(NRF):Oct86-113
Shahar, S. The Fourth Estate.
   S.P. Wemple, 589:Jan86-204
Shahîd, I. Rome and the Arabs. Byzantium and the Arabs in the Fourth Century.
   G.W. Bowersock, 123:Vol36No1-111
Shailor, B.A. Catalogue of Medieval and Renaissance Manuscripts in the Beinecke Rare Book and Manuscript Library, Yale University. (Vol 1)
   A.I. Doyle, 40(AEB):Vol8No4-249
Shakespeare, N. Londoners.
   J. Chernaik, 617(TLS):23Jan87-89
Shakespeare, W. All's Well That Ends Well. (R. Fraser, ed)
   M. Bream, 364:Nov86-112
   G. Monsarrat, 189(EA):Apr-Jun87-201
Shakespeare, W. The Complete Works: Original-Spelling Edition. (S. Wells & G. Taylor, general eds)
   L. Potter, 617(TLS):10Apr87-389
Shakespeare, W. Hamlet.* (H. Jenkins, ed)
   G.B. Evans, 402(MLR):Jul86-710
Shakespeare, W. Hamlet, Prince of Denmark.* (P. Edwards, ed)
   D. Mehl, 156(ShJW):Jahrbuch1986-209
   G. Monsarrat, 189(EA):Apr-Jun87-201
Shakespeare, W. Julius Caesar.* (A. Humphreys, ed) Titus Andronicus.* (E.M. Waith, ed)
   M. Hattaway, 541(RES):Feb86-86
   A. Thompson, 402(MLR):Apr87-444
Shakespeare, W. King Richard II.* (A. Gurr, ed)
   E.A.J. Honigmann, 402(MLR):Jul86-707
   D. Mehl, 156(ShJW):Jahrbuch1986-209
Shakespeare, W. Othello.* (N. Sanders, ed) Romeo and Juliet.* (G.B. Evans, ed) The Taming of the Shrew.* (A. Thompson, ed) A Midsummer Night's Dream.* (R.A. Foakes, ed)
   E.A.J. Honigmann, 402(MLR):Jul86-707
   D. Mehl, 156(ShJW):Jahrbuch1986-208
Shakespeare, W. Romeo and Juliet. (W.T. Betken, ed)
   T.W. Craik, 161(DUJ):Jun86-374
   M. Grivelet, 189(EA):Jan-Mar87-113
Shakespeare, W. William Shakespeare: The Complete Works.* (S. Wells & G. Taylor, eds)
   M. Dodsworth, 175:Autumn86-305
   L. Potter, 617(TLS):10Apr87-389
Shakespeare, W. Shakespeare's Plays in Quarto.* (M.J.B. Allen & K. Muir, eds)
   P. Bertram, 551(RenQ):Spring86-137
Shakespeare, W. The Sonnets [and] A Lover's Complaint. (J. Kerrigan, ed)
   G. Bradshaw, 617(TLS):30Oct-5Nov87-1199
Shakespeare, W. The Taming of the Shrew.* (B. Morris, ed)
   G.B. Evans, 402(MLR):Jan86-167

Shakespeare, W. Twelfth Night. (E.S. Donno, ed)
   G. Monsarrat, 189(EA):Apr-Jun87-201
"Shakespeare Survey."* (Vol 36) (S. Wells, ed)
   S. Chaudhuri, 447(N&Q):Mar85-108
   D. Rolle, 156(ShJW):Jahrbuch1986-248
"Shakespeare Survey."* (Vol 37) (S. Wells, ed)
   H. Hunt, 610:Spring86-65
   D. Rolle, 156(ShJW):Jahrbuch1986-248
"Shakespeare Survey."* (Vol 38) (S. Wells, ed)
   M. Grivelet, 189(EA):Apr-Jun87-208
"Shakespeare Survey." (Vol 39) (S. Wells, ed)
   J. Wilders, 617(TLS):30Oct-5Nov87-1197
Shand, G.B. & R.C. Shady, eds. Play-Texts in Old Spelling.*
   T.L. Berger, 539:Nov86-382
   J.L. Halio, 301(JEGP):Apr86-258
   W.P. Williams, 570(SQ):Summer86-280
Shaner, D.E. The Bodymind Experience in Japanese Buddhism.
   Y. Saito, 293(JASt):Aug86-843
Shange, N. For Colored Girls Who Have Considered Suicide/When the Rainbow Is Enuf.
   V.M. Patraka, 385(MQR):Winter87-285
Shangold, M. & G. Mirkin. The Complete Sports Medicine Book for Women.
   639(VQR):Winter86-31
Shanker, S., ed. Ludwig Wittgenstein.
   483:Oct86-554
Shankman, S. Pope's "Iliad."*
   R.L. Bogue, 131(CL):Summer86-299
Shannon, T.A. What Are They Saying about Genetic Engineering?
   S.P., 185:Jan87-511
Shapcott, T. Hotel Bellevue.*
   P. Lewis, 364:Dec86/Jan87-152
   P. Lewis, 565:Autumn86-71
Shapcott, T. Travel Dice.
   C. James, 617(TLS):27Nov-3Dec87-1327
Shapin, S. & S. Schaffer. Leviathan and the Air-Pump.
   C. Webster, 617(TLS):13Mar87-281
Shapiro, A. Happy Hour.
   J.D. McClatchy, 441:26Jul87-9
Shapiro, B.J. Probability and Certainty in Seventeenth-Century England.*
   C.W. Brooks, 161(DUJ):Dec85-178
Shapiro, G. & A. Sica, eds. Hermeneutics.
   C.O. Schrag, 480(P&R):Vol19No2-142
Shapiro, H. & P. Tumay. Murder in Soho.
   N. Callendar, 441:22Nov87-45
Shapiro, K.J. Bodily Reflective Modes.
   R. Skelton, 323:May86-201
Shapiro, L. Perfection Salad.*
   639(VQR):Autumn86-138
Shapiro, M. The Sense of Grammar.*
   N. Garver, 619:Winter86-68
   J. Lyne, 480(P&R):Vol19No1-76
Shapiro, N. & B. Pollack. Popular Music, 1920-1979. (Vols 1-3) (rev)
   D.E. McGinty, 91:Fall86-309
Shapiro, R. Origins.*
   P. Atkins, 617(TLS):30Jan87-103
Shapiro, W.F. Eddie Black.
   K. Kalfus, 441:1Mar87-20
Sharaf, M. Fury on Earth.
   R. Colp, Jr., 77:Winter86-87
Sharkey, T. Jack the Ripper.
   B. Woolley, 362:17&24Dec87-54

Sharma, A. The Hindu Gītā.
  B.S. Miller, 617(TLS):17Jul87-776
Sharma, B.R., ed. Puṣpasūtra.
  L. Rowell, 318(JAOS):Apr/Jun85-386
Sharma, J.K. Time and T.S. Eliot.
  M. Moran, 27(AL):Mar86-114
Sharot, S. Messianism, Mysticism, and
Magic.
  D. Glanz, 390:Oct86-54
Sharp, B. Bob Sharp's Cattle Country.
  L. Milazzo, 584(SWR):Spring86-257
Sharp, R.A. Friendship and Literature.*
  P. Hampl, 344:Winter87-135
Sharpe, E.J. The Universal Gītā.
  B.S. Miller, 617(TLS):17Jul87-776
Sharpe, K., ed. Faction and Parliament.
  L. Stone, 453(NYRB):26Feb87-38
Sharpe, P. Lost Goods & Stray Beasts.
  R. Pybus, 565:Spring86-71
Sharpe, R.A. Contemporary Aesthetics.
  W. Charlton, 483:Apr86-253
Sharpe, T. Indecent Exposure.
  S. Hathaway, 441:17May87-50
Sharples, R.W. - see Alexander of Aphrodis-
ias
Sharrock, R. Saints, Sinners and Come-
dians.*
  K. Wilson, 529(QQ):Spring86-203
Shatto, S. & M. Shaw - see Tennyson, A.
Shattuck, R. The Innocent Eye.*
  P. Brady, 478:Apr86-98
Shatyn, B. A Private War.*
  A. Lupack, 497(PolR):Vol31No1-98
Shavit, Z. Poetics of Children's Litera-
ture.*
  S. Drain, 150(DR):Fall86-386
Shaw, A. The Jazz Age.
  P. Keepnews, 441:25Oct87-57
Shaw, B., ed. Seagate II.
  A. Smith, 161(DUJ):Jun86-388
Shaw, G.B. Agitations.* (D.H. Laurence &
J. Rambeau, eds)
  B.F. Dukore, 615(TJ):Oct86-385
Shaw, G.B. Shaw on Dickens.* (D.H.
Laurence & M. Quinn, eds)
  G.M. Crane, 615(TJ):Dec86-511
Shaw, H.E. The Forms of Historical Fic-
tion.*
  A. Easson, 366:Autumn86-258
  K.M. Sroka, 571(ScLJ):Summer86-7
  J.W. Turner, 125:Fall85-91
  D. Whitmore, 405(MP):Aug86-94
Shaw, J. Taking Leave.
  R. Cohen, 441:14Jun87-28
Shaw, J. The Uncle and Other Stories.
  J. Helbert, 649(WAL):Aug86-185
Shaw, J.F. Raspberry Vinegar.
  J-P. Durix, 102(CanL):Summer86-130
  M. Goldman, 376:Jun86-121
  M. Micros, 198:Spring86-98
Shaw, R. The Arts and the People.
  M. Laski, 362:22Jan87-26
Shaw, R.B. The Call of God.
  P. Palmer, 677(YES):Vol16-247
Shaw, R.W. Abbott and Avery.
  D.R. Slavitt, 441:4Oct87-19
Shaw, W.D. The Lucid Veil.
  I. Armstrong, 617(TLS):21Aug87-903
Shawcross, J.T. With Mortal Voice.*
  D.H. Burden, 447(N&Q):Mar85-119
al-Shaykh, H. The Story of Zahra.*
  K. Fitzlyon, 364:Jul86-101

"Anatoly and Avital Shcharansky."
  D.K. Shipler, 441:4Jan87-19
Sheard, S. Almost Japanese.
  K. Jones, 441:16Aug87-23
  C. Rooke, 376:Mar86-125
Shears, R. & I. Gidley. The Rainbow War-
rior Affair.*
  P. Jones, 529(QQ):Autumn86-707
Shearston, T. White Lies.
  H. Jacobson, 617(TLS):27Nov-3Dec87-
  1307
Shechner, M. After the Revolution.
  E. Rothstein, 441:10May87-14
Sheed, W. The Boys of Winter.
  H. Gold, 441:2Aug87-3
  442(NY):19Oct87-120
Sheehan, R. Boy With an Injured Eye.
  J. Byrne, 532(RCF):Summer86-148
Shehadi, F. Metaphysics in Islamic Philos-
ophy.
  D. Burrell, 438:Summer86-375
Sheldon, R. Selected Songs. Short Songs.
Concert Songs. Assorted Songs.
  F. Candelaria, 648(WCR):Jun86-99
Sheldon, S. Windmills of the Gods.
  S.S. Wells, 441:8Feb87-25
Shell, M. Money, Language, and Thought.*
  P. Haidu, 107(CRCL):Sep86-424
Shelley, M. Frankenstein; or The Modern
Prometheus.* (B. Moser, illustrator)
  W. Veeder, 405(MP):Feb87-329
Shelley, M. The Journals of Mary Shelley
1814-1844. (P.R. Feldman & D. Scott-
Kilvert, eds)
  C. Baldick, 617(TLS):7Aug87-842
  C. Tomalin, 453(NYRB):19Nov87-35
Shelp, E.E., ed. Theology and Bioethics.
  S.P., 185:Jan87-511
Shelp, E.E., ed. Virtue and Medicine.
  J.G.H., 185:Oct86-308
  D.N. Walton, 154:Winter86-808
Shelston, A., ed. Charles Dickens:
"Dombey and Son" and "Little Dorrit."*
  S. Monod, 189(EA):Jul-Sep86-374
Shelston, A., ed. Henry James, "Washington
Square" and "The Portrait of a Lady."
  S. Bush, Jr., 402(MLR):Apr87-458
Shelton, R. No Direction Home.*
  R. Tillinghast, 385(MQR):Summer87-567
Shenker, I. Coat of Many Colors.
  M.J. Merowitz, 390:Jan86-60
Shepard, L. The Jaguar Hunter.
  G. Jonas, 441:7Jun87-19
Shepard, P. & B. Sanders. The Sacred Paw.*
  D. Lachapelle, 649(WAL):Feb87-366
Shepard, R.N. & L.A. Cooper. Mental Images
and their Transformations.
  V. Cobb-Stevens, 258:Mar86-87
Shepard, S. Seven Plays.
  B. Grantham, 157:No159-47
Shepers, H., W. Schneiders & W. Kabitz -
see Leibniz, G.W.
Shepherd, N. The Zealous Intruders.
  R. Irwin, 617(TLS):9-15Oct87-1102
Shepherd, S. Amazons and Warrior Women.
  D. Brooks-Davies, 677(YES):Vol16-264
Shepherd, W.C. To Secure the Blessings of
Liberty.
  S.P., 185:Jul87-901
Sheppard, G. & A. Yanacopoulo. Signé
Hubert Aquin.
  P-Y. Mocquais, 627(UTQ):Fall86-226

Sheppard, R., ed. Die Schriften des Neuen Clubs 1908-1914. (Vol 2)
  W. Paulsen, 133:Band19Heft3/4-364
"Sheppard's Book Dealers in The British Isles, 1987." (12th ed)
  D. Chambers, 503:Summer86-94
Sher, R.B. Church and University in the Scottish Enlightenment.*
  A.C. Chitnis, 83:Autumn86-206
Sherbo, A. The Birth of Shakespeare Studies.
  T. Hawkes, 617(TLS):10Apr87-390
Shere, L.R. Chez Panisse Desserts.
  W. & C. Cowen, 639(VQR):Autumn86-140
Shergold, N.D. & J.E. Varey, eds. Genealogía, origen y noticias de los comediantes de España.
  J.M. Ruano de la Haza, 402(MLR):Oct87-998
Sheridan, A. Discours, sexualité et pouvoir. (P. Miller, ed & trans)
  J.N. Kaufmann, 154:Winter86-780
Sheridan, M. & J.W. Salaff, eds. Lives.
  M.B. Young, 293(JASt):May86-567
Sheridan, R.B. Doctors and Slaves.
  T.L. Savitt, 656(WMQ):Jul86-499
Sherman, K. Black Flamingo.
  B. Carey, 526:Autumn86-91
Sherman, S. The Maple Sugar Murders.
  N. Callendar, 441:1Nov87-34
Sherwin-White, A.N. Roman Foreign Policy in the East, 168 B.C. to A.D. 1.*
  G.M. Paul, 487:Summer86-223
Sherwood, J. Flowers of Evil.
  T.J. Binyon, 617(TLS):28Aug87-929
Sherwood, J.C. R.S. Crane.
  R.J. Merrett, 107(CRCL):Dec86-655
Sherwood, T.G. Fulfilling the Circle.*
  G.R. Evans, 541(RES):May86-306
  D.R. Shore, 178:Dec86-455
  J.J. Smith, 402(MLR):Apr87-447
Sherzer, D. Representation in Contemporary French Fiction.
  M. LaVallee-Williams, 295(JML):Nov86-381
  B. Stoltzfus, 268(IFR):Winter87-54
  A. Thiher, 395(MFS):Winter86-679
Sherzer, J. Kuna Ways of Speaking.*
  A. Wiget, 650(WF):Jan86-46
Shesgreen, S. Hogarth and the Times-of-the-Day Tradition.*
  A.S. Gourlay, 481(PQ):Summer86-410
Sheth, N. The Divinity of Krishna.
  R. De Smet, 485(PE&W):Jul86-305
  D.L. Haberman, 293(JASt):Nov85-185
Shevoroshkin, V.V. & T.L. Markey, eds. Typology, Relationship, and Time.
  A.R. Bomhard, 159:Fall86-269
Shewey, D. & S. Shacter. Caught in the Act.
  L. Liebmann, 441:4Jan87-19
Shi Qun, comp. Riben xingming cidian: jiamingxu. Riben xingming cidian: ladingxu. Riben xingming cidian: hanzixu.
  R. Borgen, 116:Jul85-199
Shibamoto, J.S. Japanese Women's Language.
  R. King, 350:Mar87-194
  S.K. Maynard, 293(JASt):Aug86-860
Shideler, R. Per Olov Enquist.
  J.E. Bellquist, 563(SS):Winter86-85
Shizue Ishimoto. Facing Two Ways.
  C.I. Mulhern, 293(JASt):Nov85-146

Shields, C. Various Miracles.*
  M. Micros, 198:Spring86-98
  G. Whitlock, 102(CanL):Fall86-157
Shiff, R. Cézanne and the End of Impressionism.*
  J. House, 59:Sep86-369
  R. Thomson, 90:Apr86-297
Shiga Naoya. The Paper Door.
  Hiroaki Sato, 441:5Apr87-16
Shigeo, N. - see under Nishimura Shigeo
Shilts, R. And the Band Played On.
  H.J. Geiger, 441:8Nov87-9
  442(NY):28Dec87-124
Shimane, K. The Poetry of G.M. Hopkins.
  J-G. Ritz, 189(EA):Apr-Jun87-226
  R.K.R. Thornton, 541(RES):May86-284
Shimao Toshio. "The Sting of Death" and Other Stories by Shimao Toshio.
  V.C. Gessel, 407(MN):Autumn86-359
Shimazaki, T. - see under Toson Shimazaki
Shinar, P. Essai de bibliographie sélective et annotée sur l'Islam maghrébin contemporain.
  H.E. Kassis, 318(JAOS):Oct/Dec85-741
Shipler, D.K. Arab and Jew.*
  M. Yapp, 617(TLS):14Aug87-883
Shipley, G. A History of Samos 800-188 B.C.
  P. Cartledge, 617(TLS):2-8Oct87-1085
Shipton, A. - see Barker, D.
Shires, L.M. British Poetry of the Second World War.
  R. Smith, 150(DR):Winter85/86-585
Shirley, J. The Lady of Pleasure. (R. Huebert, ed) The Cardinal. (E.M. Yearling, ed)
  R. Gill, 617(TLS):31Jul87-814
Shirley, J.W. Thomas Harriot.
  W. Sharratt, 161(DUJ):Dec85-180
Shirley, J.W. & F.D. Hoeniger, eds. Science and the Arts in the Renaissance.*
  L.S. Dixon, 539:Nov86-386
Shizuo, M. - see under Mizukami Shizuo
Shkapich, K., ed. Mask of Medusa.
  M. Sorkin, 45:Nov86-79
Shlapentokh, V. Love, Marriage and Friendship in the Soviet Union.
  W.Z. Goldman, 550(RusR):Oct86-452
Shlee, A. Laing.
  C. Hawtree, 617(TLS):11-17Dec87-1374
Shloss, C. In Visible Light.
  A. Barnet, 441:7Jun87-31
Shnayerson, R. The Illustrated History of the Supreme Court of the United States.*
  442(NY):26Jan87-86
Shneidman, N.N. Dostoevsky and Suicide.*
  C. De Grève, 549(RLC):Jan-Mar86-110
  R. Freeborn, 575(SEER):Jul86-456
  G. Olson, 558(RLJ):Spring/Fall86-236
  C.V. Ponomareff, 627(UTQ):Fall86-143
Shoaf, R.A. Dante, Chaucer, and the Currency of the Word.*
  A. David, 589:Apr86-468
  F. Goldin, 405(MP):Feb87-308
Shoaf, R.A. Milton, Poet of Duality.*
  T. Healy, 402(MLR):Oct87-915
  C. Kendrick, 141:Spring86-213
  G. Mathis, 189(EA):Jan-Mar87-85
  I. Simon, 541(RES):Nov86-568
Shoard, M. This Land is Our Land.
  T. O'Riordan, 617(TLS):10Jul87-753
Shoemaker, S. Identity, Cause and Mind.*
  D.M. Armstrong, 63:Jun86-236

Shoemaker, S. & R. Swinburne. Personal Identity.*
    R.C. Coburn, 484(PPR):Sep86-155
    C. Lyas, 521:Oct86-329
"The Shogun Age Exhibition."*
    R.M. Bernier, 318(JAOS):Oct/Dec85-773
Shonfield, Z. The Precariously Privileged.
    G. Annan, 362:2Apr87-23
    J. Burnett, 617(TLS):11-17Sep87-995
Shopen, T., ed. Language Typology and Syntactic Description.
    B.J. Blake & G. Mallinson, 350:Sep87-606
Shopen, T. & J. Williams, eds. Style and Variables in English.
    E. Chaika, 126(CCC):Feb86-112
Shor, I. Culture Wars.
    R. Floud, 617(TLS):13Mar87-263
Shore, D.R. Spenser and the Poetics of Pastoral.
    M.P. Hannay, 604:Spring/Summer86-36
Shorley, C. Queneau's Fiction.
    J. Cruickshank, 208(FS):Apr86-236
    M.P.L., 295(JML):Nov86-532
    A. Thiher, 395(MFS):Winter86-678
    C. Toloudis, 207(FR):Mar87-544
Shorris, E. Power Sits at Another Table.
    A. Ward, 441:24May87-13
Short, I., ed. Medieval French Textual Studies in Memory of T.B.W. Reid.*
    A.J. Holden, 382(MAE):1986/1-139
    M.W. Morris, 589:Oct86-1002
    H. Shields, 208(FS):Jan86-56
Short, J-P. Racine, "Phèdre."
    A. Viala, 535(RHL):Mar-Apr86-283
Short, K.R.M. The Dynamite War.
    S. Cronin, 174(Eire):Fall86-142
Short, K.R.M., ed. Feature Films as History.
    R. Macmillan, 488:Dec86-511
"A Short-Title Catalogue of Books Printed in England, Scotland and Ireland and of English Books Printed Abroad 1475-1640." (2nd ed) (Vol 1) (W.A. Jackson, F.S. Ferguson & K.F. Pantzer, eds)
    A. Freeman, 617(TLS):13Feb87-170
"Short-Title Catalogue of Books Printed in Italy and of Italian Books Printed in Other Countries from 1465 to 1600 now in the British Library: Supplement."
"Short-Title Catalogue of Books Printed in France and of French Books Printed in Other Countries from 1470 to 1600 now in the British Library: Supplement."
    D. McKitterick, 617(TLS):26Jun87-704
Shorter, E. Bedside Manners.*
    639(VQR):Summer86-103
Shortt, H. The Giant and Hob-Nob.
    S. Drury, 203:Vol97No1-117
Shotton, M. - see Leskov, N.
Shoumatoff, A. In Southern Light.*
    J. Ure, 617(TLS):21Aug87-895
Shoumatoff, A. Jewish Aspects of "The Mountain of Names."
    D.L. Gold, 424:Dec86-408
Showalter, E. The Female Malady.*
    S. Bick, 42(AR):Spring86-242
    J.R. Reed, 637(VS):Spring87-410
    M. Warner, 617(TLS):4-11Sep87-940
Showalter, E. - see de Graffigny, F.
Showalter, E., Jr. Exiles and Strangers.*
    J. Gassin, 535(RHL):Jul-Aug86-796
    B. Stoltzfus, 210(FrF):Jan86-121

Shrader-Frechette, K.S. Science Policy, Ethics and Economic Methodology.*
    M. Sagoff, 482(PhR):Oct86-633
Shrake, B. Night Never Falls.
    M. Watkins, 441:22Nov87-32
Shrake, E. Blessed McGill.
    K. Ray, 441:28Jun87-24
Shreve, S.R. Queen of Hearts.
    J.H. Korelitz, 617(TLS):24Apr87-434
    A. McDermott, 441:11Jan87-10
Shriver, L. The Female of the Species.
    K. Bouton, 441:19Jul87-13
Shroff, H.J. The Eighteenth-Century Novel.
    M. Irwin, 541(RES):Feb86-100
Shrubsall, D. & P. Coustillas - see Hudson, W.H. & G. Gissing
Shukman, A. - see Lotman, J.M. & B.A. Uspenskij
Shukri, I. History of the Malay Kingdom of Patani (Sejarah Kerajaan Melayu Patani).
    S. Talib, 293(JASt):Aug86-901
Shulman, A.K. In Every Woman's Life...
    M.S. Willis, 441:31May87-56
Shurr, W.H. The Marriage of Emily Dickinson.*
    S. Bush, Jr., 402(MLR):Jul87-715
    J. Loving, 183(ESQ):Vol32No3-201
Shusterman, R. The Object of Literary Criticism.*
    A. Hyslop, 478:Apr86-118
    L. Kasprisin, 289:Fall86-119
Shuttle, P. The Lion from Rio.
    H. Davies, 617(TLS):13Feb87-165
Shuttleworth, S. George Eliot and Nineteenth-Century Science.*
    R. Ashton, 541(RES):Feb86-115
    T. Braun, 447(N&Q):Dec85-537
    E.M. Eigner, 402(MLR):Oct87-932
    K. Tetzeli von Rosador, 72:Band223 Heft2-415
Sicher, E. Beyond Marginality.*
    J. Klinkowitz, 594:Fall86-320
    P. Lewis, 565:Autumn86-71
    P. Storfer, 157:No162-48
Sichère, B. La Gloire du traître.
    F. Raphael, 617(TLS):3Apr87-362
Sicherman, B. Alice Hamilton: A Life in Letters.*
    A.F. Scott, 579(SAQ):Autumn86-390
Sichrovsky, P. Strangers in their Own Land.*
    R.S. Wistrich, 617(TLS):13Feb87-153
Siddons, A.R. Homeplace.
    R. Bromley, 441:30Aug87-20
Sider, G.M. Culture and Class in Anthropology and History.
    R. Stirrat, 617(TLS):27Feb87-208
Sider, R.D. - see Erasmus
Sidney, P. Sir Philip Sidney: Selected Prose and Poetry. (2nd ed) (R. Kimbrough, ed)
    K. Duncan-Jones, 447(N&Q):Jun85-261
Sidney, R. The Poems of Robert Sidney.* (P.J. Croft, ed)
    J. Gouws, 447(N&Q):Dec85-518
Sido. Lettres à sa fille.
    J.H. Stewart, 207(FR):Feb87-401
Siebert-Ott, G.M. Kontroll-Probleme in infiniten Komplementkonstruktionen.
    H. Janssen, 603:Vol10No1-247
Sieff, M. Don't Ask the Price.
    R. Davenport-Hines, 617(TLS):20Mar87-293

Siegel, P.N., ed. Shakespeare's English and Roman History Plays.*
  T. Hawkes, 617(TLS):10Apr87-390
Siegel, S.F. - see Yeats, W.B.
Siegmund, W., ed. Antiker Mythos in unserer Märchen.
  E. Moser-Rath, 196:Band27Heft3/4-370
Siemon, J.R. Shakespearean Iconoclasm.*
  D. Bevington, 570(SQ):Spring86-125
  T.W. Craik, 541(RES):Nov86-563
  J.E. Howard, 551(RenQ):Spring86-138
Siger de Brabant. Quaestiones in Metaphysicam: Edition revue da la reportation de Munich, texte inédit de la reportation de Vienne.* (W. Dunphy, ed) Quaestiones in Metaphysicam: Texte inédit de la reportation de Cambridge, édition revue de la reportation de Paris.* (A. Maurer, ed)
  S.P. Marrone, 589:Oct86-1005
Signoret, S. Adieu, Volodya.*
  S. Lardner, 442(NY):12Jan87-100
Signorini, R. Opus Hoc Tenue - la camera dipinta di Andrea Mantegna.
  C.M. Brown, 90:Feb86-148
de Sigüenza y Góngora, C. Infortunios que Alonso Ramírez, natural da la ciudad de San Juan de Puerto Rico, padeció. (J.S. Cummins & A. Soons, eds)
  C.R. Boxer, 402(MLR):Jan87-224
Siguret, F. L'Oeil surpris.
  D. Graham, 475:Vol13No25-153
  T.J. Reiss, 210(FrF):May86-232
Sigurjónsson, Á. Den politiske Laxness.*
  W. Friese, 562(Scan):May86-87
Sikorski, H. - see Nabokov, V.
Silber, E. The Sculpture of Epstein.*
  P. Fuller, 617(TLS):6Feb87-133
Silber, J. In the City.
  J. Johnson, 441:29Mar87-8
Silbergeld, J. Chinese Painting Style.
  H-Y. Shih, 302:Vol22No1-87
  A.B. Wicks, 318(JAOS):Jan/Mar85-175
Siler, D. - see Pradier, J.
Silk, D. Hold Fast.
  L. Lerner, 569(SR):Spring86-312
Silk, G. & others. Automobile and Culture.
  K.A. Marling, 658:Winter86-326
Silk, M.S. Homer: "The Iliad."
  C.H. Sisson, 617(TLS):17Apr87-419
Silkin, J. The Ship's Pasture.
  T. Dooley, 617(TLS):6Mar87-244
  J. Forth, 364:Oct86-82
Silko, L.M. & J. Wright. The Delicacy and Strength of Lace. (A. Wright, ed)
  W. Ude, 649(WAL):Feb87-377
Silliman, R. Paradise.*
  G.F. Butterick, 703:No17-154
Sills, B. & L. Linderman. Beverly.
  D. Harris, 441:31May87-28
Silman, R. The Dream Dredger.
  D. Guy, 441:4Jan87-12
Silva, C.R. - see under Ruiz Silva, C.
de Silva, G.G. - see under Gómez de Silva, G.
Silve, E. Paul Léautaud et le Mercure de France.
  J. Aeply, 450(NRF):Feb86-106
Silver, B.R., ed. Virginia Woolf's Reading Notebooks.*
  J. Marcus, 40(AEB):Vol8No4-272

Silver, C.G. The Romance of William Morris.*
  F. Kirchhoff, 403(MLS):Summer86-358
Silver, L. A Guide to Political Censorship in South Africa.
  N. Choonoo, 538(RAL):Fall86-416
Silver, L. The Paintings of Quinten Massys, with Catalogue Raisonné.
  J. Rowlands, 39:Apr86-287
Silverberg, R. Tom O'Bedlam.
  J. Clute, 617(TLS):2Jan87-21
Silverman, D. Selling Culture.
  M. Kozloff, 441:4Jan87-34
Silverman, K. The Subject of Semiotics.*
  L. Hutcheon, 153:Spring86-78
Silverman, R., ed. Athletes.
  442(NY):28Dec87-126
Silverstein, T. - see "Sir Gawain and the Green Knight"
Silvis, R. The Luckiest Man in the World.
  S. Pinsker, 577(SHR):Summer86-298
Simard, R. Postmodern Drama.*
  G. Bas, 189(EA):Jan-Mar87-100
  I. Smith, 223:Fall86-327
  T.J. Taylor, 615(TJ):Mar86-125
  H. Zapf, 397(MD):Sep86-495
Simenon, G. Maigret's War of Nerves.*
  639(VQR):Autumn86-128
Simenon, G. The Murderer.
  442(NY):12Jan87-101
Simenon, G. The Outlaw.
  G. Kaufman, 362:19Feb87-26
Simha, S.L.N. Tiruppavai of Goda.
  M.R. & U. Parameswaran, 314:Summer-Fall86-243
Simic, C. Selected Poems 1963-1983.*
  C. Bedient, 569(SR):Fall86-657
  L. Rector, 249(HudR):Autumn86-511
  P. Stitt, 219(GaR):Summer86-557
Simic, C. The Uncertain Certainty.
  L. Rector, 249(HudR):Autumn86-512
Simic, C. Unending Blues.
  S. Dobyns, 441:18Oct87-46
Simis, K.M. USSR.
  R.A. Cooper, 390:Mar86-61
Simmonds, N.E. The Decline of Juridical Reason.*
  R.A. Shiner, 518:Apr86-124
Simmonds, P. Pure Posy.
  D.J. Enright, 617(TLS):18-24Dec87-1399
Simmons, C. The Belles Lettres Papers.
  P-L. Adams, 61:Aug87-84
  T. Brown, 617(TLS):13-19Nov87-1249
  K. Kimball, 362:3Sep87-28
  S. Schiff, 441:24May87-10
  442(NY):20Jul87-91
Simmons, H.G. From Asylum to Welfare.
  C. Howell, 529(QQ):Spring86-19
Simmons, J. Sean O'Casey.
  N. Grene, 447(N&Q):Sep85-408
Simmons, J. Poems 1956-1986.
  P. Forbes, 362:5Mar87-28
  J. Mole, 176:Mar87-58
Simmons, J. The Railways of Britain.
  D. Luckhurst, 324:Jul87-618
Simmons, J.C. Passionate Pilgrims.
  442(NY):7Sep87-112
Simmons, M. New Mexico.
  R.M. Adams, 453(NYRB):12Mar87-28
Simmons, M. & J. Myers. Along the Santa Fe Trail.
  R.M. Adams, 453(NYRB):12Mar87-28

Simocatta, T. - see under Theophylactus
Simocatta
Simon, E. Festivals of Attica.*
  J.N. Bremmer, 394:Vol39fasc3/4-543
Simon, K. A Wider World.*
  639(VQR):Summer86-84
Simon, L. Thornton Wilder.
  R.S. Smith, 106:Winter86-469
Simon, M. The Enchanted Room.
  L. McMahon, 441:19Apr87-20
Simon, M. Verus Israel.
  C.R. Phillips 3d, 124:Jul-Aug87-448
Simon, M.E. A Practical Guide for Teachers
of Elementary Japanese.
  P.J. Wetzel, 399(MLJ):Summer86-168
Simon, R.K. The Labyrinth of the Comic.
  A.M. Duckworth, 637(VS):Summer87-524
Simon of Faversham. Quaestiones super
Libro elenchorum. (S. Ebbesen & others,
eds)
  M.D. Jordan, 589:Jan86-251
Simón Díaz, J. El libro español antiguo.
  D.W. Cruickshank, 86(BHS):Apr86-157
Simon-Pelanda, H. Schein, Realität und
Utopie.
  H-J. Behr, 684(ZDA):Band115Heft4-158
  D.H. Green, 402(MLR):Jan86-243
Simonet, B. Franchise Militaire.
  J. Aeply, 450(NRF):Jul-Aug86-184
Simonin, M. - see Boaistuau, P.
Simonin, M. - see du Perron, J.D.
Simons, K. The Ludic Imagination.*
  B.E. Teets, 177(ELT):Vol29No1-101
Simons, K. Jacques Réattu, Peintre de la
Révolution Française.
  P. Bordes, 90:Jun86-436
Simons, L.M. Worth Dying For.
  R.J. Kessler, 441:6Sep87-8
Simons, W.B. & S. White, eds. The Party
Statutes of the Communist World.
  G. Kolankiewicz, 575(SEER):Jul86-483
Simonsen, D.F. Diktet og makten.
  H. Forsås-Scott, 172(Edda):1986/3-286
  N.M. Knutsen, 172(Edda):1986/3-285
Simonsen, M. Le Conte populaire.
  H. Shields, 208(FS):Apr86-244
  J. Simpson, 203:Vol97No1-118
Simonsen, M. Hekse, trolde og bondeknolde.
  S. Knudsen, 172(Edda):1986/3-283
Simpkin, R.E. Race to the Swift.
  M.R.D. Foot, 176:Feb87-46
"Simpliciana." (Band 6/7)
  H. Wagener, 133:Band19Heft3/4-334
Simpson, C. Artful Partners. (British
title: The Partnership.)
  F. Haskell, 617(TLS):5Jun87-595
  J. Pope-Hennessy, 453(NYRB):12Mar87-19
  J. Updike, 441:29Mar87-1
Simpson, C.M. A Good Southerner.
  639(VQR):Winter86-10
Simpson, D. Element of Doubt.
  T.J. Binyon, 617(TLS):9-15Oct87-1124
  G. Kaufman, 362:2Jul87-31
Simpson, D., ed. German Aesthetic and
Literary Criticism. (Vol 2)
  A.A. Kuzniar, 221(GQ):Winter86-117
  H.M. Schueller, 290(JAAC):Spring87-301
  K. Wright, 222(GR):Spring86-80
Simpson, D. Last Seen Alive.
  639(VQR):Summer86-93

Simpson, D. The Politics of American
English, 1776-1850.*
  R. Bridgman, 27(AL):Dec86-623
  W.N. Francis, 350:Sep87-674
  639(VQR):Summer86-87
Simpson, D. Wordsworth and the Figurings
of the Real.
  S. Wolfson, 591(SIR):Spring86-131
Simpson, E. Orphans.
  P-L. Adams, 61:Sep87-102
  S. Ballantyne, 441:19Jul87-1
  442(NY):10Aug87-79
Simpson, G.G. Discoverers of the Lost
World.
  C.B. Fleming, 37:Jan-Feb86-59
Simpson, J. & J. Bennett. The Disapppeared
and the Mothers of the Plaza.* (British
title: The Disappeared.)
  639(VQR):Summer86-96
Simpson, J. & G. Martin. The Canadian
Guide to Britain. (Vol 1)
  W.N., 102(CanL):Spring86-202
Simpson, J.A., ed. The Concise Oxford
Dictionary of Proverbs.
  M-M. Dubois, 189(EA):Jul-Sep86-317
  S. Lawson, 35(AS):Winter86-352
Simpson, J.R. & others. Technological
Change in Japan's Beef Industry.
  P. Francks, 293(JASt):Aug86-862
Simpson, K.G., ed. Henry Fielding.*
  C.A. Knight, 566:Autumn86-59
Simpson, L. People Live Here.*
  W. Scammell, 364:Jun86-61
Simpson, M. Anywhere but Here.
  A. Beevor, 617(TLS):26Jun87-698
  L.A. Schreiber, 441:11Jan87-7
Sims, G.E. The Little Man's Big Friend.
  D.W. Grantham, 585(SoQ):Winter87-154
Sims, J.H. & L. Ryken, eds. Milton and
Scriptural Tradition.*
  A-L. Cary, 179(ES):Jun86-269
  G.R. Evans, 541(RES):Aug86-414
  J.B. Gabel, 579(SAQ):Winter86-106
Sims, W.L. Two Hundred Years of History
and Evolution of Woodworking Machinery.
  R. Grant, 324:Dec86-80
von Simson, G. Sanskrit-Wörterbuch der
buddhistischen Texte aus den Turfan-
Funden. (Pt 4) (M. Schmidt, ed)
  J.W. de Jong, 259(IIJ):Jan86-59
Sinclair, A. Madrid Newspapers 1661-1870.
  D.L. Shaw, 402(MLR):Jul86-772
Sinclair, A. The Red and the Blue.*
  A. Burgess, 61:May87-92
  S. Koch, 441:8Mar87-12
  D. Sexton, 364:Aug/Sep86-144
Sinclair, A. Spiegel.
  A. Walker, 617(TLS):18-24Dec87-1398
Sinclair, C. Diaspora Blues.
  B. Wasserstein, 617(TLS):3Jul87-709
Sinclair, I. White Chappell, Scarlet Trac-
ings.
  J. Clute, 617(TLS):30Oct-5Nov87-1193
Sinclair, K.V., ed. The Hospitallers'
"Riwle" (Miracula et Regula Hospitalis
Sancti Johannis Jerosolimitani).
  A.J. Holden, 554:Vol105No4-573
  L. Morini, 379(MedR):Dec86-438
  W. Rothwell, 402(MLR):Apr86-476
Sindell, G. - see Miller, H.
Sinden, D., ed. The Everyman Book of The-
atrical Anecdotes.
  P. Cotes, 324:Sep87-786

"Słownik Artystów Polskich i obcych w
Polsce Dzialajacych (zmarłych przed 1966
R.) – Malarze, Rzeźbiarze, Graficy."
(Vol 4)
  A.S. Ciechanowiecki, 90:Dec86–910
Sluijter, E.J. De "Heydensche Fabulen" in
de Noordnederlandse Schilderkunst, circa
1590–1670.
  I. Gaskell, 90:Aug86–612
Slusser, G.E. & E.S. Rabkin, eds. Hard
Science Fiction.
  L. Olsen, 395(MFS):Winter86–704
Slusser, G.E. & E.S. Rabkin, eds. Shadows
of the Magic Lamp.
  A. Gordon, 561(SFS):Mar86–89
Šmahel, F. La révolution hussite.
  H. Kaminsky, 589:Jul86–704
Small, D. The River in Winter.
  L. Zeidner, 441:25Jan87–8
  442(NY):23Mar87–100
Smallman, B. The Music of Heinrich Schütz,
1585–1672.*
  J.H., 412:Aug85–215
Smart, C. The Poetical Works of Christo-
pher Smart.* (Vol 2) (M. Walsh & K. Wil-
liamson, eds)
  C. Rawson, 83:Spring86–108
Smart, C. The Poetical Works of Christo-
pher Smart. (Vol 3, ed by M. Walsh; Vol
4, ed by K. Williamson)
  K. Walker, 617(TLS):16–22Oct87–1144
Smart, J.J.C. Ethics, Persuasion and
Truth.
  D. McNaughton, 518:Jan86–56
Smart, R.A. The Nonfiction Novel.
  C. Caramello, 395(MFS):Summer86–345
Smead, H. Blood Justice.
  A. Schmitz, 441:11Jan87–19
Smedley, A. Daughter of Earth.
  M. Jehlen, 441:23Aug87–14
Smeed, J.W. German Song and Its Poetry
1740–1900.
  E. Sams, 617(TLS):20–26Nov87–1290
Smeed, J.W. The Theophrastan "Character."
  J. Moore, 568(SCN):Fall86–44
  639(VQR):Summer86–86
Smeets, J.R. – see de Belleperche, G.
Smidt, K. Unconformities in Shakespeare's
Early Comedies.
  T. Hawkes, 617(TLS):10Apr87–390
Smiley, J. The Age of Grief.
  A. Bernays, 441:6Sep87–12
Smirnov, I.P. Khudozhestvennyy smysl i
evolyutsiya poeticheskikh sistem. Dia-
khronicheskiye transformatsii literatur-
nykh zhanrov i motivov.
  J. Graffy, 575(SEER):Jan86–117
Smith, A. Elegy on Independence Day.*
  T. Swiss, 569(SR):Spring86–302
  639(VQR):Spring86–60
Smith, A. Gobineau et l'histoire natur-
elle.*
  R. Béziau, 535(RHL):Jul–Aug86–774
  M. Biddiss, 208(FS):Oct86–477
  R.T. Denommé, 207(FR):Oct86–127
Smith, A.D. The Ethnic Origins of Nations.
  A. Kuper, 617(TLS):12Jun87–630
Smith, A.G.L. Eve Tempted.
  T. Martin, 594:Winter86–450
Smith, A.J. Literary Love.*
  W. Weiss, 156(ShJW):Jahrbuch1986–198

Smith, A.J. The Metaphysics of Love.
  J.F.S. Post, 551(RenQ):Autumn86–539
  R.H. Wells, 278(IS):Vol41–137
Smith, B. European Vision and the South
Pacific.* (2nd ed)
  J. Parker, 173(ECS):Spring87–392
Smith, B. Silver and Information.
  639(VQR):Winter86–30
Smith, B.C. After the Revolution.
  42(AR):Spring86–246
Smith, B.F. The War's Long Shadow.
  J.L. Gaddis, 617(TLS):8May87–479
Smith, B.G. Confessions of a Concierge.*
  M–C.W. Koop, 207(FR):Dec86–277
  E. Weber, 31(ASch):Summer86–418
  42(AR):Fall86–490
Smith, C. Jean Anouilh.
  E. Freeman, 208(FS):Oct86–491
Smith, C. The Making of the "Poema de mio
Cid."*
  D.G. Pattison, 382(MAE):1986/2–330
Smith, C.D. The Early Career of Lord
North, the Prime Minister.
  L. Mitchell, 447(N&Q):Mar85–131
Smith, C.R. Interior Design in 20th–Century
America.
  P.L. Brown, 441:26Jul87–16
Smith, C.S. Chicago and the American Lit-
erary Imagination, 1880–1920.*
  M. Gidley, 366:Spring86–125
Smith, D. Let Us Rise!
  N. Wiseman, 298:Spring86–144
Smith, D. Local Assays.*
  M. Ford, 617(TLS):22May87–557
Smith, D. Prisoners of God.
  M. Yapp, 617(TLS):14Aug87–883
Smith, D. The Roundhouse Voices.*
  C. Bedient, 569(SR):Fall86–657
  M. Jarman, 249(HudR):Summer86–345
  639(VQR):Winter86–27
Smith, D. Gilles Vigneault, conteur et
poète.
  P. Hébert, 627(UTQ):Fall86–225
Smith, D., with others. Gilbert La Rocque.
  N.B. Bishop, 627(UTQ):Fall86–223
Smith, D.C. H.G. Wells.*
  J.R. Reed, 637(VS):Summer87–540
Smith, D.L. – see Tirso de Molina
Smith, D.M. Cavour.*
  F.J. Coppa, 275(IQ):Spring86–121
Smith, D.W. Serious Crimes.
  T.J. Binyon, 617(TLS):9–15Oct87–1124
Smith, E.C. American Surnames.
  K.H., 424:Sep86–337
Smith, G. The Achievement of Graham
Greene.*
  H–P. Breuer, 395(MFS):Winter86–665
Smith, G. The Champion.
  P–L. Adams, 61:Apr87–91
Smith, G. Morality, Reason and Power.*
  639(VQR):Autumn86–129
Smith, G. The Novel and Society.*
  R.C. Schweik, 301(JEGP):Jul86–459
Smith, G. "The Waste Land."*
  S.B., 675(YER):Vol8No1/2–146
  B. Bergonzi, 402(MLR):Apr87–462
  R. Beum, 569(SR):Winter86–124
  D. Crane, 161(DUJ):Dec85–207
  W. Harmon, 569(SR):Summer86–510
  J. Wordsworth, 541(RES):Feb86–125
Smith, G. – see Benjamin, W.
Smith, G.B. The Devil in the Dooryard.*
  D. Montrose, 617(TLS):19Jun87–668

Smith, G.S. Songs To Seven Strings.*
  D.C. Gillespie, 575(SEER):Apr86-286
  W. Noll, 187:Spring/Summer87-355
  D. Skillen, 402(MLR):Jul86-812
Smith, H.L., ed. War and Social Change.
  P. Renshaw, 617(TLS):15May87-510
Smith, I.C. In the Middle of the Wood.
  I. Bamforth, 617(TLS):5Jun87-611
  M. Pacey, 362:4Jun87-46
Smith, I.C. Selected Poems.
  H. Buckingham, 565:Summer86-64
Smith, I.C. Towards the Human.
  I. Bamforth, 617(TLS):5Jun87-611
Smith, J. The Complete Works of Captain
John Smith.* (P.L. Barbour, ed)
  J.A.L. Lemay, 578:Fall87-113
Smith, J. Huckleberry Fiend.
  N. Callendar, 441:1Nov87-34
Smith, J. A Masculine Ending.
  T.J. Binyon, 617(TLS):17Jul87-778
  G. Kaufman, 362:2Jul87-31
Smith, J. One Hundred Most Frightening
Things.
  B. Almon, 102(CanL):Spring86-177
Smith, J.A. Printers and Press Freedom.
  F. Abrams, 441:1Nov87-30
Smith, J.A. Schoenberg and His Circle.
  R. Craft, 453(NYRB):5Nov87-30
Smith, J.B. - see Delius, F. & E. Munch
Smith, J.F. Slavery and Rice Culture in
Low Country Georgia, 1750-1860.
  B. Wood, 656(WMQ):Oct86-677
  639(VQR):Spring86-52
Smith, J.H. & W. Kerrigan, eds. Pragma-
tism's Freud.
  N. Lukacher, 400(MLN):Dec86-1286
  R. Shusterman, 290(JAAC):Summer87-427
Smith, J.L. - see Boucicault, D.
Smith, J.R. The Speckled Monster.
  R. Porter, 617(TLS):6-12Nov87-1219
Smith, K. Decoys and Other Stories.
  E. McGraw, 455:Mar86-69
  D.E. Wylder, 649(WAL):Aug86-164
Smith, K. Terra.
  T. Dooley, 617(TLS):20Mar87-301
Smith, K. Wormwood. A Book of Chinese
Whispers.
  M. Ford, 617(TLS):18-24Dec87-1394
Smith, L.B. Treason in Tudor England.*
  C. Hill, 453(NYRB):7May87-36
  R. Kaye, 441:15Feb87-21
Smith, L.W. Jane Austen and the Drama of
Woman.
  P. Honan, 83:Spring86-99
  J. Thompson, 536(Rev):Vol8-21
Smith, M. Daydreams.
  N. Callendar, 441:16Aug87-21
Smith, M. - see Chesterton, G.K.
Smith, M-A.T. Lament for a Silver-Eyed
Woman.
  D. Leimbach, 441:20Sep87-26
Smith, M.V. & D. Maclennan, eds. Olive
Schreiner and After.*
  D. Walder, 538(RAL):Fall86-401
Smith, N.B. & T.G. Bergin. An Old Proven-
çal Primer.*
  M.B. Booth, 402(MLR):Apr86-474
  F.R. Hamlin, 589:Apr86-472
Smith, O. The Politics of Language, 1791-
1819.*
  G. Claeys, 366:Autumn86-257
  C. Fierobe, 189(EA):Jul-Sep87-353
                              [continued]

[continuing]
  J. Klancher, 250(HLQ):Autumn86-409
  A. Louvre, 506(PSt):May86-78
  M. Philp, 83:Autumn86-244
  D. Simpson, 88:Fall86-63
Smith, P., ed. Perspectives on Contempo-
rary Legend.
  J. Simpson, 203:Vol97No1-120
Smith, P. Public and Private Value.*
  N. Bradbury, 541(RES):May86-272
  D. Feldmann, 72:Band223Heft2-413
  A. Kennedy, 627(UTQ):Spring87-443
Smith, P. & O.R. Jones. The Philosophy of
Mind.
  P. Snowdon, 617(TLS):15May87-528
Smith, P.J. Highlights of the Off-Season.
  R. Kaveney, 617(TLS):6Mar87-246
Smith, P.M. Language, the Sexes and
Society.
  M. Deuchar, 297(JL):Mar86-243
  B. Schräpel, 603:Vol10No2-551
Smith, P.M. & I.D. McFarlane, eds. Litera-
ture and the Arts in the Reign of Francis
I.
  J. Braybrook, 208(FS):Apr86-196
  R.D. Cottrell, 210(FrF):May86-228
  A. Moss, 402(MLR):Jul87-734
Smith, P.S. Andy Warhol's Art and Film.
  P. Core, 617(TLS):1May87-466
Smith, P.T. Policing Victorian London.
  D. Philips, 637(VS):Autumn86-143
Smith, R. Alkan. (Vol 2)
  W. Mellers, 617(TLS):16-22Oct87-1134
Smith, R.A. Late Georgian and Regency
England 1760-1837.
  J.R. Dinwiddy, 83:Spring86-86
Smith, R.C. & J. Lounibos, eds. Pagan and
Christian Anxiety.
  R.J. Lane Fox, 313:Vol76-304
Smith, R.E.F. & D. Christian. Bread and
Salt.*
  H. Leeming, 575(SEER):Jan86-132
  C. Stevens, 550(RusR):Jan86-65
Smith, R.G. Travels in the Land of the
Gods. (V. Manthorpe, ed)
  P-L. Adams, 61:Jan87-90
  442(NY):23Mar87-101
Smith, R.J., ed. The Ways We Live Now.
  C. Baxter, 385(MQR):Fall87-803
Smith, R.M., ed. Land, Kinship and Life-
Cycle.
  D. Herlihy, 551(RenQ):Autumn86-520
Smith, S. W.H. Auden.*
  639(VQR):Autumn86-118
Smith, S. Edward Thomas.
  K. Bucknell, 617(TLS):27Feb87-217
Smith, S.A. Myth, Media, and the Southern
Mind.
  C.L. Kell, 583:Fall86-92
Smith, S.A., ed. Oktyabr'skaya Revolutsiya
i Fabzavkomy (The October Revolution
and the Factory Committees).
  Z. Galili y Garcia, 550(RusR):Oct86-442
Smith, S.H. Masks in Modern Drama.
  J.W. Flannery, 615(TJ):May86-245
Smith, S.M. & D.M. - see Mullett, A.B.
Smith, S.V.H. Masks in Modern Drama.
  R. Simard, 397(MD):Dec86-628
Smith, S.W.R. Samuel Richardson.
  I. Grundy, 566:Autumn86-66
Smith, T. Thinking Like a Communist.
  W.G. Hyland, 441:23Aug87-9

Smith, T.D. Montague Summers.
   H. Ormsby-Lennon, 677(YES):Vol16-354
Smith, V., ed. Australian Poetry 1986.
   C. James, 617(TLS):27Nov-3Dec87-1327
Smith, V. Carpentier, "Los pasos perdi-
   dos."
   W.B. Berg, 72:Band223Heft2-456
   R.K. Britton, 402(MLR):Apr86-520
   A. McDermott, 86(BHS):Jul86-304
Smith, V. Selected Poems.*
   G. Catalano, 381:Mar86-103
   N. Rowe, 581:Jun86-178
Smith, W.J. & F.D. Reeve - see Voznesensky,
   A.
Smith, W.S. The Closest of Enemies.
   J.G. Castaneda, 441:1Mar87-18
   W. La Feber, 61:Mar87-92
Smither, E. Professor Musgrove's Canary.
   J. Penberthy, 617(TLS):31Jul87-823
Smither, H.E. A History of the Oratorio.
   (Vol 3)
   W. Dean, 617(TLS):30Oct-5Nov87-1187
Smits, E.R. - see Abelard, P.
Smollett, T. Humphry Clinker. (J.L. Thor-
   son, ed)
   P-G. Boucé, 541(RES):Feb86-103
   J.V. Price, 447(N&Q):Jun85-266
Smullyan, R. Forever Undecided.
   G. Johnson, 441:21Jun87-35
Smyth, D.E. Quilt.
   H. Porter, 296(JCF):No35/36-178
Smyth, E. The Memoirs of Ethel Smyth. (R.
   Crichton, ed)
   H. Spurling, 617(TLS):3Jul87-712
Smyth, R.A. Forms of Intuition.
   A. Broadie, 342:Band77Heft2-256
Snead, J.A. Figures of Division.
   K.J. Phillips, 268(IFR):Summer87-104
Snell, B. Griechische Metrik. (4th ed)
   C.M.J. Sicking, 394:Vol39fasc3/4-423
Snelling, T. - see under Hutton, L.
Sneyd, B. Riding High. (P. Barstow, ed)
   P-L. Adams, 61:May87-94
Snipes, K. Robert Penn Warren.*
   M.R. Winchell, 106:Winter86-483
Snodgrass, A. The Symbolism of the Stūpa.
   J. Fontein, 293(JASt):Aug86-812
Snodgrass, W.D. Selected Poems 1957-1987.
   G. Ewart, 441:13Sep87-52
Snoke, A.W. Hospitals, Health and People.
   R. Porter, 617(TLS):7Aug87-843
Snorri Sturluson. Edda.* (A. Faulkes, ed)
   T. Krömmelbein, 684(ZDA):Band115Heft2-
   51
Snow, J.T. "Celestina" by Fernando de
   Rojas.
   D.P. Seniff, 304(JHP):Winter86-184
Snowden, F.M. Violence and Great Estates
   in the South of Italy.
   P. Ginsborg, 617(TLS):20Feb87-189
Snowman, D. The World of Plácido Domingo.*
   W. Lonsdale, 465:Spring86-128
Snoy, P., ed. Ethnologie und Geschichte.
   W.L. Smith, 318(JAOS):Oct/Dec85-782
Snyder, J. Northern Renaissance Art.*
   S.N. Blum, 551(RenQ):Spring86-115
Soave, V. Il fondo antico spagnolo della
   Biblioteca Estense di Modena.
   D.W. Cruickshank, 402(MLR):Oct87-996
Sobejano, G. Clarín en su obra ejemplar.
   L. Bonet, 240(HR):Summer86-350
   J. Rutherford, 402(MLR):Oct87-1007
   N.M. Valis, 238:Sep86-544

Sobejano, G. - see Delibes, M.
Sobel, M.I. Light.
   J. Cornell, 441:27Sep87-32
Sobel, R. RCA.
   J. Quinlan, 441:1Mar87-21
Sober, E. The Nature of Selection.*
   R.N. Brandon, 482(PhR):Oct86-614
   A. Manser, 518:Apr86-126
Sobhan, R. The Crisis of External Depen-
   dence.
   J.P. Thorp, 293(JASt):Aug86-789
   R.J. Young, 318(JAOS):Oct/Dec85-809
"Sociolinguistique des langues romanes."
   D.E. Ager, 208(FS):Oct86-501
Sodenkamp, A. C'est au feu que je par-
   donne.
   T. Greene, 207(FR):Oct86-171
Sohnle, W.P., ed. Stefan George und der
   Symbolismus.*
   F. Claudon, 549(RLC):Jan-Mar86-115
Sojcher, J. & G. Hottois, eds. Philoso-
   phies non chrétiennes et christianisme.
   R. Bodéüs, 154:Spring86-198
Sojka, G.S. Ernest Hemingway.
   S. Pinsker, 395(MFS):Winter86-614
Sokol, E. Russian Poetry for Children.*
   A. Pyman, 402(MLR):Jan86-271
Sokolowski, R. Moral Action.
   E. Pols, 543:Dec86-399
   M.D.S., 185:Apr87-678
Sola Castaño, E. Libro de las maravillas
   del Oriente.
   A. Ricón, 552(REH):May86-130
Solà-Solé, J.M. Sobre árabes, judíos y
   marranos y su impacto en la lengua y la
   literatura españolas.*
   W. Mettmann, 547(RF):Band98Heft1/2-
   184
Soldateschi, J. - see Ungaretti, G.
Solecki, S., ed. Spider Blues.
   A. Van Wart, 105:Fall/Winter86-112
Solèr, C. & T. Ebneter, comps. Schweizer
   Dialekte in Text und Ton.
   E. Diekmann, 72:Band223Heft1-202
Sollers, P. Théorie des Exceptions.
   P-L. Rey, 450(NRF):Apr86-99
Sollers, P. Writing and the Experience of
   Limits. (D. Hayman, ed)
   D. Brewer, 405(MP):Aug86-112
Sollors, W. Beyond Ethnicity.
   N. Baym, 432(NEQ):Dec86-574
Šoloja, S. & F. Han, eds & trans. La
   Poésie paysanne de Serbie.
   L. Kovacs, 450(NRF):Oct86-116
Solomon, B.M. In the Company of Educated
   Women.*
   D.L. Eder, 152(UDQ):Winter87-107
Solomon, D. Jackson Pollock.
   M. Brenson, 441:18Oct87-24
Solomon, E. & S. Arkin - see Weiss, D.
Solomon, H.A. The Exercise Myth.*
   L. Wolfe, 529(QQ):Spring86-191
Solomon, L. Power at What Cost?
   M. Love, 529(QQ):Spring86-218
Solomon, M. The Art of Typography.
   K. Schmidt, 507:Jul/Aug86-304
Solomon, R.C. In the Spirit of Hegel.*
   M. Rosen, 482(PhR):Jan86-115
Solomon, S. The Fall of Hitler: or, Where
   is Thy Peace?
   B. Grantham, 157:No159-47

Solomon, S.G., ed. Pluralism in the Soviet
Union.*
    J. de Bardeleben, 550(RusR):Jul86-326
Solotaroff, T. A Few Good Voices in My
Head.
    R. Minkoff, 441:22Nov87-33
Solotorevsky, M. José Donoso.
    P. Bacarisse, 86(BHS):Oct86-382
Soloveitchik, J.B. The Halakhic Mind.
    J.M. Elukin, 441:22Feb87-29
Solta, G.R. Einführung in die Balkanlin-
guistik mit besonderer Berücksichtigung
des Substrats und des Balkanlateinischen.
    K.H. Schmidt, 685(ZDL):2/1986-274
Somary, F. The Raven of Zürich.
    R.J. Overy, 617(TLS):19Jun87-659
Somerville, E.O. & M. Ross. The Real
Charlotte. (V. Beards, ed)
    K.Q.Z., 295(JML):Nov86-539
Somerville-Large, P. Cappaghglass.*
    M. Koenig, 272(IUR):Spring86-86
Somerville-Large, P. To the Navel of the
World.
    C. von Fürer-Haimendorf, 617(TLS):
3Jul87-711
Sommer, D. & others, eds. Lesserfahrung –
Lebenserfahrung.
    D. Kliche, 654(WB):3/1986-492
Sommerstein, A.H. – see Aristophanes
Sonenscher, M. The Hatters of Eighteenth-
Century France.
    A. Forrest, 617(TLS):11–17Sep87-983
Soniat, K. Notes of Departure.
    A.C. Bromley, 502(PrS):Winter86-114
Sonnenfeldt, H., ed. Soviet Politics in
the 1980s.
    S.M. Terry, 550(RusR):Jul86-320
Sonnichsen, C.L. – see Farris, F.B.
Sontag, F. The Elements of Philosophy.
    W. Gerber, 543:Sep86-141
Soong, S.C. & J. Minford, eds. Trees on
the Mountain.
    C.H. Wang, 293(JASt):Feb86-389
Soop, H. The Power and the Glory.
    I. Rosell, 341:Vol55No4-173
von Soosten, J. – see Bonhoeffer, J.
Soper, K. Humanism and Anti-Humanism.
    N.S.L., 185:Jul87-894
Soper, P. A Theory of Law.*
    J. Cottingham, 518:Oct86-250
    D.G. Rèaume, 529(QQ):Spring86-194
    W.H. Wilcox, 482(PhR):Apr86-282
Sophocles. Sophoclis Tragoediae. (Vol 1)
(2nd ed) (R.D. Dawe, ed)
    H. Lloyd-Jones, 123:Vol36No1-10
Sophocles. Sophoclis Tragoediae. (Vol 2)
(2nd ed) (R.D. Dawe, ed)
    H. Lloyd-Jones, 123:Vol36No2-305
Sorabji, R. Time, Creation and the Con-
tinuum.*
    S.W. Broadie, 41:Fall85-349
    R.M. Dancy, 482(PhR):Apr86-290
Sordi, M. The Christians and the Roman
Empire.
    M. Beard, 617(TLS):20Feb87-179
Sordi, M. La Sicilia dal 368/367 al
337/336.
    J. Laborderie, 555:Vol59fasc2-292
Sorell, T. Hobbes.
    R. Tuck, 617(TLS):17Apr87-420
Sorelli, F. La santità imitabile.
    J. Howe, 589:Oct86-1035

Sørensen, B.A. Herrschaft und Zärtlich-
keit.*
    G. Hillen, 301(JEGP):Jan86-77
    R. Koc, 222(GR):Summer86-120
    W.D. Wilson, 221(GQ):Spring86-307
    W. Wittkowski, 133:Band19Heft3/4-343
Sørensen, F. La formation des mots en
français moderne.
    S. Fleischman, 545(RPh):Aug86-88
    C. Heldner, 597(SN):Vol58No1-139
Sørensen, K. Charles Dickens: Linguistic
Innovator.
    K.C. Phillipps, 179(ES):Jun86-276
Sørensen, K. St. St. Blicher.
    M. Brøndsted, 562(Scan):May86-78
Sørensen, V. Seneca.*
    N. Ingwersen, 562(Scan):Nov86-217
Sorescu, M. The Biggest Egg in the World.
    P. Forbes, 362:25Jun87-31
    V. Nemoianu, 617(TLS):9–15Oct87-1121
Sorescu, M. The Thirst of the Salt Moun-
tain.
    B. Grantham, 157:No159-47
Sorescu, M. Vlad Dracula, the Impaler.
The Youth of Don Quixote.
    V. Nemoianu, 617(TLS):9–15Oct87-1121
Sorestad, G. Hold the Rain in Your Hands.*
    G. Woodcock, 102(CanL):Winter85-174
Sorg, B. Das lyrische Ich.
    R.E. Lorbe, 301(JEGP):Jan86-72
    D.D. Stewart, 564:Sep86-255
    K. Weissenberger, 133:Band19Heft3/4-340
Söring, J. Tragödie.
    R. Galle, 52:Band21Heft3-302
Sorley, C.H. The Collected Poems of
Charles Hamilton Sorley.* (J.M. Wilson,
ed)
    L.K. Uffelman 177(ELT):Vol29No4-451
Sorrentino, G. Odd Number.
    G. Green, 532(RCF):Spring86-200
    G. Kearns, 249(HudR):Spring86-130
Sorrentino, G. Rose Theatre.
    R. Cohen, 441:20Dec87-16
Sorrentino, G. Something Said.
    C. Dowell, 532(RCF):Spring86-198
Sosin, J.M. English America and Imperial
Inconstancy.
    E.R. Sheridan, 656(WMQ):Jul86-483
Soskice, J.M. Metaphor and Religious Lan-
guage.
    E.T. Long, 543:Dec86-402
    R.A. Sharpe, 89(BJA):Spring86-184
Sötemann, A.L. Over poetica en poëzie.
    J. Goedegebuure, 204(FdL):Sep86-226
Souchal, F. French Sculptors of the Seven-
teenth and Eighteenth Centuries. (Vol 3)
    M. Jordan, 617(TLS):21Aug87-902
Soulez, A., ed & trans. Manifeste du
Cercle de Vienne et autres écrits.*
    A. Boyer, 192(EP):Oct–Dec86-584
    P. Engel, 542:Jan–Mar86-147
Soulis, G.C. The Serbs and Byzantium dur-
ing the Reign of Tsar Stephen Dušan
(1331–1355) and His Successors.
    D.M. Nicol, 575(SEER):Oct86-606
"Sources and Analogues of Old English
Poetry."* (Vol 2) (D.G. Calder &
others, trans)
    D.N. Dumville, 447(N&Q):Dec85-509
    D.K. Fry, 589:Jan86-228
    J.D. Pheifer, 541(RES):Feb86-68
    E.G. Stanley, 402(MLR):Apr87-432

de Sousa Rebelo, L. A tradição clássica na literatura portuguesa.
  T. Earle, 86(BHS):Apr86-182
Souster, R. Flight of the Roller Coaster. (R. Woollatt, ed)
  529(QQ):Winter86-946
Souster, R. It Takes All Kinds.
  S. Scobie, 376:Dec86-140
Souster, R. Jubilee of Death.
  D. Precosky, 198:Spring86-91
  L.M. York, 102(CanL):Spring86-157
Southam, B., ed. Jane Austen: The Critical Heritage. (Vol 2)
  D. Nokes, 617(TLS):6-12Nov87-1216
Southern, D.W. Gunnar Myrdal and Black-White Relations.
  J.B. Childs, 441:17May87-51
  D.M. Kennedy, 61:May87-86
Southern, E. The Music of Black Americans. (2nd ed)
  D.E. McGinty, 91:Spring86-185
Southern, R.W. Robert Grosseteste.
  A. Murray, 617(TLS):1May87-455
Southey, R. Mr. Rowlandson's England. (J. Steel, ed)
  C. Fox, 90:Dec86-908
Souza, M. The Emperor of the Amazon.
  S. White, 448:Vol24No3-95
de Souza Filho, D.M. - see under Marcondes de Souza Filho, D.
Sowa, C.A. Traditional Themes and the "Homeric Hymns."*
  N. Postlethwaite, 303(JoHS):Vol106-203
Sowards, J.K. - see Erasmus
Sowayan, S.A. Nabaṭi Poetry.
  S.K. Webster, 292(JAF):Jul/Sep86-331
Sowell, T. A Conflict of Visions.
  F. Barnes, 441:25Jan87-14
Sowell, T. Marxism.
  D.R. Steele, 258:Jun86-201
Sowinski, B. Textlinguistik.
  J. Macha, 685(ZDL):3/1986-380
Sozzi, L. L'Italia di Stendhal.
  S. Serodes, 535(RHL):Mar-Apr86-300
Spacks, P.M. Gossip.*
  J. Gordon, 400(MLN):Dec86-1273
  S.G. Kellman, 639(VQR):Winter86-150
  617(TLS):30Jan87-120
Spacks, P.M. & W.B. Carnochan. A Distant Prospect.
  A.J. Sambrook, 677(YES):Vol16-255
Spada, J. Grace.
  V. Glendinning, 617(TLS):24Jul87-792
  H. Neill, 362:16Jul87-24
  E. Stein, 441:19Jul87-21
Spaeth, D. Mies van der Rohe.*
  T.S. Hines, 505:Apr86-211
  A.W., 90:Feb86-157
Spaggiari, W. - see Borsieri, P.
Spahr, B.L. - see Ulrich, A.
Spalding, F. British Art Since 1900.*
  P. Fuller, 90:Oct86-756
  T. Phillips, 617(TLS):6Feb87-139
  A. Ross, 364:Aug/Sep86-140
Spalding, P. The History of the Medical College of Georgia.
  R. Porter, 617(TLS):7Aug87-843
Spang, K. Ritmo y versificación: Teoría y práctica del análisis métrico y rítmico.*
  W. Ferguson, 240(HR):Autumn86-459
Spang, R. Das Flussgebiet der Saar.
  A. Greule, 260(IF):Band91-425

Spanidou, I. God's Snake.*
  J. Mellors, 362:28May87-26
  M. Sanderson, 617(TLS):3Jul87-715
"The Spanish Civil War: A History in Pictures."*
  B. Knox, 453(NYRB):26Mar87-21
Spanos, W.V., P.A. Bové & D. O'Hara, eds. The Question of Textuality.
  L. Hutcheon, 107(CRCL):Sep86-461
Spariosu, M. Literature, Mimesis and Play.*
  M. Calinescu, 131(CL):Winter86-87
Spark, D., ed. 20 under 30.*
  W.C. Hamlin, 573(SSF):Fall86-455
Spark, M. Mary Shelley.
  P-L. Adams, 61:Aug87-84
  S. Gubar, 441:6Sep87-7
  C. Tomalin, 453(NYRB):19Nov87-35
  442(NY):5Oct87-127
Spark, M. The Stories of Muriel Spark.
  S. Mackay, 617(TLS):12Jun87-627
  V. Shaw, 362:30Apr87-31
Sparkes, I.G. Dictionary of Collective Nouns and Group Terms. (2nd ed)
  K.B. Harder, 424:Dec86-405
Sparling, S.L. The Glass Mountain.
  R.S. Diotte, 102(CanL):Spring86-169
Sparshott, F. The Theory of the Arts.
  R.A. Shiner, 154:Autumn86-533
Spater, G. William Cobbett.
  A.J. Sambrook, 677(YES):Vol16-281
Spatt, B. Writing from Sources.
  R.A. Eden, 126(CCC):May86-252
Spear, H.D. "Wuthering Heights" by Emily Brontë.
  K. Sutherland, 402(MLR):Oct87-927
Spear, J.L. Dreams of an English Eden.*
  C. Brooks, 326:Autumn86-55
  R.E. Fitch, 301(JEGP):Apr86-285
  M. Hardman, 402(MLR):Jul87-711
  J. Hayman, 401(MLQ):Mar85-98
Spearing, A.C. Medieval to Renaissance in English Poetry.
  A. Crépin, 189(EA):Apr-Jun87-198
  T. Davenport, 175:Summer86-159
  L. Ensminger, 588(SSL):Vol21-373
Spears, M.K. American Ambitions.
  S. Shanker, 441:14Jun87-29
Spears, R.A. & others, eds. Diccionario Básico Norteamericano.
  E. Gonzales-Berry, 399(MLJ):Winter86-447
Specht, J. & J. Fields. Frank Hurley in Papua.
  J. Povey, 2(AfrA):Nov85-83
Spechtler, F.V., ed. Lyrik des ausgehenden 14. und des 15. Jahrhunderts.*
  J.W. Thomas, 133:Band18Heft4-362
"Spectacular Helmets of Japan: 16th-19th Century."
  J. Polster, 139:Jun/Jul86-14
Speidel, M., ed. Japanische Architektur.
  U. Kultermann, 576:Sep86-315
Speier, H. German White-Collar Workers and the Rise of Hitler.
  D. Blackbourn, 617(TLS):15May87-522
Spence, J. Putting Myself in the Picture.
  A. Graham-Dixon, 362:26Feb87-19
Spence, J.D. The Memory Palace of Matteo Ricci.
  T. Brook, 293(JASt):Aug86-831
Spencer, E. The Light in the Piazza.
  K. Tudor, 198:Fall86-94

Spencer, H. Heinrich Heine.*
  F. Futterknecht, 564:May86-172
Spencer, H.M. A History of the School of
  Chemistry at the University of Virginia,
  1825-1943.
    639(VQR):Winter86-8
Spencer, J. The Rise of the Woman Novel-
  ist.
    L. Fletcher, 617(TLS):13Feb87-157
Spencer, J.P. The Red Earl. (P. Gordon,
  ed)
    R. Foster, 617(TLS):25Sep-1Oct87-1038
Spencer, R.H. Kirby's Last Circus.
    N. Callendar, 441:12Jul87-29
Spencer, S. O.G. Rejlander.
    B. Jay, 637(VS):Spring87-439
Spencer, S.I. Le Dilemme du roman marivau-
  dien.
    C. Bonfils, 535(RHL):Sep-Oct86-918
    R.C. Rosbottom, 207(FR):May87-861
Spencer, S.I., ed. French Women and The
  Age of Enlightenment.
    N. Aronson, 207(FR):Dec86-275
    A. Blum, 577(SHR):Spring86-186
    C.C. Lougee, 173(ECS):Spring87-368
Spender, D., ed. The Education Papers.
    J. Lewis, 617(TLS):30Oct-5Nov87-1184
Spender, D. Mothers of the Novel.*
    T.C. Holyoke, 42(AR):Fall86-488
Spender, D. & C. Hayman, eds. How the
  Vote Was Won.
    B. Grantham, 157:No160-47
Spender, S. Collected Poems 1928-1985.*
    R. Jones, 639(VQR):Autumn86-725
    J.D. McClatchy, 491:Oct86-31
    J. Whitehead, 184(EIC):Apr86-186
Spender, S. Journals, 1939-1983.* (J.
  Goldsmith, ed)
    R. Jones, 639(VQR):Autumn86-725
"Spenser Studies." (Vol 4) (P. Cullen &
  T.P. Roche, Jr., eds)
    G. Morgan, 402(MLR):Apr87-441
    P. Thomson, 541(RES):May86-305
Sperber, A.M. Murrow.*
    N. Lemann, 617(TLS):17Apr87-404
    R. Mayne, 176:Apr87-54
    B. Morton, 362:12Feb87-24
Sperber, D. A Dictionary of Greek and
  Latin Legal Terms in Rabbinic Literature.
    P.W. van der Horst, 394:Vol39fasc3/4-
    568
Speroni, C. & C.L. Golino. Basic Italian.
  (6th ed)
    G. Faustini, 399(MLJ):Autumn86-320
Spevack, M. & J.W. Binns, general eds.
  Renaissance Latin Drama in England.
  (1st Ser, Vols 7, 9, 11-13)
    C. Davies, 123:Vol36No2-356
Spica, I. Le Statut romanesque de "Bouvard
  et Pécuchet" de Flaubert.*
    E.F. Gray, 446(NCFS):Spring87-325
Spiegel, S.L. The Other Arab-Israeli Con-
  flict.*
    M. Rubner, 390:Jan86-55
Spiegelberg, H. Steppingstones toward an
  Ethics for Fellow Existers.
    S.P., 185:Jul87-885
Spiegelman, A. Maus.*
    R. Gehr, 62:Feb87-10
    M. Kohn, 362:10Sep87-24
Spiegelman, W. Wordsworth's Heroes.
    L. Newlyn, 617(TLS):15May87-525

Spiegl, F. The Joy of Words.
    D.J. Enright, 176:May87-70
Spierenburg, P. The Spectacle of Suffer-
  ing.
    L. Martines, 551(RenQ):Spring86-109
Spieser, J-M. Thessalonique et ses
  monuments du IVe au VIe siècle.
    R. Cormack, 303(JoHS):Vol106-265
Spiess, R. The Bold Silverfish and Tall
  River Junction.
    P.O. Williams, 404:Autumn86-58
Spillane, J.D. Medical Travellers.
    J. Black, 83:Autumn86-233
Spillard, A. The Cartomancer.
    C. Hawtree, 617(TLS):18-24Sep87-1026
Spini, G. & A. Casali. Firenze.
    C.F. Delzell, 275(IQ):Summer86-123
Spinner, T.J., Jr. A Political and Social
  History of Guyana, 1945-1983.
    D.J. Ramnarine, 529(QQ):Winter86-925
Spinoza, B. The Collected Works of
  Spinoza.* (Vol 1) (E. Curley, ed &
  trans)
    S.H. Daniel, 568(SCN):Spring-Summer86-
    19
Spinrad, N. Little Heroes.
    G. Jonas, 441:18Oct87-36
Spires, E. Swan's Island.*
    M. Jarman, 249(HudR):Summer86-337
    P. Stitt, 491:May86-101
    639(VQR):Spring86-61
Spires, R.C. Beyond the Metafictional
  Mode.*
    M. Bieder, 395(MFS):Summer86-337
    L. Hickey, 402(MLR):Jul86-775
    G. Pérez Firmat, 240(HR):Winter86-102
    K.M. Vernon, 400(MLN):Mar86-447
Spisak, J.W. & W. Matthews - see Malory,
  T.
Spitz, E.H. Art and Psyche.*
    J.J. Spector, 290(JAAC):Fall86-91
Spitz, L.W. The Protestant Reformation:
  1517-1559.*
    R.P-C. Hsia, 551(RenQ):Spring86-99
Spivey, T.R. Revival.
    M. Kreyling, 578:Spring87-102
Spivey, T.R. The Writer as Shaman.
    M. Pearson, 578:Spring87-108
Spleth, J. Léopold Sédar Senghor.
    C. Wake, 402(MLR):Oct87-984
Spore, P. Études toponymiques I.
    D. Evans, 208(FS):Jul86-374
Spore, P. Études toponymiques II.
    D. Evans, 208(FS):Jul86-374
    P. Fabre, 545(RPh):Aug86-98
Spores, R. The Mixtecs in Ancient and
  Colonial Times.
    J. Pohl, 263(RIB):Vol36No2-189
Spörk, I. Studien zu ausgewählten Märchen
  der Brüder Grimm.
    M. Diehr, 196:Band27Heft1/2-139
Spoto, D. The Kindness of Strangers.*
    T.H. Pauly, 615(TJ):Mar86-124
    C.P. Ryan, 157:No159-53
"Die Sprache des Rechts und der Verwalt-
  ung."
    W. Brandt, 685(ZDL):1/1986-105
"Sprachlehr- und Sprachlernforschung."
    C. Kramsch, 399(MLJ):Summer86-169
Spratt, J.S., Sr. Thurber, Texas.
    L. Milazzo, 584(SWR):Autumn86-538
Sprecher, T. Felix Krull und Goethe.
    H. Siefken, 402(MLR):Apr87-525

Sprengel, P. Gerhart Hauptmann.
R.C. Cowen, 406:Winter86-514
P. Skrine, 402(MLR):Jul87-793
Sprengel, P. - see Brahm, O. & G. Hauptmann
Spriano, P. Le Passioni di un decennio (1946-1956).
M. d'Amico, 617(TLS):27Mar87-314
Sprigge, T.L.S. Theories of Existence.*
M. Partridge, 479(PhQ):Jul86-448
Sprigge, T.L.S. The Vindication of Absolute Idealism.*
A.C. Grayling, 479(PhQ):Jan86-85
Spring, J. The Whole Art Thing.
J. McCulloch, 441:8Mar87-20
Springer, M. Hardy's Use of Allusion.*
R.P. Draper, 447(N&Q):Dec85-540
Springer, R. Le blues authentique.
A. Prévos, 91:Spring86-189
Springhall, J., B. Fraser & M. Hoare. Sure and Stedfast.
J.S. Galbraith, 637(VS):Winter87-295
Sproat, R. Stunning the Punters.*
W. Lesser, 249(HudR):Autumn86-479
Spuler, R. "Germanistik" in America.*
G. Friesen, 564:Nov86-336
Spurlin, P.M. The French Enlightenment in America.*
J. Gury, 549(RLC):Apr-Jun86-243
T.V. Kaufman-Osborn, 478:Apr86-124
J.H. Shennan, 208(FS):Apr86-217
Spurling, H. Ivy.*
R. Leiter, 31(ASch):Winter85/86-140
Spurrell, M., ed. Stow Church Restored.
R. Warde, 637(VS):Summer87-520
Squarotti, G.B. - see under Bàrberi Squarotti, G.
Squier, S.M. Virginia Woolf and London.*
E.W. Mellown, 579(SAQ):Autumn86-406
Squires, M. The Creation of "Lady Chatterley's Lover."*
H. Baron, 184(EIC):Apr86-166
D. Pickering, 599:Fall86-435
J. Worthen, 447(N&Q):Dec85-544
Squires, M. & D. Jackson, eds. D.H. Lawrence's "Lady."*
A. Blayac, 189(EA):Apr-Jun87-232
P.D. Morrow, 577(SHR):Fall86-385
Sri, P.S. T.S. Eliot.
R.S. Kennedy, 295(JML):Nov86-462
Ssu-ch'eng, L. - see under Liang Ssu-ch'eng
Ssu-ma Ch'ien. Syma Tsyan, Istoricheskie Zapiski (Shi Tsi). (Vol 3) (R.V. Viatkin, ed & trans)
D. Bodde, 293(JASt):Nov85-130
Ssu-t'ung, T. - see under T'an Ssu-t'ung
Staal, F. Agni.
D.M. Knipe, 293(JASt):Feb86-355
R. Schechner, 293(JASt):Feb86-359
Staar, R.F. USSR.
H. Hanak, 575(SEER):Oct86-648
Stableford, B. Scientific Romance in Britain: 1890-1950.*
W.J. Scheick, 177(ELT):Vol29No4-449
Stachel, J. - see Einstein, A.
Stachura, P.D., ed. Unemployment and the Great Depression in Weimar Germany.
B. Blackbourn, 617(TLS):15May87-522
Stack, F. Pope and Horace.*
H. Weber, 566:Spring87-177
von Stackelberg, J. Übersetzungen aus zweiter Hand.
B. Guthmüller, 52:Band21Heft2-210

Stacpoole, A., ed. Vatican II.
P. Hebblethwaite, 617(TLS):9Jan87-35
Stadler, I. Contemporary Art and Its Philosophical Problems.
D. Carrier, 617(TLS):6-12Nov87-1230
Stadler, K.R., ed. Sozialistenprozesse - Politische Justiz in Österreich, 1870-1936.
F.L. Carsten, 575(SEER):Oct86-615
Stadter, P.A. Arrian of Nicomedia.
C.P.T. Naudé, 394:Vol39fascl/2-172
Madame de Staël. Corinne ou l'Italie. (S. Balayé, ed)
D. Wood, 208(FS):Jul86-338
Madame de Staël. Correspondance générale. (Vol 5, Pt 2) (B. Jasinski, ed)
J. Gaulmier, 535(RHL):Sep-Oct86-927
Madame de Staël. Réflexions sur le suicide.
N. King, 535(RHL):Jul-Aug86-764
Staerman, E.M. Die Agrarfrage und die senatorische Opposition in der römischen Kaiserzeit.
E. Champlin, 124:Mar-Apr87-326
P.W. de Neeve, 394:Vol39fasc3/4-565
Staffel, M. She Wanted Something Else.
H. Zinnes, 441:20Dec87-17
Stafford, B.M. Voyage into Substance.*
M. Pointon, 89(BJA):Winter86-82
C.J. Schneer, 54:Dec86-682
Stafford, W.T. - see James, H.
Stagg, J.C.A. Mr. Madison's War.
D.P. Peeler, 106:Summer86-201
Ståhl, E-B. Vilhelm Ekelunds estetiska mysticism.
I. Scobbie, 562(Scan):Nov86-241
Stahl, H-P. Propertius: "Love" and "War."*
N.P. Gross, 124:May-Jun87-383
Stähli, M. Handschriften der Ratsbücherei Lüneburg. (Vol 3)
T. Frenz, 684(ZDA):Band115Heft1-1
"Stained Glass Before 1700 in American Collections: New England and New York."
P. Hetherington, 39:Nov86-461
Staines, D., ed. The Callaghan Symposium.
B. Pell, 296(JCF):No35/36-138
Staines, D. Tennyson's Camelot.*
M. Lambert, 402(MLR):Jul87-709
S. Shatto, 447(N&Q):Jun85-279
Stainton, L. Turner's Venice.*
C. Hartley, 90:May86-363
R. Kingzett, 39:Mar86-218
Stalberg, R.H. China's Puppets.*
U. Roberts, 60:Mar-Apr86-124
Stalley, R. The Cistercian Monasteries of Ireland.
J. Harvey, 617(TLS):31Jul87-825
Stallworthy, J. The Anzac Sonata.*
S. Knight, 364:Dec86/Jan87-131
Stalnaker, R.C. Inquiry.*
J. Barwise, 482(PhR):Jul86-429
G. Currie, 479(PhQ):Oct86-569
H. Field, 486:Sep86-425
E.J. Lowe, 518:Apr86-101
Stameshkin, D.M. The Town's College.
T.K. Meier, 432(NEQ):Jun86-310
Stamp, G. & A. Goulancourt. The English House, 1860-1914.*
D. Bowen, 324:Jun87-535
V. Powell, 39:Nov86-459
Stamp, T. Stamp Album.
A. Hislop, 617(TLS):3Jul87-712
M. Wandor, 362:17Sep87-26

Steadman, J.M. The Hill and the Labyrinth.*
  H.R. Asals, 551(RenQ):Summer86-356
  J. Egan, 568(SCN):Spring-Summer86-6
  C. Hill, 366:Spring86-111
  F.L. Huntley, 301(JEGP):Apr86-269
  A. Snider, 405(MP):Aug86-82
Steadman, J.M. Milton's Biblical and Classical Imagery.*
  G.R. Evans, 541(RES):Nov86-624
Steadman, J.M. The Wall of Paradise.
  A. Fowler, 617(TLS):30Jan87-115
Steadman, R. Between the Eyes.
  D. Hill, 441:11Jan87-19
Stearman, A.M. Camba and Kolla.
  D.B. Heath, 263(RIB):Vol36No1-69
Stearns, M., Jr. Crimean Gothic.
  W.G. Moulton, 685(ZDL):2/1986-211
Stebbins, S. Studien zur Tradition und Rezeption der Bildlichkeit in der "Eneide" Heinrichs von Veldeke.
  R.J. Cormier, 382(MAE):1986/2-338
Steel, B. A Textbook of Colloquial Spanish.
  J. Shreve, 238:Dec86-896
Steel, D. Fine Things.
  L. Prinz, 441:19Apr87-16
Steel, D. Kaleidoscope.
  R.L. Bray, 441:15Nov87-26
Steel, J. - see Hogg, J.
Steel, J. - see Southey, R.
Steele, B. - see Lawrence, D.H.
Steele, E. Virginia Woolf's Literary Sources and Allusions.
  J. Marcus, 40(AEB):Vol8No4-272
Steele, G.L., Jr. & others. The Hacker's Dictionary.
  R.A. Spears, 35(AS):Fall86-273
Steele, P.W. Ozark Tales and Superstitions.
  G.E. Lankford, 292(JAF):Jul/Sep86-326
Steele, R. & J. Gaillard, eds. L'Express.*
  F.G. Healey, 402(MLR):Jul87-731
  W. Wrage, 399(MLJ):Spring86-67
Steele, T. Sapphics against Anger, and Other Poems.
  R.S. Gwynn, 434:Autumn86-111
  B. King, 598(SoR):Winter87-224
  W. Logan, 441:18Jan87-13
  D. Shapiro, 491:Mar87-342
Steen, N. The Charm of Old Roses.
  A. Lacy, 441:6Dec87-34
Steen, S.J. - see Brome, R.
Stefan, J. Laures.
  C.L. Kaplan, 207(FR):Dec86-298
Stefani, G. Der Spaziergänger.
  G. Kurscheidt, 680(ZDP):Band105Heft4-622
  M. Pender, 402(MLR):Apr87-521
Steffler, J. The Grey Islands.*
  A. Brooks, 102(CanL):Spring86-175
Steger, H., ed. Soziolinguistik.*
  A. Beyrer, 682(ZPSK):Band39Heft3-398
Steghart, P. The Lawful Rights of Mankind.
  M.A.P., 185:Jan87-507
Stegner, W. Crossing to Safety.
  D. Grumbach, 441:20Sep87-14
  442(NY):7Dec87-191
Stegner, W., ed. This is Dinosaur.
  P. Schullery, 649(WAL):Nov86-256
Stehling, T. - see "Medieval Latin Poems of Male Love and Friendship"

Steiger, K.P. Vom Misterienspiel zum Stuart-Drama.
  K. Otten, 72:Band223Heft2-411
  H-J. Weckermann, 156(ShJW):Jahrbuch1986-240
Stein, A.F. After the Vows Were Spoken.*
  E. Ammons, 26(ALR):Fall86-92
  A. Habegger, 27(AL):Oct86-451
Stein, B. Her Only Sin.
  D. Johnson, 18:Sep87-67
Stein, G. Operas and Plays.
  R. Howard, 441:24May87-9
Stein, G. & C. Van Vechten. The Letters of Gertrude Stein and Carl Van Vechten.* (E. Burns, ed)
  H. Goldgar, 598(SoR):Summer87-719
  M.J. Hoffman, 395(MFS):Winter86-611
  I.B.N., 295(JML):Nov86-391
Stein, J.B. From H-Bombs to Star Wars.
  A.C., 185:Jan87-510
Stein, P. Kreolisch und Französisch.*
  S.M. Embleton, 350:Jun87-446
Stein, R. & others. Major Modern Dramatists. (Vol 2)
  V.K., 295(JML):Nov86-353
Stein, R. & F. Rickert, eds. Major Modern Dramatists. (Vol 1)
  P. Merivale, 397(MD):Jun86-358
Steinberg, L. The Sexuality of Christ in Renaissance Art and in Modern Oblivion.*
  C. Gould, 39:Apr86-292
Steinberg, M.P. - see Broch, H.
Steinberg, M.W. - see Klein, A.M.
Steinecke, H. Literaturkritik des Jungen Deutschland.
  G. Benda, 406:Fall86-406
Steiner, E. Die Entwicklung des Britischen Kontextualismus.
  D. Nehls, 257(IRAL):May86-179
Steiner, G. Das Abenteuer der Regression.*
  O. Ehrismann, 224(GRM):Band36Heft1-106
Steiner, G. Antigones.*
  E. Crim, 31(ASch):Spring86-258
  P.E. Easterling, 123:Vol36No1-14
  C. Garton, 402(MLR):Jan87-158
  P. Gottfried, 569(SR):Spring86-xxxvi
  H.J. Hansford, 541(RES):May86-303
  I. Hassan, 560:Spring-Summer86-316
Steiner, G. A Reading Against Shakespeare.
  J. Wilders, 617(TLS):30Oct-5Nov87-1197
Steiner, G. George Steiner: A Reader.*
  I. Hassan, 560:Spring-Summer86-316
Steiner, G. Tolstoy or Dostoevsky.
  E. Wasiolek, 268(IFR):Winter87-57
Steiner, G.Y. Constitutional Inequality.
  C.C., 185:Apr87-702
Steiner, P., ed. The Prague School.
  R. Wellek, 402(MLR):Jul86-693
Steiner, P. Russian Formalism.*
  M. Ehre, 131(CL):Winter86-90
  I. Paperno, 279:Vol33-141
Steiner, W. The Colors of Rhetoric.*
  W. Holmes, 567:Vol59No1/2-177
Steingräber, E. The Alte Pinakothek Munich.
  E. Young, 39:May86-367
Steinhagen, H. & B. von Wiese, eds. Deutsche Dichter des 17. Jahrhunderts.
  G. Hoffmeister, 597(SN):Vol58No1-132
  H. Langer, 654(WB):6/1986-1047
Steinhauer, H., ed & trans. Deutsche Erzählungen.
  E. Glass, 399(MLJ):Spring86-69

Stocking, G.W., Jr., ed. Malinowski,
Rivers, Benedict and Others.
J.W. Burrow, 617(TLS):18-24Dec87-1391
Stocking, G.W., Jr. Victorian Anthropol-
ogy.
J.W. Burrow, 617(TLS):18-24Dec87-1391
G. Levine, 441:1Mar87-22
Stockman, D.A. The Triumph of Politics.*
J.P.D., 185:Jul87-904
Stoddard, E. The Morgesons and Other Writ-
ings, Published and Unpublished. (L.
Buell & S.A. Zagarell, eds)
L. Pannill, 534(RALS):Spring-Autumn84-
178
Stoddard, H. Le Mendiant de l'Amdo.
E. Gellner, 617(TLS):6Mar87-234
Stoddard, W.S. Sculptors of the West
Portals of Chartres Cathedral.
R. Minkoff, 441:19Jul87-21
Stoddart, D.R. On Geography.
W. George, 617(TLS):29May87-585
Stoekl, A. Politics, Writing, Mutilation.
A. Thiher, 395(MFS):Winter86-679
Stoelzel, M. Die Anfänge vierhändiger
Klaviermusik.
L. Plantinga, 410(M&L):Jan86-71
Stoica, I. Gates of the Moment.
D. McDuff, 565:Winter85/86-72
Stokes, E. Hawthorne's Influence on Dick-
ens and George Eliot.
H. McNeil, 617(TLS):22May87-553
Stokes, M. Justice and Mercy in "Piers
Plowman."
A. Baldwin, 382(MAE):1986/2-290
S.S. Hussey, 402(MLR):Apr87-437
P.M. Kean, 541(RES):Feb86-79
Stokes, M.C. Plato's Socratic Conversa-
tions.
M. Nussbaum, 617(TLS):7Aug87-850
Stokesbury, L. The Drifting Away.
R.S. Gwynn, 434:Autumn86-111
Stoler, A.L. Capitalism and Confrontation
in Sumatra's Plantation Belt, 1870-1979.*
T. Bigalke, 293(JASt):Aug86-918
Stoler, P. The War Against the Press.
T. Winship, 441:18Jan87-12
442(NY):2Feb87-99
Stoljar, M.M. Poetry and Song in Late
Eighteenth-Century Germany.
P. Branscombe, 410(M&L):Apr86-205
E. Sams, 415:Sep86-500
D. Seaton, 173(ECS):Spring87-382
J.W. Smeed, 161(DUJ):Dec85-197
Stoltzfus, B. Alain Robbe-Grillet.*
R.R. Brock, 594:Spring86-109
L.M. Porter, 395(MFS):Summer86-332
Stolyar, A.A. Introduction to Elementary
Mathematical Logic.
D. Resek, 316:Sep86-830
Stolz, B.A., I.R. Titunik & L. Doležel,
eds. Language and Literary Theory in
Honor of Ladislav Matejka.
V.M. Du Feu, 402(MLR):Jul87-806
Stommel, H. Lost Islands.
H.P. Schwarcz, 529(QQ):Winter86-882
Stone, A.E. Autobiographical Occasions and
Original Acts.*
C. Bush, 402(MLR):Jan87-186
H.W. Emerson, Jr., 366:Spring86-129
Stone, B. The French Parlements and the
Crisis of the Old Régime.
J. Rogister, 617(TLS):18-24Dec87-1411

Stone, C. Power in the Caribbean Basin.
B.B. Levine, 263(RIB):Vol36No2-190
Stone, D., Jr. Mellin de Saint-Gelais and
Literary History.*
E.M. Duval, 207(FR):Apr87-704
Stone, D.A. The Disabled State.
J.R., 185:Jan87-506
Stone, G. & D. Worth, eds. The Formation
of the Slavonic Literary Languages.
E. Vrabie, 574(SEEJ):Spring86-125
Stone, G.W., Jr., ed. The Stage and the
Page.
H. Love, 677(YES):Vol16-256
Stone, H. - see Dickens, C.
Stone, I. Canal Irrigation in British
India.
E. Whitcombe, 293(JASt):Aug86-892
Stone, L. The Past and the Present.
N.F. Partner, 589:Jan86-90
Stone, M.E., ed. The Armenian Inscriptions
from the Sinai.
J.A.C. Greppin, 318(JAOS):Oct/Dec85-738
Stone, R. Children of Light.*
D. Johnson, 18:Sep87-67
W. Lesser, 249(HudR):Autumn86-482
Stone-Blackburn, S. Robertson Davies,
Playwright.
N. Carson, 102(CanL):Spring86-189
M. Tait, 627(UTQ):Fall86-179
A. Wagner, 108:Summer86-147
Stoneman, R. Across the Hellespont.
J.A. Cuddon, 617(TLS):18-24Sep87-1010
Stoneman, R. Daphne into Laurel.*
D. Hopkins, 402(MLR):Oct86-972
Stoneman, R. Land of Lost Gods.
W. St. Clair, 617(TLS):31Jul87-824
Stoppard, T. Rosencrantz and Guildenstern
are Dead. (B. Reitz, ed)
C. Jansohn, 72:Band223Heft1-185
Stoppard, T. Rough Crossing.
B. Grantham, 157:No159-47
Stoppelli, P. - see Vignali, A.
Stopponi, S., ed. Case e palazzi
d'Etruria.
N. Spivey, 313:Vol76-281
Stopponi, S. La tomba della "Scrofa nera."
R. Adam, 555:Vol59fasc2-338
Stora-Sandor, J. L'humour juif dans la
littérature de Job à Woody Allen.
D. Tollet, 549(RLC):Apr-Jun86-255
Storace, P. Heredity.
S. Santos, 441:8Nov87-68
Storey, E. A Right to Song.*
E. Strickland, 591(SIR):Spring86-154
Storey, G. Dickens: "Bleak House."
C.H. Sisson, 617(TLS):17Apr87-419
Storey, M. - see Clare, J.
Storey, R. Pierrots on the Stage of
Desire.*
D.B., 295(JML):Nov86-369
J.O. Burdick, 615(TJ):Mar86-120
S.B. John, 402(MLR):Jul87-744
M.G. Rose, 130:Summer86-175
Storry, D. "Second Country."
J. McMullen, 617(TLS):20-26Nov87-1277
Story, G. It Never Pays To Laugh Too
Much.*
L. Mathews, 102(CanL):Winter85-140
Stotz, C.M. Outposts of the War for
Empire.*
B.D. Hoffstot, 45:Sep86-77
Stout, H.S. The New England Soul.*
S. Bush, Jr., 165(EAL):Spring87-133

Strong, R. Henry Prince of Wales and England's Lost Renaissance.*
D.G.C.A., 324:Jun87-539
S. Foister, 90:Oct86-751
Strosetzki, C. Rhétorique de la conversation.*
R. Zuber, 535(RHL):Mar-Apr86-283
Stroud, B. The Significance of Philosophical Scepticism.*
R. Feldman, 482(PhR):Apr86-305
A.P. Griffiths, 262:Sep86-377
J. Heil, 484(PPR):Dec86-331
P.K. Moser, 84:Jun86-235
R. Squires, 479(PhQ):Oct86-558
Stroud, C. Close Pursuit.
D. Uhnak, 441:12Apr87-28
Stroud, D. Sir John Soane, Architect.*
P.D. du Prey, 576:Mar86-71
Stróżewski, W. Dialektyka Twórczości.
P. Taranczewski, 543:Sep86-143
Struc, R. & J.C. Yardley, eds. Franz Kafka (1883-1983).
K.J. Fickert, 268(IFR):Winter87-47
Strugatsky, A. & B. The Time Wanderers.
G. Jonas, 441:8Mar87-30
Struminsky, B.A. Pseudo-Meleško.
L. Hughes, 575(SEER):Oct86-589
Struthers, B. Censored Letters.*
L. Irvine, 102(CanL):Winter85-120
Struthers, J.R., ed. The Montreal Story Tellers.*
529(QQ):Winter86-950
Strutz, J. & J., eds. Robert Musil – Theater, Bildung, Kritik.
M. Meister, 602:Band17Heft1-116
Struve, G.P., N.A. Struve & B.A. Filippov – see Axmatova, A.
Struve, W. Die Republik Texas, Bremen und das Hildesheimische.
D.H. Tolzmann, 406:Winter86-525
Struzyk, B. Leben auf der Kippe.
K. Schuhmann, 601(SuF):Mar-Apr86-439
Stuart, I. Sandscreen.
N. Callendar, 441:8Mar87-29
Stuart, L. Memoire of Frances, Lady Douglas. (J. Rubenstein, ed)
W.A. Craik, 571(ScLJ):Summer86-12
M.E.S., 506(PSt):May86-87
529(QQ):Autumn86-717
Stubblebine, J.H. Assisi and the Rise of Vernacular Art.
J. White, 90:Nov86-828
Stubbs, J. Tobacco on the Periphery.
H. Klein, 263(RIB):Vol36No1-70
Stubbs, M. Discourse Analysis.*
J.F. Kess, 320(CJL):Spring86-98
M. Toolan, 307:Aug86-151
Stubbs, M., ed. The Other Languages of England.
R. Grillo, 617(TLS):23Jan87-94
Stuckenberg, J.W.H. The Life of Immanuel Kant.
R. George, 484(PPR):Mar87-485
Stuckey, S. Slave Culture.
J. Haskins, 441:26Apr87-25
Stucky, R.A. Tribune d'Echmoun.
G.B. Waywell, 303(JoHS):Vol106-249
"Studia Spinozana." (Vol 1)
W. Bartuschat, 53(AGP):Band68Heft3-309
"Studies in Eighteenth-Century Culture."* (Vol 12) (H.C. Payne, ed)
J. McLaverty, 447(N&Q):Mar85-126

"Studies in Eighteenth-Century Culture." (Vol 13) (O.M. Brack, Jr., ed)
S. Varey, 83:Autumn86-256
"Studies in Eighteenth-Century Culture." (Vol 14) (O.M. Brack, Jr., ed)
W.H. Barber, 402(MLR):Apr87-427
"Studies on Voltaire and the Eighteenth Century." (Vol 208)
N. Wagner, 535(RHL):Jan-Feb86-145
"Studies on Voltaire and the Eighteenth Century." (Vol 212) (H. Mason, ed)
M.H. Waddicor, 208(FS):Jan86-78
"Studies on Voltaire and the Eighteenth Century." (Vol 215)
M. Menemencioglu, 535(RHL):Jan-Feb86-146
"Studies on Voltaire and the Eighteenth Century." (Vol 217) (H. Mason, ed)
G. Haroche-Bouzinac, 535(RHL):Jul-Aug86-759
M.H. Waddicor, 208(FS):Oct86-462
"Studies on Voltaire and the Eighteenth Century." (Vol 219) (H. Mason, ed)
G. Gargett, 208(FS):Oct86-463
G. Haroche-Bouzinac, 535(RHL):Mar-Apr86-289
Stull, W.L., ed. Literature and Religion.
P. Cheney, 568(SCN):Spring-Summer86-7
Stump, D.V. & others, eds. Hamartia.*
A. Schmitt, 52:Band21Heft2-205
Sturgess, K. Jacobean Private Theatre.
R. Gill, 617(TLS):31Jul87-814
Sturgess, K., ed. Three Elizabethan Domestic Tragedies.
M. Dodsworth, 175:Spring86-107
Sturluson, S. – see under Snorri Sturluson
Sturm, T. – see "Christopher Brennan"
Sturm-Maddox, S. Petrarch's Metamorphoses.
P. Hainsworth, 402(MLR):Apr87-487
Stürmer, M. Dissonanzen des Fortschritts.
G.A. Craig, 453(NYRB):15Jan87-16
Stussi, A., ed. La critica del testo.
M. Bonafin, 379(MedR):Apr86-121
Stutman, S. – see Wolfe, T. & A. Bernstein
Styan, J.L. Max Reinhardt.
A.M. Nagler, 402(MLR):Jul86-803
Styan, J.L. Restoration Comedy in Performance.
J. Hérou, 189(EA):Jul-Sep87-351
Stylianou, A. & J.A. The Painted Churches of Cyprus.
R. Cormack, 90:Jan86-39
P. Hetherington, 39:Mar86-217
Suárez, J.A. The Mesoamerican Indian Languages.*
E.H. Casad, 603:Vol10No2-475
Suarez, M. Requiem of Cerro Maravilla.
J. Traub, 441:20Dec87-17
Subiotto, A. – see "Hans Magnus Enzensberger"
Sudau, R. Werkbearbeitung, Dichterfiguren.
G. Divers, 133:Band19Heft3/4-374
Suerbaum, U., U. Broich & R. Borgmeier. Science Fiction.
D. Petzold, 38:Band104Heft3/4-540
Suevus, S. Erbauungsschriften; Spiegel des Meschlichen Lebens; Eine Auswahl. (M.A. van den Broek, ed)
N.F. Palmer, 447(N&Q):Dec85-514
Suggs, H.L., ed. The Black Press in the South, 1865-1979.
J.L. Franklin, 9(AlaR):Apr86-148

Sutherland, L. Politics and Finance in the Eighteenth Century. (A. Newman, ed)
    J. Black, 161(DUJ):Dec85-182
    H.V. Bowen, 83:Autumn86-217
Sutherland, L.S. & L.G. Mitchell, eds. The History of the University of Oxford. (Vol 5)
    L. Colley, 617(TLS):13Mar87-261
Sutherland, S. Men Change Too.
    J. Barron, 362:19Nov87-31
    A. Storr, 617(TLS):24Jul87-801
Sutherland, S.P. Masques in Jacobean Tragedy.*
    R. Dutton, 402(MLR):Oct87-913
Sutherland, S.R. God, Jesus and Belief.
    P. Helm, 483:Jan86-131
Sutton, D. Edgar Degas.
    P-L. Adams, 61:Apr87-91
    M.S. Young, 39:Dec86-563
Sutton, D. Flints.
    J. Mole, 176:Mar87-59
    G. Tiffin, 617(TLS):23Jan87-92
Sutton, D.F. The Lost Sophocles.*
    A.L. Brown, 303(JoHS):Vol106-210
    J. Wilkins, 123:Vol36No1-12
Sutton, W.A. - see Anderson, S.
Suvin, D. To Brecht and Beyond.*
    J. Reinelt, 615(TJ):Oct86-378
Suvin, D. Victorian Science Fiction in the UK.*
    G.K. Wolfe, 395(MFS):Spring86-133
Suzuki, H., R. Banham & K. Kobayashi. Contemporary Architecture of Japan 1958-1984.
    C. Vorreiter-Wajed, 46:Sep86-109
Svantesson, J-O. Kammu Phonology and Morphology.
    G.F. Meier, 682(ZPSK):Band39Heft1-139
Sveinsson, G. - see Pálsson, G.
Sveistrup, H. & A. von Zahn-Harnack, eds. Die Frauenfrage in Deutschland. (3rd ed)
    P. Herminghouse, 406:Summer86-228
Svensen, A. Tekstens mønstre.
    A. Lien, 172(Edda):1986/4-369
Svensson, C. The Construction of Poetic Meaning.
    A. Pettersson, 452(NJL):Vol9No2-207
Svenungsen, N. Det norske fjeldsprog.
    E. Haugen, 563(SS):Spring86-198
Svoboda, F.J. Hemingway and "The Sun Also Rises."*
    R.W. Lewis, 587(SAF):Spring86-110
Svoboda, T. All Aberration.
    639(VQR):Summer86-98
"Svodnyj katalog slavjano-russkix rukopisnyx knig, xranjaščixsja v SSSR. XI-XIII vv."
    R. Marti, 559:Vol10No3-333
Swaggart, J. Catholicism and Christianity.
    M. Gardner, 453(NYRB):13Aug87-17
Swaggart, J., with R.P. Lamb. To Cross a River.
    M. Gardner, 453(NYRB):13Aug87-17
Swales, J. Episodes in ESP.
    J.W. Ney, 399(MLJ):Autumn86-339
Swales, M. & E. Adalbert Stifter.*
    R.K. Angress, 221(GQ):Winter86-150
    E.A. Blackall, 222(GR):Spring86-78
    C.O. Sjögren, 301(JEGP):Apr86-310
Swan, G. Carnival for the Gods.*
    T.E. Kennedy, 569(SR):Fall86-lxxxviii

Swan, O.E. A Concise Grammar of Polish.* (2nd ed)
    R.A. Rothstein, 399(MLJ):Winter86-435
Swan, S. The Biggest Modern Woman of the World.*
    D. Barbour, 168(ECW):Fall86-136
    K. Thompson, 198:Summer86-87
Swander, M. Driving the Body Back.*
    R. McDowell, 249(HudR):Winter87-675
    P. Stitt, 491:May86-100
Swann, B. Song of the Sky.*
    B. Cavanagh, 529(QQ):Winter86-904
    P.K. Kett, 649(WAL):Nov86-278
Swannell, G. State of Affairs.
    B. Grantham, 157:No159-47
Swanson, G.R. & W.B. Thesing, eds. Conversations with South Carolina Poets.
    R. Moran, 580(SCR):Fall86-87
Swanwick, M. Vacuum Flowers.
    G. Jonas, 441:8Mar87-30
Swarbrick, A., ed. The Art of Oliver Goldsmith.*
    W.B. Hutchings, 83:Spring86-106
Sward, R. Half a Life's History.
    D. McCarthy, 168(ECW):Fall86-198
Swarthout, G. The Old Colts.
    K.W. Scott, 649(WAL):Aug86-167
Swartz, M. The Politics of British Foreign Policy in the Era of Disraeli and Gladstone.
    R. Adelson, 637(VS):Autumn86-136
Swartz, R.M., H.J. Perkinson & S.G. Edgerton. Knowledge and Fallibilism.
    I. Slade, 488:Jun86-271
Sweeney, J.G. 3d. Jonson and the Psychology of Public Theater.*
    R. Dutton, 402(MLR):Oct87-913
    R.C. Jones, 130:Fall86-275
    D. McPherson, 481(PQ):Spring86-281
    K.E. Maus, 651(WHR):Autumn86-272
Sweeney, M. The Lame Waltzer.*
    M. O'Neill, 493:Jun86-110
Sweet, J.D. Dances of the Tewa Indians.
    G.P. Kurath, 187:Spring/Summer87-358
Sweets, J.F. Choices in Vichy France.
    D. Pryce-Jones, 617(TLS):3Apr87-367
    639(VQR):Autumn86-119
Sweezy, N. Raised in Clay.*
    J.A. Burrison, 292(JAF):Jan/Mar86-99
Swietochowski, T. Russian Azerbaijan, 1905-1920.
    D.S.M. Williams, 575(SEER):Oct86-618
Swift, J. The Account Books of Jonathan Swift. (P.V. & D.J. Thompson, eds)
    J.A. Downie, 83:Autumn86-268
    M. Treadwell, 541(RES):May86-268
Swift, J. Călătoriile lui Gulliver, Povestea Unui Poloboc si Alte Satire.
    V. Nemoianu, 566:Spring87-135
Swift, J. The Complete Poems.* (P. Rogers, ed)
    P-G. Boucé, 189(EA):Jul-Sep86-342
    D.C. Mell, Jr., 402(MLR):Jan86-172
Swift, J. A Tale of a Tub and Other Works. (A. Ross & D. Woolley, eds)
    A. Morvan, 189(EA):Apr-Jun87-214
    566:Spring87-195
Swift, R. & S. Gilley, eds. The Irish in the Victorian City.
    D. Clark, 637(VS):Winter87-273

Swiggers, P., ed. Grammaire et méthode au XVIIe siècle.
    G. Kleiber, 553(RLiR):Jan-Jun86-190
    J. Rooryck, 567:Vol60No3/4-343
Swiggers, P. Grammaire et théorie du langage au 18e siècle.
    J.E. Joseph, 350:Dec87-916
Swinburne, R. The Evolution of the Soul.
    A. Cussins, 617(TLS):11-17Dec87-1383
Swindells, J. Victorian Writing and Working Women.
    E. Yeo, 637(VS):Summer87-529
Swinfen, A. In Defence of Fantasy.*
    T.A. Shippey, 541(RES):Feb86-127
Switten, M.L. The Cansos of Raimon de Miraval.*
    M-D. Audbourg-Popin, 537:Vol72No1-141
Syme, R. The Augustan Aristocracy.
    J.A. Crook, 617(TLS):12Jun87-640
Syme, R. Fictional History, Old and New.
    F.C. Mench, Jr., 124:Jan-Feb87-227
Symeonoglou, S. The Topography of Thebes from the Bronze Age to Modern Times.
    W.R. Biers, 124:Jul-Aug87-454
    H. Tzavella-Evjen, 121(CJ):Feb-Mar87-267
Symington, R. - see Fairley, B.
Symonds, J.A. The Memoirs of John Addington Symonds.* (P. Grosskurth, ed)
    C. Markgraf, 177(ELT):Vol29No1-100
Symons, J. Dashiell Hammett.*
    A. Boyer, 395(MFS):Winter86-631
    W. Marling, 50(ArQ):Winter86-376
Synan, E.A. - see Campsall, R.
Synge, J.M. The Collected Letters of John Millington Synge.* (A. Saddlemyer, ed) (Vols 1 & 2)
    D. Kiberd, 541(RES):May86-288
Synge, L., ed. The Royal School of Needlework Book of Needlework & Embroidery.
    B. Scott, 39:Nov86-457
Synodinoy, K. Eoika-eikos chai syngenika apo ton Homēro ōs ton Aristophanē.
    C.J. Ruijgh, 394:Vol39fasc1/2-153
Syréhn, G. Makten och ensamheten.
    F.J. Marker, 397(MD):Sep86-499
Szambien, W. Jean-Nicholas-Louis Durand, 1760-1834.*
    A. Pérez-Gómez, 576:Dec86-419
Szanto, G. Not Working.
    C.R. Steele, 102(CanL):Summer86-128
Szarota, E.M., ed. Das Jesuitendrama im deutschen Sprachgebiet.* (Vol 3)
    L. Petzoldt, 196:Band27Heft1/2-142
Szasz, T. Insanity.
    D. Sobel, 441:15Mar87-22
Szasz, T. Karl Kraus et les docteurs de l'âme.
    J-L. Coatalem, 450(NRF):Jan86-107
Szávai, J. The Autobiography.
    J. Voisine, 549(RLC):Jul-Sep86-348
Szczepanski, J. Litteratur om Gustaf Fröding.
    J.E. Bellquist, 563(SS):Autumn86-457
Szechi, D. Jacobitism and Tory Politics 1710-14.*
    J.A. Downie, 83:Autumn86-224
    F.J. McLynn, 161(DUJ):Jun86-364
Szemerényi, O. Richtungen der modernen Sprachwissenschaft. (Pt 2)
    H. Galton, 688(ZSP):Band45Heft2-455
    P. Kosta, 260(IF):Band91-326
Sziborsky, L. - see Schelling, F.W.J.

Szilassy, Z. American Theater of the 1960s.
    P.J. Egan, 130:Winter86/87-364
    V.K., 295(JML):Nov86-431
Szirmai, J.C., ed. La Bible anonyme du ms. Paris BN f. fr. 763.
    I.D. McFarlane, 402(MLR):Jul87-733
    G. Roques, 553(RLiR):Jul-Dec86-641
Szirtes, G. The Photographer in Winter.*
    S. O'Brien, 493:Jun86-104
    S. Rae, 364:Aug/Sep86-132
Szlek, S. Logisch-semantische Untersuchungen zu ausgewählten Handlungsverben im Deutschen.
    K-H. Jäger, 406:Summer86-215
Szogyi, A. Molière abstrait.
    M. Gutwirth, 475:Vol13No25-157
    P.A. Wadsworth, 207(FR):Feb87-393
Szondi, P. On Textual Understanding and Other Essays. Theory of the Modern Drama. (M. Hays, ed & trans)
    M. Sprinker, 617(TLS):9-15Oct87-1105
Szporluk, R. The Political Thought of Thomas G. Masaryk.
    T. Thomas, 575(SEER):Jul86-477
Szyrocki, M. Geschichte der deutschsprachigen Literatur vom Ausgang des 19. Jahrhunderts bis 1945.
    Z. Swiatłowski, 654(WB):1/1986-151
Szyszkowska, M. Teorie prawa natury XX wieku w Polsce.
    W.J. Wagner, 497(PolR):Vol31No2/3-193

Tabachnick, S.E., ed. The T.E. Lawrence Puzzle.*
    A.D.B., 506(PSt):May86-88
Tabucchi, A. Il filo dell'orizzonte.
    A.L. Lepschy, 617(TLS):9-15Oct87-1115
Tabucchi, A. Letter from Casablanca.*
    I. Malin, 532(RCF):Fall86-142
Tabucchi, A. Little Misunderstandings of No Importance.
    D. Aldan, 441:4Oct87-28
Taccola, M. De rebus militaribus (De machina, 1449). (E. Knobloch, ed & trans)
    L.V.R., 568(SCN):Winter86-80
Tachikawa, M., with T. Kelsang & S. Onoda. Catalogue of the United States Library of Congress Collection of Tibetan Literature in Microfiche.
    R. Wiles, 259(IIJ):Apr86-147
Tackett, T. Religion, Revolution and Regional Culture in Eighteenth-Century France.
    W. Scott, 617(TLS):13Feb87-158
Tadié, J-Y. Proust.
    G.J. Barberet, 207(FR):Oct86-129
Tadié, J-Y. - see "Études proustiennes, V"
Taeger, B. - see Behaghel, O.
Taeger, B. - see "Der Heliand"
Taeschner, T. The Sun is Feminine.
    A. Mills, 353:Vol24No4-825
Taft, M. Discovering Saskatchewan Folklore.*
    M. Korn, 650(WF):Jan86-72
Tafuri, M. Venezia e il rinascimento.*
    J.S. Ackerman, 551(RenQ):Winter86-737
Tager, J. & J.W. Ifkovic, eds. Massachusetts in the Gilded Age.
    G. Blodgett, 432(NEQ):Jun86-299

Taggart, J.M. Nahuat Myth and Social
Structure.
A. Wiget, 650(WF):Jan86–46
Tagliacozzo, G., ed. Vico.*
L. Pennachetti, 488:Jun86–274
Tagliacozzo, G., ed. Vico and Marx.*
E. Kamenka, 319:Apr87–297
Tagliacozzo, G., M. Mooney & D.P. Verene,
eds. Vico and Contemporary Thought.
L. Pennachetti, 488:Jun86–274
Taharally, K. Anthrophanies 1–4.
R.K. Singh, 314:Summer–Fall86–235
Taheri, A. Holy Terror.
D. Sewell, 362:12Mar87–24
Taḥḥān, S. al-hakawāti al-ḥalabī. al-
qaṣṣāṣ al-ḥalabī.
H. El-Shamy, 292(JAF):Oct/Dec86–477
Tahtinen, U. Indian Traditional Values.
S. Pollock, 318(JAOS):Jan/Mar85–185
Tahureau, J. Poésies complètes.* (T.
Peach, ed)
Y. Bellenger, 535(RHL):Jan–Feb86–134
C.H. Winn, 547(RF):Band98Heft1/2–204
Tait, A.L. Lunacharsky.
W. Harrison, 402(MLR):Jan87–268
Tait, H. Catalogue of the Waddesdon
Bequest in The British Museum. (Vol 1)
G. Seidmann, 324:Oct87–856
Tait, H., ed. Jewelry 7000 Years. (Brit-
ish title: Seven Thousand Years of Jewel-
lery.)
J. Appleton, 441:12Apr87–26
G. Seidmann, 324:Oct87–856
Tait, J.A. & H.F.C. "The Bibliotheck:" An
Index to Volumes 1–10 (1956–81).
B.J. McMullin, 517(PBSA):Vol80No3–397
Taiwo, O. Female Novelists of Modern
Africa.*
C.P. Sarvan, 395(MFS):Summer86–363
Tajima, M. The Syntactic Development of
the Gerund in Middle English.*
F. Chevillet, 189(EA):Jul–Sep87–332
Takahashi, N. & M. Frauman–Prickel.
Action English Pictures.
E.U. Irving, 399(MLJ):Summer86–207
Takayoshi, K. – see under Kido Takayoshi
Takeda Izumo & others. Sugawara and the
Secrets of Calligraphy.* (S.H. Jones,
Jr., ed & trans)
C.A. Gerstle, 293(JASt):Nov85–148
Takeda Kiyoko, ed. Nihon Bunka no Kakur-
eta Kata.
Sinh Vinh, 407(MN):Spring86–122
"Taking Sides in South Africa."
R. Ellsworth, 529(QQ):Winter86–885
Talbert, R.J.A., ed. Atlas of Classical
History.
J.F. Lazenby, 161(DUJ):Jun86–357
S. Mitchell, 123:Vol36No1–153
Talbert, R.J.A. The Senate of Imperial
Rome.*
T.D. Barnes, 487:Spring86–109
G.P. Burton, 123:Vol36No1–100
Talbot, E.J. Stendhal and Romantic Es-
thetics.
F. Coulont-Henderson, 605(SC):15Jan87–
216
M. Levowitz-Treu, 446(NCFS):Fall–
Winter86/87–193
C.W. Thompson, 208(FS):Oct86–472
Talbot, M. Beyond the Quantum.
L.B. Young, 441:25Jan87–11

Tall, D. The Island of the White Cow.*
A. Higgins, 364:Aug/Sep86–142
E.G. Ingersoll, 174(Éire):Winter86–158
J.H. Korelitz, 617(TLS):23Jan87–93
Tallent, E. Museum Pieces.*
W.H. Pritchard, 249(HudR):Winter87–646
D. Wellenbrock, 649(WAL):Aug86–163
Tallent, E. Time with Children.
C. See, 441:15Nov87–11
Tamarin, D. The Argentine Labor Movement,
1930–1945.
A. Ciria, 263(RIB):Vol36No1–71
Tambiah, S.J. The Buddhist Saints of the
Forest and the Cult of Amulets.
L.M. Hanks, 293(JASt):Nov85–202
Tamburini, L. Storia del Teatro Regio di
Torino. (Vol 4)
C. Duggan, 410(M&L):Jan86–73
R. Middleton, 90:Jun86–440
Tame, D. The Secret Power of Music.
412:May85–133
Tammi, P. Problems of Nabokov's Poetics.
J.W. Connolly, 402(MLR):Oct87–1052
C. Watts, 89(BJA):Autumn86–410
Tân, P.M. & T.D. Tù. Gesprächsbuch
Deutsch–Vietnamesisch.
G.F. Meier, 682(ZPSK):Band39Heft5–622
T'an Ssu-t'ung. An Exposition of Benevo-
lence.* (Chan Sin-wai, trans)
S. Young, 485(PE&W):Oct86–419
Taney, R.M. Restoration Revivals on the
British Stage (1944–1979).
D. Meyer-Dinkgräfe, 610:Autumn86–272
Tani, S. The Doomed Detective.*
U. Schulz-Buschhaus, 490:Band18Heft1/2–
185
Tanindi, Z. Siyer-i Nebi.
N.M. Titley, 463:Autumn86–296
Tanizaki, J. Naomi.*
K.K. Ito, 407(MN):Autumn86–356
G. Kearns, 249(HudR):Spring86–132
C.I. Mulhern, 293(JASt):Aug86–863
Tannen, D., ed. Coherence in Spoken and
Written Discourse.
R.C. Henze, 355(LSoc):Sep86–404
Tannen, D. Conversational Style.*
P.R. Randall, 35(AS):Fall86–262
K. Tracy, 355(LSoc):Sep86–399
Tannen, D. That's Not What I Meant.
S.H. Elgin, 350:Mar87–200
J.S. Mayher, 186(ETC.):Fall86–306
Tannenbaum, L. Biblical Tradition in
Blake's Early Prophecies.*
D.R.M. Wilkinson, 677(YES):Vol16–286
Tanner, R.L. The Humor of Irony and Satire
in the "Tradiciones peruanas."
P. Rodriguez-Peralta, 263(RIB):
Vol36No2–191
Tanner, S.L. Ken Kesey.
J. Hoy, 649(WAL):May86–79
Tanner, T. Jane Austen.
N. Fruman, 617(TLS):16–22Oct87–1144
P. Goubert, 189(EA):Oct–Dec87–491
F. Weldon, 362:1Jan87–22
Tanner, T. The Writer and His Work: Henry
James.
D.R. Baldwin, 573(SSF):Fall86–464
N. Baym, 432(NEQ):Mar86–138
G. Bishop, 141:Summer86–352
C. Higgins, 27(AL):Oct86–449
J. Rambeau, 395(MFS):Winter86–604
639(VQR):Summer86–89

Tannery, C. Malraux l'Agnostique absolu ou
La Métamorphose comme Loi du Monde.
P-L. Rey, 450(NRF):May86-102
"Tao Te Ching."* (D.C. Lau, trans)
W.G. Boltz, 318(JAOS):Jan/Mar85-176
Tapert, A., ed. Lines of Battle.
D. Murray, 441:28Jun87-25
Tapply, W.G. Dead Meat.
N. Callendar, 441:21Jun87-36
Tappy, J-F. - see "Ernst Bloch/Romain
Rolland, Lettres (1911-1933)"
Tarasov, N. Ballet Technique for the Male
Dancer.
J. Lobenthal, 151:Mar86-91
Tarde, J. A la rencontre de Galilée, Deux
voyages en Italie. (F. Moureau & M.
Tetel, eds)
J. Pineaux, 535(RHL):Jul-Aug86-738
Tardieu, J. Margeries.
D. Leuwers, 450(NRF):Jun86-69
Tardy, W.T. Easy Spanish Reader. (rev)
M.P. Mellgren, 399(MLJ):Winter86-447
Tardy, W.T. Treasury of Children's
Classics in Spanish and English.
L.A. Larew, 399(MLJ):Autumn86-334
Taring, R.D. Daughter of Tibet.
P. Kemp, 617(TLS):13-19Nov87-1258
Tarkovsky, A. Sculpting in Time.
A. Insdorf, 441:20Sep87-20
K. Rosenberg, 707:Summer86-213
Z. Zinik, 617(TLS):9Jan87-45
Tarniewski, M. Płonie Komitet (Grudzień
1970-Czerwiec 1976).
J. Woodall, 575(SEER):Apr86-314
Tarrant, H. Scepticism or Platonism?*
J. Barnes, 123:Vol36No1-75
Tarrant, J., ed. Extrauagantes Iohannis
XXII.
G. Silano, 589:Jul86-708
Tarrant, R.J., ed. Seneca's "Thyestes."*
[shown in prev under Seneca]
G.W.M. Harrison, 124:Jan-Feb87-219
Tárrega, F.A. El prado de Valencia. (J.L.
Canet Valles, ed)
R.L. Fiore, 304(JHP):Spring86-265
Tarrow, S. Exile from the Kingdom.*
J. Cruickshank, 208(FS):Jul86-362
Tartaglia, G.D.D. - see under De' Mantelli
di Canobio detto Tartaglia, G.
Tasso, T. Creation of the World.* (J.
Tusiani, trans; G. Cipolla, ed)
C. Siani, 275(IQ):Summer86-113
"Torquato Tasso tra letteratura, musica,
teatro e arti figurative."
C. Gould, 39:Jun86-441
F. Pivont, 356(LR):May86-171
Tatar, E. Nineteenth Century Hawaiian
Chant.
J.W. Kealiinohomoku, 187:Winter87-143
Tatar, M. The Hard Facts of the Grimms'
Fairy Tales.
H. Carpenter, 441:15Nov87-28
J.A. Smith, 453(NYRB):3Dec87-22
Tate, A. The Poetry Reviews of Allen Tate,
1924-1944. (A. Brown & F.N. Cheney, eds)
R. Godden, 447(N&Q):Dec85-554
M.R. Winchell, 106:Winter86-483
Tate, D. The East German Novel.
T.C. Fox, 221(GQ):Fall86-673
M.N. Love, 395(MFS):Summer86-335
G. Opie, 402(MLR):Jan86-259
Tate, J. Constant Defender.
D. Revell, 29(APR):Jan/Feb87-43

Tate, J. Reckoner.
J. Ash, 441:1Mar87-26
Tatia, N. & M.M. Kumar. Aspects of Jaina
Monasticism.
N. Balbir, 318(JAOS):Oct/Dec85-780
Tatlock, L. Willibald Alexis' "Zeitroman
Das Haus Düsterweg" and the Vormärz.
G.K. Hart, 221(GQ):Summer86-487
Tatman, S.L. & R.W. Moss. Biographical
Dictionary of Philadelphia Architects:
1700-1930.
F. Toker, 576:Dec86-424
Tauber, W. - see Konrad von Haslau
Taubert, S. & P. Weidhaas, eds. The Book
Trade of the World. (Vol 4: Africa.)
I. Sternberg, 538(RAL):Spring86-147
Taubes, G. Nobel Dreams.
L.B. Young, 441:25Jan87-11
Tave, S. - see Bage, R.
Tavernier-Courbin, J., ed. Critical Essays
on Jack London.
G. Beauchamp, 106:Spring86-69
Tavoni, M. Latino, grammatica, volgare.
E. Fumagalli, 275(IQ):Spring86-104
Tavor, E. Scepticism, Society and the
Eighteenth-Century Novel.
J. Mullan, 617(TLS):24Jul87-803
Tavoulareas, W.P. Fighting Back.
639(VQR):Autumn86-136
Tavuzzi, M.M. Existential Judgment and
Transcendental Reduction.
U. Melle, 323:Jan86-100
Tawa, N. A Music for the Millions.
P. Dickinson, 410(M&L):Jul86-304
C. Small, 187:Winter87-145
Tax, P.W. & R.H. Lawson, eds. Arthur
Schnitzler and His Age.
S. Liptzin, 221(GQ):Spring86-326
Taylor, A. He Rau Aroha.
J.R. Chamberlain, Jr., 441:3May87-44
Taylor, A. An Old School Tie.
442(NY):9Mar87-106
Taylor, A. Visions of Harmony.
S. Fender, 362:13Aug87-19
Taylor, B. Modes of Occurrence.*
G. Stahl, 542:Jul-Sep86-406
J.E. Tiles, 518:Jul86-171
Taylor, B. & E. Brewer. The Return of King
Arthur.*
M. Lambert, 402(MLR):Jul87-709
E.D. Mackerness, 447(N&Q):Sep85-421
Taylor, C. Nkore-Kiga.
J. Goldsmith, 350:Jun87-439
Taylor, D.J. Great Eastern Land.*
C. Goodrich, 441:6Sep87-17
Taylor, E. Blush. A Wreath of Roses.
P. Craig, 617(TLS):18-24Sep87-1026
Taylor, E.H. A Life with Alan.
H. Carpenter, 617(TLS):31Jul87-828
Taylor, F.C., with G. Cook. Alberta
Hunter.
L. Birnbaum, 441:12Apr87-27
Taylor, G. To Analyze Delight.
J.L. Styan, 405(MP):Feb87-311
Taylor, G. - see Foote, S. & A. Murphy
Taylor, G. & M. Warren, eds. The Division
of the Kingdoms.*
K. Bartenschlager, 38:Band104Heft1/2-
229
M. Hattaway, 541(RES):May86-256

Taylor, H. The Flying Change.*
    L. Rector, 249(HudR):Autumn86-515
    D. Shapiro, 491:Mar87-348
    455:Dec86-64
Taylor, H. - see Dent, E.J.
Taylor, I. Victorian Sisters.
    P-L. Adams, 61:Sep87-102
    J. Burnett, 617(TLS):11-17Sep87-995
Taylor, J. English Historical Literature
    in the Fourteenth Century.
    J.A. Burrow, 617(TLS):11-17Sep87-990
Taylor, J., ed. Notebooks/Memoirs/
    Archives.
    M. Del Sapio, 402(MLR):Apr86-469
Taylor, J. Beatrix Potter.*
    L.S. Marcus, 441:26Apr87-25
Taylor, J. Storming the Magic Kingdom.
    D. McClintick, 441:10May87-1
    442(NY):1Jun87-111
Taylor, J.G. The Social World of Batavia.
    T.G. McGee, 293(JASt):Nov85-203
Taylor, J.G., ed. Tributes to Paul Dirac.
    B. Pippard, 617(TLS):18-24Sep87-1011
Taylor, J.H.M., ed. Dies Illa.*
    P.S. Noble, 382(MAE):1986/1-129
Taylor, L. & B. Mullan. Uninvited Guests.*
    362:17Sep87-24
Taylor, M. Shakespeare's Darker Purpose.
    L.S. Champion, 402(MLR):Oct86-986
Taylor, M.C. Errance.
    A. Reix, 542:Jan-Mar86-149
Taylor, M.C. Erring.
    G.D. Atkins, 478:Apr86-130
    G.G. Harpham, 141:Winter86-117
    R. Penaskovic, 577(SHR):Winter86-98
Taylor, O., ed. Nature of Communication
    Disorders in Culturally and Linguisti-
    cally Diverse Populations.
    V. Benmaman, 399(MLJ):Autumn86-303
Taylor, P. Gogolian Interludes.
    J. Warrack, 410(M&L):Apr86-199
Taylor, P. The Old Forest.*
    P. Lewis, 565:Spring86-38
Taylor, P. Private Domain.
    L. Kirstein, 453(NYRB):11Jun87-30
    A. Kisselgoff, 441:17May87-9
Taylor, P. A Summons to Memphis.*
    D. Robinson, 598(SoR):Summer87-754
    M. Wood, 617(TLS):1May87-458
Taylor, P.W. Respect for Nature.
    P.L., 185:Jul87-903
Taylor, R. Ethics, Faith and Reason.
    M. Durrant, 518:Jan86-59
Taylor, R. - see "Six German Romantic
    Tales"
Taylor, R., Jr. Loving Belle Starr.*
    E. Morin, 219(GaR):Summer86-579
Taylor, R.H. - see Thein Pe Myint
Taylor, S. - see "The Anglo-Saxon Chron-
    icle: A Collaborative Edition; MS B"
Taylor, T. Plays by Tom Taylor. (M.
    Banham, ed)
    B. Kalikoff, 637(VS):Summer87-519
Taylor, W. Faulkner's Search for a South.*
    K.L. Fulton, 106:Spring86-119
    C. Werner, 403(MLS):Summer86-329
Tcachuk, A. En el mundo de las negocios.
    R.V. Teschner, 399(MLJ):Autumn86-335
Tcherkézoff, S. Le Roi Nyamwezi, la Droite
    et la Gauche.*
    W. MacGaffey, 538(RAL):Summer86-304

Teaford, J.C. The Twentieth-Century Amer-
    ican City.
    42(AR):Summer86-377
"El teatro en Madrid (1583-1925)."
    J.E. Varey, 86(BHS):Apr86-163
Tebbutt, C.F. Huntingdonshire Folklore.
    S. Drury, 203:Vol97No1-117
Te Brake, W.H. Medieval Frontier.
    K. Biddick, 589:Jul86-709
Tec, N. When Light Pierced the Darkness.*
    R.C. Lukas, 497(PolR):Vol31No2/3-202
Teclaff, L.A. Economic Roots of Oppres-
    sion.
    T.J. Smith, 497(PolR):Vol31No2/3-200
Tedlock, D. The Spoken Word and the Work
    of Interpretation.*
    S.U. Philips, 350:Sep87-664
Tedlock, D. - see "Popol Vuh"
Teele, J.W., ed. The Meeting House on the
    Green.
    R.E. Miller, 432(NEQ):Jun86-289
Teeuw, A. & S.O. Robson - see Mpu Dusun
Tefs, W. The Cartier Street Contract.
    K. Tudor, 198:Fall86-96
Tefs, W. Figures on a Wharf.
    J.M. Kertzer, 168(ECW):Fall86-133
    P. Klovan, 102(CanL):Winter85-144
Tegethoff, W. Mies van der Rohe: The
    Villas and Country Houses.* (German
    title: Mies van der Rohe: Die Villen
    und Landhausprojekte.)
    W.J.R. Curtis, 617(TLS):2-8Oct87-1084
    T.S. Hines, 505:Apr86-211
Teichgraeber, R.F. 3d. "Free Trade" and
    Moral Philosophy.
    J. Robertson, 617(TLS):22May87-545
Teichman, J. Pacifism and the Just War.
    J.P. Dolan, 441:26Apr87-30
    B. Paskins, 617(TLS):13Feb87-154
Teillet, S. Des Goths à la nation goth-
    ique.
    J.H.W.G. Liebeschuetz, 123:Vol36No2-
    335
Tejera, V. History as a Human Science.*
    P. Zampini, 619:Winter86-79
Telotte, J.P. Dreams of Darkness.*
    M. Langer, 529(QQ):Winter86-891
Temko, N. To Win or to Die.
    H.D.S. Greenway, 441:16Aug87-23
de Tencin, C.A.G. Mémoires du comte de
    Comminge.
    V. Mylne, 83:Spring86-121
Tenenbaum, J., comp. Dena'ina Sukdu'a.
    (M.J. McGary, ed)
    C. Mishler, 292(JAF):Jul/Sep86-329
Tenèze, M-L. Le Conte populaire français.
    (Vol 4, Pt 1)
    R. Schenda, 196:Band27Heft1/2-145
Tengström, E. A Latin Funeral Oration from
    Early 18th Century Sweden.
    A. Thill, 555:Vol59fasc2-347
Tennant, E. Black Marina.*
    P. Lewis, 565:Spring86-38,
Tennant, E. The House of Hospitalities.
    A. Haverty, 617(TLS):18-24Sep87-1025
    J. Mann, 362:8Oct87-25
Tennant, I. Frank Worrell.
    M.B. Carter, 617(TLS):18-24Dec87-1412
Tennenhouse, L. Power on Display.
    T. Hawkes, 617(TLS):10Apr87-390
Tennyson, A. In Memoriam. (S. Shatto & M.
    Shaw, eds)
    K. McSweeney, 677(YES):Vol16-318

Tennyson, A. The Letters of Alfred Lord
Tennyson. (Vol 2) (C.Y. Lang & E.F.
Shannon, eds)
    G. Lindop, 617(TLS):18-24Dec87-1395
    R.B. Martin, 453(NYRB):22Oct87-17
Tennyson, A. The Poems of Tennyson.
(2nd ed) (C. Ricks, ed)
    G. Lindop, 617(TLS):18-24Dec87-1395
Tennyson, G.B. - see Carlyle, T.
Teodorsson, S.V. Anaxagoras' Theory of
Matter.
    G.B. Kerferd, 41:Fall85-307
Tepilit Ole Saitoti. Worlds of a Maasai
Warrior.
    Chinweizu, 617(TLS):14Aug87-871
de Terán, L.S. Black Idol.
    M. Seymour, 617(TLS):25Sep-1Oct87-
    1053
Terdiman, R. Discourse/Counter-Discourse.
    C.R. Besser, 207(FR):May87-865
    C. Prendergast, 208(FS):Jul86-345
    P. Schofer, 446(NCFS):Spring87-351
    639(VQR):Winter86-19
Terenzio, S. The Prints of Robert Mother-
well.
    J. Lewison, 90:Jan86-47
Terhune, A.K. & A.B. - see Fitz Gerald, E.
Terjék, J. - see Csoma de Kőrös, A.
Terlecki, T. Stanisław Wyspiański.*
    D. Pirie, 575(SEER):Apr86-269
Ter Minassian, A. La Question armenienne.
    R.G. Suny, 550(RusR):Jan86-92
Ternes, E., ed. Lautzeichen und ihre An-
wendung in verschiedenen Sprachgebieten.
    W.J.G. Möhlig, 685(ZDL):2/1986-237
Terpening, R.H. Charon and the Crossing.
    H. King, 123:Vol36No2-355
    J.M. Steadman, 551(RenQ):Autumn86-533
Terras, V., ed. Handbook of Russian Liter-
ature.*
    V. Grebenščikov, 558(RLJ):Spring/Fall
    86-224
    M.R. Katz, 104(CASS):Spring-Summer86-
    183
    A. McMillin, 402(MLR):Jan87-264
    J.E. Malmstad, 550(RusR):Jan86-43
    D. Parrott, 481(PQ):Summer86-403
    D. Patterson, 365:Spring/Summer86-184
    J.T. Shaw, 574(SEEJ):Spring86-103
Terras, V. Vladimir Mayakovsky.*
    H. Stephan, 574(SEEJ):Spring86-113
Terrell, C.F. A Companion to the "Cantos"
of Ezra Pound.* (Vol 2)
    S.M. Gall, 301(JEGP):Oct86-593
    W. Harmon, 569(SR):Fall86-630
Terrie, H. - see James, H.
Terrill, R. The Australians.
    P-L. Adams, 61:Sep87-102
    S. Lawson, 617(TLS):27Nov-3Dec87-1329
    J. Perlez, 441:20Sep87-16
Terry, G.M. East European Languages and
Literatures. (Vol 3)
    G. Thomas, 402(MLR):Jul87-812
Terry, J. Miss Abigail's Part or Version
and Diversion.
    C. Matthews, 376:Sep86-155
Terry, J. Version and Diversion.
    M. Corrigan, 441:1Mar87-20
Terry, M., ed. Prize Stories.
    L. Milazzo, 584(SWR):Summer86-402
Terry, M. Ringer.
    K. Ray, 441:29Nov87-20

Terry, M. & J.A. Metcalf. Mollie Bailey's
Traveling Family Circus.
    V.M. Patraka, 385(MQR):Winter87-286
Terry, S.M., ed. Soviet Policy in Eastern
Europe.*
    M. Croan, 550(RusR):Jul86-319
Terson, P. Strippers.
    B. Grantham, 157:No160-47
Tesauro, P., ed. Libro de Miseria de
Omne.*
    J. Rodríguez Puértolas, 86(BHS):Jul86-
    274
Teschner, R.V. Spanish Orthography, Mor-
phology and Syntax for Bilingual Educa-
tors.
    R. Muños, 238:Sep86-565
    R. Otheguy, 399(MLJ):Summer86-179
Těšitelová, M. & others. Kvantitativní
charakteristiky současné češtiny.
    J. Krámsky, 353:Vol24No6-1121
Tessa, D. L'è el dì di Mort, alegher! (D.
Isella, ed)
    E. Bonora, 228(GSLI):Vol163fasc523-431
Tessonneau, R. - see Joubert, J.
Testard, M. - see Saint Ambrose
Tester, S.J. A History of Western Astrol-
ogy.
    J. Henry, 617(TLS):27Nov-3Dec87-1316
Tetel, M. Lectures scéviennes.*
    F. Lecercle, 535(RHL):Mar-Apr86-262
Tetel, M. Montaigne.
    R.R. Nunn, 546(RR):Nov86-457
Tetzeli von Rosador, K. - see Grimald, N.
Teubner, C. & J. Charrette. Cakes and
Pastries.
    W. & C. Cowen, 639(VQR):Autumn86-141
Teveth, S. Ben-Gurion.
    M. Gilbert, 441:21Jun87-3
Teveth, S. Ben-Gurion and the Palestinian
Arabs.*
    W. Kluback, 390:Nov86-53
"The Texas Cowboy."
    L. Milazzo, 584(SWR):Summer86-402
de Texeda, J. Gramática de la lengua
española. (J.M. Lope Blanch, ed)
    C. Schmitt, 553(RLiR):Jul-Dec86-574
Texier, C. Love Me Tender.
    E. Prager, 441:7Jun87-13
"Text." (Vol 1) (D.C. Greetham & W.S.
Hill, eds)
    P. Davison, 541(RES):Nov86-607
    C. Fahy, 354:Sep86-270
"Texte." (Vol 3)
    U. Schulz-Buschhaus, 547(RF):Band98-
    Heft1/2-187
Tezcan, H. & S. Delibas. Topkapı: Cos-
tumes, Embroideries and Other Textiles.
(J.M. Rogers, ed & trans)
    G. Goodwin, 617(TLS):6Mar87-249
    J. Russell, 441:31May87-11
Tezenas du Montcel, H. L'Université.
    H. Sutton, 207(FR):Dec86-280
Thacker, C. The Wildness Pleases.*
    E.D. Mackerness, 447(N&Q):Jun85-271
von Thadden, R. La Prusse en question.
    A. Clerval, 450(NRF):Apr86-105
Thalberg, I. Misconceptions of Mind and
Freedom.*
    D. Mitchell, 63:Mar86-108
Thalmann, W.G. Conventions of Form and
Thought in Early Greek Epic Poetry.*
    R.L. Fowler, 487:Summer86-206

Thaning, K. Grundtvig.*
  J.I. Jensen, 562(Scan):Nov86-231
Thao, T.D. - see under Trán Duc Thao
Thaxton, C.B., W.L. Bradley & R.L. Olson.
  The Mystery of Life's Origins.
  C. Devine, 258:Mar86-92
Thaxton, J. Natural Attractions.
  E. Newby, 441:31May87-49
Theakston, K. Junior Ministers in British
  Government.
  V. Bogdanor, 617(TLS):4-11Sep87-944
"Le Théâtre dans l'Europe des Lumières."
  A. Tissier, 549(RLC):Oct-Dec86-473
Thein Pe Myint. Marxism and Resistance in
  Burma, 1942-1945. (R.H. Taylor, ed &
  trans)
  J. Badgley, 293(JASt):Feb86-469
Theiss, W. Schwank.
  W. Wunderlich, 196:Band27Heft1/2-147
Theodoridis, C., ed. Photii patriarchae
  lexicon.* (Vol 1)
  J. Schneider, 555:Vol59fasc2-301
  N.G. Wilson, 123:Vol36No2-223
Theophylactus Simocatta. The History of
  Theophylact Simocatta. (M. & M. Whitby,
  eds & trans)
  M. Di Maio, Jr., 124:Mar-Apr87-324
Thérel, M-L. Le Triomphe de la Vierge-
  Eglise.
  N. Coldstream, 90:Jul86-510
"Yves Thériault se raconte."
  B-Z. Shek, 627(UTQ):Fall86-215
Thernstrom, A.M. Whose Votes Count?
  A. Clymer, 441:18Oct87-40
Theroux, A. An Adultery.
  R. Hansen, 441:18Oct87-11
Theroux, P. Night Lights.
  N. Mairs, 441:15Mar87-13
Theroux, P. O-Zone.*
  S. Lardner, 442(NY):16Feb87-108
  J. Mellors, 364:Dec86/Jan87-149
Thesiger, W. The Life of My Choice.
  A. Hourani, 617(TLS):4-11Sep87-941
Thesing, W.B. The London Muse.*
  L. Manley, 402(MLR):Jan87-184
Thesleff, H. Studies in Platonic Chronol-
  ogy.
  S.R. Slings, 394:Vol39fasc3/4-476
Theunissen, M. The Other.
  G. Schufreider, 543:Mar87-596
Thevet, A. Cosmographie de Levant.* (F.
  Lestringant, ed)
  A.P. Stabler, 551(RenQ):Spring86-103
Thevet, A. André Thevet's North America.
  M. Abley, 617(TLS):19Jun87-654
Theweleit, K. Male Fantasies. (Vol 1)
  P. Robinson, 441:21Jun87-14
Thiébaux, M. Ellen Glasgow.*
  R. Gray, 677(YES):Vol16-353
Thiel-Horstmann, M. Crossing the Ocean of
  Existence.
  R.K. Barz, 259(IIJ):Apr86-133
Thierry, A. - see d'Aubigné, A.
Thieuloy, J. Voltigeur de la lune.
  A. Moorhead, 207(FR):Dec86-299
Thiher, A. Raymond Queneau.
  C. Toloudis, 207(FR):Mar87-545
Thiher, A. Words in Reflection.*
  L. Orr, 395(MFS):Summer86-351
Thillet, P. - see Alexander of Aphrodisias
wa Thiong'o, N. - see under Ngugi wa
  Thiong'o

Thistlewood, D. Herbert Read.*
  J. Keel, 709:Fall86-55
  P. Meeson, 289:Summer86-107
Thite, G.U. Medicine.
  K.G. Zysk, 318(JAOS):Oct/Dec85-808
Thody, P. & H. Evans. Faux Amis and Key
  Words.
  D.E. Ager, 402(MLR):Apr86-471
Thody, P. & H. Evans. Mistakable French.
  G. Crouse, 399(MLJ):Spring86-68
Tholfsen, T.R. Ideology and Revolution in
  Modern Europe.*
  K.R. Hoover, 125:Winter86-238
Thom, M., with C. Duvernoy & G. Pourchot -
  see Contejean, C.
Thom, P. The Syllogism.
  A. Menne, 53(AGP):Band68Heft2-203
Thom, V.M. Birds in Scotland.
  C. Perrins, 617(TLS):13Mar87-280
Thomas, A. Goodbye Harold, Good Luck.
  R. Hatch, 99:Aug/Sep86-34
Thomas, A. Intertidal Life.*
  529(QQ):Summer86-459
Thomas, A. Riding the Dolphin.
  B. Tritel, 441:23Aug87-16
Thomas, A.R. Areal Analysis of Dialect
  Data by Computer.
  W. Viereck, 685(ZDL):3/1986-409
Thomas, B. James Joyce's "Ulysses."
  P. Lawley, 402(MLR):Jan87-187
Thomas, C. L'Ashram de l'Amour.
  K. Schomer, 318(JAOS):Oct/Dec85-809
Thomas, C. Winter Hawk.
  K. Kalfus, 441:28Jun87-24
Thomas, C., with G. Tremlett. Caitlin.*
  F. Simon, 441:29Mar87-23
  362:31Dec87-22
Thomas, D. Robert Browning.
  L.A. Rubel, 403(MLS):Summer86-318
Thomas, D. The Collected Letters of Dylan
  Thomas.* (P. Ferris, ed)
  J. MacVean, 4:Summer86-69
  D. Rigal, 189(EA):Apr-Jun87-238
Thomas, D. Henrik Ibsen.*
  K. Kvam, 610:Spring86-74
  H. Rønning, 402(MLR):Jan86-260
Thomas, D. Dylan Thomas: The Collected
  Stories.*
  R.F. Peterson, 573(SSF):Spring86-206
Thomas, D. & J. Compton Mackenzie.
  A. Bell, 617(TLS):16Jan87-71
Thomas, D.M. Sphinx.*
  D.J. Enright, 453(NYRB):9Apr87-23
  G. Stade, 441:18Jan87-6
Thomas, D.M. Summit.
  L. Chamberlain, 617(TLS):26Jun87-698
Thomas, E.M. Reindeer Moon.
  P-L. Adams, 61:Mar87-94
  G.A. Dillin, 441:22Mar87-28
  J. Updike, 442(NY):30Mar87-122
Thomas, G. Les deux traditions.*
  P. Dube, 102(CanL):Winter85-139
Thomas, G.S. The Complete Flower Paint-
  ings and Drawings of Graham Stuart
  Thomas.
  A. Lacy, 441:6Dec87-32
Thomas, H. Armed Truce.
  T.G. Ash, 453(NYRB):11Jun87-44
  J.L. Gaddis, 617(TLS):8May87-479
  H.G. Pitt, 364:Dec86/Jan87-144
  M.D. Shulman, 441:1Mar87-1
  442(NY):23Mar87-100

Thomas, H. The Spanish Civil War.*
  B. Knox, 453(NYRB):26Mar87-21
Thomas, J. The Art of the Actor-Manager.*
  B. Kalikoff, 637(VS):Summer87-519
Thomas, J. Pictures, Moving.*
  M. Kreyling, 573(SSF):Spring86-215
  J. Matthews, 651(WHR):Summer86-184
Thomas, J., ed. Pirandello und die Natur-
  alismus-Diskussion.
  R. Zaiser, 547(RF):Band98Heft3/4-468
Thomas, J.L. Alternative America.*
  D. Macleod, 106:Summer86-235
Thomas, J.W., ed & trans. The Best Novel-
  las of Medieval Germany.*
  S.L. Wailes, 564:Feb86-88
  R.W. Walker, 399(MLJ):Spring86-70
Thomas, M. Antonia Saw the Oryx First.
  M. Gorra, 441:7Jun87-12
Thomas, M. Come to Africa and Save Your
  Marriage.
  B. Thompson, 441:11Oct87-11
Thomas, M. & R. Escoffey. The Penguin
  French Dictionary.
  R.J. Steiner, 207(FR):Feb87-441
Thomas, M., C. Mainguy & S. Pommier. Tex-
  tile Art.
  B. Scott, 39:Mar86-220
Thomas, M.M. The Ropespinner Conspiracy.
  V. Patrick, 441:11Jan87-9
Thomas, N. The Narrative Works of Günter
  Grass.
  J.W. Rohlfs, 402(MLR):Oct86-1047
Thomas, N. & R. Towell, ed. Interpreting
  as a Lanuage Teaching Technique.
  M.T. Krause, 399(MLJ):Autumn86-304
Thomas, N.K. Henry Vaughan.
  A. Rudrum, 617(TLS):27Mar87-316
Thomas, P.D.G. The Townshend Duties
  Crisis.
  J. Derry, 617(TLS):30Oct-5Nov87-1186
Thomas, R. The Latin Masks of Ezra Pound.
  S.J. Adams, 106:Fall86-367
Thomas, R. Out on the Rim.
  442(NY):7Dec87-194
Thomas, R. Strangers.
  N. Ramsey, 441:12Jul87-20
Thomas, R.G. Edward Thomas.*
  J.H.J., 636(VP):Autumn86-349
  J. Lucas, 637(VS):Spring87-436
  K. Wilson, 529(QQ):Winter86-906
Thomas, R.G.C. Indian Security Policy.
  S. Khilnani, 617(TLS):12Jun87-631
Thomas, R.S. Experimenting with an Amen.*
  J. Mole, 176:Mar87-63
Thomas, R.S. Ingrowing Thoughts.*
  H. Buckingham, 565:Summer86-64
  J. Hamard, 189(EA):Apr-Jun87-244
Thomas, R.S. Later Poems 1972-1982.
  J. Saunders, 565:Summer86-74
Thomas, R.S. Welsh Airs.
  S. Medcalf, 617(TLS):17Apr87-418
Thomas, S.D. The Last Navigator.
  N. Miller, 441:7Jun87-31
Thomas, V. The Moral Universe of Shake-
  speare's Problem Plays.
  J. Wilders, 617(TLS):30Oct-5Nov87-1197
Thomas Aquinas - see under Aquinas, T.
"Thomas of Erceldoune."* (I. Nixon, ed)
  K. Bitterling, 38:Band104Heft3/4-501
  J.M. Cowen, 447(N&Q):Dec85-512
  A.A. MacDonald, 179(ES):Apr86-184

"Thomasin von Zerclaere, 'Der Welsche
  Gast.'" (F.W. von Kries, ed)
  D.H. Green, 402(MLR):Apr87-509
  W.C.M., 400(MLN):Apr86-737
Thomason, B.C. Making Sense of Reifica-
  tion.
  L. Langsdorf, 488:Jun86-262
Thomason, M.V.R. Trying Times.
  W.B. Gatewood, Jr., 9(AlaR):Oct86-302
Thomasseau, J-M. Le Mélodrame.
  P. Frantz, 535(RHL):Sep-Oct86-930
  W.D. Howarth, 208(FS):Jul86-369
Thomières, D., ed. Le citoyen de demain et
  les langues.
  L.L. Harlow, 399(MLJ):Summer86-164
Thompson, A. - see Shakespeare, W.
Thompson, A.A. Hirst and Rhodes.
  D. Durrant, 364:Jul86-110
Thompson, D. An Introduction to Piran-
  dello's "Sei personaggi in cerca
  d'autore."
  A. Bullock, 278(IS):Vol41-165
Thompson, D., ed. The Leavises.*
  T.L. Jeffers, 651(WHR):Spring86-83
  C. Norris, 577(SHR):Summer86-269
  R. Wellek, 402(MLR):Jul87-725
Thompson, E.A. Saint Germanus of Auxerre
  and the End of Roman Britain.
  A.A. Barrett, 124:Mar-Apr87-323
  M. Brooke, 123:Vol36No1-160
  W. Goffart, 589:Jan86-213
  J. Harries, 313:Vol76-315
Thompson, E.P. The Heavy Dancers.
  W. Phillips, 473(PR):Vol53No2-288
Thompson, G.R. - see Poe, E.A.
Thompson, H. The News Quiz Book of the
  News.
  D.J. Enright, 617(TLS):18-24Dec87-1399
Thompson, I.E. Being and Meaning.
  F.M. Mangrum, 543:Sep86-145
Thompson, J. East is West of Here.
  A. Hornaday, 441:13Sep87-34
Thompson, J. The Getaway. The Grifters.
  A Hell of a Woman. The Killer Inside Me.
  Nothing More than Murder. Pop. 1280.
  Recoil.
  B. Gifford, 649(WAL):May86-55
Thompson, J. How to Enter the River.
  E. Pankey, 389(MQ):Autumn86-141
Thompson, J. Through Cyprus with the Cam-
  era, in the Autumn of 1878.
  R. Higgins, 39:Jan86-63
Thompson, J. & P. Scoones. Orwell's
  London.
  R.J. Voorhees, 395(MFS):Summer86-319
Thompson, J.A. Manual of Curatorship.
  J. Walsh, 617(TLS):16Jan87-58
Thompson, J.H., with A. Seager. Canada,
  1922-1939.
  C. Armstrong, 529(QQ):Summer86-401
Thompson, J.R. Thomas Lovell Beddoes.
  L.M. Jones, 340(KSJ):Vol35-188
Thompson, K. Exporting Entertainment.*
  S. Street, 707:Summer86-216
Thompson, K. A Local Hanging and Other
  Stories.
  L. Mathews, 102(CanL):Winter85-140
Thompson, K.W., ed. Diplomacy and Values.
  P. Pastor, 497(PolR):Vol31No1-84
Thompson, K.W., ed. Ethics and Interna-
  tional Relations.
  D.L., 185:Oct86-306

Thompson, L. The Political Mythology of
Apartheid.*
D.F. Gordon, 385(MQR):Summer87-553
W.G. James, 529(QQ):Autumn86-484
639(VQR):Summer86-97
Thompson, M.S. The "Spider Web."
639(VQR):Summer86-79
Thompson, N. Wellington after Waterloo.
B. Fothergill, 617(TLS):15May87-509
Thompson, P. The Ghosts of Who We Were.
455:Dec86-63
Thompson, P.V. & D.J. - see Swift, J.
Thompson, R. Sex in Middlesex.
L. Handlin, 432(NEQ):Dec86-577
Thompson, R.H. The Return from Avalon.*
R. Cochran, 481(PQ):Fall86-537
Thomsen, M-L. The Sumerian Language.
J.V. Kinnier Wilson, 361:Sep86-74
Thomson, A. Barbary and Enlightenment.
A. Hamilton, 617(TLS):23-29Oct87-1161
Thomson, C., ed. Georg Lukács et la
théorie littéraire contemporaine.
G. Good, 107(CRCL):Mar86-89
Thomson, D. Warren Beatty.
D. Coward, 617(TLS):24Jul87-792
J. Wyver, 362:23Apr87-27
Thomson, D., ed. An Edition of the Middle
English Grammatical Texts.
M. Irvine, 589:Oct86-1036
A. Ward, 541(RES):Feb86-75
Thomson, D. Suspects.*
T. McGonigle, 532(RCF):Summer86-155
Thomson, D.C. Jean Lesage and the Quiet
Revolution.
W. Irvine, 529(QQ):Autumn86-700
Thomson, J. "Liberty," "The Castle of
Indolence" and Other Poems. (J. Sam-
brook, ed)
P. Rogers, 617(TLS):23Jan87-80
Thomson, J. No Flowers, by Request.
T.J. Binyon, 617(TLS):25Sep-1Oct87-
1052
G. Kaufman, 362:2Jul87-31
Thomson, P. Shakespeare's Theatre.*
D.G. Watson, 536(Rev):Vol8-59
Thomson, P. - see Boucicault, D.
Thomson, P. & G. Salgado. The Everyman
Companion to the Theatre.*
O. Trilling, 157:No160-48
Thomson, R. Dreams of Leaving.
W. Brandmark, 362:16Jul87-23
A. Hislop, 617(TLS):17Jul87-766
Thomson, R. Seurat.*
K. Adler, 90:May86-364
M. Clarke, 39:Aug86-141
Thong, H.S. - see Du, N.
Thoreau, H.D. The Illustrated "A Week on
the Concord and Merrimack Rivers." (C.F.
Hovde, W.L. Howarth & E.H. Witherell,
eds)
R.W. Harvey, 106:Summer86-211
Thoreau, H.D. A Week on the Concord and
Merrimack Rivers; Walden, or Life in the
Woods; The Maine Woods; Cape Cod.* (R.F.
Sayre, ed)
G. O'Brien, 453(NYRB):15Jan87-46
Thoreau, H.D. The Winged Life. (R. Bly,
ed)
G. O'Brien, 453(NYRB):15Jan87-46
Thormahlen, M. Eliot's Animals.
R. Snape, 161(DUJ):Jun86-385

Thorn, J., ed. The Armchair Book of Base-
ball.
639(VQR):Winter86-30
Thornbury, B.E. Sukeroku's Double Iden-
tity.
C.A. Gerstle, 302:Vol22No1-105
Thorne, C. The Issue of War.*
639(VQR):Summer86-79
Thornton, A. Homer's "Iliad."
P.V. Jones, 123:Vol36No1-4
Thornton, L. Imagining Argentina.
L. Hafrey, 441:20Sep87-11
442(NY):7Dec87-190
Thornton, L. Unbodied Hope.*
M.A. Masse, 454:Winter87-180
Thornton, P. Authentic Decor.*
D.B., 45:Apr86-65
G.J. Stops, 90:Jul86-517
Thornton, R. Frame of Darkness.
C.R. Steele, 102(CanL):Summer86-119
Thornton, R. The Hewed Out Light.*
D.A. Macdonald, 102(CanL):Winter85-157
Thornton, R.K.R. The Decadent Dilemma.*
H. Tucker, 385(MQR):Spring87-421
Thornton, T.K. Die Thematik von Selbstaus-
löschung und Selbstbewahrung in den
Werken Peter Handkes.
T.F. Barry, 221(GQ):Summer86-499
Thorold, H. Collins Guide to Cathedrals,
Abbeys and Priories of England and Wales.
G. Cavaliero, 324:Jan87-166
Thorpe, J.D. John Milton.*
A. Burnett, 447(N&Q):Jun85-262
Thorpe, M. Out of the Storm.
B. Whiteman, 198:Summer86-85
Thorslev, P.L., Jr. Romantic Contraries.*
S. Curran, 661(WC):Autumn86-192
J. Engell, 401(MLQ):Jun85-212
D. Punter, 88:Fall86-60
J.R. Reed, 591(SIR):Spring86-156
A. Robinson, 541(RES):May86-269
F.W. Shilstone, 577(SHR):Summer86-282
Thorson, J.J. - see Smollett, T.
Thoss, D. & U. Jenni - see Pächt, O.
Thoursie, S.A.O. Die Verbalflexion eines
südbairischen Autographs aus dem Jahre
1464.
R. Peilicke, 682(ZPSK):Band39Heft1-143
Threatte, L. The Grammar of Antic Inscrip-
tions. (Vol 1)
C.J. Ruijgh, 394:Vol39fasc3/4-448
"Three Plays on a Domestic Theme."
P. Storfer, 157:No162-46
Thubron, C. Behind the Wall.
J. Mirsky, 617(TLS):11-17Sep87-973
P. Taylor-Martin, 362:24Sep87-22
Thuillier, P. Socrate fonctionnaire.
J. Largeault, 542:Jan-Mar86-92
Thulstrup, N. Commentary on Kierkegaard's
"Concluding Unscientific Postscript" With
a New Introduction.
G.D. Marino, 543:Mar87-599
Thun, N. Puschkinbilder - Bulgakow -
Tynjanow - Platonow - Soschtschenko -
Zwetajewa.
G. Dudek, 654(WB):3/1986-513
Thurley, G. Counter-Modernism in Current
Critical Theory.
J.M. Ellis, 131(CL):Fall86-374
N. Jacobs, 447(N&Q):Dec85-564
Thurlow, R. Fascism in Britain.
D. Cannadine, 362:26Feb87-23

Thurm, M. Walking Distance.
   D. Mason, 441:10May87-9
   442(NY):1Jun87-110
Thurm, S. Deutscher Glockenatlas. (Vol 4)
   I.S. Weber, 683:Band49Heft3-421
Thurn, H. Die Handschriften der Universi-
   tätsbibliothek Wurzburg. (Vol 3, Pt 1)
   R. Weigand, 684(ZDA):Band115Heft2-82
Thurston, A.F. Enemies of the People.
   M. Goldman, 441:22Feb87-3
Thwaite, A. Edmund Gosse.*
   A.F.T. Lurcock, 541(RES):Feb86-123
   S. Pickering, 569(SR):Spring86-284
Thwaite, A. Letter from Tokyo.
   D. Dunn, 176:Jun87-50
Thwaite, A. Poems 1953-1983.
   J. Saunders, 565:Summer86-74
Thwaite, A. Poetry Today.*
   A. Haberer, 189(EA):Jan-Mar87-98
   A. Swarbrick, 148:Autumn86-109
Thynne, J. & M. Two Elizabethan Women.
   (A.D. Wall, ed)
   K. Duncan-Jones, 447(N&Q):Mar85-105
Tibiletti, G. Le lettere private nei
   papiri greci del III e IV secolo d.C.
   P.J. Parsons, 123:Vol36No2-353
Tice, R. Station Stop.
   R. Bodner, 649(WAL):Nov86-276
   R. Spiess, 404:Summer86-45
Tichá, Z. Cesta starší české literatury.
   R.B. Pynsent, 575(SEER):Jul86-452
Tichi, C. Shifting Gears.
   A. Mars-Jones, 617(TLS):4-10Dec87-
   1358
   A. Nehamas, 441:19Apr87-9
Tidholm, H. The Dialect of Egton in North
   Yorkshire.
   M. Durrell, 685(ZDL):1/1986-120
Tidrick, K. Heart-beguiling Araby.
   M. Manzalaoui, 677(YES):Vol16-334
Tiefenbach, H. Xanten - Essen - Köln.
   F.G. Banta, 221(GQ):Fall86-640
   K.L. Hibbert, 402(MLR):Oct86-1030
van Tieghem, P. - see "Dictionnaire des
littératures"
"Domenico Tiepolo, the Punchinello Draw-
   ings."
   B. Ford, 90:Dec86-907
Tierney, F.M. - see Sangster, C.
Tiersma, P.M. Frisian Reference Grammar.
   T.S. Parker, 350:Dec87-917
Tietz, M. & V. Kapp, eds. La Pensée reli-
   gieuse dans la littérature et la civili-
   sation du XVIIe siècle en France.*
   F. Delforge, 535(RHL):Nov-Dec86-1126
Tietze, K-P. Szuch'uan vom 7. bis 10.
   Jahrhundert.
   C. Schirokauer, 318(JAOS):Oct/Dec85-
   764
Tiger, L. The Manufacture of Evil.
   L. Marx, 441:23Aug87-10
Tilcher, T. Der orientalische Traum der
   Schriftstellergeneration von 1848.
   L. Netter, 549(RLC):Oct-Dec86-479
Tiles, J.E. Things That Happen.
   L.N. Oaklander, 449:Mar86-111
Tiles, M. Bachelard.
   J.G. Clark, 402(MLR):Apr86-492
   T. Rockmore, 84:Dec86-529
   S. Sayers, 518:Jan86-41
   S. Schaffer, 208(FS):Jan86-106

Tilghman, B.R. But is it Art?*
   W. Charlton, 483:Apr86-253
   G. Currie, 63:Jun86-231
   G. Iseminger, 289:Fall86-115
   C. Lord, 290(JAAC):Winter86-203
Tillman, L. Haunted Houses.
   L. Gordon, 441:8Feb87-24
Tillotson, G.H.R. The Rajput Palaces.
   A. Topsfield, 617(TLS):23-29Oct87-1160
Tilly, C. The Contentious French.*
   639(VQR):Summer86-80
"Timaios of Locri, On the Nature of the
   World and the Soul." (T.H. Tobin, ed and
   trans)
   J. Hershbell, 41:Spring85-126
"Timarion."* (B. Baldwin, trans)
   A.R. Dyck, 122:Oct86-358
   E.A. Fisher, 487:Summer86-239
Timko, M., F. Kaplan & E. Guiliano - see
   "Dickens Studies Annual"
Timmerman, J.H. John Steinbeck's Fiction.
   J. Ditsky, 268(IFR):Summer87-109
Timmins, T.C.B. - see Chandler, J.
Timms, E. & D. Kelley, eds. Unreal City.*
   G. Josipovici, 208(FS):Jul86-373
   A.S.L., 295(JML):Nov86-370
   J.M. Ritchie, 402(MLR):Apr87-431
Tindall, G. To the City.
   J-A. Goodwin, 617(TLS):8May87-488
   L. Taylor, 362:7May87-25
Tingay, G. - see Vergil
Tinniswood, P. Uncle Mort's North Country.
   R. Hattersley, 362:1Jan87-21
Tintner, A.R. The Museum World of Henry
   James.*
   L. Auchincloss, 453(NYRB):9Apr87-29
   S.B. Daugherty, 26(ALR):Winter87-94
   J.W. Tuttleton, 395(MFS):Winter86-597
Tipping, R.K. Nearer By Far.
   C. James, 617(TLS):27Nov-3Dec87-1327
Tirman, J., ed. Empty Promise.
   Lord Zuckerman, 453(NYRB):9Apr87-35
Tirso de Molina. La huerta de Juan Fernán-
   dez. (B. Pallares, ed)
   M. Wilson, 402(MLR):Oct86-1021
Tirso de Molina. La mujer que manda en
   casa. (D.L. Smith, ed)
   M.C. Quintero, 238:Dec86-869
Tirso de Molina. La villana de la Sagra;
   El colmenero divino. (B. Pallares, ed)
   T.A. O'Connor, 240(HR):Summer86-340
   M. Wilson, 402(MLR):Oct86-1021
Tiruchelvam, N. The Ideology of Popular
   Justice in Sri Lanka.
   R.M. Hayden, 293(JASt):Nov85-186
Tischbein, J-H-W. Idyllen. (P. Reindl,
   ed)
   J-R. Mantion, 98:Apr86-355
Tischler, B.L. An American Music.*
   W. Mellers, 617(TLS):9Jan87-39
Tischler, H., ed. The Earliest Motets (to
   circa 1270).
   T. Karp, 589:Jul86-711
   N.E. Smith, 317:Spring86-169
Tischler, J. Hethitisches etymologisches
   Glossar. (Pt 4)
   E. Neu, 260(IF):Band91-375
Tisdale, S. Harvest Moon.
   K. Teltsch, 441:13Sep87-35
Tišma, A. L'Usage de l'homme.
   L. Kovacs, 450(NRF):Jan86-110

Tison-Braun, M. Ce Monstre incomparable...
T.J. Kline, 207(FR):Dec86-266
C. Moatti, 535(RHL):Mar-Apr86-347
Tison-Braun, M. Marguerite Duras.
N. Bailey, 208(FS):Jul86-364
D. Meakin, 402(MLR):Apr86-494
Tissoni Benvenuti, A. L'Orfeo del Poliz-
iano.
A. Buck, 547(RF):Band98Heft3/4-459
Titone, R. & M. Danesi. Applied Psycholin-
guistics.*
J. Arabski, 257(IRAL):Nov86-340
Titone, V. Vecchie e nuove storie Sicili-
ane. Le notti della Kalsa di Palermo.
H.G. Koenigsberger, 617(TLS):18-
24Dec87-1410
Tittensor, J. Year One.
A. Knopf, 441:2Aug87-17
Tittler, J. Narrative Irony in the Contem-
porary Spanish-American Novel.*
P. Hulme, 86(BHS):Oct86-382
Tivnan, E. The Lobby.
B. Gwertzman, 441:17May87-24
S. Hoffmann, 453(NYRB):8Oct87-8
Tiwari, K.N. Comparative Religion.
J.D. Redington, 318(JAOS):Oct/Dec85-816
Tixonov, A.N. Slovoobrazovatel'nyj slovar'
russkogo jazyka v dvux tomax.
F.Y. Gladney, 574(SEEJ):Winter86-596
Tobin, R.B. Vincent of Beauvais' "De
eruditione filiorum nobilium."
G.G. Guzman, 589:Oct86-1007
Tobin, R.W., ed. Littérature et gastron-
omie.
J-P. Dens, 207(FR):May87-856
Tobin, T.H. - see "Timaios of Locri, On the
Nature of the World and the Soul."
Tocci, L.M. - see under Michelini Tocci, L.
de Tocqueville, A. Selected Letters on
Politics and Society.* (R. Boesche, ed)
L. Groopman, 31(ASch):Spring86-267
K.G. Long, 396(ModA):Summer/Fall86-310
Todd, C.L. The "Sittin' Stone."
J.B. Reinstein, 440:Summer-Fall86-165
Todd, J., ed. Jane Austen.*
J.A. Dussinger, 402(MLR):Oct87-923
J. Thompson, 536(Rev):Vol8-21
Todd, J., ed. A Dictionary of British and
American Women Writers 1660-1800.*
J.K. Kribbs, 27(AL):Mar86-122
J. Simons, 541(RES):Aug86-452
H. Wilcox, 83:Autumn86-249
Todd, J. Sensibility.
W.B. Carnochan, 617(TLS):27Feb87-218
J. Hamard, 189(EA):Oct-Dec87-490
Todd, L. Cameroon.
H. Ulherr, 38:Band104Heft1/2-170
Todd, L. Modern Englishes.*
D. Bickerton, 361:Mar86-273
L.D. Carrington, 355(LSoc):Mar86-105
J.J. Kohn, 399(MLJ):Spring86-92
J.P. Williams, 350:Jun87-445
Todd, W.B. A Bibliography of Edmund Burke.
F.P. Lock, 677(YES):Vol16-278
Todd, W.M. 3d. Fiction and Society in the
Age of Pushkin.
T.J. Binyon, 617(TLS):8May87-485
E. Wasiolek, 268(IFR):Winter87-51
Todisco, A. Ma che lingua parliamo.
T.G. Griffith, 402(MLR):Apr86-495
Todorov, T. Mikhail Bakhtin.*
C. Emerson, 131(CL):Fall86-370
[continued]

[continuing]
J. O'Brien, 402(MLR):Jul86-811
D.H. Richter, 599:Fall86-411
Todorov, T. Frêle bonheur.
T. Cordellier, 450(NRF):Jan86-98
Todorov, T. Symbolism and Interpretation.*
D.H., 355(LSoc):Mar86-141
Toff, N. The Flute Book.
N. O'Loughlin, 415:Jun86-338
Toffin, G. Société et Religion chez les
Néwar du Népal.
T. Riccardi, 293(JASt):Aug86-894
Togeby, K. Grammaire française. (Vols 2 &
3)
H. Bonnard, 209(FM):Apr86-110
Togeby, K. Grammaire française. (Vol 4)
H. Bonnard, 209(FM):Apr86-110
D. Gaatone, 545(RPh):May87-502
Tognelli, J. Presunto diletto.
G. Wedel, 275(IQ):Summer86-120
Toland, J. Occupation.
S. Kellerman, 441:8Nov87-26
Toledano, H. Judicial Practice and Family
Law in Morocco.
H.E. Kassis, 318(JAOS):Jan/Mar85-160
Tolkien, J.R.R. The Old English "Exodus."*
(J. Turville-Petre, ed)
N.F. Blake, 402(MLR):Apr86-439
Tolley, A.T. The Poetry of the Forties in
Britain.*
R. Smith, 150(DR):Winter85/86-585
Tolstaya, T. "Na zolotom kryl'tse sideli
..."
S. Laird, 617(TLS):26Jun87-696
Tolstoy, N. The Tolstoys.
A. Woronzoff, 550(RusR):Jan86-60
Tomalin, C. Katherine Mansfield.
M. Walters, 362:5Nov87-31
Tomalin, M. The Fortunes of the Warrior
Heroine in Italian Literature.
K.W. Hempfer, 547(RF):Band98Heft3/4-
452
Tomalin, R. W.H. Hudson.
C. Watts, 402(MLR):Jul86-730
de Tomás García, J.L. La otra orilla de
la droga.
K.M. Glenn, 238:May86-312
Tomasek, T. Die Utopie im "Tristan"
Gotfrids von Strassburg.
D.H. Green, 402(MLR):Jan87-236
Tomaselli, S. & R. Porter, eds. Rape.
E. Showalter, 441:4Jan87-11
Tomasello, A. Music and Ritual at Papal
Avignon, 1309-1403.
P. Jeffery, 589:Jan86-215
Tomberlin, J.E. & P. van Inwagen, eds.
Alvin Plantinga.
H.E. Baber, 258:Sep86-301
R. Swinburne, 484(PPR):Mar87-511
Tomin, Z. The Coast of Bohemia.
L. Chamberlain, 617(TLS):11-17Dec87-
1375
Tomlinson, C. Notes from New York and
Other Poems.*
L. Lerner, 569(SR):Spring86-312
Tomlinson, C. Poetry and Metamorphosis.*
E. Longley, 447(N&Q):Sep85-413
Tomlinson, G. Monteverdi and the End of
the Renaissance.
D. Stevens, 617(TLS):7Aug87-845
Tompkins, J. Sensational Designs.*
P.F. Gura, 183(ESQ):Vol32No1-68
[continued]

368

[continuing]

T. Martin, 27(AL):Dec86-626

M. Oriard, 594:Winter86-451

E.S. Watts, 115:Summer86-415

Toncheva, E. The Velikij Skit (Skit Mare) Monastery.

S.H., 412:Nov85-306

Tonelli, F. Sophocles' "Oedipus" and the Tale of the Theatre.

S. Goldhill, 303(JoHS):Vol106-209

Tønnesson, S. The Outbreak of the War in Indochina, 1946.

A.L.A. Patti, 293(JASt):Nov85-206

Took, J.F. "L'etterno piacer."

S. Botterill, 402(MLR):Jul86-755

L. Pertile, 382(MAE):1986/2-327

Toole, J.K. La Conjuration des Imbéciles.

H. Cronel, 450(NRF):Jul-Aug86-192

Tooley, M. Abortion and Infanticide.*

G. Lloyd, 63:Jun86(supp)-144

Top, S. Komt Vrienden, luistert naar mijn lied.

W.H.F. Nicholaisen, 292(JAF):Jul/Sep86-342

Topitsch, E. Stalin's War.

A. Dallin, 441:15Nov87-35

Topliss, H. Tom Roberts, 1856-1931.*

A. Gray, 617(TLS):27Feb87-216

K. McConkey, 90:Sep86-685

Topper, U., ed. Märchen der Berber.

U. Marzolph, 196:Band27Heft3/4-372

Toranska, T. "Them."

A. Walicki, 441:17May87-15

Torchiana, D.T. Backgrounds for Joyce's "Dubliners."

M.P.L., 295(JML):Nov86-496

K.E. Marre, 395(MFS):Winter86-660

272(IUR):Autumn86-254

Torelli, M. Lavinio e Roma.

M.N.S. Sellers, 313:Vol76-298

Torgovnick, M. The Visual Arts, Pictorialism and the Novel.*

R.L. Flaxman, 454:Spring87-283

Torjusen, B. - see Munch, E.

Tornow, S. Die häufigsten Akzenttypen in der russischen Flexion.

S. Kempgen, 559:Vol10No2-246

de Toro, F. & P. Roster. Bibliografía del teatro hispanoamericano contemporáneo (1900-1980).

G. Luzuriaga, 352(LATR):Fall86-115

de Torre, E. José Hierro.

I-J. López, 240(HR):Autumn86-487

Torrente Ballester, G. Compostela y su ángel.

J. Pérez, 238:Mar86-105

Torres-Alcalá, A. Don Enrique de Villena.*

C. de Nigris, 379(MedR):Apr86-157

Torrey, E.F. The Roots of Treason.*

D. Smith, 106:Winter86-509

Torroella, R.S. - see under Santos Torroella, R.

Tort, P. La Pensée hiérarchique et l'évolution.

A.C. Vila, 400(MLN):Sep86-941

Tosel, A. Praxis.

A. Reix, 542:Jan-Mar86-130

Toshikuni, H. - see under Hihara Toshikuni

Toshio, S. - see under Shimao Toshio

Toscano, T.R. - see Rossetti, G.

Toso Rodinis, G. Il teatro di Emmanuel Roblès.

E. Sellin, 403(MLS):Summer86-321

Toson Shimazaki. Before the Dawn.

B. Leithauser, 442(NY):3Aug87-72

E. McClellan, 441:18Oct87-44

Totaro, L. - see Piccolomini, E.S.

Toth, E., ed. Regionalism and the Female Imagination.

L.L. Doan, 395(MFS):Winter86-627

S. Koppelman, 115:Summer86-427

Totman, C. The Origins of Japan's Modern Forests.*

Toshio Hara, 293(JASt):Feb86-417

Tottie, G. & I. Bäcklund, eds. English in Speech and Writing.

J. Pauchard, 189(EA):Jul-Sep87-340

Toulmin, S. The Return to Cosmology.*

C. Hartshorne, 480(P&R):Vol19No4-266

Toulouse, G. L'Imposteur.

S. Smith, 207(FR):Mar87-562

Tourangeau, R., ed. 125 ans de théâtre au Séminaire de Trois-Rivières.

L-E. Doucette, 627(UTQ):Fall86-186

Tournier, M. Gilles and Jeanne.* (French title: Gilles et Jeanne.)

N. Irving, 617(TLS):30Oct-5Nov87-1192

Tournier, M. The Golden Droplet.

R. Sieburth, 441:1Nov87-37

Tournier, M. La Goutte d'or.

T. Dey, 450(NRF):Apr86-91

S. Petit, 207(FR):Apr87-731

Tournon, A. Montaigne: la glose et l'essai.

F. Lestringant, 535(RHL):Jul-Aug86-729

Toussaint, J-P. Monsieur.

G. Delannoi, 98:Nov86-1147

D. Gunn, 617(TLS):7Aug87-856

Toussaint, J-P. La Salle de bain.*

L. Ferrara, 207(FR):Apr87-732

D. Gunn, 617(TLS):7Aug87-856

Toussaint, M. Contre l'arbitraire du signe.

R. Harris, 355(LSoc):Sep86-444

Tov, E. The Text-Critical Use of the Septuagint in Biblical Research.

M.K.H. Peters, 318(JAOS):Jan/Mar85-159

Tovar, A. Relatos y Dialogos de los Matacos.

M.T. Viñas Urquiza, 269(IJAL):Jul86-312

Tovar, A. & C. Larrucea de Tovar. Catálogo de las lenguas de la América del Sur con clasificaciones, indicaciones tipológicas, bibliografía y mapas. (new ed)

J. Caudmont, 260(IF):Band91-432

Tower, J., E.S. Muskie & B. Scowcroft. Report of the President's Special Review Board. The Tower Commission Report.

S. Hoffmann, 453(NYRB):7May87-9

Townsend, C. The Great Backpacking Adventure.

E. Newby, 441:31May87-49

Townsend, C.E. Czech through Russian.

H.E. Marquess, 574(SEEJ):Spring86-130

Townshend, A. The Poems and Masques of Aurelian Townshend, with Music by Henry Lawes and William Webb. (C.C. Brown, ed)

P. Walls, 541(RES):Feb86-90

Toye, W., ed. The Oxford Companion to Canadian Literature.*

J. Ferns, 402(MLR):Oct87-946

S. Jackel, 107(CRCL):Dec86-697

J. Schäfer, 38:Band104Heft3/4-548

Traba, M. Mothers and Shadows.

S. White, 448:Vol24No2-95

Tracey, G. - see Newman, J.H.

Tracy, J.D. A Financial Revolution in the Habsburg Netherlands.*
  H.H. Rowen, 551(RenQ):Winter86-773
Tracy, W. Letters of Credit.*
  B. Crutchley, 324:Mar87-336
Trager, J. West of Fifth.
  D.W. Dunlap, 441:1Mar87-21
Tragesser, R.S. Husserl and Realism in Logic and Mathematics.*
  D. Bell, 518:Jan86-31
Traglia, A. & G. Aricò - see Statius
Train, J. The Midas Touch.
  J. Grigsby, 441:31May87-57
Trainer, Y. Everything Happens at Once.
  N. Besner, 647:Fall86-112
Traister, B.H. Heavenly Necromancers.*
  M.J.B. Allen, 401(MLQ):Mar85-92
  L.S. Champion, 179(ES):Aug86-370
  R. Gill, 541(RES):Nov86-555
  N.H. Wright, 570(SQ):Summer86-266
Trakl, G. Werke; Entwürfe; Briefe.* (H-G. Kemper & F.R. Max, eds)
  M. Winkler, 133:Band19Heft1-88
Traldi, A. Fascismo e narrativa.
  P. Aragno, 276:Winter86-411
Trán Duc Thao. Investigations into the Origin of Language and Consciousness.
  G.W. Hewes, 355(LSoc):Jun86-280
Tran Tu Binh. The Red Earth. (D. Marr, ed)
  Nguyen The Anh, 293(JASt):Aug86-920
Tranoy, A. La Galice romaine.
  J.C. Edmondson, 313:Vol76-316
Tranquille, H. Des lettres sur nos lettres.
  P. Collet, 627(UTQ):Fall86-210
"Transactions of the Association of Russian-American Scholars in the U.S.A." (Vol 15) (N. Jernakoff, ed)
  C. Lodder, 575(SEER):Jan86-133
"Transactions of the Association of Russian-American Scholars in the U.S.A." (Vol 16) (N. Jernakoff, ed)
  A.R. Durkin, 550(RusR):Oct86-433
Trapido, J., with E.A. Langhans & J.R. Brandon, eds. An International Dictionary of Theatre Language.
  O. Trilling, 157:No162-52
  A. Woods, 615(TJ):Oct86-382
Traugott, M. Armies of the Poor.
  E.L. Newman, 446(NCFS):Fall-Winter 86/87-228
"Travaux de Linguistique." (Vols 9 & 10)
  J. Chaurand, 209(FM):Oct86-262
"Travaux 2: le passif."
  T.J. Cox, 207(FR):Mar87-571
"Travaux 3: Les Relations syntaxiques."
  A. Azoulay-Vicente, 207(FR):Apr87-737
Travers, M.P.A. German Novels on the First World War and their Ideological Implications, 1918-1933.
  A.F. Bance, 402(MLR):Jul87-798
Travers, T. The Killing Ground.
  B. Bond, 617(TLS):4-10Dec87-1347
Traversi, D. The Literary Imagination.*
  C. Garton, 402(MLR):Jul86-703
Travier, D. & J-N. Pelen. Le temps cévenol. (Pt 3, Vol 2)
  J.P. Piniès, 196:Band27Heft3/4-374
Travis, J. In Defense of the Faith.
  D.J. Constantelos, 589:Oct86-1037

"Tre Architetture degli Anni Trenta a Firenze."
  N. Miller, 576:Mar86-74
"Tre artisti nella Bologna dei Bentivoglio."
  C. Gould, 39:Jun86-441
Treadgold, W., ed. Renaissances before the Renaissance.
  M.L. Colish, 589:Apr86-477
Treder, U. Von der Hexe zur Hysterikerin.
  D. Lund, 133:Band19Heft1-93
Trefil, J. Meditations at Sunset.
  J. Weiner, 441:12Jul87-7
Trefulka, J. Hommage aux fous.
  L. Kovacs, 450(NRF):Jun86-97
Trefusis, V. Broderie Anglaise.
  639(VQR):Summer86-87
Treharne, R.F. Simon de Montfort and Baronial Reform. (E.B. Fryde, ed)
  M.T. Clanchy, 617(TLS):16-22Oct87-1148
Treherne, J. Mangrove Chronicle.*
  J. Mellors, 364:Jul86-103
Treherne, J. The Trap.
  P. Glasser, 441:22Feb87-28
Treip, M. "Descend from Heav'n Urania."
  R. Flannagan, 391:May86-55
Trejo, A.R. - see under Ramírez Trejo, A.
Tremain, R. The Animal's Who's Who.
  K.B. Harder, 424:Mar86-107
Tremain, R. The Garden of the Villa Mollini and Other Stories.
  V. Shaw, 362:11Jun87-29
  L. Taylor, 617(TLS):12Jun87-626
Tremayne, P. Under Helicon.
  P.L. Fermor, 617(TLS):21Aug87-895
Tremblay, B. Duhamel.
  B. Shlain, 441:25Jan87-15
Tremblay, M. Albertine en cinq temps.
  E. Hamblet, 207(FR):Apr87-732
Tremp, E., ed. Liber donationum Altaeripae.
  C.H. Berman, 589:Oct86-1008
Trench, R. Arabian Travellers.
  442(NY):19Jan87-93
Trend, M. The Music Makers.*
  D.R.P., 412:Feb85-68
Trendall, A.D. & A. Cambitoglou. The Red-Figured Vases of Apulia. First Supplement to the Red-Figured Vases of Apulia.
  M. Schmidt, 303(JoHS):Vol106-253
Trenhaile, J. The Mahjong Spies.
  P. Vansittart, 364:Jun86-94
Trenner, F. Richard Strauss.
  M. Kennedy, 410(M&L):Jul86-294
Trento, J.J. Prescription for Disaster.
  B. Woolley, 362:22Oct87-32
Treuil, R. Le Néolithique et le Bronze Ancien égéens.
  J.D. Evans, 303(JoHS):Vol106-244
Trevelyan, R. The Golden Oriole.
  J. Morris, 441:22Nov87-3
  A. Ross, 617(TLS):5Jun87-596
Treverton, G.F. Covert Action.
  S. Hoffmann, 441:29Nov87-3
Trevor, J. Dwarf Goes to Oxford.
  D. Pownall, 362:5Mar87-27
Trevor, W. Nights at the Alexandra.
  P. Craig, 617(TLS):30Oct-5Nov87-1192
  M. Pacey, 362:12Nov87-29
Trevor-Roper, H. Renaissance Essays.*
  125:Winter86-236
  639(VQR):Winter86-10

Trewin, W. & J.C. The Arts Theatre,
London, 1927-1981.
   E. Shorter, 157:No162-50
Tribe, I.M. Mountaineer Jamboree.*
   C.S. Guthrie, 650(WF):Jul86-236
Tribe, L.H. Constitutional Choices.*
   J.M. O'Fallon, 185:Jan87-486
Trible, P. Texts of Terror.
   M. Bal, 153:Winter86-71
Tricot, B. & R. Hadas-Lebel. Les Institu-
tions politiques françaises.
   A. Prévos, 207(FR):Apr87-745
Trier, J. Wege der Etymologie. (H.
Schwarz, ed)
   H. Beckers, 680(ZDP):Band105Heft1-145
Trigeaud, J-M. Humanisme de la liberté et
Philosophie de la justice. (Vol 1)
   M. Adam, 542:Apr-Jun86-276
Trigg, R. Understanding Social Science.*
   R. Attfield, 483:Oct86-544
   J-M. Gabaude, 542:Jan-Mar86-155
Trigger, B.G. Natives and Newcomers.
   G. Botting, 529(QQ):Summer86-404
   W.J. Eccles, 656(WMQ):Jul86-480
Triggs, K. The Stars and the Stillness.
   R. Mayne, 176:Apr87-52
Trillin, C. If You Can't Say Something
Nice.
   M. Russell, 441:8Nov87-11
Trimble, L. English for Science and Tech-
nology.
   D. Payne, 350:Jun87-452
Trimborn, K. Syntaktisch-stilistische
Untersuchungen zu Chrétiens "Yvain" und
Hartmanns "Iwein."
   D.H. Green, 402(MLR):Oct86-1034
Trimpi, W. Muses of One Mind.*
   M. Murrin, 122:Jul86-274
Trinh, P.C. - see under Phan Chu Trinh
Tripp, R.P., Jr., ed & trans. More About
the Fight with the Dragon.*
   R.H. Bremmer, Jr., 179(ES):Aug86-364
Tristan, F. Le Fils de Babel.
   M. Fougères, 207(FR):May87-915
"Flora Tristan (1803-1844)." (S. Michaud,
ed)
   B. Rigby, 208(FS):Apr86-224
Tristram, H.L.C. Tense and Time in Early
Irish Narrative.
   B. Ó Cuív, 112:Vol18-222
   K.H. Schmidt, 260(IF):Band91-401
Trivedi, H.V., ed. Inscriptions of the
Paramāras, Chandēllas, Kachchapaghātas
and Two Minor Dynasties. (Pt 2)
   R. Salomon, 318(JAOS):Oct/Dec85-786
Troisi, D. La finta notte.
   C. Di Biase, 275(IQ):Spring86-63
Troll, C.W. - see "Islam in India"
Trollope, A. The Letters of Anthony Trol-
lope.* (N.J. Hall, with N. Burgis, eds)
   W. Baker, 179(ES):Jun86-277
   J. McMaster, 301(JEGP):Apr86-282
   R.C. Terry, 536(Rev):Vol8-215
Trollope, A. North America.
   M. Mudrick, 249(HudR):Winter87-657
Tromly, A. The Cover of the Mask.*
   W.A. Craik, 447(N&Q):Dec85-536
Tronchetti, C. Ceramica attica a figure
nere.
   R. Adam, 555:Vol59fasc2-340
Trott, S. Sightings.
   V. Gladstone, 441:9Aug87-21

Trousdale, M. Shakespeare and the Rhetori-
cians. *
   N. Lindheim, 402(MLR):Oct86-983
Trousson, R., ed. Michel de Ghelderode,
dramaturge et conteur.
   M. Corvin, 535(RHL):Mar-Apr86-346
Trousson, R., ed. Les Relations littér-
aires franco-belges de 1890 à 1914.
   I. Higgins, 208(FS):Apr86-235
   H-J. Lope, 547(RF):Band98Heft3/4-449
Trousson, R. Le tison et le flambeau.
   V. Mylne, 208(FS):Jan86-85
Troyat, H. Chekhov.*
   H. Gifford, 617(TLS):8May87-484
   M. Pacey, 362:23Apr87-24
Troyat, H. Peter the Great.
   F.D. Reeve, 441:13Sep87-62
de Troyes, C. - see under Chrétien de
Troyes
Truchet, P. - see Rostand, E.
Trudeau, G. Downtown Doonesbury, Death
of a Party Animal. That's Doctor
Sinatra, You Little Bimbo!
   M. Richler, 441:3May87-35
Trudgill, P. Dialects in Contact.
   I. Smith, 350:Sep87-675
Trudgill, P., ed. Language in the British
Isles.*
   H.F. Nielsen, 300:Apr86-132
   H. Rogers, 320(CJL):Summer86-193
Trudgill, P. On Dialect.*
   W. Viereck, 38:Band104Heft1/2-166
   R. Young, 355(LSoc):Mar86-141
Truesdell, C. An Idiot's Fugitive Essays
on Science.
   M. Bunge, 84:Dec86-520
Truesdell, C. Rational Thermodynamics.
(2nd ed)
   M. Bunge, 486:Jun86-305
Truffaut, F. Hitchcock. (rev)
   J. Richards, 176:Jan87-51
Truffaut, F. Truffaut by Truffaut. (D.
Rabourdin, ed)
   D. Jacobs, 441:4Oct87-28
Truman, M. Murder in the CIA.
   N. Callendar, 441:27Dec87-13
Truman, M. Bess W. Truman.*
   639(VQR):Autumn86-125
Trump, D.J., with T. Schwartz. Trump.
   T. Morgan, 441:20Dec87-7
Tryon, T. All That Glitters.*
   D. Johnson, 18:Sep87-67
Trypucko, J. Pięć lat językoznawstwa
polskiego, 1966-1970.
   M.Z. Brooks, 574(SEEJ):Spring86-129
Tsagarakis, O. Form and Content in Homer.
   C.J. Ruijgh, 394:Vol39fasc3/4-466
Tscheer, R. Guzmán de Alfarache bei Mateo
Alemán und bei Juan Martí.
   A. San Miguel, 86(BHS):Apr86-161
Tseng, H. - see under Hsiao Tseng
Tshe-ring, M-M. - see under Mdo-mkhar
Tshe-ring
Tsitsikli, D. Historia Apollonii Regis
Tyri.
   G.A.A. Kortekaas, 394:Vol39fasc1/2-200
Tsong Khapa. Tsong Khapa's Speech of
Gold in the Essence of True Eloquence.
   M. Kapstein, 485(PE&W):Apr86-184
   K. Lang, 293(JASt):May86-580

"Uneeda Review."
   M. Moseley, 569(SR):Spring86–xliii
Ungar, S. Roland Barthes.*
   J. Adamson, 567:Vol61No3/4–325
   G.H. Bauer, 567:Vol60No3/4–351
   A. Brown, 208(FS):Jul86–365
   S.F.R., 131(CL):Spring86–191
   L.S. Roudiez, 535(RHL):Sep–Oct86–958
Ungar, S.J., ed. Estrangement.*
   R.W. Malcolmson, 529(QQ):Summer86–452
Ungaretti, G. Lettere a Enrico Pea. (J.
   Soldateschi, ed)
   J.P. Welle, 276:Winter86–412
Unger, D. Leaving the Land.*
   J. Jacobson, 271:Spring–Summer86–193
   D.D. Quantic, 649(WAL):May86–57
Unger, L. Eliot's Compound Ghost.
   A.V.C. Schmidt, 402(MLR):Jan86–188
   C.K. Stead, 675(YER):Vol8No1/2–125
Unger, P. Philosophical Relativity.*
   A.L. Brueckner, 311(JP):Sep86–509
   J. Koethe, 482(PhR):Jan86–141
Unger, R. Friedrich Hölderlin.
   H. Gaskill, 133:Band19Heft1–77
   E.E. George, 222(GR):Spring86–85
Ungerer, F. & others. Grammatik des
   heutigen Englisch.
   D. Nehls, 257(IRAL):Aug86–269
Unglaub, E. "Das mit Fingern deutende
   Publicum."
   H.S. Madland, 221(GQ):Winter86–137
Unrau, J. Ruskin and St. Mark's.*
   J.G. Bernasconi, 278(IS):Vol41–164
   K.O. Garrigan, 576:Jun86–175
   M.A. Stankiewicz, 289:Fall86–117
Unrue, D.H. Truth and Vision in Katherine
   Anne Porter's Fiction.
   M.B., 295(JML):Nov86–528
   R.H. Brinkmeyer, Jr., 392:Winter85/86–
   84
   J.N. Gretlund, 585(SoQ):Winter87–146
   G. Hendrick, 301(JEGP):Jul86–475
   C. MacCurdy, 27(AL):Oct86–457
Unschuld, P.U. Medicine in China.
   R. Porter, 617(TLS):30Jan87–118
Unseld, J. Franz Kafka.
   J. Rolleston, 400(MLN):Apr86–722
Unsworth, B. Stone Virgin.*
   P. Lewis, 565:Spring86–38
Unsworth, C. The Politics of Mental Health
   Legislation.
   S. Lee, 617(TLS):3Jul87–710
Untermann, J. & B. Brogyanyi, eds. Das
   Germanische und die Rekonstruktion der
   indogermanischen Grundsprache.
   T.F. Shannon, 159:Spring86–121
Unterreitmeier, H. Tristan als Retter.
   D.H. Green, 402(MLR):Jan87–236
Untracht, O. Jewelry Concepts and Technol-
   ogy.
   G. Seidmann, 324:Jan87–167
Updike, J. Facing Nature.*
   A. Suied, 98:Oct86–1057
   639(VQR):Winter86–28
Updike, J. Roger's Version.*
   J. Bowen, 364:Dec86/Jan87–147
   42(AR):Fall86–495
Updike, J. Trust Me.
   M. Robinson, 441:26Apr87–1
   M. Wood, 617(TLS):9–15Oct87–1106
Uphaus, R.W. Beyond Tragedy.
   R.A. Foakes, 677(YES):Vol16–242

Upright, D. Morris Louis: The Complete
   Paintings.*
   A. Kingsley, 90:Nov86–834
Upward, E. The Night Walk and Other
   Stories.
   K. Bucknell, 617(TLS):4–10Dec87–1348
Urban, M. Emil Nolde. (Vol 1)
   S.S. Prawer, 617(TLS):9–15Oct87–1100
Urban, P.A. & E.M. Schortman, eds. The
   Southeast Maya Periphery.
   W.T. Sanders, 263(RIB):Vol36No4–501
Urdang, C. Lucha.
   S. Wood, 441:11Jan87–18
Urdang, L., ed. Modifiers.
   E.N. Stanley, 447(N&Q):Mar85–85
Urdang, L. & F. Abate. Idioms and Phrases
   Index.*
   E.G. Stanley, 447(N&Q):Mar85–87
Urdang, L. & F. Abate, eds. Literary, Rhe-
   torical, and Linguistic Terms Index.*
   Loanwords Index.
   E.S.C. Weiner, 447(N&Q):Mar85–86
Urdang, L. & F.P. Abate, eds. Fine and
   Applied Arts Terms Index.*
   E.N. Stanley, 447(N&Q):Mar85–85
Urdang, L. & A. Humez, eds. Prefixes and
   Other Word–Initial Elements of English.*
   E.N. Stanley, 447(N&Q):Mar85–85
Urdang, L., with W.W. Hunsinger, eds. Pic-
   turesque Expressions.
   K.B. Harder, 424:Sep86–330
Urdang, L. & C.D. Robbins, eds. Slogans.
   K.B. Harder, 424:Mar86–112
Urdang, L. & F.G. Ruffner, Jr., eds. Allu-
   sions – Biblical and Historical. (2nd
   ed)
   K.B. Harder, 424:Sep86–330
Urdang, L., with A. Ryle & T.H. Lee, eds.
   –Ologies and –Isms. (3rd ed)
   R.R.B., 35(AS):Fall86–280
   K.B. Harder, 424:Sep86–330
Ureland, P.S. & I. Clarkson, eds. Scandi-
   navian Language Contacts.
   E. Haugen, 355(LSoc):Mar86–115
Urey, D.F. Galdós and the Irony of Lan-
   guage.
   J. Labanyi, 402(MLR):Jan87–225
Uris, L. The Haj.
   J. Lowin, 287:Oct86–22
Urquhart, B. A Life in Peace and War.
   A. Hertzberg, 453(NYRB):5Nov87–27
   C.W. Maynes, 441:27Sep87–14
Urquhart, F. & G. Gordon, eds. Modern
   Scottish Short Stories.
   D. Groves, 588(SSL):Vol21–352
Urquhart, T. Sir Thomas Urquhart of Cro-
   marty: "The Jewel."* (R.D.S. Jack & R.J.
   Lyall, eds)
   T. Willard, 402(MLR):Oct87–917
Usborne, K. "Elizabeth."*
   A. Fitzlyon, 364:Dec86/Jan87–140
Usborne, R. Rossini.
   362:26Nov87–30
Usmiani, R. Michel Tremblay.
   D. Salter, 397(MD):Jun86–354
Uspensky, V.A. Post's Machine.
   T.T. Robinson, 316:Mar86–253
Utley, J.G. Going to War with Japan, 1937–
   1941.
   M.A. Barnhart, 293(JASt):Aug86–865
Utley, R.M. Four Fighters of Lincoln
   County.
   R.M. Adams, 453(NYRB):12Mar87–28

Utley, R.M. If These Walls Could Speak.
  L. Milazzo, 584(SWR):Winter86-123
Utrera, R. García Lorca y el cinema.
  M. Laffranque, 92(BH):Jan-Jun85-210
Utz, P. Die ausgehöhlte Gasse.
  R. Spuler, 221(GQ):Summer86-481

Väänänen, V. Recherches et récréations
latino-romanes.
  Y. Malkiel, 545(RPh):May87-493
de Vabres, J.D. - see under Donnedieu de
Vabres, J.
Vachss, A. Strega.
  N. Callendar, 441:31May87-45
Vaculik, L. A Cup of Coffee With My
Interrogator.
  J. Laber, 441:23Aug87-17
Vaget, H.R. Goethe.
  C.E. Schweitzer, 406:Spring86-106
Vaget, H.R. Thomas-Mann-Kommentar: zu
sämtlichen Erzählungen.*
  G. Bridges, 221(GQ):Spring86-330
  F.A. Lubich, 222(GR):Summer86-122
  D. Lund & E. Schwarz, 133:Band18Heft4-
    382
  J.M. McGlathery, 301(JEGP):Apr86-314
  H. Siefken, 402(MLR):Jan86-256
Vailati, V. 1943-1944, La Storia nascosta.
  D.M. Smith, 617(TLS):7Aug87-844
Vailland, R. Chronique des Années Folles à
la Libération, 1928-1945. (R. Ballet,
ed)
  J. Sénégas, 535(RHL):Jul-Aug86-799
Vailland, R. Un Jeune Homme seul. (J.E.
Flower & C.H.R. Niven, eds)
  D. Nott, 402(MLR):Jan87-208
Vaisey, D. - see Turner, T.
Vaizey, J. Scenes from Institutional Life
and Other Writings.
  T. Blackstone, 362:29Jan87-24
  B. Trend, 617(TLS):13Mar87-260
Valdés, J. Lecturas básicas.* (3rd ed)
  A. Dias, 238:Mar86-124
Valdés, M.J. Shadows in the Cave.*
  D. Fernandez-Morera, 107(CRCL):Mar86-
    87
Valdés, M.J. & O. Miller, eds. Identity of
the Literary Text.
  J. Adamson, 178:Jun86-246
  H. Bertens, 549(RLC):Oct-Dec86-466
  N.N. Feltes, 627(UTQ):Fall86-119
  H. Kellner, 400(MLN):Dec86-1249
  J.H. Petersen, 52:Band21Heft3-290
Valdés Fernández, M. Arquitectura mudéjar
en León y Castilla.
  M. Lillo, 48:Oct-Dec86-425
de Valdivielso, J. Romancero espiritual.
(J.M. Aguirre, ed)
  J.M. Díez Borque, 240(HR):Autumn86-
    472
Valdivieso, D.E. & J.M. Serrera. Historia
de la Pintura Española: Pintura Sevillana
del primer tercio del siglo XVII.
  E. Young, 90:Aug86-612
Valdman, A. & others. En Route.
  K.E. Kintz, 207(FR):Dec86-305
Vale, B. Albion.
  P. Faulkner, 326:Spring87-33
Vale, L.J. The Limits of Civil Defence in
the USA, Switzerland, Britain and the
Soviet Union.
  M. Ceadel, 617(TLS):23-29Oct87-1162

Valender, J. Cernuda y el poema en prosa.
  S.M. Hart, 402(MLR):Jan87-229
  I. Paraíso, 547(RF):Band98Heft1/2-234
  C.C. Soufas, 238:Dec86-875
Valentin, J-M. Le Théâtre des Jésuites
dans les pays de langue allemande.*
  T.G.M. van Oorschot, 133:Band18Heft4-
    363
Valentin, J-M., ed. Volk - Volksstück -
Volkstheater im deutschen Sprachraum des
18.-20. Jahrhunderts.
  I.F. Roe, 402(MLR):Jul87-777
Valentine, J.W., ed. Phanerozoic Diversity
Patterns.
  W. George, 617(TLS):22May87-565
Valentini, A. Leopardi.
  M. Caesar, 402(MLR):Jul86-756
Valenze, D.M. Prophetic Sons and Daugh-
ters.
  J.F.C. Harrison, 637(VS):Winter87-281
Valenzuela, L. The Lizard's Tail.
  J. Byrne, 532(RCF):Summer86-146
Valenzuela, V.M. Fernando Alegría.
  S. Rojas, 263(RIB):Vol36No2-192
de Valera, D. Doctrinal de príncipes. (S.
Monti, ed)
  I.A. Corfis, 240(HR):Winter86-89
Valera, J. 151 Cartas inéditas a Gumer-
sindo Laverde. (M. Brey de Rodríguez
Moñino, ed)
  C. De Coster, 240(HR):Summer86-346
  G. Paolini, 238:Sep86-543
Valeriani, R. & D. di Castro. Il valore
delle porcellane europee.
  G. Wills, 39:May86-368
"Paul Valéry, teoria e ricerca poetica."
  N. Celeyrette-Pietri, 535(RHL):Jan-
    Feb86-162
Valette, J-P., G.S. Kupferschmid & R.
Valette. Con Mucho Gusto. (2nd ed)
  R. Moody, 399(MLJ):Summer86-202
Valfells, S. & J.E. Cathey. Old Icelandic.
  H. Fix, 680(ZDP):Band105Heft1-129
Valgardson, W.D. Red Dust.
  L. Hutcheon, 296(JCF):No35/36-165
Valin, J. Fire Lake.
  N. Callendar, 441:1Nov87-34
Vallee, L. & R. Findlay - see Osiński, Z.
Vallejo, A.B. - see under Buero Vallejo, A.
Vallès, J. L'Insurgé. (R. Bellet, ed)
  W. Redfern, 402(MLR):Oct87-969
Valles, J.L.C. - see under Canet Valles,
J.L.
Vallette-Hémery, M. Yuan Hongdao, Theorie
et pratique litteraires.
  C-P. Chou, 116:Jul85-188
Vallières, M. Comme un simple voyageur.
  K. Meadwell, 102(CanL):Winter85-158
Vallone, A. & L. Scorrano - see Dante
Alighieri
Van Antwerp, M.A. & S. Johns, eds. Dictio-
nary of Literary Biography Documentary
Series.* (Vol 4: Tennessee Williams.)
  R.A. Martin, 115:Summer86-419
Van Beek, S. & L.I. Tettoni. The Arts of
Thailand.
  U. Roberts, 60:Jul-Aug86-124
Vance, E. Mervelous Signals.
  N. Mann, 617(TLS):14Aug87-880
Vance, J.A. Samuel Johnson and the Sense
of History.*
  J.L. Battersby, 536(Rev):Vol8-157
[continued]

[continuing]

D. Flower, 249(HudR):Summer86-316
J. Mellors, 364:Nov86-102
639(VQR):Summer86-92
Vargas Llosa, M. The War of the End of the World.* (Spanish title: La Guerra del Fin del Mundo.)
L. Gorman, 532(RCF):Fall86-149
Vargas Llosa, M. Who Killed Palomino Molero?
P-L. Adams, 61:Aug87-84
R. Lourie, 441:31May87-13
J. Updike, 442(NY):24Aug87-83
Vargish, T. The Providential Aesthetic in Victorian Fiction.
G. Cunningham, 541(RES):Nov86-601
D. David, 637(VS):Winter87-279
R.J. Dunn, 594:Fall86-328
639(VQR):Spring86-44
Varnedoe, K. Gustave Caillebotte.
R. Cork, 362:22Oct87-26
E. Cowling, 617(TLS):13-19Nov87-1247
J. Russell, 441:6Dec87-11
Varnedoe, K. Duane Hanson.
R. Bass, 55:Sep86-38
Varnedoe, K. Northern Light.
B. Morton, 362:31Dec87-22
Varnhagen von Ense, K.A. Kommentare zum Zeitgeschehen. (W. Greiling, ed)
T.H. Pickett, 221(GQ):Spring86-323
Varro. Varron, "Satires Ménippées." (fasc 7) (J-P. Cèbe, ed & trans)
R. Astbury, 123:Vol36No2-315
Varro, G. La Femme transplantée.
A. Sonnenfeld, 207(FR):Oct86-150
Vasbinder, S.H. Scientific Attitudes in Mary Shelley's "Frankenstein."
D. Ketterer, 561(SFS):Nov86-395
Vasey, L. - see Lawrence, D.H.
Vasil, D. The Ethical Pragmatism of Albert Camus.
J.B. Romeiser, 207(FR):Apr87-717
Vasoli, C. - see Zabarellae, J.
Vassallo, P. Byron.
F.L. Beaty, 661(WC):Autumn86-242
Vassanji, M.G., ed. A Meeting of Streams.
W.J. Howard, 627(UTQ):Fall86-240
G.D. Killam, 529(QQ):Summer86-428
G. Woodcock, 102(CanL):Winter85-149
Vassberg, D.E. Land and Society in Golden Age Castile.*
J. Casey, 86(BHS):Jul86-278
Vassiltchikov, M. Berlin Diaries, 1940-1945.* (G. Vassiltchikov, ed)
G. Annan, 453(NYRB):9Apr87-7
G.A. Craig, 441:5Apr87-6
W. Maxwell, 442(NY):25May87-113
Vatai, F.L. Intellectuals in Politics in the Greek World, from Early Times to the Hellenistic Age.*
F.J. Frost, 487:Spring86-124
J.E. Ziolkowski, 124:Sep-Oct86-61
Vater, H. Das System der Artikelformen im gegenwärtigen Deutsch. (2nd ed)
R. Harnisch, 685(ZDL):3/1986-385
Vater, M.G. - see Schelling, F.W.J.
Vatsyayan, K. The Square and the Circle of the Indian Arts.
C.R. Jones, 293(JASt):May86-641
Vattanky, J. Gaṅgeśa's Philosophy of God.
R. De Smet, 485(PE&W):Oct86-429

Vattimo, G. Les Aventures de la différence. Introduction à Heidegger.
F. Wybrands, 450(NRF):Mar86-92
Vaughan, E. The Ordeal of Elizabeth Vaughan. (C.M. Petillo, ed)
G.K. Goodman, 293(JASt):Feb86-461
639(VQR):Winter86-13
Vaughan, E.C. Some Desperate Glory.
B. Bond, 617(TLS):4-10Dec87-1347
Vaughan, F. The Inward Arc.
639(VQR):Autumn86-137
Vaughan, R. Herbert von Karajan.*
W. Sutton, 415:Jul86-389
Vaughan, T. The Works of Thomas Vaughan.* (A. Rudrum, with J. Drake-Brockman, eds)
M.H. Keefer, 178:Mar86-108
Vaughn, W.P. The Antimasonic Party in the United States, 1826-1843.
D.P. Peeler, 106:Summer86-201
de Vaulchier, H. Charles Nodier et la lexicographie française 1808-1844.
J. Chaurand, 209(FM):Oct86-237
Vavra, R. Vavra's Cats.
P-L. Adams, 61:Jan87-90
Vax, L. La poésie philosophique.
P. Somville, 542:Apr-Jun86-270
Vázquez, J.A. & A. D. Kossoff - see under Amor y Vázquez, J. & A.D. Kossoff
Veatch, H.B. Human Rights.
J.B., 185:Jul87-884
D. Gordon, 258:Dec86-404
P. Simpson, 543:Mar87-601
Vecchi Galli, P. - see Vergerio, P.P., Jr.
Vecchio, F. Textos de ayer y de hoy.*
V. Arizpe, 399(MLJ):Spring86-88
Veeder, W. Mary Shelley and Frankenstein.
C. Baldick, 617(TLS):1May87-471
Veen, H-J., ed. From Brezhnev to Gorbachev.
A. Brown, 617(TLS):6-12Nov87-1214
Vega, B.G. - see under García Vega, B.
de la Vega, G.L. - see under Lasso de la Vega, G.
de la Vega, S.L. & C. Salazar - see under Lequerica de la Vega, S. & C. Salazar
de Vega Carpio, L. Cartas.* (N. Marín, ed)
B.M. Damiani, 238:Dec86-866
P.W. Evans, 402(MLR):Oct87-999
de Vega Carpio, L. Los celos de Rodamonte. (S.G. Maglione, ed)
M. McGaha, 552(REH):Oct86-124
de Vega Carpio, L. La Dorotea. (A.S. Trueblood & E. Honig, trans)
P.W. Evans, 402(MLR):Oct87-999
de Vega Carpio, L. La Gatomaquia.* (C. Sabor de Cortázar, ed)
A.A. Heathcote, 86(BHS):Oct86-387
de Vega Carpio, L. Las hazañas del segundo David.* (J.B. Avalle-Arce & G. Cervantes Martín, eds)
V. Dixon, 240(HR):Spring86-220
de Vega Carpio, L. El mayor prodigio y purgatorio en la vida. (M. Grazia Profeti, ed)
J. Espadas, 552(REH):Jan86-137
Vegas, F. Venezuelan Vernacular.
J.V. Iovine, 45:Feb86-77
Vegas, L.C. - see under Castelfranchi Vegas, L.
Vegetti, M., ed. Il Sapere degli Antichi.
J. Barnes, 520:Vol31No1-98

Veith, D.M., ed. Essential Articles for the Study of Jonathan Swift's Poetry.
P. Rogers, 83:Autumn86-260
Veith, W.H. Der Kleine Deutsche Sprach-atlas als Arbeitsmittel.
K. Spangenberg, 682(ZPSK):Band39Heft3-400
P. Wiesinger, 133:Band19Heft3/4-325
Veith, W.H. & W. Putschke, with L. Hummel, comps. Kleiner deutscher Sprachatlas.* (Vol 1, Pt 1)
P. Wiesinger, 133:Band19Heft3/4-325
Vela, A.R. - see under Rubio Vela, A.
Vélez, J.F. Cinco ensayos sobre "Chambú."
R.L. Williams, 238:May86-318
Velimirović, M., ed. Studies in Eastern Chant. (Vol 4)
S.H., 412:Nov85-306
Veliz, Z., ed & trans. Artists' Techniques in Golden Age Spain.
E. Harris, 617(TLS):25-31Dec87-1426
Veljanovski, C., with M. Bentley. Selling the State.
V. Borooah, 617(TLS):6-12Nov87-1221
Velleius. Velleius Paterculus: The Caesar-ian and Augustan Narrative (2.41-93).* (A.J. Woodman, ed)
B.M. Levick, 123:Vol36No1-53
R.J. Starr, 487:Summer86-246
Veloudis, G. Germanograecia.
E. Mathiopoulos-Tornaritou, 52:Band21 Heft1-97
Veltrusky, J.F. A Sacred Farce from Medie-val Bohemia: Mastičkář.
J.M. Burian, 610:Autumn86-248
G.M. Cummins, 574(SEEJ):Winter86-589
R.B. Pynsent, 402(MLR):Apr87-540
Velz, J.W. & F.N. Teague - see Crosby, J.
Vence, C., S. Lermon & S. Mallet, eds. Cuisine du Terroir.
A. Davidson, 617(TLS):18-24Dec87-1401
Vendler, H., ed. The Harvard Book of Con-temporary American Poetry.* (British title: The Faber Book of Contemporary American Poetry.)
P. Forbes, 362:12Feb87-26
P. Hainsworth, 617(TLS):1May87-459
J.P. Warren, 577(SHR):Fall86-390
639(VQR):Spring86-62
Vendler, H. The Odes of John Keats.*
D. Birch, 541(RES):Feb86-110
S.M. Sperry, 403(MLS):Summer86-342
Vendler, Z. The Matter of Minds.
J. Heal, 518:Jul86-181
P. Kitcher, 311(JP):Sep86-504
W. Matson, 483:Jan86-135
Venegas, D. Las aventuras de don Chipote o Cuando los pericos mamen.
E. Gonzales-Berry, 238:Dec86-892
Venetus, P. - see under Paulus Venetus
Veneziani, P. La tipografia a Brescia nel XV secolo.
D.E. Rhodes, 354:Dec86-375
Vennemann, T., ed. Silben, Segmente, Akzente.
I. Werlen, 685(ZDL):3/1986-381
Vennemann, T. & J. Jacobs. Sprache und Grammatik.
F. Hundsnurscher, 685(ZDL):1/1986-80
Venturi, F. Settecento riformatore.* (Vol 4, Pt 2)
D. Beales, 617(TLS):6Mar87-237

Venturi, R. & D. Scott Brown. A View from the Campidoglio. (P. Arnell, T. Bickford and C. Bergart, eds)
J. Iovine, 45:May86-75
Verani, H.J. Octavio Paz.*
R.D. Woods, 238:Mar86-115
Vercier, B. & J. Lecarme. La littérature en France depuis 1948.
G. Cesbron, 356(LR):May86-189
Verde, A.F. Lo Studio Fiorentino 1473-1503. (Vol 4) (E. Garin, ed)
M. Pozzi, 228(GSLI):Vol163fasc524-613
Verdenius, W.J. A Commentary on Hesiod, "Works and Days," vv. 1-382.
G.P. Edwards, 303(JoHS):Vol106-203
D. Sider, 124:Jul-Aug87-446
Verdès-Leroux, J. Le Réveil des somnam-bules.
J-F. Revel, 176:Jul/Aug87-25
Verdi, G. Ernani. (C. Gallico, ed)
E. Downes, 465:Spring86-107
Verdier, G. Charles Sorel.
M. Bannister, 402(MLR):Oct86-1001
R.G. Hodgson, 475:Vol13No24-421
D. Kuizenga, 207(FR):Dec86-254
J. Trethewey, 208(FS):Jul86-328
Verdon, M. The Abutia Ewe of West Africa.
J.R. Rayfield, 488:Jun86-269
Verdon, R. The Enlightened Cuisine.
W. & C. Cowen, 639(VQR):Spring86-66
Verdon, T.G., with J. Dally, eds. Monas-ticism and the Arts.*
P. Hetherington, 39:Feb86-137
Verdonk, R.A. La lengua española en Flandes en el siglo XVII.
V. Marrero, 553(RLiR):Jan-Jun86-222
Verdugo, P. & C. Orrego. Detenidos-Desaparecidos.
E. Moya-Raggio, 385(MQR):Winter87-272
Verene, D.P. Hegel's Recollection.*
D. Breazeale, 319:Oct87-608
G. Shapiro, 125:Summer86-438
P.A. Simpson, 400(MLN):Dec86-1270
Verene, D.P. Vico's Science of Imagina-tion.
L. Pennachetti, 488:Jun86-274
Verger, J., ed. Histoire des Universités en France.
P. & A. Higonnet, 617(TLS):30Oct-5Nov87-1183
Vergerio, P.P., Jr. Comedia Vergeria. (P. Vecchi Galli, ed)
P. Frassica, 545(RPh):Aug86-126
Vergil. Virgil: Selections from the "Aeneid." (G. Tingay, ed & trans)
W. Moskalew, 124:Jul-Aug87-459
Vergil. P. Vergilii Maronis Aeneidos liber quartus. (R.G. Austin, ed)
P.F. Hovingh, 394:Vol39fasc3/4-513
Vergnolle, E. Saint-Benoît-sur-Loire et la sculpture du XIe siécle.
G. Zarnecki, 90:Jul86-509
Verhaar, J.W.M., ed. Towards a Description of Contemporary Indonesian: Preliminary Studies, II.
M. Durie, 350:Mar87-190
Verhagen, A. Linguistic Theory and the Function of Word Order in Dutch.
B.J. Hoff, 204(FdL):Sep86-231
Verheyen, E. - see Heckscher, W.S.
Veriphantor - see Gorgias, J.

Vermazen, B. & M.B. Hintikka, eds. Essays on Davidson.*
  J. Hornsby, 479(PhQ):Apr86-296
  D.J. Shaw, 518:Jul86-174
  L.T., 185:Jul87-893
Vermes, G., F. Millar & M. Goodman - see Schürer, E.
Vernai, P., ed. Les Littératures de Langues Européennes au Tournant du Siècle.
  S.J. Rabinowitz, 574(SEEJ):Fall86-447
Vernes, J-R. Critique de la raison aléatoire ou Descartes contre Kant.
  J. Ferrari, 342:Band77Heft3-379
Vernier, R. Yves Bonnefoy ou les mots comme le ciel.
  R. Little, 402(MLR):Jan87-211
  S. Winspur, 546(RR):Mar86-155
Vernon, F. Privileged Children.
  F. Simon, 441:9Aug87-25
Vernon, J. Lindbergh's Son.
  P-L. Adams, 61:Dec87-110
Vernon, J. Money and Fiction.*
  M. Allott, 541(RES):Nov86-599
  J.J. Burke, Jr., 594:Winter86-454
  S. Connor, 155:Summer86-108
Vernon, R. Citizenship and Order.
  B.J.S., 185:Apr87-696
"Le verre d'époque romaine au musée archéologique de Strasbourg."
  V.T-B., 90:Jul86-519
von Verschuer, C. Les Relations Officielles du Japon avec la Chine aux VIIIe et IXe Siècles.
  R. Borgen, 407(MN):Winter86-502
Verschueren, J. What People Say They Do With Words.
  G. Urban, 350:Mar87-164
Vert, F. - see Bacon, F.
Vertone, T. Rythme, dualité et création poétique dans l'oeuvre de François Villon.
  C. Jordens, 356(LR):Feb86-71
Vertov, D. Kino-Eye.* (A. Michelson, ed)
  N. Kolchevska, 574(SEEJ):Spring86-118
de Verville, B. - see Béroalde de Verville
Vespertino Rodríguez, A., ed. Leyendas aljamiadas y moriscas sobre personajes bíblicos.
  R. Kontzi, 547(RF):Band98Heft1/2-222
  C.I. Nepaulsingh, 545(RPh):Aug86-129
Vester, E. Instrument and Manner Expressions in Latin.*
  O. Wenskus, 260(IF):Band91-392
Vester, F. Flute Music of the 18th Century.
  N. O'Loughlin, 415:Jul86-388
Veyne, P., ed. A History of Private Life. (Vol 1)
  H. Chadwick, 441:3May87-14
  B. Knox, 61:May87-90
Vial, C. Délos indépendante (314-167 avant J-C.).
  P.M. Fraser, 303(JoHS):Vol106-241
  L. Migeotte, 487:Spring86-97
Viala, A. Naissance de l'écrivain.
  P. Desan, 207(FR):Oct86-147
Viale Ferrero, M. Storia del Teatro Regio di Torino. (Vol 3)
  C. Duggan, 410(M&L):Jan86-73
Vian, F. & É. Battegay. Lexique de Quintus de Smyrne.
  M.L. West, 123:Vol36No2-310
Viatkin, R.V. - see Ssu-ma Ch'ien

Viatte, A. Histoire comparée des littératures francophones.
  M. Dorsinville, 107(CRCL):Mar86-108
de Viau, T. Théophile de Viau: Oeuvres complètes. (Vol 1) (G. Saba, ed)
  C. Abraham, 210(FrF):Jan86-104
  S. Warman, 208(FS):Apr86-204
de Viau, T. Théophile de Viau: Oeuvres complètes. (Vols 2-4) (G. Saba, ed)
  J-P. Chauveau, 475:Vol13No24-423
Vicinus, M. Independent Women.
  S. Fletcher, 637(VS):Spring87-409
Vickers, B., ed. Arbeit Musse Meditation.
  L.V.R., 568(SCN):Winter86-78
Vickers, B., ed. Occult and Scientific Mentalities in the Renaissance.
  F.L. Borchardt, 551(RenQ):Spring86-73
  R.H. Popkin, 319:Oct87-598
Vickers, H. Cecil Beaton.*
  O. Stuart, 151:Dec86-74
Vickery, W.N. & B.B. Sagatov, eds. Aleksandr Blok Centennial Conference.*
  J. Graffy, 575(SEER):Jul86-460
Vidal, A.P. - see under Pérez Vidal, A.
Vidal, G. Armageddon?
  S. Fender, 362:17&24Dec87-50
  Z. Leader, 617(TLS):20-26Nov87-1271
Vidal, G. Empire.
  S. Fender, 362:17&24Dec87-50
  J. Kaplan, 441:14Jun87-1
  Z. Leader, 617(TLS):20-26Nov87-1271
  R. Poirier, 453(NYRB):24Sep87-31
Vidal, G. Myra Breckinridge and Myron. (rev)
  Z. Leader, 617(TLS):20-26Nov87-1271
Vidal Sephiha, H. Le ladino (judéo-espagnol calque).
  L. Combet, 92(BH):Jan-Jun85-225
Vidén, G. The Roman Chancery Tradition.
  T. Honoré, 123:Vol36No2-324
Viegas Brauer-Figueiredo, M.D. - see Vieiras, A.
Vieira, N.H., ed. Roads to Today's Portugal.
  F. Cota Fagundes, 238:Mar86-109
Vieiras, A. António Vieiras "Sermão do Esposo da Mãe de Deus S. José." (M. de Fátima Viegas Brauer-Figueiredo, ed)
  N. Griffin, 86(BHS):Jul86-300
  R. Nagel, 72:Band223Heft1-237
Viel, M. La notion de "marque" chez Trubetzkoy et Jakobson.
  J.E. Joseph, 350:Sep87-665
Viereck, W., ed. Focus on: England and Wales.
  F. Chevillet, 189(EA):Jul-Sep86-330
Viereck, W., E.W. Schneider & M. Görlach, eds. Bibliography of Writings on Varieties of English, 1965-1983.*
  J.B. McMillan, 300:Apr86-135
Vieregg, A., ed. Peter Huchel: Materialien.
  S. Parker, 402(MLR):Oct87-1045
Vieregg, A. - see Huchel, P.
Vieth, D.M. Rochester Studies, 1925-1982.*
  P. Hammond, 541(RES):May86-263
Viezzer, M. & D. Chungara. Let Me Speak. (Spanish title: Si Me Permiten Hablar...)
  E. Moya-Raggio, 385(MQR):Winter87-272
Vig, N.J. & S.E. Schier, eds. Political Economy in Western Democracies.
  K.K.T., 185:Apr87-685

Vignali, A. La Cazzaria. (P. Stoppelli, ed)
  C. Di Fusco, 708:Vol12fasc2-269
Vigner, G. L'exercice dans la classe de français.*
  D. Legros, 209(FM):Oct86-257
Vigorelli, G., ed. Vita e processo di suor Virginia Maria de Leyva Monaca di Monza.
  E. Bonora, 228(GSLI):Vol163fasc524-593
Vijn, J.P. Carlyle and Jean Paul.*
  R. Ashton, 402(MLR):Jan87-176
  F. Burwick, 131(CL):Spring86-203
Villa, N. & M. Danesi, eds. Studies in Italian Applied Linguistics.
  C. Rosen, 276:Summer86-194
Villar, F. Ergatividad, Acusatividad y Genero en la Familia Lingüística Indo-europea.
  K.H. Schmidt, 260(IF):Band91-344
Villaret, B. - see Colette
Villegas, J. Teoría de historia literaria y poesía lírica.
  J.M. Marcos, 238:Mar86-110
Villemaire, Y. La constellation du cygne.
  T. Vuong-Riddick, 102(CanL):Fall86-122
Villeneuve, G. - see Woolf, V.
Villon, F. Poésies.* (J. Dufournet, ed)
  E. Du Bruck, 201:Vol11-165
Villon, F. Le Testament Villon, Le Lais Villon et les poèmes variés. (J. Rychner & A. Henry, eds)
  G. Roques, 553(RLiR):Jul-Dec86-645
Vilmure, D. Life in the Land of the Living.
  G. McFall, 441:18Oct87-30
Vinaver, E. Entretiens sur Racine.*
  R.L. Barnett, 207(FR):Oct86-120
  J. Morel, 535(RHL):Jul-Aug86-743
  R.W. Tobin, 475:Vol13No24-428
Vince, R.W. Ancient and Medieval Theatre.*
  O.G. Brockett, 610:Summer86-152
Vince, R.W. Renaissance Theatre.
  O.G. Brockett, 610:Summer86-152
  G.U. de Sousa, 570(SQ):Winter86-541
Vincent, A. & R. Plant. Philosophy, Politics and Citizenship.
  R.J. Halliday, 637(VS):Spring87-412
  J.R., 185:Jan87-502
Vine, B. A Fatal Inversion.
  G. Kaufman, 362:2Apr87-24
Vining, J. The Authoritative and the Authoritarian.
  T.D. Eisele, 185:Jul87-873
Vinson, J. & D. Kirkpatrick, eds. Contemporary Foreign Language Writers.
  K. Burke, 532(RCF):Spring86-204
Viorst, M. Sands of Sorrow.
  J. Feron, 441:2Aug87-17
Virgil - see under Vergil
Virgillo, C. & N. Lindstrom, eds. Woman as Myth and Metaphor in Latin American Literature.
  S. Magnarelli, 395(MFS):Autumn86-477
  G. Mora, 238:Dec86-886
Virtue, N. The Redemption of Elsdon Bird.
  H. Neill, 362:28May87-27
Viscusi, R. Max Beerbohm, or The Dandy Dante/Rereading with Mirrors.
  P. Boytinck, 529(QQ):Autumn86-688
  G.A.O., 295(JML):Nov86-443
  H. Orel, 177(ELT):Vol29No4-437
  K. Powell, 637(VS):Summer87-558
                                    [continued]

[continuing]
  H.W., 636(VP):Autumn86-349
  639(VQR):Autumn86-123
Visentini, M.A. L'orto botanico e il giardino del Rinascimento.
  J. Bury, 90:Jul86-514
Visvanathan, S. Organizing for Science.
  R.S. Anderson, 293(JASt):Aug86-896
"Vital Arts, Vital Libraries."
  J.J. Lauer, 2(AfrA):Aug86-84
Vitello, A. Giuseppe Tomasi di Lampedusa.
  D. Davis, 617(TLS):2-8Oct87-1083
Vitse, M. & others. Horror y tragedia en el teatro del Siglo de Oro.
  N.D. Shergold, 402(MLR):Apr86-510
Vitu, A. Le Corsaire-Satan en silhouette. (G. Robb, ed)
  M.A. Wégimont, 446(NCFS):Fall-Winter 86/87-209
Viudas Camarasa, A. Diccionario extremeño.
  R. Pellen, 553(RLiR):Jan-Jun86-224
Vivaldi, A. Ottone in villa.
  B.L. Glixon, 143:Issue39-74
Vivan, I. Tessere per un mosaico africano.
  J. Wilkinson, 538(RAL):Fall86-425
Vivante, P. Homer.*
  J.T. Barbarese, 569(SR):Spring86-xxxix
Vladislav, J. - see Havel, V.
Vlasopolos, A. The Symbolic Method of Coleridge, Baudelaire, and Yeats.*
  H. Adams, 403(MLS):Fall86-93
Vlasselaers, J. Literair bewustzijn in Vlaanderen 1840-1893.
  J. Goedegebuure, 204(FdL):Mar86-61
Vlastos, S. Peasant Protests and Uprisings in Tokugawa Japan.
  J.W. White, 407(MN):Winter86-509
Vliet, R.G. Scorpio Rising.*
  G. Davenport, 569(SR):Spring86-296
  F.K. Foster, 649(WAL):May86-84
Vliet, R.G. Soledad or Solitudes.
  B.J. Frye, 649(WAL):Feb87-359
Vodola, E. Excommunication in the Middle Ages.
  J. Bossy, 617(TLS):6Mar87-250
Voegelin, E. From Enlightenment to Revolution. (J.H. Hallowell, ed)
  G. Gillespie, 131(CL):Summer86-289
Vogan, S. Scenes from the Homefront.
  M. Peacock, 441:2Aug87-20
Vogel, E.F. Comeback, Case by Case.
  K. Taira, 293(JASt):May86-616
Vogel, S.M. African Aesthetics.*
  J. Nunley, 2(AfrA):Aug86-78
Vogel, V.J. Indian Names in Michigan.
  E.A. Callary, 424:Dec86-391
Vogel, V.J. Iowa Place Names of Indian Origin.
  L.E. Seits, 424:Jun86-214
Vogeler, M.S. Frederic Harrison.
  W.L. Arnstein, 635(VPR):Summer86-76
  P. Coustillas, 189(EA):Apr-Jun87-172
  T.R. Wright, 161(DUJ):Dec85-172
Vogelsang, B. Funde und Befunde zur schlesischen Theatergeschichte. (Vol 2)
  P. Skrine, 402(MLR):Apr86-534
Vogt, H. Flagstad.
  M. Tanner, 617(TLS):25-31Dec87-1441
Voidy, J. Les Contes de la source perdue.
  K. O'Donnell, 296(JCF):No35/36-175
Voigt, E.B. The Forces of Plenty.
  C. Wright, 363(LitR):Fall86-118

380

Voigt, E.B. The Lotus Flowers.
E. Hirsch, 441:23Aug87-20
Voigt, E-M. - see "Lexikon des frühgriech-
ischen Epos"
Voigt-Langenberger, P. Antifaschistische
Lyrik in Frankreich, 1930-1945.*
C. Bevernis, 535(RHL):Mar-Apr86-343
M. Cranston, 207(FR):May87-872
Voinovich, V. Moscow 2042.
P-L. Adams, 61:Aug87-84
M. Bradbury, 441:7Jun87-1
Voitle, R. The Third Earl of Shaftesbury,
1671-1713.*
P. Jones, 89(BJA):Summer86-284
Volk, P. Johann Baptist Straub.
A. Laing, 90:Jan86-44
Volk, P. White Light.
N. Ramsey, 441:29Nov87-20
Volk, P., with others. Bayerische Rokoko-
plastik.
A. Laing, 90:Jan86-44
Volk, R. Gesundheitswesen und Wohltätig-
keit im Spiegel der byzantinischen
Klostertypika.
L.J. Patsavos, 589:Oct86-1040
Volk. S. Gothic.
R. Clarke, 362:4Jun87-48
Volkmann-Schluck, K.H. Von der Wahrheit
der Dichtung. (W. Janke & R. Weyers,
eds)
P. Somville, 542:Apr-Jun86-271
Volland, B. Französische Entlehnungen im
Deutschen.
M. Pfister, 547(RF):Band98Heft3/4-401
Vollenweider, M-L. Deliciae Leonis, Antike
geschnittene Steine und Ringe aus einer
Privatsammlung.
J. Boardman, 123:Vol36No1-164
Vollmann, W.T. You Bright and Risen
Angels.
G. Pool, 441:21Jun87-10
Volokh, A., with M. Manus. The Art of
Russian Cuisine.
K.L. Nalibow, 574(SEEJ):Fall86-468
Vološinov, V.N. Marxism and the Philosophy
of Language.* Freudianism.
D.H. Richter, 599:Fall86-411
de Voltaire, F.M.A. Corpus des notes
marginales de Voltaire. (Vol 3)
W.H. Barber, 208(FS):Apr86-212
de Voltaire, F.M.A. Correspondance. (Vol
9) (T. Besterman, ed)
J.H. Brumfitt, 208(FS):Apr86-213
de Voltaire, F.M.A. La Défense de mon
oncle. (J-M. Moureaux, ed)
J. Hellegouarc'h, 535(RHL):Sep-Oct86-
920
E.D. James, 402(MLR):Oct86-1007
Vonnegut, K. Bluebeard.
J. Moynahan, 441:18Oct87-12
Voris, R. Peter Handke: "Kaspar."
M.E. Ward, 221(GQ):Summer86-502
Voris, R. Adolf Muschg.
M. Burkhard, 221(GQ):Fall86-670
Vorländer, K. Immanuel Kant. (2nd ed) (F.
Malter, with K. Kopper, eds)
R. George, 484(PPR):Mar87-485
Vos, A. Aquinas, Calvin, and Contemporary
Protestant Thought.
J. de Boer, 543:Dec86-406
Voslensky, M.S. Nomenklatura.
A.J. Matejko, 497(PolR):Vol31No4-327

Vosmar, J. J.P. Jacobsens digtning.
N.L. Jensen, 562(Scan):Nov86-235
Voss, B. Slips of the Ear.
C.J. James, 399(MLJ):Autumn86-317
Voss, L. Literarische Präfiguration dar-
gestellter Wirklichkeit bei Fontane.
H.R. Klieneberger, 402(MLR):Jul87-789
Vossenkuhl, W. Anatomie des Sprachge-
brauchs.*
A. Radl, 489(PJGG):Band93Heft1-202
Voyat, G. Cognitive Development Among
Sioux Children.
P.G. Patel, 320(CJL):Fall86-292
Voznesensky, A. An Arrow in the Wall.
(W.J. Smith & F.D. Reeve, eds)
J. Bayley, 441:29Mar87-7
E. Feinstein, 453(NYRB):3Dec87-36
Vranich, S.B. Obra completa de don Juan de
Arguijo (1567-1622).
C. Iranzo, 241:May86-76
Vranich, S.B. - see de Arguijo, J.
Vreuls, D. Let Us Know.*
639(VQR):Summer86-94
Vroon, R. Velimir Khlebnikov's Shorter
Poems.*
M. Klefter, 558(RLJ):Spring/Fall86-239
M.B. Kreps, 550(RusR):Oct86-432
Vuarnet, J-N. - see Bruno, G.
Vuillemin, J. Nécessité ou contingence.*
J. Barnes, 123:Vol36No1-77
Vuillemin, J. What Are Philosophical Sys-
tems?
D.M. Hamlyn, 617(TLS):27Feb87-222
Vygotski, L.S. Pensée et langage.
J-M. Gabuade, 542:Apr-Jun86-261
de Vylder, S. Agriculture in Chains.
J.P. Thorp, 293(JASt):Aug86-789

Waage, F.O. "The White Devil" Discover'd.
P. Hyland, 568(SCN):Spring-Summer86-16
Wacher, J., ed. The Roman World.
M. Henig, 617(TLS):21Aug87-906
Wachinger, B. - see Hartmann von Aue
Wacholder, B.Z. The Dawn of Qumran.
J.A. Sanders, 318(JAOS):Jan/Mar85-147
Waddell, L.M., J.L. Tottenham & D.H. Kent -
see Bouquet, H.
Waddington, M. Collected Works.
R. Johnson, 99:Oct86-38
Wade, B. & others. The Book of the World
Championship.
C. Russ, 617(TLS):30Jan87-106
Wade, B.C. Khyāl.
J. Katz, 410(M&L):Jul86-295
Wade, N. A World Beyond Healing.
R.P. Gale, 441:19Jul87-11
Wade, R.A. Red Guards and Workers'
Militias in the Russian Revolution.*
R.V. Daniels, 550(RusR):Jan86-82
Wade, T. & N. White, eds. Russia Today.
N.J. Brown, 575(SEER):Oct86-584
Wade, W.C. The Fiery Cross.
D. Chalmers, 617(TLS):20-26Nov87-1272
B. Morton, 362:17Sep87-22
T. Rosengarten, 441:26Apr87-32
van der Waerden, B.L. Geometry and Algebra
in Ancient Civilization.
J.L. Berggren, 41:Fall85-305
Wagar, W.W. Terminal Visions.
D. Ketterer, 107(CRCL):Sep86-492

Wagenknecht, E. American Profile, 1900–
1909.
D. Macleod, 106:Summer86–235
Wagenknecht, E. Daughters of the Covenant.
B.H. Gelfant, 106:Fall86–355
Wagenknecht, E. The Novels of Henry
James.*
P.B. Armstrong, 284:Winter85–148
Wagenknecht, E. The Tales of Henry James.
P. Buitenhuis, 284:Fall86–76
J.W. Gargano, 573(SSF):Winter86–128
Waggoner, B.A. & G.A., comps. Universities
of the Caribbean Region.
A.J. Payne, 263(RIB):Vol36No2–194
Waggoner, H.H. American Poets from the
Puritans to the Present. (rev)
C. Clausen, 569(SR):Winter86–vi
Waggoner, N.M. Early Greek Coins from the
Collection of Jonathon P. Rosen.
A. Johnston, 303(JoHS):Vol106–258
Waghorne, J.P. & N. Cutler, with V. Nara-
yanan, eds. Gods of Flesh, Gods of
Stone.
L.A. Babb, 293(JASt):May86–642
Wagner, A., ed. Contemporary Canadian
Theatre.*
U. Kareda, 627(UTQ):Fall86–180
R.P. Knowles, 102(CanL):Summer86–137
C. McCaughey, 476:Winter87–83
Wagner, A.M. Jean-Baptiste Carpeaux.*
M. Yorke, 324:Apr87–404
Wagner, G. The Chocolate Conscience.
B. Fothergill, 617(TLS):11–17Dec87–1371
D. Stein, 362:15Oct87–29
Wagner, H.R. – see Schutz, A.
Wagner, H.R., with I. Srubar. A Bergsonian
Bridge to Phenomenological Psychology
R.J. Anderson, 323:May86–203
Wagner, M.L. The Lotus Boat.
J.R. Allen 3d, 116:Jul85–164
D. Bryant, 244(HJAS):Dec86–619
E.H. Kaplan, 134(CP):Vol19–134
M.K. Spring, 293(JASt):Feb86–390
Wagner, M.M. – see Anneke, M.F.
Wagner, R. My Life. (M. Whittall, ed)
W.A. Bebbington, 317:Fall86–663
Wagner, R. Ferdinand Raimund.
P. Branscombe, 402(MLR):Jul87–783
Wagner, R. Wagner: Prelude and Transfigu-
ration from Tristan and Isolde. (R.
Bailey, ed)
R. Anderson, 415:Sep86–499
Wagner, R.G. Reenacting the Heavenly
Vision.
K. Bernhardt, 293(JASt):Aug86–834
Wagner-Martin, L. Sylvia Plath.
I. Hamilton, 441:25Oct87–12
Wagoner, M. Tobias Smollett.*
J.V. Price, 588(SSL):Vol21–325
Wagy, T.R. Governor LeRoy Collins of
Florida.
R.C. McMath, Jr., 9(AlaR):Jul86–233
Wah, F. Waiting for Saskatchewan.
S. Scobie, 376:Mar86–125
Wahba, M., ed. Samuel Johnson.
A. Pailler, 189(EA):Apr–Jun87–243
Wain, J. Dear Shadows.*
W. Boyd, 364:Apr/May86–154
Wain, J. Open Country.
A. Haverty, 617(TLS):20–26Nov87–1275
Wain, J. – see Johnson, S.
Wainright, C.S. Distant Mountain.
A. Kenny, 404:Winter–Spring86–60

Wainwright, J. Selected Poems.*
H. Buckingham, 565:Summer86–64
Wainwright, J. The Tenth Interview.
442(NY):1Jun87–112
Waite, P.B. The Man from Halifax.*
J.R. Miller, 529(QQ):Autumn86–646
G.W., 102(CanL):Summer86–173
Waith, E.M. – see Shakespeare, W.
Wakabayashi, B.T. Anti-Foreignism and
Western Learning in Early-Modern Japan.
C. Dunn, 617(TLS):22May87–542
Wakefield, D. French Eighteenth-Century
Painting.*
M.R. Michel, 90:May86–362
Wakefield, L. & others. Time Pieces. (M.
Wandor, ed)
V.M. Patraka, 385(MQR):Winter87–286
Walbank, F.W. & others, eds. Cambridge
Ancient History.* (2nd ed) (Vol 7, Pt 1)
S. Hornblower, 123:Vol36No1–85
Walberg, G. Provincial Middle Minoan
Pottery.*
J.A. MacGillivray, 303(JoHS):Vol106–249
Walbruck, H.A. Lustige Dialoge.
J.D. Arendt, 399(MLJ):Autumn86–318
Walcott, D. The Arkansas Testament.
M. Rudman, 441:20Dec87–12
Walcott, D. Collected Poems 1948–1984.*
P. Balakian, 491:Jun86–169
P. Forbes, 493:Oct86–14
B. King, 598(SoR):Summer87–741
Walcott, D. Three Plays.
B. King, 598(SoR):Summer87–741
Wald, A.M. The New York Intellectuals.
D.M. Oshinsky, 441:7Jun87–24
Wald, H., ed. Spanish at a Glance.
G.A. Olivier, 399(MLJ):Winter86–448
Walden, H. Ice Cream.
W. & C. Cowen, 639(VQR):Spring86–69
Walden, K. Visions of Order.*
D. Harrison, 102(CanL):Winter85–130
Walden, S. The Ravished Image.*
T. Bajou, 39:Jan86–60
S. Whitfield, 176:Feb87–53
Waldenfels, B. In den Netzen der Lebens-
welt.*
T. Bettendorf, 687:Oct–Dec86–649
Walder, D. Athol Fugard.
S. Gray, 538(RAL):Summer86–281
Waldoff, L. Keats and the Silent Work of
Imagination.
B. Schapiro, 191(ELN):Dec86–74
S. Wolfson, 340(KSJ):Vol35–193
Waldron, A. Close Connections.
D. Betts, 441:15Nov87–18
Waldrop, M.M. Man-Made Minds.
E. Dobb, 441:4Oct87–29
Waldrop, R. The Hanky of Pippin's Daugh-
ter.
R. Weinreich, 441:1Mar87–12
Walesa, L. A Way of Hope.
L. Kolakowski, 441:13Dec87–3
Waley, P. – see "Curial and Guelfa"
Walker, A. The Color Purple.
D. Pinckney, 453(NYRB):29Jan87–17
Walker, A. National Heroes.*
J. Boorman, 707:Winter85/86–55
Walker, A. Vivien.
V. Glendinning, 617(TLS):24Jul87–792
Walker, B.G. The Crone.*
639(VQR):Summer86–104
Walker, D. The Transparent Lyric.*
M. Dickie, 402(MLR):Oct87–944

Walker, D.C. The Pronunciation of Canadian French.
A. Fancy, 399(MLJ):Summer86-186
B.E. Gesner, 207(FR):Feb87-443
Walker, I. - see Plato
Walker, I.M., ed. Edgar Allan Poe: The Critical Heritage.
H. Beaver, 617(TLS):2Jan87-8
Walker, J. Metaphysics and Aesthetics in the Works of Eduardo Barrios.*
M.S. Arrington, Jr., 345:Nov86-508
P.R. Beardsell, 86(BHS):Jul86-303
L. Monguió, 240(HR):Spring86-244
L. Pollmann, 547(RF):Band98Heft1/2-236
D.L. Shaw, 402(MLR):Apr86-519
Walker, J.M. Fugitive Angels.*
T. Swiss, 569(SR):Spring86-302
Walker, J.R. Lakota Myth. (E.A. Jahner, ed)
J. Rice, 649(WAL):May86-91
Walker, K. - see Dryden, J.
Walker, K. - see Lord Rochester
Walker, M. The Literature of the United States of America.
J.A.L. Lemay, 402(MLR):Oct87-939
Walker, M. Old Somerset Customs.
S. Drury, 203:Vol97No1-117
Walker, M. The Waking Giant.
T. Omestad, 441:12Apr87-27
A.B. Ulam, 617(TLS):6Feb87-129
442(NY):13Apr87-105
Walker, P. Zola.*
E.F. Gray, 395(MFS):Winter86-677
L. Kamm, 207(FR):Feb87-399
R. Lethbridge, 402(MLR):Jul87-745
D.E. Speirs, 446(NCFS):Fall-Winter 86/87-214
Walker, P.D. "Germinal" and Zola's Philosophical and Religious Thought.*
E.F. Gray, 395(MFS):Summer86-331
M.A. O'Neil, 478:Oct86-335
G. Woollen, 402(MLR):Apr86-488
Walker, R. Regency Portraits.*
K. Garlick, 39:Jul86-65
Walker, R.M. - see "El cavallero Pláçidas (MS Esc. h-I-13)"
Walker, S., ed. Buying Time.
S. Minot, 455:Mar86-76
Walker, T. In Spain.
X. Fielding, 617(TLS):11-17Dec87-1385
Walkiewicz, E.P. John Barth.
R.F. Kiernan, 268(IFR):Summer87-113
Wall, A.D. - see Thynne, J. & M.
Wall, M. The Complete Fursey.
M. Harmon, 272(IUR):Spring86-77
Wall, R.E. Blackrobe.
G. Decarie, 296(JCF):No35/36-190
Wallace, A.F.C. St. Clair.
R. Rosenzweig, 441:18Oct87-15
Wallace, B. Common Magic.
A. Archer, 529(QQ):Autumn86-663
G. Boire, 102(CanL):Fall86-130
Wallace, C.M. The Design of "Biographia Literaria."*
E.D. Mackerness, 447(N&Q):Jun85-277
Wallace, D. Chaucer and the Early Writings of Boccaccio.*
J.D. Burnley, 541(RES):Nov86-552
J. Dean, 481(PQ):Summer86-407
M. Marcus, 276:Autumn86-315
Wallace, D.F. The Broom of the System.
C. James, 441:1Mar87-22

Wallace, I. The Writing of One Novel.
A.M., 125:Spring86-338
Wallace, J.D. Early Cooper and His Audience.*
M.D. Bell, 165(EAL):Vol22No3-334
M.T. Gilmore, 27(AL):Oct86-437
639(VQR):Autumn86-115
Wallace, K.Y., ed. La Estoire de Seint Aedward le Rei.*
B.J. Levy, 382(MAE):1986/2-272
J.H. Marshall, 402(MLR):Oct86-999
Wallace, R. Beethoven's Critics.
L. Langley, 617(TLS):13Feb87-159
Wallace, R. God Be with the Clown.*
D.L. Macdonald, 106:Fall86-381
Wallace, R., ed. Light Year '86.
D. Galef, 448:Vol24No1-103
639(VQR):Winter86-30
Wallace, R. Tunes for Bears to Dance To.
F. Pollak, 448:Vol24No1-106
Wallace, W.A. Galileo and His Sources.*
D. Gruender, 319:Jul87-445
Wallace-Hadrill, A. Suetonius.*
A.B. Breebaart, 394:Vol39fasc1/2-187
R.C. Lounsbury, 121(CJ):Dec86-Jan87-159
Waller, D. The Motown Story.
D.E. McGinty, 91:Fall86-309
Waller, P.J. Town, City and Nation.
K. Tiller, 447(N&Q):Dec85-566
Wallis, P.J. & R.V., with T.D. Whittet. Eighteenth-Century Medics.
R. Porter, 83:Autumn86-231
Wallon, H. L'enfant turbulent.
E. Jalley, 542:Apr-Jun86-263
Walpole, H. Memoirs of King George II by Horace Walpole.* (J. Brooke, ed)
M. Kallich, 173(ECS):Summer87-509
L.E. Troide, 566:Autumn86-75
529(QQ):Spring86-222
Walpole, R.N., ed. Le Turpin français, dit le Turpin I.*
I. Short, 402(MLR):Oct87-949
M.E. Winters, 207(FR):Apr87-705
Walser, G. Hellas und Iran.
K.H. Kinzl, 487:Summer86-244
E. Will, 555:Vol59fasc2-290
Walser, M. Breakers.
S. Ruta, 441:1Nov87-43
Walser, M. The Inner Man.
J. Mellors, 364:Jul86-103
Walsh, D. The Mysticism of Innerworldy Fulfillment.
D.A. Freeman, 396(ModA):Spring86-180
Walsh, G.B. The Varieties of Enchantment.*
D.E. Gerber, 41:Vol6-199
I.J.F. de Jong, 394:Vol39fasc3/4-419
Walsh, J.P. Lapsing.
L. Taylor, 362:8Jan87-22
Walsh, M. - see Smart, C.
Walsh, M. & K. Williamson - see Smart, C.
Walsh, M.E.W. Jean Stafford.
W. Leary, 649(WAL):Nov86-259
Walsh, R. The Mycroft Memoranda.
639(VQR):Winter86-21
Walter, H.A. Deutsche Exilliteratur 1933-1950. (Vol 2)
H. Lehnert, 221(GQ):Winter86-157
Walton, D.N. Physician-Patient Decision-Making.
R.V., 185:Oct86-308

Walton, D.N. Topical Relevance in Argumentation.
  D. Hitchcock, 154:Winter86-819
Walton, H., Jr. Invisible Politics.
  D.J. Garrow, 579(SAQ):Summer86-310
Walton, J.M. The Greek Sense of Theatre.
  D. Bain, 123:Vol36No1-140
  E.M. Craik, 303(JoHS):Vol106-223
  M.W. Edwards, 529(QQ):Spring86-184
  G. Giesekam, 610:Spring86-61
Walz, E.P. François Truffaut.
  K.A. Reader, 208(FS):Jan86-117
Walzer, M. Exodus and Revolution.
  H. Levine, 639(VQR):Summer86-531
Walzer, M. Interpretation and Social
Criticism.
  J.P. Diggins, 441:15Mar87-11
Walzer, M. Spheres of Justice.*
  J. Cohen, 311(JP):Aug86-457
Wambaugh, J. Echoes in the Darkness.
  L. Franks, 441:1Mar87-12
Wamberg, B., ed. Out of Denmark.
  A. Svensen, 562(Scan):Nov86-251
Wandor, M. Gardens of Eden.
  H. Buckingham, 565:Summer86-64
Wandor, M., ed. On Gender and Writing.*
  J. Todd, 402(MLR):Apr87-464
Wandor, M. - see Dayley, G.
Wandor, M. - see Luckham, C.
Wandor, M. - see Wakefield, L. & others
Wang Meng-ou, ed. T'ang-jen hsiao-shuo
chiao-shih.
  F.K.H. So, 116:Jul85-209
Waniek, K. Die Mundart von Ratiborhammer.
  A.R. Rowley, 685(ZDL):2/1986-264
Wanniski, J., ed. The 1987 Mediaguide.
  J.D. Atwater, 441:12Jul87-15
Wansell, G. Tycoon.
  G. Daugherty, 441:25Oct87-38
  R. Davenport-Hines, 617(TLS):25-
31Dec87-1421
Wantrup, J. Australian Rare Books 1788-
1900.
  A. Payne, 617(TLS):19Jun87-670
Wapner, J.A. A View from the Bench.
  M.E. Gale, 441:13Dec87-19
Ward, G.W.R. and W.N. Hosley, Jr., eds.
The Great River.
  B.C. Smith, 432(NEQ):Dec86-588
Ward, Mrs. H. Marcella.
  T.C. Holyoke, 42(AR):Winter86-119
Ward, J.A. American Silences.*
  M.A. Cohen, 27(AL):Mar86-140
Ward, J.F. Language, Form, and Inquiry.
  D. Rucker, 619:Winter86-74
Ward, J.P. Wordsworth's Language of Men.
  J. Chandler, 661(WC):Autumn86-207
  D. Gervais, 97(CQ):Vol15No2-148
  W.J.B. Owen, 541(RES):May86-273
Ward, P. Travels in Oman.
  P. Hodson, 617(TLS):4-11Sep87-942
Ward-Jackson, C.H. & D.E. Harvey. The
English Gypsy Caravan.
  S. Walrond, 324:Jun87-537
Warden, J., ed. Orpheus.
  M. Mueller, 107(CRCL):Mar86-116
Warden, M.R. The Shadow of Wings.
  S. Brady, 649(WAL):Nov86-273
Warder, A.K. Introduction to Pali. (2nd
ed)
  J.W. de Jong, 259(IIJ):Oct86-325
Warder, A.K. - see Ñāṇamoli, B.

Wardhaugh, R. How Conversation Works.*
  A. Garnham, 307:Aug86-153
  K. Tracy, 355(LSoc):Sep86-399
Wardman, A. Religion and Statecraft among
the Romans.
  J.A. North, 313:Vol76-251
Wardropper, B.W., ed. Historia y crítica
de la literatura española. (Vol 3)
  J.A. Whitenack, 403(MLS):Fall86-91
Warhol, A. 25 Cats Name Sam and One Blue
Pussy. Holy Cats by Andy Warhol's
Mother.
  J. Russell, 441:6Dec87-89
Waringhien, G., ed & trans. La Romantika
Periodo.
  K.M. Hall, 208(FS):Jan86-82
Warland, B. Open Is Broken.
  D. Bennett, 102(CanL):Winter85-152
Warme, L.G. Per Olof Sundman.
  M.J. Blackwell, 221(GQ):Winter86-165
  R. Wright, 563(SS):Winter86-83
Warminski, A. Reading in Interpretation.
  M. Sprinker, 400(MLN):Dec86-1226
Warmus, W. Emile Gallé.
  G.E. Baker, 658:Spring86-88
Warner, A., ed. Traditional American Folk
Songs from the Anne and Frank Warner
Collection.*
  L.C. Jones, 440:Summer-Fall86-170
  A.C. Rotola, 377:Jul86-147
Warner, E. Woolf: "The Waves."
  C.H. Sisson, 617(TLS):17Apr87-419
Warner, J.A. Blake and the Language of
Art.*
  K. Mulhallen, 661(WC):Autumn86-202
Warner, K.P. Thomas Otway.
  M. Jones, 447(N&Q):Mar85-122
Warner, K.Q. Kaiso! the Trinidad Calypso.
  J.C. Dje Dje, 91:Fall86-306
Warner, K.Q., ed. Voix françaises du monde
noir.
  R. Bjornson, 399(MLJ):Autumn86-310
Warner, M. Monuments and Maidens.*
  639(VQR):Spring86-44
Warner, P. Lord's: 1787-1945.
  617(TLS):7Aug87-854
Warner, S. The Wide, Wide World.
  S. Mitchell, 441:10May87-16
Warner, V. Before Lunch.
  W. Bedford, 4:Summer86-89
  E. Larrissy, 493:Jun86-108
Warner, W. Knute, and Knute Again.
  J. Prindle, 441:2Aug87-16
Warnke, M. Hofkünstler.
  N. Hammerstein, 224(GRM):Band36Heft4-
466
Warnock, M. A Question of Life.
  D.C., 185:Jan87-512
  J. Harris, 518:Oct86-238
Warren, B. Classifying Adjectives.*
  G.N. Carlson, 361:Jun86-188
Warren, J.W. The American Narcissus.*
  E.B. Jordan, 395(MFS):Summer86-358
Warren, M.A. Gendercide.
  C.C., 185:Apr87-703
Warren, N.H. New Mexico Style.
  R.M. Adams, 453(NYRB):26Mar87-32
Warren, R.P. New and Selected Poems, 1923-
1985.*
  639(VQR):Winter86-26
Warren, W.L. The Governance of Norman
and Angevin England 1086-1272.
  M. Prestwich, 617(TLS):16-22Oct87-1148

Washburn, Y.M. Juan José Arreola.
  R. Fiddian, 402(MLR):Apr86-522
Washington, J. Alain Locke and Philosophy.
  I.M.Y., 185:Jul87-895
Washington, J.M. - see King, M.L.
Washington, M.H. Invented Lives.
  H.L. Gates, Jr., 441:4Oct87-3
Wasiolek, E., ed. Critical Essays on
  Tolstoy.
  V.D. Mihailovich, 268(IFR):Summer87-105
Wasiolek, E. L.N. Tolstoy.
  M.J.D. Holman, 402(MLR):Jul87-809
Wasserman, J., ed. Modern Canadian Plays.*
  A. Messenger, 102(CanL):Winter85-125
  B. Parker, 397(MD):Mar86-151
Wasserstein, D. The Rise and Fall of the
  Party-Kings.
  A.J. Forey, 161(DUJ):Jun86-359
Waswo, R. Language and Meaning in the
  Renaissance.
  L. Jardine, 617(TLS):18-24Dec87-1408
Waterlow, S. Nature, Change, and Agency in
  Aristotle's "Physics."
  I. Mueller, 53(AGP):Band68Heft2-193
Waterlow, S. Passage and Possibility.*
  R. Smith, 41:Spring85-67
Waterman, A. Selected Poems.
  J. Mole, 176:Mar87-58
Waterman, R.H., Jr. The Renewal Factor.
  D. Diamond, 441:25Oct87-38
Waters, F. Flight from Fiesta.
  C.L. Adams, 649(WAL):Nov86-231
  J. Sullivan, 441:30Aug87-20
Waters, F. Frank Waters: A Retrospective
  Anthology. (C.L. Adams, ed)
  T.A. Tanner, 649(WAL):Aug86-147
Waters, K.H. Herodotus the Historian.
  S. West, 123:Vol36No1-130
  H.D. Westlake, 303(JoHS):Vol106-207
Waterston, E., ed. John Galt.
  A.A. Den Otter, 102(CanL):Summer86-
  139
Watkin, D. A History of Western Architec-
  ture.*
  J.M. Richards, 617(TLS):13Feb87-152
Watkin, D. The Royal Interiors of Regency
  England.*
  G.J. Stops, 90:Jul86-517
Watkins, C., ed. The American Heritage
  Dictionary of Indo-European Roots. (rev)
  P.H. Salus, 350:Mar87-182
Watkins, F.C. Then & Now.*
  R. Belflower, 541(RES):Feb86-133
  H. Claridge, 447(N&Q):Dec85-556
Watkins, G. Dickens in Search of Himself.
  S. Wall, 617(TLS):11-17Dec87-1380
Watkins, G. Dylan Thomas and Vernon
  Watkins.
  M.B., 295(JML):Nov86-395
Watkins, G. - see d'India, S.
Watkins, J. Science and Scepticism.*
  R.J. Ackermann, 518:Jan86-50
  I. Levi, 311(JP):Jul86-402
  A. O'Hear, 84:Sep86-363
  M. Williams, 486:Jun86-302
Watkins, V. The Collected Poems.
  A. Motion, 617(TLS):3Jul87-716
Watmough, D. Fury.*
  D. Carpenter, 102(CanL):Spring86-166
Watrous, J. A Century of American Print-
  making, 1880-1980.
  B. Reilly, 658:Spring86-90

Watson, A. The Evolution of Law.*
  R.A. Bauman, 24:Winter86-603
  J.F. Oates, 124:Jul-Aug87-463
Watson, A. - see Butterfield, H.
Watson, A.G. Catalogue of Dated and
  Datable Manuscripts c. 435-1600 in
  Oxford Libraries.
  A.I. Doyle, 354:Dec86-373
  78(BC):Summer86-145
Watson, B., ed and trans. The Columbia
  Book of Chinese Poetry: From Early Times
  to the Thirteenth Century.*
  H.H. Frankel, 244(HJAS):Jun86-238
  E.H. Kaplan, 134(CP):Vol19-134
  P.W. Kroll, 293(JASt):Nov85-131
  J.P. Seaton, 116:Jul85-151
Watson, C.M. Prologue.
  N. Harris, 395(MFS):Summer86-283
Watson, D. Caledonia Australis.
  J. McCalman, 381:Mar86-69
Watson, J.B. Tairora Culture.
  J.M. Blythe, 293(JASt):Aug86-797
Watson, J.R. English Poetry of the Roman-
  tic Period: 1789-1830.
  J. Blondel, 189(EA):Jul-Sep86-348
Watson, J.R., ed. An Infinite Complexity.*
  F. Piquet, 189(EA):Jul-Sep86-349
  N. Roe, 447(N&Q):Jun85-272
Watson, J.R. Wordsworth's Vital Soul.*
  P. Larkin, 677(YES):Vol16-289
Watson, L. The Dreams of Dragons.
  R. Lewis, 441:10May87-28
Watson, R. The Literature of Scotland.*
  T. Crawford, 571(ScLJ):Winter86-27
  K. Sutherland, 541(RES):Aug86-425
Watson, R. MacDiarmid.
  A. Haberer, 189(EA):Jan-Mar87-97
Watson, R. Macmillan History of Litera-
  ture.
  L. Hartveit, 179(ES):Feb86-90
Watson, R. The Philosopher's Diet.
  S.C., 219(GaR):Summer86-588
Watson, R.D., Jr. The Cavalier in Virginia
  Fiction.
  R. Brinkmeyer, 579(SAQ):Autumn86-409
  P. Castille, 594:Spring86-111
  W.L. Frank, 27(AL):May86-302
Watson, R.N. Shakespeare and the Hazards
  of Ambition.
  H. Smith, 570(SQ):Summer86-255
Watson, S. Five Stories.
  D. Ingham, 102(CanL):Fall86-156
Watson, S. - see Mandel, M.
Watson, W. Tang and Liao Ceramics.*
  90:Apr86-304
Watson, W.H., ed. Black Folk Medicine.
  S.B. Thiederman, 650(WF):Oct86-299
Watt, D.E.R. - see Bower, W.
Watt, F.B. In All Respects Ready.
  D.B. Dodds, 529(QQ):Autumn86-655
Watt, G. The Fallen Woman in the Nine-
  teenth-Century English Novel.*
  E. Jay, 447(N&Q):Sep85-404
  A. Murphy, 158:Dec86-194
  S.M. Smith, 402(MLR):Jul87-712
Watt, W.S. - see Cicero
Wattenberg, B.J. The Birth Dearth.
  T. Jacoby, 441:12Jul87-9
de Watteville, V. Speak to the Earth.
  T. Swick, 441:28Jun87-25
Watthée-Delmotte, M. Villiers de l'Isle-
  Adam et l'hégélianisme.
  J. Decottignies, 535(RHL):Sep-Oct86-942

Watts, C. – see Conrad, J.
Waugh, E. The Essays, Articles and Reviews of Evelyn Waugh.* (D. Gallagher, ed)
  A. Blayac, 189(EA):Jan–Mar87–98
Waugh, E. Evelyn Waugh, Apprentice. (R.M. Davis, ed)
  M.P.L., 295(JML):Nov86–549
Waugh, P. Metafiction.*
  H. Bertens, 549(RLC):Jan–Mar86–98
Waxman, C.I. America's Jews in Transition.
  L. Grossman, 390:Jan86–62
Wayman, T. The Face of Jack Monro.
  S. Scobie, 376:Dec86–141
  B. Serafin, 648(WCR):Oct86–76
Wayman, T., ed. Going for Coffee.
  R. Hedin, 649(WAL):Nov86–249
Wayne, D.E. Penshurst.*
  M.G. Brennan, 541(RES):Nov86–612
  S. Bygrave, 89(BJA):Spring86–178
  R. Dutton, 402(MLR):Oct87–913
  S.M. Kurland, 405(MP):Nov86–219
Wayne, M. The Reshaping of Plantation Society.
  P. Lachance, 106:Winter86–449
Weales, G. Canned Goods as Caviar.*
  E.L. Galligan, 569(SR):Fall86–lxxxv
Weales, G. Odets the Playwright.
  H.T.B., 295(JML):Nov86–520
Wearing, J.P. The London Stage, 1920–1929.*
  K. Beckson, 365:Winter86–68
Wearne, A. Nightmarkets. Out Here.
  C. James, 617(TLS):27Nov–3Dec87–1327
Weatherhead, A.K. The British Dissonance.
  R. Bowen, 131(CL):Winter86–110
Weatherilt, M. – see Champfleury
Weaver, J.H. The World of Physics.
  D.J.R. Bruckner, 441:27Sep87–36
Weaver, R., ed. Canadian Short Stories. (4th Ser)
  S.R. MacGillivray, 628(UWR):Spring–Summer86–65
Weaver, S.A. John Fielden and the Politics of Popular Radicalism 1832–1847.
  D. Thompson, 617(TLS):11–17Dec87–1371
Webb, A. Hot Light, Half-Made Worlds.
  A. Ross, 364:Aug/Sep86–140
Webb, J.C. Mechanism, Mentalism, and Metamathematics.
  S. Shapiro, 316:Jun86–472
Webb, P. Water and Light.
  J. Hulcoop, 102(CanL):Summer86–151
Webb, P., with R. Short. Hans Bellmer.*
  J. Brun, 192(EP):Oct–Dec86–553
Webb, S. Pestis 18.
  N. Callendar, 441:26Apr87–37
Webb, S.S. 1676.*
  J.M. Murrin, 656(WMQ):Jan86–119
Webb, T., ed. English Romantic Hellenism 1700–1824.*
  C. Martindale, 402(MLR):Jan86–175
Webber, J.L., ed. Song of the Birds.
  R. Anderson, 415:May86–280
Weber, D.J., ed & trans. Arms, Indians, and the Mismanagement of New Mexico.
  L. Milazzo, 584(SWR):Summer86–402
Weber, E. France, Fin de Siècle.*
  42(AR):Fall86–490
Weber, E. & C. Mithal. Deutsche Originalromane zwischen 1680 und 1780.
  J.W. Van Cleve, 406:Winter86–531

Weber, J. Customs Violation.
  P-L. Adams, 61:Nov87–123
  D. Finkle, 441:20Sep87–26
Weber, R. Seeing Earth.*
  S.T. Arnold, 561(SFS):Jul86–211
Weber, S. Institution and Interpretation.
  C.M. Hurlbert, 590:Jun87–64
Weber, W. & I. Auf den Spuren des göttlichen Schelms.
  K. Reichl, 72:Band223Heft1–229
"Webster's Ninth New Collegiate Dictionary."
  G-J. Forgue, 189(EA):Jul–Sep87–342
Wechsler, H.J. Offerings of Jade and Silk.
  J.L. Dull, 293(JASt):May86–581
Wecker, C., ed. American-German Literary Interrelations in the Nineteenth Century.
  E-M. Kröller, 107(CRCL):Jun86–309
Wedde, I. Tales of Gotham City.
  R. Pybus, 565:Spring86–71
Wedekind-Schwertner, B. "Dass ich eins und doppelt bin."
  F.A. Lubich, 222(GR):Spring86–82
Wedel, J. The Private Poland.
  A. Husarska, 441:8Mar87–21
Weeks, A. Comprehensive Schools.
  R. Floud, 617(TLS):13Mar87–263
Weems, J.E. "If You Don't Like the Weather..."
  L. Milazzo, 584(SWR):Summer86–402
Weesner, T. The True Detective.
  J. Coleman, 441:26Apr87–20
Wegehaupt, H. Alte deutsche Kinderbücher.
  H-J. Uther, 196:Band27Heft3/4–376
Wegelin, C. – see James, H.
Wegner, U. Afrikanische Saiteninstrumente.
  V. Erlmann, 187:Winter87–147
Wegstein, W. Studien zum "Summarium Heinrici."
  R. Hildebrandt, 684(ZDA):Band115Heft3–120
Wehr, H. A Dictionary of Modern Written Arabic. (4th ed) (J.M. Cowan, ed)
  P. Cachia, 318(JAOS):Oct/Dec85–742
Wehrli, M. Literatur im deutschen Mittelalter.*
  J. Heinzle, 684(ZDA):Band115Heft3–117
  W. McConnell, 221(GQ):Winter86–127
Wei, K.T. Women in China.
  W. Hu, 87(BB):Dec86–262
Wei-liang, H. – see under Huang Wei-liang
Weidemann, T., ed. Thucydides: The Peloponnesian War, Book I – Book II.
  B.M. Lavelle, 124:May–Jun87–388
Weidert, A. Tonologie.
  W.G. Moulton, 685(ZDL):2/1986–247
Weides-Mallmann, G. Swifts satirische "Persona."
  B. Nugel, 566:Autumn86–6
Weidman, J. Praying for Rain.*
  C. Sigal, 617(TLS):18–24Sep87–1022
Weidmann, H. Heinrich von Kleist – Glück und Aufbegehren.
  M. Harman, 221(GQ):Spring86–319
  W. Wittkowski, 133:Band19Heft3/4–351
Weigel, G. Tranquillitas Ordinis.
  J.P. Dolan, 441:26Apr87–30
Weigel, J.A. Patrick White.
  B. Kiernan, 71(ALS):May86–417
Weigl, B. The Monkey Wars.*
  T.R. Hummer, 651(WHR):Spring86–69

Weigle, M., ed. New Mexicans in Cameo and Camera.
L. Milazzo, 584(SWR):Summer86-402
Weil, E. La philosophie de Pietro Pomponazzi.
A. Reix, 542:Oct-Dec86-523
Weil, S. Formative Writings. (D.T. McFarland & W. Van Ness, eds)
E. Young-Bruehl, 441:2Aug87-19
Weimann, G. & C. Winn. Hate on Trial.
R. Clements, 99:Aug/Sep86-28
Weinberg, F.M. Gargantua in a Convex Mirror.
P. Nykrog, 402(MLR):Oct87-952
Weinberg, H.B. The American Pupils of Jean-Léon Gérôme.*
H. Adams, 90:Sep86-683
Weinberg, S.L., ed. Ramtha.
M. Gardner, 453(NYRB):9Apr87-16
Weinberger, J. Science, Faith, and Politics.
D.G., 185:Jan87-504
Weinblatt, A. T.S. Eliot and the Myth of Adequation.
W. Harmon, 569(SR):Summer86-510
Weiner, E. Decade of the Year.
E. Weiner, 441:30Aug87-21
Weiner, J. En busca de la justicia social.
D.L. Heiple, 304(JHP):Spring86-261
Weingarten, R. Shadow Shadow.
D. Shapiro, 491:Mar87-341
Weingartner, R., ed & trans. "Graelent" and "Guingamor."
S. Kay, 208(FS):Jan86-58
S. Sturm-Maddox, 589:Jul86-748
Weinreb, B. & C. Hibbert, eds. The London Encyclopaedia.
M.H. Port, 447(N&Q):Sep85-386
Weinsheimer, J.C. Gadamer's Hermeneutics.
J.J. Baker, 223:Summer86-193
S. Connor, 402(MLR):Jul87-686
M.W. Gullick, 89(BJA):Summer86-289
Weinstein, A. Fictions of the Self: 1550-1800.
J. Frank, 569(SR):Fall86-650
Weinstein, J. A Collector's Guide to Judaica.
K. Guth-Dreyfus, 39:Jun86-442
Weinstein, N. Listen & Say It Right in English!
J.M. Hendrickson, 399(MLJ):Autumn86-340
Weinstein, P.M. The Semantics of Desire.*
R. Chambers, 301(JEGP):Jan86-144
D. David, 158:Dec86-186
R. Kiely, 401(MLQ):Jun85-221
Weintraub, S. The Unexpected Shaw.*
J. Stokes, 677(YES):Vol16-340
Weintraub, S. Victoria.
D. Cannadine, 453(NYRB):23Apr87-30
R.B. Henkle, 441:22Mar87-16
R. Mayne, 176:Apr87-52
R.T. Shannon, 617(TLS):15May87-509
M. Wandor, 362:21May87-27
Weir, B. & C., with D. Benson. Hostage Bound, Hostage Free.
L. Kennedy, 441:14Jun87-18
Weir, D. The Bhopal Syndrome.
J.R. Luoma, 441:29Nov87-16
Weis, E. & J. Belton, eds. Film Sound.
T. Elsaesser, 707:Autumn86-246
Weisberg, R.H. The Failure of the Word.*
W.W. Holdheim, 52:Band21Heft3-324

Weisgerber, J., ed. Les Avant-gardes littéraires au XXème siècle.
B. Morrissette, 149(CLS):Spring86-82
M. Perloff, 402(MLR):Apr86-426
Weishaupt, J. Die Märchenbrüder.
S. Ude-Koeller, 196:Band27Heft3/4-378
Weisman, J. Blood Cries.
S. Kellerman, 441:19Jul87-20
Weiss, A. Chaucer's Native Heritage.
N.F. Blake, 179(ES):Feb86-72
J.D. Burnley, 541(RES):Nov86-552
G. Kane, 589:Oct86-1011
Weiss, B. The Hell of the English.
P. Beer, 617(TLS):11-17Dec87-1380
Weiss, B. Wie finde ich Literatur zur Geschichte der Naturwissenschaft und Technik?
H. Breger, 706:Band18Heft1-112
Weiss, C. Griechische Flussgottheiten in vorhellenistischer Zeit.
S. Woodford, 303(JoHS):Vol106-259
Weiss, C. Seh-Texte.
E. Vos, 204(FdL):Mar86-68
Weiss, D. The Critic Agonistes.* (E. Solomon & S. Arkin, eds)
F.R. Cunningham, 27(AL):May86-295
J. Hunter, 434:Winter86-242
Weiss, H.F. Funde und Studien zu Heinrich von Kleist.
H.M. Brown, 402(MLR):Jul86-787
J.M. McGlathery, 301(JEGP):Apr86-309
W. Wittkowski, 133:Band19Heft3/4-353
Weiss, M. No Go on Jackson Street.
N. Callendar, 441:30Aug87-29
Weiss, P. Philosophy in Process. (Vol 7, Pt 2)
T. Krettek, 543:Jun87-798
A. Reix, 542:Jan-Mar86-96
Weiss, P. Toward a Perfected State.
R.B. Marcin, 543:Mar87-603
Weiss, R.L. & C. Butterworth - see Maimonides, M.
Weiss, T. The Man from Porlock.
P. Makin, 402(MLR):Oct86-992
Weiss, W., ed. Die englische Satire.*
B. Nugel, 566:Spring87-130
Weisser, M.R. A Brotherhood of Memory.*
B. Levine, 287:Aug-Sep86-27
Weissmann, G. They All Laughed at Christopher Columbus.
M.W. Lear, 441:5Apr87-39
Weitz, M.C. Femmes.
M.B. Sarde, 207(FR):Feb87-410
Weitze, K.J. California's Mission Revival.*
P. Borsook, 45:May86-73
C. Robertson, 658:Winter86-315
Weitzenhoffer, F. The Havemeyers.
J. Russell, 441:31May87-11
Weitzmann, K. & H.L. Kessler. The Cotton Genesis.
R. Cormack, 617(TLS):14Aug87-878
Weitzmann-Fiedler, J. Romanische gravierte Bronzeschalen, Berlin.
E.J. Beer, 683:Band49Heft1-96
Weixlmann, J. & C.J. Fontenot, eds. Studies in Black American Literature. (Vol 2)
N. Harris, 395(MFS):Winter86-635
von Weizsäcker, R. A Voice From Germany.*
G.A. Craig, 453(NYRB):8Oct87-38

Wekker, H. & L. Haegeman. A Modern Course
in English Syntax.
　　R.R. van Oirsouw, 353:Vol24No4-836
　　Seok Choong Song, 660(Word):Dec86-219
Welch, C.B. Liberty and Utility.*
　　B.G. Garnham, 83:Autumn86-242
Welch, D. Fragments of a Life Story. (M.
De-la-Noy, ed)
　　C. Hawtree, 617(TLS):8May87-488
Welch, R. Hand & Machine.
　　B. Beaumont-Nesbitt, 324:Mar87-335
Welch, R.E., Jr. Response to Revolution.
　　R.B. Gray, 263(RIB):Vol36No2-195
　　639(VQR):Spring86-53
Welch, S.C. India: Art and Culture 1300-
1900.*
　　42(AR):Spring86-248
Welch, T.L., comp. Bibliografía de la
literatura uruguaya.
　　S. de Mundo Lo, 263(RIB):Vol36No1-72
Weldon, F. The Heart of the Country.
　　C. Chanteau, 362:5Feb87-28
　　J.K.L. Walker, 617(TLS):13Feb87-164
Weldon, F. The Hearts and Lives of Men.
　　L. Heron, 362:17Sep87-25
　　S. Mackay, 617(TLS):11-17Sep87-977
Weldon, F. Letters to Alice.*
　　L.D. Mitchell, 95(CLAJ):Sep86-104
Weldon, F. Polaris and Other Stories.*
　　G. Finn, 99:Aug/Sep86-36
Weldon, F. The Rules of Life.
　　E. Leider, 441:2Aug87-16
　　S. Mackay, 617(TLS):11-17Sep87-977
Weldon, F. The Shrapnel Academy.*
　　C. Sigal, 441:26Apr87-14
Weldon, F. Rebecca West.
　　A. Crozier, 395(MFS):Winter86-671
Wellas, M.B. Griechisches aus dem Umkreis
Kaiser Friedrichs II.
　　J.M. Powell, 589:Apr86-481
Wellbery, D.E. Lessing's "Laocoon."*
　　A.A. Kuzniar, 564:Nov86-327
　　E. Methuen, 83:Autumn86-242
　　M. Morton, 221(GQ):Spring86-311
　　L. Weissberg, 400(MLN):Apr86-725
Wellek, R. The Attack on Literature and
Other Essays.
　　S.G. Nichols, 107(CRCL):Sep86-465
　　R. Selden, 402(MLR):Apr86-419
Wellek, R. Four Critics.
　　G. Bisztray, 107(CRCL):Jun86-263
Wellek, R. A History of Modern Criticism,
1750-1950.* (Vol 5)
　　C. Baldick, 617(TLS):18-24Dec87-1406
　　V. Nemoianu, 400(MLN):Dec86-1245
　　639(VQR):Summer86-88
Wellek, R. A History of Modern Criticism,
1750-1950.* (Vol 6)
　　C. Baldick, 617(TLS):18-24Dec87-1406
　　V. Nemoianu, 400(MLN):Dec86-1245
　　639(VQR):Summer86-89
Weller, A.S. Lorado in Paris.
　　H. Adams, 658:Summer/Autumn86-209
　　A.A. McLees, 207(FR):Mar87-578
Wellershoff, D. Winner Takes All.
　　J. Brooks, 441:4Jan87-20
Welliver, W. Dante in Hell.
　　G. Costa, 545(RPh):Nov86-215
Wellman, C. A Theory of Rights.
　　J. Waldron, 185:Jan87-474
Wellman, C. Welfare Rights.
　　V. Held, 482(PhR):Jan86-150

Wellmer, A. Zur Dialektik von Moderne und
Postmoderne.*
　　R. Rochlitz, 98:Jan-Feb86-7
Wells, C.J. German.
　　M. Durrell, 402(MLR):Oct87-1015
Wells, H.G. The Future in America.
　　H. Beaver, 617(TLS):18-24Sep87-1020
Wells, H.G. The Man With a Nose and Other
Uncollected Short Stories of H.G. Wells.
(J.R. Hammond, ed)
　　J. Huntington, 561(SFS):Jul86-200
Wells, R.H. Shakespeare, Politics and the
State.
　　T. Hawkes, 617(TLS):10Apr87-390
Wells, S., ed. The Cambridge Companion to
Shakespeare Studies.
　　J. Wilders, 617(TLS):30Oct-5Nov87-1197
Wells, S. Re-Editing Shakespeare for the
Modern Reader.*
　　D. Bevington, 402(MLR):Jul87-704
　　P. Edwards, 40(AEB):Vol8No4-260
　　P.C. McGuire, 115:Summer86-423
　　D. Mehl, 72:Band223Heft2-470
　　L. Scragg, 148:Autumn86-102
Wells, S. Shakespeare.*
　　M. Willems, 189(EA):Jan-Mar87-81
Wells, S. - see "Shakespeare Survey"
Wells, S. & G. Taylor - see Shakespeare, W.
Welsh, A. George Eliot and Blackmail.*
　　D. Carroll, 637(VS):Winter87-266
　　D. Cottom, 594:Fall86-338
　　D.P. Deneau, 268(IFR):Winter87-45
　　G. Levine, 454:Spring87-279
Welskopf, E.C. Soziale Typenbegriffe im
alten Griechenland und ihr Fortleben in
den Sprachen der Welt. (Vols 1 & 2)
　　T.J. Saunders, 123:Vol36No2-330
Welt, E. Berlin Wild.*
　　J. Mellors, 364:Jul86-103
Welty, E. One Writer's Beginnings.*
　　E. Alarcón, 152(UDQ):Fall86-155
　　P.W. Prenshaw, 534(RALS):Spring-
　　Autumn84-259
Welzig, W., ed. Katalog gedruckter
deutschsprachiger katholischer Predigt-
sammlungen. (Vol 1)
　　C. Daxelmüller, 196:Band27Heft1/2-148
Welzig, W. & others - see Schnitzler, A.
Wen Mei-hui, ed. Studies in Scott.
　　Peng Fumin, 588(SSL):Vol21-369
Wendorf, R., ed. Articulate Images.*
　　C.L. Brooks, 541(RES):Feb86-128
Wennberg, R.N. Life in the Balance.
　　R.S., 185:Oct86-307
Wennergren, E.B., C.H. Antholt & M.D. Whit-
aker. Agricultural Development in Bang-
ladesh.
　　J.P. Thorp, 293(JASt):Aug86-789
Wensberg, P.C. Land's Polaroid.
　　T. Goldwasser, 441:25Oct87-39
Wentworth, M. James Tissot.*
　　R. Thomson, 59:Mar86-108
Wentzlaff-Eggebert, F-W. & E. Andreas
Gryphius 1616-1664.
　　K.F. Otto, Jr., 406:Fall86-397
Wenzel, H-E. Lied vom wilden Mohn.*
　　B. Leistner, 601(SuF):Sep-Oct85-1094
Wenzel, S. Preachers, Poets, and the Early
English Lyric.
　　J.V. Fleming, 344:Summer87-150
Werenskiold, M. The Concept of Expression-
ism.
　　J. Lloyd, 90:Jul86-516

van der Werf, H. The Extant Troubadour
Melodies. (G.A. Bond, ed)
  M. Switten, 317:Summer86-381
Werhane, P. & K. D'Andrade, eds. Profit
and Responsibility.
  S.C., 185:Oct86-310
Werkmeister, W.H. Kant.
  D.E. Christensen, 543:Dec86-339
Werkmeister, W.H. Kant's Silent Decade.
  E.C. Sandberg, 342:Band77Heft2-252
Werlen, I. Gebrauch und Bedeutung der
Modalverben in alemannischen Dialekten.
  W.P. Ahrens, 350:Mar87-187
Werner, E. The Sacred Bridge. (Vol 2)
  J.A. Smith, 410(M&L):Jul86-316
Werth, P. Focus, Coherence and Emphasis.
  G. Brown, 307:Aug86-142
  N. Erteschik-Shir, 297(JL):Mar86-208
  M.S. Rochemont, 320(CJL):Summer86-189
Wertheim, A.F. American Popular Culture.
  P.Z. Du Bois, 87(BB):Dec86-260
Wertsch, J.V., ed. Culture, Communication
and Cognition.
  P.G. Patel, 320(CJL):Winter86-377
Wesling, D., ed. Internal Resistances.*
  L. Bartlett, 649(WAL):Nov86-250
Wessel, F. Probleme der Metaphorik und die
Minnemetaphorik in Gottfrieds von Strass-
burg "Tristan und Isolde."
  D.H. Green, 402(MLR):Apr86-527
  T. Tomasek, 684(ZDA):Band115Heft4-175
Wessel, H. Logik.
  J. Dölling, 682(ZPSK):Band39Heft3-401
Wessell, L.P., Jr. The Philosophical Back-
ground to Friedrich Schiller's Aesthetics
of Living Form.*
  J.F. Hyde, Jr., 406:Fall86-399
Wessels, H-F., ed. Aufklärung.
  C.P. Magill, 83:Spring86-121
  G. Mieth, 654(WB):3/1986-520
  T.G. Sauer, 221(GQ):Spring86-309
Wessely, O., ed. Bruckner Symposium "Die
österreichische Symphonie nach Anton
Bruckner."
  P. Banks, 410(M&L):Jan86-77
Wessely, O. & E. Kanduth – see de Monte, P.
West, B. Epic, Folk, and Christian Tradi-
tions in the "Poema de Fernán González."*
  G. West, 402(MLR):Jul86-761
West, C. Routine Complications.
  W.A. Kretzschmar, Jr., 35(AS):Fall86-
277
West, D. The Living is Easy.
  H. Eley, 617(TLS):17Apr87-410
West, F. Gilbert Murray.*
  L. Greenspan, 556:Summer86-79
West, I. Pride Against Prejudice.
  L. Ryan, 381:Mar86-49
West, J. The State of Stony Lonesome.
  P. Henetz, 649(WAL):Nov86-240
West, J.L.W. 3d, ed. Conversations with
William Styron.
  F.C. Watkins, 395(MFS):Winter86-623
West, J.L.W. 3d. A "Sister Carrie" Port-
folio.
  H.J. Dawson, 26(ALR):Spring87-91
  R.W. Dowell, 395(MFS):Summer86-263
  42(AR):Spring86-248
West, M.L. Greek Metre.
  M.W. Haslam, 122:Jan86-90
  C.M.J. Sicking, 394:Vol39fasc3/4-423

West, M.L. The Hesiodic "Catalogue of
Women."
  M. Davies, 123:Vol36No1-6
  G.P. Edwards, 303(JoHS):Vol106-204
West, M.L. The Orphic Poems.*
  R. Janko, 122:Apr86-154
West, N. Molehunt.
  N. Hiley, 617(TLS):22May87-539
West, P. Sheer Fiction.
  D. Sacks, 441:9Aug87-21
West, R. Cousin Rosamund.*
  W. Lesser, 249(HudR):Autumn86-481
  42(AR):Summer86-380
West, R. Family Memories. (F. Evans, ed)
  F. Donaldson, 617(TLS):20-26Nov87-
1277
West, R. Sunflower.*
  P-L. Adams, 61:Mar87-94
  T. Mallon, 441:15Feb87-26
West, R. & J.E. Trevelyan. Alternative
Medicine.
  K. Brewer, 87(BB):Dec86-262
West, R.H. Reginald Scot and Renaissance
Writings on Witchcraft. (A.F. Kinney,
ed)
  W. Shumaker, 551(RenQ):Summer86-323
  B.H. Traister, 570(SQ):Winter86-543
West, T.G. & G.S. – see "Plato and Aris-
tophanes: Four Texts on Socrates"
West, W.J. Truth Betrayed.
  S. Hood, 362:12Nov87-28
Westbrook, M. Oregon or Bust.
  L. Sanazaro, 649(WAL):May86-86
Westen, D. Self and Society.
  R.E.G., 185:Jan87-495
Westenholz, A. Den glemte abe.
  E. Cederborg, 172(Edda):1986/1-91
Westerberg, K. Cypriote Ships from the
Bronze Age to c. 500 B.C.
  V. Tatton-Brown, 123:Vol36No1-162
Westerdijk, P. African Metal Implements.
  B. Jarocki, 2(AfrA):Nov85-85
Westergaard, K. State and Rural Society in
Bangladesh.
  J.P. Thorp, 293(JASt):Aug86-789
Westermeyer, J. Poppies, Pipes, and
People.
  J.M. Halpern, 293(JASt):Feb86-472
Westerweel, B. Patterns and Patterning.
  S. Gottlieb, 551(RenQ):Winter86-816
Westhover, J.G. – see McCarthy, J.
Westlake, M. Imaginary Women.
  S. Bradfield, 617(TLS):11-17Dec87-1374
Westling, C. Idealismens estetik.
  M.J. Blackwell, 563(SS):Autumn86-437
Westling, L. Sacred Groves and Ravaged
Gardens.*
  R.H. Brinkmeyer, Jr., 27(AL):May86-301
  B.L. Clark, 454:Winter87-188
  C. Kahane, 301(JEGP):Oct86-595
  G.W. Koon, 573(SSF):Winter86-132
  N. Polk, 594:Winter86-456
  D. Roberts, 184(EIC):Apr86-180
Westlund, J. Shakespeare's Reparative
Comedies.*
  R.N. Watson, 405(MP):Nov86-216
  D. Willbern, 570(SQ):Spring86-126
Weston, J. The Real American Cowboy.
  L. Clayton, 649(WAL):Aug86-146
Westphal, P.B., M.W. Conner & N. Choat,
eds. Meeting the Call for Excellence in
the Foreign Language Classroom.
  F.W. Medley, Jr., 399(MLJ):Winter86-422

Westphall, V. Mercedes Reales.
R.M. Adams, 453(NYRB):12Mar87-28
Weststeijn, W.G. Velimir Chlebnikov and
the Development of Poetical Language in
Russian Symbolism and Futurism.*
R.R. Milner-Gulland, 402(MLR):Apr86-541
Wetherbee, W. Chaucer and the Poets.*
N.F. Blake, 402(MLR):Oct86-974
P. Boitani, 589:Jul86-716
J.D. Burnley, 541(RES):Aug86-404
R.A. Shoaf, 301(JEGP):Jan86-102
Wetherell, W.D. The Man Who Loved Levit-
town.*
E. McGraw, 455:Mar86-69
D. Madden, 598(SoR):Summer87-728
Wetherill, P.M., ed. "L'Éducation senti-
mentale."
C. Wake, 402(MLR):Apr87-481
Wetherill, P.M. - see Flaubert, G.
Wetzel, K.M. Autonomie und Authentizität.
J. Köhler, 489(PJGG):Band3Heft1-204
Wetzels, L. & E. Sezer, eds. Studies in
Compensatory Lengthening.
J. Goldsmith, 350:Jun87-401
Wevers, L. - see Hyde, R.
Wexler, A. Emma Goldman.*
W.L. Frazer, 534(RALS):Spring-Autumn84-
198
Wexler, J. The Bequest and Other Stories.*
R.W. Harvey, 102(CanL):Winter85-170
Weydt, H., ed. Partikeln und Interaktion.*
U. Brausse & R. Pasch, 682(ZPSK):
Band39Heft4-513
Whalen, T. Philip Larkin and English
Poetry.
L. Mackinnon, 617(TLS):3Jul87-717
Whaling, F. The Rise of the Religious
Significance of Rāma.
R.W. Lariviere, 318(JAOS):Jan/Mar85-183
Whalley, G. Studies in Literature and the
Humanities.* (B. Crick & J. Ferns, eds)
S. Lukits, 529(QQ):Summer86-419
Whalley, G. - see Coleridge, S.T.
Whalley, P. Bandits.
T.J. Binyon, 617(TLS):9Jan87-42
Wharton, T.F. Samuel Johnson and the Theme
of Hope.*
J.H. Pittock, 83:Spring86-105
Wharton, W. Tidings.
S. Kenney, 441:6Dec87-18
Wheeler, J.A. & W.H. Zurek, eds. Quantum
Theory and Measurement.*
J.F. Tobar, 606:Jun86-527
Wheeler, K., ed. German Aesthetic and Lit-
erary Criticism. (Vol 3)
L. Dietrick, 564:Nov86-338
N.D.B. Saul, 83:Autumn86-296
H.M. Schueller, 290(JAAC):Spring87-301
Wheeler, L.W., ed. Ten Northeast Poets.
K. McCarra, 571(ScLJ):Winter86-37
Wheeler, M. English Fiction of the Victo-
rian Period, 1830-1890.*
M. Dodsworth, 175:Spring86-104
L. Hartveit, 179(ES):Oct86-460
S. Monod, 189(EA):Jul-Sep86-357
Wheeler, M. - see "The Oxford Russian-
English Dictionary"
Wheeler, R. Sword over Richmond.*
639(VQR):Summer86-78
Wheeler, R.P. Shakespeare's Development
and the Problem Comedies.
F.W. Brownlow, 402(MLR):Jan86-170

Wheelis, A. The Doctor of Desire.
B.L. Knapp, 441:10May87-20
Whelan, F.G. Order and Artifice in Hume's
Political Philosophy.*
N. Capaldi, 319:Oct87-604
J. Robertson, 173(ECS):Winter86/87-238
639(VQR):Winter86-16
Whelan, R. Robert Capa.*
H. Martin, 507:Jul/Aug86-303
Whelan, R. & C. Capa - see "Robert Capa:
Photographs"
Whenham, J., ed. Claudio Monteverdi:
"Orfeo."
W. Edwards, 617(TLS):13Feb87-159
Whiffen, M. & C. Breeze. Pueblo Deco.*
D. Gebhard, 576:Sep86-313
J.V. Iovine, 45:Feb86-77
Whigham, F. Ambition and Privilege.*
A. Thompson, 506(PSt):May86-75
125:Winter86-235
Whinnom, K. The Spanish Sentimental
Romance 1440-1550.*
A. Gier, 72:Band223Heft2-475
Whipple, A.B.C. The Challenge.
T. Gibbs, 441:26Jul87-6
Whipple, G. Life Cycle.*
D. Precosky, 198:Spring86-91
Whisnant, D.E. All That is Native and
Fine.*
R.A. Banes, 106:Spring86-93
D.J. Dyen, 187:Spring/Summer87-365
Whitaker, B. The Global Connection.
J. Ryle, 617(TLS):23-29Oct87-1163
Whitaker, M. Arthur's Kingdom of Adven-
ture.
J.D. Burnley, 179(ES):Feb86-81
P.J.C. Field, 382(MAE):1986/2-304
M. Halsall, 178:Mar86-101
Whitaker, M. The Crystal Fountain and
Other Stories.
P. Craig, 617(TLS):18-24Sep87-1026
Whitaker, P. Brecht's Poetry.*
E. Boa, 402(MLR):Oct87-1040
Whitaker, T. Tom Stoppard.*
E. Diamond, 130:Spring86-79
Whitby, M. & M. - see Theophylactus Simo-
catta
White, A. Schelling.*
M.G. Vater, 319:Apr87-302
White, A.R. Grounds of Liability.
J.H. Bogart, 185:Apr87-673
White, A.R. Rights.*
J.E. Bickenbach, 483:Jan86-128
N.E. Bowie, 484(PPR):Sep86-165
S.M. Uniacke, 63:Jun86-241
White, B.R. The Forgotten Cattle King.
L. Milazzo, 584(SWR):Summer86-402
White, C. The Pictures in the Collection
of Her Majesty the Queen: The Dutch Pic-
tures.*
K. Andrews, 39:May86-364
White, C. Rembrandt.*
P.C. Sutton, 90:Sep86-680
White, C. Peter Paul Rubens.
J. Russell, 441:6Dec87-11
White, C. Giovanni Battista Viotti (1755-
1824).
S. McVeigh, 410(M&L):Oct86-397
White, D. Cyrene. (Vol 1)
R.A. Tomlinson, 303(JoHS):Vol106-246
White, E.M. Teaching and Assessing Writ-
ing.*
G. Brossell, 126(CCC):Oct86-354

Wiles, D. The Early Plays of Robin Hood.*
 C. Fees, 203:Vol97No1-114
Wiles, D. Shakespeare's Clown.
 J. Wilders, 617(TLS):30Oct-5Nov87-1197
Wiles, M. God's Action in the World.
 G. Jantzen, 617(TLS):20Mar87-305
Wiley, N. The Great State Fair of Texas.
 L. Milazzo, 584(SWR):Autumn86-538
Wilhelm, F. - see Straus, O.
Wilhelm, J.J. The American Roots of Ezra
Pound.
 M.B., 295(JML):Nov86-529
 W. Harmon, 569(SR):Fall86-630
 M. Moran, 27(AL):Mar86-114
Wilken, R.L. The Christians as the Romans
Saw Them.*
 A. Wasserstein, 313:Vol76-302
Wilkes, L. The Aesthetic Obsession.
 W. Charlton, 89(BJA):Autumn86-406
Wilkie, A. Biedermeier.
 J. Russell, 441:6Dec87-89
Wilkins, C.L. & H.M. - see López de Ayala,
P.
Wilkins, T. Cherokee Tragedy. (2nd ed)
 D.R. Lewis, 649(WAL):Nov86-266
 L. Milazzo, 584(SWR):Summer86-402
Wilkinson, C.F. American Indians, Time,
and the Law.
 A. Boyer, 441:8Mar87-21
Wilkinson, M. Hemingway and Turgenev.
 M. Sacharoff, 295(JML):Nov86-485
Wilks, M., ed. The World of John of Salis-
bury.
 F.R. Swietek & M.D. Jordan, 319:Jul87-
444
Will, E. Histoire politique du monde
hellénistique (323-30 av J.C.), II.
 G.J.D. Aalders H. Wzn., 394:Vol39
fasc1/2-217
Willan, B. Sol Plaatje.
 D. Kennedy, 637(VS):Spring87-422
 N.C. Manganyi, 538(RAL):Fall86-393
Willard, C.C. Christine de Pizan.*
 D.R. Howard, 551(RenQ):Spring86-69
 A.J. Kennedy, 208(FS):Jul86-315
Willard, D. Logic and the Objectivity of
Knowledge.*
 V. Pietersma, 484(PPR):Jun87-688
 R.S. Tragesser, 482(PhR):Oct86-611
Willcox, W.B. - see Franklin, B.
Wille, G. Der Aufbau der Werke des Tac-
itus.
 J. Hellegouarc'h, 555:Vol59fasc2-320
Willeford, C. Sideswipe.
 N. Callendar, 441:19Apr87-22
442(NY):23Feb87-136
Willemart, P. O Manuscrito em Gustave
Flaubert.
 M.A. Esteban, 446(NCFS):Fall-Winter
86/87-213
Willemen, C. The Chinese Hevajratantra.
 J.W. de Jong, 259(IIJ):Jan86-65
Willett, J. Brecht in Context.*
 R.J. Goebel, 222(GR):Winter86-38
Willett, J. The Weimar Years.*
 V. Jirat-Wasiutyński, 529(QQ):Summer86-
339
Willett, J. & R. Manheim - see Brecht, B.
William VII. The Poetry of William VII,
Count of Poitiers, IX Duke of Aquitaine.*
(G.A. Bond, ed & trans)
 S. Kay, 382(MAE):1986/1-142

William of Lucca. Wilhelmus Lucensis, "Co-
mentum in tertiam ierarchiam Dionisii que
est de divinis nominibus." (F. Gastal-
delli, ed)
 T.M. Tomasic, 589:Jan86-252
Williams, A. Prophetic Strain.*
 D. Brooks-Davies, 83:Autumn86-258
 A.J. Weitzman, 173(ECS):Fall86-101
 D. Womersley, 541(RES):Nov86-572
Williams, A.D. - see Galbraith, J.K.
Williams, A.S. The Rich Man and the Dis-
eased Poor in Early Victorian Literature.
 P. Beer, 617(TLS):11-17Dec87-1380
Williams, B. Ethics and the Limits of
Philosophy.*
 S. Blackburn, 518:Oct86-193
 H. Harriott, 258:Mar86-98
 J. McDowell, 393(Mind):Jul86-377
 J.A. Miller, 396(ModA):Winter86-67
 S. Morrison, 529(QQ):Autumn86-696
 T. Nagel, 311(JP):Jun86-351
 S. Wolf, 185:Jul87-821
Williams, C.K. Flesh and Blood.
 E. Hirsch, 441:23Aug87-20
Williams, D. Eye of the Father.
 M. Frutkin, 99:Jun/Jul86-43
 T.B. Vincent, 198:Summer86-83
Williams, D. The India Office, 1858-1869.
 L. Zastoupil, 293(JASt):Feb86-434
Williams, D. Treasure in Roubles.
 T.J. Binyon, 617(TLS):17Apr87-411
Williams, D.R. Duff.
 P.E. Roy, 529(QQ):Spring86-167
Williams, F. Elementary Classical Greek.
 J.E. Rexine, 399(MLJ):Spring86-71
Williams, F.B., Jr., ed. The Gardyners
Passetaunce [c. 1512].*
 K.F. Pantzer, 78(BC):Summer86-247
Williams, G. "Macbeth."*
 R.L. Smallwood, 611(TN):Vol40No3-137
Williams, G. Harri Tudur a Chymry/Henry
Tudor and Wales.
 B. Ó Cuív, 112:Vol18-219
Williams, H. Rousseau and Romantic Auto-
biography.
 J.F. Hamilton, 207(FR):Oct86-123
 J. Voisine, 535(RHL):Mar-Apr86-291
Williams, J., ed. Eyes on the Prize.
 J. Haskins, 441:25Jan87-20
Williams, J.A. Jacob's Ladder.
 G. Packer, 441:15Nov87-26
Williams, J.A., ed. Themes of Islamic
Civilization.
 W.R. Roff, 302:Vol22No1-124
Williams, M. Black Theatre in the 1960s
and 1970s.
 D.W. Beams, 615(TJ):May86-247
Williams, M. Women in the English Novel,
1800-1900.
 A. Murphy, 158:Dec86-194
Williams, M.I., ed. A Directory of Rare
Books and Special Collections in the
United Kingdom and the Republic of
Ireland.
 D.J. Shaw, 354:Dec86-390
 J.H. Wiener, 635(VPR):Fall86-111
Williams, N. My Brother's Keeper?
 B. Grantham, 157:No159-47
Williams, N. The Unlovely Child.*
 J.D. McClatchy, 491:Oct86-31
Williams, N. Witchcraft.
 W. Brandmark, 362:4Jun87-48
 J. Melmoth, 617(TLS):12Jun87-626

Williams, N.D. A Lexicon for the Poetical Books.
  S. Kaufman, 318(JAOS):Oct/Dec85-800
Williams, P., ed. Bach, Handel, Scarlatti.
  G.J. Buelow, 410(M&L):Jul86-290
  E. Cross, 83:Autumn86-301
  G.B. Stauffer, 414:Vol72No2-272
Williams, P. The Organ Music of J-S. Bach.* (Vol 3) [entry in prev was of Vols 1-3]
  G. Guillard, 537:Vol72No2-292
Williams, R. Loyalties.
  S. Manley, 441:22Mar87-28
Williams, R.C. Klaus Fuchs, Atom Spy.
  Z. Steiner, 441:13Dec87-9
  S. Toulmin, 453(NYRB):19Nov87-54
Williams, R.C. The Other Bolsheviks.
  R. Service, 617(TLS):6-12Nov87-1213
Williams, R.L., ed. Ensayos de literatura colombiana.
  B. Torres Caballero, 240(HR):Summer86-363
Williams, R.L. Gabriel García Márquez.
  R. Janes, 238:Mar86-117
  E. Skinner, 395(MFS):Winter86-646
  B. Torres Caballero, 240(HR):Autumn86-492
Williams, R.L. Mario Vargas Llosa.
  G.R. McMurray, 268(IFR):Summer87-103
Williams, S. Conflict of Interest.
  R.G., 185:Oct86-305
Williams, S. Diocletian and the Roman Recovery.
  T.H. Watkins, 124:May-Jun87-386
Williams, S. German Actors of the Eighteenth and Nineteenth Centuries.
  G. Flaherty, 301(JEGP):Oct86-630
  C.R. Mueller, 610:Autumn86-251
Williams, S.A. Dessa Rose.*
  K. Bucknell, 617(TLS):17Jul87-765
  E.B. Kelly, 95(CLAJ):Jun87-515
Williams, S.Y. American Feasts.
  W. & C. Cowen, 639(VQR):Spring86-67
Williams, T. Collected Stories.
  P.T. Nolan, 573(SSF):Spring86-205
  639(VQR):Summer86-92
Williams, T. The Moon Pinnace.*
  W.H. Pritchard, 249(HudR):Winter87-653
Williams, U. & W. Williams-Knapp, eds. Die "Elsässische Legenda Aurea." (Vol 1)
  K. Gärtner, 684(ZDA):Band115Heft1-22
Williams, W.C. The Collected Poems 1909-1939. (A.W. Litz & C. MacGowan, eds)
  J. Mole, 176:Jul/Aug87-46
  R. Pinsky, 441:4Jan87-3
Williams, W.C. The Doctor Stories.* (R. Coles, ed)
  I. Bamforth, 617(TLS):22May87-558
Williams, W.C. Something to Say. (J.E.B. Breslin, ed)
  42(AR):Spring86-248
Williams, W.J. Voice of the Whirlwind.
  G. Jonas, 441:2Aug87-25
Williams, W.L. The Spirit and the Flesh.
  E. Gregersen, 441:29Mar87-10
Williams, W.P. & C.S. Abbott. An Introduction to Bibliographical and Textual Studies.*
  H. Amory, 517(PBSA):Vol80No2-243
  P-G. Boucé, 189(EA):Jan-Mar87-78
Williams-Krapp, W. Überlieferung und Gattung.
  E. Catholy, 133:Band18Heft4-360

Williamson, A. Introspection and Contemporary Poetry.*
  T. Gardner, 219(GaR):Winter86-1016
  A. Golding, 405(MP):Nov86-235
  W.H. Pritchard, 31(ASch):Autumn86-553
Williamson, C., Jr. Desert Light.
  N. Callendar, 441:12Jul87-29
Williamson, E. The Half-Way House of Fiction.
  J.B. Hall, 304(JHP):Spring86-258
  F. Pierce, 402(MLR):Jul86-766
Williamson, H. The Illustrated Tarka the Otter.
  J.W. Blench, 161(DUJ):Jun86-389
Williamson, J. The Crucible of Race.*
  J.G. Taylor, 9(AlaR):Jan86-74
Williamson, K. - see Smart, C.
Williamson, P. Catalogue of Romanesque Sculpture.
  P. Hetherington, 39:Feb86-137
Williamson, R.K. Introduction to Hegel's Philosophy of Religion.
  K. Hart, 63:Jun86-227
Willinger, D., ed. An Anthology of Contemporary Belgian Plays 1970-1982.
  R. Trousson, 535(RHL):Nov-Dec86-1152
Willis, C. Lincoln's Dreams.
  G. Jonas, 441:7Jun87-18
Willis, J. - see Martianus Capella
Willis, M.S. Only Great Changes.
  J. Volkmer, 502(PrS):Fall86-134
Willis, P.C - see Moore, M.
Willis, S. Marguerite Duras.
  D. Coward, 617(TLS):10Jul87-741
Willmot, R. The Ribs of Dragonfly.*
  P. O'Brien, 102(CanL):Fall86-135
  B. Whiteman, 526:Summer86-98
Wills, G. Reagan's America.
  J. Beatty, 61:Mar87-90
  A. Brinkley, 617(TLS):22May87-535
  S. Hoffmann, 453(NYRB):28May87-3
  C.V. Woodward, 441:11Jan87-1
  442(NY):23Feb87-135
Wills, J.E., Jr. Embassies and Illusions.
  L.D. Kessler, 293(JASt):Nov85-134
Wilmerding, J., ed. In Honor of Paul Mellon, Collector and Benefactor.
  G. Reynolds, 39:Jun86-438
Wilmerding, J. Andrew Wyeth: The Helga Pictures.
  P-L. Adams, 61:Aug87-84
Wilmet, M. La détermination nominale.
  J.E. Joseph, 350:Jun87-434
Wilmet, M., ed. Sémantique Lexicale et Sémantique Grammaticale en Moyen Français.
  M. Stasse, 209(FM):Apr86-120
Wilmeth, D.B. & R. Cullen - see Daly, A.
Wilmut, R. From Fringe to Flying Circus.
  A.F. Sponberg, 615(TJ):May86-248
Wilmut, R. Kindly Leave the Stage!
  G. Robinson, 611(TN):Vol40No3-141
  O. Trilling, 157:No159-51
Wilshere, A.D. - see Saint Edmund of Abingdon
Wilson, A. The Collected Stories.
  M. Casserley, 617(TLS):6-12Nov87-1226
Wilson, A. & J.L. A Medieval Mirror.*
  A.,Henry, 354:Jun86-169
  E. Silber, 90:Aug86-609
  78(BC):Summer86-145

Wineman, S. The Politics of Human Serv-
ices.
C. Bradshaw, 529(QQ):Autumn86-704
Wing, D. Short-Title Catalogue of Books
Printed in England, Scotland, Ireland,
Wales, and British America and of English
Books Printed in Other Countries 1641-
1700. (Vol 2) (T.J. Crist, ed)
A. Mason, 517(PBSA):Vol80No2-255
Wing, N. The Limits of Narrative.
G.W. Ireland, 617(TLS):11-17Dec87-1381
Winks, R., ed. Colloquium on Crime.
P. Wolfe, 395(MFS):Winter86-707
639(VQR):Autumn86-136
Winks, R.W. Cloak and Gown.
G. Hodgson, 441:16Aug87-7
Winn, C. Legal Daisy Spacing.
529(QQ):Winter86-951
Winn, C.H. Jean de Sponde.*
D.L. Rubin, 551(RenQ):Summer86-321
Winn, J.A. John Dryden and His World.
A. Burgess, 61:Nov87-116
Winn, M.B. - see de Saint-Gelais, O.
Winner, A. Characters in the Twilight.
Y. Chevrel, 549(RLC):Jan-Mar86-71
Winner, L. The Whale and the Reactor.
R.E.G., 185:Apr87-704
Winnicott, D.W. Holding and Interpreta-
tion.*
O. Sacks, 441:24May87-3
Winnicott, D.W. The Spontaneous Gesture.
(F.R. Rodman, ed)
P. Lomas, 617(TLS):24Jul87-798
O. Sacks, 441:24May87-3
Winnifrith, T. - see Brontë, C.
Winnifrith, T. - see Brontë, P.B.
Winnifrith, T., P. Murray & K.W. Gransden,
eds. Aspects of the Epic.
G.D. Lord, 402(MLR):Jan87-153
Winnington-Ingram, R.P. Studies in Aes-
chylus.*
A.N. Michelini, 122:Apr86-163
Winograd, T. & G.F. Flores. Understanding
Computers and Cognition.
G.H. Morris, 583:Spring87-337
Winquist, C.E. Epiphanies of Darkness.
S.E.H., 185:Jul87-906
Winson, J. Brain and Psyche.
J.J. Ratey, 529(QQ):Autumn86-690
Winston, D. & J. Dillon. Two Treatises of
Philo of Alexandria.
J. Mansfeld, 394:Vol39fasc3/4-491
Winter, D.E. Stephen King.
G.K. Wolfe, 395(MFS):Spring86-133
Winter, J.M. The Great War and the British
People.
P. Renshaw, 617(TLS):15May87-510
Winter, K.H. Marietta Holley.*
E. Hedges, 534(RALS):Spring-Autumn84-
186
Winter, R. The California Bungalow.
C. Robertson, 658:Winter86-315
Winterbottom, M., ed. The "Minor Declama-
tions" Ascribed to Quintilian.
H.M. Hine, 123:Vol36No1-58
Winternitz, H. East Along the Equator.
G. Overholser, 441:20Sep87-30
442(NY):16Nov87-160
Winters, A. The Key to the City.
J.D. McClatchy, 491:Oct86-31
L. Rector, 249(HudR):Autumn86-514
Winters, M., ed. The Romance of Hunbaut.
G.S. Giauque, 589:Oct86-1012

"Winter's Tales."* (new ser, Vol 2) (R.
Baird-Smith, ed)
J. Mellors, 362:1Jan87-22
Winterson, J. Oranges Are Not the Only
Fruit.
U. Hegi, 441:8Nov87-26
Winterson, J. The Passion.
A. Duchêne, 617(TLS):26Jun87-697
Wintle, S. - see Kipling, R.
Winton, T. Minimum of Two.
H. Jacobson, 617(TLS):27Nov-3Dec87-
1307
Winton, T. An Open Swimmer.
B. Matthews, 381:Mar86-83
Winton, T. Scisson and Other Stories.
H. Jacobson, 617(TLS):27Nov-3Dec87-
1307
B. Matthews, 381:Mar86-83
Winton, T. Shallows.*
B. Matthews, 381:Mar86-83
442(NY):12Jan87-101
Winton, T. That Eye, the Sky.*
G. Epps, 441:17May87-50
B. Matthews, 381:Mar86-83
Wippel, J.F. Metaphysical Themes in Thomas
Aquinas.*
J.F. Ross, 319:Oct87-592
Wirsung, C. Die Celestina-Übersetzungen
von Christof Wirsung. (K.V. Kisch & U.
Ritzenhoff, eds)
J.T. Snow, 551(RenQ):Autumn86-556
Wirth, G. Studien zur Alexandergeschichte.
S. Hornblower, 123:Vol36No2-330
Wirth, J.R., ed. Beyond the Sentence.*
G.D. Prideaux, 320(CJL):Summer86-185
S.A. Thompson, 355(LSoc):Sep86-407
Wiseman, J. A History of the British Pig.*
C. Hawtree, 364:Aug/Sep86-155
Wiseman, T.P. Catullus and his World.
P.Y. Forsyth, 487:Summer86-220
Wishard, A. Oral Formulaic Composition in
the Spielmannsepik.
D.H. Green, 402(MLR):Jan86-243
Wishart, T. On Sonic Art.
C. Fox, 607:Jun86-37
Wismann, H., ed. Walter Benjamin et Paris.
R. Rochlitz, 98:Dec86-1182
Wisniewski, R. Kreuzzugsdichtung.
H. Bekker, 221(GQ):Spring86-299
Wisse, R.R., ed. A Shtetl and other Yid-
dish Novellas.
M. Roshwald, 268(IFR):Summer87-117
Withers, C.W.J. Gaelic in Scotland 1698-
1981.*
S. Watson, 355(LSoc):Sep86-421
Witt, M.A.F. Existential Prisons.*
E. Gelfand, 210(FrF):Jan86-123
L.M. Porter, 395(MFS):Summer86-332
D.H. Walker, 402(MLR):Oct87-977
Wittes, C., ed. Behind the Scenes.
P. Leonard, 108:Winter86-138
Wittgenstein, L. Remarques mêlées.
C. Chauviré, 98:Dec86-1159
Wittkowski, W., ed. Goethe im Kontext.*
S. Atkins, 406:Fall86-369
D.F. Mahoney, 221(GQ):Spring86-315
Wittlin, C.J. - see López de Ayala, P.
Wittmann, R., ed. Bücherkataloge als
buchgeschichtliche Quellen in der frühen
Neuzeit.
J.L. Flood, 354:Sep86-277

Wittreich, J. "Image of that Horror."*
L.S. Champion, 179(ES):Aug86-370
R.E. Fortin, 301(JEGP):Jul86-448
R.S. White, 161(DUJ):Dec85-189
Wittreich, J. Interpreting Samson Agonis-
tes.
R. Rollin, 580(SCR):Spring87-59
Wittrock, W. Toulouse-Lautrec, the Com-
plete Prints.*
D.P. Becker, 90:Sep86-684
Witvliet, T. The Way of the Black Messiah.
D. Martin, 617(TLS):11-17Sep87-997
Wodak, R. Hilflose Nähe?*
G.E. Speidel, 355(LSoc):Sep86-410
Woesler, W. - see Heine, H.
Woffinden, B. Miscarriages of Justice.
C. Price, 362:29Oct87-27
Wogaman, J.P. Economics and Ethics.
P.F.C., 185:Apr87-685
Wohl, M. Techniques for Writing. (rev)
J.J. Kohn, 399(MLJ):Winter86-452
Wohlfart, G. Der spekulative Satz.*
M. Rosen, 192(EP):Jan-Mar86-135
Wolandt, G., ed. Kunst und Kunstforschung.
P. Somville, 542:Apr-Jun86-271
Wolf, B.J. Romantic Re-Vision.*
D.C. Miller, 403(MLS):Fall86-72
R. Thacker, 106:Spring86-51
Wolf, C. Cassandra.* (German title: Kas-
sandra.)
R. Buckeye, 532(RCF):Spring86-210
E. Waldstein, 221(GQ):Summer86-503
Wolf, C. Die Dimension des Autors.
M. Fulbrook, 617(TLS):2-8Oct87-1075
Wolf, F.A. Prolegomena to Homer 1795. (A.
Grafton, G.W. Most & J.E.G. Zetzel, eds &
trans)
M.W. Edwards, 24:Winter86-590
Wolf, G. & R. Rosenstein, eds. The Poetry
of Cercamon and Jaufré Rudel.*
S. Kay, 382(MAE):1986/1-142
S. Spence, 589:Apr86-486
"Konrad Wolf im Dialog." (D. Heinze & L.
Hoffmann, eds)
K. Kändler, 654(WB):9/1986-1575
Wolf, L. Le français régional d'Alsace.
N.C.W. Spence, 208(FS):Jan86-121
Wolf, M. Revolution Postponed.
N. Diamond, 293(JASt):Nov85-135
Wolf, R. & A. Terzani. Japan: The Beauty
of Food.
G. Greene, 441:13Dec87-28
Wolf, U. Das Problem des moralischen
Sollens.*
R. Bittner, 687:Jan-Mar86-142
Wolfe, C. The Rise of Modern Judicial
Review.
R.M., 185:Jan87-504
639(VQR):Summer86-94
Wolfe, G. The Urth of the New Sun.
G. Jonas, 441:20Dec87-18
Wolfe, M. Jolts.
B. Hayne, 627(UTQ):Fall86-244
Wolfe, P. Laden Choirs.
B. Kiernan, 71(ALS):May86-417
Wolfe, P. Something More Than Night.
L.D. Harred, 395(MFS):Summer86-370
Wolfe, P. - see Naudé, G.
Wolfe, T. The Bonfire of the Vanities.
F. Conroy, 441:1Nov87-1
N. Lemann, 61:Dec87-104

Wolfe, T. The Complete Short Stories of
Thomas Wolfe. (F.E. Skipp, ed)
M.K. Spears, 453(NYRB):24Sep87-34
Wolfe, T. Mannerhouse. (L.D. Rubin, Jr. &
J.L. Idol, Jr., eds)
S. Stutman, 580(SCR):Fall86-94
Wolfe, T. & A. Bernstein. My Other
Loneliness.* (S. Stutman, ed)
L. Willson, 569(SR):Winter86-131
Wolfe, T. & E. Nowell. Beyond Love and
Loyalty.* (R.S. Kennedy, ed)
L. Willson, 569(SR):Winter86-131
Wolff, C. Magnus Hirschfield.*
P. Parker, 364:Jun86-105
Wolff, C. Nouvelles pièces sur les erreurs
prétendues de la philosophie de Mons.
Wolff.
J. Ecole, 192(EP):Oct-Dec86-575
Wolff, C. Oratio de Sinarum philosophia
practica. (M. Albrecht, ed & trans)
D.E. Mungello, 706:Band18Heft1-120
Wolff, C.G. Emily Dickinson.*
C. Benfey, 453(NYRB):26Mar87-46
Wolff, F. Socrate.
M. Adam, 542:Oct-Dec86-509
Wolff, G. Providence.*
D. Flower, 249(HudR):Summer86-314
Wolff, J. Rilkes Grabschrift.*
U.K. Goldsmith, 406:Winter86-539
O. Olzien, 224(GRM):Band36Heft2-238
Wolff, R., ed. Heinrich Mann: Werk und
Wirkung. Heinrich Mann: Das Werk im
Exil.
H.F. Pfanner, 221(GQ):Summer86-491
Wolff, R.L. Nineteenth-Century Fiction.*
(Vol 4)
W.E. Smith, 517(PBSA):Vol80No2-274
Wolff, R.L. Nineteenth-Century Fiction.
(Vol 5)
W.E. Smith, 517(PBSA):Vol80No4-512
J. Sutherland, 617(TLS):16Jan87-66
Wolff, R.P. Understanding Marx.*
D. Schweickart, 311(JP):Dec86-729
Wolff, T. Back in the World.*
T. De Pietro, 249(HudR):Autumn86-487
J. Saari, 42(AR):Winter86-118
Wolff, T. The Barracks Thief and Selected
Stories.
M. Boruch, 434:Autumn86-98
L. Taylor, 617(TLS):6-12Nov87-1227
Wölfflin, H. Renaissance and Baroque.
C. Gould, 39:Nov86-451
"Heinrich Wölfflin: Autobiographie, Tage-
bücher und Briefe." (2nd ed) (J.
Gantner, ed)
M. Podro, 90:Apr86-299
Wolfram of Eschenbach. Titurel. (C.E.
Passage, ed & trans)
S.M. Johnson, 301(JEGP):Jul86-421
Wolfram von Eschenbach. Willehalm. (M.E.
Gibbs & S.M. Johnson, trans)
S.L. Clark, 221(GQ):Summer86-474
W. Crossgrove, 301(JEGP):Oct86-617
Wolfson, N. & E. Judd, eds. Sociolinguis-
tics and Language Acquisition.
M. Eisenstein, 355(LSoc):Mar86-99
Wolfzettel, F. Einführung in die franzö-
sische Literaturgeschichtsschreibung.*
C. Jordens, 356(LR):May86-168
U. Schulz-Buschhaus, 224(GRM):Band36
Heft1-117
Wolicka, E. Byt i Znak.
A.N. Woznicki, 543:Dec86-408

Woods, S. Under the Lake.
M. Stasio, 441:7Jun87-30
Woods, S.H., Jr. Oliver Goldsmith.
P. Dixon, 677(YES):Vol16-277
Woodson, T., L.N. Smith & N.H. Pearson –
see Hawthorne, N.
Woodward, B. Veil.
D.C. Martin, 441:18Oct87-1
T. Powers, 453(NYRB):19Nov87-8
M. Tingay, 362:5Nov87-28
Woodward, C.V. Thinking Back.*
B. Maine, 125:Spring86-339
Wooldridge, T.R. Concordance du Thresor de
la Langue Françoyse de Jean Nicot.
G. Roques, 553(RLiR):Jan-Jun86-245
Woolf, V. Beau Brummell et autres essais.
(G. Villeneuve, ed & trans)
F. Coblence, 98:Apr86-341
Woolf, V. The Complete Shorter Fiction of
Virginia Woolf.* (S. Dick, ed)
C.R. Miller, 627(UTQ):Fall86-113
639(VQR):Autumn86-125
Woolf, V. The Essays of Virginia Woolf.*
(Vol 1) (A. McNeillie, ed)
W. Maxwell, 442(NY):13Apr87-100
Woolf, V. The Essays of Virginia Woolf.
(Vol 2) (A. McNeillie, ed)
P.N. Furbank, 617(TLS):9-15Oct87-1107
Woolf, V. Melymbrosia. (L.A. De Salvo,
ed) Pointz Hall. (M.A. Leaska, ed)
J. Marcus, 40(AEB):Vol8No4-272
Woollatt, R. – see Souster, R.
Woolley, B. Time & Place.
M. Terry, 649(WAL):Aug86-140
Woolley, P. Child of the Northern Spring.
D.G. Hartwell, 441:16Aug87-16
Woolrich, C. Darkness at Dawn.
P. Wolfe, 573(SSF):Spring86-208
Woolverton, J.F. Colonial Anglicanism in
North America.*
B.E. Steiner, 656(WMQ):Apr86-319
Woozley, A.D. Law and Obedience.
G. Lesses, 41:Fall85-318
Wordsworth, D. Letters of Dorothy Words-
worth.* (A.G. Hill, ed)
R. Sheets, 637(VS):Autumn86-145
639(VQR):Spring86-46
Wordsworth, J., M.C. Jaye & R. Woof. Wil-
liam Wordsworth and the Age of English
Romanticism.
C. Rosen, 453(NYRB):17Dec87-22
Wordsworth, W. The Borderers.* (R.
Osborn, ed)
J.K. Chandler, 405(MP):Nov86-196
R. Langbaum, 591(SIR):Winter86-571
Wordsworth, W. The Cornell Wordsworth.
(S.M. Parrish, ed)
C. Rosen, 453(NYRB):17Dec87-22
Wordsworth, W. An Evening Walk. (J. Ave-
rill, ed) Descriptive Sketches. (E.
Birdsall, with P.M. Zall, eds)
J.K. Chandler, 405(MP):Nov86-196
P.D. Sheats, 661(WC):Autumn86-214
Wordsworth, W. The Fourteen-Book "Pre-
lude" by William Wordsworth. (W.J.B.
Owen, ed)
S.J. Wolfson, 661(WC):Autumn86-209
Wordsworth, W. The Manuscript of William
Wordsworth's Poems. (W.H. Kelliher, ed)
A.R. Jones, 354:Jun86-184
Wordsworth, W. The Oxford Authors: Wil-
liam Wordsworth. (S. Gill, ed)
P. Drew, 402(MLR):Apr87-454

Wordsworth, W. Peter Bell.* (J.E. Jordan,
ed)
W.J.B. Owen, 541(RES):Nov86-578
Wordsworth, W. The Salisbury Plain Poems
of William Wordsworth. (S. Gill, ed)
The Ruined Cottage [and] The Pedlar. (J.
Butler, ed)
J.K. Chandler, 405(MP):Nov86-196
Wordsworth, W. & D. The Letters of William
and Dorothy Wordsworth.* (Vol 6, Pt 3)
(2nd ed) (A.G. Hill, ed)
J.H. Averill, 591(SIR):Summer86-286
P.H. Butter, 402(MLR):Jul86-724
Working, R. Resurrectionists.
B.A. Bannon, 441:19Apr87-16
Woronzoff, A. Andrej Belyj's "Petersburg,"
James Joyce's "Ulysses," and the Symbol-
ist Movement.
R.S. Struc, 107(CRCL):Dec86-687
Worster, D. Nature's Economy.
T. Hatley, 579(SAQ):Summer86-306
Worth, D.S. The Origins of Russian
Grammar.
V. Živov, 559:Vol10No1-73
Worth, K. Oscar Wilde.*
A. Cameron, 610:Spring86-78
J. Stokes, 677(YES):Vol16-338
Worthen, J. – see Lawrence, D.H.
Worthen, T.D., with R.L. Cherry – see
Ayers, D.M.
Worthen, W.B. The Idea of the Actor.*
E. Hill, 610:Summer86-166
J. Norwood, 615(TJ):May86-239
L. Woods, 612(ThS):May/Nov86-169
Wos, L. & others. Automated Reasoning.
M.J. Beeson, 316:Jun86-464
Wotton, G. Thomas Hardy.
W.E. Davis, 395(MFS):Winter86-658
Woudhuysen, H.R., with D. Trotter – see
Kipling, R.
Wray, W.D. Mitsubishi and the N.Y.K.,
1870-1914.
W.D. Hoover, 293(JASt):Aug86-867
Wreen, M.J. & D.M. Callen – see Beardsley,
M.C.
Wreggitt, A. Man at Stellaco River.
P.M. St. Pierre, 102(CanL):Summer86-121
Wren, K. Vigny: "Les Destinées."
C. Crossley, 402(MLR):Jul86-743
S. Haig, 446(NCFS):Spring87-321
N. Rinsler, 208(FS):Jan86-82
Wren, R.M. Achebe's World.
D. Carroll, 447(N&Q):Dec85-574
Wren, R.M. J.P. Clark.
T.R. Knipp, 538(RAL):Summer86-278
Wretö, T. Folkvisans upptäckare.
S.H. Rossel, 301(JEGP):Jul86-428
G.C. Schoolfield, 133:Band19Heft2-170
Wrigglesworth, J.L. Libertarian Conflicts
in Social Choice.
R.E.G., 185:Apr87-681
Wright, A. – see Silko, L.M. & J. Wright
Wright, B. Black Robes, White Justice.
E.R. Shipp, 441:18Oct87-31
Wright, B. & T. Mellors – see Fromentin, E.
& P. Bataillard
Wright, B. & D.H.T. Scott. Baudelaire:
"La Fanfarlo" and "Le Spleen de Paris."
G. Chesters, 402(MLR):Oct86-1011
Wright, C., ed. Frege.
M. Espinoza, 542:Jan-Mar86-150

Wright, C. Frege's Conception of Numbers as Objects.*
P. Smith, 521:Apr86-152
Wright, C. The French Painters of the Seventeenth Century.*
E. Young, 39:Apr86-290
Wright, C. Premonitions of an Uneasy Guest.
R. Pybus, 565:Spring86-71
Wright, C. Realism, Meaning and Truth.
S. Blackburn, 617(TLS):27Feb87-221
Wright, C.D. Further Adventures with You.
455:Dec86-63
Wright, E. Franklin of Philadelphia.*
639(VQR):Autumn86-123
Wright, E. Psychoanalytic Criticism.*
B. Jordan, 402(MLR):Apr86-417
D. Knight, 208(FS):Jan86-109
"Frank Lloyd Wright Letters Trilogy." (B.B. Pfeiffer, ed)
A.L. Huxtable, 441:15Feb87-3
Wright, G. Blood Enemies.
N. Callendar, 441:2Aug87-29
Wright, G.C. Life Behind a Veil.
639(VQR):Summer86-80
von Wright, G.H. Erklären und Verstehen.
P. Engel, 542:Oct-Dec86-546
von Wright, G.H. Philosophical Logic.
S.J. Wagner, 482(PhR):Jul86-427
von Wright, G.H. Philosophical Papers. (Vol 3)
J-L. Gardies, 542:Oct-Dec86-546
Wright, J. Phantom Dwelling.
C. James, 617(TLS):27Nov-3Dec87-1327
J.P. Ward, 493:Oct86-48
Wright, J.P. The Sceptical Realism of David Hume.*
F. Wilson, 154:Winter86-747
Wright, L.R. Among Friends.
R. Thacker, 102(CanL):Winter85-136
Wright, L.R. Sleep While I Sing.
T.J. Binyon, 617(TLS):21Aug87-910
T.J. Binyon, 617(TLS):9-15Oct87-1124
G. Kaufman, 362:2Jul87-31
Wright, M.I. & R.J. Sullivan. The Rhode Island Atlas.
K.B. Harder, 424:Mar86-121
Wright, M.R. - see Empedocles
Wright, N., ed. The Historia Regum Britannie of Geoffrey of Monmouth: 1.
J.D. Burnley, 179(ES):Oct86-450
Wright, P. A Brittle Glory.
A. Hartley, 176:Apr87-59
Wright, P. Spycatcher.
C. Andrew, 441:16Aug87-13
N. Annan, 453(NYRB):24Sep87-47
Wright, R. Late Latin and Early Romance in Spain and Carolingian France.*
T.J. Walsh, 545(RPh):Nov86-199
Wright, R. On Fiji Islands.*
J. Clifford, 617(TLS):25Sep-1Oct87-1041
Wright, R. Veracruz.*
639(VQR):Autumn86-126
Wright, R.B. Tourists.
J. Ferns, 102(CanL):Winter85-123
Wright, S. Evolution. (W.B. Provine, ed)
J. Secord, 617(TLS):11-17Dec87-1370
Wright, S. Randall Jarrell.
J.A. Bryant, Jr., 569(SR):Fall86-lxxvi
Wright, T. Coal Mining in China's Economy and Society, 1895-1937.
W.C. Kirby, 293(JASt):May86-583

Wright, T. The Passions of the Mind in General. (W.W. Newbold, ed)
B. Vickers, 617(TLS):24Jul87-788
Wright, T. "Tess of the D'Urbervilles."
D. Trotter, 617(TLS):17Apr87-419
Wright, T.R. The Religion of Humanity.*
A. Jumeau, 189(EA):Apr-Jun87-225
M.S. Vogeler, 637(VS):Summer87-543
Wright, W. Lillian Hellman.*
J. Lahr, 362:28May87-24
J. Rubins, 617(TLS):10Jul87-749
442(NY):26Jan87-86
Wrigley, C.J., ed. A History of British Industrial Relations. (Vol 2)
F. Cairncross, 617(TLS):24Apr87-447
Wrigley, E.A. People, Cities and Wealth.
E. Gellner, 617(TLS):11-17Sep87-980
Wrigley, E.A. & D. Souden - see Malthus, R.
Wroth, M. The Poems of Lady Mary Wroth.* (J.A. Roberts, ed)
M.G. Brennan, 447(N&Q):Mar85-114
Wroth, W. - see "Russell Lee's FSA Photographs of Chamisal and Penasco, New Mexico"
Wu Jiaqian & others, comps. Riben xingshi renming dacidian.
R. Borgen, 116:Jul85-199
Wührl, P-W. Das deutsche Kunstmärchen.
H-H. Ewers, 52:Band21Heft3-317
Wulff, D.M. Drama as a Mode of Religious Realization.
N. Hein, 293(JASt):Feb86-434
Wülfing, W. Schlagworte des Jungen Deutschland.
M.E. Geisler, 406:Fall86-407
Wulstan, D. Tudor Music.*
J.H.B., 412:Nov85-307
D. Stevens, 415:Jun86-336
Wunenburger, J-J. Sigmund Freud.
M. Adam, 542:Apr-Jun86-265
M. Erman, 98:Mar86-284
Würffel, S.B. Ophelia.
S. Michaud, 549(RLC):Oct-Dec86-469
Wurgaft, L.D. The Imperial Imagination.*
H. Brogan, 324:Jun87-537
Wurlitzer, R. Slow Fade.*
D. Johnson, 18:Sep87-67
Wurm, S.A. & P. Mühlhäusler, eds. Handbook of Tok Pisin.
E. Woolford, 350:Sep87-648
Würzbach, N. Anfänge und gattungstypische Ausformung der englischen Strassenballade 1550-1650.
W.G. Müller, 38:Band104Heft1/2-219
Wurzel, W.U. Flexionsmorphologie und Natürlichkeit.*
J. Klausenburger, 320(CJL):Winter86-327
Wyatt, D. The Fall into Eden.
P. Lagayette, 189(EA):Oct-Dec87-486
V. Norwood, 344:Winter87-129
Wyatt, D.K. Thailand.
A. Ramsay, 293(JASt):Feb86-473
Wyatt, J. Against Capitulation.*
J. Matthias, 598(SoR):Winter87-206
Wyatt, V. Shapes of their Thoughts.
J.C. Berlo, 2(AfrA):Nov85-82
Wyatt-Brown, B. Yankee Saints and Southern Sinners.*
G. Morrison, 396(ModA):Summer/Fall86-312
639(VQR):Summer86-78

Wyclif, J. On Universals. (A. Kenny, trans) Tractatus De Universalibus. (I.J. Mueller, ed)
S. MacDonald, 518:Oct86-208
Wyczynski, P. Louis-Joseph Béliveau et la vie littéraire de son temps.
D.M. Hayne, 627(UTQ):Fall86-222
Wyden, P. The Unknown Iacocca.
A.B. Fisher, 441:25Oct87-38
Wygant, F. Art in American Schools in the Nineteenth Century.
M. Di Blasio, 289:Summer86-109
Wylie, H., E. Julien & R.J. Linnemann, eds. Contemporary African Literature.
J.I. Okonkwo, 538(RAL):Fall86-445
Wyman, D.S. The Abandonment of the Jews.*
H. Ziff, 152(UDQ):Winter87-96
Wyndham, F. The Other Garden.
R. Cobb, 617(TLS):2-8Oct87-1073
L. Heron, 362:31Dec87-24
Wyndham, H., ed. Famous Potatoes.
J.H. Maguire, 649(WAL):Feb87-368
Wysling, H. Narzissmus und illusionäre Existenzform.*
H.R. Vaget, 406:Summer86-243
Wytrzens, G. Die slavischen und Slavica betreffenden Drucke der Wiener Mechitharisten.
A. Hetzer, 602:Band17Heft2-311

Xenocrates & Hermodorus. Senocrate-Ermodoro: Frammenti. (M. Isnardi Parenti, ed & trans)
H.B. Gottschalk, 123:Vol36No1-79
Xingpei, Y. & Hou Zhongyi - see under Yuan Xingpei & Hou Zhongyi
Xinxin, Z. & Sang Ye - see under Zhang Xinxin & Sang Ye

Yadel, M. "La Chute" von Albert Camus.
M. Zobel-Finger, 72:Band223Heft2-474
Yagi, T. Le Mahābhāṣya ad Pāṇini 6.4.1-19.
R. Rocher, 318(JAOS):Oct/Dec85-815
Yahuda, M. Towards the End of Isolationism.
M. Ng-Quinn, 293(JASt):Aug86-836
Yalom, M. Maternity, Mortality, and the Literature of Madness.
R. Asselineau, 549(RLC):Oct-Dec86-463
Yamal, R. Sistema y visión de la poesía de Nicanor Parra.
M. Gottlieb, 238:Dec86-884
J. Higgins, 86(BHS):Oct86-381
Yancy, P.M. The Afro-American Short Story.
C. Werner, 395(MFS):Winter86-638
Yang, A.A., ed. Crime and Criminality in British India.
S. Lewandowski, 293(JASt):Aug86-898
Yang, J. - see under Jiang Yang
Yang, P.F-M. Chinese Dialectology.
W.G. Boltz, 116:Jul85-216
Yaniv, A. Dilemmas of Security.
M. Widlanski, 441:4Oct87-40
Yanovskaya, L. Tvorcheskii put' Mikhaila Bulgakova.
J. Grayson, 575(SEER):Apr86-282
Yanowitch, M. Work in the Soviet Union.
D. Filtzer, 575(SEER):Oct86-640
P. Hollander, 550(RusR):Oct86-454

Yarmolinsky, J.V. Angels Without Wings.
G. Wolff, 441:25Oct87-14
Yarshater, E. - see "Encyclopaedia Iranica"
Yartz, F.J. Ancient Greek Philosophy.
J.S. Murray, 41:Vol6-236
Yates, G.G. - see Martineau, H.
Yates, J. Teenager to Young Adult.
A. Myers, 617(TLS):1May87-472
Yates, R. Cold Spring Harbor.*
J. Clute, 617(TLS):14Aug87-873
W.H. Pritchard, 249(HudR):Winter87-652
Yates, R. Young Hearts Crying.*
P. Iyer, 473(PR):Vol53No1-132
Yates, W.E. & J.R.P. McKenzie, eds. Viennese Popular Theatre.
H. Zohn, 402(MLR):Jul86-792
Yathay, P. & J. Mann - see under Pin Yathay & J. Mann
Yazawa, M. From Colonies to Commonwealth.
R.W. Beales, Jr., 656(WMQ):Jul86-503
R.H. Bloch, 173(ECS):Winter86/87-262
M.B. Norton, 432(NEQ):Mar86-155
Yeager, J. & D. Rutan, with P. Patton. Voyager.
M. Collins, 441:27Dec87-10
"The Yearbook of English Studies." (Vol 9) (G.K. Hunter & C.J. Rawson, eds)
C. Price, 447(N&Q):Sep85-413
"The Yearbook of English Studies." (Vol 13 ed by G.K. Hunter & C.J. Rawson; Vol 14 ed by C.J. Rawson)
W.B. Carnochan, 402(MLR):Jan86-162
"The Yearbook of English Studies." (Vol 15) (C.J. Rawson & J. Mezciems, eds)
A. Varty, 541(RES):Nov86-609
Yearling, E.M. - see Shirley, J.
Yeats, W.B. The Collected Letters of W.B. Yeats.* (Vol 1) (J. Kelly, with E. Domville, eds)
M. Dodsworth, 175:Spring86-109
R. Fuller, 364:Apr/May86-145
M. Harmon, 272(IUR):Spring86-101
H. Vendler, 442(NY):16Mar87-96
639(VQR):Autumn86-122
Yeats, W.B. Poems of W.B. Yeats.* (A.N. Jeffares, ed)
A. Swarbrick, 148:Autumn86-109
K. Worth, 541(RES):May86-287
Yeats, W.B. Purgatory. (S.F. Siegel, ed)
D.T.O., 295(JML):Nov86-559
Yeats, W.B. W.B. Yeats: The Early Poetry. (Vol 1) (G. Bornstein, ed)
C. Rawson, 617(TLS):24Jul87-783
Yeats, W.B. W.B. Yeats: The Poems.* (R.J. Finneran, ed)
G. Bornstein, 403(MLS):Spring86-82
Yeats, W.B. - see also Cullingford, E.
"Yeats Annual No. 1."* (R.J. Finneran, ed)
C.W. Barrow, 174(Éire):Fall86-157
"Yeats Annual No. 2."* (R.J. Finneran, ed)
R.E. Ward, 174(Éire):Spring86-151
"Yeats Annual No. 4." (W. Gould, ed)
D. Kiberd, 617(TLS):13Feb87-166
C. Rawson, 617(TLS):24Jul87-783
Yeazell, R.B., ed. Sex, Politics, and Science in the Nineteenth-Century Novel.
E.B. Jordan, 395(MFS):Summer86-358
Yehoshua, A.B. The Lover. A Late Divorce.
M.A. Abidor, 287:Jan86-26
Yellin, J.F. - see Jacobs, H.A.

Yenal, E.   Charles d'Orléans.
   M-J. Arn, 179(ES):Feb86-75
   D.A. Fein, 207(FR):Dec86-253
   J. Fox, 402(MLR):Apr86-478
   A.T. Harrison, 589:Jan86-253
   S. Spence, 545(RPh):Feb87-418
Yerkes, D., ed.   The Old English Life of
Machutus.*
   P.J. Lucas, 382(MAE):1986/2-267
   J. Roberts, 627(UTQ):Summer87-588
Yerkes, D.   Syntax and Style in Old
English.*
   P.S. Baker, 402(MLR):Apr86-438
Yevtushenko, Y.   Almost at the End.
   M. Carlson, 441:28Jun87-12
Yezierska, A.   Hungry Hearts and Other
Stories.
   P. Craig, 617(TLS):18-24Sep87-1026
Yglesias, H.   The Saviors.
   T. Talbot, 441:16Aug87-14
Yglesias, J.   Home Again.
   C. Reynolds, 441:1Nov87-28
Ying, H. & J.M. Brown.   Speaking Chinese in
China.
   T. Light, 399(MLJ):Winter86-423
Ying-ming, H. - see under Hung Ying-ming
Yizhong, C. - see under Cheng Yizhong
Yokoyama, T.   Japan in the Victorian Mind.
   C. Blacker, 617(TLS):14Aug87-869
Yolen, J., ed.   Favorite Folktales from
Around the World.
   B.L. Clark, 441:25Jan87-12
Yolton, J.W.   Locke.
   R.W. Dyson, 83:Autumn86-246
   E. Matthews, 479(PhQ):Jul86-420
   A. Morvan, 189(EA):Apr-Jun87-213
   I. Tipton, 518:Oct86-214
Yolton, J.W.   Perceptual Acquaintance from
Descartes to Reid.*
   B. Gower, 83:Autumn86-292
   J.M. Hill, 566:Autumn86-72
   E. Matthews, 479(PhQ):Jul86-420
   C. Wilson, 482(PhR):Jan86-105
Yolton, J.W.   Thinking Matter.*
   J. Agassi, 488:Dec86-526
   J.M. Hill, 566:Autumn86-72
   N. Jolley, 482(PhR):Jan86-111
   E. Matthews, 479(PhQ):Jul86-420
Yonekura, H.   The Language of the Wycliff-
ite Bible.
   K. Sørensen, 179(ES):Feb86-78
Yonnet, P.   Jeux, Modes et Masses (1945-
1985).
   H. Cronel, 450(NRF):Nov86-105
   J-F. Fourny, 207(FR):Apr87-744
York, R.A.   The Poem as Utterance.
   A. Haberer, 189(EA):Jan-Mar87-112
Yorke, M.   Evidence to Destroy.
   T.J. Binyon, 617(TLS):2-8Oct87-1074
Yorkey, R.C. & others.   New Intercom 1-4.
(2nd ed)
   S.J. Gaies, 399(MLJ):Spring86-93
Yoshida, K.   Tanrokubon.*   (M.A. Harbison,
ed & trans)
   A.L. Markus, 293(JASt):Nov85-158
Yoshida Mitsuru.   Requiem for Battleship
Yamato.
   R.H. Mitchell, 293(JASt):Aug86-868
Young, A.   Tudor and Jacobean Tourna-
ments.
   S. Anglo, 617(TLS):10Jul87-750
Young, A. - see Caudwell, C.

Young, B.A.   The Rattigan Version.*
   B. Nightingale, 617(TLS):21Aug87-908
Young, B.M.   Ueda Akinari.
   C.A. Gerstle, 302:Vol22No1-106
Young, C.R.   The Royal Forests of Medieval
England.
   P.D.A. Harvey, 161(DUJ):Dec85-177
Young, D.C.   The Olympian Myth of Greek
Amateur Athletics.
   H.D. Evjen, 121(CJ):Feb-Mar87-268
   S. Instone, 303(JoHS):Vol106-238
   J.C. Traupman, 124:Jul-Aug87-456
Young, E.   A Vindication of Providence.*
   P-G. Boucé, 189(EA):Jul-Sep86-371
Young, G.   Slow Boats Home.
   J.A. West, 441:22Feb87-29
Young, G.   Worlds Apart.
   J. Ure, 617(TLS):7Aug87-840
Young, G.V.C. & C.R. Clewer.   Føroysk-Ensk
Ordabók/Faroese-English Dictionary.*
   W.B. Lockwood, 402(MLR):Oct86-1048
Young, J.Z.   Philosophy and the Brain.
   S. Sutherland, 617(TLS):8May87-489
Young, M.W.   Magicians of Manumanua.
   E. Brandewie, 650(WF):Jan86-54
Young, P.   Hawthorne's Secret.*
   J. Seelye, 579(SAQ):Summer86-311
Young, P.   Melancholy Ain't No Baby.
   L. Rogers, 376:Mar86-133
Young, R.A.   Carpentier, "El reino de este
mundo."
   W.B. Berg, 72:Band223Heft2-456
   R.K. Britton, 402(MLR):Apr86-520
   A. McDermott, 86(BHS):Jul86-304
Young, R.F.   Resistant Hinduism.
   R.W. Lariviere, 318(JAOS):Jan/Mar85-182
Young, R.M.   Darwin's Metaphor.*
   G. Levine, 637(VS):Winter87-253
Young, R.V.   Richard Crashaw and the
Spanish Golden Age.*
   G. Hammond, 402(MLR):Jul86-719
   A. Terry, 86(BHS):Apr86-171
Young, T.D., ed.   Conversations with
Malcolm Cowley.
   S.P., 295(JML):Nov86-454
Young, T.D. & G. Core - see Ransom, J.C.
Young, T.D. & J. Hindle - see Ransom, J.C.
Young, T.D. & J.J. Hindle - see Bishop,
J.P. & A. Tate
Youngblood, D.J.   Soviet Cinema in the
Silent Era, 1918-1935.
   P. Kenez, 104(CASS):Spring-Summer86-
   181
Youngson, A.J.   The Prince and the Pre-
tender.
   F.J. McLynn, 161(DUJ):Dec85-183
Yourcenar, M., ed & trans.   Blues et
gospels.
   A.P., 91:Spring86-191
Yourcenar, M.   Mishima.*   (French title:
Mishima ou la vision du vide.)
   L. Allen, 617(TLS):27Mar87-320
Yourcenar, M.   Two Lives and a Dream.
   J. Sturrock, 441:19Apr87-18
Yourgrau, B.   Wearing Dad's Head.
   K. Acker, 441:8Nov87-7
Yovel, Y.   Kant and the Philosophy of His-
tory.
   D.E. Christensen, 543:Dec86-339
   V. Gerhardt, 342:Band77Heft3-375
Yu, A.C., ed & trans.   The Journey to the
West.   (Vols 1-3)
   V.B. Cass, 293(JASt):Aug86-837

Yu, A.C., ed & trans. The Journey to the West. (Vol 4)
 V.B. Cass, 293(JASt):Aug86-837
 R.E. Hegel, 116:Jul85-215
Yu, W-D. Max Frischs "Andorra."
 G.B. Pickar, 221(GQ):Winter86-161
Yu Zhuoyun. Palaces of the Forbidden City. "Skipjack," 463:Winter86/87-414
Yuan, G. - see under Gao Yuan
Yuan Xingpei & Hou Zhongyi, comps. Zhongguo wenyan xiaoshuo shumu.
 J.B. Brennan, 116:Jul85-179
Yudelman, D. The Emergence of Modern South Africa.*
 W.G. James, 529(QQ):Autumn86-484
"Fukuzawa Yukichi on Education" - see under Fukuzawa
Yule, G. The Study of Language.
 J. Aitchison, 353:Vol24No6-1131
Yule, H. & A.C. Burnell. Hobson-Jobson.* (2nd ed, ed by W. Crooke)
 W.B. Frere, 364:Apr/May86-178
 J. Suraiya, 453(NYRB):19Nov87-44
Yung, K.K., ed. Samuel Johnson 1709-94.
 J.H. Pittock, 83:Spring86-105
Yvancos, J.M.P. - see under Pozuelo Yvancos, J.M.

de Zabaleta, J. El día de fiesta por la mañana y por la tarde.* (C. Cuevas García, ed)
 N. Griffin, 402(MLR):Oct87-1003
 T.R.A. Mason, 86(BHS):Jul86-284
Zabarellae, J. De Methodis libri quatuor - Liber de Regressu. (C. Vasoli, ed)
 J. Jolivet, 542:Oct-Dec86-521
Zach, W. Poetic Justice.
 M. Bernsen, 490:Band18Heft3/4-358
Zachary, H. The Venus Venture.*
 42(AR):Summer86-380
Zaehner, R.C. Mystik.
 G. Becker, 489(PJGG):Band93Heft1-212
Zafran, E.M. French Salon Paintings from Southern Collections.
 R. Thomson, 59:Mar86-108
Zagajewski, A. Tremor.
 D.J. Enright, 617(TLS):27Mar87-315
 P. Forbes, 362:25Jun87-31
Zagarell, A. The Prehistory of the Northeast Bahtiyari Mountains, Iran.
 E.C. Stone, 318(JAOS):Apr/Jun85-335
Zagona, H.G. Flaubert's "Roman philosophique" and the Voltairian Heritage.
 C.A. Mossman, 446(NCFS):Fall-Winter 86/87-211
 A. Tooke, 208(FS):Apr86-225
Zak, W.F. Sovereign Shame.*
 J. Reibetanz, 401(MLQ):Jun85-181
Zaknic, I. - see Le Corbusier
Zaleski, C.G. Otherworld Journeys.
 N. Lemann, 61:Jul87-96
 R.A. Shweder, 441:14Jun87-3
Zaliznjak, A.A. Ot praslavjanskoj akcentuacii k russkoj.
 R.F. Feldstein, 574(SEEJ):Winter86-594
Zaller, R. The Cliffs of Solitude.
 D.H., 355(LSoc):Mar86-142
Zalta, E.N. Abstract Objects.
 M. Byrd, 316:Mar86-246
Załuska-Strömberg, A. Grammatik des Altisländischen.
 H. Fix, 680(ZDP):Band105Heft1-127

Zambelli, P., ed. "Astrologi hallucinati."
 P. Curry, 617(TLS):5Jun87-603
Zambon, F. Robert de Boron e i segreti del Graal.
 F. Suard, 554:Vol105No4-583
Zambrano, M. Les clairières du bois.
 A. Reix, 542:Jan-Mar86-97
Zameenzad, A. The Thirteenth House.
 A. Bery, 617(TLS):3Jul87-714
Zander, H. Shakespeare "bearbeitet."*
 M. Brunkhorst, 156(ShJW):Jahrbuch1986-252
Zanger, V.V. Exploración intercultural.
 M.J. Cousino, 399(MLJ):Winter86-449
 L.J. Walker, 238:Mar86-127
Zanger, V.V. Face to Face.
 R.W. Fairchild, 399(MLJ):Autumn86-340
Zangrilli, F. Bonaviri e il mistero cosmico.
 E. Gioanola, 275(IQ):Winter86-126
 F. Manca, 276:Winter86-413
Zanzotto, A. Le Galaté au bois.
 G. Quinsat, 450(NRF):Oct86-110
Zanzotto, A. Idioma.
 P. Hainsworth, 617(TLS):2-8Oct87-1083
Zarader, M. Heidegger et les paroles de l'origine.
 F. Wybrands, 450(NRF):Dec86-93
Zarate, G. Enseigner une culture étrangère.
 E.C. Knox, 207(FR):May87-889
Zardini, M. The Architecture of Mario Botta.
 S. Holt, 45:Oct86-75
Zaret, D. The Heavenly Contract.*
 C.R. Davis, 568(SCN):Winter86-69
Zarrilli, P. The Kathakali Complex.
 C. Martin, 293(JASt):Aug86-900
Zaslowsky, D. & others. These American Lands.
 M. Norman, 441:11Jan87-18
Zatlin, L.G. The Nineteenth-Century Anglo-Jewish Novel.
 M.F. Schulz, 402(MLR):Jan86-181
Zatlin-Boring, P. Jaime Salom.
 H. Cazorla, 552(REH):May86-124
"Zbornik u čast Petru Skoku."
 M. Frederic, 209(FM):Oct86-259
Zeami Motokiyo. On the Art of the Nō Drama.* (J.T. Rimer & Yamazaki Masakazu, trans)
 J. Goff, 244(HJAS):Jun86-295
Zebrowski, M. Deccani Painting.
 A. Schimmel, 318(JAOS):Apr/Jun85-357
Zee, A. Fearful Symmetry.
 R. Kahn, 441:8Feb87-18
 M. Lebowitz, 344:Fall87-142
van der Zee, J. The Gate.
 J. Giovannini, 441:8Mar87-20
Zeffirelli, F. Zeffirelli.*
 J. Richards, 176:Jan87-53
"Zeit der Ernte (Le temps de la moisson)."
 M. Piclin, 192(EP):Oct-Dec86-586
Zeitler, W.M. Entscheidungsfreiheit bei Platon.
 R.W. Sharples, 303(JoHS):Vol106-215
Zeitlin, F.I. Under the Sign of the Shield.*
 S. Murnaghan, 124:Mar-Apr87-330
Zeitlin, I.M. Ancient Judaism.*
 H.W. Basser, 529(QQ):Winter86-935
Žekulin, N.G. Turgenev.
 A.V. Knowles, 402(MLR):Oct87-1049

WITHDRAWAL